BLACK LITERATURE
C R I T I C I S M

Classic and Emerging Authors since 1950

Guide to Gale Literary Criticism Series

For criticism on	Consult these Gale series
Authors now living or who died after December 31, 1999	*CONTEMPORARY LITERARY CRITICISM (CLC)*
Authors who died between 1900 and 1999	*TWENTIETH-CENTURY LITERARY CRITICISM (TCLC)*
Authors who died between 1800 and 1899	*NINETEENTH-CENTURY LITERATURE CRITICISM (NCLC)*
Authors who died between 1400 and 1799	*LITERATURE CRITICISM FROM 1400 TO 1800 (LC)* *SHAKESPEAREAN CRITICISM (SC)*
Authors who died before 1400	*CLASSICAL AND MEDIEVAL LITERATURE CRITICISM (CMLC)*
Authors of books for children and young adults	*CHILDREN'S LITERATURE REVIEW (CLR)*
Dramatists	*DRAMA CRITICISM (DC)*
Poets	*POETRY CRITICISM (PC)*
Short story writers	*SHORT STORY CRITICISM (SSC)*
Literary topics and movements	*HARLEM RENAISSANCE: A GALE CRITICAL COMPANION (HR)* *THE BEAT GENERATION: A GALE CRITICAL COMPANION (BG)* *FEMINISM IN LITERATURE: A GALE CRITICAL COMPANION (FL)* *GOTHIC LITERATURE: A GALE CRITICAL COMPANION (GL)*
Asian American writers of the last two hundred years	*ASIAN AMERICAN LITERATURE (AAL)*
Black writers of the past two hundred years	*BLACK LITERATURE CRITICISM (BLC)* *BLACK LITERATURE CRITICISM SUPPLEMENT (BLCS)*
Hispanic writers of the late nineteenth and twentieth centuries	*HISPANIC LITERATURE CRITICISM (HLC)* *HISPANIC LITERATURE CRITICISM SUPPLEMENT (HLCS)*
Native North American writers and orators of the eighteenth, nineteenth, and twentieth centuries	*NATIVE NORTH AMERICAN LITERATURE (NNAL)*
Major authors from the Renaissance to the present	*WORLD LITERATURE CRITICISM, 1500 TO THE PRESENT (WLC)* *WORLD LITERATURE CRITICISM SUPPLEMENT (WLCS)*

BLACK LITERATURE
CRITICISM

Classic and Emerging Authors since 1950

VOLUME 3: Mackey-Zobel

Foreword by Howard Dodson

Jelena O. Krstović, Project Editor

GALE
CENGAGE Learning™

Detroit • New York • San Francisco • New Haven, Conn • Waterville, Maine • London

GALE
CENGAGE Learning™

Black Literature Criticism: Classic and Emerging Authors since 1950, Vol. 3

Project Editor: Jelena O. Krstović

Editorial: Niesha Amos, Dana Ramel Barnes, Tom Burns, Elizabeth A. Cranston, Kathy D. Darrow, Kristen A. Dorsch, Jaclyn Hermesmeyer, Jeffrey W. Hunter, Jelena O. Krstović, Michelle Lee, Thomas J. Schoenberg, Lawrence J. Trudeau, and Russel Whitaker

Data Capture: Frances Monroe, Gwen Tucker

Indexing Services: Factiva®, a Dow Jones and Reuters Company

Rights and Acquisitions: Beth Beaufore, Vernon English, Jackie Jones, Jaqueline Key, Tracie Richardson, Jhanay Williams

Imaging and Multimedia: Lezlie Light, Robyn Young

Composition and Electronic Capture: Gary Leach, Gary Oudersluys

Manufacturing: Cynde Bishop

Product Manager: Janet Witalec

For product information and technology assistance, contact us at **Gale Customer Support, 1-800-877-4253.**
For permission to use material from this text or product, submit all requests online at **www.cengage.com/permissions.**
Further permissions questions can be emailed to **permissionrequest@cengage.com**

Gale
27500 Drake Rd.
Farmington Hills, MI, 48331-3535

LIBRARY OF CONGRESS CATALOG CARD NUMBER 88-641014

ISBN-13: 978-1-4144-3170-3 (3-volume set)
ISBN-10: 1-4144-3170-8
ISBN-13: 978-1-4144-3173-4 (Vol. 3)
ISBN-10: 1-4144-3173-2

Printed in the United States of America
1 2 3 4 5 6 7 12 11 10 09 08

Contents of Volume 3

Foreword by Howard Dodson vii

Introduction ix

Acknowledgments xiii

Authors Included in *BLC: Classic and Emerging Authors* xvii

Foreword

Sixteen years ago (1992), Gale published *Black Literature Criticism: Excerpts from Criticism of the Most Significant Works of Black Authors over the Past 200 Years*. The three-volume work, the first of its kind, published excerpts from criticism on the work of 123 black writers primarily African American but including selected African and Caribbean writers. A one-volume supplement, published in 1999, provided more extended criticism of an additional 26 black writers. Together, the four-volume set offered readers a representative sampling of the critical perspectives of critics of African American literature. Authors whose works dated from the 18th and 19th centuries were included in the four volumes. Poets, novelists and playwrights were among the writers whose works were under review. While all the writers surveyed were people of African descent, critics were black and white and included journalists, professional book reviewers and academic critics as well as fellow writers. Literary texts reviewed or critiqued included works published through 1998. Most, however, had been published prior to the 1950s.

This second edition, *Black Literature Criticism: Classic and Emerging Authors*, focuses on writers and works published since 1950. Like the previous volumes, the majority of the authors surveyed are African American, but representative African and Caribbean authors are also included. Given the proliferation of literature published by African Americans especially since the 1960s, and the even more vast volume of criticism it has generated, this compilation is necessarily selective. Writers whose works have found their way into the dynamic and evolving canon of African American literature and have been subjected to extensive critiques that did not appear in the previous series have been selected for inclusion. So have writers whose works have been published in major anthologies and encyclopedias of African American literature. In affording easy access to criticism of these writers' works, *Black Literature Criticism: Classic and Emerging Authors* provides students, teachers, writers and other readers of the literature with resources for making their own critical assessments of the writers and their work. *Black Literature Criticism: Classic and Emerging Authors* also provides its users with access to the at times heated discourses around the nature and character of African American literature; what distinguishes it aesthetically, intellectually and politically from other literatures; and what has been its relationship to and impact on American literature.

Prior to the 1960s, most mainstream American literary organizations and literary magazines did not admit African American writers, critique their works or publish African American writers or critics. African American newspapers and magazines dating back to the 19th century often featured reviews and critiques of African American literature. During the 1920s, *Crisis* and *Opportunity*, the official magazines of the NAACP and the National Urban League, provided national forums for African American Literary criticism as did on occasion the *Journal of Negro History* and the *Journal of Negro Education*.

Denied full access to the Modern Language Association and other professional American literary organizations until the 1970s, African American writers and critics formed the College Language Association (CLA) in 1939. The CLA at its annual conference provided a forum where specialists in African American literature could present their assessments of African American writers and their works as well as overall evaluations of the evolving field of African American literature. The *CLA Journal* became a principal forum for publishing this work. It was joined by Johnson Publication's *Negro Digest* (and its successor *Black World*) in 1941. *Negro Digest/Black World* catered to a more general audience and played a major role in reporting African American literary developments and publishing African American literature and criticism. By the 1960s *Negro Digest/Black World* were joined by the *Black Literature Forum, the Journal of Black Poetry, Callaloo, The Black Theater Review* and a host of other African American Literary publications that focused on African American literature, literary history and criticism.

During the 1940s and 1950s a few African American writers—notably novelists Richard Wright and Ralph Ellison, Pulitzer prize-winning poet Gwendolyn Brooks, and Tony Award-winning playwright Lorraine Hansberry—came to the critical attention of the American literary establishment. Not until the emergence of African American studies programs and departments on American college and university campuses during the late 1960s and 1970s, however, did African American writers and their works as well as African American literature as a field enter the mainstream academy and literary profession. Previously published out of print works by African American writers were reprinted and distributed by publishing houses interested in cashing in on the Black Studies bonanza. Writers whose works had been turned down again and again by mainstream publishers suddenly found themselves courted by them. New black publishing houses such as Broadside, Third World Press, and Amistad Press published the works of writers from the black arts movement. And mainstream publishers, realizing that blacks do read and buy books, started new black imprints to publish black works.

Beginning in the 1970s, the pages of mainstream literary publications began to open to black writers and black critics. The MLA and other previously all-white literary organizations both opened membership to blacks and included panels on black literature in their annual programs. Black writers and critics even became officers in these organizations, including president. During the 1970s, black writers and their works began to find a place in college, university and grade school classrooms, in black bookstores and with mainstream booksellers. Gradually, African American literary critics—black, white and otherwise—found their reviews and critiques in print—in great abundance.

This abundant and diverse body of criticism of the works of African American, Caribbean and African writers has been scattered in the thousands of publishing outlets used by critics in this expansive period of literary production. *Black Literature Criticism: Classic and Emerging Authors* brings together a selection of this work and makes it available in an easily accessible format. The Schomburg Center for Research in Black Culture of The New York Public Library is pleased to join with Gale and the writers and critics whose work appears here in making this valuable resource available to all who seek knowledge of black writers' literary sojourn over the last half century.

Howard Dodson
Director
Schomburg Center for Research in
Black Culture of the New York Public Library

Introduction

A Comprehensive Information Source on Black Literature

*B*lack Literature Criticism: Classic and Emerging Authors since 1950 (*BLC: Classic and Emerging Authors*) complements two earlier publications from Gale in the subject area: the three-volume *Black Literature Criticism* (*BLC*; 1992) and the one-volume *Black Literature Criticism Supplement* (*BLCS*; 1999). Designed to meet the needs of university students, upper high school students, general readers, and teachers, *BLC: Classic and Emerging Authors* provides a wealth of information on major black writers of the past 50 years. Featured in this new three-volume set is a broad selection of the best criticism from the last several decades of the twentieth century and the first decade of the twenty-first century. With an emphasis on contemporary and global authors, *BLC: Classic and Emerging Authors* includes 80 writers, 48 of whom have not previously been covered in *BLC*. Among the authors included in *BLC: Classic and Emerging Authors* are: Nigerian novelist, short story writer, and poet Chinua Achebe; Cameroonian novelist and short story writer Calixthe Beyala; Haitian-born American novelist and short story writer Edwidge Danticat; American poet Yusef Komunyakaa; South African novelist and playwright Zakes Mda; American children's author Walter Dean Myers; Senegalese screenwriter and novelist Ousmane Sembène; Ghanian playwright Efua Sutherland; and Martinican novelist Joseph Zobel. The scope of *BLC: Classic and Emerging Authors* is wide, with authors spanning several genres and representing many nations, including Nigeria, Ghana, Senegal, Barbados, Zimbabwe, Haiti, South Africa, Kenya, Guyana, Algiers, and the United States.

Coverage and Inclusion Criteria

BLC: Classic and Emerging Authors was developed in response to numerous requests from students, librarians, and other readers for information on major black authors not covered in the first edition of the *BLC* series and the *Supplement*. Authors were selected for inclusion in *BLC: Classic and Emerging Authors* based on the range and amount of critical material available as well as on the advice of an advisory board of scholars led by Howard Dodson, Director, Schomburg Center for Research in Black Culture of the New York Public Library. About 40% of *BLC: Classic and Emerging Authors* entries were selected for updating from the first edition of *BLC* and the *Supplement*; typically, the revisions are extensive, including all new criticism and completely rewritten author introductions. A special effort was made to identify important new writers as well as the authors most frequently studied in high school and academic programs.

Each author entry in *BLC: Classic and Emerging Authors* presents a sampling of current, full-text critical responses to the author's works. Criticism ranges from initial responses, later selections that document any rise or decline in literary reputations, and retrospective analyses. Interviews are also included in many entries. Thus, *BLC: Classic and Emerging Authors* is both timely and comprehensive.

Organization of Author Entries

Information about authors and their works is presented through eight key access points:

- The **Author Heading** cites the name under which the author most commonly wrote, followed by birth and death dates. Uncertain birth or death dates are indicated by question marks. Name variations, including full birth names when available, are given in parentheses on the first line of the Biographical and Critical Introduction.

- The **Biographical and Critical Introduction** contains background information about the life and works of the author. Emphasis is given to four main areas: 1) biographical details that help reveal the life, character, and personality of the author; 2) overviews of the major literary interests of the author—for example, novel writing, autobiography, social reform, documentary, etc.; 3) descriptions and summaries of the author's best-known works; and 4) critical commentary about the author's achievement, stature, and importance.

- Many *BLC: Classic and Emerging Authors* entries include an **Author Portrait**.

- The **List of Principal Works** is chronological by date of first book publication and identifies the genre of each work. For non-English language authors whose works have been translated into English, the title and date of the first English-language edition are given in brackets following the foreign language listing. Unless otherwise indicated, dramas are dated by first performance rather than first publication.

- **Criticism** is arranged chronologically in each author entry to provide a useful perspective on changes in critical evaluation over the years. Entries include book reviews, studies of individual works, and comparative examinations. To ensure timeliness, current views are most often presented. For the purpose of easy identification, the critic's name and the date of the critical work are given at the beginning of each piece of criticism. Unsigned criticism is preceded by the title of the source in which it appeared. Within the criticism, titles of works by the author are printed in boldface type. Publication information (such as publisher names and book prices) has been deleted at the editor's discretion to provide smoother reading of the text.

- Critical essays are prefaced by **Explanatory Notes** as an additional aid to readers of *BLC: Classic and Emerging Authors*. These notes may provide several types of valuable information, including: 1) the perceived importance of the critical work; 2) the commentator's approach to the author's work; 3) the apparent purpose of the criticism; or 4) changes in critical trends regarding the author.

- A complete **Bibliographical Citation** of the original essay or book precedes each piece of criticism.

- An annotated **Further Reading List** appears at the end of most entries and suggests resources for additional study. In addition, boxed text directs readers to other Gale series containing information about the author.

Other Features

BLC: Classic and Emerging Authors contains three distinct indexes to help readers find information quickly and easily:

The **Author Index** lists all the authors appearing in *BLC*, *BLCS*, and *BLC: Classic and Emerging Authors*. To ensure easy access, name variations and name changes are fully cross-indexed.

The **Nationality Index** lists all authors featured in *BLC*, *BLCS*, and *BLC: Classic and Emerging Authors* by nationality. For expatriate authors and authors identified with more than one nation, multiple listings are offered.

The **Title Index** lists in alphabetical order all individual works by the authors appearing in *BLC*, *BLCS*, and *BLC: Classic and Emerging Authors*. English language translations of original foreign-language titles are cross-referenced to the foreign titles so that all references to a work are combined in one listing.

Citing *Black Literature Criticism: Classic and Emerging Authors*

When citing criticism reprinted in *BLC: Classic and Emerging Authors*, students should provide complete bibliographic information so that the cited essay can be located in the original print or electronic source. Students who quote directly from reprinted criticism may use any accepted bibliographic format, such as University of Chicago Press style or Modern Language Association (MLA) style. Both the MLA and the University of Chicago formats are acceptable and recognized as being the current standards for citations. It is important, however, to choose one format for all citations; do not mix the two formats within a list of citations.

The examples below follow recommendations for preparing a bibliography set forth in *The Chicago Manual of Style*, 15th ed. (Chicago: The University of Chicago Press, 2006); the first example pertains to material drawn from periodicals, the second to material reprinted from books:

Hancock, Hug W. "Condé's *I, Tituba, Black Witch of Salem.*" *Explicator 59.* no. 3 (spring 2001): 165-67. Reprinted in *Black Literature Criticism: Classic and Emerging Authors since 1950*, Vol. 1, edited by Jelena O. Krstović, 346-47. Detroit: Gale, 2008.

Pereira, Malin. "*Museum* and Cosmopolitanism." In *Rita Dove's Cosmopolitanism*, pp. 74-90. Urbana: University of Illinois Press, 2003. Reprinted in *Black Literature Criticism: Classic and Emerging Authors since 1950*, Vol. 1, edited by Jelena O. Krstović, 493-502. Detroit: Gale, 2008.

The examples below follow recommendations for preparing a works cited list set forth in the *MLA Handbook for Writers of Research Papers*, 6th ed. (New York: The Modern Language Association of America, 2003); the first example pertains to material drawn from periodicals, the second to material reprinted from books:

Hiddleston, Jane. "Feminism and the Question of 'Woman' in Assia Djebar's *Vaste est la prison.*" *Research in African Studies* 35.4 (winter 2004): 91-104. Reprinted in *Black Literature Criticism: Classic and Emerging Authors since 1950*. Ed. Jelena O. Krstović. Vol. 1. Detroit: Gale, 2008. 463-71.

Booker, M. Keith and Dubravka Juraga. "Merle Collins: *Angel.*" *The Caribbean Novel in English: An Introduction.* Portsmouth, N.H.: Heinemann, 2001. Reprinted in *Black Literature Criticism: Classic and Emerging Authors since 1950*. Ed. Jelena O. Krstović. Vol. 1. Detroit: Gale, 2008. 340-43.

Acknowledgments

The editor wishes to acknowledge the valuable contributions of the many librarians, authors, and scholars who assisted in the compilation of *BLC: Classic and Emerging Authors* with their responses to telephone and e-mail inquiries. Special thanks are offered to the three chief advisors for *BLC: Classic and Emerging Authors*: Howard Dodson, Director, Schomburg Center for Research in Black Culture of the New York Public Library; Maryemma Graham, Professor of English, Kansas University; and Abena P. A. Busia, Associate Professor of English, Rutgers.

Comments Are Welcome

The editor hopes that readers will find *BLC: Classic and Emerging Authors* to be a useful reference tool and welcomes comments and suggestions about the work. You are cordially invited to call, write, or fax the Product Manager:

Product Manager, *BLC: Classic and Emerging Authors*
Gale
27500 Drake Rd.
Farmington Hills, MI 48331-3535
1-800-347-4253 (GALE)
Fax: 248-699-8054

Acknowledgments

The editor wishes to thank the copyright holders of the excerpted criticism included in this volume and the permissions managers of many book and magazine publishing companies for assisting us in securing reproduction rights. Following is a list of the copyright holders who have granted us permission to reproduce material in this volume of *BLC*. Every effort has been made to trace copyright, but if omissions have been made, please let us know.

COPYRIGHTED MATERIAL IN *BLC*, VOLUME 3, WAS REPRODUCED FROM THE FOLLOWING PERIODICALS:

African American Review, v. 34, 2000 for review of *"Like the Singing Coming off the Drums"* by Yoshinobu Hakutani. © 2000 Yoshinobu Hakutani. Reproduced by permission of the author. / v. 34, 2000 for review of "Two Cities" by Kimberly Ruffin. © 2000 Kimberly Ruffin. Reproduced by permission of the author./ v. 34, fall, 2000 for review of *"Whatsaid Serif"* by Mark Scroggins. Copyright © Mark Scroggins. Reproduced by permission of the author./ v. 35, 2001 for review of *"Bruised Hibiscus"* by Sandra Adell. Copyright © 2001 Sandra Adell. Reproduced by permission of the author. / v. 35, 2001 for "The Shaman's Apprentice: Ecstasy and Economy in Wilson's *Joe Turner*" by James R. Keller. © 2001 James R. Keller. Reproduced by permission of the author. / v. 36, fall, 2002 for "Miles and Me: An Interview with Quincy Troupe" by Douglas Turner. © 2002 Douglas Turner. Reproduced by permission of the author. / v. 40, summer, 2006 for "The Urban Gothic Vision of Colson Whitehead's *The Intuitionist* (1999)" by Saundra Liggins. © 2006 Saundra Liggins. Reproduced by permission of the author.—*American Poetry Review,* v. 34, March/April , 2005 for "Quincy Troupe: An Interview by Jan Garden Castro'. Reproduced by permission of the author.—*Antioch Review,* v. 65, spring, 2007. Copyright © 2007 by the Antioch Review Inc. Reproduced by permission of the Editors.—*BOMB,* summer, 2001. Reproduced by permission.—*Callaloo,* v. 15, winter, 1992; v. 22, summer, 1999; v. 25, 2002; v. 28, winter, 2005.Copyright © 1992, 1999, 2002, 2005 by Charles H. Rowell. All reproduced by permission of The Johns Hopkins University Press.— *CLA Journal,*v. XLVIII, September, 2004. Copyright, 2004 by The College Language Association. All rights reserved. Used by permission of The College Language Association.—*Contemporary Literature,* v. 45, No. 1, spring, 2004. Copyright © 2004 by the Board of Regents of the University of Wisconsin System. Reproduced by permission.—*Critique,* v. 43, winter, 2002. Copyright © 2002 by Helen Dwight Reid Educational Foundation. Reproduced with permission of the Helen Dwight Reid Educational Foundation, published by Heldref Publications, 1319 18th Street, NW, Washington, DC 20036-1802.—*TDR/The Drama Review,* v. 34:1, T125-spring, 1990. Copyright © 1990 New York University and the Massachusetts Institute of Technology. Reproduced by permission of The MIT Press, Cambridge, MA.—*English in Africa,* v. 30, May, 2003. Reproduced by permission.—*English Studies,* v. 87, December, 2006. Copyright © 2006 Swets & Zeitlinger. Reproduced by permission.—*English Studies in Africa,* v. 44, 2001 for "'Kenyan Sherocs': Women and Nationalism in Ngugi's Novels" by Sam Raditlhalo. Copyright © Witwatersrand University Press 2001. Reproduced by permission of the publisher and the author.—*Journal of Black Studies,* v. 32, May, 2002. Copyright © 2002 Sage Publications. Reproduced by permission of Sage Publications, Inc.—*L'Esprit Créateur,* v. 47, 2007. © L'Esprit Createur 2007. Reproduced by permission of The Johns Hopkins University Press. —*Literature/Film Quarterly,* v. 30, 2002. Copyright © 2002 Salisbury State College. Reproduced by permission.—*MELUS,* v. 23, fall, 1998; v. 28, winter, 2003. Copyright *MELUS: The Society for the Study of Multi-Ethnic Literature of the United States*, 1998, 2003. Both reproduced by permission.—*Modern Drama,* v. XLI, winter, 1998; v. XLV, fall, 2002 Copyright © 1998, 2002 by the University of Toronto, Graduate Centre for Study of Drama. Both reproduced by permission.—*Narrative,* v. 9, May, 2001. Copyright © 2001 by the Ohio State University Press. All rights reserved. Reproduced by permission.—*The Nation,* v. 250, January 29, 1990 for "The Serpent's Tooth" by Gene Santoro. Reproduced by permission of the author. First published in Dancing In Your Head. Copyright 1994. Oxford University Press./ v. 277, December 15, 2003. Copyright © 2003 by The Nation magazine/ The Nation Company, Inc. Reproduced by permission.—*Neohelicon,* v. XXXI, 2004 for "Season of Anomy—Postmodernism and Development Discourse" by Wale Oyedele. Copyright © Akademiai Kiado. Reproduced with kind permission from Springer Science and Business Media and the author.—*New Statesman & Society,* v. 3, January 5, 1990. Copyright © 1990 New Statesman, Ltd. Reproduced by permission.—*New York Times Book Review,* September 29, 2002. Copyright © 2002 by The New York Times Company. Reprinted with permission.—*Research in African Literatures,* v. 19, summer, 1988; v. 26, autumn, 1995; v. 29, summer, 1998; v. 30, summer, 1999; v. 34, fall, 2003; v. 35, winter, 2004; v. 36, spring, 2005; v. 37, winter, 2006. Copyright © 1988, 1995, 1998, 1999, 2003, 2004, 2005, 2006 Indiana University Press. All reproduced by permission.—*School Library Journal,* v. 48, January, 2002. Copyright © 2002. Reproduced from *School Library Journal.* A Cahners/R. R. Bowker Publication, by permission.—*Southern Literary Journal,* v. 33, spring, 2001. Copyright © 2001 by the University of North Carolina Press. Used by permission.—*Theatre Journal,* v. 51, 1999; v. 58, March,

COPYRIGHTED MATERIAL IN *BLC,* VOLUME 3, WAS REPRODUCED FROM THE FOLLOWING BOOKS:

PHOTOGRAPHS APPEARING IN *BLC*, VOLUME 3, WERE RECEIVED FROM THE FOLLOWING SOURCES:

Authors Included in *Black Literature Criticism:*
Classic and Emerging Authors since 1950

Chinua Achebe 1930-

Chimamanda Ngozi Adichie 1977-

Raymond Andrews 1934-1991

Tina McElroy Ansa 1949-

Kofi Anyidoho 1947-

Ayi Kwei Armah 1939-

Mariama Bâ 1929-1981

James Baldwin 1924-1987

Toni Cade Bambara 1939-1995

Amiri Baraka 1934-

Calixthe Beyala 1961-

Edward Kamau Brathwaite 1930-

Gwendolyn Brooks 1917-2000

Abena P. A. Busia 1953-

Octavia Butler 1947-2006

Bebe Moore Campbell 1950-2006

Martin Carter 1927-1997

Barbara Chase-Riboud 1939-

Lucille Clifton 1936-

Merle Collins 1950-

Maryse Condé 1937-

Jayne Cortez 1936-

Fred D'Aguiar 1960-

Tsitsi Dangarembga 1959-

Edwidge Danticat 1969-

Amma Darko 1956-

Assia Djebar 1936-

Rita Dove 1952-

Henry Dumas 1934-1968

Ralph Ellison 1914-1994

Nawal El Saadawi 1931-

Nuruddin Farah 1945-

Lorna Goodison 1947-

Charles Gordone 1925-1995

Michael S. Harper 1938-

Wilson Harris 1921-

Bessie Head 1937-1986

Merle Hodge 1944-

Chenjerai Hove 1956-

Charles Johnson 1948-

Edward P. Jones 1950-

William Melvin Kelley 1937-

Randall Kenan 1963-

John Oliver Killens 1916-1987

Jamaica Kincaid 1949-

Yusef Komunyakaa 1947-

George Lamming 1927-

Julius Lester 1939-

Werewere Liking 1950-

Audre Lorde 1934-1992

Nathaniel Mackey 1947-

Paule Marshall 1929-

Zakes Mda 1948-

Gcina Mhlophe 1960-

Toni Morrison 1931-

Albert Murray 1916-

Walter Dean Myers 1937-

Lauretta Ngcobo 1931-

Ngugi wa Thiong'o 1938-

Elizabeth Nunez 1944-

Ben Okri 1959-

Niyi Osundare 1947-

Suzan-Lori Parks 1964-

Sonia Sanchez 1934-

Ousmane Sembène 1923-2007

Ntozake Shange 1948-

Wole Soyinka 1934-

Efua Sutherland 1924-1996

Véronique Tadjo 1955-s

Quincy Troupe 1943-

Amos Tutuola 1920-1997

Derek Walcott 1930-

Alice Walker 1944-

Colson Whitehead 1969-

Zoë Wicomb 1948-

John Edgar Wideman 1941-

August Wilson 1945-2005

Benjamin Zephaniah 1958-

Joseph Zobel 1915-2006

Nathaniel Mackey
1947-

(Full name Nathaniel Ernest Mackey) American poet, novelist, critic, and editor.

INTRODUCTION

Mackey is known for poetry and prose that encompass themes and rhythms from multiple cultures, most notably incorporating the musical qualities and spontaneity of improvisational American jazz. One of his best-known works, *Song of the Andoumboulou,* is a serial poem that began in his 1985 volume, *Eroding Witness,* and has been published in subsequent units since then. In his role as longtime editor of the literary journal *Hambone,* Mackey nurtures innovation and cross-cultural connections in the creative arts by publishing the work of both young and established writers, visual artists, and musicians, spanning a wide spectrum of ethnic traditions. Mackey further develops the relationship between world music and poetry by sharing his knowledge of African American and Third World musical movements through radio broadcasts, lectures, readings, and workshops.

BIOGRAPHICAL INFORMATION

Mackey was born in 1947 in Miami, Florida, and grew up in California. He moved there with his mother and siblings after his parents separated, when Mackey was four years old. Although initially interested in mathematics and science, he developed an interest in reading poetry and in music, especially improvisational jazz. This interest was bolstered and influenced by listening to jazz pioneers like Miles Davis and by his family's involvement in a Baptist church, where Mackey noticed that the response people had to music in a spiritual setting was different than the way they responded in a more formal concert setting. His subsequent perception of the affinity among music, spirituality, and the search for cultural identity became an abiding theme in his poetry and fiction. As he entered Princeton University, Mackey began to take his own writing more seriously and his work was published in some of Princeton's literary magazines. After graduating in 1969 Mackey taught mathematics at a public school in Pasadena, California, then began his doctoral studies in English and American literature at Stanford University. After receiving his doctorate from Stanford in 1975, he taught at the University of Wisconsin-Madison and the University of Southern California before accepting a post at the University of California, Santa Cruz, in 1979. In 1993 Mackey won the Whiting Writer's Award, and in 2006 he won the National Book Award for poetry for the collection *Splay Anthem* (2006).

MAJOR WORKS

Mackey's poetry does not exhibit a consistent voice or textual style; instead, fragmented, fleeting voices, not unlike instruments heard in improvisational jazz, are used experimentally to produce an effect of complex spontaneity and intertextuality. His first poetry collections are the chapbooks *Four for Trane,* published in 1978, and *Septet for the End of Time,* which appeared in 1983. The title of the first volume honors legendary jazz saxophonist John Coltrane, signaling the aesthetics of jazz as a key influence in the poet's work. The second volume draws on a wide spectrum of cultural influences including the Koran, the society of West Africa, and the Pyramid texts of Unas, introducing themes of cross-culturality that are characteristic throughout Mackey's poetry. *Eroding Witness* (1985) was Mackey's first major collection of poetry. It was a National Poetry Series selection the year it was published. The serial poems "Mu" and *Song of the Andoumboulou,* for which Mackey has become well known, each began in this volume, which also includes the poet's earliest chapbook works. The "Mu" series continues in *Outlantish*

(1992) and *School of Udhra* (1993). *Song of the Andoumboulou* continues in the latter, as well as in *Song of the Andoumboulou: 18-20* (1994) and *Whatsaid Serif* (1998). *Splay Anthem* extends and intertwines individual poems from both epic series.

Mackey has also published four books of experimental fiction, including *Bedouin Hornbook* (1986), *Djbot Baghostus's Run* (1993), *Atet, A. D.* (2001), and *Bass Cathedral* (2008). Together, these novels form the *From a Broken Bottle Traces of Perfume Still Emanate* series, which focuses on the Mystic Horn Society and is composed of letters written by the jazz composer/musician "N" to the mysterious "Angel of Dust." Mackey has also written two volumes of essays and literary criticism, *Discrepant Engagement* (1993) and *Paracritical Hinge* (2005). Throughout Mackey's writings the search for cultural foundations and identity is a recurring theme.

CRITICAL RECEPTION

Influenced by the various aesthetics of jazz, world music, and the works of twentieth-century writers like Robert Duncan, William Carlos Williams, Henry Dumas, and Langston Hughes, Mackey's works are regarded as a unique contribution to the tradition of American modernist and postmodernist innovative poetry. Critical discussion has revolved around Mackey's treatment of identity and history, and his blending and juxtaposition of a variety of cultural elements, including music, religion, and geography. Despite the fact that some commentators have labeled his writings difficult and abstract, many scholars commend Mackey's linguistic innovation, praising especially his wordplay, which involves an extensive vocabulary of real words combined with an inventive use of made-up words. In addition, critics have generally applauded his stylistic experimentation, pointing out the unconventional spacing between lines of verse, the jagged and irregular left and right margins, and the frequent use of narrative fragments and repetitive words and phrases that appear in Mackey's work. Acknowledging the complexity of both his fiction and his poetry, other observers have discussed how Mackey reifies language, developing it into a "thing," and how his writings work simultaneously on several different levels and involve multiple layers of meaning.

PRINCIPAL WORKS

Four for Trane (poetry) 1978
Septet for the End of Time (poetry) 1983
Eroding Witness (poetry) 1985
Bedouin Hornbook (novel) 1986

Outlantish: "Mu" Fourth Part-Eleventh Part (poetry) 1992
Discrepant Engagement: Dissonance, Cross-Culturality, and Experimental Writing (critical essays) 1993
Djbot Baghostus's Run (novel) 1993
Moment's Notice: Jazz in Poetry and Prose [coeditor with Art Lange] (poetry and prose) 1993
School of Udhra (poetry) 1993
Song of the Andoumboulou: 18-20 (poetry) 1994
Strick: Song of the Andoumboulou 16-25 (recorded poetry) 1995
Whatsaid Serif: Song of the Andoumboulou 16-35 (poetry) 1998
American Poetry: The Twentieth Century. 2 vols. [coeditor with Carolyn Kizer, John Hollander, Robert Hass, and Marjorie Perloff] (poetry) 2000
Atet, A. D. (novel) 2001
Paracritical Hinge: Essays, Talks, Notes, Interviews (essays and prose) 2005
Splay Anthem (poetry) 2006
Bass Cathedral (novel) 2008

*These four novels constitute volumes 1 through 4 of Mackey's fictional epistolary series entitled *From a Broken Bottle Traces of Perfume Still Emanate.*

CRITICISM

Mark Scroggins (review date 2000)

SOURCE: Scroggins, Mark. Review of *Whatsaid Serif,* by Nathaniel Mackey. *African American Review* 34, no. 3 (2000): 555-58.

[*In the essay that follows, Scroggins commends the poems in* Whatsaid Serif, *and suggests that the verses are "about change, movement, and becoming."*]

Whatsaid Serif, Nathaniel Mackey's third full-length volume of poetry, presents us with twenty-one new installments of the innovative, ongoing serial poem *Song of the Andoumboulou,* a work whose earlier movements appeared in Mackey's first two books of poetry, *Eroding Witness* and *School of Udhra.* The Andoumboulou are a somewhat shadowy people alluded to in the cosmology of the Dogon people of Mali. Originally dwelling in an area later to be settled by the Dogon, the Andoumboulou were small red people, "an earlier, flawed or failed form of human being"—or, as Mackey tends to think of them, "a rough draft of human beings." The Andoumboulou are incomplete, unfinished, and thereby reflect a wider human condition: As Mackey puts it, "the Andoumboulou are in fact us; we're the rough draft." *Whatsaid Serif,* then, is a book of poems about change, movement, and becoming. Mackey's is not a conventional poetic; he works within the avant-garde tradition of modernist and postmodernist poetry, in the vein of early Amiri Baraka (LeRoi Jones) and Clarence Major, or—to deploy the musical analogies of which he himself is fond—in the tradition of cutting-edge jazz players such as Anthony Braxton and Pharoah Sanders. Mackey's poetry is "difficult" for those who demand that poetry present a straightforward record of experience and emotion. But for those willing to follow Mackey's work in its musical twists, cross-cultural swoops, and self-relexive coils, *Whatsaid Serif* offers an exhilarating ride.

Whatsaid Serif's very title exemplifies Mackey's eclectic poetic practice. *Whatsaid* evokes that what-sayer storyteller of the Carib-speaking Kalapalo people of Brazil. The what-sayer appears again and again in *Whatsaid Serif,* sometimes as a questioning figure ("except the what-sayer, / obsessed, asking what. 'Was it a woman / he once was in love with?' 'Was it a lie / he'd long since put it all behind?'"), sometimes as a humorous one ("I was the what-sayer. / Whatever he said I would / say so what"; or, "He said he would say / nothing. I whatever popped into my / head"). *Serif* is a word of obscure origin, denoting one of those fiddly lines at the top or bottom of a printed letter. *Seriff,* however, is a variant of *Shereef,* an Arabic word of deep resonance: It literally means 'noble, glorious,' and denotes a descendant of Muhamet and, by implication, a Muslim priest, the ruler of Morocco or one of his provincial subordinates, a Muslim prince in general, and the chief magistrate of Mecca. In one phrase—*Whatsaid Serif*—Mackey encompasses cultures Arabic, African, and Brazilian, as well as deeply rooted indigenous narrative practices and the irreducibly graphic nature of writing and, by poststructuralist implication, language itself. (Mackey has spoken of what he sees as "the Dogon emphasis on signs, traces, drawings, 'graphicity.'")

In the poems of *Whatsaid Serif,* the word itself is migratory, shifting. Everything, in fact, is on the move, for this is a book of passages, of migration, of *hejira.* The "speaker" of the poems—and his very identity is mobile, evanescent—sits in bars, lounges, and other places of transcience ("the Long / Night Lounge," "Wrack Tavern / Inn of Many Monikers") simultaneously moving ("It was a train we were on / peripatetic tavern we / were in, mind unremittingly elsewhere"). Places shift, as do modes of transportation: "It was a train / in southern Spain we / were on. . . . It was a train outside São / Paulo on our way to Algeciras we / were on. . . . A train / less of though than of quantum / solace, quantum locale . . . train / gotten on in Miami"—Mackey's own birthplace—"long since gone." But "What had been a train was now a / bus between Fez and Tetuan," a bus which shifts bewilderingly back to a train, bus again, and then boat: "Whatever it was it / was a boat we were on, bus we were / on, sat on a train orbiting abject / Earth. . . ." The itinerary of this journey—spiritual, cultural, sexual—is one of the imagination rather than

of Rand McNally (there are no bus lines, heaven knows, running between São Paulo and Algeciras!). The travelers' destination isn't quite clear: It may be the "eventual city known as By-and-By," it may be Zar ("the lazy asymptotic arrival we / glimpsed," also known as "Raz," "Arz," and "Zra"), or it may be some Star, which shifts to "Rast," "Tsar," and, in the title of *Whatsaid Serif*'s second section, "Stra." And throughout this journey, playing from the tape machine or from unnamed sources, there is music—blues music, jazz, Brazilian music, Arabic music—which itself *is* the motion:

> Gnostic sleeper stowed
> away on
> the boat we rode, runaway sunship, Trane's
> namesake music's runaway ghost . . .
> Posthumous
> music made us almost weep, wander,
> Soon-Come Congress we'd other wise have
> been, sung to if not by Lenore by
> Eronel,
> every which way, on our way
> out

In these shifting names and place-names (Leonore/ Eronel, Zar/Raz/Arz/Zra), Mackey further develops the "anagrammatic scat" he first explored in *School of Udhra,* a reshuffling of letters and phonemes that foregrounds the tangible, graphic nature of the word, even as it evokes the manner in which a master jazz musician will elaborate and improvise on a tune until the "head" is left far behind. *Crib* becomes "C'rib," and the African American vernacular for one's home merges in an abbreviation for "Carib." The bus on which the speaker rides becomes "B'us," shorthand for 'be us,' which later we learn "was code for buzz." *Whatsaid Serif* deploys a number of individual words in an almost leitmotific manner, introducing them and reintroducing them in different order and garb: "whatsaid" itself, and its variations—"what-sayer," "say what," and so forth; "strick," which refers to pieces of fiber or hemp before they are made into rope, though Mackey hears much more in a word ("I hear the word *stick,* I hear the word *strike,* I hear the word *struck,* and I hear the word *strict.* I hear those words which are not really pronounced in that word, but there are overtones and undertones of those words, harmonics of those words. The word *strick,* then, is like a musical chord in which these words are otherwise not present are present."); and the "loquat" fruit, which here takes on a range of sexual and gnostic meanings, ranging from the fruit of knowledge of good and evil of Genesis 1 to an extended and hilariously obscene pun on "loquat/low squat."

The speaker of the poems is en route on both a spiritual and cultural *hejira* and a sexual pursuit. The object of his seduction—or perhaps his seducer, for roles, like everything else, shift continually in this volume—is introduced as "Wide-eyed Anuncia," a portmanteau word containing both the Virgin Mary's annunciation and the spider-trickster figure Ananse. Later she will become "Sophia," Greek for 'knowledge,' and the speaker's pursuit of her will take on increasingly gnostic overtones. Wherever the train-bus-boat-spaceship of *Whatsaid Serif* and its what-saying passenger are headed, one of the ultimate "asymptotic" goals is knowledge or *gnosis,* which shows itself in glimpses and erotic flashes, and then disappears again around the bend.

Multiculturalism is enjoying a much-deserved vogue in the academy, with long-overdue attention being paid writers of a vibrant array of once-marginalized groups. One would advance Mackey as something of an exemplary poster poet for multiculturalism, if one did not sense that the term itself, as it's all too often used, does violence to the complex and compelling vision of his poetry. Multiculturalism, that is, too often is simply a code word for spicing up the bland dish of white American writing with a generous dash of non-white color. Mackey's preferred term for his own scholarly studies, whose subjects range from the African American poets Amiri Baraka and Clarence Major, to the Caribbean writers Wilson Harris and Kamau Brathwaite, to the white avant-gardists Charles Olson and Robert Duncan, is *cross-culturality* (as in the title of his *Discrepant Engagement: Dissonance, Cross-Culturality, and Experimental Writing*). The term captures, as *multiculturalism* no longer does, Mackey's sense of the interpenetration of various cultures, of how musical, mythical, and poetic forms migrate between regions, nations, and races, taking on ever-shifting significances even as they retain the traces of their origins.

This interpenetration is beautifully exemplified in the passages of *Whatsaid Serif* that explore the theme of the *cante moro,* or "Moorish song." Federico García Lorca, a poet of immense importance for the "New American Poetry" of the 1960s, traced the roots of his own *cante jondo* ('deep song') to the marginalized African elements in Spanish music. As the Gypsy singer Manuel Torre told Lorca in 1927, "What you much search for, and find, is the black torso of the Pharoah." What this means, Mackey explains in his essay **"Cante Moro,"** is that "you have to root your voice in fabulous origins, find your voice in the dark, among the dead." The journey of *Whatsaid Serif,* then, is a journey across cultures, down *routes* which are as well *roots,* filiations of musical form, of cultural emotion, and of spiritual experience. The speaker of these poems continually seeks *gnosis,* knowledge, but that knowledge—never entirely achieved—cannot be the knowledge of some singular place of origin, but must be the knowledge of an epoch- and world-wide web of intertangled inheritance. As the journey draws near its end (at least for this particular volume of Mackey's work), there is an edge of despair at one's prolonged "waywardness, / atlessness":

> Freight of wind and waywardness,
> atlessness, drift,   Draped and enjambed
>   hasp of
> heaven, short of heaven, moot condolences
> coaxed out of stricken wood . . .

One senses, however, that Mackey's unique, challenging, and exhilarating journey will continue. Is it not, by its very definition, endless?

Megan Simpson (essay date winter 2003)

SOURCE: Simpson, Megan. "Trickster Poetics: Multiculturalism and Collectivity in Nathaniel Mackey's *Song of the Andoumboulou.*" *MELUS* 28, no. 4 (winter 2003): 35-54.

[*In the following essay, Simpson suggests that the trickster figure appears throughout the ongoing poem* Song of the Andoumboulou—*not as a physical presence, but on the level of discourse.*]

Over the course of his twenty-five-year publishing career, Nathaniel Mackey has authored five poetry chapbooks and three full-length collections of poetry, including **Eroding Witness** (selected for the National Poetry Series by Michael Harper, 1985), **School of Udhra** (1993), and **Whatsaid Serif** (1998). His work of serial fiction, **From a Broken Bottle Traces of Perfume Still Emanate,** has appeared in two installments to date: **Bedouin Hornbook** (1986) and **Djbot Baghostus's Run** (1993). In addition to his creative pursuits, Mackey has established his reputation as a scholar with his book, **Discrepant Engagement: Dissonance, Cross-Culturality, and Experimental Writing** (1993), and numerous periodical articles in which he examines the writing he finds most compelling: that of contemporary Caribbean and African American experimental writers such as Edward Kamau Brathwaite, Wilson Harris, and Clarence Major as well as the Black Mountain poets Robert Duncan, Charles Olson, and Robert Creeley. With Art Lange, Mackey edited the anthology **Moment's Notice: Jazz in Poetry and Prose** (1993). Born in Miami in 1947, Mackey has taught at the University of California at Santa Cruz since 1979 and continues to edit the journal *Hambone.*

Mackey works at the intersection of the African American vernacular and Euro-American "open form" poetics, a rich intersection, but one not often recognized as such, and in which we can locate the projects of few other African American poets. Amiri Baraka comes to mind, representing the generation before Mackey, as do a few of the young innovators whose work is often contextualized with that of the "language writers," such as Will Alexander, Erica Hunt, and Harryette Mullen. Although the much-needed critical vocabulary for talking about postmodern African American writing has begun to be developed by scholars such as Aldon Lynn

Nielsen in his book *Black Chant,* contemporary American poetry scholarship and publishing have yet to adequately account for linguistically innovative African American poetry. Thus, placing Mackey's writing in any one literary tradition or context is difficult since his poetry itself is "difficult." But significant critical engagements with Mackey's work have appeared, most notably in a recent special issue of *Callaloo* (2000) and in Paul Naylor's *Poetic Investigations: Singing the Holes in History.*

Mackey's ongoing sequence poem, ***Song of the Andoumboulou,*** is published to date in more than forty numbered sections, the first seven appearing in 1985 in ***Eroding Witness.*** Other installments appear in ***School of Udhra,*** and ***Whatsaid Serif*** is comprised wholly of ***Song of the Andoumboulou,*** sections 16-35, many of which had previously been published in literary journals such as *Sulfur, Conjunctions,* and *apex of the M*; subsequent sections continue to appear in *Callaloo* and other periodical venues. In 1995 Mackey made a CD recording of sections 16-25, entitled *Strick,* with jazz/world music artists Royal Hartigan and Hafez Modirzadeh. The series is an improvisational work of sometimes jarring dissonance and startling connections, rife with noise and punctuated by deep silences.

The title of the series, ***Song of the Andoumboulou,*** refers to a traditional funeral song of the Dogon people of West Africa that invokes what in their complex cosmology is an earlier, flawed form of human being. Mackey was initially inspired, upon hearing a sound recording of the song, not so much by the meaning of its words or to what they refer, but by the harsh and "raspy" texture of the singing itself ("Interview," O'Leary 40). Mackey emulates this rasp in his poetic sequence by means of various formal and stylistic gestures, including radical word play, sonic devices, ragged left and right margins, irregular spacing within and between lines, frequent use of ellipses, repetition, and enigmatic fragments of narrative stitched to one another with what seem to be the sinewy innards of language itself.

Song of the Andoumboulou begins with an epigraph from Marcel Griaule's *Conversations with Ogotemmêli,* an anthropologist's account of Dogon cosmology and culture garnered through interviews with a single tribal elder, and the first few sections of the series stay close to this particular source in terms of theme and specific references. But the series quickly expands its scope, shifting emphasis and admitting more and different cultural "source" materials as it continually evolves. The various musical, poetic, and cultural elements that find their way into Mackey's sequence include West African myth (Yorubá and Dogon in particular), Haitian deities, voudoun, flamenco, Moroccan and Andalusian influences, Arabic and Islamic traditions, gnosticism, reggae, jazz, and blues.

Most critical assessments treat the series as investigative (of either history, identity, or both); virtually all

analyze the implications of the poem's cultural roaming and inclusiveness; and several even hone in on Mackey's apparent interest in collective identity in the work, a theme I too will be taking up in my analysis. But none has traced these aspects of ***Song of the Andoumboulou*** to the active presence of a trickster aesthetic, by which I mean writing that privileges and seeks to embody in its formal and thematic gestures the behaviors and effects of the trickster figure found in the folklore of oral cultures throughout the world.

Appearing in the tales and myths of many different and widely separated oral cultures, tricksters nonetheless do share certain common features across cultures. They function as cultural heroes, as in the Native American creation tale in which the trickster coyote is responsible for teaching the "New People" all they need to live and survive (Hyde 8-9), while also challenging the norms and laws of the culture. Indeed, trickster's behavior is at times extremely transgressive, as in the Winnebago trickster cycle in which trickster actually kills a group of children (Hyde 40). Tricksters embody opposites in many different ways and on many different levels. In West African traditions, the spider trickster Anansi of the Ashanti people "speaks the truth by dissembling" and the Fon's trickster Legba "is at once an agent of disruption and an agent of reconciliation" (Pelton 2, 75). A given trickster may behave foolishly in one tale, bravely and wisely in the next. For instance, in a widespread North American Indian tale, Coyote gets his head stuck in an elk skull, then bumbles about until he falls into a river and is washed away (Hyde 39-40). In another story, Coyote cleverly builds a fish trap by designing it to take advantage of the salmon's instinct to swim upstream to spawn (Hyde 18-19). Tricksters almost always serve a mediating function, particularly between the human and divine realms, and their role, among others, is to ensure the survival of their culture (Smith 4). In the Tsimshian Raven cycle, for example, the Raven trickster serves both functions simultaneously when he steals light from heaven to illuminate the previously dark world of the humans (Hyde 25).

No longer relegated to orality, tricksters have extended their territory to include contemporary written literatures, especially works by authors writing from historically marginalized cultural positions. In many such works, including Mackey's, the trickster's allegiance is not so much to one traditionally defined "culture" as it is to cross-culturality itself. Tricksters in these postmodern texts do not always appear as characters or figures; although trickster figures are mentioned in Mackey's ***Song of the Andoumboulou,*** the trickster functions in the work primarily on the level of discourse itself, as a kind of trickster discourse. In "Trickster Discourse: Comic Holotropes and Language Games," Chippewa writer Gerald Vizenor defines trickster discourse as that in which the trickster functions as "a semiotic sign" whose narrative functions—the deployment of irony, chance, and difference—are better understood through the lens of linguistics than that of sociology (189). Vizenor defines the trickster as "communal signification and a discourse with imagination" and "a language game" in which trickster is "disembodied in a narrative" (87, 196). While for Vizenor trickster discourse is closely associated with narrative expression, it could just as well be engaged in lyric or poetic forms, understood as a particular approach to language use, one which admits and emphasizes trickster's linguistic antics. Here, Henry Louis Gates, Jr. is helpful: in identifying the pan-African trickster figure Esu-Elegbara as the central trope of an African American literary and critical tradition, he emphasizes Esu's linguistic abilities, including "the function of interpretation," and his affinity for indeterminacy and figurative language (6).

Mackey knows all about Esu and makes direct reference to him in both his creative and his theoretical/critical writings. In his essay **"Sound and Sentiment, Sound and Symbol,"** Mackey explores the nature of his own intellectual interest in Esu-Elegbara in a discussion of "Legba," by which name Esu is known in Fon-Yorubá folklore. Here, Mackey reads a range of cross-cultural literary and musical gestures—found in writing as diverse as William Carlos Williams' poetry, Ralph Ellison's *Invisible Man,* and the fiction of Wilson Harris—in terms of Legba's limp ("a play of difference") and his role as one who "presides over gateways, intersections, thresholds, wherever different realms or regions come into contact" (*Discrepant* 244). Paul Hoover, in his analysis of Mackey's fictional work *Bedouin Hornbook,* identifies the narrator as well as a character known variously as Heidi (a Northern European? Perhaps the character of the popular children's book? The name a play on "hide"?) and Aunt Nancy (Anansi, the spider of African folklore?) as trickster figures. Hoover finds Mackey himself "playing the trickster for moral purpose" in this work by "conflat[ing] black and white cultural icons" (745). Esu also has a clear presence in *Song of the Andoumboulou,* in which Mackey makes constant reference to the African and African diaspora cultures in which Esu thrives, and Esu himself is mentioned, though sparingly, in **"Song of the Andoumboulou: 12"** as Eshu and as Legba in **"Song of the Andoumboulou: 13"** (*School* 9, 11).

But how, exactly, does the trickster function in Mackey's *Song of the Andoumboulou,* and how can our understanding of that work be deepened by exploring this presence? I argue that approaching Mackey's *Song of the Andoumboulou* as a kind of trickster discourse can enable a deeper understanding of how the poem's disjunctive formal characteristics function in relation to one of the work's central concerns: the possibility of a collective subjectivity that might allow the poem's ex-

plorers to partake of the "discrepant engagement" necessary for the realization of a cross-cultural identity, neither essentialist nor assimilationist, but improvisational.

Locating trickster's presence in the work on the level of discourse might profitably begin with a tracing of the operations of the "what-sayer" at play throughout the volume *Whatsaid Serif.* The what-sayer appears at times as a trickster-like character, whose first appearance in the book is as one "obsessed, asking what" (15). He has a keen interest in language and meaning, pointing always to the limitations of the first and the impossibility of the latter:

> [. . .] "What does 'Language
> is a fruit of which the
>   skin
>   is called chatter' mean?" he
>   asked [. . .]
>   (19)

But even when the what-sayer appears as an agent, he is not confined to a single character. In **"Song of the Andoumboulou: 20,"** he inhabits the poem's speaker: "I was the what-sayer. / Whatever he said I would / say so what" (22). At other times the what-sayer is not embodied at all: language itself is doing the what-saying, as in the passage in which the speaker is in conversation with an entity identified as "what the book went on to say" (19). As the book's title suggests, what-saying goes on quite well without an agent or specific "what-sayer": things simply get "what-said" by the writing itself; by *serif,* a printing term derived from the Latin *scribere,* to write. The word's homonym, *seraph,* brings to the book's title the implication that writing functions on more than a mundane level and is neither transparent nor unproblematic. The what-sayer trickster is a kind of deconstructive angel, the one who continually challenges, thwarts assertion, perceives the gaps and artifice present in any description or expression, "insisting a story lay / behind the story he complained he / couldn't begin to infer" (38). The what-sayer's task is never done in *Song of the Andoumboulou,* a text whose principal gestures are juxtaposition, dissonance, contrast, and palimpsest.

One of the most significant effects of these gestures is the bringing together of disparate materials—place names, music, deities, objects, all from a wide range of cultural sources—locating the work in a kind of energy field of cross-cultural contact. One important implication of this gesture is the calling into question of essentialist views of culture. In interviews Mackey has addressed this as a concern in his work, especially regarding "the cultures of marginalized peoples" which "tend to be subjected to oversimplification . . . made into monolithic and often homogenous entities that in actual fact they are not." Mackey wants to "acknowledge the complexity of black culture," in particular, what he calls "its variousness and its several-sidedness" ("Interview," Foster 59).

Of course in bringing together diverse cultural elements, even if they are mostly from "black" cultures, Mackey not only combines them in new ways, but also shifts contexts, alters, and re-creates these elements. For instance, in **"Song of the Andoumboulou: 12,"** the Osanyin, a group of Voudoun deities, share the page with several Yorubá figures and traditions such as Eshu himself and an *egungun,* a ritual mascarade performance. These two different traditional cultures are put into relation with one another at the same time that both come in contact with globalism: King Sunny Adé, the Yoruba juju music band leader of Nigeria who became a world famous pop icon in the late twentieth century, shows up in the poem a few lines later. In **"Song of the Andoumboulou: 16,"** Mackey explores the cultural reach of "duende," a kind of unrequited longing most often associated with the work of Spanish poets, by overlaying a discussion of it with references to ancient Islamic artistic expression in the form of "the oud's complaint," and "ya habibi echoing / endlessly [. . .]" (**Whatsaid** 3, 7). Mackey resists the notion that to recombine elements from disparate sources somehow harms or destabilizes the cultures from which they are culled, for, as he explains, "these traditions—the mythology, the lore—are not being gone to as some kind of fixed, given entity that one then has to have a subservient relationship to. They are active and unfinished; they are subject to change; they are themselves in the process of transformation and transition" ("Interview," O'Leary 35).

Trickster is a steady presence in cultural transformation. But according to Jeanne Rosier Smith, that tricksters are "culture builders" and so appear "at moments of . . . crisis" does not mean that they restore a disrupted culture to a former ideal state (9). Rather, they "preserve *and transform*" (emphasis mine), much like a jazz improvisationist (4). What Smith calls "the trickster aesthetic" thus "challenges an ethnocentric view," allowing that no one culture is unmediated, "natural," or whole (11). Mackey does not seem as interested in what gets transformed into what when a culture is in transition as he is in the very fact that such transition is always already ongoing. This gives him permission to extract, combine, and overlay elements from different cultural contexts in his poem. Certainly, in *Song of the Andoumboulou,* no one culture is central, for the scene of the poem is not only constantly in flux, but cultures, even geographic locations, overlap and inhabit one another.

In **"Song of the Andoumboulou: 21,"** the speaker and his unidentified companions are on a train "in southern Spain" while listening to Brazilian music. They feel themselves to be in two places at once, as if the music

                   [. . .] put one
             place atop another,

                                          brought
                Brazil in, air as much of
             it as earth, even more, an ear
                we'd have called inner unexpectedly
                out . . . Neither all in our
             heads nor was the world an array
                                          less
             random than we'd have
                                    thought . . .

                                  (**Whatsaid** 30)

Mackey's poem, in this passage and others, suggests that "the world," including one's cultural location in it, is neither completely random nor completely subjective. Yet whatever order there is in the "array" that becomes apparent to the speaker and his companions seems facilitated by the act of listening to music from one culture while traveling through the physical geography of another. Identity itself, in this context, must be shaped by a similar ongoing reciprocal process of personal and cultural construction and deconstruction. As Andrew Wiget indicates in his overview of Native American trickster tales: "Trickster functions not so much to call cultural categories into question as to demonstrate the artificiality of culture itself. Thus he makes available for discussion the very basis of social order, individual and communal identity" (94).

Individual identity is very much part of the discussion in *Song of the Andoumboulou,* most notably evident in what Joseph Donahue has termed "the elided first person" (63) that figures so prominently in *Song of the Andoumboulou,* and which the title of Mackey's first collection, *Eroding Witness,* posits. Donahue notes that Mackey's avoidance of the grammatical sentence, "the site where actor and acted upon are locked into place," allows him to resist the dualistic logic that defines object in relation to subject (63). In an interview with Edward Foster, Mackey discusses his wariness of the subject/object duality in terms of "the Cartesian separation of the ego from the rest of the world" and his desire to achieve a kind of subjectivity that both avoids and critiques the "I" of Western colonialism (49).

This attempt is everywhere evident in *Song of the Andoumboulou,* in which, although sentences and clauses do appear, the first person pronoun rarely occupies the subject position in them. Personal agents are often avoided altogether in favor of human expression or utterance itself, as in "Cries of thousands / cut in on the music" (**Whatsaid** 6). Similarly, the presence of the "I" is often communicated through its absence, as when it is implied rather than stated. Verb phrases without any identified subject, punctuated as complete sentences, often have this effect, such as "Feasted on ghost- / lore, leavings" (**Whatsaid** 7) and "Sat up sleepless in the Long Night Lounge" (**School** 13). This particular syntactic pattern is common throughout the series. Another frequently employed technique is to suppress the first person pronoun into modifying structures, so that the self is subordinated, embedded within phrases. The first two stanzas of **"Song of the Andoumboulou: 12"** rely on this strategy: "Weathered raft I saw myself / adrift on. // Battered wood I dreamt I / drummed on, driven" (**School** 9). Mackey suppresses the first person not only into modifying noun phrases as in these examples, but also into adverb clauses, as in "Bedouin / glimpse of what once I reach after it / vanishes" (**School** 12). The self is also frequently present in its possessive or object form, as in "my mouth" or "what held me" (**Eroding** 40, 48). Thus, the "I" never actually disappears, but its status as a fixed, self-contained independent agent gives way to a self comprised of "communal and collective inheritance" (Mackey, "Interview," Foster 48). In place of the "Bound I," Mackey posits an "Insubordinate / us" (**School** 10).

This, again, is the province of the trickster, who, according to Vizenor, *is* "communal signification" (187), and who, according to Smith, "play[s] a central role in the connection of self and culture" (4). When the "culture" in which the trickster functions is an expanded cross-culturality, it becomes possible to "expand" or "widen" subjectivity as well, thus making the self resistant to what Mackey calls "the reduction to a state of non-entity" that often results from the processes of social othering in a hegemonic society ("Interview," Foster 53). The "self" in Mackey's *Song of the Andoumboulou* is expanded in part as a consequence of traveling through geography, cultures, and history, from Dogon myth to twentieth century American jazz to pre-Islamic North Africa. The series' speaker and his (similarly) unidentified companions might be productively viewed as voyagers or wanderers. In **"Song of the Andoumboulou: 20,"** even when they are in a tavern, they are not still, for it's a "peripatetic tavern." And not only do the wanderers' feet keep moving, but their thoughts, too, run ahead; a "mind unremittingly / elsewhere" is a mind in motion (**Whatsaid** 22).

Significantly, tricksters are often depicted as itinerant, a condition which enables them to maintain the liminal status necessary to perform their functions of mediation, unification, and transformation (Gates 6, Blaeser 140). But I am not suggesting that the wanderers in Mackey's poem are themselves trickster figures; rather, the poem's trickster discourse is a wandering discourse, continually dislocating and relocating the poem's speaker(s) with its "Rumble underfoot," like a "Train / pulling in, pulling out" (**Whatsaid** 10). Indeed, it often seems that the geography through which the speaker and his companions (as well as the poem's readers) move is that of discourse itself, the conventions of narrative and storytelling that function to make time a place that can be inhabited momentarily:

> Came now to a place was more
> time than place, nonsonant
> music's tipped acquittal,

> long-known place known as
> By-and-By . . .

(Whatsaid 79)

Song of Andoumboulou wanders formally as well: as a serial poem its boundaries are continually extending and its twists and turns are potentially never ending. It is an open-ended serial whose boundaries permeate and are permeated by other of Mackey's works. For instance, the first letter to Angle of Dust (a series of such letters comprise his epistolary novel **Bedouin Hornbook**) appears in **Eroding Witness** as part of **"Song of the Andoumboulou: 7."** The continual movement in and of the poem, from place to time to sound, and the "expanded" subjectivity that it implies—the sense that the self is never fixed in a single time or location—seems to facilitate Mackey's poetic quest for what Jeffrey Gray calls "a viable first-person plural identity (622), and what Mackey himself refers to in the poem variously as "two-ness" or "the / we they might've been" (**Whatsaid** 11, 9).

This quest also includes what Paul Naylor views as Mackey's "poetic investigations" of various cultural valuations of collectivity, from the "Simonians," disciples of Simon Magus who sought "to become we," named in Mackey's epigraph to **"Song of the Andoumboulou: 17"** (**Whatsaid** 9) to the "lost twinness" that figures in Dogon cosmology. In his reading of *Conversations with Ogotommêli,* Mackey discovered that the Andoumboulou were flawed because they resulted from a divine incestuous union, an act which also disrupted the "principle of twin births" which had been originally established by the God Amma and his wife earth with their offspring, the twin spirits Nummo, "inventive beings who construct the world and bring to it the first spoken words" (Griaule 23). The Nummo (though spelled "Nommo") figure in Mackey's *Song of the Andoumboulou* right from the start of the series in a reference to the first words being brought to earth concealed in a woven garment, a passage in which there is

> [. . .] a longing
> to unveil what's underneath,

> the Word the Nommo
>   put inside the fabric's
> woven secret

(Eroding 40)

The associations between plurality, creativity, and language implied by this religious myth offer resonance to the connections Mackey forges in *Song of the Andoumboulou* among linguistic experimentation, mysticism, and collective subjectivity.

Mackey not only eschews normative syntax, linked as it is to the Cartesian "I," but also tries to "test and break the limits of what can be said," as Brent Hayes Edwards puts it (572), a gesture which might result in what Mackey himself calls "a telling inarticulacy" (*Discrepant* 253). Trickster is not only most at home in a borderlands of linguistic indeterminacy and ambiguity, but also is, according to Vizenor, "that wild space over and between sounds, words, sentences and narratives" (196). In *Song of the Andoumboulou,* Mackey explores this wild space in his reference to words which "pointed / not beside the point though almost," and those which were "wanting not to be / words" (*Whatsaid* 15, 16): these are trickster words, indeed, mischievously thwarting or resisting the process of signification itself. Mackey seeks instead a "wordless / rapport," and strives toward alternative ways of seeing and knowing (i.e. "the intuitive, the uncanny, the oneiric, the sympathetic, the coincidental, the ecstatic, the intangible, the paradoxical, the oceanic, the quirky, the psychosomatic, the quixotic, the religio-erotic and so on") that Mackey associates with mysticism and Western heterodox traditions (*Whatsaid* 13-14; "Interview," Naylor 646; "Interview," Foster 49). Consistent with this effort are Mackey's phrases "sophic / belly, sophic butt," which seem less anomalous when we recognize that they embody an attempt on the level of language itself to locate knowledge in the body rather than in a disembodied lògos (*Whatsaid* 19).

That Mackey also seeks "a telling inarticulacy" throughout *Song of the Andoumboulou* is evidenced by the frequent appearance of various wordless sounds as well as the fragmented, interrupted, incomplete quality to the writing in general. Wordless sounds include non-linguistic expression such as musicality itself, as in the numerous references to song, musical instruments, and musical forms: "endless refrain," "the oud's complaint," "flamenco strings," "Davidic / harp," and so on (*Whatsaid* 5, 3, 12). Multiple incomplete and indeterminate vocalities can be heard in the series as well, from "Ethiopian moan" and "Cries of thousands" to "Muttering" and "The slight / rub of untongued / voices" (*Whatsaid* 12, 6, 4; *Eroding* 46). Non-vocal sounds also proliferate and even speak: "Whoosh" "Flutter spoke / next," "Swirl spoke, so / did whir" (*Whatsaid* 12, 9, 6).

But it is not so much these frequent references to inarticulacy as the texture of the poem itself that functions as a telling inarticulacy. No sooner than a particular scene, narrative line, image, or syntactic structure begins to develop or become apparent, is it dropped, thwarted, interrupted, or sent suddenly in another direction. Take the following excerpt from **"Song of the Andoumboulou: 16,"** for example:

  Hummed. "Tell me," so
 disdainfully it stung . . .
      Raw-throated
  singer beating time with a
   dry stick . . .

Is the one who hums the same who speaks the quoted imperative? And who feels the sting? We have a partially developed interpersonal interaction, but without complete expressions or identified participants. Ellipses indicate that the exchange continues, but elsewhere, not here in the poem for us to follow. Instead, we are suddenly confronted with a singer, presented in a noun phrase so that narrative action is only implied by the verbal "beating" but not realized or completed. Again ellipses signify a kind of fade-out.

In the next line we enter a narrative already underway; the agent is absent or has been suppressed, and we come in on the finite verb:

    Feasted on ghost-
 lore, leavings, "whither thou
  goest . . ." In another house
 dwelt far beyond sight. That
  they were there, anywhere
       at all,
  ever the heist it had
 always been . . . [. . .]

Who is feasting, dwelling? Who addresses whom as "thou"? That "ghost" rhymes with "goest" causes the quoted phrase to suggest simultaneously the image of a withered ghost and a wandering, as if whoever is doing the wandering has only a suggested, or ghostly, presence. Indeed, the presences are always elsewhere, "in another house" and "out of sight." It seems uncertain that "they" are anywhere at all, as if they are in fact a kind of "heist," embodying, impossibly, their stolen, and thus absent, selves. "Brute / pointlessness bearing / down," the passage continues, as if in self-reference to the continuous inarticulacy that seems somehow nonetheless to propel the poem onward, from one fragmented expression to the next (*Whatsaid* 7).

For Mackey, inarticulacy is closely linked to collective subjectivity, as this passage illustrates:

   A wuh
 sound sounding like dove-warble
  worked his throat, the we
 he, she and I were haunted by.

      (*Whatsaid* 19)

The singular pronouns are "haunted" by a "we," suggesting the individuals are inhabited or possessed by an otherworldly, or at least non-normative, plurality. To be "haunted by" also implies a desire for what is not (yet, perhaps) solidly manifest in daily reality. The grammar of this passage is interesting, too: an independent clause is followed by a noun phrase set off by a comma, i.e. a noun phrase appositive. But what noun in the main clause is the appositive, whose core noun is "we," renaming? According to linguistic convention, it should be "throat," the noun immediately preceding it, in which case "throat," the site of verbal expression, is equated with plural subjectivity. Add to this that the throat is in the process of being "worked" by "a wuh sound," the initial phoneme in the word "we," a "we" that wants to be spoken, is on the verge of being named as such, and we arrive at the implication that from such inarticulacy arises the suggestion of a multivalent, multicultural collectivity, linking linguistic experimentation and creativity with plurality (*Whatsaid* 12).

No one is more interested in language than trickster. Gates notes that "Much of Esu's literature concerns the origin, the nature, and the function of interpretation and language use 'above' that of ordinary language" (6). Trickster's own communal function and multivocality are closely linked to extending and exceeding the capabilities of language. Together these tendencies comprise what Smith sees as "trickster's biggest contribution to the postmodern [. . .] the notion that identity can be multiplicitous and that the deconstruction of a falsely unitary language need not lead to incoherence" (17). While it could be argued that in *Song of the Andoumboulou* trickster's antics do in fact result in incoherence, in the most literal sense of the word, that incoherence is nonetheless meaningful, an intentional push beyond the bounds of the sayable and the confines of the singular.

Trickster's plurality, indeterminacy, and multivocality are very much features of the mediating function trickster serves, whether that be between "the realm of the gods" and "our human world" (Gates 6), or "between self and other . . . male and female . . . real and fantastic . . . story and audience" (Smith 21). Mackey's trickster discourse allows for boundary crossing on a number of fronts, so that elements that would not normally appear in the same context, do, in what Naylor calls "the representation of the moment . . . when traditions cross paths, and sameness yields to diversity to achieve a more rather than less creative encounter" (71).

In addition to the cross-cultural blendings and juxtapositions I have already mentioned, Mackey's text also permeates temporal boundaries. The "Remnant of an alternate / life" referred to in **"Song of the Andoumboulou: 18"** might indicate a kind of historical recovery or at least an encounter in the present with traces of the past (*Whatsaid* 18). Similarly, encounters with the "obsolete"—including the constant engagement with those most obsolete of beings, the Andoumboulou—in the present of the poem which itself seems to have "Rethought what Andoumboulou / meant," keep the portal open between then and now. Mackey also swings the poem wildly into the future and back again in his play with verb tenses, such as the future past perfect combined with the conjunctive in the lines, "We who will have been / compost could wood be / water" (*Whatsaid* 27). Consistent with these gestures, time in the poem seems circular, folding back on itself rather than progressing linearly, further blurring

the distinction between what was and what is: "Endless night now / ended, / rebegun" (*School* 11). The circularity is seemingly doubled in this example, with "endless" and "rebegun" functioning simultaneously as redundancy and contradiction.

Another boundary regularly breached in *Song of the Andoumboulou* is that between the human and the spiritual realms. This boundary is trickster's primary residence, and Esu even walks with a limp, one leg shorter than the other, because "he keeps one anchored in the realm of the gods" (Gates 6). The "chthonic / stir" in **"Song of the Andoumboulou: 17"** indicates the audible presence of the underworld within the text, whose trickster discourse is itself the "conduit" between these realms (*Whatsaid* 9). Both the temporal and the spiritual border-crossings such as these that occur throughout the poem have a significant feature in common: the transgressed boundary in both cases is that between the apparent and the hidden, thus admitting elements that conventional western thinking in its insistence on solid distinctions between past and present, the spiritual and the material, and so on, would deem extraneous or divergent.

Giving access to such heterogeneous elements results in what Mackey calls "noise," a positive term for "whatever the signifiying system, in a particular situation, is not intended to transmit" (*Discrepant* 20). Thus, it is a potentially radical, transformative act to admit this noise. To understand how noise functions in relation to the poem's reach toward collective subjectivity, we must view words such as "Andoumboulou," "chthonic," "Ogun" (a Yorubá diety), "Udhrite" (the adjectival form of Udhra, a pre-Islamic school of poetry) that appear in the poem as neither references nor allusions, but *presences*. Like the Yorubán egungun mask, which invokes a family's ancestors and thus permits a temporary commingling of the dead with the living (Drewal 175), itself mentioned by Mackey in **"Song of the Andoumboulou: 12,"** the disparate elements brought together in the poem, be they from other times, cultures, or spiritual planes, cohabit in the poem's moment.

Robert Plant Armstrong describes what he terms "syndetic" processes as central to Yorubá culture. While synthesis involves the resolution of opposites, syndesis is marked by "accretion": rather than one meaning giving way to the next, the past to the present, and so on, contradictory meanings and moments add to one another (13). In his analysis of David Bradley's novel *The Chaneysville Incident,* Edward Pavlić not only argues that "West African syndetic processes are present in contemporary African American culture," but also uses Armstrong's analysis of syndesis to show how Bradley's novel posits a syndetic, "inter-subjective and improvisational" African American identity (167). This idea is easily extended to Mackey's poem, in which the collective subjectivity the poem's travelers seek is certainly syndetic, admitting noise, dissonance, indeterminacy, improvisation. In an interview, Mackey defines improvisation as "a metaphor for . . . processes of cultural and social revaluation (O'Leary 36), in other words, an interpretive process. Thus, Mackey's *Song of the Andoumboulou* might be productively viewed as more of a reading than a statement to be read, an engagement with the very process over which the trickster Esu rules, according to Gates: "the uncertainties of explication [. . .] a process that is never-ending and that is dominated by multiplicity" (21).

Reading the poem this way, as a kind of trickster discourse, makes it evident just how complex and, indeed, tricky, is the conception of collective identity posited by it. Mackey's invented word "Ouadada" first appears in **"Song of the Andoumboulou: 18"** of *Whatsaid Serif,* where it seems to refer to the first person plural:

> [. . .] Monophysite
> lament, one we, Ouadada, that
> we would include, not reduce to us . . .
> He to him, she to her, they to them,
>   opaque
> pronouns, "persons" whether or not we
> knew who they were . . .
>
>   (14)

Ouadada seems to be "one we," one version of collectivity, which the poem's speaker(s) "would include" but "not reduce" to an "us." It is a we-ness that allows or perhaps requires a certain amount of slippage, remaining evocative and open, inclusive of a range of cultural elements. The origins of the word are unknown, but it contains echoes consistent with the thematics of the poem as well as the poetics of its author: the oud, a North African lute, which already has a pronounced presence in *Song of the Andoumboulou,* is evoked in the word. Could "dada" be a reference to the European avant garde movement that so privileged nonsense play and has an important place in the lineage of experimental writing in which we must also place Mackey? And what about Ouadda, a city in the Central African Republic? The word "Ouadada" appears variously as a destination of sorts: in **"Song of the Andoumboulou: 20"** the speakers are "on our way to Ouadada," but uncertain about "when it would / be Ouadada" (*Whatsaid* 22-23). In **"Song of the Andoumboulou: 25,"** Oudada is simply "sought" (*Whatsaid* 45). Does Ouadada name a place? A state of being? Certainly the object of a quest, but one that shifts and morphs with each reference. In its third occurrence in **"Song of the Andoumboulou: 20,"** it names a kind of intimate contact or merging with the / an other(s): "the collective kiss we / called Ouadada" (*Whatsaid* 24).

However difficult it is to achieve or arrive at Ouadada, remaining as it does just out of reach throughout *Song of the Andoumboulou,* with trickster as guide, readers might begin to participate in the quest, to at least imagine the possibility of a collective cross-cultural identity that would allow "the incorporation of diversities into the psyche" (Ong 7) and thus move beyond the logics of "us and "them" so often underlying current conceptions of literary as well as social multiculturalism.

Works Cited

Armstrong, Robert Plant. *The Powers of Presence: Consciousness, Myth, and Affecting Presence.* Philadelphia: U Pennsylvania P, 1981.

Blaeser, Kimberly M. *Gerald Vizenor: Writing in the Oral Tradition.* Norman OK: U of Oklahoma P, 1996.

Donahue, Joseph. "Sprung Polity: On Nathanial Mackey's Recent Work." *Talisman* 9 (1992): 62-65.

Drewal, Henry John, John Pemberton III, and Rowland Abiodun. *Yorubá: Nine Centuries of African Art and Thought.* New York: Center for African Art, 1989.

Edwards, Brent Hayes. "Notes on Poetics Regarding Mackey's *Song.*" *Callaloo* 23.2 (2000): 572-91.

Gates, Henry Louis, Jr. *The Signifying Monkey: A Theory of African-American Literary Criticism.* New York: Oxford UP, 1988.

Gray, Jeffrey. "'Beyond the Letter': Identity, Song, and *Strick.*" *Callaloo* 23.2 (2000): 621-39.

Griaule, Marcel. *Conversations with Ogotemmêli: An Introduction to Dogon Religious Ideas.* Trans. R. Butler, et al. New York: Oxford UP, 1965.

Hoover, Paul. "Pair of Figures for Eshu . . ." *Callaloo* 23.2 (2000): 728-48.

Hyde, Lewis. *Trickster Makes This World: Mischief, Myth, and Art.* New York: Farrar, 1998.

Mackey, Nathaniel. *Bedouin Hornbook.* Lexington KY: Callaloo Fiction Series, 1986.

———. *Discrepant Engagement: Dissonance, Cross-Culturality, and Experimental Writing.* Tuscaloosa: U of Alabama P, 1993.

———. *Djobot Baghostus's Run.* Los Angeles: Sun and Moon, 1993.

———. *Eroding Witness.* Urbana: U of Illinois P, 1984.

———. "An Interview with Nathaniel Mackey." By Edward Foster. *Talisman* 9 (1992): 48-61.

———. "An Interview with Nathaniel Mackey." By Paul Naylor. *Callaloo* 23.2 (2000): 645-63.

———. "An Interview with Nathaniel Mackey." By Peter O'Leary. *Chicago Review* 43.1 (1997): 30-46.

———and Art Lange, eds. *Moment's Notice: Jazz in Poetry and Prose.* Minneapolis MN: Coffee House, 1993.

———. *School of Udhra.* San Francisco: City Lights, 1993.

————. *Strick: Song of the Andoumboulou 16-25*. With Royal Hartigan and Hafez Modirzadeh. Spoken Engine, 7 90807 16252 9, 1995.

————. *Whatsaid Serif*. San Francisco: City Lights, 1998.

Naylor, Paul. *Poetic Investigations: Singing the Holes in History*. Evanston IL: Northwestern UP, 1999.

Nielson, Aldon Lynn. *Black Chant: Languages of African-American Postmodernism*. Cambridge UK: Cambridge UP, 1997.

Ong, Walter. "Introduction: On Saying We and Us to Literature." *Three American Literatures: Essays in Chicano, Native American, and Asian-American Literature for Teachers of American Literature*. Ed. Houston A. Baker, Jr. New York: MLA, 1982. 3-7.

Pavlić, Edward. "Syndetic Redemption: Above-Underground *Emergence* in David Bradley's *The Chaneysville Incident*." *African American Review* 30.2 (1996): 165-84.

Pelton, Robert D. *The Trickster in West Africa: A Study of Mythic Irony and Sacred Delight*. Berkeley: U of California P, 1980.

Smith, Jeanne Rosier. *Writing Tricksters: Mythic Gambols in American Ethnic Literature*. Berkeley: U of California P, 1997.

Vizenor, Gerald. "Trickster Discourse: Comic Holotropes and Language Games." *Narrative Chance: Postmodern Discourse on Native American Indian Literatures*. Ed. Gerald Vizenor. Norman: U of Oklahoma P, 1989. 187-211.

Wiget, Andrew. "His Life in His Tail: The Native American Trickster and the Literature of Possibility." *Redefining American Literary History*. Ed. A. LaVonne Brown Ruoff and Jerry W. Ward, Jr. New York: MLA, 1990. 83-96.

J. Edward Mallot (essay date spring 2004)

SOURCE: Mallot, J. Edward. "Sacrificial Limbs, Lambs, Iambs, and I Ams: Nathaniel Mackey's Mythology of Loss." *Contemporary Literature* 45, no. 1 (spring 2004): 135-64.

[*In this essay, Mallot argues that the multivolume* From a Broken Bottle Traces of Perfume Still Emanate *"seems to reject classification of any order, preferring to revel in the possibilities—more than in the full realizations—of a text that offers letters, song lyrics, convoluted diagrams, and accounts of dreams that rattle and hum meanings, a cacophony that somehow sounds correct."*]

> Perhaps Wilson Harris is right. There are musics which haunt us like a phantom limb. Thus the abrupt breaking off. Therefore the "of course." No more than the ache

of some such would-be extension. Still, I'm not so sure anymore. I'm not so sure all this recent insistence of mine on absence isn't couvade after all. (Please don't tell me you told me so.)

Nathaniel Mackey, ***Bedouin Hornbook***

Nathaniel Mackey's ***Bedouin Hornbook*** rejects easy classification, despite the temptation to screw the text into preexisting sets of literary acceptance. There are genres which haunt us, to echo Mackey's protagonist N., like phantom limits; thus the gentle slide into academic pigeonholing, therefore the "of course that's what it is." Poetic in sound and image, the ***Hornbook*** is not poetry. While novelesque in narrative scope and concern, the text does not follow the parameters of a conventional novel, opting instead to slip within N.'s ongoing correspondence, a half exchange that, at best, half answers a handful of issues before the book concludes. Mackey himself shies away from referring to his multivolume ***From a Broken Bottle Traces of Perfume Still Emanate*** as "novels," telling Paul Naylor, "For a long time I was uncomfortable with them being called fiction and with the individual volumes being called novels, but I eventually got used to it" ("Interview" [Naylor] 651). To dismiss the argument of genre by claiming the ***Hornbook*** an epistolary fiction is to ignore a number of features of this narrative type. First, the lack of authorial intrusion in an epistolary work grants an immediacy of experience with those who "author" the letters, so much so that the reader may suffer from the absence of an omniscient viewpoint; in Mackey's text the question of distance between Mackey himself and the "N." that writes the letters is constantly up for reexamination. Not surprisingly, Mackey offers scant explanation of how to distinguish between N. and Nathaniel: "N. and I have some things in common. We overlap. . . . Shared experiences. Some shared proclivities" ("Interview" [O'Leary] 46). Second, the tone of the text suggests an interchange of thought between N. and the recipient of the letters, the remarkably ambiguous Angel of Dust, without providing either the Angel's letters or much assurance that interchange is actually taking place. Ultimately, the text seems to reject classification of any order, preferring to revel in the possibilities—more than in the full realizations—of a text that offers letters, song lyrics, convoluted diagrams, and accounts of dreams that rattle and hum meanings, a cacophony that somehow sounds correct.

Joseph Allen, attempting to find a prevailing structure to the multivolume work, argues: "The letters blur boundaries between fiction and theory, narration and critique, presence and absence, music and discourse. N., as well as the reader, must create theoretical cultural fictions to fill the perceived gaps of meaning among the letters" (205). The words demand such an aggressive mode of interpretation, in part, precisely because the Angel remains absent, a felt presence at every turn but with no speaking role. This silence seems appropriate for a text obsessed with absence, challenging its characters to see "what isn't there" and to examine the means by which something is both instantly lost and constantly found. That we feel we have lost something recalls N.'s "ache of some such would-be extension" (**Hornbook** 1); remove enough layers, however, disentangle enough knots, and the past—or the present, or the memory, or whatever "phantom limbs" we're seeking—may yet be found. Thus the plays on homonyms and synesthetic puns; therefore the "of course" of recognition sudden and sweeping. Interestingly, it is loss that makes possible the slippages between memory and rememory, between death and rebirth, between isolation and communion. This loss is often a transubstantiation of experience that presents metonymy in reincarnated form, as if the spirit of the amputated figure drifts to a new mode, or "plane," of expression.

The suggestion of reality as a palimpsest of planes of possibility—each true at any given moment, with emphasis placed on the gaps between states as much as the states themselves—recalls the "thousand plateaus" model posited by French philosophers Gilles Deleuze and Félix Guattari. All meaning, according to this model, rests on relation, the collision of planes of possibility that erode as they shift past each other. Extraneous factors can complicate or make impossible otherwise desirable connection; in Mackey's case, these factors include distance, language, physicality, social constraints, and death. To "kill off" these constraints allows for more direct communication, and in the **Hornbook** sacrifice predicates survival. That something has been severed, importantly, does not mean that it remains forever inaccessible, but that it becomes another absent layer in the palimpsest of our existence, a phantom limb or lamb or iamb that replaces the real arm or body or word we knew before. Indeed, the introduction of a phantom limb, physical or textual or otherwise, may strengthen the body as a whole—the Angel of Dust may, arguably, assume a more potent narrative stance in silence; the protagonist may gain more potential with a name that's only a letter.

The plateau model works for Mackey's project in a number of ways. Musically, the model functions as a scale, the evocation of a single note the implication of an entire scale: one hears the note C but infers D, E, and so forth. Meaning is only truly generated either by the acknowledgment of the entire chord or by charting the progression of notes along a scale. Mackey's penchant for adding a capital *D* to names that begin with *J*—a device fully exploited in the **Hornbook**'s sequel, ***Djbot Baghostus's Run***—reflects what can happen when a prior plane is revisited; molecules can shift over time and place, generating an altered past that suffers mediation but, nevertheless, refuses to disappear entirely. As bodies can possess phantom limbs, Mackey's thousand plateaus include phantom planes, levels of meaning and discourse that remain temporarily silent only to reassert themselves later, a percussive undercurrent never heard but always there.

Still, Deleuze and Guattari's plateaus project fails to fully explain Mackey's epistolary enterprise. The original model resembles a stack of parallel planes, but N. finds that his world is not a smooth, regular series of strata. Instead, his sense of order can become complicated by any number of outside pressures, including individual grief, collective infighting, racial discrimination, public rejection, distance, time, and history. These separate problems suggest that the texture of reality is much rougher than in a smooth, striated model, as each of these "outside pressures" can add another "plane" from various angles. The result, for N., is not a stack of planes but a geometric nightmare, a crazy quilt of self and environment. It is perhaps this texture of the problem of loss and recovery that leads Mackey to refer to his work as weaving, as warp and weft seeking a kinship but remaining, simultaneously, discrete threads. If the **Hornbook** and the **Run** are, indeed, indicative of a thousand plateaus, one might conclude that these planes *intersect each other,* complicating the goal of recovery but expanding the potential of something strange and wonderful in its own creaky creation.

SOMETHING LOST

The first sentence of **Bedouin Hornbook**—"You should've heard me in the dream last night" (1)—assumes familiarity with both "you" and "me." In truth, we know neither. It seems shocking—given that the entire volume is written by N., given N.'s tendency to go on and on about himself, betraying his hopes and fears and insecurities, given his apparent project of writing as a kind of intellectual catharsis—how little we actually know about the narrator. One may assume that N. is male, that N. is black, that N. is heterosexual, that N. is part of a jazz-blues band, that N. is somewhat talented; but these "facts" are ultimately only assumptions. We cannot even claim N.'s name. If anything, the **Hornbook**'s opening words suggest the degree to which the narrator relies on an exchange of discourse, even though that exchange seems undercut by the Angel of Dust's absence. This nonpresence opens a wide variety of possible identities for the letters' recipient. It also places the reader in literary terrain virtually impossible to navigate: we have a writer we do not know, communicating to a blank recipient we neither see nor hear. We have word, but no world; text, but little context.

Furthermore, the relationship between the two is unquestionably complicated. One gathers as much from the opening section alone, which ends with N. edging toward severance:

> I'm not at all sure this won't be the last letter you'll receive from me. As much as I hate to say so, this dialogue of ours seems hopelessly enmeshed in the very "ontology of loss" of which you've insisted I disburden myself. I know I've been known to cut you loose be-

fore, but this time I think I really mean it. I'll send tapes of the band, of course, but please don't expect anything more in the way of words.

Love, N.

(3)

The suggestion of tapes to follow and the closing "Love" should signal that this break may be only temporary, and indeed some ten months later N. will resume contact, opening the **Hornbook**'s second letter with an apology: "I'm sorry to have taken so long answering your letter, though I'd have thought you'd be the last person to be bothered by those sorts of questions" (4). This will hardly be the first time N. feels compelled to apologize for a lapse in communication; a quick survey of the dated epistles demonstrates that exchange either flowed heavily or hardly at all. **Djbot Baghostus's Run** begins on a similar note: "Sorry to've taken so long getting back to you. I've been meaning to write for some time but it seems one thing or another has managed to get in the way. . . . For the time being, though, I prefer not to talk too directly about what I'm doing" (7). While N. frequently apologizes for his failure to connect, later in the **Run** he'd "begun to wonder why I hadn't heard from you for so long" (48). That N. maintains a dialogue with the Angel is important, for he relies on the Angel as audience and critic. Letters frequently end with a request akin to "Tell me what you think" (**Hornbook** 16), only to complain in other segments that "(here you can say you told me so again)" (**Hornbook** 17). At certain points N. clearly feels that the Angel not only misunderstands him but unfairly manipulates his ideas; at other points he feels an absolute affinity: "Thank you for the tape. It's as though we shared a single set of ears. It's not only that I'd already heard the piece you sent (I have the record it's on in fact), but it's the very cut I like most on the album" (**Hornbook** 138). N. and the Angel even read the same texts simultaneously, pondering the same questions: "I too was puzzled by the passage you point out in Bastide's book" (**Run** 74).

One could, arguably, infer from the name of his correspondent that N.'s letters are transcripts of drug-induced states, the Angel a muse of abuse that guides his intellectual "trip." That the Angel never speaks, lacks a "name," appears with inconsistent frequency, and is, at times, sworn off by N. suggests that the Angel may reflect an addiction and not an individual. Alternatively, one could just as easily argue that the Angel is a more traditional type of muse, one that creates magic out of dust, visits the recipient of divine art—in this case, N.—and returns to dust at the conclusion of N.'s "song." This would hold particular weight in the context of Mackey's ongoing poetry series **Song of the Andoumboulou,** where N. confers with the muse during the construction of his songs. Then again, the Angel could stand in for a specific outside friend and critic of Mackey's work, one helpful enough to garner the epi-

thet "angel" while granted anonymity within the published text. The Angel could, obliquely, refer to Mackey's readers, the text then a dialogue with the readership in which Mackey's replies are supplied entirely in advance. Finally, Mackey could be conversing with himself, an example of what he might call "autoconstitutive stress" (**Hornbook** 61), in which a writer must rely on metadiscourse to make true progress.

Regardless of what self-referentiality might be traced in the letters, Mackey seems to insist that the Angel figure represents a need to reconnect with others, particularly individuals from the past:

> I acknowledge in the very first of the Angel of Dust letters . . . the correspondence, the letter form, the sense of being in conversation with the dead . . . that one is writing beyond one's self or at least aspiring to write beyond one's self. . . . You know, in language we inherit the voices of the dead. Language is passed on to us by people who are now in their graves and brings with it access to history, tradition, times and places that are not at all immediate to our own immediate and particular occasion whether we look at it individually and personally or whether we look at it in a more collective way and talk about a specific community.
>
> ("Interview" [Foster] 54)

The palimpsest that becomes the Angel of Dust—the layers of possibility that refuse to collapse into a simple, static entity—parallels the realms of communication that can and do permeate our daily lives, involving the living and the dead, the seen and the invisible. Curiously, to enter this palimpsest of communication requires both a wandering from the self and a dialogue with others. The latter is usually attained through song; while we may perform a solo, we engage in a tonal affinity by entering a realm of shared sound, playing to an audience that, although sometimes invisible, is always attentive. Mackey opens the **Song of the Andoumboulou** sessions with a curiously self-reflexive assertion: "The song says the / dead will not / ascend without song" (**Eroding Witness** 33). Dream sections of the **Hornbook,** like many of the performances, underscore the notion of songs as séances, either direct or inferred. The coexistence of the there and not there becomes at one point expressed in the musical paraphrasing practice of "dubbing": "In fact, the alternation between absence and availability, the evocation of something there but not there that one gets from 'dub,' was very much what Shango seemed to be after—a skeletal promise or a spectral insistence of a sort that the organ seemed to be played by a ghost" (**Hornbook** 87). In this light, N.'s opening words in the **Hornbook** might be not only a wishful longing for the Angel's company but a simple statement of fact. If the Angel represents both the dead and the living, who conquer verbal and physical distance to achieve a constant, if not constantly obvious, communion, the figure should have "heard me in the dream last night."

Because the dead seem irrevocably tied to the power of music performance, those who seek to communicate through the conduits of voice and instrument must offer a form of personal sacrifice. Pain bears promise, and N. eventually wonders if the pain in his brow—presumably caused by cowrie shells lodged in his head—is somehow necessary for his music to shine: "Are the attacks a self-sentencing conviction the music fosters and feeds, even if only as the occasion for a reprieve? Are self-sentencing conviction and self-commuting sentence merely symbiotic halves of a self-cycling ordeal? Do I knock myself down in order to be picked up?" (**Run** 18). The cowrie-shell pains are the latest in a long line of references to pain as the occasion of birth and rebirth, of bodily harm as the mechanism that allows the music and the dead to speak. The image of bloodletting as that which causes the pen to fountain occurs in the **Hornbook**'s opening letter, where N.'s "thinking hovered around the figure of a cloth-enshrouded, enormously protective Thigh. The needle pricked a vein and what blood flowed out was an ending, the ending of a song I went on to write" (14). The concept of veins as reflective of a continuum, a linearity of music and time, is echoed in the opening chapter of the **Run**:

> In this, of course, he works the vein opened up by such people as Milford Graves, Sunny Murray and Rashied Ali. And by "vein" I mean exactly that, for what he does (or so it seemed to me that night) is insist upon a hemorrhaging, a dilation of one's way of looking at time. What struck me most was his playing's apparently absent yet all the more convincing regard for linearity, his having collapse and consolidation, qualm and quanta, find their way to one another.
>
> (8)

A vein opening to allow a song to be heard conveys several messages at once: that both the dead and their song are somehow within us; that their appearance requires some loss, whether of bodily or psychological self, on our part; that music floats above bodies, space, and time. Images of blood and sacrifice become more fully realized in the composition N. entitles "Meat of My Brother's Thigh." The story concerns two brothers starving in the forest. To ensure that his brother can finish the journey, the elder secretly cuts away and serves part of his own thigh. Upon finding their way out, the younger realizes the sacrifice his brother has made and vows to serve him forever (**Hornbook** 89). Assuming that the elder brother symbolizes those people like Graves, Murray, and Ali as well as writing influences such as Wilson Harris and Amiri Baraka, N./Mackey opens up veins not only to the muse of poetry but to the muses of artistic ancestry as well. Sacrifice pays homage to the past, provides food for the present, and preserves ground for the future.

Barry Powell's work on ancient myths around the world suggests that sacrificial motifs—including castration and circumcision—indicate a transcultural belief that death was a prerequisite to life, that a pruning of the human body generated a smaller, tighter, more productive whole: "[F]or many peoples, sacrifice was necessary to appease the divine powers that ruled the world. Human beings were felt to be in debt to the gods and to the angry ghosts, who had to be bought off at any price. The value of sacrifice was gauged by the pain it caused those who made it" (220-21). Powell concludes, "the continuing fertility of the earth cannot be separated from the inevitable presence of death" (237). Indeed, myths from Greece, Rome, ancient Africa, and pre-Christian Mesopotamia all share, though in variegated forms, rituals of sacrifice, practiced for a multiplicity of ends: to ensure a good harvest, to guarantee success in war, to save mankind. Osiris, an Egyptian god referenced in Mackey's prose, stands as a ready example. He manages to procreate after death; his postmortem, ubiquitous phallus ensures political power for the pharaoh; his coffin grants the world continual prosperity, bought at the expense of Osiris's own death and his wife's grief.

Osiris is not the only African figure to transmit energy and prosperity after death. Mackey's attention to "the creaking of the word" in Marcel Griaule's *Conversations with Ogotemmêli* reflects an extended, complex relationship between N.'s letters and basic tenets of the Dogon peoples. A number of Ogotemmêli's teachings find echoes in the **Hornbook,** including the transformation from sacrifice to survival. As Griaule explains:

> In all its different forms, whether of consecration, expiation, divination, purification, upholding the invisible or securing salvation for one's self, sacrifice for the Dogon had one unchanging effect—the redistribution of life-force.
>
> But it was not simply a matter of taking a victim's life-force to put it somewhere else, or to increase the life-force of some other being, visible or invisible. The object was rather to create a movement of forces within a circuit composed of the sacrificer, the victim, the altar and the power invoked.
>
> (131)

Although the Dogon model presents relatively static representations for the "nouns"—the victim, the altar, and so forth—it still requires rather liquid "verbs" for the magic and message to arise from Griaule's "circuit." Intriguingly, these verbs take the very forms Mackey uses in sections such as "Meat of My Brother's Thigh"—bleeding and speaking. In Dogon rituals of sacrifice, Griaule continues,

> At the critical moment, that is to say, when the blood flows, the man utters a prayer, by which he invokes the power, for example the Nummo, and explains what he is doing. The prayer is spoken aloud. It is therefore itself an expulsion of force, which follows the lines of the breath issuing from the speaker's mouth. This force

serves, in the first place, to arouse the Nummo and, in the second place, to direct the force that flows from the wounded throat of the victim and pours out on to the altar.

(131)

If the sacrificed, sacrificed by, and sacrificed to provide what Griaule terms a "circuit" of transformation, blood and speech provide the conduits by which transformation occurs. Something lost, something gained: Mackey's epistolary works, in a fashion somewhat mysterious and somewhat metafictive, enact the same formula. The Dogon rituals of sacrifice, stripped of their precise, original context, become resurrected in a more universal form, one gained through N.'s willingness to pour out literal and metaphoric blood. In Mackey's interpretation, "[i]t's a transformation":

> And it's a case in point of the fact that these traditions—the mythology, the lore—are not being gone to as some kind of fixed, given entity that one then has to have a subservient relationship to. They are active and unfinished; they are subject to change; they are themselves in the process of transformation and transition. They speak to an open and open-ended possibility that the poetics that I've been involved in very much speaks to as well. To see cracks and incompleteness as not only inevitable but opportune.
>
> ("Interview" [O'Leary] 35)

Within the *Hornbook,* the something-lost-something-gained equation works in a number of ways. The pain of separation from a loved one becomes the occasion for song. The sacrifice of opening up a vein or "opening up" on a page becomes the catharsis necessary for genuine expression. The missing letters on a wall of graffiti become, for one of N.'s fellow musicians, an "enabling confusion concerning the singular and the plural," a "vacillation between the claims of the one and the counterclaims of the other" (*Hornbook* 26); for another, this same wall of grammatical errata becomes "an invitation into an area of *un*common sense, and . . . the dislocations they visited upon so-called proper English were manifestly of an invasive, mediumistic order" (27). That something becomes verbally missing does not diminish the power of the message; if anything, the remaining phonemes and phonics gain areas of potential power, exploring what isn't said by refusing to utter it. This may explain, to some extent, the silence of the Angel; by not allowing the recipient of the letters to reply directly, Mackey may be offering volumes of commentary in its wake. Certainly, the Angel's present nonpresence opens up a number of interpretive options, each expanding the text's ability to "speak."

Harryette Mullen, on the other hand, sees in the Angel's silence a much more politically charged statement, one in which absence is a gesture toward the oppression that has silenced African Americans for generations:

> The accumulated images of castration/amputation in *Bedouin Hornbook* are related to the persistent association of African Americans with both coerced silence

and strategic inarticulateness, although what Mackey investigates is the relative stress placed on either articulation or disarticulation as oppositional values within and between cultures. The discursive representation of the African as *alogos* in Western culture becomes, for Mackey, the background of a series of meditations on music, myth, mastery, and masculinity. Just as the individual seeking through literacy to distinguish himself from the "voiceless" mass learns the value of secrecy and indiscretion . . . so also the need, within traditional black communities, to shroud African spirituality in secrecy has contributed to the elusiveness, evasiveness, and enigmatic quality of African cultural practices in regard to a Western context of misunderstanding, oppression, and often deliberate distortion.

(37-38)

Like Baraka and Ishmael Reed before him, Mackey engages in occasionally optioned silence and coerced grammar to create an impression that challenges the world order of the word. For Mullen, "The supposed lack of precision associated with aesthetic and spiritual traditions of the African diaspora is transformed into a positive value, rather than a deficit. What might sound like faulty grammar or blurred pronunciation of standard English is . . . accurate in its signification of a profound difference in world view" (39). Self-sacrifice of word and gesture becomes, for Mackey, more than an outward motive; the cut and the shift stretch toward both cultural and personal bounds, while testing the limits of aesthetic expression. If poetry, according to Mackey's collection of essays *Discrepant Engagement,* represents "language owning up to being an orphan" (234), it is music that both mourns and heals. Song becomes "wounded kinship's last resort . . . [it] bears witness to what is left out of that concept of reality, or, if not exactly what, to the fact that something *is* left out" (232).

One useful exploration of music as an acknowledgment of something lost and something gained can be gleaned from N.'s meditations on the falsetto, a manner of singing in which the primary voice is deliberately muted to allow a higher register to take precedence, as if the lower key is sacrificed to recover it. "What is it in the falsetto," N. asks, "that thins and threatens to abolish the voice but the wear of so much reaching for heaven?" (*Hornbook* 52). N. begins to think of the falsetto in terms of the moan or shout, two methods of speaking that manage to convey more in their wordlessness than more conventionally articulate methods could accomplish: "Like the moan or the shout, I'm suggesting, the falsetto explores a redemptive, unworded realm—a meta-word, if you will—where the implied critique or the momentary eclipse of the word curiously rescues, restores and renews it: new word, new world" (*Hornbook* 52). If history, as the Angel suggests, is merely a "manner of speaking," N. could hardly be accused of "trying to out-shout or shut history up" (*Hornbook* 70); a more complicated politics of voice and message is involved than simply offering a counterdiscourse. On a psychological level, to begin, the falsetto reminds us of our other selves, our other avenues of language and song, which were always inside us but rarely outside.

The troubling of the voice precipitated by the invocation of the falsetto echoes a second phantom voice, the duende, defined by Mackey as "a conversation with the dead, intimacy with death and with the dead" ("Cante Moro" 197), one that only occurs when the possibility of death becomes evident. "The word *duende*," he explains, "means spirit, a kind of gremlin, a gremlinlike, troubling spirit. One of the things that marks the arrival of *duende* in flamenco singing is a sound of trouble in the voice. The voice becomes troubled. Its eloquence becomes eloquence of another order, a broken, problematic, self-problematizing eloquence" (195). Mackey turns to the work of Federico García Lorca to more fully explain the sacrifice required and potential promised in evoking duende. One section of García Lorca's *Deep Song and Other Prose* describes a flamenco singer who, although technically sound, fails to truly affect her audience, a limitation she can overcome only by sacrificing tonality for more textual depth:

> As though crazy, torn like a medieval weeper, La Niña de los Peines got to her feet, tossed off a big glass of firewater and began to sing with a scorched throat, without voice, without breath or color, but with *duende*. She was able to kill all the scaffolding of the song and leave way for a furious, enslaving *duende*, friend of sand winds, who made the listeners rip their clothes with the same rhythm as do the blacks of the Antilles when, in the "lucumí" rite, they huddle in heaps before the statue of Santa Bárbara.
>
> (45-46; qtd. by Mackey, **"Cante Moro"** 196)

Mackey elaborates:

> Lorca does not so much define *duende* as grope after it, wrestle with it, evoke it through strain, insist on struggle. He says, for example, that "one must awaken the *duende* in the remotest mansions of the blood." He says that "the *duende* loves the rim of the wound" and that it "draws near places where forms fuse together into a yearning superior to their visible expression." He writes, "Each art has a *duende* different in form and style but their roots all meet in the place where the black sounds of Manuel Torre come from—the essence, the uncontrollable, quivering, common base of wood, sound, canvas, and word."
>
> (**"Cante Moro"** 196-97)

Again, concepts of sacrifice find their potency from death itself. Both the literal word and the corporeal body suffer, bleed, even disappear entirely in order to find a modified, more energized form in reincarnation. For Richard Quinn, "*Duende* appears as the recouping of loss, a re-establishment of multiform collectivity. Absence, loss, limping, and impairment become abundance rather than deficit" (618). In this sense, the "absent" elements of N.'s letters become way stations of

physical and psychic potency, generating multiplicity by killing singularity. The abandonment of the static body and word allows a host of tangential relations to sing along; the falsetto and the duende produce not synonyms but symbiosis:

> This wooing of another voice, an alternate voice, that is so important to duende has as one of its aspects or analogs in poetry that state of entering the language in such a way that one is into an area of implication, resonance, and connotation that is manifold, many-meaninged, polysemous. One has worked beyond oneself. It is as if the language itself takes over. Something beyond the will, the conscious design or desire of the poet, is active, something that goes beyond univocal, unequivocal control. . . . Bound reference, univocal meaning, is no solution to the riddle of language.
>
> (**"Cante Moro"** 199)

This "riddle" challenges the reader to acknowledge that what is not is part of what is, that the seeming opposite actually reflects teeming homonyms of sound and sense.

In a similar vein, the members of the band discuss the relative worth of searching for a drummer, one that will provide an undercurrent for the others. The men of the group will spend a great deal of time in the **Run** dreaming of the mystical Djeannine, a shared dream-answer to a shared band problem. Aunt Nancy, on the other hand, argues near the end of the **Hornbook** that such a search is essentially unnecessary, that percussion is constantly taking place, "that the absence and/or presence of the drum could never be taken literally, that either was also the other as a genetically dislocated aspect of itself. This, she insisted, was the heterodox beauty of our conception, the hybrid (as against 'highbred') pedigree of our percussive concept, the resiliency which made such retrieval as Lambert proposed altogether redundant, not to say absurd" (134). Acknowledging that opposites are simply the flip side of "this side," the **Run** takes up the question of the relationship of opposites, of whether flip side is highly integral to the present state or only occasionally relevant; the inability to decide leaves N. muttering "flipside so near so far" (45) over and over again. What remains clear is that opposites are what make us whole, that absences make the present felt more sincerely, that the past is always with us and will catch up with us over the history of our futures. Sacrifice and pain can make us more acutely aware of what has been lost and what remains to be recovered. This does not mean that N. exhorts his audience to undergo self-mutilation for aesthetic gain, what the Angel calls "a thinly veiled romance of distantiation." Rather, sacrifice symbolizes what N. calls a "'broken' claim to connection" (**Hornbook** 34), a fragmented whole that speaks both to the entire group and to each disjointed member. Here, N. visualizes the collection of parts as a "rickety bridge (sometimes a rickety boat)," the planks claiming at once a kinship with each other and a uniqueness of their own, an object that creaks its group song of longing and togetherness. N. begins to see himself as somehow floating above the texture of the rickety boat: "I felt my anchorlessness as a lack, as an inured, eventually visible pit up from which I floated, looking down on what debris looking into it left" (*Hornbook* 34). N. has now assumed the role of the book's title—the Bedouin unattached to an overly deterministic sense of place, time, identity, or meaning, a wanderer of art and semantics. What remains to be learned from the *Hornbook* is the meaning of the title's second word—what information can be gleaned from a hornbook for the wanderer, how that information can be accessed, and whether this "primer" is a self-contained unit or dependent on the reader-wanderer's ability to see what else might be contained. According to Mackey, this process must come from recognizing and reclaiming a sense of the in-between:

> The dynamic quality of a tone is a statement of its incompleteness, its will to completion. To hear a tone as dynamic quality, as a direction, a pointing, means hearing at the same time beyond it, beyond it in the direction of its will, and going toward the expected next tone. . . . We are always *between* the tones, *on the way* from tone to tone; our hearing does not remain with the tone, it reaches through it and beyond it.
>
> . . . (how much does "limb" have to do with "liminal"?)
>
> (*Hornbook* 15-16)

SOMETHING GAINED

Consistently, *Bedouin Hornbook* and *Djbot Baghostus's Run* present music as a tiered process of becoming—even in repeated performances of the same piece—rather than a fixed, static identity. Little wonder that music is commonly referred to as arrangement; the argument, according to N.'s band, is that the process of moving the molecules of music gives each note an electric, temporal charge, one that gains its strength only in relation to other notes. The musicians draw this conclusion when they read John Miller Chernoff's *African Rhythm and African Sensibility*:

> [Aunt Nancy's] preoccupation with "absence" and "presence" (more exactly with a coupling or a structured cohabiting of one with the other) no doubt recognized its pedigree in such passages as this: *"The music is perhaps best considered as an arrangement of gaps where one may add a rhythm, rather than as a dense pattern of sound. In the conflict of the rhythms, it is the space between the notes from which the dynamic tension comes, and it is the silence which constitutes the musical form as much as does the sound"* (Chernoff's emphasis).
>
> I was even more struck by the point the book makes to the effect that polyrhythmic drumming implies an absent, additional rhythm, a furtive beat one's listening supplies or one's dancing echoes.
>
> (*Hornbook* 144-45)

But while "[p]olyrhythmicity accents absence" (*Hornbook* 145), it's absence that makes polyrythmicity possible, a symbiosis of sound and silence that allows

each to exploit its individual power. The silences are golden, pregnant pauses that generate possibilities for the next note. Chernoff argues in his groundbreaking study that well-constructed rhythms in African music deliberately contain "absence" in order to foster a more collective "presence": "A good rhythm, if it is to enhance itself, should both fill a gap in the other rhythms and create an emptiness that may be similarly filled" (114). If another performer fails to fill this gap, the audience may do so themselves; in fact, "[i]n African music, it is the listener or dancer who has to supply the beat: the listener must be *actively engaged* in making sense of the music" (50). Everything in African music, from participants to rhythms to individual notes, gains its power only in the context of everything (and everyone) around it; gaps are not losses but invitations. Thus the "plane" each musical note occupies can never gain full autonomy, but merely a relational reality by means of the other notes; we may think we hear a single note but always mentally register an entire chord.

Mackey illustrates his chord-within-a-note concept at various points in the *Run,* as band members and audiences suddenly awake to the realization that repetition has birthed multiplicity. One example concerns Frank Wright, who performs "a tuneless, ultra-out wall of sound (no head, no recognizable structure), a raucous, free-for-all cacophony which at times had the feel of an assault" (61). During the intermission, Aunt Nancy asks him to play "China":

> [He] said, "No problem." The second set, however, went just like the first, equally tuneless, equally nonstop, equally without a head or a recognizable structure, coming nowhere near the melody line of "China." The one difference was that about forty-five minutes into the set Wright let the tenor fall from his mouth and hang by its strap, cupped his hands in front of his mouth like a megaphone and yelled, "China! China! China!" He then took the tenor back to his mouth for another twenty or so no-letup minutes of squeaks, honks, moans, growls and screeches.
>
> (62)

Wright's composition, like all song, encloses every song within its invisible range; the audience may only hear certain notes but unconsciously recognizes the continuum of music as a piece unfolds. For Jarred Bottle, the chord of sound also includes place and sex: his girlfriend has recently become infatuated with a woman named China. That he and Aunt Nancy are composing a piece entitled "Not Here, No There" speaks to the world of difference—and, at other moments, the absolute irrelevancy—of tones and places. We hear a single note, but synesthetically we experience a world. Wright's performance reverberates in N.'s monotonous "letter to the world" near the close of the *Run*:

> I began by playing the same note, C, over and over again, a back-to-basics move or approach by way of which I underscored my start from scratch. I jumped

octaves and varied placement and duration but the only note I played was C. I played it long, I played it short, I played it staccato, I played it spaced, I played it soft, I played it loud. C was my letter to the world.

The world's reply was at first a cool one, almost no reply at all.

(178-79)

"The world" follows by bringing out, en masse, 3-D glasses to wear, the answer to N.'s single tone (although expressed in a chord of possible expressions) a chord of their own. The communion is not, importantly, a one-to-one correspondence, but an addition—or, more accurately, a recognition—of a simultaneous, parallel plane of thought.

Literary critics have already begun to theorize Mackey's works as systems of multiple planes; Adalaide Morris, for example, considers his writing "stereoscopic," "that is, like the optical instrument which creates three-dimensional illusions by bringing into a single focus photographs of the same scene taken from slightly different angles. The flash of depth—the stereoscopic moment—occurs in the instant the viewer's eye makes one picture out of two or more angles" (749). Somewhat similarly, David C. Kress suggests that Mackey's works again and again concern "the potential multiplicity of thought" (765) and the process of "becoming" (766). Kress even turns briefly to Deleuze and Guattari, who emphasize the vast promise of the rhizome (775). Indeed, the French philosophers' own multivolume project, entitled *Capitalism and Schizophrenia,* shares much more with Mackey's prose than what Kress's analysis affords. *A Thousand Plateaus* opens, appropriately, with what appears to be a schizophrenic musical composition, a scale of jagged lines and wild loops that run over the page. Deleuze and Guattari's gesture speaks not only to the incompleteness of any one note in a chord of possible meanings but to the essential notion of movement along notes as that which generates meaning, a meaning constantly bound to notions of relativity. The crazy arcs and vectors that seem to distort the scale actually give it clarity, explaining the messy process of becoming, the journey to realization that music embraces. Each note, each horizontal bar of the scale represents a mode of thinking; meaning is generated in the space between the two. The French philosophers verbally describe their project as a study of plateaus of engagement:

> For example, a book composed of chapters has culmination and termination points. What takes place in a book composed instead of plateaus that communicate with one another across microfissures, as in a brain? We call a "plateau" any multiplicity connected to other multiplicities by superficial underground stems in such a way as to form or extend a rhizome. We are writing this book as a rhizome. It is composed of plateaus. . . . Each morning we would wake up, and each of us would ask himself what plateau he was going to tackle, writing five lines here, ten there. We had hallucinatory ex-

periences, we watched lines leave one plateau and proceed to another like columns of tiny ants. We made circles of convergence. Each plateau can be read starting anywhere and can be related to any other plateau.

(22)

Translator Brian Massumi, in somewhat similarly convoluted fashion, explains:

> In Deleuze and Guattari, a plateau is reached when circumstances combine to bring an activity to a pitch of intensity that is not automatically dissipated in a climax. The heightening of energies is sustained long enough to leave a kind of afterimage of its dynamism that can be reactivated or injected into other activities, creating a fabric of intensive states between which any number of connecting routes could exist. Each section of *A Thousand Plateaus* tries to combine conceptual bricks in such a way as to construct this kind of intensive state of thought. The way the combination is made is an example of what Deleuze and Guattari call consistency—not in the sense of a homogeneity, but as a holding together of disparate elements.

(xiv)

In other words, plateaus symbolize modes in rhizome-like fashion, bringing us out of our static, incomplete sensations to more holistic forms of understanding.

In this context, it is highly appropriate for the jazz function of Mackey's text—the literal performances, the almost-connections between characters' dreams and desires, the constant invocations of call and response that infuse song with interpretive power—to become such a powerful motif; each performer, each dreamer provides another "plane" in what stretches toward a concept of the "holistic text." Each call, aware of its own incompleteness, asks for the response of a different, but related, plane, an opposition to deconstruct and reconstruct its own signification. Thus jazz soloists are expected not to repeat the exact melody, but to generate an altered same, a repetition with a difference. Thus N. seems entirely right to contribute only a "body and soul" murmuring to the Crossroads Choir performance; thus an audience can truly reply to a persistent C with 3-D glasses. The call and the response, while eroding past each other as planes and eroding each other as "witnesses," make the counterpoints that much more resilient. N. demonstrates the process early in the *Hornbook*:

> "I don't know you but I know your father. I don't know your father but I know your father's father. I don't know your father's father but I know your father's grandfather. I don't know your father's grandfather but I know your grandfather's grandfather. I don't know your grandfather's grandfather but I know your great-great-grandfather's father. I don't know your great-great-grandfather's father but I know your great-great-grandfather's grandfather. I don't know your great-great-grandfather's grandfather but I know your great-great-grandfather's great-great grandfather. I don't know your great-great-grandfather's great-great-grandfather but I know your great-great-grandfather's great-great-grandfather . . ." And so on.

I was after something similar. Not so much a stutter in any precise sense of the term as a curve of articulation which whenever it asserted would instantly qualify, even contradict itself. That sense of a receding, self-correcting withdrawal into a cave of ancestors I found immensely attractive, a curious borderline stance between the compelling and the merely compulsive.

(23-24)

In the sense of "a thousand plateaus," N. here has called and responded to history, both as an individual and as part of a collective; each plane of possibility not only "erodes" the plane before but also completes it. The plateaus of prose invite both the performers within and the readers without to add their own plane, to participate in not so much a group stutter as a collective harmony, to add a limb to our societal phantom limb. Even the reader becomes implicated in the process of this universal enterprise, expected not to unlock all of Mackey's meanings but to produce a new plane in his/her own interpretive experience. The improvisation of "China" seems a failure only to those who insist that meaning resides in only one plane of thinking at one time; in truth China is a place and all places, a woman and all women, a song and all songs.

Our inclination should be to instinctively reach beyond any one understanding of China, to constantly stretch toward other plateaus. Our minds should be desperate for the counterpoints of both-and, acknowledging that either-or is a notion passé and pointless; our hands should be desperate for thumbs, oppositions that make the fingers work. N. elaborates on the motif of the hand and the thumb as an essential plane of counterpoint in his piece entitled "Opposable Thumb at the Water's Edge":

> Its basic theme I'd put this way: Graspability is a self-incriminating thirst utterly native to every hand, an indigenous court from which only the drowned hope to win an acquittal. The piece makes use of two triadic phrases which I call utility riffs: "whatever beginnings go back to" and "an exegetic refusal to be done with desire." These generate a subtheme which could be put as follows: Thirst is by its nature unquenchable, the blue lips of a muse whose refusals roughen our throats with *duende*.

(*Hornbook* 43)

In a reply that is somehow both magical and inevitable, Penguin produces what N. calls "an extraordinary occurrence":

> At that point Penguin (whom I'd vaguely noticed fingering an imaginary horn towards the end of the piece, and who, by the time I finished, had taken his oboe from its case, inserted the mouthpiece and wet the reeds with his tongue and lips) embarked on a solo in which he held forth on what he said was a rapport he sensed—"a shadowy congress" he called it—between Opposable Thumb and an extremely ancient, primeval Egyptian god by the name of Temu. In the course of his solo he presented an impressive, all but overwhelming rush of corroborative data.

(*Hornbook* 44)

Not to be silenced, Aunt Nancy and Djamilaa begin to "play" a critique of phallocentricity—not countered effectively at all by Lambert's suggestion of the hand as a vulva enclosing the thumb / phallus—and produce "a symbiosis from which every horizon [that] had fallen away sought to extend itself" (*Hornbook* 49). In light of Deleuze and Guattari's planes of meaning, the opposition of the thumb becomes the necessity for discourse, any one avenue of approach only a start. It may be for this reason that the *Run* emphasizes that "have not" is, in essence, "halve not" (11)—a warning not to threaten the totality by disparaging any contributing singularity, a call to accept the completeness of being.

The *Run* often "breaks down" any seeming unit into dissected elements, to generate an accordion out of a single plane. Djamilaa begins this process in relating the search for a name to the striated meanings of a dream:

> "Speaking of names though," Djamilaa added after a pause, "the dream I dreamt last night had a strange tripartite power. It was able to 1) name without announcing or announce in such a way that to announce was to show, 2) show in such a way that to show was to tell, and 3) tell in such a way as to dictate its own reception, dictate and read itself at the same time."

(38)

Djamilaa offers her audience three planes of interpretation, each relying on a different mode of thought; the movement from one plane to another rests, in large part, on "verbing" from one to the other, on sacrificing the prior method of analysis, on stripping the self of the stasis of that thought process and recovering its traces in the next level. The tripartite method also allows for the certainty that, while dream, dreamer, and Djamilaa's audience may be working with the same materials or the same terms, their individual planes remain composed of separate elements, of dissimilar proclivities. Hence the need for telling "in such a way as to dictate its own reception"; hence Mackey's insistence that N. is neither the reader nor himself, but a figure "we overlap." Reception counts for as much as production in Mackey's world, unleashing the terrifying possibility that, even if we were all to understand the usefulness of the "thousand plateaus" model, we would not see or use the same multiplicity in the same way.

This conclusion finds further support within the context of Djamilaa's dream, appropriately subtitled "Synaesthetic Serenade." The record playing is "Pennies from Heaven," but the dream-character Penny "*could've sworn they were chanting, 'Penny's from heaven'*" (*Run* 39). Unlike the playful, chordal qualities of homonyms that N. normally employs, the distinction here becomes almost ominous: "*Penny had warned him against confusing the girl with the song he assumed she inspired, against the presumption of any across-the-board equation. She'd said it before and she'd say it again:* PENNY'S *wasn't the same as* PENNIES. PENNY'S *meant* PENNY IS. PENNIES *meant* PENNY AIN'T. *The difference was one her life depended on"* (40). The consequences of slippage become critical, begetting contradictory interpretations that strike to the heart of Penny's self-perception and Othered-reception. One choice among a sound plane of homonyms requires a move to another plane in a different system and in an opposite direction, and for Penny herself the implications seem far more than merely semantic.

Djamilaa's dream continues to add at least three other planes to the "pennies" homonym. The speaker introduces a chord of temporality: *"Penny's was indeed a dance of near collapse and last-minute recovery, a felt advance beyond impairment and limitation which amounted to a meeting of the here-and-now with the hereafter"* (***Run*** 41-42). She utilizes a second word chord:

> *Again the door hinges creaked. Penny's dance, the implied wind insisted, rested on a tenuous, tottering "chord" in which like-sounding*
>
> IMPAIRMENT
>
> *"notes" were all sounded at once.* EMPOWERMENT *made for rickety,*
>
> IMPEDIMENT
>
> *resilient limbs, each of which appeared stilted, possessed of a studied awkwardness; each of which, while crippled, was itself a crutch.*
>
> (42)

Finally, Djamilaa experiences a chord of emotion: *"What I felt was a lulling, alarming blend of complacency and pleasure—comforting and disconcerting at the same time. Never even in a dream had I thought death would be so playful, yet death, I reflected nonchalantly, was obviously what this was"* (42). The full song of her dream, then, is composed of at least four planes of analysis, each its own instrument and related to the others. Movement along and among planes, so widely and wildly demonstrated in the ***Hornbook,*** becomes in the ***Run*** only part of what's actually going on in the meaning of meaning, for any single set of plateaus is extended and compressed, dictating and dictated by other sets. Where the ***Hornbook*** often stretches one layer of meaning into an entire accordion, the ***Run*** reveals more of the according to.

A possible model of this new paradigm occurs on page 109 of the ***Run,*** a "Suspect-Symmetrical Structure of Misconceptual Seed's Parallactic Dispatch". . . . At first glance, the diagram may seem to resemble the plateaus model, allowing one to move in a variety of ways from one plane involving "Misconceived Root (Pampas)" and "Buenos Aires" and a second that includes "Circumstantial Ground (Silverlake)" and "Elysian Park." But the diagonal vectors that connect these

highly ambiguous plateaus suggest visually that longing not only moves one between planes but establishes its own striation of planes that stretch vertically. This complements the apparently more "established" horizontal lines and results in the circle of "Esq/Est," itself characterized by simultaneous movement to and from the center vertically, back and forth horizontally. Even more frustratingly, the outward posts of the diagrams are all their own striated systems, such as the "demonic he/she/it" of "Implied Horizon." Finally, the inability of any set of parallel lines to be constantly "dotted" or "straight" refuses the observer any chance to establish a hierarchy among systems; one does not know where to begin or how to proceed. Given Mackey's ongoing textual conversation with contemporary jazz, "Suspect-Symmetrical Structure" might well be a reply to composer Anthony Braxton, whose compositions are "titled" by geometric diagrams. Early in his career, Braxton began assigning visual representations to particular sounds, a synesthetic process he has called "conceptual grafting" (Lock 3). The idea was to consider space and sound together; hence Braxton has described his Composition 96 as "an attempt to integrate horizontal structural formings into the forward space of the music" (Lock 4). By Composition 160, Braxton's vision had become even more complicated, "Moving out of the science space and more into the poetic space. I'm no longer interested in a definition of music that's only in one space" (Lock 1). Mackey's diagram, in contrast, presents a structure too convoluted to prove effective. Not surprisingly, N. himself asks whether any structure is "anything but an after-the-fact heuristic seed, a misleading, misconceptual sleep inside which to walk is to begin to wake up? Like it or not, we're marked by whatever window we look thru. The stigmata, luckily, turn out not to be static" (***Run*** 108).

One may argue, given the nightmarish quality of the diagram, whether the movement of stigmata is, indeed, lucky. N. seems quite reasonable, however, to point out the impossibility of locking a text into any closed schema. As richly complex as Deleuze and Guattari's model may be, as much as it illuminates Mackey's prose, the entirety of the text refuses to support it; too many factors, stemming from too many sources, stretching in too many directions, will not allow one single set of planes to contain the whole. For that matter, any conformity to form strikes N. as a twofold threat. First, there exists the danger of intellectually diminishing returns; "[o]ne way to state it would be to say that I'm troubled by the apparent fatalism intrinsic to form, the threat of a conservatism the centralness of 'form' to 'conformity' seems to imply" (***Hornbook*** 77). All meanings, past and future, tend to collapse into a masterview of text; in this context, N.'s letters and the world in which he lives lose their unpredictability and vitality. The point of textual sacrifice, of course, is to kill the interpretive self of these stifling demands for structural sameness. Second, and perhaps more damaging, the pressure to re-form, but not reform, pushes everything that refuses to fit into the silences of marginalia. This tendency is condemned quite early in the *Hornbook,* as a crowd in a record shop demands that N.'s band recontextualize its aims within "the whole culture," allowing music listeners to appropriately assign their contributions a rightful place. "All I can say," Aunt Nancy replies, "is that the culture you're calling 'whole' has yet to assume itself to be so except at the expense of a whole lot of other folks, except by presuming that what they were up to could be ignored at no great loss" (12). Othered expressions become either stifled or silenced entirely. In the case of the thousand plateaus, Aunt Nancy's argument bears some truth; one must, after all, decide where to begin with the model, what direction the connecting tangents will travel and what single narrative might emerge in the end. "What," asks N., "could free the future from every flat, formulaic 'outcome,' from its own investment in the contested shape of an otherness disfigured by its excursion thru the world?" (*Hornbook* 100).

If one is still to use Deleuze and Guattari's model, one might begin with the acknowledgment that any one "flat, formulaic" set of plateaus is merely a single set—that a host of competing factors and complicated agendas, each with its own strata, function at cross-purposes, resulting in a multidimensional arrangement of meanings across time, space, words, and peoples. One example of this modified model can be seen in a dance group's performance:

> Aunt Nancy, as we watched the dancers go thru their routine, whispered into my ear that she was struck by the interplay and the counterpoint between the upward thrust of the surrounding buildings and the dancers' answering exploration of horizontality, their insistence, variegated as it was, on "getting down." I in fact had been similarly struck, had taken note of the same thing.
>
> (*Run* 110-11)

The reader immediately notices the performative matrix that brings together the horizontality of the dancers and the verticality of the buildings but somehow refuses to connect them. Instead, the upness and the acrossness of the competing sets of planes seem to suggest, if anything, a texture, a tapestry of threads of individuality and intentionality.

As Mackey asserts in *Discrepant Engagement,* "Creative kinship and the lines of affinity it effects are much more complex, jagged, and indissociable than the totalizing pretensions of canon formation tend to acknowledge" (3). The title of his collection of essays, he explains, comes from Wilson Harris:

> It is an expression coined in reference to practices that, in the interest of opening presumably closed orders of identity and signification, accent fissure, fracture, incongruity, the rickety, imperfect fit between word and world. Such practices highlight—indeed inhabit—dis-

crepancy, engage rather than seek to ignore it. Recalling the derivation of the word *discrepant* from a root meaning "to rattle, creak," I relate discrepant engagement to the name the Dogon of West Africa give their weaving block, the base on which the loom they weave upon sits. They call it the "creaking of the word." It is the noise upon which the word is based, the discrepant foundation of all coherence and articulation, of the purchase upon the world fabrication affords. Discrepant engagement, rather than suppressing or seeking to silence that noise, acknowledges it.

> (19)

N. spends a fair amount of time in the *Hornbook* trying to come to terms with the creaking of the Word, and even plans a speech on the topic: "The sense I get from this is that a) we can't help but be involved in fabrication, b) a case can be made for leaving loose ends loose, and c) we find ourselves caught in a rickety confession no matter what" (*Hornbook* 116). Our commitment—however willing or unwilling—to participating in the fabrication, to compulsive confessions and loose ends that refuse to fit, is twofold. First, we are all speakers and spoken to, all bound to a process of communication that seeks enough commonality to keep "Pennies" from "Penny's." But regardless of the breadth of our worldview, our struggles for accommodation, our models of complexity, someone or something will slip away, while exceptions will permeate inward. Second, we are all subject to the mythologies and mysteries of loss, rendering our lives not realms of solid experience but webs of connections and fissures; "[w]e not only can but should speak of 'loss' or, to avoid, quotation marks notwithstanding, any such inkling of self-pity, speak of *absence* as unavoidably an inherence in the texture of things (dreamseed, habitual cloth)" (*Eroding Witness* 50).

Mark Scroggins remarks in his work on *Septet for the End of Time* that a number of factors threaten to erode the variety of witnesses in Mackey's work, each potentially seen as pressing down on the warp and the weft that give us identity while locking us within it. The self in Mackey's projects, Scroggins argues, is "an eroding witness": "the self can recognize its cultural, spiritual roots only as eroding traces in the works of others, and that recognizing self is in turn eroded, like the figure on the cover of *Bedouin Hornbook,* by the forces of history, change, distance, and time itself" (44). He later elaborates:

> The speakers of these poems wake up again and again, not from dreams to waking "reality," but from dreams to dreams, from one order of language to another—from an order of music to that of its mythic equivalent, and back again, from an order of death to life-in-death and death-in-life . . . the orders of reality—orders which are as much spiritual as they are historical—are embodied and embraced in the culturally structured orders of speech. While these speakers may desire to

awaken from the "nightmare" of history, their repeated awakenings are a reiteration of the self's utter entanglement in the network of cultural traces that constitute it.

(45)

By the time the reader meets N., he has already well acknowledged the "network of cultural traces" that compose his own life; further, he is already on his way to recognizing the specific forces—time, space, history, and so forth—that constitute his subject position. Where N. succeeds is his awareness of two concepts: first, that significance is almost defiantly relational, verb-al, stubbornly refusing to hold the same meaning for all people at all times. The trick lies in inhabiting the fissures between planes, in seeing meaning as what happens in the cracks. Somewhere between two similar words—for example, "card" and "cord"—is the precise point of distinction between the two, the electrical charge that gives both their individual potency; somewhere within "cord" is a chord, an entire realm of sound and sense, silence and nonsense. Second, a wide range of elements threatens the stability and the success of our lives, leaving us with a life-cloth that lacks certain fibers, that speaks to its own incompleteness. The key lies in understanding the pressures on warp and weft, the absences that bring us power as well as loss. Gaps become places to invent, to lament, to howl; external pressures beget ex-pressions of grief and belief.

Mackey insists in his essay **"Other: From Noun to Verb"** that linguistic riffs and shifts merely echo the "grammar" of life that defines and confines our existence:

> But a revolution of the word can be only a beginning. It initiates a break while remaining overshadowed by the conditions it seeks to go beyond. The shadow such conditions cast makes for a brooding humor that straddles laughter and lament, allows no easy, unequivocal foothold in either. Oppositional speech is only partly oppositional. Cramp and obstruction have to do with it as well.

(58)

In other words, the pressures of warp and weft are a highly intricate matrix of directional pressures, each with their own agendas but often working together to make us fixed, static, marginalized "nouns." Thus the need to "highlight the dynamics of agency and attribution by way of which otherness is brought about and maintained, the fact that *other* is something people do, more importantly a verb than an adjective or a noun" (51). Weaving, on a societal scale, can serve to bind any marginalized person or people within the centralized confines of power, economics, or artistic categorization. On an individual scale, however, the creaking that the word always allows—the interstices and fissures that make any fabric, literal or societal, a breathable, permeable structure—permits the artist the potential of reply, of producing a "difficult" or even "unreadable" work that both cuts against the conventional grain and argues that that grain is, for the marginalized, both "difficult" and "unreadable" itself. Thus the staunch resistance to academic typecasting, therefore the "of course that's what it's not." Mackey and fellow writers may resort to sacrificial limbs to lament sacrificial lambs, to kill the sense of iamb to recover the I Am.

Works Cited

Allen, Joseph. "Nathaniel Mackey's Unit Structures." *Black Orpheus: Music in African American Fiction from the Harlem Renaissance to Toni Morrison*. Ed. Saadi A. Simawe. New York: Garland, 2000. 205-29.

Chernoff, John Miller. *African Rhythm and African Sensibility: Aesthetics and Social Action in African Musical Idioms*. Chicago: U of Chicago P, 1979.

Deleuze, Gilles, and Félix Guattari. *A Thousand Plateaus: Capitalism and Schizophrenia*. Trans. Brian Massumi. Minneapolis: U of Minnesota P, 1987.

García Lorca, Federico. *Deep Song and Other Prose*. Ed. and trans. Christopher Maurer. 1975. New York: New Directions, 1980.

Griaule, Marcel. *Conversations with Ogotemmêli: An Introduction to Dogon Religious Ideas*. London: Oxford UP, 1965.

Kress, David C. "Middle Voice Moves in Nathaniel Mackey's *Djbot Baghostus' Run*." *Callaloo* 23 (2000): 765-83.

Lock, Graham. Liner Notes. *Anthony Braxton: Willisau (Quartet) 1991*. Hat Hut Records Ltd, 2002.

Mackey, Nathaniel. *Bedouin Hornbook*. Callaloo Fiction Ser. Lexington: U of Kentucky P, 1986.

———. "Cante Moro." *Sound States: Innovative Poetics and Acoustical Technologies*. Ed. Adalaide Morris. Chapel Hill: U of North Carolina P, 1997. 194-212.

———. *Discrepant Engagement: Dissonance, Cross-Culturality, and Experimental Writing*. Cambridge: Cambridge UP, 1993.

———. *Djbot Baghostus's Run*. New American Fiction 29. Los Angeles: Sun and Moon, 1993.

———. *Eroding Witness*. Urbana: U of Illinois P, 1985.

———. "An Interview with Nathaniel Mackey." Conducted by Edward Foster. *Talisman* 9 (1992): 48-61.

———. "An Interview with Nathaniel Mackey." Conducted by Paul Naylor. *Callaloo* 23 (2000): 645-63.

———. "An Interview with Nathaniel Mackey." Conducted by Peter O'Leary. *Chicago Review* 43.1 (1997): 30-46.

———. "Other: From Noun to Verb." *Representations* 39 (1992): 51-70.

Massumi, Brian. "Translator's Foreword: Pleasures of Philosophy." Deleuze and Guattari ix-xv.

Morris, Adalaide. "Angles of Incidence/Angels of Dust: Operatic Tilt in the Poetics of H.D. and Nathaniel Mackey." *Callaloo* 23 (2000): 749-64.

Mullen, Harryette. "Phantom Pain: Nathaniel Mackey's *Bedouin Hornbook*." *Talisman* 9 (1992): 37-43.

Powell, Barry B. *Classical Myth.* 2nd ed. Upper Saddle River, NJ: Prentice-Hall, 1998.

Quinn, Richard. "The Creak of Categories: Nathaniel Mackey's *Strick: Song of the Andoumboulou 16-25.*" *Callaloo* 23 (2000): 608-20.

Scroggins, Mark. "The Master of Speech and Speech Itself: Nathaniel Mackey's 'Septet for the End of Time.'" *Talisman* 9 (1992): 44-47.

FURTHER READING

Criticism

Gray, Jeffrey. "Travel and Difference: Lyn Hejinian and Nathaniel Mackey." In *Mastery's End: Travel and Postwar American Poetry,* pp. 212-33. Athens: University of Georgia Press, 2005.

Discusses the travel poems of Hejinian and Mackey, asserting that the verse of both writers chronicles "the expedition to locate an elusive and estranged identity."

Hoover, Paul. "Pair of Figures for Eshu: Doubling of Consciousness in the Work of Kerry James Marshall and Nathaniel Mackey." In *Fables of Representation: Essays,* pp. 26-55. Ann Arbor: University of Michigan Press, 2004.

Explores the theme of "double consciousness" in Mackey's *Bedouin Hornbook* and in the paintings of Kerry James Marshall.

Lavery, Matthew A. "The Ontogeny and Phylogeny of Mackey's *Song of the Andoumboulou.*" *African American Review* 38, no. 4 (winter 2004): 683-94.

Considers how in Mackey's poetry, especially in the serial poem *The Song of the Andoumboulou,* the author conducts an "anthromorphism of language into a physical form, bringing it into the world as a thing, as a human body."

Zamsky, Robert L. "A Poetics of Radical Musicality: Nathaniel Mackey's '-Mu' Series." *Arizona Quarterly* 62, no. 1 (spring 2006): 113-40.

Centers on the significance of the relationship between musicality and poetics in Mackey's writings, in particular in the "Mu" series.

Additional coverage of Mackey's life and career is contained in the following sources published by Gale: *Contemporary Authors,* **Vol. 153;** *Contemporary Authors New Revision Series,* **Vol. 114;** *Contemporary Poets,* **Eds. 6, 7;** *Dictionary of Literary Biography,* **Vol. 169;** *Literature Resource Center***; and** *Poetry Criticism,* **Vol. 49.**

Paule Marshall
1929-

AP Images

(Born Valenza Pauline Burke) American novelist and short story writer.

For additional information on Marshall's career, see *Black Literature Criticism,* Ed. 1.

INTRODUCTION

Regarded as a major voice in contemporary American literature, Marshall is recognized as one of the first authors to explore the psychological trials and concerns of black American women. Drawing upon her experiences as a black woman of Barbadian heritage, she embodies the cultural dichotomy that provides the major tensions in her fiction. Although her writing deals primarily with black and feminist issues, critics note that the power and importance of her work transcends color and sexual barriers and speaks to all individuals.

BIOGRAPHICAL INFORMATION

Marshall was born in 1929 in Brooklyn, New York, to Barbadian parents. As a young girl, she was profoundly influenced by the conversations she overheard between her mother and the other women of Brooklyn's Barbadian community. The power these women wielded with their words, their sharp character analyses, and the poetic rhythms of their Barbadian dialect instilled in Marshall a desire to capture some of this "magic" on paper. However, it was only after reading a volume of poetry by Paul Laurence Dunbar that Marshall realized that a literary forum existed which, in her own words, "validated the black experience"; she then began to seek out the work of such African American writers as Zora Neale Hurston, Gwendolyn Brooks, and Ralph Ellison. After graduating from Brooklyn College in 1953, Marshall began working as a researcher for a small magazine, *Our World*. She was soon promoted to staff writer and sent to Brazil and the Caribbean on assignments; she would later draw upon these experiences in her fiction. In 1959 Marshall embarked upon her career as a novelist with the publication of *Brown Girl, Brownstones,* a work that was commercially unviable, but proved to be a critical success. Her subsequent books earned her a larger reading audience. She has received several awards for her work, including a Guggenheim Fellowship, a National Endowment for the Arts Fellowship, and a McArthur Fellowship in 1992. In addition, Marshall has taught creative writing courses at Yale University, Columbia University, the University of Iowa, and the University of California at Berkeley. She resides alternately in the United States and in Africa.

MAJOR WORKS

Marshall's first novel, *Brown Girl, Brownstones,* is a frank depiction of a young black girl's search for identity and of her increasing sexual awareness. Autobiographical in tone, the story is about Brooklyn-born Selina, the daughter of Barbadian immigrants Silla and Deighton. When Selina's charming father, Deighton, inherits some island land, he wants to return there and build a home; her ambitious mother, Silla, however, wants to sell the land and use the money to purchase the family's rented brownstone. The marital conflict that follows forces Selina to reassess her own identity and consider her own future. Although critics often discuss *Brown Girl, Brownstones* as a female *bildungsroman* detailing Selina's physical and emotional growth, the novel also chronicles Silla's confrontations with her spendthrift husband as she tries to become assimilated to American culture and, as the owner of a brownstone house, a participant in the American dream.

Comprised of explorations of psychological struggle and enlightenment, the stories in *Soul Clap Hands and Sing* (1961), Marshall's next work, deal with aging men who are forced to come to terms with their emotional and spiritual decline. In her second novel, *The Chosen Place, The Timeless People* (1969), Marshall explored issues of group and individual identity. Saul Amron, a Jewish American anthropologist, becomes embroiled in the political struggles of a primitive agricultural community on the West Indian island of Bournehills. Critics have noted that Saul's position is ironic because although he is a representative of the white patriarchy, he is also, as a Jew, a member of a group that historically has been the victim of prejudice. Often considered Marshall's most political novel, *The Chosen Place, The Timeless People* has been praised for examining the problems facing many Third World countries in their struggle to establish a national identity. In *Reena and Other Stories* (1983), republished as *Merle* (1984), Marshall again focused on women's attempts to overcome sexual and racial discrimination and on the difficulties women face in personal relationships.

Marshall's best-known novel, *Praisesong for the Widow* (1983), treats themes of acculturation and identity. Avatar (Avey) Johnson is a successful widow who has lost touch with her West Indian-African American roots. While on her annual luxury cruise through the West Indies, Avey has disturbing dreams and decides to leave the cruise and fly home. While stranded and waiting for a flight, she meets a local shopkeeper on the island of Grenada and begins a life-changing spiritual journey. *Praisesong for the Widow* was a commercial and critical success and garnered an American Book Award in 1984. Written from a female perspective, Marshall's novel *Daughters* (1991) chronicles a daughter's struggle to address her ambivalent feelings about her domineering father. When Ursa-Bea MacKenzie, a West Indian native living in New York City, returns home to participate in her father's reelection campaign for prime minister, she realizes the depths of his machinations and sabotages his campaign. Marshall's 2000 novel, *The Fisher King,* also explores issues of family, heritage, displacement, and identity. The narrative follows the multigenerational story of two American families torn apart by conflict. After Sonny-Rett and Cherisse marry and abandon their classical music careers to become jazz musicians in Paris, their families blame each other. Only when Sonny-Rett and Cherisse's grandson, Sonny, comes back to Brooklyn years later does the rift begin to heal.

CRITICAL RECEPTION

Marshall is regarded as one of the leading American authors writing about the African diasporic experience. Reviewers praise her artistry, particularly her complex characters, fluid narrative style, and sense of humor and irony. They also commend her finely crafted language and skillful rendering of West Indian dialect. Exploring themes of assimilation, alienation, displacement, family and cultural ties, and collective and individual identity, Marshall is viewed by commentators as an authentic voice that concentrates on the struggle of women to deal with gender, family, and cultural roles and maintain a healthy sense of self in a demanding and confusing world. Critics point out the diversity of female characters in her work and laud her ability to create a wide canvas of compelling and complex women in her fiction. Autobiographical aspects of her work are also a recurring topic for commentators, with many noting that her own recognition and celebration of her West Indian heritage and resultant spiritual journey parallels the stories of several of her characters. Critics concur that her insightful explorations of the complexities and challenges of the diasporic experience provide a valuable contribution to American literature.

PRINCIPAL WORKS

Brown Girl, Brownstones (novel) 1959
Soul Clap Hands and Sing (short stories) 1961
The Chosen Place, The Timeless People (novel) 1969
Praisesong for the Widow (novel) 1983
Reena and Other Stories (short stories) 1983; also published as *Merle: A Novella and Other Stories,* 1984
Daughters (novel) 1991
Language Is the Only Homeland: Bajan Poets Abroad (nonfiction) 1995
The Fisher King (novel) 2000

CRITICISM

Joyce Pettis (essay date 1995)

SOURCE: Pettis, Joyce. Introduction to *Toward Wholeness in Paule Marshall's Fiction*, pp. 1-8. Charlottesville: University Press of Virginia, 1995.

[*In the following essay, Pettis notes that the idea of a journey is a unifying motif in Marshall's literary oeuvre, contending that "the most significant travel establishes cultural connections among people of the African diaspora and advances the traveler from spiritual morbundity to spiritual reclamation."*]

Progression, momentum, and culmination form the concept of a journey and are useful in thinking about Paule Marshall's fiction. Journeys are significant for many characters in *Brown Girl, Brownstones*; *Soul Clap Hands and Sing*; *The Chosen Place, the Timeless People*; *Praisesong for the Widow*; and *Daughters.* The most significant travel establishes cultural connections among people of the African diaspora and advances the traveler from spiritual moribundity to spiritual reclamation. Through multidimensional characters and situations in the United States and the Caribbean, each work reproduces patterns of race, gender, and class along with other forces that fracture the psyche. Marshall uses the journey motif to communicate the necessity of movement away from the debilitation caused by fracturing. Her characters travel, literally and metaphorically, but only one of them reaches the desired destination at the novel's end. In *Praisesong,* Avatara Johnson, an elderly widow, finally reaches the goal toward which Marshall's fiction has journeyed for twenty-four years. It is a small island named Carriacou, where remnants of West Africa are remembered and form an active part of the islanders' customs. It is where spiritual reintegration occurs. This book [*Toward Wholeness in Paule Marshall's Fiction*] will examine Marshall's canon as her provocative passage to culmination, where psychic transformation becomes possible.

Daughters confirms that the spiritual journey of Avatara Johnson in *Praisesong* brings closure to a particular vision that has animated Marshall's work. Although fragmented characters exist in this novel, its focus shifts away from their spiritual recovery. Its psychically centered characters are not limited to those spiritually whole ancestors who appear in earlier novels. *Daughters* is nonetheless a significant part of this work because it continues to explore the consequences of colonialism in the Caribbean, the intersections of race, gender, and class, and the behavior of psychically whole characters as positive agents of community.

The fractured psyche, defined and discussed in chapter 1 [of *Toward Wholeness in Paule Marshall's Fiction*], identifies a motif that, like the journey, has constituted a primary concept in Marshall's work. The presence of the fractured psyche has increased the richness and multidimensionality of the experiences she chronicles and has helped to anchor her work historically. Her inclusive fiction incorporates subjects such as men and women in urban and rural labor forces, the individual and the community, immigrants and assimilation in adopted countries, and conflicts between illusion and

reality. Her work offers insight into personal relations, including those between husbands and wives, same-sex friends, mothers and daughters, and fathers and daughters.[1] These relationships are complicated by fracturing, particularly in the areas of individual and cultural identity, individual and cultural alienation, and spiritual moribundity.

The journey motif complements and enhances the geographic sweep of Marshall's fiction and becomes crucial in the reciprocity between her texts and the cultures represented in them.[2] The West Indians in *Brown Girl* are immigrants from Barbados; an American research team in *The Chosen Place* relocates to the fictional island of Bourne; the Afro-Caribbean protagonist Merle Kinbona immigrates to London for her college education and many years later plans to travel to East Africa; the Connecticut-born Estelle establishes her life on the Caribbean island of Triunion and sends her Triunion-born daughter to Connecticut during her adolescence; Avatara's vacation cruise from New York places her in Grenada and Carriacou. The novellas of *Soul Clap Hands and Sing* are set in North America, South America, and the Caribbean. This geographic sweep is central to Marshall's fiction in emphasizing the widespread nature of fracturing that originated with a displaced West African population during the slave trade.[3]

The Chosen Place expands in scope to include an exploration of the fates of the white descendants of traders. Are these people, whose economic and class position was secured through the purchase and sale of Africans and related import and export industries, ignorant about or unscarred by that history? How might they redeem themselves, although they had no direct role in the accretion of their wealth and inherited power? Through Harriet Amron, a WASP from New England whose inheritance originated with profits from the trade, Marshall depicts an angle that is often underrepresented. As a member of the research team traveling to Bourne Island, Harriet personally journeys back, but she arrives at an impasse between the personal and historical.

Marshall stated that in designing *The Chosen Place,* she wanted "to have a kind of vehicle that looked at the relationship of the West to the rest of us. So I hoped that the novel would not solely be seen as a novel about the West Indies, even though it's set there, but a novel that reflects what is happening to all of us in the Diaspora in our encounter with these metropolitan powers, the power of Europe and the power of America."[4] Using character, ritual, and symbols of technology, Bourne Island becomes one of many places in Marshall's canon where she dissects intricate relationships that produce fracturing. The diversity of this topographic representation underscores Marshall's commitment to education about the African diaspora and her acknowledgment of a worldwide black community of African descendants.[5] Although she does not situate characters in West Africa, its presence hovers as the origin of cultural identity.

This book is structured to follow Marshall's movement toward spiritual wholeness. Fragmentation is located in the historical experiences of black people of the African diaspora, and the fractured psyche is defined as the rending and mutilation of human spirit, a process that represents an unavoidable consequence of traumatic cultural displacement. The continuing presence of the fractured psyche indicates progressive alienation in a culture hostile to African Americans and Afro-Caribbeans. This perpetual conflict originates in the difference between European cosmological systems and African systems. The social reality for descendants of West Africans in the United States and the Caribbean, defined by European cosmology, privileges qualities that are alien to an African cultural orientation.

Evidence of fracturing and alienation that can be linked to opposition between Eurocentric culture and African-derived culture is supported by the research of numerous psychologists who work from an Afrocentric perspective. The work of Na'im Akbar and Joseph A. Baldwin underpins cultural analysis of Marshall's fractured men and women in conflict with their social reality. Akbar's and Baldwin's research, discussed in chapter 1, also verifies the consequences of these problems. This volume also cites the work of Gerald Gregory Jackson, who links evidence of fracturing with cultural differences between Africans and Europeans. Robert Blauner's study of differences between immigrants and colonized people lends credibility to the discussion of the sociocultural results of displacement and bondage.

Several words describe the ideal postfractured state—*spiritual wholeness, regeneration, reintegration,* and *reclamation.* All of these terms speak to the restoration of wholeness, which means that the spirit is gathered up, healed, and revealed unto itself (see chapters 1 and 4). Marshall's trilogy—**Brown Girl, The Chosen Place,** and **Praisesong**—is discrete not only in its trajectory toward this ideal but also in its location of the healing within the black cultural and communal matrix. The emphasis on Marshall's progressive thematic vision is substantiated by the female protagonists in her trilogy. The journey is instrumental to all of them, but in the first two books the protagonists only stand poised for their most significant travel at the conclusion of the text. Not until Avatara Johnson's extensive literal and metaphorical travels in **Praisesong** does Marshall culminate journeying with embracing one's cultural origins and healing a fractured psyche. Spiritual wholeness is finally attained.

Spiritual wholeness, reintegration, reclamation, and *spirituality* are used interchangeably in this discussion to designate the desirable end of a splintered psyche. The term *spirituality* is employed in its West African cultural sense as an embodiment of dynamic energy separate from the physical body but essential to its well-being, both physically and emotionally. Spirituality is acknowledged by psychologists and others who study traditional African culture. In chapter 1 [of *Toward Wholeness in Paule Marshall's Fiction*], the research of Linda James Myers and Dominique Zahan confirms intellectually that spirituality is a dynamic entity in the experience of descendants of Africans. Margaret Washington Creel links spirituality with the African worldview, writing that it "affected one's whole system of being, embracing the consciousness, social interactions, and attitudes, fears and dispositions of the community at large" (72). The significance of the term *spiritual wholeness* within this context justifies its appropriation as the desired goal in the journeys undertaken in Marshall's fiction.

Several theoretical perspectives shape my reading of the novels discussed here. I am primarily indebted to black feminist practice and feminist literary theory. The historical and cultural resources that invigorate my readings of Marshall's fiction—my contextual focus, in other words—reflects Deborah McDowell's idea that a study of black women's literature should "expose the conditions under which literature is produced, published, and reviewed." This procedure is "not only useful but necessary to Black feminist critics" ("New Directions," 192). Establishing the cultural context and identifying the forces that shape the existence of black men and women is an essential step in their representation in criticism. Paula Giddings's *When and Where I Enter,* Patricia Hill Collins's *Black Feminist Thought,* Jacqueline Jones's *Labor of Love, Labor of Sorrow,* Deborah K. King's "Multiple Jeopardy, Multiple Consciousness," and Bonnie Thornton Dill's essays all prove vital in sustaining a black feminist perspective and in incorporating historical and sociological findings to inform literary analysis. Just as important, these studies were instrumental in furthering the identification of race, gender, and class inequities. Because significant parts of this book emphasize black workers as exploited and therefore fractured, Marxist feminist criticism also offers viable ways of interpreting the relationship between labor and exploitation and of drawing conclusions about the state of the psyche in that connection. Josephine Donovan's *Feminist Theory: The Intellectual Traditions of American Feminism* provides useful insights into Marxist feminist ideology.

Marshall's status in American literature constitutes an underlying motivation for this book. Scholars of

African-American and Afro-Caribbean literature, avid readers of these works, and many contemporary American novelists consider her among the premier American writers. Her work is taught internationally. Nevertheless, significant numbers of Americans knowledgeable about literature remain ignorant of Marshall. Consequently, this volume seeks to increase her much-deserved visibility to a multicultural audience. In the afterword to *Brown Girl, Brownstones,* Mary Helen Washington wrote that "just now—in the 1980s—[Marshall is] being discovered," although by that time she had authored three major books (323). Since 1981, Marshall has published two more substantial novels, and black women's fiction has received increased critical attention, some of which has been directed at Marshall's sustained and serious work. Based on her inclusion in theses and dissertations and in chapters in book-length critical studies, particularly those whose terrain includes the diaspora, interest in her work is accelerating. *Daughters* has perhaps introduced her to another audience, both through television appearances—where Marshall talked about her work—and through its publication during a period of lively interest in fiction by black women. Most significantly, receiving the prestigious MacArthur Award in 1992 has certainly enhanced her status in American letters.

Marshall's membership in both the Afro-Caribbean and African-American communities appreciably widens her audience. Carol Davies, Daryl Dance, and Edward Brathwaite, all cited in chapter 1, are among those who claim her cross-culturally. Brathwaite, in fact, cites *The Chosen Place* as "a significant contribution to the literature of the West Indies" and praises its scope and value ("Rehabilitations," 126).

One means of evaluating Marshall's status in the tradition of African-American letters is to view her fiction in relation to her fellow writers. Therefore, this book will juxtapose Marshall's work with the fiction of other women writers and discuss its articulation within a women's literary tradition. The authors with whom she is compared include Pauline Hopkins, Frances Ellen Watkins Harper, Nella Larsen, Jessie Fauset, Zora Neale Hurston (representing an early tradition in black women's fiction) and Ann Petry, Gwendolyn Brooks, Kristin Hunter, Sarah Wright, and Toni Morrison (evoking later style). Although several themes, images, and situations in the fiction of these writers mesh with Marshall's work, her distinction among them is established through the unity of her measured tread toward psychic reintegration and through her inclusion of the African diaspora. This comparative assessment is essential to a claim for enhancing Marshall's status in American and African-American letters.

Although Marshall's vision of spiritual wholeness serves as the unifying entity of her work, her fiction is neither parochial nor myopic. Thus, this book deliberately avoids analyzing her fiction chronologically and follows instead a topical approach.

Chapter 1 establishes the perspective for an investigation of the fractured psyche in Marshall's fiction, notes the phenomenon's presence in the work of other writers, and points out Marshall's distinctiveness in her development of it. Relevant biographical and literary connections are established because they underscore pertinent diasporic connections in the novels. Her position among women writers in African-American literary tradition is also discussed.

Chapter 2 has its basis in the initial disruption of African communities. Community as a vital entity in the experiences of black people is equally important in Marshall's fiction. Where people group themselves, how they identify with the land in Third World settings, and how they manage their survival in merciless urban cities is connected with the well-being of the psyche. Marshall's characters identify certain spaces as psychological havens; that is, the seclusion and psychocultural safety of the setting outweighs its physicality. The chapter also examines configurations of ritual, legacy, history, and survival in the community in *The Chosen Place* and explores the relationship among geography, cultural dislocation, and survival by juxtaposing First and Third World communities in *Daughters.*

Gender, race, and class comprise a dynamic that is often underestimated in its power to perpetuate psychic fracturing. Chapter 3 analyzes the workings of these forces in Marshall's fiction. The alienated men in *Soul Clap Hands and Sing* function as early examples of different kinds of fracturing and the subsequent failure of survival. One section identifies selected images of capitalism and discusses the threat posed to the psyche in the world of work. Merle Kinbona's psychic stabilization through the culturally rich practice of talk, an art in black communities, revealingly counters the failed men of *Soul Clap Hands.* Situating Merle's recovery in a community-based behavior is an important precursor to the role of community and heritage in achieving spiritual wholeness.

Chapter 4 explores the attaining of spiritual wholeness in *Praisesong,* the culmination of a particular vision that compelled Marshall's fiction beginning in the mid-1950s. The first section compares her development of materialism and labor with that of other black women writers who have depicted the destructiveness of materialism and of race, gender, and class but have not envisioned a means of salvaging the fractured psyche. The chapter also analyzes the role of elders or ancestors—Aunt Cuney and Lebert Joseph in *Praisesong,* Miss Thompson in *Brown Girl,* and Leesy in *The Chosen Place*—exponents of psychic wholeness in Marshall's fiction. Spiritual wholeness may replace fracturing when the character reclaims self from the killing impulses of capitalism-materialism and consciously participates in redefining them; when suspicion and misplaced ethnocentrism among displaced people of African descent are replaced by the acknowledgment of cultural connectedness, regardless of physical domicile; and when myth and ritual become privileged rather than suspect.

The last chapter focuses on Marshall's most recent novel, *Daughters.* This chapter continues a discussion begun in chapter 2 in which black male and female partnership is posited as essential to salvaging and preserving the community. Sons of the community are tractable in Caribbean neocolonialist and American postslavery games of political domination. Daughters are more likely to have attained spirituality and are also more likely to return their service to the community. Several female characters in *Daughters* demonstrate characteristics of wholeness and thus move beyond its quest. This chapter analyzes their involvement in community and their personal lives in light of that accomplishment.

Notes

1. See, for example, Leela Kapai, "Dominant Themes and Techniques in Paule Marshall's Fiction," *CLA Journal* 26 (1972): 49-59; Marcia Keizs, "Themes and Styles in the Works of Paule Marshall," *Negro American Literature Forum* 9 (1975): 67, 71-75; and Kimberly W. Benston, "Architectural Imagery and Unity in Paule Marshall's *Brown Girl, Brownstones,*" *Negro American Literature Forum* 9 (1975): 67-70.

2. In the section on Marshall in *Black Women Novelists,* Barbara Christian subordinates the characters of *The Chosen Place* to the culture of Bournehills. She further equates the concept of time, both fluid and static, with the people and their culture, all rhythmically bound together (104-8).

3. In *There Is a River: The Black Struggle for Freedom in America* (New York: Vintage, 1983), Vincent Harding points out the euphemistic employment of the term "the Trade" to encapsulate the business of flesh stealing and selling in specific ports "from the Guinea coast to Barbados and Jamaica, to Charleston and Norfolk" (8).

4. Pettis, 123-24. Although Jean Carey Bond's review of *The Chosen Place* praises several features of the novel, it ignores the convergence of

diaspora communities as one of the novel's primary components. Marshall's studied attention to communities of African descendants and her references to other displaced and exploited people connected by history and legacy are strangely omitted among a generally favorable review. See "Allegorical Novel by Talented Storyteller," *Freedomways* 10 (1970): 76-78.

5. See Joseph E. Holloway, ed., *Africanisms in American Culture* (Bloomington: Indiana Univ. Press, 1990). Margaret Washington Creel's essay, "Gullah Attitudes toward Life and Death" offers particularly pertinent information concerning community and spirituality that is reflected in Marshall's fiction and is useful for a conceptual analysis of *Praisesong* and *The Chosen People.*

Bibliography

Brathwaite, Edward. "Rehabilitations: West Indian History and Society in the Art of Paule Marshall's Novel." *Caribbean Studies* 10 (1970): 125-34.

Christian, Barbara. *Black Women Novelists: The Development of a Tradition, 1892-1976.* Westport, Conn.: Greenwood, 1980.

Creel, Margaret Washington. "Gullah Attitudes toward Life and Death." In *Africanisms in American Culture,* ed. Joseph E. Holloway, 69-97. Bloomington: Indiana Univ. Press, 1990.

McDowell, Deborah. "New Directions for Black Feminist Criticism." In *Feminist Criticism,* ed. Elaine Showalter, 186-99. New York: Pantheon Books, 1985.

Pettis, Joyce. "A *MELUS* Interview: Paule Marshall." *MELUS* 17 (1992): 117-30.

Washington, Mary Helen. Afterword to *Brown Girl, Brownstones,* by Paule Marshall. 1959; New York: Feminist Press, 1981.

Adele S. Newson-Horst (review date summer/autumn 2001)

SOURCE: Newson-Horst, Adele S. Review of *The Fisher King,* by Paule Marshall. *World Literature Today* 75, no. 3/4 (summer/autumn 2001): 148.

[*In the review that follows, Newson-Horst offers a laudatory assessment of* The Fisher King.]

Paule Marshall's fifth novel is a wonderful rendering of the African diaspora (from Brooklyn to Paris) in its many complexities. Set against the backdrop of a triangular relationship, *The Fisher King* at once celebrates and delineates the nuances of diaspora interactions—a reality perhaps best captured by the musical form of jazz. The work exceeds the scope of the novel of development, the novel of exile, as well as the novel of the émigrée to reach a new height in diaspora writings. Sketching both petty warfare and cultural innovations, it tells the story of a man who is able to capture the soul of his listeners with his new music.

Hattie Carmichael, a city girl, placed in foster care in a central Brooklyn neighborhood, proves to be the base of the triangle that holds together the lives and later the memories of Everett Carlyle Payne (a.k.a. Sonny-Rett Payne) and Cherisse McCullum Payne for a now-interested world. Described as the "motherfathersisterbrother" of the grandson of the couple, in the present (early spring 1984), Hattie raises Sonny (named for his grandfather) in Paris, where African vendors do not accost her, having dubbed her "une Américaine noire. A non-believer."

Lured back to America to attend a concert which commemorates the fifteenth anniversary of Sonny-Rett's death and celebrates his music, Hattie takes the eight-year-old Sonny to Brooklyn for a two-week visit. An African American-West Indian feud is personified in the form of the maternal and paternal grandmothers. Both live on Macon Street, the venue of grand brownstones, many of which are currently being renovated by Edgar DeC Payne and his Three R's Housing Group of Central Brooklyn (Reclamation, Restoration, Rebirth). Sonny's brother Edgar is the architect of the concert and, significantly, a man who recognizes "Nothing's pure. Nothing's wholly selfless"; his success is, in part, an understanding that "sometimes shaking hands with the right folks" and a plastered smile "can make a big difference in this life."

From the first of the seventeen chapters, the petty feud between the American family of Cherisse McCullum and the West Indian family of Everett Payne is foregrounded, a dilemma of the diaspora person. Florence Varina McCullum-Jones comes from a Southern family which at the time of Reconstruction could boast landownership in Varina, Georgia and economic success. Compelled to leave due to racist threats, her father relocated his family and the seed of a magnolia tree to Brooklyn. Hers, then, is a genteel, rooted American family. Yet her disdain of her neighbors, the West Indian families, is disturbing.

Ulene Agatha Cummings is an emigrant from a village in the West Indies. She travels to America after the first "white people war finish" and prides herself on her ability to "cut and contrive," something she perceives the other American grandmother is unable to do. The mother of both Edgar and Sonny-Rett, she raises the latter to be a concert pianist who would one day play at Carnegie Hall. When he makes his foray into jazz and marries Florence Varina's daughter (Cherisse), then moves to Paris never to return, her heart is both broken and hardened.

The child wishes to alienate neither of his proud and willful great-grandmothers. Ulene is the emigrant; Florence Varina is the migrant, and the child the personification of the diaspora element which might effect the healing. He too, like his grandfather, is an artist in his own right. His sketches of castles in which he situates himself as a guard posted on the outside to protect his grandfather on the inside are quite compelling.

In his youth, Sonny (the grandfather) was persecuted for his inclinations and preoccupations concerning jazz. Ulene applied the whip regularly, yet he "never uttered a word, never cried, never begged her to stop." He found understanding in Hattie, who at the time was an employee at a local record store. She kept him informed of the latest trends in music, and later she became the perfect audience and trusted critic. The author's account of how Sonny-Rett won both his name and the beginning of his fame is reminiscent of James Baldwin's short story "Sonny's Blues":

> Everett Payne took his time paying his respects to the tune as written, and once that was done, he hunched closer to the piano, angled his head sharply to the left, completely closed the curtain of his gaze, and with his hands commanding the length and breadth of the keyboard he unleashed a dazzling pyrotechnic of chords (you could almost see their colors), polyrhythms, seemingly unrelated harmonies, and ideas—fresh, brash, outrageous ideas. It was an outpouring of ideas and feelings informed by his own brand of lyricism and lit from time to time by flashes of the recognizable melody. He continued to acknowledge the little simpleminded tune, while at the same time furiously recasting and reinventing it in an image all his own.

Marshall's novel is a national treasure as much as the musical form it employs to tell the story of the diaspora. Like Florence Varina's assessment of her great-grandson, the novel has "some of all of us in [it]." The epigraph at the start of each chapter brilliantly provides the marker for character, diaspora character types, and a larger sense of the neighborhood, "the timeless, familiar vocabulary of around the block." The novel functions as a metaphor for a larger African hyphenated community in which people are measured by how neighborly they can actually be and families aren't always a function of direct blood lines.

Beverly A. Johnson (lecture date November 2001)

SOURCE: Johnson, Beverly A. "Revolutionary Solutions: Challenging Colonialist Attitudes in the Works of Paule Marshall." *CLA Journal* 45, no. 4 (June 2002): 460-76.

[*In the essay below, originally presented as a lecture in November 2001, Johnson investigates how characters*

*in Marshall's literary works challenge colonialist atti-
tudes and work to solve conflicts.*]

Paule Marshall is an author who is adept at understanding and illustrating the complexities of life in particular
for young and older female characters within novels
such as **Brown Girl, Brownstones**; **The Chosen Place,
The Timeless People**; and **Daughters.**[1] Many of her
characters are confronted with the challenge of resisting
gender-, ethnic-, and immigrant-based categories that
restrict or limit ways in which they can define and redefine their lives. Scholarly attention certainly has been
given to her characters' sense of historical awareness
and internal development of self that attempt at the very
least to resist colonialist patterns of being. More recent
scholarly attention has focused on Marshall's female
protagonists from the standpoint of exposing the concerns of identity from individualist and group perspectives while reemphasizing a spiritually oriented past as
a guide of understanding and progressing in the future.[2]
However, several critics also point out that Marshall's
works are effective in exposing relevant conflicts that
exist in efforts to merge themes of identity and ethnicity.
Yet critics are keen on emphasizing that the attempt to
merge both themes tend to remain unresolved. Martin
Japtok, for example, asserts in his study of Marshall's
first novel how protagonist Selina Boyce's journey to
self-discovery is hindered by a need to merge both her
individual and group identity.[3] In addition, a critical essay by Gavin Jones acknowledges Marshall's use of sea
imagery as a "constantly shifting quality" that can aid
in understanding Selina Boyce's ambivalence in her
search for wholeness and self-discovery.[4] Scholar Moira
Ferguson's analysis of Marshall's novel **Daughters** provides one of the most striking discussions in identity in
that it positions Marshall's female protagonist and main
female characters ultimately as leaders with ancestral
"star" powers.[5] The characters' journeys, according to
Ferguson, lead them to better paths of exploring awareness of self through political and social resistance to
discrimination and inequality.[6] Ferguson's assertion that
Ursa Mackenzie (by the novel's conclusion) takes on a
similar role as Congo Jane and thus becomes a leader
in her own right is a message that can be applicable to
some extent to Marshall's protagonists Selina Boyce
and Merle Kinbona.[7] With these critical perspectives in
mind, I believe that an analysis of how select works of
Marshall not only address but also challenge colonialist
attitudes with revolutionary solutions is quite relevant
to the contribution of scholarly materials that currently
exist. This essay therefore explores how select protagonists are effective in conveying strategies to move toward solving rather than simply exposing existing conflicts.

One similar idea present in Marshall's works **Brown
Girl, Brownstones**; **The Chosen Place, The Timeless
People**; and **Daughters** is that the actions of each protagonist can be understood from a global rather than a
national context. The protagonists in these novels are
therefore equipped with methods to resist colonialist
mentalities that are designed to stifle rather than promote self-awareness in both Caribbean and American
societies. Yet protagonists such as Selina Boyce, Merle
Kinbona, and Ursa Mackenzie face many conflicts
throughout their present journeys, confront their pasts
intentionally, and create better opportunities for themselves before the novels' conclusions in spite of the
colonialist attitudes that on the surface tend to be dominant forces in their lives. One of the most resourceful
methods of understanding how these protagonists ultimately create these better opportunities for themselves—by resisting a colonialist mentality—is through
an appropriate ideology that establishes three essential
steps designed to challenge the core belief systems of
individuals or groups. Thus, political critic Stephen
Carter's essay "The Insufficiency of Honesty" provides
a rather insightful approach to viewing integrity rather
than honesty as a more valued weapon of resistance
based on the following standpoints: (1) being able to
determine what is right and wrong, (2) acting on what
one discerns even at personal cost, and (3) admitting
openly that one is acting on his or her understanding of
right and wrong.[8] In using Carter's approach as a
framework,[9] we can see that Marshall's female protagonists promote revolutionary solutions on three distinct
levels. First, Marshall advocates through her protagonists a sense of morality that emphasizes the need to
have and to act with integrity rather than simple honesty. Second, Marshall's protagonists target solutions
that will allow them to claim or reclaim a stronger sense
of self-identity. Third, the actions of these protagonists
indicate that people can reject or, at the very least, control their desire for power that in most cases provides
only a false sense of temporary gratification. Selina
Boyce, Merle Kinbona, and Ursa Mackenzie represent
women of color who choose to discover revolutionary
solutions not just to survive but to gain some measure
of contentment out of the awareness of controlling their
lives in spite of colonialist efforts designed to deny
them the opportunities to do so in their environments.

Since Marshall's novels are keen on emphasizing one's
values and belief systems rather than a simplistic view
of external behaviors and actions, I believe it is necessary to discuss each protagonist through an examination
of the ways each one incorporates integrity in her life
rather than assert simple honesty, particularly while she
is in the midst of major conflicts. The utilization of
Carter's steps are viable in efforts to understand how

these three protagonists move toward revolutionary solutions in their resistance to colonialist attitudes presented during the course of their personal development within Marshall's works.

SELINA BOYCE (BROWN GIRL, BROWNSTONES)

Selina Boyce is the youngest of Marshall's protagonists whose personal growth and experiences provide readers with a keen vision of revolutionary solutions that challenge colonialist mentalities. Her solutions are twofold in conveying that one must have integrity rather than honesty in order to validate any choice or decision, and redefining power on one's own accord can allow her inner spirit to control and shape her external life: one that is easily exposed to colonialist values. One dominant way to view how Selina Boyce incorporates Carter's approach in moving from fake honesty to a strong sense of integrity is through exploring the relationship she has with her mother, Silla Boyce.[10] For it is through this conflicting relationship that Selina not only develops integrity on levels to resist colonialist mentalities but also makes the effort to move Silla in this direction as well. Gavin Jones highlights the fact that much of the criticism of Selina's character is categorized as a personal development story or one that highlights the conflicts of the black experience from a Bajan immigrant's familial perspective. Yet while Jones goes much further in his analysis to emphasize the real challenge of defining oneself with "frequently conflicting definitions," his perspectives can be expanded to reveal not only an exposure of the problems but also to include the solutions to colonialist attitudes indicative of Selina Boyce's internal spirit and external choices.[11]

In a general sense, Marshall's first novel begins with her protagonist understanding on a very basic level that her parents' ideals and identities for their children are vastly different. Deighton Boyce's ideal family environment is on the island of Barbados while Silla Boyce wants to achieve some measure of the American Dream by "buying [a] house" in Brooklyn. Yet at the novel's beginning young Selina is not afraid to voice her opinions based on her sense of right and wrong. She believes at this time that her father has a right to at least imagine a different life for his family while also strongly believing that her mother's memories, which detailed a life of suffering, deserve a respectful audience (Marshall, *Brown Girl* 45-46). Thus, in Book One, a-ten-year-old Selina honestly states to her mother that she has taken the father's position in being pleased with having land in Barbados. After Silla describes her poignant struggles in life as a young child and teenager growing up in Birmshire, she expects Selina to change her perspective about the place, yet Selina reasserts, "I still think I'd like it" (46). This is one of the initial signs that Selina is moving forward in gaining a sense of integrity that will enable her to resist colonialist attitudes. Equally

significant is the mother's response at the end of Book One that foreshadows Selina's move toward integrity in contrast to the mother's lack of integrity during the course of the novel. Silla's comment, "Look how I has gone and brought something into this world to whip me" (47), can be interpreted not so much as to show the distance between Silla and Selina but to suggest that Silla as a mother can learn as much from her daughter's honesty as her daughter can learn from her mother's honest intentions.

In Books Two and Three—entitled "Pastorale" and "The War," respectively—Selina slowly understands that honesty cannot substitute for integrity based on the outcome of the dominant familial conflict. Viewing her mother as morally wrong for wanting to take Deighton's land, Selina decides to tell everyone who she believes can help stop the mother's act. Although her actions are to some degree in vain, she has attempted what Carter suggests are the three steps needed to establish integrity.[12] First, she clearly discerns who is right and wrong by believing the mother has no right to sell her husband's property (94). Secondly, she voices and acts on her beliefs even at personal cost by disregarding Miss Thompson's warning that her parents' issues do not concern her (94). Thirdly, she verbally confronts her mother at the factory site (95-101). During this time, Marshall positions the protagonist to challenge the mother's materialism through their brief debate about money and love. Although skeptically and in opposition to her mother, Selina establishes an early belief that the internal values of love and freedom are more important than industrialized, materialistic values of mainstream society that Silla tries to instill in her (103-04). These values for Selina become more sustainable by the novel's conclusion.

By the end of "The War" Selina and her sister Ina observe a mother who develops what Carter deems a fake honesty, for although she reveals to Deighton the plan and her reasons for selling his land (113-14) and is even blatantly honest in wanting him deported, she does not offer her children a strong example of a mother who has integrity. Unlike Selina, Silla never took the time to seriously contemplate whether what she believed was "good, right or true."[13] Silla's desire for revenge and to fit into a Barbadian community intent on assimilating into mainstream society at the expense of her daughters keeps the conflicts between Selina and the mother an essential part of the plot. This point is relevant because it shows Selina in a growth process of modeling herself through those traits of her mother that she resists rather than focusing only on the ones that the mother accepts for herself.

Even though it should be acknowledged that Selina temporarily becomes deceptive about her relationship with Clive Springer and her intent to join the Barbadian Association, it is clear that she ultimately moves beyond a shallow sense of honesty and regains a stronger sense of integrity based on three dominant decisions: ending her relationship with Springer, refusing to accept the Barbadian Association's scholarship money, and deciding to chart her own path towards Barbados instead of following the career plans that her mother wants for her in America. These three decisions suggest that with integrity one can become a revolutionary in her or his own right and for the right reasons. For Selina, it is critical to recognize that her mother has adopted to some extent a colonialist mind-set in light of what she wants for her family. Selina's actions in openly telling her mother what she believes, even at the cost of jeopardizing their relationship, highlights the fact that one must always consider resisting or challenging people they may be closest to. Selina decides to base her decision to leave Clive Springer not so much on the mother's rejection of him, but rather on her own realization that she had outgrown him.

Selina continues to articulate these ideas when she confronts her peers with a negative view of their organization, which debates the inclusion of all people of color. She condemns them because of her belief that their organization promotes rather than resists any form of colonialist attitudes; she asserts, "[I]t's the result of living by the most shameful codes possible—dog eat dog, exploitation, the strong over the weak, the end justifies the means—the whole kit and caboodle" (227). Similarly, by the novel's end Selina's integrity allows her to speak with courage to the Barbadian association and to tell her mother that knowing what one does not want for oneself is a key step to discovering a more authentic self-identity. At age seventeen, a more reflective and courageous Selina asserts:

> "Now that I'm less of a child I'm beginning to understand. . . . But still I can't accept the award." . . .
> "Oh, not only because I don't deserve it, but because it also means something I don't want for myself. . . ."
>
> (303)

Although Selina's future may be uncertain, her acts of resistance—in claiming her own voice based on integrity and on her ability to redefine true power on her own terms—suggest viable revolutionary solutions to colonialist attitudes prevalent in both mainstream society and in the ethnic communities. In addition, Selina's expression of self is in a manner that is based more on integrity than on blatant honesty, and this type of self-expression promotes real empowerment for her rather than a false and temporary sense of gratification.

MERLE KINBONA (THE CHOSEN PLACE, THE TIMELESS PEOPLE)

Marshall's most effective effort toward creating characters that promote revolutionary solutions is most evident in her development of protagonist Merle Kinbona. Numerous publications, including one by scholar Jane Olmstead, focus on the protagonist's ability to communicate resistance on various levels, such as body language, speech, and ties to the Bournehills community (252).[14] My interest similarly focuses on Kinbona's progression in articulating the detrimental nature of colonialist attitudes and on offering revolutionary solutions from two parallel standpoints: her mental lapses and her role as a community activist. For with each mental lapse the protagonist endures, she gains the strength to become more resistant to people and ideas that threaten her integrity and that of the Bournehills community.

At the beginning of the novel, Marshall sets an interesting tone with Merle's physical description that suggests to some extent that the dominant character will have to measure her self-worth based on her resistance to colonialist attitudes that challenge her integrity with respect to her own life and her community (Marshall, *Timeless* 5). Initially, readers learn about Merle through the characters Leesy Walkes and Allen Fuso. Their comments about her allow the reader to know that the community sees Merle as one whom they trust and as a character who fights for what she believes in. For instance, in Book One Leesy Walkes reveals that Merle has suffered from a psychological ailment brought on by her refusal to teach her students only about the English and their history (32). Merle's decision to incorporate in her classes the history of Cuffee Ned and the Bournehills island resulted in her being fired from her teaching position (33). With this early form of resistance defining her character to some extent, Leesy's depiction of Merle's first mental lapse provides further context for Merle's growth as one with integrity. For each time Merle is characterized as acting or behaving in an insane manner, she progresses with hope and determination to make some major change in her life.

Merle's dear friend Allen Fuso further describes her to Saul Amron as a woman with a troubled past that includes the loss of her husband and daughter, yet he asserts, "She hasn't gone under, she's still Merle; herself and kind of special" (17). By describing Merle as also being symbolic in understanding the island, Allen indirectly highlights the attributes of a woman who ultimately replaces honesty with a consistent measure of integrity in order to not simply remain alive but to live with a sense of clarity and vision, which she uses to reclaim herself. At the core of her existence is the resis-

tance to colonialist mentalities through a clear understanding that basing one's actions on a consistent
integrity is one of the best ways to achieve real progress
for Bournehills. Thus in Books Three and Four, entitled
"Carnival and Whitsun," Kinbona's empowerment of
self becomes more tangible for the reader based on
three major events: the Carnival, the closing of Cane
Vale, and Merle's confrontation with Harriet Amron.[15]

During the first two events of the Carnival and the closing of Cane Vale, Merle is not only in the process of
helping herself but of also helping Saul Amron realize
that his mission in helping others cannot be fulfilled as
he would like until he gains a stronger sense of integrity. Even before the Carnival event, Merle aids Saul in
exploring how he is clearly representative of the
colonialist system despite his efforts to support the
Bournehills people (226-27). Thus, through observing
Merle's active commitment to celebrating the past
struggles of her people during the Carnival, Saul realizes even more that the understanding of one's history
will lead to solving problems rather than creating them
(315). Based on their honest relationship with one another, both characters are able to come to terms with
the most painful parts of their past in order to effectively remedy the problems facing the Bournehills community. Thus Merle's tirade during the temporary closing of Cane Vale makes the truth even clearer for him.
She exclaims, "You know what your trouble is? Do you
know? . . . You can't see for looking, that's what. Or
maybe deep down you don't want to see" (389-90).
Merle's further criticism of Saul highlights what she
perceives to be the colonialist attitudes that have kept
her community from progressing as a people. Yet the
most significant solution she offers to Saul during her
tirade is the integrity that is not built on monetary quick
fixes but on an examination of the psychological devastation of colonialist attitudes. She yells at him:

> "Well, open your eyes damn you and look. It's there
> for a blind man to see. Look at those poor people stand-
> ing out there like they've turned to stone, afraid to set
> foot inside the gate when they should be overrunning
> this place and burning it the hell down, or better yet,
> taking it over and running it themselves. Talk about
> change? That's the kind we need down here bo."
>
> (388)

Even though Merle's verbal confrontation with Saul
leads to her final mental lapse, she becomes stronger by
the novel's conclusion as a result of applying the three
key steps of integrity, as Carter prescribes, in fighting
her inner battle of being separated from her child, one
of the most painful parts of her past. She is able, therefore, to defeat Harriet Amron with the following revelation:

> I can't be bought or bribed. . . . And I don't accept
> handouts. Not anymore at least. I use to. You might
> have [doubts] about that, but I did. And for the longest
> time. And because of it I lost two people who meant
> life itself to me. I've grown wise in my old age. . . .
> Poor as the devil, but proud.
>
> (441)

Merle is indirectly admitting in her anger to Harriet that
her sexual relationship with Saul was not in anyone's
best interest, yet it was a viable lesson to her because
she learned that being intimate with him was more an
attempt on her part to recover or to reclaim a part of
her past that she realized she could not find in the arms
of another woman's husband but rather in bold resistance to the core source of colonialist power embodied
in both the Englishwoman and Harriet Amron. In contrast to Harriet, Merle is able to progress as a dimen-
sional character by not suppressing or fearing her past
and present, but through an honest, reflective analysis
of it.

In a broader and more extensive context than that of
Selina Boyce, Merle offers two key solutions in her efforts to resist colonialist attitudes, from both a personal
and universal perspective. First, one must be an active
teacher in exposing truths and facts rather than illusions
of them. Second, self-purification is necessary to make
change and can be achieved more appropriately with integrity than without it. Merle is able to see her future
more clearly by the novel's end as an activist who is intent on making a difference in her home environment
(468). She tells Saul:

> But I'll be coming back to Bournehills. This is home.
> Whatever little I can do that will matter for something
> must be done here. A person can run for years but
> sooner or later he has to take a stand in the place for
> better or worse, he calls home, do what he can to
> change things there.
>
> (468)

Merle's progress as an individual and as a community
leader who tries and succeeds ultimately at not only being honest about her past but also valuing her sense of
morality in order to find peace enables her to map out a
better existence for her future and the future of her
community. In a similar fashion as Merle Kinbona, Ursa
Mackenzie is another protagonist who reiterates the
same message.

URSA MACKENZIE (*DAUGHTERS*)

In his critique of Washington's policies in *Souls of Black
Folks,* W. E. B. Du Bois asserts, "The hushing of the
criticism of honest opponents is a dangerous thing."[16] It
is this message that evolves as a collective stance for
the major female characters in Marshall's 1991 novel

entitled *Daughters*.[17] The novel promotes feminist forms of activism and revolutionary solutions that support rather than impede the progress of poor and lower-class people on the island of Triunion. Based primarily on the lives of protagonist Ursa Mackenzie, her mother, Estelle Mackenzie, and Ursa's best friend, Vincereta (Viney) Daniels, the novel shows how women can reaffirm for one another a collective vision of empowerment through a keen determination to improve the quality of their lives. Estelle and Viney are instrumental, therefore, in Ursa's development of an inner spirit that ultimately comes to shape her external life and allows her to reclaim her voice.

Most of the first three chapters that focus on the protagonist highlight a young woman who is uncertain about her future from economic and educational perspectives. In addition, Ursa is unable to admit that her dependency on her father at times clouds her honest criticism of him as a political figure. Yet in efforts to take control over her own life, she develops a favorable approach that suggests she is a person of integrity. For example, she does not regard money as more important than people when she turns down a lucrative job as the Associate Director of Research at the National Consumer Research Corporation (*Daughters* 46-48). She goes even further to externally reject white mainstream values by selling her apartment, car, furniture, and "NCRC" suits, and she also braids her hair in a style that reflects her Caribbean upbringing (48). However, when targeting her relationships with boyfriend Lowell Carruthers and father Primus Mackenzie, Ursa is quite hesitant to make permanent changes that are needed to promote favorable self-development. Ironically, Lowell Carruthers' blatant honesty in his negative assessment of Ursa and her father's relationship is exactly what helps Ursa obtain the integrity needed to critically view her father's political aims and to bring closure eventually to her relationship with Carruthers (45-46). Ursa poignantly exposes Lowell's indictment of Primus' ineffective leadership in his district when she decides to begin a new job conducting a follow-up study of the Midland City mayoral race (274-76). Her two separate visits with Mayor Lawson and his former campaign manager, Mae Ryland, exposes Ursa to the reality that Lawson simply caters to the interests of white politicians and businessmen rather than the needs of the black people who voted him into office (296). Ursa realizes also that the forces that perpetuate the impoverished areas of Midland City, New Jersey, are quite identical to the forces that leave the Morland District of Triunion overcrowded and economically crippled (332-33). Although reluctant at first, she returns to the island, and with her mother as a guiding force, she delivers the

resort-scheme prospectus to her father's political rival, Justin Beaufils, who uses it against Primus and thus wins the election (390-91).

Ursa does not silence the criticism of an honest opponent to her father, for she comes to understand that Primus' opponent is not just his political rival Justin Beaufils; his true opponents, from a familial and community standpoint, are his wife and daughter. This is important because Ursa's decision to aid Beaufils shows that she recognizes, as Selina Boyce does, that being critical of loved ones is sometimes necessary when resisting colonial attitudes and behaviors. Thus it is significant to point out also that although Estelle's overall impact upon Ursa's life is subtle, it is more effective than Primus's influences by the novel's conclusion because Estelle has more integrity than her husband. She is most successful in teaching her daughter (in the spirit of ancient leaders Congo Jane and Will Cudjoe) that having integrity and the moral reflectiveness to maintain it when faced with difficult decisions will be essential in challenging colonialist attitudes and systems (362-64). Thus Ursa is ultimately able to see clearly her dependent ties to her father and to see him as a political figure and a father who has flaws that should be corrected, whether he wants them to be or not. Ursa and Estelle reclaim their voices indirectly in a familial context and believe that their actions are based on a commitment to the community and themselves rather than on any false sense of political power.

In a fashion similar to Estelle, Ursa's best friend Viney plays a critical role in shaping Ursa's outlook on her relationship with Lowell and her parents. The strong bond of these two women enables Viney, in particular, to push Ursa to critically examine her relationship with Lowell (102-03). Viney simply asks Ursa whether Lowell is useful (102-03), because she is skeptical of his commitment to Ursa, his community, and his culture. In short, Viney wants Ursa to have favorable relationships with a man who has integrity (111-12). She tells Ursa:

> "You remind me of a cat with a string of tin cans and some bones from a graveyard tied to its tail when it comes to your folks. . . . All that stuff about them and that island stays on your mind. . . . The cans and bones keep up such a racket that you can't hear yourself, your own voice trying to tell you which way to go, and what to do with your life. You can't hear Ursa. You know what you're gonna have to do with all that stuff, don't you?"
>
> (112)

Ursa's return to Triunion is indicative of her attempt to bury the "cans and bones" that have perpetuated instability for her. With Viney's help, Ursa sees her family and Triunion society from a new perspective. She is able to validate, eventually, her actions and choices based on her own beliefs rather than through efforts to please others—especially her father. She understands that her father, Primus, has never taken the time to reflect on his values in a manner that would create a clearer, more objective progression for his people. Ursa, Estelle, and Viney suggest through their relationships that collectivism is key in any form of revolutionary solutions that are long-term.[18] They have also learned that one may find the answer to resistance not so much in waging battle with the traditional colonialists but with one's relatives or even one's self: a lesson that each of Marshall's protagonists discover throughout their experiences.

Marshall's novels **Brown Girl, Brownstones, The Chosen Place, The Timeless People,** and **Daughters** are quite instrumental in conveying revolutionary solutions to colonialist attitudes based on the final positions of the protagonists in her works. Each protagonist (Selina, Merle, and Ursa) is able to create better opportunities for herself in spite of the colonialist attitudes that are prevalent in their lives. With integrity rather than honesty as a core foundation of their inner being, these characters find revolutionary solutions in claiming their voice and rejecting power that is based on a false sense of external gratification. For these three protagonists, this is where the real power of truth exists.

Notes

Author's note: This paper was presented at the International Conference on Caribbean Literature in Trois Ilets, Martinique (Nov. 7-9, 2001).

1. Paule Marshall, *Brown Girl, Brownstones* (New York: Feminist Press, 1981); *Daughters* (New York: Plume, 1991); and *The Chosen Place, The Timeless People* (New York: Vintage, 1992). Hereafter, each novel is cited parenthetically in the text.

2. See Dorothy Denniston, *The Fiction of Paule Marshall: Reconstructions of History, Culture, and Gender* (Knoxville, U of Tennessee P, 1995) and Joyce Pettis, *Toward Wholeness in Paule Marshall's Fiction* (Charlottesville: UP of Virginia, 1995).

3. Martin Japtok, "Paule Marshall's *Brown Girl, Brownstones:* Reconciling Ethnicity and Individualism," *African American Review* 32:4 (1998): 306-15.

4. Gavin Jones, "The Sea Ain't Got No Back Door: The Problem with Black Consciousness in Paul Marshall's *Brown Girl, Brownstones*," *African American Review* 32:4 (1998): 599.

5. Moira Ferguson, "Of Bears and Bearings: Paule Marshall's Diverse Daughters," *MELUS* 24:1 (1999): 177-93.

6. Ferguson 178-79.

7. Ferguson 190. Ferguson offers an optimistic view for Ursa's Mackenzie's future because of her resistance to colonial powers and adherence to her maternal ancestral forces. Similar to Mackenzie, Selina Boyce and Merle Kinbona are protagonists whose futures are favorable in light of their methods of resistance to colonialist attitudes.

8. Stephen Carter, "The Insufficiency of Honesty," *The Writer's Presence: A Pool of Essays,* ed. Donald McQuade and Robert Atwan (Boston: Bedford, 2000) 328.

9. Carter's assertion that honesty is a "poor substitute for integrity" makes his steps of defining integrity applicable to those protagonists intent on exploring solutions to their past conflicts steeped in colonialist mentalities.

10. In her afterword to the novel, Mary Helen Washington discusses Silla as a dominant guide for Selina, yet reveals her development as a dominant character through Selina's eyes (afterword, *Brown Girl, Brownstones* [New York: Feminist Press, 1981] 315).

11. Jones, 601ff.

12. Carter 329.

13. Carter 329. Silla's revenge-based actions are not necessarily preceded by a clear moral judgment. Even though she is honest about her intentions, her course of action is dictated much more by self-interest and image than by integrity.

14. See Jane Olmstead, "The Pull of Memory and the Language of Place in Paule Marshall's *The Chosen Place, The Timeless People* and *Praisesong for the Widow*," *African American Review* 31:2 (1997): 252. In addition to Olmstead's work, see Joseph Skerrett, "Paule Marshall and the Crisis of Middle Years: *The Chosen Place, The Timeless People,*" *Callaloo* 6 (1983); Sascha Talmor, "Merle of Bournehills," *Durham University Journal* 80 December (1987); and Missy Dehn Kubitschek, "Paule Marshall's Women on a Quest," *Black American Literature Forum* 21 (1987).

15. Although these events highlight a progressive relationship of honesty and trust between Merle Kinbona and Saul Amron, my focal point is not only to establish how they aid each other but also to suggest that each event is key in positioning Merle Kinbona as coming closer to dealing with her past, which she has left unresolved for many years.

16. W. E. B. Du Bois, "Of Mr. Booker T. Washington and Others," from *The Souls of Black Folk,* in *The*

Norton Anthology of African American Literature, ed. Henry Louis Gates, Jr., and Nellie McKay (New York: Norton, 1997) 635.

17. Du Bois's criticism of Washington is relevant in a discussion of these characters because it reminds us that internal criticism within groups, families, and communities can be more favorable than detrimental to relevant political and social causes intent on promoting progress rather than hindering it.

18. See Ferguson 177-93.

FURTHER READING

Criticism

Benjamin, Shanna Greene. "Weaving the Web of Reintegration: Locating Aunt Nancy in *Praisesong for the Widow.*" *MELUS* 30, no. 1 (spring 2005): 49-67.

Contends that Marshall's use of West African myth in *Praisesong for the Widow* gives the author the opportunity "to reach beyond the material reality of race, class, and gender oppression and delve into the psychological and spiritual desires of black women."

DeLamotte, Eugenia C. *Places of Silence, Journeys of Freedom: The Fiction of Paule Marshall.* Philadelphia: University of Pennsylvania Press, 1998, 198 p.

Critical study of Marshall's short stories and novels, focusing specifically on the interconnectedness of power, memory, and speech in her works.

Japtok, Martin. "Sugarcane as History in Paule Marshall's 'To Da-Duh, in Memoriam.'" *African American Review* 34, no. 3 (fall 2000): 475-82.

Explores the symbolism of sugarcane in the short story "To Da-Duh, in Memoriam."

Zakes Mda
1948-

(Born Zanemvula Kizito Gatyeni Mda) South African playwright, novelist, poet, and nonfiction writer.

INTRODUCTION

A prolific author of works in a variety of genres, Mda is considered one of the foremost writers in post-apartheid South Africa. Born into the apartheid system—which, from 1948 to 1990, legally mandated racial segregation and the subservience of blacks to whites in all aspects of social and political intercourse—Mda witnessed its malevolence firsthand. In his writings he explores both the causes and the effects of a society organized in terms of racial dominance and exploitation, as well as the spirit of revolt that eventually led to its dismantling.

BIOGRAPHICAL INFORMATION

Mda was born in 1948 in the Herschel District of the Eastern Cape Province of South Africa. His paternal grandfather, Charles Mda, was a petty chief whose job was to enforce apartheid laws. His father, A. P. Mda, was a founding member of the African National Congress Youth League, where he worked with Nelson Mandela, before leaving that group to join the more radical liberationist Pan Africanist Congress. His mother, Nompumelelo Rose Mda, was a nurse. Because of his father's political involvement, the young Mda came into regular contact with some of South Africa's leading activists, and for a brief period he lived in Mandela's home, Orlando. In 1963 Mda's father was forced into exile in the Basotholand Protectorate—later the independent Kingdom of Lesotho—and a year later, Mda crossed the border to join him; two years later, the rest of the family followed. The move forced the family to learn a new language and Mda's feelings of inadequacy in both his native tongue and that of his new country led him to begin writing his creative works in English when he was in high school. Mda went to schools in Lesotho and Switzerland before moving to the United States to pursue a master's degree in theater at Ohio University, after his first published volume of plays, *We Shall Sing for the Fatherland and Other Plays* (1980) met with great acclaim. Mda next received a master's degree in mass communication, also from Ohio University.

In 1985 he returned to Lesotho to work for the country's National Broadcasting Corporation Television Project while continuing to write and produce plays. Shortly thereafter, Mda took a position at the University of Lesotho as a professor of English; in 1991 he became head of the university's English department, after receiving his doctoral degree from the University of Capetown in South Africa in 1990. Upon his return to Lesotho, Mda co-founded the Martholi Traveling Theatre—with which he went, with his students, to rural mountain villages to help the residents express themselves through drama—and was director of the Theatre for Development program at the university. In 1992 Mda received a fellowship from Yale University's South African Research Program; he remained in the United States, teaching at various universities, until 1994, when he returned to South Africa to serve as a visiting professor at Witwatersrand University's School of Dramatic Art. In 1996 Mda took over the directorship of Thapama Productions, a motion picture and television production company, in Johannesburg. In 1998 he took part in a cultural exchange program in Reykjavik, Iceland, called Shuttle 99, conducting workshops in children's literature for South African and Scandinavian writers. In the early 2000s Mda began dividing his time between the United States, where he teaches creative writing at Ohio University, and South Africa, where he directs the Southern African Multimedia AIDS Trust, produces plays at the Market Theatre in Johannesburg, and works as a beekeeper in the eastern Cape region.

MAJOR WORKS

In his plays and novels Mda investigates apartheid and all its attendant social ills: forced relocation, migrant labor, poverty, violence, and unjust land distribution. He also examines problems with the post-apartheid system and postcolonial governments in Africa. In his first published play, *We Shall Sing for the Fatherland,* Mda confronts the disillusionment of soldiers who have fought in the liberation of a fictional African country. After fighting in their country's war for independence, two soldiers return to civilian life, but have neither homes nor jobs. They commit minor burglaries and live in a city park, maintaining the militaristic demeanor they learned in the war to deflect their alienation from the new society they have helped to create. In *And the Girls in Their Sunday Dresses* (1993), Mda again addresses what happens to a country's people after liberation. Two women—identified in the play as The Lady and The Woman—wait to buy rice at a government aid food depot. Although the interaction between the women seems simple, through their conversation the audience learns of the inefficient, corrupt bureaucracy that has sprung up in their newly independent country, which in many ways is even worse than the exploitative colonial rulers. In another early play, *The Hill* (1990), two migrant workers, disenfranchised by the collapse of South Africa's agricultural economy, await word on whether they will be hired as laborers in the country's gold mines. Trapped in a kind of limbo, the men develop what Mda reveals to be a diseased and degrading relationship of chronic one-upmanship, even comparing the relative size of their stools. Meanwhile, the work in the mines, which the men believe will bring them great wealth, turns out to be just as dehumanizing as their joblessness—in fact, Mda portrays migrant labor as little more than modern slavery.

In his novel *Ways of Dying* (1995) Mda again focuses on South African social problems, this time portraying the country's violence in the lead-up to the anti-apartheid revolution as largely self-inflicted among poor blacks—the self-imposed "ways of dying" of the book's title. *The Heart of Redness* (2000) examines how black South Africans responded to their new freedoms just after the end of apartheid. In this novel, residents of a village in the eastern Cape must decide whether to accept the proposal of a black empowerment firm that wants to capitalize on post-apartheid possibilities by turning the village into a tourist destination. Mda addresses the many meanings of "progress" and contrasts the native experience of Africa with Joseph Conrad's white European view of it in his novella *The Heart of Darkness*. In his next novel, *The Madonna of Excelsior* (2002), Mda takes up the subject of miscegenation. The book is based on an actual 1971 court case in South Africa in which nineteen blacks in the town of Excelsior were charged with violating the country's Immorality Act, which outlawed sexual encounters between blacks and whites. In *The Whale Caller* (2005), Mda explores the range of human love relationships in a story of a man who is torn between his love for a woman and his obsession and fascination with a whale. Mda's most recent novel, *Cion* (2007), continues the story of the protagonist of *Ways of Dying* after he has moved to the United States and attempts to negotiate the seemingly strange habits of his new culture.

CRITICAL RECEPTION

Mda has received numerous accolades and honors both as a playwright and as a novelist. He is considered one of the leading voices in South African letters, particu-larly for his acknowledgment of the ambivalent nature of liberation in African countries. Of this quality, Chijioke Uwah noted: "Mda's creativity and foresight have never been in doubt. At a time when playwrights were concerned with the evils of apartheid he had the foresight and courage to deal with issues beyond the demise of apartheid." In 2003 Mda became engaged in a public spat with the American novelist Norman Rush, who (in a January, 2003 *New York Review of Books* article) excoriated Mda in a review of *The Heart of Redness,* accusing him of clinging to a "culturally backward-looking ideology" and of ignoring the African AIDS pandemic in his novels. Mda, for his part, responded with outrage over the expectation that he should include a comprehensive analysis of AIDS in all of his books, noting that Rush did not take white South African writers to task for not discussing AIDS. Mda has also sometimes been censured for the violence, hopelessness, and predictable characterizations (especially of whites) in his works, but he continues to be esteemed for his passionate and imaginative portrayals of life in contemporary Africa.

PRINCIPAL WORKS

*We Shall Sing for the Fatherland and Other Plays (plays) 1980

Bits of Debris: The Poetry of Zakes Mda (poetry) 1986

The Hill (play) 1990

†The Plays of Zakes Mda (plays) 1990

‡And the Girls in Their Sunday Dresses: Four Works (plays and dramatic poetry) 1993

When People Play People: Development Communication through Theatre (nonfiction) 1993

Ways of Dying (novel) 1995

Melville 67: A Novella for Youth (novella) 1997

The Role of Culture in the Process of Reconciliation in South Africa (nonfiction) 1997

She Plays with the Darkness: A Novel (novel) 1999

The Heart of Redness (novel) 2000

The Madonna of Excelsior (novel) 2002

§Fools, Bells, and the Habit of Eating: Three Satires (plays) 2002

The Whale Caller (novel) 2005

Cion (novel) 2007

*Includes *We Shall Sing for the Fatherland, Dead End,* and *Dark Voices Ring.*

†Includes *Dead End, We Shall Sing for the Fatherland, Dark Voices Ring, The Hill,* and *The Road.*

‡Includes *And the Girls in Their Sunday Dresses, The Final Dance, Banned,* and *Joys of War.*

§Includes *The Mother of All Eating, You Fool, How Can the Sky Fall?,* and *The Bells of Amersfoort.*

CRITICISM

Chijioke Uwah (essay date May 2003)

SOURCE: Uwah, Chijioke. "The Theme of Political Betrayal in the Plays of Zakes Mda." *English in Africa* 30, no. 1 (May 2003): 135-44.

[In the following essay, Uwah analyzes Mda's stance on the political stagnation and broken promises that followed rebellion and liberation in many African countries.]

Africa's political history has been a continuous song of promises and betrayal. Mike van Graan captures this sad reality very eloquently in his paper titled "Theatre in the New South Africa: Sellout or Vanguard":

> Utopia is a relative state of being. For many in oppressive situations, the kingdom which they pray might come has for so long been 'a pie in the sky when you die.' Many died, and for those left behind, the demise of the immediate tyranny which drove them to prayer in the first place has been confused with the notion that the kingdom has come. Yet for many post-colonial Africans, for many post-military junta Latin Americans, for many post-communist dictatorship East Europeans, the kingdom which they at one stage thought was nigh, is not among them, has still not come and may indeed be further away.
>
> But maybe for some it has come. Either new elites have emerged or old elites have continued to enjoy their privileges, but now with greater legitimacy as the tyranny under which they acquired their privileges has been cast on the scrap heap of history and the cocktail party and caviar boundaries have been redrawn to accommodate a few former victims.
>
> (1991, 23)

This summary of the realities of the third world political landscape forms the bedrock of Zakes Mda's political vision in most of his plays in the seventies and eighties. His scepticism about the political future of South Africa is rooted in the perception that many African countries that acquired independence are no better off now. Will South Africa be any different? Broken promises seem to be the rule rather than the exception in all of these countries. He articulated his disillusionment in an interview with Myles Holloway: "Yes, I am disillusioned with independent Africa. I don't see any overt independence at all. Most liberated countries have just taken over the colonial structures" (Holloway 1989, 86).

His disillusionment found expression in *We Shall Sing for the Fatherland,* a play produced in 1978 in which he accurately predicted the state of the common man in a post-independent South Africa. It is a play that concretely demonstrates the concept of betrayal, for—like millions of other Africans—the South African masses

represented by the two hoboes would find out that all their sweat and blood for the liberation of their country was in vain. Like other Africans north of the Limpopo, they would find out that independence has merely been a changing of the guard; only this time the new guard happens to be black. Mafutha, a character in the play who is representative of the new ruling elite, demonstrates his lack of concern for the welfare of his people. While the veterans Sergeant and Janabari were trying to reach out to him, he was busy negotiating with the white banker, symbolic of Western neo-colonial institutions, for a position in the country's Stock Exchange. The sense of betrayal prompts the veterans to ask the all-important question:

SERGEANT:

> We are the men who sacrificed our sweat and blood for the cause. Was it for this, Janabari?

JANABARI:

> We made the sacrifice. Our only mistake was to come out of it alive.
>
> (Mda 1980, 7)

Mda's intention in this play is to explore the idea of betrayal in the lives of the common people. Throughout the play he exposes the veterans to all kinds of ill-treatment reminiscent of the colonial days. Firstly, there is Cabinet, the highest policy-maker in the land whose sole aim should be the welfare of the poor masses. Its callous eviction of the veterans from the park, which can only be compared to the land-grabbing tendencies of the colonial masters, is the first blow to the veterans' dream of an egalitarian society.

OFISIRI:

> Cabinet is interested in you insofar as it wants your type cleared off the streets. *(Brandishing the letter.)* Our country is chairing an international conference on Environment. Delegates from all over the world will be flocking all over the city. Tours will be conducted for them throughout our beautiful city, and as I told you before, you are not anyone's idea of a tourist attraction.
>
> (16)

The thematic similarity between this incident and another that takes place in Ngugi wa Thiong'o's play, *This Time Tomorrow* (1972), needs to be emphasised. Mda has repeatedly stated that his inspiration—and, perhaps, scepticism—came from reading Ngugi's works about Kenya. In *This Time Tomorrow* Ngugi also highlights the plight of the common man in post-independence Kenya. Thousands of poor people were callously evicted from their slum dwelling in Nairobi because as Kiongo, the city council health inspector declared, they represent an eyesore and embarrassment to the government in the eyes of the world: "'By twelve o'clock today these shacks must be demolished. They are a great shame on our city. Tourists from America,

Britain and West Germany are disgusted with the dirt that is slowly creeping into a city that used to be the pearl of Africa'" (Ngugi 1972, 193).

The similarity in reasons given by officials for the eviction of their people in both **We Shall Sing for the Fatherland** and *This Time Tomorrow* is very conspicuous. In both cases the interests of visiting European and American tourists come before those of the masses of the people.

Later on in the play Mda presents the audience with the cumulative effect of the suffering and the feeling of betrayal by the veterans. He articulates their loss of patriotic zeal through their inability to sing for the fatherland:

SERGEANT:

Come Janabari, let us sing for the fatherland. The land we liberated with our sweat and blood. Our fatherland. *(They stand together, and then open their mouths wide, trying to sing. But the voices won't come out. In frustration they stop trying and sit down.)* It is of no use, Janabari.

JANABARI:

Our voices are gone.

SERGEANT:

And we can't sing for the fatherland before we sleep.

JANABARI:

Let us sleep without the song.

(Mda 1980, 23)

The song element is important here because it represents patriotism and love for one's country. In the European tradition, the national anthem is supposed to stir up the spirit of love and commitment to one's country. In the African tradition, a song is used to demonstrate joy and happiness. There is always a song for every occasion. The fact that the veterans are unable to sing for their fatherland means that they have lost their love and patriotic zeal for their country.

If there is one character that Mda uses effectively to portray the theme of betrayal it is Mafutha, who, as mentioned earlier, is symbolic of the new leadership in post-independent Africa. This is the leader upon whose shoulders rest the hopes and aspirations of millions of people who have suffered at the hands of their colonial masters. What Mda portrays in the character of Mafutha is the metamorphosis that takes place in the mind-set and attitude of African leaders after independence. Thus we see an example of self-centred, egocentric and corrupt leadership. Mda represents these qualities through Mafutha's actions. When he comes across the veterans in the park, he ignores them:

JANABARI:

Good morning, sir, Mr Mafutha.

SERGEANT:

How are you, Mr Mafutha?

(Businessman looks the other way and walks on with offended pomposity . . .)

JANABARI:

Mm, Serge. It is our people who snub us.

(14)

In the African tradition, and especially in black communities in South Africa, greeting is a very important aspect of social relationship. When people greet each other, it is a symbol of respect and of communal values. It shows that the people respect and care for one another. When people fail to greet, it is regarded as arrogance and lack of respect. Mda draws from this aspect of African tradition to highlight the gross neglect of the masses of the people by the leadership. The fact that Mafutha was negotiating his political future with a foreign power reflects his lack of sensitivity to his people's needs.

Frantz Fanon highlights this point in his book *The Wretched of the Earth* when he says:

Before independence, the leader generally embodies the aspirations of the people for independence, political liberty and national dignity. But as soon as independence is declared, far from embodying in concrete form the needs of the people in what touches bread, land and restoration of the country to the sacred hands of the people, the leader will reveal his inner purpose: to become the General President of that company of profiteers impatient for their returns which constitutes the national bourgeoisie.

(Fanon 1961, 133)

It is important to point out that Mda's indictment of the post-colonial situation is based on socialist principles. His distaste for capitalist exploitation is voiced later by Janabari, who says:

We are not getting our share of whatever there is to be shared. That is what the learned ones call Capitalism. It has no place for us . . . Only for the likes of Mr Mafutha and the other fat ones at the Chamber of Commerce and Stock Exchange. Serge, I have been trying to tell you that our wars were not merely to replace a white face with a black one but to change a system which exploits us, to replace it with one which will give us a share in the wealth of this country. What we need is another war of freedom, Serge, a war which will put the land back in the hands of the people.

(Mda 1980, 22)

An understanding of class conflict marks off Mda's social criticism from that of the broad African nationalism of the time. Mda locates the source of oppression at the conjuncture of class, race, and capital. According to Myles Holloway:

Mda's political vision, particularly in *We Shall Sing for the Fatherland,* is more comprehensive than the dichotomy of black heroism and white oppression that characterises a great deal of black theatre. Mda attempts to encompass in dramatic terms the complex interaction of race, class and capital as the determinants of oppression and exploitation.

(1989, 30)

In Mda's view, oppression is the prerogative of the rich and powerful—but frightened—class who are paranoid about losing everything. It doesn't matter whether they are the colonial masters or the new black elite. It is usually the poor and the helpless who suffer.

If Mda was predicting political betrayal in independent South Africa in *We Shall Sing for the Fatherland,* he has followed through forcefully in *Mother of All Eating* (first produced in 1992). 'Eating' (slang for embezzlement and corruption) has become rampant in post-1994 South Africa and surpasses the scale of corruption predicted in *We Shall Sing for the Fatherland.*

Mda must certainly feel betrayed, and his scepticism—which was prompted by his experiences in other African countries (in particular Lesotho, where he spent the greater part of his life), and which he articulates in *We Shall Sing for the Fatherland*—seems to be vindicated by tendencies in the new South African democracy. *Mother of All Eating* centres on the activities of 'the Man,' a Principal Secretary in the government's Health Ministry. Through the actions and dialogue of this character, Mda exposes the extent of corruption and betrayal of the poor masses by government bureaucracy in the post-independence era. The audience will certainly react with shock at the level of corruption being portrayed on stage, but as the Man rightly points out, this is no time to point accusing fingers or gasp in horror, because everyone in society is guilty of corruption in one way or another:

> I hear your whispers and snide remarks. Who of you here can claim to have clean hands? Now tell me! Did you buy those BMs and Benzes that you drive with your meagre salaries? I am no different from any one of you. The word that we use here at home is that 'we eat.' Our culture today is that of eating. *Re ne re ja soft.* Everybody eats. From the most junior civil servant to the most senior guy.

(Mda 1995, 9)

Using the character-audience interaction device, which again is drawn from the traditional African theatrical repertoire, Mda points out that because the society is rotten, no one should sit in judgement. The audience here sits in judgement not only of the characters on stage but of themselves as well. Mda's intention in this play is to shock the audience with the reality of political independence in Africa—and South Africa in particular. He presents this play using direct symbolism, a departure from the vague and ambiguous symbolism he applied in *We Shall Sing for the Fatherland*:

MAN:

> Oh, it is you, Mr Director of Department of tenders . . . Ah, so you have received the five thou that I left in your pigeon-hole at the club. That's very nice, isn't it? . . . Well, it is true that we chose that particular tender because the contractor promised to pay us ten percent kickback if we gave him the contract . . . Yes, the contract was tendered at 10 million rands. Yes of course one percent of ten million is one million . . . let's not kill the goose just yet, we are going to get lots and lots of golden eggs from it.

(7)

The use of this kind of direct symbolism demonstrates the playwright's anger at the turn of events in the 'new' South Africa. He had warned in *We Shall Sing for the Fatherland* that the South African masses may not reap the fruits of independence. His scepticism seems to have been vindicated by the high levels of corruption demonstrated by officials of the present government. The main character describes the extent of corruption in the ministry:

> You see, in government, when they discover your corruption, they promote you. There are two reasons for that. The first is that they want to shut your mouth so that you won't reveal what you know which may expose some of the top dogs in government. The next reason which is more important is that they appreciate your brains and want to bring you up there so that they may benefit from your expertise in corruption.

(140)

The theme of corruption and betrayal of the poor is further emphasised by Mda's use of contrasts. He presents another character, Joe, who is a close friend of the main character. Joe is a model citizen. He is committed, patriotic and exceptionally honest in the discharge of his duties, but the irony here is that he is regarded as a villain because of his honesty. He is fired from his job and finds it difficult to secure other jobs. When he manages to secure jobs he is fired from each of them because of his honesty:

> Man: Well, the big guns had had enough of Joe and his holier-than-thou attitude towards our noble tradition of 'eating.' They fired him. After being kicked from Power Supply, Joe moved from job to job. Every time he gets a good job with a lot of prospects for 'eating' he tries to be honest. So they kick him out. I have told him, "Wake up, Joe, wake up!" But Joe will never wake up. Right now he is unemployed.

(24)

Another of Mda's recent plays that highlight the theme of political betrayal is *You Fool, How Can the Sky Fall?* First produced in 1995, the play portrays the illusions of petty dictatorship in a country that has just achieved political independence and exposes the extent of nepotism in government. The play also shows how a preoccupation with power can hamper the normal running of a country, causing chaos. In his review of the play, Raeford Daniel remarks:

Zakes Mda's play *You Fool, How Can the Sky Fall?* was written, I understand, sometime before the new dispensation came about in South Africa. So, while some of the situations contained therein may be deemed painfully close to the bone, one can only hope that the playwright was not being overly prophetic.

(1995, 16)

The play centres on a small band of cabinet ministers confined in what looks like a prison cell. They spend their time paying sycophantic court to the benevolent President, lusting after the female minister among them and suspecting each other of betraying the cause. Significantly, throughout the play the ministers never discuss anything regarding the improvement of standards of living among the people. In the course of the play the ministers are taken away one after another to be interrogated and tortured by some unnamed power referred to simply as 'them.' At the end, the traitor is revealed to be the benevolent dictatorial President and he gets his due punishment.

Presented in the form of a comedy, this play bears a close resemblance to *We Shall Sing for the Fatherland,* for it makes far-reaching comments on the ugly state of affairs in post-independence Africa using a combination of satire and symbolism. Thus, while the audience will be amused by the dialogue on stage, the message will nevertheless be clear to them:

> You remember when the daughter of the Honourable Minister of Agriculture was getting married? Yes, the wedding of the year . . . or was it the decade now? The wise one, the father of the nation, instructed the Honourable Minister of Information to decree that for the whole of that week nothing newsworthy in the country and indeed in the world would happen. Those who were going to commit murder and rape waited in eagerness for the week to end. All international struggle and natural disasters were on hold. All the news on radio, on television and in the newspapers was about the wedding and only the wedding was to be reported . . . and in meticulous detail too.

(6)

It is this pre-occupation with trivial issues to the total neglect of the real issues affecting the life of the ordinary man in the street that dominates this play and forms the central theme. Mda here suggests that there is something irresponsibly carefree about post-independence Africa. He jokes about how lightly cabinet takes its responsibilities. He presents a cabinet on whose shoulders rest the hopes and aspirations of the majority of the people, but who are more concerned with trivial matters to bother about this very important responsibility as demonstrated here by the Culture and Agriculture Ministers fighting over the affection of the Minister of Culture, a woman who seems to enjoy the attention as well.

CULTURE:

> May I wash your feet, beautiful princess?

HEALTH:

> (amused) We don't have any water here.

CULTURE:

> With my tongue. (To Agriculture) See if you can top that.

AGRICULTURE:

> Me, I don't lick your feet. I give you the time of your life as only a man can do. (He pinches her bottom.)

HEALTH:

> You do that again I am going to cut your thing, which is already not there in any case.

(22)

While the Ministers of Agriculture and Culture struggle over the affection of the Minister of Health, the Minister of Health is revered for his numerous money-spinning contracts he had brought the way of the Honourable Cabinet Ministers: "Justice: Why would we wish him dead? We all admired him. We all owe our wealth to his resourcefulness" (11).

The concept of deception which goes hand in glove with betrayal is emphasised with symbolism. Mda did this in *We Shall Sing for the Fatherland,* where the removal of the hoboes from the city streets and parks was done to present a façade of prosperity and cleanliness to visiting delegates of an environment conference. In this play Mda shows how cabinet manipulates the perceptions of the public, using its influence to deceive and betray. For example, they use the frontage of film-set housing to deceive investors into perceiving prosperity. The daughters of the revolution represent the only real threat to the dominance of the president and his cabinet. Mda uses them to symbolise the suffering masses who have had enough of the neglect and oppression that characterise post-independence Africa. The shrapnel wounds on their naked bodies symbolise the wounds of colonialism, oppression, poverty, lack of dignity and the struggle for liberation. The fact that these wounds have not healed shows that oppression, poverty and lack of dignity, which were characteristic of their lives in the colonial era, continue even in the post-independence era and highlights the corruption, dictatorship and insensitivity that characterise the post-independence era. The fact that their wounds have only healed on the surface points to the disappointment felt by the masses, who have sacrificed so much for independence only to be betrayed by their own people who they fought to put in place.

HEALTH:

> You said when you saw the naked women they had scars . . . healed scars.

YOUR MAN:

> Scars . . . wounds . . . Ma'am, I tell you they may look like scars, but inside they are dripping with the agony of freshness.

(66)

It is these scars dripping with the agony of betrayal that characterise life in post-independence Africa—and, by extension, South Africa. It is important to note that when one looks at the political situation in this country, Mda's criticism of post-independence Africa is very close to the situation at home. The theme of betrayal is especially relevant to South Africa when one considers the fact that South Africa should have learnt useful lessons from the political situation in other African countries. What we see here, however, is a situation where the real heroes of independence are abandoned to a life of hopelessness and despair while the black elite, having achieved power through the sacrifice of these poor masses, abandon them to a life of poverty—the same situation they suffered under apartheid. In an article in *City Press* in June 2001, Mpumelelo Mkhabela writes that, after sacrificing their youth for freedom, thousands of ex-soldiers are now faced with a bleak future: "Seven years into the new dispensation, there are thousands of former cadres roaming the streets unemployed with no hope for the future as the 25th anniversary of June 16 approaches" (2001, 21).

It is a credit to Mda that he could foresee the situation before it arose. This emphasises the fact that theatre needs to play a more active role in criticising the corruption of the political elite and portraying the plight of the poor. As Robert Kavanagh so rightly put it some time ago: "The changed political atmosphere in the country makes a revaluation of the function of the theatre in South Africa a painful necessity" (1979, 38). He was, of course, talking about post-Soweto South Africa, but his point is as pertinent today as it was then.

Mda himself pointed out that a truly South African theatre will not be that which is the sole privilege of the dominant classes but that in which peasants and workers are active participants in its production and enjoyment (1992, 216). Mda's creativity and foresight have never been in doubt. At a time when playwrights were concerned with the evils of apartheid he had the foresight and courage to deal with issues beyond the demise of apartheid.

Works Cited

Daniel, Raeford. 1995. Rev. of *You Fool, How Can the Sky Fall?*, Zakes Mda. *The Citizen* Feb.: 16.

Fanon, Frantz. 1961. *The Wretched of the Earth.* London: Penguin.

Holloway, Myles. 1989. "Zakes Mda: An Interview with Myles Holloway." *South African Theatre Journal* 2: 81-88.

Holloway, Myles. 1989. "Social Commentary and Artistic Mediation in Zakes Mda's Early Plays." *English Academy Review* 6: 28-41.

Kavanagh, Robert. 1979. *After Soweto: People's Theatre and Political Struggle in South Africa.* London: TQ Publications.

Mda, Zakes. 1980. *We Shall Sing for the Fatherland and Other Plays.* Johannesburg: Ravan Press.

———. 1992. "Politics and the Theatre: Current Trends in South Africa." *Theatre and Change in South Africa.* Ed. Geoffrey Davis and Ann Fuchs. Harwood Academic: Amsterdam. 193-218.

———. 1995. "Mother of All Eating" (unpublished typescript).

———. 1995. "You Fool, How Can the Sky Fall?" (unpublished typescript).

Mkhabela, Mpumelelo. 2001. "Was the War for Liberation Really Won?" *City Press* 10 June: 21-22.

Ngugi wa Thiong'o. 1972. *This Time Tomorrow.* London: Heinemann.

Van Graan, Mike. 1991. "Theatre in the New South Africa: Sellout or Vanguard?" Southern African Association for Drama and Youth Theatre (23pp.).

Sten Pultz Moslund (essay date 2003)

SOURCE: Moslund, Sten Pultz. "Zakes Mda: *Ways of Dying.*" In *Making Use of History in New South African Fiction: An Analysis of the Purposes of Historical Perspectives in Three Post-Apartheid Novels,* pp. 90-113. Copenhagen, Denmark: Museum Tusculanum Press, 2003.

[*In the following essay, Moslund examines Mda's use of the apocalyptic and the carnivalesque in* Ways of Dying *to portray the political and social conditions of South Africa just after the end of apartheid.*]

All the historical elements in **Ways of Dying** evolve from the story of two village cousins, Noria and Toloki, who meet again in adulthood after a long spell of separation; both having been away from home and having led their lives independently since adolescence. Gradually, as they confide in each other about their pasts, a picture emerges of two different, but rather emblematic, lives torn by the course of South African history. Both protagonists left the countryside to seek their fortunes in the city, only to be sucked into a whirlpool of squalor, rejection, dejection and violence. Toloki, as a result, has retreated to a hermetic life of homelessness after an elapse of abuse and ostracism and Noria has lost the magical powers she possessed back in the village of evoking happiness around her with her laughter and song. She has turned into an empty shell after a failed marriage, prostitution and the loss of two sons of whom the latter is said to have been the reincarnation of the former. The first son, Vutha, was chained to a pole by his father and died of starvation. The second son, Vutha the Second, whose father is unknown, is executed by the liberation movement, accused of being an informer of the rival ethnic group, despite his age of five.

As Noria and Toloki reacquaint themselves with each other and fall in love, they learn to combine their strengths, revived from their creative minds and innocent fascination with life, to vindicate ways of living despite the life-negating realities of squatter camp existence and the prevalence of the violence and destruction that pervade their surroundings.

With *Ways of Dying,* we stay within recent South African history. The narrative time, although vague through the absence of any specific reference to time and place, can be identified as the transition years of the early 1990s. Notably, the historical focus is on the problems of violence that spilled over into the transition from the South Africa of the 1980s that Serote and Nicol characterise. Instead of a relief from violence with the beginning of negotiations between the warring factions, the country seemed on the brink of disintegrating into a hellish scenario of uncompromising racial and ethnic antagonism, arbitrary killings and pervasive lawlessness. This is illustrated in Mda with the historical accuracy and biting realism we saw in Serote. Clashes between youth and police continue and *tsotsis* and state-sponsored vigilantes are savaging train commuters and the townships relentlessly. The Third Force continues its covert tyranny, supplemented by an upsurge in right-wing assaults on random black victims. And ethnic violence, orchestrated by the apartheid police force and spearheaded by Mangosuthu Buthelezi (alluded to in the story as "the tribal chief"), is threatening to plunge the country into a bloody civil war (17, 169, 170, 88-9, 132-34). The latter is evidently an expression of the fear that was generated by the death tolls in ethnic hostilities which amounted to 6.000 in the years between 1990 and 1995 (Maphai, 1995: 73).

However, the tropes that run through the novel to capture the essence of this society imaginatively are surprisingly ambivalent, wavering, as Johan van Wyk observes, between the apocalyptic and the carnivalesque (van Wyk, 1997: 80). The apocalyptic revolves around an imagery of all-consuming death that spreads from the war between the state and its resistance, to the killing of children and the killing of birth itself. The final stage represents the doom of halted fertility and is referred to symbolically on several occasions. It is followed through in the images of murders of innocent children, of men being forced to make love to corpses, and it culminates in the symbolic scene at the massacre in the squatter camp by the police and tribal agitators where a pregnant woman is stabbed with a spear. In the minutes before she dies, her labour begins, but as soon as the baby's head appears it is chopped off (170). "Soon we shall experience the death of birth itself", is the germane reaction to the whole situation when the funeral orator, the "nurse", is obituarising Noria's second son, the reincarnation of her first child, on the birthday of Christ at the beginning of the novel (5). If fecundity is squelched, the only thing that is given life

is death. At another funeral, of a father who was murdered at his son's funeral, the nurse closes the circle of national self-destruction: "funerals acquire a life of their own, and give birth to other funerals" (149).

The carnivalesque interrupts to offer a strange but welcome relief to the otherwise grim picture. Whereas the apocalyptic images suggest death-in-life, the relief is to be found in its antonymic coinage life-in-death, as a whole range of examples confirm the presence of a courageous spirit in the face of death. These reveal themselves as an element of comedy that fuses with times of deadly seriousness. At one point several funeral parties fill the entire cemetery with laughter as the nurse at one of the graves passes a joke about the deceased. Likewise the novel opens with slapstick humour, when the funeral procession of Noria's son collides with a merry wedding procession; and a comedy of errors evolves when two bodies are mistakenly swopped in a morgue (152-3, 7, 17). But the components of life-in-death run deeper than mere comedy.

A notable manifestation of the carnivalesque is in the character of Toloki who himself encompasses the dual representation of thanatos and libido. Since childhood he has always been associated with death-in-life. Growing up in the village, he was treated cruelly as a social outcast. People regarded him as ugly with the looks of "something that has come to fetch us from the other world" (64). The strong link with the other world is maintained in his adult life. He establishes himself as a professional funeral mourner in the city and apart from being referred to by others as smelling of death (50, 90), he forges the otherworldly connexion himself by stating that "death continues every day. Death becomes me, it is part of me" (106). Yet his professional costume evokes as much of the burlesque as solemnity in relation to his vocation. Bought a long time ago in a shop that rented out strange and fanciful costumes for parties, Toloki's all-black scarecrow outfit with tight pants, cape and top hat (21), is evocative, as van Wyk points out, of New Year carnivals as much as of the terror of Halloween: death is contextualised with the games and fun of imagination (van Wyk, 1997: 88). In addition, Toloki is one of the most zealous characters in the novel. Notwithstanding his solemn companionship with the dead, the principle of life-in-death is expressed in both his witty allusions to his austere occupation as well as in the fact that he makes a living out of other people's mortality. As he puts it: "As long as there are funerals I'll survive" (46).

The ambivalence thus surrounding the representation of the country's violent history will be explained in this analysis by, once again, turning to the two functions of literature identified by Njabulo Ndebele. To recount what has been said about Ndebele so far, he operates with literature as a medium that may inform as well as involve its readers; literature may serve to display a recognisable picture of reality, or history, and it may serve to bring about a transformation of reader consciousness. Although the latter appears as the nobler purpose in Ndebele's criticism, in that it contributes to the development of such human preferences as sensitivity, subtlety and critical insight on which the perfection of any society depends, and although Ndebele has criticised resistance literature for being superficially sensationalist because its authors were preoccupied with informing without involving, both functions of literature must be regarded as relevant (see Ndebele, 1994: 40-53, 73).

Translating the mentioned doublesidedness in Mda's representation of the past into Ndebele's terminology, it is arguable that the very realistic and uncompromising depiction of violence and its metaphorical support in the apocalyptic strand of the novel corresponds to Ndebele's notions of supplying the reader with a recognisable reality. Mda seeks to communicate a picture of the violence of the past with an imagery and a realism that is as palpable as that in Serote where the unpleasantness of the past is to be mirrored in no uncertain terms. Conversely, the carnivalesque involves the reader by inviting a change of consciousness, not unlike Lindi's song in *Gods of Our Time,* that may result in socially and culturally constructive ways of dealing with an otherwise malignant past. These two sides to the novel will be followed through in turn. To start off with the informative presentation of history, Mda provides the reader with a familiar picture of how several dynamics have contributed to a particularly harsh brutalisation of the people of the country's social periphery, all leading to a state of social, cultural and moral dislocation in the novel's present.

As Toloki and Noria re-familiarize themselves with each other, we are provided with a multitude of flashbacks and digressions from the main story that explain how the present came to be through a dismembering past of western intrusion and apartheid tyranny. Already in their youth, the stronger forces of western modernisation begin in make themselves felt in the violent clashes between old and new value systems. Competition arises between traditional religion and Christianity, embodied respectively in Noria's mother, That Mountain Woman, who works as a *sangoma* and in the Archbishop's independent church (96-7). Similarly, Napu, Noria's lover, is enabled by the opportunity of wage labour to acquire a status of individual independence and break loose from the traditional system of bride wealth liability towards the family-in-laws. Instead of paying *lobola,* he takes the pregnant Noria away to get married before the magistrate (69). Lured by the bright lights, they seek their fortune in the promises of the new values of the city. But the promises, of course, turn out to be illusory: "There were no diamonds", Noria relates, "nor was there gold. Only mud and open sewers" (126). Napu is not able to provide for

his wife and son and their marriage sinks with the material and spiritual deprivation of their lives. The final stage of bereavement is reached when Noria prostitutes herself in order to survive. As she sums it up bleakly herself: "I have been chewed, Toloki. Chewed and then spewed" (135). When we meet her again in the squatter camp, she has lost the magical laughter that evoked immediate happiness around her in the distant time and place of the village. Libido has been reduced to a faint will merely to stay alive.

Toloki follows the same path from a traditional rural past to the disillusion of modernisation, although his passage is qualitatively different from Noria's. Whereas the story of Noria illustrates the social and cultural uprooting of black South Africa, Toloki's delineates the moral disintegration of the apartheid society into a chaos of callous violence. He flees the village after having been brutally assaulted by his father but his ensuing quest for "love and fortune" is "dogged by deaths and funerals throughout" (58). From the countryside, where white farmhands set alight their black colleagues for the fun of it and a whole community abominates itself by cruelly murdering ten bandits in a moment of raging mass-justice, he moves to the city where death and apathy are "even more plentiful", as described at the beginning of this analysis (57). Life has become worthless as apartheid and its multiple consequences breed an inferno of obduracy, abuse and anarchy. In the words of a nurse:

> Normal deaths are those deaths that we have become accustomed to, deaths that happen everyday. They are deaths of the gun, and the knife, and torture and gore. We don't normally see people who die of illness or of old age.
>
> (146-7)

This remark seems closely coupled with the central phrase of the novel which touches on the self-enforcing catalyst of social, cultural and moral depravity:

> Death lives with us everyday. Indeed our ways of dying are our ways of living. Or should I say our ways of living are our ways of dying?
>
> (89)

The normality of murder, torture and gore referred to by the nurse further contaminates the already bleak ways of living, which in turn precipitates more death in an endless vicious circle. It is the sign of a prideless society that has turned in on itself in a thrust of self-destruction where even innocence kills and is killed. As in the case of Vutha the Second who is necklaced by the youth of the resistance movement and set alight by his playmate (177).

The sociologist Dumisane Ngcobo, in addressing the social, cultural and moral upheaval that has been sketched in the realist strand of Mda's novel, speaks of an aftermath of nihilism, mass psychological depression and social despair among large sections of the black South African community (Ngcobo, 1999: 139). Their willing or forced acceptance of alien Eurocentric worldviews in the modernisation process has resulted in Africans being de-centred to the fringes of a basically European civilisation. This denigration, Ngcobo goes on, "is carried out through a denial of blacks of their own history and thus a denial of their humanity . . ." (140). To further explicate Ngcobo's contention, non-western people in their representation in Euro-centric discourse is characterised by their "lessness". According to Frantz Fanon, Eurocentric discourse has pervaded every sphere of life in the postcolonial world as a legacy of colonialism. African children, for example, are brought up to see the world from an almost exclusively Western perspective. The education they receive is European through and through. Even entertainment is produced in the west, with Tarzan or Crusoe against the savage world as the archetypal hero-villain structure. Western bias is stigmatised even on word level to impose itself on consciousness: black is "evil", "dirty", "diabolic"; white is "innocent", "bright", "clean", "pure" (Fanon, 1967: 189). From childhood, black identity is thus subconsciously subordinated, or "socially appropriated", in Foucaultian terms, by the endless reproduction of the European ideal (Fanon, 1967: 146-9 and Foucault, 1972: 227). Transferred to Jackson's theories on story-telling, such representation is devastating to self-perception. Drawing on Jean-Paul Sartre's observations, he states that shame and self-negation arise

> . . . when the recognition of who one is ceases to be mirrored by those one loves, and comes to be determined by one's appearance in the eyes of others, filled with indifference or hate. . . . [A]ny inner reflections on *who* one is are eclipsed by the external definition of *what* one is in the eyes of others. No longer a subject for-oneself, one is reduced to being an object—isolated, exposed, fixed, categorised, and judged by the Other.

(Jackson, 2002: 58)

In South Africa, Ngcobo says, the imposition of alien and rather self-centred norms and world views at the expense of a culturally imbedded value system coupled with the undermining of society by violence have entailed "a near eclipse of hope and collapse of meaning" (141). Certainly this has long been the state of affairs in the squatter camps depicted by Mda, which have remained a monument of economic exploitation and socio-cultural ostracism ever since Toloki acquainted himself with them eighteen years ago (138).

Against such circumstances of absolute public and private self-negation, the only remedy, says Ngcobo, is "a new black leadership grounded in African culture and capable of removing the defeatist attitude from amongst the black periphery" (153). In other words, a self-generated discourse is needed in which people are al-lowed to fashion a positive self-image and are allowed the necessary amount of autonomy of the definition of reality it takes to influence and to change reality.

This is precisely where the second, the consciousness-raising element of Mda's fiction sets in. Whereas a recognisable picture of the South African transition and the socio-cultural causes that lead up to its dismal disposition represent the historical thread in the novel, the aforementioned life-in-death qualities run as a strong ahistoric or imagined undercurrent of the narration. As in the case of Serote's psychological probe into the consciousness of the struggle and Lindi's song, the imagined domain supplies the historical information with a conjectural vestige of how to counteract the historical reality. As in Serote, creativity plays a crucial role in dignifying the ways of living and dying in the face of ugliness and abomination. Indeed Toloki and Noria, in drawing, singing and in their artistic construction of Noria's tin shack, manage to humanise the most inhuman conditions. The shack, in their eyes, becomes a piece of art and it is the power of imagination, too, that enables them to "see beauty where there is none" in the scene where the couple transcend the depressing reality of their surroundings by envisioning another, prettier world with comforts and a garden on the walls papered with bright pictures cut from glossy magazines (103-4). However, in contrast to Serote, the consciousness-raising mechanisms in Mda's novel are much more concerned with an explicitly cultural revival, as if responding directly to Albie Sach's request in 1989 for a development of an "artistic and cultural vision" that corresponds to the political development of South Africa" (Sachs, 1998: 239). To elaborate briefly on Ndebele's literary theory, he agrees with Ngcobo that cultural recuperation among the oppressed in South Africa is essential in rejuvenating a sense of social positivism. He qualifies the literature of involvement as a literature that frees the social and cultural imagination, to reconstruct an African aesthetic and value system after the disruptions caused by European hegemony:

> The material life of Africans should be given a new forward articulation that will enlarge intellectual interest and expand the possibilities of imagination. It is a re-evaluation which, I believe, should result in a profound philosophical transformation of the African consciousness, a consciousness that should and must endure.

(Ndebele, 1994: 161)

Mda returns to the same idea in his visions for the genre that has earned him his renown, the Theatre for Development, by proposing that ". . . Development is meaningful only if it allows for the empowerment of local communities . . . to promote a spirit of self-reliance among the marginalised" (quoted in Mervis, 1998: 39). In this respect creative works play the crucial role of "enrich[ing] and expand[ing] people's own forms of expression". A play or a piece of literature thereby "strengthens the point of view of the most progressive section of the people; and it roots itself in tradition and develops this in a positive manner" (quoted in Mervis, 1998: 44). As it has been shown, Serote does move beyond the stage of mere informing to involve the reader in a scrutiny of the psychological depth of subjugation. However, in spite of his own appeal in an interview to rearticulate the "wisdoms, gems and treasures of African culture", there is little of this in *Gods of Our Time,* apart from in Lindi's song at the end (Solberg, 1998: 84). Conversely, the theme of life-in-death in *Ways of Dying,* the ways of living, that particularly Toloki and Noria are searching for, is often intricately associated with an attempt to reconnect themselves with a humanist value system that, to a large extent, is rooted in the African tradition they were born into. Another way of putting this is that Serote's preoccupation with political empowerment is shifted in Mda to a preoccupation with social and cultural empowerment. And in a manner of speaking, the absence of a survival language in Serote's characters, and the tentative suggestions of its recovery in a self-reliant form of expression, is to be found in Mda in the explicit reconnection of life with African tradition and ethos.

Hence, a version of the Ubuntu philosophy is to be found in the squatter camp community which is surviving history on mutual caring and assistance, generosity and selflessness (42-3, 60-2, 125-6). Moreover, values are frequently drawn from pools of traditional wisdom. Proverbs, for instance, soothe people not to despair by the burden of hardship: "Our elders say", Toloki is reminded by Noria, "that an elephant does not find its own trunk heavy" and "In our language there is a proverb which says the greatest death is laughter" (157 and 153). Likewise there is the reassurance of tradition in the metaphor of Toloki and Noria's way of sleeping. According to custom, they curl up in a foetal position, thus suggesting the auspicious quality of shared cultural values. Not only do they reassure the community a sense of togetherness and belonging, they produce a promise of life and regeneration, signalled in the connotations of the unborn child and rebirth every morning that may be affirmed even in the midst of death and destruction. In that light, the coinage "Our ways of dying are our ways of living" and "our ways of living are our ways of dying", becomes positively ambivalent by also inviting a change of consciousness that diminishes the weight of affliction. It becomes possible to humanise the ways of dying, if the ways of living are generated from the larger body of the community as well as from the accumulation of knowledge and experience that is expressed through its cultural idioms. Or, to contextualise the central lines with Ndebele, the transformation of consciousness, from that of self-destruction to regeneration, relies on "a forward articulation" of "African social and cultural consciousness".

At a metanarrative level, the novel itself underscores the urge to overcome "the defeatist attitude" among black South Africans that Ngcobo speaks of in that several formal strategies are adopted to articulate an African aesthetic. First of all there is the narrative voice. The narrators, the plural "we", explicitly assign their authority to the oral tradition:

> Just like back in the village, we live our lives together as one. We know everything about everybody. We even know things that happened when we were not there. . . . We are the all-seeing eye of the village gossip. When in our orature the storyteller begins the story, 'They say it happened . . .' we are the 'they'. No individual is the owner of the story. The community is the owner of the story, and it can tell it the way it deems it fit. We would not be needing to justify the communal voice that tells this story if you had not wondered how we became so omniscient in the affairs of Toloki and Noria.

> (8)

In this way the indigenous techniques of story telling are foregrounded in the otherwise alien form of the written novel and the western literary concept of the "omniscient narrator" is amusingly concretized by constituting a participatory, physical presence in the story.

The structure of the narration shares similar features from orature. The main storyline digresses with flashbacks of other stories in what Margaret Mervis calls a "disjunctive style" which, she says, "negates linear time, reflecting rather the cyclical nature of oral narrative" (Mervis, 1998: 50). One may even elaborate on Mervis' observation and argue that the time structure of *Ways of Dying* is spiral more than cyclical. The return to the trope of rebirth at the end of the novel, for example, where Toloki and Noria wake up on New Year's Day from sleeping naked in the foetal position, has been pushed in a positive or upward direction in comparison with the starting point of the narrative circle on Christmas Day (9, 181-2). The renewal of life implied at the end of the novel is not shaded by the burial of new life as it is at its beginning and likewise the still burning tyres at the New Year celebrations, which carry the connotations of necklacing and the killing of Vutha, release only the smell of "pure wholesome rubber" without "the sickly stench of roasting human flesh" (199).

Thirdly, Mda's application of the English language invites the imposition of local mastery of the foreign medium. As mentioned in the analysis of *The Ibis Tapestry,* language, to Bakhtin, is "overpopulated with the intentions of others". The implications of this propagation are but aggravated when the value-laden language is that of a former coloniser with a long history of subordinating indigenous modes of expression. In the face of this, Mda overcomes the stigmatisation in the master language of otherness and subordination by adapting English to a local colour. The text which is richly interspersed with African proverbs, expressions and idioms, comprises an altogether African South African English (see: 3, 6, 22, 56, 68). Against this background it is arguable that Achmat Dangor misses the mark when he in his harsh critique of **Ways of Dying** dismisses Mda's language as "laboured" and proliferated with "badly constructed sentences and malapropisms" (Dangor, 1996: 22). In fact any interest in standardising English in accord with metropolitan dictum is bound to be outvoiced in the future South Africa. Hitting the nail on the head, Guy Butler predicts that "twenty million blacks will use English for their own interests and ends, without worrying much about the views of less than two million English-speaking South Africans" (quoted in Ndebele, 1994: 99).

In inseparable closeness to Ndebele's twin paradigms of a consciousness-raising literature and the revival of African culture is, of course, the embrace in Mda's novel of magical realism. Magical realism itself is, as Michael Chapman has aptly demonstrated, an integral part of African orature in which "imagination conjures up a plentitude of possibility in the emotion-saturated, surprising language of dream and desire" (Chapman, 1996: 48 and 40-9). At the same time there is in magical realism, as an independent contemporary form, an inherent appeal to the validity of traditional cosmologies, which only reinforces its faculty for cultural revival. According to Gabrielle Foreman, Magical realism bypasses what may seem as the "total negation of faith and tradition" in modern civilisation. Magical realism, she says:

> . . . presumes that the individual requires a bond with the traditions and the faith of the community, that s/he is historically constructed and connected. Echoing Alejo Carpentier, who first named the phenomenon, critic Marguerite Suárez-Murias contends that 'the marvellous . . . presupposes an element of faith on the part of the author or the audience.'
>
> (Foreman, 1995: 286)

Hence a connection is drawn between gusto and the traditional past, as in the metaphor of the figurines made by Toloki's father Jwara which bring bliss and amusement to the children of the squatter camp at the end of the novel (197-8). The figurines were created by an amalgamation of two forces, Noria's magical singing and Jwara's dreams (23, 25). Bearing in mind that dreams in African oral tradition are often associated with messages from ancestors (see van Wyk, 1997: 83), there is a promise of restored placidity, symbolised in the township children's laughter, by cultivating a creative link between the traditions of the past and the present. The figurines, it should be noted, too, are brought to the squatter camp by the otherwise anaemic undertaker Nefodolodwhe whose financial success has made him discard all connections with his "backward" and "indolent" people. At one point, his westernized consciousness recedes as he is forced to make a tribute of recognition towards his kinsmen after Jwara's ghost

has haunted him with the demand that he find the figurines in the village and return them (189-94). The magic that is offered in African folklore also helps Noria surmount the tyrannical presence of history in a much more subtle, and perhaps for that reason a much more successful and convincing way. After her first son, Vuthi, falls victim to the state of depravity that is forced upon the squatter camp environment, in that he is kidnapped by his morose father and dies tied to a pole without food and water, it is through the magic of divine conception and reincarnation that she overcomes the loss (139-40). Whether the magic is to be interpreted as ontological, as reality being magic, or epistemological, as Noria's worldview being magic, the fact remains that her African heritage tenders an alternative reality that defiantly slips through the claws of history (for ontological and epistemological magic see Faris, 1995: 165)[1].

At this stage it is appropriate to insert the caveat that Mda, despite his emphasis on cultural self-determination, does not present an uncritical embrace of African tradition or advocate a new form of cultural chauvinism in South Africa. As it is, he incorporates in the novel a resistance to its own form. This is primarily expressed in the narrative voice which, on the one hand, is self-critical of the community it represents and, on the other, not always reliable. In regard of the sexual escapades of That Mountain Woman (who is from another village), the narrators say: "We told the story over and over again, and we laughed and we said, 'That Mountain Woman has no shame'". After which it is confessed: "But one could detect a smack of envy in our voices when we said that. Those were adventures that would never be seen in our conservative village" (34). As concerns the cruel treatment by the community of Toloki in his childhood who would mercilessly be chased away for his ugliness when everybody enjoyed Noria's laughter, the unreliability of the narrators reveals itself when they claim always to have been happy when Toloki and Noria were happy and felt the pain when they were hurt (8)[2]. Instead, the cultural regeneration that Mda offers, is to evolve from a non-essentialist and non-static dialogue between the values of tradition and contemporary needs and as long as Africans recover from the defeatist attitude about their own tradition, the ideal of hybridising African culture with all other cultures in South Africa is not rejected. This idea is in many ways illustrated in Toloki's vocation which is soundly rooted in and in touch with traditional African practices, yet greatly inspired and moulded by so many other cultures and religions, from Hinduism to Christianity (see 125)[3]. Similarly it has been shown how the novel itself forms a great hybrid between a modern, western tradition and African traditions of storytelling.

In addition to the culturally transformative elements that have been analysed, the insertion of magical realism into a historical novel may also be interpreted in terms of Coetzee's notions of a literature in rivalry with the discourse of history. Accordingly, it is the argument here that *Ways of Dying,* in addition to applying to Ndebele's theory of a literature informing and involving, reaches beyond the kind of supplementary historical fiction that merely adds to history a certain density of observation or lived experience[4]. Just as the magic fences off the tyrannical presence of history in Noria's story of divine conception, the tyrannical presence of the discourse of history is fenced off by magical realism as a creative mode in assertion of an entirely independent literary discourse.

The fusion of magic with reality in the novel, such as Noria's second pregnancy or Toloki's ability to remember his father's death before he has heard of it (van Wyk, 1997: 101), is as disruptive of the conventional discourse of history with its foundations in western rationality and logic as Nicol's deconstruction of narrative authority and objectivity. And like Nicol's postmodern ventures, the magic in *Ways of Dying* opens up another discursive universe distinct from that of the traditional historical novel insofar as it offers an alternative epistemology, in oxymoronic rivalry with the historical material that is presented. In this respect, Faris and Zamora claim that:

> . . . magical realism is a mode suited to exploring—and transgressing—boundaries, whether the boundaries are ontological, political, geographical or generic. Magical realism often facilitates the fusion, or coexistence, of possible worlds, spaces, systems that would be irreconcilable in other modes of fiction. The propensity of magical realist texts to admit a plurality of worlds means that they often situate themselves on laminal territory between or among those worlds—in phenomenal and spiritual regions where transformation, metamorphosis, dissolution are common, where magic is a branch of naturalism, or pragmatism.
>
> (5-6)

In other words, Mda is able to set up a parallel discourse of promise that coexists ahistorically with and in rivalry to the historical discourse, the realism, of the novel. Whereas the discourse of history and rationality, employed in the novel's realistic representations of history, offers only a bleak life-negating predictability of cause and effect gathering a momentum of misery, the elements of the fantastic explode the confines of that very discourse by inviting us, like *The Ibis Tapestry,* to *think* differently from the dominant meaning-making systems. Only with another language of extended possibilities does it become feasible to deal with and thus to counteract the course of history. Hence multiple historical causes effect the death of Noria's son, but magic brings him back to her; multiple historical forces turn Nefodolodwhe against his own people, but magic, the return of Jwara's ghost in his dreams, forces him to reconnect: and multiple historical forces sentence Noria and Toloki to a squalid existence and also deprive Noria of her second child, but magic, or at least epistemologi-

cal magic, conjures up another mindset between the two of them that helps them conquer these realities. The discourse of magic, to sum up, defies the inevitable defeat that permeates the discourse of history. The mode of loss is countered with a mode of replenishment.

A question that comes to mind when considering the depiction of suffering in *Ways of Dying* is whether the blend of carnivalesque and magical ingredients does not diminish the drabness of the realism. One argument that may be launched against the aesthetic elements in the novel is definitely that beauty may take the sting out of suffering and consequently erode the political message of calling attention to the injustice committed against the destitute in South Africa, then as well as now. The beauty that Toloki and Noria are able to conjure out of their drab reality, for example, as well as magical realism itself, could foster an unintentional romanticization of the squatter camps where a hard-hitting realism would have had an uncompromising effect. However, as André Brink argues, creativity and imagination are in many instances required to make suffering palpable. As a sobering contrast, Brink calls attention to the mind-numbing effect of the persistent realistic reportage of violence on television, which was also what inhibited Poley in *The Ibis Tapestry* (Brink, 1998: 19-21). In alignment with Brink's argument, it may be maintained that it is not sheer beauty but a certain *tragedy* in the beauty, when, for example, Toloki and Noria wander in their imagined and materially unobtainable garden. This generates a sense of deflation lurking right below the surface of the thrill of the moment. Similarly it is the duality in the book of history and the human responses that makes us recognise at one and the same time the inhumanity of life in the squatter camps and the humanity of those bawdy, miserable people who are so easily dehumanised.

In further accord with Brink's contention, many critics share the conviction that magical realism may be seen as "an antidote to the exhausted forms of expression", such as natural realism and post-modernism (Zamora and Faris, 1995: 7). So the ambiguous representation of the past in *Ways of Dying,* which simultaneously confirms a well-known picture of reality and disrupts our normative perceptions of reality, enforces on the reader a new and fresh engagement with the history before him or her. In other words, it provokes an attention-drawing and, with its metaphorical potency, consciousness-raising actuality, which urges the centre of society to reconsider its derisive perception of the periphery.

To return briefly to the constellations in the novel between the discourse of history and the discourse of literature, these become all the clearer when *Ways of Dying* is interpreted as a future history. Whereas the historical material in the novel represents a world of facts, the counter-historical discourse of magic represents a world of utopian longings. Michael Green maintains that in contrast to historians who are reluctant or unwilling to make predictions about the future:

> . . . novelists are precisely able to ignore the caution of the historian because their enterprise carries, quite obviously, a different emphasis. Their concern is to make the present meaningful in terms of its possible outcome; the imaginative effort invested in this is not to be measured in terms of their literal ability correctly to foresee the outcome, but rather in their ability to use a particular literary strategy to intervene in the present.
>
> (257-8)

Accordingly the magical realist components of *Ways of Dying* disrupt the discourse of history, that so blatantly mirrors poor South Africans in a world of denial and destruction, and offer instead a discourse of opportunity by means of which the dystopian direction of history can be changed to a utopian direction. At the same time, it is arguable that the capacity of magical realism for disrupting our normative perceptions of reality is a prerequisite for the change of consciousness it takes to acknowledge the utopian allusions of the novel as other than outrageous. In Coetzeean terms of a rival aesthetic, the magical universe in *Ways of Dying* and its utopian implications empower the novel to "evolve its own paradigms" and "issue its own terms", independently of the discourse of history, in a way that forces upon us a reassessment of what is considered socially, politically and economically plausible. In the words of André Brink, we are urged to:

> . . . imagine what has previously been impossible: to grapple, exuberantly and adventurously, with the limits of the possible. . . . [as] only by dreaming and writing the impossible can life be made possible.
>
> (Brink, 1993: 2)

It is the utopian aspirations and their very probability in alternity which impinge themselves on present reality and keeps us in touch with the very sources of revolutionary energy in the midst of a worldwide supremacy of conservative politics (see also Jameson quoted in Green, 1997: 248-9).

With that, it is fitting to delve further into that Other historical discourse of the novel, off-limits to the ordinary historian, the implied visions of the future, which also come in other forms than the magical.

Green explains about future histories that they:

> . . . seek to comment upon the past and present by projecting the implications of the past and the present forward in time. In this way they reverse the standard techniques of historical fiction, but remain directly related to them. In any event, attempts to give meaning to the past generally involve . . . an implied or explicit appeal to the future.
>
> (244)

This appeal to the future, he continues, can involve either a desire or a warning, a utopia or a dystopia (264). As it has been indicated, history in Mda's novel contains a projection of both in correspondence with double entendre of the imagery; that of the carnivalesque and that of nightmarish terror.

To outline briefly the utopian allusions, which have already been suggested in the analyses of the consciousness-raising dynamics of the novel and its rival mode, there is a utopian desire embodied in Toloki, Noria and their good neighbours to overcome the burdens of the past by recreating a social fabric woven by moral, cultural, communal and humanist positivism. This will engender an all-inclusive society based on a shared set of values, including economic, racial and gender equality, social responsibility and pacifism. In short, a society constructed on a social conscience similar to the philosophy of Ubuntu that disallows any form of human abuse or undesirable marginalisation. As has also been stated, it is not only their political inferiority that Serote is concerned with, but the social and cultural deprivation of the majority of the South African population that must undergo resuscitative treatment, if they are to have any democratic right of independently participating in shaping society. Only then, says Ndebele, will the oppressed discover a "new, rich and very complex social language of their own" (1994: 119).

The dystopian indications in *Ways of Dying* evidently centre on the further disintegration of society into an anarchy of violence, civil war and utter self-destruction, if no counter is generated to stop it. The emphasis in the novel on the "tribal chief", for example, and his ability to animate an imagined and aggressive ethnicity warns of the destructive potential of group politics coupled with political intolerance and a zero-sum orientation (e.g. see 47-9). Similarly post-apartheid South Africa is experiencing a taste of the dystopian vision of the novel. Hein Marais, for instance, refers to the phenomenon of a "lost generation" of South African youth "with little education, poor job prospects, and prone—en masse, it seem[s]—to violence and other 'anti-social' behaviour" (110; see also Deegan, 1999: 173). The crime statistics speak for themselves: more than 20,000 South Africans were murdered in 1995 and 36,888 cases of rape or attempted rape were reported. The same year, there were 12,531 cases of vehicle hijackings and 1996 counted 481 crime syndicates operating in the country. Moreover, cases of burglary, robbery, assaults and drug trafficking in South Africa continue to hover among the highest numbers in the world (Marais, 1998: 107, 109). Again this can be contextualised with the disappearance of the enemy for the combat-minded youth in *Gods of Our Time* who, adding insult to injury, have no other skills than fighting and are offered no alternative livelihood.

Obviously the development of the spiritual culture of the country—intellectualism, ideas, feelings, ethics—to counter this dystopian advance is far from adequate to stop the tide of disintegration. There is a compelling need for the development of the material culture as well; for as long as scarcity exists for the masses, there is a breeding ground for animosities, be they based on race, class or ethnicity.

If navigated by utopian aspirations, post-apartheid South Africa will relieve the squatters of their material misery through economical redistribution. But *Ways of Dying* presents a past that is very prone to confer upon the country a drive in the direction of dystopia. First of all there is a brief mention of the rich whites at the tourist centre of the city who:

> "don't pay any particular attention to [Toloki], except of course to make sure that their wallets and handbags are safe. But then that is what they do every time they see someone who does not look quite like them."
>
> (183)

In this snapshot description, superimposed on the background of the squatter camps, the entire question of future redistribution is encompassed. It points forward in time towards the indecisive resolution of the battle over South Africa, which has led Jay Reddy to comment that "the end of apartheid seems to represent for the white minority a defeat in which they have lost nothing" (quoted in Ndebele, 1994: 156). In other words, the negotiated settlement has guaranteed no material concessions on the side of the privileged for the sake of the underprivileged[5]. This is to be seen in the light that post-apartheid South Africa is still described by the World Bank as one of the most unequal economies in the world with a gini coefficient of no less than 0,68 (Marais, 1998: 106).

The implication of underlining the indifference of the rich to the poverty around them while not mentioning the question of guilt throughout the novel, seems, then, to agree with Ndebele when he, instead of guilt, demands that those who prospered on apartheid should accommodate the need for redistribution: "Guilt is irrelevant, but it crops up because the struggle was unresolved. Those who have lost should properly experience loss, not guilt" (156). Guilt, he goes on to say, is a personal flagellation that leads to humility which is not a good sight on a national scale. On the contrary, justice, understood as paying back, is a "decisive corrective action" that "leads to knowledge and responsibility". Although Mike Nicol in *The Ibis Tapestry* radically dismisses any alleviation of guilt for the sake of remembering, he shares with Ndebele and Mda the idea that the offenders are indebted to the offended, illustrated in Sarra's devotion to Salma's recovery. However, as was also shown in the analysis of *The Ibis Tapestry,* the *wealthy parts* of the white community are "ensconced in so much political and economical privilege" that they are able to barricade themselves and their riches behind barbed wired walls with "armed response" signs, from where it is easy to ignore the anguish of the periphery. Even if this may ultimately change the white phobia expressed in J. M. Coetzee's *Disgrace* of being "raped" through race-related retribution from a dormant to an actual peril.

There is also an appeal in *Ways of Dying* to the current incumbents. If the beneficiaries of apartheid are not ready to take direct responsibility, the initiative lies with the government. In this respect, the future African leadership is represented in a manner that may foretell rapture as well as agitation. It is a taste of utopia that the high-ranking leaders of the resistance movement visit absolutely the lowest end of the social scale to listen to their grievances. But the fact that the leaders arrive in a big, black Mercedes Benz, "high powered" and "bejewelled", already signals great distance (161-2). And aloofness is further emphasised when the leaders ask Noria, in perfect anticipation of the ANC's attempt to censor history as discussed in the Serote analysis, to keep silent about the execution of her son as it will weaken the outward image of the movement (166-7).

The question, then, is whether the leaders, once in power, will take the masses into consideration who bled for the common cause. Initially, the democratically elected government of 1994 set up the so-called Reconstruction and Development Programme for rapid redress of past inequalities, which, among other things, resulted in the extension of water and electricity supplies to many remote and poor areas of the country as well as the construction of one million houses. However, after less than two years, that ambitious programme was abandoned in favour of the current supply-side strategy, GEAR (Growth, Employment and Redistribution), that aims not at forthright redistribution, but at creating the most lucrative conditions for the private economy in the hope of bringing about a "trickle down effect" while cutting government spending and reducing state assets (Lundahl, 1998: 29-31). Similarly, there is clearly a government reluctance to implement even the recommendations of compensation and rehabilitation made by the Truth and Reconciliation Commission in its final report. The report suggests among other things that the beneficiaries of apartheid, and especially big business, should pay a reparations tax for the development of poor South Africa (see Krog, 1998: 432-3). As Annette Lansink says, none of the recommendations have materialised in government policy, and the funding of the Truth Commission's Reparations Committee is so severely curtailed that the majority of victims who were promised compensation are still waiting for it (Lansink, 2000: 9; see also Matlou, 2001 and Merten, 2001).

Above all the government and office holders appear more interested in careerism and in uniting the elite within the existing order rather than stirring up the masses with expectations of fast deliverance. Whatever it may be, it is certainly not the utopia embedded in Mda's history that dictates the direction of the near future in South Africa. The restraint in the country on the subject of social justice, among the privileged as among the government, is staggering when one considers the compelling and inescapable everyday signs of the wrongs of the past: the violence and the deprivation in the townships and squatter camps.

A third dimension that is included in Mda's future history of dystopia concerns the antithesis to the cultural flowering that was mentioned as part of the utopia. In the absence of a strong will to consciously develop independently along culturally connected lines, the alternative is an obdurate society of individuals bent on materialist self-gain. The representative of this future scenario is the undertaker Nefodolodwhe who has chosen an uncompromising denial of his rural past and developed an avaricious scavenger-mentality in looking forward to the fatal misfortune of his fellow men (see: 116-7).

Ndebele maintains that depriving the oppressed of any meaningful spiritual life of their own, as referred to earlier, has also deprived them of any control of their own fate. In correspondence with Ngcobo's argument that blacks have been denied their own history and humanity and Jackson's observations on discursive objectification, they are doomed to respond to history instead of initiating it (1994: 159). If this is not made up for, as in Mda's vision of a reaffirmation of African values, oppression will continue, although masked to the extent that the oppressed do not perceive their own oppression. The glitter of apartheid, Ndebele says, like materialistic extravagance, rich neighbourhoods, institutions of financial power, which previously represented exclusion and repulsive, exploitative white power, now represent "opportunity and possible fulfilment". And so the "brazen oppression of the past is now replaced with the seductive oppression of having to build and consolidate and enjoy what was achieved at our expense". Instead of a "self-created reality" the only option for the disempowered is then one of absorption and accommodation like Nefodolodwhe (153-4). Society will continue along the lines of the old order of the African being contained within a western pre-eminence rather than a new order of African self-determination in a truly free society. Instead of freedom, Ndebele concludes, spiritual emptiness will prevail at the expense of constructive content (136-7).

So, all in all, the past as it is represented in **Ways of Dying** contains a host of indications that point towards an undesirable future in South Africa and a continuation of the dystopian development that has gathered increasing impetus throughout the apartheid years and, earlier still, since the western disruption of the African civilisation. In order to turn the tide of historical cause and effect it is necessary, accordingly, to imagine the

impossible. Hence the utopian innuendoes of a truly egalitarian society brought about by social and cultural self-determination are forwarded as an indismissable alternative, which, in the light of a discourse of expanded possibility, ought to appear all the less improbable.

Note

1. It should be noted that the vindication of African culture and aesthetics that is so explicitly suggested in *Ways of Dying* seems only possible now that the retribalisation policies of the National Party are gone. During apartheid, it was considered an almost pro-government statement to claim one's ethnic heritage. Hence the outspoken self-negations of the *Drum* magazine at the height of the resistance:

> Tribal music! Tribal history! Chiefs! We don't care about chiefs! Give us . . . anything American. You can cut out this junk about kraals and folk-tales and Basutos in blankets—forget it! You're just trying to keep us backward, that's what!

The reconsideration of this mentality in *Ways of Dying* is not an isolated case. Can Temba says: "Those of us who have been detribalised and caught in the characterless world of belonging nowhere have a bitter sense of loss (quoted in Gready, 1990: 147)."

In post-apartheid South Africa even white authors have used the change to reimagine Afrikaner or English identity by forging a cultural connection with indigenous tradition in a thrust to finally take root on the continent as Africans. The story of Krotoä, for instance, a Khoi-San woman who married and had children with the Danish surgeon Pieter van Meerhoff in the 17th century, resurfaces again in Afrikaner memory after its apartheid repression, as a myth of the unifying foremother, *onse ma,* who has fostered a fundamentally hybrid race (see Coetzee, 1998: 112-15). And in terms of literary form, works like Brink's *Imaginings of Sand* and Etienne van Heerden's *Ancestral Voices* are joining Zakes Mda by revalidating African traditions of story-telling and magic and mixing those with oral traditions among Afrikaners and the English settlers.

2. In the same way an uneasiness deriving from repression of the truth may be detected in the case of Noria's second pregnancy. The narrators never question her claim to divine conception despite the gossip of Noria seeing other men and gossip being one of the primary sources of the narrator's omniscience (140 and 8). Of course the possibility of a divine pregnancy serves the principle of presenting South African ontology as magic by taking magic for granted, or, as Faris puts it, to make it "grow organically out of reality" (106). How-

ever, the context of Noria's pregnancy invites an unnerving ambiguity. Just as much as the incident may be genuinely magic, the magic may also prove to be Noria's mind playing a self-deceiving trick. Considering the ambivalence of her many "dreams" of strangers that arrive to make love to her before she falls pregnant, the magical conception may turn out to be the poignant sign of a mental defence mechanism that is protecting Noria from the painful memory of being raped.

Antjie Krog refers to an almost conspiratorial silence about the issue of rape during the hearings of the Truth Commission:

> There seems to be a bizarre collusion between the rapist and the raped. Although rumors abound about rape, all these mutterings are trapped behind closed doors. Apparently high-profile women, among them cabinet ministers, parliamentarians and businesswomen, were raped and sexually abused under the previous dispensation— and not only by the regime, but by their own comrades in the townships and liberation camps. But no one will utter an audible word about it.

(277)

Although Noria of course belongs to a different level than the career-minded ministers and businesswomen, many reasons for keeping silent may be the same. A clinical psychologist, Nomfundo Walaza, adds "[w]ho have been raped know that if they talk about it in public they will lose something again—privacy, maybe respect" (277). The fact is that the silence of the public, which, in this interpretation, is represented in *Ways of Dying* in the absence of any response from the narrators to Noria's pregnancy, endorsing or rejecting the magic, preserves the issue of rape as a taboo or a violation that women have to endure privately. Even Serote's novel, which is so concerned with a female perspective of the past, is conspicuously silent about rape. Although the crime itself and the almost ritual repression of it in public, are, of course, far from problems that are confined to African societies, the culturally specific addressal in *Ways of Dying* concerns a skepticism towards the communal voice and its silences, and a skepticism towards self-righteousness alignments by the same voices behind a pretense of Africanism as a moral high ground (see for instance Malungana, 1999 for an example of how uncritical Africanism can be exploited to championing a silencing of women).

3. The ideal way of instituting social modernization and development was touched upon by Bessie Head who stressed the necessity of indigenous incorporation—especially when the impulse of change was as foreign as the European. She made the following observation in Botswana:

> If one wishes to reach back into ancient Africa, the quality of its life has been preserved almost intact in Botswana . . . . Anything that falls into its depth is absorbed. No new idea stands sharply aloof from the social body, declaiming its superiority. It is absorbed and transformed until it emerges somewhere along the line as 'our traditional custom'. Everything is touched by 'our traditional custom'—British Imperialism, English, Independence, new educational methods, progress, and foreigners. It all belongs.

(Head, 1990: 15)

4. At this juncture it would be appealing to amalgamate Coetzee and Ndebele's theories by stating that Ndebele's literature of involvement corresponds to Coetzee's rival mode. A consequence of such an argument would be that Ndebele's literature of informing equates the information that is passed on to the reader through the discourse of history. The parallels between Ndebele and Coetzee in this respect are pronounced but not convincing. First of all historical discourse may be as involving as informing in that there are consciousness-raising potential in the historian's choice of perspective for any given historical period. It may be argued, for instance, that the probes into the psychology in Serote's characters and Lindi's attempts to redress the tormented minds around her add to the historical material a certain and engaging depth without taking up arms against the discourse of history itself.

5. It can be asserted against this argument that redistributive concessions have been imposed on the privileged after all, in the form of increased tax-rates (which prior to the year 2000 reform, in regard to income tax, amount to 45% for the highest salaried groups (see South African Revenue Service: www.sars.gov.za/Default.htm). However, the new budget as presented by Minister of Finance, Trevor Manuel in February 2000 compromises these measures to a certain extent with new tax breaks for the employed. Jay Reddy's comment could furthermore be defended when arguing that taxing customarily loads the burden of redistribution unevenly on the middle-class and lower middle-class when considering the advantages of tax deductions that are always enjoyed by the wealthy. As it was phrased in the editorial of the Mail & Guardian on the 25th of February 2000, in reference to Trevor Manual's promise of an asset sales tax directed against the rich (a cushion against the left-wingers' response to the tax reductions): ". . . the rich can afford to pay cunning accountants to help them avoid the worst stric-

tures of the capital gains tax" (*The Mail & Guardian,* 2000; see also Barrell, 2000). In that light the greatest beneficiaries of the apartheid system are still able to circumvent their social responsibilities.

Bibliography

Barrell, Howard: "Budget Backs Business for Growth" in *Daily Mail & Guardian,* February 25, 2000 (www.mg.co.za/mg/news/2000feb2/ 15feb-budget2.html).

Brink, André: "To re-imagine our history" in *The Weekly Mail & Guardian,* Review of Books, September 24-30, 1993 (pp. 1-2).

Brink, André: "Interrogating Silence: New Possibilities Faced by South African Literature" in *Writing South Africa. Literature, apartheid, and democracy 1970-95.* UK: Cambridge University Press, 1998, (pp. 43-54).

Chapman, Michael: *Southern African Literatures.* London and New York: Longman Limited Group, 1996.

Coetzee, Carli: "Krotoä remembered: a mother of unity, a mother of sorrows?" in Sarah Nuttal and Carli Coetzee (eds.): *Negotiating the past: The making of memory in South Africa.* Oxford and Cape Town: Oxford University PRess, 1998, (pp. 112-19).

Coetzee, J. M.: *Disgrace.* South Africa: Random House (Pty), 2000 (First published in Great Britain by Martin Secker & Warburg, 1999).

Dangor, Achmat: "Just Before We Shall Sing" in *The Sunday Independent,* 4 February, 1996, (p. 22).

Deegan, Heather: *South Africa Reborn.* London: UCL Press, 1999.

Faris, Wendy B.: "Scheherazade's Children: Magical Realism and Postmodern Fiction" in Lois Parkinson Zamora and Wendy B. Faris (eds.): *Magical Realism. Theory, History, Community.* Durham and London: Duke University Press, 1995 (pp. 163-89).

Foreman, Gabrielle P.: "Past-On Stories: History and the Magically Real, Morrison and Allende on Call" in Lois Parkinson Zamora and Wendy B. Faris (eds.): *Magical Realism. Theory, History, Community.* Durham and London: Duke University Press, 1995 (pp. 285-303).

Gready, Paul: "The Sophiatown Writers of the Fifties: the Unreal Reality of Their World" in *Journal of South African Studies,* Vol. 16, No. 1, March, 1990 (pp. 139-65).

Green, Michael: *Novel Histories. Past, Present, and Future in South African Fiction.* Johannesburg: Witwatersrand University Press, 1997.

Head, Bessie: "Social and Political Pressures that Shape Literature in Southern Africa" in Cecil Abrahams (ed.): *The Tragic Life: Bessie Head and Literature in Southern Africa.* New Jersey: Africa World Press, Inc., 1990 (pp. 11-17).

Krog, Antjie: *Country of My Skull.* UK and South Africa: Random House, 1999 (first published in South Africa by Random House, 1998).

Lansink, Annette: "Forget revenge . . . what about compensation?" in *Sowetan,* 29 March, p. 9.

Lundahl, Mats: "The Post-Apartheid Economy, and After?" in Lennart Petersson (ed.): *Post-Apartheid Southern Africa. Economic Challenges and Policies for the Future.* London: Routledge, 1998.

Malungana, S. J.: "The Relevance of Xitsonga Oral Tradition" in *Altern*ation, Vol. 6, 1999, (37-54).

Maphai, Vincent T.: "Liberal Democracy and Ethnic Conflict in South Africa" in Harvey Glickman (ed.): *Ethnic Conflict and Democratization in Africa.* Georgia: The African Studies Association Press, 1998.

Marais, Hein: *South Africa: Limits to Change. The Political Economy of Transition.* South Africa: University of Cape Town Press, 1998.

Mervis, Margaret: "Fiction for Development: Zakes Mda's *Ways of Dying*" in *Current Writing,* Vol. 10, No. 1, 1998 (pp. 39-55).

Mda, Zakes: *Ways of Dying.* Oxford and Cape Town: Oxford University Press, 1995.

Ndebele, Njabulo: *South African Literature and Culture. Rediscovery of the Ordinary.* Manchester and New York: Manchester University Press, 1994.

Ngcobo, Dumisane: "Nihilism in Black South Africa: the New South Africa and the Destruction of the Black Domestic Periphery" in *Alternation,* Vol. 6, No. 1, 1999 (138-54).

Nicol, Mike: *The Ibis Tapestry.* New York: Alfred A. Knopf, Inc., 1998.

Solberg, Rolf: "Interview with Mongane Wally Serote" in *Writing South Africa. Literature, apartheid, and democracy 1970-95.* UK: Cambridge University Press, 1998, (pp. 180-6).

van Wyk, Johan: "Catastrophe and Beauty: *Ways of Dying,* Zakes Mda's Novel of the Transition" in *Literator* 18 (3), Nov. 1997, pp. 79-90.

Zamora, Lois Parkinson and Faris, Wendy B.: "Introduction: Daiquiri Birds and Flaubertian Parrot(ie)s" in Lois Parkinson Zamora and Wendy B. Faris (eds.): *Magical Realism: Theory, History, Community.* Durham and London: Duke University Press, 1995 (pp. 1-11).

FURTHER READING

Criticism

Bell, Madison Smartt. "Mammals in Love." *New York Times Book Review* (8 January 2006): 9.

Review of *The Whale Caller* that finds the book superficially charming but missing what Bell considers Mda's usual complexity.

Donadio, Rachel. "Post-Apartheid Fiction." *New York Times Magazine* (3 December 2006): 48-53.
Includes Mda in an analysis of major young fiction writers in post-apartheid South Africa.

Farred, Grant. "Mourning the Postapartheid State Already? The Poetics of Loss in Zakes Mda's *Ways of Dying*." *Modern Fiction Studies* 46, no. 1 (spring 2000): 183-206.
Concludes that *Ways of Dying* fails as a work of post-apartheid literature.

Goodman, Ralph. "De-Scribing the Centre: Satiric and Postcolonial Strategies in *The Madonna of Excelsior*." *Journal of Literary Studies* 20, nos. 1-2 (June 2004): 62-70.
An exploration of Mda's use of satire and postcolonial discourse as a means of liberating "the subject from the power of hegemonic language."

McLaren, Joseph. Review of *The Heart of Redness: A Novel,* by Zakes Mda. *Africa Today* 51, no. 3 (spring 2005): 134-36.
Reviews *The Heart of Redness* and praises Mda's use of metaphor to portray post-apartheid South Africa.

Mngadi, Sikhumbuzo. "Some Thoughts on Black Male Homosexualities in South African Writing: Zakes Mda's *The Hill* and Kaizer Nyatsumba's 'In Happiness and Sorrow'." *English in Africa* 32, no. 2 (October 2005): 155-68.
Examines homosexuality among black men in South Africa as Mda presents it in his play *The Hill*.

Zulu, N. S. "The Collective Voice in *The Madonna of Excelsior*: Narrating Transformative Possibilities." *Literator* 27, no. 7 (April 2006): 107-26.
Discusses what Mda's use of a collective voice in his novel *The Madonna of Excelsior* reveals about South Africa's transformation from a society of institutional racism to one in transition.

Additional coverage of Mda's life and career is contained in the following sources published by Gale: *Contemporary Authors,* Vol. 205; *Contemporary Authors New Revision Series,* Vol. 151; *Contemporary Dramatists,* Eds. 5, 6; *Dictionary of Literary Biography,* Vol. 225; and *Literature Resource Center.*

Gcina Mhlophe
1960-

(Full name Nokugcina Mhlophe) South African playwright, poet, short story writer, and children's writer.

INTRODUCTION

Mhlophe is an award-winning playwright, children's writer, stage and screen actress, storyteller, poet, and director. Her most famous drama, *Have You Seen Zandile?*, was first produced in Johannesburg, South Africa, in 1986 and has since been performed in Scotland, Switzerland, England, Holland, Germany, and the United States. Mhlophe is dedicated to preserving the art of storytelling, finding in the oral tradition a means of preserving the indigenous South African folktales, myths, worldviews, history, and values. With this goal in mind, she has established "Zanendaba" ("Bring Me a Story"), a program that trains storytellers as professionals and provides them with avenues for performing, including in schools and other organizations. In addition to giving a voice to the often-silenced women who have experienced the oppressive systems of apartheid and their own patriarchal society, Zanendaba also serves to educate the country's youngsters, many of whom cannot read and have been separated from the histories of their own cultures by colonial institutions that were dismissive of and discouraged oral practices. Mhlophe has won several accolades, including an Obie Award for her performance in *Born in the RSA* (1987); a Noma Award nomination for her children's book *Queen of the Tortoises* (1990); and a BBC Africa Service Award for radio drama, the Sony Award in Britain for best actress in a radio drama, and the Fringe First Award at the Edinburgh Festival, all for *Have You Seen Zandile?*.

BIOGRAPHICAL INFORMATION

Mhlophe was born in 1960 in Hammarsdale, near Durban, in KwaZulu-Natal, a province of South Africa. From an early age she was profoundly influenced by an elderly aunt and her paternal grandmother, both of whom inspired her imagination and passed along their passion for storytelling. She was raised by her paternal grandmother in the city of Durban, where she learned to speak Zulu. At the age of ten she was abruptly taken away by her mother to live in the rural area of the Transkei, South Africa, where she resided until she turned eighteen. While in high school, Mhlophe began writing fiction and verse in Xhosa, the language taught at the local school. By 1979 she had moved to Johannesburg, where she began writing in English and working variously as a household servant, a newsreader for such outlets as BBC Radio, and a writer for *Learn and Teach,* a literacy magazine. One of her first stories, "My Dear Madam," was published in 1981; its emphasis on Mhlophe's personal experience (her work as a servant) reflects what would become a rich source for her writings. She began performing in the theater in 1982, appearing in Maishe Maponya's play *Umongikazi* in 1983, and acting in film, playing a role in the movie *Place of Weeping* in 1986. Mhlophe wrote her first full-length play—the autobiographical *Have You Seen Zandile?*—around this same time. By the late 1980s she had begun producing books for children, including *The Snake with Seven Heads* (1989), and in March of 1989 began working as resident director at the Market Theatre in Johannesburg, the first woman and the first black individual to hold that position. In 1991 she began focusing her energies on storytelling, combining this interest with her devotion to the issue of childhood literacy. To this end she has traveled throughout the rural areas of South Africa, visiting schools with her "reading road show." In addition, she has provided narration for *Gift of the Tortoise,* a recording released by the internationally known Zulu a cappella group, Ladysmith Black Mambazo, in 1993; performed her own stories and written the musical accompaniment for the television series *Gcina and Friends* for SABC-TV; released the storytelling CD *Fudukazi's Magic* in 2000; and performed in television shows and documentaries, including *Art Works, Literacy Alive,* and *Songololo.* She is the recipient of honorary doctorates from London Open University and the University of Natal, and has lectured at several universities.

MAJOR WORKS

In Mhlophe's best-known work, *Have You Seen Zandile?,* the author explores such themes as how one's identity is defined by one's relationships to others, the correlation between identity and language, the centrality of women as custodians of the African storytelling tradition, and the vital importance of an oral community. Though Mhlophe is listed as the primary author of the play, she collaborated on it with playwrights Maralin Van Renen and Thembi Mtshali. *Zandile* opened at the Market Theatre in Johannesburg in 1986. The play is written in three languages, Zulu, Xhosa, and English, and revolves around the title character's mutually dependent relationship with her paternal grandmother, Gogo, a loving Zulu woman who imparts to her grand-daughter a deep appreciation for storytelling. When the play opens in mid-1960s apartheid South Africa, Zandile is eight years old, living with Gogo in the modern city of Durban, enjoying time for stories, creativity, and play. As the narrative progresses, Zandile is abducted by her mother, Lulama, and taken to an entirely different world—an agrarian world filled with hard work and the crushed dreams of her emotionally vacuous mother, who was forced to abandon her own dream of becoming a singer due to government policies and gender restrictions. Although Zandile attempts to communicate with her grandmother through letters, these are destroyed by Lulama; in the meantime, her grandmother desperately shows photographs and pleads: "Have you seen Zandile?" The play ends as Zandile, who has survived all these years on the stories and memories instilled in her by her grandmother, finally returns to Durban to reunite with Gogo, only to discover that she has passed away.

Among Mhlophe's many short stories is "The Toilet" (1987), an often quoted tale about the act of writing. In the story, the narrator hides in the back room of the house in which her sister works in order to avoid being discovered by her sister's white employers. After she finds a job in a factory, the narrator must leave the house hours before she starts work—again to avoid detection—and searches out a place where she can await her starting time. Finding refuge in a public toilet that is hardly ever used, the narrator begins lingering there, then begins to write, reflecting that "the walls were wonderfully close to me—it felt like it was made to fit me alone." The tale revolves around the narrator's need to venture beyond the "safe" confines of cultural notions that teach her to be quiet and obedient, and to begin to publicly express herself. Mhlophe is also the author of several children's books, including *Queen of the Tortoises, The Singing Dog,* (1992), *Hi, Zoleka!* (1994), and *Stories of Africa* (2003), many of which reflect her belief in the educational and moral value of traditional African folk tales. *Our Story Magic,* published in 2006, consists of original fairytales and fables written by Mhlophe in the ancient tradition of South African folk tales.

CRITICAL RECEPTION

Although Mhlophe's writing has been praised as lyrical and her play *Have You Seen Zandile?* lauded for the universality of its themes, Mhlophe has most often been criticized for not writing more overtly political pieces. Mhlophe has responded by stating that she articulates a political statement each time she writes about her life as a South African woman, communicating a story that does not often get told by the Western-dominated press. Several commentators echo this sentiment and view her

emphasis on the personal as a means of defying those who defend apartheid, who advocate the depiction of blacks as part of an anonymous mass—one-dimensional and stereotypical. Several observers add that her focus on the particular, or local, simultaneously addresses universal themes that permeate across cultural, gender, class, and political boundaries. Above all, she is applauded for her efforts at promoting and encouraging the tradition of storytelling, which has benefitted both South African youth and South African women. According to Marcia Blumberg, "Mhlophe's storytelling . . . energizes women's voices in South Africa, making them audible and valuable; it also helps to restore them to the community at large, where they have been mostly silenced yet have always belonged."

PRINCIPAL WORKS

Have You Seen Zandile?: A Play Originated by Gcina Mhlophe, Based on Her Childhood (play) 1986
The Snake with Seven Heads (for children) 1989
Somdaka [and director] (play) 1989
Queen of the Tortoises (for children) 1990
The Singing Dog (for children) 1992
Hi, Zoleka! (for children) 1994
Durban: Impressions of an African City [with Paul Weinberg and David Robbins] (nonfiction) 2002
Love Child (short stories) 2002
Stories of Africa (short stories for children) 2003
Our Story Magic (short stories for children) 2006

CRITICISM

Gcina Mhlophe with Linda Parris-Bailey and Patrick Kagan-Moore (interview date February 1989)

SOURCE: Mhlophe, Gcina, Linda Parris-Bailey, and Patrick Kagan-Moore. "The *Zandile* Project: A Collaboration between UT, Carpetbag Theatre, and South African Playwright Gcina Mhlophe." *Drama Review* 34, no. 1 (spring 1990): 115-30.

[*In the following interview, conducted in February 1989 by Kagan-Moore, Mhlophe and Parris-Bailey, cofounder of Carpetbag Theatre, discuss such topics as the inception of* Have You Seen Zandile?; *their mutual desire to preserve the tradition of storytelling; the political nature of* Zandile; *race relations in South Africa; the importance of music to the play; and Mhlophe's role as director.*]

In 1987, Tom Cooke returned to the University of Tennessee as chair of the Department of Theatre. Since then, Cooke and Phillip Arnoult, founder and director of the Baltimore Theatre Project, have made Knoxville the site of a series of collaborations between foreign and American theatre artists. These projects represent an alliance among professional, academic, and alternative performance agencies; they signify Cooke and Arnoult's intent to build an international theatre research center at UT. In the latest of these efforts, 29-year-old South African playwright, performer, and poet Gcina Mhlophe was brought in . . . to stage her play *Have You Seen Zandile?* with actresses from Carpetbag Theatre, a professional black theatre company from Knoxville. The production previewed at UT, moved to Baltimore for a month-long engagement at the Theatre Project, and remains in the Carpetbag repertory.

Have You Seen Zandile?, first produced at the Market Theatre in Johannesburg in 1986, is an autobiographical treatment of Mhlophe's childhood in South Africa. Until she was 10 years old, Mhlophe was raised by her paternal grandmother in Durban, a city on the southeast coast of South Africa. Stolen away by her mother, she was taken to live in the rural Transkei, where she spent the next eight years of her life. The play chronicles the life of Zandile, the central character, from the age of 8 through her young womanhood at age 18. Following its performances at the Market Theatre, *Zandile* traveled to the Edinburgh Theatre Festival, winning the 1987 Fringe First Award. Subsequent performances included trips to Zurich, London, Holland, Germany, and Chicago.

Linda Parris-Bailey, cofounder of Carpetbag Theatre, described the Knoxville collaboration as a venture that had been under consideration for over a year, since Arnoult had brought an Argentinian theatre troupe to Knoxville:

> We had been talking about working with Baltimore Theatre Project, building a relationship, since they worked with Teatro del Sur. And Phillip [Arnoult], having seen *Zandile* at Edinburgh, suggested to us that it might be of interest.

Arnoult, an adjunct professor at UT, sees the *Zandile* project and other collaborations as important to the development of training programs at UT:

> We brought Teatro del Sur, six months later we had [Soviet designer] Nikolai Vagin, and now *Zandile,* and next year we're bringing in Gerry Mulgrew to direct the Clarence Brown company in *Blood Wedding*. And what I'd like to get out of this is to see that stand-alone collaboration seep in and around the ongoing training that goes on at UT—to make that pedagogical link.

While all of these collaborations center upon artists outside academic settings, Arnoult sees the facilities and climate provided by the university to be critical factors in organizing such events:

> I've worked for international theatre organizations for over 15 years. It's my opinion that the real place that meaningful change can happen is in the university setting as opposed to the regional theatre setting where agendas are so tightly drawn that risks are getting less and less easy to take. So it's fitting that this should happen here at the university, and it'll probably have a greater long-term impact.

Cooke agrees and sees long-term university-based collaborations as an alternative to shorter ventures at international festivals: "This kind of thing can't happen at festivals; I mean we're going to try to make it happen at our festival [in Fall 1990], but the way it's set up now it doesn't happen." As Cooke sees it, the *Zandile* collaboration exemplifies much of what he'd like to do in the future, particularly in its benefits to the locally based Carpetbag company.

> The centerpiece of the research institute was the idea of trying to get important international artists to spend time with American companies, American artists, in a place to create things, to work together, and share. This project is an ideal example of that—it is giving a local black company an opportunity to work with an important South African playwright.

And Arnoult sees the collaboration benefiting international artists as well:

> When Gcina [Mhlophe] was in Edinburgh, she was downstairs at the Travers, and I might have seen *Zandile* with all of 40 other people in this tiny theatre. And then it was in Chicago. But now it'll go into the repertory of the Carpetbag Theatre; it has a chance to be around for awhile. That's one of the things I like about Linda Parris-Bailey, and one of the reasons I wanted her company for this collaboration. She doesn't do disposable theatre.

Describing their goals for the research center, Arnoult and Cooke outline several:

> 1. Artistic collaboration, with particular emphasis on giving a boost to smaller companies.
>
> 2. Greater exposure for little-known artists, both foreign and domestic.
>
> 3. Pedagogical linkage with UT training programs.
>
> 4. Scholarship, research, and documentation.
>
> 5. Service to other departments within the university.
>
> 6. Service to the community through local and regional performances, including touring groups and Knoxville-based festivals.

I was invited to Knoxville in February 1989 by Phillip Arnoult to see a rehearsal and speak to the artists.

[*Kagan-Moore*]: *How did you come to write* **Have You Seen Zandile?**

[Mhlophe]: When I started acting I was mostly doing poetry. I do poetry with song and dance. It's called praise poetry. And I wrote in Xhosa because that's where I went to school. It wasn't a conscious decision to say, "Now I'm going to write a play." I just wanted to do this story. I wanted to do another story, really, but it was going to demand a cast of fourteen, and we didn't have money. And so I had to think of something smaller; and then came the idea of doing *Zandile.*

You were acting at the time?

[Mhlophe]: Yes, I was doing a lot of workshop theatre where actors, say six actors, meet for the first time, they hardly know each other, and talk, and decide "What do you want to be?"—"I want to be a truck driver"—OK, and somebody else would be a nurse, or anything under the sun. You can choose any character you want to play. And then we find stories for those kind of characters, and find how they're going to meet, all those people.

This was in Johannesburg?

[Mhlophe]: Yes. At the Market Theatre. So that was my training in terms of writing plays. I've done something like three or four plays now where I wrote my own lines. You go out and search and realize things you never thought about, you know. And you watch people in the streets. So when I began to write plays, of course, that helped a lot. That workshop helped a lot.

Where have you found common ground in your collaboration?

[Parris-Bailey]: Our work in Carpetbag has a very strong base in storytelling. It's rooted in telling one's own story and telling it honestly. And that's one thing that we share in terms of our attitude about our work. Also that, in telling those stories, we're very much involved in a community, where relationships between parents, grandparents, family are highly respected.

[Mhlophe]: As she is saying, it's something that's very special for me, storytelling. It's very much a part of our culture. Storytelling which is all about animals and things like that, which is all about being able to speak, and also stories that are real and historical.

In Carpetbag then, you rely on oral accounts in constructing your performances?

[Parris-Bailey]: Yes. Very definitely. Both of our current pieces are based heavily on interviews, particularly our new piece, *Red Summer.* And obviously we draw on newspaper accounts, written accounts, those sorts of things, but our work is very heavily based on oral accounts of the incident, and how people felt about that community. It was interesting, I didn't know it when I met Gcina, but I found out that she's also a storyteller.

Are you a storyteller as well?

[Parris-Bailey]: I'm basically a performer and writer. I tell stories in the context of our show. But the two other women in the company are individual storytellers.

What other things do you share? Besides a tradition of storytelling?

[Mhlophe]: I'd like to say that the first half of the play happens on the southeast coast of South Africa, in a place called Durban. The lifestyle Zandile's living is fairly modern. She wears these beautiful dresses, she's having ice creams, time to play. And the second half of the play happens in the Transkei, which is a very rural area, and there's no time at all to play. There's work, work, work, and she has to learn all these things, and she's constantly being told that she's being groomed to be married off. So there are those two different things as well. And I know that you live in modern houses compared to the kind of houses we live in—having water inside the house, and not having to go and fetch firewood from the river, but there are places that are quite rural in the United States as well. I think that there is common ground there, too.

This division she speaks of, between urban and rural setting—is that a particular focus for the Carpetbag Theatre? Politically?

[Parris-Bailey]: Not specifically. A lot of our work is historically based. *Red Summer* is our latest piece and it looks at an historical event and deals with the strength and power of the community. But not in an urban versus rural context. It talks about racial conflict in an area that was historically seen as being very rural, very balanced, very open—in a sense enlightened. We're trying to get people to see that such a perception was based on some very dangerous ideas: paternalism . . . and when these two communities confronted each other, there was a violent clash.

The other piece we do, *Dark Cowgirls and Prairie Queens,* is also historically based. It's about black women who settled and traveled throughout the Southeast and Southwest between 1830 and 1890 looking for freedom. It's about how they created an environment that was liveable for themselves, created changes in the country. It's a kind of hero-worship piece, in a sense, but it talks about people who are lesser known, tells their stories. And the purpose of telling those stories is to empower people, to make people understand that these were common people, just like any of us, and when they were confronted with things that had to be done, they did them.

Is the **Zandile** *work consistent with these other pieces?*

[Parris-Bailey]: It's consistent in that some of the questions we ask ourselves in our work are, "Whose story are we telling?" and, "Are we telling it correctly?" and, "What's the purpose of telling that story?" And when we looked at **Zandile** the story was being told by the person most intimately knowledgeable about the experience. And because it had the ability to touch us all, and to make us understand those involved, we began to feel as if we understood more about South Africa, more about another community.

Is that one of your goals? To educate us about South Africa?

[Mhlophe]: Yes. Because somehow South Africa looks so small in the news, it just becomes "South Africa." But it's a big country, very big. Sections of South Africa are very different from each other and all kinds of things happen there every day. And I've found, since I started acting in 1982, I've done plays that deal with the political conflicts and with the police and the shooting and the dying and detentions and everything. Every single play I've done—this is the first different play. And I've found that in people's minds they read the newspapers, they see the news on television, they listen to the radio, and that's all they know about South Africa. It was to a point where I was getting quite angry and thinking, "Do you think we spend our lives marching in the streets?" You know. As I'd say to them, "We do washing sometimes, sometimes we fall in love, sometimes children get born." There's all kinds of things that happen in the middle of all that. And those are things that can be easily overlooked while they're busy dealing with the conflict, the political situation.

[Parris-Bailey]: And I think for people who care, who want to assist, it sometimes becomes overwhelming, so that when they begin to relate to *Zandile* on a personal level, then their concern is rooted much more deeply. Because it's difficult to understand the things that go on in South Africa and be able to imagine people having normal lives, and when I say normal I mean having experiences that we also have. So in a very peculiar way, things get dehumanized.

[Mhlophe]: It becomes like what happens in the movies.

How would you like American audiences to respond to your work?

[Mhlophe]: I'd like to simply be accepted as a person, in the way I've said I'll accept them as people. And the other things of where you come from, background, and other things—those simple dynamics—just being people. That's what I wish for. *Zandile* does something altogether different than when we're performing political plays. It's not a particularly mental play.

Do you see it as political in any sense?

[Mhlophe]: In a certain way; you find things like children thinking that they're going to grow up to be white. You see, Zandile lives in a fairly small surrounding in the Transkei. She's not enjoying the standard of living of white people. And she thinks she's fine where she is,

because she's black, but when she grows up she can be white, and she can get all those things. So those things are very—always they go on there; all the time.

[Parris-Bailey]: There are a couple of things I'd like to be sure to say here, and one is that I think it's a mistake to separate things out and say some things are and aren't "political." It's very political to tell your own story because our stories don't get told.

[Mhlophe]: Yes. That's right.

[Parris-Bailey]: So the act of telling that story is in itself political. That's the first thing, and the other thing is, and I heard this from Gcina, when you open your door and write about what you see in South Africa, then it becomes political, because that's what the environment is. Because, I would hate for anybody to say that *Zandile* is unimportant because it's not political. That's definitely not the case.

In climates of severe repression, doesn't the oral tradition take on added political importance?

[Mhlophe]: Yes.

Did you experience that growing up?

[Mhlophe]: For us, storytelling is something to teach children right from wrong. And then there are stories about history; history is passed on. I don't remember having such a lot of time to speak to my father when I was younger. But once I went back, after this experience in the Transkei, when I went back to Durban, we got this very close bond. And my father is telling me wonderful things about my family, about where they came from, about how that house we lived in was built, what happened, why our name is not Shlophe, our name is Mhlophe—things I would never have known. There is no book that is going to describe that to me. Nothing like that has been written; so that's storytelling. Sit down with my father, and he tells me why his name is Msgaiza; all of that. Our names have meanings; and when you're told the meaning of your name, when you meet other people, that's the beginning of the conversation—"What's your name?" And it's, "How did you get a name like that?" And then comes the whole story of what happened to the parents, and there's all of that. Which maybe is why we hated it at school when we were forced to take English names because the inspectors could not speak our language. They couldn't pronounce our names, so they gave us English names. You have a name, you don't even know what it means. Mary Jane, my God. What am I going to do with a name like that?

So, having your own name is a political act?

[Parris-Bailey]: And that's said in the piece; it's very funny, but Zandile is teaching the flowers to sing. And as she teaches them, she shares with them her school experience. She talks about the fact that the inspector can't speak her language, so they're going to have to take English names. And you get all kinds of wonderful names, like Violet.

[Mhlophe]: And Sunflower.

[Parris-Bailey]: And again, it lets you understand what that experience is about for a child.

[Mhlophe]: I don't know about here, but at home, white children are terrified of a strange black man. Not only children—the mothers are terrified when the husband is at work and there's a black man knocking at the door. It could be the lover of the woman who works for them, he could be her husband. But he's a strange black man, and that's scary. We grew up terrified of all strange white men driving into our neighborhood. Terrified.

That's built into the culture, then. Fear of the other.

[Mhlophe]: Yes. And then after school, I went to live in Johannesburg and got a job as a domestic worker looking after these children—four children. And the woman, this Irish woman, was lovely. She wasn't the usual white woman "madam." We used to sit and speak, and she took it as an advantage that I'm able to speak English. But the children couldn't understand that. They kept saying, "What kind of nanny are you? Our nanny never used to wear clothes like those. Our nanny never used to do her hair like that." And it took them quite a while to get used to this new kind of nanny they've got. That I speak English and I can play games with them. Normally they want a *maaba*, a grown-up person; someone they can ridicule, perhaps, because she can't speak English. But on the other hand they grow close to that woman, you know? Many times the mother is not at home and they are brought up by this strange black woman. And they grow to be quite close to this woman. And then, she could be fired, anything could happen, they could go to college, and they won't speak to her whatever happens.

Was your perception of the political climate different in the Transkei than it was in Johannesburg?

[Mhlophe]: In the Transkei it's very different. People still live a life that's fairly traditional. The way it was. I hated my stay there. I spent eight years there. I hated it, I dreamt of going away. Now I realize, I find a surprise in my writing, that it's still based out there in the Transkei. It's physically very beautiful. And maybe it was at a time in my life when my mind was ready to learn—I've learned a lot by living in the Transkei. And also having to survive. When things are not easy you seem to grow a shell to protect yourself, and your mind is all you have left to survive. So things are difficult, but in another way. There is a hard life in Johannesburg, and survival, and police raids at four o'clock in the morning, and all those hazards. But these things are very different.

You've mentioned acting in political plays. How political are you allowed to be? Is there censorship of the theatre?

[Mhlophe]: There is censorship, of course. The government sends people to come and see plays, and they read scripts and all kinds of things. But we have learned that—if they decide they want to ban a play—you are never sure, they keep you on your toes. They are not predictable in terms of what play they're going to ban and which they're going to let go. So all you can do is make sure your play is good, and if they decide to ban it, you change a few things and change the name and hit the stage again. You just keep going.

You've spoken about the need for greater support and nurturance of young black artists in South Africa.

[Mhlophe]: Yes. Not a lot of people are interested in theatre. Theatre is not something that's encouraged by family. You can't say to a young artist that you can get rich. It's very rare to get rich. It's always an advantage to be able to do something else besides acting. And those things I never hide from the young people that I work with. But my biggest thing is that people who feel comfortable now in theatre should be able to do it. I'm against building superstars. I hope that won't happen in South Africa. People you can't touch. I wouldn't like to have bodyguards, so that people wouldn't be able to speak to me. So I'm hoping that there is a big enough number of people thinking in that direction, wishing to help other people. And the universities—I don't know how many black people have tried to get into universities where they do drama, and have fallen and gotten out because it just wasn't worth it. It wasn't the kind of theatre they wanted to learn.

In what way? It represented another culture?

[Mhlophe]: Yes. I'd rather go and learn theatre in some workshop. So we need to help each other and help young people.

Many of your concerns are similar to those expressed by American artists, particularly black performers.

[Parris-Bailey]: Yes. We have to support the right of artists to not be superstars but to work and live in a community, in a region, and to develop there. It's very important to our company, and I think it's very important to people who are involved in the regional theatre movement. And I'm not talking about the large companies—I'm talking about community-based theatres in the South, Midwest—those theatres that are trying to work in the community context.

An alternative context?

[Parris-Bailey]: If you choose. I don't like that term. I prefer the term community-based, because of what we do. We serve a specific community, speak from a specific community. And we make no apologies for that at all. We hope to nurture community-based artists. And community can mean many things. We're part of the community of Knoxville, of the Southeastern region, of the black community that is worldwide. So those are the places that we speak from; those are our communities. So we believe, as Gcina does, that we need to nurture artists, help them work, help them live, help them . . .

[Mhlophe]: And prepare them to deal with problems we've had. I've been writing for quite a number of years. And it's only recently that I've found myself being paid for published work. All these nice people who think the work is wonderful, and yet who come and take it away, and I'm supposed to be pleased that it's in print, that's payment enough. So because I've been through that, I wouldn't like a younger person to go through it if I can help it. It's like a mother protecting a child.

[Parris-Bailey]: And for me, I want them to understand that the work we do is very important. We want to teach them respect for the work, and the responsibility that goes along with it. Because our work does influence people in ways that are very tangible and ways that are intangible; people who come to sit in a theatre are moved by an experience, and they don't leave that experience behind. Particularly in the communities that we serve, which are not theatre-going communities full of people who go to a play every three weeks. That just doesn't happen. People that we tour to have made a tremendous effort to get us there; and what they know about our work is what we want to talk about. And that's why they trust us to come to their communities. We don't do *Fences*. When our work goes out, what we send out is "this is what our play is about." And that's what people want from us. So we have a responsibility that goes along with that.

Let's talk a little about **Zandile.** *This is a work with lots of singing, dancing.*

[Mhlophe]: Yes. But . . . it's not like a musical. There's very little singing compared to a whole lot of other shows I've done. But there is singing, and it goes as part of the history. There's a very strong reason why those songs are there.

[Parris-Bailey]: Yes. That's another thing we share in common. Our company doesn't do musicals, but we do plays with music.

[Mhlophe]: Music—if you're going to deal with the political theatre—is unavoidable. It becomes people's strength. One thing I realized—we went to this Martin Luther King gathering one day—is that the singing is not as passionate as it is at home. People put their hearts to the singing, and some of the songs are based on traditional dance songs, so they change the lyrics to suit

whatever occasion. And it's really hard to stop people once they start singing, to carry on to the next speaker. So it's unavoidable that political theatre will always have that thread of music.

[Parris-Bailey]: Yes. And broad political movements in this country have always had strong music; and I think that's consistent with giving that kind of inspiration to a movement.

Your actresses are learning South African songs . . .

[Mhlophe]: Yeah. They most certainly are.

[Parris-Bailey]: Uh-huh. She was making fun of us this morning [*laughter*].

As I watched the rehearsal, I felt the movement was important as well, the movement that accompanies the song.

[Mhlophe]: Well, the movement is just part of the enjoyment of the song. When I work with people that are not from South Africa, I have to look at myself in the mirror, because they try and copy what I'm doing. I realize that it's something that just comes with the songs, and I never thought about it before.

You don't think of it as dancing or choreography?

[Mhlophe]: Oh no.

What was it like teaching the movement to the actresses?

[Mhlophe]: Very interesting. Especially with somebody like Edris [Cooper] who plays Zandile. She's a very good actress, and she dances well, and suddenly she's out of place dancing South African steps with this song. It's like Michael Jackson is known to be such a beautiful dancer, but if you made him do a Zulu dance, I'm convinced it would take time. The rhythms are different.

You worked on the songs and dances separately from the rest of the text?

[Mhlophe]: Yes. But I also tried to put the songs in context in terms of where the songs come from. You know, one of the songs is a very popular wedding song. And you can place the song, explain to them what time the song comes in, the culture behind it. And that has taken a lot of our time. But I don't see it as wasted time. Sharing those things.

Many passages of the text are in Zulu.

[Mhlophe]: We translated those.

All of them?

[Mhlophe]: Most.

The ones you've not translated, the actresses learned those as they would learn a song?

[Mhlophe]: Yes. And also when people speak in a different language, they lose . . . it's like asking me to do a play with Spanish paragraphs in it. It's good that I'm here to guide them—tell them how to say that, tell them what it means in English, and where it comes from. So you can't literally translate things, but you can explain the background, where it comes from.

So they can communicate the situation, if not the language?

[Mhlophe]: Yes.

One of the images that struck me as I watched the rehearsal was the two South African girls, Zandile and Lindiwe, singing "Sugar, Sugar." I felt I was watching two American actresses pretending to be South African teenagers who were pretending to be American teenagers singing top-40 hits.

[Mhlophe]: They were top-40 hits in South Africa as well. We listen a lot to American music.

How much of city culture is determined by influences outside Johannesburg? It's an international city?

[Mhlophe]: It is international. It's the cultural heart of South Africa. Music, new fashions, theatre. I come from Durban, and you find that the majority of people in Johannesburg now, who arc making it in show business, are from Durban or Capetown or other parts of South Africa. It's all happening there.

Much like L.A. or New York or Chicago here.

[Mhlophe]: Yes.

What's the importance of working together as black women in this project?

[Mhlophe]: First of all, the only thing I can say is that I'm very relaxed working with them, and I hope they find it relaxing working with me. I like that. I don't know, maybe it's the fashion in which we work, maybe we had something in common somewhere, even before we met. I don't like rules; so I don't enjoy working like that, receiving rules or giving out rules. So I find a lot of flexibility in the way they work. And I hope as a director, I'm being as flexible as possible. Being women together, there are a whole lot of dimensions, all kinds of wonderful conversations we can have, and I like that. I like to have fun while I'm working, and that's probably why I'm in show business. I don't think I could stay in a factory all day making clothes, clothes that are not mine, just carrying on.

[Parris-Bailey]: Gcina is a very nurturing person as a director, and we've had a ball working with her. We've really developed a relationship in a short period of time

that is . . . I'd be reluctant to say that all this wouldn't be possible if Gcina were a man, but there is this kind of camaraderie—I don't know what to call it.

[Mhlophe]: Yes. To find that kind of harmony with people you don't know . . . How far is South Africa from Knoxville? Different backgrounds and different languages and things like that . . . but I'm really glad that there's that kind of common ground.

Is the piece still changing?

[Mhlophe]: Yes. We're still working on the mother. It's the most difficult part in the play. I've had a very, very difficult relationship with my mother, and all kinds of things could have grown from that. And when the play was first presented at the Market Theatre, it was a very hard script on the mother. So when I rewrote the script, I wanted to work on that.

*Is this the first performance of **Zandile** that you haven't appeared in?*

[Mhlophe]: Yes. And I don't have any reason to feel that it won't be carried across.

What's it like for you to let go of it in this way?

[Mhlophe]: I said the first day I arrived here, "I'm glad that somebody else is going to be able to do this." And maybe that means a longer life for the play. As a performer, I know the problem is that the play is so personal. It really eats at me sometimes. Sometimes I get so emotionally drained after the show that I find it difficult to come out from backstage. So maybe it's better for somebody who's not so personally involved to work with it.

What have you drawn on in working on the role of the grandmother?

[Parris-Bailey]: A couple of things. One, of course, is my experience with my own grandmother—and with my mother. But the real understanding of Gogo comes from Gcina. You sometimes meet people who you know have been given a tremendous gift in terms of their love and compassion for other people. My sense of Gogo I get through Gcina, and I understand the person who gave her this gift. And that's really what I draw on.

You've collaborated on this piece before, is that right?

[Mhlophe]: Yes, I have, with the Chicago theatre company. They went out shopping for plays to bring to their festival; apparently they saw the play the same time Phillip [Arnoult] saw it.

In what ways is this production different?

[Mhlophe]: I think that a person's character, no matter how much you tell yourself you're acting, sort of seeps through. People are very different; the woman who acted the grandmother in Chicago was about 53 years old, her knees pained her, so that added something altogether different to the play, something I wasn't prepared for. So I'm always ready for new things. And also, I didn't cast the people who are in this show.

You didn't cast the Knoxville production?

[Parris-Bailey]: That's right, she inherited all of us.

[Mhlophe]: And I was nervous. I didn't know what to expect. And on the other hand, I'm not exactly the kind of person who is into auditions; I've never had the misfortune of having to go and audition. I've always found they phone me, say please can you come and do this show; people say, come and do that, that part would suit you. I've been very lucky, in that sense. And being in Chicago watching the people who came to audition was a strange feeling. Realizing how much they give to it; there were 16 women onstage vying for the parts. And we're just going to choose 2 people out of the 16, and all of them are doing their best. And I realized even more how lucky I've been that I've never had to do this. So I chose the people that I wanted to work with. And even then, after I had chosen them, having had this whole selection, I remember phoning Michael—the producer of the play in Chicago. I realized that there's a whole section that deals with the size of the . . . of the breasts. And I realized that I didn't look at that in the woman I had cast. So I called Michael frantic in the morning: "Michael, does she have any boobs?" Things like that show how inexperienced I am, auditioning. So I think I would have been nervous anyway, if I had come and chosen people.

Had the company auditioned with the text at all?

[Parris-Bailey]: No. All the women in the show are in the company. The company consists of five actors, three women and two men. And there are also two other women who float in and out of the company, and one of the men. So Gcina inherited all of us, like family.

[Mhlophe]: And it's working out.

Do you have other projects lined up? What happens after **Zandile** *goes to Baltimore?*

[Mhlophe]: I've just accepted a job at the Market Theatre, as a resident director for a whole year, beginning in March 1989. While I'm in office, I'm going to produce three plays. One is a children's show. I've written a children's book called **The Snake with Seven Heads.** Very colorful. A book of folktales, from my grandmother's collection. I've written the script, but I'm not happy with it. I'm going to rewrite it, and the music is not strong enough. I'm hoping to open my first play in May, and go from there.

Your position with the Market Theatre—you're the first woman and the first black person to achieve such a post?

[Mhlophe]: Yes I am. Some people gave money to help a young black director. And people voted for me, and so that's why I'm taking the job. I'm looking forward to it.

Do you have further plans for **Zandile***?*

[Mhlophe]: Yes, possibly. We haven't toured such a lot in South Africa. Very little. People are still complaining that **Have You Seen Zandile?** has been all over the world—Germany, Holland, Switzerland, England, and now in the States, and now others are doing it—they're complaining that they haven't seen it. And I have a lot of friends in Capetown. There are people who wrote to me a few times, wanting to do **Zandile** if I can't do it. So there is that possibility, touring little towns in South Africa. I don't know, we'll see.

Would you perform in it there?

[Mhlophe]: No. I'd stage it to tour.

What have you learned about the play by producing it in so many places?

[Mhlophe]: That the play—it could have happened to anybody. The story could have happened to anybody. And that's a wonderful thing for me to have experienced, to find that when people come to me after the show, they don't say to me "Oh, it's terrible what those people are doing to you in South Africa"—the sorts of things that they usually say when they see political plays. Suddenly people start coming to me as people and start telling me stories—I don't know what the guy's name is, and he starts telling me about his grandmother. You know, he kind of just holds you.

Devarakshanam Betty Govinden (essay date 1998)

SOURCE: Govinden, Devarakshanam Betty. "'While she watered the morning glories': Evaluating the Literary Achievement of Gcina Mhlophe."[1] In *Childhood in African Literature*, edited by Eldred Durosimi Jones, pp. 69-81. Trenton, N.J.: Africa World Press, 1998.

[*In the following essay, Govinden offers an overview of Mhlophe's writings, concentrating specifically on how the author's use of personal experiences as a source for her art extends into universal themes involving issues of gender, race, and politics.*]

While the feminist debate about 'the subject', or sense of self, is illuminated in the works of several South African women writers, both black and white, it is in the writings of black women that the question of a sense of self straddles issues of race, class and gender. Black women writers such as Ellen Kuzwayo and Miriam Tlali reveal in their work the interplay of competing assumptions about the identity and role of woman and mother, intermeshed in varying strands of theoretical, feminist and nationalist discourses. In her analysis of black women writers, and with particular reference to Kuzwayo, Dorothy Driver notes that 'some space is being claimed for the voices of women beyond the careful definitions of mother in the discourse of Black Consciousness . . .' and suggests that this 'space' is taken up by Gcina Mhlophe, projecting the 'figure of "new" black woman'.[2] In this essay I shall consider the writing of Gcina Mhlophe, with a particular analysis of *Have You Seen Zandile?*,[3] in her development of an independent and critical voice.

Gcina Mhlophe [her full first name is Nokugcina] was born in KwaZulu-Natal in 1958, and developed her talents for writing at primary school and at high school. In her writings she draws from her own experience. The story **"My Dear Madam"**[4] published in 1981, was composed from diary entries she had made when she worked for a woman for 37 days. *Have You Seen Zandile?* has autobiographical elements, with the story of her life with an elderly aunt (depicted as a grandmother in the play) and mother. Her aunt, who was a good storyteller, had a major benevolent maternal influence on her. Gcina Mhlophe's experiences included working at film making, news reading, journalism and writing for a worker audience. She states that she has a special feeling for words and for working with words, and wishes to dispel stereotypes one may have of black performance: 'Sometimes people have this assumption that if something is black, then it must have music, it must have dancing. I love words, I think there is so much you can do in connecting with the audience without having music'.[5] While *Have You Seen Zandile?* does have song and music, Gcina Mhlophe notes that the songs are not racy but intimate, between a girl and her grandmother—'nothing to do with the usual energetic stuff'.[6] She also points to the significance of teenage dances in the play, where the young people are conscious of their bodies. The need to love oneself, to love one's body is important, as Mhlophe points out. With children there is less self-consciousness about the body, and more readiness at 'abandoning the body'.[7]

Gcina Mhlophe is clear that she wishes to claim a personal space or self as person/writer/performer. With the pressure to write about the masses, about larger political themes, and produce 'political theatre', she records that she has been criticized for concentrating on private concerns. Her reply is significant, for it shows that one cannot separate the personal and public: 'I argue that if I am allowed to talk about the rest of South Africa, I'm more than allowed to talk about myself. *I am one of those masses* we talk about all the time, why not talk about me specifically. . . . My writing centres around

people more than the movements . . . .'.[8] She finds a public self or voice ironically by being herself.

Her independent voice is illustrated in a piece entitled *Somdaka*;[9] it is about a man Mhlophe met in Mt Frere, who was not the typical black worker in the migrant labour system. She states that she could have 'set it up in protest style', with the use of authentic migrant workers, and the help of the Mineworkers' Union. The play, *Somdaka,* is not overtly political with all the dramatic effects of spectacle, such as marching, and revolutionary songs, and shouts of 'amandlas'. But as the playwright explains, she 'wanted to get to the heart of the man'.[10]

Njabulo Ndebele has made important critical statements, that resonate immediately with Gcina Mhlophe's purposes. He has stressed the need to present the interior lives of black people and has lamented that 'writers can themselves be encapsulated by the material and intellectual culture of oppression'.[11] He called for less prescriptive approaches in black writing and the need for critical distance. He makes the important point that writers are trapped in the very society they are criticizing, with the result that they unwittingly normalize apartheid. His dictum, the 'rediscovery of the ordinary', has become a critical touchstone in South African literary criticism, where he calls for the depiction of black lives in their particularity rather than the 'human anonymity' that is, in fact, a dimension of the oppressor's strategy.[12] Ndebele's call for a radical displacement of the white oppressor as an active, dominant player in the imagination of the oppressed[13] is well illustrated in Gcina Mhlophe's approach to her art and her sense of self.

What Gcina Mhlophe does is side-step the power games involved in cultural resistance to apartheid; she forges a 'liberated zone' through her writing, outside the regimes of truth of apartheid. She resists packaging one-dimensional, reductionist caricatures of political history. While she goes back to the wellsprings of culture, lost through urbanization, this is not a romanticized life of a remote past, but a life that is very contemporary. The tendency to compartmentalize people into rural and urban is resisted, as Gcina Mhlophe shows the way in which the lives of people from these two sectors are inextricably linked. In bridging the gap between rural and urban naturally, she dispels stereotypes of rural women. Lauretta Ngcobo notes that when rural women are mentioned there is a response such as: 'You mean the ones who carry wood on their heads?'.[14] Of Gcina Mhlophe she observes, 'I think it is her rural background that makes her as rich as she is . . .'[15] Nor is rural life idealized. In **"Nokulunga's Wedding"**[16] Mhlophe uses irony to show the entrapment of a black woman in traditional black society: 'There is nothing to be done'. Driver argues that in this short story Gcina Mhlophe 'exposes the voices of patriarchy that preside over the oral tradition, and thus exposes the voice of communal orality as a voice which curbs and controls female desire'.[17] One reads the silences of the text, its inevitability, critically.

Gcina Mhlophe draws from black women's experiences. Elaine Showalter[18] distinguishes between feminine (imitative of men's writing), feminist (protest against oppression) and female writing (the use of female experience as the source of their art). Gcina Mhlophe uses female experience as the context to protest against oppression, devising various strategies that are in keeping with the circumstances of women. Cecily Lockett refers to Mhlophe as 'probably the most overtly feminist of the black poets now writing'.[19] In the poem **'Say No'** Mhlophe is strident that women should resist all forms of oppression:

> Say No, Black Woman
> Say No
> When they give you a back seat
> in the liberation wagon
> Say No
> Yes Black Woman
> a Big NO[20]

A different resolution is sought in her piece **'The Toilet'**,[21] which relates the problems a black woman encounters in finding a physical and metaphorical space in which to write. She draws from autobiographical details as she herself was confined to a back room in the house where her sister was a domestic employee. The story highlights the importance of making choices, and that black women cannot be passive, but must become agents of their own destiny. In **'The Toilet'** Gcina Mhlophe does not project a 'victim-image' of black women but shows their determination to overcome obstacles. The physical problem of finding space to write is general for black women: 'Living, in this our country, has made massive cultural and historical demands on us, so that the mere act of writing, of finding time, let alone space to do so, is in itself an act of monumental significance'.[22]

The underlying significance of finding a writing-space is noted by Driver, who states that 'Mhlophe's narrative . . . is about finding a position from which to write, which is to say about constructing an identity from which to speak, a place from which she may both view herself (as writer) and her sister (she who forbids writing) and from which she may dream of a world which offers, through acting, the assumption of many more roles than a wife who makes baby clothes and does not read too much'.[23] In the short story she feels the pull of the womb of security provided by the toilet: 'the walls were wonderfully close to me—it felt like it was made to fit me alone'.[24] Yet if she is to grow into her own person, become a writer, she must move beyond the safe confines of such enclosure, and seek the open spaces of the wider world. This means not accepting the 'law of

the father which demands her absence and silence' but engaging in nurturing oneself, to use the maternal metaphor, in one's emergence as a writer.[25]

Mhlophe's claiming of her freedom as a person and as a writer has echoes in Zoe Wicomb's depiction of Frieda in *You Can't Get Lost in Cape Town*[26], where Frieda moves from the foetal position when she hides under the kitchen table, in the short story, 'Bowl like Hole', to developing into an independent writer in the later stories.[27]

The disposition to find a unique and individual response to South African township life is shown in the short piece, **'It's Quiet Now'**.[28] The narrator is depicted as a self, alone, at the window, in the middle of the night, reflecting on an earlier scene of violence. While maintaining a certain distance, she is not detached, but reflective, finding a space between a sense of self and the affairs of the community. She does not set up any binary or hierarchical divisions, and resists the fashionable preoccupation to extol 'the struggle' and the macro freedom story of black South Africans.

This shifting link between the personal and political, and Gcina Mhlophe's claiming of an individual as well as a communal voice is well illustrated in **Have You Seen Zandile?** While the play is attributed to Mhlophe, as the principal author, the script actually developed experimentally, with Mhlophe collaborating with two other women playwrights, Maralin Van Renen and Thembi Mtshali. The play begins with Zandile alone on stage, singing about MOTHERS who will be coming home bringing their children sweets, rice and meat (p. 1). We note the difference between fantasy and reality, when the imaginary sweet becomes the real stone, in her mouth. Her dreamworld is conjured up with Bongi, the imaginary companion, and concerns the important elements in her world of experience—dresses, school, and beating . . . Zandile is eight years old at this point, and the inevitable question of what she will become when she grows up (p. 4) crops up. Zandile dreams for Bongi: she will become 'a white lady with long hair like that, and you will have nice clothes and nice shoes with high heels. . . . And Bongi, we can speak English . . . you can also have a car!' (pp. 4-5). The content of her life is controlled by a distant white world, and is underlined once again when Zandile asks: 'Gogo, I love this doll but why do they always make them pink?' (p. 8). Fanon's classic observations of colonial and colonized continue to have grim validity here.

The important element of the play is that it revolves around Zandile's relationship with the women in her life. The identity of women is not connected with male figures, as in Buchi Emecheta's *The Joys of Motherhood* or Flora Nwapa's *Efuru*. While this is a world where men are absent,[29] the patriarchal world still remains intact. Her mother reminds her that she cannot perform traditional ceremonies without the male figures, and the ideal is still marrying a man, and raising children. Even Gogo sees this as the ultimate goal for Zandile: 'I can even see my little Zandile, wearing a white dress, walking slowly out of church with her husband and smiling with those dimples that I like' (p. 26). Male values also dominate education, as they study the 'white man's' history. We note the aversion to the study of this history (and biology) at school.

The absence of men, however, has the ironic value of empowering women. Women are able to provide love and an atmosphere for personal growth for other women; women provide the security to develop a positive self-image, especially when one's sense of self is undermined. To adapt the concept of *ubuntu,* one may assert that 'a woman is a woman because of another woman'. This bonding especially takes place in the context of story-telling between Zandile and Gogo, the grandmother. Kuzwayo points to the centrality of women in African folklore: 'and in all this it was the women, the mothers and the grandmothers who did the communicating, the teaching'.[30] Trinh Minh'ha also points out that 'Every woman partakes in the chain of guardianship and transmission'.[31] Gcina Mhlophe shows how each thrives on this relationship.

Other writers, such as Maya Angelou and Ama Ata Aidoo, have also depicted in their writings the pivotal role of 'the grandmother', as survivor of the extended family.[32] In Mhlophe's story the grandmother gives the child the great gift of stories and the magic to tell them, and the child gives the grandmother a purpose (p. 11). We realize later that when the grandmother dies this is due to her bereftness at Zandile's absence. The life shared between Gogo and Zandile is one of sufficiency, if not of plenty. There is no sense of abject poverty, both materially and emotionally, and the continuity in and with an oral literary community is depicted naturally. Their lives are like the '"eet-sum-more" biscuits, the tin never goes empty . . .' (p. 3) It is ironic that the picture of the HAPPY FAMILY is a consumer image on the Mazawatee Tea tin, and the words on the 'Zulu Mottoes'—'you are the love of my heart' (p. 15) are, in fact, true. Eva Hunter and Dorothy Driver caution us, however, from claiming a special link between women and orality, illustrating their point of view with reference to Mhlophe's **"Nokulunga's Wedding,"** where the predominant voice is a patriarchal one curbing the expression and will of 'female desire'.[33]

One of the stories that Gogo tells is of a woman who faces difficulties in her life, and has to work on Sundays. We have an evocative picture of a madonna figure, with a child and dog of many colours. This story links women to the origins of the cosmos unobtrusively, as the woman in the story was translated to the moon. This seems to be consonant with the 'yang' principle, of origins of life and culture, rather than the western 'man in the moon' concept. During the story-telling that transports Zandile into another, wider world, Zandile goes off to sleep in the warmth of her grandmother's words, and is undergirded by the concluding prayer, 'uJehova unguMalusi wami' which is an interesting collocation between the 'missionary faith' that arrived in the last century and the reclaiming of an earlier, older spirituality.

Zandile's imaginary experience includes lessons to her grandmother's flower-bed as a class of children, with herself as teacher. In her imagination, she will have the children's eyes gouged out (p. 19) if they do not obey her, the teacher. In her new dress with patterns of goats, giraffes and elephants, she again shows the extent that they are ruled by values from a white world—they have to change their names to white names, as they await the arrival of the white supervisor. It is ironic that the children are like sunflowers—wanting to grow—but, Zandile, styling herself along the behaviour of her own teachers, is breaking the flowers—ten years before the Soweto Revolt. Gogo reminds Zandile of the sanctity of all life—including plants (p. 23). It is ironic that it is for this educational system that Gogo is prepared to sacrifice, to give Zandile an opportunity to study. As she says: 'even if I have to die doing it, I'm keeping Zandile at school' (p. 9). The Soweto youth were prepared to die rather than continue in apartheid schools.

Zandile is forcibly removed from her world with her grandmother when the feared white car does arrive and she is snatched away to live in the Transkei with her mother, Lulama. Zandile writes letters to Gogo in the sand, hoping the birds will carry her message to her. She writes to Gogo, recalling that she used to put Zambuk on her blisters (p. 34), 'but they don't have Zambuk here . . .' (p. 34). There is a significant relational difference between Zandile and Lulama, the mother, signifying two different worlds. As Lulama point out, 'This is not Durban, this is the Transkei' (p. 38). The mother, hardened by the circumstances of her life, wants to develop a tenacious personality in Zandile. The mother also tells her 'stories', but they are of the stark reality of her own struggle to survive. 'When I was your age I cut the grass for every roof in this house' (p. 39), she points out grimly. She loves to have her daughter with her, but has been the victim of tradition and circumstances, in marrying early, and with the responsibilities of caring for four children at the age of twenty two.

It is the stories of the imagination that have helped them survive the ravages of apartheid, stories set in a rural situation rather than the urban. A victim of bureaucracy and discrimination against women, Lulama had to give up her career as a singer, and is robbed of the creative energies that sustain the imagination; Gogo had escaped the debilitating effects of this truncated living. One is aware of a romantically promising picture of the life that Lulama had, being dashed to the ground, and this constrains her to teach Zandile to work to survive, 'That is why I have learnt not to live on hopes, that is why I am teaching you to work . . .' (p. 41). Lulama's life is emotionally denuded, without dream and story. In her poem, **'The Dancer'**, Gcina Mhlophe writes to her 'Mama', and there are overtones with her depiction of Lulama, the mother, in *Have You Seen Zandile?*, as in her own life:

> Mama
> they tell me you were a dancer
> they tell me you had long
> beautiful legs to carry your graceful body
> they tell me you were a dancer
>
> Mama
> they tell me you sang beautiful solos
> they tell me you closed your eyes
> always when the feeling of the song
> was right, and lifted your face up to the sky
> they tell me you were an enchanting dancer
>
> Mama
> they tell me you were always so gentle
> they talk of a willow tree
> swaying lovingly over clear running water
> in early Spring when they talk of you
> they tell me you were a slow dancer
>
> Mama
> they tell me you were a wedding dancer
> they tell me you smiled and closed your eyes
> your arms curving outward just a little
> and your feet shuffling in the sand;
> tshi tshi tshitshitsha tshitshi tshitshitshitsha
> o hee! how I wish I was there to see you
> they tell me you were a pleasure to watch
>
> Mama
> they tell me I am a dancer too
> but I don't know . . .
> I don't know for sure what a wedding dancer is
> there are no more weddings
> but many, many funerals
>
> where we sing and dance
> running fast with the coffin
> of a would-be bride or would-be groom
> strange smiles have replaced our tears
> our eyes are full of vengeance, Mama
>
> Dear, dear Mama
> they tell me I am a funeral dancer.

(1985-1988)[34]

Gcina Mhlophe paints the image of a 'prima donna', wafting on the promise of a bright future, but unable to realize her dreams. Alice Walker, in *In Search of our Mothers' Gardens,* also draws attention to the way women's hopes to become creative artists and to write about beauty are dissipated. Through the life of one individual she also shows the tragedy of the whole community, with hopes of life turned to death, in the decades that followed. In contrast to the life of the grandmother, we see the effects of urbanization on Lulama. The myth of 'Mother Africa', of which her own mother is an individual example, is explored as women are caught in the wider forces of oppression. In her poem, **'We Are at War'**, Mhlophe writes:

> Forces of exploitation
> degrade mother Africa
> as well as us, her daughters
> Her motherly smile is ridiculed
> She has seen her children sold
> Her chains of slavery are centuries old
> There is not time to cry now . . .[35]

Miriam Tlali, among other black women writers, has also drawn attention to the tendency to confuse 'Mother Africa' with the role of African mothers, when she states, 'It is a problem when men want to call you Mother Africa and put you on a pedestal, because they want you to stay there forever without asking your opinion—and unhappy you if you want to come down as an equal human being'.[36]

The other main relationship in the play is that between Zandile and her friend Lindiwe. They share 'stories' of their adolescent experiences, and these are in contrast with those between Zandile and her grandmother and mother. The stories are of boys and of menstruation, of the new myths of growing up—that babies came from the aeroplane—and obsessions with being fat. Zandile regrets that she cannot ask her mother for answers to her burning questions. They look forward to reading BONA and DRUM—magazines from the alternative culture—which will provide them with further 'stories'—the 'real' knowledge they desire—not the history and other subjects that are dispensed at school. Zandile notes: 'I hate history. The great trek, great trek every year it's the same, the great trek' (p. 49). Trinh Minh'ha notes that 'when history is separated itself from story, it started indulging in accumulation and facts'.[37]

The myth of an alluring life in distant Johannesburg is especially strong for Lindiwe, who dreams of meeting 'sophisticated men' there. The irony is that this is 1976, and the world of Soweto is also part of that reality. The pulp culture of Barbara Cartland is pervasive, and of American pop music, epitomized by the song 'Sugar-sugar, honey-honey, you are my candy girl', which also shows the way women are possessed by men. Zandile, however, does not see fulfilment in her life necessarily culminating in love and marriage, and this is confirmed by the promise of a different kind, as suggested in the concluding scene.

The poignant ending shows Zandile holding up a photograph, set in a Bible, and a suitcase full of presents. She holds up the dresses that her grandmother had been saving up for her, showing a longing to encapsulate her world in the beauty of childhood, of not losing one's innocence with the passage into adulthood. They also signify the timeless gift of storytelling which is the grandmother's real gift to Zandile (and to Mhlophe), and the celebration of this through the play, *Have You Seen Zandile?* Mhlophe has also subverted the 'gift' that was confined to storytelling in the (female) domestic domain by transporting it, with much acclaim, to the (male) public space of performance. It is important to note, then, that while Mhlophe weaves autobiographical elements in her writing, especially of her growing up experiences in the play, she, like Zoe Wicomb in *You Can't Get Lost in Cape Town* is not presenting an 'autobiography of nostalgia', that is directed towards some idealized past. In presenting both positive and negative experiences Mhlophe is producing 'survivor-knowledge', and creating the future.[38]

By depicting dramatically different worlds in Zandile's relationships with three central women in her life, Mhlophe is problematizing the concept of 'sisterhood' and 'motherhood' among black women, given the differences among individuals, within families, communities, and between age groups. M. J. Daymond's point that '"motherhood" in South African writing and criticism functions as a profoundly disruptive and simultaneously reintegrative metaphor',[39] is evident in Mhlophe, but in a different, and unique configuration of relationships. Mhlophe is depicting a black woman who is developing an independence from maternal influences, as well as acknowledging a maternal figure (epitomized in the character of Gogo) as an important formative influence. In her depiction of Lulama, she is critical, too, of the 'controlling image' that all black women are 'natural' mothers.[40]

Given the closeness to details of Mhlophe's own life, and her point that the play is her way of 'exploring memory and disruption in a woman's life',[41] we see the intersection of the personal and artistic, in the effort to recuperate and assert selfhood, agency and subjectivity, rather than 'blame herself on history'.

When we compare Mhlophe with say Kuzwayo and Tlali, we notice that black women writers depict a 'variety of subjectivities'; the tendency to homogenize African women is resisted.[42] In constructing an independent, autonomous space Mhlophe has worked with the experience of 'difference' without fetishizing and celebrating it for itself.[43]

The discourse of identity and difference within feminism, based on constructed binaries and linearity between men and women, and between white and black women is modulated, even disrupted, as we consider its fluid, dynamic nature, and as we consider difference within 'difference'. In embodying a multiplicity of influences, all in interaction with one another, and projecting a complex self, as depicted in the character of Zandile, Mhlophe illustrates well the 'hyphenated identities and hybrid realities' that Trinh Minh'ha speaks of.[44]

At the same time, Mhlophe does not discount the place of solidarity among all women. In her poem **'We Are at War',** already referred to, she sees that 'women of my country / mother Africa's loved daughters / black and white' face a common enemy.[45] Mhlophe is stridently feminist in what she believes women can achieve from within a common solidarity shared by all women, both black and white. Yet she is claiming such a feminist position within the sphere of indigenous African, rather than western experience, and is far from producing a 'colourless' feminism.

Mhlophe's purposes are wide-ranging and critical, as she explores questions of politics, gender and race in the light of experience, and expressed through the 'participatory literature of liberation' based on the African communal experience. Her identities as writer, black woman, Third World woman, global woman are intricately interwoven in a particular temporal and spatial context. She has developed her own storytelling project (called *Zanendaba*—*'Bring me a Story'*) in the context of local culture, and has also extended this art to draw from the rich heritage of folklore among the traditional literatures of the world. Mhlophe expresses a particular wish to 'reclaim Africa'. This is one of the challenges of reading and writing in the new South Africa. As Tony Voss notes 'The civil imaginary, the cultural space, the *kgotla*: much of our humanity, much of what we are able to contribute to the world will depend on our rootedness in Africa'.[46]

Gcina Mhlophe points out that when she travels she uses a translator, since her play, *Have You Seen Zandile?* is in three languages—English, Xhosa and Zulu. She wrote it naturally switching from one language to another, and the overall effect is that of a 'bridge' since it is more inclusive than if it were only in one language. In the mixing of languages she is drawing from her own language experiences, having learnt Zulu in KwaZulu-Natal from her father's family, and Xhosa in the Transkei, when she moved to be with her mother. She is able to incorporate the multi-dimensional character of the languages, and thus shows up the artificial boundaries that were set up to justify the creation of Bantustans in pursuance of 'grand apartheid'. Mhlophe's point that 'Language is who you are, it is important to say "this is my language"'—shows the multi-faceted sense of selfhood that she is forging. She embodies the merging of different local languages and cultures, with a strong individuality in the context of her life's experiences, bridging traditional black culture and western forms, in all their heterogeneity.

In an interesting way Mhlophe is locating her work in the local and particular, and in this way reaching to the universal, across cultures and traditions. The transglobal culture that she is creating is not that of the commodity-ridden culture of Coca-Cola and Zambuk, but that of the fabric of community life, and of cultural memory, straddling rural and urban experience. Writing in another time and place, but describing Gcina Mhlophe's experiences well, Silko records: 'I grew up with storytelling. My earliest memories are of my grandmother telling me stories while she watered the morning-glories in her yard'.[47] In this way Gcina Mhlophe is contributing significantly to developing a critical feminism, an alternative new internationalism and a vibrant heterogeneous post-colonial literary culture.

Notes

1. Leslie Marmon Silko, quoted in Trinh T. Minh'ha, *Woman, Native, Other—Writing Postcoloniality and Feminism* (Bloomington: Indiana, 1989): 135.

2. Dorothy Driver, in M. J. Daymond, Introduction to *Feminists Reading South Africa, 1990-1994,* p. 14 (forthcoming).

3. Mhlophe, Gcina, T. Mtshali and M. van Renen, *Have You Seen Zandile?* (Johannesburg: Skotaville, 1988).

4. Gcina Mhlophe, *My Dear Madam,* in Mothobi Mutloase, *Reconstruction* (Johannesburg: Ravan Press, 1981): 180-98.

5. Gcina Mhlophe, in Interview with Dennis Walder, 'The Number of Girls is Growing', in *Contemporary Theatre Review* [Special Issue on South African Drama], November, 1995 p. 3.

6. Walder: 5.

7. Walder: 5.

8. Walder: 5.

9. *Somdaka* was written and directed by Mhlophe, at the Market Theatre, in Johannesburg, in 1989.

10. Walder: 6.

11. Njabulo Ndebele, *Rediscovery of the Ordinary— Essays on South African Literature and Culture* (Johannesburg: Congress of South African Writers [COSAW], 1991): 63.

12. Ndebele: 23.

13. Ndebele.

14. M. J. Daymond, 'Some Thoughts on South Africa, 1992: Interview with Lauretta Ngcobo', in *Current Writing* 4.1 (1992): 85-97.

15. *Current Writing.*

16. Gcina Mhlophe, *Nokulunga's Wedding,* in Susan Brown et al (eds), *LIP: from Southern African Women* (Johannesburg: Skotaville, 1987): 82-6.

17. Dorothy Driver, 'M'a-Ngoana, O Tsoare Thipa ka Bohaleng—The Child's Mother Grabs the Sharp End of the Knife: Women as Mothers, Women as Writers', in *Rendering Things Visible—Essays on South African Literary Culture,* ed. Martin Trump (Johannesburg: Ravan Press, 1990): 250.

18. Elaine Showalter, 'Towards a Feminist Poetics', in *The New Feminist Criticism,* ed. Elaine Showalter (London: Virago, 1993): 125-143.

19. *Breaking the Silence—A Century of South African Women's Poetry,* ed. Cecily Locket (Johannesburg: Ad Donker, 1990): 36.

20. Susan Brown, Isabel Hofmeyr, Susan Rosenberg (eds), *LIP from Southern African Women* (Johannesburg: Ravan Press, 1983): 164-5.

21. Gcina Mhlophe, 'The Toilet', in *Sometimes When it Rains: Writings by South African Women,* ed. Ann Oosthuizen (London: Pandora, 1987): 1-7.

22. Publisher's note in *Women in South Africa: From the Heart—An Anthology* (Johannesburg: Seriti sa Sechaba Publishers, 1988): 6.

23. Driver: 251.

24. *Sometimes When it Rains: Writings by South African Women,* ed. Ann Oosthuizen (London: Pandora, 1987).

25. See Joan Meterlerkamp, Ruth Miller: 'Father's Law or Mother's Lore?', *Current Writing* 4 (1992): 57-71.

26. Zoe Wicomb, *You Can't Get Lost in Cape Town* (London: Virago, 1987).

27. Rob Gaylard, 'Exile and Homecoming: An Approach to Zoe Wicomb's *You Can't Get Lost in Cape Town,* paper presented at the Association of University English Teachers of South Africa [AUETSA] Conference, Transkei, 1994.

28. Gcina Mhlope, 'It's Quiet Now', in Oosthuizen: 8-9.

29. Demographic figures on 'male absenteeism' in South Africa have pointed to its particular incidence in KwaZulu-Natal and the former Transkei.

30. An Introduction to *Women in South Africa: From the Heart—An Anthology* (Johannesburg: Seriti sa Sechaba Publishers, 1988): 6.

31. Minh-ha: 121.

32. See Mildred Hill-Lubin, 'The Grandmother in African and African-American Literature', in *Ngambika—Studies in Women in African Literature,* eds Carol Boyce Davies & Anne Adams (Trenton, New Jersey: Africa World Press, 1986): 241-56.

33. Eva Hunter, 'A Mother is Nothing but a Backbone—Tradition and Change', in Miriam Tlali's *Footprints in the Quag, Current Writing* 5.1: 60-75.

34. ed. Lockett: 352-3.

35. Brown: 159-60.

36. Quoted in Mineke Schipper, 'Mother Africa on a Pedestal: the Male Heritage in African Literature and Criticism', in *African Literature Today,* 7 (1987): 35-54.

37. Minh-ha: 119.

38. Janet Varner Gunn, '"Border-Crossing" and the Cross-Cultural Study of Autobiography', paper presented at the Association of University English Teachers Association of Southern Africa [AUETSA] Conference, 1994.

39. M. J. Daymond, *Feminists Reading South Africa, 1990-1994: Writing, Theory and Criticism,* p. 9 (forthcoming).

40. Patricia Hill Collins, *Black Feminist Thought: Knowledge, Consciousness, and the Politics of Empowerment* (Boston: Unwin Hyman, 1990): 70.

41. Walder: 8.

42. Hunter: 72.

43. Edward Said draws attention to this trend among those who have been 'othered': 'Representing the Colonised: Anthropology's Interlocutors, *Critical Inquiry* 15 (Winter 1989): 213.

44. *When the Moon Waxes Red: Representation, Gender and Cultural Politics* (London: Routledge, 1991): 73.

45. Brown: 159-60.

46. Tony Voss, 'Reading and Writing in the New South Africa', *Current Writing* 4.1 (1992): 8.

47. Leslie Marmon Silko in Minh'ha: 135.

Marcia Blumberg (essay date 1999)

SOURCE: Blumberg, Marcia. "Revaluing Women's Storytelling in South African Theatre." In *South African Theatre as/and Intervention,* edited by Marcia Blumberg and Dennis Walder, pp. 137-46. Amsterdam, The Netherlands: Rodopi, 1999.

[*In the essay below, Blumberg surveys Mhlophe's efforts to perpetuate the art of storytelling among South Africans and evaluates the role storytelling plays in* Have You Seen Zandile? *in preserving the rituals, personal relationships, and personal histories of its female characters.*]

There was a time in African culture when the setting of the sun announced that it was time for story-telling [. . .] The television and the radio and the disco are taking over [. . .] That kills something of the child's imagination [. . .] Our stories are fresh because they've been suppressed for so long.[1]

When women "spin a story" they illustrate the political significance of personal narratives for performance theory [. . .] In their story-telling process, women come to see that their personal experiences have social origins.[2]

To tell a story is to activate a dream.[3]

Three women in South African theatre shared an engagement with their work during the London conference, treating us to diverse modes of storytelling in

their performances. I would like here to make yet another voice audible, that of Gcina Mhlophe, who received an honorary doctorate from the Open University in 1994. At that time, Dennis Walder's presentation attested to her participation in many facets of South African theatre, emphasizing her use of storytelling in different forms and venues as a vehicle of intervention:

It is for her contribution as a writer and artist to that larger struggle [. . .] to be heard [. . .] that we honour Gcina Mhlophe [. . .] She performs in schools and fringe theatre venues around the world, and now lives by storytelling [. . .] for Gcina and her group of self-taught traditional story-tellers, Zanendaba ["Bring me a story"], it means tellling the truths which have been lost, which have not yet been heard [. . .] They help others to tell *their* stories, the stories of their lives but also the stories of their people.[4]

The involvement of Mhlophe and women from Zanendaba[5] in storytelling is a recuperative practice directed at oral history and South African culture. The individual and sometimes collective empowerment of the women makes this performative form a vital aspect for the en-gendering of voice in South Africa.

Mhlophe's activities have brought a greater awareness of the art of storytelling and have widened its appeal and value, especially for black South Africans, who, Ellen Kuzwayo reminds us, "have owned [their] stories while owning so little else."[6] Mhlophe is keenly aware of the valorization of written stories and particular narratives exemplifying the might of colonial structures that simultaneously devalue, and sometimes erase, the practices of the oral tradition. Prizing the repository of stories, values, history, mythology, and a world view of a particular culture, she knows it requires ongoing performance to facilitate its transmission:

TV and going to the moon are great, but storytelling is number one. There is that person-to-person contact, which is crucial, and it has spirituality. I have yet to meet a storyteller who wants to compete. There's no competition: I tell you that story of my people, you tell the story of your people.[7]

In foregrounding the communication between storyteller and listener, Mhlophe not only points to the dynamic of sharing amongst equals, she also appreciates the opportunity stories provide both to learn and to improve understanding, since stories, amongst their many attributes, carry personal and community histories.

Analyzing the material conditions for production of these performances, Mhlophe pragmatically asserts their benefits: "people of different political persuasions could share in storytelling. And children of different financial standing could be reached very cheaply [. . .] It's very cost effective."[8] The practical effect of minimal costs translates into accessibility for audiences of all ages and political stripe; levelling the economic considerations brings inclusivity. Mhlophe utilizes traditional folk-tales but also creates new stories to maintain freshness and engage her listeners. She also realizes how much the context for storytelling has altered over the decades and emphasizes the need to be always aware of the particular audience: "I often tell stories in a theatre or classroom. My grandmother told me stories around the fire at home."[9] Nokwanda Sithole considers that

> the stories have changed territorially because of changing audiences and environments. Mhlophe has also done a lot of adapting in her different projects: You can tell the same story to university, high school, primary and little children, but have to do it differently for each group.[10]

These varying occasions for the performance of stories nevertheless provide rich opportunities for reconnecting with traditions and narratives of the past and for revaluing them within the context of a country in flux.

As an interventionary practice in another mode, "Mhlophe believes that storytelling can play a role in redressing distortions to African history and pride—particularly for young children who cannot read."[11] Storytelling offers one method to combat the poor educational practices, and the perhaps even poorer relationships between students and their teacher, which are the legacy of apartheid; it also provides a more creative, participatory, less authoritarian approach. Yet the question of intervention raises other problems when we consider the contrast between the engagement of storytellers as performers and that of academics whose research involves collecting stories. One journalist cautions: "In scholarly hands, [. . .] the record is dry, flat and often incorrect."[12] Sithole also warns that recently

> there has been a conscious drive by black people to record black history, but this has happened to a limited extent. There has also been a tendency towards an academic approach—not accessible to the majority of people for whom the exercise is meant.[13]

These issues of who speaks for and to whom, and of the quality of listening, as well as such related problems as the dynamics of sisterhood, require sensitive analysis.

How do stories work in order for them to be recaptured and transformed? Women's "spinstorying" has been regarded as "a rich and intricate verbal art [that] combines different story types and different ways of telling stories,"[14] and conceptualized as the often private performance of personal narratives. Mhlophe's storytelling workshops transform the private into a more public form, yet still provide a supportive environment. As women participate in the narratives of other women's lives, they perceive commonalties and assess differences; most importantly, they feel part of a community rather than dealing with various oppressive conditions in isolation.

> Spin suggests the curvilinear structure of kernel stories that spiral from conversation to story to conversation to story. Personal narratives spin connections and inter-

> weave women's lives [. . .] Women focus on personal narratives because they cannot draw upon a shared history at a social level when their history is particularized, depreciated, regulated, and silenced.[15]

"Spinstorying" exemplifies the dynamics of communication between women and the performance of stories imbricated in their lives and histories. Across many cultures, patriarchal systems have silenced and regulated women in oppressive ways. Mhlophe's storytelling therefore energizes women's voices in South Africa, making them audible and valuable; it also helps to restore them to the community at large, where they have been mostly silenced yet have always belonged.

How does Mhlophe employ the practice of storytelling in her own theatrical stagings? Central to Mhlophe's play *Have You Seen Zandile?*[16] is the performance of words rendered concrete in the practices of storytelling, the ritual of praise poetry, the recuperation and narrativization of personal history. From the vantage-point of young adulthood, Zandile remembers and revalues her personal history, which forms a significant part of the extended silence, the unspoken, forgotten, or neglected stories, of her community. The recall and shaping of memory translates into its narrativization in the plays. Zandile's quest for the memories of childhood directly relates to her absence from and desire for a reunion with her grandmother; Gogo, in turn, searches for Zandile over many years and retains her grandchild's artefacts and gifts, which constitute a personal memory-bank and a cultural treasure-trove.

Zandile's enactment of scenes from her youth comprises fourteen discrete fragments set in the context of apartheid South Africa over two decades from the mid-Sixties. While the larger political picture informs her situation, the play stresses the personal as political. Zandile's world is turned upside-down when she is abducted by her Xhosa mother and removed from the city and her Zulu granny's loving care. Zandile is unacquainted with the Xhosa language and culture and unused to rural traditional ways, but her alienation is somewhat ameliorated by her desperate attempts to communicate with Gogo and her determination to learn all about her people and their history. In fact, the play renders concrete the contention that "the personal is not only political, as feminists have said, but sociological and historical as well."[17] All of these facets obtain in what has sometimes been dismissively regarded as a "woman's story." The deliberate mix of languages, Zulu, English, and Xhosa, emphasizes the rich cultural heritage that signifies Zandile's history and that of her creator, but also reminds spectators that these are three of eleven official languages in South Africa, all of which represent the stories of many diverse peoples.

The title, *Have You Seen Zandile?,* precedes a phrase, "a play originated by Gcina Mhlophe, based on her childhood," then names three women, Mhlophe, Maralin

Vanrenen, and Thembi Mtshali. These markers, as well as the dedication "to the memory of my grandmother, Gogo, who deserves praise for the storyteller in me," point to the collaboration of the three women and to a different kind of collaborative inspirational work through memory, the spiritual presence, and the love for the techniques of storytelling instilled by Mhlophe's grandmother. The acknowledgement that the play is "based on" her childhood takes spectators into the liminal space of autobiography, suggesting that her life-story is a starting-point for the stories in the play, much as her storytelling employs, reworks, and renews folk-tales. It is instructive to assess the play in the light of Jane Watts's rationale for what she sees as a common writing practice among black South African writers:

> whatever genre they take up is likely to be used as a *vehicle for this autobiographical search* [. . .] Writing becomes a request for reassurance that they in fact *have* an identity, that they have rescued the fragments and shards of a personality from the systematic official attempt to eradicate it.[18]

Watts's perspective offers a very narrow view of black writers and devalues the autobiographical genre, denying the creativity of the writers and the range of material produced in South Africa. Mhlophe's play deliberately employs aspects of the genre that provide the writer with tools of self-discovery and at the same time extends the process to concerns wider than cultural and gender implications.

The play also realizes the argument that "self-definition in relation to significant others [. . .] is the most pervasive characteristic of the female autobiography [. . .] for women it is relational."[19] Zandile's relationships with Gogo, her mother, her invented and actual friends, and other women constitute the dramatic and emotional structuring of the play. Even scenes that feature one actor on stage include other female interlocutors, so that relationality "is the most pervasive charactcristic." Zandile's abrupt, unwanted relocation and separation from Gogo provide opportunities for this internal dialogue, which is at once personal and representative of issues and cultural practices within the communities.

Miki Flockemann's admiration for the dynamic of *Have You Seen Zandile?* as a "sort of 'counter discourse' to what has been called protest theatre, because of the way it goes into area of personal life and experience" elicits Mhlophe's printed response: "If I could write about the masses I can also write about myself, I'm one of the masses!"[20] Challenges that her play lacked relevance since it seemed to eschew the liberation struggle provoked a rejoinder from Mhlophe:

> I've done plays that deal with the political conflicts and with the police and the shooting and the dying and detentions [. . .] [T]his is the first different play [. . .] I was getting quite angry, "Do you think we spend our lives marching in the streets?" [. . .] "We do washing sometimes, sometimes we fall in love, sometimes children get born."[21]

This response came at the same time as Albie Sachs's controversial paper "Preparing ourselves for freedom" reacted to a rather narrow focus on the politics of liberation as the *sine qua non* of artistic work.[22] Furthermore, Flockemann's contextualization of the play's setting stressed the relevance of its trajectory in the present:

> First workshopped then performed [. . .] in 1986, the play is set in the period between 1966 and 1976—though the "horizon" of the play seems more in keeping with developments in the 1990's, transcending the post-Sharpeville, pre-Soweto period of the actual time of the play.[23]

This speaks directly to the opposite dynamic in Athol Fugard's *The Road to Mecca* (1985) and *Playland* (1992), which, while written in the past decade (the latter even set in 1990), depict attitudes and mind-sets reminiscent of the Sixties.

The play begins with an empty stage but is soon occupied with Zandile's performance as an eight-year-old child in dialogue with a newly invented friend. There is an obvious depth of affection between herself and Gogo, and the importance of storytelling is brought out as Gogo performs the story of the woman on the moon. The latter staging realizes storytelling not only as a formative influence on the young Zandile but also as an integral component of their tradition. Spectators witness the interaction of the teller's performance and the listeners' participation, see the educative potential, and realize how the story acts as a *caveat* about moral choices: a mother's desire to care for her baby supervenes over a prohibition about Sunday work, for which she and her baby are cruelly punished with banishment to the moon and permanent separation from the rest of the family. This story provides an ironic parallel with Zandile's situation later in the play: her mother kidnaps her, removing her permanently from contact with her beloved Gogo. Yet the mythic mother does everything she can for her baby, who remains with her although they are both banished.

Another scene combines the comic and the serious in a significant demonstration of the effects of storytelling as Zandile performs for the putative pupils, flowers in Gogo's garden. She enacts multiple roles: the teacher, Miss Zandile; herself and her imagined friend, Bongi, as schoolgirls; and, in addition, the pupils' response. Reiterating Gogo's cautionary tale about the danger of the white car that arrives and takes naughty children "to a far away place and nobody's going to see you ever again,"[24] she emulates the authoritarian structures of her school. Comedy arises from self-reflexive strategizing for her class when they receive a visit from the school inspector. Exhibiting an understanding of role-playing and appeasement, Zandile informs the students about the inspector's linguistic handicap—he can only understand English. As she assigns "white names" to the flowers, she observes in amazement: "Do you know what name the inspector gave me today? Elsie. And I don't even look like an Elsie!" (20). Mhlophe explains how her father's stories taught her the significance of names: "Our names have meanings; and when you're told the meaning of your name, when you meet other people, that's the beginning of the conversation."[25] In other words, their African names provide a genealogy and place the interlocutors in specific contexts, which the assumed English names erase. The final tableau represents Zandile's frustration at the students' mistakes in the rendering of a Zulu song and her violent reaction as she breaks the flowers (students). In contrast to the harsh education system, which spawns violence, Gogo lovingly remonstrates with her: "Everything that grows has feelings" (23).

The arrival of the white car at the end of the school term violently disrupts the anticipated vacation, as the vehicle facilitates her abduction. Scenes from the Transkei evoke linguistic and cultural alienation; Zandile alleviates her unhappiness by telling stories to the children in the fields, but, most importantly, she tells her story to Gogo in the form of letters that are destroyed by her mother. Between Zandile's attempts to reach her, Gogo shows the photographs and asks spectators, "Have you seen Zandile?" (34). This question, which reverberates with the significance of its function as title, places audience members in a disturbing scenario of complicity, since they have witnessed the abduction and do know the answer but are bound by theatrical convention to remain silent in response to Gogo's desperate plea. Perhaps, at this moment, the dilemma of the spectator, who finds herself in a morally untenable situation, partly replicates but also exposes the difference in the situations of many South Africans, who knew to a greater or lesser degree about the intolerable conditions and injustice of apartheid, yet were complicitous in their silence and inaction.

Zandile's proudest moment also involves storytelling, as she invokes her grandmother and recites a praise poem in Xhosa for her teacher on his retirement. That this scene derives from personal experience is confirmed by Mhlophe's joy at the memory of her discovery of the ritual of praise poetry, "That's the poetry that I grew up on. That's the poetry that inspired me to become a writer."[26] Zandile's pride in her performance of the praise poem is evident, but is contrasted with the appearance of Gogo on the other side of the stage in an isolating spotlit area. Gogo's gifts mark her continued affection for Zandile, as does her anticipation of their meeting sometime; as she places these presents in a suitcase, this bag and its contents become an overdetermined signifier for their once-loving relationship and its loss, as well as a repository for her childhood dreams.

The final scene represents Zandile's return to Durban to search for Gogo, but her dreams of an anticipated re-

union are shattered when she hears about her granmother's recent death. As Gogo had taken solace in storytelling about her granddaughter, so Zandile sustained herself on stories in the absence of her grandmother through the presence of her transmitted tradition. This final tableau is the most poignant moment of the play: Zandile, isolated in a pool of light, opens Gogo's suitcase and takes out the wrapped gifts, which she places on one side while she unpacks in turn the three dresses from her childhood. "*She then holds all three dresses closely to her, hugging them and sobbing. The lights slowly fade to black*" (77). The gestures and images, the dramatic structure of bonding, forced separation, and a discovery that creates a certain finality but no emotional resolution—these are, indeed, aspects that are immediately understood despite cultural difference. So, too, is the pain of multiple losses: that of her cherished grandmother, her childhood, the missed years of non-communication, and the never-to-be-restored bond with her mentor and muse. Peggy Phelan's interrogation of the conjunction of objects, memory, and loss is especially pertinent to this situation:

> The speech act of memory and description [can] become a performative expression [. . .] The description itself does not reproduce the object, it rather helps us to restage and restate the effort to remember what is lost. The descriptions remind us how loss acquires meaning and generates recovery—not only of and for the object, but for the one who remembers.[27]

The dresses signify Zandile's lost innocence, the abruptly terminated joy of childhood, and the painful separation and now final loss of her Gogo. Spectators are assured that this "loss acquires meaning and generates recovery" by Mhlophe's construction of her story as that of Zandile, and her avowed intention to devote time and energy to storytelling.

The specificities of the South African situation create a complex problematic and demand closer attention. As Susan Bennett remarks in another context, "cultural baggage is not an optional extra; it must be carried everywhere."[28] Gogo's suitcase is a repository of artefacts for Zandile, but the dresses are the most significant items, since they are metonymic of her life and are also among the few possessions that she calls her own. Her positioning at the conjunction of issues of race, class, gender and economics marks her transformation from a child to a young black woman restricted by structures of apartheid, customary law, and patriarchy. These dresses thus signify her dreams and their enforced curtailment. Zandile's allusion to Gogo's gift of a new dress as she performs the role of Miss Zandile signifies her aspirations for a career as a teacher—one possible option for a well-educated young black woman in South Africa in 1966, in contrast to the millions of black women employed as domestic workers. In addition, Zandile's separation from the dresses, which represent one component of her urban life and its potential, foregrounds some of the material effects of her abduction and the coercion to adopt the practices and fulfil the expectations of a traditional rural life. That Zandile is prohibited from wearing shoes to supposedly facilitate her work in the fields is of a piece with Lulama's explanation that her daughter's dreams of teaching are inappropriate: "Are you going to teach the goats?" (38). Quite apart from their more universal implications, the dresses, as a marker of Zandile's disrupted childhood, serve as a vehicle for manifold factors which stage interventions specific to South Africa.

In South Africa and on international stages, Mhlophe's performance of storytelling is invested with the force of the personal as political and the extended force of the personal as a metonym of the community and its politics. As the oppressive structures and their attendant silences break down, so the voices engendered in storytelling can articulate and activate new dreams. Will spectators be listening attentively and feel empowered?

Notes

1. Gcina Mhlophe, quoted in Tyrone August, "Interview with Gcina Mhlophe," *Journal of Southern African Studies* 16.2 (June 1990): 330-31.

2. Kristen M. Langellier & Eric E. Peterson, "Spinstorying: An Analysis of Women Storytelling," in *Performance, Culture, and Identity,* ed. Elizabeth C. Fine & Jean Haskell Speer (Westport CT: Frederick J. Praeger, 1992): 157-60.

3. Breyten Breytenbach, "Why are Writers Always the Last to Know?" *New York Times Book Review* (28 March 1993): 16.

4. Dennis Walder, "Presentation of Gcina Mhlope for an honorary degree of Doctor of the Open University" (April 1994); unpublished MS.

5. Gcina Mhlophe prioritizes the following for Zanendaba: training a core of professional storytellers; conducting in-house workshops, sending storytellers to organizations and schools upon request; building the resources of the Institute in order to conduct research into African folklore; hosting exchanges between storytellers from around the world and especially with Africa; holding regular storytelling performances and creating an annual festival (*South African Outlook,* 54).

6. Ellen Kuzwayo, *Sit Down and Listen* (Claremont, S.A.: David Philip, 1990): ix.

7. Gcina Mhlophe, quoted in Yvonne Fontyn, "The world is listening to Gcina's tales," *Weekly Mail & Guardian* 10.20 (20-26 May 1994): 36.

8. Mhlophe, quoted in Tyrone August, "Interview with Gcina Mhlophe (1993)," *Politics and Performance: Theatre, Poetry and Song in Southern Africa,* ed. Liz Gunner (Johannesburg: Witwatersrand UP, 1994): 280.

9. Mhlophe, quoted in Bobby Rodwell, "Gcina Mhlophe," *Speak* 37 (1991): 6.

10. Nokwanda Sithole, "Once Upon a Time," *Tribute* (November 1989): 20.

11. Sithole, "Once Upon a Time," 18.

12. *South African Outlook* 121.4 (May 1991): 53.

13. Sithole, "Once Upon a Time," 18. Desiree Lewis's reminder, "the right to interpret black experience in South Africa has been a white right. Blacks may have emotions and display their experience, but cannot be credited with self-knowledge or interpretation" ("The Politics of FEMINISM in South Africa," *Staffrider* 10.3 [1992]: 20), challenges critics and academics to reflect more carefully on their practices. My approach utilizes the playwrights' statements to bring their voices to the fore in a dialogue with their playtexts and the writing of other critics; yet I am ever mindful of my situation as a mediator as I listen to the various voices, interpret the different texts, and shape my own writings.

14. Langellier & Peterson, "Spinstorying: An Analysis of Women Storytelling," 157. Sincere thanks to Dennis Walder for drawing my attention to this article and for sharing his then unpublished manuscripts and other material on the work of Gcina Mhlophe.

15. Langellier & Peterson, "Spinstorying," 173-74.

16. *Have You Seen Zandile?* premiered at the Market Theatre, Johannesburg in February 1986 and returned in July 1987. It won a Fringe Festival Award at the Edinburgh Festival in 1987 and toured to Basel, Zurich, and London. Its American premiere in Chicago in 1988 was followed by a season in 1989 in Baltimore and Knoxville, Tennessee, with the Carpetbag Company. My thanks to Gcina Mhlophe for talking with me about her work in London in 1993 and on subsequent occasions in Toronto. Most of all I thank her for challenging me to think long and hard about my positioning and role in this work.

17. Wini Breines, *Young, White and Miserable: Growing Up Female in the Fifties* (Boston MA: Beacon, 1992): x.

18. Jane Watts, *Black Writers from South Africa: Towards a Discourse of Liberation* (London: Macmillan, 1989): 115 (my emphasis).

19. Bella Brodski & Celeste Schenck, ed. "The Other Voice," *Life/Lines: Theorizing Women's Autobiography* (Ithaca NY: Cornell UP, 1988): 8, 9.

20. These citations are taken from an unedited version of "Gcina Mhlophe in conversation with Miki Flockemann and Thuli Mazibuko, Cape Town, 2 August 1994" (forthcoming in *Contemporary Theatre,* 1999). My thanks to the editor, Lizbeth Goodman, for providing this material.

21. Quoted in Patrick Kagan-Moore, "The *Zandile* Project: A Collaboration Between UT, Carpetbag Theatre, and South African Playwright Gcina Mhlophe; An Interview," *Drama Review* 34.1 (Spring 1990): 119-20.

22. Albie Sachs,"Preparing ourselves for freedom," in *Spring is Rebellious: Arguments About Cultural Freedom by Albie Sachs and Respondents,* ed. Ingrid de Kok & Karen Press (Cape Town: Buchu, 1990): 19-29.

23. Miki Flockemann, "*Have You Seen Zandile?* English or english—An Approach to Teaching Literature in Postapartheid South Africa," *AUETSA [Association of University English Teachers of Southern Africa]* (Fort Hare & Potchefstroom, S.A., 1991): 510-11.

24. Gcina Mhlophe, Maralin Vanrenen & Thembi Mtshali, *Have You Seen Zandile?* (London: Heinemann/Methuen, 1988): 19. Further page references are in the text.

25. Quoted in Patrick Kagan-Moore, "The *Zandile* Project," 122.

26. Quoted in Peter Gzowski, "Gcina Mhlophe interviewed on CBC," *Morningside* (18 May 1995): 1, 2. Thanks to the CBC for supplying the transcript of the radio interview.

27. Peggy Phelan, *Unmarked: The Politics of Peformance* (London: Routledge, 1993): 147.

28. Susan Bennett, "Mother Tongue: Colonized Bodies and Performing Cultures," *Contemporary Theatre Review* 2:3 (1995): 108.

Works Cited

August, Tyrone. "Interview with Gcina Mhlophe," *Journal of Southern African Studies* 16.2 (June 1990): 329-35.

Bennett, Susan. "Mother Tongue: Colonized Bodies and Performing Cultures," *Contemporary Theatre Review* 2:3 (1995): 101-109.

Breines, Wini. *Young, White and Miserable: Growing Up Female in the Fifties.* Boston MA: Beacon, 1992.

Breytenbach, Breyten. "Why are Writers Always the Last to Know?," *New York Times Review of Books* (March 28, 1993): 1; 15-17.

Brodski, Bella, & Celeste Schenck, ed. "The Other Voice," *Life/Lines: Theorizing Women's Autobiography.* Ithaca NY: Cornell UP, 1988.

Flockemann, Miki. "*Have You Seen Zandile?* English or english: An Approach to Teaching Literature in Postapartheid South Africa," *AUETSA [Association of University English Teachers of Southern Africa]* (Fort Hare/Potchefstroom, 1991): 509-23.

Fontyn, Yvonne. "The world is listening to Gcina's tales," *Weekly Mail & Guardian* 10.20 (May 20-26, 1994): 36.

Gzowski, Peter. "Gcina Mhlophe interviewed on CBC," *Morningside* (May 8, 1995): 1-6.

Kagan-Moore, Patrick. "The *Zandile* Project: A Collaboration Between UT, Carpetbag Theatre, and South African Playwright Gcina Mhlophe; An Interview," *Drama Review* 34.1 (Spring 1990): 115-30.

Kuzwayo, Ellen. *Sit Down and Listen.* Claremont, S.A.: David Philip, 1990.

Langellier, Kristen M., & Eric E. Peterson. "Spinstorying: An Analysis of Women Storytelling." *Performance, Culture, and Identity,* ed. Elizabeth C. Fine & Jean Haskell Speer (Westport CT: Praeger, 1992): 157-79.

Lewis, Desiree. "The Politics of FEMINISM in South Africa," *Staffrider* 10.3 (1992): 15-21.

Mhlophe, Gcina, Maralin Vanrenen & Thembi Mtshali. *Have You Seen Zandile?* London: Heinemann/Methuen, 1988.

Phelan, Peggy. *Unmarked: The Politics of Peformance.* London: Routledge, 1993.

Rodwell, Bobby. "Gcina Mhlophe," *Speak* 37 (1991): 6-8.

Sachs, Albie."Preparing ourselves for freedom," in *Spring is Rebellious: Arguments About Cultural Freedom by Albie Sachs and Respondents,* ed. Ingrid de Kok & Karen Press (Cape Town: Buchu, 1990): 19-29.

Sithole, Nokwanda. "Once Upon a Time," *Tribute* (November 1989): 18-21.

Walder, Dennis. "Presentation of Gcina Mhlophe for an honorary degree of Doctor of the Open University" (April 1994); unpublished MS.

Watts, Jane. *Black Writers from South Africa: Towards a Discourse of Liberation.* London: Macmillan, 1989.

FURTHER READING

Criticism

Driver, Dorothy. "M'a-Ngoana O Tŝoare Thipa ka Bohaleng—The Child's Mother Grabs the Sharp End of the Knife: Women as Mothers, Women as Writers." In *Rendering Things Visible: Essays on South African Literary Culture,* edited by Martin Trump, pp. 225-55. Athens: Ohio University Press, 1990.

    Includes a brief discussion of Mhlophe's short stories "The Toilet," "Nokulunga's Wedding," and "It's Quiet Now."

Mhlope, Gcina, and Tyrone August. "Interview with Gcina Mhlope." *Journal of Southern African Studies* 16, no. 2 (June 1990): 329-35.

An interview in which Mhlophe offers insight into such issues as her use of African languages along with English, the educational and moral value of traditional folktales, her role as a woman writer, the mixing of politics and art, and the importance of bringing the theatre into rural areas.

Toni Morrison
1931-

© Katy Winn/Corbis

(Born Chloe Anthony Wofford) American novelist, editor, playwright, librettist, and children's book writer.

For additional information on Morrison's career, see *Black Literature Criticism*, Ed. 1.

INTRODUCTION

Morrison was awarded the 1993 Nobel Prize in Literature, making her the first African American to win this honor. Her novels explore issues of African American female identity in stories that integrate elements of oral tradition, postmodern literary techniques, and magical realism to give voice to the experiences of women living on the margins of white American society. Given her status as a best-selling African American female author, Morrison's work is viewed as having achieved a breakthrough for other black women novelists trying to succeed in the mainstream publishing industry. Her work has won several of modern literature's most prestigious honors, including the National Book Critics Circle Award and the American Academy and Institute of Arts and Letters Award for *Song of Solomon* (1977); the Pulitzer Prize in fiction and the American Book Award for *Beloved* (1987); the 1996 National Book Foundation Medal for Distinguished Contribution to American Letters; the National Humanities Medal in 2001; and the Coretta Scott King Book Award for *Remember* (2004).

BIOGRAPHICAL INFORMATION

Morrison was born in 1931 in Lorain, Ohio, where her father worked as a ship welder. She is very close in age to her sister, with whom she formed a strong bond that has continued throughout her life. Morrison was encouraged by her family to read and spent much of her childhood at the local library. She graduated with a B.A. from Howard University in 1953 and went on to complete an M.A. in English literature at Cornell University in 1955. In the late 1950s and early 1960s, she worked as an instructor at Texas Southern University in Houston and at Howard University in Washington, D.C. She worked as an editor for Random House publishers from 1965 to 1983. Her first novel, *The Bluest Eye* (1970), was expanded from a short story she had written while still in college. Although *The Bluest Eye* received scant critical attention when it was first published, Morrison's career as a nationally recognized author was launched with the success of *Sula* (1973), her second novel, following which *The Bluest Eye* was retrospectively given renewed consideration as an important work of fiction. While continuing to write novels and children's books, as well as editing several essay collections on issues of race in America, Morrison has taught as a guest professor in English and humanities at a number of colleges and universities, including the State University of New York at Albany and at Purchase, Yale University, Bard College, Harvard University, and Trinity College at Cambridge University in England. Since 1989, she has held a post as professor of humanities at Princeton University.

MAJOR WORKS

Morrison's overarching thematic concern throughout her oeuvre revolves around issues of African American female identity in the contemporary world. Her novels offer complex examinations of problems within the African American community, power dynamics between men and women, and issues of racism in relations between black and white America. Her fictions are self-consciously concerned with myth, legend, storytelling, and the oral tradition, as well as with memory, history, and historiography, and have thus been recognized as postmodern metanarratives. They are also conscious of the African cultural heritage as well as African American history, thus demonstrating the importance of the past to the struggles of contemporary African Americans. Her novels often employ elements of magic, fantasy, and the supernatural, such as the character in *Song of Solomon* who can fly, or the ghost of a dead child who appears in *Beloved. The Bluest Eye,* her first novel, is set in the 1940s and addresses issues of race and beauty standards through the figure of Pecola Breedlove, an eleven-year-old African American girl who dreams of having blue eyes and long, blond hair. After Pecola is raped and becomes pregnant, she descends into insanity and insists that she has "the bluest eyes in the whole world."

Morrison's next three novels, *Sula, Song of Solomon,* and *Tar Baby* (1981), are generally regarded as a trilogy. *Sula* centers on the powerful bonds of friendship between Sula and Nel, who meet as girls and maintain their friendship into adulthood. This bond is ruptured, however, when Nel finds her husband in bed with Sula. Reviewers note that in the novel Morrison explores the importance of female friendship in the formation of individual identity, which in reality is often superseded by women's relationships with men. *Song of Solomon* turns on the character of Milkman Dead, who is born in the North but journeys to the South, where he discovers that he is a descendant of Solomon, a member of a mythical West African tribe whose members can fly. According to legend, these Africans, captured and enslaved in America, escaped their bondage by flying back to Africa. *Tar Baby* is set on the Isle de Chevaliers in the Caribbean, in contemporary times. Through the character of Jadine Childs, a successful fashion model and student of art history, *Tar Baby* examines the dilemmas of assimilation and cultural identity among middle-class African Americans.

Morrison's subsequent three novels, *Beloved, Jazz* (1992), and *Paradise* (1998), are often loosely grouped as another trilogy, each set in a different period of African American history: *Beloved* takes place during the post-Civil Rights era, with flashbacks to the years of slavery in the South; *Jazz* is set during the Harlem Renaissance of the 1920s; and *Paradise* is set during the Civil Rights era of the 1960s and 1970s. *Beloved* combines elements of magical realism with the tradition of the African American slave narrative in the story of Sethe, a former slave struggling to raise her children in post-Civil War America. Sethe once killed her own infant in order to save it from a life of slavery, and the ghost of this dead child comes back to haunt her home as an adolescent girl called Baby Suggs. *Jazz* concerns a romantic triangle between a woman named Violet, her husband Joe, and an eighteen-year-old girl named Dorcas, with whom Joe falls in love. Joe's passion for Dorcas ultimately results in his shooting and killing her. *Paradise* explores the tensions between the all-black town of Ruby and an all-female convent located on the outskirts of the town. Threatened by the empowerment of women within the convent community, the men of Ruby invade it and massacre the women living there.

In Morrison's 2003 novel, *Love,* she once again touches on the bonds of female friendship and the damage inflicted by a patriarchal society that exploits young girls. Narrated by L., the former cook at a once-luxurious resort catering to African American visitors, the novel concerns the internecine struggles between two childhood friends, Heed and Christine, over the affections of Bill Cosey, the now-deceased owner of the resort. Heed and Christine's friendship is torn apart when Cosey, Christine's fifty-two-year-old grandfather, purchases the eleven-year-old Heed from her parents in order to take her as his child bride. Heed and Christine, now old women, both live in the mansion of the closed-down resort, fiercely battling one another over the ambiguous will Cosey had scribbled on a restaurant menu. In addition to her novels, Morrison has written several children's books with her son, Slade Morrison, and a libretto for the opera *Margaret Garner* (2005), with music composed by Richard Danielpour. The opera is based on the story of escaped African American slave Margaret Garner, which also was the basis for Morrison's novel *Beloved.*

CRITICAL RECEPTION

Morrison holds a unique and central role in the American literary canon, having achieved commercial success along with critical acclaim for her work. Her novels have been almost universally praised by reviewers, and have been the subject of numerous academic books and essays in the fields of gender studies, ethnic studies, postmodern theory, literary theory, and cultural studies. Several scholarly discussions revolve around the lyrical quality of her prose, which has been described as precise, rich, vivid, and powerful. Other analyses focus on her use of Black English as well as her incorporation of multiple narrative voices, which critics identify as key elements of her work. Her style of storytelling has often been described as "gifted," and her writing is admired for embodying many of the rituals and rhythms of the African oral tradition. Morrison is also singled out for her realistic and powerful portrayals of marginalized black women, and is lauded for her ability to depict the entire range of African American experience, from the brutalities and oppression of slavery to the richness and communal spirit of African American culture. Another area of critical study is Morrison's narrative tendency to mix the fantastic with the realistic. Critics have noted the importance of the elder or ancestral figure in her fiction, linking this character to the folklore and beliefs of traditional African culture, in which the supernatural holds power and portent. Still other scholars have commended Morrison's treatment of issues of African American identity, finding that the quest for the self is a motivating and organizing device in her fiction.

PRINCIPAL WORKS

The Bluest Eye (novel) 1970

Sula (novel) 1973

The Black Book [editor] (nonfiction) 1974

Song of Solomon (novel) 1977

Tar Baby (novel) 1981

Dreaming Emmett (play) 1986

Beloved (novel) 1987

Jazz (novel) 1992

Playing in the Dark: Whiteness and the Literary Imagination (essays) 1992

Race-ing Justice, En-Gendering Power: Essays on Anita Hill, Clarence Thomas and the Construction of Social Reality [editor and author of introduction] (essays) 1992

Paradise (novel) 1998

The Big Box [with Slade Morrison; illustrations by Giselle Potter] (juvenilia) 1999

I See You, I See Myself: The Young Life of Jacob Lawrence [with Deba Foxley Leach, Suzanne Wright, and Deborah J. Leach] (juvenilia) 2001

Book of Mean People [with Slade Morrison; illustrations by Pascal Lemaître] (juvenilia) 2002

Love (novel) 2003

Who's Got Game? The Ant or the Grasshopper? [with Slade Morrison; illustrations by Pascal Lemaître] (juvenilia) 2003

Who's Got Game? The Lion or the Mouse? [with Slade Morrison; illustrations by Pascal Lemaître] (juvenilia) 2003

Remember: The Journey to School Integration (juvenilia) 2004

Who's Got Game? The Poppy or the Snake? [with Slade Morrison; illustrations by Pascal Lemaître] (juvenilia) 2004

Margaret Garner: An Opera [music by Richard Danielpour] (libretto) 2005

Toni Morrison: Conversations (nonfiction) 2008

What Moves at the Margin: Selected Nonfiction (nonfiction) 2008

CRITICISM

Yeonman Kim (essay date spring 2001)

SOURCE: Kim, Yeonman. "Involuntary Vulnerability and the Felix Culpa in Toni Morrison's *Jazz*." *Southern Literary Journal* 33, no. 2 (spring 2001): 124-33.

[*In the following essay, Kim contends that even though the characters in* Jazz *are depicted as helpless victims in the face of harsh external forces involving economics, race, gender, and politics, each one undergoes a "restorative transformation" as the novel progresses.*]

Given that jazz is "an interplay of voices improvising on the basic themes or motifs" (Jones 200) and Toni Morrison's *Jazz* is often considered a textualized piece of jazz, the characters' involuntary vulnerability to harsh outside circumstances is fundamentally reiterated and varied throughout the novel. The recurrent tunes of the motif are intricately intertwined with a variety of other thematic elements—such as "the mystery of love" that involves jealousy and forgiveness (*Jazz* 5), the history of southern blacks' migration to northern cities, and their quest for identity by seeking their parents. The narrative of *Jazz* thus weaves the motif of the turn-of-the-century African American characters' involuntary vulnerability and its improvised variations, synchronizing distinct levels of structure and textuality with jazz-like flexibility and fluidity. On the superficial level, the narrator interweaves both negative and positive natures of the characters. The reader may easily find the characters' disordered aspects—carnal desire, jealousy, lack of morality, injury, murder, and the like; yet, with a bit more care, their affirmative aspects also become clear.

Instead of giving a moral assessment of their binary behaviors, however, *Jazz* turns its attention toward a deeper level, starting to seriously examine the question of "who shot whom" (6). The narrator now traces the concealed forces that govern and victimize the characters' psyches stealthily but dominantly. She indicates the existence of manipulating external circumstances, which make them "crack" involuntarily in terms of morality, as Richard Hardack observes:

> The implicit connection between transcendental/ Modernist fragmentation, violence, and the site of the involuntary has been recently reinforced and rendered explicit in Morrison's *Jazz*. Morrison asserts that the violent fragmentation of the American character—in Melville's Pierre, who loses control of his body, and in Billy Budd, who kills without intention, in Norris' McTeague or De Lillo's Axton in *The Names*, or in any of a plethora of American characters who are defined by what is in some context an act of involuntary or unconscious violence—is foremost a projected attribute of American blackness.

(452)

The deviant conduct of the characters in *Jazz* is involuntary and, perhaps, inevitable. They are inevitably fragmented by outer forces such as the seducing City and its music, the unreliable narrator, as well as social, political, and economic conditions. Morrison, therefore, does not assert that these involuntarily victimized, pathetic characters are to blame for their extraordinary behaviors; rather, she gives them a chance to redeem themselves, exhorting them to forgive and love each other and to be careful in order not to be trapped by the manipulating circumstances. "Sth" (3), the novel's opening word, serves to elicit attention from the listener/reader and may well launch this exploration of the text with an emphasis on the main characters—Joe Trace, Violet, Dorcas Manfred, and Golden Gray.

Throughout the novel, the characters exhibit the duplicity of the human mind: while they display aberrant behaviors such as murder, injury, and misunderstanding, they are also neighborly and kind. The narrative begins with their extraordinary transgressions, which might make the reader consider the characters as morally/mentally corrupt. Above all, Joe is a dreamer desirous to take a bite of the forbidden apple—that is, Dorcas. Although "he *knew* wrong wasn't right," his vain impulse to taste the apple keeps growing intense (74). And he appears to have fulfilled this desire in the sense that he could date the young Dorcas, but the affair ends up with his shooting Dorcas because of the unsatisfied desire to possess her as his own. Even after her death, Joe's aspiration for Dorcas is still operating: dreaming of Dorcas, he quits his job and pays little attention to his wife. He has lost all sense of reality. His wife Violet is almost a lunatic when she tries to take revenge by attacking Dorcas in the coffin. She is also one who seems to hardly realize what goes on. Rather than blaming Dorcas, she continually looks at her photograph on the fireplace and is jealous of her youth and amiability, wishing to be "white, light, young again" (208).

Dorcas is an indiscreet girl to whom "everything was like a picture show" (202). What does love mean to her? It is simply a secret and thrilling game, or a fight to win someone. In her relationship with Acton, her new lover after leaving Joe, she is very impudent and insincere about love: enjoying other girls' jealousy, she says, "I won him. I won!" (216). In other words, what she might have regarded as love for Acton is far from the notion of love, but is instead vanity for satisfying her own desire to lord a popular man over other girls.

And Golden Gray is described as an egoistic racist when his story is first told. Possibly because of his white color, Wild abruptly turns to run away and knocks herself against the tree. Then, the narrator, in a contemptuous tone, emphasizes the order of Golden Gray's interest: after the collision, the horse, trunk, and other belongings come to his eyes first, and, at last, the wounded woman Wild. To Gray, his horse and trunk are more important than the pregnant woman who is knocked down and bleeding from the head because of him.

Nevertheless, the characters in *Jazz* are not always negatively depicted as examined above. Morrison's novel would not simply draw on a pack of stereotypical stock characters, but rather depicts a complex working of the characters' psychological and behavioral patterns. In relation to Morrison's characterization, Jan Furman points out:

> If they are not psychopaths (and they never are in Morrison's work), then they are merely interesting people and extraordinary specimens of the human condition: they are good people who do bad things. "The combination of virtue and flaw, of good intentions gone awry, of wickedness cleansed and people made whole again," interests Morrison. She does not judge characters by "the worst that they have done" or by the best, but the "combinations . . . are the best part of writing novels."
>
> (86)[1]

As such, instead of condemning the characters' disorderly conducts and transgressions, Morrison sophisticatedly lays out their positive aspects in the text from time to time. As for Joe, for example, the narrator says, "A nice neighborly, everybody-knows-him man. The kind you let in your house because he was not dangerous, because you . . . never heard a scrap of gossip about him doing wrong" (73). Violet also "had been a snappy, determined girl and a hardworking young woman, with the snatch-gossip tongue of a beautician" (23).

In this discourse of the human mind, the simple dichotomy of good and evil does not concern Morrison. She does not assert that it is natural that human beings have both good and bad aspects, but posits other relevant questions—why and how the characters are "good people who do bad things" (Furman 86). Do the neighborly and hardworking characters deliberately commit transgressions? Or, are there more crucial factors that paralyze their moral consciousness? The narrative makes it evident that the characters are induced to do wrong by seducing, misleading, and oppressive external forces to which they are involuntarily vulnerable.

The City is one of the misleading forces, involving the historical situation surrounding it. The temporal setting of *Jazz* is the late-nineteenth and early-twentieth centuries, when southern blacks moved to the North in the hope of greater freedom and wealth. When Violet and Joe came to the City, "they both knew right away that perfect was not the word. It was better than that" (107). And their dreams appeared to come true, since the City might give them better opportunity:

> The money to be earned for doing light work—standing in front of a door, carrying food on a tray, even cleaning strangers' shoes—got you in a day more money than any of them had earned in one whole har-

vest. White people literally threw money at you—just being neighborly: opening a taxi door, picking up a package. . . . Steel cars sped down the streets and if you saved up, they said, you could get you one and drive as long as there was road.

(106)

In actuality, however, to make an easy fortune and own a fancy car would turn out to be a hard to achieve dream. The apparently affirmative aspects of the City are not much pertinent to understanding the City life depicted in *Jazz*. Furman explains, "In *Jazz* there is the seductive New York" (96). Clearly, the City in the text has a bewitching and controlling power on its inhabitants. Its manipulative dominance over the characters is so strong that the narrator emphatically says in relation to Joe's attitude of being "free to do something wild": "Take my word for it, he is bound to the track. It pulls him like a needle through the groove of a Bluebird record. Round and round about the town. That's the way the City spins you. Makes you do what it wants, go where the laid-out roads say to. . . . You can't get off the track a City lays for you" (120). Its music operates as a similar seducing mechanism. Dorcas, for example, has lived in "a City seeping music that begged and challenged each and every day. 'Come,' it said. 'Come and do wrong' " (67). The City people are directly exposed to the overwhelming temptation of crime and the carnal "appetite" of its seductive music.

Furthermore, the City forces its people to lose their way of life and receive its own way of living, manipulative and unproductive. It is merely the place that, with "fascination, permanent and out of control" (35), makes Joe forget:

> little pebbly creeks and apple trees so old they lay their branches along the ground and you have to reach down or stoop to pick the fruit. He forgets a sun that used to slide up like the yolk of a good country egg, thick and red-orange at the bottom of the sky, and he doesn't miss it, doesn't look up to see what happened to it or to stars made irrelevant by the light of thrilling, wasteful street lamps.

(34)

Life in the City is not only economically consumptive to the inhabitants, but also mentally destructive. It is the process of forgetting from where they come. They are seduced to put their place of origin into cognitive oblivion, away from the generative power of nature and under the sway of the consumptive state of the City.

The characters are also vulnerable to the unreliability of the unnamed narrator in *Jazz*. The narrator is a first-person voice that is omnipresent, but not omniscient. She can travel from place to place and from time to time, but does not know or anticipate all the relevant information for the narration of her characters. In reference to herself, she says, "I watch everything and everyone and try to figure out their plans, their reasonings, long before they do," but she too is "exposed to all sorts of ignorance and criminality" (8).

By saying this, the narrator is now "taking precaution" (8) for both readers and writers. On the one hand, it is a warning for the reader who might not attend to the fallibility of the narrator and/or writers in general, and who, therefore, tends to believe in the absolute credibility of printed matter such as a history book. However, what if it turns out that the history book is written with a mind biased against a particular group, like black women, as has often happened? So, Morrison, in a recent interview, strongly urges:

> You had to stay alert to political changes, because you never knew what people were going to do at any moment. So you had to be always on guard and be able to adjust quickly. That ability was a double entendre: at the same time accommodating the grid we felt and the determination not to let life beat us up completely— you know, that instinct for survival plus "joie de vivre" was very important.

("Toni Morrison" 41)

An individual marginalized under the pressure of politics and power relations ought not to be a negligent onlooker of human history but an active agent ready to pinpoint and fight back socio-political injustice inflicted, much as the reader should be critically alert to the probable unreliability of the narrator/author.

On the other hand, the narrator's indication of her possible "ignorance and criminality" is a mindful warning for herself and, perhaps, writers in general. What if the narrator of *Jazz* does not realize her faults in describing Golden Gray? What if Morrison has merely overlooked the occasional absurdity of the narrator? She herself "believes in the artist's measure of responsibility for engendering cultural coherence and cohesion by retrieving and interpreting the past—what she calls 'bear[ing] witness' " (Furman 4).[2] It implies that writers must be careful in transmitting their views of the world, and feel responsible for them for the sake of society.

The characters under consideration all hunger in common for father/mother figures who are crucial to retrieving their identity.[3] Joe has eagerly looked for his mother Wild, who hid herself in the forest. Violet remembers her mother Rose Dear, who jumped to death down a well shaft. Dorcas is missing her Mama, who was killed in a fire. Golden Gray is seeking his father Hunter's Hunter. It is intriguing to ask what has separated and kept the parents and children so far apart. *Jazz* demonstrates that the separations were made by the unfairness of race, gender, and class, not by their will.

Why did Wild get wild and come to live in the woods with "blue-black birds"? Wild's wildness was "all caused by class exploitation and race and/or gender oppression" (Mbalia 625). Raped, impregnated, and left alone without any caring hand, she could not avoid becoming "wild" and isolating herself in the wilderness only with wild birds. Why did Violet lose Rose Dear in early childhood? She had no choice but to commit suicide, because, despite her struggle for life, the suffering was too overwhelming and severe to endure: her husband left the family, and the unjust sheriff took everything, even the chair she was sitting on. And Dorcas' Mama burned to death while the fire engine was kept "polished and poised in another part of town" (38), just as the ambulance did not come for Dorcas "really because it was colored people calling" (210). As for Golden Gray, he was compelled to live "one-armed" without his father's affectionate love for the reason that his mother, Vera Louise Gray, was a daughter of a rich white landlord, while his father was "a black-skinned nigger" (145). Such a complex working of race, gender, and class, along with brutal economic circumstances, has forcefully pushed the characters toward extreme wretchedness.

As examined so far, the turn-of-the century African American characters in *Jazz* are inevitably exposed and vulnerable to those harsh conditions of the City and its seductive music, the unreliable narrator, and the oppression of class, race, and gender. They are "brought to the edge of endurance and then asked to endure more; sometimes they crack" (Furman 5). In this sense, Morrison no longer leaves the pathetic characters victimized under the control of such hard to endure circumstances, as Hardack points out that she "has often returned to essentially humanistic verities at the close of the polemical novels" (466). Her characters now need to be healed and restored to a joyous stage.[4]

The process of deliverance from their vulnerable state is diversified and dramatized. In Golden Gray's case, the restoration takes place naturally through the narrator's recognition of her fallibility: "What was I thinking of? How could I have imagined him so poorly? . . . I have been careless and stupid and it infuriates me to discover (again) how unreliable I am" (160). Then she starts to reconsider Gray:

> Now I have to think this through, carefully, even though I may be doomed to another misunderstanding. I have to do it and not break down. Not hating him is not enough; liking, loving him is not useful. I have to alter things. I have to be a shadow who wishes him well, like the smiles of the dead left over from their lives. I want to dream a nice dream for him, and another of him. Lie down next to him, a wrinkle in the sheet, and contemplate his pain and by doing so ease it, diminish

> it. I want to be the language that wishes him well, speaks his name, wakes him when his eyes need to be open.
>
> (161)

The person of Gray that the narrator describes highly differs from that of the former egoistic Gray. The narrator at this moment sees him as a humane person who shows warm affection to Wild. So, the modified description of the character of Golden Gray is possibly meant to reshape the reader's conception of him.

As for Violet, her restorative transformation begins earlier than Joe's. She brings Dorcas' picture back to her aunt Alice Manfred and, to keep Dorcas from precipitating her jealousy, affirms that "she was ugly. Outside and in" (205). After that resolution, she is now hesitant about whether to take or leave Joe, saying indecisively, "Do I stay with him? I want to, I think. I want . . . well, I didn't always . . . now I want. I want some fat in this life" (110). This hesitation is soon stopped by Alice Manfred, who, with a keen insight and sense of reality, advises Violet, "Wake up. Fat or lean, you got just one. This is it" (110). Violet's anxiety about life is gradually relieved through a series of conversations with the motherly woman Alice. Reconciliation and sisterhood thus come to sprout between Violet and Alice, who otherwise might have had a lifelong feud due to Dorcas' death.

In Joe's case, it takes a long time to resume a sense of reality on account of his persistent attachment to Dorcas. Ironically enough, however, Dorcas plays the restorative role through her friend Felice. In other words, not until Felice delivers her friend's last words does Joe show a positive change in his relationship with his wife. Dorcas says right before her death, "There's only one apple. . . . Just one. Tell Joe" (213), just as her aunt addresses to Violet, "you got just one" (110). He consequently realizes that his only apple should be his wife Violet.

Dorcas' dying words, nevertheless, do not imply that she does not love Joe. The opposite case can be inferred from Felice's comment given to Joe. "See? You were the last thing on her mind. . . . She let herself die" (213). Despite her usual self-serving egotism, Dorcas, at the last moment of life, realizes the true meaning of love and, thereby, chooses to sacrifice herself for the sake of Joe. Eusebio L. Rodrigues comments on this point: "Her love is so generous and self-sacrificial that she allows herself to bleed to death rather than reveal his name for the police to find him" (747). This sacrificial love is an important clue to understanding "the mystery of love" (5). Happiness and delightful moments have now returned to the house of Joe and

Violet, which was gloomy, enough to enjoy music: "Mr. Trace moved his head to the rhythm and his wife snapped her fingers in time. She did a little step in front of him and he smiled. By and by they were dancing" (214).

By presenting the revitalizing moments with Felice, Joe, and Violet together at the dinner table toward the end of the novel, *Jazz* takes on a mystic and dramatic method by appropriating the Miltonic, Christian concept of the *felix culpa* (happy fault).[5] In brief, the term signifies that even though Adam and Eve, by taking of the "apple of good and evil," are cast out of Eden, the fault in turn brings out the great happiness that "a fairer Paradise is found now" (Milton, *Paradise Regained* 44.613) through the sacrificial death and resurrection of Jesus. Felice, as her name implies "happiness," assumes a similar, restorative role in *Jazz.*

Concerning the naming of the characters, Morrison says, "I'm trying to reflect the milieu. At least I use the names that black people are willing to accept for themselves" ("Interview" 460). If the name Felice is used for a certain ramification and Joe's remark—"Felice. They named you right. Remember that" (215)—takes credit, Felice obviously serves as the mediator figure, an agent who restores Joe and Violet's love and merriment that have been broken on account of their past culpability. Also, the narrator of *Jazz* mysteriously suggests that Felice is "another true-as-life Dorcas" (197), and similarly says, "I saw the three of them, Felice, Joe and Violet, and they looked to me like a mirror image of Dorcas, Joe and Violet" (221). Felice is depicted as an incarnate Dorcas in the narrative of *Jazz.*[6] It might imply that Felice could be regarded as a transformed Dorcas, who, after a redemptive death, helps Joe and Violet to find their lost love and happiness.

Jazz contains Morrison's diagnosis of the extraordinary behaviors of the ordinary people Joe, Violet, Dorcas, and Golden Gray, and, at the same time, avails her restorative treatment of them with an emphasis on sacrificial love. In spite of their intrinsic goodness, they commit bizarre acts such as injury and murder, for they have been involuntarily exposed to the misleading circumstances of the City and its music, the unreliability of the narrator, and the oppressive conditions of class, race, and gender. So, "What turned out different was who shot whom" (6). Nobody shot anybody. Rather, they were shot by harsh circumstances and conditions. The treatment for curing the victimized and wounded characters is prescribed to be forgiveness and love between each other. In addition, Morrison admonishes her people to be wide awake and careful not to be induced or seduced by those harmful circumstances. As the griot cautions—"When Violet isn't paying attention she stumbles onto these cracks" (23)—her people ought to be attentive and, if needed, rebellious to manipulative narrator/authors and seductive cities as well as to the oppressive exploitation and based on class, race, and gender prejudices. "Wake up" (110).

Notes

1. See Nellie Y. McKay, "Interview with Toni Morrison," *Contemporary Literature* 24 (1983): 413-429. Rpt in *Toni Morrison: Critical Perspectives Past and Present,* ed. Henry Louis Gates, Jr. and K. A. Appiah (New York: Amistad, 1993), 405.

2. See Thomas LcClair, " 'The Language Must Not Sweat': A Conversation with Toni Morrison," *New Republic* 184 (21 March 1981): 26.

3. Michelle C. Loris points out, from the perspective of child psychology, that the characters' loss of their mother and/or father in childhood plays a seminal role in *Jazz*. She indicates that their early loss of parental love, as a result of gender and race-related adversity, is closely related to Joe's search for Dorcas as his oedipal mother figure and Dorcas' positive reaction to Joe as her fantasized father replacement (56).

4. Similarly, Loris sees *Jazz* as a process in which the characters (Joe, Violet, and Dorcas, in this case) regain their True Selves from the past False Selves (62).

5. On the concept of the *felix culpa* and its literary application to John Milton's *Paradise Lost,* see Arthur O. Lovejoy, "Milton and the Paradox of the Fortunate Fall" in *Essays in the History of Ideas* (New York: George Braziller, 1995), 277-295.

6. Tabitha, whose Greek name was Dorcas, was a woman who spent her life making robes and other clothing for the poor. Later, she experienced a revival of life. When she became sick and died, her family called for Peter, since he stayed near her town of Joppa. Then a miraculous event happened: "Turning toward the dead woman, he said, 'Tabitha, get up.' She opened her eyes, and seeing Peter she sat up" (Acts 9:32).

Works Cited

Furman, Jan. *Toni Morrison's Fiction.* Columbia: U of South Carolina P, 1996.

Hardack, Richard. " 'A Music Seeking Its Words': Double-Timing and Double-Consciousness in Toni Morrison's *Jazz*." *Callaloo* 18 (1995): 451-471.

Jones, Gayl. *Liberating Voices: Oral Tradition in African American Literature.* Cambridge: Harvard UP, 1991.

Loris, Michelle C. "Self and Mutuality: Romantic Love, Desire, Race, and Gender in Toni Morrison's *Jazz*." *Sacred Heart University Review* 14.1-2 (1993-1994): 53-62.

Mbalia, Doreatha Drummond. "Women Who Run with Wild: The Need for Sisterhoods in *Jazz*." *Modern Fiction Studies* 39 (1993): 623-646.

Milton, John. Paradise Lost *and* Paradise Regained. Ed. Christopher Ricks. New York: Signet, 1968.

Morrison, Toni. "Interview with Toni Morrison." *The Massachusetts Review* 36 (1995): 455-473.

———. *Jazz*. New York: Plume, 1993.

———. "Toni Morrison." Interview. *Belles Lettres: A Review of Books by Women* 10.2 (1995): 40-43.

Rodrigues, Eusebio L. "Experiencing *Jazz*." *Modern Fiction Studies* 39 (1993): 733-754.

James Mayo (essay date summer 2002)

SOURCE: Mayo, James. "Morrison's *The Bluest Eye*." *Explicator* 60, no. 4 (summer 2002): 231-34.

[*In the essay that follows, Mayo suggests that Claudia, the narrator of* The Bluest Eye, *may have been a victim of sexual assault.*]

Toni Morrison's **The Bluest Eye** presents readers with a variety of thematic concerns, including dealing with or repressing guilt, shame, and violence; coming to terms with society's image of ideal beauty (both feminine and masculine); racial self-loathing; and, in a narrative sense, dealing with memories of the past that correspond to those themes. Claudia, the novel's narrator, reflects on one summer of her childhood, relating to readers her sense of shame and guilt over the incestuous rape of 11-year-old Pecola Breedlove. Although most criticism of the novel focuses on Pecola's life, as filtered through Claudia's memory-narrative, Morrison gives readers a subtle clue that Claudia herself is a victim of rape and has repressed the memory. Readers should thus consider Claudia's sense of guilt over the death of Pecola's child in a different light.

After her rape, Pecola eventually makes her way to Soaphead Church, a West Indian mystic/prophet. Angry at God for ignoring the wishes of this small, "pitifully unattractive" child (173), anger that he directly expresses in a letter to God. Soaphead Church grants Pecola's wish, giving her the blue eyes she longs for, even though "[n]o one else will see her blue eyes" (182). Soaphead Church is a self-admitted child molester, a man abandoned by his wife years before his arrival in Lorain and his encounter with Pecola. Morrison

describes Church as a man who "[a]ll his life had a fondness for things" (165). At some point, perhaps after his wife deserts him, Church's "attentions [. . .] gradually settled on those humans whose bodies were least offensive—children" (166), specifically the bodies of "little girls," whom he finds "usually manageable and frequently seductive" (166).

The hints that Morrison gives readers that Claudia may in fact be one of the "little girls" that Church finds attractive appear in Church's letter to God and in the beginning of the following chapter (the first chapter of the "Summer" section). Church writes in his letter to God. "I couldn't [. . .] keep my hands, my mouth, off them. Salt-sweet. Like not quite ripe strawberries covered with the light salt sweat of running days and hopping, skipping, jumping hours" (179). In the following chapter, as the narrative voice again becomes Claudia's, the sexual symbol of the strawberries is revisited. The chapter begins with Claudia's reminiscing about summer, and she relates that she only has "to break into the tightness of a strawberry" (187) to see summer. Morrison then mixes the symbol to further suggest that Claudia, like many other young girls in Lorain, was a victim of Soaphead Church's pedophilia, as Claudia links strawberries and summer to "dust and lowering skies" (187). Claudia explains that, for her, summer is "a season of storms. The parched days and sticky nights are undistinguished in my mind, but the storms, the violent sudden storms, both frightened and quenched me" (187). The language here is clear: "strawberry," "tightness," and "quenched" offer sexual imagery, whereas "violent," "sudden," "storms," and "frightened" suggest the violence and trauma that a victim of pedophilia would experience.

Morrison also gives readers a subtle clue as to how Claudia may have fallen victim to Soaphead Church. Church, in his confessional, yet blasphemous, letter to God, describes his method of luring the girls into his lair: "I gave them mints, money, and they'd eat ice cream with their legs open while I played with them. It was like a party" (181). Throughout the novel Claudia, Frieda, and Pecola, as would any child growing up poor, long for candy and ice cream. Mr. Henry, who boards with Claudia's family, uses the promise of candy and ice cream as an enticement to keep the girls from telling their parents that he has brought the "whores" into the home while the family is away, thus establishing the relationship between material gifts and sex. Claudia also relates to readers that she and her sister sold seeds throughout the summer of Pecola's pregnancy, ignoring their mother's advice to go only to the homes of people they knew and going, instead, from door to door (188).

Again, the sexual reference in the language ("seeds") is clear, and Claudia and Frieda could have, like Pecola, found their way to the door of Soaphead Church.

All of this may lead readers to question why, if she or her sister had indeed been raped by Soaphead Church, Claudia does not reveal that fact in the course of her narration. Two explanations are possible. Claudia, after describing the relationship between strawberries and summer, goes on to say in the same paragraph that her "memory is uncertain" (187). Claudia remembers a story her mother told her of a tornado that struck Lorain in 1929. Over the years. Claudia's and her mother's separate stories have blended, and she states, "I mix up her summer with my own" (187). Naturally, this could be offered as an explanation for Claudia's failure to mention her own rape. Perhaps Claudia has chosen not to remember or accept her ordeal, as Pecola does after she "receives" blue eyes. As Pecola descends into insanity, she has completely repressed the memory of her own rape, and Claudia could have done the same.

Another possibility concerning the omission points to a theme of the novel that many critics have noted, the keeping of secrets. Pecola keeps the secret of her rape: Pecola's mother does not make public the fact that her daughter was raped by her own father; Pecola's mother also chooses not to make public the fact that her husband beats her. J. Brooks Bouson argues that Morrison protects readers from the "traumatic, shame-laden subject matter of her novel" by making them part of the conspiracy, by "invoking the 'back fence' world of 'illicit gossip'" (Bouson 26). "Conspiracy" implies that the characters, indeed the victims, are committed to keeping the traumatic events of their lives secret, only revealing them in an intimate, trusting manner with the reader. The fact that they would want to keep such traumatic events secret only makes sense. The self-loathing they feel could be made worse if their secrets were revealed.

Claudia expresses the feelings of guilt that she and her sister experience over the death of Pecola's child and Pecola's insanity. Claudia feels that the fact that the seeds they planted do not grow somehow implicates her in the death of the child. She and her sister, like the other members of the community, do not do enough to save Pecola, but perhaps Claudia's feelings should be viewed in a different light. It is possible that, as a victim of rape herself, Claudia shares in Pecola's trauma and shame in a more direct manner.

Works Cited

Bouson, J. Brooks, *Quiet as It's Kept: Shame, Trauma, and Race in the Novels of Toni Morrison*. Albany: State University of New York Press, 2000.

Morrison, Toni. *The Bluest Eye*. New York: Plume, 1994.

Monika M. Elbert (essay date 2003)

SOURCE: Elbert, Monika M. "Toni Morrison's *Beloved* (1987): Maternal Possibilities, Sisterly Bonding." In *Women in Literature: Reading through the Lens of Gender,* edited by Jerilyn Fisher and Ellen S. Silber, pp. 38-40. Westport, Conn.: Greenwood Press, 2003.

[*In the essay below, Elbert underscores the central role of strong women in* Beloved.]

Although published in 1987, Toni Morrison's most widely acclaimed and Pulitzer Prize-winning novel ***Beloved*** may just as well have been written in the nineteenth century. A modern-day rendition of the nineteenth-century genre of the slave narrative, it is a fictional account based on the true story of Margaret Garner, an escaped slave. Escaped slaves were never safe in the United States, especially after the Fugitive Slave Act was passed in 1850, a law which permitted slave masters to pursue runaway slaves across state lines. It would be foolhardy to discuss gender roles in this novel without taking into account the "peculiar institution" (as slavery was called in the nineteenth century) of slavery as the framework. It is helpful to juxtapose Morrison's novel with Frederick Douglass' *Narrative of the Life of Frederick Douglass: An American Slave* (1845) and Harriet Jacobs' *Incidents in the Life of a Slave Girl* (1861), although Morrison's account shows a more gender-balanced attitude toward the suffering of both male and female slaves. Morrison is concerned with the suffering inflicted upon both sexes; the oppression or suffering under slavery has no gender preference. The injury to slave men and fathers, like Paul D. or Sethe's husband Halle, is just as egregious as the sacrilege to slave mothers and daughters, like Beloved, the one daughter Sethe manages to murder when Schoolteacher comes to retrieve the escaped mother and children.

Morrison's ***Beloved*** falls in the tradition of Harriet Beecher Stowe's *Uncle Tom's Cabin* (1852): They both explore maternal possibilities that will effect radical social change. Stowe's readers were the sympathetic Northern mothers, who would react emotionally to the violence done to family life under slavery and then use their influence over their husbands to change the system. Morrison points to the influence of the mothers and grandmothers, the guardians of the community, to exorcise "124" of its ghost. Both authors know that the past needs to be exorcised or healed for there to be a future or for there to be a reconciliation of the sexes (in the case of *Beloved* through a happy marriage between Sethe and Paul D.). The haunted "124" Bluestone Road needs to be put in order—on both a familial and a national level—for Sethe to be reborn and have another chance at finding peace. Tellingly, *Beloved* opens with the ghosts of the past still haunting "124" even though it is 1873, well into Reconstruction and 18 years after Sethe's murder of Beloved.

The quintessentially strong Morrison female protagonist, Sethe withstands the atrocities to herself and to her children and still survives. Spurred on by Schoolteacher's Nephews' desecration of her maternal milk, Sethe is resolved to see that her children find safety and freedom. At the end of the narrative, all the injured mothers, alive and dead, exorcise the ghost of Beloved, representative of all lost children, and come to terms with any sense of guilt for their aborted motherhood by uniting in spiritual communion and song, the words of which resist any white patriarchal framework, represented by the "Word." Sethe and the community are cured by the singing women: "the voices of women searched for the right combination, the key, the code, the sound that broke the back of words. . . . It broke over Sethe and she trembled like the baptized in its wash" (261).

Sethe's personal odyssey involves a rediscovery of the community and of her own power. Initially, she can only identify herself in her maternal role; she proclaims that her children are her "own best thing." Paul D. ("a singing male"), the healing male energy, teaches her about her value as an individual and guides her toward autonomy, as he asserts, "You your best thing, Sethe." But Sethe, too, is able to heal Paul D. through her love, "Only this woman Sethe could have left him his manhood like that. He wants to put his story next to hers" (273). Sethe recovers from the victim role of wounded mother and daughter through Paul D.'s love. In fact, Sethe has learned that, as Paul D. claims, her maternal love is "too thick" and that she needs to replace that with self-love and self-respect. The middle of the text, comprising a dialogue between Sethe, Beloved, and Denver, shows the real danger of merging identities, as it ends with a cacophonous and frenzied pitch (so different from the final cleansing tone of the community), "Beloved / You are my sister / You are my daughter / You are my face; you are me" (216). This attitude shows both Sethe's narcissism and her vulnerability; after all, the devouring demon child returned from the dead also tries to possess Sethe.

Morrison's canon favors women who find emotional equilibrium, and even before Sethe reaches this point, there are two positive female role models: Baby Suggs and Sethe's last child, Denver. Baby Suggs, Sethe's mother-in-law, as a wise woman preacher, provides the community with food for the soul, until the terrible day upon which Beloved is killed. She understands the value of self-love and communal nurturance, and her legacy is passed down to Denver. The granddaughter Denver knows about the dangerous boundaries formed by overidentification as well as the limitations of sisterhood. When Beloved threatens to destroy both her mother and herself, Denver reaches out to the community and works outside "124" to find self-sustenance and to provide for her family. Fully integrated in the neighborhood, Denver begins to bring the healing process home to her mother. The key to happiness for the Morrison protagonist, regardless of one's gender, is a spiritual celebration of oneself, which then makes possible acts of kindness and love to one's family and one's larger community. The beloved is finally oneself.

Students might want to discuss what makes the quintessential Morrison female protagonist so strong. Self-sustaining women with great fortitude, wisdom, and self-respect are revered in the Morrison canon, and she draws much of her inspiration from strong women she has known in her own life. Celebrating generations of strong, capable women in her family, Morrison proclaims, "they believed in their dignity. They believed they were people of value, and they had to pass that on" (Moyers 59). Even though the novel's ending ironically belies the fact, *Beloved,* too, is a story to pass on—as a triumph of the human spirit, students should try to answer the riddle of why the story is so important to pass on, what that means in terms of the American awareness of the past, or in terms of a characteristic historical amnesia among Americans.

Works Cited

Morrison, Toni. *Beloved.* New York: Plume, 1987.

———. Interview. "Toni Morrison, Novelist." With Bill Moyers. *Bill Moyers: A World of Ideas, II, Public Opinions from Private Citizens.* Ed. Andie Tucher. New York: Doubleday, 1990, 54-63.

FURTHER READING

Criticism

Aguiar, Sarah Appleton. "'Passing On' Death: Stealing Life in Toni Morrison's *Paradise.*" *African American Review* 38, no. 3 (fall 2004): 513-19.

> Discusses the cycle of life theme found in Morrison's trilogy—*Beloved, Jazz,* and *Paradise*— arguing that the final novel centers dramatically on

the journeys into death experienced by its female characters and "demonstrates unequivocally that death is a necessary condition of and for life."

Eckstein, Lars. "A Love Supreme: Jazzthetic Strategies in Toni Morrison's *Beloved*." *African American Review* 40, no. 2 (summer 2006): 271-83.

Examines how the improvisational style, rhythms, and sounds of jazz music inform the narrative of *Beloved*.

Werrlein, Debra T. "Not So Fast, Dick and Jane: Reimagining Childhood and Nation in *The Bluest Eye*." *MELUS* 30, no. 4 (winter 2005): 53-72.

Explores the connection between childhood innocence and the ideology of American innocence, and claims that in *The Bluest Eye* Morrison exposed this concept of patriotic innocence as not only false, but also oppressive and degrading, especially to African American youth.

Additional coverage of Morrison's life and career is contained in the following sources published by Gale: *African American Writers*, Eds. 1, 2; *American Writers: The Classics*, Vol. 1; *American Writers Supplement*, Vol. 3; *Authors and Artists for Young Adults*, Vols. 1, 22, 61; *Beacham's Encyclopedia of Popular Fiction: Biography & Resources*, Vol. 2; *Black Literature Criticism*, Ed. 1:3; *Black Writers*, Eds. 2, 3; *Children's Literature Review*, Vol. 99; *Concise Dictionary of American Literary Biography*, 1968-1988; *Concise Major 21st-Century Writers*, Ed. 1; *Contemporary Authors*, Vol. 29-32R; *Contemporary Authors New Revision Series*, Vols. 27, 42, 67, 113, 124; *Contemporary Literary Criticism*, Vols. 4, 10, 22, 55, 81, 87, 173, 194; *Contemporary Novelists*, Eds. 3, 4, 5, 6, 7; *Contemporary Popular Writers*; *Dictionary of Literary Biography*, Vols. 6, 33, 143, 331; *Dictionary of Literary Biography Yearbook*, 1981; *DISCovering Authors*; *DISCovering Authors 3.0*; *DISCovering Authors: British*; *DISCovering Authors: Canadian Edition*; *DISCovering Authors Modules: Most-Studied Authors, Multicultural Authors, Novelists, and Popular and Genre Writers*; *Encyclopedia of World Literature in the 20th Century*; *Exploring Novels*; *Feminism in Literature: A Gale Critical Companion*, Ed. 1:6; *Feminist Writers*; *Gothic Literature: A Gale Critical Companion*, Ed. 3; *Literary Movements for Students*, Vol. 2; *Literature and Its Times*, Vols. 2, 4; *Literature and Its Times Supplement*, Ed. 1:2; *Literature Resource Center*; *Major 20th-Century Writers*, Eds. 1, 2; *Major 21st-Century Writers* (eBook), 2005; *Modern American Literature*, Ed. 5; *Modern American Women Writers*; *Novels for Students*, Vols. 1, 6, 8, 14; *Reference Guide to American Literature*, Ed. 4; *Short Stories for Students*, Vol. 5; *Something about the Author*, Vols. 57, 144; *St. James Guide to Young Adult Writers*; *Twayne Companion to Contemporary Literature in English*, Ed. 1:2; *Twayne's United States Authors*; *20th Century Romance and Historical Writers*; and *World Literature Criticism*, Vol. 4.

Albert Murray
1916-

© *Christopher Felver/Corbis*

American critic, essayist, novelist, and poet.

INTRODUCTION

Murray is considered one of the foremost cultural critics of the mid- to late-twentieth and early twenty-first centuries. Focusing largely on the influence of African American musical forms on the American culture and psyche—of both blacks and whites—Murray identified what he termed a "blues idiom," suggesting that it is this quality that lends the United States its unique character.

BIOGRAPHICAL INFORMATION

Murray was born in Nokomis, Alabama, in 1916. His mother was young and unmarried, so Murray was raised by a couple in Mobile. In grade school his teachers rec-

ognized his intelligence and academic capacity, and he was sent to the Mobile County Training School, where he was deeply influenced by his teachers. Murray earned his bachelor's degree from the prestigious Tuskegee Institute (now Tuskegee University) in 1939. He briefly pursued graduate studies at the University of Michigan and Northwestern University before returning to teach at Tuskegee. Murray joined the U.S. Army Air Corps in 1943 and served until 1946 when he transferred to the U.S. Air Force reserves. In 1948, he earned his master's degree from New York University, then returned once again to teach at Tuskegee. Following some postgraduate study at the Sorbonne in Paris in 1950, Murray was recalled to active duty in 1951. He rose to the rank of major before retiring from the military in 1962. At that time he moved with his family to Harlem to begin his writing career. His first book, a collection of essays entitled *The Omni-Americans,* was published in 1970. Murray's other writings of the 1970s included *Train Whistle Guitar* (1974), the first novel of what would eventually become a four-part fictional autobiography. Although he considered himself first and foremost a fiction writer, Murray's abiding interest in music shaped his work and led to his reputation as a premier cultural observer. In the 1980s his focus on jazz and blues as uniquely American art forms propelled him to venture beyond fiction writing into the world of music. He collaborated with the legendary jazz bandleader Count Basie on an autobiography, *Good Morning Blues,* published in 1985. Murray also established, with jazz musician Wynton Marsalis, the concert series Jazz at Lincoln Center, and serves on its board of directors; this major musical institution presents jazz as an art form comparable to classical symphonic music and opera. In the 1990s Murray resumed writing, finishing two more novels in his four-part series—*The Spyglass Tree* (1991), *The Seven League Boots* (1996)—and publishing a volume of poetry, a book of essays, and a collection of letters he had exchanged with his former Tuskegee schoolmate Ralph Ellison. Murray continued to write and received numerous honorary doctoral degrees and symposia on his life and work. In 1996 he was presented with a Lifetime Achievement Award from the National Book Critics' Circle. Murray completed his four-part series with the publication of *The Magic Keys* in 2005.

MAJOR WORKS

In Murray's seminal work, the essay collection *The Omni-Americans,* he put forth an idea that would shape much of his further thinking, as well as his reputation among black intellectuals: the American racial categories "black" and "white" are artificially constructed notions that ultimately damage both groups. Equally opposed to both the black nationalists of the time who advocated separatism and the white social and economic theorists who purported that black Americans were victims of white exploitation and of their own pathological tendencies, Murray argued that full racial integration was the only way to heal the damage done by institutional racism. He wrote in *The Omni-Americans,* "The so-called black and so-called white people of the United States resemble nobody else in the world so much as they resemble each other." In his next book, the travel narrative *South to a Very Old Place* (1972), Murray examined black culture in the South through the lens of a trip he took to southern cities that had made a strong impression on him, including Mobile, Tuskegee, and Memphis. Murray's first novel, *Train Whistle Guitar*—along with its sequels, *The Spyglass Tree, The Seven League Boots,* and *The Magic Keys* —follows the story of an intelligent young black boy named Scooter as he grows up in Mobile, Alabama, in the 1920s. In the second and third volumes, Scooter moves to Tuskegee and joins a swing-era jazz band. The fourth installment, *The Magic Keys,* finds Scooter newly married and a graduate student at New York University. While living in Manhattan, he is profoundly influenced by the people around him, particularly writers and musicians. Scooter's story concludes, in classic *bildungsroman* fashion, with his return to Alabama and a life of great promise.

In two books of music theory, *The Hero and the Blues* (1973) and *Stomping the Blues* (1976), Murray outlines a blues and jazz aesthetic that centers on the figure of a hero who, according to Murray, is not simply a musician but the embodiment of black American experience and values. He also maintains that improvisation—the essential element of jazz music—is a major factor in a communal tradition that was critical to the spirit of confrontation that spawned the movement to improve living conditions for blacks in the United States. Murray expanded his blues hypothesis in the volume *The Blue Devils of Nada* (1996), in which he argues that blues is the quintessential musical idiom that has animated the spirit of American life itself, offering inspiration not only to black Americans beset by racism, but to anyone troubled by the existential conundrums of modern life. In 2001 Murray published a volume of poetry, *Conjugations and Reiterations,* in which he uses elements of jazz, blues, and gospel music, as well as folk mythology, in lyrical poems that explore aspects of the American experience ranging from improvisational art to the wisdom of the gospels. *From the Briarpatch File* (2001) is a collection of essays, reviews, and interviews in which Murray reveals details of his personal journey as a writer, his admiration for the achievements of such legendary artists as Duke Ellington and William Faulkner, and further elucidates his thoughts on the role of the blues in American life.

CRITICAL RECEPTION

Murray is universally admired in literary circles for the erudition, provocativeness, and lyricism of his writings. Considered one of the foremost American men of letters of the twentieth century, he has influenced several generations of black thinkers, encouraging African Americans to embrace the vibrancy of their culture rather than what Murray called in *The Omni-Americans* the "social science fiction" of damage and victimization that sociologists often attribute to black American life. Critics have noted Murray's refusal to adhere to any one ideology in explaining the African American experience as a major factor in the success of his works with both academic and popular readers. Additionally, he is considered a significant influence in the jazz and blues music industries both because of his philosophical writings on those subjects and because of his practical involvement in bringing performances to the public with the acclaimed Jazz at Lincoln Center series.

PRINCIPAL WORKS

The Omni-Americans (essays) 1970
South to a Very Old Place (travelogue) 1972
The Hero and the Blues (criticism) 1973
Train Whistle Guitar (novel) 1974
Stomping the Blues (criticism) 1976
Good Morning Blues: The Autobiography of Count Basie, as Told to Albert Murray (biography) 1985
Reflections on Logic, Politics, and Reality: A Challenge to the Sacred Consensus of Contemporary American Thinking (nonfiction) 1989
The Spyglass Tree (novel) 1991
The Blue Devils of Nada (nonfiction) 1996
The Seven League Boots (novel) 1996
Trading Twelves: Selected Letters of Ralph Ellison and Albert Murray [editor, with John F. Callahan] (letters) 2000
Conjugations and Reiterations: Poems (poetry) 2001
From the Briarpatch File (essays) 2001
The Magic Keys (novel) 2005

CRITICISM

Sanford Pinsker (essay date autumn 1996)

SOURCE: Pinsker, Sanford. "Albert Murray: The Black Intellectuals' Maverick Patriarch." *Virginia Quarterly Review* 72, no. 4 (autumn 1996): 678-84.

[*In the following essay, Pinsker discusses Murray's role as a black American intellectual, emphasizing his independence of mind.*]

If the public intellectual is best defined as a specialist in being a non-specialist, maverick intellectuals add a certain amount of unpredictability to the formula, for they tend to regard group-think of any sort with suspicion. And nowhere is the inclination stronger than when public intellectuals operate in ways that remind maverick types of Harold Rosenberg's famous description of the New York intellectuals as a "herd of independent minds." Saul Bellow, for example, makes it his habit to distrust nearly anything that too many "deep thinkers" agree about—partly because he thinks of himself as a writer rather than as a socio-political type, and partly because genuinely independent types are not likely to feel comfortable hammering out a consensus.

Albert Murray, the black critic-writer, is a kindred spirit, not only because, at 77, he brings nearly as much accumulated experience to cultural matters as does the octogenarian Bellow but also because he has made it his business to swim against the tides of fashion. The difference, of course, is that Bellow, for all the battles fought and lumps taken, never suffered from the cruelest sting of all: anonymity. From *The Dangling Man* (1944) onward, his novels were widely reviewed and often lavishly praised. New, ever more prestigious awards seemed to follow effortlessly on the heels of earlier ones; and for at least two generations of reader-critics, Bellow's cultural pronouncements have had the heft of holy writ. By contrast, the arc of Murray's career has a very different trajectory. His first collection, *The Omni-Americans* (1970), argued that the language of social science inadequately—and insufficiently— captures the richness of the black American experience. Indeed, by concentrating on versions of black pathology and the fits of shame, self-hatred, and rage that these engender, opinion-makers such as Daniel Patrick Moynihan and Kenneth Clark sell black culture short. For the truth is that this vibrant, multi-faceted culture is no less complex than that of any other group (to write it off as disorganized and emasculated by centuries of white oppression is dangerously reductive), but also that it has produced, in Murray's words, "the most complicated culture and therefore the most complicated sensibility in the modern world."

The Omni-Americans threw off such maverick insights easily, and by the fistful. The rub, of course, is that they were very much against the grain of that time, that place. Murray, for example, still clung to the word "Negro" at a cultural moment when Black was the operative word—not only as a adjective defining a new sense of "power," but also of aesthetics. Worse, in an age of the afro, he could even manage to call up a few kind words on behalf of hair straighteners. What he meant to celebrate was a vision of America as "incontestably mulatto" and to argue for a halt to the facile ways in which white norms were contrasted with black deviations: ". . . the so-called black and so-called white people of the United States resemble nobody else in the world so much as they resemble each other."

Granted, black communities have their own styles, and these are best represented in the jazz and blues traditions. Where others rode through black ghettos and saw only the despair of poverty and the thumbprints of pathology, Murray argues for the effortless aristocracy of a Duke Ellington or Count Basie, and for the sheer resilience of black life per se: "its elastic individuality . . . its esthetic receptivity, and its unique blend of warmth, sensitivity, nonsense, vitality and elegance." None of these things, he rightly points out, suggests emasculation, much less adds up to the smoldering rage that found its most articulate spokesman in James Baldwin.

In fact, Murray was as complicated a social critic as American blacks were as a people. He could luxuriate in the best examples of black culture without for a moment embracing the angry case being made for separatism, just as he could look evidences of racism squarely in the eye without losing faith in the promises made to all Americans in the documents of our Founding Fathers:

> The Declaration of Independence and the Constitution are the social, economic, and political heritage of all Americans. . . . So far as white people are concerned, the most revolutionary, radical and devastating action any U.S. Negro can engage in is to compete with other Americans for status, employment, total social equality, and basic political power.

Not surprisingly, many reviewers, black as well as white, were in no mood to take Murray's vision seriously. Did he really believe, Saunders Redding asked, that the WASP ethic works as well for blacks as it is generally believed to work for whites? What seemed like a rhetorical question 26 years ago now has more than a measure of legitimacy because blacks in significant numbers have, in fact, joined the middle class. One could argue, of course, that this is the result of the Civil Rights Movement and that would be true in part; but the greater part, I would submit, has to do with the positive, upbeat qualities of black life that Murray isolated in *The Omni-Americans.*

I am not much attracted to the word "denial," largely because it is psychobabble and usually because when it is trotted out stiff counter-arguments are called for; but *denial* is probably the best (probably the *only*) way to account for Murray's virtual anonymity as a mainstream black intellectual. That the black community *knew* him and in varying degrees, took him seriously is true enough, but it is even truer that the abiding influence of Murray's vision had to wait until 1980, when Stanley Crouch, his feisty, free-wheeling protégé, wrote a piece entitled "Chittlins at the Waldorf: The Work of Albert Murray." As Crouch's star shot into the stratosphere (*Notes of a Hanging Judge* [1990], a collection of cultural essays that includes the piece on Murray and that won the National Book Award, was followed by a second collection (*The All-American Skin Game* [1995]) and what can only be called media celebrity), Murray suddenly became a figure to reckon with. Henry Louis Gates, Jr. profiled him in the pages of *The New Yorker* ("King of Cats" [April 8, 1996]), and in short order the intellectual community was divided between those busily "rediscovering" his work and those, like myself, who found themselves scrambling to read whole swathes of Murray for the first time.

No doubt Murray must find much of this ironic, for if he labored many years under Ralph Ellison's very long shadow (they were classmates at Tuskegee, close friends as the arc of their respective careers took very different turns, and finally, prideful antagonists when the line between master and disciple, influencer and influenced, gradually blurred), he now finds himself mentioned in the same breath with Stanley Crouch, a man both more famous and many years his junior.

When the voluminous Ellison-Murray correspondence is eventually published, we will move beyond gossip to something closer to the truth about their complicated relationship; and no doubt their respective biographies, surely warranted, will shed their shares of light. Meanwhile, what we have is the portrait of a man of letters, for Murray is equally comfortable as a novelist, music critic, and cultural analyst. Indeed, the apparently disparate interests converge into a single vision of black life as richer, more complicated, and finally of such singular importance to the very rhythms of the republic. Each is an extension, rather than a diminishment, of the possibilities of the other, with the result that Murray's work often seems to pluck at a single string.

But what a string, and what notes it nonetheless manages to make! For Murray simply never bought into the narrow view of racism-and-rage that has been the dominant mode of most black literature since Richard Wright's *Native Son* (1940). If there are a few good voices rattling around in his head, they belong to Thomas Jefferson and Abraham Lincoln, Ernest Hemingway and James Joyce—and of course a whole retinue of jazz men like Jelly Roll Morton, King Oliver, Charlie Parker, Dizzie Gillespie, Miles Davis, and Thelonius Monk. Taken together, what they articulate is jazz, an idiom at once authentically black and deeply American. What Murray knew to his very bones some 30 years ago— and that he has been embroidering ever since—is that black writers and critics "have mostly been preoccupied with the literal document as agitprop journalism, so much so that for all the realistic details to make the reader feel that all this really happens, their stories seldom rise above the level of one-dimensional patently partisan social case histories." Murray made these remarks during a 1977 interview, but the words ring as true now as they did then.

Indeed, the very fact that he chooses to preface his latest collection, *The Blue Devils of Nada,* with talk about the limitations of realism and the more expansive possi-

bilities of the lyrical mode suggest something about what it means for a black maverick intellectual to stay the course. Then, as now, the race for attention has often gone to the loudest voice insisting on this-or-that stance as a litmus test for authentic blackness. Generally, the stances of choice have been political (a clenched fist, an Afro, a dashiki), but at bottom what they come to are futile exercises in romanticism—at best, distractions from the main business of consensus-building; at worst, dangerous efforts to destabilize the republic. The black aesthetic movement was, of course, Black Power's cultural wing, and while its early practitioners fairly dripped with sound-and-fury, they have produced no Faulkners. Indeed, what must have galled those who turned their collective backs on the white devil's bookshelf is that Ellison's *Invisible Man* (1952) remains one of our century's most accomplished novels, made possible precisely because its author cobbled what he learned from Eliot and Joyce, Conrad and Mann, to what he knew from the streets and the jazz rhythms doing riffs inside his soul.

And it is here that the paths of Murray and Ellison meet, for Murray's essays are at once a defense of an Ellison increasingly under attack (by refusing to hew the party line, Ellison's novel earned an unparalleled enmity among black critics who refused to recognize the greatness under their very eyes) and a justification of his own fiction, jazz criticism, and cultural commentary. But where Ellison's essays cultivated an elegance of expression, or put another way, the cool disinterestedness of an intellectual in his booklined study, Murray's prose often had the earmarks of a scrapper. He said it as it was, long before Howard Cosell turned the phrase into a grammatically inept trademark, and long before Stanley Crouch learned to trade vivid one-liners on "The Charlie Rose Show." Here, for example, is how Murray responded to an interviewer asking him if he thought "many critics today are receptive to, or aware of, the changes going on in black fiction":

> Critics? Man, most critics feel that unless brownskin U.S. writers are pissing and moaning about injustice they have nothing to say. In any case, it seems that they find it much easier to praise such writers for being angry (which requires no talent, not to mention genius) than for being innovative or insightful.

One of the critics Murray surely had in mind was Irving Howe, a man who believed that the conditions of black life could not help but produce social realism of a certain stripe. Ellison's strongly worded demurral (contained in his essay, "The World and the Jug") is well known, dozens of Murray's essays, essentially elaborating on the same point, are less so; but what they share is a belief that narrowed expectations lead inevitably to diminished results, and that the path to genuine liberation is likely to be as complicated as it is fiercely individual. Murray, who was much attracted to sagas of herohood (see *The Hero and the Blues,* 1973), felt that most biographies of black folk left out everything that makes black life rich, and a transcendent black art possible: "style in general and stylish clothes in particular, all of the manifest love of good cooking and festive music and dancing and communal good times (both secular and sacred), all of the notorious linguistic exuberance, humor, and outrageous nonsense, not to mention all of the preoccupation with love and lovemaking (that blues lyrics are so full of)"—these, captured in the very riffs and glides of Murray's own *style,* are the stuff that, taken together, make up the black lifestyle and that its best artists capture in their music, and sometimes in their prose.

By contrast, most writing about blacks seems a pale carbon copy of the genuine article, one driven by special agendas that wring the life out of the very thing it attempts to capture. Hence,

> . . . most biographies and autobiographies of so-called U.S. black folks tend to read like case histories or monographs written to illustrate some very special (and often very narrow) political theory, or ideology of blackness, or to promote some special political program. Such writing serves a very useful purpose, to be sure. But the approach does tend to oversimplify character, situation, and motive in the interest of social and political issues as such, and in the process human beings at best become sociopolitical abstractions. At worst they are reduced to clichés.

We have learned to settle for one-dimensional portraits of black life—and, to our collective shame, even learned how to praise them. In this sense, a maverick type like Murray is an important player in the ongoing dialogue about what is worthy of serious regard and what is decidedly slimmer goods. It is, after all, still possible for certain black intellectuals to make a splash with books that talk about hip-hop in the language of semiotics and deconstruction. What Murray provides is an alternative, one confident that Ellington and Basie's music will last—and matter—long after Snoop Doggy Dogg has long been forgotten, and that the thickly textured passages of memoir contained in Murray's **South to a Very Old Place** (1971) will continue to captivate so long as there are people who care about the suppleness of well-wrought paragraphs.

America has been blessed with maverick intellectuals at least since the days of Emerson and Thoreau. They tend to be larger in impact than they are in raw numbers. For a very long time, the number of black intellectuals could be counted on the fingers of a single hand, with W.E. B Dubois so dwarfing the competition that many were not even aware that there *was* competition. But even as we note with pride that a critical mass of black public intellectuals now exists, the number of maverick black intellectuals, those with a genuine independence of mind and equal measures of spunk remains quite small. To them, Albert Murray stands as a patriarch, with all the adoration and resistance that the term properly inspires.

More important, though, for Americans of all colors, his work speaks to the best we are and the even richer possibilities of what we might become.

Paul Devlin (essay date spring 2007)

SOURCE: Devlin, Paul. "Albert Murray at Ninety." *Antioch Review* 65, no. 2 (spring 2007): 256-65.

[*In the following essay, Devlin provides a retrospective of Murray's life and works.*]

> There is only the ultimate actuality of entropy . . . *of the void,* upon which we impose such metaphorical devices as AND, as in (andoneandtwoandthreeandfourand) and one, and two, and three, and four and so forth and so on from which we also get "*and it came to pass and so on it went time after time after time.*" as has been recorded here, there, and elsewhere.
>
> —Albert Murray, *The Magic Keys,* 2005

Albert Murray turned ninety in May 2006 (the month that also marked his sixty-fifth year of marriage to his wife, Mozelle). He has had one of the most impressive and influential literary careers of the last fifty years, yet he has failed to find fame with the public at large, though almost all of his thirteen books are still in print, with major trade presses. It has been said that his work is difficult. Perhaps this is because he is among the most original literary stylists in English during the past fifty years, a claim supported by even casual perusal of his quartet novels or travelogue-memoir **South to a Very Old Place,** which are narrated in a highly unusual, distinctively Southern voice that orchestrates idiomatic down-home African-American speech through the high modernist masters who formed the core of Murray's literary influences. It's not for nothing that he is a member of the American Academy of Arts and Letters, and recipient of a lifetime achievement award from the National Book Critics Circle.

An "African-American" from Mobile, Alabama, Murray prefers the word *Negro,* which was the respectful term when he was growing up. Murray has emphasized the "incontestably mulatto" nature of American culture, following Constance Rourke's claim that the American character is part Yankee, Negro, Backwoodsman, and Indian. How can the man who wrote **The Omni-Americans** be African-American?

At the Mobile County Training School, Murray was a good baseball player and star student, winning scholarships to Tuskegee Institute (B.S., 1939). He went on to study at Northwestern, the University of Michigan, New York University (M.A., 1948), the Sorbonne, and Air University. Though he taught English and directed the theater at Tuskegee, he also had another career as Major Murray, United States Air Force, from which he retired in 1962. He did not publish his first book, **The**

Omni-Americans, a collection of essays and articles he wrote in the mid to late 1960s, until 1970, at age fifty-four; for this reason, his turning ninety may seem to have come out of the blue and it is all the more cause for celebration. He was not, like his contemporaries Saul Bellow, Arthur Miller, or Arthur Schlesinger, Jr., on the scene from the late 1940s onward. It should also be noted that Murray's story is proof positive that it is possible, with the luck of good health, to start over, lead two lives, have two successful careers, and that a retirement need not be dull.

The Omni-Americans was first subtitled "Black Experience and American Culture." The subtitle of a later edition of this attack on social scientific approaches to race and culture in America much better explains Murray's views: "Alternatives to the Folklore of White Supremacy and the Fakelore of Black Pathology." *The Omni-Americans* received wide and immediate attention when it was published (making the cover of *The Washington Post Book World*). In a review the novelist Walker Percy called it "a book about race and the United States that fits no ideology, resists all abstractions, offends orthodox liberals and conservatives, attacks social scientists and Governor Wallace in the same breath, sees all the faults of the country, and holds out hope in the end." In *The Omni-Americans,* Murray rejects African cultural patrimony for African-Americans; riffing on Thomas Mann's pragmatic approach to the measurement of time in the prelude, "Joseph and His Brothers," Murray dates African-American dimension of American culture primarily to the middle passage. He writes that "there is truly no urgent reason to trace the origin of U.S. Negro style and manner any farther back in time than . . . 1619—if indeed that far." As a character in Murray's novel *The Seven League Boots* remarks, "Africa? Hey that's alright with me about the great-grandaddy of my drums and the grandmammy of the mellow brown in my complexion. . . . This music ain't got nothing to do with sending no messages to some chief across the river somewhere over yonder. This music we play is about going somewhere and getting on sometime in the United States of America."

What followed was an impressive and ambitious parade of books, which includes, aside from his novels and memoir, a group of what he called "literary notes," worth about a warehouse full of dissertations, which re-think farce, the blues, and the hero-image (*The Hero and the Blues,* 1973), a poetics and anthropology of jazz (*Stomping the Blues,* 1976), an as-told-to biography of Count Basie (*Good Morning Blues,* 1986), two essay collections (*The Blue Devils of Nada,* 1996 and *From the Briarpatch File,* 2001), a uniquely Murrayan book of poetry (*Conjugations and Reiterations,* 2001), not to mention a lively and learned letter exchange with Ralph Ellison (*Trading Twelves,* 2000).

"Endless negation," wrote Ralph Waldo Emerson, "is a flat affair." "Who," he asked in a lecture condemning slavery, "can long continue to feel an interest in condemning homicide, or counterfeiting, or wife beating?" For anyone who feels they will sleep longer than Rip Van Winkle next time they hear the word *critique,* Murray offers a sort of cosmic stoicism delivered with barbershop humor while wearing a tuxedo, standing in front of a big band. For Murray, who grew up in Mobile knowing ex-slaves and even some who had been personally brought over from Africa on the last slave ship to arrive in the U.S. (the *Clotilde*), affirmation certainly does not include acceptance of injustice but rather an orientation toward dealing with it. In *The Hero and the Blues,* Murray advocates regarding obstacles in terms of "adventure and romance" rather than in terms of social science or what we would today call critical theory (the Marx-Freud derived). It makes a better story. A better work of art. The other stuff cannot swing. To affirm life is to aim for elegance in spite of entropy. As he wrote in *The Blue Devils of Nada,* "the affirmative disposition toward the harsh actualities of human existence . . . is characteristic of the fully orchestrated blues statement." For Murray the world is a briarpatch and the hero like the rabbit, whether Brer Rabbit or Duke Ellington's "Cottontail," who must maintain a dapper fur coat. The man who wrote *Stomping the Blues,* winner of the ASCAP award for music criticism in 1977, meant "stomping" euphemistically: to "stomp" the blues is to elegantly dance them away, not to smash them into the ground. (Murray illustrated this on CSPAN in 2002. The blues thrive on the clenched fist but cannot withstand a snap on the afterbeat.) In the words of Duke Ellington, who called Murray "the unsquarest person I know," "it don't mean a thing if it ain't got that swing"—a phrase that has long been Murray's mantra. In Murray's words, expressed in a 1996 interview with *The New York Observer,* "the question . . . is whether life is worth living. Are you going to wake up one morning and cut your throat or go stomping at the Savoy? You know what I'm goin' do!"

Murray was born in Nokomis, Alabama, in 1916 and raised by adoptive parents in Magazine Point on the outskirts of Mobile; even the small town of his inauspicious, illegitimate birth recalls greatness in American literature. Remember Longfellow: "by the shining big sea water / stood the wigwam of Nokomis." In the cosmopolitan seaport of Mobile and segregation of central Alabama at Tuskegee Institute, Murray's mind formed in those years of the Depression a unique outlook on American history and culture, which may serve as a guide for all the world, regardless of time and place. Murray's life has taken him throughout the deep South, to Paris, Morocco, Los Angeles, and finally to the "beanstalk castle town" of New York, where he has left his mark on some of the city's most august cultural institutions.

As a novelist, Murray's achievement is less recognized than it should be, but not less than any novelist of the last fifty years. In a quartet of semi-autobiographical novels, *Train Whistle Guitar* (1974), *The Spyglass Tree* (1991), *The Seven League Boots* (1996), and *The Magic Keys* (2005), Murray chronicles the adventures of Scooter, a promising young man from Gasoline Point, Alabama. The cheerful narrator, who is always playing with time and memory, could have dedicated these books to Stendhal's "happy few." Representation of victimization or the effects of racism and oppression on the young hero are nowhere to be found, though they do appear as aspects of the larger world, most especially in *The Spyglass Tree.* Scooter succeeds not by making a lot of money or advancing a political program or telling the white man that he feels something is amiss, but by becoming comfortable with his own consciousness. They are like novels that are "after the novel" as a historicized genre, yet "before" it as well, with roots in the epic and fairy tale (note the special objects as titles) and possibly in some prose works of the classical world, the gospels in particular. There are more than a few analogies between the four novels and the four gospels, which may explain why they do not read at all like typical novels. (Like Guillermo Cabrera-Infante, Murray is particularly interested in plot.) For instance, tones and emphases change slightly from book to book. Characters come and go and repeat with slight difference, as if four different narrators each purported to narrate a different section of Scooter's story. Ultimately, these novels (in which no character's speech is in quotation marks) form something like a novelized fairy tale, a picaresque adventure that owes little in style or structure to the great nineteenth-century novels or even much to the important modernist works that influenced Murray so strongly (though the influence of Joyce, Mann, Proust, and Malraux are there just under the surface, alongside the countless Uncle, or "Unka," Remuses of Murray's boyhood). These novels are highly original not just for their lilting lyrical choreography, but in the sense that they are structured along the lines of jazz compositions. As Murray has remarked in interviews, he learned from Thomas Mann's literary use of some of the elements of European art music, such as leitmotifs, that he could use elements of American art music (jazz), such as vamps, breaks, riffs, and tags, to structure a novel.

In *Train Whistle Guitar,* Scooter has a wide array of adventures around the outskirts of Mobile, learning valuable lessons from a host of charismatic characters, including an outspoken World War I veteran, a star piano player whom Scooter watches defy the orders of a white sheriff, and his greatest hero, a freight-train-hopping guitar player who catches him attempting to run away and stops him, encouraging him to go to school. Scooter's take on sports, American history, personalities around town, and various childhood topics rings completely true. In *The Spyglass Tree,* Scooter goes off to school at a college similar to Tuskegee. The title is a metaphor for college and thus for education itself: a high vantage point from which to regard one's

own experience. Scooter is not really shown learning in the classroom, but rather around it—from his mysterious polymath roommate; from a local blues singer, Hortense Hightower; in the library; and from successful African American businessmen in town—as the book flashes back and forth from his earlier days to his current situation. Scooter's willingness to perform an act of selfless heroism in a racial conflict leads to Hortense Hightower's arranging for him to obtain a bass fiddle. By the next book, *The Seven League Boots,* which the *Los Angeles Times* called a "rich and moving song of the human spirit," Scooter is playing in the band of the Bossman, a Duke Ellingtonesque band leader. He spends time in New York and Los Angeles with the band, dates a movie star, visits Europe, and does all sorts of hip things in a sleek version of the late 1930s. The style of *The Seven League Boots* evokes its posh settings as perfectly as *Train Whistle Guitar*'s style evokes the gritty and folksy outskirts of Mobile circa 1920. In *The Magic Keys,* Scooter has (temporarily?) abandoned music, having settled down with his college sweetheart, and is going to graduate school and getting reacquainted with an old college pal, Taft Edison (Ralph Ellison). Most importantly, as the quarter draws to a close, Scooter is gearing up to write the biography ("The Dancing of an Attitude: The Foot Notes of the One and Only Royal Highness") of one of his many mentors, a tap dancer known as Royal Highness, formerly known as Kid Stomp the Royal High Stepper and Kid Royal King of the Stompers. ("Who says I ain't?")

His 1971 travelogue-memoir, *South to a Very Old Place,* was included in the Modern Library in 1995. The book starts in midtown Manhattan, where Murray notes that first one must go North to go South, and proceeds to give an unforgettable portrait of Harlem (his home since 1962). Next he heads a bit further north, to New Haven, then begins the journey "down the way" to North Carolina, Atlanta, Tuskegee, Mobile, New Orleans, and Memphis, visiting, talking, signifying, and speculating on how the South has changed or not changed in the wake of the civil rights movement. As Murray remarks to a journalist over dinner in Atlanta, "I'm not down here to run any statistics but just to see how it feels. I'm operating on my literary radar . . . my metaphor finder—how about that?" He talks to blacks and whites of large reputation and no reputation. Reports of his talks with Robert Penn Warren, C. Vann Woodward, and Walker Percy exist alongside analysis such as this, from an old man in Mobile, during an "after-supper back porch rocking-chair session in the fig-tree-fresh, damp-clay-scented twilight":

> its going to take one of these old Confederate bush-whackers from right down through in here to go up against these old southern white folks when they get mad. My daddy used to say it over and over again. So when Lyndon Johnson got in there on a humble—and boy that's the onliest way he coulda made it in there—I was watching with my fingers crossed. . . . [H]e was

one of them and if they made him mad he was subject to do some of that rowdy cracker cussing right back at them, and some of that old cowboy stuff to boot. When they commence to telling me about how mean he is, I say that's exactly what we need, some mean old crackers on our side for a change. . . . That's why I got to give old Lyndon Johnson credit. Because all he had to do was let them know he was going to hold the line on the black man and he could've stayed up there as long as he wanted to. . . . That's why I got to give him credit don't care who don't. Because I know what he coulda done and I remember what he did for a fact. He got up there in front of everybody and said we shall overcome. Boy that's enough to scare white folks worse than the Indians, boy.

Another substantial work of nonfiction is *The Blue Devils of Nada: A Contemporary American Approach to Aesthetic Statement.* This collection of essays, written mainly in the 1980s and 1990s, contains indispensable insights on Duke Ellington, Louis Armstrong, Romare Bearden, and Count Basie, but the shining masterpiece in the book is the eighty-page essay (which reads more like a rollicking, impassioned sermon), "The Storyteller as Blues Singer: Ernest Hemingway Swinging the Blues and Taking Nothing." Here Murray argues persuasively for Hemingway's inclusion in the blues tradition and makes the case that the philosophy of the blues, as he sees it, was intuited and written by Hemingway, especially in the short stories.

Not slowing down for a moment, in 2001 Murray published a highly original book of poetry, *Conjugations and Reiterations,* and another book of essays, *From the Briarpatch File: On Context, Procedure, and American Identity.* In his poetry, inspired by W. H. Auden, T. S. Eliot, Marianne Moore, and Wallace Stevens no more or less than the blues, Murray presents an unexpected patchwork quilt of styles and topics, from twelve-bar blues stanzas about hopping freight trains to a long, Faulknerian rumination on Faulkner, to a celebration of Louis Armstrong and an Armstrongesque mock sermon. *From the Briarpatch File* is a miscellany that not only includes some of Murray's most abstract thoughts on the nature of art, but also important essays on Duke Ellington and Louis Armstrong and two of his most in-depth and unguarded interviews.

Without Albert Murray, the story of American culture (and the African-American influence on it in particular) of the last fifty years might be, for the worse, very different. Murray's impact on culture comes not just from his contributions to world belle-lettres but, not unlike Pound (on Pound's better days), from his generosity and behind-the-scenes curating and coaching. Who knows where some of his close friends, such as Romare Bearden, Ralph Ellison, or Wynton Marsalis, would have been without Murray's voice of humor and learning, shared downhome-modernist aesthetic, and shared experience to steady them in their endeavors? Murray's

as-told-to autobiography of Count Basie is one of the most highly regarded jazz memoirs, not just for its historical value but for Murray's authentic capture of Basie's voice and manner. The Murray-Bearden collaboration, in which Murray served as all-around literary adviser (naming paintings, suggesting themes and series, ghost-writing prose pieces, writing catalog essays), helped Bearden (who was already successful when Murray moved to New York and renewed the friendship made in Paris in 1950) shoot into the stratosphere in the 1960s and beyond. Who knows what musical direction his friend Wynton Marsalis might have taken, or if Marsalis's Jazz Lincoln Center would stand as it does today as the defender and conservatory of classic jazz? In the 1970s, Murray worked closely with Martin Williams to develop the Smithsonian Jazz programs. This heroic act of cultural preservation and reclamation eventually grew into what became in 1996 a full constituent of Lincoln Center, Jazz Lincoln Center, where Murray has been closely involved since its inception as a concert series in 1987 and continues on the board today. It should be noted, considering the traditional "blackness" of Jazz Lincoln Center, that Murray has been accused of promoting an ethnic essentialism as regards the performance of jazz music. But that notion has grown out of a lazy interpretation of Murray's claim that the formal structure of the music contains specifically American inflections and variations and it helps to have been, as many African-American musicians are (and always have been), raised in church to have a more complete grasp of the whole vocabulary, not to mention a tendency to put the proper feeling into the music. By no means, for Murray, can white musicians not measure up; but, especially years ago, there was sometimes a bit of a disconnect between the assessments of the formal appreciators (many white) and white musicians.

Because of their shared concerns and similar outlooks on American culture, and also because Murray, though only two years younger, emerged on the scene two decades later, he is often looked at as synonymous with and/or a protégé of his friend Ralph Ellison. Though together (and also with Harold Cruse) their work comprises a formidable attack on Pan-Africanism (any by extension pan-anythingism: Slavism, Germanism, or whatever), Ellison and Murray are quite different. Reading their 1950-1960 letter exchange, *Trading Twelves,* dispels notions of Ellison's having influenced Murray and reveals two mature thinkers and artists riffing and joking on all sorts of subjects. Also, for instance, in their writings on jazz, Murray is much more focused on the ritual and anthropological dimensions than Ellison. Murray had a somewhat different reading list than Ellison and was a much more serious and substantive reader of Thomas Mann, not to mention Hermann Broch. In their novels, Murray is a sunny Tolstoy to Ellison's dark Doestoevsky. Murray's "shimmering summer sunshine blueness" which meant "whistling time and rambling time. And also baseball time," a joyous feeling that permeates his novels (even when the action takes place at night), contrasts sharply with the dark humor and nightmarish surrealism of Ellison's *Invisible Man* and parts of *Juneteenth*. The critic Van Wyck Brooks once had a theory about Mark Twain: that he laughed so hard he cried. Twain's laughter is closer to Ellison's, who laughed at the American scene to keep from exploding. Swift, Voltaire, Twain, and Ellison all laughed the laugh of the satirical reformer. Murray's laughter is closer to the uproarious Rabelais, who also had a thing or two to say about farce.

Today the ideas Murray espoused (along with Ralph Ellison, to be fair) about the "mulatto" nature of American culture have become commonplace. Prominent African American baby boom writers and/or professors such as Henry Louis Gates, Cornel West, the late August Wilson, Charles Johnson, James Alan McPherson, Robert O'Meally, and Stanley Crouch, who were all around in the maelstrom of the 1960s, listened to the steady voices of writers from their parents' generation and they all basically ended up subscribing (more or less) to the Murray-Ellison vision of American culture. This is the vision that won out (partially, perhaps, through Murray's personal accessibility and friendly guidance) and why you see some of these gentlemen on PBS and widely dispersed throughout contemporary culture, instead of, say, Ron Karenga, Ekwueme Michael Thelwell, Amiri Baraka, Leonard Jeffries, or their disciples. Though the Murray-Ellison line of inclusion, hybrid mixed-up tangled identity, may have looked conservative or wacky in 1970, today it looks like the appropriate vision for our globalized world—a vision, particularly in Murray's case, that nicely balances local particulars with cosmopolitan tastes. Indeed, what someone recently said of Henri Bergson may apply to Murray as regards his "incontestably mulatto" America: late in life Bergson no longer seemed especially original because stunning ideas he espoused forty years earlier "thoroughly saturated the times conceptions." Meanwhile, perspectives on race and identity aside, *Stomping the Blues,* with its emphasis on the centrality of swing and the blues in jazz, in addition to some of his other writings on music, has largely shaped the broad vision of Jazz Lincoln Center, to say nothing of other institutions. Murray's novels will find their audience, even if they must wait as long as John Donne's poetry, though I suspect it will not take quite that long. His nonfiction critical prose, *The Hero and the Blues,* and his essays, monuments of fearlessly original literary thinking about the most fundamental topics—such as *How should one regard obstacles? What does America mean? What is the relationship of art to life?*—will enthrall anyone who would try to go beyond contemporary cynicism on such topics. Art, for Murray, following Suzanne K. Langer, is the life of human feeling. In contemporary academic discourse, feeling is often derided as having led to the twentieth century's worst atrocities,

but Murray comes from a group on whom atrocities were inflicted, who had to preserve feeling, and most importantly, complex humor, alongside which high-handed political ideologies can hardly compete, which is also perhaps why Murray and Ellison won out over the pseudo-piety and dull rage of the figures mentioned above.

Murray's fierce common sense, his rigorous pragmatism, his recognition of the farcical shadow play behind all action and the iron law of entropy, yet Malrauvian commitment to art in spite of it, is a worldview for any century. The answers Murray gives are from a man who first published at fifty-four and now is ninety, a man who grew up without electricity in Mobile, Alabama, knew former slaves and freight-train-hopping blues players, went to college on scholarships, read the Western canon and more backwards and forwards, became an expert on the music he lived in terms of, served his country for twenty years, and traversed the globe, slowly formulating ideas and working out a style, until settling in Harlem to write it all down—and thank goodness he did, because his work, no less than an Armstrong solo or Bearden collage, is one of the best antidotes to the blues there is. This is useful because, as the epilogue to *Stomping the Blues* states, "Nor has anybody ever been able to get rid of the blues forever. . . . You can only drive them away and keep them at bay for the time being. Because they are always there, waiting and watching. So retirement is out of the question . . . all you have to do to keep them in their proper place, which is deep in the dozens, is to pat your feet and snap your fingers." And darned if his paragraphs aren't orchestrated for that effect!

FURTHER READING

Criticism

Borshuk, Michael. "Albert Murray Brings It on Home: Revisioning Black Modernism in *Train Whistle Guitar.*" In *Swinging the Vernacular: Jazz and African American Modernist Literature,* pp. 159-85. New York: Routledge, 2006.

Analyzes the ways in which Murray foregrounds the black vernacular in American culture through his use of older jazz styles.

Karrer, Wolfgang. "The Novel as Blues: Albert Murray's *Train Whistle Guitar* (1974)." In *The Afro-American Novel since 1960,* edited by Peter Bruck and Wolfgang Karrer, pp. 237-62. Philadelphia: John Benjamins North America, Inc., 1982.

Examines the mythical and musical aspects of *Train Whistle Guitar.*

Pinsker, Sanford. "'The Bluesteel, Rawhide, Patent-Leather Implications of Fairy Tales': A Conversation with Albert Murray." *Georgia Review* LI, no. 2 (summer 1997): 205-21.

Interview in which Murray discusses major influences on his fiction, the role of jazz music in African American literature, and his decision to choose a life in letters.

Additional information on Murray's life and works is contained in the following sources published by Gale: *Black Writers*, Ed. 2; *Concise Major 21st-Century Writers*, Ed. 1; *Contemporary Authors*, Vols. 49-52; *Contemporary Authors New Revision Series*, Vols. 26, 52, 78; *Contemporary Literary Criticism*, Vols. 73; *Contemporary Novelists*, Ed. 7; *Contemporary Southern Writers*; *Dictionary of Literary Biography*, Vol. 38; *Literature Resource Center*; **and** *Major 21st-Century Writers* (eBook), Ed. 2005.

Walter Dean Myers
1937-

© *Jerry Bauer*

(Born Walter Milton Myers; has also published as Walter M. Myers.) American novelist, poet, and author of works for children and young adults.

For additional information on Myers's career, see *Black Literature Criticism,* Ed. 1.

INTRODUCTION

Myers is included among premier American authors of fiction for young adults and his books have won dozens of awards, including several Coretta Scott King awards and two Newbery Honor Book citations. Using realism and urban vernacular to reach underrepresented adolescent readers, Myers not only recreates many of the difficult scenarios confronting modern youth—including teen pregnancy, gangs, drug use, sexual relationships, crime, and school violence—but also examines at length the ties of family and friendship in black communities. While Myers is perhaps best known for his novels that explore the lives of young Harlem blacks, he is equally adept at producing modern fairy tales, ghost stories, and adventure sagas. In addition, he has developed a reputation as a skilled author of histories for juvenile audiences, penning biographies of such notable figures as Malcolm X, Martin Luther King, Jr., and Muhammad Ali.

BIOGRAPHICAL INFORMATION

Myers was born into an impoverished family in Martinsburg, West Virginia, in 1937. When he was two years old, his mother died in childbirth. His father subsequently struggled as a single parent during the Great Depression, until Herbert and Florence Dean, friends of Myers's parents, offered to care for Walter and two of his seven siblings. The Deans, a hard-working couple with children of their own, moved the family to the Harlem district of New York City and found blue-collar jobs to support the children. Myers's foster parents treated him kindly; his new mother enjoyed hearing him read aloud, and his new father delighted in telling him scary stories, and sometimes acting them out as well. Myers's elementary school was integrated, and he grew up with Irish and Jewish friends. He faced some difficulties in childhood, however. He was plagued by a speech impediment, and other youngsters teased him about it. Speaking in front of a class was particularly difficult, until one of his teachers suggested that he recite something that he wrote himself—and which avoided the words he found difficult to pronounce. As a result, Myers began writing poetry. Recognizing his literary talent, his teachers placed him in college preparatory classes. He won several awards for his essays and poetry, but recalls feeling frustrated as his family made light of his academic achievements and encouraged him to accept that his opportunities were limited by race and economic status. Although he was accepted at Stuyvesant High School, a prestigious magnet school within the New York City public school system, he dropped out when he realized that his family could not afford to pay for college. He subsequently joined the army at the age of seventeen. Throughout his three-year enlistment, including a tour of duty in Vietnam, he read avidly and continued writing. After his discharge from the service, he worked in a variety of positions, including postal clerk, interoffice messenger, and interviewer in a factory, and began submitting poetry and short stories to various magazines. He also attended a writing class led by author Lajos Egri, who encouraged Myers to become a professional writer.

Myers's writing career advanced significantly after he entered a contest sponsored by the Council on Interracial Books for Children. His entry won, and in 1969 his first book, *Where Does the Day Go?*, was released under his birth name, Walter M. Myers. From then on he published under the name Walter Dean Myers, in honor of his adoptive parents. After attending a writer's workshop at Columbia University taught by John Oliver Killens, Myers secured a job as an acquisitions editor at Bobbs-Merrill Publishing. While working at Bobbs-Merrill, he continued to periodically publish picture books until his agent suggested that Myers's writing might be better suited for the young adult market. Myers passed along one of his short stories to an editor at Viking, who said he enjoyed "the first chapter" and requested a chance to see the rest of the manuscript. The story, fleshed out into a full-length novel, became *Fast Sam, Cool Clyde, and Stuff* (1975), which displays all of the characteristics that would later become hallmarks of Myers's prose style—wit, street language, and strong African American leads. During this period, Myers married his second wife, Constance Brendel, with whom he had a son, Christopher. Myers later collaborated with Christopher, a noted children's book illustrator, on several titles, including *Harlem* (1997), *A Time to Love* (2002), and *Autobiography of My Dead Brother* (2005), and *Tribute* (2008). In 1977 Myers left Bobbs-Merrill and became a full-time writer. In the early 1980s, he went back to school and graduated with a B.A. from Empire State College.

MAJOR WORKS

Myers's familiarity with the lives of inner-city children has provided him with keen insight into the lives of his readers. While his books confront the myriad difficulties presented to young urban African Americans, Myers is unique in his ability to portray his protagonists as fully realized persons. His emphasis on realism provides an innate draw for reluctant readers, yet at the same time his writings contain a moral subtext in which Myers attempts to offer instruction and alternative decision-making possibilities. His heroes speak with a genuineness, using curses, slang, and rough terminology, while his narratives strive to connect choice and action with personal and moral responsibility, addressing broader themes including broken families, gambling, imprisonment, gangs, homelessness, youth violence, and drug use in specific terms, without shying away from their unpleasant realities. But even while dealing with adverse situations and subject matter, Myers maintains a level of sophistication in his writing, filling his stories with humor and love. His characters have support systems of friends, extended family, and community who provide counsel and a larger sense of purpose. For example, in *Hoops* (1981), teenager Lonnie Jackson is a Harlem high school basketball star, preparing for the citywide Tournament of Champions. His coach, Cal, is a former pro-basketball player, who lost everything after getting involved in a points-shaving scandal. After Lonnie discovers that several big-time gamblers are betting on the tournament, Cal counsels Lonnie to avoid the mistakes he once made himself. In *Motown and Didi* (1984), two teenaged protagonists are able to overcome a confrontation with the neighborhood drug dealer with one another's help, ultimately finding a measure of their dreams through the power of their love for each other.

While a number of Myers's young adult novels are set in Harlem, several also reflect his military experience, generally narrated by characters who reveal the African American perspective of serving in the armed forces. Perhaps Myers's most famous and widely read novel, *Fallen Angels* (1988) tells the tale of seventeen-year-old Richie Perry, who chooses the Army over college in 1967 in order to provide financially for his mother and brother back in Harlem. Sent to fight in the closing days of the Vietnam War, Richie confronts racism, the immorality of war, and the value of friendship under the worst possible conditions. *Fallen Angels* describes Richie's tour of duty in graphic detail, highlighting the horrors of war and the effect that such violence has on young soldiers, particularly in terms of psychological trauma and drug addiction. Though Myers's young adult novels remain his most popular works to date, the author has expanded his repertoire by authoring several works of biography and history for juvenile audiences, including *A Place Called Heartbreak: A Story of Vietnam* (1992), *Malcolm X: By Any Means Necessary* (1993), *Toussaint L'Ouverture: The Fight for Haiti's Freedom* (1996), and *I've Seen the Promised Land: The Life of Dr. Martin Luther King, Jr.* (2004). As in his fiction, Myers stresses the impact of cause and effect on the lives of individuals, citing historical examples of the hardships faced as a result of one's personal convictions.

CRITICAL RECEPTION

Myers has been consistently lauded for his realistic portrayal of inner-city life in his young adult novels. Widely regarded as a talented storyteller, he is also uniquely skilled at creating plausible and multidimensional characters, many of whom defy the traditional notion that black youth suffer from low self-esteem. On the contrary, Myers's protagonists are celebrated for their fortitude; their ability to hang onto their moral integrity even in the midst of violence, danger, or the temptation of money or prestige; their willingness to reach for higher levels of personal awareness and understanding; and their determination to not be defeated by the negative influences surrounding them. Several commentators stress that Myers's talent for characterization allows his readers to identify with the individual and his situation first, while putting race and ethnicity second; thus, although Myers's stories revolve around inner-city African Americans, they appeal to readers of all races and class. Despite the nearly universal positive reception of Myers's works by teachers and critics, many parent associations have taken issue with the author's graphic use of imagery and language, debating whether such realistic depictions are appropriate for young audiences. This has led some to call for the removal of several of Myers's texts, particularly *Fallen Angels,* from school and children's libraries. Others have labeled such attempts blatant censorship. Because of these actions, in 2003, Myers was ranked eighth overall on the American Library Association's list of threatened novelists, joining such other authors as Robert Cormier, Judy Blume, Toni Morrison, and Katherine Patterson, all of whom have been noted for their broadly realistic narratives.

PRINCIPAL WORKS

Where Does the Day Go? [as Walter M. Myers; illustrated by Leo Carty] (picture book) 1969

The Dancers [illustrated by Anne Rockwell] (picture book) 1972

The Dragon Takes a Wife [illustrated by Ann Grifalconi] (picture book) 1972; revised edition, illustrated by Fiona French, 1995

Fly, Jimmy, Fly! [illustrated by Moneta Barnett] (picture book) 1974

Fast Sam, Cool Clyde, and Stuff (young adult novel) 1975

The World of Work: A Guide to Choosing a Career (young adult nonfiction) 1975

Brainstorm (young adult novel) 1977

Mojo and the Russians (young adult novel) 1977

It Ain't All for Nothin' (young adult novel) 1978

The Young Landlords (young adult novel) 1979

Hoops (young adult novel) 1981

The Legend of Tarik (young adult novel) 1981

Won't Know till I Get There (young adult novel) 1982

The Nicholas Factor (young adult novel) 1983

Tales of a Dead King (young adult novel) 1983

Motown and Didi: A Love Story (young adult novel) 1984

Mr. Monkey and the Gotcha Bird: An Original Tale [illustrated by Leslie Morrill] (juvenile fiction) 1984

The Outside Shot (young adult novel) 1984

Adventure in Granada (young adult novel) 1985

Ambush in the Amazon (young adult novel) 1986

Crystal (young adult novel) 1987

Shadow of the Red Moon (young adult novel) 1987

Sweet Illusions (young adult novel) 1987

Fallen Angels (young adult novel) 1988

Scorpions (young adult novel) 1988

The Mouse Rap (young adult novel) 1990

Now Is Your Time!: The African-American Struggle for Freedom (young adult nonfiction) 1991

A Place Called Heartbreak: A Story of Vietnam [illustrated by Frederick Porter] (young adult nonfiction) 1992

Somewhere in the Darkness (young adult novel) 1992

Young Martin's Promise (young adult nonfiction) 1992

The Great Migration: An American Story [paintings by Jacob Lawrence] (poetry) 1993

Malcolm X: By Any Means Necessary (young adult nonfiction) 1993

Remember Us Well: An Album of Pictures and Verse (young adult nonfiction) 1993

Young Martin's Promise [illustrated by Barbara Higgins Bond] (juvenile biography) 1993

The Glory Field (young adult novel) 1994

Glorious Angels: A Celebration of Children (poetry) 1995

The Story of the Three Kingdoms [illustrated by Ashley Bryan] (juvenile fiction) 1995

How Mr. Monkey Saw the Whole World [illustrated by Synthia Saint James] (picture book) 1996

One More River to Cross: An African-American Photograph Album (young adult nonfiction) 1996

Slam! (young adult novel) 1996

Toussaint L'Ouverture: The Fight for Haiti's Freedom (young adult nonfiction) 1996

Harlem [illustrated by Christopher Myers] (poetry) 1997

Amistad: A Long Road to Freedom (young adult nonfiction) 1998

Angel to Angel: A Mother's Gift of Love (poetry) 1998

At Her Majesty's Request: An African Princess in Victorian England (young adult biography) 1999

The Journal of Joshua Loper: A Black Cowboy (young adult fiction) 1999

The Journal of Scott Pendleton Collins: A World War II Soldier (young adult fiction) 1999

Monster [illustrated by Christopher Myers] (young adult novel) 1999

145th Street: Short Stories (young adult short stories) 2000

The Blues of Flats Brown [illustrated by Nina Laden] (picture book) 2000

Malcolm X: A Fire Burning Brightly [illustrated by Leonard Jenkins] (young adult biography) 2000

Bad Boy: A Memoir (young adult memoir) 2001

blues journey [illustrated by Christopher Myers] (poetry) 2001

The Greatest: Muhammad Ali (young adult biography) 2001

The Journal of Biddy Owens, the Negro Leagues (young adult fiction) 2001

Patrol: An American Soldier in Vietnam [illustrated by Ann Grifalconi] (young adult novel) 2001

Three Swords for Granada [illustrated by John Speirs] (young adult novel) 2002

A *Time to Love: Tales from the Old Testament* [illustrated by Christopher Myers] (young adult nonfiction) 2002

The Beast (young adult novel) 2003

Blues Journey [illustrated by Christopher Myers] (picture book) 2003

The Dream Bearer (young adult novel) 2003

Antarctica: Journeys to the South Pole [illustrated by Christopher Myers] (young adult nonfiction) 2004

Here in Harlem: Poems in Many Voices (poetry) 2004

I've Seen the Promised Land: The Life of Dr. Martin Luther King, Jr. [illustrated by Leonard Jenkins] (young adult biography) 2004

Shooter (young adult novel) 2004

USS Constellation: Pride of the American Navy (juvenile nonfiction) 2004

Voices from Harlem (poetry) 2004

Autobiography of My Dead Brother [illustrated by Christopher Myers] (young adult novel) 2005

The Harlem Hellfighters: When Pride Met Courage [with William Miles] (young adult nonfiction) 2006

Jazz [illustrated by Christopher Myers] (nonfiction picture book) 2006

Street Love (young adult novel) 2006

Harlem Summer (young adult novel) 2007

What They Found: Love on 145th Street (young adult short stories) 2007

Game (young adult novel) 2008

Sunrise over Fallujah (young adult novel) 2008

Tribute [illustrated by Christopher Myers] (children's poetry) 2008

CRITICISM

Beth Murray (essay date 2002)

SOURCE: Murray, Beth. "Defending *Fallen Angels* by Walter Dean Myers: Framing—Not Taming—Controversy." In *Censored Books II: Critical Viewpoints, 1985-2000,* edited by Nicholas J. Karolides, pp. 167-72. Lanham, Md.: Scarecrow Press, 2002.

[*In the following essay, Murray points out that although some readers may take offense at the raw language, racial tensions, and violent subject matter of* Fallen Angels, *the multilayered novel merits reading since it addresses not only the coming-of-age of its protagonist, but also such universal issues as war, peace, grief, comradeship, death, oppression, and patriotism.*]

The plot of *Fallen Angels,* by Walter Dean Myers, is not extraordinary in its skeletal form: a young army soldier from Harlem flies to Vietnam, encounters challenges, builds alliances, sustains injuries, loses comrades, and ultimately returns home; plane to plane. It's a war story, after all. However, Walter Dean Myers's artistic choices in creating this particular story as one soldier's vivid narrative of feelings, thoughts, and observations fleshes out the tale with immediacy and the inevitable controversy that seems to shadow immediacy. In choosing to write a Vietnam War story at all, Walter Dean Myers strode knowingly toward controversy. In choosing to tell the story through Richard Perry, a soldier on the front lines, Myers stood squarely in the complex immediacy of controversy. This is not a "war book" aiming only to clarify military strategy and events, though it does so to some extent. Readers spend a great deal of time inside the mind of Richard Perry, looking out through his eyes, listening through his ears—feeling his feelings. Perspective and depth lean upon each other.

Perry and his comrades refer to their lives and families in the states as being "back in the world." This phrase underscores the enormity of Myers's task as a writer: transporting readers to a different world, in place and time. Today's teen readers categorize a Vietnam War novel as a work of historical fiction. Richard Perry guides the historical journey. Though Perry narrates in the first person, the story relies heavily upon dialogue among multiple characters with varying and often opposing perspectives. The story plays as a movie: episodic, with flashbacks, interior monologues, and a vast cast of characters.

However, the very same narrative element that brings immediacy also brings protection. Myers is careful to cushion the read within Perry's perspective of a pensive young man taking care, questioning, quietly defending, stretching to understand, and learning to live with the emotional paradoxes of war and of life. The most controversial elements are often Perry's observations, not his own actions or words. Perry's perceptions and preconceptions emerge through these observations, on behalf of the reticent reader. In time, the war problematizes many of Perry's prejudgments. As Perry's categorization of his world grows more complex, the reader must wonder past stereotypes as well.

Teaching *Fallen Angels* (or sharing it with teens) invites exploration of censorship issues on multiple levels. In this book, there is something to challenge anyone's thinking. Of course, some readers construe challenges as opportunities to be offended. This book will "offend" almost anyone seeking a reason to be offended. First, it is a war story set largely in Vietnam. Those opposed to that particular conflict or violence in books for young people might oppose this book, despite its acclaimed accuracy. Second, it takes a close look at a multiraced platoon and personifies the "battle within the battle" faced by soldiers of color. Those opposed to plain talk about sometimes divisive racial tension in books for young people might oppose this book. Those opposed to any questioning of the military might oppose this book. Third, this book relies upon an ensemble of characters to spin its story. Most of these characters are soldiers on the front lines of a war. They speak as any range of soldiers might: some formally, some informally, some derogatorily, and some religiously. Characters utter racial slurs, sexual innuendo, homophobic comments, and "cuss" words between their playful banter and professions of solemn support. Those who oppose "offensive" language in books for young people might oppose this book. Those who oppose open prayer might oppose this book. One could choose to view such elements as controversial enough to keep the book available on the shelf, marginally significant enough to entrust it to the hands of a few who could mediate it themselves, or important enough to share it at the center of a broad classroom inquiry into the construction of perspectives and perceptions. Myers lays the groundwork to support such brave inquiry.

In teaching a controversial book, we often anticipate—sometimes tensely—reactions in young readers: the flush of giggles over the allusion to the human anatomy in chapter 10, or the exchanged glances and raised eyebrows as one character blurts out "hell" or "fuck" in the midst of a fiery tirade. Profanity and racial slurs arrest attention as they hope to stereotype, intimate, taunt, and dehumanize. We wait to see if the controversial moment lures or alienates readers. Myers doesn't make us wait in *Fallen Angels.* By page three, the "enemy" Vietnamese are dehumanized and objectified as "Congs." By page 6, the sergeant taunts soldiers with language that would make most people blush. By page 7 the same sergeant has stereotyped and estranged the entire gay population. By page 12, there is a triangle of racial tension involving a Vietnamese cleaning woman, an African American soldier, and a White soldier filled with derogatory labels and knee-jerk bravado, brinking on violence.

So why bother with this book at all? The story is broader and deeper than its necessarily coarse language and imagery. The timeless tensions it explores merit close study. The instructional challenge then becomes gauging comfort levels with explicitness and creating contexts where everything can be interrogated, including discomfort. Myers did not write this book to place readers at ease. The reader is challenged to unpack the battles within battles, the histories and motivations. These tensions are not new nor are they unique to the Vietnam War. They are patterns in human history. Myers tries to help readers find their place in history through Perry's struggles. It is both a war story and a coming-of-age story.

Sometimes the coming-of-age story supersedes the war story. This book is part of a larger mission on Myers's part to share voices formerly unheard and inspire readers formerly unmirrored in literature for young people on their rites of passage. *Scorpions* (1988) and *Monster* (1999) are examples of two other titles working toward that career-long mission. Perry is searching, as are many young people who would be drawn to this text. He just

happens to be a soldier. The immediacy of Perry's first-person view pushes the book, through war, toward more universal struggles. Thus the text is doubly rich as the poignant, complex lessons Perry and Peewee, Perry's newfound comrade, and the others learn as they come of age are inextricably bound up with the complex lessons of the Vietnam War. The lines between boyhood and manhood are as blurred as the borders between war and peace. The parallel exploration of personal and global treacherous, unsettled terrain sets this story above other adolescent novels in which the journey is not nearly so plural.

Hostile actions are vital to the authenticity of this tale. However, Myers focuses less on how people die and more on the emotional aftermath, as in the case of Jenkins's death.

> "You know him?"
>
> "No," I said, "I just met him at the replacement company."
>
> "Sometimes it goes like that," Monaco said. He started to say something else then shrugged it off, and left.
>
> I wanted to say more to him. I wanted to say that the only dead person I had seen before had been my grandmother. . . . But Jenkins was different. Jenkins had been walking with me and talking with me only hours before. Seeing him lying there like that, his mouth and eyes open, had grabbed something inside my chest and twisted it hard.
>
> (43)

When the platoon commanding officer dies, the aftermath is again more central than the physical demise. Perry has aged over the pages between the deaths. His perspective broadens to collective rather than individual grief.

> Shock. Pain. Nobody wanted to look at anybody else. Nobody wanted to talk. There was nothing to say. Lieutenant Carroll's death was close. It hung around our shoulders and filled the spaces between us. Lieutenant Carroll had sat with us, had been afraid with us, had worried about us. Now he was dead.
>
> (120)

As Perry wrote the tragic letter to Mrs. Carroll, Myers broadened the range of perspectives yet again: "I know that it is not much comfort to you that your husband died bravely, or honorably, but he did. All of the guys in the squad who served under him are grateful for his leadership and for having known him"(131).

Other deaths followed, including the loss of comrade and enemy lives—though the line between is increasingly blurred, a hallmark of war, particularly the Vietnamese conflict. Myers wasted not one death as statistic or set dressing. Each was an opportunity to consider another perspective, or deepen the understanding of a familiar one.

Unlike textbook accounts and television coverage of war, which most often focus on acts of aggression, well-written trade books focus on the results of aggression—the uprooted and ruined lives, the suffering from pain and sadness, and the waste of lives and energy, and resources. If the violence in these stories can convince young people that they must find peaceful ways to settle their differences, then it is justified.

(Tomlinson, 45)

Hostile words are also vital for authenticity. No character in this story is simply good or evil, rather an emerging negotiation of perspectives. Take Peewee, for instance, the fast-talking little guy from Chicago whose conversations often turn to verbal boxing matches. Finding a spic-and-span sentence uttered by this character is nearly impossible. However, he is deeper than a foul-mouthed runt. Early in the book, we learn a great deal about Peewee "back in the world" in a few of his own words.

> [T]his is the first place I ever been in my life where I got what everybody else got . . . anything anybody got in the army, I got. You got a gun. I got a gun. You got boots, I got boots. You eat this lousy-ass chip beef on toast, guess what I eat?"

(15)

He is a central player in most name-calling volleys. Perry often runs interference for Peewee when he gets too deep with someone too large. In the should-Monaco-marry-the-girl-back-home discussion, Peewee meets our expectations of smart-aleck superficiality by asking: "Is she pregnant?" and "What's she look like?" Then he surprises us as the first romantic in the crowd to say: "I vote for the marriage." When Perry breaks down after a near-death brush with a Vietcong soldier, it's Peewee who comforts him.

Similarly, Peewee internalizes the struggle faced by the young children in their war-torn country. Wanting to help in some way, he starts making a doll with items he finds in the immediate area. As he completes the doll, the platoon watches the smiling woman hand her child—for whom the doll was intended—to an American soldier. The child had been mined. The soldier, the child, and the child's family die instantly. When others check in on Peewee later, clearly shaken and withdrawn, the exterior emerges again.

> "Hey Peewee," I said, "it's okay to feel bad about what's going on over here, man. It's really okay."
>
> "Me? Feel bad?" Peewee turned over in his bunk and pulled his sheet up around his shoulders. "Never happen."

The words—profane, profound, and mundane—are all part of a larger, more complex context.

The initial categories of censorship concern (war, racial tension, coarse language) pervade the entire book; however, just as Perry and his platoon evolve, so do the categories. War becomes more complicated than "kickin' butt" and being American. Patriotism emerges along a continuum, interpreted variably among characters and situations. Racial lines blur as soldiers lean on each other for platoon survival (though the strongest link is shared between Perry and Peewee, two African Americans). Coarse language begins to sound commonplace for its frequency. The words between carry the memorable meanings. These potentially contentious elements, considered together, mirror the journey of the *Fallen Angels* cast. All are vital to its compelling telling.

This is a valuable book for capable and interested young readers to experience individually. Most teachers and librarians find comfort in an individual approach, given the "lively" language and stark subject matter. However, this book screams for conversation and invites exploration beyond its bindings. What was life for those "back in the world?" What about the Vietnamese perspective? What do veterans, politicians, and protesters think about the event retrospectively? What challenges do we still face? What poetry grew out of this era? What songs? What patterns from this era persist and recur today? What is oppression and who were the oppressors in the Vietnam conflict? What types of oppression does the military fight against? What types of oppression does it support and reward? How do veterans return home? How does a war-torn country adapt to "peace"? Who is this book for? Whom might it offend? Why? How might some story events be described through the eyes of another character, real or imagined, within or beyond *Fallen Angels*?

Imposing this text on young people would do them and the story a disservice. The layers, levels, and perspectives demand committed exploration. The reader needs to be the explorer. Using the text as a vehicle for critical examination of a hotly contested historical period considered from a variety of perspectives would offer all involved a learning experience. The art becomes harnessing the controversy that swirls around this text, framing and naming the subtle levels of controversy, not taming them.

Works Cited

Myers, Walter Dean. *Monster*. New York: Harper Collins, 1999.

———. *Fallen Angels*. New York: Scholastic, 1988.

———. *Scorpions*. New York: Harper Trophy, 1988.

Tomlinson, Carl. (1995). "Justifying Violence in Children's Literature." In *Battling Dragons: Issues and Controversy in Children's Literature,* ed. Susan Lehr. Portsmouth, N.H.: Heinemann, 1995.

Walter Dean Myers with Olubunmi Ishola (interview date January 2007)

SOURCE: Myers, Walter Dean, and Olubunmi Ishola. "An Interview with Walter Dean Myers." *World Literature Today* 81, no. 3 (May-June 2007): 63-5.

[*In the following interview, conducted in January 2007, Myers discusses such topics as the inspiration for* Harlem Summer; *his interest in jazz; his collaborative efforts with his son, illustrator Christopher Myers; and his work as a poet.*]

[*Ishola*]: *Your new book,* **Harlem Summer,** *is about a young African American boy, Mark Purvis. Mark is in a jazz band with some of his friends and becomes involved with jazz musicians and jazz poets throughout the course of the novel. Your books are known for providing a compelling perspective on hard-hitting issues faced by at-risk youth. You also seek to portray the beauty of the African American experience, requiring young adults to question their values and decisions. What message do you feel jazz has to offer at-risk youth, especially those in the African American community? What do you want young adults to question and think about as they read* **Harlem Summer***?*

[*Myers*]: All art involves the interplay of discipline and creativity. In *Harlem Summer,* my young protagonist comes to realize that what he sees as a casual activity, the jazz explosion of 1920s Harlem, actually represents a seriousness and work that is belied by the joy of performance. As he sees the characters from the Harlem Renaissance pass through the office of *The Crisis,* he begins to understand that there are young people in the world very much like him but who have adopted a seriousness and maturity that he hasn't seen previously. I would like young people to realize that the different levels of life are self-generated and not dependent on race or economic status.

In **Harlem Summer,** *many historical figures are brought to life: Countee Cullen, Langston Hughes, W. E. B. Du Bois, Jessie Fauset, Fats Waller, Queenie, Bumpy Johnson, and others are all connected through sixteen-year-old Mark Purvis. I know that, while growing up in Harlem, you also rubbed shoulders with many such figures. Is this book, in some way, autobiographical?*

The idea of *Harlem Summer* came from stories I heard at home in Harlem. My dad worked occasionally for the notorious gangster Dutch Schultz. Schultz had, beside his numbers business and other illegal enterprises, several legitimate companies. One of them was a moving company located a few blocks from where I lived and down the street from Fats Waller. My father worked on Schultz's moving vans. My parents attended rent parties in which Fats played and regaled his audience with his humor and songs.

How much research did you undertake in re-creating these characters? Was your goal to depict their personalities as historically accurate as possible, or did you take creative liberties?

I did quite a bit of research in putting this story together. I have the major black newspaper of the day, the *Amsterdam News,* on microfilm and could follow what was going on in the black world on a weekly basis through that paper. I also have all of the issues of *The Crisis,* the magazine at which my hero worked, so I knew what was being published in 1925 and by whom. I also consulted the biography of Langston Hughes, who came to my church to read and sell his books, as well as a number of books on the Harlem Renaissance.

Besides young-adult novels, you've written a great deal of poetry. **Here in Harlem: Poems in Many Voices,** **Harlem,** *and* **Blues Journey** *are all compelling pieces that invoke a musical feeling with their words. Similarly, jazz poetry demonstrates jazz-like rhythms, tone color, or the feel of improvisation through literary style. How would you define jazz poetry? Would you call yourself a jazz poet?*

Jazz poetry tries to emulate some of the complex rhythms of jazz and uses a musical vocabulary. I don't consider myself a jazz poet, but rather a poet whose works reflect his cultural heritage. Since my heritage is both African American and European, my poetry varies accordingly and is also affected by what I'm reading at the time.

What do you feel is vital about the dialogue jazz provides between the artist and audience?

Jazz is meant to be physically interactive. The musician wants his listener to respond to the music by feeling the rhythm and at least wanting to move with it. Many old-time jazz musicians considered their performances to be most successful when people got up and started dancing.

To follow up the previous question, you've collaborated with your son, Christopher Myers, on **Jazz** *and* **Blues Journey,** *two books that seek to express music in words and pictures. How is that collaboration between words and art, and the dialogue it creates, similar to the dialogue between artist and audience? How does it differ?*

Most picture books are done with the writer and artist far away from each other. In these instances, it's the editor bringing the work together into one creative endeavor. This is good, but when I work with my son, Chris, we feed off each other. I'll present a text and then Chris will respond to that text with his art. He doesn't just want to illustrate my words but to contribute his own vision to the overall piece. When I see what he's done, the nuances he brings to the work, I'll often change the text to add accents to his images. Sometimes, as we discuss ideas that we might like to work on in the future (a constant conversation) I will try to build a vocabulary around his visual concepts or try to change the rhythm of my text to contrast with his style.

You've called jazz "America's gift to the world"; it is probably one of the few things that can be considered an integral part of American culture. However, jazz lacks some of the popular appeal that other styles of music have. Why do you think this is so?

Music in the United States has been heavily influenced by changing media as well as production costs. The big bands of the 1940s and 1950s were too expensive by the mid-1960s. The rise of the rap artists can be attributed largely to inexpensive production costs. Getting performers into a studio or on a set for a day and producing a video that doesn't have to have high production values is relatively risk free. Getting professional classical or jazz musicians into a performance where production values are very demanding is very expensive and therefore risky.

Of the different styles of jazz—ragtime, big band, bebop, modal, cool, fusion, free, etc.—which is your favorite? Who are some of your favorite jazz artists?

I first attended jazz performances during the Count Basie and Duke Ellington period, so the big band era remains a favorite. I've always loved Louis Armstrong and the pianists of the renaissance period—Fats Waller and James P. Johnson were great. I'm most recently influenced by some of the fusion stuff from the Miles Davis-Keith Jarrett hard-rock period of the 1970s. I like the challenges the music presents, and I see myself as fusing writing styles.

Is there a recent book that has captured your interest?

I'm currently reading *The Psychology of Action,* by Peter Gollwitzer and John Bargh, which discusses how people make decisions to act as opposed to internal decisions of preference. I believe that not enough attention is being paid to the differences between preferences and actions as it applies to inner-city kids. I'm also reading *Grace Under Fire: Letters of Faith in Times of War,* edited by Andrew Carroll, a fascinating and uplifting book.

What outside the realm of literature has drawn your attention of late?

I'm more and more interested in the ways young people develop their values and the difficulties that so many inner-city kids face when forced to make adult decisions at an early age.

What current writing projects do you have underway or have planned for the near future?

I am in the middle of a book on the war in Iraq, which is filling my head and soul with its challenges. I'm also planning a book on African American dance with the same format as *Jazz.*

FURTHER READING

Criticism

Lane, R. D. "'Keepin' It Real': Walter Dean Myers and the Promise of African-American Children's Literature." *African American Review* 32, no. 1 (spring 1998): 125-38.

An in-depth examination of Myers's influence in the field of literature aimed at black youth, focusing specifically on the novel *Somewhere in the Darkness,* which demonstrates the author's skill at depicting realistic and authentic black male characters who defy mainstream notions of what constitutes black masculinity.

Vellucci, Dennis. "Man to Man: Portraits of the Male Adolescent in the Novels of Walter Dean Myers." In *African-American Voices in Young Adult Literature: Tradition, Transition, Transformation,* edited by Karen Patricia Smith, pp. 193-223. Metuchen, N.J.: Scarecrow Press, 1994.

Calls Myers's young male protagonists "remarkable," citing their capacity to remain morally upright despite their hostile and dangerous environments, and recognizing the vital role played by other males—fathers, brothers, surrogate fathers—who offer support and guidance to the adolescent boys.

Additional coverage of Myers's life and career is contained in the following sources published by Gale: *Authors and Artists for Young Adults,* Vols. 4, 23; *Beacham's Guide to Literature for Young Adults,* Vols. 6, 8, 11; *Black Literature Criticism,* Ed. 1:3; *Black Writers,* Ed. 2; *Children's Literature Review,* Vols. 4, 16, 35, 110; *Contemporary Authors,* Vol. 33-36R; *Contemporary Authors New Revision Series,* Vols. 20, 42, 67, 108; *Contemporary Literary Criticism,* Vol. 35; *Dictionary of Literary Biography,* Vol. 33; *DISCovering Authors Modules,* Eds. MULT, NOV; *Junior DISCovering Authors; Literature and Its Times,* Vol. 5; *Literature Resource Center; Major Authors and Illustrators for Children and Young Adults,* Eds. 1, 2; *Major Authors and Illustrators for Children and Young Adults Supplement,* Ed. 1; *Major 20th-Century Writers,* Ed. 2; *Major 21st-Century Writers* (eBook), ed. 2005; *Something about the Author,* Vols. 41, 71, 109, 157; *Something about the Author Autobiography Series,* Vol. 2; *Something about the Author—Brief Entry,* Vol. 27; *St. James Guide to Young Adult Writers;* and *Writers for Young Adults.*

Lauretta Ngcobo
1931-

South African novelist, editor, and children's book author.

INTRODUCTION

Ngcobo is a South African novelist whose work articulates her long-standing concern with economic, social, and political justice. Reviewers maintain that her novels are imbued with her own experiences struggling against the injustices of the apartheid system in South Africa in the second half of the twentieth century. Ngcobo is lauded for her ability to provide a much needed voice for black South African rural women, who battle economic forces, social customs, and oppressive political policies with passion and dignity in their fight for equality within a patriarchal and racially discriminatory Africa.

BIOGRAPHICAL INFORMATION

Ngcobo was born in 1931 in rural Ixopo, South Africa. Born during the apartheid era, she grew up experiencing racial discrimination and became politically active as a young woman. She was a member of the Pan-African Congress, a political group that was banned by the white South African government. Her husband, Abednego, was a founding member of the Pan-African Congress and was subsequently imprisoned for several years. Because of her political activities and her fight against the government's apartheid policies, she too became a target for South African security forces and narrowly escaped arrest. In 1963 she fled with her three children to Swaziland and stayed briefly in Tanzania and Zambia before immigrating to London in 1969. She found work as a teacher in London and decided to settle there. Alienated from the struggle back home, she began to write a novel that explored her experiences as an activist. Her first novel, *Cross of Gold,* was published in 1981. She is also the editor of a 1987 anthology entitled *Let It Be Told,* which contains essays by black British women writers including Marsha Prescod and Julie Pearn. In 1990 Ngcobo's second novel, *And They Didn't Die,* was published. A year later Ngcobo returned to South Africa, where she became a member of the KwaZulu-Natal Provincial legislature.

MAJOR WORKS

Ngcobo's fiction is informed by the turbulent political situation in her native South Africa and her participation in the political and social movement to end the discriminatory policies of apartheid. In her first novel, *Cross of Gold,* she touches on the role of black women in the struggle in South Africa. The novel opens with the shooting of a political activist, Sindisiwe Zidoke, as she tries to escape to Botswana with her young sons. Surviving the shooting, Sindisiwe is motivated to become a freedom fighter; her actions, however, lead to her violent death at the hands of government security forces. The story then shifts to the story of her son Mandla, who continues the fight against apartheid. By the time of her second novel, however, Ngcobo was ready to more fully explore the heroism of black rural women in the struggle against apartheid and confront the conflicting economic, political, and cultural forces that shaped the South African black female experience during that era. In *And They Didn't Die* Jezile, a rural South African black woman, is beset by political and cultural forces; not only must she deal with the oppression of apartheid, she must also conform to cultural mores that dictate her obedience to her husband, Siyalo, as well as to her meddling mother-in-law. When a crippling drought and other economic factors force Siyalo to work in the city—and only return home for two weeks out of the year—the couple's relationship is threatened not only by the distance, but by Jezile's inability to conceive a child during his brief stays. While visiting her husband in Durban, Jezile witnesses the political activism of urban women as they fight for better living conditions and fair wages and feels a sense of kinship with them. When Siyalo is arrested and sentenced to ten years in prison for stealing milk to feed their starving child, Jezile is forced to take a job as a domestic servant in a white household and is subsequently raped by her white employer. Now pregnant, she returns to her village, but is disowned by her in-laws for bearing the child of a white man. When a soldier breaks into her house and attempts to rape her daughter, S'naye, Jezile kills the soldier and must face the consequences of her actions. Ngcobo has also written a children's book, *Fiki Learns to Like Other People* (1993).

CRITICAL RECEPTION

Ngcobo's novels have attracted critical attention for their poignant and compassionate depiction of the challenges and suffering of black South African women under the repressive apartheid system and traditional South African patriarchal customs. Critics trace the development of Ngcobo's portrayal of the female characters in her novels as evidence of the novelist's own growing racial and feminist consciousness: in her first book, *Cross of Gold,* she killed off her female character, Sindisiwe, because she found it difficult to view African women as capable of effecting change; by her second novel, *And They Didn't Die,* she was able to more fully develop a strong, if not tragic, female protagonist who undergoes her own brave journey toward political and social activism, even if it comes at great cost. Ngcobo's inability to sustain a female protagonist in *Cross of Gold* is viewed by critics as an accurate reflection of the privileged role of men in the struggle against apartheid. Other commentators note that her fiction also addresses the economic disempowerment and cultural dislocation imposed on the black population, particularly black rural women, by industrialization, colonialism, migrant labor, and the apartheid system.

PRINCIPAL WORKS

Cross of Gold (novel) 1981
Let It Be Told: Essays by Black Women in Britain [editor] (essays) 1987
And They Didn't Die (novel) 1990
Fiki Learns to Like Other People (juvenilia) 1993

CRITICISM

Cherry Clayton (essay date 2000)

SOURCE: Clayton, Cherry. "Rural Women and African Resistance: Lauretta Ngcobo's Novel *And They Didn't Die.*" In *Postcolonizing the Commonwealth: Studies in Literature and Culture,* edited by Rowland Smith, pp. 115-32. Waterloo, Ontario: Wilfrid Laurier University Press, 2000.

[*In this essay, Clayton maintains that* And They Didn't Die *presents a characterization of a strong rural woman, Jezile, who faces a series of racial, sociopolitical, cultural, and economic forces that work against her and other South African women.*]

> How was it that laws were so clear cut, when the lives they governed were so muddled?
>
> —Ngcobo 1991:226

> The hand that rocks the cradle should also rock the boat.
>
> —South African women's slogan

CULTURE, IDEOLOGY AND REPRESENTATION

Debates about the relationship of culture, ideology and the politics of literary representation are complex. Frantz Fanon wrote in *Toward the African Revolution* that the process of industrialization camouflaged racism: "the perfecting of the means of production inevitably brings about the camouflage of the techniques by which man is exploited, hence of the forms of racism" (1967:35). These essays evoke the spirit of the 1958 Accra conference on African strategy and unity as a historical unravelling of the 1884 Berlin conference, which carved up continents in the name and spirit of European imperialism. Fanon goes on to say that "The advent of peoples, unknown only yesterday, onto the stage of history, their determination to participate in the building of a civilization that has its place in the world of today give to the contemporary period a decisive importance in the world process of humanization" (1967:146). A black South African writer, Lauretta Ngcobo, echoes this thought when she says: "there is another victory to be won, if South Africa is to be restored to her space in Africa. The cultural battle. There is no other place in the continent which is less African than South Africa" (1994:570).

The humanist discourse which emerges in relation to the decolonization of Africa now co-exists with a deconstructive discourse which problematizes cultural identity, critiques the development and enlightenment paradigms for Africa, and insists on contradiction and difference in the cultural articulation of African and Afro-American identities.[1] Henry Louis Gates, Jr., argues that the heritage of each black text in a Western language is "a double heritage, two-toned" and that writers of African descent "occupy spaces in at least two traditions: a European or American literary tradition, and one of the several related but distinct black traditions" (1984:4). While "the very act of writing has been a political act for the black author (Gates 1984:5), the structure of the black text has been repressed and treated as if it were transparent (Gates 1984:6). Black people have always been "masters of the figurative"; saying one thing and meaning another has been "basic to black survival in oppressive Western cultures" (Gates 1984:6).

Critics working within African and Afro-American feminism have also wanted to stress repetition and revision in black women's texts. Barbara Johnson, writing on Zora Neale Hurston, argues that Hurston's protagonist needs to "assume and articulate the incompatible forces involved in her own division. The sign of authentic voice is thus not self-identity but self-difference" 1984:212). Houston Baker, Jr., situates narration within "a world that is itself constituted by a repertoire of 'stories'" (1984:224). Susan Willis, writing on Toni Morrison, says that "sexuality converges with history and functions as a register for the experience of change, i.e. historical transition" (1984:263). Morrison, like Ngcobo, "develops the social and psychological aspects that characterize the lived experience of historical transition" and its consequences, "the alienation produced by the transition to wage labour" (Willis 1984:265). Domestic service constitutes only a marginal incorporation as wage labour, and in Morrison's fiction "individual genealogy evokes the history of black migration and the chain of economic expropriation from hinterland to village, and village to metropolis" (Willis 1984:265). Individual differences between women function to test the social dynamic within the group and society at large (Willis 1984:279). Jane Bryce, discussing African women's writing in a "post-Negritude, postcolonial reading of culture" suggests that recent writing is marked by a "self-conscious disjunction" (1994:619) between tradition and modernity. African women writers' use of English and of the novel genre "may be seen as an implicit assertion of distance from the nostalgia for origins, a recognition of the need for a revisioning of culture and their relationship to it from a postcolonial perspective" (Bryce 1994:620-21).

When Lauretta Ngcobo contextualizes her own literary production, she also points to multiple, often conflicting allegiances. Born in 1931 in rural Natal, she was forced to flee South Africa in 1963 after persecution by the South African government and police harassment.[2] Her husband was in the first executive of the Pan-Africanist Congress, a radical group that broke away from the African National Congress in 1959 and organized the pass resistance that led to the Sharpeville massacre in 1960. He was sent to jail along with people like Sobukwe (leader of the PAC) and Mandela. Ngcobo's husband was involved in the lengthy Treason Trials which began in 1956. He was then in prison between 1960 and 1963, and a militant activist until 1969, when the couple eventually settled in England with their three children, and where Lauretta began her first novel, *Cross of Gold* (1981), a novel in which she found it difficult to keep her female protagonist alive as a focal centre (Hunter 1994:102). Sindisiwe dies because at the time "death and destruction" were all-pervasive; "such has been the history of our struggle in South Africa" (Hunter 1994:107). At the time of writing her first novel Ngcobo found it difficult to see African women as capable of effecting change:

> In South Africa . . . a black woman is oppressed by law, which has calcified around the old traditional customs. Under the Natal Code, for instance, a woman is a perpetual minor who cannot perform at law even when her husband is dead. She's equally incapacitated socially, economically, all round.
>
> (Bush 1984:7)

Ngcobo has also expressed ambivalence about feminism and the freedom that Western women aspire to, while being agents of racial oppression themselves, whether in South Africa or England: "I am not referring

to the structure of institutionalised power, but to the yoke of daily injustice, to the bitterness of everyday living" (Vivan 1989:111). She calls attention to a range of levels of oppression and draws a comparison between oppression by African men and white women: "through our man we feel the weight of the system, as well as that of law and tradition. An analogous thing happens to us in respect of the white woman: it is through her that a variety of oppressions befall us" (Vivan 1989:112). Yet she acknowledges that white women have won rights which will benefit African women after democratization. This has been the case in South Africa, where women represented in Parliament now constitute 33-1/3 percent of the total, moving from 130th in the world to 10th place (Davis 1994:587).

In attempting to define her place in relation to Western and African traditions, Ngcobo admits that "Our women are caught up in a hybrid world of the old and the new; the African and the alien locked in the struggle to integrate contradictions into a meaningful new whole" (Ngcobo 1986:82). African women had been cardboard figures in a written tradition that created contradictory images of idolized mothers and the realities of wifehood.[3] The oral tradition, though she cites a moving instance of its performance by her grandfather at her own birth, also "extolled the virtues of humility, silent endurance and self-effacing patterns of behaviour for our girls" (Ngcobo 1986:81). During her growing years and education she was made to feel marginalized in the educational system (35 women to 500 men when she attended university) (Ngcobo 1986:85). At school and university she observed the cultural clash between rural and city ways and people: "I began to feel a disfigurement of outlook, a mutilation within" (Ngcobo 1986:85). This may account for the strong presence she gives to rural women, and their powers of resistance, in her later novel, *And They Didn't Die,* in which the title signals defiance and survival.

In her autobiographical writing, essays and interviews Ngcobo relates the fragmentation of cultural traditions to political processes, especially industrialization and migrant labour. The introduction of scripted literature divided society into an educated elite and an uneducated mass, and became a source of alienation. The system of migrant labour "altered beyond recognition the structures of our societies" and affected women who had traditionally played a prominent role in the transmission of oral literature (Ngcobo 1986:84). Urbanization in the gendered form of migrant labour for men "created . . . hardened divisions between men and women" (Ngcobo 1986:85). The story of *And They Didn't Die,* which relates the different but politically inflected trials of an African couple, Jezile and Siyalo, sundered by multiple factors deriving from poverty, migrant labour, political activism and prison, customary law and gendered oppression, becomes the vehicle for conveying this process of "hardened division" between the sexes. The stories of their different trajectories into city life, patterns of disillusionment, economic struggle and politicization, become representative stories illuminating the complex intersections of capitalism, race and gender in South African life and their effects on rural people.[4] Ngcobo's self-positioning in relation to literary traditions is also complex, acknowledging hybridity and multiple affiliations. She acknowledges her special feeling for Thomas Hardy's fiction, and this may have affected her creation of dignified rural people who are crushed by political and economic conditions as if by fate, and the passing away of rural communities (Vivan 1989:106). She has also mentioned the attraction of the novel form: "The only form that I get on well with is the novel, but I want to capture the feel of South Africa at this particular time of transition" (Daymond 1996:85). However, she feels that her emphasis on one central character and action is derived from an African tradition:

> our folklore which always pivots around the story of an individual, an important person of our tradition. The importance of the plot is created around one single character. . . . Each character has a certain gamut of options, which are drawn from an objective reality, even if it is then partly invented in the story.

> (Vivan 1989:109)

Thematically African novels are restricted, because topics like land or factory ownership have no relevance, so the themes of European fiction become "arid, senseless, useless material" (Vivan 1989:110). "The black writer is forced to limit himself to a few themes which deal with a society scarred by poverty and restrictions" (Vivan 1989:110). But there is a broader theme of historical suffering: "the fundamental themes which are for us of common interest, and ask for an answer to the feelings of our people" (Vivan 1989:110).

In her introduction to Miriam Tlali's *Footprints in the Quag* (1989), Ngcobo traces the movement in black South African writing from a literature of cultural assimilation to protest. As literature tried to deal with industrialization and migratory labour, writers were bewildered: "These writers were faced with the paradox of creating or fashioning a new indigenous character, while the dynamics of the situation pointed to the destruction of the culture in which that character had to be rooted and flourish" (Ngcobo 1989:xi). The consolidation of white power with the Union of the provinces in 1910 "marks the Africans' first awareness of themselves as an oppressed people" (Ngcobo 1989:xii). A new spirit emerged dramatically in the 1970s and within that mood Miriam Tlali "writes from the heart of those turbulent cities" (Ngcobo 1989:xv), expressing "the wounds sustained in the collapse of our societies" (Ngcobo 1989:xvii), especially through women's eyes. As a result, Tlali tends to see tradition as a salvation for African people, whereas Ngcobo is much more critical of African custom. With regard to political purpose,

Ngcobo says that her writing is "a social/political comment": "I believe books by the oppressed people can, ever so subtly, restore the desire for freedom and the will to achieve this" in the face of the psychological introjection of colonial images of inferiority (Bush 1984:8).[5]

RURAL WOMEN, GENDER AND RACIAL POLITICS

In *And They Didn't Die* Ngcobo's purpose was to show "how country women cope and resist the pressures of the law, how the laws of the country disadvantage them" (Bush 1984:6). Rural women, the traditional food producers, have been without tilling and land tenure rights. Yet women have often rallied to oppose injustice: they fought against the imposition of passes in the late 1950s; against the problem of dipping their dying cattle (dipping tanks were introduced to control disease), and the government's policy of building beerhalls for men, while not providing facilities for child care (Bush 1984:8). Multiple grievances led to defiance by women, erupting in different regions of Natal in 1959. About 1,000 women were arrested. These events, the context for the first section of the novel, record the emergence of "a vast new political constituency. No understanding of the radicalisation of black politics in those years would be complete without a knowledge of the emergence and behaviour of this constituency" (Lodge 1983: 150).[6] Jezile's husband is in Durban while she struggles with her mother-in-law's persecution for her infertility. Siyalo is politicized in Durban by the evidence of social injustice, overcrowding and exploitation of labour, and is soon identified as a troublemaker. During Jezile's visit she experiences the humiliations of her husband's hostel life, but is also given a glimpse of the activism of urban women who storm the beerhalls in protest. She feels a bond with city women: "how similar their situations were" (Ngcobo 1991:30).

Historical activities by the ANC Women's League are represented in a woman doctor and leader, Nosizwe, who illuminates aspects of political leadership during the build-up of popular resistance. The problems of traditional lifestyles are illustrated by Jezile's friend Zenzile, who dies in childbirth. We see the contradictions of Jezile's life and her growing awareness of her husband's involvement in an African patriarchal system. The difficulties of parenting are shown when both parents are imprisoned for periods of time. The contradictions of government policy, destroying rural communities while trying to preserve them artificially, are shown in intimate detail, as are impossible economic conditions in the countryside.

In the second phase of Jezile's life she is incorporated into urban domestic service while her husband is in prison. The transition from a fairly stable though distant family life to a single-mother household suggests the contradictions of human sexuality and family life in rural and urban South Africa. Jezile is accused by her mother-in-law (the custodian of customary law) of infidelity when she returns pregnant from a brief prison sentence. After Siyalo's prison sentence she is drawn into a single women's culture which supports her. She takes on domestic service in a white household and is then raped by her employer, who sends her home with the child to protect himself from arrest. Once back in the village she is disowned by her in-laws for having mothered a "white" child. After Siyalo's release from prison he claims his daughters, but he and Jezile are separated by customary law. The compounded force of racial oppression and customary law is vividly illustrated in these ironic plot twists.

In the last, compressed section of the narrative, Jezile and her children move through the turbulent political clashes of the 1976 countrywide insurgency and the emergency period of the mid-1980s. Jezile's daughter Ndondo becomes a political activist and flees the country. Her son Lungi, the child of mixed race, becomes a leader at his coloured school and is paralyzed from the waist down in a police shooting incident. When her daughter Ndondo visits her secretly during the emergency period, a soldier storms their house and attempts to rape Jezile's other daughter, S'naye. Jezile kills the soldier. Jezile now goes to her husband with an account of her own rape by her employer and they realize that at the moment of a possible reunion they will be sundered by another prison sentence. The final scene is complex in its evocation of a historical abyss, the abyss of the combined historical damage of industrialization, the apartheid system and racialized sexual abuse: "He swung around to face her, carnage in his mind, and looked at her wordlessly, penetrating those eyes, mind to mind, heart to heart. Together they drifted back in reverse into a vortex beyond recovery, in a kind of falling away" (Ngcobo 1991:245). This ending also counters any emancipatory or enlightenment narrative, constituting a critique of the liberal ideology which sees modernization as inevitably progressive.[7] Ngcobo's narration during the transitional period in South Africa thus involves a memory of the complexity of historical damage to individuals, the family and the collectivity of the oppressed. Her novel is an implicit answer to the question Said poses as central to a decolonizing imagination: "How does a culture seeking to become independent of imperialism imagine its own past?" (Said 1993:214).

While the narrative moves toward a violent crisis and sense of historical loss, the seizing of subjectivity by those who have traditionally been seen as objects and a "subordinate race despised by all" (Wicomb 1992:18) manifests "the material reality of people's lives" in a way which Wicomb calls moving beyond "the legacy of victims" (1992:15). Ngcobo's novel demonstrates a complex relationship between social structures and subjectivity, particularly in Jezile's fully rendered consciousness as she struggles with the changing political and cultural contexts that surround her, with what

Belinda Bozzoli calls "the changing material world" as "a decision-making existential being" (Bozzoli with Nkotsoe 1991:236). The novel is well suited to displaying the tension between internal and external struggles, conflicts between generations and genders. ***And They Didn't Die*** is thus anti-essentialist in effect, recognizing, like Foucault, "the manifold structures of power" with their varied forms and multiplicity of "localized resistances and counter-offensives" (Escobar 1984-85:381) and thus also recognizing that "women, far from being powerless, are agents in their own fates" (Udayagiri 1995:161). In Jezile's successful defence of her daughter's body the materiality of women's oppression is recognized and partly resolved. Female sexuality mediates systems of power, but the generational progression from Jezile to S'naye shows how self-defence is the lesson of female experience. In defending her daughter, Jezile defends herself in an action that testifies to the consciousness-raising she has undergone in both racial and gender politics.

Discourse, Labour and African Renewal

Ngcobo has argued that in South Africa women's quarrel is primarily with the state, and that this differentiates their feminist struggle from many others (Bush 1984:8). Because of her characters' involvement in radical political action her fiction could be said to be part of the discourse of the Pan-Africanist Congress. Graham Pechey characterizes two counter-texts to the Freedom Charter of 1955 and its broad universalizing humanism: the Pan-Africanist Congress and Black Consciousness (1994:28). The PAC critique of 1959, he argues (the point in time where Ngcobo's second novel begins) "is founded in an anti-modernist narrative that reduces everything to a story of repossession" (1994:28). ***And They Didn't Die*** could be said to participate in this anti-modernist discourse and in the radical politics of the PAC, but it feminizes this discourse and offers a critique of liberal discourse and earlier women's writing in South Africa by revisioning key tropes. Instead of the seduced and abandoned white settler women who characterize the novels of Olive Schreiner and Pauline Smith, and whose stories are played out in terms of white settler hegemony and patriarchal social codes for settler women, Ngcobo's protagonist Jezile is politicized by multiple forms of gender and racial oppression to the point of militancy and an act of violence. Seduction is replaced by rape, indicating the structural and personal violence the state inflicts on African women, and their economic and personal vulnerability in domestic labour.[8]

The liberal use of the adoptive situation in Schreiner's novel *From Man to Man* (1926), where a white woman adopts the child of her husband's liaison with a coloured servant, is also revised when Jezile bears a coloured child from her employer's rape and the child becomes an activist in radical clashes with the state and the military. This situation allegorizes the national situation:

European interbreeding with an indigenous and slave population produced the people whose partial alliance with Black Consciousness helped to oust them from power. Ngcobo's reworking of this narrative trope inverts Sarah Gertrude Millin's notorious use of mixed blood as the sign of laxity and degeneration (see Coetzee 1988). The revised adoptive family evokes the spirit of non-racial resistance that marked the 1980s in South Africa and the rise of associations such as the United Democratic Front.

And They Didn't Die thus evokes the existential dimension of the cultural dislocations, land expropriations and economic disempowerment imposed by colonialism, industrialization and migrant labour. By appropriating narrative, one of the forms of cultural control, and subverting it to oppositional purposes, South African writers circulate new histories, in this case making rural women's consciousness in previously "hidden struggles" available to new readerships (see Beinart and Bundy 1987). The intersections of customary law, African patriarchy and apartheid legislation are revealed in the detailed emotional texture of family life.[9] The destructive personal effects of migrant labour are graphically presented: sexual loneliness, enforced adultery, arrest for those politicized in the cities, the degradation of the physical and social environment, "a hopeless patchwork of effort, determination, and failure" (Ngcobo 1991:221; see Ramphele 1991). The slow collapse of subsistence agriculture is the context of the opening chapters, and the women's grievances are related to the extension of influx control legislation in the Bantustan (homeland) policy designed to prevent permanent African settlement and thus political franchise in the cities (Walker 1982).

At the same time the novel provides a fictional record of the construction of patterns of resistance and solidarity, the ways in which currents of freedom rippled through rural communities and in moments of private reflection and understanding:

> she knew she had taken a decision that she should have taken ages before. Nobody would ever take that power away from her—not his mother, not her own mother, not anyone. Both mothers had had such a hold on her precisely because they had never had that power over their own lives.

> (Ngcobo 1991:11)

The lifting of women's local resistance to new levels is shown in the prison experience of the village women:

> Then suddenly, somewhere in the deepest part of that jail, they heard a different kind of song. It pierced the prison air and shattered the silence of the vast corridors. The women in the cells listened for a few moments. Then they knew it was Nosizwe. They picked up her song and sang it with gusto. Her song was not a hymn, it was a political song that throbbed in the gut. Their voices returned to them full of strength and defiance. They grew strong and threw off the feeling of inadequacy that had gripped them.

> (Ngcobo 1991:100-101)

The links between the 1950s decade, which Ngcobo describes as the beginning of "political confrontation with the oppressor" (1989:xii), and thus of a new type of literature, and the township uprisings of the 1970s and 1980s are telescoped in the last section of the novel, in the story of Jezile's children (see Mzamane 1985). Ngcobo's position within the generation of writers produced by Sharpeville and its political contexts is unique, as Mzamane has pointed out, because she carries to an English-speaking audience the rural experiences and subjectivities usually produced in indigenous languages or in the liberal, patriarchal, morally recuperative format of Alan Paton's *Cry, the Beloved Country* (Mzamane 1985:40). The English language and the multi-generational realistic family saga are adapted to become the vehicles of a South African narrative of dispossession and resistance. Ngcobo adopts the documentary devices of incorporating political speeches, lists of grievances, historical dates and protests, devices that have been central to historical fiction and its use by South African novelists such as Nadine Gordimer (see Clingman 1986:187-88). Rural families living on the reserves are made into what Raymond Williams calls a "knowable community," shaped by a novelist "in such a way as to give it identity, presence, ways of reusable articulation" (Williams 1990:165-82).

Ngcobo's insistence on a cumulative plot movement toward an act of violent retaliation against sexual violence suggests the role played by gender awareness in black South African women's writing, and its relationship to State violence and the aftermath of colonialism (see Head 1977; Mvula 1988; Qakisa 1988; Tlali 1989). The conclusion of the novel, while evoking solidarity between Jezile and Siyalo, also draws the limits of the body as metaphor.[10] The body, writes Jean Comaroff, is "a tangible frame of selfhood" which "mediates all action upon the world and simultaneously constitutes both the self and the universe of social and natural relations of which it is a part" (1985:6-7). The South African legacy is still immured in forms of violent control and aggression inflicted on women (Hansson 1991). The tragic "vortex" that concludes the novel is an index to the semi-occlusion of rural African predicaments in the mass migrations to the cities, under apartheid, and in the emergence of an educated, urban African elite.

The story Ngcobo tells is also the story of African women's labour: "the country women are the backbone of the South African superstructure" (Bush 1984:8). They maintain homes for absent husbands, supplement meagre wages, produce and raise the next generation of workers (Bush 1984:8). The labour of serfs generally, as J. M. Coetzee has pointed out, was elided in the late-nineteenth-century South African pastoral. The rural labour of African women has been doubly elided in white South African fiction, except for occasional glimpses, such as the one we get in Gordimer's *July's People* (1981), which is in a displaced futuristic setting. Ngcobo makes visible what Njabulo Ndebele calls "the unacknowledged presence of Black labour and the legitimacy of the political claims based upon that labour" (1994:4). The differentiated process of labour incorporation for men and women, and the different costs, are detailed within a family setting which is repeatedly shattered by punitive state interventions.

Ndebele has pointed out that the role of literature in the crisis of transition is not an easy one: "It throws up a problematic of its own within the broad cultural crisis" (1994:9). Ngcobo's novel, written within that crisis, looks backward and forward, finding an avenue "in the history of the survival culture of the people" (Ndebele 1994:8). Though *And They Didn't Die,* as Eva Hunter has argued, works within a broad framework of historical and social referentiality (Hunter 1994:120), subjectivity is shown as constructed within what Benita Parry calls "antagonistic forces and heterogeneous signifying practices, solicited and situated by conflicting ideological addresses" (Parry 1994:22). These ideological addresses include radical PAC politics, racialized gender violence, anti-apartheid activism and a critique of customary African law. Ngcobo's novel is a form of antipastoral that looks backward over fifty years to Sol Plaatje's noble Barolong couple, Mhudi and Ra-Thaga, embedded in visionary pastoral romance. The insistent narrative focus on Jezile and her shifting subjectivity "affirm cultural identity as a new and insurgent subjectivity that has been fought for and reconstructed in the process of struggle" (Parry 1994:22). The story Ngcobo tells in *And They Didn't Die* is the story of what cannot afford to be forgotten in the construction of a democratic future for South Africa. Ngcobo is in accord with Fanon's pan-African vision when she writes of the relationship between South Africa and the rest of Africa: "Where the white government sees state barriers, we see gates, not to enter and pillage or encroach on other people's territories but to enter in good will, and together with fellow Africans we shall create a new impregnable African Continent" (Ngcobo 1991:199).

Notes

1. Mridula Udayagiri writes that "development has been a problematic concept, because it perpetuates unequal relations in the global economy, and ignores perceptions of progress that may be very different from those of policy-makers" (1995:160). She also suggests that theories of development and underdevelopment "remain firmly anchored in emancipatory paradigms that emerged in the Age of Enlightenment" (1995:160).

2. Biographical details are taken from the interview by Robert Bush (1984:5-8).

3. Zoe Wicomb says ambivalent social attitudes towards women are rather like those that characterize writing itself: "the consecration of women as virgins or mothers or other fetishization of Woman which at the same time allows women as human beings to be treated with contempt" (1994:574).

4. Margaret Daymond writes in her introduction to *South African Feminisms* that the essays in the collection "begin to uncover a history of complicity between apartheid ideology and the patriarchalism of nineteenth-century Calvinism, tracing an overlap between the institutionalisation of racial 'apartness' and masculinist epistemology" (1996:x-xi).

5. Carol Boyce Davies describes African feminism as "a hybrid of sorts"; there is "a struggle against women's own internalised oppression" (Boyce Davies and Graves 1986:241). For Ngcobo this struggle clearly took place over time in her increasing confidence in representing rural women's lives in fiction.

6. Brian Worsfold gives an excellent account of the political context for the novel in his article on Ngcobo in *Altered State: Writing and South Africa* (1994).

7. Ngcobo had been pressured by her first publisher, Longmans, to add an optimistic epilogue to *Cross of Gold* (Bush 1984:7).

8. Jackie Cock (1987) discusses the South African domestic worker as one instance of the "trapped worker."

9. Customary law offered forms of protection but at the cost of the woman's loss of autonomy in communally identified functions within marriage and childbearing (see Nhlapo 1991). Independence, migration and incorporation into urban wage labour brought a new set of problems, economic insecurity and often a neo-colonial repackaging of patriarchy (see Jochelson 1995; also Cheater and Gaidzwana 1996).

10. Grant Farred cites the inscriptions on the body of forms of male power, and discusses different sites of oppression and resistance in his article on *And They Didn't Die* (1993).

References

Baker, Houston A., Jr.

1984 "To Move without Moving: Creativity and Commerce in Ralph Ellison's Trueblood Episode." In Henry Louis Gates, Jr., ed., *Black Literature and Literary Theory,* 221-48. New York: Methuen.

Bazilli, Susan, ed.

1991 *Putting Women on the Agenda.* Johannesburg: Ravan Press.

Beinart, William, and Colin Bundy

1987 *Hidden Struggles in Rural South Africa.* London: James Currey.

Boehmer, Elleke, Laura Chrisman and Kenneth Parker, eds.

1994 *Altered State? Writing and South Africa.* Mundelstrup: Dangaroo Press.

Boyce Davies, Carole, and Anne Adams Graves

1986 *Ngambika: Studies of Women in African Literature.* Trenton, NJ: Africa World Press.

Bozzoli, Belinda, with Mmantho Nkotsoe

1991 *Women of Phokeng: Consciousness, Life Strategy and Migrancy in South Africa, 1900-1983.* Portsmouth: Heinemann.

Bryce, Jane

1994 "Writing as Power in the Narratives of African Women." In Anna Rutherford, Lars Jensen and Shirley Chew, eds., *Into the Nineties: Post-Colonial Women's Writing,* 618-25. Mundelstrup: Dangaroo Press.

Bush, Robert

1984 "Do Books Alter Lives?" *Wasafiri* 1, 1:5-8.

Cheater, A. P., and R. B. Gaidzwana

1996 "Citizenship in Neo-Patrilineal States: Gender and Mobility in Southern Africa." *Journal of Southern African Studies* 22, 2:189-200.

Clingman, Stephen

1986 *The Novels of Nadine Gordimer: History from the Inside.* Johannesburg: Ravan Press.

Cock, Jacklyn

1987 "Trapped Workers: Constraints and Contradictions Experienced by Black Women in Contemporary South Africa." *Women's Studies International Forum* 10, 2:133-40.

Coetzee, J. M.

1988 *White Writing: On the Culture of Letters in South Africa.* New Haven: Yale University Press.

Comaroff, Jean

1985 *Body of Power, Spirit of Resistance.* Chicago: University of Chicago Press.

Davis, Geoffrey

1994 "I Speak as a Woman Person: Geoffrey Davis Interviews Emma Mashinini." In Anna Rutherford, Lars Jensen and Shirley Chew, eds., *Into the Nineties: Post-Colonial Women's Writing,* 579-97. Mundelstrup: Dangaroo Press.

Daymond, M. J., ed.

1996 *South African Feminisms: Writing, Theory and Criticism 1990-1994.* New York and London: Garland.

1992 "Some Thoughts on South Africa, 1992: Interview with Lauretta Ngcobo." *Current Writing* 4, 1:85-97.

Escobar, A.

1984-85 "Discourse and Power in Development: Michel Foucault and the Relevance of His Work to the Third World." *Alternatives* 10, 3:377-400.

Farred, Grant

1993 "'Not Like Women at All': Black Female Subjectivity in Lauretta Ngcobo's *And They Didn't Die.*" *Genders* 16:94-112.

Fanon, Frantz

1967 *Toward the African Revolution.* Translated by Haakon Chevalier. New York: Grove Press.

Gates, Henry Louis, Jr., ed.

1984 *Black Literature and Literary Theory.* New York: Methuen.

Gordimer, Nadine

1982 *July's People.* London: Penguin, 1982. Originally published in 1981.

Hansson, Desiree

1991 "Working against Violence against Women." In Susan Bazilli, ed., *Putting Women on the Agenda,* 180-93. Johannesburg: Ravan Press.

Head, Bessie

1977 *The Collector of Treasures.* London: Heinemann.

Hunter, Eva

1994 "'We Have to Defend Ourselves': Women, Tradition and Change in Lauretta Ngcobo's *And They Didn't Die.*" *Tulsa Studies in Women's Literature* 13, 1 (Spring) :113-26.

Hunter, Eva, and Craig Mackenzie, eds.

1993 "Lauretta Ngcobo" (1980 interview). In *Between the Lines II,* 97-116. Interviews with Nadine Gordimer, Menan du Plessis, Zoe Wicomb, Lauretta Ngcobo. Grahamstown: NELM.

Jochelson, Karen

1995 "Women, Migrancy and Morality: A Problem of Perspective." *Journal of Southern African Studies* 21, 2:323-32.

Johnson, Barbara

1984 "Metaphor, Metonymy and Voice in *Their Eyes Were Watching God.*" In Henry Louis Gates, Jr., ed., *Black Literature and Literary Theory,* 205-19. New York: Methuen.

Lodge, Tom

1983 *Black Politics in South Africa since 1945.* Harlow: Longman.

Marchand, Marianne H., and Jane L. Parpart, eds.

1995 *Feminism, Postmodernism, Development.* London: Routledge.

Millin, S. G.

1986 *God's Stepchildren.* Johannesburg: Ad. Donker. Originally published in 1914.

Mzamane, Mbulelo

1985 "Sharpeville and Its Aftermath: The Novels of Richard Rive, Peter Abrahams, Alex la Guma and Lauretta Ngcobo." *Ariel* 16, 2:31-44.

Mvula, Kefiloe Tryphina

1988 "The Naked Night." In *Women in South Africa: From the Heart—An Anthology,* 45-51. Johannesburg: seriti sa sechaba.

Ndebele, Njabulo

1994 "Liberation and the Crisis of Culture." In Elleke Boehmer, Laura Chrisman and Kenneth Parker, eds., *Altered State? Writing and South Africa,* 1-9. Mundelstrup: Dangaroo Press.

Ngcobo, Lauretta

1981 *Cross of Gold.* London: Longmans.

1986 "The African Woman Writer" and "My Life and My Writing." In Kirsten Holst Petersen and Anna Rutherford, eds., *A Double Colonization: Colonial and Post-Colonial Women's Writing,* 81-82 and 83-86. Mundelstrup: Dangaroo Press.

1989 Introduction to *Footprints in the Quag: Stories and Dialogues from Soweto.* Cape Town: David Philip.

1991 "A Black South African Woman Writing Long after Schreiner." In Itala Vivan, ed., *The Flawed Diamond: Essays on Olive Schreiner,* 189-99. Mundelstrup: Dangaroo Press.

1991 *And They Didn't Die.* New York: George Braziller.

1994 "Now That We're Free." In Anna Rutherford, Lars Jensen and Shirley Chew, eds., *Into the Nineties: Post-Colonial Women's Writing,* 568-70. Mundelstrup: Dangaroo Press.

Nhlapo, Thandabantu

1991 "Women's Rights and the Family in Traditional and Customary Law." In Susan Bazilli, ed., *Putting Women on the Agenda,* 111-23. Johannesburg: Ravan Press.

Parry, Benita

1994 "Some Provisional Speculations on the Critique of 'Resistance' Literature." In Elleke Boehmer, Laura Chrisman and Kenneth Parker, eds., *Altered State? Writing and South Africa,* 11-24. Mundelstrup: Dangaroo Press.

Paton, Alan

1948 *Cry, the Beloved Country.* New York: Charles Scribner's.

Pechey, Graham

1994 "'Cultural Struggle' and the Narratives of South African Freedom." In Elleke Boehmer, Laura Chrisman and Kenneth Parker, eds., *Altered State? Writing and South Africa,* 25-35. Mundelstrup: Dangaroo Press.

Plaatje, Sol T.

1957 *Mhudi.* Lovedale: Lovedale Press. Originally published in 1930.

Qakisa, Mpine

1988 "Storm on the Minedumps." In *Women in South Africa: From the Heart—An Anthology,* 154-60. Johannesburg: seriti sa sechaba.

Ramphele, Mamphela, with Chris McDowell

1991 *Restoring the Land: Environment and Change in Post-Apartheid South Africa.* London: Panos.

Rutherford, Anna, Lars Jensen and Shirley Chew, eds.

1994 *Into the Nineties: Post-Colonial Women's Writing.* Mundelstrup: Dangaroo Press.

Said, Edward

1993 *Culture and Imperialism.* New York: Knopf.

Schreiner, Olive

1985 *From Man to Man.* London: Virago. Originally published in 1926.

Tlali, Miriam

1989 *Footprints in the Quag: Stories and Dialogues from Soweto.* Cape Town: David Philip.

Udayagiri, Mridula

1995 "Challenging Modernization: Gender and Development, Postmodern Feminism and Activism." In Marianne H. Marchand and Jane L. Parpart, eds., *Feminism, Postmodernism, Development,* 159-77. London: Routledge.

Vivan, Itala, ed.

1989 *The Flawed Diamond: Essays on Olive Schreiner.* Mundelstrup: Dangaroo Press.

Walker, Cherryl

1982 *Women and Resistance in South Africa.* London: Onyx Press.

Wicomb, Zoe

1994 "Why I Write" and "Comment on Return to South Africa." In Anna Rutherford, Lars Jensen and Shirley Chew, eds., *Into the Nineties: Post-Colonial Women's Writing,* 573-76. Mundelstrup: Dangaroo Press.

1992 "Nation, Race and Ethnicity: Beyond the Legacy of Victims." *Current Writing* 4:15-20.

Williams, Raymond

1970 *The English Novel from Dickens to Lawrence.* New York: Oxford University Press.

Willis, Susan

1984 "Eruptions of Funk: Historicizing Toni Morrison." In Henry Louis Gates, Jr., ed., *Black Literature and Literary Theory,* 263-83. New York: Methuen.

Worsfold, Brian

1994 "Black South African Countrywomen in Lauretta Ngcobo's Long Prose Works." In Elleke Boehmer, Laura Chrisman and Kenneth Parker, eds., *Altered State? Writing and South Africa,* 111-19. Mundelstrup: Dangaroo Press.

Stacey M. Floyd-Thomas and Laura Gillman (essay date May 2002)

SOURCE: Floyd-Thomas, Stacey M., and Laura Gillman. "Subverting Forced Identities, Violent Acts, and the Narrativity of Race: A Diasporic Analysis of Black Women's Radical Subjectivity in Three Novel Acts." *Journal of Black Studies* 32, no. 5 (May 2002): 528-56.

[*In the essay below, Floyd-Thomas and Gillman offer a detailed analysis of the development of radical subjectivity among the black female characters of three novels: Alice Walker's* The Color Purple, *Michelle Cliff's* No Telephone to Heaven, *and Ngcobo's* And They Didn't Die.]

> We return to "identity" and "culture" for relocation, linked to political practice—identity that is not informed by a narrow cultural nationalism masking continued fascination with the power of the white hegemonic other. Instead identity is evoked as a stage in a process wherein one constructs radical black subjectivity. Recent critical reflections on static notions of black identity urge transformation of our sense of who we can be and still be black. Assimilation, imitation, or assuming the role of rebellious exotic other are not the only available options and never have been. This is why it is crucial to radically revise notions of identity politics, to explore marginal locations as spaces where we can best become whatever we want to be while remaining committed to liberatory black liberation struggle.
>
> —bell hooks (1990, p. 20)

This article aims to explore the making of Black women's radical subjectivity as it is interrogated in Black women's writings. It further examines how Black women through their "fictions" imagine and create a space for both the subversion of oppressive sociopolitical structures and the possibility for liberatory self-determination. Black women's radical subjectivity shatters the boundaries of geopolitical spaces that traditionally have been defined through citizenship and creates alternative social imaginaries that represent a space where home and belongingness may be attained and self-determination realized. It is from the examination of Black women's textualities that we can detect this upheaval of nation-state racial formations that subverts the policing power of the state to force and essentialize racial identities. In this article, we trace the process of subverting forced identities, violent acts, and the narrativity of race. We analyze the lives, the movements, and the actions of the Black female protagonists from three geopolitical contexts as portrayed in the following novels: African American author Alice Walker's (1982) *The Color Purple,* Caribbean author Michelle Cliff's (1987) *No Telephone to Heaven,* and South African author Lauretta Ngcobo's (1999) ***And They Didn't Die.*** In what follows, and before engaging further in a theoretical articulation and analysis, we provide a summary of these novels.

SUMMARY OF THE NOVELS

THE COLOR PURPLE

The Color Purple (Walker, 1982) traces the liberation of the African American woman and her reality during the post-reconstruction Jim and Jane Crow South. It represents a reclaiming of a past that articulates at once a personal and historical transition for the Black woman and her community. As a way to establish intimacy between women, Walker uses an epistolary structure laced with diaries, letters, and prayers as forms of female expression.

The novel principally centers on the liberatory struggles of four Black women. The narrative voice is spoken through the voice of Celie, who writes letters to God and later her sister Nettie. This is the only way that she can share her secrets: being raped by her father, watching her mother's death without being able to tell her of her victimization, protecting her sister from incest and rape, and bearing the brunt of everyone's contempt and pity, most particularly Pa's and her new husband's, Mr. __, who saw her as no more than a beast of burden. Walker's second character, Shug Avery, is a prodigal daughter who gets thrown out of her Baptist minister father's home for bringing shame to her family. She is a juke-joint singer whose claim to fame is not just her voice but her profane reputation, one that is saturated in good times, lovers, and luxury. Sofia, the novel's third character, enters as the "amazon" woman who is fiery and self-directed. Strong-willed and independent, she fights with and eventually leaves her husband Harpo, curses the mayor's wife, and confronts Celie when Celie turns against her. Nettie is Celie's confident sister who, thanks only to Celie's sacrifices, is able to complete some basic studies and eventually escape from the incestual threat of Pa and the seemingly inevitable rape of Mr. __ . Never forgetting the debt that she feels compelled to repay to her sister, Nettie becomes employed by a missionary and his wife to serve as a nanny to their children, who are later discovered to be Celie's. During the more than 20-year separation of these two sisters, Nettie remains a source of love and support either through Celie's memory of her or her letters. The novel retraces the interconnecting lives of these four women as each evolves from victim-survivor into a self-actualized woman.

NO TELEPHONE TO HEAVEN

No Telephone to Heaven (Cliff, 1987) is a coming-of-age novel set in neocolonialist Jamaica. The female protagonist, Clare Savage, undergoes several rites of passage in her quest for personal integrity as she confronts racial politics, stereotypes, and myths embedded within the cultures she travels among and between—Jamaica, Britain, and the United States. In the course of the novel, Cliff traces the ongoing identity crises facing this migrating Jamaican, light-skinned girl. The novel charts Clare's travels to New York with her family, to

England for her university education, around Europe with a lover, and her eventual return to Jamaica where she becomes a cultural-nationalist revolutionary. The novel weaves back and forth from the beginning of Clare's life as an unwitting Jamaican girl who eventually learns the ways in which she has been appropriated and defined as "other." This sociopolitical coming-of-age process culminates in her participation in an armed guerrilla group and an early and tragic demise.

AND THEY DIDN'T DIE

And They Didn't Die (Ngcobo, 1999) is a fictional account of the effects of the 1913 and subsequent Land Acts in Apartheid South Africa. Set in the Sabelweni valley, it spans the late 1950s to the 1980s. It pays homage to the women of rural KawaZulu-Natal who struggle to retain control of their land and preserve their families while their husbands are carried miles away to the city of Durban. Under the Apartheid regime, the Zulu women merely have a reproductive function: to produce migrant labor. At the same time, with their husbands absent, it also becomes incumbent on them to tend the land and the livestock. The untold story that Ngcobo exposes is this traditional culture's relentless suffering in the face of the Apartheid state's determination to destroy their lifestyle, culture, and families. Ngcobo portrays Jezile Majola's struggle against two interacting forms of power that control her and the other Zulu women of Sigageni: the Apartheid state on the one hand and the traditional Zulu culture on the other. The story traces Jezile's process of political consciousness as she strives to preserve her family's survival.

OBJECTIVES

By bringing these three novels into intertextual dialogue with one another, we conceive a Diasporic political site that does the following: (a) reveals a common location in consciousness that is not geographically bound and (b) evokes analogous liberatory processes undertaken by Black women and their communities throughout the African Diaspora. One may wonder why Black women's writings should be privileged for the enacting of radical Black subjectivity and the imagining of a Black Diasporic political site. We contend that Black women's literary tradition is a primary repository of the Black communal experience because it is bound to the origins of Black people and their historical context of struggle within specific locations, times, and experiences. Black women writers who engage in literary compositions hold themselves accountable not to their individual whims or personalized localized consciousnesses but rather to the collective values of Black history and culture (Cannon, 1988). The identity formation of the Diasporic imagined community is constituted at the crossroads of each society's everyday material life as it is lived and transformed through individual and collective memory and rememory, chronicled in the canon of Black women's writings (Brah, 1996).

When taking their writings into account collectively, Black women's textualities, we are proposing, should be read as a "series of boundary crossings and not as a fixed geographical, ethnically, or nationally bound category of writing" (Boyce Davies, 1994, p. 4). Therefore, together the writings of these three authors offer us a snapshot of a Black Diasporic political site. In this site, Black people redefine identity away from exclusion and marginality as they reconnect to and remember Black experiences that are otherwise dislocated and sequestered by the geopolitics of nation, space, and time.

As we forge these new Diasporic constellations, it is important also to take into consideration not just the common experiences of oppression among Black peoples but also the historically variable forms of relationality among Black peoples within and between Diasporic formations. Upon studying the intersections of specific spaces, nations, and historical contexts, we want to do a faithful rendering of how each community and the individuals within them are inserted into their own particular sociopolitical context and set of social relations (e.g., the interlocking systems of class, culture, ethnicity, and gender). In analyzing narrativities of race, it is important to take note of both the diversity of experiences as well as the common components of Black struggle. Herein, we may analytically conceptualize a confluent narrativity of race from which emerges a Diasporic community unified in struggle without falling into overgeneralizations that discount the diverse experiences of each Black culture's realities (Brah, 1996). If we were not to take into account the diversity of Black culture, we would be identifying with hegemony.

Indeed, so much of what Blackness is has been described through a hegemonic view so that it still becomes mandatory to articulate a subjective understanding of what Blackness is through the lens of those marginalized voices who embody it. By using the terms *Black* and *Blackness,* we are not upholding or espousing a politicized agenda of pan-Africanism, negritude, or Afrocentrism per se. Rather, our intentionality in referring to these groups of African-descended peoples is merely to address the diverse realities of people within certain social locations in the legacy of colonization. Therefore, *Blackness* is relationally and provisionally used herein to describe Black people's plight in the face of the White supremacist agenda of colonization. As Carol Boyce Davies (1994) stated, *Black* should be provisionally used in the ongoing search to find the language to articulate the experiences of Black peoples' encounters with overwhelming Whiteness and Eurocentricity.

The validity of this linguistic project of naming stems from the power that we give language to make visible and demystify the unmarked yet historical legacy of pervasive White racism throughout the Black Diaspora. That having been said, if we were to see Blackness solely as an identity marker articulated by the colonialist agenda, we would interfere with subjective Black identity formation and thus would erase, ignore, or speak for the ways in which Black people have fomented countercultures separate and apart from the gaze of hegemonic normativity. It is in this counter-hegemonic marginal space that radical Black subjectivity can be seen rather than overseen by an authoritative nation-state that claims to know Black people better than Black people know themselves (hooks, 1990). In other words, it is only through bringing to the center voices that are otherwise marginalized that we can grasp radical Black subjectivity and its identity formation separate and apart from the term *Black* as generically applied to African descendants. This ability to locate Black subjectivity as it exists in multiple and diverse locations helps us to see the inner workings of how Black consciousness can traverse imposed boundaries instituted to keep margins contained and alliances from being formed. It is with this conscientization that we take Black women's subjective experiences as a departure point for our analysis, as illustrated in the aforementioned novels.

GENERATIVE THEMES AND LITERARY ILLUSTRATIONS

The task of grasping radical Black subjectivity as an imaginary Diasporic political site is to understand as central the struggle of Black women who have wrested their identity from the strongholds of hegemonic normativity as revealed in the lives of the protagonists. These acts and the problems they pose for Black women within the Diaspora culminate in the following three themes: the problem of identity, the problem of the maternal/home, and the novel acts that subvert such problems, namely, speaking truth to power.

THE PROBLEM OF IDENTITY

The problem of identity is the problem of seeing oneself through the eyes of the other. W. E. B. DuBois (1903/1982) tackled the notion of seeing and being seen as a dialectic that makes the Black individual self-conscious about her existence within a White supremacist hegemonic order. He referred to a cultural experience where Black self-definition is not possible in the face of colonization, but rather one understands herself through a dialectical account of being Black and citizen. DuBois's illustration of this experience is haunting. He stated that the Black individual has

> a peculiar sensation, the double-consciousness, the sense of always looking at oneself through the eyes of the other, of measuring one's soul by the tape of a world that looks on in amused contempt and pity. One ever feels [this] twoness . . . two souls, two thoughts, two unreconciled strivings; two warring ideals in one dark body, whose dogged strength alone keeps it from being torn asunder.
>
> (pp. 8-9)

This dialectical understanding of identity has become the standardized matrix through which Black people's understanding of self has become crystallized in the

minds of society (Anderson, 1995). We contend that to foment radical Black subjectivity within a Diasporic community, we must move beyond this legacy of ontological Blackness, the Blackness that Whiteness created.

These novelists move beyond ontological Blackness by representing radical Black subjectivity as an identity politics that is a process of self-discovery and actualization rather than a static reified artifact. The essential attributes that come from the experiences of Black people as a group, these novels show, can be used progressively within that group for the goal of empowerment independently from views taken outside of that group. In reshifting the ontology of Blackness from one exclusively delimited by dialectical entrapment to one that embraces a range of responses leading from self-hatred to self-actualization, the novelists elaborate several subthemes posed by the problem of identity. The subthemes include internalized oppression in the forms of horizontal violence and intraracial prejudice and the protagonists' acts of radical Black subjectivity that subvert such problems.

HORIZONTAL VIOLENCE

When we think about violence, we primarily focus on control and domination from an outside force (whether it be economic, social, or political) over a particular group by a superior organization of power and domination. The act of colonization, as it has had its effects on Black communities and nations throughout the world, is a key example of this. Within a colonial agenda, power is organized and violence is exercised within a system that maintains control over Black people. But it is those more internalized forms of oppression that add further injury to the acts of violence. The genius of colonization as a form of institutionalized violence is such that the architects of it no longer need to be present for its effects to take root. The very gatekeepers and attendants of colonized violence are its victims (Woodson, 1977). In this regard, Black people, through acts of horizontal violence, mediate relationships that force subjugated identities, thus preserving and perpetuating existing power relations based on racist and sexist politics.

Horizontal violence is a central theme in these three novels. Celie, the most powerless of figures in *The Color Purple* (Walker, 1982), is the one who enacts horizontal violence. Plagued with her own inability to respond to her husband Mr. __'s beatings and constant belittling, Celie reacts to her stepson Harpo's light-hearted bewilderment at his wife Sofia's strong-willed nature to do what she wants and say what she feels. When Harpo asks her what he should do to "make her mind," Celie reflects on Sofia's free-willed nature as well as Sofia's pity for Celie's compliance to Mr. __'s abuse. Celie then replies: "Beat her" (p. 43). Celie does not want to focus on how Sofia's boldness is something her husband admires still, after 3 years of marriage. Al-

120

though Celie knows that Harpo and Sofia are blissful in their relationship, what matters to her is that other women feel the pain that she feels. In this manner, Celie will be confident that her own subjugated identity is not one that she has chosen for herself but one that is forced on her. And thus by understanding her forced identity as a predetermined lot for all women, Celie takes solace in her suffering and that of other women. According to Celie's logic, Sofia's disregard for such subjugation needed to be punished because otherwise, if left unpunished, it would expose to Celie the absurdity of her complicity with her own subjugation.

In *The Color Purple* (Walker, 1982), Celie used someone else's hands to enact her horizontal violence against Sofia. In *No Telephone to Heaven* (Cliff, 1987), Christopher, an orphaned house laborer for a Jamaican upperclass family, uses his own agency to carry out horizontal violence. He does this to exact vengeance for being forced to abide by the lowly station to which he had been assigned. Christopher seeks to find a plot in which he can bury his grandmother in order for her spirit to rest. He feels that the best source of aid in this painstaking quest is Mas' Charles, his employer, the father of Paul, his childhood friend. He goes to ask Mas' Charles and his wife if she can be buried in their family gravesite. Christopher ignores the warnings of Mavis, the maid and his lover, that it was past midnight and therefore inappropriate for him to be in the house. He enters Mas' Charles's bedroom to make a desperate midnight plea. Mas' Charles, roused from his sleep, is offended by the intrusion. With irritation and condescension, he shakes his head at Christopher's ignorance, curses him, and then orders him out of his house. Although Christopher apologizes, the man, now incited with rage against him, curses him once again. In one instant, a sudden force takes hold of Christopher. His grandmother's spirit speaks to him and through him, telling him to be "quick of hand" (Cliff, 1987, p. 47). And he kills Mas' Charles, his wife, and later their daughter with a fiery righteous indignation that he himself does not understand.

The manifestation of horizontal violence is poignantly illustrated in Christopher's most vehement and cruelest murder—that of Mavis. Realizing that he has murdered the entire family, Christopher goes to seek out his lover to absolve his action or take refuge. Instead of consoling him however, she dismisses the "lit passion" in his eyes and tells him that he had no business to be there that time of night, no business to ask for any land, no business to believe that he was owed anything (Cliff, 1987, p. 48). As Christopher tries to explain his reasoning, she insists that he remember that his obligation is to his master and that whatever he has, he owes to him. Christopher says to himself in awe, "Lord Jesus, they were dead and she was still taking care of them. In death, as in life, their faithful servant" (Cliff, 1987, p. 48). And with his machete, he maims her like an animal, slaying her worse than his masters. He kills Mavis

because even she represents for him his inability to be anything but what he is in the eyes of the other. And it was intolerable for Christopher that Mavis, his lover and his equal, would dare look on him with the same contempt and pity as his master. It is Christopher's vengeance against those trying to subjugate his identity throughout the novel that foregrounds the demise of Clare and her fellow guerrillas at the hands of their own.

In *The Color Purple* (Walker, 1982) and *No Telephone to Heaven* (Cliff, 1987), Celie and Christopher act out horizontal violence as a response to their powerlessness, thereby perpetuating the relationships of power and submission and the forced identities that ensue for both of them as well as for the victims of their actions. In **And They Didn't Die** (Ngcobo, 1999), by contrast, the most salient example among several that reflect horizontal violence can be found in the actions of Chief Siyapi, the leader and most powerful member of the Sabelweni community. His is a peculiar form of double consciousness because he is held accountable both to the Apartheid regime that recently appropriated his power and to the Zulu community that his role requires him to represent. The scene is set in the late 1950s. The Zulu women and some of their husbands are in the midst of a boycott targeted against three sets of Apartheid legislation: laws that limited the Zulu farmers' access to the land, laws designated to regulate mobility of women (social and economic) by compelling them to carry passes, and laws intended to enforce hereditary chiefs into submission by threatening those who resisted the government's instructions with exile that subject all chiefs to the authority and the arm of the Apartheid regime, the Bantu Affairs Department (BAD).

Chief Siyapi's acts of horizontal violence are made apparent as his role changes from being the chief of the Zulu people to the instrument of the Apartheid state that annihilates the Zulu community. As his new role develops, his illusory power ultimately leads to his demise and the near demise of his people. The chief, "being anxious to demonstrate his authority to both his masters and his subjects," does double-dealing whereby he acts as informant to the BAD authorities in the Zulu peasants' political meetings by trying to find out what the pulse and plans were of the boycott (Ngcobo, 1999, p. 173). When it is time to actually appear at the most pressing planning meeting concerning the boycott, he does not show up, in fear that his power will be compromised. He reneges because he knows that his constituents were not going to falter in their plans. The crowd, realizing that Siyapi is not going to show up, started shrieking with rage. The voices of furious women and their husbands rang out: "Down with Siyapi, down with the traitor, down with the white man's stooge!" (p. 173). With anger burning in their hearts and minds, they move quickly to his mansion on the hill and satiate the flames of fiery anger that is in their hearts by burning his home, his livestock, and his family within it. And Jezile, who felt dirty although she had not participated in the flaming and burning of yet another temple, "shut her eyes tight in an effort to banish the thought of God standing there watching" (p. 174). She wonders

> God, how to get clean, how to clean the world, how to clean Sabelweni again? How to get rid of the government that poisoned the leaders, and now their people—was there nothing that was not tainted by the evil policies of the government?
>
> (p. 174)

The tragic irony of horizontal violence, as Celie, Sofia, Mavis, and Jezile's stories bring out so well, is that the forces of power from an external force are not reflected on but become internalized wherein victims become co-conspirators with their oppressors in regulating and oftentimes obliterating their own way of life. Moreover, the profound reality of horizontal violence as tragic irony is that although aware of the hypocrisy and self-destruction that they are a part of directly or by extension, these characters feel powerless in the face of such a pervasive force. In all of the examples noted earlier, these acts of horizontal violence are not random but rather culturally produced ones in which the perpetrators are brought to a double consciousness of being aligned with their oppressor or aligned with the oppressed. In this manner, these characters carry out novel yet clearly recognizable acts against those who make salient to them their forced identities.

INTRARACIAL PREJUDICE

Intraracial prejudice is the second and probably most insidious form of internalized oppression. This form of oppression highlights the ways in which pigmentocracy and colorism impact Black identity formation. Intraracial prejudice operates through a matrix of attitudes about the role in which color not character, degrees of likeness not personality, and complexion not inner spirit dictate human worth. As many scholars and cultural critics have noted, the quiet taboo of colorism and the identity complex it poses to Black individuals and communities continue to plague Black peoples' psyche and social behavior (Russell, Wilson, & Hall, 1993). An exploration of intraracial prejudice reveals that the beliefs and actions of Black people are determined by shades of color as they relate to Black status and self-worth. Thus, it is difficult to look beyond color and probe the soul of Black identity. These three novels illustrate how color matters in terms of forcing hierarchicalized identities across the Black Diaspora. Within the colonialist and neocolonialist contexts, the valuing of lightness over darkness within the Black community is the internalized manifestation of racism based on skin color found in authoritarian racist regimes. This is often articulated in the Black folk expression: "If you're light, you're right, if you're brown stick around, if you're Black, get back."

In *The Color Purple,* we can note the shades of oppression as they exist along the color line within the lives of Walker's (1982) female characters. The notion of a Black woman's attractiveness and beauty is strikingly illustrated when Harpo talks to Celie about his admiration of Sofia: "She pretty he tell me. Bright." As a point of clarification, Celie replies: "Smart?" Harpo replies: "Naw. Bright *skin*. She smart too I think" (p. 37). As further evidence of the ways in which beauty is seen along color lines, old Mr. __, Mr.__'s father, bewildered by his son's attraction to Shug Avery, scolds him by saying, "Just what is it about this Shug Avery anyway, he say. She Black as tar, she nappy-headed. She got legs like baseball bats" (p. 58). Whereas Sofia is celebrated as a beautiful woman because of her light skin, Shug is ridiculed for having physical characteristics that are attributed to Black women at large. In these two examples, we can clearly see the ways in which Black people have absorbed the aesthetic preferences of the hegemonic culture to the detriment of the community at large.

In *No Telephone to Heaven* (Cliff, 1987), we see another effect of intraracial prejudice as it confers not beauty but rather social acceptance and personal safety. As the Savage family migrates from Jamaica to New York, they stop in a Southern town in Georgia to look for lodging. Boy Savage, Clare's father, leaves his family in the car and enters the motel office to check in. Immediately upon seeing him, the White motel keeper asks Boy where he comes from: "His tone suggested challenge, rather than mere curiosity—concerned, no doubt, about the stranger's apricot color, which Boy would have explained as a suntan, given the chance—and the unfamiliar cadence of his voice." Boy replies that they had recently arrived from Jamaica "in his most, Jesuit-educated manner." Pressed by the motel keeper on whether or not he was colored, Boy acts confused about the query and asks for clarity. Frustrated by Boy's evasiveness, the motel keeper replies, "Niggers! . . . Because if you're niggers you can't stay here. You ain't welcome. It ain't legal. . . . It don't matter where you come from." Boy, the "bluefoot" replies, "we're not . . . ah, what you said." And he was "glad that the Black car with the slightly darker wife and mango and guava daughters was parked out of sight" (p. 55). The innkeeper had a great suspicion because Boy had not used the N word, and he further baited his perspective guest.

> He cast his trained eye across the stranger's face. Thin lips—but dark curly hair. Large nose—but no tinge to the voice. Colored skin—but a manner that was quite white. If this was a Negro, he had never encountered one of his ilk before. . . . What should I say to this man? Boy wondered. A lesson from the third form on the history of Jamaica sprang to mind: Mulatto, offspring of African and white; sambo, offspring of African and mulatto; quadroon, offspring of mulatto and white; mestee, offspring of quadroon and white; mestefeena, offspring of mestee and white. Am I re-

membering it right? he asked himself. These Aristotelian categories taught by a Jesuit determined they should know who they were—and fortunate at that. In the Spanish colonies, there were 128 categories to be memorized. The class of multicolored boys rose and recited in unison.

(p. 56)

After reflecting on his memories of caste stratifications, Boy assures the motel keeper that he is of the right ilk by replying: "I am a white man. My ancestors owned sugar plantations" (Cliff, 1987, p. 57). He does not mention that he was a descendent of slaves, of course, and probably a product of miscegenation. The innkeeper, still hesitant and distracted by the skin tone of Boy, welcomes him to Georgia and the Red Clay Motel by giving him the key. After entertaining the option that was available to the lightest of light-skinned Blacks, Boy decides to pass for White to attain the social and economic mobility and access that he was seeking. Boy realizes that color is the only door of opportunity available for him to realize his hope of a more economically thriving life for himself and his family. Ironically, however, as he further delves into the lie that passing presupposes in one's everyday life, he removes himself not only from his cultural identity but also from family and friends who could in any way expose the White mask that he was wearing. Such a situation leads, ultimately, to the separation of the family along color lines. His darker wife and darker still daughter return to Jamaica. The mother, submitting to the hierarchy that the husband has created, leaves Clare, the lighter skinned, to tend to the father and takes the daughter that favors her back to Jamaica, never to return. This notion of imposable Blackness and honorary Whiteness based on the color line is posed as the quintessential coming-of-age experience for Clare, one that shatters any hope of ever creating an identity separate and apart from her color. She comes to assume a "White" identity during her adolescence that has not only been forced on her by society but reinforced to her by her father as well.

The problem of intraracial prejudice becomes even more glaring when double consciousness becomes physically embodied because one parent is Black and the other is White. Such is the case of Jezile's son, Lungu, who is the product of Jezile's rape at the hands of her White employer. Jezile is victimized a first time by her White employer through the rape and then is victimized a second time when he fires her because it is illegal for her to give birth to a White child. Upon her return to her community, she is victimized for a third time. She is met not with understanding and empathy but rather is treated disdainfully and ultimately excommunicated from the village of not only her husband's family but of her maternal family as well. She finally endures the cruelest punishment when her husband's family takes her other children away from her because she is now perceived as an unfit mother.

Alone now with Lungu, Jezile triumphs over the hate inflicted on her by both the White and Black communities, the oppressors and the oppressed alike. She refuses to have her child internalize the community's hatred by accepting an identity that is forced on him. In the face of this hostility,

Jezile's white child grew bigger every day. . . . His skin remained remarkably white, in spite of the long days in the sun, and his eyes were grey. His hair, though short and African in texture, was blond. He had his mother's full sensuous lips and like her, he was steady and deliberate in everything he did. (Ngcobo, 1999, pp. 222-223)

[Jezile] squandered all her love on him. She felt deeply for the child and often had wondered how he would bear the burden of his life. He was caught between two warring worlds.

(p. 228)

The subthemes of horizontal violence and intraracial prejudice make explicit the ways in which Blackness is created and identities are forced on Black people, making self-determination seemingly impossible. Internalized oppression is mediated through acts of horizontal violence and intraracial prejudice wherein Black people themselves perpetuate their own subjugated identities as a compensatory act: to survive the powerless situation that they perceive themselves to be in inasmuch as they can only see themselves in the eyes of the other. In such efforts to survive, the result proves ultimately to run counter to their efforts, leading often to the destruction of self-reflection and communal empowerment. In the next two sections, we will see how the female protagonists subvert forced identities as they create a radical Black subjectivity of their own.

THE PROBLEM OF THE MATERNAL/HOME

Much of the problem of identity is further elucidated when we look at the ways in which the maternal impacts the definition of home and motherland within specific cultural contexts. We find these definitions in identity narratives such as the novels we are analyzing herein. Identity narratives are literary expressions of specific forms of cultural representations of both individual and collective identities that constitute commonalities and differences between self and others. A special feature focuses on the reinvention or reinstating of tradition as a means to thwart cultural amnesia. Here, the motif of home—including relations between mothers and children in the family—is crucial. Moreover, it is significant to note that there is a close relationship between identity narratives and familial processes. Identity narratives that focus on the maternal role make explicit the ways in which the mother figure cultivates a sociopolitical disposition within the family as a means to support or transform the power structures of society. The maternal can thus be so influential as to even transform history and reorganize present human groups.

Thus, the maternal as an identity narrative can alter cultures both past and present in order to usher forth new interpretations of home and motherland (Yuval-Davis, 1997).

Understanding Black women's identity narratives entails gauging the frequency with which Black women use these themes of the maternal to articulate their remembering of home in the formation of their subjective identity. Identity narratives, as they are elaborated in Black women's writings, deal with becoming, which is primarily linked to the source of home and mother. In these iconographies of radical Black subjectivity, images of mothers and home conventionally suggest one's origins: birth—the start of one's being, hearth—the context of one's nurturing, and roots—the geographical and genealogical legacy that links an individual to people and places (Nasta, 1992).

Whereas internalized oppression, horizontal violence, and intraracial prejudice constitute the colonialist and neocolonialist legacy that perpetuates Black women's subordination and disempowerment, it is possible nonetheless to subvert such devastating social effects. The female characters in their memories and remembering of the maternal/home enact a series of strategies that allow them to move beyond such a legacy toward personal and collective empowerment. We define the maternal/home as self-love, communal support, and solidarity. In an effort to remember home, the authors of these novels create a sociopolitical testimony of what it means to be motherless and homeless. In all three novels, each female protagonist's self-empowerment is directly related to her ability or inability to mother or be mothered and to having a home as a context in which such a sacred process can take root. Initially, what we bear witness to is the disruption that occurs in the identity formation of these female characters at the hands of patriarchal forces that have permeated the sacredness of the maternal home.

The processes by which the female characters of the respective novels try to claim their mothering roles or actual ties with their mother are ones in which the mother that they want to be is bound to the redeeming of their lost mothers and motherlands. The role of the mother in the context of the home is linked to cultural traditions and expectations of competing societies: the colonizer's and the colonized. To make recognizable the contribution of rural women to the resistance struggles of the Apartheid regime, Ngcobo (1999) situated her narrative in a complex relationship not only to the colonialist regime but also to the traditions of African culture in which Jezile and her family must live. The colonialist culture's demand for cheap labor and the racism that it perpetuates on the one hand and the traditions of African culture as a means to undermine that hegemonic order on the other were equally scrutinized by Ngcobo. This author highlighted the ways in which both the prescriptions of a racist Apartheid regime and the tradi-

tional patriarchal culture come into conflict with the emancipatory struggle of these Zulu women.

Jezile's life is testimony to this type of conflict. As a prospective mother, she is torn between abiding by the values of Zulu culture governing women (that demand that she bear children) and the migratory practices set up by the Apartheid regime (that forbid her to be with her husband). Trying to reconcile or escape these contradictions further exacerbates Jezile's plight. As she tries to secure a pass to Durban (an identity document through which White authority controls the movements of Black people) to conceive a child with her husband, she finds herself "trapped between the impositions of customary law, state law, and migratory practices" (Ngcobo, 1999, p. 40). Here, Jezile reflects on her effort to conceive as an act of betrayal against her own people. Her determination to visit her husband has led her not only to succumb to Apartheid impositions but also to defy the cultural covenants made with the Zulu women of Sigageni, who had made a pact to refuse to accept the passes forced on them as a means of social and political control.

Although the control of mobility exercised by the Apartheid regime creates a roadblock for Jezile's realization to become a mother, it is within her own culture that her identity as a mother is defined and controlled. This is most evident as we see her try to create an identity for herself separate and apart from the scrutiny of her every movement by her mother-in-law, MaBiyela. In the Zulu culture, the fulfillment of a woman's life depends solely on her success as a mother. Every woman was born "to be a mother; every girl was born to be a mother" (Ngcobo, 1999, p. 55). Throughout Jezile's childhood, she "trained hard for the role" (p. 55). This posed great hardship in imagining a sense of home for Jezile:

> What was difficult to understand was that despite the formidable position of power that being a mother implied, in reality, young mothers were truly powerless. Being a mother did not put a woman centrally at the home. . . . She could decide nothing about her life; where to live, where to go, with whom and when. Her position of power as a mother could only be exercised from the outside. Essentially, she was in a permanent state of dependency and estrangement.
>
> (p. 55)

This outside force and feeling of alienation for Jezile, and for all Zulu women, was her mother-in-law. It was only when she could go to her mother's home that Jezile could be herself, not her father's child or her child's mother. She could eat the foods she wanted to, she could walk with her head uncovered, and laugh loudly. Such was the extent to which Jezile was controlled by MaBiyela, the mother that matters most. She was controlled to such an extent that whether or not her husband was present, it was MaBiyela's dictates that governed her identity.

Once excommunicated from the home of the mother that matters most because of a pregnancy that resulted from the rape of her White employer, Jezile is finally free to be the mother she wants to be. In this act of becoming, she is now also able to remember home. Although the Majolas take away from her the two Majola children, S'naye and Ndondo, Jezile transcends the tragedy in order to make possible a freer role for herself as mother and a better home for Lungu, the only child that she can mother. She knew that the rift with the family and the cause of his birth would certainly make his burden heavier by having to negotiate two warring worlds. She attempted to ameliorate that burden:

> She sought to cushion that discovery with love, for there was no doubt that his little life, in spite of its innocence, bore the responsibility for the great pain that the family had suffered. Jezile was determined that she would teach him the importance of justice as a virtue, for he was one of those whose own life had known no justice.
>
> (Ngcobo, 1999, p. 228)

Life at their new exilic home at Luve allowed Jezile to remember home for herself and her son. It is not the home of her mother where they could be carefree and happy, and neither is it the one governed by the unyielding dictates of the Majola family. Rather, it is a home steeped in the reality of the pain that Jezile and her son face at the hands of their multiple oppressors mingled with the home that they hope for in the name of justice.

Here at the new home, Jezile envisions a new maternal role and Lungu's obligation to fight for the life they wanted:

> Life at Luve was a training ground for that fight for justice, for even before the dawn of understanding [Lungu] felt it as he played with the other children in the absence of the father, in the lonely struggles of his mother. . . . He soon learned that by virtue of his birth, he had been disinherited from all sources of power—the white world, and his place in the African male structure. This soon opened his eyes to the needs of others who were oppressed by power.
>
> (Ngcobo, 1999, p. 228)

The only "home" that Celie ever knew and recorded in her letters to God was one in which she experienced both maternal loss and the imposition on her of the role of the substitute mother. She is motherless and homeless, unable to undergo a typical process of development through nurturing. When her mother becomes ill and is no longer able to fulfill the sexual needs of her husband, Pa turns to Celie to serve as her mother's surrogate. It also falls on Celie to cook, keep the house, and mind the children. Celie recounts that in the midst of this changing of roles, her mother becomes angry with her, noting her pregnancies, and interrogates her about the identity of the father. Celie replies that the father is God. Celie knows that the incestuous truth about her father's children would kill her mother, whether by her own inability to do anything about it or her inability to live with it. Pa, moreover, silences her with this very threat: "You better not never tell nobody but God. It'd kill your mammy" (Walker, 1982, p. 11).

The role of maternal surrogacy is linked to the understanding of home throughout this novel, first as a phenomenon that evokes disempowerment, but ultimately as one that empowers. As surrogate mother to her mother's children, to Mr. __'s children, and to her sister Nettie (by protecting her from the advances of both Pa and Mr. __), Celie is stripped of her capacity to be a real mother. This is mirrored in the other female characters as well, Squeak, Sofia, and Sister Corrine. What we realize in the lives of all of the women in *The Color Purple* (Walker, 1982) is that they are all homeless and have been driven into roles of maternal surrogacy as they lived in the homes that belonged to others.

Ultimately, however, these women, through their perseverance and survival struggles, are able to remember home. After Celie's father dies, several hidden truths are revealed to her: Pa is not her biological father but her stepfather, and the home she always knew as Pa's was not his home but hers and Nettie's, left to them by their biological father and mother. Celie now realizes that she no longer has to be a homeless person, subsumed by the forced identities that others have imposed on her. She further realizes just what she had inherited from her mother's pain and her unknown father and states in her letter: "Oh, Nettie, us have a house! A house big enough for us and our children, for your husband, and Shug. Now you can come home cause you have a home to come to!" (Walker, 1982, p. 217). As Celie acquires a house, she envisions a home, a home where she and Nettie can be rejoined as mothers to their children and as mothers with a home.

Like Celie, Clare too is motherless and travels from place to place in search of a home. Clare becomes motherless when still residing in New York. She first suffers the abandonment of her mother, who decided to leave her and her father to return to Jamaica. Several years later, she suffers a permanent loss when her mother dies. Resonating with her mother's feelings of being a stranger in a foreign land, America, in spite of the years that she had resided there, Clare grows increasingly discontent with the home that her father is trying to make for her. Yearning to connect with her absent mother, Clare rereads one of the last letters from her mother before her death, in which she wrote:

> "I hope some day you make something of yourself, and some day help your people." A reminder, daughter— never forget who your people are. Your responsibilities lie beyond me, beyond yourself. There is a space between who you are and who you will become. Fill it.
>
> (Cliff, 1987, p. 103)

With each phase in Clare's life, whether it be her studies in London, her romantic interloping/friendship with Harry/Harriet, or her love affair with the Vietnam vet, Bobby, Clare always wondered if her actions "would have pleased her mother. She did not know" (Cliff, 1987, p. 117). Just as with Celie, it is her loss and her yearning that prevent her from forming a true self. Although Clare knew that her mother would be happy with her education or her seeking friends and lovers to fill the voids in her life, she also knew that her mother's words were beckoning her to right the wrongs that had been acted on her, her mother, and her motherland. All of her efforts to fulfill her mother's hope and her dreams, by extension, fail. Clare returns to the island and eventually joins a group of armed guerrillas, whose mission is to destabilize the power of the Jamaican government that is aligned with the American tourist and film industries.

She accepts her calling to be a mother warrior. Following her grandmother's death and the realization that she herself cannot have children, Clare wonders what to do with the home that she has acquired. Having no family of her own to help her remember, revive, or fill it, she opens it up to her new family, the group of fellow guerrillas. She uses it as a sanctuary from which to recreate home, in memory of her mother and a motherland free from the forces that seek their destruction. In her search to recover ties to her mother and to remember her motherland, Clare embarks on a journey that, although riddled with tribulation, eventually empowers her to be able to attain a sense of who she is and where she belongs. And with this action, she knew her mother would have been pleased.

THE NOVEL ACTS OF RADICAL BLACK SUBJECTIVITY

Once a person enacts radical Black subjectivity, her life is no longer anonymous or private. Her action of subverting oppression holds in the balance the lives of those who have endured similar oppression and is testimony of the oppression and the possibility of subverting it. She represents a courage to come forward and disclose an otherwise silent but nonetheless painful truth, a courage that allows many others to be given voice. At this point, a transformation of life comes about where the person who enacts radical Black subjectivity becomes bound up with others who she might or might not know and to whom she grows exponentially accountable. Her burden is thus converted into a blessing of advocacies for others. The enacting of subverting forced identities is the seed of radical Black subjectivity and its activism, whereby someone confronts the injustices of a system of oppression that has the power at best to circumscribe her agency and at worst to annihilate her very existence. This is a necessary action whereby Black women strive not only to survive a tragedy but also to transcend it for themselves or others. This is not an endeavor that is taken lightly, for such novel acts provoke further attacks. This becomes evident in the three novels under scrutiny.

Clare takes a brave first step in transforming her life when she confronts her father regarding his scorn toward her because she, like her mother, has refused to accept America as her home. In addition, upon her mother's death, her father feels that she has not cried for her sufficiently to please him. He scolds her:

> "You callous little bitch. I suppose you have more feeling for niggers than for your own mother." Out it slid. The fury he had been holding in him escaped—the cause of his loss. Again, he aligned his daughter with his wife, who had abandoned him to strangers, and died without a word.
>
> (Cliff, 1987, p. 104)

Furious at him and his blatant self-hatred that he wanted her to embrace, Clare looks at him defiantly and says, "My mother was a nigger." He strikes her on her face. Weeping in shock, she states with the same intent, "And so am I" (Cliff, 1987, p. 104).

Clare's radical Black subjectivity is further illustrated during her studies in art history at a London university. While in class, Clare and her classmates are distracted by a demonstration of the National Front taking place outside of their classroom window. Racial epithets are being shouted in the streets: "KAFFIRS! NIGGERS! WOGS! PAKIES! GET OUT! A banner-white bed sheet with black paint—went past. KEEP BRITAIN WHITE!" (Cliff, 1987, p. 137). Clare sat still, wishing that they would clear out. A classmate that Clare barely knows mutters towards her, "I say, those nig-nogs are a witty lot" and later refers to Idi Amin as a great ape. Clare, subtly turning to the woman, retorts: "Why don't you go fuck yourself?" and then departs (p. 138). Later, Liz, a White colleague and friend of Clare's, is wondering why Clare seems down. Having just been informed that the National Front demonstration had taken place, Liz states that she does not know why Clare would be so upset about such an event. Clare responds: I am "by blood . . . the sort they . . . were ranting about" (p. 139). Her friend assures her that her "blood has thinned, or thickened, or whatever it does . . . you know what I mean." In this incident Clare realizes again that she is not home, that she does not fit in or belong.

The two moments of insight described earlier, in which Clare acts out her conscientization, serve as the crystallizing moments that foreground her radical Black subjectivity as a guerrilla warrior. In the interrogation process with the guerrilla leaders, she must prove her worth and her loyalty to them, the mission, and the land. But more importantly, she must prove herself to her mother and finally put to rest the feelings of powerlessness that have prevented her from righting the wrongs she had faced. They question her about her motives for joining their group and what drew her to this political group. She responds that the cause of her desire to want to be a guerrilla who challenges, takes over, and reclaims her land is for "my own needs, for the most part . . . I return to this island . . . to bury . . . my mother . . . I return to this island because there is nowhere else. . . . I could live no longer in borrowed countries on borrowed time" (Cliff, 1987, pp. 192-193). Then, they press her again, probably curious about her selfish desire, and she replies: "My mother told me to help my people. At the moment this is the closest I can come" (p. 196). With this conviction, Clare sets out to free her people and herself.

Jezile's acts of radical Black subjectivity are dispersed throughout the entirety of the novel, born out of necessity. Confronting hardship after hardship at the hands of the Bantu Authority, Jezile and the Sigageni women had no fear because they were "people who owed allegiance to another order" (Ngcobo, 1999, p. 80). So they listed their grievances to the BAD forces even without fear of attacks. Grievances included: not wanting to live without their husbands in their lives; wanting the right to visit them when there was a need to do so or to live with them in the cities where they worked; demanding living wages for their free labor; demanding the need for more land to raise crops and feed their families; demanding to feed their livestock that were dying; wanting clinics for their sick children; wanting chief leadership without the influence of Bantu authorities; wanting reconciliation with those members of the community who had been moved out because they had no land for the crops; and demanding the abolishment of passes that kept them and their men enslaved (Ngcobo, 1999). These women, who had once waited for their husbands to take action or their chiefs to lead them or their mothers-in-law to advocate for them, "were making decisions and they were going to implement them. They were facing white intruders and screaming hell into their faces" (pp. 81-82).

It is this type of unwavering courage that fomented the rebellion of the Sigageni women that led to Jezile's final and most novel act. In this act, Jezile finds that her daughter is about to be raped at the hands of a White government guard. Flashing back to her own experience of being in the same compromising act that had excommunicated her from her way of life and removed her from her family at the hands of a government guard, Jezile is determined not to have the cycle of violence repeated. With no one there to take on the task of saving her daughter, "Jezile recalled in an instant her own struggle with Potgeiter [her White rapist]. And the memory stung her into action" (Ngcobo, 1999, p. 242). Jezile leaps to the knives on the table, "in an instant she had plunged the sharpest one deep into the left side of the depraved soldier" (p. 242). She had killed him. She turns to her own daughter who she has now saved from what was Jezile's own miserable plight and says: "'Look, he's dead. It was bound to happen at some time or other; we have to fight back. I couldn't let him do it to you.' . . . Something akin to peace settled on her face . . . an air of achievement about her" (p. 242).

Whereas Clare and Jezile enact their radical Black subjectivity through the committing of violent acts that result in the deaths of their enemies, Celie speaks truth to power in such a manner that transcends the violence at the moment that she informs Mr. __ that she is leaving him and going to Memphis with Shug and Mary Agnes. In avoiding violence, she thus leaves open the possibility not only for her to be saved but for her oppressor's transformation as well. Having spared Mr. __'s life on one occasion while shaving him and being saved by Shug from committing an act that would have led to the demise of oppressor and victim, Celie escapes a cycle of violence. However, it should be noted that Clare and Jezile's victims were not ones of their own community. They were White people who did not see them and their community as human or worthy of life. In the case of Celie and her efforts to bring about Black liberation, she knows that because her oppressor looks like her (and is also a victim), there might be hope for his transformation as well, or at least the chance for his life to be spared yet again.

Much like Clare's guerrilla group and Jezile's women's community, Celie's womenfolk form a community that fosters the development of radical Black subjectivity. This development is epitomized in Celie's decision to leave Mr. __. At a family gathering when all of the women are in attendance except for Nettie, who is still in Africa, Shug states that Celie is leaving Mr. __ and going home to Memphis with her. Startled and disgusted, he looks at her and says, "I thought you was finally happy. What wrong now?" And Celie replies with all of the vehemence and pride that she has never been able to express to anyone but God:

> You a low down dog is what's wrong. . . . It's time to leave you and enter into the Creation. And your dead body just the welcome mat I need. . . . You took my sister Nettie away from me . . . and she was the only person loved me in the world . . . but Nettie and my children coming home soon. . . . And when she do, all us together gon wup your ass. . . . I got children. . . . Being brought up in Africa. Good schools, lots of fresh air and exercise. Turning out a heap better than the fools you didn't even try to raise.
>
> (Walker, 1982, p. 181)

As she gets in the car to leave, Celie asks Mr. __ if she has received any more letters from Nettie. Laughingly he says he would not give them to her if they had arrived. In her departing moment from the house that was never her home and from the man who was never her husband, Celie shouts the words for the women in these novels as if expressing Jezile's outrage against the BAD authorities and as if expressing Clare's vengeance against those who had bled Jamaica, her mother, and herself:

> I curse you. . . . Until you do right by me, everything you touch will crumble. . . . Until you do right by me . . . everything you even dream about will fail. Every lick you hit me you will suffer twice. . . . The jail you plan for me is the one in which you will rot.
>
> (p. 187)

And as the car pulled off and the dust raised up from the ground, Celie explains in celebration and new-found freedom: "I'm pore, I'm Black, I may be ugly and can't cook. . . . But I'm here" (p. 187). And we all rejoice with her and all these women who found their freedom by resonating with Shug's final words: "Amen, amen" (p. 187).

CONCLUSION

Radical Black subjectivity, as illustrated in the three novel acts of Celie, Clare, and Jezile, speak poignantly to the subversive acts that have been fomented across the Black Diaspora. By bringing these three novels into intertextual dialogue with one another, we conceive a new political space in which there can be cultivated a shared political consciousness, one that is not geographically bound. This radical Black subjectivity that was once only imagined and hoped for by these three women and their female cohorts becomes real through their acts. This radical subjective space facilitates the emancipation of Black women and their communities from their diverse yet common experiences of racialized gendered oppression. In this space and through these acts, these women model strategies for subverting colonialist and neocolonialist practices. These novel acts and the women who carry them out demystify forced identities by speaking truth to power in order to foreground the ways in which Black people can implement a liberatory struggle that transcends the problems posed by forced identities.

References

Anderson, V. (1995). *Beyond ontological Blackness: An essay on African American religious and cultural criticism.* New York: Continuum.

Boyce Davies, C. (1994). *Black women, writing and identity: Migrations of the subject.* London: Routledge.

Brah, A. (1996). *Cartographies of Diaspora: Contesting identities.* London: Routledge.

Cannon, K. (1988). *Black womanist ethics.* Atlanta: Scholars Press.

Cliff, M. (1987). *No telephone to heaven.* New York: Vintage.

DuBois, W. E. B. (1982). *The souls of Black folk.* New York: New American Library. (Original work published 1903)

hooks, b. (1990). *Yearning: Race, gender and cultural politics.* Boston: South End Press.

Nasta, S. (Ed.). (1992). *Motherlands: Black women's writing from Africa, the Caribbean and South Asia.* New Brunswick, NJ: Rutgers University Press.

Ngcobo, L. (1999). *And they didn't die.* New York: Feminist Press.

Russell, K., Wilson, M., & Hall, R. (1993). *The color complex: The politics of skin color among African Americans.* New York: Doubleday.

Walker, A. (1982). *The color purple.* New York: Washington Square Press.

Woodson, C. G. (1977). *The miseducation of the Negro.* New York: AMS Press.

Yuval-Davis, N. (1997). *Gender and nation.* London: Sage.

FURTHER READING

Criticism

Hunter, Eva. "'We Have to Defend Ourselves': Women, Tradition, and Change in Lauretta Ngcobo's *And They Didn't Die*." *Tulsa Studies in Women's Literature* 13, no. 1 (spring 1994): 113-26.

Claims that *And They Didn't Die* differs from other novels by South African women writers because it utilizes Western narrative models and because it conveys a strong and outspoken statement of opposition to South African customs that repress and punish women.

Miller, Margaret. "Forms of Resistance: South African Women's Writing during Apartheid." *Hecate* 24, no. 1 (May 1998): 118-44.

Examines how several South African women writers, including Ngcobo, have depicted the activism and political resistance of black women during the apartheid era.

Additional coverage of Ngcobo's life and career is contained in the following sources published by Gale: *Contemporary Authors,* **Vol. 165; and** *Literature Resource Center.*

Ngugi wa Thiong'o
1938-

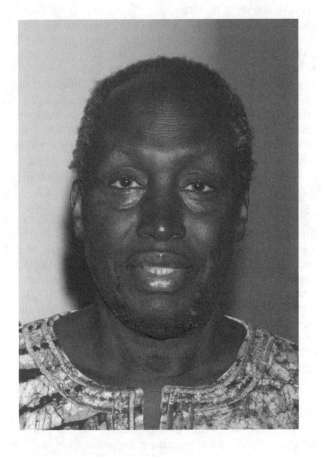

(Born James Thiong'o Ngugi; also transliterated as Ngũgĩ; also published as James T. Ngugi.) Kenyan novelist, playwright, essayist, short story writer, children's writer, and critic.

For additional information on Ngugi's career, see *Black Literature Criticism,* Ed. 1.

INTRODUCTION

Ngugi is widely regarded as one of the most significant contemporary African writers. His first novel, *Weep Not, Child* (1964), was the first English-language novel to be published by an East African and his account of Kenya's Mau Mau Emergency—an eight-year uprising by rebels against the British colonial government—in his novel *A Grain of Wheat* (1967; revised 1986) pre-

sented an African perspective on the revolt for the very first time. Additionally, Ngugi's *Caitaani Mutharabaini* (1980; *Devil on the Cross*) is the first modern novel written in Gikuyu (or Kikuyu), a Kenyan language in which the author intends to continue writing his creative works. Ngugi has also been influential in the field of education in East Africa and is recognized as a humanist who is deeply interested in the growth and well-being of his people and country.

BIOGRAPHICAL INFORMATION

Born in 1938 in Limuru, Kenya, to Ngugi to Thiong'o wa Nduucu and Wanjika wa Ngugi, Ngugi is the fifth child of the third of his father's four wives. He was one of the few students from Limuru to attend the elite Alliance High School. While at Alliance, he participated in a debate in which he contended that a Western education is harmful to African students; the headmaster subsequently counseled Ngugi against becoming a political agitator. Ngugi next attended Makerere University in Uganda and later the University of Leeds in England, where he was exposed to West-Indian-born social theorist Frantz Fanon's *The Wretched of the Earth,* a highly controversial treatise that maintains that political independence for oppressed peoples must be won—often violently—before genuine social and economic change can be achieved. Ngugi was also influenced by the writings of Karl Marx and Friedrich Engels, developing an ardent opposition to colonialism, Christianity, and other non-African elements in Kenya. During this period, he also began to write plays and novels criticizing Kenyan society and politics. In 1962 his first full-length play, *The Black Hermit,* was performed at the Uganda National Theatre. In the early 1960s he worked as a regular columnist for the *Sunday Post, Daily Nation,* and *Sunday Nation.* Ngugi wrote his first novel, *Weep Not, Child,* while he was a student at Makerere. In 1969 Ngugi—then an instructor at the University of Nairobi—and several colleagues mounted a successful campaign to transform the school's English Department into the Department of African Languages and Literature. After the publication of *A Grain of Wheat,* Ngugi rejected his Christian name, James, and began writing under the name Ngugi wa Thiong'o. He also began translating his play *The Trial of Dedan Kimathi* (1976) into Gikuyu, under the title *Mzalendo Kimathi.* Ngugi published his last English-language novel, *Petals of Blood,* in 1977.

Because of his vocal opposition to the injustice perpetrated by the postcolonial Kenyan government, Ngugi was arrested and imprisoned without charge in the

Kamoto Maximum Security Prison from 1977 to 1978. There Ngugi wrote a memoir, *Detained: A Writer's Prison Diary* (1981) and vowed to write only in the Gikuyu language. He began writing his first novel in Gikuyu, *Devil on the Cross,* on sheets of toilet paper while in prison. The group Amnesty International named Ngugi a prisoner of conscience in 1977 and he was released from prison the following year. Upon his release, Ngugi lost his position at the University of Nairobi. When his theater group was banned by Kenyan officials in 1982, Ngugi, fearing further reprisals, left Kenya and went into self-imposed exile. After the release of *Matigari ma Njiruungi* in 1986, the Kenyan government issued a warrant for the arrest of the main character, believing Matigari was a real person. Eventually realizing their mistake, the government confiscated all copies of the novel and prevented it from being sold in Kenyan bookshops from 1986 to 1996. Upon leaving Kenya, Ngugi lived primarily in London until he moved to the United States in 1989. He has since taught at several universities, including Yale, New York University, and the University of California, Irvine, as well as holding a visiting professorship at the consortium of colleges that includes Amherst, Mount Holyoke, New Hampshire, Smith, and East Massachusetts. In August 2004 Ngugi returned to Kenya for the first time since 1982. Within a week his apartment was broken into by armed gunmen and Ngugi and his wife were brutally attacked. They returned to California shortly thereafter, but have continued to travel to Kenya in the hope of prosecuting their attackers.

MAJOR WORKS

Ngugi's fiction reflects his concern for the poor of Kenya who have been displaced by white colonialists and by African opportunists who seized power after independence. His early novels, *Weep Not, Child, The River Between* (1965), and *A Grain of Wheat,* all explore the detrimental effects of imperialism. In *Petals of Blood* Ngugi offered a scathing critique of capitalism and accused wealthy landowners and bureaucrats of exploiting the poor and working classes. *Devil on the Cross* focuses on four protagonists who meet on a bus on their way to attend, as spectators, a "Competition in Theft and Robbery," in which the competitors all boast of the ways they have exploited the masses in the past and outline new plans for doing so in the future. One of Ngugi's most controversial novels because of its advocacy of armed rebellion against repression, *Matigari* follows an African rebel whose name means "the patriot who survived the bullets" in Gikuyu. In 2004 Ngugi published his first novel in nearly two decades, *Murogi was Kagogo* (*Wizard of the Crow*). A satirical portrayal of events in twentieth-century Africa, the novel tells the story of the people of the fictional Free Republic of Aburiria, for whose souls four different but equally sinister powers battle to control.

Ngugi began his playwriting career with *The Black Hermit,* but his two most widely recognized theatrical works are *The Trial of Dedan Kimathi* and *Ngaahika Ndeenda: Ithaako ria Ngerekano* (1977; *I Will Marry When I Want*). The former play was written in response to a 1974 play by Kenneth Watene that characterized Kimathi, the leader of the Mau Mau uprising, as a crazed and brutal paranoiac. The content of Ngugi's play derives from the actual trial of Kimathi after his betrayal and capture in 1956, but Ngugi makes extensive use of mime, dance, and Gikuyu song to portray Kimathi as a courageous freedom fighter struggling against the forces of imperialism. The symbolic focus of *I Will Marry When I Want* is the framed deed to one and a half acres of land that hangs in the house of a farm laborer, Kiguunda wa Gathoni, and his wife, Wangeci. The story shows how Kiguunda's employer, Kioi, a wealthy Christian businessman, gains possession of the land—to build a foreign-owned insecticide factory—by persuading Kiguunda to join the church.

Ngugi's nonfiction explores subject matter familiar from his novels, including the cultural and linguistic imperialism of the West, the loss of traditional African cultures, and the effect of Christianity on tribal communities. The essays in *Homecoming: Essays on African and Caribbean Literature, Culture, and Politics* (1972) emphasize the important social functions of African literature. *Writers in Politics* (1981) and *Decolonising the Mind: The Politics of Language in African Literature* (1986) present essays that explore Kenya's myriad social and political problems and stress the need for radical, fundamental reform. Though both works underscore the need for African writers to use their native languages, rather than the languages of colonizers, *Decolonising the Mind* also contains Ngugi's pledge to write solely in Gikuyu, calling the collection his "farewell to the English language." Ngugi's has not written any fiction since that time in English, although he has released nonfiction works in English. *Moving the Centre: The Struggle for Cultural Freedoms* (1992) examines such social issues as the importance of language to national identity, the effects of globalization on native cultures, and Ngugi's hope for a strong and united Africa. Based on a series of lectures that Ngugi delivered at Oxford University in 1996, the essays in *Penpoints, Gunpoints, and Dreams: Toward a Critical Theory of the Arts and the State in Africa* (1998) discuss the role of the writer in contemporary African society and the complex relationship between art and the state.

CRITICAL RECEPTION

Critics have consistently acknowledged Ngugi as one of the most important voices in African letters. His fiction is noted for its overtly political agenda, its attempts to give a literary voice to the poor of Kenya, and its persistent critique of colonialism and oppressive regimes. Critics have also praised Ngugi's role as an influential postcolonial African writer, particularly in his portrayal of corrupt post-liberation African governments—a topic rarely explored from within the continent because of the controversy engendered when Africans criticize their hard-won postcolonial governments. Ngugi's essays and critical works have been acclaimed as powerful and insightful explorations of relevant political, social, and literary issues in Africa. Moreover, reviewers have asserted that his nonfiction work has provided a much-needed African perspective on world affairs.

PRINCIPAL WORKS

The Black Hermit [as James T. Ngugi] (play) 1962

Weep Not, Child [as James T. Ngugi] (novel) 1964

The River Between [as James T. Ngugi] (novel) 1965

A Grain of Wheat [as James T. Ngugi] (novel) 1967; revised edition [as Ngugi wa Thiong'o], 1986

*This Time Tomorrow: Three Plays (plays) 1970

Homecoming: Essays on African and Caribbean Literature, Culture, and Politics (essays) 1972

Secret Lives and Other Stories (short stories) 1975

†The Trial of Dedan Kimathi [with Micere Githae-Mugol] (play) 1976

Ngaahika Ndeenda: Ithaako ria Ngerekano [*I Will Marry When I Want*] (play) 1977

Petals of Blood (novel) 1977

Caitaani Mutharaba-ini [*Devil on the Cross*] (novel) 1980

Detained: A Writer's Prison Diary (diary) 1981

Writers in Politics (essays) 1981

Njamba Nene na Mbaathi I Mathagu [*Njamba Nene and the Flying Bus*] (juvenilia) 1982

Barrel of a Pen: Resistance to Repression in Neo-Colonial Kenya (essays) 1983

Bathitoora ya Njamba Nene [*Njamba Nene's Pistol*] (juvenilia) 1984

Decolonising the Mind: The Politics of Language in African Literature (essays) 1986

Matigari ma Njiruungi [*Matigari*] (novel) 1986

Njamba Nene na Chibu King'ang'i [*Mjamba Nene and the Cruel Chief*] (juvenilia) 1986

Writing against Neocolonialism (essays and criticism) 1986

Moving the Centre: The Struggle for Cultural Freedoms (essays and criticism) 1992

Writers in Politics: A Re-Engagement with Issues of Literature and Society (essays and criticism) 1997

Penpoints, Gunpoints, and Dreams: Toward a Critical Theory of the Arts and the State in Africa (essays and criticism) 1998

Murogi was Kagogo [*Wizard of the Crow*] (novel) 2004

*Includes *This Time Tomorrow*, *The Reels*, and *The Wound in the Heart.*

†Ngugi later translated this work into Gikuya under the title *Mzalendo Kimathi.*

CRITICISM

Sam Raditlhalo (essay date 2001)

SOURCE: Raditlhalo, Sam. "'Kenyan Sheroes': Women and Nationalism in Ngugi's Novels." *English Studies in Africa* 44, no. 1 (2001): 1-11.

[*In the following essay, Raditlhalo maintains that Ngugi's female characters represent Kenya's best hope for establishing a viable postcolonial existence through their fervent political and cultural nationalism.*]

Women in Ngugi's novels are, in the main, nationalists whose presentation/*re*-presentation forms the basis of this essay. A political and social intrusion such as colonialism did not affect men *only*, but also seriously affected the status and economy of women in precolonial societies (Presley 13-31). In so far as the Crown assumed jurisdiction over governance, the legal system, taxation, choice of work, and location of work, it seriously undermined the domestic production of women in the Central Province of modern-day Kenya and elsewhere. Our interest lies in how Ngugi handles the issue of women in colonial and post-colonial Kenya with respect to their nationalistic fervour in his novels, specifically in *The River Between* (1965), *A Grain of Wheat* (1967), and *Petals of Blood* (1977).

Ngugi, starting with *The River Between* (1965), has written with a strong sense of history and a keen understanding of patriarchy. Ngugi is not 'structurally incapable' of recognising the evils of patriarchy, as he demonstrated in *The River Between.* In this text, in which change is wrought by imperialistic tendencies and resistance to such intrusion, the death of Muthoni comes about because her father, with expressive eurochristian zeal, ostracises her at home but is unable to sever links with their culture (36). Her seemingly simplistic statement—'I want to be a woman' (26)—is not as simple as it may appear. Ngugi shows an understanding of this complexity: human beings can and will strive to realise an ideal even at the cost of death. Muthoni is hardly a nationalist. But if, as we understand, nationalism almost always begins in the cultural terrain, then *she is a cultural nationalist.* By asserting her culture she reclaims her right to be part of the changes that occur in her community, while still appreciating the significance of some of the community values. In reading *The River Between* we are thrown back to the period of cultural nationalism in Kenya. We bear in mind the historical specificities of the interaction between cultural and political interventions in Kenya. This interaction relates to the circumcision dispute which occurred in the late 1920s. Waiyaki, as protagonist in this text, promotes Independent schools because those children whose parents rejected enforced Christianity were barred from missionary schools. Since such children had to be circumcised, and the missionaries framed this practice as 'barbaric', independent schools became necessary. In promoting the schools, Waiyaki represents the political dimension of the intervention. The elders have invested in him a hopeful, ultimately triumphant outcome of 'conquering the missionaries, the traders, *the Government*' (98; emphasis added). The government can only realise that a political solution had to be found for a problem begun on the cultural terrain. The Gikuyu revolt against missionary interference was started precisely on this contested terrain, as evidenced by the Kikuyu Central Association's anti-missionary leaning in late 1929. This prompted the Native Commissioner in 1930 to comment on the level of greater political activity which grew out of the events of 1929 (Presley 94). So while Waiyaki represents the political dimension of this struggle, it is Muthoni who succinctly expresses its cultural dimension. For, as Simon During has noted, nationalism has often existed as a mode of freedom (here, the Independent Schools) and its most powerful form—cultural nationalism—was in fact developed *against* imperialism (138-39).

In **The River Between** Ngugi is able to show the importance of a female character as a potentially unifying and dividing force from the historical and nationalist viewpoint. Through Muthoni, Ngugi recognises that the (then nebulous) nation is both a subject and an agency of *ambivalent* narration that holds culture at its most productive position, as a force for 'subordination, fracturing, diffusing, reproducing, as much as producing, creating, forcing, guiding' (Bhabha 308). Ngugi shows how this ambivalence leads to Muthoni's untimely death as she dies from a septic circumcision would but with infinite pride in her stance.

Given the above, I fail to understand the kind of 'engineered disputation' that underlies Elleke Boehmer's criticism of this death. Boehmer holds that in death Muthoni almost achieves the beatific state, a glorified woman submitting to the ancient laws of the elders (193). For her, in this instance Ngugi (un)consciously upholds patriarchy. But then Ngugi's handling of Muthoni's choice indicates that, for him, at least at this stage in his writing, he is concerned more with the 'morality of action', the logic behind the kind of individual choices that people make, than with creating allegorical tropes. The novelist shapes the character to elucidate the workings of his character's mind and feelings. With Boehmer, however, Muthoni's right to make *her own decision* about whether to accept circumcision is subordinated to the spectacle of disputation and the assumption that 'We Are All Sisters In Struggle'. This assump-

tion seems to bind women together in a sociological notion of the 'sameness' of their oppression, a viewpoint that Chandra Mohanty has decried (337). While the victimisation of women in particular societies cannot be ignored, smoothed over or condoned, Boehmer's analysis fails to take cognisance of the historical development in Kenyan nationalism outlined, for instance, by Likimani, Kanogo and Presley. The treatment of African women as a single entity obscures significant variations found among them and contributes to the continual misunderstanding of women and their position.

O'Barr notes that new research on Kenyan nationalism points to the diversity that existed within each ethnic group. For Mohanty, while it is true that the potential of male violence against women circumscribes and elucidates their social position, to define women continually as archetypical victims freezes them into 'objects who defend themselves', men into 'subjects who perpetrate violence', and thus every society into polar positions of the powerless (read: women) and the powerful (read: men). This makes it unnecessary to theorize on male violence and occludes the interpretation of such violence within specific societies, both in order to understand it better, as well as in order to change it (339). For Boehmer, Ngugi tends to 'set up his women characters as icons—allegorical figures representing all that is resilient and strong in the Kenyan people' (189). A careful analysis of these characters should therefore be our starting point.

Having begun with cultural nationalism, in his next novel Ngugi gradually introduces the core contributions of women in the liberation struggle. In **A Grain of Wheat** the most formidable nationalist woman is undoubtedly Wambui. She is described appropriately as an 'enigma', an integral part of the 'Passive' Wing of the Mau Mau fighters. We learn how, during the emergency, 'she carried secrets from the villages to the forest and back to the villages and towns. She knew the underground movements in Nakuru, Njoro, Elburgon and other places in and around the Rift Valley', showing her to be anything but 'passive' (19). Ngugi's portrayal here reveals both the commitment of Wambui and the wide-ranging activities which were entrusted to her. Then again we realise the extent of the area that had given the forest fighters support from 'villages and towns', nullifying the perception that the revolt originated *only* in the urban areas. But does Wambui then become an icon? If so, is this in and of itself a reprehensible representation? While we cannot charge Ngugi with a *re-creation* of the historical Wambui, surely we can grant him the right to use Kenya's material history? The historical Wambui Wagarama, past president of the Mumbi Central Association (*Kiama Kia Mumbi*) interviewed by Presley (127), was a rural woman of formidable qualities.[1] Two features emerging from the interview about the MCA are important: one, that the women used the same tactics, as initiators, as men to organize themselves; secondly, that they did not see themselves as outside the concerns of the nationalist movement, but rather as concerned, politicized Gikuyu (118). Muthoni Likimani observes how nothing could have been achieved without the concerted help from women. It was the women who hazarded their lives to gain back a country by steering loyalists into traps, stealing guns and ammunition, transporting the same to the forests; spying for, hiding and feeding the freedom fighters (114). Ngugi probably pays homage to a historical figure such as Wambui Wagarama, but to read this homage as an allegory seems to de-historicise his literary concerns.

I think Ngugi only begins to become allegorical in his representations of women after *A Grain of Wheat.* Quite apart from anything else, Kenyan women played a vital role in often forcing issues with the colonial government. Fictively, in *A Grain of Wheat* Ngugi also relates how, because of the imprisonment of Harry Thuku, women took the lead in trying to free him for his agitation about taxation, land alienation and forced female labour (issues that women passionately identified with). This episode comes quite early in the text and is not easily erased from the mind of the reader as the marchers fall (14). Historically, in the organized attempt to release Harry Thuku, the first woman to fall was Mary Nyanjiru, the mother of female political protest (Presley 7). In another interesting parallel, Kanogo observes that the crowd which had gathered outside the police station seemed to be getting restive because of seemingly weak male leadership. Crucially, when the male leadership attempted to disperse the crowd the women were enraged at this perceived male compromise. They resorted to taunting the men, and one Mary Nyanjiru even performed the *Guturama,* the exposure of female genitalia as the ultimate articulation of simultaneous feelings of anger, frustration, humiliation or revenge (Kanogo 82; cf. *Grain of Wheat* 157). Ngugi uses the material history of Kenya, not to create 'icons' or 'allegorical' figures, but to reveal a confluence of the cultural and political issues expressed by the women who remain committed nationalists.

Probably the weakest and tritest criticism of Ngugi's women characters relates to the sexual relations in which they are enmeshed. In Boehmer's analysis, Ngugi seemingly has a penchant for resorting to the patriarchal monolithicism which he rhetorically seeks to demolish:

> In the field of sexual relations, certainly, the willing submission of women is the order of the day. The texts are unabashedly frank: from *The River Between* to *Petals of Blood,* all descriptions of sexual encounters invariably and emphatically cast the man in the dominant position. The woman, whether she is the adoring Nyokabi, or the self-sufficient Wanja, is passive, openly subordinate, 'exhilaratingly weak', and apart from the raped Dr Lynd, consistently transported by phallic power.
>
> (193-94)

The fallacy of a phrase such as 'unabashedly frank' is that it is posited without any contextualisation and a virulent streak of textual under-reading. Emmanuel Ngara shows that this is not a case of being 'unabashedly frank' but simply of being realistic and in keeping with what Ngugi sees as the canons of linguistic behaviour in the characters concerned (84-85). For Ngara, there is less control in dialogue involving characters such as Githua and Koinandu, since the author realistically records the turn of mind in such characters. Even in describing the sexual act, the reader perceives beauty in it rather than shock or disgust.

The claim that women characters in Ngugi's texts submit to men's advances so willingly that this may be characterised as being 'the order of the day', (hence) as oversexed individuals, and with men in the 'dominant position', is inconsistent both with the texts themselves and with what is a given social reality. Although Boehmer never clarifies exactly what she means by 'dominant position' one can only surmise that she means that men actually initiate the sexual encounters. To begin with, and with regard to the first statement, it must be observed that Mumbi's skilful choice of Gikonyo (*Grain of Wheat* 80), as an example, is *her choice, her decision.* Mumbi chooses the more reticent, doubtful Gikonyo over the flamboyant Karanja. A *re-reading* of the text shows that when Karanja outruns Gikonyo as they race for the train station, it is Mumbi who turns this seeming defeat to her advantage. Walking through the forest, Gikonyo suddenly realises that the prize of the race was never the train, but Mumbi's undivided attention—the giveaway is the mischievous glint in her eyes (79). Later, in taking advantage of Mumbi, Karanja sees it as just revenge arising from his long-held grudge.

In *Petals of Blood,* it is *Wanja's decision* to initiate sexual relations with Munira. As she contemplates her position, Wanja acknowledges her strength, knowing how weak men could become before her, a power that sometimes frightened her (56). Her encounter with Munira is also on her own terms, part of her scheme: 'Come Mwalimu, take me for a walk, just a little walk. I have a knot only you can untie!' (63). She is the one who decides on the appropriate time for their coitus: 'The moon . . . the orange moon. Please, Mwalimu . . . stay here tonight . . . Break the moon over me.' (66) And clearly, when she allows Munira to touch her again after the Karega debacle and her failed business venture, she sets both tone and pace: 'He was about to jump into bed with her when she suddenly turned cold and chilly, and her voice was menacing. "'No, Mwalimu. No free things in Kenya. A hundred shillings on the table if you want high-class treatment'" (279).

What is most significant is that we are required to psychologically close these episodes, invalidating the 'unabashedly frank' claim of Boehmer, and validating Ngara's claim about the reticence of Ngugi about sexual relations in his texts. Ngugi's stated philosophical undertaking is to dismantle the oppressive structures in society, and women play a major part in this. And yet, importantly, it is not a forced depiction, as the characters Ngugi portrays in the countryside of Kenya adequately show.

In addition to some women's influence in love and sexual relations, we need to understand that Ngugi exposes the present unfair and unequal treatment of women by the state. It is important to realise that the notion of citizenship focuses on the way the *state* acts upon the *individual* and does not address the problem of the way in which the state itself forms its political programme (Anthias and Yuval-Davis 132). By focusing on women, Ngugi is selecting an area in which pretentious state propaganda proclaims how the state cares for all its citizens, including women, while simultaneously undermining the very social fabric in which women live. In *Petals of Blood* it is the women who play a crucial part in transmitting the idea of collectivity. For instance, they have a profound understanding of *thengeta,* which state functionaries undermine in a thoroughly callous way, thereby showing themselves to be indifferent to the traditional community and to the role of women within it. If the nation-state is the basic political unit by which modernity reproduces itself, to denigrate the very citizens for which a state is supposed to care is to be less than modern (During 139). Ngugi's women are nationalists because Kenya—materially, culturally and politically—has become a battleground with women as a powerful and significant group of contestants (in real life, Charity Ngilu standing as a presidential candidate in the December 1997 General Elections is a case in point). In articulating women's struggles in Kenya, Ngugi thus began to link the social and political reality. The post-colonial texts of Ngugi on Kenya reveal an attempt at mapping possible futures through the intertwining of individual character with the body politic.

If Boehmer's criticism has *any* merit, it is with Ngugi's post-colonial texts. In them Ngugi allows his ideological standpoint to hold sway over his characterisation. James Ogude observes that the debate on gender relations in Kenya has tended to fall into two theoretical categories (153). On the one hand we have scholars who place great emphasis on women as an homogeneous group exploited by men and by a system controlled by men, and on the other we have scholars who see women as part of the broad labouring people consisting of workers and peasants. These categories suffer from their privileging of one category over the other and of regarding themselves as self-sufficient analytical categories. These contradictions are apparent in Ngugi's *Petals of Blood.*

Petals of Blood begins in the present, yet maps out the Kenyan landscape from possibly the twelfth century, with the incursions of Arabic and Portuguese traders and invaders. It is a present fraught with difficulties such as Africa's perennial drought, corruption in high places and legalised lawlessness. The natural phenomena, in the text, reverberate as the drought of morality and the insensitivity of the African ruling class. Ngugi centres his analysis of the African condition on the village of Ilmorog, and by extension, on all the villages in which the African peasants languish in poverty and misery. It is a village in the midst of a country where restiveness, repression and fear are discernible (42). Against this background of what is essentially a power struggle in its material, political, educational and gender forms and the concomitant repression, Ngugi draws women who will change in their lives. The formidable Nyakinyua has to contend with the modern-day Kenya on its own terms. With this character, Ngugi challenges our notion of patriotism and 'matriotism'. Nationalism enables both. Nyakinyua's intention espouses the hard path of struggle to be rid of modern *marimus* and in this instance she is a matriot. If nationalism can be understood from myriad routes, so can patriotism and matriotism. Matriotism and patriotism mean an affection for one's country, loyalty to its institutions and zeal in its defence, and is a sentiment known to all men and women (Kedourie 49). The crucial difference, in an oppressive country, is to delineate which institutions claim one's loyalties. For characters such as Nyakinyua and Karega in *Petals of Blood,* Muturi, Wangari and Wariinga in *Devil on the Cross,* and Matigari in *Matigari* (1987), the institution of *wananchi,* its egalitarian values and mores, claims their loyalty. Ngugi's characters show that it is possible to be loyal to one's countrymen and women, displaying a tremendous sense of 'a community in anonymity' which is the hallmark of classical nationalism. Surely such loyalty to, and love for one's country and *wananchi* is equal to a search for liberty, independence, peace, and social happiness! This is unlike the more rabid form of patriotism centred on the State and practised by allegiances to flags, national colours and the armed forces. Since the 'organisational bourgeoisie' is definitely beyond the pale in their close association with the State, Nyakinyua's loyalty cannot then involve the presidency, the various state apparatuses and its personalities. Her intention is to have a say in the lives of *wananchi,* and to this extent she is a matriot. It is she who correctly perceives that despair and nonchalance at their neglect by Nderi wa Riera is not only foolish, but self-defeating. She sees the episode as allowing the city to dance, for once, to the tune of those 'of us who sweat, of us who feel the pain of bearing' (115-16). Like Wambui in *A Grain of Wheat,* Nyakinyua is placed at the centre of the decision-making process in what is a major undertaking for the community.

Metaphorically Nyakinyua presents her relationship to the state as a disgruntled citizen. All she did was to produce more citizens, but she never got anything out of it and even lost her children to the state. Her role here is not only as a link with the past but also to display the ability to posit a possible future for the Ilmorogians in the 'leaky boat' of the Kenyan state. Ngugi gives her more significance, because a grandmother plays many parts in traditional African society. She preserves the extended family, family history, wisdom and lore, in an individual and personal way. All this enhances her status and that of her community (Hill-Lubin 258). Ngugi's women characters eschew corruption for the enhancement of the community. By virtue of her long life, Nyakinyua is able to draw a parallel between the colonialists and the new national bourgeoisie, between colonialism and neo-colonialism (Lebdai 115-16; cf. *Petals of Blood* 86). In Mohanty's view, women are 'constituted as women through a complex interaction between class, culture, religion, gender relations and other ideological frameworks' (340). The role played by Nyakinua as an oral historian, a repository of individual and collective memories, a cultural broker, as well as a family and social member brings to the fore some of the complexities suggested by Mohanty. Another interesting character is Wanja, who epitomises the Kenyan ethic in her search for prosperity, and no matter how anti-social her morals, fits into this category of being willing to enhance the community through sacrifice. More than any other character, her willingness to 're-make' her community stems from her experiences of the evils of patriarchy and its exploitative form. Her fulminations about the life of a barmaid-cum-commercial sex worker reveal the extent of her alienation in the state (128-34).

The correlation between prosperity and prostitution in Kenya is incisively portrayed in *Petals of Blood.* Wanja's loss of status, social standing and esteem forces her into a situation where, to regain the monetary power she had initially wielded, she resorts to commercialised sex. To this extent, in *Petals of Blood* the moral focus rests on Ngugi's premise that the Kenyan postcolonial government is nurturing a state of such dependency on tourists that it creates a nation of prostitutes, servants, cooks, shoeshine boys, bed makers and porters. In Wanja we come to realise the validity of G. C. M. Mutiso's assertion that the most liberated women are not represented as the most admirable in terms of moral values (72). Yet, crucially, they know their own minds.

Ngugi opens himself up to criticism in his ambivalent portrayal of Wanja. Instead of a balanced reading of Wanja's position as a prostitute, Ngugi moralises the issue by questioning her prostitution as a method of freeing herself and ultimately rejects the possibility of any form of struggle within the limits of a repressive patriarchal society. We feel for Wanja when the morally uptight Karega condemns her and in anguish she dismisses

his ideological arrogance (327). Ogude observes how contentious the issues are in gender studies that Ngugi pursues at this point: the role of colonialism and capitalism in the liberation of women, and whether prostitution offers women any form of liberation within a patriarchal system (167-68). A form of nationalism in which love for one's country overrides one's impulse to despair motivates Muthoni, Wambui, Nyakinyua and Wanja. But, as O'Barr has observed, it is with characters such as Nyakinyua and Wanja that Ngugi 'describes women's participation as emerging from their maternal attributes', which (un)intentionally 'genders' them (12). And yet what Ngugi does show is that to seek to control women, in this post-modern moment, under the weight of custom and oppressive reactionary tendencies—'what we have always done!' (Obbo 110)—is as foolhardy as trying to keep women out of any arena in which their lives will be affected. The most striking detail of the devaluation of nationalism and sheroism in post-colonial Kenya is the bawdy song at the gathering by the 'organisational bourgeoisie' which we read about as Munira goes in search of help for the sick child. Such a return to the regressive nativism of 'custom' and 'tradition' misleads the unwary critic-cum-scholar into seeing the apparent seamlessness of cultural practices, where culture is seen as static, thus mummified.

What is wrongly interpreted as the erotics of nationalism in the early novels is now depicted by Ngugi quite seriously as the erotics of sexuality in the postcolony in which sex acts as a viable currency for women. During, in quoting Heine, alerts us to the fact that sexuality and nationalism have been used as analogous for a long time, which should not now be seen as the preserve of Africans (145). Heine, while contemplating English nationalism and the national identity it acquires after the French Revolution, sardonically waxes lyrical about how British beauties are: wholesome, nourishing, substantial and inartistic, yet as excellent as good Old England's simple, honest fare: roast beef, roast mutton, pudding in flaming brandy, boiled vegetables in water (with two kinds of sauces, one of which is melted in butter). It is such analogies that help to form a mutant culture. This conflation of sexuality and nationalism in the postcolony is what Ngugi questions when Wanja secures her freedom from Kimeria wa Kamianja (*aka* Hawkins Kimeria) with unsolicited sex (which is really rape). It is crucial to point out that whereas Wanja is brutally raped, in her article Boehmer hardly sees this as worthy of consideration. She merely mentions that Wanja is 'equipped with an extremely durable vagina' (193). Wanja's later descent into commercialised sex is as a result of the fickle nature of 'the promised land' of the pre-independence phase of nationalism. In that phase women were valued as important components of society and *bona fide* nationalists, not as sex machines. It is precisely for such reasons that Ogude's observation about whether prostitution offers women any form of liberation in the postcolony, remains valid. It remains an unresolved issue of the post-colonial period in Ngugi's fiction given such rigid categorisations within which postcolonial nationalism is framed.

If a 'national chorus' of the oppressed and the 'liberated woman' is an ideal for which Ngugi strives, it is because nationalism is still a potent force in African societies which seek to question their state apparatuses. These societies have, in retrospect, worsened with time. While women remain nationalists in those Ngugi texts set both in the colonial and post-colonial eras, in the latter era they do so only by joining in the class struggles of their compatriots. The opposite of such a representation, as the case of Wanja clearly shows, is authorial condemnation, with redemption being possible only when Wanja decides to take a stand in the struggle. Significantly, we are made to understand that she begins to feel 'the stirrings of a new person' after giving up prostitution (337). If prostitution is allegorical of the decadent state of the nation, then motherhood is allegorical of national rebirth and regeneration. In the end the whore image is transformed into a mother Africa trope (Ogude 168). As Ogude succinctly observes, in these post-colonial texts there exists no other struggle except the class war. This necessarily leads to an ideological *laager* for no democratic spaces exist outside class struggle (173).

While Ngugi shows a marked sensitivity to women as nationalists in pre-independent Kenya, after independence, particularly with **Petals of Blood** and **Devil on the Cross,** he privileges class over the exigencies of other categories that constitute women. Although he strives to reveal the inter-connectedness of race, class and sex oppression, it is within the class paradigm that Ngugi mediates this intertwinement and posits only one outcome. Thus the *newer* phase of nationalism significantly 'genders' women, over and above the 'birth pangs of national consciousness' that the pre-independence women characters display.

Note

1. The Mumbi Central Association is an important association since it was formed in 1920 by women tired of their exclusion from the decision-making process within the then radical Kikuyu Central Association. The association's objectives were similar to those of the KCA: land, labour, taxation and education (see Presley 117-19).

Works Cited

Anthias, Floya and Nira Yuval-Davis. 'Women and the Nation-State'. *Nationalism.* Ed. John Hutchinson & Anthony D. Smith. Oxford: Oxford University Press, 1994. 312-316.

Bhabha, Homi. 'Narrating the Nation'. *Nationalism.* Ed. John Hutchinson & Anthony D. Smith. Oxford: Oxford University Press, 1994. 306-312.

Boehmer, Elleke. 'The Master's Dance to the Master's Voice: Revolutionary Nationalism and the Presentation of Women in the Writing of Ngugi wa Thiong'o'. *Journal of Commonwealth Literature* xxvi.1 (1991): 188-197.

During, Simon. 'Literature—Nationalism's other? The case for revision'. *Nation and Narration.* Ed. Homi K. Bhabha. London & New York: Routledge, 1990. 138-153.

Hill-Lubin, Mildred A. 'The Grandmother in African and African-American Literature: A Survivor of the African Extended Family'. *Ngambika: Studies of Women in African Literature.* Ed. Carole Boyce Davis & Ann Adams Graves. Trenton: Africa World Express, 1990. 257-270.

Kanogo, Tabitha. 'Kikuyu women and the politics of protest: Mau Mau'. *Images of Women in Peace and War: Cross-cultural and Historical Perspectives.* Ed. Sharon Macdonald. London: Macmillan, 1987. 78-99.

Kedourie, Elie. 'Nationalism and Self-Determination'. *Nationalism.* 49-55.

Lebdai, Benaouda. 'Rachid Boudjedra and Ngugi wa Thiong'o: A Comparative Study of Two Post-Independence African Writers'. Diss. University of Essex, 1987.

Likimani, Muthoni. *Passbook F.47927: Women and Mau Mau in Kenya.* London: Macmillan, 1985.

Mohanty, Chandra Talpade. 'Under Western Eyes: Feminist Scholarship and Colonial Discourses'. *Boundary* 2 (xii), 3(xiii) 1984: 333-358.

Mutiso, G-C. M. *Socio-Political Thought in African Literature: Weusi?* London: Macmillan, 1974.

Ngara, Emmanuel. *Stylistic Criticism and the African Novel: A Study of the Language, Art and Content of of African Fiction.* London: Heinemann, 1982.

Ngugi wa Thiong'o. *The River Between.* London: Heinemann, 1965.

———. *A Grain of Wheat.* London: Heinemann, 1967.

———. *Petals of Blood.* London: Heinemann, 1977.

———. *[Caitaani Muthabaraini] Devil on the Cross.* London: Heinemann, 1982.

O'Barr, Jean. Introductory Essay. *Passbook F.47927: Women and Mau Mau in Kenya.* London: Macmillan, 1985.

Obbo, Christine. *African Women—Their Struggle for Economic Independence.* Johannesburg: Ravan, 1981.

Ogude, James. 'Ngugi's Concept of History and Character Portrayal in his Post-colonial Novels.' Diss. University of the Witwatersrand, 1996.

Presley, Cora Ann. *Kikuyu Women, the Mau Mau Rebellion, and Social Change in Kenya.* Boulder: Westview Press, 1992.

Jacqueline Bardolph (essay date 2002)

SOURCE: Bardolph, Jacqueline. "Moving away from the Mission: Ngugi wa Thiong'o's Versions of *A Grain of Wheat*." In *Missions of Interdependence: A Literary Directory,* edited by Gerhard Stilz, pp. 133-41. Amsterdam, The Netherlands: Rodopi, 2002.

[*In the following essay, Bardolph contrasts Ngugi's first edition of* A Grain of Wheat, *which he wrote as James Ngugi, with his later revised edition, written after he renounced Christianity, his Anglicized name, and what he considered the trappings of colonialism.*]

When Ngugi finished writing **A Grain of Wheat** in November 1966, he was in Leeds doing postgraduate studies. The date corresponds to a moment of qualified optimism in African history: Nkrumah was still in power. Obote had not yet taken over in Uganda. That same year, Oginga Odinga published *Not Yet Uhuru,* a socialist analysis of the way in which he considered the rural masses were being cheated of the benefits of independence. Ngugi was educated in a religious context before going to university at Makerere. One must also underline that during the years of Emergency, the churches as a whole were on the side of the British government, in particular helping with the propaganda that described Mau Mau as terrorists, violent outsiders refusing Christian and human values for the sake of atavistic regression. The villagers, suspected of helping the forest guerrillas, and the inmates in detention camps, were subjected to intensive re-education, told to confess, to seek rehabilitation. Moral Rearmament was explicitly involved in the campaign to cultivate guilt feelings among the people, and pacifist Revivalist currents encouraged them to 'see the light' at public meetings. The detainees who agreed to begin new lives were gradually restored to freedom, "going through the pipe-line," their card symbolically changing from black to grey and to white.

With this in mind, one can read **A Grain of Wheat** (published in 1967)[1] as a novel written by the man still called James Ngugi. The revised edition produced twenty years later by Ngugi wa Thiong'o (1986) paradoxically helps one realize how strong some Christian elements were for the more politically aware mature writer who, by that time, had grown to consider them as unacceptable. Under the phrase "Christian elements," we include here several levels: the beliefs and practices of ordinary people of the time, the picture of the struggle as indicated by the combination of government and official churches, and the overall Christian vision that shapes the book, whether as expression of belief or as convenient parable.

The novel published by Heinemann seems at first to fit into the pattern set by Achebe's village novels. When one examines what has been cut out from the original manuscript (kept at the School of Oriental and African Studies in London), whether as a change of mind or under guidance from the publisher, several features become apparent. The early text has an even more nightmarish quality than the final version. Eliminated passages show characters suffering from one another's sneers or mocking gaze. Disgust is stressed in sentences that speak of bad smells, excrement and slime. The drop that moves towards Mugo's eyes in his opening dream is also a slug.[2] Physical repulsion is connected with humiliation, and the humiliation is always of a sexual nature. The main elements which did not find their way into the published book have to do with rape fantasies of a twisted nature. The novel is framed by two instances when Mugo feels anger and disgust towards an old lady, first the aunt that brought him up, then at the end the old woman, the mother of the deaf and mute that was shot. These figures with their potential evil eyes are close to castrating witches. The early text adds a weird element to Mugo's irrational emotions. When he feels like throttling the aunt, the imaginary assault is told in terms of climax and release. He sees her with her legs in the air.[3] At the end of the book he kills an old lady, in the same paroxystic mood, and sets her on a stool "burying her feet wide apart in the ashes."[4] Another very long passage, in fact a whole chapter, dealing mostly with Thompson, has been eliminated. The man feels horribly guilty because he once saw a little girl sleeping on a bed in London and felt a strong desire to take her then and there. Years later in Kenya, ashamed of this fantasy, he starts scribbling at night in a notebook, wanting to confess and feel free again. His confession also includes the tortures inflicted as he was responsible for the detention camp of Rira. His exalted mood when he wants to liberate himself by this written account is described in the same terms as that of Mugo.[5] The parallel is so strong that some terms could apply to either character. The intricate black and white pair, both feeling guilty and afraid of the other's sneer is not very far from the Munira/Inspector Godfrey pair at the beginning of **Petals of Blood.** Both are involved in the writing down of guilt, as a mode of atonement. Mugo has several nocturnal doubles, Kihika, Karanja, or Thompson, in fantasmatic couples which are clear echoes of Conrad. On the whole, the world in the early manuscript is more irrational, more anguished. All the characters, colonized or colonizers, are locked in nightmares and guilt, distrustful of one another—the parallel between the two adulterous couples, Gikonyo and Mumbi, Thompson and his wife, is underlined—and ultimately alone with their shameful past and oppressive fantasies.[6]

The published novel focuses on a group of people of the same generation. There are three men, Karanja, Mugo, and Gikonyo, and one woman, Mumbi, a pattern that will be repeated in **Petals of Blood,** as will be the confession theme. The others are peripheral to this central plot devoted to ordinary rural young people. There is the group of rebels, Koinandu, General R, Kihika, the politicians of the Party, and the whites. The older generation are here witnesses more than actors. Several fathers are missing or contested. The general atmosphere is one of fear, guilt and exhaustion on the eve of the independence. The village is coming to terms with the meaning of loyalty, courage and betrayal after a period where sides had to be taken but distinctions were often blurred. The process is helped by a chain of confessions, first private then public that help words to regain their meaning as they liberate the actors of this troubled period one after the other.

In 1986, Ngugi, who had not returned to Kenya since 1982, was well-known for his fiction and for the cultural and political positions contained in his collections of essays. Writing directly on an early copy of *A Grain of Wheat,* he brought several types of changes to bear on the novel. The situation of the 1950s and the 1960s is analysed differently. The simple terms, which were close to the world view of the villagers then, are replaced by more general terms: The Party, which is too close to Kenyatta's politics, is replaced by the Movement, which is of a more general nature. The pair of "traitors and collaborators" recurs repeatedly: There is no half-judgment (25, 60). Some elements of economic analysis are added, in particular concerning the relationship with Asians and Europeans. The possibility of ambivalent assessments is reduced through complete changes in some characters. In the first version, Gatu, a strange man in the detention camp, is full of wisdom, courage, but also despair, a kind of sad clown who commits suicide. His bleak assessment of human capacities is now replaced by certainties. The character who so disturbed Gikonyo is killed by the camp authorities who try to pass this as suicide. General R is, like all rebels in the early novel, a frightening figure (think of Boro in *Weep Not Child*). The novelist has been at pains to find motivations for the violence of the forest fighters. In the 1967 version, General R who used to be a tailor, is an outcast because he has committed a major transgression by hitting his father. He is no longer part of his community. His motive for fighting is connected to personal pride and an inflated sense of honour. In the 1986 version, this disappears from the presentation of the character who becomes an articulate anti-colonial fighter. Koinandu is so altered that, in the 1986 version, he gets a new name, Koina. In 1966, Ngugi was trying to understand the violence committed against white people. He presented the rape of an unattractive spinster by her houseboy as such an extreme case, caused by envy, greed and a distorted sense of manhood.[7] The odd thing is that, although such rapes featured widely in the anti-Mau Mau propaganda of the time, I have not been able to find historical accounts that would match the story. It is as if the young Ngugi still saw the guerrillas as they were presented by propaganda, as creatures totally beyond moral redemption, and tried to find motives and attenuating circumstances. Yet Koinandu remains a thug to the end, motivated by envy and fear. The new Koina does not rape Mrs. Lynd. He just hacks her dog to pieces and finds equalitarian justifications for his resentment.

There is however a very significant change. In the 1967 version, the Reverend Jackson is a minister, a true believer. He is respected by all, in particular the elders and preaches against Mau Mau. He becomes involved in the Revivalist movement. His position is described in a rather non-committal way, close to the point of view of the villagers. He dies at the hands of General R in a manner which can be read as martyrdom, and haunts the conscience of the ex-guerrilla. He is one of the Christ figures of the book, an element in the collective suffering. Any ambiguity there might have been in the interpretation of this important character is lifted by the way Ngugi modifies his presentation radically twenty years after. In 1986, the church minister who has been an informer is justly executed. The recent version is firmly didactic and shows as far as possible the people as more conscious, more united. The charismatic forest leader, Kihika, is no longer a marginal or ambivalent figure, a man his sister refused to see avenged.[8] He is closer to the full national hero, Dedan Kimathi, as presented in the 1977 play.

The modifications point at some of the elements in the 1967 novel, which perhaps readers at the time had not analysed in the same way. Let us read again the system of values which is represented there and the part played by Christian churches and their teaching. It is obvious now, especially if one compares this with the unpublished extracts, that the main value system rests on manhood.[9] When the moment of decision comes, a man tests whether he is true to his circumcision. The characters feel threatened by the laughter of young women and the all-seeing eyes of old ones, the sneers and sexual taunting on the part of white people. Kihika is admired for his courage in tackling a whiteman singlehanded. Both Karanja and Mugo are grateful at some point to a white man who has saved them from humiliation, while at others they feel debased, un-manned by their oppression. Humiliation in the hands of representatives of the colonial power is always shown here as sexual in nature; all examples of torture are to do with castration and penetration. Virility, the capacity to engender males and look after one's honour is the core value. The young people do not seem to have other ethical codes to guide their behaviour. They often live in a spiritual vacuum, especially at the end of the years of Emergency. The novel is about spiritual drought, the kind of moral lassitude one sees after conflicts which in some aspects were a form of civil strife, as in the postwar fiction of Zimbabwe. Mumbi has "no words. No feelings. Nothing" (181). She wants Mugo to forget about the dead, but to "Speak to the living. Tell them about those whom the war maimed, left naked and scarred: the orphans, the widows" (161). There is no definite political consciousness in any of the ordinary people, whether they are loyalists, rebels or ordinary people caught in between. The central couple, Gikonyo and Mumbi, named after the mythical founding couple of the Kikuyu, have gone through the terrible period by trying to survive, both attempting to save some personal happiness in the chaos.

What, then, is the part played by organized religion and by the Christian vision in the overall narrative? The experience told is that of a community, and it is described in the terms used by the majority in their discussions, comments and songs. The Bible, the Old Testament in particular, plays an important part in the way people perceive themselves and give shape to their predicament. Mumbi sees herself as Ruth, an earth figure waiting for a child (69). The songs quoted are those sung at the time. From the beginning, anti-colonial attitudes were expressed in Biblical terms: The oppressed were the people of Israel, and Kenyatta was to be the Moses who would deliver them. The whole economy of sacrifice is close to what is left of the Kikuyu traditional religion and to a sombre view of the Christian message which stresses suffering and sin more than beatitude. The Revivalist movement is described in a non-committal way, as a new development that helps some individuals. The violent figure of Kihika is redeemed by the fact that he always quotes from his Bible, which is true of his historical model. In such characters, the values of manhood can be reconciled with the Biblical vision.

The syncretic conception that equates Ngai with the Christian god and Gikuyu and Mumbi with Adam and Eve is part of the efforts of the missions to reconcile two visions and also part of the creed of the nationalist independent churches. In later works, Ngugi will use a more revolutionary mythical ancestor in Ndemi, an active Promethean figure. But here, the vision of the land to be fertilized again or of the allegorical woman to be impregnated is part of the agricultural rhetoric of the title. It is, however, to be noted that none of the main characters suffers from the loss of their land although repossessing land was the central claim for the people who rose against the power of the settlers.

At a deeper level, the narrative seems to be still permeated by the guilt feelings induced by the propaganda. We have seen how close the picture of the terrorists is to the way the rebellion was presented in Kenya and England, even if the young novelist tries to explain the humiliations and unjust treatments that drove some fighters to the forest. In a puritanical vision, sin is equated most of the time with the sin of the flesh. Suffering seems to be the only way forward, a system of atonement that can provide a fresh start when the world as it was known has collapsed. The image of crucifixion is used several times (152, 157). This is a major trope for Ngugi even when it appears in an inverted form in *Devil on the Cross*. The major characters go through a phase of soul-searching, then of confession that is close to the Revivalist method (86, 98). Ngugi's fascination with such emotional type of belief appears again, in a clearly distanced manner in the character of the barmaid in *Petals of Blood.*

Later in his career, when he publicly declared he was not a Christian and changed his name, Ngugi said he used the Bible as a source of metaphors and parables close to the culture of his people. It is true that, in the 1960s, a period when written literary Kikuyu was used essentially for the translation of the Good Book, references to the Bible served to establish a strong link between English, which he enjoyed in a guilty manner, and the popular rhetoric in his own language. The lyrical passages, the agricultural metaphors that give dignity to the simple English used here owe much to the psalms and parables, as well as to the songs composed at the time of the Emergency (75, 85, 126).

The enigmatic character of Mugo can thus be explained by the ambivalent attitude to the power and poetry of the Biblical text. When he speaks like a Messiah, a Moses, he is clearly deluded by a sense of his lonely elite position, like other similar protagonists in Ngugi's fiction. The pastiche of prophetic pronouncements is blasphemous in a man who knows his guilt, whereas others think of him as a saint, who is able to talk with God (108, 110, 112, 139, 164, 173, 188). His betrayal echoes all the other betrayals, however: Mumbi had no real excuse to give herself to Karanja; Gikonyo betrayed the oath because he had a wife to love, a selfish human motive for an act that weighs on them later. Mugo is more ambivalent, excessive in his courage and in his cowardice. Paradoxically, he betrays Kihika in order to save himself for his destiny as a saviour. There is no doubt yet that he is a fraud, and he knows it. He accepts in advance the trial and judgment by the couple of ex-fighters, even if they are not very positive figures. But somehow the book seems to imply that, for all his delusions and weaknesses, he ultimately embodies the major values of the community. His confession is the sacrificial act that allows regeneration: Mumbi and Gikonyo can come together again. And, in his choice to offer himself as a sacrificial victim, "he is a man of courage" who comes close to the manly virtue of a circumcised man. In some ways, Mugo's confession and his feeling of indignity are duplicated by the writing of the book itself. The long conflict has profoundly shaken everyone, divided families, encouraged individual acts of survival at the expense of solidarity. If one refers to similar situations around the world one sees how silence—Kenyatta's "Forget and Forgive!"—can be in itself destructive. The worse moments have to be faced, spoken about, and when one thinks how close to the actual events the 1967 novel is, one can only admire the courage of the young man who chose to give such an image of his people. Later on, political tools were acquired that helped him to analyse the factors differently and present a more militant text based on a clear idealization of fighters as opposed to "traitors and collaborators." It is much easier to see the choices that could have been made, the reasons that could have been given.

The first title of *A Grain of Wheat* was to have been *Wrestling with God,* a phrase taken from the struggle between Tobias and the angel as quoted in a letter by Conrad, referring to the act of fictional creation.[10] The book does not just refer to the world view of Christian villagers seen from a detached position. It is written in the margins and between the lines of the Bible. It reflects some aspects of the colonizer's ideology as taught in a school system that conveyed good and bad together, the vision of the missions, the visions of independent churches and the syncretic popular narratives. But it mostly creates a highly personal world, the tortured self-searching and ironical distance of one who worked on Conrad and found there a pessimism to which he could relate. The end is very bleak, with isolated figures in the drizzle. In detention, Gikonyo has come to the conclusion that "to live and die alone was the ultimate truth" (102). On his return he finds it difficult to regain any kind of faith. All the heroes, even the near mythical couple, are at a loss. The only fruit of the period is an illegitimate child, but he is there, he is ill and needs attending to. The sick child, like in *Petals of Blood,* is an image of the pain of the world. In spite of the rewriting of *A Grain of Wheat* in 1986 to give positive examples to people in their present resistance, the novel remains complex, alive and fraught with deep contradictions. The Christian mode of narrative, whether a grand metaphor or the expression of a deep belief, is the only element that makes sense in this picture of a world that suffers spiritually from its division more than from external oppression.

Notes

1. Ngugi wa Thiong'o, *A Grain of Wheat* (London: Heinemann, 1967). All page references to this edition unless otherwise indicated.

2. "A slug started moving towards him" (MS 3).

3. "He watched her struggles like a fly in a spider's hands, saw her kick her legs in the air" (MS 14).

4. "The new rage now fully possessed him, his body shook violently. But as in the meeting, he was clear about his next action. He knew he would put

his hand around his neck. Would she groan? Anyway he would press, harder, and she would feel the power of his hands. He felt almost triumphant as he beheld the future, this little future he had just planned.

And that is what he did.

The old woman did not scream.

She fell from his hands onto the ground as if she had died at his touch . . . He bent down and raised the inert body from the ground. He placed it on the stool near the fire-place, making her head and hands rest on the stone. He then buried her feet, wide apart into the ashes. He stood back to survey the work of his hands" (MS 351).

5. "He wrote in fury. Images flowed, merged, clashed. It was as if he had only a few minutes to live and wanted to purge his soul of filth, a confession to a priest before the gallows fell" (MS 267).

6. Robson (who becomes Thompson): "I want to know what went wrong that even my wife laughs secretly at me" (MS 264). On Mugo: "At night, in the morning, I saw the grin, the sneer, the secret laughter, the face was everywhere" (MS 267). Mugo: "Mugo felt the woman look at him with a glint, the glint as of a puzzled recognition transformed her into Mugo's idea of a witch. The luridness seemed to ooze from her eyes and creep towards his flesh" (MS 10).

7. "He found his tongue and revealed his thoughts to other people: she was alone, it was not right for a woman to live alone, Man, I'll break her in. I'll swim in that hole. The others laughed at Koinandu's delightful tongue" (185).

8. "But she did not want anybody to die or come to harm because of her brother" (181).

9. Cf. pages 25, 31, 32, 106, 130, 157.

10. Jacqueline Bardolph, "Ngugi wa Thiong'o's *A Grain of Wheat* and *Petals of Blood* as Readings of Conrad's *Under Western Eyes and Victory,*" *The Conradian* 12.1 (1987): 32-49.

Works Cited

Bardolph, Jacqueline. "Ngugi wa Thiong'o's *A Grain of Wheat* and *Petals of Blood* as Readings of Conrad's *Under Western Eyes* and *Victory,*" *The Conradian* 12.1 (1987): 32-49.

Ngugi wa Thiong'o. *Devil on the Cross,* tr. from Gikuyu by the author (London: Heinemann, 1982).

———. "A Grain of Wheat" (original MS, kept at the School of Oriental and African Studies in London).

―――. *A Grain of Wheat* (London: Heinemann, 1967).

―――. *A Grain of Wheat* (London: Heinemann, rev. ed. 1986).

―――. *Petals of Blood* (London: Heinemann, 1977).

―――. *Weep Not Child* (London: Heinemann, 1964).

Odinga, Oginga. *Not Yet Uhuru* (London: Heinemann, 1966).

Evan Mwangi (essay date winter 2004)

SOURCE: Mwangi, Evan. "The Gendered Politics of Untranslated Language and Aporia in Ngugi wa Thiongo'o's *Petals of Blood*." *Research in African Literatures* 35, no. 4 (winter 2004): 66-74.

[*In the following essay, Mwangi relates Ngugi's use of untranslated Gikuyu passages and expressions in* Petals of Blood *to the problematic status of women in postcolonial Kenya.*]

Ngugi wa Thiong'o's *Petals of Blood* occupies a unique position in his oeuvre because it is the last novel he wrote in English. But unlike its predecessors, in which non-English expressions are stylistically integrated into English and subordinated to the English discourse, *Petals of Blood* contains numerous non-English expressions that are left either untranslated or loosely hanging in the sentence structure in a way that would suggest the narrative's ideal reader to be a person who is competent in both English and Gikuyu. Although critics have acclaimed the novel's political thrust and stylistic innovations as a culmination of Ngugi's gradual development from his earlier work, little attention has been paid to the untranslated language in the text and the novel's structural contradictions. This paper reads the untranslated moments as metonymic of the frustrated struggles to convert revolution into final liberation. The metonymy of untranslated language is backed by structural and gendered contradictions to draw our attention to the narrative's demand to be read against the grain. While the use of untranslated terms conforms to the narrative's desire to forge a decolonized English, it also ironically reveals how deeply colonial and patriarchal hegemonies are entrenched in the very articulations against them. My aim is to advance the conversation started by Craig V. Smith in his brief comments on the "frequent, prominent and sometimes untranslated use of African words, sayings and especially songs" (95) in *Petals of Blood* and his observation that the world presented in the text is "strongly gendered" (93). I want to relate gender to the untranslated language and further propose that this relationship complements structural contradictions in figuring the failed conditions of the postcolony, and I argue that Ngugi textualizes the postindependence condition as untranslated and sexualized, but the text does not step out of the patriarchal and colonial hegemony despite its use of elements of an African language.

Set in the rustic village of Ilmorog in postindependence Kenya, *Petals of Blood* is basically the story of the murder of three millionaires associated with the neocolonial government in exploiting the people. The narrative highlights the subsequent arrest of four friends as the police try to solve the mystery of the triple murder. These arrested characters are Munira, a teacher in a rural school whose diary at the police station forms the bulk of the narrative; Wanja, a prostitute exiled from the village by her family when she becomes pregnant, now returned to Ilmorog and staying with her grandmother, Nyakinyua; Karega, a politically naive school teacher who develops into a politically conscious activist and trade unionist; and Abdullah, an itinerant trader who fought in the guerilla war for Kenyan independence and became crippled. The epic narrative begins with the arrest of the suspects and uses flashbacks to recount the life stories of the characters until the deadly fire in which the millionaires die in Wanja's brothel. The use of the diary form, stories-within-the-story technique, and multiple flashbacks to bring together the various narratives and lay bare the evils of neocolonialism as a form of prostitution of the nation by its elites gives the anticolonial novel a rich texture. But patriarchy and colonialism remain deeply entrenched in the narrative's use of untranslated language and gendered tropes.

Petals of Blood is one of the numerous African novels that disturb the creative/critical dichotomy by theorizing their own content and form in a metafictional vein. This is evident in instances where we encounter artists and art as subjects in artistic works or where fictional audiences engage in the interpretation of texts. The metafictional impulse in *Petals of Blood* is accentuated by the narrative's presentation of multiple other narratives that concatenate in the story and its suggestion that the major characters are painters, performers, or critics of the social condition. A self-consciously political novel, *Petals of Blood* presents art as not only a means by which we understand our circumstances and narrate ourselves into existence but a reflection of the concrete conditions around us of which we perhaps might be unaware. Even the most trivial artistic production invoked in the novel suggests the material and political conditions in which we dwell, just the way the untranslated language and aporia express the condition in the postcolony. In the story, this is best articulated in an untranslated moment when children habitually enunciate the conditions of the postcolony in banal songs that remind them of the rank and gritty reality that defines their lives in Ilmorog. Through their teacher

Munira's observation about their artistic production and material practice, we are shown the inextricable artistic bonding between the real self and the banality of habitual articulations:

> They also sang: *Kamau wa Njoroge ena ndutu kuguru*; and thought of their own jiggers eating their toes and scratched them against the floor in earnest.
>
> (10)

The narrator, presenting events to the reader from Munira's center of consciousness, assumes that the reader understands Gikuyu language and therefore leaves the non-English words untranslated. They literally translate into "Kamau son of Njoroge has jiggers on his foot." Even if this is a frivolous children's song from the common storehouse of oral traditions—the type that the text calls "nonsense songs" (20) and "nonsense work songs" (264)—it reminds the children of their own specific conditions. They in turn engage in self-reflexive projects of scratching their jigger-infected toes.

The novel contains numerous untranslated taboo words. These are expressions that are not used in polite society because they refer to intimate parts of the body, infallible beings, or phenomena whose mention would portend bad luck. Generally writers avoid taboo words by using euphemisms or truncated versions of the words. It is intriguing that that **Petals of Blood** is more articulate in translated taboo words, even when those words are a transcription from a pre-existing oral text. This implies the exultation of evil in the postcolony that is now defined by dirtiness and degeneracy. To be sure, the novel employs taboo words to underline its outrage with the arrested decolonization. In **Petals of Blood,** Ngugi inscribes swear words within the register of the male. To give an example, women in lawyer Chui's home sing a sexually innocuous, but politically laden, song to the effect that Irish potatoes are peeled at First Lady Ngina's home. When their male counterparts take over the poetic expression, they sing a circumcision song that uses taboo expressions that the author cannot reproduce in his mother tongue; the taboo expressions are reproduced in English but truncated with dashes to suppress their offensiveness. The narrator seems to be happy with the song in that he describes the taboo parts as "juicy sections." Oddly, the text sees juiciness in the offensive words it cannot reproduce unless it is in translation. The words cannot be articulated in the language of the self although their voicing is possible in English as an Other language.

Similarly, after the Ilmorog residents partake of the traditional brew, they utter obscenities openly in the traditional songs they perform. The taboo words are either unscripted or euphemized in translation. Njuguna and

Nyakinyua, Ilmorog male and female elders, respectively, are particularly notorious in the parts of the song they vocalizes (207-09). Their enunciations are translated into English, albeit in words that are not as strongly taboo as the ones used in the traditional circumcision song that the characters would be singing in Gikuyu. When the same song appear before in the text and are given to the reader in Gikuyu as well, the taboo words are truncated and euphemized in the English translation (150). What is apparent here is the text's attempt to clean up the obscenities of the traditional culture while invoking it as a gesture against a debasing capitalistic modernity. The euphemisms and silences do not fully depose patriarchy and its obsessions. When debating who between male and female categories is more important than the other, Njuguna says: "Is it not a man who sleeps, *hmmm! hmmm!* You know where?" (162). The expression *Hmmm! Hmmm!* is a substitute for a taboo expression that refers to sexual activity. The new expression is cheekier than what it substitutes. The expression pretends to differ from what it is intended to express, but it is only deferring meaning for greater effect, a consequence Njuguna deems amusing, revealing how acceptable is the position that he presents.

For his part, Abdulla takes pleasure in repeating an Indian's Swahili swear words that refer to a mother's genitalia (253). The expression collocates the Swahili word for the female genitalia (*k*; truncation ours) and the Gikuyu word *Nyukua,* a derogate term for "mother." The text gives women, too, taboo expressions. When Munira's mucus accidentally flies into Nyakinyua's face, the words the old woman uses in reaction are taboo (7), designating a woman's sexual organ. They are in Gikuyu language, and no translation is given because their foulness cannot be expressed in any other language. They are foregrounded on the printed page by italicization to draw the reader's attention to their indecency and the outrage that frames Nyakinyua's response to the modernity that Munira and his school symbolize in the dilapidated Ilmorog. Abdulla jokingly uses a worse version of the taboo expression when ordering a beer for Munira (11); the untranslated expression, too, is a variant term for the female genitalia. In the postcolony, it appears that women have become a derogate category to such an extent that even positively drawn characters would habitually tap into antiwomen vulgarity to express themselves without the text fearing compromising the ideal reader's attitude towards the characters.

Through untranslated language and gendered self-contradiction, Ngugi's narrative presents to the reader women who derogate themselves by viewing their natural sexuality in negative terms. This is especially seen in the way some of the untranslated expressions tie up with bodily effluents to suggest that the nation is not yet fully liberated. Wanja, the principal female character, is one of the earliest rounded characters by a male writer in the history of African literature. Bonnie Roos succinctly summarizes the novelty in Ngugi's creation of Wanja when she says that "we find Wanja a refreshing change from the traditional, passive, melodramatic, male-dependent, lackluster heroines" (154). She reads Wanja as a trope and recognizes the "archetypal nature of her construction."

A cautious appropriation of Fredric Jameson's reading of postcolonial characters as allegorical representations of the condition and the fate of the nation is in order here to help us see how the characters represent untranslated desires. For Jameson, allegory as the structuring principle in narratives is used in a special way in postcolonial literature to inscribe a more communal mindset than would be found in the more individualistic western narratives. In the essay "Third World Literature and the Era of Multinational Capital," Jameson urges us to read the story of individual characters in Third World literature as national allegories of the embattled situation formerly colonized people find themselves in (69). He sees Third World texts to deploy the destiny of the private individual to allegorize the public cultural, economic and cultural domain. His theory has been criticized most articulately by Aijaz Ahmed because of what Ahmed sees as Jameson's essentializing and tendentious generalization. Rosemary M. George sees Jameson's typology as infused with an outsider's misunderstanding of texts he is reading from locations that are not his own. We would further criticize the theory in the sense that a text like *Petals of Blood* contains many individual characters with varied destinies. If we were to use Jameson's universalizing model, we might ask who, among Karega, Wanja, Munira, Abdulla, and the battery of other characters, does the text use as an allegory of the nation? David Punter cautions us that even while critiquing Jameson's "self-evident reductivism," it would be hard to extricate these texts from allegorical references to history (55). Although modern African literature is generally seen to be a development from—and of—traditional oral literature that is highly allegorical, the discomfort with Jameson's claim could be as a result of looking at allegory as comprising a "naïve mode of one-to-one mapping" (Szeman 806). But Jameson himself noted in the much debated essay that the kind of allegory that he is talking about is "profoundly discontinuous, a matter of breaks and heterogeneities, of the multiple polysemia" (73). These, of course, are elements that would be found in any literature, the only difference being that in the Third World texts, the characteristics are used to ground the text in the concrete cultural and political dynamics of the society presented. Reading postcolonial Indian narratives, Peter Morey proposes that the national allegory is not expressed by an individual text or character but is

"instead accretional, cumulative and continually being created and worked out" (163). Within an individual text, attempts to map an imaginary nation are made through different characters whose variegated destinies point to a multiplicity of the possibilities of the postcolonial "destination." The main characters in *Petals of Blood* suggest possibilities of the nation. But it is Wanja whose anxieties and condition most closely resembles the prostituted fate of the untranslated nationhood. In fact, the text invites the reader to see Wanja as a metonym of the state of the disintegrating nation (Boehmer 193; McLuskie and Innes 4; Ogude 118; Palmer 263; Roscoe 298; Stratton 48). Her body translates into the site upon which Ngugi records the mistranslation of the nation and recodes the nation to conform to her as a fictional personality. It is little wonder that her sad fate is tied to the capitalist forces the text links to the deterioration of the nation.

Wanja, the symbol of the nation, views her sexuality as a curse that ties her inextricably to her fate as a prostitute (293). She registers her anger through the use taboo expletives. But it is the way the narrative presents Nyakinyua's husband using similarly untranslated language that most forcefully creates the impression that femininity is a weakness to be shunned in favor of masculinity. Nyakinyua thinks one would have to be feminine to betray the fighting spirit. When her husband volunteers to dig a grave for young men killed by the colonialist Waitina Mzungu, she deprecates her husband as effeminate before she understands he intends to kill the colonial administrator:

> And I was so ashamed: I was so ashamed I wept: so my man was a woman after all? To get a jembe to dig a grave of the young?
>
> (325)

This underlines Njamba Nene's heroism through suspense and dramatic irony in that he is fully aware about his own intentions while the other characters and the readers are in the dark. It also inadvertently reveals, however, its anchorage of patriotism to patriarchy in the sense that Nyakinyua, and the text, would condemn Njamba Nene (Gikuyu for the Great Hero) as a woman had he not shown patriotism in attempting to kill the colonialist. Even if he does not kill the colonial officer because the gun jams with age and rust, he is a patriot and, in the text's gendered hierarchy, qualifies to be seen as a man.

Nyakinyua equates her husband's initial "womanish" response with "urine and shit in his bones" (325). It is productive here to recall Simon Gikandi's cogent reading of the image of body effluents as "the metaphor for postcolonial failure" (95). Although Gikandi's focus is on the failure of the former colony to liberate itself fully, it is this motif that Ngugi employs here in structuring Nyakinyua's husband in the pre-independence struggle. Julia Kristeva shows the use of body effluents as semiotic symbols through which otherness is expressed, saying that "excrement and its equivalents (decay, infection, disease, corpse) stand for the danger from outside: the ego threatened by non-ego, society threatened by its outside, life by death" (71). Wanja's name means one who belongs to the periphery, and it is no wonder that in certain politically symbolized games such as football matches, she can only be a spectator, although that role still puts her in trouble with her parents. At work in Nyakinyua's words in refiguring her husband is the view of the woman as a death-trafficking non-ego. In the image the text evokes through Nyakinyua's expression, the threat to masculinity and nationhood is figured as excrement. The conflation of the figurative expression with womanhood confirms the patriarchal view of men as the society and women as its outside. Nyakinyua's husband is the ego, which should be fighting for the nation, while the colonial power and women are the non-egos to be fought and mastered if the nation is to realize itself. Further, the old man's intervention is a culmination of his childhood belief that "the flower of Ilmorog manhood" has been trampled underfoot when colonialists subdued the natives (324). This intervention concretizes men's representation of colonialism as enervation of masculinity and recalls the despoiled flowers of the novel's title.

It is particularly through intertextuality that the polluting non-ego aspect of Nyakinyua is crystallized. To protest the pollution of her traditions by the modernity that Munira and his school represent to her, the old woman defecates on the compound of the institution. Supported by untranslated language and the contradiction in the other characters' ability to access this private act, her protest ties her to the murdered capitalists. These are people who, in the overall philosophy of the narrative, are seen to have defecated, as it were, on the nation. In Gikuyu, her physical act would be described as *kumia nja* (emptying one's bowels on the compound). The reference bands her with Hawkins Kimeria's father, *Kamia Nja,* whose name translates into the Gikuyu for "the diminutive one who defecates on the compound." Kamia Nja has collaborated with the colonialists to exploit his own people. Nyakinyua is anticolonialist like her husband, Njamba Nene in the sense that she is the one who rouses the community against neocolonialism when the bank tries to sell their land to reclaim the loans it had cheated the public into.

The aporiae that suggest arrested translation reach a head through the anachronies that structure the narrative. By aporiae we mean moments of self-contradiction, silences, and narrative breaks. We can read these moments in **Petals of Blood** as highly gendered and political. To fully appreciate the aporiae, concepts that help us work out the structural contradictions in the novel must be clarified. In structuralist terms, an anachrony is the discrepancy between story-order (the sequence events take in the real world as created in the text) and text-order (the sequence in which events follow one another in the text). It is such a disjunction that causes a flashback or a flash-forward (Rimmon-Kenan 46). The anachronies in **Petals of Blood** reveal subterranean patriarchal and colonial values against which the narrative struggles long after its end. Female characters that may appear positive are revealed to be lacking when we come to terms with the anachronies that structure their appearance and actions in the narrative. A case in point is Wanja's mother, who is shown as developing in the text-order in the sense that she is a negative character when we meet her for the first time in the novel and has improved tremendously the last time she appears in the narrative. As the novel closes, Wanja's mother is a positive character, and the text uses her to show an ideal revolutionary who rejects her husband's alignment with the oppressor. Despite her husband's protest, she continues to see her sister who is reputed to have links with freedom fighters (233). He supports the colonial government despite the fact that it killed his father. While the husband of his wife's sister uses the skills he acquired in World War Two to make guns for freedom fighters, Wanja's father is busy amassing wealth at the expense of his family and country as a whole (233). Despite its negative portrayal of her husband, the text does not redeem Wanja's mother. In portraying her positively, the text is not so much interested in showing the reader her good nature as her husband's retrogressive ideas. To be sure, in the "actual" world outside the text, Wanja's mother is the admirable character we see in this instance long before the postindependence moment when she exiles her daughter. In the postindependence era, we never get to see her as the politically conscious woman she was during the fight for freedom.

When she appears next in the postindependence era, the text is silent whether the "now aged mother" has been transformed fully (337). Her heart goes to Wanja, but because the narrative is relayed to us through a hallucinating Wanja, it is not clear whether the mother is any different. When she and Wanja weep, the narrator uses the adverb *maybe* to describe the reason for crying, signaling to the readers that they should not be overly optimistic that the mother has changed from the dragon she acted when she sent Wanja to exile as a prostitute. She still remains a blindly religious woman with "faith in the mercy and in the infinite justice of Christ" (337). The text has already laughed at this predisposition in its female characters. Through Karega's reflection on the use of religion to enthrall the people's minds, the text pokes fun at religious crusades "in which girls claimed that they could speak in tongues, communicate with

Jesus and heal by faith" (305). Such a performance is expressed earlier in an untranslated Gikuyu locution in which Karega's mother sings "kuu iguru gutiri mathina," which would translate into the naïve belief that "in heaven there are no problems"; so we should tolerate the problems on earth as we wait for the afterlife. By making Wanja's mother, like Karega's dead mother, a character who is still wearing religious blinkers, the novel completely silences the possibility of women shaking off the yokes of their slavery.

In a metafictional self-presentation it enunciates through Karega's theory of art, **Petals of Blood** express a desire to be different from critical realist texts that express the conditions of the postcolony without offering hope out of the situation (200). Through Karega, again, the novel criticizes the postcolonial tendencies to hide in sectarian groupings and "linguistic enclaves" (304). Ironically, however, the text is caught up in similar situations that it criticizes. Admittedly, Ngugi's texts in Gikuyu contain expressions, fairly elaborate passages, and signs reproduced to the reader in English and untranslated into Gikuyu. For example, **Matigari ma Njiruungi** (translated as **Matigari** by Wangui Goro) has a scene in which Kabuuru (Settler) William and Njooni Mbooi (John Boy, Jr.) dialogue in directly in English in a way that would be incomprehensible to a Gikuyu-speaking reader who does not understand English because the words are untranslated. Similarly, the Gikuyu texts, especially the children's book **Njamba Nene na Mbaathi I Mathagu** (first published in 1982 and published in the English translation as **Njamba Nene and the Flying Bus**), mimic English texts that can be understood fully by a Gikuyu reader who understands English and has experienced the parodied texts in English language. The anticolonial discourse is so haunted by a deep sense of Englishness that the Gikuyu of the texts is conterminous with the colonial language, indicating the ubiquity of the colonialism in the postindependence present; but the untranslated English in Gikuyu texts are not as gendered as the untranslated Gikuyu in English texts. It is a fair conclusion that Ngugi's **Petals of Blood** uses untranslated language in pointedly gendered terms to express disillusionment with the postcolonial order. The very structure of the narrative seems to echo the unfulfilled expectations that the novel thematizes, expressing in its untranslated language what Biodun Jeyifo would call "arrested decolonization" in the sense that the struggles for independence have not been translated into human freedoms in Africa. Ironically, if it is lack of translations into English from Gikuyu that expresses metonymically that failure of revolution to translate into independence, it is its use of English that enables it to express the vulgarity of the postcolony.

Works Cited

Ahmad, Aijaz. "Jameson's Rhetoric of Otherness and the National Allegory." *In Theory: Classes, Nations, Literatures.* London: Verso, 1992.

Boehmer, Elleke. "The Master's Dance to the Master's Voice: Revolutionary Nationalism and the Representation of Women in the Writing of Ngugi wa Thiong'o." *Journal of Commonwealth Literature* 26.1 (1991): 188-97.

Gikandi, Simon. "Reading the Referent: Postcolonialism and the Writing of Modernity." Ed. Shusheila Nasta. *Reading the 'New' Literatures in a Postcolonial Era.* Cambridge: D. S. Brewer, 2000. 87-104.

Jameson, Fredric. "Third World Literature in the Era of Multinational Corporations." *Social Text* 15 (1986): 65-88

Jeyifo Biodun. "The Nature of Things: Arrested Decolonization and Critical Theory." *Research in African Literatures* 21.1 (1990): 33-48.

Kristeva, Julia. *Powers of Horror.* Columbia UP, 1982.

McLuskie, Kathleen and Lynn Innes. "Women and African Literature." *Wasafiri* 8 (1988): 3-7.

Ngugi wa Thiong'o. *Devil on the Cross.* Nairobi: East African Educational Publisher, 1980.

———. *Matigari ma Njirungi.* [Matigari]. Nairobi: East African Educational Publishers, 1986.

———. *Njamba Nene na Mbaathi I Mathagu* [Njamba Nene and the Flying Bus]. Nairobi: East African Educational Publishers, 1982.

———. *Petals of Blood.* London: Heinemann, 1977.

Ogude, James. *Ngugi's Novels and African History: Narrating the Nation.* London: Pluto, 1999.

Palmer, Eustice. "Ngugi's *Petals of Blood.*" *Critical Perspectives on Ngugi wa Thiong'o.* Ed. G. D. Killam. Washington: Three Continents, 1984. 271-84.

Punter, David. *Postcolonial Imaginings: Fictions of a New World Order.* Edinburgh: Edinburgh UP, 2000.

Richards, Ivor A. *The Philosophy of Rhetoric.* 1936. New York: Oxford UP, 1965.

Rimmon-Kenan, Shlomith. *Narrative Fiction: Contemporary Poetics* London: Routledge, 1983.

Roos, Bonnie. "Re-Historicizing the Conflicted Figure of Woman in Ngugi's *Petals of Blood. Research in African Literatures.* 33.2 (2002): 154-70.

Roscoe, Adrian. *Uhuru's Fire.* London: Heinemann, 1985.

Smith, Craig V. "Rainbow Memories of Gain and Loss": *Petals of Blood* and the New Resistance." *The World of Ngugi wa Thiong'o.* Ed. Charles Cantalupo, Trenton: Africa World P, 1995. 93-108.

Stratton, Florence. *Contemporary African Literature and the Politics of Gender.* London: Routledge, 1994.

Szeman, Imre. "Who's Afraid of National Allegory? Jameson, Literary Criticism, Globalization." *The Southern Atlantic Quarterly* 100.3 (2001): 803 27.

FURTHER READING

Criticism

Gikandi, Simon. *Ngugi wa Thiong'o.* Cambridge: Cambridge University Press, 2000, 328 p.

Literary critique of Ngugi's role in postcolonial Kenyan literature.

Ngugi wa Thiong'o and Angela Lamas Rodrigues. "Beyond Nativism: An Interview with Ngugi wa Thiong'o." *Research in African Literatures* 35, no. 3 (fall 2004): 161-67.

Interview in which Ngugi discusses his plans to return to Kenya from exile, the impact of globalization on Africa, and the role of the writer in preserving a historical sensibility and native languages.

Uraizee, Joya F. "'Flowers in All Their Colours': *Nations* and Communities in Ngugi wa Thiong'o's *Petals of Blood.*" *International Fiction Review* 31 (2004): 27-38.

Examines the idea of nations and local seats of government in *Petals of Blood,* highlighting contrasts throughout the novel that Ngugi uses to develop his themes.

Uskalis, Eriks. "Allegory and the Retrieval of History: Ngugi wa Thiong'o's *The River Between* and *Matigari.*" *ARIEL* 36, nos. 3-4 (July 1, 2005): 85-102.

Argues that Ngugi uses allegory as a mode of dissent in *The River Between* and *Matigari.*

Elizabeth Nunez
1944-

(Also wrote as Elizabeth Nunez-Harrell) Trinidadian-born American novelist.

INTRODUCTION

Nunez is a respected humanities scholar and English professor who, from 1986 to 2000, directed the National Black Writers Conference, the panelists for which have included such notable black authors as Maya Angelou, Alice Walker, Gwendolyn Brooks, and Derek Walcott. Chair of the PEN American Open Book Committee, which focuses on providing people of color access to the publishing industry, Nunez is also the author of several novels, including *Beyond the Limbo Silence* (1998), which received the Independent Publishers Book Award in 1999, and *Bruised Hibiscus* (1994), which won the American Book Award in 2001.

BIOGRAPHICAL INFORMATION

Born in 1944 in Cocorite, Trinidad, Nunez was raised in a family of eleven children. She immigrated to the United States at the age of nineteen, after finishing high school, then earned an undergraduate degree from Marian College in 1967. She subsequently entered New York University, earning a master's degree in 1971 and a Ph.D. in 1977, both in English. She became affiliated with the City University of New York (CUNY) in 1972, where she has been credited with creating and initiating a variety of academic programs, and where she holds the position of Distinguished Professor of English at Medgar Evers College. In addition to her teaching duties, she has also served as executive producer for the CUNY television series *Black Writers in America.* She is the recipient of several awards, including the Sojourner Truth Award from the National Association of Black Business and Professional Women's Clubs, the 1999 Carter G. Woodson Outstanding Teacher of the Year Award, and the 2003 Caribbean American Heritage Award. She has also received an honorary doctorate in humane letters from Marian College for her contributions to the arts and education.

MAJOR WORKS

Nunez's first novel, *When Rocks Dance* (1986), is set in Trinidad during the colonial era, and treats such themes as power, wealth, education, the patriarchy, ritual sacrifices, the spiritual realm, freedom, land ownership, and African tradition. The novel opens with the story of Emilia, a native woman whose lover is an Englishman. His wife is barren, and he promises Emilia a tract of land if she can provide him with an heir. Emilia subsequently gives birth three separate times to sets of twins, yet all die at birth, a result of Emilia's having been cursed by the Igbo spirits. In order to break the spell she must sacrifice her fourth set of twins, who are born alive. She offers them to the gods by leaving them in the forest to die. Emilia then has a ninth child, a girl she names Marina, who displays the strengths of all her siblings before her. She is beautiful, strong, and seemingly immune from the illnesses and pitfalls of life. *Bruised Hibiscus* is set in a Trinidad village in the 1950s and involves murder and sexual violence. The main characters, Rosa and Zuela, who were close for a time during adolescence, are reunited amid the widespread terror that results from two shocking and monstrous murders. *Beyond the Limbo Silence* is told from the first-person point of view of emotionally fragile Sara Edgehill, a college student from the Caribbean who is awarded a scholarship to attend a Catholic college in Wisconsin. Exploring relationships between blacks from diverse cultural and political backgrounds, the novel relates how Sara falls in love with one of the few other blacks at the school, Sam Maxwell, an African American law student and political activist who leaves her for Mississippi, where his colleagues, the real-life Michael Schwerner, Andrew Goodman, and James Earl Chaney, disappear. During the course of the novel, another student, Courtney, is transmogrified into an Obeahwoman, and helps Sara reclaim her African and Caribbean heritage.

Discretion (2002) is the story of man torn between two worlds, neither of which he can give up. Oufoula Sindede is a diplomat from an unnamed African country. Schooled in Western ways as a child, Oufoula is a Christian who learned to love Shakespeare and play tennis. He has a traditional marriage to his wife, Nerida, whom he loves, and a decades-long passion for Marguerite, a Jamaican-born painter who lives in New York City, and who refuses to engage in an affair with the married man. Over the twenty years since they first met, he has been unable to put her out of his mind. The story opens with Oufoula, at fifty-five, reconnecting with Marguerite. *Grace* (2003) also features a male protagonist, Justin Peters, a black Trinidadian and Harvard graduate who teaches at a small college in Brooklyn. Justin is criticized by Afrocentric colleagues for his concentration on the works of "Dead White Men"; his wife, Sally, a Harlem-born poet and teacher, tries to recapture her reason for living as she suffers from the memories of her physician father being killed by the Ku Klux Klan, and her mother's mental breakdown in the aftermath. The one thing the couple have in common is their love for their young daughter. When Sally, confused and depressed, moves out of the house and in with a female friend, Justin is bewildered by Sally's actions and fears that she will ultimately leave him. *Prospero's Daughter* (2006) is a retelling of Shakespeare's *The Tempest*. Set on Chacachacare, a small island off the coast of Trinidad, the novel revolves around the depraved and racist Doctor Peter Gardner, who has hidden himself and his young daughter, Virginia, on the sparsely populated island to avoid prosecution for the often-deadly experiments he has conducted on unsuspecting human victims. Taking over the home and land of the dark-skinned orphan Carlos, who is being cared for by a terminally ill woman, the doctor amuses himself by attempting to "civilize" the boy, who eventually falls in love with Gardner's daughter. The enraged doctor then accuses Carlos of attempted rape.

CRITICAL RECEPTION

Overall, Nunez's novels have been praised and highly recommended by reviewers. Many critics regard her writing as symbolically and metaphorically rich, and laud her multilayered and complex plots, many of which address sociocultural issues revolving around race, gender, and class. She has been singled out for her evocation of the Caribbean landscape and is noted as a major contributor to the field of Caribbean literature. In addition to discussing Nunez as a feminist writer, focusing on her treatment of women and their resistance to colonial oppression, several observers note the spiritual dimension in her work, finding its source in the indigenous Trinidadian culture. Some view this aspect of her fiction as the author's condemnation of Western society, while others argue that it expresses the idea that black individuals can survive in American culture only by preserving traditional African and Caribbean religious and social beliefs. Many other scholars commend her contribution to African diaspora literature, and favorably compare her writing style to that of Toni Morrison and Alice Walker.

PRINCIPAL WORKS

When Rocks Dance [as Elizabeth Nunez-Harrell] (novel) 1986
Bruised Hibiscus (novel) 1994
Beyond the Limbo Silence (novel) 1998
Defining Ourselves: Black Writers in the 90s [coeditor with Brenda M. Greene] (essays) 1999
Discretion (novel) 2002
Grace (novel) 2003
Stories from Blue Latitudes: Caribbean Women Writers at Home and Abroad [coeditor with Jennifer Sparrow] 2005
Prospero's Daughter (novel) 2006

CRITICISM

Leah Creque-Harris (essay date 1990)

SOURCE: Creque-Harris, Leah. "*When Rocks Dance*: An Evaluation." In *Caribbean Women Writers: Essays from the First International Conference,* edited by Selwyn R. Cudjoe, pp. 159-63. Wellesley, Mass.: Calaloux Publications, 1990.

[*In the essay that follows, Creque-Harris offers an overview of* When Rocks Dance, *focusing on how the author intermixes thematic concerns—colonialism, African tradition, capitalism, ritual sacrifice, and power—with the novel's questions of gender, race, and social status.*]

When Rocks Dance is Elizabeth Nuñez-Harrell's first novel set in her native Trinidad that describes the resistance of three women to their disfranchised condition during the colonialist era of the late nineteenth century. Historically, this postslavery epoch in Trinidadian history was characterized by the economic change from a society dependent upon the production of cocoa and sugar cane to the discovery of oil, the source of the nation's wealth and impetus for multinational exploitation and of the industrialization of the society. Despite the emergence of an international identity of a second-generation population descended from African slaves, Asian indentured servants, and European colonists, there was no place for the black woman in this society. The struggle of these Afro-Caribbean women is intricately linked with the oppression of other ethnic groups, the indigenous Indians whose people have been annihilated and banished to the borders of Venezuela and the indentured class of Asians represented by the East Indian overseer, Ranjit.

The triple dynamics of race, gender, and class greatly affected the lives of the three central characters. Women had no legal rights or access to the traditional measures of wealth without benefit of marriage or inheritance. Emilia's quest for power through land ownership, the predominant conflict of this novel, is a reaction of protest to her experience as the concubine of two European landowners in succession upon whom she is totally dependent for basic survival.

Education also was a privilege denied to women of this era. Virginia, adopted by a childless European couple, attained the coveted ability to read and write, as well as an affinity for Shakespeare through the auspices of her white foster mother, who endeavored to erase Virginia's ethnic origin through acculturation.

Although these two women come from different backgrounds (Emilia is uneducated, uncultured, and amoral, while Virginia is well-bred), their life experiences have taught them how precarious and unstable their status is and how important power and wealth are for their survival. Both women were orphaned in childhood and would have been homeless but for the patronage of whites (Emilia as the concubine of Hrothgar and Virginia as the foster child of the Smiths). Both women were subjected to abuse as the sex objects of men. Emilia becomes a concubine at age twelve to maintain a roof over her head, and Virginia's foster father begins to lust after her in her adolescence, which causes her foster mother to remove her from their home via an arranged marriage to a Portuguese planter. From this experience, Emilia learned the importance of land ownership. Virginia, who already possessed land from her "dowry" and late husband, knew the importance of prestige and status.

The theme of land ownership and prestige as a life's goal is in keeping with the literary tradition of Caribbean women writers as exemplified in Paule Marshall's *Browngirl, Brownstones*. In this tradition, land ownership refers to the ancestral memory of African kinship with the earth and the brutal displacement of African people by slavery. Beyond economic security, property ownership is a legal mode to protest to the violation of one's inherent rights. Nuñez-Harrell keeps this ancestral memory alive throughout the text with accurate accounts of the middle passage experience and the genocide of the native Indians. Secondarily, this quest for land symbolizes the stereotypical feminine trait in nature to seek a nest, a home for the shelter, and security of her offspring.

Emilia endures the pain and humiliation of several unsuccessful pregnancies ending in stillbirths due scientifically to strangulation on the umbilical chord and metaphysically to the Ibo taboo of bearing twins, to reclaim the land for her own security, her progeny, and her people. Hrothgar, in desperate need of an heir, promises that she will inherit his cocoa estate if she bears him a son who lives.

Thus begins her quest for autonomy and power—the ability to control and shape one's environment. In this patriarchal, colonialist setting, power is attained through economic wealth, political might through organized numbers, armed struggle, or spiritual acumen by transcending the oppression of the physical realm to effect change.

Emilia begins to suspect through her continual failure to validate herself as a woman through motherhood that she is indeed cursed according to the Ibo legend. It becomes obvious that she cannot attain her desired economic security without first acknowledging the religion and spiritual powers of her African ancestors as syncretized in the new world in the form of obeah (or in Christian terms, first seeking the kingdom of God).

In this call for authenticity and loyalty to one's heritage, Emilia begins to seek salvation through a spiritual journey back to her African homeland. This marks an important juncture in the novel when Nuñez-Harrell presents a reordering of the universe revolving around a theology of liberation where African gods preside alongside Christian rituals to heal the particular sociopolitical condition of colonized people.

The Ibo priest who administered to Emilia's condition warned that her curse could only be lifted through the sacrifice of her soon-to-be-born twin sons. After this ritualistic sacrifice she will bear a child who will be destined for wealth. With the assistance of the Warao Indian whose animistic religion confirmed the obeah prophecy, Emilia sacrifices her first opportunity to be a mother and gives birth to a beautiful mulatta daughter, Marina, who grows up to scorn her mother's plight yet embraces her thirst for land ownership. This sacrifice, though it appears savage, is analogous to the Christian sacrifice of God's "only begotten son so that others may live."

Marina's destiny is linked with Antonio de Balboa, her future husband and the son of Virginia and the Portuguese planter, Vasco de Balboa. As was true for her mother, her birthright of wealth and security from the de Balboa estate is dependent upon her giving birth to a child. She must first, however, break the curse on Antonio, whose first three wives died in childbirth. It is implied that since she embodied the spirits of her eight brothers, she is strong enough to survive this curse without harm.

Although Marina's physicality is female she is, in essence, a male. Is it the author's intent that it would take a masculine identity to possess such power? Or is there strength in the union of genders? This may refer to the obeah or voodoo practice of indiscriminate possession by deities regardless of sex.

Both Antonio and Marina are "children of the damned," of parents who sold their souls rather than live in truth. Here again, when one violates their authenticity, they are condemned. The motif of the sins of the father being visited upon the son is reenacted. Antonio's father was a Roman Catholic priest who defected for academic freedom and became further disillusioned after witnessing the atrocities of slavery. He married and impregnated Virginia only to realize his sin and thereafter ceased to perform as her husband, rendering her a bitter and lonely woman perversely clinging to her relationship with her son. In the telling of this story Nuñez-Harrell introduces the proverbial myth of Oedipus, which the early Greeks created to understand the complexity of their existence and the notion of kinship.

Virginia's demands for Antonio's attention and affection are a frustrated enactment of power over her domicile that cannot be enacted in this patriarchal society. Marina's presence as her daughter-in-law threatens not only her domain but also her European convention. Moreover, Virginia fears Marina's reputed powers and is repelled by the presence of obeah that she discovers in her home. She assumes that Marina, like her mother, is a practitioner of obeah. In reality, what caused Virginia's hysteria at the discovery of obeah in her home was her deep-rooted racial ambivalence as a black female raised by a white woman.

Eventually, Antonio's curse threatens Marina's life when she becomes ill while pregnant with twins. Emilia intervenes with obeah to save her daughter's life. Like her mother in her younger days, Marina is reluctant to use obeah but finally yields to its promise.

Through an eclectic use of spiritual powers which defy science and make a mockery of modern medicine, Marina safely delivers twins, one boy and one girl, and the lives of Emilia and Virginia are restored to order. The trinity archetype as a symbol of divine power is used throughout the unfolding of this drama. The trio of characters alternately represents the three branches of the trinity in this three-tiered examination of women's quest for power in this island whose name is derived from its topological representation of the trinity—one mountain with three peaks. At the moment of greatest danger, when Marina is at the brink of death, these three strong-willed, disparate women are united in their belief and affirmation of African tradition as the source of their salvation. Alternately, each represents the forces of the trinity: Emilia displays the reproductive power of God, the Mother/Father. As God the daughter/son, Marina's life exemplifies the divine aspect of humankind as a way of life. Her destiny as a woman of wealth and power is the fulfillment of divine promise as a devotee of a New World religion. Then there is God the Holy consummate Spirit moving in and through humanity giving knowledge where there is none. Through this spirit, Virginia surrenders to seek obeah after the medical doctor that she summoned, using her white connections, failed to heal Marina.

The obeah ritual that saved Marina's life was achieved through a male medium, who went into a trance to bring the body of Christ to Marina. Antonio had to participate in this ritual by going to a Catholic Mass, receiving communion to bring the unbroken host to Alma, the Diviner, as penance for his father's sin of breaking the vows of chastity and deserting the priesthood. This ritual, which mingles the sacrament of the Catholic church with the obeah ritual, is significant as a mechanism for paying homage to obeah. Again sacrifice is the element of salvation, and Marina's life is saved through the sacrifice of a male. The medium never returns to life from his trancelike state.

At the closing of this story all of the men who are pivotal characters in this story diminish in importance. Antonio is compelled to leave Marina after burning Smith's home to get Marina's property back. Virginia's foster father dies, and the Warao retreats to Venezuela having completed the cycle to wrench the land from the white man's hands. All the men have wielded their limited powers leaving the women as survivors. The Trinidadian expression from which the title is derived, "What right have eggs among rocks when they are dancing?" aptly describes why the fragile and cowardly men in the novel moved out of the way to allow the triumph of strong women. None of the male-female relationships in this book are romantically fulfilling.

The ultimate success of these women in attaining control over their lives can be attributed to the bonding that takes place among them as they become united in their struggle to secure the promise of the future through Marina and her children. It is through these mother-daughter bonds that these women develop their autonomy. In the absence of real mothers, Emilia and Virginia discover their identities through mother Africa. Marina develops the characteristics of self-determination and independence from her mother's transmission of these values, as is often the case with black women worldwide. Although many mothers of the black race would not claim to be feminists, their approach to survival is decidedly feminist.

Elizabeth Nuñez-Harrell has crafted an engaging narrative rich in symbolism and metaphor that is a composite of familiar and traditional themes and of literary devices. As an accomplished scholar in the humanities, she has blended such familiar themes as the tragic mulatto, the noble savage, and the oedipal conflict with the romanticism of the African past contrasted with a critique on the destructiveness of colonialism and capitalism. Although these contrivances along with the superimposed feminist point of view make the telling of the story self-conscious, these devices are appropriately used to handle the complex weaving of issues on race, gender, and class in a multicultural society.

Thelma B. Thompson-Deloatch (essay date 1999)

SOURCE: Thompson-Deloatch, Thelma B. "Fire and Ice: The Socioeconomics of Romantic Love in *When the Rocks Dance* by Elizabeth Nunez-Harrell." In *Arms*

Akimbo: Africana Women in Contemporary Literature, edited by Janice Lee Liddell and Yakini Belinda Kemp, pp. 117-29. Gainesville: University Press of Florida, 1999.

[*In this essay, Thompson-Deloatch studies how the ownership of land in* When Rocks Dance *is connected to economic independence and power, and how "the land supplants the love bond in marriages and unions."*]

Somewhere among the older Jamaican rhymes and quips is, or was, this couplet:

> Men are dogs, they are made to roam
> Women are cats to stay at home.

To the Caribbean woman writer, the deeper cultural norm that supports such a notion is well known and well examined. It is the basis for Susheila Nasta's observation that "the post-colonial woman writer is not only involved in making herself heard, in changing the architecture of male-centered ideologies and languages. . . . [S]he has also to subvert and demythologize indigenous male writings and traditions which seek to label her" (xv).

Critical exegeses on Caribbean women's writings are replete with examinations of the contrasting issues represented in this literature: past/present/future, oppressor/victim, youth/age, native/foreign. But one focus that marks the emergence of Caribbean women's fiction as significant is the varied responses to the female dilemma and their varied strategies for resistance and survival.

In Elizabeth Nunez-Harrell's novel *When Rocks Dance,* seemingly, a conscious effort is made to include the various oppositional forces that tend to appear in the postcolonial writings. The novel takes its integrity from conflicts whose roots rest in the colonial system; race; and gender, class, politics, religion, culture, history, and geography. Romantic in the classical sense, the novel balances the mythical with the historic and sociological concepts of womanhood and seeks to resolve selected conflicts through very old methods of land tenure now seized by new hands—the black woman's hands.

The ownership of land has been a fundamental manifestation of power in most societies. The land, mother earth, has been the source of economic, social, and political might, as well as a cause for war for eons, and it is Ileana Rodriguez who best captures the concept as it relates to colonial societies. She writes, "In all writings on 'nation,' there is a truth which some locate in the strict terrain of language and words . . . [O]thers, like myself, situate [this truth] in the discussion of land, territory, and land tenure, that is, in the political arena of struggle. . . . Both theories, one linguistic, the other political, fight for the representation of nation. But this 'nation' . . . is a nation in which neither Indians, nor blacks nor women have a space" (4).

Elizabeth Nunez-Harrell and other female Caribbean writers are settling the linguistic notion, but the political fight for recognition and representation is often explored in fictional constructs such as *When Rocks Dance.* In this case, the land supplants the love bond in marriages and unions. Used as a substitute for romantic love and its attendant features, the possession of land fails as a sustaining basis for family life, even if it offers socioeconomic place or space to the characters. In some significant way, by grounding the novel in the land, Nunez-Harrell calls attention to the most enduring recorded problem of humankind, the cause of feuds, disputes, and wars, ancient and modern—land, territory, borders, the economic significance to individuals and nations, and the national "love" relationships based upon resources.

When Rocks Dance is an essentially feminist novel, taking its name from an African proverb that posits that men are like eggs while women are the rocks of society. It asks, also, "when rocks dance, what right have you among them if you are an egg?" (298), suggesting a selective fraternization of the sexes. The plot reveals women who maintain equilibrium, while the male characters suffer emotional disintegration as the complex pressures of Caribbean life become personal. This classical, romantic novel explores "the region's historical conflicts" through romantic love and exposes the eternal cultural resistance to colonial hegemony that exists and persists in most colonized states regardless of the pronouncements of love, church, and government.

The novel opens with the common-law relationship of an old English cocoa planter, Hrothgar, and a young, shrewd Trinidadian woman, Emilia, who becomes his lover two months after her twelfth birthday and after the death of her mother, the cook. "He promised that if she would bear him a son, old man that he was, he would will his cocoa estate and his house to her upon his death. . . . That promise made her endure long nights of his body pressing roughly into hers. . . . She stayed in Hrothgar's bed to reclaim the land" (*WRD* [*When Rocks Dance*] 12, 13). The image of the oppressor is a vivid one and the idea of the colonist as a material rapist has been well discussed elsewhere in postcolonial nonfiction.

Such situations give rise to critical observations such as that of Rodriguez, who observes that, "tied more to Independence and the Founding Fathers of the land, the modern woman finds that the only exit possible is through money. Capital/dowry provides the vocabulary for discussing the relation of a marriage/nation-state" (xv). The truism of the interrelatedness of socioeconomics and romantic unions is carried out from the beginning of the novel with Emilia's resolve, to the end with Virginia's visit to the landowning Indian.

Founded upon utilitarian principles, Emilia's and Hrothgar's relationship epitomizes the crux of colonialism, exploitation, and greed. It is not surprising that

Emilia's eight sons (four pairs of twins) die, or that upon the advice of the Ibo obeah man they are abandoned soon after their birth. The only child Emilia manages to raise is a daughter, Marina, who survives because she is imbued with the spirit of eight men—her dead brothers, given back to the land.

Beyond the fact that twins die because children need love to survive emotionally, Emilia's twin boys are used as currency, "blood money" to purchase the valued cocoa land from the perceived "oppressor." Emilia's aim now is to reclaim from Hrothgar that which he has seized—mother earth and herself, the boys' birth mother. Emilia's daughter—without realizing that her mother's lot was not by choice, as hers is—later reminds Emilia that there is a name for women who exact a price for their sexual services.

Unaware of Emilia's needs, the proud and elated Hrothgar, the aged father of twin sons for the fourth time, held high hopes that these boys would continue his tradition. Hrothgar "called them his cocoa planters. He made them over-seers. . . . Hrothgar penned his will. . . . The boys would be his heirs. They would send the 'Portogee' trader to the devil and make the Negroes till the soil" (18). Knowing from the obeah man, however, that these boys would not live, Emilia leaves them in the forest in an attempt to rid herself of a curse. She seduces Hrothgar with obeah and in the heat of his passion informs him that the twins are "sleeping in the cocoa patch." This knowledge turns the old man's love to hate even as his hope turns to madness and hers to despair, for male heirs are never to be his and the land was never to be hers. Her contract to deliver live sons is as broken as her husband's last hope of having heirs. The nothingness of Hrothgar's later life then manifests itself in hatred and bitterness toward Emilia and the girl child, Marina. What began as nurturing, cooking food, mutual convenience, dreams unfulfilled—"a marriage" based on market principles—becomes a relationship in atrophy, withered, sick, and dead.

To Hrothgar, the females (wife and child) are not factors in the land tenure system. He feels no responsibility for their well-being, nor does the larger society, including the church, which acts as facilitator for the total and cyclical abuse of the female in this novel.

The female Caribbean fiction writer may be at an observation point at which cultural realities overcome any instinct to label the genesis of the devalued female in Caribbean society. Critics such as Carole Boyce Davies and Elaine Savory Fido point to the Caribbean's cultural history as possible fictional fodder. They record, "There were numerous signs of the conditions of women which were depressing: street insult and verbal and physical beatings from men; women with scores of children who were forced to beg the 'children's father' for support at his workplace on pay day before the money was spent; girls of promise getting pregnant and

thereafter losing all the brilliance they had previously shown, sinking into a round of baby-making for men who saw sex as recreation and women as conquests; all this crowned by an oral culture which endorsed this behavior" (xiv).

In response to this literary "burden," newer female Caribbean writers are addressing the topic. Pamela Mordecai and Betty Wilson identify a positive response that focuses on the value of ordinary human beings, "the worth of male to female persons and vice versa; the worth of black persons (or other persons of color) to other black persons and to white persons" (Her True-True Name xiii). Although from the perspective of the fictional, white, colonial man, the women were chattel for his comforts and of little emotional significance to him, Emilia was not passive in victim status. She valued herself and her child and became proactive to ensure her daughter's economic well-being. What Ileana Rodriguez found to be true in Teresa de la Parra's Ifigenia applies to Marina's portrayal: "Without money, the future vanishes, for the absence of money is poverty and poverty means 'complete dependency' and 'humiliation and pain' . . . happiness, freedom and success are synonyms for money" (62). Also, Rodriguez reports, "Body is capital. The poor, declassé, disinherited and dowryless woman must think in terms of the best use of that capital" (65).

This thinking is manifested in Emilia's own life of total dependency and, naturally, forms the frame of reference for her daughter's future. Emilia's daughter, Marina—spirit child, at once European and African, stereotypically materialistic, sensual and mysterious—marries Antonio de Balboa for his land, despite a curse upon him that causes his three previous wives to perish in childbirth. "Marina's mind clung to just one word that she had heard. Land. de Balboa had land. . . . 'How can I meet him?' Emilia sighed, relieved. 'It will be arranged,' she said" (43).

Equally self-centered, Antonio de Balboa, preoccupied with "a will to live, an innate desire to reproduce, a muffled drumming from the world of his African ancestors that told him without logic or understanding that Marina would save him . . . married the woman" (55). Struck silent by Marina's height and arrogance, her golden hair, grey eyes, almost white skin, "breasts projecting forward ready for an argument, [and] a backside high and rigid," Antonio marries Marina not only because of physical attraction, but "because in the sanctum of his brain where his mind was free from the primitive grappling of the intellect, he knew passionately that this woman would save him" (56).

Proceeding from these motivations, the union of Marina and Antonio is plagued with several conflicts: differences in religion, interferences by mothers-in-law, periodic rejection, problems of self-esteem, problems of class differences, difference of opinions on the purpose and value of land and of heritage, and lack of a unified vision. Although Marina does survive the difficult delivery of her twin children and succeeds in breaking the curse on young de Balboa, her relationship with her husband is merely a physical one. The emotional and psychological distance that separates this couple is enough to lead each of them to the harsh introspection and loneliness attendant to unions founded without love. Marina's constant fear that Antonio's mother will sell the fifteen acres of oil-drenched cocoa land pushes her to torment and taunt her husband about his seemingly incestuous relationship with his mother, his restrictive religion, and worse yet, about his motivation for his marriage to her. Marina fails to see the familial similarities; that like her mother and like her husband, she too is confused about romantic love and the benefits that accrue therefrom. Her major motive for marriage was economics; his, social acceptance.

Antonio de Balboa, the product of a loveless marriage, is twice cursed. His father, an excommunicated Portuguese priest, marries his mother, Virginia, the Black adopted daughter of a white English couple. Distressed at the adoptive father's advances to the regal Virginia, Mrs. Smith, the mother, arranges to give to the ex-priest, de Balboa, a handsome dowry of land if he would marry her adopted daughter and, thus, remove the carnal temptation from her husband's presence. On the following one-sided agreement, the union was made and de Balboa tells Virginia his terms: "I'll not sleep with you as man and wife. I won't share your bed. You may do as you please, I will not have her sell you to me like a lump of coal. I'll have no hand in her slave traffic. Your color offends her. I'll give you the land too. It's your right as her daughter" (60).

Yet the reader realizes that Virginia pays a much higher price to enter this marriage than the dowry her "mother" gave. Her new husband could not keep all his promises. Indeed, on the wedding night, "his stoic detachment oozing swiftly out of his soul," he took her in a "frenzy . . . as though he had lost every ounce of his rational self, his Christian morality" (61).

This is the story of Antonio's conception and the only sexual encounter between his parents and practically the only connection. Years later, the embittered Virginia realizes that her son, Antonio, has forgiven his father for the twelve years of silence and rejection. She challenges her son, "Tell me what should I have understood. You talked to him. Tell me . . . tell me, how do you think he intended for us to live? To eat? . . . I managed. I sold chickens, ducks. I taught school. I managed" (68, 69). It is significant that Virginia focuses on the economics of their existence, not on the emotional and physical needs.

Raised in the darkness and discomfort of his parents' loveless marriage and caught, forever, in his attempt to compensate to his mother for his father's shortcomings,

Antonio is overwhelmed by the problems in his own relationship. Cerebral and idealistic, he loses focus, loses control of his life, loses touch with his environment, and learns that good intentions cannot sustain a relationship. When he sets sail for Europe it is not as an adventurer, but as a felon, a loser, a deserter—a man who has failed in his most important ventures in life, a man who tried to establish his sons' economic security through desperate reaction rather than rational proaction. He, a father, a son, a husband, once a respected school principal, must "return," as his father could never do, to Europe, where he will be nothing. His twin sons are left to be raised as he and Marina were raised: fatherless, by a mother who will have to "father" them, despite the fact that a birth father is alive.

Antonio leaves the country, however, with an understanding that could come only from personal experience: "He wished he could tell her [his mother] yes, his father was a he-goat, a ram goat, a hypocritical, self-righteous ram-goat, but he could not. Was it because he too understood how the flesh, the human condition, could so mercilessly remind a man that he is a man, not a god who can control his passion. . . . Was it that he understood that his father was a man although a priest? Antonio's long weeks of abstinence, self-denial, his refusal to make love to Marina had taught him that the body could betray the mind and desire what the mind had decided it would not choose" (210).

How did Antonio arrive at this position from where he was at the beginning of his union with Marina, when "the heavens saw the son of that Portuguese religious dissenter . . . make love without restraint or caution as though the very act and the woman he penetrated were all that gave his life meaning?" (121) One answer is found in Edward Kamau Brathwaite's theory of the duality of love. In his musings on developing a Caribbean aesthetic, Brathwaite invented the term "the love axe/l" (186). This concept of love as a central Caribbean driving force, the central emotion that moves life along (self-love included), also embraces the idea that love acts as an axe, a tool that cuts, chops, breaks open, damages, and reveals an inner core, and that may even "draw blood." Romantic love as represented in Nunez-Harrell's novel bears out Brathwaite's musings. At the core of the novel, as well as at the periphery, the plot and subplots, the major and minor characters, are all connected by romantic love (an axel); yet it is romantic love that fails, that goes to a state of atrophy—axed.

In the cases of the three female characters under discussion, the modern feminine perspective is at once dramatized and negated. While the women are left to any means possible for their survival and that of their offspring, they are somewhat unhappily free from restrictive notions of marriage. Davies and Fido observe that the "strength of the [Caribbean] women surely comes from necessity, from being unable to walk away from being left to raise the children" (xv). Mark A. McWatt, also writing of the Caribbean wife and mother, found that "it is a painfully ambiguous role, for it is that towards which the woman generally aspire, and yet, it is the role that most relentlessly traps and diminishes them [*sic*]" (228).

In her critical evaluation of **When Rocks Dance,** Leah Creque-Harris observes that "none of the male-female relationships in this book are romantically fulfilling" (163). What was not mentioned is that neither the male nor the female characters seemed disturbed about the romantic atrophy in their lives. The women, however, constantly contemplate the material hardships. The consistent irony on the romantic love axel of the plot is the successful demonstration that each of the partners in a union has experienced sexual fulfillment with the mate, and in Virginia's case, outside the marriage. It seems, then, that there is deliberate effort to show, first, that sexual fulfillment by itself is not sufficient to sustain a marriage or a union. Second, the developments demonstrate that the romantic attraction was not the grounds for these unions; therefore that rubric can hardly be used to evaluate their success or failure. It is the land and its significance upon which these unions were erected, and as the land went so, too, did the "love." Finally, the novel overtly shows the impossibility for romantic love to thrive in the presence of other overwhelming personal, social, and economic problems. The fictional landscape in the individual lives mirrors the larger political and cultural dilemma of the Caribbean, captured well by Antonio Benitez-Rojo when he sets forth the dilemma:

> I start from the belief that "Caribbeanness" is a system full of noise and opacity . . . a chaotic system beyond the total reach of any specific kind of knowledge or interpretation of the world. To my way of thinking, no perspective of human thought . . . can by itself define the Caribbean's complex sociocultural interplay. We need all of them at the same time. . . . [I]f . . . we study the Caribbean by paying attention only to the impact of Afro-Caribbean beliefs upon its social and political structures, we are only looking at one among many of the area's fundamental aspects. Moreover, if we were to study the Caribbean's cultural history only in terms of the clash of two discourses that speak in terms of race, or class, or colonialism, or economic development, we would be also studying dynamics that are fundamental to the system. . . . [C]onstruction of these polarized models constitutes a reduction that is characteristic of modernity, but it is a reduction that had persisted with uncommon tenacity in the area's histography and its literature.

(255, 256)

When Rocks Dance gives credence to Benitez-Rojo's theory of chaos and helps to provide reasons for a Caribbean dialectic that ignores established paradigms reserved for more homogeneous societies. Furthermore, the chaos theory provides grounds for Merle Hodge's more pointed conclusions expressed in her landmark essay, "The Shadow of the Whip: A Comment on Male-Female Relations in the Caribbean." Hodge posits that as a residue of slavery and continued colonialism, mutual respect was lost between enslaved men and women and their offspring. The man, unable to provide for his family and take leadership in his affairs, was reduced to the single role of impregnating. The children were/are left to be raised by a female, a mother, grandmother, older sister, aunt, or stranger. "Women became mother and father to the race" (115).

In exploring the complications of romantic love, **When Rocks Dance** extends itself to include the Indian. The fictional situation supports the thesis that Indians, too, suffered from the cultural mores relevant to gender and class. They, too—brought to the Caribbean as indentured labor, to work on sugar plantations—suffered dislocation of family and other humiliations.

On the fringes of the novel, the ambitious East Indian character, Ranjit, becomes interested in learning to read. For one year, under the private tutelage of schoolteacher Virginia de Balboa, he learns much and falls in love with her vitality. Like the other love unions in the novel, Ranjit's marriage is also in that dreaded state of catastrophe. The narrator summarizes his condition and his wife's: "Indira, Ranjit's wife, bore the pain of gossip well. Her job was to bear children, something she also did well. She never spoke to her husband on any topic other than food, clothing, and shelter. . . . None of the East Indian women around her thought that their husband's business was any of theirs. The women had their role and the men theirs" (**WRD** 131). Social practice and the inferiority placed upon Indians in that society had bred such misconception "that the possibility of romantic love between Virginia and Ranjit was not ever a consideration. . . . A Negro woman and an Indian man just didn't see each other that way" (**WRD** 131).

Nunez-Harrell breaks the false barrier of interracial love in several directions and, for a brief moment, shows that some of the characters are caught by the "love axe/l." Aware of the atrophy that has set into their lives, they further realize that it is "what they call love" that has died, but not themselves as lovers. Thus, Nunez-Harrell reveals the naked axel of love in atrophy, the naked truth of human beings who are alive yet dead. The narrator provides again a front seat to this scenario, emphasizing at once the emotional neediness and the capacity to find ecstasy that ironically resides in these outwardly "cold" characters. The tension in the plot is heightened by this and other contradictions. Here, the women characters are juxtaposed for emphasis: "Indira didn't count on the longing for something more than a bed partner that festered in her husband's heart. Nor could she know the pain of loneliness that Virginia suffered because she . . . had no bed partner. . . . For one short evening, with her husband wandering on the beach . . . indifferent to his wife's activities, Virginia knew sexual fulfillment. . . . They [Virginia and Ranjit] clung to each other like lost souls adrift on a raging sea. Unbridled passion, emotions pent up in marriages that they both thought had cooled desire, raged through them. . . . [S]he too felt the flow, the burning fire, the sweet indescribable pleasure" (131).

Experiencing cold, empty marriages, each of the characters in this novel is portrayed, at least once, as a person fully equipped and capable of enjoying "love" physically. The novelist goes to great pains to disclose possible underlying reasons for the "loveless" situations that exist. These, besides the focus on economics and land, range from Father de Balboa's rejection of his slavery-supporting church, his renunciation and denunciation of that church, to his son Antonio's confusion about his role in life. While the novel depicts women as primary "sufferers"—an important Caribbean term—there is no doubt that Nunez-Harrell attempts to capture the torment of the men, the husbands, thereby attempting to present the entire picture of pain. The axe of love dictates and mothers are left with the children, who, like Antonio and Marina, endure the pain of both their parents, the pain of a burdened, bitter mother, and an "absent," maybe idealized, father. This experience is indelible and the outcome unsure, although there is a suggestion in the novel that the pattern is cyclical.

Dubem Okafor, writing of West Indian and West African fiction, calls for a change to be effected only by a "death" of the old ways: "The quest for a unity of being, for psychic and cultural identity, for social and moral redemption . . . will avail us nothing, if at the end of the journeys . . . we are made to begin again because we lack love. It seems that West Africa and the West Indies are bound together by the common fate of the absence of love and the frantic quest for it. . . . Hence a second death is necessary for a realization of the promise of fulfillment, for the unification of being, complete psychic and social regeneration . . . divested of all racial and cultural antagonism and polarization" (172).

It seems that Nunez-Harrell has begun to effect that death of which Okafor speaks. By reaffirming and respecting Emilia's African roots and reality, returning the Amerindian to his territory, and returning Antonio to his "father's land" (Europe); by anchoring Marina on land, revitalizing Virginia, and returning her to the farm, the land, and to Ranjit's love; some death/healing is in process. This is not only the psychological unity of the characters' being but also a revitalization of the self brought about by acceptance of the self, love of the self, respect for and by the self and, thus, of others. This rebirth or epiphany achieves what the Caribbean poet/prophet Brathwaite describes as "those who are no longer concerned with colonial despair, with our having 'nothing,' our 'exile' but with a total roots directed (Emilia) redefinition of ourselves: an aesthetic: word

act, vision, value system. The results are still tentative . . . the race between achievement and chaos is still very much on. But the gate is there, broken but open" (185). The economic factor is de-emphasized. Reconciliation to "having nothing" may be a more healthy basis for romance.

Elizabeth Nunez-Harrell helps to make a track through Brathwaite's "gate." By focusing on the economics of love, its mutations and connections, she performs an autopsy on the dead relationships, not so much in hopes of reviving the dead, but to assist the living. Even from the dust of the marriages discussed, some love arises. It may be the love of self. Deceptively, the Caribbean, a naturally beautiful yet economically impoverished region beset by lingering problems and human misery, remains a port of call for the "Love Boat"—those who are seeking love, those who have it, lost it, found it, or desire it. Each may join in the "kumina," when rocks dance. Frail "eggs" may shatter, but the weak may—like Ranjit and Antonio—survive and join Virginia, Emilia, and Marina. They may grow strong from the exercise of love. They may find their own steps and rhythm in the dance; they may hear the music through their experiences; and, most important, they will know that there is no score, no stage directions, no ringmaster save themselves. Like the fire and ice of love, the axe and axe/l of love, the dance must end if another is to begin. And each dancer must take his or her own step to and with the partner, regardless of the setting, be it ballroom or backyard bacchanal.

The symbolism inherent in the title of the novel can then be interpreted on yet another level to mean that continuous breaking of eggs will reduce the ability to provide new life. After all, a rock is tough, but it is lifeless. The dance polishes the rocks, smooths them, refines them externally, but leaves them encrusted with lost life elements, old possibilities resting upon sharp-edged broken shells. The ideal outcome is to soften rocks and harden eggshells, to reevaluate the attempt to decode natural love by economic laws.

In his commentary on the background of the West Indian novel, Kenneth Ramchand makes the following prescriptive observation: "Instead of creating characters whose positioning on one side or other of the region's historical conflicts consolidates those conflicts and does violence to the make-up of 'the person,' the West Indian novelist should set out to visualize a fulfillment, a reconciliation in the person and throughout society, of the parts of a heritage of broken cultures. . . . This vision and a conception of wider possibilities and relationships still remains [sic] unfulfilled today in the Caribbean" (10). **When Rocks Dance** takes up Ramchand's old gauntlet through its treatment of romantic love. After exposing conflicting motivations and stormy violence in several relationships founded upon materialism, the novel, through subtle moral decoding, settles some storms and attempts to effect reconciliations. And it does so not so much with mates, but with the self, where both healing and fulfillment begin, as all the characters learn.

Works Cited

Brathwaite, Edward Kamau. "The Love Axe/l: Developing a Caribbean Aesthetic." *Bim* (June 1978): 186.

Benitez-Rojo, Antonio. "The Polyrhythmic Paradigm: The Caribbean and the Postmodern Era." *Race, Discourse, and the Origins of the Americas*. Ed. Vera L. Hyatt and Rex Nettleford. Washington, D.C., and London: Smithsonian Institution Press, 1995. 255-67.

Creque-Harris, Leah. "*When Rocks Dance*: An Evaluation." *Caribbean Women Writers: Essays from the First International Conference*. Ed. Selwyn R. Cudjoe. Wellesley: Calaloux Publications, 1990. 159-63.

Davies, Carole Boyce, and Elaine Savory Fido, eds. *Out of the Kumbla: Caribbean Women and Literature*. Trenton: Africa World Press, 1990.

Hodge, Merle. "The Shadow of the Whip: A Comment On Male-Female Relations in the Caribbean." *Is Massa Day Dead: Black Moods in The Caribbean*. Ed. Orde Combs. Garden City: Anchor Books, 1974. 111-18.

McWatt, Mark A. "Wives and Other Victims." Davies and Fido. 223-35.

Mordecai, Pamela, and Betty Wilson, eds. *Her True-True Name: An Anthology of Women's Writing from the Caribbean*. Portsmouth: Heinemann, 1990.

Nasta, Susheila, ed. *Motherlands: Black Women's Writings from Africa, the Caribbean and South Asia*. New Brunswick: Rutgers University Press, 1992.

Nunez-Harrell, Elizabeth. *When Rocks Dance*. New York: G. P. Putnam's Sons, 1986.

Okafor, Dubem. "The Themes of Disintegration and Regeneration in the West Indian and West African Novel." *Bim* (June 1978): 158-73.

Ramchand, Kenneth. *The West Indian Novel and Its Background*. Exeter, N.H.: Heinemann, 1983.

Rodriguez, Ileana. *House/Garden/Nation: Space, Gender, and Ethnicity in Postcolonial Latin American Literatures by Women*. Translated by Robert Carr and Ileana Rodriguez. Durham and London: Duke University Press, 1994.

Sandra Adell (review date winter 2001)

SOURCE: Adell, Sandra. Review of *Bruised Hibiscus*, by Elizabeth Nuñez. *African American Review* 35, no. 4 (winter 2001): 679-81.

[*In the following favorable assessment of* Bruised Hibiscus, *Adell presents a brief summary of the novel's story-line, commenting specifically on the author's fictional use of the spirit world—in particular Obeah practices—which the critic states recurs throughout Nunez's novels.*]

With the publication of **Bruised Hibiscus,** Elizabeth Nuñez has greatly enriched the rapidly developing field of African diaspora literature. In this novel Nuñez weaves such a rich and well-crafted tapestry of legend, myth, and history that one cannot help comparing her to Toni Morrison, whose *Song of Solomon* stands out as a masterpiece among novels of the African diaspora. Set in Trinidad, where Nuñez was born, **Bruised Hibiscus** tells a story of passion, sexual repression, adultery, class conflict, and murder. The novel's two principal characters, Rosa and Zuela, were, for a brief period during their adolescence, inseparable. But time, circumstances, and social class set them apart as adults until two heinous murders—crimes of passion—and the terror that grips the women of the island in their wake, cause Rosa to transgress the social stratification that separates people along caste, class, and color lines and seek out Zuela as the one person who can help her ease the torment gnawing at her soul.

The novel opens with the grisly discovery, by a fisherman in the village of Otahiti, of the remains of a white woman that have been stuffed in a brown burlap coconut bag and dumped into the sea. The year is 1954. Trinidad is still a British colony and the debilitating effects of British colonialism and exploitation are symbolized by familial relations. Rosa's mother Clara Appleton is left to languish like other wives of British sugar cane planters and overseers while their husbands satisfy their sexual desires with native women and—sometimes—with men. Rosa's husband Cedric lives with the humiliating knowledge that his father committed suicide by walking into the sea and drowning after his British lover broke off their relationship. Cedric also lives with the frustration of always being seen as inferior in the eyes of whites, no matter how well-read and intellectual he proves himself to be. Clara Appleton is the sole exception. Cedric's position as headmaster of the local secondary school makes him a perfect match for Rosa, the youngest of her three daughters, who at age twenty-eight, is considered too old and therefore unsuitable for marriage to an Englishman or white Trinidadian. Despite her racism and class-consciousness, Clara Appleton consents to her daughter's marriage to the son of a black fisherwoman and the East Indian man who worked for her husband in order to keep her own indiscretions from being revealed. Rosa accepts Cedric's proposal purely to satisfy her sexual desires—her middle name is Nymphia—and Cedric marries Rosa out of revenge for his suffering as one of the "Queen's darker subjects."

The discovery of the murdered and mutilated white woman coincides with an abrupt change in Rosa's passion. After three years of marriage, she no longer desires Cedric. As speculation spreads that the woman was murdered because her husband, an East Indian doctor, caught her *in flagrante delicto,* Cedric becomes increasingly obsessed with the idea that his wife is being unfaithful to him. The news of a second vicious murder—this time of a black woman by two Trinidadian brothers—and Cedric's ever menacing and irrational behavior cause Rosa to make a pilgrimage to the Shrine of Our Lady of Fatima in the impoverished village of Laventille. It is on the hill leading to the Shrine that Rosa encounters Zuela, whose life-script is linked to hers by their shared childhood memory of looking through an hibiscus bush and witnessing the sexual assault of a young brown girl by "a man old enough to be the girl-child's father."

The image of the young girl behind the hibiscus bush is one of several recurring images that contribute to the lyrical, almost incantatory quality of *Bruised Hibiscus.* They are disturbing images: images of a notorious gangster, Boysie Singh, who the islanders believe murders and cuts out the hearts of young women to rub on the hooves of his racehorses to make them run faster; of two pigs devouring the butchered body of a woman named Melda; of the opium-addicted Chinaman's recurring nightmares of his wife and daughter being slaughtered back in China; of Zuela, not much older than the "girl-child" behind the hibiscus bush, being bargained over by her father and the Chinaman who came to her village in Venezuela "to buy alpagats [sandals] for his store and took her, too." The Chinaman promised Zuela's father that he would treat her like a daughter. Shortly thereafter, he made her his wife. By the time she and Rosa meet on the hill to the Shrine of Our Lady of Fatima, Zuela is a worn out, twenty-nine-year-old woman with ten children and a murderous rage against her tyrannical husband boiling inside her, brought on by the news traveling by word of mouth that women are being killed. Zuela is able to act upon her rage and escape a marriage that was a virtual prison. Rosa tries but cannot escape. The forces of evil are much too great, even for Mary Christophe, the ancestral figure/Obeahwoman who tries, but fails, to stem the tide of events that send Rosa to her fate in the sea.

In the "Author's Notes" at the end of the novel, Nuñez lists two murders, one occurring in 1954, the other in the 1960s, and the 1977 Black Power revolution in Trinidad as real events upon which *Bruised Hibiscus* is loosely based. But these facts are only the framework. A very gifted novelist, Nuñez never falls into mere reportage. She keeps her distance and lets her imagination and beautiful writing prevail. The result is a stunning and often chilling work of fiction that one will find hard to put down or to forget.

Bruised Hibiscus is Nuñez's third novel. She published her first, *When Rocks Dance,* in 1986. Set in Trinidad near the end of the colonial period, *When Rocks Dance* is a haunting tale of a beautiful Trinidadian woman's obsession with owning land. It also tells of a society in transition, where religious beliefs, conflicts of class, and intraracial racism play themselves out against a lush natural background that harbors an invisible world of spirits whose presence affects, often with devastating results, the lives of those the spirits claim to protect.

The belief in an invisible world of spirits and in Obeah, a Yoruba-derived religion similar to Haitian Voudun, is a theme that runs throughout Nuñez's fiction. In her second novel, *Beyond the Limbo Silence* (which won the 1999 Independent Press Award for Multicultural Fiction), Obeah is embodied in Courtney, one of three young women from the Caribbean who earn scholarships to a small Catholic college in rural Wisconsin as an experiment in integration. Told from the first-person perspective of Sara Edgehill and based loosely on Nuñez's own experiences as a college student in Oshkosh, Wisconsin, in 1963, Nuñez exposes the hypocrisy of white integrationist sponsors of black students. She also plays out a drama of cultural differences between blacks from the Caribbean environment and African Americans through the relationship between Sara and Sam, a young black man from Milwaukee. When Sara becomes deeply depressed, first over Sam's departure to Mississippi to join the voters rights campaign, and later over her pregnancy, it is Courtney, transmogrified into an Obeahwoman, who induces the dream state that reconnects Sara to Africa and Trinidad and the myths of sea cows and mermaids that regularly invaded her imagination when she was a child.

It is evident from her novels that Elizabeth Nuñez's imagination is likewise a storehouse of stories, legends, and myths. She is an accomplished writer who is creating a memorable space for herself in African diaspora literature. She is one of those rare novelists who *must* be read.

FURTHER READING

Criticism

Nunez, Elizabeth, and Barbara Lewis. "Negotiating Multiple Worlds: A Public Interview with Elizabeth Nunez." *Black Renaissance/Renaissance Noire* (summer-fall 2002): 202-13.

In an interview conducted in April 2002, Nunez discusses her novels, particularly *Discretion* and *Beyond the Limbo Silence*; offers insight into her writing process and her thematic concerns; and expounds on the topics of marriage and technology.

Rahming, Melvin B. "Theorizing Spirit: The Critical Challenge of Elizabeth Nunez's *When Rocks Dance* and *Beyond the Limbo Silence*." *Studies in the Literary Imagination* 37, no. 2 (fall 2004): 1-19.

Describes a "spirit-centered" approach to literary criticism and emphasizes its importance when dis-

cussing such works as *When Rocks Dance* and *Beyond the Limbo Silence*—novels that center on spiritual matters.

Tejani, Bahadur. "*When Rocks Dance*: Historical Vision in Elizabeth Nunez-Harrell's First Novel." *World Literature Today* 68, no. 1 (winter 1994): 53-58.

Detailed overview of *When Rocks Dance* in which the critic praises "the fact that it provides Trinidadians with a cultural synthesis which is operative today and which includes elements of the traditions of the island's three major groups."

Additional coverage of Nunez's life and career is contained in the following source published by Gale: *Contemporary Authors,* Vol. 223; and *Literature Resource Center.*

Ben Okri
1959-

Dave M. Benett/Getty Images Entertainment/Getty Images

Nigerian novelist, poet, and short story writer.

INTRODUCTION

Okri is an award-winning novelist, poet, and short story writer who continually seeks in his writings to describe the social and political turmoil of his native Nigeria, including that country's civil war and its ensuing violence and transformation. He is best-known for his trilogy of novels—*The Famished Road* (1991), *Songs of Enchantment* (1993), and *Infinite Riches* (1999)—which explores the phenomenon of *abiku*, or spirit child, from a postcolonial perspective. Critics often concentrate on Okri's incorporation of elements of magical realism in his fiction, and compare him to such prominent writers as Gabriel García Márquez and fellow Nigerian Chinua Achebe.

BIOGRAPHICAL INFORMATION

Okri was born in 1959 in Minna, Nigeria. He spent his early years in England, where his father was a law student, and around the age of seven returned to Nigeria with his parents. In 1967 he entered the Children's Home School in Sapele, Nigeria, then later transferred to Christ's High School in Ibadan. Inspired by music and by Greek, German, Roman, and African myths and folktales, he began to write stories when he was around twelve years of age. In 1970 he entered Urhobo College in Warri, Nigeria, but left to join his family in Lagos in 1975. A year later, he began writing his first novel, *Flowers and Shadows,* which was eventually published in 1980. Okri moved to England in 1978, where he lived with an uncle and worked as a librarian and writer for the periodical *Afroscope.* At that same time he studied literature at Goldsmiths College in London before being awarded in 1980 a Nigerian government scholarship, which he used to enroll at the University of Essex, where he completed his undergraduate degree in comparative literature. In the early 1980s he was named poetry editor for *West Africa* magazine, a position he held until 1987. During the mid-1980s he also worked for the British Broadcasting Corporation (BBC) African Service, hosting the *Network Africa* program. When the Arts Council of Great Britain granted him a bursary, he turned his focus to writing fiction. He concentrated on the short story genre, composing the tales that would later be published in the collections *Incidents at the Shrine* (1986) and *Stars of the New Curfew* (1988). In 1991 his novel *The Famished Road* was awarded the prestigious Booker Prize for Fiction. He has received numerous other honors, including the Commonwealth Writers' Prize for Africa in 1987; the *Paris Review* Aga Khan prize for fiction in 1987; the Premio Grinzane Cavour in 1994; and the Crystal Award in 1995. He was named a fellow in the Royal Society of Literature in 1997, and in 2001 was named a member of the Order of the British Empire (OBE). Okri served as a visiting fellow at Trinity College, Cambridge, from 1991 to 1993. He lives in London.

MAJOR WORKS

Critics contend that Okri's writing is characterized by nightmarish imagery and bizarre distortions of reality in the tradition of surrealist and magical realist authors. Difficult as his writings are to comprehend by those outside his native country, Okri maintains that the supernatural elements in his works are realistic representations of life inside Nigeria, demonstrating the continuity between the realistic and mystical realms of experience that exists for Nigerians. Okri's first published work, the novel *Flowers and Shadows,* portrays the dichotomy of Nigeria's rich and poor neighborhoods as the backdrop to the story of a spoiled rich child who learns the unpleasant truth behind his family's wealth. This work has been described as a postcolonial *bildungsroman* with similarities to Chinua Achebe's *Things Fall Apart* and Salman Rushdie's *Midnight's Children.* In Okri's second novel, *The Landscapes Within* (1981), an artist struggles to create aesthetic beauty in an African country wracked by corruption, violence, cruelty, and despair. With the publication of the celebrated novel *The Famished Road,* Okri received considerable critical acclaim for his astute and imaginative exploration of the *abiku* theme. The novel chronicles the story of Azaro, a child who, as an *abiku,* can choose to leave his earthly life for the spirit world from which he came and whose inhabitants repeatedly encourage his return. In *Songs of Enchantment,* Okri continued Azaro's story. In the novel, Azaro finds that he is able to enter the dreams of other people and beings and begins to grapple with the oppressive economic and social forces that threaten his family and his community. The third novel of the "Famished Road" trilogy, *Infinite Riches,* once again follows Azaro's struggle to mediate the real and spirit worlds and deal with the demands and struggles of the material world. In Okri's next novel, *Astonishing the Gods* (1995), an unnamed protagonist undertakes a quest to become invisible after he learns to read and realizes that his people are not represented in history textbooks. Along the way, he undergoes a spiritual journey and eventually attains perfect invisibility. *Dangerous Love* (1996) is a reworking of Okri's second novel, *The Landscapes Within.* In *Dangerous Love,* Omovo, a young clerk at a chemical company, spends his free time painting his bleak ghetto surroundings. Critics describe the novel as a *künstlerroman* that explores the role of artists in Nigerian society. Okri's 2002 novel, *In Arcadia,* chronicles the adventures of a television film crew as they travel around Europe in search of a modern-day Arcadia, or paradise.

CRITICAL RECEPTION

Okri is regarded as a highly imaginative novelist and short story writer. Reviewers consistently commend his attention to Nigeria's natural beauty and to the challenges faced by its people. They laud his poignant portrayals of Nigerian people struggling with economic, social, and political forces that threaten to tear apart families and communities. His use of surrealism and oral tradition has generated a mixed reaction from reviewers, many of whom maintain that his work can be difficult to read. His language, however, has continued

to receive critical acclaim, with scholars praising it as graceful, controlled, and spare. He is often compared to fellow Nigerian author Chinua Achebe for his examination of his homeland, to magical realist Gabriel García Márquez in his use of surrealism and oral tradition, and to *künstlerroman* authors James Joyce and Ayi Kwei Armah for his chronicling of his protagonists' growth, as in *The Landscapes Within.* Scholars of Okri's oeuvre consider *The Famished Road* as a milestone publication in the author's career, signifying a dramatic advance in his abilities as a fiction writer. While a number of critics view Okri's subsequent novels as inferior works, many find much to recommend in his later fiction, even if it is not at the same level of achievement as *The Famished Road.* Despite the mixed critical assessments of these later writings, many scholars concur that *The Famished Road* has provided a valuable contribution to modern African literature.

PRINCIPAL WORKS

Flowers and Shadows (novel) 1980
The Landscapes Within (novel) 1981
Incidents at the Shrine (short stories) 1986
Stars of the New Curfew (short stories) 1988
*The Famished Road (novel) 1991
An African Elegy (poetry) 1992
*Songs of Enchantment (novel) 1993
Astonishing the Gods (novel) 1995
Birds of Heaven (essays) 1996
Dangerous Love (novel) 1996
A Way of Being Free (essays) 1997
*Infinite Riches (novel) 1999
Mental Fight: An Anti-Spell for the 21st Century (poetry) 1999
In Arcadia (novel) 2002

*These novels are often referred to as the "Famished Road" trilogy.

CRITICISM

Bode Sowande (lecture date 7 June 1994)

SOURCE: Sowande, Bode. "The Metaphysics of *Abiku*: A Literary Heritage in Ben Okri's *The Famished Road.*" In *No Condition Is Permanent: Nigerian Writing and the Struggle for Democracy,* edited by Holger Ehling and Claus-Peter Holste-von Mutius, pp. 73-81. Amsterdam: Rodopi, 2001.

[*In the essay that follows, originally delivered as a lecture on 7 June 1994, Sowande investigates the rich African literary heritage—particularly that involving African mythology—that influenced* The Famished Road.]

Like Abiku's fragmentation of one soul, strung into many lives spanning perhaps centuries,[1] Ben Okri's novel *The Famished Road*[2] is a story of many stories whose narrative style springs from an African literary heritage, already celebrated by many storytellers. Fagunwa, in the Yoruba language,[3] and Tutuola in English, have made the road between humans and spirits, the homestead and the forest, the canon of mythology by which modern man can find meaning to his life. It is a physical road, as well as a spiritual and psychic way to other levels of consciousness, abundantly acknowledged as part of Yoruba cosmology.

The gods have their pantheon, the dead their world, the unborn their void, the spirits of all the elements the space which they share or contest with humans.

Wole Soyinka, in "The Fourth Stage,"[4] the essay which gives a Yoruba meaning to tragic theatre within the context of a pan-human experience, explains to us the numinous transition which is the road between the levels of consciousness of the gods, the unborn, the dead and the living.

And it is in the world of the living that we experience a common space, a common time shared or fiercely contested by man and spirits.

At the homestead, the spirit-child intrudes as the incarnation of the deity Abiku. The child's boast to life is the nagging tragedy of his parents as he also claims a right to death at short and rapid intervals. He returns always to the same parents. He defies all rituals of supplication to his spirit, as we see in Soyinka's poem "Abiku":

> In vain your bangles cast
> Charmed circles at my feet
> I am Abiku, calling for the first
> And the repeated time.
> Must I weep for goats and cowries
> For palm oil and the sprinkled ash?
> Yams do not sprout in amulets
> To earth Abiku's limbs
> So when the snail is burnt in his shell,
> Whet the heated fragment, brand me
> Deeply on the heart. You must know him
> When Abiku calls again.[5]

With Azaro, the *abiku* in Okri's *The Famished Road,* his coming "the repeated time" is an act of will on his part, and it is a determined claim to life. However, once in this particular incarnation, he wills himself on the road back to his spirit-world, reverting to the stubbornness of the *abiku*-child celebrated in Wole Soyinka's poem.

Azaro's homecoming to his spirit-world, chaperoned by the three-headed spirit (325-40), is held up by two weeks of ritual sacrifices and observance performed by his mother and father, with little pause and with acute emotional anguish. Azaro, the *abiku,* after his return from this two-week excursion, unwittingly proclaims himself a conscious apprentice of human life.

If Azaro wills himself to life, his mother and father hover around with silent prayers and wishes that are not the sharp admonition that we find in J. P. Clark's "Abiku." This is a poem that describes the toils and frustrations of having an *abiku* and the ultimate parental cry that that spirit-child should permanently decide the world of his choice; that of the spirits or that of the living.

> Coming and going these several seasons,
> Do stay out on the baobab tree,
> Follow where you please your kindred spirits
> If indoors it is not enough for you.
>   . . . . .
> But step in and stay
> For good. We know the knife-scars
> Serrating down your back and front
> Like beak of the sword-fish
>   . . . . .
> Then step in, step in and stay
> For her body is tired,
> Tired, her milk going sour
> Where many more months gladden the heart.[6]

The frustrations of Azaro's parents find echoes in the cries of many mothers, as celebrated earlier in J. P. Clark's poems;

> "If a spirit calls you," Mum said, "don't go, you hear? Think of us. Think of your father who suffers every day to feed us. And think of me who carried you in my womb for more than nine months and who walks the streets because of you."
>
> "Yes, think of us," Dad added.
>
> I nodded.
>
>   (306)

The characterization of Azaro has already been crafted by the signature of the spirit-child in the contemporary Yoruba belief-system. If Soyinka describes the rebellious and daring *abiku,* and if J. P. Clark explores the frustration of the *abiku*'s loved ones, what Okri adds is the use of *abiku* metaphysics to explain individual fate, societal fate, and human fate; a microcosm as defined by his family life, and a macrocosm which encircles all destinies as the ripening of repeated incarnations. Individuals are as *abiku* in spirit as nations are *abiku* in metaphor (325-40, 487-88).

It is this prodigy of vision as seen in the neophyte experience of Azaro's father (a mouthpiece for the author) and in the innocence of Azaro that is characterized by the king of spirit-children, the cosmic gang-leader of all *abikus*, Ajantala.

Okri's aim in pushing Azaro's father to the limits of his physical and psychic groping for life's meaning through suffering, and the continuous expansion of Azaro's vision within the same space occupied by spirits and men—this becomes the description of Ajantala consciousness.

D. O. Fagunwa presents a satirical vignette of Ajantala in his novel *Ogboju Ode Ninu Igbo Irumale,* and when this vignette is held up in relief against Okri's Azaro we search for a respite of humour in Okri's dark vision of human tragedy:

> Fagunwa's Ajantala, the leader of all spirit children, knows the weaknesses and tragedies of human life, and his contemplation includes man as the willing culprit of all vices, and for this what man needs is a thorough thrashing! And so when Ajantala is born, he has the complete vision of the infinite past, the present and the infinite future. He grows, walks, talks the day he is born and inflicts deserved punishment on man. Alarmed, it is Obatala the god of creation who sends a messenger to bring Ajantala back to heaven.[7]

Ajantala's strains are found in Soyinka's "Abiku," and it is Ajantala's shadow that is dreaded in Clark's "Abiku," but Okri's *abiku* is a painstaking exploration of this Ajantala complex as glimpsed by Azaro, who, though he is a spirit-child, lacks the daring will anticipated by Ajantala. However, Okri contents himself with an epic romance of this complex as the spirits wade into everyday human existence, insisting on their claim to Azaro, and sharing the same time-scale with the living, when they please, as they please.

This wandering of the spirit-consciousness in Azaro veers between the exotica of dreams, as acutely characterized by the 'innocence' of the child, and the allegory of the road and the forests of life.

Again, the road is mapped for Okri as it was mapped for Fagunwa, Tutuola, and Soyinka by Yoruba cosmology, whose primordial divine task is to clear the road between creation and man.

The first act was the construction of the road of destinies that the gods must tread in their primordial leadership of man, and in this cosmology it is Ogun who performs this duty, celebrated poetically by Soyinka as being the elder brother of Dionysos and Prometheus, and contrasting in tragic heroism with the lucid Apollonian wisdom of Obatola.[8]

* * *

Azaro wanders along so many roads of minor fates, and takes us down one major road that is akin to that described in the creation-myth; and it is this journey of Azaro that is Okri's pageant of life's infinite history, mythologies, divergent destinies, all uniting in a cosmic soul. Azaro is on the road homeward to the spirits; Azaro is also on his sick-bed. The road he treads in his spirit-self is the primordial road of elemental beginnings (325-40). This pageant links Okri's Azaro with other travellers of the road, in Fagunwa's Akara-ogun,[9] the storyteller of Tutuola's *My Life in the Bush of Ghosts,*[10] the town dwellers being witnessed by the forest dwellers in Soyinka's *A Dance of the Forest.*[11]

All of these co-travellers are on the road to their respective destinies, passing through their respective forests to understand and master their individual or collective human fate. The road is here a metaphor of life, its metaphysical import championed by the "Professor" in Soyinka's play *The Road.*[12]

There is an implicit need for guidance on the road, and it is from the invocation in Soyinka's poem "Death in the Dawn" that Okri derives the title of his novel:

> And the mother prayed, Child
> May you never walk
> When the road waits, famished.[13]

We encounter the same prayer on life's road, like a repeated litany, in the play *The Road*: "Samson: May we never walk when the road waits famished."[14] In Fagunwa, Akara-ogun invokes a similar prayer in his tragic confrontation with the daemon Agbako; "Spirits of the woods! Pilgrims of the road!—hasten to my rescue!"[15]

In this combat, Fagunwa's hero calls on the road to be an ally, although the same road helps the two adversaries to equalize the chances of the fighting opponents:

> I ordered the road to seize him and it seized him and cast him in the bush. But even as the road obeyed me, so did it leave me also, and I found myself right in front of Agbako.[16]

The road in Fagunwa is an impartial medium of fate leading to Mount Langbodo, the summit of human quest, and equally leading to the forest of all spirits and the dome of heaven.[17]

Okri's road and forest are on the map of the contemporary Yoruba cosmos, but Okri has chosen to give Azaro a road that has an insatiable lust for lives—lust in the sensual sense of the word, as characterized by Madame Koto, and lust in the sense of a vampire medium, inherent in the predatory corruption of man against man.

* * *

It is the folk-tale narrated to Azaro by his father that gives us the perfect description of Okri's hungry road; it is the story of the king of the road (258-61). This king will never be satisfied by the sacrifices of his people on the altar of his own greed; in desperation, they conspire against him, only for him to thwart their efforts. He eats some of his people up to satisfy his hunger and slake his thirst. The people in turn poison his food, which he consumes with the same relish that he applies in devouring the human delegation. The poison increases his hunger, and he devours trees, the bush, the rocks and a part of the earth; yet without satisfaction. Then he turns on himself and eats up his entire self, leaving only the stomach, which in turn is melted by a terrible rainstorm. The stomach is swallowed by the road, becoming part of all the roads on the face of the earth. All travellers on the road request protection and blessings by leaving ritual sacrifices on it before they set out.

The dread and the ethos of this famished road are crystallized in the prayer of Soyinka's poem "Death in the Dawn," and in this prayer the sacrifice is to Ogun, the god who created the primeval road:

> Traveller, you must set forth
> At dawn
> I promise marvels of the holy hour
> Presages as the white cock's flapped
> Perverse impalement—as who would dare
> The wrathful wings of man's progression. . . .[18]

Our return to Ogun the Yoruba god of the binary forces of creativity and war will explain the dark shadow that is cast on Azaro's road. From its beginnings in the infinite genesis of Ifa,[19] the road possesses a binary essence which demands the virtue of balance. The instrument that first clears it is wrought through the alchemy of fire, air, and solid mass by the genius of Ogun, patron god of the hunter, the poet, the sculptor, the surgeon, the warrior and all who use iron; and this road therefore contains an interflux of forces that are as creative as they are destructive.

If we explore the possibilities of Ogun's manifestations in human life, we begin to understand the road as an equipoise of power—life is held in balance there. We find a "good eternal" and its opposite, and they resolve themselves in the god Ogun.

In Okri's **The Famished Road,** the author contemplates the shadow on the road rather than the light on it, even though, by implication, we do understand that the creeping darkness of this road is an absence of light.

* * *

In Azaro's pageant through the spirit-world, in the parade of the spirits dissolving around humans, in the community of the *abiku*-child at home, at play and on the wandering road—what we encounter is life as a crossroads of many existences. Azaro's life is a flux of activities at crossroads. We see the earth as a meeting-point of many worlds, but Okri's prime focus is the road trodden by spirits.

Tutuola and Fagunwa, at these crossroads, interpret humans as being creatures with an inferior philosophy of life in comparison with the spirits, who in turn regard humans with pity, contempt and condescension. An apt description is provided in Akara-ogun's encounter in *The Forest of a Thousand Daemons*:

> Even so do you children of earth behave, you who have turned kindness sour to the charitable. We watch you, you whose eyes do not stay long in one place, you who chase emptiness all your life. Those who already boast a full stomach continue to seek glorified positions, seek to live like kings, forgetting that the fingers of the hand are unequal. And it is also in your nature that your minds are never at peace; those who find happiness today ensure that their neighbours find no peace the day following; death today, tomorrow disease; war today, confusion tomorrow; tears today, tomorrow sorrow—such is the common pursuit of you children of earth. And when we think of your plight, we pity you. . . .[20]

It is his love for his parents that makes him choose to stay, but Azaro's spirit-friends hold the human race in disdain, while Azaro's father labours to understand what it is in human nature that denies man a charitable destiny:

> He kept asking: WHY? After eons he asked: WHAT MUST WE DO? And then he asked: HOW DO WE BRING IT ABOUT? Pressing on, he wanted to know; WHEN? Relentlessly, twisting and turning, he demanded: WHAT IS THE BEST WAY?
>
> (494)

If the child's father labours to resolve the contradictions of life, whose metaphor is the road, he coexists with characters whose main concern is to prey on their fellowmen, and it is through this coexistence that Okri's subplot of a political quest is woven into the story.

Africa's problems of leadership come to the fore. The author paints a grim picture, with the political party of the rich pitted against the party of the poor. Madame Koto, a lady lustful for power, money and the craft of evil, uses her drinking bar as a beehive of politics, sex, violence and fetish-worship, while the spirits find the bar suitable for their orgies of sensualities. The madame is the hostess of all that is negative in the relentless power-grabbing characteristic of Africa today.

At the same crossroads is the "spirit man," an old, blind minstrel whose music destroys all principles of melody; in the spirit-world he has two heads: the visible head has blind eyes, the invisible head seeing eyes. This blind man is a witness for Azaro's spirit-friends, and belongs to the same category of witnesses as the beggars, one of whom is the four-headed spirit sent to lead Azaro back to his roots.

Poised against these malevolent characters is the heroic political fugitive, chronicling in his photographs the exploitation of the poor by the rich, intervening as mentor to Azaro.

In the dream-world, energies are pitched against each other in an epic struggle between life on the road of humans and life on the road of the spirit-world. Indeed, the dream is the landscape of various crossroads.

The wrestling opponents of Azaro's father—Yellow Jaguar, Green Leopard, the man in the snow-white suit—all continue to battle against the father in dream-consciousness, and each victory of Azaro's father is an initiatory elevation towards the political truth and idealism that crown him with confidence at the end of the narrative.

For Azaro's mother, the crossroads that we see through her dreams is the road of the healer, a road of suffering, patience, deep understanding of the healing elements, a road bordered by the vegetation of healing herbs, a road lit by prayer-candles and sweetened by clouds of incense, a road of endless prayers of supplication, pure with perseverance. In her dream-world, she always succeeds in calling back the soul from its flight of departure. She is a suffering woman at prayer, close to the priests and priestesses but lacking the power of priesthood.

With great ease, Azaro enters into these dreams either during the night or during his waking hours, but here the dreams of the day are lucid experiences for the *abiku*-child, who as a spirit has three eyes and one ear. And it is Madame Koto (350) and the blind old man (334-35) who dread seeing Azaro in their individual dreams. But later, in her ambition for greater power, Madame Koto begs Azaro in his dream for his own young blood in order to prolong her life, since, in the world of witchery, she is two hundred years old. The *abiku* rejects her plea;

> One night she appeared to me in my sleep and begged me to give her some of my youth.
>
> "Why?" I asked.
>
> And she replied:
>
> "I am two hundred years old and unless I get your young blood I will die soon."
>
> (496)

This is the lust that rules on Azaro's road: the lust for blood, politicians killing their people through unending exploitation, the abiku's travails, mercilessly inflicted on him by his kindred spirits, the wretchedness of his parents' lives, as described by the *abiku*'s mother; "My life is like a pit. I dig it and it stays the same. I fill it and it empties" (443).

* * *

The despair in the story is overwhelming. The insistence of the *abiku* on staying alive is heroic in the face of such deprivation, but the ethos is faith, the eternal faith that propels man through his history amd mythology. Despair and faith rekindle the emotions of Ogun morality—that, like Sisyphus, Okri's *abiku* will find his moments of triumph over his kindred spirits in our world of the living, which always awaits a new birth.

* * *

Held up against Yoruba cosmology, *The Famished Road* becomes a compass by which man rediscovers his origins and by which he constructs his present for a better future; this is Okri's prevalent use of paradox as the enigma of life, an enigma whose lucid resolution is found in opposing energies. *The Famished Road* brings *irunmale* to the homestead—*irunmale* here being an evocation of all the spirits of the earth.

Irunmale is that unseen world in which dwell the multitudes of life-forces, all incarnated by spirits, and *irunmale* is the crossroads world between man and heaven, man and the gods, innocence and wisdom, an environment in the cosmos of Ifa. Azaro is a willing exile from *irunmale*.

Growing up as children, the Yoruba are entertained by the stories of this *irunmale*, and always it is the storyteller's art to present a didactic account within the aesthetic of oral performance; with the use of brief episodes spiced by song and dance. This tradition of oral narrative is the Fagunwa/Tutuola legacy in Nigerian literature.

The storyteller, as in Okri's Azaro, employs a lucid narrative whose strength is determined by an ability to portray depth and complexity with a fascination for the mysterious as the very seed of life, and a fascination for life as the seed of mystery. This is the poetic of the stories that bring *irunmale* onto the road to the living. Okri's *The Famished Road* is faithful to this literary tradition; in addition to a canon of Yoruba mythology, Okri employs a creative mythology crafted from the actualities of modern man. Okri's major achievement is to reverse the journey of the road from the homestead of the living towards *irunmale*, and make the *abiku*, the self-exile of *irunmale*, undertake a journey from *irunmale* to the living world. It is the reverse process of folk heroism, which inevitably opens up a book of lessons for man. This reverse process, however, overburdens the reader, compelling him to unrelieved contemplation of the tragedy of man. And here Okri differs from Fagunwa, Tutuola and Soyinka despite the common heritage of their works, with their roots in African cosmology; in this case, the Yoruba example.

Notes

1. Lecture given on 7 June 1994, Iwalewa-Haus, University of Bayreuth, Germany, "Identität in Afrika."

2. Ben Okri, *The Famished Road* (1991; London: Random House/Vintage, 1992). All references are from this text.

3. D. O. Fagunwa, *Ogboju Ode Ninu Igbo Irunmale,* tr. Wole Soyinka as *The Forest of a Thousand Daemons* (Lagos: Nelson Panafrica Library, 1968, 1982). Amos Tutuola's novels in English are of this tradition. A good example is *My Life in the Bush of Ghosts* (London: Faber & Faber, 1954, 1982). In 1990 Tutola's *Bush of Ghosts* was presented on stage; see Bode Sowande, "Bringing Amos Tutuola to the Theatre Stage," in *Palaver,* ed. Bernard Hickey (Lecce: Università degli Studi di Lecce, 1991): 111-15.

4. Wole Soyinka, "Appendix: The Fourth Stage," in *Myth, Literature and the African World* (Cambridge: Cambridge UP, 1976).

5. Wole Soyinka, "Abiku," in *Modern Poetry from Africa,* ed. Gerald Moore & Ulli Beier (1963; Harmondsworth: Penguin, 1975): 153.

6. J. P. Clark, "Abiku," in *Modern Poetry from Africa,* ed. Moore & Beier, 117.

7. Fagunwa, *The Forest of a Thousand Daemons,* 107-14.

8. Soyinka, "Appendix: The Fourth Stage."

9. Fagunwa, *The Forest of a Thousand Daemons,* 107-14.

10. Amos Tutuola, *My Life in the Bush of Ghosts.*

11. Wole Soyinka, "A Dance of the Forests," in *Collected Plays* (London: Oxford UP, 1973), vol.1: 1-77.

12. Wole Soyinka, "The Road," in *Collected Plays* vol.1, 147-232.

13. Wole Soyinka, "Death in the Dawn," in *Modern Poetry from Africa,* ed. Moore & Beier, 145-46.

14. Soyinka, "The Road," in *Collected Plays* I, 199.

15. Fagunwa, *The Forest of a Thousand Daemons,* 25.

16. Fagunwa, *The Forest of a Thousand Daemons,* 22, 23.

17. Fagunwa, *The Forest of a Thousand Daemons,* 14.

18. Soyinka, "Death in the Dawn," 146.

19. Ifa is an actual pre-Christian, pre-Islamic Yoruba belief system flexibly divided into the healing arts, the literary arts, the magical or talismanic arts, the oracular arts, and an all-binding philosophical afflatus. It is noted for its non-dogmatic essence, and it is therefore a perfectly progressive belief-system for the Yoruba.

20. Fagunwa, *The Forest of a Thousand Daemons,* 19.

Robert Fraser (essay date 2002)

SOURCE: Fraser, Robert. "Responsibilities: Fictions, 1978-1982." In *Ben Okri: Towards the Invisible City,* pp. 23-36. Devon, U.K.: Northcote House, 2002.

[*In the following essay, Fraser examines the central themes of* Flowers and Shadows *and* The Landscapes Within, *arguing that the novels deserve a wider audience "partly because these books are of intrinsic worth, and partly because they are the seed from which [Okri's] later, more confidently original work arose."*]

If I don't learn to shut my mouth I'll soon go to hell,
I, Okigbo, town-crier, together with my iron bell.

(Christopher Okigbo, 'Hurrah for Thunder')

. . . what the dickens his name is.

(Shakespeare, *The Merry Wives of Windsor,* III. ii)

Over the last few years Okri's first two novels—*Flowers and Shadows,* written in the mid- to late 1970s, though not published until 1980, and *The Landscapes*

Within, issued late the following year—have largely been eclipsed by *The Famished Road* and the books that came after it. It is important to correct this imbalance, partly because these books are of intrinsic worth, and partly because they are the seed from which the later, more confidently original work arose.

Interestingly, each of these works takes hold of an adage or quotation, turns it over in the palm of its hand, and asks, '*Is* this true?'; 'If so, in what sense?'; 'What, if we pursued this lesson to its logical extent, would the consequences be: for me, for you, for society, for the world?' Even more promisingly, each novel probes the nature and the limits of stories: what they can and cannot do, the differences between fiction and fantasy, or between both and so-called 'reality'. Both are placed in Africa—in a recognizable Lagos—yet, in a manner typical of this author, neither is consumed by its setting. Its location is a mode of being, one illustration of a set of human responses that run much deeper: at a subterranean, almost a sub-fictive level. Both books, moreover, posit much the same difficult question. What, they ask, does it mean to be responsible: as a citizen, an artist, or, more broadly, as a human being?

Both books describe the lives of young male Lagos dwellers. But Jeffia Okwe, the idealistic only son of a self-made businessman, and Omovo, the dreamy painter from the slums, are altogether different characters facing distinct, if related, problems. *Flowers and Shadows* is a study of privilege. Its young protagonist Jeffia possesses much that is supposed to make life sweet. He is intelligent, well qualified, healthy, even handsome—and he lives with his parents in the opulent district of Ikoyi. By the end of the novel his businessman father and his best friend are both dead, and he has moved with his mother to the less-favoured district of Alaba. This is not because they have failed, nor because Jeffia has had any great mental revelation: resolutions that belong to a different sort of fiction. True, there are epiphanies— 'showings forth'—of a sort in this finely wrought book. But these, as we shall see, are of a subtle variety: the kind maybe that you might achieve by turning over one of the flowers of the title and examining its petals from beneath.

Much can be gleaned from an episode early in the tale, one that is echoed not only elsewhere in the book but also in its immediate successor, and at other moments in Okri's later fiction as well. It describes the tormenting of a 'brown and white puppy' (*FS* [*Flowers and Shadows*] 4-6). Jeffia observes this atrocity while strolling back home at night from his schoolfriend Ode's house, where they have been discussing the morality of intervention. The perpetrators are a couple of ragged boys a little younger than Jeffia. His first reaction is to pose a question: 'Why are these boys being cruel to it like that?' Jeffia does not, as many in his position might, condemn the boys vocally or mentally for their callousness. He accepts at face value the younger boy's excuse, delivered in pleading pidgin, 'My father was jailed—they say he thief, what can a poor man do? If man no die, he no rotten'. Jeffia looks no further into this half-explained misery: he is not a revolutionary, social analyst, or animal-rights activist. Unconsciously, nonetheless, he recognizes the psychology behind the cruelty: 'he understood that those who knew pain lived pain.' He also instinctively knows what he can do to ease the dog's suffering. After a brief and playful bargaining, he buys the animal and takes it home.

This transaction assumes for Jeffia the aspect of a compassionate adventure, whose wider implications he only partially admits to. Yet the episode also disturbs him quite deeply. He is disoriented by it, just as he is by the sight of a man idly throwing stones at nesting birds, whom he observes a few pages further on (*FS* 20). This is the first of a series of parallels or sequels to the dog-tormenting episode that recur in the story. The puppy turns out to belong to Juliet, one of the discarded mistresses of Jeffia's father, Jonan. When, having elicited that she is the owner as a result of a newspaper advertisement, Jeffia visits her to return her pet, an unsuspected aspect of his father's squalid past is laid bare. The dog molesting is also obliquely connected to Jonan in quite a different way, through the younger tormentor's claim that his father has been framed for theft. This is more or less what has happened to the father of Cynthia, the young nurse with whom Jeffia takes up halfway through the narrative. In this instance, it is a commercial agent of Jonan's who has performed the framing. Juliet, Cynthia's father—indirectly Cynthia as well—the dog-harassing urchins of that early scene: all feature as victims. In every case the source of their discomfiture turns out to lie uncomfortably close to Jeffia himself.

These diverse strands in the plot combine to raise an essential and unifying question: the nature in this—or indeed in any—society of moral and civic responsibility. Why, the book seems to ask, is life like this, and who—or what—is to blame? The text offers no simple answer. At moments indeed, the writing almost gives the impression of passively accepting a destiny that nobody can control. It sustains this almost-attitude partly through Jeffia's behaviour, an 'unintentional indifference' (*FS* 119), which at times seems non-judgemental almost to a fault. It reinforces this sense of helplessness through a series of unhappy flukes, the causes of which lie beyond strict personal accountability. The most obvious case is the death early on of Ode, crushed by a lorry whose driver has not heard the young man's cries. Jeffia's reaction to this tragedy—like his mother's—is to call it 'unbelievable'. The adjective may mean that they both consider the lorry driver to have been incredibly negligent; their general attitude, however, suggests that they regard the accident as another example of a malevolent—or indifferent—fate (*FS* 72).

The impression of cosmic powerlessness is beautifully underscored at points by images of psychedelic inten-

sity. Two recur in quick succession in chapters fourteen and fifteen. The first describes a run-over dog, its entrails spread luridly across the road (*FS* 124), a symbol clearly connected with the dog-hurting incident at the beginning. The second describes a baby beetle stranded in the garden of Jeffia's house while tiny ants swarm all over it (*FS* 129). There is a premonition of both these inadvertent deaths earlier in the story. One night, whilst driving home in the dark, Jeffia drives over a frog (*FS* 50). Typically, his reaction is not to question his own driving, but to identify with the amphibian: 'Deep down inside himself. He felt that someone had stepped on his quiet life.' Jeffia observes all of these spectacles of supine suffering with lingering curiosity etched with moral concern. He does not, however, explicitly interpret them as elements within a wider pattern. Is Jeffia therefore deficient?

In vivid contrast to this quietism, there are elements in the book that turn it almost into a detective story, with Jeffia as the industrious sleuth, and his father as the culprit. Jeffia learns quite a lot about his father during the months covered by the action. One lesson—though not I think the most important—is that Jonan's relative success in business has been facilitated by shady dealings that have laid waste everything—and almost everyone—around him. Jonan's victims stretch out endlessly. As well as Juliet and Cynthia's unnamed father there is Sowho, Jonan's estranged half brother. This relation has actively contributed to the commercial success of Jonan's enterprises, but has been cheated out of his share. Jonan lives in fear of his turning up on the doorstep and demanding his cut. When he does so, the resulting car chase kills both men (*FS* 176). Another victim is a former employee who knows too much about the nefarious aspects of the firm. Jonan hires a group of thugs to kill him. Fortuitously his murder leads Jeffia to Cynthia. He observes the assault while driving home, and meets his girlfriend-to-be whilst crouching over the victim's bruised and dying body (*FS* 66).

Various explanations are available for all this visible distress—what Okri in a telling phrase calls 'the unacceptable continuum of the unfortunate' (*FS* 189). Jeffia vacillates between them. The first, and least plausible, is to see all this misery as symptomatic of the corruption and nastiness strangling Nigeria. This is the line taken, for example, by Okri's friend Adewale Maja-Pierce in his introduction to the Longman African Classics edition of the novel. Maja-Pierce views the cumulative suffering in the book as a comment on the venality gripping the country during the oil boom of the 1970s, when Nigeria languished beneath Gowon's military heel. He thus connects the book with a number of 'state-of-the-nation' novels published during this period by writers such as Festus Iyayi, Kole Omotoso, Ifeoma Okoye, and Bode Sowande (*FS* xiii). True, there are satirical scenes that favour this interpretation, notably one that Maja-Pierce cites: an observation of Lagos's soldiery on traffic duty (*FS* 97). Such incidents, though, are few and far between. Their relative scarcity suggests to me that Okri was already a very different kind of novelist from his immediate Nigerian contemporaries.

The second alternative would be to adopt Jeffia's own temperamental quietism by regarding all these phenomena—military thuggishness, commercial malpractice, the suffering of animals—as products of unpitying destiny. At one point Okri underpins this point of view by applying to Ode's untimely death a fragment from the Greek dramatist Menander: 'those whom the gods love, die young.' This received and pessimistic view is occasionally hinted at by Okri's style, over which his sensibility seems not yet to be fully in control. The result is a series of rhetorical, limp-wristed phrases that might be grouped under the heading 'the novel wringing its hands'. Such is the sentence in chapter one about the winds being 'eavesdropping messengers of the gods' (*FS* 7), or the 'hells' in which Cynthia's father is regarded as living, swamping her justified feelings of indignation beneath 'a feeling of futility' (*FS* 82).

The third and most persuasive option is to interpret the action of the novel through its central human relationships: the complementary but very different rapports that Jeffia achieves with his parents. Jonan, after all, is the apparent source of much of the suffering in the book, while his wife, whom he continues commendably to protect, is arguably his most intimate victim. Jeffia's attitudes towards the world are mostly refracted through this double focus. Despite the dispiriting discoveries he comes across during the course of the story, he continues to feel affection for his father. It is an inarticulate love, a baffled love, possibly a remnant from an earlier phase of emotional development, but it is nonetheless intense. Nowhere does this emerge more clearly than in the scene, recognizable to all teenage readers, in which Jonan rails at his son for being out late (*FS* 69-70). His bluster collapses after a few seconds. Jonan can terrify his employees; his wrath cannot convince his boy. There is an unspoken empathy between them that compels Jonan to be lenient with Jeffia even when his moral meddling almost gets both of them into trouble with the police. As a result, Jeffia can see right through his father's irate front. Like many tyrants, Jonan is fundamentally a weak man. Furthermore, he is culturally confused, espousing modernity whilst furtively communing with *juju* spirits. Maja-Pierce interprets this reliance on traditional remedies as connecting him with evil in some way. Actually—in every available sense—it is viewed as pathetic.

The clue to Jonan's temperament lies in his relationship with his own father, a subsistence farmer from a remote village in Urholand who lived a life of near destitution. Eventually Jeffia's grandfather had succumbed to a wasting disease that there was no money to treat. His last words to Jonan were 'My son . . . poverty is a curse' (*FS* 111). The memory of that ignominious end—of his father's 'dying face, crushed and wasted'—haunts Jonan, rushing back to torment him at inconvenient moments. The recollection fills him with 'melancholy', but it also spurs him on. 'It had always been a driving part of his life' comments the narrator. 'It gave him energy.'

Just as Jonan's ruthless pursuit of business success is motivated by his father's economic failure, so his wife's tenacity, her loyalty, maternal instincts, and touching trust, are products of insecurities in her own very different background. An orphan, she has been abused mentally and physically as a child and a young woman. Jonan has rescued her from a destructive earlier relationship, and given her the warmth, material comfort, and self-respect she so desperately craved. Unsurprisingly she is devoted to him, and their only child is the apple of her eye. Through her we perceive a different Jonan, a person for whom the 'state-of-the-nation' version of the story—or the opposed fatalistic reading—have no room: someone affectionate, practical, and, in the private realm at any rate, pretty effective.

In essence, Jonan is a decent man undermined by a combination of his own history and of economic circumstances. A vital clue to his mental make-up—and to the novel's theme of social inequity—occurs in chapter twelve when a beggar who has materialized out of the crowd in downtown Lagos attempts to clean the windscreen of his chauffeur-driven Mercedes with a cloth. The beggar is a picture of destitution, 'a travesty of a man' (*FS* 100), and the rag is filthy. Jonan buys him off with a hastily flung naira note, yet all the way back to the office his face remains 'screwed up'. With precocious restraint, Okri refrains from telling us why this is so. It is left for the reader to work out that the beggar represents everything the plutocrat loathes and dreads. He is the man Jonan fears he might have become.

With uncanny insight, Jeffia understands much of this. His insight partly explains the tentativeness—as well as the affability—of his filial nature. It also enables him to contemplate the significance of the second Mosaic commandment with its well-known corollary 'for the sins of the fathers are visited upon the children'. Jeffia's preoccupation with this adage is of a kind with the quiet pessimism of his personality, but it also transcends it. The 'sin', if you remember your Exodus, was idolatry.[1] Jonan is not altogether a sinner, and the danger of Jeffia being swamped by his legacy is, I think, offset by his shrewdness. Nevertheless, it is before the idol of Mammon that Jonan has bowed. Like his biblical near-namesake Jonah, he has been swallowed up.

The advantage of this critical approach to the novel is that it enables us to construe it as a generational tragedy in the style of Chinua Achebe, rather than a surface satire—or diatribe—after the school of Omotoso or

Ijayi. The brittle heroism of Okonkwo, protagonist of Achebe's first novel *Things Fall Apart,* one remembers, was a reaction against the comparative ineffectiveness of his father, the gentle, flute-playing Unoka.[2] *Flowers and Shadows* harks back to such influences, but it also anticipates Okri's later fiction. In chapter fifteen, for example, Jeffia recalls Ode and himself participating in a school debate on international capitalism, environmental vandalism, and racial politics (*FS* 131-2). The discussion looks right forward to the story **'Stars on the New Curfew'** in the volume of that title, and to Okri's sixth novel, *Infinite Riches.*

The mutual indebtedness of Okri's books, and the organic coherence of his evolving *œuvre,* are even clearer in his second novel, the book reissued in revised form in 1996 as *Dangerous Love,* but which originally appeared in 1981 under the title *The Landscapes Within.*[3] Okri was just 21 when in March 1980 he finished writing this first version, in which, he later declared, he had wanted to celebrate 'the small details of life as well as the great' and 'to be faithful to life as lived in the round, and yet to tell a worthwhile story' (*DL* [*Dangerous Love*] 325). As he later saw it, such aims were too ambitious for his skill at the time. Hence the revision. However, the first version richly repays analysis. In it, Okri was to confess, 'I came to see . . . the key to much of my past work, and perhaps also to my future.'

Like *Flowers and Shadows, Landscapes Within* begins with a premonition (*LW* [*Landscapes Within*] 3), this time in the form of two dreams (reduced to one in *DL* 1), the first of which features a murdered girl. These nightmares—recounted in the notebook of the artist-hero Omovo—themselves relate to a series of horrific recalls of the Nigerian Civil War by several characters in the book. Their further significance remains unexplored until chapter seven, when the protagonist Omovo goes walking with his friend Keme along a moonlit Lagos beach (*LW* 54-60; *DL* 43-7). They find the corpse of a girl who has been murdered and mutilated in some kind of perverted rite. Later on, the dream prognostication is fulfilled once again when Omovo's girlfriend Ifeyinwa is killed, as a result partly of mistaken identity, partly of an ongoing tribal tiff, during a return trip to her village (*LW* 265); in *Dangerous Love* she is called 'Ifeyiwa' and her death is related even more starkly (*DL* 281-2). Like the girl in Omovo's dream, all of these women are victims. As in the previous novel, we are prompted to enquire, of what or of whom?

Omovo, who lives in Alaba with his drunken, woebegone father and his resentful stepmother Blackie, makes an unsatisfactory living as a junior clerk in a chemicals firm, from which he is eventually sacked. His passion and vocation, however, are painting (the 'dangerous love' to which the title of the 1996 revision partially alludes). It may be significant that Okri, a one-time employee of ICI, had once toyed with the idea of taking up art as a career. In any case, throughout the book painting serves as a metaphor for all art forms, including literature. An important theme throughout is *mimesis,* or the representation of reality. What, the novel seems to enquire, is the exact relationship between the representation of the world observed in art forms, dreams, fantasies, and the everyday world that we perceive around us? Are art and dream and fantasy all distortions? If so, are they the *same kind* of distortion?

Omovo completes several paintings during the course of the story, one of which is stolen, another lost, and yet another confiscated by the authorities. The most startling, *Drift,* depicts a large pool of stagnant water festering outside his house (*LW* 33; *DL* 26). The intensification of reality in this work has already been alluded to (p. 17). The text here refers to its 'oblique shapes and heads with intent and glittering eyes.' 'He knew now what he wanted,' the narrative adds, 'and he was pleased.' But, when the painting is exhibited at the local 'Ebony' art gallery, the military authorities confiscate it because they think it presents an unflattering impression of Nigeria (*LW* 50; *DL* 39-40). This provocative action is important because, though overbearing, insensitive, and philistine, it is not strictly speaking irrational. In essence, the authorities espouse a Stalinist understanding of art as *agitprop.* For them art is tolerable only if it endorses the official policies of the state. Yet that is also a classical, Platonic view. For the Greek philosopher Plato, artists were of two kinds: those who praised the ideals espoused by the rulers, and those who insisted on representing wickedness. The former were to be supported by the government. The latter, on the other hand, were likely to unsettle the citizens by saying, or perhaps painting, inconvenient things. To prevent this happening, Socrates—Plato's mouthpiece in *The Republic*—demands that they quit the city.[4] Omovo then is in good company. But so one might say—playing devil's advocate for a moment—is the government.

When feeling discouraged, Omovo strolls round to visit a friend and mentor of his, an older artist named Dr Okocha. It is Okocha who provides a middle road in the argument about art and life—and incidentally encapsulates many of the themes of the novel—by quoting the statement 'In dreams begin responsibilities (*LW* 118; *DL* 101). Dr Okocha attributes these suggestive words to 'an Indian poet'; in fact they make up the second epigraph to the volume *Responsibilities* (1918) by the Irish poet, W. B. Yeats.[5] No source has been found for this quotation; the current opinion among scholars is that the words are Yeats's own. Yet this paradoxical formulation distils the predicament of many artists in Ireland, Nigeria, or any other postcolonial state. Artists, as both Okocha and Omovo are aware, can operate effectively only through a process of free association, a controlled self-disorientation akin to dreaming (in *Dangerous Love,* Okocha prefers the term 'visions'). In many cases they induce this condition in themselves consciously and deliberately. Others—critics preeminently—interpret the effect as they will, but it is hopelessly naive of the originator to disclaim all responsibility for the result. Thus the confiscating authorities were quite justified in asking Omovo 'Why did you do that painting?' (*LW* 50). But Omovo himself was both strictly within his rights—but also somewhat ingenuous—when he replied, 'I just did it. I painted what I had to paint.'

There is a parallel to be drawn here with a novel that Omovo is desultorily reading throughout the story: Wole Soyinka's 1965 study of post-independence manners, *The Interpreters.*[6] That book too centres on a painter, Kola, who is working on a group portrait of several of his friends, all of whom are characters in the plot. Kola has associated each one of these acquaintances visually with an *orisa,* one of the deities of the traditional Yoruba pantheon. His canvas is viewed by Soyinka as a vision—or, as the title of the book implies, an *interpretation*—of the Nigeria of the time, a period some thirteen years before that covered by *The Landscapes Within.* The difference between Kola and Omovo is that the first is quite conscious of what he is doing, whereas Omovo seems to have drifted into his role as social interpreter with a sort of awe-struck insouciance. Why then is he so threatening?

One clue is given in a passage where Omovo is telling Keme about an episode during his childhood when his beloved mother scolded him for staring too hard at a cobweb:

> When I was young, I can't remember how old, I remember my mother beating me with a comb and then with the heel of her shoe. She beat me because I sat for a long time staring at a mass of cobwebs and trying to draw them. She was afraid of cobwebs and said that there was something wrong with me and why should I look at something as strange as a cobweb. I looked at cobwebs and things not only to draw them but to know them. Too many people are afraid to look at cobwebs and other things. That's the problem.
>
> (*LW* 153-4; *DL* 152)

The interesting aspect of this reminiscence is the different perspective on reality possessed by mother and child. The mother's reprimand is a product of fear and incomprehension, but she is also convinced that the child is actively drawn to nastiness, a perverse preference that she attempts to beat out of him. Yet the growing Omovo, like his older self, is drawn to the unkempt and unsightly facets of his world not because they are out-of-bounds but, as he tells Keme, simply in order to *know* them, to absorb their essence, to interpret their nature, perhaps as a preliminary to painting—or here drawing—them. For Omovo the conventional distinction between beauty and ugliness—an evaluative assessment quite irrelevant to artistic representation as he understands it—simply does not exist. If his mother makes one kind of mistake in construing his motives, the authorities make a second. They assume that Omovo's concentration on the less seemly aspects of

social reality—stagnant pools, cobwebs, traffic jams—is a form of criticism. It is not intended as such. Omovo fastens on these sights because they possess a rich visual potential. Above all, he depicts them simply because they exist.

If there is one characteristic that Omovo shares with Jeffia from *Flowers and Shadows,* it is his innocence. Like Jeffia, he has a tendency to accept everything around him with passivity laced with mild curiosity. This, for example, is the attitude that he adopts to the drastic haircut received at the hands of an apprentice barber at the beginning of the book (*LW* 6-7; *DL* 5). Omovo drifts off to sleep and, while he is dozing, the hairdresser cuts off more hair than expected. Jolted into consciousness, Omovo observes the result with interest. In a mood of playful experimentation, he urges the man to continue until he is bald. For the rest of the book Omovo's bare and shining scalp is the subject of intrigued derision by everyone else in the compound. He does not anticipate this reaction; he accepts it nonetheless. In a sense he regards the resulting social obloquy as a new and unaccustomed element in his existence, something of which, like the cobwebs and traffic jams, he must take intelligent account, simply to know it for what it is.

It is this kind of ethical neutrality, viewed by others as amoral, that constantly lands Omovo in trouble, both with the powers-that-be and with his prying, judgemental neighbours. The clash of values is exacerbated when, with a typical lack of foresight, Omovo drifts into an adulterous affair with Ifi, the young country-bred wife of his middle-aged neighbour, Takpo. It is Ifi who enacts yet another parallel with *Flowers and Shadows* when she rescues a lame stray dog from the unwelcome attentions of passers-by (*LW* 228-9, *DL* 228-9). Like so many of the characters in that earlier book, she too is a victim, a product of a broken home whose misery has given her an insight into the sufferings of others. She is attracted to Omovo partly because of his sensitivity, and partly because his oddity makes him stand out. (She is the only person around, for example, who appreciates his unusual hairdo.) The growing bond between them is not, however, strong enough to prevent her eventually running away to her village, where she is casually murdered when mistaken for somebody else.

In *Landscapes Within* the somewhat fragmentary and undeveloped account of Ifi's and Omovo's amours reads too much like added romantic interest to be entirely convincing. By the time Okri came to revise the story as *Dangerous Love,* he had come to see this strand as a major element to the story, as the new title implies. Yet already in the first version there is much that is instructive about this painful entanglement, above all in the parity between Omovo's attitude towards it and the implied attitude adopted by the narrative voice. Both regard it with suspended judgement. In Omovo's case, this is because his sympathy for, and attraction towards,

OKRI

BLC: CLASSIC AND EMERGING AUTHORS, Vol. 3

Ifi dwarf all other considerations. Is he, we wonder with relevant persistence, irresponsible in what he does? In the narrator's case, tolerance is impelled by a recognition of at least two of the parties—Ifi and Takpo—as victims. Admittedly Takpo is a truly brutish husband: overbearing, violent, and coarse. Yet the most moving scene in the book is that in which this seeming ogre takes his bewildered young spouse to the bush, and begs her to show him love and respect (*LW* 232-5; *DL* 231-6). There is an unflinching authenticity about this moment that enables us to see Takpo as tragic, and that mitigates even Ifi's dismay and disgust with something approaching pity. When all are so damaged, what place is there for indictment or moralizing of any kind?

The book achieves this even stance through the honesty with which events are recounted, a candour that mirrors Omovo's own attentiveness. One of the recurrent epithets in the narrative is 'clear'. When Omovo looks at the houses of Alaba in the morning light, 'all were clear to him', 'His mind was clear' (*LW* 114). When Omovo and Okocha part company after a meeting of minds, 'The road was clear. Everything was clear' (*LW* 30). In Omovo's painting of a traffic jam, 'People were walking in the background and foreground—and they were very clear' (*LW* 155). When he executes four swift miniatures of a boy's face, 'The drawings were beautiful and clear and sensitively shaded' (*LW* 165). As he observes the to-ings and fro-ings at the chemicals factory where he works, 'everything became clear and definite and clear-cut' (*LW* 193). In the last resort, it is this very lucidity that proves threatening.

Another recurrent term is 'silence'. Time and time again in the book, busy or halting conversations peter out into wordless transcendence. When Omovo and Ifi first make love, 'The silence between them was like a presence' (*LW* 211). The erotic hush is momentarily interrupted by a cloud of mosquitoes, droning 'like small badly tuned pocket transistor radios'. Afterwards they get dressed 'in a different kind of silence' (*LW* 215). Pauses such as these are so much more highly charged than the book's occasionally prosaic dialogue that they carry much of the meaning.

The Landscapes Within is a book that reflects what one might call the subversiveness of reticence. Society disapproves of Omovo because he is quiet and paints what he sees. The narrative of the novel too is quiet in its overall manner. It too relates what it observes. In so far as the work has a message, that is it: the menace—and the sustained responsibility—of such self-contained, undemonstrative watchfulness.

These concerns were to remain with Okri, and inform his later work. To some extent they remain integral to his thinking. In the second part of **'The Joys of Storytelling',** he turns to consider the potential implicit in all narratives for 'transgression'. His suggestion—the cumulative result of two decades at unemphatic odds

with the social and political status quo—is that the resistance to the way the world offered by fiction as against more direct forms of social action frequently takes the form, not of a statement, but of mild interrogation. Indeed the writer is sometimes most subversive when his enquiry does not even proceed as far as an implied question mark. Self-standing loveliness can be just as effective in its mute indictment of brutality: 'Transgression', writes Okri, 'can also reside in creating a beautiful thing. Sometimes the creation of a beautiful thing in a broken resentful age can be an affront to the living, a denial of suffering. Sometimes beauty can be accusatory' (*WBF* [*A Way of Being Free*] 65). It is just this sort of composed and intelligent query in the face of chaos and corruption that the young Okri offers us in his first two novels.

Notes

1. Exod. 20: 4.

2. Chinua Achebe, *Things Fall Apart* (London: Heinemann, 1958), 3-6. The parallel with Jonan's father is uncanny: 'When Unoka died,' we read on page 6, 'he had taken no title at all, and he was heavily in debt'.

3. In the following discussion the wording of the quotations is, by and large, taken from *The Landscapes Within*. I discuss the effect of the stylistic changes in *Dangerous Love* in Chapter 8 [of *Ben Okri: Towards the Invisible City*] below.

4. Plato, *The Republic,* bk III, 398. One should add, in fairness to Plato, that Socrates insists on the dissident poet being treated with the utmost courtesy, anointed with myrrh, and crowned with fillets of wool—before being asked to leave.

5. *Yeats's Poems,* ed. A. N. Jeffares with an appendix by Warwick Gould (London: Macmillan, 1989), 196. Yeats attributes the saying 'to an old play', which, however, has never been discovered.

6. Wole Soyinka, *The Interpreters* (London: Heinemann, 1965).

David C. L. Lim (essay date 2005)

SOURCE: Lim, David C. L. "*Songs of Enchantment.*" In *The Infinite Longing for Home: Desire and the Nation in Selected Writings of Ben Okri and K. S. Maniam,* pp. 89-99. Amsterdam: Rodopi, 2005.

[*In this essay, Lim explores how Okri depicts Africa historically, socially, and spiritually in his writings, commenting specifically on the author's portrayal of Africa's relationship with the Western world and how his vision of a "universal civilization" differs from that envisioned by Léopold Sédar Senghor.*]

MATHEMATICS OF DESTINY

Where *TFR* [*The Famished Road*] closes on an elevated note, *Songs of Enchantment* (*SOE*) opens to a portentous future. As if to remind us of the impossibility of completion and to caution us against hastily equating Dad's transformations in the first book of the trilogy with 'arrival', Azaro says early in *SOE* that nothing is ever finished and struggles are never truly concluded. With his *abiku* foresight, he reveals that the political chaos brought on by the coming independence is fast spreading. It is already amidst the compound people, "waiting to burst into flames" and destroy lives (*SOE* 3). Children will die from water poisoning. Around the country, dissension will grow fat and many who have hitherto opposed the corrupt Party of the Rich will succumb to accepting its patronage. They will be defeated by hunger, unable to wait any longer for justice to come. Ade will die in a car crash and his father will go insane and be killed by thugs from the Party of the Rich. Madame Koto will be stabbed (but her death postponed until *IR* [*Infinite Riches*]) and countless other calamities will befall the nation-people before *SOE* runs its course. Interestingly, although the unborn nation is fast disintegrating in *SOE,* Okri does not see it as a "dark" novel:

> My books that seem to be books of light are actually books of despair, and I always say that, with the passing of time, *Astonishing the Gods,* which is seen as the book of light, will grow darker, and a book like *Songs of Enchantment,* which is seen as a dark book, will grow lighter. It will change over time.[1]

Okri offers no elaboration on how *SOE* might be seen as growing lighter in time, but the answer is already implicit in our earlier explication of the 'twisted' logic of the impossible: 'the greater the lack, the more there is to overcome, and the more levels of self-transcendence there are to achieve'. Darkness is light in the same way that every failure is a secret victory, a prepared ground for the active re-invention of a higher order. In the context of *SOE,* we might say that the darkness overshadowing the lives of the compound people is a prelude to the emergence of a higher political order. This "mathematics of destiny,"[2] the way in which things will somehow work out for those who persevere when the time is right, applies as much to the trilogy as it does to Nigeria and Africa.

"Things peak at different times for different people," says Okri.[3] "Africa has gone through its own stage of civilisation a thousand years ago and gone into a decline. It's like Greece." Elsewhere, Okri has suggested a reason for the decline of a civilization: "It's possible that one has been travelling on one road for too long."[4] As a result, one has forgotten the reason for travelling. Forgetting, as we know from the road-builders in *TFR,* is the first step towards decline. Applying this logic to postcolonial Africa, it might be said that the people's challenge to stay alive (within the global economic system) and to stay intact (as a nation in a world divided by ethnonationalist upsurges) need not extend into bad infinity. Similarly, the prevalent image of Africa as a perpetually starving and naturally backward continent "inhabited not by human beings but by a monstrous

variation of black insects" (*IR* 203) cannot be said to be the culmination of the continent's destiny. Nor can it be said that Africa's present decline suggests, as "contemporary peakers" believe, that its people "never had a peak" and that "all they had was dark ages."[5] Okri laments people's general tendency to overlook Africa's resilience of spirit and overemphasize the negative impact of colonialism. Is it not possible, Okri asks, that colonialism did not penetrate the kernel of Africa, "our spiritual and aesthetic and mythic internal structures, the way in which we perceive the world"?[6] Of course, he says, the "African ways have their flaws" and colonialism had been "a hugely negative thing in many ways—particularly its effect on the self-perception of the people."[7] It made them see themselves as less than what they were. But does that mean that the damage is irreparable or that Africa's resilience is less worthy of attention in comparison to its brief nightmare of colonization?

Okri's contestation of the metanarrative of the West as the privileged agent of history and the bearer of light to Africa is not a new enterprise. Others before him have asked whether scholars, including even well-meaning Africanist historiographers and anthropologists, have not themselves perpetuated the distorted image of the continent in their haste to grasp and explain away its failures. Similarly, the relationship between colonizer and colonized has been debated ever since Senghor, Fanon, and Memmi. Much of this has been discussed elsewhere, so, to avoid needless repetition, this short [essay] will limit its focus to just one question: where does Okri sit in this familiar landscape? We might begin by noting that, in spite of evident postcolonial concerns in his writings, Okri himself is not keen on the label. He states emphatically in an interview:

> I reject utterly the way in which my work is placed within the whole context of the margin, the periphery, postcolonial and stuff like that. I think those are very poor descriptions of the work that some of us are trying to do. Because it completely situates the work within a time/historical context and not within the context of the self and inner necessity, which is bigger and beyond that. And there are affinities between writers that have more to do with that than they have to do with the fact that they both come from so-called ex-colonial nations. When people do that they're not seeing what I'm doing and they're completely missing the point and I feel sad about that.[8]

Here one might perhaps be tempted to read Okri's self-distancing from the "postcolonial and stuff like that" with a pinch of salt. After all, according to the standard cynical view, writers almost never fail to bemoan the ways in which their works are misunderstood, which is reason enough to treat their outbursts as a kind of writerly posturing that ultimately has little if any bearing on the writings themselves. It is true that writers sometimes overlook the textuality of their texts, except that here Okri's texts *are* at odds with certain textbook prescriptions of postcolonial theorizing. Negritude, for instance, is usually dismissed as a 'stupid', even racist, essentialist myth, a defensive-reactionary appeal to some ahistorical essence that does not exist. But is it nothing but a self-defeating response to colonialism, an attempt to cover up Africa's inferiority complex and the shame of its colonizability? Could it, instead, be a kind of 'necessary lie' to be used to "free us from our smallness" and "help us get to our true reality"?⁹ These are some of the key issues we will be examining in relation to Okri's endeavour to revalidate Africa's relationship with the rest of the world.

THE AFRICAN WAY

In *SOE,* as in *TFR,* Dad continues to propound in the same feverish style his fantastic political visions and the novel ways in which he is "going to rule this country" (119). But it is in *SOE,* instead of *TFR,* that his visions attain density and historical-contextual specificity. Consider, for example, the episode set in Madame Koto's bar where Dad is found sounding off his political ideas to Azaro and goes on for so long and so vigorously that Azaro, already growing edgy, is invaded by all kinds of insects. Although this scene is not much different from the others where Dad talks about wondrous political possibilities, it is particularly worth noting because Dad's ideals are for the first time explicitly referred to (by Azaro) as visions of an "African utopia," in which "we would pool all our secret wisdom, distil our philosophies, conquer our bad history, and make our people glorious in the world of continents" (124). Africa, continues Dad, "is the home of the world" that "could be the garden of the earth" (126). But "look at how we live in this world," he laments, pointing to all that is wrong with the continent. Dad's emphasis on Africa is amplified by Azaro's account of a momentous spirit-event secretly taking place amidst the nation's political chaos. With his *abiku* eyes, Azaro sights in the sky "the slow migration of the great spirits of Africa" (26). He is initially unable to comprehend what he sees, since what he sees appears locked and coded in gnomic riddles. It is only after a few sightings that he begins to understand that the innumerable great spirits of the continent and master-spirits from all over the world are "coming together for their mighty convocation" (40-41). They are trailed by "representatives of our forgotten gods, our transformative ancestors" (159), and behind them, representatives from the spirit-world who had lived

> The African Way—The Way of compassion and fire and serenity: The Way of freedom and power and imaginative life; The Way that keeps the mind open to the existences beyond our earthly sphere, that keeps the spirit pure and primed to all the rich possibilities of living [. . .] The Way that preaches attunement with all the higher worlds, that believes in forgiveness and generosity of spirit, always receptive, always listening, always kindling the understanding of signs [. . .] The Way that always, like a river, flows into and flows out of the myriad Ways of the world.

> (*SOE* 159-60)

From Azaro we learn that the African Way, also referred to as "the Original Way" (*SOE* 160), is a way of being in the world, a spiritual mode of existence through which "forgotten and undiscovered" ancestral knowledge was produced (161). Ancestral knowledge here encompasses

> legends and moments of history [. . .] wonderful forms of divination by numbers and cowries and signs, numerological systems for summoning the gods, [. . .] the stories and myths and philosophical disquisitions on the relativities of African Time and Space [. . .] astronomical incidents: the date of a stellar explosion, a supernova bursting over the intense dream of the continent, heralding, according to a king's soothsayer, a brief nightmare of colonization, and an eventual, surprising, renaissance.

> (*IR* 113-14)

There is certainly poetic beauty in Okri's description of the African Way, but his valorization of it nonetheless brings him dangerously close to the essentialist trap that Senghor is said to have fallen into when he promoted the much derided Pan-African philosophy of Negritude. Is Okri heading in the same direction as Senghor, ideationally? Is he advocating some kind of return to the idealized purity of precolonial Africa? To answer these questions, one should perhaps begin by noting that the most unfortunate thing about Negritude is that the popular view of its being theoretically suspect is also the most inaccurate. Negritude, which has many overlooked variants ranging from the aggressive to the conciliatory and inventive, has been rejected en bloc for relying on African blackness as justification for everything, for homogenizing the heterogeneous Africa, and for setting up false binaries: "Negro emotion confronting Hellenistic reason; intuitive Negro reasoning through participation facing European analytical thinking through utilization."¹⁰ Negritude has also been criticized by the likes of Ayi Kwei Armah, Wole Soyinka, and Ezekiel Mphahlele as an unfortunate theory that romanticizes Africa, glosses over its ugly and violent side, and makes the black man look ridiculous by portraying him as having "insect antennas" and "mystic emotion."¹¹ Are these fair accusations? Let us examine two passages from Senghor's *On African Socialism*:

> In contrast to the classic European, the Negro African does not draw a line between himself and the object; he does not hold it at a distance, nor does he merely look at it and analyze it. After holding it at a distance, after scanning it without analyzing it, he takes it vibrant in his hands, careful not to kill or fix it. He touches it, feels it, *smells* it.
>
> [. . .]
>
> Thus the Negro African [. . .] abandons his personality to become identified with the Other, dies to be reborn in the Other. He does not assimilate; he is assimilated. He lives a common life with the Other; he lives a symbiosis [. . .] he 'knows ["is born with"] the Other'. Subjects and objects are dialectically face to face in the very act of knowledge.¹²

Of the two passages, the first is clearly romantic. It paints the Negro African as a native endowed with the mythical ability to perceive secret interconnectivity between all things, and to experience harmonic oneness with the world. The second passage, by contrast, is not only perfectly reasonable but also, one is tempted to argue, Lacanian in implication: the Other is not external to the subject's identity but is intimately external or 'extimate'. The subject always by default misrecognizes the truth about this extimate relationship. That is why it is only when the subject abandons his personality (his *agalma,* what is most precious to him) to become identified with the Other (recognize that he has always already been the Author of his Fate), that he will be symbolically reborn in the place where the Other always already was (become a self-recognizing subject of drive). Reading the second passage from a Lacanian standpoint, we might also say that reality is not a pre-discursive object but something that has to be found "in the very act of knowledge,"[13] in the traversal of one's fundamental fantasy.

It is not mentioned often enough that Senghor was keenly aware of the hostile reception given his ideas. In defence of his position, he points out in "Negritude: A Humanism of the Twentieth Century" that all he is saying is that Africa has gone through history in ways that are distinct from Europe, and that, because of these differences, Africa has come to possess certain historically conditioned and culturally encoded sensibilities which are neither irrelevant nor inferior simply because they differ from the European norm. The fundamentals of Senghor's vision are not lost on scholars like V. Y. Mudimbe who argue that the dominant view of Negritude as promoting false binarisms "seems quite wrong."[14] Senghor's philosophy, Mudimbe argues, can be understood through a challenging proposition Senghor offered to the Senegalese Socialist Party in July 1963: "Finally, what too many Africans lack, is the awareness of our poverty and creative imagination, I mean the spirit of resourcefulness."[15] Is this not also the same point Okri makes when he says that Africa should not overlook its resilience of spirit and great capacity to dream?

In the *abiku* trilogy, Okri not only insists on the resilience of the African Way, he also insists that those who attempt to negate it would only end up negating themselves. To borrow the words of the reformed Governor-General in *IR,* because imperialists "set out to dominate the world, they are condemned to live with the negative facts of their domination. They will be changed by the world that they set out to colonize" (*IR* 161). This subversive logic of 'he who thinks he penetrates Africa is, unbeknownst to him, always already penetrated by it' (to adapt Lacan's 'the one who counts is always already included in the account') is nicely illustrated by Cezair-Thompson in her reading of the 'famished road' motif. Cezair-Thompson contrasts Okri's road of creation with the road in Joyce Cary's *Mister Johnson.* The latter, she

argues, represents the path "which the colonizers impose upon Africa, and which symbolically appropriates the natives' rights to 'imagine' their own destiny, map their own terrain and tell their own story."[16] Okri's road, on the other hand, is mythic-creative in origin, created by no one, always transforming itself and elusive of all attempts to pin it down. It is perpetually hungry and ever ready to devour those who travel on it without first offering the proper sacrifices. In *TFR,* one of its victims is the white man in Mum's story. The white man in the tale was once an important figure in the colonial government of the unborn nation. When independence troubles started, he tried unsuccessfully for three years to leave the country. Even taking a plane out was futile; when he got off the plane, he found himself back in the same place. It was only later he discovered that "the only way to get out of Africa is to get Africa out of you" (*TFR* 483). The moral of Mum's story is this: the white man—representative of "short-sighted conquerors of the times' (*SOE* 160)—may colonize the continent, extract its riches and wreak havoc upon it, but ultimately it is he who is swallowed by Africa, as is Mr Kurtz in Joseph Conrad's *Heart of Darkness.*

If we concede that Okri's Senghorian African Way is not 'stupid' essentialism, how, then, does it compare to, say, the Asian Way, an ideology propounded by East Asian leaders like Singapore's Lee Kuan Yew and Malaysia's Mahathir Mohamad? How do they compare, beyond the fact that they reject the West's self-representation as the body of universal values and posit themselves as a way of healing the wounded psyches of their once-colonized people? One might note that the Asian Way, which asserts its particularity as a synthesis of 'ours' ('Asian values') and 'theirs' (Western capitalist-economic rationalism), is in the last instance a cynical ideology strategically employed by the political class in East Asia to restrict civil rights, inculcate blind obedience to authority, cover up corrupt practices and perpetuate existing relations of oppression. It is a kind of reverse racism constituted strictly on the basis of pure difference, whereby any transaction between self and Other can only occur with the former being perpetually tormented by a deep fear of being contaminated by the Other or robbed of its superior indigenous Thing. By contrast, Okri's African Way is closer to another Way: namely, that developed by Ayi Kwei Armah in his novel *Two Thousand Seasons,* insofar as they both aim at "preserving knowledge of who we are, knowledge of the best way we have found to relate to each other, each to all, ourselves to other peoples, all to our surroundings."[17] The crucial difference is that Okri's Way is not, like Armah's Way and the Asian Way, a particularity posited in a purely differential relation with other particularities. Although it has its distinctive, culturally and historically shaped expressions (forms, divinations, rituals, stories, myths, and so on), it does not close in upon itself or posit itself as the best or only Way, but "always, like a river, flows into and flows out of the myriad Ways of the world" (*SOE* 160). Furthermore, although Okri's Way promises self-empowerment, it does not, like the aforementioned Ways, prescribe a return to ancestral practices for its own sake (as if Africans must only stick to doing African things if they aim to be empowered), or promote unquestioning deference to authority. What it simply asks of the subject is to "say yes to destiny and illumination" (*TFR* 487), to rekindle what Senghor refers to as Africa's "spirit of resourcefulness." Put another way, it asks that the subject replace his cynical-defeatist attitude of thought with one that keeps the mind open to possibility in impossibility, in self-transcendence and nation-building.

To clarify this with an illustration, we might imagine the subject in search of healing via Okri's African Way as having to "make a parabolic journey" (*SOE* 281) to the presupposed other side where the Cure is believed to lie waiting. The twist here is that if and when the subject eventually makes the journey and crosses the threshold, he will discover that, contrary to what he had hitherto assumed, the Cure is not 'out there', external to himself, to be found in ancestral rituals or some such thing, but lies, rather, within himself. Rituals, if they are noble, are only there to help the subject cope with the "fire and ice of being born" (131) and to recognize that "OUR DESTINY IS [and has always been] IN OUR HANDS" (279). This perhaps explains the significance of the novel's title and the reason why Okri sees *SOE* as a book of light rather than darkness. *SOE* celebrates the enchantment and redivination of the self, and this celebration is made possible, ironically enough, by the powers that are attempting to negate it: namely, the corrupt political class of the would-be nation as well as "those whose hunger had been defeated by the promise of wealth and instant protection" and "who didn't want to suffer and wait for justice any more" (111). This is ultimately the same as saying that *SOE* 'celebrates' political strife—not by perversely revelling in it but in recognizing that it is, in the final account, a secret opportunity to surmount the seven mountains of life and, in doing so, surmount oneself.

ALL THINGS ARE LINKED: OKRI, SENGHOR AND THE UNIVERSAL CIVILIZATION

Okri's African Way is but one of the many Ways flowing in and out of each other like the river of creation which became a road which then branched out to the whole world. In Okri's philosophy, all Ways flow into the great sea of humanity to constitute what he calls the "universal civilization."[18] This notion of "universal civilization" has not received as much scholarly attention as the *abiku* and famished-road motifs, but it is pivotal to, if not the culmination of, Okri's vision in which "All things are linked" (483). It is mentioned perhaps for the first time in his essay **"Redreaming the World,"** where, by way of clearing the ground for the introduction of the term, he reminds contemporary victors not to forget the mathematics of destiny, that "to swallow

the history of others into your own history is to expect to be constipated with the history of others."[19] To "strangled nations" and "wounded peoples," he asks them not to "hold themselves down with rage about their historical past or their intolerable present" but instead to find the humility and strength to distil their experience into the highest creativity. It is only when people recognize the logic of the rise and fall of things, Okri writes, that there may be hope "for us all to create the beginnings of the first true universal civilization in the history of recorded and unrecorded time." The idea surfaces next in Okri's essay **"Time to Dream the Best Dream of All,"** where he urges the United Nations to commit itself steadfastly to its "universal goal": "the realisation of the human potential, the eradication of poverty, the enhancement of liberty, and the triumph of justice."[20] Despite the UN's shortcomings, Okri says, it is today "the only organisation still vaguely capable of articulating the notion of one world, a sort of symphony of humanity." It is not until *Astonishing the Gods* (*ATG*), though, that the notion receives its fullest treatment. From the allegorical novel, we learn that the dream of the Invisibles is to "initiate on earth the first universal civilisation where love and wisdom would be as food and air" (*ATG* 131), a place where

> the most ordinary goal was living the fullest life, in which creativity in all spheres of endeavour was the basic alphabet, and in which the most sublime lessons possible were always learned and relearned from the unforgettable suffering which was the bedrock of their great new civilisation.
>
> (*ATG* 28)

After *ATG*, 'universal civilization' is invoked in several other works. In his essay **"The Joys of Story-Telling I,"** for instance, Okri reflects on the postmodern collapse of the great systems (in whose name nations and individuals have wreaked violence upon others), and how it is *celebrated* rather than mourned by strong poets, "albeit with some sadness in their hearts," because they know that the last remaining towers of certainty must collapse before "a true world history and genius" can begin.[21] Only then, he writes, "might the world hope as one and struggle as one, towards the first universal golden age."[22] In *IR*, the third book of the *abiku* trilogy, the notion surfaces as the "grand picture of humanity" (112-13), a composite of "the great jigsaw that the creator spread all over the diverse peoples of the earth, hinting that no one race or people can have the complete picture or monopoly of the ultimate possibilities of the human genius alone" (112).

Even from these few examples it is clear that the 'universal civilization' is a central constant in Okri's writings. What is perhaps not so evident is how much it recalls, if not has its roots in, Senghor's lesser-known Negritudist conception of the "Civilization of the Universal."[23] For Senghor, the universal civilization is the reconciled totality of the inherently *equal* parts of a divided but interdependent world. It is a pan-human order, to be achieved through a world-historical "dynamic symbiosis" wherein only the fecund elements of each part are retained and the harmful discarded.[24] Senghor also believes, rightly or wrongly, that Africa stands to benefit from "an infusion of the inquisitive spirit and a higher development of analytical reason," while "Western Europe, now locked in a dehumanizing worship of machines and material wealth, will benefit from the African contribution of its greater emotional and spiritual development, vitality, and understanding of the interconnectedness of all life in the universe."[25] Although there are essentialist moments in Senghor's conception here that would furrow the brows of postcolonial critics, it would serve us well not to throw out the baby (Senghor's attempt to validate Africa's place in the world) with the bathwater (his essentialist view of the inherent differences between the West and Africa). In any case, Okri, despite being influenced by Senghor, does not draw wholesale from him but radicalizes his ideas. For instance, where Senghor envisages the realization of the universal civilization as a distant but actual possibility,[26] Okri sees it more as an impossible ideal to be pursued but never to be fully attained, as attainment would only lead to the cessation of the infinite overcoming of self-limitations. Like the road-builders' Heaven in *ATG,* Okri's universal civilization is a transgressive utopia which, instead of insisting on arrival, celebrates process over product.

Notes

1. Falconer, "Whispering of the Gods," 49.

2. Okri, in Falconer, "Whispering of the Gods," 46.

3. Hattersley, "Ben Okri: A Man in Two Minds," 6.

4. Martin Linton, "Dreams of Utopia on Road to Reform," *Guardian* (London; 4 November 1991).

5. Okri, in Hattersley, "Ben Okri: A Man in Two Minds," 6.

6. Wilkinson, *Talking with African Writers,* 86.

7. Hattersley, "Ben Okri: A Man in Two Minds," 6.

8. Falconer, "Whispering of the Gods," 44.

9. Okri, *Mental Fight,* 5.

10. V. Y. Mudimbe, *The Invention of Africa: Gnosis, Philosophy, and the Order of Knowledge* (Bloomington: Indiana UP, 1988): 94.

11. Léopold Sédar Senghor, *On African Socialism,* tr. & intro. Mercer Cook (London & Dunmow: Pall Mall, 1964): 74.

12. Senghor, *On African Socialism,* 72-73.

13. *On African Socialism,* 73.

14. Mudimbe, *The Invention of Africa,* 94.

15. Mudimbe, *The Invention of Africa,* 94.

16. Cezair-Thompson, "Beyond the Postcolonial Novel," 35.

17. Ayi Kwei Armah, *Two Thousand Seasons* (1973; London & Ibadan: Heinemann, 1979): 39.

18. Okri, "Redreaming the World."

19. "Redreaming the World."

20. Ben Okri, "Time to Dream the Best Dream of All," *Guardian* (London; 7 January 1995).

21. Okri, *A Way of Being Free,* 30.

22. *A Way of Being Free,* 31.

23. Léopold Sédar Senghor, "Negritude: A Humanism of the Twentieth Century," in *The Africa Reader: Independent Africa* (New York: Random House, 1970): 187-88.

24. Senghor, *On African Socialism,* 49-50.

25. Janet G. Vaillant, *Black, French and African: A Life of Léopold Sédar Senghor* (Cambridge MA & London: Harvard UP, 1990): 266.

26. Senghor rejects Jean-Paul Sartre's Marxist reading of Negritude, which argues that Africa's black cultural values will be cancelled out when the grand symbiosis of cultures occurs. Africa, he argues, will remain African, true to the culture of Negritude and the goal of African socialism which is to create a society in which the human personality can reach its potential.

Works Cited

Armah, Ayi Kwei. *Two Thousand Seasons* (1973; London & Ibadan: Heinemann, 1979).

Cezair-Thompson, Margaret. "Beyond the Postcolonial Novel: Ben Okri's *The Famished Road* and its 'Abiku' Traveller," *Journal of Commonwealth Literature* 31.2 (Summer 1996): 33-45.

Falconer, Delia. "Whispering of the Gods: An Interview with Ben Okri," *Island* 71 (1997): 43-51.

Hattersley, Roy. "Ben Okri: A Man in Two Minds," *Guardian* (London; 21 August 1999), Guardian Profile: 6. <http://www.guardian.co.uk/saturday_review/story/0,3605,268270,00.html>, accessed 21 August 1999.

Linton, Martin. "Dreams of Utopia on Road to Reform," *Guardian* (London; 4 November 1991).

Mudimbe, V. Y. *The Invention of Africa: Gnosis, Philosophy, and the Order of Knowledge* (Bloomington: Indiana UP, 1988).

Okri, Ben. *Birds of Heaven* (London: Phoenix, 1996).

———. "The Catastrophe Now Facing Nigeria," *Guardian* (London; 6 September 1994).

———. *The Famished Road* (1991; London: Vintage, 1992).

———. *Infinite Riches* (London: Phoenix, 1998).

———. *Mental Fight: An Anti-Spell for the 21st Century* (London: Phoenix, 1999).

———. "Redreaming the World: An Essay for Chinua Achebe," *Guardian* (London; 9 August 1990), Review: 14.

———. "Plea for Somalia," *Guardian* (London; 3 September 1992).

———. *Songs of Enchantment* (1993; London: Vintage, 1994).

———. "Time to Dream the Best Dream of All," *Guardian* (London; 7 January 1995).

———. *A Way of Being Free* (London: Phoenix, 1997).

Senghor, Léopold Sédar. *On African Socialism,* tr. & intro. Mercer Cook (London & Dunmow: Pall Mall, 1964).

———. "Negritude: A Humanism of the Twentieth Century," in *The Africa Reader: Independent Africa* (New York: Random House, 1970): 179-92.

Vaillant, Janet G. *Black, French and African: A Life of Léopold Sédar Senghor* (Cambridge MA & London: Harvard UP, 1990).

Wilkinson, Jane. *Talking with African Writers: Interviews with African Poets, Playwrights and Novelists* (London: James Currey, 1992).

FURTHER READING

Criticism

Cezair-Thompson, Margaret. "Beyond the Postcolonial Novel: Ben Okri's *The Famished Road* and its 'Abiku' Traveller." *Journal of Commonwealth Literature* 31, no. 2 (1996): 33-45.

Considers *The Famished Road* to be representative of African "decolonized fiction" based on its novel approach to the symbolic import of both the "road" and the character of the *abiku*.

Hawley, John C. "Ben Okri's Spirit-Child: *Abiku* Migration and Postmodernity." *Research in African Literatures* 26, no. 1 (spring 1995): 30-9.
Contends that Okri's use of the *abiku* narrator in both *The Famished Road* and *Songs of Enchantment* signals a shift in African fiction toward postmodernism.

Hemminger, Bill. "The Way of the Spirit." *Research in African Literatures* 32, no. 1 (spring 2001): 66-82.
Describes the worldview Okri established in *The Famished Road* and *Songs of Enchantment* as "being-in-the-world," and claims that both novels "argue for increased interplay between physical and spiritual in a modern technologized world."

McCabe, Douglas. "'Higher Realities': New Age Spirituality in Ben Okri's *The Famished Road.*" *Research in African Literatures* 36, no. 4 (winter 2005): 1-21.
Detailed analysis of how the principles of New Age spirituality inform the characters, themes, and narrative techniques of *The Famished Road.*

Moh, Felicia Alu. *Ben Okri: An Introduction to His Early Fiction.* Enugu, Nigeria: Fourth Dimension Publishing, 2001, 160 p.
Full-length study of Okri's early fiction.

Ogunsanwo, Olatubosun. "Intertexuality and Post-Colonial Literature in Ben Okri's *The Famished Road.*" *Research in African Literatures* 26, no. 1 (spring 1995): 40-52.
Argues that the narrative intertexts employed by Okri in *The Famished Road* form a discursive cross-culturality that challenges the dominant Eurocentric worldview.

Additional coverage of Okri's life and career is contained in the following sources published by Gale: *African Writers*; *Black Writers,* Eds. 2, 3; *British Writers Supplement,* Vol. 5; *Concise Major 21st-Century Writers,* Ed. 1; *Contemporary Authors,* Vol. 138; *Contemporary Authors New Revision Series,* Vols. 65, 128; *Contemporary Literary Criticism,* Vols. 87, 223; *Contemporary Novelists,* Eds. 5, 6, 7; *Dictionary of Literary Biography,* Vols. 157, 231, 319, 326; *Encyclopedia of World Literature in the 20th Century,* Ed. 3; *Literature Resource Center*; *Major 20th-Century Writers,* Ed. 2; *Major 21st-Century Writers* (eBook), Ed. 2005.; *Reference Guide to Short Fiction,* Ed. 2; *Short Stories for Students,* Vol. 20; *World Literature and Its Times,* Vol. 2; and *World Writers in English,* Vol. 1.

Niyi Osundare
1947-

Nigerian poet, essayist, playwright, and nonfiction writer.

INTRODUCTION

Compared with writers as diverse as Walt Whitman, Bertolt Brecht, and Pablo Neruda, Osundare is one of the most admired African Anglophone poets of his generation. Exploring themes such as the importance of respect for nature, the imperative of historical preservation, and the dignity bestowed by hard work and perseverance, Osundare has produced poetry that speaks to both an academic and a popular readership. Osundare has won many awards for his work, including the Commonwealth Poetry Prize, two Cadbury Prizes, the Fonlon-Nichols Award, and the Noma Award, which is Africa's equivalent of the Nobel Prize for literature.

BIOGRAPHICAL INFORMATION

Osundare was born in 1947 in Ikerri, a village in western Nigeria. In his poem "Farmer-Born," he describes himself as "farmer-born peasant-bred." Osundare's father was a noted village musician, and his paternal grandfather was a diviner-physician. As a child Osundare would accompany his grandfather into the forest to gather roots and herbs to cure all manner of ailments. An integral part of the healing process was the use of incantations to stir the medicines to life. Thus, he became acquainted at an early age with the power and importance of nature and language. Osundare attended local Christian schools and Ibadan University, from which he graduated in 1972 with honors in English. From there he moved to England to pursue a master's degree at the University of Leeds, and later moved to Toronto to attend York University, where he earned a doctorate. In 1982 he returned to Nigeria to join the teaching staff at Ibadan University. In 1990 Osundare won the first of two Fulbright scholar-in-residence fellowships to work at the University of Wisconsin. His second fellowship was to the University of New Orleans, where he became a full professor of English in 1997. In August 2005 Osundare and his wife were among the tens of thousands of victims of Hurricane Katrina and the subsequent flooding of New Orleans. The couple were nearly swept away in the flood waters, but they managed to climb to safety in their attic, where they remained for twenty-six hours until a neighbor heard their cries for help and rescued them. Having lost all of their belongings—including all of Osundare's manuscripts—they were homeless for the next two weeks before being taken in by a family in Alabama. While living temporarily in the family's basement, Osundare received an e-mail message from Franklin Pierce College in New Hampshire, offering him a teaching position. Since then, Osundare has lived with his wife in Rindge, New Hampshire.

MAJOR WORKS

Musicality is one of the most essential elements of Osundare's poetry. In his later work he often includes musical directions because he believes poetry should be experienced orally. He has said: "When I perform in Nigeria, I have a number of musicians backing me up with different kinds of drums. Each drum has its own kind of symbolic message. The drums are very important as tools of expression and interpretation. Poetry flows, it is rhythm. And the rhythm is in every word, every syllable. My language, Yoruba, is music." Osundare's first published collection, *Songs of the Marketplace* (1983), evidences these values. The volume's title is a reference to the vibrancy of African markets, which are gathering places for community socializing as well as places of commerce. Nevertheless, despite the book's implicit emphasis on African music and culture, its individual poems are highly critical of the social and political realities that plague modern Nigeria. In the poem "Excursion" Osundare presents a litany of portraits of African poverty, and then contrasts them with the callousness of the rich and powerful: "Several government people / have passed through these streets / several Mercedes tyres have drenched / gaunt road liners in sewer water." In his second volume, *Village Voices* (1984), Osundare continued to lament social and economic inequality in Nigeria, particularly after the oil industry brought fabulous wealth to the upper classes along with unprecedented governmental corruption and greed through the 1970s and 1980s. In *The Writer as Righter: The African Literary Artist and His Social Obligations,* a book-length essay published in 1986, Osundare detailed his thoughts on the role of writers in spotlighting social ills in Africa. With *A Nib in the Pond* (1986) Osundare returned to poetry, this time with an explicitly socialist agenda, dedicating many poems to such leaders as Fidel Castro and Agostinho Neto. With *The Eye of the Earth* (1986) Osundare began to address environmental issues in his poetry—a concern that continues throughout his body of work. In *Songs of the Season* (1990) Osundare took a different approach, deliberately couching his poetic observations in simple, accessible language to appeal to as wide an audience as possible. The subjects of the poems are national and international events of the time, in the form of satires, dialogues, tributes, and parables. The poems in *Waiting Laughters,* for which Osundare won the Noma Prize in 1990, are meant to be performed and accompanied by music. The work has been described as an "experimental orchestration around a major theme." In *Midlife* (1993) Osundare turned to more personal subject matter, exploring the arrested development of his homeland through his own experiences as a middle-aged man. *Horses of Memory* (1998) contains more poems inspired by Nigeria's desperate need for political change and the country's collective memory of its troubles. In *The Word Is an Egg* (2000) Osundare's awareness of the power of language comes to the fore, with poems that focus on writing in the language of one's colonizers, the role of words in the formation of personal and national identity, and the social and political abuse of language in the forms of censorship and illiteracy. Osundare's most recent volume of poetry, the post-Katrina *Tender Moments* (2006), departs from his characteristic focus on politics and social ills and addresses instead the intricacies of human relationships.

CRITICAL RECEPTION

Osundare is revered as a poet who examines the social and political condition of modern Africa with musicality and a sense of humor despite his often-grim subject matter. Critics often comment on the human quality of his work, particularly in his evocation of history and memory through the use of traditional African literary and musical elements that appeal to ordinary people. In a November, 2002 interview for *Poetry International Web,* Osundare commented on the essential role of the writer in dramatizing Africa's problems: "You cannot keep quiet about the situation in the kind of countries we find ourselves in, in Africa. When you wake up and there is no running water, when you have a massive power outage for days and nights, no food on the table, no hospital for the sick, no peace of mind; when the image of the ruler you see everywhere is that of a dictator with a gun in his hand; and, on the international level, when you live in a world in which your continent is consigned to the margin, a world in which the colour of your skin is a constant disadvantage, everywhere you go—then there is no other way than to write about this, in an attempt to change the situation for the better."

PRINCIPAL WORKS

Songs of the Marketplace (poetry) 1983
Village Voices (poetry) 1984

The Eye of the Earth (poetry) 1986
A Nib in the Pond (poetry) 1986
The Writer as Righter: The African Literary Artist and His Social Obligations (nonfiction) 1986
Moonsongs (poetry) 1988
Songs of the Season (poetry) 1990
Waiting Laughters: A Long Song in Many Voices (poetry) 1990
Selected Poems (poetry) 1992
African Literature and the Crisis of Poststructuralist Theorizing (nonfiction) 1993
Midlife (poetry) 1993
Seize the Day and Other Poems for the Junior (poetry) 1995
Horses of Memory (poetry) 1998
Pages from the Book of the Sun: New and Selected Poems (poetry) 2000
Thread in the Loom: Essays on African Literature and Culture (essays) 2000
The World Is an Egg (poetry) 2000
The State Visit (drama) 2002
Two Plays (drama) 2005
Tender Moments (poetry) 2006

CRITICISM

J. O. J. Nwachukwu-Agbada (essay date 1996)

SOURCE: Nwachukwu-Agbada, J. O. J. "Lore & Other in Niyi Osundare's Poetry." In *New Trends & Generations in African Literature,* edited by Eldred Durosimi Jones, pp. 73-86. Trenton, N.J.: Africa World Press, 1996.

[*In the following essay, Nwachukwu-Agbada explores Osundare's rejection of European-influenced dogmatic poetry in favor of socially conscious folk poetry about ordinary people.*]

For a writer to merit a mention in literary history there are a number of criteria he/she must meet. One is his/her position in the tradition; another is the uniqueness of his/her artistic virtues; and yet another is the configuration of emphases to which his/her *oeuvre* is regularly returning. Niyi Osundare seemed to have been aware of these literary dictates before he set to work. To be sure, in each of his poems so far, his artistic anchor seems to be a recourse to lore, particularly the lore of his Yoruba people and a diagnosis of the social conditions of the ordinary person in society. Before his generation, poetry in Nigeria was essentially privatist; even though much of it recorded public issues, it was rendered in personalist terms with the aim of excluding the majority of its potential audience and cultivating a small coterie of connoisseurs (Chinweizu *et al.*;

Osundare, 'A Distant Call'; Aiyejina, 'Recent Nigerian Poetry'; Nwachukwu-Agbada, 'Matter and Form'). Niyi Osundare is not just a pioneer of the age who has sought to counter the trend in Nigerian poetry, he is probably the most prolific and consistent in his use of folk resources and the examination of the lives of ordinary people.

A proof of his awareness of his direction from the outset is to be found in two of his poems, **'The Poet'** and **'Poetry Is'.** As artistic manifestos, they are a deliberate contradiction of the school of poetry which insists that 'a poem must be "pure" and never "soiled" with "thought" (Knickerbocker and Reninger, p. 224). An examination of the poetry of the major Nigerian poets before Osundare shows that they were not averse to the thinking of this school. The dogmatic position of this poetic movement in Europe is encapsulated in Laurence Lerner's famous poem entitled, 'This Poem' in which poetry is said to be a 'mask' meant to conceal the poet's thought. A poem in Lerner's consideration is not supposed to reflect reality because it is essentially a 'fiction' which 'disfigures' and 'distorts' (pp. 105-6). In other words, poetry is neither a cognitive object nor a didactic medium outside of itself. According to Wilbur Scott, poets and critics of this persuasion 'shun all material such as the personal or social conditions behind the composition, the moral implications . . . so long as these are "extrinsic"—that is tangential to an understanding of the poem' (p. 181). Lerner was of course articulating in verse the view of a poetic stance pioneered by Wordsworth, Coleridge, Keats, Shelley, Mill etc. and brought to its peak by such modernist poets as Hopkins, Lorca, Mallarmé, Cowley, Tagore, Pound, Eliot and Thomas.

In Osundare's **'The Poet'** (*A Nib,* pp. 9-10). poetry must be infused with social consciousness. Here the poet 'is not a gadfly' who can afford urbane disinterestedness when 'urgent' social issues need to be commented upon. In other words, the poet cannot remain aloof, 'refine himself out of existence, paring his fingernails' like a Joycean god when all over the place there are 'soiled streets' calling for 'collective action'. This position locates Osundare's poetry in the socialist realm. The socialist artist by orientation does not believe in 'the "magic" qualities of art works and the unique features of the artist's mind' (Caudwell, p. 127). Rather he believes that an artist must proffer a specific social and cultural philosophy 'towards the field of action'. The poet ought not be a 'prophet' or 'God's hollow ventriloquist' who remains superior to others on account of his possession of the so-called special innate traits. Osundare's **'The Poet'** argues that since 'the poet's eyes are washed in the common spring' he must therefore serve as a social activist and salvage society from its own decadence. The belief is that,

> Literature is a social institution, using as its medium language, a social creation. Such traditional literary devices as symbolism and metre are social in their very

nature. . . . The poet himself is a member of society, possessed of a specific social status: he receives some degree of social recognition and reward; he addresses an audience, however hypothetical . . .

> (Wellek and Warren, p. 94)

Anybody reading Osundare's **'The Poet'** or his **'Poetry Is'** against Laurence Lerner's articulation of the 'purist' school in 'This Poem' may conclude that the former is not bothered by form. But in an interview with Sanya Oni, Osundare dismisses any misconceptions as to his notion of art: 'One is not asking for a simplistic kind of art, but for art that is accessible, relevant and beautiful' (p. 7). The truth is that in spite of the ideological intent of socialist art, an attention to form is equally important. Leon Trotsky, one of the Leninist faithfuls in socialist Russia in the 1920s, is known to have taken Mayakovsky to task over his *oeuvre* which the former says have 'no peaks, they are not disciplined internally. The parts refuse to obey the whole. Each part tries to be separate' (p. 152). However, in articulating the social conditions of the underprivileged in the historical development of the Nigerian society, Osundare has chosen to work within the oral tradition to which poetry is no stranger. He achieves two things by this choice: he convinces us that he is a cultural nationalist, what with his employment of the oral technique which is in fact an enduring African contribution to literary stylistics; secondly, he symbolizes his declared empathy for the condition of the ordinary man in the street by returning to a thought and speech pattern to which this class may easily respond.

I

It was William Bascom who had sought to distinguish between verbal art and literature by his observation that 'verbal art is composed and transmitted verbally, while literature is composed in writing and transmitted in writing.' However, he never failed to have the two linked up when he said:

> Yet it is obvious that these two traditions have not followed independent courses, but have intermingled and influenced one another. One result has been reworked tales, proverbs or other forms of verbal art which have reworked and adapted to literary standards of style and propriety, and thereafter transmitted by writing or printing.

> (p. 249)

Niyi Osundare is one such writer who has not only reworked folklore but has also deployed folk items[1] for the purposes of enhancing his writing and projecting his ideological predisposition. It is clear from his revelatory preface to *The Eye of the Earth* (1986) that he is able to unite orality and writing because of his rich cultural background, he being 'farmer-born, peasant-bred', and having 'encountered dawn in the enchanted corridors of the forest, suckled on the delicate aroma of healing herbs, and the pearly drops of generous moons' (p. *ix*).

Any wonder then that the titles of his collections either bear out his love for lore (*Songs of the Marketplace, Village Voices* and *Moonsongs*) or indicate at once that advocacy would be an essential element in his verse (*A Nib in the Pond, The Eye of the Earth, Waiting Laughters* and *Songs of the Season*).

In his '**Poetry Is**', a poem we have described as one of his artistic manifestos, the very first line takes us to the associativeness of a folkloristic heritage, particularly when it objects to 'esoteric whisper / of an excluding tongue'. For him, poetry is not 'a learned quiz / entombed in Grecoroman lore'; instead it is the 'eloquence of the gong / the lyric of the marketplace' (*Marketplace*, p. 3). The 'lyric of the marketplace' subsumes musicality and collectivity because a marketplace in folk history is a gathering point, the heart of the village; the spirits of selling and buying come together here. In his important poems, lore and one human predicament or the other are brought together with an artistry that makes his work very memorable. In '**Excursions**' (*Marketplace*, p. 7), the sundry commentator is either a folk or a folk sympathizer because of the manner in which he cultivates our emotion in favour of the ordinary person:

> in city fringes pregnant women
> rummage garbage heaps for
> the rotting remnants of city tables
> above, hawks and cultures hovering
> for their turn
>
>   (p. 8)

His most touching line in '**Excursions**' is where he calls attention to 'the family head' who 'roams the bush / trapping rats and insects'. This is a picture of poverty and underutilization of one's energy. The trapping of rats and insects is a folk chore meant for children in the villages, but when an adult engages in such an activity he is either mentally underdeveloped or abjectly improvident. Because the folks constitute the 'other' in his poetic vintage, Osundare is always reflecting their sordid lives in terms which either bespeak of their wretchedness and helplessness or their ignorance.

In '**Reflections**' (p. 37), he objects to the way the world is socially structured and likens it to 'the Solel Boneh's steam-shovel' because 'it scoops earth from one place / To fill up the hole in another' (p. 38). What the rich gain is the loss of the poor; poverty is the aftermath of someone else's affluence. Often Osundare's metaphor for the poor is sheep, while wolf is his idea of the rich who savour the helpless in order to survive doubly. In '**Ignorance**' (p. 33), he asks, 'how could sheep all agree / to give their crown to a wolf?' (p. 34). This is a side-step to the animal' story in which the wolf seeks the co-operation of the very creatures it regularly feeds upon. In '**To the Dinosaur**' (p. 41), a folkloric, prehistorical animal is employed as a metaphor for the African tyrant's emptiness; the metaphor is a sarcastic reference

to African rulers who adopt ancient, undemocratic postures in order to retain their places for life. One of their strategies is to dispose 'two million / skeletons to purchase a gilded skull' (p. 41). This issue of sheep ignorantly ministering unto the wolf is re-echoed here

. . . . .

> Knowing neither
> You have torn down the gate
> and asked wolves to tend your sheep
>
>   (p. 41)

The 'leopards', the whites, take over the places of wolves in '**Namibia Talks**' (p. 49) but the sheep remain Africa and Africans. The poet-persona chides fellow Africans:

> For so long we mistrusted our sheep
> to the care of leopards
> we have woken to the whitened skeleton
> of talkative folly
>
>   (p. 50)

Osundare, a folk commentator, utilizes diachronic terms and divests them of their archaic denotation. Words and clichés which ordinarily would have been regarded as worn-out are refurbished for the sole purpose of creating original humour. Name-calling and term-twisting as we know are very common in folk life. The *oriki* singers in Yoruba culture invest beauty on their composition through action-imagery, alliteration, pitching and morphological innovations. A few examples of his neologism will suffice.

Let us begin with what he has done with the word 'archaic'. In more poems than one he has shown his aversion for stilted academicism because it is pretentious. Those who are guilty of this belong to the 'archaidemia' (*Marketplace*, p. 27). Other nonce words of his include, 'kwashiorkored children' (*Marketplace*, p. 3) for malnourished children; 'mercedesed Pharoahs' (*A Nib*, p. 15) for important people in Mercedes cars; 'kiwi-ed boot' (*Moonsongs*, p. 32) for boots polished with kiwi polish; 'darkdom' for kingdom (*The Eye*, p. 25); 'executhieves' (*The Eye*, p. 46) for people in executive positions who steal from government coffers; and 'kolatera' (*Village Voices*, p. 50) for collateral (but the poet here plays on 'kola', the Nigerian euphemism for bribe). Others are word distortion and inversion. These are copious in *A Nib*: 'comrades or comeraids / trailblazers or blaze-trailers' (p. 21); 'from democracy to demoncrazy / from conscience to con-science' (p. 21); 'allies or all lies / adultery or adult tree / message or mess age' (p. 21); 'suffrage or suffer age' (p. 22); 'of statesmen and statemen'.

Osundare copiously uses metaphors and images that point to the past for purposes of making a contemporary statement on various issues which affect the lives of the ordinary person. In '**The Horseman Cometh**'

(*Marketplace,* p. 45), the horseman is the military tyrant who 'will build arsenals / in place of barns / and prod the poor / to gorge on bullets'. Apart from 'horseman', a term which takes our minds to antiquity, the word 'cometh' is on its own an archaic item. However, in the employment of these words, the poet is playing with the synecdoche of modern African anachronism when unelected individuals snatch power by force:

> A horseman gallops to power
> and tyrants of all the world rejoice
> torture chambers multiply apace
> and the noose thickens, descending

(p. 45)

His references to sword in **'Killing without a Sword'** (*Village Voices,* p. 13), **'The Land of Unease'** (*Village Voices,* p. 45), **'The Rocks Rose to Meet Me'** (*The Eye,* p. 14) or the words closely associated with the sword such as 'scalpel', 'knife', 'matchet', 'mattock' etc. are his metaphors for mindless eating. It is 'mindless eating' which leads to the request for 'a fruit deliciously beyond our reach' in **'Killing without a Sword'.** In **'The Land of Unease',** the persona castigates men that 'forge unequal knives / . . . with machetes greedier / than Esimuda's sword'. These are men who want to have everything to themselves. They are the prodigal in **'Eating Tomorrow's Yam'** (*Village Voices,* p. 16) who 'calls for a knife' when 'there is only one yam left / in the village barn'. The point here is that the word 'sword' and associated words take us to the time of gladiators who amused by being reckless.

The aura of lore which suffuses Osundare's poetry is justified by his decision from the outset to explore the pool of communal memories. His stance as the conscience of the folk after all accords well with the role of the artist of old whose bounden duty it was to 'wear courage like a shield / telling kings their fart / chokes the village nose' (*Village Voices,* p. 1). The 'other' in whose favour he has chosen to resolve his art is the folk whose concept of the earth is gradually being distorted by 'executhieves'. In *The Eye of the Earth,* for instance, the autobiography is collective rather than private. According to Funso Aiyejina, 'the animistic energy with which the volume is charged does not originate from the poet as an individual but rather as the sensitive heir to, and interpreter of a complex tradition and a collective philosophy' (**'To Plough'**, p. 2106).

In performing this role, Osundare chooses to be a griot, but a modern one. Unlike the griots of old who

> . . . conserved the constitutions of kingdoms by memory work alone; each princely family had its griots appointed to preserve tradition.

(Niane, p. *vii*)

Osundare would like that which is worthy such as the earth's ecology to be conserved and our capitalist tradition which is retrogressive to be done away with. In **'Forest Echoes',** the persona recalls the time when,

> Bouncing boughs interlock overhead
> like wristwrestlers straining muscularly
> on a canvas of leaves wounded
> by the fists of time

(*The Eye,* p. 3)

The poet chooses a journey motif very common in folktales. The trip is towards the forest comparable to that undertaken by D. O. Fagunwa's hero in *The Forest of a Thousand Daemons* or Amos Tutuola's *Palm-wine Drinkard*. The poet's allusion to Fagunwa's protagonist's journey in,

> Here they are
> midget and monster still
>
> . . . . .
>
> A forest of a million trees, this,
> a forest of milling trees

(p. 5)

is revealing. In **'The Rocks Rose to Meet Me',** the Romantic picture of a communion with the elements is complete. Here the Rocks—Olosunta and Oroole—are personified: 'Olosunta spoke first / the riddling one whose belly is wrestling ground / for god and gold' (p. 13). After Olosunta, spoke Oroole: 'Oroole came next / his ancient voice tremulous in the morning air' (p. 15). We may interpret this interlocution between man and the rocks at the metaphorical level to mean a reading of their history and the process of disintegration they might have experienced as a result of the 'plundering' to which they had been exposed over the years, yet in folklore, animate/inanimate communication is realistic. The desolation which has visited the forest in recent times is due to the impact of capitalistic exploitation of resources and the nuclear experimentation which have tended to undermine the original status of the earth:

> a lake is killed by the arsenic urine
> from the bladder of profit factories
> a poisoned stream staggers down the hills
> coughing chaos in the sickly sea
> the wailing whale, belly up like a frying fish
> crests the chilling swansong of parting waters.

(p. 50)

Like a typical traditional bard, Osundare employs forms of folklore in varying proportions. Apart from the songs (*orin*) which still retain part of their original Yoruba structure, proverbs (*owe*), curses (*epe*), incantations (*ofo*), riddles (*alo apamo*) and myths (*itan*) are largely reworked, and in most cases built in snippets into the lines. In Segment IV of *Moonsongs* he instructs that the poem be read 'to the accompaniment of the song: *Osupa oi yuwa mi o, osupa o, i yeyin mi . . .*' (p. 8). He does not supply the Yoruba song, not even in a glossary. In most of the poems the musical instruments to be used are suggested: omele, gbedu, ibembe, bata, adan, agba, ogbele, woro, reso, gangan (all types of drums), gong, shekere, the flute etc. are recommended for various poems. Outside the songs, these other folk-loric forms are integrated into the poems so that it becomes difficult to draw lines in their usage. For example, *Moonsongs* which flows like an *ijala* verse (Yoruba hunter's incantation) has several stanzas in which bits of these oral forms are incorporated in varying proportions:

How many hours will make a minute
How many oceans total one drop
Of elusive water
How many forests will make one tree
In regions of meticulous showers
How many . . . ?

(*Moonsongs*, p. 17)

In **'Under the Mango Tree'** (*Moonsongs*, pp. 49-50) alliteration, tongue-twisters, punning and word reformulation are easily noticeable in a passage such as this:

the mortal murmurs of musing mangoes,
of crude climbers and missiles
from starving quivers;
and suddenly, each fruit a toll
of expiring winds
each toll a tale
each tale a tail of coiling snakes
ah! mangoes man goes. Man

(p. 50)

Direct Yoruba terms and expressions in his lines show his fidelity to lore and orality. In all his collections so far Yoruba interjections are quite numerous. Many of these are glossed but there are indications that they might be direct borrowings from local songsters who use them in their various compositions: Expressions such as '*Iya jajeji l'Egbe / Ile eni I'eso ye'ni*' (suffering afflicts the stranger in a strange land / One is most important in one's own home) in *Songs of the Market-place* (p. 40); '*Ogeere amokoyeri*' (the one that shaves his head with the hoe) in *The Eye of the Earth* (p. 1); '*Ise losupa nse lalede orun, lalede orun / Is losupa nse* . . . (Busy is the moon in the compound of the sky / busy is the moon) in *Moonsongs* (p. 21). However, some of the words and expressions are apparently used for their musical effect since they are not explained. In *Moonsongs*, there are '*agbamurere*' (p. 1), '*kiriji kiriji kiriji pepelupe*' (p. 1) and '*Teregungu maja gungun*' which the poet in fact says is only a 'rhythmic refrain, it has no meaning' (p. 44).

II

The other major prong of his poetry is the 'other', referring to the social condition of the African and Nigerian citizenry. In his assessment of Osundare, Biodun Jeyifo has remarked that,

In all of modern African poetry, all, I repeat, only in the poetry of Agostinho Neto and David Diop will you find the same depth and passion and lyricism in solidarity with the oppressed, the down-trodden, the dis-

possessed, and a corresponding faith in their aspiration and will to revolutionary change as we confront in Osundare's poetry. The dispossession of the majority of our people, and more specifically of the rural producers, may, in fact, be said to be the grand theme of Osundare's poetry.

(pp. 317-18)

The tendency on his part to let the burdens of the ordinary man take over the prop of his poetic vintage is justified in **'The Poet'** in which he projects the view that,

The poet's pen is
the cactus by the stream
(shorn of its forbidding thorns)
each stem a rib
towards the field of action
its sap the ink of succour
when doubt's drought
assaults the wall

(*A Nib*, p. 10)

The implication of the above poetic programme of action is that the poet believes in a poetic mediation whose content is ideological, whose resolution favours civic causes.

To be able to perform this crucial function for the ordinary citizen, Osundare's poetic stance is modelled on the town-crier. Fortunately this stance is not far from a griot's with which we have also associated him. In the words of Griot Mamadou Kouyate, griots 'are vessels of speech . . . the memory of mankind' (Niane, I). But Osundare's town-crier is in addition the conscienceman. This is perhaps one obvious example of his debt to the late Christopher Okigbo who called himself 'town-crier with my iron bell'. In **'I Wake up This Morning'**, Osundare's persona says:

I have borrowed the earful clamour
of the towncrier
gained the unkillable clarion
of the gong

. . . . .

when I sing ears shall bend my way

(*Village Voices*, I)

Having adopted this posture, the poet-protagonist is then able to call attention to the contradictions in society to which the common man is easily a victim. One of these contradictions is the disadvantage which the ordinary person suffers as a result of his position in the social and economic relations network. Often his means of existence is threatened as the poet observes in **'Eating with All the Fingers'** because whereas members of the privileged class in society can afford to 'eat with all the fingers', the poor are not usually so lucky. The poet-persona, having deployed himself as the spokesman of the people, intones:

we will raise our voices
and tell the world

we will not be watchers
of others eating

(*Village Voices*, p. 15)

This position is restated in **'Unequal Fingers'** in which the speaker says,

Let no-one tell us again
that fingers are not equal
for we know
how the thumb grew fatter
than all the others

(*Village Voices*, p. 60)

Poems such as **'The New Farmer's Bank'**, **'A Farmer on Seeing Cocoa House, Ibadan'**, **'The Eunuch's Child'**, **'A Villager's Protest'**, **'The Politician's Two Mouths'**, **'Akintunde, Come Home'**, **'Chicken Story'** are the voicing of these issues which daily agitate the minds of peasants. **'The New Farmer's Bank'** (*Village Voices*, p. 50) is a satirical thrust at the contradiction in establishing agricultural credit banks all over the country to which the grassroots farmers have little or no access:

Then go till your land
with closed fists
how can you borrow government money
without *Kolatera*

'A Villager's Protest' and **'The Politician's Two Mouths'** are swipes at the politician who would make promises upon promises before election time only to fool the villagers who voted him into office. The truth is that if,

A politician tells you to wait
and you heed his words
ah! friend
your sole will tell you
the biting pains of folly

(*Village Voices*, p. 57)

Rather than fulfil his promises, the politician will seek his own pleasure. Listen to **'A Villager's Protest'**:

Now in
and promises forgotten
fat cars, juicy damsels
and the best there is

(*Village Voices*, p. 48)

'Excursions' (*Marketplace*, pp. 7-15) is a searing indictment of society for structures which ensure that the poor are perpetually held to their miserable places. All over the land, poverty, ignorance, want and disguised slavery are evident:

halfnude, toughbiceped labourers
troop in tipperfuls from sweatfields
drilled by foremen soulless like
a slavemaster, a few kobo greet

the miserly homecoming
of a pilgrimage of misery

(p. 8)

Even in the churches, the oppression of the poor goes on through deceit and cant:

between belches the plump preacher
extols the virtue of want,
the only ticket to the wealth beyond

(p. 9)

And in the markets, greedy businessmen, now overnight millionaires, are making their money simply by being

exporters
importers
emergency contractors
manufacturers' representatives
buying cheap
selling dear

(p. 15)

'Sule Chase' (*Marketplace,* pp. 16-18) equally indicts society for its tendency to react to social symptoms rather than cast a lingering look at their causes. Sule who is chased even by dishonest and unpatriotic members of the various strata of society on account of his pilferage of a piece of bread is no more than a victim of a heartless capitalist orientation. Yet, unlike Sule, his chasers are guilty of even more heinous crimes against society:

The race gathers more legs
In every lane
Tailors with giant scissors
Permsecs with PENDING files
Barristers with fused bulbs
Telephonists in dead head-sets
The doctor with his chair aloft . . .

(p. 16)

Even those who merely hear Sule has stolen join in the chase without actually knowing what he stole until they stone him to death and behold 'they arrest Sule's corpse / His left hand clutching / A rumpled three kobo loaf' (p. 18).

Osundare's town-crier model is further advanced in *The Eye* and *Moonsongs*. To begin with the social issues in each are fused and continuous, story-like in fact. And secondly in each case one voice is heard throughout. In *The Eye*, the poet is still concerned with the plight of the people, but this time his concept of people is global. Here he is no longer addressing the local chieftains running their country like a personal estate, but all those in influential places world-wide whose duty it is to ensure that 'our earth . . . neither wastes nor wants'. The earth is described as the 'breadbasket / and compost bed / rocks and rivers / muds and mountains'. The entire collection calls attention to the dwindling state of forests, rocks and rain resulting from the bizarre approach of the earth's inhabitants to the survival of plant and animal life. The volume is also a surreptitious ideological banter on capitalists and multinationals, scattered in different parts of the world, busy plundering rather than ploughing the earth. In **'Ours to Plough, Not to Plunder'**, the poet beckons the inmates of the earth to 'let gold rush from her deep unseeable mines / hitch up a ladder to the dodging sky / let's put a sun in every night' (p. 48).

The central symbol in *Moonsongs* is the moon; like 'the eye' in *The Eye* the moon is here a watchman, an observer, the one who oversees the earth. The moon is 'the eye of the sky', the 'hourglass', the 'serenade of the storm', the 'lymph of the lore', the 'historian's if' (pp. 24-5). It is the harbinger of new seasons and the signal of the passage of years. It is also a mask through which the poet is able to make sundry statements about the joys and chaos of the seasons, about night and day, sea and sky, the poor and the prosperous. The intention of the poet is civic since all these things affect the ordinary person. The most transparent and graphic of the poems in *Moonsongs* are those addressing the fate of the other person, the underprivileged. An example will suffice. In Segment XXII, the poet contrasts the experience of the moon in Ikoyi with what is observed in Ajegunle, both parts of Nigeria's Lagos now metaphors for affluence and squalor respectively. In Ikoyi, 'the moon . . . is a laundered lawn / its grass the softness of infant fluff' whereas in Ajegunle 'the moon / is a jungle / sad like a forgotten beard / with tensioned climbers (p. 42). By this comparison, the poet is able to strike our ire and win our sympathy for the misery of a large section of the world's populace.

III

Niyi Osundare is not only the most prolific of Nigeria's post-Civil War poets, he is the most consistent in the manner in which he employs folkways to advance public advocacy. Often the pose of his persona is folkloric, rather quixotic and prattling, relying so much on the oral stylistic technique and morphological inventiveness, two crucial elements in folk speech and drama. Since his first collection of poems was published in 1983, the quality of poetic mediation in his *oeuvre* has continued to improve. *The Eye of the Earth,* his fourth volume, epitomizes the success of his poetic career because here content and form are conjoint; here too he shows that accessible language need not lead to doggerel. However, in *Moonsongs* the symmetry of scope of concern and artistic language is awfully absent;[2] the poet who had in his various pronouncements denounced the recondite language of pre-Civil War Nigerian poetry here allows his language to tilt upwards with the result that whereas he employs various dimensions of lore and discusses the fate of the people as in the other collections, his linguistic medium is more complex, more obscure as he piles images, metaphors and symbols which

ordinarily have little associations.[3] Be that as it may, Osundare will remain an unforgettable member of the post-war Nigerian revolutionary poetic vanguard who daily carve anguish out of the simple words our elders taught us.

Notes

1. Alan Dundes considers as folklore all the activities of the folk, written and unwritten. See his 'What is Folklore?' in *The Study of Folklore,* ed. Alan Dundes (New Jersey: Prentice-Hall, 1965): 1-3.

2. Chinyere Nwahunanya has said so too. In a paper he presented at the 1989 Modern Language Association of Nigeria Conference held at the University of Nigeria Nsukka entitled, 'Osundare's New Esotericism: The Genesis of Poetic Disintegration', Nwahunanya warned that if the new trend of obscurity continued in his poetry, 'Osundare would be cultivating the same problems which made the troika (Chinweizu *et al.*) scream at the Okigbos, the Soyinkas and their ilk. Most importantly, instead of leading to poetic growth, it would result in an obscurantism that would mark the beginning of his distintegration as a poet.' (p. 12).

3. During a chat with Niyi Osundare in his office on 29 January 1990 he freely accepted that *Moonsongs* was largely obscure, but attributed it to the pains he suffered from the multiple head injuries he received in 1986 from a robbery attack which took place right on the University of Ibadan campus. According to him, the poems were written on the hospital bed against the advice of his doctor. Luckily, his post *Moonsongs* collections—*Songs of the Season* (Ibadan: Heinemann, 1990) and *Waiting Laughters* (Lagos: Malthouse, 1991)—belong to the mainstream of the Osundare tenor.

Works Cited

Aiyejina, F. 'Recent Nigerian Poetry in English: An Alternative Tradition.' In *Perspectives on Nigerian Literature: 1700 to the Present,* Vol. I. Ed. Yemi Ogunbiyi. Lagos: Guardian Books, 1988.

———. 'To Plough, not to Plunder.' A review of *The Eye of the Earth* in *West Africa* (London) 6 October 1986.

Bascom, W. R. 'Verbal Art.' *Journal of American Folklore* 68 (1955).

Caudwell, C. *Illusion and Reality.* London: Lawrence and Wishart, 1977 (1937).

Chinweizu, Onwuchekwa Jemie and Ihechukwu Madubuike. *Toward the Decolonization of African Literature.* Enugu: Fourth Dimension Publishers, 1980.

Jeyifo, B. 'Niyi Osundare.' In *Perspectives on Nigerian Literature: 1700 to the Present* Vol. 2. Ed. Yemi Ogunbiyi. Lagos: Guardian Books, 1988.

Knickerbocker, K. I. and Reninger, H. W. *Interpreting Literature: Preliminaries to Literary Judgement.* New York: Holt, Rinehart and Winston, 1979 (1955).

Lerner, L. 'This Poem.' In *New Lines II: An Anthology.* Ed. Robert Conquest. London: Macmillan, 1963.

Niane, D. T. *Sundiata: An Epic of Old Mali.* Trans. G. D. Pickett. London: Longman, 1965 (1960).

Nwachukwu-Agbada, J. O. J. 'Matter and Form in Post-War Nigerian Poetry (1970-1985).' MA Dissertation, University of Ibadan, 1986.

Oni, S. 'Osundare, Poet of the Marketplace.' *National Concord,* 24 June 1988.

Osundare, N. 'A Distant Call.' *West Africa* (London) 4 November 1985.

———. *A Nib in the Pond.* Ife: Ife Monograph Series, 1986.

———. *Moonsongs.* Ibadan: Spectrum, 1988.

———. *Songs of the Marketplace.* Ibadan: New Horn Press, 1983.

———. *The Eye of the Earth.* Ibadan: Heinemann, 1986.

———. *Village Voices.* Ibadan: Evans Brothers, 1984.

Scott, W. *Five Approaches to Literary Criticism.* New York: Collier Macmillan Publishers, 1962.

Trotsky, L. D. *Literature and Revolutions.* Ann Arbor: University of Michigan, 1960.

Wellek, R. and Warren, A. *Theory of Literature.* Harmondsworth: Penguin Books, 1973 (1949).

Christine Fioupou (essay date 2001)

SOURCE: Fioupou, Christine. "Poetry as a 'Metaphorical Guillotine' in the Works of Niyi Osundare." In *Telling Stories: Postcolonial Short Fiction in English,* edited by Jacqueline Bardolph, pp. 277-90. Amsterdam: Rodopi, 2001.

[*In the following essay, Fioupou examines the impact and influence of Osundare's politically charged poetry.*]

This essay will not be dealing with short fiction as such but with poetry and short fiction, or, to put it more clearly, with poetry and, as it were, 'short' faction—faction not only in the sense of the literature which fuses fact and fiction but also in the sense of rebellion through alternative literary forms. Niyi Osundare belongs to the second generation of Nigerian poets from the University of Ibadan who call themselves the "alternative" tradition,[1] as they see their verse as an 'alternative' to the more complex poetry of the first generation of writers: also, they use the 'native' tradition of orature and 'alter' it to make it their written and oral contemporary own. In a penetrating and provocative article,

Stephen Arnold used the five-hour interview he had with the writer to reveal "the full autobiographical and mythopoetic significance"[2] of Osundare's poetry and its "rootedness" in Ikere-Ekiti, Yorubaland, where the author was born in 1947. Talking about his early life and the origin of his love of satire, Osundare recalls:

Hence the title of this essay. I shall use Osundare's words—alluding to the functions of songs in his father's oral tradition as "a metaphorical guillotine"—to focus on his own poetry. It would be too ambitious here to consider the theoretical issue of satire, given the author's prolific production—his nine 'collections' of poems range from the socially committed to the more private. So I shall be examining some of the poems that relate to satire, studying how they function both as individual pieces and as part of a wider dynamic structure: if poetry is a kind of guillotine that can hurt and kill metaphorically, then the power of the word and the power of the pen can be a form of "political action [taking] an artistic form" for those who, like Niyi Osundare, are still in the country and take the risk of speaking out.

SONGS OF THE SEASON IN SEASONS OF ANOMY

Songs of the Season is a selection of poems "with a definable style and purpose"[3] which Niyi Osundare has been writing for his weekly column in the *Sunday Tribune* since 1985, an experiment with what he calls verse journalism. Indeed, if some Nigerian writers choose the short story or various forms of short fiction to deal with vital political and social issues, Osundare tends to privilege the verse form.

Roughly speaking, the poems included in **Songs of the Season** are those written between 1985 and 1990, thus spanning two military dictatorships—the end of the Buhari Regime (1984-1985) and five years of the Babangida Administration (1985-1993). The introductory section, called *isihun*—meaning 'voice-opener' in Yoruba—is made up of a single poem called **"A Song for My Land,"** subtitled "For Nigeria at 25" (hence written in 1985), which aptly conveys the topical tone of the collection.

The first section, called *Songs* (7-36), engages in satire against, for instance, pompous professors and grovelling dons, opportunists and pandering poets, reckless drivers and ruthless tax-gatherers, murderous tyrants and kangaroo courts:

> In our country's court there's a Kangaroo
> [. . .] He mangles the Law with his haughty hoof
> And tilts the scales with a lode of lies
>
> He leaps through our past with marsupial magic
> He sees a lion and hails a lamb
>
> **("Song of the Kangaroo," 21)**

The last poem of this set, **"Shout of the People"** (34-36), is subtitled "In memory of Nigeria's fifth coup d'état." It refers to Babangida's coup—which toppled Buhari—and is presented as just another remake of a sterile charade parading as salvation:

> 2We have heard so many dawn crows
> And brave pledges from cocky throats
> But their rooster has never laid an egg
> And our brood waits, bereft
> Of a hatchery of hopes
>
> And shout the PEOPLE
> Behold we starve

The couplet, a rejoinder to the false promises made by post-Independence self-proclaimed khaki kings, is used as a refrain throughout the poem. In the last stanza—"We have been trampled" (36)—the shout of the people turns into a more urgent cry of protest that abruptly closes the first *Songs*:

> And shout the PEOPLE
> Break these chains!
> For we bleed

The second section; called *Dialogue* (37-59); is shorter but more varied in form and mood, as it includes a moving **"Song of Life"** (52-57)—a warm tribute to the late actor Femi Johnson, his love of life, yams and wine—as well as satirical pieces based on debates—or the lack of them. For example, **"'Only Four': A Song for Obtuse Angle"** (51) dramatizes with grim irony the vindication of a university man who proclaims that he is responsible for the killing of "only" four students and not for what the press called a "senseless massacre":

> When I become an emperor
> I will slay the press
> And hang all editors by their itchy pens.
>
> [. . .] The students assailed my comfort
> For just a few hours
> And I called the police to quell the row
> My guests fired their guns
> (After all the mob too fired
> Their volleys of noisy chants)
> And a few students decided to die.
>
> (51)

Variations on the lethal fire of guns pitted against the metaphorical "volleys" of students' "noisy chants" or against the journalists' "itchy pens" are woven into the satirical poems of the third section: *Tributes* (60-100) exposes repressive systems and simultaneously pays homage to the victims of the powers that be. In his **"Letter to Fawehinmi"** (70-72), Osundare addresses Gani Fawehinmi, the civil-rights champion and critic of the military authorities for over thirty years. An indomitable public-spirited man, this lawyer is called the "conscience of the common man." He has been sent to jail more than nineteen times, and was in prison when

Osundare wrote his tribute in 1989 ("Dear Gani, / I wonder where you are now," 70). From what I gather, he was back in jail until recently, for, as the first line of the stanza hammered throughout the poem grimly anticipates,

> These, still, are seasons of terror
> Of blind hunters and forests
> Of savage guns
>
> (71)

Osundare assures "Gani" that he is a model for those who can claim "WE are not a people / without a voice / without a vision / without a spine [. . .] / WE are not scoundrels who swallow their tongues / To save their mouths" (71). The letter then ends on a note of hope for the tireless fighter who was jailed because he had "Proffered a bountiful harvest of OTHER ways":

> . . . Look beyond the walls
> Beyond the shuttered screams of incarcerated con-
>   science
> Beyond the emperors who seal our fate
> In their national stomachs
> Look . . . beyond . . .
> The brittleness of office,
> The transience of POWER
> Look . . . beyond . . .
>
> (72)

The mood of **"For Dele Giwa"** (73-76) is more threnodic, as it is dedicated to the editor of *Newswatch*, killed by a letter bomb in 1986. The circumstances of his death are rendered, dirge-like, through animal tales and proverbial sayings:

> The hyena's laugh is cackle of death
> ah! the hyena's laughter
> is ploy before the pounce:
> whoever takes the lion's spoor
> for the snail's offenceless track
> let him count again
> the absent fangs of a giggling mouth.
> And the hyena laughed its fire laugh
> And Giwa crossed the other bank.
>
> [. . .]   Dele Giwa has crossed the river
>
> (73)

The grief felt by Osundare for the loss of a friend and colleague is described as being shared by the murdered journalist's pen, paper and ink: the very physical personification of the social critic's writing 'weapons' deepens the sense of waste and sterility, pain and frustration, miscarried hopes and aborted dreams:

> the pen prostrate now
> like a labouring bull, its womb swollen with inks
> of unmediated birth;
> the nib lies face up like a tool bereft,

its tongue askew, its point one staring shadow
of flowless metal,
in the closet a teeming forest of virgin paper
awaiting the quickening touch
of the pricking pen.

[. . .]　　　Dele Giwa has crossed the river.

(75)

Apparently, Dele Giwa's critical pen had become too powerful for the Babangida regime and had to be stopped lest it fertilize unwanted ground and yield "baskets of ripening truth . . ." (74).

The satirical pieces of the fourth section, *Parables* (101-27), are deeply rooted in Yoruba oral tradition. Parables, animal fables—which here often come close to short fiction—proverbs and praise-songs are appropriated as part of the author's debunking strategy. For example, following the fairy-tale pattern, **"The King and the Poet"** (124-25) illustrates two bards' different reactions to kingship and tyranny. Osundare sides with the poet who "vanished into a bottomless dungeon" because he refused to comply with the king's "craving [for] the velvety caress / Of plastic truths" (125) and rejects the grovelling praise-singer who helps perpetuate repressive systems:

Our bard saw a funeral in every street
But told stories of fanciful fairs

He sang and sang and sang
The king sinking deeper into orgasmic coma
He saw himself, not only a king now,
But also a god, thunder with a million bolts.

(126)

Yet the poem ends on the awakening of the despotic king to the harsh reality announced by a swordless guard:

His message was brief and very brutal:
　"Your Majesty, there is a raging sea
　Right at the palace gate."

(126)

It is precisely Osundare's sympathy with a "raging sea at the palace gate" that spurs him to go on with his "Sunday strivings," as the title of the last set of the collection—*Sundry strivings* (128-50)—seems to suggest. Indeed, *Songs of the Season* ends on a pun on sundry/Sunday, and the last poem of the movement is significantly called **"Song for All Seasons"**: thus, by recycling daily struggles for his Sunday column, the poet sings not only for the season but for *all* seasons and for all and sundry, relentlessly struggling against **"Seasons of Anomy."**[4]

Songs of the Season could, then, be called "Songs of Resistance" or, to adapt Soyinka's words once again, 'guerrilla poetry.' Soyinka's influence on the younger generation of writers is undeniable—Osundare headed his **"Song of the Tyrant"** (22-29) with a quotation from *Kongi's Harvest*, Soyinka's first satirical play to deal directly with military dictatorship. And when one thinks of "metaphorical guillotines," one cannot help thinking of Soyinka's own 'agit prop' theatre, which he calls "guerrilla theatre" or "shotgun theatre": in 1983, when Shagari—then President of the civilian regime of the Second Republic—came to deliver his election speech at Ifé, Soyinka and his Guerrilla Theatre Unit—composed of actors, singers and musicians—performed their "Etika Revolution," scathing satirical sketches in a mixture of pidgin English and standard English that exposed the corruption and violence of the Shagari Administration. Soyinka defines his 'guerrilla theatre' as a political weapon that allows the theatre company to "aim, shoot and go" for—as Edgar Allan Poe would say about the short story—"a certain unique or single effect," as it were. The songs, collected on an LP under the title *Unlimited Liability Company*,[5] soon became very popular in Nigeria. They spread as the anthem of the opposition and were widely played on the radio when, ironically enough, Buhari first came to power:

I love my country I no go lie
Na inside am I go live and die
I love my country I no go lie
Na im and me go yap till I die.

I can testify that this refrain is sung in Lagos and beyond by people from all walks of life. Apparently, it has been in everybody's head for years, known even by those who cannot read. The chorus is repeated, the tune appropriated, and new songs adapted from it. When reading some of his poems from ***Songs of the Season,*** Niyi Osundare insists on borrowing the tune from Soyinka's "I love my country" in **"The Road to Abuja"** (23-24) or **"And Cometh the Bulldozer"** (17-18), to name but two poems. In the last example,—referring to the Keep-the-Country-Clean campaign in 1984-85 that ruthlessly demolished shops and house—the song is remoulded as:

A roar and rumble in our starving streets
Down came our huts and shambling shacks
The wind now our robe the sky our roof
But this abyss is not a place to die

Surely not a place to die

(18)

which is an ironical variation of Soyinka's "na inside am I go live and die." What is remarkable is the cross-fertilization of these various oral and written literary genres—theatre, journalism, short fiction, popular songs and poetry—that reverberate in Nigeria as means of survival when "Silence buries truth in its abyss of fear" (**"For Dele Giwa,"** 74).

THE POWER OF THE WORD: *WAITING LAUGHTERS*
OR "WAITING FOR THE BASTILLE". . . .

"Farmer-born, peasant-bred,"[6] Osundare extensively uses images of sowing and harvesting in all his collections: as the farm is planted with seeds that will sprout, so words will scatter their grain and fertilize the page or the ear, as the opening poem of *Village Voices* suggests:

> [. . .] My words will not lie like a eunuch wind
> fluttering leaves in a barren forest
>
> [. . .] I shall rise with tomorrow's sun
> and plant more songs in the ears
> of a waking world
>
> then plant them like a yam seedling
> which multiplies the original breed.[7]

Village Voices, published in 1984, is dedicated to the poet's father—"a conversationalist / who savours the flavour of words / a singer / whose throat is honey to the heart" (vii)—who could also, as we know, provoke the fall of a king with a "metaphorical guillotine." Many of Osundare's poems capture the transfiguring power of songs and music, and of words: words can be endowed with quasi-magical qualities, can both soothe and hurt, as when the poet/singer uses the traditional 'poetry of abuse' to deflate his opponent:

> [. . .] Bees hum peacefully in a fallowing farm
> A restless boy punctures their hive
> With a crooked stick
>
> You have poked your crooked finger
> In the hive of my mouth
> A chorus of bees would have stung
> Were this my season song
>
> Yes, I would have told you
> About your swollen testicles
> Which crook your legs like miserable bows,
> And your lips thick like hippo skin;

("**Not in My Season of Songs,**" 9-10)

In his study of satire in Irish literature, Vivian Mercier claims that "'Sticks and stones may break my bones, / But words will never hurt me' is one English proverb that has never had much currency in Ireland."[8] We could say the same about Africa but also about any place— England included—where words are considered as potent weapons. This view is illustrated in the title-poem of *A Nib in the Pond,* collected in 1983:

> We read your lines
> opening up the earth
> like a book of paths [. . .]
>
> You who throw a nib
> in the pond of silence
> the ripples in your inkpot
> convulse barracks and powerbrothels
> overturning plots of plunder

> lying on calculating tables
> like bowls of poison[9]

The incongruity of the title comes from the unexpected association of the nib of the pen, connected with the act of writing, with the more rural pond into which the nib is not only dipped but thrown provocatively to break the "silence." Similarly, in **"The Word,"** where "the word / is a pod / quick with unspoken seeds / exploding in the dry season / of occasion" (12), poetry is not synonymous with neutrality or remoteness from the world. It can be a rhythmical call for action, particularly in the face of unbearable situations:

> Not standing still
> is the beginning of battle
> he will never pluck the fruit
> whose back caresses the earth
>
> The circle which has a beginning
> also has an end
> a little patience is what it needs
> the stammerer will call
> his father's name.[10]

The last stanza rejects despair by exploding the fateful sense of closure associated with the circle and revitalizes the proverbial saying about the stammerer, which reappears as a positive leitmotiv throughout *A Nib in the Pond.* For instance, in the poem **"When We Write the Epitaph of Apartheid"** (1983), dedicated to Nelson Mandela, the cumulative repetition announces an inevitable positive outcome:

> Time it may take
> the stammerer will call
> his father's name
>
> Time it may take
> The sun will rise
> Above the trees

(43)

> [. . .] We will see you
> When our struggle
> blooms into victory
>
> . . . When in lurid colours
> We write the epitaph of apartheid
>
> for
> Time it may take
> the stammerer will call
> his father's name
> Time it may take
> The sun will rise
> Above the trees.

(45)

These lines have a prophetic ring indeed, now that the vicious circle of apartheid has historically come to an end, now that, after much "stammering," its epitaph is written. Hence, Osundare's incantatory words prompt the reader/listener not to give up the struggle, preparing the ground and loosening up the soil for "seeds of change" (51).

Waiting Laughters, published in 1990, also explores the various forms of waiting, capturing them through humour, wit and laughter, going "beyond wails, beyond walls"[11] to counter "monologues / of talkative triggers."[12] **"Waiting Like the Bastille"** is, of course, an illustration of the *literal* guillotine of the French Revolution to which Osundare alluded in his interview:

> Waiting
> like the Bastille, for the screaming stones
> of turbulent streets;
> their bread is stone
> their dessert garnished sand from the kitchen
> of heartless seasons
> And when the humble axe finally heeds its noble task,
> the head descends, lumpen dust in its royal mouth
>
> Behold the wonder
> the crown is only a cap!
>
> (22)

Here, the poet crosses boundaries to look ironically again at "the transience of power"; he relishes antitheses like "humble" and "noble" as well as the polysemy of "lumpen" associated with "royal," thus deflating all power-mongers who, whether kings or generals, should know they are as vulnerably human as any pariah. The poem carries the debunking process further with a Yoruba chant that derides dishonourable rulers; then—with mocking repetitions that echo children's songs or nursery rhymes—it demystifies the king's body and emblems of power:

> The king's brave legs are bone and flesh
> Bone and flesh, bone and flesh
> The castle is a house of mortar and stone
> Mortar and stone, mortar and stone
> A chair is wood which becomes a throne.
>
> (22)

The last two lines of the poem—

> Oh teach us the patience of the Rain
> which eats the rock in toothless silence
>
> (23)

—are in fact repeated throughout the book, and it soon becomes obvious that ***Waiting Laughters***—subtitled "a long song in many voices"—is much more than a mere collection of poems or a sum of fragments. Osundare himself calls most of his works "composed volumes, not collections,"[13] as collections would imply that the poems have been written independently, without a clear thread linking them together. Apparently, the poems are orchestrated in such a way that they can be read as a kind of subversive symphony—to deflate "sin-phoneys"?[14]—punctuated by obsessive refrains that in the end form the lyrical backbone of the piece. The

words, relentlessly repeated throughout, become so many obsessive chants that reverberate or are reappropriated from one composition to another, sticking in the reader's memory. The rhythmical repetition of key lines allow the poems to become chanting performance more than ordinary recitation, all the more so as very specific musical accompaniments are provided as a kind of 'stage directions' at the beginning of each section of ***Waiting Laughters.*** This suggests that Osundare's written poetry is also meant to be the kind of performance poetry that can initiate the public into a new type of communal experience. And even if it can be argued that "phrases never concentrate themselves into the shape of a dagger,"[15] that searing words or "metaphorical guillotines" are impotent in the face of parcel bombs and fire-guns, the debate on whether artists can directly influence the course of history is still open. At least, in Nigeria, they can become instrumental in further strengthening the resilient stuff their public is made of. Meanwhile, writers will go on with the "quickening touch" of their pens, mediating ***Village Voices*** or **"Odes to Anger"**:

> [. . .] Do not take away my anger
> A volcano is gathering in the pit of my stomach
> Let me erupt in fables and fire songs
>
> Dreams are dying, waters wailing
> Medieval monarchs decree our lives from rocky
>   heights
> Justice dangles on common gallows
>
> [. . .] Do not take my anger away
> My stubborn noun, my adjective which,
> Like the scorpion, carries a burning tale

The middle stanza from this poem—published by Osundare in January 1997 in the Nigerian *Post Express*—could allude to "the judicial crime" which the Abacha military government committed against writer Ken Saro-Wiwa and eight other Ogoni activists. When he was in detention, Saro-Wiwa had managed to send a letter to the editor of the London *Guardian* in which he stated that, when after a year in prison, "sixty five days in chains, weeks of starvation, months of mental torture," he was taken to appear before a kangaroo court, he knew that "a sentence of death against which there is no appeal is a certainty." Yet his claim, used as the title of his letter, was that "In Nigeria the pen is still mightier than the sword," for

> The men who ordain and supervise this show of shame, this tragic charade, are frightened by the word, the power of ideas, the power of the pen; by the demand of social justice and the rights of man. Nor do they have a sense of history. They are so scared by the power of the word, that they do not read. And that is their funeral.[16]

Saro-Wiwa also accused the governments which supply "arms and credit to the military dictators of Nigeria" and pilloried all those who "denigrate humanity" worldwide, yet he remained hopeful because he knew there were people committed to fighting them. And this allowed him to write; "Whether I live or die is immaterial." Ken Saro-Wiwa—with his eight companions—was hanged on November 10, 1995. And though the hangman's noose was not metaphorical, his words have survived as writers and journalists keep fighting with "the barrel of a pen" (Ngugi), hammering out their anger to their readers or listeners. Niyi Osundare stated that "[Ken Saro-Wiwa]'s pen was getting too large, his images too disturbing" for the powers that be.[17] Wole Soyinka was also becoming too mighty for the government, and went into exile in November 1994. He was subsequently charged with treason by the Nigerian military; if he had stayed in the country, he stated, he would have faced a fate similar to that of Ken Saro-Wiwa.[18] Already, in 1988, during the Symposium on African Literatures organized in Lagos in honour of his Nobel Prize, Soyinka—in his keynote address, "Power and Creative Strategies," broadcast on Nigerian Television—had called for the end of all dictatorships, "this denigration of the popular will":

> "The divine right of kings" which ended with the decapitation of crowned heads of Europe several centuries ago has—need I state the obvious?—been replaced by the "divine right of the gun" on this continent.[19]
>
> A coup later, with new "pampered emperors on purchased thrones," we have come full circle . . .[20]

To conclude, and to make a long story short or various long poems-cum-symphonies into one short story for "a certain unique or single effect," I shall stammer once more, quoting again from Niyi Osundare's "medley of voices" and "metaphorical guillotines":

> The circle which has a beginning
> also has an end[21]
>
> Time it may take
> The stammerer will call
> his father's name[22]
>
> Waiting
> like the Bastille, for the screaming stones
> of turbulent streets[23]
>
> Waiting
> like the tyrant for his noose[24]
>
> Oh teach us the patience of the rain
> which eats the rock in toothless silence[25]

Notes

1. Biodun Jeyifo, "Introduction" to Niyi Osundare's *Songs of the Marketplace* (Ibadan: New Horn, 1987): vii.

2. Stephen Arnold, "A Peopled Persona: Autobiography, Post-Modernism and the Poetry of Niyi Osundare," in *Autobiographical Genres in Africa,* ed. Janos Riesz & Ulla Schild (Berlin: Dietrich Reimer, 1996): 150.

3. Osundare, "Preface," *Songs of the Season* (Ibadan: Heinemann Frontline, 1990): v.

4. Adapted, of course, from Wole Soyinka's novel *Season of Anomy.*

5. Soyinka, *Unlimited Liability Company,* Featuring Tunji Oyelana and his Benders; music & lyrics by Wole Soyinka (Nigeria: Ewuro, 1983).

6. Osundare, *The Eye of the Earth* (Ibadan: Heinemann Nigeria, 1986): ix.

7. Osundare, "I wake up this morning," in *Village Voices* (Ibadan: Evans Nigeria, 1984): 1-2.

8. Vivian Mercier, *The Irish Comic Tradition* (Oxford: Clarendon, 1962): 107.

9. Osundare, *A Nib in the Pond* (collected in 1983; Ifé Monograph on Literature and Culture, 4th series, no. 6; University of Ifé, 1986): 12.

10. Osundare, "Not Standing Still," *A Nib in the Pond,* 12.

11. Osundare, *Waiting Laughters* (Lagos & Oxford: Malthouse Press, 1990): 25.

12. Osundare, *Midlife* (Ibadan: Heinemann Frontline, 1993): 66.

13. Arnold, "A Peopled Persona," 144.

14. Osundare, *Nib,* 42.

15. Mercier, *The Irish Comic Tradition,* 182.

16. Ken Saro-Wiwa, "In Nigeria the pen is still mightier than the sword," *Guardian Weekly* (May 28, 1995): 2.

17. Osundare, "The Longest Day," *Newswatch* (November 18, 1996): 44-45.

18. *Herald Tribune* (March 15-16, 1997).

19. "Power and Creative Strategies," *Index on Censorship* 17.7 (August 1988): 8.

20. Osundare, *Midlife,* 66.

21. Osundare, *A Nib,* 12.

22. *A Nib,* 43.

23. Osundare, *Waiting Laughters,* 22.

24. *Waiting Laughters,* 14.

25. *Waiting Laughters,* 23.

Works Cited

ARNOLD, Stephen. "A Peopled Persona: Autobiography, Post-Modernism and the Poetry of Niyi Osundare," *Autobiographical Genres in Africa,* ed. Janos Riesz & Ulla Schild (Berlin: Dietrich Reimer, 1996): 142-65.

JEYIFO, Biodun. "Introduction" to Niyi Osundare's *Songs of the Marketplace* (Ibadan: New Horn, 1987): vii-xv.

MERCIER, Vivian. *The Irish Comic Tradition* (Oxford: Clarendon, 1962).

OSUNDARE, Niyi. "Celebrating Soyinka," *ANA Review* (October-December 1996): 26.

————. *The Eye of the Earth* (Ibadan: Heinemann Nigeria, 1986).

————. "For Kunle Ajibade," *Post Express* (January 11, 1997): 15.

————. "The Longest Day," *Newswatch* (November 18, 1996): 44-45.

————. *Midlife* (Ibadan: Heinemann Frontline, 1993).

————. *Moonsongs* (Ibadan: Spectrum, 1988).

————. *A Nib in the Pond* (collected in 1983; Ifé Monograph on Literature and Culture, 4th series, no. 6; University of Ifé, 1986).

————. "Ode to anger," *Post Express* (January 11, 1997): 15.

————. *Seize the Day and Other Poems for the Junior* (Ibadan: Agbo Areo, 1995).

————. *Selected Poems* (London: Heinemann, 1992).

————. *Songs of a Season* (Ibadan: Heinemann Frontline series, 1990).

————. *Songs of the Marketplace* (1983; Ibadan: New Horn, 1987).

————. "Theatre of the Beaded Curtain: Nigerian Drama and the Kabiyesi Syndrome," *Okike* 27-28 (March 1988): 99-113.

————. *Village Voices* (Ibadan: Evans Nigeria, 1984).

————. *Waiting Laughters* (Lagos & Oxford: Malthouse Press, 1990).

SARO-WIWA, Ken. "In Nigeria the pen is still mightier than the sword," *Guardian Weekly* (May 28, 1995): 2.

SOYINKA, Wole. *Unlimited Liability Company,* featuring Tunji Oyelana and his Benders; music & lyrics by Wole Soyinka (Nigeria: Ewuro, 1983). Gramophone record.

Tanure Ojaide (essay date 2003)

SOURCE: Ojaide, Tanure. "Niyi Osundare and His Poetic Choices." In *The People's Poet: Emerging Perspectives on Niyi Osundare,* edited by Abdul-Rasheed Na'Allah, pp. 17-26. Trenton, N.J.: Africa World Press, 2003.

[In the following essay, Ojaide explores Osundare's responses to various influences in his poetry.]

Niyi Osundare has published a body of poems, which deserves serious study, over the past two decades that have acquired a pattern of what he does and does not do. The poet's Yoruba background, his university education, and the Zeitgeist and Volkgist of the late 1960s through the 1970s in particular, combine with other factors to shape the direction of his poetic explorations. It is in light of these factors that I intend to examine his poetic choices and how these choices impact on his work. To the poet, many poetic choices are made available, depending on one's interests and objectives. Some of these aims affect thematic and aesthetic considerations. Like an explorer, the poet's interests determine the choices of what to experience. With Osundare, some choices appear forced upon him by conditions of the time, as others arise from personal options and considerations. Thus he is influenced at certain times to "imitate" and at other times to react against. Admiring or disliking somebody or something elicits various responses, which can be seen as aspects of influence. For example, if admiring the later poetry of Christopher Okigbo makes Osundare musical, and if disliking Wole Soyinka's obscure and difficult poetry in *Idanre* makes him write what he considers to be accessible to the generality of poetry readers, there is a strong influence of both writers. Like every artist in one way or the other, Osundare makes such choices that he feels will meet the demands of fulfilling his poetic role and expectations.

A prime molder of Osundare as a poet is the education he received at the University of Ibadan from 1969 to 1972. It is not that the other universities he attended much later for graduate studies, such as Leeds and York, did not influence him, but his formative years as a poet were spent at Ibadan. Having the personal experience at the University of Ibadan at about the same time as him and knowing Osundare as a fellow student in the same English department, I know that the university curriculum and student activities of the time have had a lasting impact on him. In the English department, we had started to read African literature primarily side by side with British literature. There were courses in African literature, such as modern African poetry taught by Dan Izevbaye, modern African drama taught by Oyin Ogunba, and modern African fiction taught by Theo Vincent. These modern African literature courses were taught along with modernist poets, like T. S. Eliot, Ezra Pound, and W. B. Yeats, courses on Shakespeare, metaphysical poets, and other areas and periods of English literature.

There was a strong interest in modern African poetry that was written by J. P. Clark Bekederemo, Christopher Okigbo, and Wole Soyinka, among others who did not have the advantage we enjoyed of reading African literature. I can recollect in lecture halls, tutorials, and the creative writing club that there were heated discussions about these three Nigerian poets. Most of us seem to have chosen models from among them. Okigbo's untimely death in the war gave a great boost to the popularity of his poetry among young students of English. Soyinka's detention during the war also made him very popular among us. Niyi Osundare, no doubt, was part of this group who was fascinated by the poetic persona cut by Okigbo, the musicality, and word play of his poetry. One can adduce Osundare's interest in poetic musicality, in the forms of chant-like rhythms and the use of figures of sound—especially alliterations, to this Okigboesque disposition of most of us "budding" undergraduate poets at the University of Ibadan in the late 1960s and early 1970s. Okigbo's last poems, "Path of Thunder: Poems prophesying War" and the experiments, such as his elegiac homage to W. B. Yeats, were familiar reading materials among undergraduates of English then. What could be a stronger echo of Okigbo's "The General is up . . . the General is up . . . commandments . . . / the General is up the General is up the General is up—" than Osundare's "The general is up, up, up / The general is up . . ." in *Moonsongs*? (*Okigbo,* 69 and *Selected Poems,* 68).

The use of incantation rhythms, alliterative sounds, and word play has become part of Osundare's poetic signature. The **"Eye of the Earth"** best illustrates this aspect of Osundare's poetic choice. Here is **"Earth"**:

> Temporary basement
> and lasting roof
>
> first clayey coyness
> and last alluvial joy
>
> breadbasket
> and compost bed
>
> rocks and rivers
> muds and mountains
>
> silence of the twilight sea
> echoes of the noonsome tide
>
> milk of mellowing moon
> fire of tropical hearth
>
> spouse of the roving sky
> virgin of a thousand offsprings
>
> Ogeere amokoyeri

(p. 1).

In using incantation rhythms, Osundare balances one line against another as each couplet further reinforces the previous one. He also uses oriki rhythms in *Moonsongs.* While later I will talk of Osundare choosing simplicity over difficulty and obscurity, as in Soyinka's *Idanre,* this use of Yoruba poetic models has been attempted earlier by Wole Soyinka in poems like "Koko Oloro" in *Idanre* and "Muhammad Ali at the Ringside, 1985" in *Mandela's Earth.* Here, both poets share experiences of poetic forms of their native culture.

Closely related to the poetic infatuation with Okigbo's musicality and play on words is a certain resistance to obscurity and difficulty of African poetry as in Soyinka's *Idanre* phase. Many young Nigerian poets of the early 1970s might agree with some of the points made by

Chinweizu in *Towards the Decolonization of African Literature* about the euromodernist excesses of modern African poetry even though criticisms were made. In the English department of the University of Ibadan, during the period of Osundare's undergraduate program, lecturers and students had wondered what Soyinka meant in many of the poems—especially the title poem. Most of us left the classroom to the creative writing club and carried with us, from one place to the other, arguments as to what poetry should be. As much as we respected Wole Soyinka to the point of reverence, many of us did not want to write poetry in his manner. As I said earlier, the model was usually Okigbo and sometimes J. P. Clark-Bekederemo. A "budding" dramatist like Shadrack Agbagbarha might have had a better inclination to Soyinka's drama, but plays like *A Dance of the Forests* and *The Road* might not have endeared to some of us because of their perceived difficulty.

The obvious reaction to the euro-modernist aspects of modern African poetry, as in Soyinka's worst cases in *Idanre,* no doubt geared Osundare and many other undergraduate poets to write more comprehensible poetry, as in J. P. Clark Bekederemo's "A Reed in the Tide." One way Osundare has shown this aspect in his writing is the conscious choice of simplicity in collections, such as *Village Voices, Songs of the Marketplace,* and *The Eye of the Earth.* To Osundare, "[T]he simple word / is the shortest distance / between two minds" (*Selected Poems,* 3). In fact, his **"Poetry Is"** can be seen as a poetic manifesto of the younger generation of Nigerian poets of the early 1970s and as an indirect jibe at Soyinka's type of poetry. Among my coevals at Ibadan, including Osundare, the deep respect that extends to reverence for Soyinka did not endear many of us too much with his *Idanre* phase of poetry. Osundare's poetic choice at the beginning of his poetic career was for poetry that communicates directly. To him,

> "Poetry is
> not the esoteric whisper
> of an excluding tongue
> not a claptrap
> for a wondering audience
> not a learned quiz
> entombed in Grecoroman lore
>
> Poetry is
> a lifespring
> which gathers timbre
> the more throats it plucks
> harbinger of action
> the more minds it stirs
>
> Poetry is
> the hawker's ditty
> the eloquence of the gong
> the lyric of the marketplace
> the luminous ray
> on the grass's morning dew

Poetry is
what the soft wind
musics to the dancing leaf
what the sole tells the dusty path
what the bee hums to the alluring nectar
what rainfall croons to the lowering eaves

Poetry is
no oracle's kernel
for a sole philosopher's stone

Poetry
is
man
meaning
to
man

(Songs of the Marketplace, 4).

World politics of the Cold War era, diverse implications for Africa, non alignment, and Marxism also helped to shape Osundare's poetic direction. Osundare's days at Ibadan involved radicalized student union politics. There were frequent demonstrations against policies of European or North American governments that ran contrary to African interests. Students were bussed to Lagos to demonstrate when Portuguese mercenaries invaded Guinea Bissau. Most students seem to have aligned on the part of revolution, no matter how well they understood its implications. This infatuation with revolution was manifested in student union politics in 1970 when Osinowo ran for the secretarial position, which he won by distributing posters emblazoned with "Osinowo, Revolution." I believe most of us voted for him because he stood for revolution. The death of Kunle Adepoju in a student demonstration in 1971 was perhaps the apogee of this student radicalism against their administrators and anti-African interests.

Osundare imbibed many Marxist ideas, and in fact, he declared himself a Marxist in the 1970s and early 1980s. Although he declared himself a Marxist, Osundare was not an ideologue for all its implications like Biodun Jeyifo, Tunde Fatoba, and Festus Iyayi. In any case, his proletarian ideas form part of the bedrock of *Village Voices, Songs of the Marketplace,* and *Moonsongs.* Most of the poems in these collections are people/masses-oriented. **"I Sing of Change"** is illustrative of a classless society:

I sing
of the beauty of Athens
without its slaves

Of a world free
of kings and queens
and other remnants
of an arbitrary past

Of earth
with no
sharp north
or deep south

without blind curtains
or iron walls
. . . . .

I sing of a world reshaped

(Songs of the Marketplace, 90).

Unlike the earlier generation, with poets like Clark-Bekederemo, Okigbo, and Soyinka, the major conflict now had nothing to do with African and Western influences but with class. This class conflict stared Osundare in the eye in two areas of Lagos:

Ikoyi
The moon here
is a laundered lawn
its grass the softness of infant fluff;
silence grazes like a joyous lamb,
doors romp on lazy hinges
the ceiling is a sky
weighted down by chandeliers
Ajegunle
here the moon
is a jungle
sad like a forgotten beard
with tensioned climbers
and undergrowths of cancerous fury
cobras of anger spit in every brook
and nights are one long prowl
of swindled leopards

(p. 73).

The contradictions of society, as expressed in Marxism, became more glaring after the energy crisis of the early 1970s and after the political corruption worsened the economic plight of the common people.

Osundare adopts a communal voice, rather than an individual voice, in many of his poems in *Village Voices* and *Songs of the Marketplace.* Osundare's poetry does not appear to be personal. It is rare for him to write about a personal experience or for him to be confessional. There are no poems about his relationships—no love poems, for instance. He distances himself from the personal, but he, nonetheless, still expresses himself. One would expect personal poems in *Midlife,* but there are none. It is not that every poet must write about his or her relationships, but I have not seen an Osundare love poem. Love poetry could oftentimes show much of the sensibility, passion, and humanity of a poet. Poets like Pablo Neruda and Odysseus Elytis in recent times have been involved and distanced in their poems. The choice should not be so much between being involved and being distanced, as in a relationship, but should involve being completely human. Thus, is the paradox that while he attempts to be a literary pop artist by using the communal voice and simple language, Osundare disengages from the personal, which coalesces into pop art, and shows much of one's humanity.

Consequent upon his Marxist infatuation and a materialist approach to life, Osundare rejects the primacy of myths and the kabiyesi syndrome of Yoruba dramatists like Soyinka and Femi Osofisan. He is very selective of his use of Yoruba folklore. Unlike Soyinka, associated with Ogun and Osofisan with Eshu, Osundare has so far avoided being tagged with any party of the Yoruba pantheon. So how Yoruba a poet is he as we can say of Yoruba being the essence of Wole Soyinka and to a large extent of Osofisan? These two are more dramatists than poets, but still there is overwhelming presence of Yoruba divinity in their works. Osundare avoids the company of gods in his poetry.

But I am not saying Osundare is not a Yoruba writer. His choices are informed by ideological and political considerations, as he wants to be seen as ranging on the side of the people—as down-to-earth. Here and there are elements of Yoruba folklore, but not the myths that form the backcloth of Soyinka's and Osofisan's writings. In *The Eye of the Earth,* for instance, Osundare talks of "the one that shaves his head with the hoe." In *Moonsongs,* he no doubt employs the image of the moon of his youth as revealed in Yoruba mythology: "The moon pounds her yam / in the apron of the night" (*Moonsongs,* 1988: 29). There appears to be a growing use of materials from Yoruba folklore but not from the pantheon. *Waiting Laughters*'s strength comes from the use of Yoruba axioms, proverbs, and myths:

> I have not told a bulbous tale
> in the presence of asopa
>
> I have not shouted "Nine!"
> In the backyard of the one with a missing finger
>
> (p. 70).

"Asopa" is one with swollen scrotum.

And yet Osundare models some of his poems on oriki rhythms as **"Earth,"** in *The Eye of the Earth,* quoted in full earlier and other poems in *Moonsongs.* His musicality is a blending of alliterative sounds and Yoruba rhythmic patterns—ijala and oriki.

Osundare's choice of certain figures of speech and sound is also very significant on the nature of his poetic style. The copious use of metaphors, personifications, epithets, and alliterations give a certain robust sing-song identity to his poetry. In *Moonsongs,* "The moon this night is an infinity of smiles" (p. 43). Furthermore, he addresses the moon:

> Oh moon, matron, master, eternal maiden
> The bounce of your bosm
> The miracle of your cheeks
> Your smile which ripens the forests
> Your frown which wrinkles the dusk
> The youth of your age
> The age of your youth . . .
>
> (*Selected Poems,* 55).

Metaphors and personifications make poetry not only exude sensuous delight but also concreteness. Here,

Osundare sidetracks the weaker similes for stronger metaphors and personifications that give vitality to the poet's style.

Osundare has many poetic choices regarding style. In **"Forest Echoes,"**

> Palm-bound, scalpel-toothed,
> the squirrel pierces the tasty iris
> of stubborn nuts;
> adzeman of the forest,
> those who marvel the canine fire
> in your mouth,
> let them seek refuge in the fluffy grace
> of your restless tail
>
> (*Eye of the Earth,* 8).

In many other poems, epithets appear in alliterative clusters, such as "A bevy of birds" and "A barrack of beasts." Here, Osundare appears to have been influenced by the popular trio of J. P. Clark-Bekederemo, Christopher Okigbo, and Wole Soyinka, whose poetry relished metaphors, epithets, assonances, alliterations, and hyphenated words.

One of the controversial aspects of the "new African poetry" is the accusation that it pays too much attention to content at the expense of form. The critic, Ken Goodwin, has written about this particular aspect. With too many African writers, the didactic side seems to have been more emphasized at the expense of the craft. While it favors meaning, the African oral tradition does not neglect craft. This modern African literature of engagement was carried to its limits in the 1970s and 1980s during the Marxist phase. At the same time, there was a writer, like the francophone Labou Tansi who reacted in the opposite direction. For Tansi, according to Jonathan Ngarte, "[T]he emphasis now had to be put not on writing only in order to say something but rather on writing as a mode of invention, as a way of writing oneself into being with words that are so many pieces of one's own flesh; for him there can be no other aesthetic or thematic approach in a world in which mankind seems determined to kill life" (p. 132). Thus, there appears to be a binary attitude, as if African literature has to emphasize either themes or aesthetics.

It is here that Osundare stands out as bridging this unnecessary gap between "saying something" and "writing as a mode of invention." He says a lot in his work in a very artistic way. What could be more thematically engaging than **"The Eyes of the Earth?"** And yet the poem is aesthetically fulfilling. Osundare's choice, therefore, is to synthesize aspects of themes and form.

So far in his poetic career, Niyi Osundare has made many poetic choices that have given a certain character and identity to his poetry. There is no doubt that his being a Yoruba, the socio-political atmosphere of his years of adulthood, and his training in the English department at the University of Ibadan influenced him to take models and reject some artistic directions. His simple, people-oriented poetry, his musicality, his rejection of Yoruba pantheon for a Marxist materialist stance, his conscious attention to craft, and his lack of very personal, confessional poetry are results of his poetic choices. These choices have not just assigned him an identity, but these choices have also given poetic strength to his poetic opus.

References

Clark-Bekederemo, John Pepper. *A Reed in the Tide.* London: Longman, 1965.

———. *Casualties.* London: Longman, 1970.

Ngate, Jonathan. *Francophone African Fiction: Reading a Literary Tradition.* Trenton, NJ: Africa World Press, 1988.

Okigbo, Christopher. *Labyrinths.* London: Heinemann, 1971.

Ojaide, Tanure. *Poetic Imagination in Black Africa: Essays on African Poetry.* Durham, NC: Carolina Academic Press, 1996.

Osofisan, Femi. *The Oriki of a Grasshopper and Other Plays.* Washington, DC: Howard UP, 1995.

Osundare, Niyi. *Songs of the Marketplace.* Ibadan: New Horn, 1983.

———. *Village Voices.* Ibadan: Evans, 1984.

———. *The Eye of the Earth.* Ibadan: Heinemann, 1986.

———. *Moonsongs.* Ibadan: Spectrum, 1988.

———. *Waiting Laughters.* Lagos: Malthouse, 1990.

———. *Selected Poems.* Oxford: Heinemann, 1992.

———. *Midlife.* Ibadan: Heinemann, 1993.

Soyinka, Wole. *Idanre and other Poems.* London: Methuen, 1967.

Additional coverage of Osundare's life and career is available in the following sources published by Gale: *African Writers*; *Black Writers,* **Ed. 3**; *Contemporary Authors,* **Vol. 176**; *Contemporary Poets,* **Ed. 7**; *Dictionary of Literary Biography,* **Vol. 157**; **and** *Literature Resource Center.*

Suzan-Lori Parks
1964-

AP Images

American playwright, screenwriter, and novelist.

INTRODUCTION

Winner of the 2002 Pulitzer Prize for drama for her play *Topdog/Underdog* (2001), Parks is one of the most highly acclaimed African American woman playwrights in contemporary theater. Her use of "rep & rev" (repetition and revision) to reexamine and reconfigure Eurocentric historical episodes is lauded for providing an afrocentric history and identity to historical events—elements that are largely missing from the Eurocentric historical record. Innovative and at times controversial, Parks uses language reminiscent of African American dialects and vernacular to give multiple meanings to the spoken word and expose the hidden message behind the dialogue of her characters. Often depicting and exaggerating black stereotypes, Parks draws attention to their invalidity and the ignorance upon which they are based. Parks's plays are noted for their originality, nonlinear progression of time, poetic dialogue, political and social agendas, and depiction of the search for identity.

BIOGRAPHICAL INFORMATION

Parks was born in Fort Knox, Kentucky, in 1964 to Francis McMillan and Donald Parks. Because of her father's career as a U.S. Army officer, the family relocated frequently during her childhood, including to the former West Germany, where her parents enrolled her in the local German school system rather than the school set up for the children of American military personnel. This immersion in the German language gave Parks a valuable perspective on her native language that was to inform the dialogue she would later write for her plays. Returning to the United States, she enrolled at Mount Holyoke College, Massachusetts, initially to pursue a degree in chemistry; she later switched her major to English and German literature. While at Holyoke she enrolled in a fiction writing course at nearby Hampshire College taught by esteemed American writer James Baldwin. Baldwin, after hearing Parks read her work aloud (she often acted out the parts herself), encouraged her to pursue writing plays as a profession. Parks remembers that instance as a turning point in her life. She subsequently delved into the work of Adrienne Kennedy and Ntozake Shange, two dramatists whose works were free from conventional theater restraints and addressed contemporary social issues. Her first play, *The Sinner's Place* (1984), helped her receive honors for her English degree but was rejected for staging by Mount Holyoke because it was too innovative for the drama department. After graduating in 1985, Parks enrolled in the Yale University School of Drama, hoping to learn the craft of playwriting by training as an actor. After one year she departed for New York, where she produced *Betting on the Dust Commander* in 1987 and *Imperceptible Mutabilities in the Third Kingdom* in 1989, which won the Obie award for the best Off-Broadway play of 1989. Parks's subsequent awards have included several grants and fellowships, a PEN-Laura Pels Award for Excellence in Playwriting in 2000, and a second Obie award, for the play *Venus* (1996). Parks has taught at many colleges and universities, including Yale University, the University of Michigan, New York University, and Northeastern Illinois University, and in 2000 was named director of the California Institute of the Arts performance program. She continues to write plays and screenplays and has ventured into fiction, publishing her first novel, *Getting Mother's Body,* in 2003. In 2006 she released *365 Days / 365 Plays,* the culmination of an ambitious undertaking in which Parks wrote a play a day for one entire year. In 2001 Parks married noted blues musician Paul Oscher.

MAJOR WORKS

Since her first play, *The Sinner's Place,* Parks has demonstrated a passion for searching for knowledge, history, and identity. In her first play to be produced in New York City, *Betting on the Dust Commander,* she examined family relations, upheaval, and movement. This work has been attributed to Parks's constant relocation during childhood. She gained critical and popular attention with her next production, *Imperceptible Mutabilities in the Third Kingdom,* a tetralogy of four short plays—*Snails, The Third Kingdom, Open House,* and *Greeks.* In *Snails* a white naturalist disguises himself as an exterminator so he can "bug" the home where three African American women live, thereby gaining insight into the actions of these women in a nonwhite-influenced surrounding. Through this "study" the women lose identity and respect and become objects to manipulate and examine. *The Third Kingdom* reenacts the Middle Passage across the Atlantic Ocean. In lieu of the dearth of known history from these subjugated people, Parks provides memories and cultural references that create a new, solid history for African Americans to follow. In *Open House* Blanca, a former slave, is dying and her memories are being stolen from her—symbolized by continuous tooth extractions—linking her loss with African Americans' loss of culture, identity, and voice. In *Greeks* Parks further elaborates on the assertion that African Americans have an unsure link with the past and therefore have a difficult time understanding their present. Parks continued the search for an African American past in her next play, *The Death of the Last Black Man in the Whole Entire World* (1990). In this play, the main character, Black Man with Watermelon, is continually beaten, enslaved, and killed, yet always returns to the stage to tell his story. Parks highlighted the importance of "telling the story" as a way to fight the negation of African Americans, whose literary silencing during the years of the slave trade has rendered their story almost forgotten. For *The America Play,* which premiered in New York City in 1994, Parks created a protagonist who grows to adulthood obsessed with the life and death of U.S. president Abraham Lincoln, who was assassinated while viewing a theater performance by actor John Wilkes Booth in 1865. This protagonist, dubbed the "Foundling Father," finds work as a carnival sideshow attraction in which he sits in an ersatz theater chair wearing "whiteface" paint—a reversal of the early twentieth-century minstrel shows in which white comedians wore "blackface" paint in order to imitate and denigrate African Americans. For a small sum, arcade visitors can take a shot at the Foundling Father with a cap gun.

Parks recreated the sideshow atmosphere in *Venus* (1996), a fictionalized account of the curious case of Saartjie Baartman, a South African Khoi-San woman brought to England in 1810 as a sideshow attraction and dubbed the "Venus Hottentot" due to her exaggerated female form. In *Venus* Parks rewrote this history, casting Baartman not as a docile pawn but as an accomplice in her fame and destiny. A willing participant, Venus uses her African "otherness" to obtain wealth and love. Parks explored Nathaniel Hawthorne's *The Scarlet Letter* in her next two plays, *In the Blood* (1999) and *F———A* (2000). In the comi-tragic *In the Blood,* Hester, a homeless single mother, lives under an overpass with her five multi-ethnic, illegitimate children. The play stresses that identity and culture are becoming increasingly difficult to discover and claim, a condition that leads to disillusionment and diaspora. For *F———A*'s Hester, the "A" stands for Abortionist. This play, like the former, ends in tragedy as Hester's son, who was a sweet youth, transforms into a violent and brutal man. Parks's next work, *Topdog/Underdog,* won the Pulitzer Prize, making Parks the first African American woman to receive the award. In the play, which Parks wrote in a matter of days, two brothers, named Lincoln and Booth, struggle to succeed in life. Lincoln, a sad figure who was once a skilled purveyor of three-card monte—until his partner was shot—now works in an arcade shooting booth costumed as Abraham Lincoln, paralleling Parks's Foundling Father in *The America Play.* Booth, a skilled shoplifter, ridicules his brother's job and tries to convince him to return to the far more lucrative monte game. The two share a rundown tenement room, where they drink and quarrel to the point of violence. In 2003 Parks released her first novel, *Getting Mother's Body,* about a black family from Texas during the 1960s. In the novel, sixteen-year-old Billy Beede, pregnant and abandoned by her coffin-maker lover, attempts to dig up her mother's corpse in order to retrieve the diamond ring and pearl necklace with which she was supposedly buried. Among the novel's colorful characters are Billy's churchless minister uncle; his one-legged wife; and Dill, a lesbian who was once Billy's mother's lover. In late 2006, Parks's *365 Days / 365 Plays* premiered; about seven hundred theaters across the United States each committed to producing one week's worth of the plays, so that by the end of a year's time, all 365 plays would have been performed somewhere in the country. Among the playlets are brief monologues and dialogues; short plays treating broad subjects like war as well as minute trivial details of a single day; pieces involving the deaths of notable figures like Barry White or Johnny Cash; and scripts that simply list stage directions.

CRITICAL RECEPTION

Critical response to Parks's plays has been largely favorable. Although some commentators charge that she reinforces racial misconceptions with her use of stereotypical language and gestures, most reviewers contend that her over-the-top depiction of stereotypes is meant to lampoon these misconceptions and make a farce out of the underlying prejudices that drive stereotyping. She is applauded for her attempts to fill in the gaps of African American memory and history, and for her refusal to rely on the Eurocentric history that has been dominant for centuries. Her innovative use of plot and language—especially black English—has prompted debate, with some observers calling her dramatic works powerful and her dialogue poetic, and others criticizing the storylines as fragmented and her language as dense and unintelligible. Several scholars emphasize the musicality of her writings, commenting on her use of a rhythmic repetition of words or phrases, a technique outlined by Henry Louis Gates, Jr. in his seminal work *The Signifying Monkey*. This method, called "rep & rev," has its origin in the improvisational nature of jazz, in which a line or phrase is revised in some way each time it is repeated. Commentators have also associated this "improvisational" quality with Parks's "openness" with regard to the arrangement and organization of the performance of her scripts. In what Jennifer Johung called her "specifically unspecific writerly marks," Parks often leaves directing, acting, and staging directions vague and ambiguous. Still other critics have focused on Parks's controversial decision in *Venus* to portray Baartman as a willing accomplice to her own exploitation. While some reviewers found the award-winning play monotonous in its repetition of well-worn themes of sexual and race exploitation, others have praised it as a significant achievement that is both comical and horrifying in its depiction of the pain of racial and sexual humiliation.

PRINCIPAL WORKS

The Sinner's Place (play) 1984

Betting on the Dust Commander (play) 1987

Fishes (play) 1987

*Imperceptible Mutabilities in the Third Kingdom (play) 1989

Anemone Me (screenplay) 1990

The Death of the Last Black Man in the Whole Entire World (play) 1990

Greeks (play) 1990

Pickling (radio play) 1990

The Third Kingdom (radio play) 1990

Devotees in the Garden of Love (play) 1991

Locomotive (radio play) 1991

The America Play (play) 1994

The America Play and Other Works (plays) 1995

Girl 6 (screenplay) 1996

Venus (play) 1996

In the Blood (play) 1999

F———A (play) 2000

Red Letter Plays (plays) 2001

Topdog/Underdog (play) 2001

Getting Mother's Body (novel) 2003

Their Eyes Were Watching God [with Misan Gagay and Bobby Smith; adapted from the novel by Zora Neale Hurston] (screenplay) 2005

365 Days / 365 Plays (plays) 2006

*This work is a tetralogy of short plays: *Snails, The Third Kingdom, Open House,* and *Greeks.*

CRITICISM

James Frieze (essay date winter 1998)

SOURCE: Frieze, James. "*Imperceptible Mutabilities in the Third Kingdom*: Suzan-Lori Parks and the Shared Struggle to Perceive." *Modern Drama* 41, no. 4 (winter 1998): 523-32.

[*In this essay, Frieze examines Parks's use of the technique "Rep & Rev" in* Imperceptible Mutabilities in the Third Kingdom.]

[MR. SERGEANT SMITH]:

> Thus events of my destiny ssgonna fall intuh place. What events? That I dont know. But they gonna fall intuh place all right.[1]

The thinking of Mr. Sergeant Smith, would-be hero of the fourth and final section of Suzan-Lori Parks's *Imperceptible Mutabilities in the Third Kingdom,* is wishful in the extreme. He has, after all, been waiting what seems like an eternity for the Commander to honour him with that vague, but distinctly noble thing: a Distinction. Waiting for the Distinction is also the chief preoccupation of Mrs. Smith and of their children, Buffy and Muffy. The family's waiting is far from passive. In anticipation of Mr. Smith's homecoming, they clean the house, and especially father's desk. They discuss the clothes that the girls should wear for the big welcome, settling for "perm press [. . .] polka-dotted [. . .] swisses" (59). They pore over the letters that Mr. Smith sends them, searching for clues as to when the Distinction will be awarded. Though the official purpose of examining the letters is to ascertain how much favour father has managed to curry with the Army, their analysis is also driven by an unofficial purpose: to determine how much daddy is thinking of each member of his family.

To interpret correspondence with a precision appropriate to military matters, the three female Smiths have constructed a ledger, with multiple columns, which they fill in as follows. MRS. SMITH: [. . .] "Subject": uh letter. Check thuh "non bill" column. [. . .] BUFFY: "Contents"? [. . .] MRS. SMITH: Write—uh—"general news." [. . .] Slash—"report of duties" (62, intervening dialogue omitted). Then the final columns: "'Mention of Work': check: 'yes.'" When it comes to the category titled "Mention of Family," an argument ensues, since Buffy was mentioned but Muffy was not. Sandwiched in the middle of these formalities is the column titled

"Signs of Distinction." Mrs. Smith asks, "What'd we put last time." "Last letter's Signs of Distinction were 'on the horizon,'" informs Buffy. "Before that?" asks the mother. "Soon," says Buffy. "Before that," she adds, with exemplary efficiency, "he reported his Distinction to be arriving quote any day now unquote" (62-64).

To comfort her sister Muffy, who is upset at not being mentioned, Buffy tells her of a family called the Censors. "Mr. Censor," says Buffy, "is a man who won't let Sergeant Smith say certain things because certain things said may put the Effort in danger." She explains that Mr. Smith "deals in a language of codes—secret signs and signals" (64). It is no coincidence that Buffy, the most adept of the female Smiths at coordinating the ledger, is also the most deeply immersed in the lore of military intelligence. So zealously does the ledger map the place-into-which-events-can-fall that, akin to the army's "language of codes," the "signs and signals" of the ledger take on a life of their own. The interpretive codes have become more substantial than the events to which they refer.

Whether their absurd behaviour causes them to be isolated, or whether isolation makes them odd, the Smiths appear to be without friends or neighbours. Being isolated makes them very much at home, however, in the Obie Award-winning (that is, Distinguished) world mapped by Suzan-Lori Parks in her first major play. Like the Smiths, the three other groups of characters introduced during the course of the play have somehow become unhinged, not only from each other, but from origins, society, and destiny. Reacting against this unchaining of being, Parks's writing incubates a kind of collective consciousness. The characters strive to rearticulate their immediate environment with its historical and cosmic underpinnings. This striving leads them to construct surreal frames of reference in which dreams and metaphysical insights are continuous with mundane domestic details and with the methodological practices of science, organized religion, and the Army. Within these frames of reference, the characters moor themselves, semi-wittingly, to floating signifiers—objects and motifs which are psychologically rich and socially familiar: a desk; a rock; a cockroach; a boat; a gun. Parks encases these symbolic objects in multinuanced locational phrases such as "fall intuh place," "Open House," and "Third Kingdom."

In deploying these objects and tropes, Parks draws on the African-American tradition of "repetition [and] difference" that Henry Louis Gates, Jr., charts in *The Signifying Monkey*.[2] "Rep & Rev," as Parks calls it,[3] found its apotheosis in jazz composition, a central principle of which is the establishment of a particular phrase or harmonic line which is then repeated with a signal difference. Parks's theatrical application of the technique conjures up the experience of meanings changing, often barely perceptibly, over time.

Echoing Parks's "Rep & Rev," I will come back to the Smiths (at the end of this essay) via a discussion of the three other sets of characters that constitute Parks's play. While blow-by-blow chronological analysis can be a tedious and inadequate form of scrutiny, I use chronological order here because *Imperceptible Mutabilities* so provocatively links the production of chronology to the framing of identity. In the mini-essays that preface the collection of her plays, Parks comments that "Standard Time Line and Standard Plot Line are in cahoots!" She sees time as "circular,"[4] but satirizes any attempts to map time (including her own) by furnishing her essay with pseudo-scientific diagrams. "Standard Plot Line" deploys the phenomenon of foreshadowing to install linearity as the dominant temporal pattern. Foreshadowing channels nuances in a single direction. In contrast, Parks encourages multidirectional reading, the free play of intertextual nuances. "Through each line of text," she explains, "I'm rewriting the Time Line—creating history where it is and always was but has not yet been divined."[5] She writes a narrative which uncovers the effects of previous narratives.

The first section of the play features three roommates. They are named Mona, Chona, and Verona—or rather, they used to be. In the first scene of the play, Chona, now named Charlene, states that "[o]nce there was uh robber who would come over and rob us regular." A few lines later, Mona, now Molly, says: "[o]nce there was uh me named Mona who wanted to jump ship but didnt" (26). The third scene of the play begins as follows:

MOLLY:

> Once there was uh me named Mona who wondered what she'd be like if no one was watchin. You got the Help Wanteds?

CHARLENE:

> Wrapped thuh coffee grinds in um.

(27)

Like the "coffee grinds," Mona's identity is a series of residues packaged as an urban convenience. Physically and ontologically, the used coffee conjures up images of Black identity being ground down and wrapped in discourse. From her first appearance—at the very start of the play—Mona herself is, in a sense, buried beneath language. She recites a language lesson:

MOLLY [MONA]:

> [. . .] "S-K" is /sk/ as in "ask." The little-lamb-follows-closely-behind-at-Marys-heels-as-Mary-boards-the-train. Shit. Failed every test he shoves in my face. He makes me recite my mind goes blank.

(25)

After beginning, here, by showing the effects of narrative, Parks goes on to uncover those effects, to peel away accreted discursive layers in search of the sense of "me-ness" that Mona feels has been stolen from her.

The Mona/Chona scenes are interspersed with monologues by a character named The Naturalist, who discusses his strategies for researching his subjects with the aid of a "fly"—a device used by anthropologists to study subjects in their natural environment (27). The Naturalist gains entry to the Mona/Chona household in the guise of Lutzky, an "exterminator professional with uh Ph.D" (28), on whom Mona and Chona rely to treat the enormous cockroaches (a parodic rendering of the anthropologist's fly) that reside in their living-room. Pretending to wipe out their infestation problem, Lutzky infests them in the name of research.

Lutzky's claims to cleanse the living-room recall the similarly euphemistic question that The Naturalist, Lutzky's double, poses in his first appearance in the play: "How. Should. We. Best. Accommodate. Our subjects" (29). What betrays The Naturalist's purpose in this fascinating speech act is his ghettoization of each word in the sentence. Bearing in mind that the human-sized roaches in the living-room are placed there by Lutzky, his real question, exactly opposite to how it is framed, is: "how can I infiltrate my subjects?" Lutzky, like The Naturalist, does not destroy, but contains by pronouncing that he *can* destroy. Mona and Chona are impressed, not by what Lutzky does (the roaches only grow bigger), but by what his weapons can do. The remote promise of violence serves Lutzky/The Naturalist as an ingenious alternative to actual violence. It is the cover under which the Naturalist changes the things he objectifies, a process encapsulated in his symbolic changing of names—Mona to Molly, Chona to Charlene, and Verona to Veronica.

Under his (generally remote) management, the characters' living-room has become a kind of purgatory. While idealized purgatories are places of reckoning and recognition, The Naturalist wants to maintain this particular purgatory as a place of misreckoning and misrecognition. When The Naturalist visits the living-room, he struggles to maintain control as a nexus of narratives begin eerily to overlap, irrupting into the surface of Parks's text and into the consciousness of the residents, threatening to blow The Naturalist's cover. Chona/Charlene acts the dutiful hostess, accommodating everyone's needs. While assisting Lutzky in treating the roaches, she finds time to cook up a peach cobbler. Meanwhile, Verona/Veronica watches a rerun of her favourite television program, *Wild Kingdom*, narrated by her hero, Marlin Perkins. Though supposedly a rerun, the episode plays out bizarrely, Perkins wielding a gun on "thuh wild beasts" (35) while Lutzky hoses down his clients. Between two fanciful narratives of invasion, colonization, and destruction—Lutzky purportedly looking for roaches, and Perkins surveying an African jungle—Parks inserts a third narrative which is all too familiar. This third narrative springs from Verona's distress at the unexpected violence unleashed by Perkins. Verona calls the police to complain, but the po-

lice refuse to come, causing Verona to wonder if they have paid their taxes. A farcical, overblown scene mutates into one that is flatly domestic.

Downstage right,[6] Mona/Molly lies down, not quite sleeping, not quite daydreaming, in a kind of "daymare." This image of Mona frames the scene. Lying down on the ground of memory, Mona contextualizes the scene's fragments of narrative as repressed memories irrupting into consciousness. As Parks systematically dismembers reality, Mona re-members it.

One of the key uses to which Parks puts "Rep & Rev" is the establishment of a multi-temporal logic in which past and present, archaic and urbane, are wrapped together—as personified by the folding of Mona into Molly, Chona into Charlene, and Lutzky into The Naturalist. The play is not precolonial or postcolonial. It is set, in so far as it *is* "set," in the overlap between before and after, between what is determined and what is reversible. Parks provocatively ties the materialities of urban and suburban life to the archaic and the metaphysical. While the Mona/Chona/Verona scenes grow out of and recede back into domesticity, the Seers—the portentously named characters of the "Third Kingdom" scenes—inhabit a poetic limbo between the archaic and the urbane.

The second set of characters featured in the play, the Seers—Kin-Seer, Us-Seer, Over-Seer, Shark-Seer, and Soul-Seer—appear to be on a sea voyage, though only two of them, Over-Seer and Us-Seer, are convinced that the journey is indeed an aquatic one. Over-Seer's name and authoritative bearing resonate with the slave masters of the Middle Passage. Us-Seer seems to embody the home body, standing in both for those who are left behind when slaves depart and those, within the diaspora, who are themselves left behind by practices that divide to conquer. The other three—Kin-Seer, Shark-Seer, and Soul-Seer—ride an ambiguous sea of symbolism that frequently mires them in confusion. Kin-Seer, for example, announces: "Last night I dreamed of where I comed from. But where I comed from diduhnt look like nowhere like I been" (37). Questioning him, the others establish that Kin-Seer saw "2 cliffs where thuh world had cleaved intuh 2." Kin-Seer describes "wavin" at someone on a far-off cliff, someone he refers to as "my uther me." Later in the scene, Soul-Seer, whose gaze seems to be fixed straight down, sees a sight that makes him recoil. He cries out: "ssblak ssblakallblak!" Over-Seer explains to him: "Thats your *self* youre looking at! Wonder #1 of my glass-bottomed boat" (37-38).

The Seers find it hard to recognize themselves and their environment. It falls to Over-Seer to fill in the gaps in their knowledge. Over-Seer informs them that when "[h]alf the world [fell] away," a wet place was "inscribe[d]" between the two worlds called "the Third Kingdom." This topographical narrative is complicated, however, by Over-Seer's qualification that "[t]he 2nd part comes apart in 2 parts" (37-39). Breaking down parts of a binary into other parts is Parks's way of clearing a space for the examination of identity dynamics. In an essay titled "An Equation for Black People Onstage," she insists that it is not necessary to have White people on stage to portray Blackness as relational. Opposing the notion that "the Klan . . . have to be outside the door for Black people to have lives worthy of dramatic literature," Parks argues that Blackness is already in-between because relationship to the other is an integral part of the self.[7] She asserts that "[w]ithin the subject is its other."[8] To show how Black people carry the relationship to Whites within them, and to think beyond that relationship, Parks dramatizes Black people relating to each other and to themselves, trying on Blacknesses which are defining but also mutable.

In experiential terms, the Seers embody the confusion of living in limbo. In textual terms, they are a bridge—albeit rickety—between domesticity and archaism. They image a form of seeing which is unwittingly poetic, and display a visionary capacity which is startlingly vivid but horrifyingly incomplete. In the 1989 production of the play, directed by Liz Diamond, the Seers were presented as voices on tape.[9] The stage was dark, except for black-and-white slides projected onto a black screen. Historically aspecific, the slides featured fragments of bodies, hands, and feet in thick mud. The Seers are themselves icons out of focus, mangled archetypes, elliptical points of reference.

Parks challenges the supremacy of the actual as an index of truth by privileging iteration over explanation. At the beginning of the play, Mona, contemplating suicide, asks: "What should I do Chona should I jump should I jump or what?" Rather than answer Mona, Chona asks her if she wants some eggs. Though the two women continue to talk at cross-purposes, an oblique relationship emerges between "scrambled" eggs and Mona being "splat" on the ground (25). In Part Two of the play, Mona's question is echoed by Kin-Seer, who asks: "Should I jump? Shouldijumporwhut?" (40). Riffing on particular lines and phrases allows Parks not only to connect characters but to evoke the historicity of metaphor, the way in which metaphors stored in the cultural image bank are borrowed and resisted at different points in time—sometimes deliberately, sometimes less so. Each iteration surveys the distance that has been travelled since the last iteration in terms of both time and consciousness. Parks mines the gap between what has happened and what has not happened, what is lost in memory and what is over-familiar.

The central character of the central section, and symbolically a(nother) kind of middle passage, is Aretha Saxon. Aretha is enslaved to a family of Saxons—Charles Saxon and his children, Anglor and Blanca Saxon. When Aretha learns that her time as a guardian has come to an end because her "lease" has "expired," she insists on taking photographs of the family with big, "toothy" smiles (41). This task of preservation proves tricky because her subjects are confused and unwilling. Aretha is undeterred by the defectiveness of the images; it is the idea of archiving that drives her: "Dont matter none at all. You say its uh cry I say it uh smile. These photographics is for my scrapbook. Scraps uh graphy for my book." Aretha appears to have swallowed whole the rhetoric that validated slavery. Pathetically echoing Hollywood happy endings, she murmurs: "Mm gonna remember you grinnin" (54). Culture, she seems to believe, can overcome nature.

Parks chisels at the culture in which Aretha is entombed. A character named Miss Faith functions, like The Naturalist in the first section of the play, as a personification of what needs to be stripped away. Just as The Naturalist makes science his posture, a disguise in which he believes, religion gives Miss Faith an excuse for her actions. She spends her time in Christian prayer but is far from meek, and infinitely more pragmatic than she is spiritual.

Under Miss Faith's supervision—literally under it, as Miss Faith sits on a high platform overlooking her[10]—Aretha measures space to assess how many slaves they will be able to accommodate. As Aretha works, Miss Faith instills in her respect for documents, especially records and statutes (42-44). "The power of the book," Miss Faith explains, "lies in its contents. It contents are facts." Alluding to the fact that Aretha's term as a slave is about to "expire," Miss Faith "*extract[s] Aretha's teeth with a large pair of pliers.*" This diligent dentistry proceeds despite Aretha's screams.[11] Taking words out of Aretha's mouth, Miss Faith informs her patient: "if we didnt pluck them we couldnt photograph them" (46-47).

Miss Faith personifies the archivism critiqued by Michel Foucault in *The Archaeology of Knowledge.* Foucault states,

> [t]he archive is not that which, despite its immediate escape, safeguards the event of the statement, and preserves, for future memories, its status as an escapee; it is that which, at the very root of the statement-event, and in that which embodies it, defines at the outset *the system of its enunciability.*[12]

What Foucault suggests is that the contours of the "statement" are not fixed at the moment of its inception. Over time, they develop, and can mutate. This mutability betrays, for Parks as for Foucault, the duplicitous nature of archival history and theology. The public face of the archive is that which smothers the fugitive quality of the utterance by recording it. The private face is that which attaches itself, unseen, at the very moment that the statement is born. By so doing, the archive provides an invisible framework within which the statement can be read. This framework—what Foucault calls a "system of enunciability"—inscribes a logic which confines future analysis to a narrow realm of possible interpretations. Establishing the "system of enunciability" of the "statement-event" is job one for Miss Faith and for The Naturalist. Aretha's scrapbook, like the ledger kept by the Smiths, reflects Parks's belief that indoctrination is an instilling, not merely of knowledge, but of ways of knowing. For Parks, the ability to control one's own identity depends not only on redefining particular events, but on reconceiving the very systems that hold events in place.

Slowly, barely perceptibly, Parks's characters shed their ingrained ways of knowing: they begin to unlearn. Analysis of their own failure causes the characters to question ways of seeing, including their own. This retrospective questioning comes to a head in veiled epiphanies—critical visions which, for character and spectator alike, are revelatory but muffled. These fragmented visions do not burst in from outside the machine of the narrative; they are precipitated by its breakdown.

Transgressing the narrow realm of interpretations permitted by Miss Faith becomes, for both Aretha and the audience, a matter of reading signs which articulate the mundane and actual with the heightened and fantastic. In a scene prefaced (in the printed text) with the word "*Dreamtime,*" Aretha goes to meet her maker, who turns out to be her earthly master, Charles Saxon. He asks for her papers, which state that her name is also "Charles Saxon." She informs Charles that her husband is dead (44-45). A subsequent scene casts Miss Faith as a real estate agent, showing Anglor and Blanca a potential home. Aretha is cast—or, to the extent that this is her dream, casts herself—as an awkward curiosity who hovers around the house like a bad memory.

In these scenes of multiple and mis-taken identity, Parks directs attention away from the question of who is really who, inscribing (con)fusion—not only about heritage, but about the distinction between factual and metaphorical truth—as generative. Boxed in, indoctrinated, relieved of her teeth, Aretha exercises power through re-inflection. Her fragmented visions are the imposition of her idiolect upon the systems, personified by Miss Faith, that work to station her. It is an imposition which productively reveals inconsistencies in, and thereby begins to unravel, those systems. Aretha may have swallowed the rhetoric that validated slavery, but in digesting she rearranges, so that Miss Faith's book becomes more "scraps uh graphy for [her own] book."

In Parks's hands, repetition-compulsion metastasizes from a psychic into a semantic and then into a social disturbance. Merging the fantastic and the actual, Parks leads both Aretha and the spectator away from the deciphering advocated by Miss Faith, and by The Naturalist, and towards multidirectional reading. In so doing, she makes available a virtual identification between character and spectator based on the shared struggle to perceive.

Gazing upward, imagining that he has caught a man from falling out of the sky, Mr. Smith trips over a mine. He is awarded a Distinction only after, and because, he loses his legs. Later, when his children interrogate him, he asks each of them: "You one uh mines?" (70). Embedded within this pithy interrogative are several of the questions that Parks prompts her characters, and her audience, to ask. What belongs to and defines me? How does my identity trip me up? How should it conceal itself? That Mr. Smith voices these questions in four densely signifying words reflects the fact that recognition of the self depends, for Parks, on the formation and application of a personal idiom. The Distinction—both before and in the moment that it is awarded—imposes itself on Sergeant Smith. He begins, in a minor but triumphant act of signifying, to turn things around. Having been dis-membered in losing his legs, he begins to re-member himself by imposing his way of knowing. It is a kind—a horribly ironic and far from magical kind—of reversal.

For Mr. Sergeant Smith, time is initially a vista of possibility. Linear temporality furnishes him with a sense of destiny encapsulated in the epithets "on the horizon," "soon," "any day now" (63). By the end of the play, however, the character of time itself appears, from Mr. Smith's perspective, to have deteriorated:

> Time for somethin noble was yesterday. There usta be uh overlap of four hours. Hours in four when I'd say "today" and today it'd be. Them four hours usta happen together, now, they scatters theirselves all throughout thuh day. Usta be uh flap tuh slip through. Flaps gone shut.

(71)

Smith's comment on the dispersal, and increasing inhospitability, of what he experiences as "today" invokes with new clarity what the play (until this point) has cumulatively alluded to. What is insinuated by Parks's satirical portraiture of self-misrecognition, and is now stated by Mr. Smith, is the power that lies in the spatio-temporal codes on which identity relies. Time and space underlie the governance of identity, and of mechanisms, such as race, which frame identity. The very systems that purport to hold identity in place can be used to perpetrate those subtle forms of social exclusion predicated on self-exclusion and self-misrecognition.

As he reads back on his life, Mr. Smith allows the audience to read back on the characters that precede him within the history of the play. Though characters such as Mona, Chona, and the Seers are less able than Mr. Smith to articulate their experience, the characters testify through inter-articulation. Inter-articulation by the characters—of what happens in their dreams and on television with what happens in their waking interactions—evolves in parallel with Parks's radical narrative. The narrative is a perceptual template which works against the templates that station her characters.

The play ends with Mr. Smith answering questions about evolution from his son, Duffy. Duffy is confused by his father's reference to the family as turtles, an allusion to the long wait for the Distinction. Mr. Smith explains: "No, boy—Duffy—uh—Muffy, Buffy, no, we ain't even turtles. Huh. We'se slugs. Slugs" (71). Conceiving progress is about looking forward, but also about reading back. The evolutionary scale on which Mr. Smith reads back from turtles to slugs itself refers to a passage iterated twice during the "Third Kingdom" scenes (39, 55). In this passage, Shark-Seer dreams that a fish swallows him. He becomes the fish. The fish becomes a shark. The shark goes ashore and is given shoes. Parks guards against simple metaphorical correspondences by making ontology impossibly double, self-concealing. The dream evinces, not particular identity positions, but the dynamics of relational identity. In the paradigm of Shark-Seer's fish story, identity is made visible only after it has been swallowed.[13] Endowed with shoes—new possessions with which to traverse a new culture—the swallowed splits into "uh third Self made by thuh space in between" (39). Since nature and ideology both abhor a vacuum, the "space in between" is bound to be filled, to become an interstice in which a new identity is built. What Shark-Seer faces is a challenge similar to that which Parks sets before her audience: the challenge of building meaning in the crevices within temporal and spatial logic; the crevices, that is, between reading in one direction (conceived of as forward) and reading in an opposite direction (conceived of as back). The play challenges its audience to read multidirectionally.

Meeting that challenge depends on retrieving people (Buffy/Muffy; Mona/Chona; the Seers) from the systems (reflected in the names) that seem to swallow them. Parks prompts the audience to salvage substance from the forms that rise above it. Driven both by deconstructive and thetical impulses, she deploys "Rep & Rev" to put systems in their place, paving ground that can begin to accommodate subjects.

Notes

1. Suzan-Lori Parks, *Imperceptible Mutabilities in the Third Kingdom,* in *The America Play and Other Works* (New York, 1995), 58. Subsequent references appear parenthetically in the text.
2. Henry Louis Gates, Jr., *The Signifying Monkey: A Theory of Afro-American Literary Criticism* (New York, 1989), xxii-xxiv.
3. Suzan-Lori Parks, excerpt from "Elements of Style," in *The America Play and Other Works,* 9-10.

4. Ibid., 10-11.
5. Suzan-Lori Parks, "Possession," in *The America Play and Other Works,* 5.
6. *Imperceptible Mutabilities in the Third Kingdom,* by Suzan-Lori Parks, The Brooklyn Academy of Contemporary Arts Downtown, Brooklyn, NY, 26 September 1989, production detail.
7. Suzan-Lori Parks, "An Equation for Black People Onstage," in *The America Play and Other Works,* 19.
8. Ibid., paraphrasing Toni Morrison, "Black Matters." See Morrison, *Playing in the Dark: Whiteness and the Literary Imagination* (Cambridge, MA, 1992), 1-28.
9. *Imperceptible Mutabilities,* production detail. See note 6.
10. Ibid.
11. Ibid.
12. Michel Foucault, *The Archaeology of Knowledge,* trans. A. M. Sheridan Smith (New York, 1972), 129.
13. In the 1989 BACA production, the slides accompanying Shark-Seer's dream were of bejewelled and well-dressed women, lending a concreteness to the social commentary.

Jennifer Johung (essay date March 2006)

SOURCE: Johung, Jennifer. "Figuring the 'Spells' / Spelling the Figures: Suzan-Lori Parks's 'Scene of Love (?).'" *Theatre Journal* 58, no. 1 (March 2006): 39-52.

[*In the essay below, Johung analyzes the "spells" that make up the "Scene of Love (?)" in* Venus, *commenting that the "infamous [scene] necessitates an adjustment in the way that readers and producers of Parks's work think about the intersections between the activities of writing and performing, as well as the interactions between the interpretation of the written marks on the page and the embodiment of the corporeal markings of performers onstage."*]

a spell

An elongated and heightened (rest). Denoted by repetition of figures' names with no dialogue. Has a sort of architectural look.

This is a place where the figures experience their pure true simple state. While no "action" or "stage business" is necessary, directors should fill this moment as they best see fit.

The feeling: look at a daguerreotype; or: the planets are aligning and as they move we hear the music of their spheres. A spell is a place of great (unspoken) emotion. It's also a place for an emotional transition.[1]

Scene 19: A Scene of Love (?)

The Venus

The Baron Docteur

The Venus

The Baron Docteur

The Venus

The Baron Docteur

The Venus

The Baron Docteur

The Venus[2]

Suzan-Lori Parks's one-page "Scene of Love (?)" from her 1996 play, **Venus,** dares readers, performers, and directors of printed drama to ask the question—what are we to do here? A name is printed on the page of a playscript: we expect it to be followed by a line of dialogue or a stage direction, but we only have the name until the next line where another name is printed, and so on. At first glance, Parks's short scene of "spells" refuses to impart guidelines on the passage of performance time or the determination of performance space and performing bodies. But what if different guidelines apply? And what if these elusive guidelines exist outside of the accepted conventions of dramatic writing and theatrical practice? Suppose we consider this formal shift from determinacy to indeterminacy as functioning to expand, rather than confound, the frameworks through which readers and practitioners make specific interpretative decisions. Then, we can also begin considering the processes by which the material specificity of performers within a performing space can be activated, paradoxically, by refusing the particularity of one formal framework for either readerly or directorial interpretation, in order to specify the alternate material condition of specifically raced bodies.

The ostensible illegibility of this kind of formal experimentation from an African American writer has been met with criticism; as Harry Elam and Alice Rayner point out, "[Parks's] craft has been vilified by some African Americans for being incomprehensible."[3] Indeed, *New York Times* writer Monte Williams has disclosed that "some blacks have complained that Ms. Parks's work is too abstract to accurately capture the black experience."[4] Although Parks has declared that "there is no single 'Black Experience,' there is no single 'Black Aesthetic' and there is no way to write or think or feel or dream or interpret or be interpreted"[5] so as to resist the critical blind-siding of her simultaneously experimental form and material specificity,[6] certain aspects of her formal experimentation—however individualized in a singular character, narrative stand, or rhythmic structure—do seem to operate specifically alongside an African American cultural experience. In contrast to the indeterminate status and function of Parks's spells, the

language she accords her characters is highly specific, so much so, in fact, that she disregards stage directions altogether, embedding every action and emotion in the very physical digestion and delivery of the words themselves. As she says in an interview:

> The difference between "k" and "o.k." is not just what one might call black English versus standard English, for example. Or black English versus mid-Atlantic English . . . If you jump to that word faster, if you put your words together in a different order, you're feeling something differently, and it's just an attempt to try to be more specific so that I don't have to write in all these parenthetical things.[7]

Though Parks is quick to indicate that such writerly specificity is not solely an attention to the nuances in black vernacular speech, her attention to formal structure and the shift in dramatic interpretation that it entails are thus deeply intertwined. The implication here is that African American history and identity can be revised—or, more precisely, rewritten—through formal interventions.

However, while material specificity and formal experimentation may converge in Parks's dialogic constructions, the exceptionally unspecific spells and the illegibility of their function within a dramatic structure at large remain an interpretative conundrum. Thus far, **Venus** is Parks's only work to include an entire scene of spells. The scene is suspended in the middle of a play that re-members the historical figure of the South African "Hottentot Venus," Saartjie Baartman, who, because of her large buttocks and prominent genitalia, was put on show in nineteenth-century England; after her death, her body was dissected, studied, and exhibited in Paris.[8] Venus is Parks's Baartman, and the Baron Docteur is the scientist who liberates her from the freak show, becomes her lover, and instigates the precisely measured investigations of her various body parts. Their love is elusively depicted on Parks's page through the unhinging of a direct link between specifically dramatic formal constructions and the specific material conditions of scenic action, in order to open up a potential space outside of dramatic conventions that may gesture more precisely to the processes of cultural and historical revision so urgent in Parks's work as a whole. The scene of spells is not merely unspecific, but usefully so. The negotiation between formal imprecision and the alternatively precise and revisionary material conditions of the raced body of Venus in love with the presumably white, European body of the Baron Docteur may be mapped onto the continual passage between unspecific textual notation and variously specific performance interpretations. Under these terms, Parks's infamous "Scene of Love (?)" necessitates an adjustment in the way that readers and producers of Parks's work think about the intersections between the activities of writing and performing, as well as the interactions between the interpretation of the written marks on the page and the embodiment of the corporeal markings of performers onstage.

Neither dialogue nor stage direction, Parks's new writerly activity literally marks an intervention into the process of interpreting textual marks, and their figurative relationship to embodied spatial and temporal determinations in performance. Following upon the advances in textual editing as motivated by the combinations of verbal and visual codes within Modernist and avant-garde poetry, painting, music, and performance, the interpretation of both the function and the operation of Parks's new marks must also be tied to such an expanded concept of textual notation.[9] Beginning in the 1980s and led primarily by Jerome McGann, a revision of textual criticism and editing prompted the re-evaluation and subsequent revaluation of the material conditions of text.[10] McGann argued that an examination of the bibliographical codes of elements such as typography, layout design, or weight of page, for example, alongside the linguistic codes of the words themselves, was required in order to acknowledge the entwinement of verbal and visual forms of expression. Building upon McGann and writing extensively on the visuality of poetic texts, Johanna Drucker has argued that the visual logic and schema of typography, structure, and formatting act as analogues to the production of vocal sound and/or silence, their materiality participating graphically in the production of meaning.[11]

If we can consider the markings of a poetic text as matter that signifies textually as well as visually, then how can we consider those very same material codes with respect to a performance text? In his current work on print and performance, W. B. Worthen contends: "the material properties of a dramatic text—typography, layout, page and cover design—matter to the ways specific groups of readers (actors, directors, audiences, reviewers) understand its potentialities for performance, insert them into the conventional behaviours—the 'performative regimes,' so to speak—of theatre practice."[12] Calling attention to the disjuncture between the "slow reading" invoked by modern poetry to foreground the material surface of texts and the "speed reading" inferred by modern dramatic texts, Worthen offers examples within performance scripts of textual material that cannot be so easily or speedily translated into performance—moments and matter that force us to rethink the way we read and thus perform, direct, and interpret drama.[13] Harold Pinter's pauses, Patrick Marber's emphases, Sarah Kane's punctuation, David Grieg's layout, and Suzan-Lori Parks's spells all support Worthen's claim that, in considering the print-form of drama, we may begin to identify an interplay between the page and the stage that informs the way we make decisions about performance. Isolating Parks's spells, on the page and onstage, as seemingly outside of any kind of theatrical practice, Worthen writes:

> This materialization strikes me as something more like the challenge first offered to readers of *Waiting for Godot*, or perhaps to readers of "The Love Song of J. Alfred Prufrock," a material text that appears less to direct our performance than to claim a space outside contemporary conventions of reading, theatrical or otherwise.[14]

I agree that Parks's spells take us outside of not only the domains of the typically verbal performance script, but also of the theatre's determination of onstage presence and action, space and time. But I also want to suggest that these typographical challenges that operate within visual as well as verbal domains can direct an alternative means of embodying the page, albeit in an indirect manner whereby the elusiveness functions to question the very conventions that move page onto stage. At the very least, we can no longer read the spells as only linguistic determinants of speech, silence, or space, but must, in conjunction, acquire a visual articulation that expands interpretative potential by widening the conceptual frameworks that drive practical decision-making. Elizabeth Dyrud Lyman proposes that Parks is developing a new system of dramatic writing that "stands precisely at the intersection of editing and performance: the (re)distribution of dramatic information in the text, from purely verbal language to a fusion of verbal and visual languages."[15] Tracing the decisions of print interpreters (editors and publishers) as they have affected and been affected by Parks's stage interpreters (directors and performers), Lyman argues that print must finally embrace the visual logic of dramatic texts as a serious participant in the production of meaning on the page as well as in the production onstage. Along with Worthen, Lyman significantly advances the field of inquiry into the activities of writing and performing toward a much-needed convergence of the materials and methods of print notation and performance. Such an expanded notion of writing, reading, and interpreting performance print-marks could indeed benefit from a pursuit of the visual dimensions implicated in this very different relationship between the mark and its determination of body, space, movement, and time.

Nonetheless, we still do not know what exactly to do with Parks's "Scene of Love (?)." And though we may recognize that Parks's marks operate visually as well as verbally, we still do not know how to articulate and interpret them on both levels simultaneously, or why the way we interpret them is significant to the kinds of interventions that Parks is making both within and outside of the theatre. Of course, the inexactitude of this suspension outside of dramatic conventions might precisely be the point. Directors are urged by Parks to fill these moments "as they best see fit." Yet, establishing a set of formal terms and concepts capable of operating simultaneously within and across verbal and visual frameworks would enable producers of Parks's scene of spells to negotiate the transition from the verbal-visual page to the space, time, and bodies of the stage. This usefully imprecise negotiation would afford interpreters an expanded vocabulary for articulating their performance decisions.

I. To Index the Figure

In defining a set of terms conceptualizing the movement back and forth between verbal and visual determinants, operating across both page and stage, I find Rosalind Krauss's notion of the index-as-imprint especially valuable. Writing about 1970s art installations and photographic experimentations in her two "Notes on the Index," Krauss undoes the stability of the index as a marker of physical presence and linear temporality. Conventionally, an index is a graphical measurement of presence that typically serves as a guiding principle that directs the observer's perception of natural phenomena.[16] Krauss, however, reverses the terms of this convention, proposing the concept of a "presence fixed indexically," or the installation of presence by means of the index.[17] Dennis Oppenheim's large-scale 1975 installation, *Identity Stretch,* elaborates upon her argument. Oppenheim transferred the image of his own thumbprint onto a large field outside of Buffalo, New York, by magnifying it one thousand times and fixing its traces in the ground through lines of asphalt. Through the distortion of Oppenheim's thumb and the translation of its print into grooves and mounds of asphalt that the viewer walked among, the installation could be seen and experienced as an index. Instead of the index acting as a marker of presence where the original thumbprint is a direct marker of the actual surface, Krauss suggests that the index is itself capable of instantiating presence by bringing an alternative version of Oppenheim's thumb into being. In Krauss's revised concept, the conventional indexical operation of "encoding reality" becomes one of "imprinting it."[18] As an imprint, the index is both a displaced marking and a marker of displacement, whose referents are unfixed and constantly changing. Krauss explains that "[t]hough they are produced by a physical cause, the trace, the impression, the clue, are vestiges of that cause which is itself no longer present in the given sign."[19] Therefore, the presence proposed by the index-as-imprint is paradoxically not present. Instead, the index is an operation of presence—an operation that works to imprint presence in its absence.

How, then, does considering Parks's spells as indices on the page help us to understand the function of her indeterminate stage marks? In her own definition of a spell, Parks points readers to the early photographic technique of daguerreotype. Popular in America from the 1840s through the 1860s, the technology was initially intertwined with the long-established art of portraiture, producing the first exact images of people.[20] This very exactitude, however, is precisely what photography destabilizes by and through the operation of the index. Roland Barthes, from whom Krauss draws, defines the photographic image as a "message without a code." Through the activities of framing, reduction, flattening, and distorting, the photograph no longer remains in direct relation to the object, person, or scene that once existed before the lens of the camera. In his essay "Rhetoric of the Image," Barthes associates this "loss of equivalence" with "a statement of quasi-identity."[21] The photographic image then becomes an indexical imprint of the subject's absent presence, simultaneously presupposing and reinstating identity.

As a mark of simultaneous pre- and postpresence, the photographic image as index, through Krauss's reinterpretation, operates in parallel to Parks's own process of simultaneously notating the page and the stage, and perhaps more importantly to her development of an indexical concept of quasi-identity. In order to mark subjecthood indexically, Parks writes the names of what she calls stage "figures"—designated as such because they are absent in normative historical narratives but made present through the very act of Parks's imprinting.[22] Her indexical imprinting of these figures is deeply engaged with the reconstruction of African and African American identity through a history of diaspora. As defined by cultural theorist Paul Gilroy,

> [d]iaspora identifies a relational network, characteristically produced by forced dispersal and reluctant scattering. It is not just a word of movement, though purposive desperate movement is integral to it. Push factors, like war, famine, enslavement, ethnic cleansing, conquest and political repression are a dominant influence.[23]

Through this physical and psychic displacement, the linearity of the past is ruptured, as people, places, and cultural systems are lost, forgotten, and reinvented outside the borders of any one nation. Parks herself claims that she writes her figures from a "fabricated absence" that she imagines as "the story that you're told goes, 'once upon a time you weren't here.'"[24] This narrative opening that Parks parodies must be reconstructed out of the absence of a unified past, instead charting a story that must somehow begin from nothing. Founded without a beginning, the fabricated absence that Parks invokes becomes produced as well as productive, continually reconstituting itself into a presence.

If this notion of presence reimagined in the face of absence can only be a figure of presence in the light of these revisions of diasporic identity as displacement, what does it mean that Parks's spells determine, in her words, "a place where the figures experience their pure true simple state"?[25] Taking Parks's statement in conjunction with Krauss's model of the index, I propose that the relationship of the figure to her status as subject is indexical. As a figure in Parks's play, Venus is an indexical imprint of the historically real nineteenth-century Saartjie Baartman. Venus's subjecthood is a figuration that is formally displaced through the imprint of her name on the page—an imprint that, as in Krauss's reworking, instantiates her presence as a figurative presence that must then approach subjecthood by way of a relational construct between subject, figure, and name. Indeed, passing towards and away from subjectivity through the marking of more than one name, more than one time, Parks's figures can only experience their pure true simple state in repetitive alternation with another figure's name, as in the "Scene of Love (?)" between the Venus and the Baron Docteur.

In Irma Mayorga and Shannon Steen's November 1998 production of *Venus* at Stanford University, the relational construction of subjectivity that occurs in the spells was heightened by the performers' concentrated exchange of looks. In the "Scene of Love (?)" as in many of the other scenes in which she is put on show or otherwise watched, Venus was placed on an elevated and rotating platform. A birdcage-like enclosure came down from the ceiling, imprisoning her, while the Baron Docteur circled around, moving closer and then stepping further away. At all times, as each circled past the other, eye contact was maintained.[26] As Parks herself admits, "there's a lot of watching in *Venus*."[27] About an African woman who was put on show for crowds of white spectators both in her life and after her death, the play is, in Elam and Rayner's words, "a show about show business and theatricality."[28] In their essay charting the play's negotiation between narrative and spectacle, Elam and Rayner also turn their attention to the exchange of looks between performers that in turn makes evident the exchange of looks between spectators and performers. For Elam and Rayner, Parks recuperates the look as a pose: in doing so, she opens up a site of resistance in the face of the re-inscription of an oppressive and degrading spectatorial gaze. Extending Craig Owens's summary of Homi Bhabha's and Dick Hebdige's concepts of "posing," Elam and Rayner write:

> The pose is an act that paradoxically accepts and refracts the gaze of the spectator. . . . It arrests the line of sight and transfixes the one who is looking. . . . This return of the spectator's gaze, in other words, both refuses the desire of that gaze and mirrors back the absence of the object of the spectator's gaze, as if to say that "it is not me (other) you are looking at; whatever you see is your own absence." And in this sense, the pose is, paradoxically, the "representation of the representation."[29]

In this deflection of the look by the one-looked-at, the presence of the looker is instantiated through and by the presence of the other that comes back to the looker as an absence. The simultaneous instantiation of the displaced presence of the looker and the figurative presence of the one-looked-at—a process I call an indexical presencing—is dependent on the relational nature of Parks's "pure true simple state."

A spell's pure, true, and simple state can also be achieved by turning this repetitive alternation inwards, which Parks notates as the repetition of only one fig-

ure's name. For example, in a sequence that takes place before the Chorus of the Spectators approaches, looks at, and attempts to touch Venus, Parks inserts a spell for Venus alone. Thus preempting the look of the spectators, Venus poses and looks at herself, her own figurative presence always already established. In Elam and Rayner's terms, she represents her own representation, to be further indexed by the looks of the spectators.

THE VENUS

THE VENUS

THE VENUS

THE VENUS

THE CHORUS OF THE SPECTATORS

Lookie-Lookie-Lookie-Lookie

Hubba-Hubba-Hubba-Hubba

Lookie-Lookie-Lookie-Lookie

Hubba-Hubba-Hubba-Hubba[30]

In both this moment and in the "Scene of Love (?)," the spells' imprint of subjecthood is relational; it is an imprint that must exist because of and through either the boundaries of other figures or other figurations of the same figure. We can then qualify Parks's statement, since this pure true simple state is only possible in a complex moment of inter-relationships between Parks's re-membering of the nineteenth-century figure, the figure of the printed name on the page, and the figurative subjecthood embodied on the stage. Functioning as an index of historical presence as well as of subjecthood, and operating through the imprint of a name, Parks's spells mark out a concept of figurative subjectivity.

II. TO WRITE THE PERFORMING BODY

In considering this revision of presence through, by, and in the face of absence, we must also recognize that Parks's imprint is primarily a product and process of writing. I activate writing here in the Barthesian sense of "writing and not the written."[31] As neither speech nor transcription, writing negotiates the return of the body as neither "too present" nor "too absent."[32] Turning to Jacques Derrida's further examination of the longstanding binary between speech and writing that he, too, dismantles through the work of writing, I want to remain committed to Barthes's concept of the body returning as both present and absent—indexically, as it were—through the operation of writing. In order to examine why the writerly form of the spells is significant to Parks's reimagining of figurative presence, Derrida's notion of the "supplement," in supporting Krauss's focus on the visual image, extends the terminology applicable to the operation of indexicality that I have been tracing in the relationship between Parks's textual marks and their embodied status, and between the figurative presence of names and bodies.

For Derrida, writing is "the greatest sacrifice aiming at the greatest symbolic reappropriation of presence."[33] Writing is necessary to remake the absence of speech into presence; it must be added to speech to remake the failure of speech's presence into a writerly presence founded on absence. Because it is additive, writing is supplementary. It stands, as Derrida says, "*in-the-place-of*,"[34] and as such it is a substitutive presence, filling a void. But in doing so, writing also must define the void, calling attention to it as the absence of presence that marks the presence of writing. As a material mark, writing "accumulates presence," but it does so by marking the continual negotiation between presence and absence.[35] And because writing enacts the operation through which presence is resurrected through absence, writing can also enact an operation through which alternate, abandoned, or ruptured histories are reconfigured from the location of the present.

In Richard Foreman's 1996 production of **Venus** at Yale Repertory Theatre and the Public Theater in New York, writing materially framed the stage space. Describing the scenography in the *New York Times,* Ben Brantley wrote that the walls of the stage were "emblazoned with chains of words."[36] These lines of texts, according to Elam and Rayner's reading of the production, called attention to the fact that Parks's reinstantiation of Saartjie Baartman must always be trapped in the words of her historical past, a story that quite literally "shaped the stage in words."[37] By spatializing the entire performance within a framework of writing, the Foreman production conceptualized Parks's commitment to her own activity of writing as intervening decisively in the reconstruction of displaced history. Parks explains: "History is not 'was,' history is 'is.' It's present, so if you believe that history is in the present, you can also believe that the present is in the past . . . so you can fill in the blanks. You can do it now by inserting yourself into the present. You can do it for back then, too."[38] The collapsing of past with present, of absence with presence, can therefore productively activate the void of the absent past. Addressing the indeterminacy at the heart of Parks's experimentation, this kind of conceptual collapsing is at work in the formal structure of her writerly marks—a structure that continuously determines and then dismantles the imprint and embodiment of names and figures along the lines of a metonymic formation. As a discursive construction, metonymy enables the incommensurable nature of one thing to stand in for, or over, a completely different other thing. Upholding the boundaries of two defined entities in the face of their collision, metonymic operations can reconfigure the way we dismantle binary constructions through displacement rather than conflation. Parks herself uses the activity of writing and the indexical imprint of the writerly mark as impetuses for various acts of dismantling: breaking up the linear succession between the historical past and the historical present; breaking down the distinction between the absence of historical origin and the presence of individual subjecthood; breaking through the absence of speech with the presence of the material mark; and breaking in the mark of a figure's name with the embodied figure.

In their employment of naming as a discursive as well as a corporeal imprint, Parks's spells also metonymically mark a continual passage back and forth between the page and the stage. The spells are, thus, an index on the page and of the stage. They do not, however, exist between the page and the stage, but are, in my mind, both the page and the stage. The spells reimagine textual markings as simultaneously pre- and postperformance, as both incomplete and complete, empty and full, absent and present, semantic and asemantic, material and immaterial, writerly and corporeal, since—to keep Barthes in the front of our minds again—writing marks the indexical return of the body. For performance theorist Peggy Phelan, "in moving from the grammar of words to the grammar of bodies, one moves from the realm of metaphor to the realm of metonymy."[39] Phelan's notion that bodies too have a grammar which functions metonymically contributes significantly to how we understand the indeterminate status of Parks's spells as both writing and performance. Using the operation of metonymy to draw attention to the displacement between the performing body and its subjectivity, Phelan writes: "Performance uses the performer's body to pose a question about the inability to secure the relation between subjectivity and the body per se; performance uses the body to frame the lack of Being promised by and through the body—that which cannot appear without a supplement."[40] For Phelan, the body in performance is metonymic of presence: it always stands in for the subjectivity of a character or of the performer that is never fully present within itself—a subjectivity that must be made visible or readable through the body as supplement.

In Foreman's production, the actress playing Venus, Adina Porter, was costumed in a bodysuit with artificially padded, enormous, and bare buttocks. In their reading of this negotiation between the constructed body of Venus and Porter's own body, Elam and Rayner contend that the padding did not hide but rather called attention to the actress's body parts that were "not outside but literally inside the contested display of the body."[41] The black body as the object of the desiring gaze was materially shown to be an imaginary construction, since the padding covered over the actress's own buttocks, which in turn had to be read from within the supplemental ones. Thus embedded in the choice of costume design is a way to conceptualize the extension of Derrida's operation of writing to encompass the writing of performing bodies. Since the body of Parks's reinstantiated Venus costumed in a padded bodysuit framed Porter's lack of a huge posterior as present, foregrounding the presence of absence, her artificial body was therefore supplemental because it continuously placed and displaced this absence as presence.

While the absent presence of a black bottom flickered between the actress's real one and the artificially constructed one, a similar move may also occur more generally across Parks's writerly marks and the bodies they direct. In Parks's spells, the writing of the figure's name supplements—placing and displacing—the figure's body; the body in turn supplements the writing. This two-way supplemental relationship occurs simultaneously, so that writing and body index one another. The spells, then, write out the names of the figures in order to question the direct, unified relationship between the presence of the writerly mark and the presence of the performer's body, and between historical presence and the presence of individual subjecthood—relationships that Parks revises as indexical. Performers must indexically negotiate the embodiment of these figures, their own bodies becoming figurations that can never fully assume subjectivity because of their very definition as figures. As such, the spells initiate a constant negotiation back and forth—a flickering between the absent subjectivity of the historical figure and the present subjectivity of the figure in Parks's play, and between the absent subjectivity inherent in figurative presence and the material presence of the body of the performer.[42]

III. FROM IMPRECISION TO IMPROVISATION

The continual, indexical, and supplemental passage between words and bodies, text and performance, affords an endless set of options for directors to practically experiment with Parks's elusive demarcations "as they best see fit." Parks says: "I think I provide the map . . . And what I try to do is say there are 10 roads, 20, 50 roads—take one. I get a kick out of just seeing what people do. I think that the playwright provides the map. But I think a bad play only has a one-way road . . . that's not a map."[43] But in order to recognize any of these various maps, practitioners must first extend the terms through which they might be accustomed to approaching a performance text. Although the spells may seem dramatically unspecific, suspended as they are outside of the accepted conventions of dramatic writing, their imprecision nonetheless charts an alternately specific model of materiality instantiated within and through absence. Yet the expansion of a verbal-visual vocabulary applicable to a dramatic practice that also embraces the particularities of absent histories and subjects also demands an alternative means of accessing the specific spatial and temporal vocabularies implicated in this conceptualization of imprecision.

As Parks's spells require a new process of interpretation, they also chart a different kind of spatial and temporal understanding between notation and performance, offering the possibility of reinvention to each new performing body within the very marks that notate each performance. Director Liz Diamond, who collaborated with Parks on her earlier plays *Imperceptible Mutabilities in the Third Kingdom, Death of the Last Black Man in the Whole Entire World,* and *The America Play,* says that rehearsals allow her and her performers to collectively discover what to do with Parks's "dynamics." "And you can't do that," she explains, "you can't even do that reading out loud—you can only do that when everybody is up on their feet and their bodies are moving in space and you've got somebody 15 feet away from somebody else."[44] Rehearsals provide a space and a time for improvisation, for working on one's feet, for trying new things out and taking new things on, with Parks's spells reorienting the spatial and temporal starting points.

This reorientation of space and time, as activated through a shift from imprecision to improvisation, relies both formally and conceptually on the complex passage already identified in musical notations and their embodied instantiations in performance. In her article on *Venus,* Lyman cites the Virginia Live Arts production, in which director John Gibson interpreted Parks's spells as avant-garde musical notation, the space on the page equaling time in performance. "In other words," Lyman explains, "in Gibson's production an equal amount of time was devoted to 'A Scene of Love (?)' (in which there is no dialogue), as to a page from the Docteur's intermission speech (containing 313 words)."[45] As other scholars have also pointed out, musical structures—most prominently, the structures inherent in jazz—have deeply influenced Parks's writing, as even her foundational dramatic structure of "Rep and Rev" is a concept integral to jazz whereby a musical phrase is repeated and revised slightly each time.[46] While notational transcriptions are never primary documents of jazz performances because the jazz score is rarely the final authority, the structured openness of what does exist as jazz's notational and/or embodied demarcations provides a means to frame the openness afforded to producers of Parks's spells by conceptualizing indeterminacy as a productive and paradoxically specific imprecision.

Jazz composer George Russell has articulated a seemingly paradoxical theory of jazz improvisation, one that theorizes the unframing of conventional music theory within the framework of specific, improvisatory performances, thus pointing us toward certain spatial and temporal practicalities with regards to Parks's spells. According to Russell, his Lydian Chromatic Concept of Tonal Organization for Improvisation organizes tonal resources from which the musician may draw upon to create his improvised lines, "like an artist's palette: the paints and colors, in the form of scales and/or intervallic motives, waiting to be blended by the improviser."[47] The Chromatic Concept is not a system; there are no rules. Rather, it provides a structural understanding of the possibilities embedded in any musical moment. "You are free to do anything," Russell allows, "for you can resolve the most far-out melody since you always know where home is."[48] Home is, for Russell, the chromatic scale of "polymodal" tones made possible in the vertical spread of a chord, or the series of notes marked one on top of the other and sounded at the same time, each note implying another new scale of tones and thus possible horizontal or temporal progression. Although relying on a series of complex musical examples to open up new avenues for improvisation through the potential use of more than one tonal scale, Russell's notion of polymodality nonetheless provides a practical framework for reorienting the spatial and temporal contingencies that confound Parks's interpreters. If we can imagine the names of a spell as musical notes, then we can conceptualize the space of spell as a vertical spread or chord—with all names/notes sounded together—gesturing toward a horizontal progression through time—with one name/note sounded after another. Russell's polymodal possibilities for improvisatory interpretation are housed simultaneously in each name/note and in the intervals between them. Applying Russell's concept to Parks and under the terms that I have been proposing, the possibilities for improvisation can be housed in our understanding of the indexical writerly imprint of one name and its spatiotemporal relation to other names. In Russell's words, we are free to do what we want if we can locate our decisions in reference to this kind of conceptual home.

Directors and actors ultimately do have to make specific decisions. And whether they involve rotating platforms and cages, padded costumes and lines of text, or slow passages of time, these decisions temporarily embody Parks's notation according to specific yet atypically dramatic codes elaborated within each performance. As implied by Russell's concept, improvisation does not exist outside of codification, but is bound to the performer's negotiation of potentiality embedded within the codes—a negotiation that pries open the possibilities afforded by the notational marks and establishes the performer's own bodily insertion into the space and time of those marks. Parks's process of opening up marks and establishing the frameworks for their embodiment is driven by the material particularities of her conceptual re-imagining of dramatic practice. Flickering back and forth from the imprecise page to the precise stage, her spells momentarily and conditionally situate an embodied subjectivity that is figured (written, notated, imprinted) through repetitive and alternating naming on the page, and is then figured (embodied) by the performer in relation to the writerly naming of other figures (would-be characters) that, in turn, contingently figure (determine) the bodies of other performers.

So when the Venus is approached by the Baron Docteur for the first time, and their love-at-first-sight is scripted as an entire page of spells, Suzan-Lori Parks's "Scene of Love (?)" demands our attention—not only because, as readers, directors, and performers, we are not so sure what to do, but also because we are beginning to recognize the very material concepts effected in Parks's specifically unspecific writerly marks, and to understand

that any practical decision should only be a momentary specification in order to invert the spells' suspension outside of dramatic conventions as a suspension contingently embedded within dramatic reinvention. What is it that, in her words, "best fits" in this scene? I think she gives us as good an answer as we will ever get: that we can do what we think fits. A spell, for Parks, is a look, a place, a state, a moment, and a feeling. We can expand what we mean by these various possibilities and thus expand what we think fits, if we come to acknowledge both the notational and the notional possibilities invested within such inexactitude.

Notes

1. Suzan-Lori Parks, "Elements of Style," *The America Play and Other Works* (New York: Theatre Communications Group, 1995), 16-17.

2. Parks, *Venus* (New York: Theatre Communications Group, 1997), 80.

3. Harry J. Elam, Jr. and Alice Rayner, "Body Parts: Between Story and Spectacle in *Venus* by Suzan-Lori Parks," in *Staging Resistance: Essays on Political Theater,* ed. Jeanne Colleran and Jenny S. Spencer (Ann Arbor: University of Michigan Press, 1998), 275.

4. Monte Williams, "From a Planet Closer to the Sun," *New York Times,* 17 April 1996, C1, 14.

5. Parks, "An Equation for Black People Onstage," in *The America Play and Other Works,* 21.

6. For example, in a 1995 interview with Parks, Steven Drukman suggests that "critics are resistant to seeing you [Parks] as a formally innovative writer, a theoretical writer. You always have to be writing about, as you just said, 'black on black violence,' or something like that . . . I'm not quite sure why that is, what this resistance is of critics to seeing you as a formalist, or as formally experimental." See, Drukman, "Suzan-Lori Parks and Liz Diamond: Doo-a-Diddly-Dit-Dit," *TDR* [*The Drama Review*] 39, no. 3 (1995): 61. Elizabeth Dyrud Lyman quotes Parks in 1990: "Why doesn't anyone ever ask me about *form*?" See, Lyman, "The Page Refigured: The Verbal and Visual Language of Suzan-Lori Parks's *Venus,*" *Performance Research* 7, no. 1 (March 2002): 90.

7. Parks, quoted in Shelby Jiggetts, "Interview with Suzan-Lori Parks," *Callaloo* 19 (Spring 1996): 311.

8. For historical details, see Sander Gilman, "Black Bodies, White Bodies: Towards an Iconography of Female Sexuality in Late Nineteenth-Century Art, Medicine, and Literature," in *"Race," Writing, and Difference,* ed. Henry Louis Gates, Jr. (Chicago: University of Chicago Press, 1986), 223-61. At the request of president Nelson Mandela, Baartman's remains were returned from France to South Africa and buried near her birthplace in 2002.

9. Early twentieth-century experiments included figured verse, orchestral scoring, painted calligraphy, typographical experiments, and collage by such artists/writers as Guillaume Apollinaire, Filippo Tommaso Marinetti, Tristan Tzara, Marcel Duchamp, Gertrude Stein, and the Dadaists. Later twentieth-century experiments included the inscription of the performance process within the text, score, or poem by Jackson MacLow, John Cage, Charles Olson, and David Antin.

10. See Jerome McGann, *Black Riders* (Princeton: Princeton University Press, 1993); *A Critique of Modern Textual Criticism* (Charlottesville: University of Virginia Press, 1992); and *The Textual Condition* (Princeton: Princeton University Press, 1991).

11. See Johanna Drucker, "Visual Performance of the Poetic Text," in *Close Listening: Poetry and the Performed Word,* ed. Charles Bernstein (New York: Oxford University Press, 1998), 131-61.

12. W. B. Worthen, "The Imprint of Performance," in *Theorizing Practice: Redefining Theatre History,* vol. 1, ed. Worthen and Peter Holland (Houndmills: Palgrave, 2001), 214.

13. Ibid., 216.

14. Ibid., 229.

15. Lyman, "Page," 90.

16. Krauss gives the example of weathervanes that register the wind, coding its direction through the index of their arrows.

17. Rosalind Krauss, "Notes on the Index: Part 1," in *The Originality of the Avant-Garde and Other Modernist Myths* (Cambridge: MIT Press, 1985), 209.

18. Krauss, "Notes on the Index: Part 2," in *The Originality of the Avant-Garde,* 216.

19. Ibid., 217.

20. See Floyd and Marion Rinhart, *American Daguerreiean Art* (New York: Clarkson N. Potter, Inc., 1967); and *The American Daguerreotype* (Athens: University of Georgia Press, 1981).

21. Roland Barthes, "Rhetoric of the Image," in *Image Music Text,* trans. Stephen Heath (New York: Hill and Wang, 1977), 36.

22. Parks, "Elements," 16.

23. Paul Gilroy, "Diaspora and the Detours of Identity," in *Identity and Difference,* ed. Kathryn Woodward (London: Sage, 1997), 318.

24. Drukman, "Parks and Diamond," 67.

25. Parks, "Elements," 16.

26. Suzan-Lori Parks, *Venus,* dir. Irma Mayorga and Shannon Steen, Stanford University, November 1998. In a recent conversation, Steen told me that, in their production, the spells were based on the look between characters.

27. Parks, quoted in Jiggetts, "Interview," 313.

28. Elam and Rayner, "Body Parts," 268.

29. Ibid., 278-79.

30. Parks, *Venus,* 145.

31. Roland Barthes, "From Speech to Writing," in *The Grain of the Voice,* trans. Linda Coverdale (New York: Hill and Wang, 1985), 6.

32. Ibid., 7.

33. Jacques Derrida, "'. . . That Dangerous Supplement' . . . ," in *Of Grammatology,* trans. Gayatri Chakravorty Spivak (Baltimore: Johns Hopkins University Press, 1997), 142-43.

34. Ibid., 145.

35. Ibid., 144.

36. Ben Brantley, "Of an Erotic Freak Show and the Lesson Therein," *New York Times,* 3 May 1996, C3, 1.

37. Elam and Rayner, "Body Parts," 273.

38. Parks, quoted in Jiggetts, "Interview," 316.

39. Peggy Phelan, *Unmarked: The Politics of Performance* (London: Routledge, 1993), 150.

40. Ibid., 150-51.

41. Elam and Rayner, "Body Parts," 272.

42. In using the term "flickering," I am invoking the notion of alternation as well as the sudden slippage through which the "being there" of subjectivity becomes and is instantiated through its "not-being-there," so that the presence of subjectivity is only momentary, fleeting, and constructed in alternation with its absence. N. Katherine Hayles writes about the "flickering signifiers" that make up the visual display of text on computer screens, so that the displacement of presence by the pattern of codes creates the fiction of presence. It seems to me that virtual presence—constituted through flickering signifiers that are, according to Hayles, "characterized by their tendency toward unexpected metamorphoses, attenuation, and dispersion" (30)—might be another way to consider Parks's spells. In the realm of virtual reality, Hayles substitutes the term "pattern" for presence and the term "randomness" for absence. See N. Katherine Hayles, *How We Became Posthuman: Virtual Bodies in Cybernetics, Literature, and Informatics* (Chicago: University of Chicago Press, 1999).

43. Parks, quoted in Jiggetts, "Interview," 312.

44. Liz Diamond, quoted in Drukman, "Parks and Diamond," 70.

45. Lyman, "Page," 97.

46. See, for example, Drukman, "Parks and Diamond," or Louise Bernard, "The Musicality of Language:

Redefining History in Suzan-Lori Parks's 'The Death of the Last Black Man in the Whole Entire World,'" *African American Review* 31 (Winter 1997): 690.

47. George Russell, *The Lydian Chromatic Concept of Tonal Organization for Improvisation* (New York: Concept Publishing, 1959), 1.

48. Ibid., 27.

FURTHER READING

Criticism

Als, Hilton. "The Show-Woman: Profiles." *New Yorker* 82, no. 35 (30 October 2006): 74-81.

Anecdotal account of Parks's work as a playwright, touching on such topics as family influences, professional associations, thematic concerns, and writing style.

Foster, Verna A. "Nurturing and Murderous Mothers in Suzan-Lori Parks's *In the Blood* and *F———A*." *American Drama* 16, no. 1 (winter 2007): 75-89.

A psychosocial examination of the opposing feelings of love and rage experienced by the mothers in *In the Blood* and *F———A*, comparing these individuals with the maternal figures in Nathaniel Hawthorne's *The Scarlet Letter* and Toni Morrison's *Beloved,* and with the mythological sorceress Medea.

"For the First Time, the Drama Pulitzer Goes to a Black Woman." *Journal of Blacks in Higher Education,* no. 36 (summer 2002): 60.

Contains an announcement of Parks's receipt of the Pulitzer Prize for drama; also includes a brief synopsis of Parks's life.

Young, Jean. "The Re-Objectification and Re-Commodification of Saartjie Baartman in Suzan-Lori Parks's *Venus*." *African American Review* 31, no. 4 (winter 1997) 699-708.

Argues against Parks's contention in *Venus* that the main character, Saartjie Baartman, was a ready and willing participant in her own exploitation.

Additional coverage of Parks's life and career is contained in the following sources published by Gale: *Authors and Artists for Young Adults,* **Vol. 55;** *Contemporary American Dramatists; Contemporary Authors,* **Vol. 201;** *Contemporary Dramatists,* **Eds. 5, 6;** *Contemporary Women Dramatists; Drama Criticism,* **Vol. 23;** *Drama for Students,* **Vol. 22;** *Literature Resource Center; Reference Guide to American Literature,* **Ed. 4.**

Sonia Sanchez
1934-

(Born Wilsonia Benita Driver) American playwright, poet, songwriter, and children's book author.

For additional information on Sanchez's career, see *Black Literature Criticism*, Ed. 1.

INTRODUCTION

Sanchez is recognized as a chief proponent of racial and feminist concerns in the arts. In addition to her accomplishments as a poet and playwright, Sanchez has played an important role in the black studies movement. From the beginning of her literary career during the cultural revolution of the 1960s to her later successes as an author and educator, Sanchez has worked to inspire and empower those seeking an identity outside of the European American mainstream. Her experi-

mentation with the traditional structure and aesthetic of poetry and theater has contributed to the changing landscape of American literature.

BIOGRAPHICAL INFORMATION

Sanchez was born in 1934 in Birmingham, Alabama. When she was one year old, her mother died, and she was sent to live with her grandmother, with whom she resided until her grandmother's death five years later. Sanchez lived with various other relatives before moving to Harlem, New York, in 1943, joining her father, Wilson L. Driver, and his third wife. Driver, a musician, took Sanchez to hear such prominent jazz artists as Billie Holiday, Billy Eckstine, and Art Tatum. Sanchez began writing poems as an adolescent, which helped her to overcome a prominent stutter. After graduating with a B.A. in political science from Hunter College in 1955, she began graduate work at New York University, studying writing under poet Louise Bogan. Around this time Sanchez heard Malcolm X speak, and her interest in racial politics increased dramatically. She formed a writers' workshop in Greenwich Village with a group of other poets from the Black Arts Movement, most notably Amiri Baraka and Askia Muhammad Touré. By the early 1960s Sanchez had founded the "Broadside Quartet" with her husband, Etheridge Knight (whom she later divorced), Haki R. Madhubuti, and Nikki Giovanni. She taught at San Francisco State College from 1967 to 1969, where she played an integral role in developing several of the nation's first courses in black studies. In 1969 her first volume of poetry, *Home Coming,* was published. The following year she became an assistant professor at Rutgers University and began to sever ties with the "Broadside Quartet."

In the early 1970s Sanchez moved back to New York City, where she held a variety of teaching positions and produced several original plays, including *Dirty Hearts* (1971). From 1972 to 1976 she belonged to Elijah Muhammad's Nation of Islam, which she eventually left because she felt that women were relegated to a subordinate role in the organization. Throughout the 1970s she continued to publish a variety of work, including her first book of poetry for children, *It's a New Day* (1971). She received a PEN Writing Award in 1972 and the National Education Association Award in 1977. Critical recognition of her work grew in the 1980s with the publication of her poetry collection *homegirls & handgrenades* (1984), which won an American Book

Award. She was granted a PEN fellowship in the arts in 1993 and her volume of poetry *Does Your House Have Lions?* (1997) was nominated for the National Book Critics Circle Award. In addition to serving as a contributing editor of *Black Scholar* and the *Journal of African Studies,* Sanchez held the Laura Carnell Chair in English at Temple University, where she taught for twenty-two years. She received the Lindback Award for Distinguished Teaching upon her retirement from Temple in 1999.

MAJOR WORKS

The poems in *Home Coming* are a celebration of the urban lifestyle that Sanchez had left for a time during her early years as a teacher. Writing in free verse and utilizing frequent line breaks, Sanchez replicated the unique rhythm and mannerisms of the urban black dialect throughout the volume. She continued writing in an avant-garde style in her next collection of poetry, *We a BaddDDD People* (1970), with political overtones that are much stronger and more confrontational. Sanchez surprised many of her readers with her next volume, *Love Poems* (1973). In contrast to the jazz-inspired rhythms of her earlier work, *Love Poems* consists mainly of haiku and lyrical verse. Many of the poems in this introspective collection were composed during a trip to China and involve intimate subject matter and natural landscapes. Written while she was affiliated with the Nation of Islam, *A Blues Book for Blue Black Magical Women* (1974) is a prose-poem dealing with the struggle between African American ancestry and the dominant history of Western society. In this work, Sanchez examined rituals of the past and the values of modern culture, offering her readers a vision of a hopeful, integrated future.

Sanchez's next volume, *I've Been a Woman* (1978), details the personal, spiritual, and political journey of one woman as she strives to establish her own identity. Sanchez inserted herself as a character in *homegirls & handgrenades,* an autobiographical collection in which she incorporated dialogue and narration to create poetic sketches bringing to life individuals from her past. *Under a Soprano Sky* (1987) continues to develop themes of racial identity and self-empowerment while addressing such topics as loss and aging. In this collection, Sanchez's thoughts on the death of her brother from AIDS and modern young people's lack of awareness of their heritage are expressed in an elegiac tone. For *Wounded in the House of a Friend* (1995) Sanchez created a type of poetry called *sonku,* which consists of five lines with five syllables each. The symbolism in this volume is more ambiguous than that in much of her other writing, but the central theme of mistreatment of African American women by men is one of Sanchez's long-standing concerns. The poems of *Does Your House Have Lions?* feature elements of Greek tragedy and African storytelling, recounting the life of Sanchez's brother and the effect of his illness and untimely death on her family. The love poems in *Like the Singing Coming off the Drums* (1998) are highly erotic, overtly musical, and based upon Japanese verse structures. The volume also contains poetic tributes to such public figures as rapper Tupac Shakur, jazz vocalist Ella Fitzgerald, and academic Cornel West. *Shake Loose My Skin* (1999) is a selection of Sanchez's verse spanning over thirty years and includes four new pieces.

Although Sanchez is known primarily for her poetry, she has also written a number of plays and children's stories. Her first play, *The Bronx Is Next* (1968), exposes the oppression of African American women within the Black Arts Movement. Another drama, *Sister Son/ji* (1969), contains a series of highly stylized dream sequences in which a woman remembers her life as a black revolutionary. The play *Malcolm/Man Don't Live Here No Mo'* (1972), which details major events in the life of Malcolm X in verse form, was written for children. Sanchez's *The Adventures of Fathead, Smallhead, and Squarehead* (1973) began as a story that the author told her children, and highlights Sanchez's efforts to educate young people about tolerance, compassion, and self-confidence.

CRITICAL RECEPTION

Critics have commended Sanchez's versatility and unreservedness as a poet. The evolution of her style from brash, avant-garde verse to poetry characterized by nuanced intimacy and formality is applauded by reviewers, as is the celebration of cultural differences in her art. Though she has adopted many styles of writing throughout her career, critics recognize her steadfast attitude toward her political convictions and social activism. Furthermore, her emphasis on ancestral African ritual and tradition has been viewed as an important educational tool as well as an innovative literary device. Acknowledged as unique and distinctive, her work has been compared favorably to that of such notable figures as T. S. Eliot and Walt Whitman. Sanchez's plays have been recognized for their depiction of powerful females within a repressive social environment. Some of Sanchez's writing has been criticized for sacrificing artistic subtlety in favor of political rhetoric, but her profound influence on a generation of readers and students is equally noted. A renowned poet, playwright, professor, and activist, Sanchez has been a powerful and persistent voice in African American and women's literature for the past four decades.

PRINCIPAL WORKS

The Bronx Is Next (play) 1968; published in journal *Drama Review*
Home Coming: Poems (poetry) 1969

Sister Son/ji (play) 1969; published in book *New Plays from the Black Theatre: An Anthology*

We a BaddDDD People (poetry) 1970

Dirty Hearts (play) 1971; published in journal *Scripts*

It's a New Day: Poems for Young Brothas and Sistuhs (juvenilia) 1971

three hundred and sixty degrees of blackness comin at you: An Anthology of the Sonia Sanchez Writers' Workshop at Countee Cullen Library in Harlem [editor] (poetry) 1971

Malcolm/Man Don't Live Here No Mo' (play) 1972; published in journal *Black Theatre*

The Adventures of Fathead, Smallhead, and Squarehead (juvenilia) 1973

Love Poems (poetry) 1973

A Blues Book for Blue Black Magical Women (poetry) 1974

Uh Huh, But How Do It Free Us? (play) 1974

I've Been a Woman: New and Selected Poems (poetry) 1978

A Sound Investment: Short Stories for Young Readers (juvenilia) 1980

homegirls & handgrenades (poetry) 1984

Under a Soprano Sky (poetry) 1987

Wounded in the House of a Friend (poetry) 1995

Does Your House Have Lions? (poetry) 1997

Like the Singing Coming off the Drums: Love Poems (poetry) 1998

Shake Loose My Skin: New and Selected Poems (poetry) 1999

Full Moon of Sonia (songs) 2004

CRITICISM

Regina B. Jennings (essay date 1992)

SOURCE: Jennings, Regina B. "The Blue/Black Poetics of Sonia Sanchez." In *Language and Literature in the African American Imagination*, edited by Carol Aisha Blackshire-Belay, pp. 119-32. Westport, Conn.: Greenwood Press, 1992.

[*In the essay that follows, Jennings focuses on the Afrocentric perspective of Sanchez's poetry, emphasizing the poet's use of the form and structure of the blues.*]

As a poet, Sonia Sanchez has evolved since her first book *Homecoming* published in 1969 during the heart of the Black Power Movement. Back then her poetics included a strident tropology that displayed a matriarchal protection of black people. Today, after publishing twelve books of poetry, including the acclaimed *Homegirls and Handgrenades* and *Under a Soprano Sky,* one can still discover poetic conventions developed during the Black Arts Movement. The purpose of this artistic movement involved challenging the Eurocentric hegemony in art by developing a new aesthetic that represented the ethos, pathos, and expression of African Americans. These neo-renaissance artists were inspired by the rhetorical eloquence and activism of Rev. Martin Luther King, Jr. and Malcolm X. From this era of intense political activism, artists such as Sonia Sanchez wrote poems illustrating a resistance to inequality best described in "Black Art" by Imamu Amiri Baraka (1969).

It is obvious that revolutionary fervor characterized some of Sanchez's work, but it is essential for understanding her poetics, as well as the neo-aesthetic of the sixties, to recognize that anarchy was not the goal. These poets considered themselves to be word soldiers for black people, defending their right to have equality, honor, and glory. In each of Sanchez's volumes of poetry, for example, one finds the artist handling themes that include love, harmony, race unification, myth, and history. Her poetic personas are diverse, incorporating themes from China, to Nicaragua, to Africa. Yet, there is a pattern in her figurative language that blends an African connection. In this article, I shall examine the Afrocentric tropes that embody Sanchez's poetics. To use Afrocentricity in this regard is to examine aspects of traditional African culture not limited by geography in Sanchez's work. A body of theory that argues such an African commonality is in Kariamu Welsh's *The Concept of Nzuri: Towards Defining an Afrocentric Aesthetic.* Using her model will enable this kind of topological investigation.

Houston Baker, Jr. presents a different aesthetic in *Blues, Ideology, and Afro-American Literature.* This book is a point of departure from Africa, concentrating solely on discussions of African American art from a black American perspective. On the back cover of *Under a Soprano Sky,* Baker maintains that blue/black motif appears in selected works by Sanchez. Baker's definition of the blues constitutes a transitory motion found precisely in this motif. The blues manifests itself in Sanchez's prosody in varying degrees and in differing forms. It determines shape and category, directs the vernacular, and informs the work. To demonstrate this specific vitality in Sanchez's poetry, Baker's construct of a blues matrix is an apt qualifier.

One can identify the blues as matrix and Afrocentric tropology in Sanchez's literary vision when one understands the significance of her axiology. Her ethics informs not only her creativity but her essays and articles as well. Her focus is to inscribe the humanity of blacks to challenge the Eurocentric perspective of black inferiority. Her particular axiology emerged during the greatest period of social unrest between whites and blacks. In the sixties, African American artists deliberately fused politics and art to direct social change. That Sanchez's axiology influenced her ethics has to be considered in order to understand why her poetry inverts the tropology of "white" and "black." The artists of the Black Arts Movement were at war with America. Their tone and perspective encouraged black people to re-think their collective position and to seize control to di-rect their destiny. Consider this Sanchez poem entitled **"Memorial"**:

> i didn't know bobby
> hutton in fact it is
>   too hard to re
> cord all the dying
>   young/blks.
>   in this country.
> but   this i do know
>   he was
> part of a long/term/plan
>   for blk/people.
>   he was denmark
>   vesey.
>   malcolm
>   garvey. all the
>   dead/blk/men
>   of our now/time
>   and ago/time.
>   check it out. for
> bobby wd be living today.
> Panther/jacket/beret
>   and all.
> check it out & don't let
>   it happen again.
>   we got enough
> blk/martyrs for all the
>   yrs to come
>   that is, if they
>   still coming
>   after all the shit/
>   yrs of these
> white/yrs   goes down

(Sanchez 1969:30)

The ethics in **"Memorial"** involve the dichotomy be-tween "white" and "blk" (black). By positioning Bobby Hutton historically in the pantheon of heroic black men who died fighting against racial oppression, Sanchez el-evates him. In death, she has magnified the significance of how he lived. The conditionality of being black in this poem denotes heroism against tyranny. In fact, D. H. Melhem (1990) argues that heroism exists in Sanchez's poetry. In the ideology of black people, Pan-thers are resistance leaders (Foner, 1970; Brisbane, 1974). Thus, by capturing the humanity of heroes in the first five stanzas, the persona suggests to the reader that he or she too can incorporate Hutton's heroics.

The term "white" adjectivally expresses the racism in America responsible for all the "years" of heroic deaths. White is now an inverted symbol, the antithesis of its traditional meaning of purity and goodness. Imamu Amiri Baraka, one of the definers of the black aesthetic, along with Larry Neal, "modernized the black poem by fusing it with modernist and postmodernist forms and ideas (Harris, 1985:136)." William Harris writes that

poets such as Sanchez learned from Baraka to invert poetic techniques. "Even the most cursory reading of contemporary black poetry reveals the extent to which it was influenced by projective form and avant-garde" (Harris, 136). However, Sanchez herself states that her inversion of symbols derived directly from the Muslims and Malcolm X (Braxton, 1990:357). The meaning of avant-garde has to broadened to include the philosophy of Malcolm X. To adopt a projective form was crucial to the sixties poet who stood before audiences during this politically tense era. Poets such as Sanchez were in the forefront of reshaping the ideology and activism of black people. Elements of the avant-garde challenged the status quo in society and in art. Welsh writes: "the idea of art for the sake of art has firm roots in European culture. Africans, for the most part, do not believe in the concept of art for art's sake (Richards, 1985). The life force is the motivating factor in the expression and the product of art (Barrett, 1979:5)."

In **"Memorial,"** the lines "check it out & don't let it happen again" speak directly to the reader, suggesting three modes of action. First, it encourages the reader or listener to review the situation inherent in the poem. Second, it expresses the need for a defensive and offen-sive posture against oppression. Third, it speaks of black control. This utterance of action points to the passivity of the audience. In this matriarchal persona, using accu-satory language and tone in such lines as "part of a long/term/plan," Sanchez infuses the fracture that has historically wounded African American advancement. Likewise, the concept of black annihilation is in the de-notation of the final terms "goes down."

Annihilation is a seminal notion in the collective black psyche based upon African enslavement (Kardiner, 1967; Kovel, 1984; Cress-Welsing, 1991). Therefore, Sanchez's linguistic war with America comes out of the ethos of black people. Conversely, another seminal theme throughout her body of work is one of racial solidarity. Using this theme, her persona as matriarchal protector assumes mythic dimensions. The following untitled poem from *We a BaddDDD People* is an ex-ample:

> i am a blk/wooOOOOMAN
>   my face.
>   my brown
>   bamboo/colored
>   blk/berry/face
>   will spread itself over
> this western hemisphere and
>   be remembered.
>   be sunnnnnnnNNNGG.
>   for i will be called
>   QUEEN. &
>   walk/move in
>   blk/queenly/ways

(1970:6)

Here one can see that the ontology of "blk" has mytho-logical and historical advantages. Male and female deities enrich the mythology of traditional Africa. As "queen," the black woman is an avatar, possessing extraordinary powers, stretching her "face" across the continents (Thompson, 1984:79-83). To be black in this archetypal voice is to be potent, omnipotent, and good. In **"Memorial"** and in the above black woman poem, a feature of deictics, (verb tenses, adverbials, pronouns, demonstratives) (Culler, 1975:165) is similar, in particular, the concept of time. Both poems converge the timeless present with the future. However, in this black woman poem, the power of myth determines a success that will occur in the future. This sense of continuity depicts power, harmony, and victory. Welsh writes: "It is the consciousness of victory that produces in cyclical fashion an aesthetic will. The consciousness of victory will involve redefinition and reconstruction and a fundamental understanding of the creative processes, historical factors, and cultural legacies of Africa" (8-9).

In the above poem, the aesthetic will is victorious because of the "redefinition" of black that has broadened into a nationalistic "consciousness." This nationalism that challenges Eurocentricism in art and society is an utterance that welcomes its own distinctiveness. It has a concern for all black people distinguished in the gradations of hue. Pragmatics this deliberate demonstrate how deeply Sanchez's poetics emerge from the concept of race solidarity. Unlike black poets of previous decades such as Countee Cullen and Claude McKay, Sanchez finds victory in being black. The ontology of black in the poetry of Cullen and McKay, on the other hand, involves one or all of the following declensions: inferiority, shame, denial, and escape (Bell, 1989; Davis, 1974; Cooper, 1973). Form is another difference in Sanchez's poetry. She does not write poems in traditional taxonomy, imitating and revising established meter, versification, and rhyme. Her poetic patterns are avant-garde.

The theme and genre of the black woman verse show a definite African connection. This is a praise poem popular in Africa since 2000 b.c. (Lomax, 1970:xx). By writing the above poem, Sanchez gives honor to the power of the female principle which will not only be "remembered" but be "sunnnnnnnNNNGG." Song and its traditional significance in African culture has already been established (Bebey, 1975; Chernoff, 1979). From the mundane to the extraordinary, it is interwoven within traditional African culture. When a child cuts its first teeth, the people sing. When a king is coronated, the people sing. Larry Neal writes: "Most contemporary black writing of the last few years has been aimed at consolidating the African American personality. And it has not been essentially a literature of protest. It has, instead, turned its attention inward to the internal problems of the group" (*Black Fire*, 647).

Pigmentation problems have plagued African Americans since their sojourn in this country. Sanchez suggests this problem by lyrically presenting the solution.

Her presentation demonstrates the realism inherent in an Afrocentric aesthetic because it must be "representational of the ethos of black people" (Welsh, 1990:3). Sanchez continues:

            and the world
               shaken by
             my blkness
will channnNNNNNNGGGGGEEEE
         colors. and be
               reborn.
             blk. again.

                              (1970:6)

To be reborn black again is a prelude to collective self-reliance. The final two lines suggest that blacks were in power prior to whites; therefore, seeking control is in concert with past behavior. Her historical reference probably points toward the ancient Egyptians or Kemitans (Asante, 1990). This reach back to Africa for a common past is a commonality argued in *The Concept of Nzuri*: "Numerous writers have expounded on the historical and cultural bond between continental and diasporan Africans. It is not based solely on color, but the bond exists because of a common African heritage that dates back to predynastic Egypt" (3).

Sonia Sanchez's poetic voice is visionary and archetypal. She wrote the above black woman poem twenty-one years before scholars in a focused manner textualized the notion of a common African aesthetic. Another facet of this theoretical aesthetic is found in the staggered formation of letters in particular words. This formation is an element of the avant-garde, introduced during the 1960s. For example, consider the spelling of the sign "change." Its orthographic repetition signals a specificity in quality and energy of expression (Richards, 1989:11-12). Dona Richards defines this energy as *ntu*, a manifestation of the energy informing our ontology. By transforming the orthography of "change," Sanchez causes her listeners and readers to enter a textured relationship with the sign's denotation, connotation, and sound. To hear or read a word formulated this way gives an unsettling tension. This orthography for the effect of sound is a poetic praxis that demonstrates the Black Arts Movement's theory of audience involvement, which can be traced back to traditional Africa. David Miller writes that some of Sanchez's poetry is "in essence, communal chant performances in which [she] as poet, provides the necessary language for the performance. The perceptions in such poems are deliberately generalized, filtered through the shared consciousness of the urban black" (Evans, 1984:16). It is here where Sanchez's style sharply contrasts the performances of other sixties poets. Houston Baker would compare this technique to that of the blues or jazz singer making and improvising the moment simultaneously. To compare Sanchez to a more traditional poet is like comparing how singers Patti LaBelle and Paul Simon hit high notes. Thus, Sanchez's "quality of expression" as defined by Welsh, produces an energy that electrifies audiences, involving them in the experience of the performance.

An Afrocentric artist does not view society impartially because "society gives visions and perspectives to the artist" (2). This interrelationship between poet and audience can also be examined in this next poetic praxis. Sanchez prefaces her poetry in a manner that warms the audience. Before she recites, she generally talks informally to her public. By the time she actually reads a poem, they have come to know her as friend, mother, sister, or guide. The following selections demonstrate how Sanchez speaks directly to and with her audience, requesting guidance, direction, companionship, and leadership. The first short excerpt is from a poem entitled **"blk rhetoric"** and the second is from **"let us begin the real work"**:

> who's gonna make all
> that beautiful blk/rhetoric
> mean something . . .
>
> (1970:15)

* * *

> with our
> minds/hands/souls.
> with our blk/visions
> for blk/lives.
> let us begin
> the begin/en work now.
> while our
> children still
> remember us & looooooove.
>
> (1970:65)

"Blk rhetoric" begs for an answer. The reader can be silent or the listener can shout the answer. It doesn't matter; the question encourages a response. Here the poet is asking for direction and guidance. She is asking either to join or to be joined in the task of building a better future for black people. In **"let us begin the real work,"** the deictics (pronoun usage) illustrate further the nonseparation between poet and audience. The pronoun "I" is absent. Jonathan Culler writes that the artist constructs a "model of human personality and human behavior in order to construct referents for the pronouns" (1975:165). Sanchez's "human behavior" is represented in the possessive case pronouns throughout the work. They bind the artist not only to her creation, but also to her audience. She takes responsibility for the behavior she calls forth in the poem. The use of "our" in particular shows the respect and interrelatedness the artist has for the audience, and by extension, society. She is "with" them, representing their ethos and pathos in poetry and performance. Terminology such as "our" visions and "our children" creates a commonality of purpose and strongly indicates her position as one of the people. The pragmatics suggest that she is not a leader but an utterer and clarifier of what is already known. To

paraphrase Malcolm X in a 1972 film about his life, Sanchez is only telling the people what they already know.

Similarly, the blues is a creative form indigenously American that has always been known. In selected poems from Sanchez's collection, one finds, as Houston Baker points out, a blue/black motif.

> we are sudden stars
> you and i exploding in
> our blue black skins
>
> (1984:9)

To the redefinition of "black" as aesthetically and mythically good, Sanchez adds the color blue. This blue motif changes meaning in different poems, but it consistently demonstrates itself as a literary engagement issuing specific denotations to expression. Houston Baker defines the blues as matrix. It is an impetus for the search for an American form of critical inquiry. The blues is, of course, best known as a musical art form removed from linguistics and semantics. Naturally when one thinks of the blues perhaps one conjures up a grits and gravy black man fingering his guitar or a whiskey brown woman moaning about her man leaving town. Baker extends these cultural metaphors. In *Blues, Ideology, and Afro-American Literature,* his theoretical blues matrix informs African American literature, giving it inventive play in symbol and myth. Its expression gives the literature an emotive of music. The blues emerges out of black vernacular expression and history. It is the motion of the enslaved American Africans bringing coherence to experience.

In the above poem entitled **"Haiku,"** Sanchez gives us the energy of the blues "exploding" inside a distinctive American couple. Being both black and blue is an American duality that symbolizes the tragic institution of European slavery and the vital energizer that reformed the tragedy. It is significant that in Sanchez's collection of poetry, she frequently writes symbolically in sharp and brilliant haiku that form a "locus of a moment of revelation" (Culler, 175). **"Haiku"** reveals the heights of cosmological love, one boundless as the universe, with energies constantly in transformation and motion. Baker writes:

> To suggest a trope for the blues as a forceful matrix in cultural understanding is to summon an image of the black blues singer at the railway junction lustily transforming experiences of durative (increasingly oppressive) landscape into the energies of rhythmic song. The railway juncture is marked by transience.
>
> (7)

> Only a radically altered discursive prospect—one that dramatically dissociates itself from the "real"—can provide access to the blues artistry.
>
> (121)

To adjectivally describe "stars" as "sudden" marks this transience. Considering that the blues is always in motion contextualizes the differing modes of exploration that Sanchez creates when this motif appears. Using "blue" to denote mythic propensities, she creates it as a healing force, not just for her own personal self, but as a remedy for the distress that disturbs humanity. Consider this excerpt from **"Story."**

> when will they touch the godhead
> and leave the verses of the rock?
>   and i was dressed in blue
>   blue of the savior's sky.
>   soon, o soon, i would be worthy.

                                                    (1984:9)

Notice that the voice is restrained and reverent as if in prayer. The mythical elements are obvious, giving a timeless quality to the poem, but a certain deictic movement signaled by the word *when* quietly reaches back into antiquity. For a specific effect, Sanchez's typography moves inward in the final three lines. This kind of typographic movement alerts the reader that something special is occurring in those lines. It is the persona, perhaps being either ritualized or anointed for the job of saving souls. The comparison of "blue" as the color of the garment worn with the "blue" of the "savior's sky" dramatically accentuates the healing potential of "blue" as color and as spatial covering of the universe. This blues matrix is undertoned with a subtle sadness; yet it is not the sadness normally associated with the blues singer. It is more like the melancholy of a holy person relinquishing her personal wants to be able to fulfill an ordained prophecy. Larry Neal called it the Blues God that survived the Middle Passage: "The blues god is an attempt to isolate the blues element as an ancestral force, as the major ancestral force of the Afro-American. It's like an Orisha figure" (Baker, 1988:157-58).

Orisha are African deities that can interact with mortals through prayer, sacrifice, and dance. They are either male or female, each controlling specific powers that inform human existence (Thompson, 1983; Jahn, 1961). In traditional African culture, one of the ways people can become avatars is through ritual where those chosen dress in the colors of the god and adorn themselves or are adorned in natural objects of the diety's habitat. For example, the riverain goddess Oshun heals with water and carries a fan crafted in a fish motif because her spirit moves through fish. In **"Story,"** the persona's spirit is placated and made reverential through blue as motif. This shows a specific example of how the blues matrix influenced Sanchez's poetics. From the mythic to the commonplace, it can determine content, category, and form. A point of contrast is in the next selection where Sanchez writes a blues poem written in black vernacular expression.

> will you love me baby when the sun goes down
> i say will you love me baby when the sun goes
> down

> or you just a summer time man leaving fo winter
> comes
>   round.

                                                    (1987:74)

This poem entitled **"blues"** can be sung or recited in the style of a blues song. Its mimesis is in the melody and lyric of music. Repetition is a poetic as well as a blues convention reifying the stated question. The terms "i say" merely add stress, signifying the importance of the initial inquiry. Langston Hughes gave the concept of the "blues-singing black" prominence in poetry. As a folk poet or a poet of the folk Hughes's works have marks of orature. According to Richard Barksdale in *Black American Literature and Humanism,* Hughes poetry contains naming, enumerating, hyperbole, understatement, and street-talk rhyming. Plus, Hughes's has a recurring motif of a "sun down" image. Sanchez in a real sense is a disciple of the Hughesian school. In her repeated line is a signifying "sun down" image.

An examination of the deictics of verb tense demonstrates the converging of the present with the future. The speaker is asking a question that can only be answered in the future. Baker refers to blues translators as those who interpret the experiencing of experience (1974:7). The persona is allowing the readers to partake of her knowledge of distinct circumstances that ended in grief and loss.

Metaphorically ingesting her "man" demonstrates the music in lyrical and figurative language. Cannibalistically, this man is very much a part of the persona. Yet, an irony is in the final two lines: the persona is not going to suffer grief and loss again. Larry Neal writes: "even though the blues may be about so-called hard times, people generally feel better after hearing them or seeing them. They tend to be ritually liberating in that sense" (Baker, 1988:158).

Aware of experiencing experience, the persona, "sees" the probability of sorrow lying before her. In the seeing is the "liberating" because she is free to make choices about her life. She can choose to continue her present course, or she may redirect her situation, excluding the danger signal in front of her, or she may take some other mode of action, keeping the situation in tact but with some element of difference. This series of options in this folksy expression is heightened because of the final stanza.

This is the inventive play of the blues. Was the persona teasing us all along? Will she indeed start a brand new life? Will she continue to question the stability of her mate, or is she preparing him for the difference, the changes that life automatically brings? The answer rests in the mystery of the Blues God, always in motion, forever in productive transit.

The poetry of Sonia Sanchez continues to be in productive transit. She is a poet spanning over two decades, creating a new aesthetic that fused politics and art. She believes that the artist is the creator of social values (Sanchez, 1983) and her legacy and artistry indicate that single purpose. As the co-founder of the Black Studies Program at San Francisco State College, in 1967 she has been the antithesis of the ivory tower scholar. Sanchez's activism is difficult to equal. Not only did she fight for a Black Studies Program, but she is the first person to develop and teach a course concerning black women in literature. Sanchez has lived and created in an Afrocentric perspective before this way of knowing became textualized. Creating a protective matriarchal persona, she has through versification, plays, and children's books inscribed the humanity of black people. Being our champion and critic, she has forged a blue motif that cleanses, heals, mystifies, and rejoices.

References

Asante, Molefi Kete (1987) *The Afrocentric Idea.* Philadelphia: Temple University Press.

Asante, Molefi Kete (1990) "The African Essence in African American Language." In M. K. Asante and K. W. Asante, *African Culture The Rhythms of Unity,* pp. 233-252. Trenton, N.J.: Africa World Press.

Baker, Houston A., Jr. (1988) *Afro-American Poetics: Revisions of Harlem and the Black Aesthetic.* Madison: University of Wisconsin Press.

Baker, Houston A., Jr. (1984) *Blues, Ideology, and Afro-American Literature.* Chicago: University of Chicago Press.

Baker, Houston A., Jr. (1974) *A Many-colored Coat of Dreams: The Poetry of Countee Cullen.* Detroit: Broadside Press.

Bebey, Francis. (1975) *African Music: A People's Art.* New York: L. Hill.

Bell, Bernard. (1989). *The Afro-American Novel and Its Tradition.* The Amherst: University of Massachusetts Press.

Braxton, Joanne M. and Andree Nicola McLaughlin, eds. (1990) *Wild Women in the Whirlwind: Afro-American Culture and the Contemporary Literary Renaissance.* New Brunswick, N.J.: Rutgers University Press.

Brisbane, Robert H. (1974) *Black Activism: Racial Revolution in the United States, 1954-1970.* Valley Forge, PA: Judson Press.

Chernoff, John Miller. (1979) *African Rhythm and African Sensibility.* Chicago: University of Chicago Press.

Cooper, Wayne, ed. (1973) *The Passion of Claude Mckay: Selected Prose and Poetry 1912-1948.* New York: Schocken Books.

Cress-Welsing, Frances. (1991) *The Isis Papers.* Chicago: Third World Press.

Culler, Jonathan. (1975) *Structural Poetics: Structuralism, Linguistics, and the Study of Literature.* New York: Cornell University Press.

Davis, Arthur P. (1974) *From the Dark Tower: Afro-American Writers, 1900-1960.* Washington, D.C.: Howard University Press.

Evans, Marie, ed. (1984) *Black Women Writers 1950-1980: A Critical Evaluation.* New York: Anchor Books.

Foner, Philip S., ed. (1970) *The Black Panthers Speak.* New York: J. B. Lippincott.

Harris, William J. (1985) *The Poetry and Poetics of Amiri Baraka.* Columbia: University of Missouri Press.

Jahn, Janheinz. (1961) *Muntu: The New African Culture.* New York: Grove Press.

Jones, LeRoi and Larry Neal, eds. (1969) *Black Fires.* New York: William Morrow.

Kardiner, Abram and Lionel Ovesey. (1967) *The Mark of Oppression.* Cleveland, Ohio: Meridian Books.

Kovel, Joel. (1984) *White Racism: A Psychohistory.* New York: Columbia University Press.

Lomax, Alan and Raoul Abdul, eds. (1970) *3000 Years of Black Poetry.* New York: Dodd, Mead & Company.

Malcolm X. (1972) *The Autobiography of Malcolm X.* Warner Bros Studio.

Melhem, D. H. (1990) *Heroism in the New Black Poetry.* Lexington: University Press of Kentucky.

Sanchez, Sonia. (1983) *Crisis and Culture: Two Speeches by Sonia Sanchez.* New York: Black Liberation Press.

Sanchez, Sonia. (1969) *Homecoming.* Detroit: Broadside Press.

Sanchez, Sonia. (1984) *Homegirls & Handgrenades.* New York: Thunder's Mouth Press.

Sanchez, Sonia. (1987) *Under a Soprano Sky.* Trenton, N.J.: Africa World Press.

Sanchez, Sonia. (1970) *We A BaddDDD People.* Detroit: Broadside Press.

Thompson, Robert Farris. (1984) *Flash of the Spirit: African and Afro-American Art and Philosophy.* New York: Vintage Books.

Welsh, Kariamu. (1991) *The Concept of Nzuri: Towards Defining an Afrocentric Aesthetic.* Westport, C.T.: Greenwood Press.

Yoshinobu Hakutani (essay date spring 2000)

SOURCE: Hakutani, Yoshinobu. Review of *Like the Singing Coming off the Drums,* by Sonia Sanchez. *African American Review* 34, no. 1 (spring 2000): 180-81.

[*In the following review of* Like the Singing Coming off the Drums, *Hakutani contends that by adopting the style of the Japanese haiku, Sanchez "poignantly expresses a desire to transcend social and racial differences and a need to find union and harmony with nature."*]

While Sanchez is known as an activist poet, much of her poetic impulse in *Like the Singing Coming off the Drums* derives from the tradition of Japanese haiku, in which a poet pays the utmost attention to the beauty inherent in nature. A great majority of Sanchez's latest collection of poems are entitled haiku, tanka, or sonku. Reading such poems indicates that Sanchez, turning away from the moral, intellectual, social, and political problems dealt with in her other work, found in nature her latent poetic sensibility. Above all, her fine pieces of poetry show, as do classic Japanese haiku and tanka, the unity and harmony of all things, the sensibility that human beings and nature are one and inseparable. Much of Sanchez's poetry, therefore, poignantly expresses a desire to transcend social and racial differences and a need to find union and harmony with nature.

Traditionally as well, the haiku, in its portrayal of human beings' association with nature, often conveys a kind of enlightenment, a new way of looking at humanity and nature. Some of her poems in *Like the Singing Coming off the Drums* follow this tradition. In the second stanza in **"Love Poem [*for TuPac*],"** the lines "the old ones / say we don't / die we are / just passing through into another space" suggest Sanchez's fascination with the Buddhistic world view of reincarnation. The last line "let it go . . . like the wind" in this haiku,

> what is done is done
> what is not done is not done
> let it go . . . like the wind.

spontaneously expresses an enlightenment achieved in Zen philosophy. Another haiku included at the end of the first section, **"Naked in the Streets,"** also concerns the Zen-like discipline of thought:

> let us be one with
> the earth expelling anger
> spirit unbroken.

In the middle section, **"Shake Loose My Skin,"** Sanchez offers another Zen-inspired haiku:

> you are rock garden
> austere in your loving
> in exile from touch.

Although most of the short poems collected in *Like the Singing Coming off the Drums* are stylistically influenced by the poetics of haiku as well as by the aesthetics of modernist poetry, much of Sanchez's ideological concern is post-modern and post-colonial. Many of her poems aim at teaching African Americans to achieve subjectivity and value their heritage. Even such a haiku as

> mixed with day and sun
> i crouched in the earth carry
> you like a dark river.

succinctly expresses what Langston Hughes conveys in "The Negro Speaks of Rivers." Moreover, the most important thematic concern is love of humanity, an act of faith that must begin with self-love. The last poem in the collection, dedicated to Gwendolyn Brooks, is a response and rejoinder to such a poem as Brooks's "The Mother." Not only is Brooks portrayed as "a holy one," she has become a universal symbol of the mother with enduring love and humanity: "restringing her words / from city to city / so that we live and / breathe and smile and / breathe and love and / breathe her . . . / this Gwensister called life."

The penultimate poem in *Like the Singing Coming off the Drums* is dedicated to Cornel West. In contrast to the rest of the poems, it is a prose poem like Whitman's *Song of Myself.* West, a Harvard professor, is not presented as a spokesman of academia but characterized as a cultural activist like Whitman, Hughes, and Brooks, each of whom in a unique way sought to apotheosize the humanity of the land. Sanchez sees West as the foremost individual at the dawn of the twenty-first century, a spokesperson always "questioning a country that denies the sanctity, the holiness of children, people, rivers, sky, trees, earth." Sanchez urges the reader to "look at the father in him. The husband in him. The activist in him. The teacher in him. The lover in him. The truth seeker in him. The James Brown dancer in him. The reformer in him. The defender of people in him. The intellectual in him." Rather than dwelling on the racial conflict and oppression the country has suffered, Sanchez admonishes the reader to see cross-pollination in the various cultures brought together to the land. West is "this twenty-first-century traveler pulling us screaming against our will towards a future that will hold all of humankind in an embrace. He acknowledges us all. The poor. Blacks and whites. Asians and Native Americans. Jews and Muslims. Latinos and Africans. Gays and Lesbians."

Whether *Like the Singing Coming off the Drums* is Sanchez's best work will remain to be seen in the new millenium, but an effort to use diverse principles of aesthetics in molding her poetry has few precedents in American literature. Thematically, American poets such as Emerson, Dickinson, and Whitman were partly influenced by various cultural and religious traditions, just as Pound, Wallace Stevens, Gary Snyder, and Richard Wright at some points in their careers modeled their work on Eastern poetics. Sanchez, on the other hand, remains one of the few American poets intent on relying on cross-culturalism for both the style and the content of her poetry.

O i will purchase my brother's whisper.
O i will reward my brother's tongue.

In *Like the Singing Coming off the Drums* (1998), Sanchez trains her own tongue to curl around the many sounds of love. Whether they are elegiac, bluesy, romantic, sisterly, or sensual, the notes she strikes vibrate with her essence—compassion, concern, humanity, hunger for justice, vulnerability, and strength. In this volume she returns to the haiku and the tanka, which appeared earlier in *Love Poems* and *I've Been a Woman: New and Selected Poems,* and adds the blues haiku, and the sonku, an invented form. She writes:

> love between us is
> speech and breath. loving you is
> a long river running.

Almost twenty years later Sonia Sanchez more than ever deserves the incisive critique of Margaret Walker Alexander in a 1980 review in *Black Scholar* that her poetry is "consistently high artistry that reflects her womanliness—her passion, power, perfume, and prescience."

Aware of her own indebtedness to generations of women who shaped her poetic vision, Sanchez makes the final poem in *Shake Loose My Skin,* **"Aaaayeee Babo (Praise God),"** a fitting praise song to "women whose bodies exploded with flowers." From Mama Driver, from Shirley Graham Du Bois, from eighty-four-year-old Mrs. Rosalie Johnson, from the not so small voices of LaTanya, Kadesha, Shanique, from Mrs. Benita Jones, an angry black woman in Philadelphia, hounded by racism out of her home, Sonia Sanchez has extracted the sweet nectar of their lives and has it nourish and sustain her. For it is these women, and many more like them, who in "recapturing the memory of our most sacred sounds" remind Sanchez of the humanity, the peace, the community, and the purpose that she learned while encircled by the big Charles White arms of her southern upbringing.

FURTHER READING

Criticism

Curb, Rosemary K. "Pre-Feminism in the Black Revolutionary Drama of Sonia Sanchez." In *The Many Forms of Drama,* edited by Karelisa V. Hartigan, pp. 19-29. Lanham, Md.: University Press of America, 1985.

> Traces Sanchez's emerging feminist consciousness in her plays *The Bronx Is Next, Sister Son/ji,* and *Uh, Uh, But How Do It Free Us?*

Sanchez, Sonia, and Jacqueline Wood. "'This thing called playwrighting': An Interview with Sonia Sanchez on the Art of Her Drama." *African American Review* 39, nos. 1-2 (spring-summer 2005): 119-32.

> Sanchez comments on such areas as her creative process and work ethic, her concern with the issues of black women, and aspects of individual works. Includes brief synopses of several of Sanchez's plays.

——, and Danielle Alyce Rome. "An Interview with Sonia Sanchez." In *Conversations with Sonia Sanchez,* edited by Joyce A. Joyce, pp. 62-9. Jackson: University Press of Mississippi, 2007.

> Sanchez discusses such subjects as her literary ideology, her use of Black English, and her creative process.

Additional coverage of Sanchez's life and career is contained in the following sources published by Gale: *Black Literature Criticism,* **Ed. 1:3;** *Black Writers,* **Eds. 2, 3;** *Children's Literature Review,* **Vol. 18;** *Concise Major 21st-Century Writers,* **Ed. 1;** *Contemporary Authors,* **Vol. 33-36R;** *Contemporary Authors New Revision Series,* **Vols. 24, 49, 74, 115;** *Contemporary Literary Criticism,* **Vols. 5, 116, 215;** *Contemporary Poets,* **Eds. 2, 3, 4, 5, 6, 7;** *Contemporary Southern Writers; Contemporary Women Poets; Dictionary of Literary Biography,* **Vol. 41;** *Dictionary of Literary Biography Documentary Series,* **Vol. 8;** *DISCovering Authors 3.0; DISCovering Authors: Multicultural Authors; Encyclopedia of World Literature in the 20th Century,* **Ed. 3;** *Literature Resource Center; Major Authors and Illustrators for Children and Young Adults,* **Eds. 1, 2;** *Major 20th-Century Writers,* **Eds. 1, 2;** *Major 21st-Century Writers* **(eBook), 2005;** *Modern American Literature,* **Ed. 5;** *Poetry Criticism,* **Vol. 9;** *Something about the Author,* **Vols. 22, 136; and** *World Poets.*

Ousmane Sembène
1923-2007

AP Images. (Sembène is on the left.)

(Also known as Sembène Ousmane) Senegalese novelist, screenplay writer, and short fiction writer.

For additional information on Sembène's career, see *Black Literature Criticism*, Ed. 1.

INTRODUCTION

Sembène is widely considered the greatest African filmmaker of the twentieth century and is counted among that continent's most revered fiction writers. His works, which are based largely on Sembène's Marxist-Leninist ideology, typically depict underprivileged groups or individuals facing opposition from a corrupt, bureaucratic colonial system and from degrading, no less brutal traditional customs such as polygamy and female genital mutilation.

BIOGRAPHICAL INFORMATION

Sembène was born in 1923 in the Casamance region of southern Senegal. His family was from the Muslim Wolof ethnic group and Sembène attended both Islamic and French schools. When he was fourteen years old, he was expelled for fighting with his school principal. Sembène briefly tried working for his father—a fisherman—but seasickness prevented him from earning a living in that profession. In 1938 he was sent to live

with relatives in Dakar, where he performed a variety of odd jobs. In 1944 Sembène was drafted into the French colonial army to serve during World War II, participating in the Allied invasion of Italy and the movement to liberate France from Germany. On returning to Dakar in 1947, Sembène took part in the Senegalese railway strike that temporarily crippled French colonialism in West Africa and rallied African nationalism. Later in 1947, Sembène moved to Marseilles, France, where he found work as a longshoreman. In 1950 Sembène joined the French Communist Party and the following year an accident on the docks left him with a broken back; these two events were seminal to the formation of his understanding of social and political theory. Unable to do the difficult work on the docks, Sembène spent months frequenting libraries and museums, educating himself and ultimately becoming a respected intellectual figure. He channeled his experiences into writing novels and went on to join groups supporting liberation from colonial rule in Indochina and Algeria. Sembène returned to Senegal in 1960, after that country achieved independence from French rule. Although he had achieved great success with his novels internationally, Sembène realized that his writing reached only a limited readership in Senegal—where the majority of people are illiterate and speak the indigenous Wolof language—so he turned to filmmaking. He saw film as an effective medium for mass communication and spent a year studying cinematography in the Soviet Union under noted filmmaker Marc Donskol. In 1969 Sembène co-founded the Panafrican Film and Television Festival of Ouagadougou (FESPACO), held biennially in Burkina Faso. Through the 1970s Sembène's socialist themes frequently provoked the censorship of the Senegalese government. Nevertheless, he continued to denounce the Westernized elite in postcolonial Africa as well as the oppressive nature of many African customs. Sembène died in Dakar in 2007, after a long illness.

MAJOR WORKS

Sembène's works are based largely on his socialist philosophy and his experiences living and working in Africa and France. His first novel, *Le docker noir* (1956; *The Black Docker*), concerns a black dock worker who writes a book that is stolen by a white woman. While not considered one of his strongest novels, it established a pattern for his subsequent works, which depict Africans who fall victim to a corrupt social or political system. Most of Sembène's fiction is based on actual events—for example, a newspaper article on the suicide of a black maid in France became the basis of his film *Le noire de . . .* (1966; *Black Girl*), which was based on his short story of the same name and won a Cannes Film Festival Special Prize. One of Sembène's most acclaimed novels, *Les bouts de bois de Dieu* (1960; *God's Bits of Wood*) recounts the railworker strikes of 1947-48 on the Dakar-Niger line, in which Sembène participated. Sembène's films all provide glimpses into the lives of people who are socially and economically exploited, especially under colonial regimes. His first short film, *Borom Sarret* (1963), details one tragic day in the life of a Senegalese cart driver. In *Emitaï* (1971) French colonists fight a resistance group made up of native Senegalese at the end of World War II; as in other Sembène films, the women in *Emitaï* are the strongest resisters and serve as the link between past and future as they maintain and pass on tribal history and customs.

Xala (1974), based on Sembène's novel of the same name, takes up the broader issue of elitism and hypocrisy in post-independence African countries, but with a decidedly satirical tone. After appropriating government funds to finance his marriage to his third wife, the protagonist, El Hadji Abdou Kader Beye, is cursed with *xala*, or impotence, by a group of beggars he has routinely mistreated. Unable to consummate his new marriage, El Hadji loses the respect of family and colleagues. To remove the curse, he ultimately succumbs to the demands of the beggars, who spit on him while his first wife and her children watch. In *Camp de Thiaroye* (1988) Sembène returned to the historical film genre, portraying the true story of a World War II camp where Senegalese soldiers who fought with the French Resistance waited to return home, only to be cheated out of their severance pay by the French commanders. When they mutinied, the French massacred the entire camp. In *Guelwaar* (1992)—which is also based on a true story—Sembène addressed tension between Christian and Muslim Africans. When the title character dies, his body is mistakenly buried in a Muslim cemetery. When the error is discovered, the Christians attempt to take back the body.

Sembène's last three films comprise a trilogy in which he explores the ambiguous role of women in contemporary African society. In *L'heroisme au quotidian* (1999), a group of women in a small village in Senegal become empowered when they suddenly begin receiving radio signals from women outside the village on their small battery-powered radios. *Faat Kiné* (2000) tells the story of a young divorced mother negotiating life in modern Dakar while still influenced in many ways by her traditional upbringing. Sembène's most lauded film was his last. In *Moolaadé* (2004), Sembène took up the volatile subject of female genital mutilation—the traditional custom of excising, usually with a razor blade and without anesthesia, the clitoris and sometimes also sewing the labia closed until marriage. An excruciating procedure, FGM, as it is known, remains highly controversial and some African countries have outlawed it. *Moolaadé* concerns a small village where four girls have sought sanctuary with an older woman to avoid having the procedure done to them.

CRITICAL RECEPTION

Often called the "father of African cinema," Sembène was lauded for the warmth and humor he brought to difficult subject matter, particularly in films such as *Xala* and *Faat Kine*. The overall critical view is that his works were bleak yet hopeful because of their focus on the power of collective groups to enact societal change. Beginning with his second film, *Borom Sarret,* Sembène won numerous awards at international film festivals, although his works were frequently censored within Senegal. Both *Camp de Thiaroye* and *Guelwaar* won prizes at the Venice Film Festival, while *Moolaadé* was honored at Cannes and won the American Association of Film Critics' Best Foreign Film of the Year prize for 2004.

PRINCIPAL WORKS

Le docker noir [*The Black Docker*] (novel) 1956

O Pays, mon beau peuple! (novel) 1957

Les bouts de bois de Dieu [*God's Bits of Wood*] (novel) 1960

Voltaïque [*Tribal Scars and Other Stories*] (short stories) 1962

Borom Sarret (screenplay) 1963

L'Harmattan, Volume I: Référendum (novel) 1964

Niaye (screenplay) 1964

Véhi-Ciosane ou Blanche Genese, suivi du Mandat [*The Money Order, with White Genesis*] (novellas) 1965

La noire de . . . [*Black Girl*] (screenplay) 1966

Mandabi [*The Money Order*] (screenplay) 1968

Taaw (screenplay) 1970

Emitaï [*God of Thunder*] (screenplay) 1971

Xala (novel and screenplay) 1974

Ceddo (screenplay) 1976

Le dernier de l'empire. 2 vols. [*The Last of the Empire*] (novel) 1981

Niiwam suivi de Taaw (novellas) 1987

Camp de Thiaroye (screenplay) 1988

Guelwaar (screenplay) 1992

L'heroisme au quotidian (screenplay) 1999

Faat Kiné (screenplay) 2000

Moolaadé (screenplay) 2004

CRITICISM

Ousmane Sembène with Sada Niang and Samba Gadjigo (interview date autumn 1995)

SOURCE: Sembène, Ousmane, Sada Niang, and Samba Gadjigo. "Interview with Ousmane Sembène." *Research in African Literatures* 26, no. 3 (autumn 1995): 174-78.

[*In the following interview, Sembène discusses the themes of international aid to poor countries, the "Africanization" of the Catholic Church in Africa, and major characters in his film* Guelwaar.]

As far as I am concerned, I no longer support notions of purity. Purity has become a thing of the past.

On 20 February 1993, President Compaoré of Burkina Faso opened the 13th Panafrican Festival of Cinema at Ouagadougou (FESPACO) at the Stade du 4 mai, Ouagadougou's main soccer stadium, with thousands of people from around the world in attendance. This second largest film festival on the African continent was first held in 1969 as "Semaine du Cinéma Africain" with Ousmane Sembène as one of its founders. Since then, Sembène has acquired the status of a pioneer and taken part in and witnessed the mushrooming of African cinema.

His latest feature film, *Guelwaar,* was chosen for the opening ceremony at Cinema Neerwaya, in recognition of his long-standing contribution. The film, which Sembène had voluntarily withdrawn from the official festival competition, generated so much enthusiasm and controversy that it put him virtually at the epicenter of the Hotel Independance. It was there that we had the opportunity to meet and talk with him about the film and other issues in cinema and literature.

[*Niang*]: *How was* **Guelwaar** *received in Senegal?*

[*Sembène*]: *Guelwaar* has not been shown in Senegal yet. When the film arrived in the country, it coincided with the campaign for the presidential elections.[1] Perhaps they will mention it on the radio and television programs, but this is not certain. I had asked that a gala be held for its premiere in Dakar, but this was rejected. *Guelwaar* deals with the issue of state begging. Begging has existed in Senegal from times immemorial, but we have spent the last thirty years in Senegal begging for help from Europe, America, Japan, and Germany. It has been estimated that Senegal receives one billion CFA francs per day in foreign aid.[2] One does not need to do a thorough analysis of the situation to realize that there is a waste somewhere, but, above all, that the country cannot survive from begging raised into a state policy. If, for example, somebody falls near you, you may help that person to get back on his/her feet. If your neighbor's house catches fire, you may bring water to help put it out. You may even feed him/her for a day or two, and help rebuild his/her house; but it is impossible to be available to him/her and provide help all the time.

[*Niang*]: *Do you make any distinction between the Wolof "yelwaan" and the French "quémander"?[3]*

The term "yelwaan" refers to street beggars. It applies to people stricken by a physical deformity, blindness, or some type of disability and to whom others provide assistance. But when it comes to the state, it is an entirely different matter. In traditional Africa, begging was not as widespread as it is today. Some household heads would even go so far as to refuse to consume food that was offered as alms, or forbid their children to eat at their neighbor's. This being said, sterile women or women who had undergone a miscarriage were required to humble themselves through begging. Such women had to humble themselves in front of every housegate so as to defeat the spell they were suffering from. This type of begging had a symbolic value. Nowadays, in African cities, begging has become the expression of a social and economic predicament.

[*Gadjigo*]: *Is it fair to say then that while you condemn "quémander," you look more kindly to instances of "yelwaan," that is, begging brought about by a physical disability or poverty? It seems to me that, in our present context, these two concepts share a common source, don't they?*

I have dealt with this question in *Xala.* In *Guelwaar,* the act of begging is of a different kind.

[*Gadjigo*]: *Yet even in* **Xala** *you seem to suggest that the main character has been reduced to begging by a social injustice. His plight seems to point to a failure of state social and economic programs in Senegal, and you take up this theme again in* **Guelwaar.** *In fact, everything seems to hold together.*

You are right, everything holds together, but it is up to you to analyze it and make up your mind on it. In *Guelwaar,* the donations regularly made to the African continent assume the features of an economic and political program totally geared towards foreign aid. These donations are humiliating both to Africans who receive them and to those living outside the continent. We know what goes on in Somalia, in Yugoslavia, but we also know what is bound to happen in Chad, in Senegal. The situation is such that those who govern us today no longer make the effort to try and find solutions. By the same token, we also know that most of these donations—which I condemn but which are made to us—are used for political gains and for the benefit of influential voters.

[*Gadjigo*]: *The last scene of* **Guelwaar** *features, in the foreground, young people tearing open bags of food donations, and spilling the content of these on the ground,* *as a symbolic act of rejection and refusal. Up to this scene, these children had figured in the film only as props. Now, in many of your other films, it is women to whom you grant this role (rejection and refusal), thus forcing them to break out of their silence and marginal existence. Why such a change?*

In 1989, 1990, 1991, 1992, 1993, all the revolts that took place in Africa were carried out by high school children. These revolts were neither the work of political parties, churches, mosques, nor of trade unions. Children initiated them on their own.

[Niang]: **Guelwaar** *also features an opposition between an orthodox Christianity symbolized by the priest and a kind of contextualized Christianity symbolized by the children carrying a crooked cross.*

The Catholic Church is Africanizing itself by using elements borrowed from other sources, which suggests a certain cultural dynamism. When the pope goes to visit voodoo priests, imagine that there was a time when these priests would have been killed (not visited), since all African religions were considered savage. But these religions have not died off. Our ancient religions have not disappeared; they are present and have taken different shapes.

[Niang]: Are you suggesting that these conflicts do not exist as far Islam is concerned?

Islam, too, has its own problems; but one cannot deal with all these issues in the same film.

[Gadjigo]: Let us turn to the language issue. Last night, some spectators were frustrated that the version of **Guelwaar** *that had been shown was in French. Some expressed the opinion that the movie would have been more expressive if shown in Wolof.*

This was only one show. The original which you will probably have the opportunity to see is in Wolof with English subtitles. The Wolof film would have been better in Ouagadougou, but how many spectators would be able to read the subtitles?

[Niang]: Are you suggesting that, in this case, the orality of the film is more accessible in French?

Absolutely!

[Niang]: This film incorporates certain aspects of the African diaspora and of panafricanism. Everyone speaking French in it does so with an African accent. There is even a French West Indian accent in the speech of the fourth wife. What meaning do you assign to such linguistic diversity?

As far as I am concerned, I no longer support notions of purity. Purity has become a thing of the past. We have to open up to the diaspora for their and our own

sake. I constantly question myself. I am neither looking for a school nor for a solution but asking questions and making others think.

[Niang]: But you seem to have taken, in this film, a different approach. In **Camp de Thiaroye** *there was an African-American soldier, in* **Ceddo** *you had featured African captives, but in* **Guelwaar** *you opt for a woman who makes the trip back to Africa and who re-integrates herself into the Senegalese milieu. Yet, it is also this fourth wife who is least accepting of the social constraints and who rebels against these.*

She is an outsider who brings with her another culture. Some things she can accept, others she cannot accept.

[Gadjigo]: **Xala** *features what could be referred to as a "a main character": El Hadj Kader Bèye.* **Le mandat** *has Dieng. Is there a main character in* **Guelwaar***?*

Often, there is no main character in my films. They are group stories. At a given time, at a given hour, each character plays a little role and the sum of these roles make up the physiognomy of the group.

[Niang]: The imam in **Guelwaar** *is rather unusual. . . .*

I want you to know that *Guelwaar* is inspired by a true story. The burial actually took place.

[Gadjigo]: This imam corresponds totally to this type of character in your work until the moment he hits someone, utters insults, and blasphemes. It is only then that he starts acquiring a positive image and becomes a unifying element between Catholics and Muslims. It is when he stops behaving like an imam that you have assigned to him a positive value.

The imam himself states that members of both groups have grown together. The Catholic elder states, "You are a credit to humankind," and immediately positions himself outside the religious context. These two religions are perceived in this film as factors of division; they have come from the outside and break the harmony of a world in danger of "falling apart," to use Achebe's phrase.

[Gadjigo]: Oumar Faye in **O pays, mon beau peuple,** *Bakayoko in* **Les bouts de bois de Dieu,** *and Pierre Henry Thioune, alias Guelwaar, these are hard characters who sometimes forget that the men they lead are humans.*

It is because they are leaders.

[Niang]: They are also very lonely characters.

They are human and thus complex beings.

[Gadjigo]: One is struck by the tendency you have of creating characters who are ahead of their community and who grow rough whenever their communities do not follow them.

Leading a group is difficult, especially for one who wants to be responsible and stay clear-sighted.

[*Gadjigo*]: *Aren't these characters anachronistic?*

I don't know.

[*Niang*]: *What does FESPACO[4] represent for you?*

Nowhere are so many African films shown at once, nowhere do so many African filmmakers ever come together. And this event is taking place on the African continent. Besides, the organizers of this event are not politicians. One may assume any ideological tendency, any political orientation that one wishes. This gathering is neither a church congregation, nor a mosque community, nor a chapel group.

[*Gadjigo*]: *Yes, but it seems that during the Sankara years, the Burkinabe population was more involved in the organization of this event. This year, I can assure you that the local population was visibly absent.*

To each leader, his/her impact on his era. As far as we are concerned, we have seen many leaders come and go and we want to be eternal. For us, the domestic issues which crop up during the FESPACO are of secondary importance to the festival.

[*Gadjigo*]: *One often hears, "Monsieur Sembène has a good knowledge of Senegalese society." I would like to think that your work does not limit itself to reflecting the present and that you are after all a visionary, one who constructs a future.*

That is what is required of the artist. Just look at all these people jostling each other to see a film, who would like to see me as if I were in a zoo cage. The truth is that we manage to reach them somewhere inside of themselves, that we give voice to their preoccupations. We give voice to their inner screams.

[*Gadjigo*]: *What direction would you like to see African cinema take?*

My wish is that young African filmmakers assume their social responsibilities, that they become the voices of their peoples, of their time, that there might be a spirit of competitiveness among them. Someone who says, "I am like my father," or "I have done as my father has done," pays tribute to his father, but someone who says, "I have achieved more than my father has," has outgrown his father.

[*Niang*]: *Ousmane Sembène, thank you.*

Notes

1. February-March 1993 presidential elections in Senegal. Following the announcement of the results which gave the majority to the Socialist Party of Senegal led by M. Abdou Diouf, several days of rioting ensued in Dakar.

2. At the time this interview was conducted, the one hundred percent devaluation of the CFA franc had not yet taken place.

3. Even though often translated into English as "beg," this term also contains semantic features that imply deferring one's agency to the benefactor. The entrapment and humiliation that ensues is perhaps best articulated by *Mandabi*'s Dieng in the last scene of that movie. "Yelwaan," on the other hand, usually presupposes a religious (traditional or otherwise) context.

4. Festival Panafricain du Cinéma à Ouagadougou.

Josef Gugler and Oumar Cherif Diop (essay date summer 1998)

SOURCE: Gugler, Josef, and Oumar Cherif Diop. "Ousmane Sembène's *Xala*: The Novel, the Film, and Their Audiences." *Research in African Literatures* 29, no. 2 (summer 1998): 147-58.

[*In the following essay, Gugler and Diop analyze the significant differences between Sembène's novel and the film version of* Xala, *questioning the author's intention of appealing to the widest possible Senegalese film audience.*]

> The artist must in many ways be the mouth and the ears of his people. In the modern sense, this corresponds to the role of the griot in traditional African culture. The artist is like a mirror. His work reflects and synthesizes the problems, the struggles, and the hopes of his people.
>
> Ousmane Sembène, **"Filmmakers and African Culture"** 80

Ousmane Sembène is exceptional in combining two roles: the distinguished writer is also the foremost film director in Africa South of the Sahara.[1] *Xala* is perhaps the finest among his many film productions.[2] It is complex in plot, diverse in characterizations, and rich in satirically observed detail.[3] The film successfully marries the seductive lure of the medium to the director's didactic purpose. *Xala* also offers an excellent opportunity to compare Sembène's approaches to his two chosen media. Even though the film was released just one year after the publication of his novel *Xala* in 1973, it presents a major departure. Some of the differences between the novel and the film can be understood as Sembène's judicious adaptations to the different medium. But there is also a clear shift in emphasis—from denouncing the parasitic Senegalese bourgeoisie to exposing the neocolonial political regime—that defies explanation in terms of the different requirements of the two media: the artist's mirror reflects different perspectives on the problems, the struggles, and the hopes of his people—he addresses different audiences.

Novel and film both tell of affliction. The curse of the *xala* that has inflicted impotence on El Hadji Abdou Kader Bèye on his wedding night with his third wife,[4] takes on a symbolic connotation as the impotence that afflicts the emerging Senegalese bourgeoisie becomes apparent. El Hadji represents, experiences, and eventually articulates the impotence of his class. Sembène entertains us with the satirical account of El Hadji's physical impotence, but eventually confronts us with the economic and cultural impotence of the bourgeoisie that cripples the nation.[5]

The Senegalese bourgeoisie fails to accomplish a productive function. Its representatives are looking for quick profits, whatever the means. They are parasites trafficking in allotments of subsidized rice and diverting supplies intended for drought victims. These avowed businessmen got where they are by exploiting others—El Hadji defrauded his illiterate kin. Instead of making productive investments, they spend their ill-acquired resources lavishly in absurd imitations of foreign consumer culture—to the point where El Hadji bankrupts himself. Sembène's acerbic account of their transgressions makes us agree that they deserve to be spit upon.[6]

The story demonstrates that the members of the Chamber of Commerce constitute only a pseudo-bourgeoisie. The impotence of these *compradores* is poignantly portrayed in El Hadji's *cri de cœur* as he faces the expulsion from the Chamber of Commerce that will seal his ruin:[7]

> We are dirt grubbers! Who owns the banks? The insurance companies? The factories? The construction companies? The wholesale trade? The movie theaters? The book shops? The hotels? etc., etc., etc. All these and more besides are out of our control. Here, we are just crabs in a basket. We want the colonialist's place. We got it. This Chamber is the proof. What has changed, in general or in particular? Nothing. The colonialist has become stronger, more powerful, hidden inside us, as we are here assembled. He promises us the left-overs of the feast if we behave ourselves. Beware anyone who wants to upset his digestion, who wants a bigger slice of the profit. And we? . . . Dirt grubbers, agents, distributors, in our fatuity we call ourselves "businessmen." Businessmen without funds.
>
> (139, our translation)[8]

El Hadji's request for a bank loan of CFA 500,000, equivalent—allowing for two decades of inflation—to less than $10,000, conveys the limited nature of the resources of a member of the now all-African Chamber of Commerce. The ultimate decision over El Hadji's future lies with the presumably French boss of the bank official he implores.

Women are central to the story: some demonstrate the cultural alienation of the *nouveaux riches,* others present alternative models.[9] The men, in one of the rare instances where they draw on their cultural heritage, affirm their commitment to polygamy not for traditional ends—to bring labor to the kinship group and assure its continuity—but simply to enhance their status. El Hadji's second wife, Oumi N'Doye, serves to project the image of a "modern" Westernized couple, his third wife, Ngoné, to confirm his economic success.

In sharp contrast, Sembène presents two female characters of integrity, one traditional, the other modern. Adja Awa Astou, El Hadji's first wife, portrays quiet dignity, patient devotion to the principles of a Muslim marriage, loyalty to her husband even in his ruin. Rama, their daughter, embodies the future, reborn Africa, a society that will draw on its own language and culture while emancipating women from patriarchal traditions.

The beggars constitute the counterpart to the bourgeoisie.[10] Their poverty provides a telling contrast to the conspicuous consumption of the *nouveaux riches*. Reduced by the greed, abuse of power, and cultural alienation of the *arrivistes* to the status of pariahs, they can be seen to represent but the extreme image of the masses who are similarly cheated and robbed. As it turns out, the beggars have a measure of power: their blind leader Gorgui has put the *xala* on El Hadji, and he can take it away again.[11] Sembène's portrayal of the beggars echoes Fanon's faith in the revolutionary potential of the *lumpenproletariat* rather than Marx's dismissive view of it.[12]

Novel and film are similar in style. The novel is written in a naturalist genre, and the film presents the story in a realistic vein, except for the surreal opening sequence preceding the credits. Working with amateurs, Sembène had not much choice in the matter.[13] In any case, the naturalist novel and the realistic film are quite appropriate to Sembène's didactic intentions, and they are the styles he invariably chooses.

Sembène demonstrates his expertise in both media by playing to their distinct opportunities and limitations. The film offers telling images.[14] The businessmen wear Western suits without regard to the tropical heat—except in their public display of the ousting of the French from the Chamber of Commerce. Awa, Oumi, and Rama dress in strikingly different ways. The top of the wedding cake features a European couple. A bottle of Evian serves to wash El Hadji's Mercedes-Benz, another to fill its radiator. Many of the beggars are severely crippled. The freeze frame that concludes the film is not easily forgotten.

The film reduces the number of marginal characters, for example, the number of El Hadji's children and of members of the Chamber of Commerce, making it easier for the viewer to distinguish them. And it moves away from the nuanced characterizations of the novel to contrast the principal figures more sharply. In the novel Awa's son asks his father for money, in the film both her children are above such entreaty. The changes in the characterization of Rama are most significant. She has a Fiat automobile in the novel, but rides a moped more in line with the image of her austerity in the film. The novel has Rama take the part of her father in the final confrontation with the beggars, telling them to leave, but the film has Awa take on that role, thus emphasizing her loyalty. Rama is playful with her fiancé, opportunistic in the encounter with the police officer, in the novel; in the film she invariably presents an image of principled determination. Most strikingly, while the novel has Rama's fiancé, Pathé, and Awa's father, Papa Jean, the film has no major male character with positive attributes to match Awa and Rama.

The novel offers a good deal of explanation for the foreign reader. Some explanations are provided in the text, for example, that "El Hadji" and "Adja" are the honorific titles that came to them because they made the pilgrimage to Mecca. In addition, there are a dozen footnotes that translate, explain, and even comment. The novel thus explicitly addresses a foreign public. The film, in distinct contrast, makes little effort to avoid some aspects of the story being lost on foreign viewers. Thus the *badiène's* references to Ngoné as her daughter suggests to the foreigner that she is Ngoné's mother—in fact she is the sister of her father and in accord with local custom plays the principal role in her niece's marriage. The transvestite serving at the wedding party is well known to Dakarites, but his character escapes most foreigners—and they miss the irony of his subsequent comment on El Hadji's impotence: "There are no real men today." Most importantly, the Wolof songs, which constitute a major co-text, are not subtitled, as is the Wolof dialogue.[15]

The film omits major strands of the story while adding several new developments. Thus the viewer misses the story of the relationship between the *badiène* and Ngoné's parents and the *badiène's* machinations that ensnare El Hadji into marrying Ngoné. Missing from the film also is the drama of Awa's relationship with her parents after her conversion from Catholicism to Islam to become Abdou Kader Bèye's first wife. Finally, the relationship between Rama and her fiancé, Pathé, is omitted from the film.

New in the film is the reappearance of the three Frenchmen of the old Chamber of Commerce: two bringing attaché cases full of cash for the members of the new all-African Chamber of Commerce, and one of them becoming advisor to the Chamber's president; the third commanding the police detachments. An entirely new story is introduced with the peasant who has come to the city with the savings of his village to buy supplies and with the transformation of Thieli (i.e., the vulture) from thief to successor of El Hadji at the Chamber of Commerce. New is the arrest and deportation of the beggars and their long walk back to Dakar. The last two stories are linked by the introduction of the seller of

Kaddu (i.e., The Voice), the Wolof newspaper Ousmane Sembène edited with Pathé Diagne.[16]

There is thus a definite contrast between the kinds of elements Sembène has omitted and added. In the move from the novel to the film he has dropped major strands from the story that focus on family relationships. And he has added new elements that develop an explicitly political dimension. The reappearance of the three Frenchmen makes palpable the neocolonialism El Hadji comes eventually to denounce.[17] The police are shown as the ready tool of the bourgeoisie: to keep the masses away from the fruits of independence, to keep the beggars out of the affluent neighborhood, to deport them from the city, to arrest the relative El Hadji dispossessed.

If a police force at the beck and call of the bourgeoisie demonstrates state support for their interests, the connection between the Chamber of Commerce and the political establishment is made explicit by the government minister and the two "deputies." The representative's 15% cut on a government contract demonstrates the corruption of that establishment.

Subtly, the film takes the viewer a couple of steps further into a critique of the political regime. Repeated references to the President become ambiguous. We are left to wonder whether they are aimed at the President of Senegal rather than the President of the Chamber of Commerce. The Frenchman advising the Chamber's President reminds the informed viewer of Jean Collin, a naturalized Frenchman who played an eminent role in Senegalese government from the time of independence until 1990.[18] The empty slogans mouthed by the members of the Chamber of Commerce caricature the discourse of Léopold Senghor, the President of Senegal until 1981. Indeed, Françoise Pfaff suggests that the voice of the Chamber's president has the same intonation as that of Senghor (*Cinema of Ousmane Sembene* 74). The Chamber of Commerce and its members thus become emblematic of the state and its leaders. El Hadji's accusations expose not just the impotence of Senegalese businessmen but the political impotence of the newly independent nation.

The images of the abrupt take-over of the Chamber of Commerce by Africans can be seen to stand for the political take-over by Africans that came with independence in 1960. The surrealism of this sequence, not repeated anywhere else in the film, signals an underlying message. The ejection of the political symbols of the colonial order from the Chamber of Commerce suggests the political nature of that message, the surrealism of the sequence that the ejection of those symbols, and indeed of the colonial masters, is not for real.

Once the film is seen as a denunciation of not just the economic but the political regime, the peasant and his pronouncements, introduced into the film, take on their full significance. It is not just that the latest recruit to the Chamber of Commerce robbed a peasant, the entire political economy is geared toward the neglect and even outright exploitation of the peasantry, the large majority of Senegalese citizens, and the most severely deprived.

As Sembène exposes the political system, he also takes aim at its ideology. He ridicules the ideas of *négritude* so closely linked to Senghor, one of the principal founders of the *négritude* movement. The members of the Chamber of Commerce boast about their "*africanité*" as they congratulate El Hadji on his third marriage. And one of the guests at the wedding party tells of his last trip to Europe: he had gone to Switzerland rather than to Spain where there all too many Africans: "*la négritude, hé! ça voyage*" 'negritude, hey, it gets around' is the ironic comment. Masks from distant cultures are used, or rather abused: a Mossi mask from Burkina Faso serves as an object of decoration in the President's office, a Yoruba mask from Nigeria is employed to collect the ballots at the Chamber of Commerce.

Instead of the undifferentiated slogans of *négritude,* Sembène posits a selective approach to both the African and the Western heritage. Rama brings the ideals of such a synthesis alive. She makes do (in the film) with a moped, shakes hands with Modu, El Hadji's driver, refuses to drink Evian water with her father, wears African-style dress, works on the orthography of Wolof, insists on speaking Wolof, and denounces polygamy. The posters in her room claim the heritage of the anti-colonial struggles of Samory Touré and Amilcar Cabral.[19] When she confronts her father in his office, the camera focuses on her dress: it reproduces the national colors, and they match those of a map behind her, a map of an undivided Africa—in contrast to maps of Africa with its borders inherited from colonialism next to her father and at the Chamber of Commerce. The concern she expresses about her mother may also be heard as her concern about mother Africa.

The film ends on a freeze frame, and the viewer is left to imagine what might ensue. If the cleansing ritual rids El Hadji of his *xala,* will his regained potency translate beyond the family in a new role in business? Or in the political arena? If the wretched of the earth, to use the phrase coined by Fanon, can curse and cleanse, are they a political force to be reckoned with? The novel seems to preclude such a revolutionary prospect as the police outside the house raise their weapons into firing position at the end.

How to explain the shift in emphasis from the denunciation of the Senegalese bourgeoisie in the novel to an attack on the political regime and a suggestion of revolt? The threat of persecution or censorship does not provide a ready explanation. In the first decade after independence, and indeed subsequently, the Senegalese authorities tolerated a level of dissent unheard of in most African countries. Whatever Sembène might write, he was unlikely to be subjected to persecution. As for censorship, it was less of a threat to a novel published in France than to a film produced and to be shown in Senegal—as events were to show.

There was, however, another problem: Sembène needed to secure funding to produce the film. He had started out writing a film script. While waiting to find funding for his film, he transformed his script into the novel. Subsequently, from the novel, he developed a new script for the film.[20] Conceivably, a novel that attacked the political regime explicitly would have jeopardized the financial support Sembène was seeking for the film.[21] The Société Nationale de Cinéma had been established in 1972. Two years later four films were released that had been produced with its support, *Xala* among them. Sembène had begun shooting without outside support. In view of Sembène's reputation, the National Film Institute offered a 50% participation without a review of the script. Eventually the Institute financed 60% of the film (Vieyra 87).[22]

A second interpretation for the shift between the novel and the film—and the two explanations are not mutually exclusive—focuses on the different audiences Sembène was seeking to reach. In the early 1960s, Sembène had turned to the film medium so as to reach a wider African audience. In 1968, he had produced *Mandabi* in Wolof, the language widely used throughout most of Senegal. In *Xala,* he introduces some Wolof dialogue and advertises *Kaddu,* omits the translations, explanations, and comment the novel provides for the foreign reader, and makes subtle references to the political context in Senegal that are lost on the foreign viewer. That the film seeks first and foremost to reach a large Senegalese public becomes all the more evident when we take into account the songs which accompany key scenes.

The songs intertwine proverbs, popular sayings, and metaphors. They are sung by the *griot* who accompanies Gorgui, the blind beggar. While the novel and most of the dialogue in the film are in French, the *griot* sings in Wolof. He repeats his songs so that they stay with the audience, or rather, with those audiences that understand them: the songs, unlike the Wolof dialogue, are not subtitled.

The songs constitute a major co-text for Senegalese viewers. Their lyrics, written by Sembène (Ghali 90), sharpen the political message of the film. Outside El Hadji's office, just after Thiely has robbed the peasant, the *griot*'s song chastises the new rulers whose autocratic conception of government is reminiscent of the lizard who brooks nobody else around him:

> A ruler should not be like a lizard. The lizard's character is no good. If you follow him, he complains that you are stepping on his tail. If you walk side by side

with him, he questions your pretense to be his equal. And if you walk ahead of him, you hear him say, you are scaring away my insects.[23]

He sings of the necessity and the inevitability of change, equates inaction with worthlessness, and extols the courage of the lion:

> Instead of crying, you have to find a solution for your
> problems.
> The cursed ones are those whose offspring are worth-
> less.
> For everything there is a season. Everybody will have
> their turn.
> The lion cannot be deprived of the object of his desire
> for lack of
> courage.

As the beggars march to El Hadji's villa to take revenge, the *griot*'s song reenforces the metaphor of the lion whose determination and courage will triumph over the lizard:

> The lion is courageous. The lion is honest. The lion
> cannot be deprived of the object of his desire for lack
> of courage.

The songs move from the denunciation of the lizard, the epitome of autocratic rule, to praise for the lion, the symbol of selflessness and courage, and a revolutionary call for the Senegalese viewers to oppose their ruler.

The authorities let the film be shown in Senegal but imposed ten cuts. Senegalese audiences were not to see the unceremonious removal of the bust of Marianne, the symbol of the French Republic, from the Chamber of Commerce; the Frenchman ordering police to push back the crowd in front of the Chamber; the members of the Chamber opening their attaché cases to find them stuffed with cash; the Frenchman conducting the police raid on the beggars; El Hadji's statement to the members of the Chambers that they had the police and the army in their pockets; Gorgui lecturing Awa that prisoners are happier than peasants, fishermen, or workers; and the call to revolt that closes the film (see Hennebelle). With their censorship the authorities proved false the member of parliament's sarcastic claim, after El Hadji had denounced his fellow members at the Chamber of Commerce, that here they had democracy. Sembène responded by distributing flyers which detailed the scenes that had been cut.[24]

In his novel **Xala,** Sembène introduces the foreign reader to family relations among the Dakar upper-middle class even as he ridicules and denounces these *arrivistes* of early postcolonial days. In his film, Sembène departs from the novel to create powerful images and introduce song. And he recasts his story to reach first and foremost a Senegalese audience. He denounces not only the pseudo-bourgeoisie but also the political leaders in the neocolonial order a decade after independence and calls for revolutionary change.

Sembène has continued to expose and denounce, to present less than flattering mirrors to his two audiences: the Senegalese—and their former colonial masters.

Notes

1. Sembène Ousmane is the name his novels and films usually indicate. We follow here more recent convention in putting his family name last.

2. For a summary of critical comment on the film, see Pfaff (*Twenty-Five Black African Filmmakers* 212-13).

3. In his critical discussion of francophone African films, Michel Serceau mentions *Xala* as one of three films distinguished by greater complexity of characters and plot.

4. The reader/viewer skeptical of the power of the *xala* may detect that Sembène offers an alternative psychological interpretation as well. That El Hadji should be impotent on his wedding night is not all that surprising considering how Rama had denounced his polygamy, how he had been put down by Oumi, how the *badiène* and two of his fellow businessmen had questioned his virility. And El Hadji subconsciously senses the responsibility of the beggars for his affliction—he explodes in anger at the beggars at the very moment he tries to answer the question: who inflicted the *xala* on him?

5. For a study of the Senegalese business world in the late 1960s, see Samir Amin, who emphasizes the neocolonial context. Catherine Boone provides a detailed account of the relationship between business interests and the state up to the 1980s. Of particular interest to the reader/viewer of *Xala* is her account of the political crisis of 1968-70 (165-72) and of the regime's response, which included the promotion of a *rentier* class rooted in ad hoc, speculative, and state-mediated business opportunities (182-97).

One specific response was the transformation of the European-dominated Chambre de Commerce, d'Agriculture et d'Industrie de Dakar into an African-dominated Chambre de Commerce d'Industrie et d'Artisanat de la Région du Cap-Vert, i.e. of the wider Dakar region, in 1969. As in *Xala,* the transition was abrupt, even if it proceeded in a more decorous fashion. At the formal inauguration Léopold Senghor spoke of "our socialism, national and democratic, realistic and humanistic at the same time." There was remarkable continuity between the two bodies in one respect: out of seven, then eight commissions, only one met regularly: it was concerned with imports, i.e., with gaining access to government-controlled opportunities for large legitimate and illegitimate gains (Anon., Diagne and Decupper, and various *Bulletins* of the two Chambers of Commerce).

Film and novel omit altogether the Lebanese community, the third major player in the Senegalese economy to this day.

6. Lucy Fischer and Marcia Landy suggest parallels with films by Luis Buñuel such as *The Discreet Charm of the Bourgeoisie* and *Viridiana.*

7. Apart from the dependency on overseas interests, the film introduces another limitation on Senegalese businessmen. Ahmed Fall is a Mauritanian, a representative of the immigrant group that dominated the retail grocery trade until the riots against Mauritanians in 1989. El Hadji's proposal to establish retail outlets, while a blatant attempt to get his bank to provide him with liquid funds, constitutes also a nationalist project.

8. Sembène here closely echoes a statement made by the Union des Groupements Economiques Sénégalais (UNIGES) in the report of its first congress in 1968: "[Commerce, industry and banking in Senegal] are the *chasses gardées* of foreigners [resting upon] their colonial privileges while Senegalese vegetate in marginal sectors of the economy" (Boone 168). UNIGES had 2,600 members, mainly small-scale traders, transporters, and artisans, and played a major role in the 1968-70 crisis.

9. For detailed discussions of the female characters in the film, see Pfaff, *Cinema of Ousmane Sembene* 150-62 and Petty.

10. Aminata Sow Fall has focused afresh on the condition of beggars in Dakar. The title of her novel *La grève des bàttu ou les déchets humains* uses the very expression, "human rubbish," employed by the President in the film. Fall posits that a beggars' strike is effective, in an Islamic society that prescribes the giving of alms, in countering attempts to evict the beggars from the city's central administrative and business district. Peter Hawkins suggests that Sow Fall took up the topics of poverty and power addressed by Sembène in *Xala* and in *Le dernier de l'empire* not for lack of imagination but to present them from a non-Marxist perspective.

11. The contrast between the political potential of the beggars and the impotence of the bourgeoisie may be related to the contrast between images of life and creativity and images of the lifeless Other in Sembène's novels established by Christiane Ndiay.

12. Sembène's affirmation of the political potential of the *lumpenproletariat* in *Xala* contrasts with the celebration of the force of the proletariat in his *chef-d-œuvre, God's Bits of Wood.* The problems entailed in the latter's classic Marxist analysis (Gugler, "African Literature and the Uses of Theory") may well have induced Sembène to shift to a Fanonesque stance. Or perhaps he would ar-

gue the complementary political role of the workers and the *lumpen.*

13. Only one professional actor participated in the film, Douta Seck in the role of Gorgui, the blind beggar (Pfaff, *Cinema of Ousmane Sembene* 53). Samba Diabaré Samb, a *griot* highly respected in Senegal, took on the role of the *griot* accompanying Gorgui.

14. For a discussion of Sembène's technique, which includes swift cutting unusual in African films, and indeed in his earlier films, see Ukadike 180-81. Mowitt draws attention to Sembène's use of false match on action cuts in order to invert and (con)fuse narrative space. He suggests that the director uses two different syntaxes that correspond to the syntaxes of French and Wolof and that "the specific texture of *Xala* derives from the dense bilingual interplay among French and Wolof 'shots'" (81).

15. The English version of *Xala* further limits the viewer because its subtitles fail to convey whether the characters use Wolof or French and thus withhold information on language use that is central to the story.

16. A total of 23 issues of *Kaddu* were published between 1971 and 1978. They varied in size from 10 to 20 pages. The last issues, in 1976-78, included some material in languages other than Wolof: Pulaar, Seereer, Madinka, and Arabic. Today, major national newspapers carry sections in Wolof and other Senegalese languages every other week.

17. We might expect the novel to confront its foreign readers with a denunciation of their complicity in neocolonialism, and the film to direct popular opposition against the bourgeoisie and the political regime rather than a distant power well beyond its reach. There is a striking parallel here to the later work of Ngũgĩ wa Thiong'o. *Petals of Blood,* published in 1977, describes the emergence of the Kenyan bourgeoisie. Only three years later, *Caitaani Mũtharabainĩ,* expressly written, in language and in style, to be accessible to a broader, local public, embraces the neocolonialism thesis (see Gugler, "How Ngũgĩ wa Thiong'o Shifted"). Perhaps both authors felt that popular wrath is more easily raised against a regime controlled by foreigners, that nationalism is a more potent force than class consciousness.

18. Jesus Christ, as Senegalese referred to Jean Collin, drawing on his initials, was extremely powerful, by all accounts. In Senegal, he elicited strong emotions, for and against. An outside observer, *Jeune Afrique,* offered a quite positive assessment, concluding "But if Jean Collin does not deny his [French] origins, he decided a long time ago to be

Senegalese and to work for Senegal, to the extent that the French no longer consider him one of their own" (Andriamirado 13).

19. With a third poster in Rama's room Sembène pays homage to Charlie Chaplin—and, we may surmise, claims his heritage as film director and as the advocate of the little man. Elsewhere in the house, a poster advertises Sembène's first full-length feature film, *La Noire de.* . . . And in the hallway, a poster of Jimi Hendrix reminds us of the African diaspora's impact on Western music.

20. Vieyra describes the new script as "enriched" (87). Presumably the delay contributed to the complexity of the plot, the diversity in characterizations, and the riches in satirically observed detail. The novel might have benefitted from more of a delay. It appears to have been written in a hurry and to have gone into print without proper editing: the text is marred by non sequiturs and by less than felicitous turns of phrase.

21. The threat that financial support would be withheld and/or the film would be censored appears to have weighed on Sembène when the film was shot. According to Samba Diane, the resemblance between the actor playing the European commanding a police detachment and Collin, who was Minister of the Interior for more than ten years, was too close for comfort: his appearance was changed and the two scenes shot again.

22. If the cuts imposed on *Xala* indicate that the authorities were less than pleased with the product they had cosponsored, they nevertheless provided finance for *Ceddo,* Sembène's next production (Vieyra 95).

23. The text of our translation differs from the summary given by Sembène in an interview (Ghali 90) in phrasing but not in message.

24. According to Sembène, the film was very successful in Senegal, despite the cuts (see Ghali), so successful that nobody drove a Mercedes in Dakar for three months after its release (see Welsh).

Works Cited

Andriamirado, Sennen. "L'homme fort du Sénégal." *Jeune Afrique* 1374 (1987): 4-13.

Amin, Samir. *Le monde des affaires Sénégalaises.* Paris: Editions de Minuit, 1969.

Anon. "Le mystère de la Chambre de Commerce, d'Agriculture et d'Industrie de Dakar." *Africa* 43 (1968): 15-19, 69.

Boone, Catherine. *Merchant Capital and the Roots of State Power in Senegal 1930-1985.* Cambridge Studies in Comparative Politics. Cambridge: Cambridge UP, 1992.

Cruise O'Brien, Rita. "Foreign Ascendance in the Economy and State." *The Political Economy of Under-development: Dependence in Senegal.* Ed. Rita Cruise O'Brien. Sage Series on African Modernization and Development 3. Beverly Hills: Sage Publications, 1979. 100-25.

Diagne, Issa, and Joel Decupper. "La Chambre de Commerce de Dakar va-t-elle continuer à jouer les inutilités?" *Africa* 68 (1974): 29, 31, 35.

Diane, Samba. Personal communication. March 1994.

Fall, Aminata Sow. *La grève des bàttu ou les déchets humains.* Dakar: Les Nouvelles Editions Africaines, 1979.

Fanon, Frantz. *Les damnés de la terre.* Cahiers libres 27-28. Paris: François Maspero, 1961. English trans. by Constance Farrington, *The Wretched of the Earth.* New York: Grove, 1963.

Fischer, Lucy. "Xala: A Study in Black Humor." *Millenium Film Journal* 7-9 (1980): 165-72.

Ghali, Noureddine. "Ousmane Sembène, entretien." *Cinéma* 208 (1976): 83-95. English trans. by John D. H. Downing "An Interview with Sembene Ousmane." *Film and Politics in the Third World.* Ed. John D. H. Downing. Brooklyn: Autonomedia, 1987. 41-54.

Gugler, Josef. "African Literature and the Uses of Theory." *Literary Theory and African Literature. Théorie littéraire et littérature africaine.* Ed. Josef Gugler, Hans-Jürgen Lüsebrink, and Jürgen Martini. Beiträge zur Afrikaforschung 3. Münster: LIT Verlag, 1994. 1-15.

———. "How Ngũgĩ wa Thiong'o Shifted from Class Analysis to a Neo-Colonialist Perspective." *Journal of Modern African Studies* 32 (1994): 329-39.

Hawkins, Peter. "Marxist Intertext, Islamic Reinscription? Some Common Themes in the Novels of Sembène Ousmane and Aminata Sow Fall." *African Francophone Writing: A Critical Introduction.* Ed. Laïla Ibnlfassi and Nicki Hitchcott. Oxford: Berg, 1996. 163-69.

Hennebelle, Guy. "Le cinéma de Sembène Ousmane." *Ecran* 43 (1976): 41-50.

Landy, Marcia. "Political Allegory and 'Engaged Cinema': Sembène's *Xala.*" *Cinema Journal* 23.3 (1984): 31-46.

Mowitt, John. "Sembene Ousmane's *Xala:* Postcoloniality and Foreign Film Languages." *camera obscura* 31 (1993): 73-94.

Ndiaye, Christiane. "Termites et Bouts-de-bois: métaphores de l'Identité et de l'Altérité chez Ousmane Sembène." Paper presented at the Annual Meeting of the African Literature Association, Pointe-à-Pître. 1993.

Ngũgĩ wa Thiong'o. *Petals of Blood.* London: Heinemann, 1977; New York: Dutton, 1978.

———. *Caitaani Mũtharaba-inĩ.* Nairobi: Heinemann, 1980. English trans. by the author, *Devil on the Cross.* London: Heinemann, 1982.

Petty, Sheila. "Towards a Changing Africa: Women's Roles in the Films of Ousmane Sembène." *A Call to Action: The Films of Ousmane Sembène*. Ed. Sheila Petty. Westport: Praeger, 1996. 67-86.

Pfaff, Françoise. *The Cinema of Ousmane Sembene, A Pioneer of African Film*. Contributions in Afro-American and African Studies 79. Westport: Greenwood, 1984.

———. *Twenty-Five Black African Filmmakers: A Critical Study, with Filmography and Bio-Bibligraphy*. New York: Greenwood, 1988.

Sembène, Ousmane. *Les bouts de bois de Dieu: Banty mam yall*. Paris: Le Livre Contemporain, 1960. English trans. by Francis Price, *God's Bits of Wood*. Garden City: Doubleday, 1962.

———. *Xala*. Paris: Présence Africaine, 1973. English trans. by Clive Wake, *Xala*. London: Heinemann, 1976; Westport: Lawrence Hill, 1976.

———. "Filmmakers and African Culture." *Africa* 71 (1977): 80.

———. *Le dernier de l'empire: roman sénégalais*. 2 vols. Paris: L'Harmattan, 1981. English trans. by Adrian Adams, *The Last of the Empire: A Senegalese Novel*. London: Heinemann, 1983.

———. *La noire de . . . (Black Girl)*. Film written and directed by Ousmane Sembène. Paris: Les Actualités Françaises; Dakar: Films Domirev, 1966. Distributed in the US by New Yorker Films.

———. *Mandabi (The Money Order)*. Film written and directed by Ousmane Sembène. Paris: Comptoir Francçais du Film, and Dakar: Films Domirev, 1968. Distributed in the U.S. by New Yorker Films.

———. *Xala*. Film written and directed by Ousmane Sembène. Dakar: Société Nationale de Cinématographie and Films Domirev, 1974. Distributed in the U.S. by New Yorker Films.

Serceau, Michel. "Le cinéma d'Afrique noire francophone face au modèle occidental: la rançon du refus." *iris* 18 (1995): 39-46.

Ukadike, Nwachukwu Frank. *Black African Cinema*. Berkeley: U of California P, 1994.

Vieyra, Paulin Soumanou. *Le cinéma au Sénégal*. Brussels: OCIC/L'Harmattan, 1983.

Welsh, Henry. "Ousmane Sembène: 'Un film est un débat.'" *Jeune Cinéma* 99 (1976): 13-17.

David Murphy (essay date 2007)

SOURCE: Murphy, David. "Fighting for the Homeland? The Second World War in the Films of Ousmane Sembène." *L'Esprit Créateur* 47, no. 1 (2007): 56-67.

[*In the following essay, Murphy examines Sembène's treatment of the period of Vichy French occupation of Senegal during World War II in his films* Emitaï *and* Camp de Thiaroye.]

Towards the end of Ousmane Sembene's film *Emitaï* (1971), set in the Casamance region of southern Senegal during the Second World War, a messenger arrives in a village occupied by the French colonial army, which is there to requisition rice for its men. The messenger brings news of a change in regime in the metropolitan 'center' of the French Empire, resulting in the hasty removal of posters of Marshall Pétain, one of which had stood framed behind the French commander when he had earlier sent the young African conscripts off to war, and their replacement by posters of General Charles de Gaulle. The colonial troops, the *tirailleurs sénégalais,* who had led the conscripts away to the strains of *Maréchal, nous voilà,* are extremely confused at this sudden change of authority, and an indignant, disbelieving *tirailleur* (played by none other than Sembene himself) asks his African NCO to explain how a mere "Général de brigade" could possibly replace a "Maréchal": "Où tu as vu deux étoiles commander sept étoiles?" Sembene thus presents the change in regime from Vichy to Free France as entirely cosmetic, the replacement of one remote image or figurehead by another. It is no coincide that this change in regime occurs just minutes before the film's final sequence, in which the men of the village are gunned down by the colonial troops for refusing to hand over the rice. In essence, the spectator is invited to perceive a fundamental continuity between the colonial policies of Vichy and Free France.

Recent historical analysis by Eric Jennings and Ruth Ginio, amongst others, has produced a rather different picture of Vichy rule in the colonies, and has emphasised the particularly repressive form of colonialism practised by Pétain's government.[1] Historians have long commented on the pivotal role played by the Second World War as a catalyst for decolonization. However, both Jennings and Ginio move beyond the general arguments that the fall of France in 1940, and the subsequent reliance on colonial troops to liberate the 'homeland', simply led to a decline in France's prestige in the eyes of its colonized subjects. In particular, Jennings argues that "the years 1940 to 1944 contributed to decolonization in a much more tangible way, by ushering in a reductionist ideology and a new, harsher brand of colonialism, which both directly and indirectly fuelled indigenous nationalism" (Jennings 2). This article will analyse two films by Sembene that are set during the Second World War, *Emitaï* and *Camp de Thiaroye* (1988),[2] films which, by turns, both contradict and confirm the historical interpretation proposed by Jennings and Ginio. Although Sembene underlines the continuity between colonial rule under Vichy and the Free French, he is nonetheless aware that Vichy permitted the development of a more nakedly racist system, as is illustrated by the opposition between the progressive Captain Raymond and the intransigent local commanders in *Camp de Thiaroye*. However, Sembene's fundamental argument is that France's behaviour in its colonies was a profound betrayal of the allegedly 'universal' prin-

ciples of the French Republic: the excesses and ambiguities of the Vichy period merely served to reinforce
this fact.

Both films focus on the role of the *tirailleurs sénégalais,*
who, despite their name, were in fact drawn from
France's colonial territories right across the continent.[3]
The *tirailleurs sénégalais* are inherently ambiguous figures, for they can be viewed both as the agents of
French colonialism—France's African Empire was
largely built by French officers leading local recruits—
and also as its victims, especially in relation to the First
and Second World Wars, in which the *tirailleurs* gave
their lives for the metropolitan 'homeland', only to rediscover their status as mere colonial subjects once the
war was over. The figure of the *ancien tirailleur* has
long occupied an important place in both African literature and cinema.[4] One of the earliest works in French
by an African author is Bakary Diallo's *Force-Bonté*
(1926), the autobiography of an uneducated Fulani
shepherd who joins the *tirailleurs* and becomes a fervent supporter of France's civilizing mission in Africa.[5]
However, Diallo's text becomes an unconsciously ironic
commentary on French colonial hypocrisy, as he suffers
horrific injuries in the First World War but is refused
citizenship by the country that he had helped to defend.
Undoubtedly, the best-known example of the tragic
tirailleur is the character of *le fou* in Cheikh Hamidou
Kane's masterpiece, *L'Aventure ambiguë* (1961): a man
traumatized by his experience of war in Europe, *le fou*
rejects Western civilization as fundamentally dehumanizing.[6] Prior to *Emitaï,* Sembene had provided two cinematic representations of the *tirailleurs,* which fit this
model of mental trauma and victimhood. In his short
film *Niaye* (1964), Tanor has lost his mind due to the
trauma of his experiences during France's colonial wars
of the 1950s in Vietnam and Algeria; this trauma leads
Tanor, like Kane's character *le fou,* to violence, as he
murders his father, stabbing him to death with the same
efficiency with which he had no doubt killed so many
other 'natives' in Vietnam and Algeria. After the murder, there follows a dream sequence in which he imagines the village overrun by armoured cars, infantrymen,
and even parachutists. A more benign but equally tragic
image of the *tirailleur* is to be found in Sembene's first
short film, *Borom Sarret* (1962). In the film's tense climax, the cart driver is stopped by a policeman and
asked for his papers. As he takes the papers from his
pocket, a military medal falls to the ground. As the cart
driver reaches for the medal, we see in close-up the policeman's boot stamp down upon it, followed by a cut
to a low-angle shot of the cart driver looking up at his
tormentor standing over him with the high-rise homes
of the bourgeoisie in the background. His earlier sacrifices for the 'homeland' mean nothing to the new elites
of the post-independence regime. From these brief examples, it thus becomes clear that the *tirailleurs
sénégalais* have often been deployed as a conduit
through which to explore the nature and legacy of

French colonialism in Africa, and their role in both
world wars has been central to this process.

Emitaï and *Camp de Thiaroye* are the two films in
which Sembene makes the most sustained attempt to
examine the significance of the Second World War in
the decolonization of French West Africa. Both films
are centred on so-called *bavures* committed by the colonial army in Senegal: the colonizer attempts to present
such violence as an aberration, whereas, for Sembene,
it is symptomatic of colonial rule as a whole.[7] *Emitaï* is
based on a number of incidents that took place in
Casamance in 1942, in which troops murdered peasants
who refused to allow their rice harvest to be requisi-
tioned. *Camp de Thiaroye* focuses on a specific incident that took place on 1 December 1944 at the
Thiaroye demobilization camp just outside Dakar: a
dispute arose with the military authorities over their refusal to pay the African troops the same level of
demobilisation pay as their white, French counterparts,
leading the *tirailleurs* briefly to take a hostage in the
form of the head of the French West African army;
thirty-five *tirailleurs* were massacred and hundreds of
others wounded in a brutal reprisal by the army.[8] Depicting massacres that took place under both Vichy and
Free French rule, Sembene seeks explicitly to represent
what he views as the fundamental continuity in colonial
practice. This blurring of the boundaries between Vichy
and Free France is particularly evident in *Emitaï,* as
Sembene himself acknowledges:

> Je n'ai pas voulu indiquer la date exacte à laquelle les
> événements se déroulent. C'est aux alentours de 1942-
> 43-44. On ne sait si c'est au moment de la prise de
> pouvoir par de Gaulle au Sénégal ou en France. Ce que
> j'ai voulu suggérer c'est que pour nous Africains il n'y
> a pas de différence entre les deux régimes. Nous étions
> toujours des colonisés. Les méthodes, certes, ont
> quelque peu changé mais l'objectif était toujours de
> maintenir l'Empire Français. On l'a bien vu après la
> libération de la France: c'est dans le sang qu'ont été
> étouffées les revendications africaines à Thiaroye au
> Sénégal, à Grand-Bassam en Côte d'Ivoire, à Sétif et
> Guelma en Algérie, à Madagascar, pour ne rien dire
> d'Indochine.[9]

This desire to blur events leads to a certain number of
historical inaccuracies. For example, at the beginning of
the film, the conscripted African troops are sent off to
war in Europe, whereas, in fact, the many troops conscripted under Vichy saw service in Africa itself. More
worryingly, Sembene has the French commander declare, standing before a poster of Pétain, that "La France
est en guerre contre l'Allemagne," which, of course,
makes no sense in historical terms, since Pétain's regime began with France's surrender and its acceptance
of a German victory. However, the lack of historical accuracy in Sembene's film should not be taken as proof
of a cavalier attitude towards history; on the contrary,
Sembene would argue that his films represent the fundamental historical 'reality', which cannot be gleaned

through a naturalistic representation of the 'facts' (an argument to which I will return in the conclusion to this article).

The thematic connections between the two films are reinforced by a specific intertextual reference in *Camp de Thiaroye* to the events depicted in *Emitaï*. The Western-educated, civilized, and urbane Senegalese NCO, Sergeant-Major Diatta, who is originally from Casamance, is shocked to discover from his uncle that his parents have been killed by French troops in a massacre at Effok (one of the historical incidents upon which Sembene based *Emitaï*). The liberal French commander, Captain Raymond, attempts to explain the incident as a *bavure* resulting from the excesses of Vichy, but a newly radicalized Diatta equates the massacre at Effok with the Nazi atrocities at Oradour-sur-Glane (where the Nazis wiped out an entire village in retribution for an attack by the Resistance), an assertion that Raymond simply cannot accept. However, the films present quite different versions of the *tirailleurs*: the loyal servants of Empire that we see in *Emitaï* become its tragic victims (and the agents of an incipient anti-colonialism) in *Camp de Thiaroye*. I will examine the significance of this shift in Sembene's representation of the *tirailleurs* in greater detail below.

Emitaï is a slow, almost meditative film, which examines the difficulties faced by the Diola people of Casamance in coming to terms with what they perceive as their abandonment by their gods who have allowed the French to steal their food and take their sons away to fight in foreign wars. It opens with scenes of young Diola men on a lonely dirt road being captured by *tirailleurs* and, subsequently, conscripted into the colonial army bound for Europe. From the start, Sembene thus depicts the army as a repressive presence, which forces allegiance through violence. However, it is significant that there is a also a (tragi-)comic element to this sequence: the *tirailleurs* pounce from the long grass on a series of unsuspecting victims in almost slapstick fashion. Rather than the imperial rhetoric of France's Empire uniting as one against the enemies of the 'homeland', we are presented with makeshift attempts to coerce a hostile local population into supporting France's war effort. Sembene deliberately chooses to ignore those (such as himself) who volunteered to fight for France, for his aim is to make his audience reflect upon the ambiguity of French colonial practices. The white commander sends the troops off to war with the grimly ironic words "vous êtes des engagés volontaires"; the scene later jumps forward to the present as the camera pans over the war memorial in central Dakar, which features a *tirailleur* standing alongside a white, French soldier. Sembene casts his film as an invitation to the audience to go beyond such simplistic memorializing of the colonial regime in order to search for the repressed history of Empire.[10]

The film is primarily concerned with the political radicalization of women; it is they who constitute the main opposition to the colonial army, a fact comically underlined when a young girl forces a *tirailleur* to retreat, as she playfully grabs hold of his rifle. The conscription of the young men of the village leads the chief Djiméko to conclude that they must abandon their fatalistic belief in the will of the gods who, he claims, have abandoned them. He leads his men into battle against the French, only to be quickly defeated with Djiméko himself mortally wounded. After his demise, the men return to their former passivity, thus causing the women of the village to take up the mantle of resistance when the French return a year later to requisition their rice. The women hide the rice and the army punishes them by obliging all women and children in the village to sit exposed in the burning heat of the midday sun. Both the *tirailleurs* and the men of the village are presented as upholders of the colonial status quo: they accept the fact of French domination and, in their very different ways, collaborate in the exercise of colonial oppression.

The *tirailleurs* are unambiguously cast as the willing agents of colonialism. Although the troops are led by two white, French commanders, it is significant that all of the troops are Africans, and Sembene does not flinch from illustrating the soldiers' role in upholding colonial authority. The film concludes with an act of colonial violence in which the *tirailleurs* gun down the men of the village who refuse to carry the rice for them. The camera shows the *tirailleurs* in profile with guns pointing at the villagers off-screen; as the screen fades to black, we hear the sound of gunfire. *Emitaï* was made in the context of ongoing anti-colonial struggles, particularly in Lusophone Africa—in 1971, neighbouring Guinea-Bissau was still engaged in a bitter war of independence with the Portuguese. Any form of 'collaboration' with the colonial powers is unequivocally viewed as a betrayal of African independence.

However, by the late 1980s the situation had changed radically: the continent had been freed from direct colonial rule, and there was a growing willingness to explore more of the ambiguities of colonialism. Consequently, in *Camp de Thiaroye* Sembene presents the *tirailleurs* as not only victims of colonialism but also active agents of anti-colonial resistance. The film is set in an army camp established for African troops returning from the war in Europe. Sembene makes an explicit visual link between the demobilization camp and the concentration camps of Nazi Germany through the character of Pays, a man who has suffered deep psychological scars and been rendered mute by his time in Buchenwald.[11] Significantly, it is Pays who first discovers the barbed-wire fence enclosing the camp, which had previously been invisible due to the blinding white light created by the sun on the sandy landscape. While the other men settle into their quarters, Pays approaches the camp boundary. He is filmed from behind in a medium-distance shot, and is thus framed against the barbed-wire fence, which gradually becomes visible. Subsequently, there is a cut to a low-angle shot in medium close-up with the camera outside the fence looking up at Pays framed more clearly against the barbed-wire. The camera zooms in towards Pays' face and then follows his gaze, as he turns to look at four watchtowers at each corner of the camp. These subjective shots convey the sense of unease felt by Pays, which is heightened by the extra-diegetic sound of a haunting blues played on the harmonica. As the scene progresses, there is a medium shot of Pays running his hand along the barbed-wire, which then cuts to a close-up of the hand itself as it gently touches the barbs (see opposite). The sense of menace has increased, with the spectator expecting Pays to cut his fingers as he tenses his hand open and closed on the fence. The tension is broken by the arrival of the Corporal, Pays' closest friend, who picks up a handful of soil, which he then pours over Pays' hand. Taking the troubled soldier's hand in his own, the Corporal comforts him like a child, reassuring him that he has now returned to African soil and that the horrors of Buchenwald are behind him. His words succeed in calming Pays but the camera tells another story: as they walk back towards the barracks, the camera frames them both against the barbed-wire and the viewer is presented with a premonitory glimpse of the *tirailleurs* as prisoners rather than soldiers.

Unlike in *Emitaï* there is absolutely no indication that these *tirailleurs* have been conscripted into the army; on the contrary, the film is at pains to stress their allegiance to France and the sacrifices that they have made on behalf of *la patrie*. However, their experiences upon returning to Africa after their contribution to the liberation of the French 'homeland' disabuse them of their illusions about the Empire. The most remarkable (and complex) way in which Sembene presents the *tirailleurs'* resistance to colonial domination is by creating visual and narrative links between these African soldiers and the German army. These links underline the neglected fact of African suffering at the hands of the Nazis, but they also illustrate the keen awareness amongst the *tirailleurs* that their imperial masters had been subjugated by a more dominant power, which had led to France itself becoming a 'colonized' nation, subject to the indignities routinely meted out to Africans. For example, the Corporal often lapses into German when he is angry; he upbraids the chef over the poor quality of the food served to the *tirailleurs,* and he insults a driver who almost runs over two of his men. However, the most powerful link to the German army is created through the visual motif of Pays' SS helmet. The ambiguous symbolism of the helmet is demonstrated in the scene that immediately follows Pays' discovery of the barbed-wire fence. Two *tirailleurs* walk towards the fence in order to hang out their wet clothes to dry (an act that would render innocent that which, moments earlier, had appeared menacing), but their

path is blocked by Pays (in the foreground of the shot), who is now wearing an SS helmet and a great-coat. This sequence is followed by a cut to a profile shot of Pays with the imposing watchtower in the background. Day turns to night as he turns to look up at the watchtower, and there is a dissolve into black and white images from the Second World War. A German soldier peers through a pair of binoculars; then, we see three still shots of dead concentration camp prisoners hanging from or lying behind barbed-wire fences; these images are accompanied by the extra-diegetic rattle of machine-gun fire. Once again, the viewer is given a premonition of the bloody fate that awaits the *tirailleurs*.

This link between Nazi Germany and the French colonial regime in Africa contains clear echoes of the ideas elaborated by Aimé Césaire in his polemical anti-colonial essay, *Discours sur le colonialisme* (1955). For Césaire, Europe's exploitation of Africa during the slave trade and subsequently under colonization was no different from Hitler's exploitation of Europe:

> Oui, il vaudrait la peine d'étudier, cliniquement, dans le détail, les démarches d'Hitler et de l'hitlérisme et de révéler au très distingué, très humaniste, très chrétien bourgeois du XXᵉ siècle qu'il porte en lui un Hitler qui s'ignore, qu'Hitler l'*habite,* qu'Hitler est son *démon,* que s'il le vitupère, c'est par manque de logique, et qu'au fond, ce qu'il ne pardonne pas à Hitler, ce n'est pas *le crime* en soi, *le crime contre l'homme,* ce n'est pas *l'humiliation de l'homme en soi,* c'est le crime contre l'homme blanc, c'est l'humiliation de l'homme blanc, et d'avoir appliqué à l'Europe des procédés colonialistes dont ne relevaient jusqu'ici que les Arabes d'Algérie, les coolies de l'Inde et les nègres d'Afrique.[12]

Attempts to create a moral equivalence between Nazism and colonialism are, of course, fraught with danger and, in particular, risk occulting the specific ideologies, practices, and contexts that shaped them both. However, the basic point made by both Sembene and Césaire remains an extremely pertinent one: the dominant narrative of the Second World War as a battle between the *good,* democratic nations of Europe and the *bad,* fascistic ones is a simplification that appears all too apparent when viewed from the perspective of France's colonial possessions.

The *tirailleurs sénégalais* who fought for the colonial 'homeland' during the war are subsequently denied the same rights as French citizens and are forced to return to their role as mere colonial subjects. This reduction in the men's status is powerfully conveyed by Sembene in the scene in which the *tirailleurs* are obliged to part with the US army uniforms that they had been given for their return home. (The fact that the French must rely on the US for handouts is another indication of the decline in their colonial prestige.) These uniforms carry significant symbolism for the men: they are a badge that marks them out as veterans of the war in Europe; they also, temporarily, remove the men's inferior colonized status. However, the colonial army disapproves of its *indigènes* rising above their station and, although the *tirailleurs* are due to be demobilized within days, they are forced to replace their American uniforms with the distinctive red *chéchia* and white shorts of the standard *tirailleurs'* uniform, one which infantilizes them and restores the image of the *bon enfant* of *Y'a bon Banania* fame. Literally and symbolically, the men are obliged to don their former servile identity. The camera lingers on the pile of boots and trousers that the *tirailleurs* cast upon the ground; then, as Pays queues to receive his uniform, the haunting harmonica tune returns and the looming presence of the watchtower casts its shadow over the men.

Camp de Thiaroye depicts its soldiers developing a pan-African sensibility and undergoing a political radicalization: they learn that the promise of assimilation and equality that France offered to its colonial subjects is quite simply an illusion. As the historian Myron Echenberg writes: "To the ex-POWs the authoritarian manner in which they were being treated was a bitter reminder that they were returning home to an unchanged colonial system, unappreciative of the great sacrifices they and their fallen comrades had made" (Echenberg, *Conscripts,* 101). To compound matters for these war veterans, their integrity and loyalty are being questioned by white, French officers who had spent the war out of harm's reach in the colonies (a fact underlined on several occasions in the film). In order to gain equality, they are obliged to engage in active resistance against the French army, which will lead to brutal retribution.

According to the historical record, the 'mutinous' *tirailleurs* were gunned down by loyal troops, who killed 35 of their number and wounded many others. However, Sembene chooses to depart from historical accuracy; in the film, the massacre is carried out by unseen aggressors in armoured vehicles who rake the camp with machine-gun fire and shells under cover of the dead of night. Understandably, some commentators have taken issue with Sembene's decision to depart from the 'facts'. More bitingly, the critic Kenneth Harrow argues that Sembene alters the facts in order to fit the binaristic, Marxist, and pan-Africanist worldview that characterizes all of his work.[13] For Harrow, Sembene's classic realist film style refuses ambiguity in favour of narrative certainty in which the film's message is at all times evident to the audience. While I concur with Harrow's judgement that *Camp de Thiaroye* is at times a rather schematic film, whose drama is weakened by the overdetermined binaries within its narrative structure, I disagree fundamentally with his views both on the realism of Sembene's cinema and the nature of realist art in general. Harrow's article associates "the classic realist system" with a generalized "dominant ideology," and he asserts that "[t]he contemporary Western critic must

refuse all forms of dominant discourse, even those employed so brilliantly and with such anti-colonial passion, by Ousmane Sembène" (Harrow 152). In effect, Sembene is cast as an old-fashioned modernist-realist who believes in simplistic notions of Truth and Reality, the implication being that 'we' have all moved beyond such illusions and should now embrace the ambiguity and ambivalence that are central to postmodern/poststructuralist thinking.

On a very basic level, the idea that Sembene's binaristic thinking leads him to hide the fact that those who carried out the massacre were themselves Africans is deeply misleading: throughout the film, we are made aware that the camp is guarded by African soldiers who man the gates and the watchtowers; moreover, as we saw earlier in *Emitaï,* it is the *tirailleurs* who fire on the unarmed peasants at the close of the film, which indicates that Sembene was more than aware of the 'ambiguity' of colonial violence. Indeed, ironically, one might argue that *Camp de Thiaroye* in fact embraces a greater degree of ambiguity than *Emitaï,* for it marks an attempt to understand those who had in the high nationalist period of the 1960-70s been vilified as the willing servants of empire.

In order to challenge the main thrust of Harrow's critique of Sembene, it is necessary to examine in greater depth the precise nature of the filmmaker's work and the political-aesthetic choices that he makes. The postmodern/poststructuralist turn in critical thinking over the past few decades has encouraged a rejection of binary thinking in favour of the exploration of ambiguity and ambivalence. While acknowledging the invaluable corrective value of such work, which attempts to counter the intellectual shortcuts taken by certain reductive forms of political criticism, it can often seem that ambiguity, the inbetween, the hybrid, have become the necessary components of any 'right-thinking' text, in the same way that political resistance was once deemed an artistic and critical necessity in a previous era. However, by what criteria are binary oppositions inherently wrong? As Timothy Brennan has remarked in relation to the writings of Amilcar Cabral, the independence leader of Guinea-Bissau (a man whom Sembene admired greatly):

> [T]he dialectic of colonizer and colonized was simply not supposed to represent either a sociological explanation or a nuanced cultural model [for Cabral]. It was itself a focus—that is, a careful exclusion. He was not lumping difference together, nor was he unaware of multiple communities with their disparate interests. He did not emphasize the disparate because it would not then, in that project, have led to more than the impossibility of doing.[14]

Similarly, if Sembene deploys Manichean oppositions in his work, it is not because he is unaware of other positions, it is because he is attempting to mobilize people behind his vision of Africa's past, present, and future; his representations of the French colonial powers in *Emitaï* and *Camp de Thiaroye* are the most caricatured in his entire *œuvre*, but even in these cases he nevertheless presents the 'opposing' camp of the colonized in a comparatively complex fashion, highlighting internal conflicts based on gender (*Emitaï*) and loyalty to the colonial powers (*Camp de Thiaroye*). His work thus constitutes a fascinating example of a cinema that engages in the strategic use of binaries, but which is nonetheless consistently aware of the limits of fixed notions of identity and culture. Equally, the classification of his films as realist does not do justice to the full range of his filmmaking. Although the primary register of his films is often one of closely observed realism, they often contain symbolic, non-realistic or non-linear sequences, a process that is particularly pronounced in his films of the 1970s. Sembene's notion of realism is not, as is often argued, governed by a naturalistic sense of verisimilitude; on the contrary, his work is deeply informed by the Brechtian notion of realism as the deployment of form in the fashion that is most effective in revealing the fundamental reality of a situation. Semebene's films are thus a creative intervention into political and historical debates, bringing about what Charles Forsdick (via Glissant) has termed a "transformation-through-representation."[15] In the willed amnesia of the post-colonial era, Sembene challenges the official discourse of Empire and invites both Africa and France to uncover its shared history:

> On ne fait pas une histoire pour se venger, mais pour s'enraciner. Voilà pourquoi nous avons fait ce film pour le monde entier et non pas pour une race; c'est pour que vous sachiez que les noirs ont participé à la guerre, et que nous n'avons pas fini avec notre histoire qui est aussi la vôtre.[16]

The *tirailleurs sénégalais* who participated in the Second World War did so for two homelands, and it is this fundamental ambiguity that Sembene charts in these two films.

Notes

1. Eric T. Jennings, *Vichy in the Tropics: Pétain's National Revolution in Madagascar, Guadeloupe, and Indochina, 1940-1944* (Stanford, CA: Stanford U P, 2001); Ruth Ginio, *French Colonialism Unmasked: The Vichy Years in French West Africa* (Lincoln: U of Nebraska P, 2006).

2. For a more detailed analysis of both films, see David Murphy, *Sembene: Imagining Alternatives in Film and Fiction* (Oxford: James Currey; Trenton, NJ: Africa World Press, 2000), chapter 6.

3. By far the best work on the *tirailleurs sénégalais* is Myron J. Echenberg's *Colonial Conscripts: The "Tirailleurs Sénégalais" in French West Africa,*

1857-1960 (London: James Currey; Portsmouth, NH: Heinemann, 1991). Sembene was himself a *tirailleur,* who saw action in Europe in the final years of the Second World War.

4. For a comprehensive account of literary representations of the *tirailleur,* see Janos Riesz, "La 'Folie' des tirailleurs sénégalais: fait historique et thème littéraire de la littérature coloniale à la littérature africaine de langue française," in J. P. Little and Roger Little, eds, *Black Accents: Writing in French from Africa, Mauritius and the Caribbean* (London: Grant and Cutler, 1997), 139-56.

5. Bakary Diallo, *Force-Bonté* (1926; Paris: Nouvelles Éditions Africaines, 1985).

6. Cheikh Hamidou Kane, *L'Aventure ambiguë* (Paris: 10/18, 1961).

7. Charles Forsdick traces the history of representations of the colonial massacre in his article, "*Ceci n'est pas un conte, mais une histoire de chair et de sang:* Representing the Colonial Massacre in Francophone Literature and Culture," in Lorna Milne, ed., *Postcolonial Violence, Culture and Identity in Francophone West Africa, the Maghreb and the Antilles* (Frankfurt: Peter Lang, 2007), forthcoming.

8. The best account of the incidents at Thiaroye is to be found in Myron J. Echenberg, "Tragedy at Thiaroye: The Senegalese Soldiers' Uprising of 1944," in Peter C. W. Gutkind, Robin Cohen, and Jean Copans, eds., *African Labor History* (Beverly Hills, CA, London: Sage, 1978), 109-28.

9. Guy Hennebelle, "Ousmane Sembène: 'En Afrique noire nous sommes gouvernés par des enfants mongoliens du colonialisme,'" *Les Lettres Françaises* (6-12 October 1971), 16.

10. The continued existence of an 'official' French version of colonial history was underlined by the French army's attempts to block the release of both films.

11. For two recent attempts to chart the experience of black people of different nationalities imprisoned by the Nazis, see Clarence Lusane, *Hitler's Black Victims* (New York: Routledge, 2003); Serge Bilé, *Noirs dans le camps nazis* (Paris: Le Serpent à Plumes, 2005).

12. Aimé Césaire, *Discours sur le colonialisme* (Paris: Présence Africaine, 1955), 12.

13. Kenneth W. Harrow, "*Camp de Thiaroye:* Who's That Hiding in Those Tanks and How Come We Can't See Their Faces?", *iris,* 18 (1995), 147-52.

14. Timothy Brennan, *At Home in the World: Cosmopolitanism Now* (Cambridge, MA: Harvard U P, 1997), 3.

15. Forsdick, "*Ceci.*"

16. Samba Gadjigo *et al.*, eds., *Ousmane Sembène: Dialogues with Critics and Writers* (Amherst: U of Massachusetts P, 1993), 83.

FURTHER READING

Criticism

Aguiar, Marian. "Smoke of the Savannah: Traveling Modernity in Sembène Ousmane's *God's Bits of Wood*." *Modern Fiction Studies* 49, no. 2 (summer 2003): 284-305.

Argues that the Sembène's depiction of the railway system and the bodies of the Senegalese workers who built the system serves as a metaphor for the African anticolonial movements that began in the 1940s.

Jones, James A. "Fact and Fiction in *God's Bits of Wood*." *Research in African Literatures* 31, no. 2 (summer 2000): 117-31.

Examines differences between Sembène's fictional depiction of the 1947-48 railway strike in French West Africa in his novel *God's Bits of Wood* and the event's description in historical documents of the era.

Rapfogel, Jared, and Richard Porton. "The Power of Female Solidarity: An Interview with Ousmane Sembene." *Cineaste* (winter 2004): 20-5.

Interview in which Sembène discusses issues affecting women in contemporary Africa, including female genital mutilation, polygamy, and economic empowerment.

Additional information on Sembène's life and career is contained in the following sources published by Gale: *Black Literature Criticism*, **Ed. 1:3;** *Black Writers*, **Eds. 1, 3;** *Contemporary Authors*, **Vol. 125;** *Contemporary Authors—Brief Entry*, **Vol. 117;** *Contemporary Authors New Revision Series*, **Vol. 81;** *Contemporary Literary Criticism*, **Vol. 66;** *Contemporary World Writers*, **Ed. 2;** *Literature Resource Center*; **and** *Major 20th-Century Writers*, **Ed. 1.**

Ntozake Shange
1948-

(Born Paulette Linda Williams; also known as Ntozake Shange) American dramatist, novelist, poet, essayist, and children's writer.

For additional information on Shange's career, see *Black Literature Criticism,* Ed. 1.

INTRODUCTION

Shange is best known for her first dramatic production, the award-winning *for colored girls who have considered suicide / when the rainbow is enuf* (1975). A unique blend of poetry, music, dance, and drama, the play is often referred to as a "choreopoem," or "staged poetry." In her dramas, novels, and poetry—which are often amalgamations of a variety of literary forms and media—Shange draws heavily upon her experiences as a black female in America to write innovatively and passionately about racial, political, and feminist issues. She is particularly noted for her dramatic representations of African American women, and for her strong opposition to any discrimination—whether it be racial, sexual, or political—against them in American society. She has received mixed critical reaction both to the ways in which she foregrounds the intersection of race and gender oppression in the experiences of African American women, and for her depictions of the relationships between black women and men. While Shange focuses on the pain of their experiences, her characters maintain a sense of triumph over their circumstances, often through discovering their inner strength and in celebrating friendships with other women.

BIOGRAPHICAL INFORMATION

Shange was born in 1948 in Trenton, New Jersey, to Paul T. Williams, an air force surgeon, and Eloise Owens Williams, a psychiatric social worker and educator. The eldest of four children, she spent her childhood with her family in upstate New York and in St. Louis, Missouri. Hers was an intellectually and aurally stimulating childhood: the family traveled to such foreign destinations as Cuba, Haiti, Mexico, and Europe. Shange's mother was an avid reader, sharing with her children the major works of the African American canon, while her father was a drum player who at one time had his own band, loved the rich and varied musical expression of Africa. As a result of their parents' interests, the Williams children came into frequent con-

tact with many of the foremost black intellectuals and musicians of the time, including Dizzy Gillespie, Chuck Berry, Miles Davis, and W. E. B. DuBois. Shange attended Barnard College in New York and graduated with honors in 1970. She received an M.A. in American Studies in 1973 from the University of Southern California, Los Angeles. During college she went through a period of depression after separating from her first husband, attempting suicide several times before focusing her rage against society's treatment of black women. In 1971, when she was in graduate school, she changed her name to Ntozake Shange (which in Zulu means "she who comes with her own things / she walks like a lion") as a way of reaffirming her personal strength based on a self-determined identity, and as a means of connecting with her African roots. Throughout her career as a writer, performer, and director, she has taught courses in women's studies, creative writing, drama, and related subjects at colleges and universities across the United States, including the City College of the City University of New York, the University of Houston, the University of Florida, and Villanova University. Among the numerous awards she has received for her work are the 1992 Paul Robeson Achievement Award, the 1993 Living Legend Award from the National Black Theatre Festival, and the Pushcart Prize. In 2004 Shange suffered a stroke, which affected her ability to write.

MAJOR WORKS

The controversial and dramatic choreopoem *for colored girls* is the work which has defined Shange's career and reputation. Nominated for Tony, Emmy, and Grammy Awards in 1977, *for colored girls* won the Outer Circle Critics Award as well as several Obie Awards. The play, which began as a series of poems that were eventually incorporated into a single dramatic performance, presents a strong feminist statement on behalf of black women. The production is structured as a series of vignettes relayed through the poetic soliloquies, dialogue, stories, and chants of seven black actresses. These vignettes incorporate music, dance, and poetry, as each woman conveys painful experiences such as rape, illegal abortion, violence, and troubled relationships. The message of the play is ultimately hopeful, as Shange's characters conclude that African American women should look to a female god within themselves for strength, and appreciate that the "rainbow" of their own color is powerful enough to sustain them. While also emphasizing the poetic monologue, *Spell #7* (1979) has a more conventional narrative than *for colored girls,* in that the characters interact with one another in the context of a semi-developed storyline. The production's nine characters in a New York bar discuss the racism black artists contend with in the entertainment world. At one point, the all-black cast appears in overalls and minstrel-show blackface to address the pressure placed on the black artist to fit a stereotype in order to succeed. Shange's Obie Award-winning *Mother Courage and Her Children* (1980) was adapted from the Bertolt Brecht drama. While the original play was set in seventeenth-century Europe, Shange situates her characters in the post-Civil War era in the United States, where African American soldiers are employed to aid in the massacre of Native Americans in the West. Mother Courage supports herself by selling wares to white people, without concern for the moral implications of her actions.

After the production of *Mother Courage,* Shange began to concentrate on writing novels and poetry. She experimented with the conventions of fiction writing with her first full-length novel, *Sassafrass, Cypress, and Indigo* (1982), which was adapted from Shange's novella entitled *Sassafrass* (1976). Written in a pastiche style that includes recipes, magic spells, poetry, letters, and other written texts, the novel centers on sisters who find different ways to cope with their love relationships. Sassafrass is a weaver who cannot leave Mitch, a musician who abuses drugs and beats her. Cypress, a dancer in feminist productions, struggles against becoming romantically involved. Indigo, the youngest sister, retreats into her imagination, befriending her childhood dolls, seeing only the poetry and magic of the world. The novel *Betsey Brown* (1985) focuses on a middle-class adolescent girl in St. Louis in the late 1950s, when American schools were first integrated. Betsey, the main character, is bussed to a predominantly white school, where she is confronted for the first time with racial difference.

In *The Love Space Demands,* a choreopoem published in 1991, Shange returned to the blend of music, dance, poetry, and drama that characterized *for colored girls.* The volume includes poems on celibacy and sexuality, on black women's sense of abandonment by black men, on a crack-addicted mother who sells her daughter's virginity for a hit, and a pregnant woman who swallows cocaine, destroying her unborn child, to protect her man from arrest. Shange's 1994 novel, *Liliane,* again finds the author exploring the issues of race and gender in contemporary America. In the work, Liliane Lincoln undergoes psychoanalysis in an attempt to better understand the events of her life, during which she forms brief, sexual relationships with men, mourns the deaths of childhood friends, and travels in pursuit of artistic inspiration and wisdom. Shange's poetry, including *Nappy Edges* (1978), *Some Men* (1981), *A Daughter's*

Geography (1983), and *Ridin' the Moon in Texas* (1987), share with her plays and novels a concern with the experiences of African American women and a nontraditional use of language which captures the rhythms of Black English speech patterns. In the 2004 collection *The Sweet Breath of Life,* Shange combined poetry with photographs by the Kamoinge Workshop (a group of African American photographers) in an homage to *The Sweet Flypaper of Life,* which was published in 1955 by poet Langston Hughes and photographer Roy DeCarava. Beginning in the 1990s Shange expanded her oeuvre to include children's books. Among these are *Float Like a Butterfly* (2002), about boxer Muhammad Ali; *Daddy Says* (2003); *Ellington Was Not a Street* (2003); and *Whitewash* (1997), about a young African American girl who is traumatized when a gang attacks her and her brother on their way home from school and spray-paints her face white.

CRITICAL RECEPTION

Discussion of *for colored girls* has revolved around the play's unique theatrical form of the "choreopoem," its use of Black English, and the politics of race and gender which it expresses. Many reviewers have celebrated the play's innovative form, which defies the traditional, linear act/scene structure, and have praised its theatricality, linguistic style, and representation of African American experience. Other commentators, however, have found the production offensive, calling the playwright racist based in part on her unsavory depictions of black men, who are viewed as obstacles to the social and spiritual freedom of black women. Critical judgment of her work as a whole has focused in part on Shange's innovative linguistic style. Many reviewers have admired the lyrical quality of her dialogue, but others have found the inventive language to be an impediment, especially for readers of Shange's poetry and novels, who encounter spelling variations, irregular punctuation, and lowercase letters. Many other observers have emphasized the musicality of her dramas, suggesting that Shange incorporates African-based nonverbal actions like dance, song, poetry, and ritual in order to preserve and maintain ties to the black community's African culture and heritage. Her poetry, too, has been compared to jazz in such elements as its improvisation of repeated refrains and themes and Shange's use of linguistic syncopation. Her focus on the experience of black women in particular is a theme that runs through much critical commentary. In general, she is applauded for offering realistic and passionate renderings of female African Americans, depicting their imperfections as well as their strengths. She is applauded for her attempts to tear down stereotypes that devalue and diminish them, and for offering works that affirm their significance and worth.

PRINCIPAL WORKS

for colored girls who have considered suicide / when the rainbow is enuf: A Choreopoem (drama) 1975

Sassafrass (novella) 1976

Natural Disasters and Other Festive Occasions (poetry and prose) 1977

A Photograph: A Still Life with Shadows / A Photograph: A Study of Cruelty (drama) 1977; revised as *A Photograph: Lovers-in-Motion* 1979

Nappy Edges (poetry) 1978

Boogie Woogie Landscapes (drama) 1979; revised as *Black and White Two-Dimensional Planes* 1979

Spell #7: A Geechee Quick Magic Trance Manual (drama) 1979

Mother Courage and Her Children [adapted; from the drama *Mother Courage and Her Children,* by Bertolt Brecht] (drama) 1980

Some Men (poetry) 1981

Three Pieces: Spell #7; A Photograph: Lovers-in-Motion; Boogie Woogie Landscapes (dramas) 1981

Sassafrass, Cypress, and Indigo (novel) 1982

A Daughter's Geography (poetry) 1983

From Okra to Greens: Poems (poetry) 1984

See No Evil: Prefaces, Essays and Accounts (essays) 1984

Betsey Brown: A Novel (novel) 1985

Ridin' the Moon in Texas: Word Paintings (poetry) 1987

Three Views of Mt. Fuji (drama) 1987

Betsey Brown: A Rhythm and Blues Musical [with Emily Mann] (play) 1989

The Love Space Demands: A Continuing Saga (poetry) 1991

I Live in Music (poetry) 1994

Liliane: Resurrection of the Daughter (novel) 1994

Whitewash (for children) 1997

If I Can Cook You Know God Can (essays) 1998

The Beacon Best of 1999: Creative Writing by Women and Men of All Colors [editor] (poetry, short stories, and essays) 1999

Float Like a Butterfly: Muhammad Ali, the Man Who Could Float Like a Butterfly and Sting Like a Bee (for children) 2002

Daddy Says (for children) 2003

Ellington Was Not a Street (for children) 2003

The Sweet Breath of Life: A Poetic Narrative of the African-American Family (poetry) 2004

Wild Flowers [with David Murray] (poetry) 2006

CRITICISM

Philip U. Effiong (essay date 1994)

SOURCE: Effiong, Philip U. "The Subliminal to the Real: Musical Regeneration in Ntozake Shange's *Boogie Woogie Landscapes.*" *Theatre Studies* 39 (1994): 33-43.

[*In the following essay, Effiong discusses music, dance, and ritual as significant modes of African nonverbal ex-* pression, *and examines how these art forms function as instruments of healing and spiritual redemption in* Boogie Woogie Landscapes.]

The basis for Ntozake Shange's poetic style—her choreopoem—is apparent in her insistence that Black writers revive "the most revealing moments from lives spent in nonverbal activity," since it is through nonverbal activity—music, song, dance/movement, ritual— that "black people have conquered their environments / or at least their pain."[1] To preserve this ceremonial ideal, Shange creates a liberated stage space in which theatrical styles and themes are explored, overcoming the limitations of dialogue and realism. She relies on indigenous folklore by applying ritual and ceremony— "the way we worship"—to her drama.[2] Separating these components would deny African-Americans a theatrical heritage emphasizing collective participation, celebration, and action-inducing genres. To ignore them, Shange observes, would be to sell "ourselves & our legacy quite cheaply / since we are trying to make our primary statements with somebody else's life / & somebody else's idea of a perfect play."[3]

Shange recommends revising stereotypes of Blacks as singers and dancers, rather than discarding them. As Margaret Wilkerson has noted, African music, with "its complex, phonetic reproduction of words and its polyphonic and contrapuntal rhythmic structures," offers creative material for African-American dramatists seeking "new ways of conceptualizing music as an element of drama."[4] Shange seems to share this view as well as that of Barbara Ann Teer who believes that, as powerful religious forces, music and dance explicate Black people's spiritual and primal well-being.[5]

The presence of dance, song, music, poetry, and ceremony in Shange's work dramatizes a continuity of culture from Africa to Black America, citing Africa as a distant but "accessible" homeland and identity source. Assessing Shange's technique, Elizabeth Brown-Guillory writes: "not only did she popularize the choreopoem, but she brought to the American theater an art that is undeniably African."[6] Shange's drama is committed "to recuperating marginalized folk traditions of 'New World' Africans and of women in general."[7] Her choreopoem sustains the vibrant theatrical form that she prescribes and initiates a revolutionary phase in the African-American quest for a functional theatre.

In redesigning a non-linear dramatic pattern that distorts an oppressive language and dialogue tradition, Shange obscures the progression of action and character. Her adherence to non-linearity is rooted in her belief that drama can relay diverse, though related, themes through several voices and individual representations. In searching for new theatrical forms, Shange creates a musical quality offering its audience a "reverie" of the type commonly relayed during a musical performance.[8] Shange suggests:

we demolish the notion of straight theater for a decade or so. refuse to allow playwrights to work without dancers and musicians / 'coon' shows were somebody else's idea / we have integrated the notion that drama must be words / with no music & no dance / cuz that wd take away the seriousness of the event / cuz we all remember too well / the chuckles & scoffs at the notion that all niggers cd sing & dance / & most of us can sing & dance / . . . this is a cultural reality. this is why i find the most inspiring theater among us to be in the realms of music & dance.[9]

Music and dance in Shange's drama function as in traditional African performance. Apart from retaining ties with Africa, dance, like music, serves as a cathartic and freeing agent—a defense mechanism. Recalling her dance training in San Francisco, Shange claims:

> with dance I discovered my body more intimately than I had imagined possible. With the acceptance of the ethnicity of my tights & backside, came a clearer understanding of my voice as a woman & as a poet. The freedom to move in space . . . insisted that everything African, everything halfway colloquial, a grimace, a strut, an arched back over a yawn, waz mine.[10]

To fully explore Black nonverbal resources, Shange endorses a theatre of "more than verbal communication," one that appeals to all the physical senses and celebrates the "interdisciplinary culture" of Black Americans.[11] Reconstructing standard English usage, Shange uses language to bolster her theatrical liberty. She does not use a Black English or idiom comparable to Ebonics.[12] Instead, she applies a colloquial, metaphoric, rhythmic style that complements the musicality of her drama. Shange's English is not "Black," it is a personal construct avouching her own cultural, dramatic, and feminist self. She liberates herself from the language of her oppressor. After the production of *Spell #7* in 1979, Shange responded to a New York reviewer who claimed that she had done the English language much damage:

> the man who thought i wrote with intentions of outdoing the white man in the acrobatic distortions of english waz absolutely correct. i cant count the number of times i have viscerally wanted to attack deform n maim the language that i waz taught to hate myself in . . . being an afro-american writer is something to be self-conscious abt / & yes / . . . i haveta fix my tool to my needs / . . . so that the malignancies / fall away / leaving us space to literally create our own image.[13]

Sandra Richards notes how the women of Shange's *for colored girls who have considered suicide / when the rainbow is enuf* can "bypass through music and dance, the limitations of social and human existence."[14] Music, movement and song "convey layers of sensate information lying beyond or outside linguistic, cerebral dimensions of the brain."[15] Playwrights like Shange "find in music a second language that gives expression to profound anguish and joy of their vision and experience . . . finding in the dissonant tones of black music a powerful expressive mode."[16] Not always utilitarian,

Shange's music punctuates action with *life,* fashioning a *total* theatre that appeals to all the senses, stimulating audience involvement.

BOOGIE WOOGIE LANDSCAPES[17]

Structured on the boogie-woogie—a piano-playing method evolving from jazz and blues, and sometimes described as "up-tempo" blues[18]—Shange's *boogie woogie landscapes* (1979) is an expressionistic and fantasy representation filtered through the random thoughts, reveries, visions, hopes, "combat breath," internal conflicts and memories of the play's single "real" character, layla. The notion of boogie-woogie as speeded-up blues reflects the play's rendition of the central character's thought process in quick succession. Dealing with correlating themes in different parts of *landscapes,* Shange deviates from the traditional beginning, middle, and end arrangement, presenting her subject matter via the spontaneous thought process of the boogie-woogie. Her approach foregrounds random unresolved themes of color, racism, sexism, and ignorance, all of which filter through layla's mental state. Hope is eventually, but subtly, foreseen in the efficacy of music.

An adaptation of the choreopoem, *landscapes* resembles *colored girls* in its use of unreal, symbolic characters;[19] de-emphasis on dialogue; flashbacks; episodic renditions; and portrayal of themes and subthemes in imagistic monologues. As in *colored girls,* major themes center around Blacks, especially Black women and girls. Unlike *colored girls,* however, "characters" here are not only women; there are men who interact with women, and there are occasional instances of actual dialogue. So, *landscapes* is not a choreopoem in the original sense displayed in *colored girls.* This slight shift in form shows a gradual, though not strictly chronological, progression from the choreopoem to other forms, creating space to explore varied themes and skills.

While *landscapes* is technically set in layla's bedroom, the real "landscape" lies within her head. This mental process, both conscious and unconscious, grows out of a hostile racist and sexist setting and is relayed in quick, stream-of-consciousness succession, suggesting speed and kinesis. The caustic revelations handed out by layla are surprisingly direct. As Shange notes, the voices of layla's "unconsciousness" are "unspeakable realities / for no self-respecting afro-american girl wd reveal so much of herself of her own will / there is too much anger to handle assuredly / too much pain to keep on truckin / less ya bury it."[20]

Shange's unique structure shocks her reader / audience into appraising the consequences of racial abuse and the macabre results of violating women. Layla is conditioned by a racist discourse which sees America in terms of two main colors, denying her the opportunity to recognize and pursue numerous colors—the vast resources that comprise human existence. Addressing this problem, night-life companion (n.l.c.) #2 points out that "she never thought people places or ideas were anything / but black & white."[21] N.l.c. #1 further explains the insecurities, fears, and restraint of this color dilemma in layla's life: "her most serious problem is how / to stop walking on this road the / color of pitch / . . . she is trapped in black & white / without shadows / she cannot lean against anything / the earth has no depth because she cannot hold it" (114). Layla's life is empty and without substance. Although she attempts to go beyond black and white, she remains obsessed with the limitations of color and the dissonance that comes with this obsession. She either "howls / for anything red" or she "wd have a fierce yellow" (115). A restrictive color-conscious life generates self-hatred in layla who periodically detests the fact that she is Black. Her phobia for her Black self is exhibited in her constant belief that she stains anything she touches "with grime" and "a furrow of slate fingerprints" with which "she made things black" (115). N.l.c. #6 observes: "she didnt want anything as black as the palms of her hands to touch her" (115).

Layla's attempts at escaping her insecurities are relayed through flashback and mime by the n.l.c.s. While her goals are worthwhile, they are subsumed in her passion for colors. In her desire to learn more, she carries out a bizarre ritual in which she eats books, gothic novels, and "the black & white pages" of newspapers, remaining confined to her perceptions of black and white (116). While "reading" does not provide escape from layla's color-stifled life, she finds new hope in a spiritual realm when she discovers Jesus. Through Christ she seems to find a huge range of unexplored "dimensions / & hope, . . . horizons . . . different dawns" (117). For once, layla recognizes and relates to a variety of colors, accepting herself without fear and with excitement: "she studied the legs & arms of herself / the hair & lips of herself / before the burst of spirit let her hold herself" (116-7).

But layla's immersion in religion is a bland exercise devoid of profound liturgic healing. For one, she cannot escape her entrapment in color concepts. Such experimentation with "jesus" fails to erase the racist and sexist mutilations on her psyche or the psyches of her degenerate, loveless family. Her gnarled rite-of-passage away from fulfillment evolves into a nightmarish desire to save her family and Black people from the shackles of color which repress her. The n.l.c.s. express this dilemma when they recall a violent racist attack on layla's brothers and sisters. At this point, the optimistic color images associated with layla's religious gambit revert to discordant images, expunging any possibility for religious growth. Once again she becomes the black-staining organism devoid of racial confidence. Increasingly captivated by images of blood—"scarlet" and "red"—she desperately attempts to rescue the "little black things" who are "charred" by "scrawny cheap

white men" (118). The abuse and subsequent reduction of layla's siblings to a less-than-human state is reiterated in her allusion to them as "little black things." This racist attack merges the discordant images of color with the dehumanizing effects of hate on the individual and the family. As the n.l.c.s reenact the White supremacist chant—"niggahs / niggahs / go home / go home / niggahs!" (118)—the ultimate feeling of alienation is aroused, even as layla tries in vain to reassure her brothers and sisters. Again, colors evoke the permeating disenchantment. While orange and yellow are metaphors for hope, such optimism is eclipsed by more volatile and bloody images elicited by red and scarlet which comprise "a cacophony of colors" (119).

A deeper appraisal of layla's arduous and degenerate family life occurs in a flashback acted out by n.l.c.s #1, #2, and #3. Within the family, layla is introduced to racism, police harrassment, and the division of the world into colored and white. The task of raising children is left in the hands of a tiring, hostile grandma because mommy and daddy are rarely present; "mommy" finally leaves the madhouse because she cannot cope with her mischevious children and the several maids hired to stabilize her family. Within this labyrinth, layla learns to steal and peek at Regina, a maid, when she has sex with Roscoe. She learns to accept another maid, Carrie, as her role model since her own parents fail to offer her the incentive she desperately needs. She is crushed, therefore, when Carrie goes to jail for cutting someone. Memories of past family life come to this vehement halt, fitting well into the abrasive climate of the drama.

The gruesome impact of a life of racial entrapment, family disintegration, and self-hate induces a chain reaction where the simple ability to appreciate love is lost even while it is coveted. In a brief drama where n.l.c. #4 expresses love toward layla, using imagery-rich poetry to eulogize her beauty, layla's responses exemplify the loss of human affection. She incessantly reminds n.l.c. #4 that her humanity is sucked dry by race, color, violence, and sexual tensions. Her depraved history is a heavy load that she cannot shed: "i am sometimes naked / but mostly i wear my past / the pinafores & white socks that shamed me" (122). Subsumed within this debauched, bloody epoch, layla grows to accept her background as normal: "i sleep more easily now / my love in that scarlet cup" (122).

While, on one level, layla's rejection of n.l.c. #4's advances implies her self-denial of basic human traits, Shange extols this denial as a vital step toward resisting sexual molestation. Incensed by n.l.c. #4's love overtures, two women, n.l.c. #1 and n.l.c. #3, approach layla with a range of aggressive proposals for deterring rapists, proposals already being executed in "cuba where rape is treason" (123).

More poignant attention is paid to the plight of women—girls in particular—when issues of infibulation, clitorectomy, forced marriage, polygamy and incest are raised. Shange expands her theme to include Black women and women / girls from a variety of backgrounds. Her language is straightforward and coarse:

> societies usedta throw us away / or sell us / or play with our vaginas / cuz that's all girls were good for. at least women cd carry things & cook / . . . i wish it waz gd to be born a girl everywhere / then i wd know for sure that no one wd be infibulated / . . . infibulation is sewing our vaginas up with cat-gut or weeds or nylon thread to insure our virginity . . . we've been excised. had our labia removed with glass or scissors . . . we've lost our clitoris because our pleasure is profane & the presence of our naturally evolved clitoris wd disrupt the very unnatural dynamic of polygamy . . . we're sewn-up / cut-up / pared down & sore if not dead / & oozing pus / . . . & STILL . . . afraid to walk the streets or stay home at night.

> [135]

Using n.l.c. #3, Shange's sermon on the mental, physical, and social agony informing female sexual desecration voices a ritual of terror and distress in which girls are ultimate losers. Their defilement is compounded by their susceptibility to family estrangement, death, and blame. More disconcerting is the truth that "attackers / molesters & rapists . . . are proliferating at a rapid rate" and, on too many occasions, they "like raping & molesting their family members better than a girl-child they don't know yet" (136).

Female victimization persists in the ritual climb from girl to woman. In a scene where n.l.c. #3, as layla, is depicted as having undergone the passage from girl to wife, images of death and decay explicate her condition. Her husband, n.l.c. #4, describes their children as "ghost children . . . swallowed / like placenta / . . . when you rear yr young in dark closets" (136). The family is in a wretched state and layla, now bereft of her father, mother, and sisters, bears the majority of its burden, laboring to attend to her husband and children's needs. n.l.c. #4 admits:

> like a stray cat she waited on me . . . she leaned / over steaming laundry / the baby the father / & the graves . . . she waited / her hair so heavy / her head hung down to fondle the baby / warm the baby.

> [136-7]

Shange merges racism and sexism as two variations of a single phenomenon. In concentrating on gender matters, she momentarily drops her manipulation of color symbolism, refocusing on the general decay in human values. Events filtering through layla's consciousness and unconsciousness expand beyond African-American society to embrace humanity. The world is portrayed as hypocritical, pretentious, and spiritually-deficient. The daily "elegance" that we witness and appreciate is a shadow of the real depreciation: "elegant hoodlums / el-

egant intellectuals / . . . elegant derelicts / elegant surgeons / elegant trash. elegant priests / elegant dieticians / elegant nymphomaniacs / . . . elegance. elegance. elegance" (140).

In her final chant, layla's insightful alliance with the musicians and n.l.c.s provokes her awareness of a pervasive desire for harmony. She discerns the human tendency to engage in "struggle" and "merge in our eccentricity / this penchant for the right to live" (141). At the end of *landscapes* layla's trust is embedded in the attainment of a spiritual realm represented by music. Dance and music are restorative instruments of hope, strength, and the communication of key moods and tensions. Out of the six n.l.c.s four are required to sing, move and / or dance well. Layla also entertains "a trio of musicians . . . who reflect her consciousness . . . [and who] side with the night-life interlopers, attempting to refine layla's perceptions of herself and her past," rather than just entertaining her (113). The musicians and n.l.c.s suggest the presence of spirits and this fantasy dynamic evolves into concrete reality as they constantly move around and "thru the walls" of layla's bedroom (113). In this ritualized arena, the spiritual and natural worlds merge.

Music pervades the drama as a theatrical and uplifting device; it reclaims a sacred mode, healing and transcending the mundane world. At the beginning of *landscapes,* layla returns from a disco accompanied by her background theme song. She hints at music as a redeeming symbol:

> dontcha wanna be music / . . . dontcha wanna be daybreak & ease into a fog / a cosmic event like sound / & rain
>
> . . . . .
> like when a woman can walk down gold street feeling like she's moved to atlantis . . . it's what we call a marin intrusion interlopin visions & deities findin the way home cuz we dont recognize what's sacred anymore

> [113]

The refrain of "music," "fog," "cosmic event," and "rain" resurfaces throughout the play. Music is repeatedly alluded to as a source for deliverance, the only factor in the play that comes close to regaining a lost spirituality: "music offers solace / offers some kinda way to reach out / to ring bells on gold street / . . . to be free / in truth / in silence" (120).

To heighten the role of music as a participatory ceremony for change, the n.l.c.s take part in an orgiastic fanfare during which they completely immerse themselves in music as they dance, sing selected songs, chart the development of musical forms from "neo-afrikan" to "rock n roll," and mark the significance of artists like

Sun-Ra and Ike Turner (126-9). The ceremony substantiates the sacred role of music, a role that dogmatic religion does not accomplish: "shall i go to jonestown or the disco? / if jesus wont fix it / the deejay will" (138). Shange implies that, perhaps, mind and body will find salvation in the blending of music and the divine. As n.l.c. #1 puts it: "at the disco we shout the praises of the almighty / i wrap my arms around you till the end" (139). On their own, music and the divine are deficient. At the disco there is the potential to "dance myself to death" while isolated religion becomes little more than a series of downcast, barren screams: "shout hallelujah / praise the lord / shout hallelujah / praise the lord" (140). Rather than completely discredit Christianity, Shange underscores the integral need to reconstruct its structure by applying the recuperative role of music so that the religion addresses and appeals to the sensibilities and sociopolitical needs of Black people.

Music is not only a symbol, it is a pathway to the type of ceremonial drama that Shange endorses. This drama will shun trivialities and advance viable themes, just as Shange calls for the news media to eschew petty information and focus on issues like Zimbabwean independence, the isolation of White South Africans, and the education of African-American children (125-6). Music does not provide total regeneration in *landscapes,* but it remains the cardinal metaphor for ritual growth and freedom, the type of freedom Shange anticipates for all girls:

> right now being born a girl is to be born threatened; i
> want being born a girl to be a cause for celebration /
> cause for protection & nourishment of our birthright /
> . . . we pay for being born girls / but we owe no one
> anything / not our labia, not our clitoris, not our lives.
> we are born girls to live to be women who live our
> own lives / to live our lives. to have / our lives / to
> live.

[136]

CONCLUSION

Shange is a gifted dramatic poet whose feminist rhetoric blends with her entrancing musical poetry to mold a fascinating style and powerful vision. She harmonizes music, dance, poetry, and movement to express her views on the effects of racism, sexism, poverty, and spiritual decay on women, Blacks, relationships, art, and life's energies. Shange is pivotal to a growing socioartistic trend in which women of color "assert their very presence . . . become warriors raging against their own invisibility."[22]

Shange makes pronounced contributions to the Black Aesthetic and its efforts to break down conventional walls. Sandra Richards observes that Shange's deviation from conventional realistic styles is influenced, in part, by Artaud's "Theatre of Cruelty" and Baraka's "Black Revolutionary Theatre." Like both artists, Shange exhibits "a locus for emotionally charged, eruptive forces which assault social complacency to expose victims who, nevertheless, contain within themselves seeds of their own regeneration."[23] The religio-ritualistic role of music is germane to the attainment of this "emotional charge."

Music, dance/movement, and song are used profoundly "as spirit-forces . . . [which] amplify, contradict, or reaffirm the spoken word."[24] Such African-based nonverbal tools ritualize Shange's drama and guide her ritual participants—both players and observers—to new insights. This ritual approach to Black drama, a concept promoted in the 1960s, borrows and reapplies the sacred, spiritual, and communal significance of traditional African performance in a new setting. The process harmonizes with E. T. Kirby's description of indigenous African dramatic ritual as "abstract or symbolic actions arranged in a pattern and progression that approaches closer to that which is fundamentally ritual as it becomes more highly controlled and precise in execution."[25] Shange equally displays a penchant for discarding concepts of time and space as she conveys random and fragmented, yet controlled and coherent thoughts.

Moments of possession are attained as Shange's themes, language, visual and musical effects arrest the senses of her audiences, startling them into consciousness. This overall ritual impact is sustained in the incantatory and telegraphic properties of her intense musical poetry, confirming Jane Splawn's point that poetry contributes to "a more ritualistic effect than is achieved through the use of naturalistic/realistic dialogue."[26] While Shange confronts critical themes, she also mourns the loss of a strong, indigenous, religious culture which her theatre strives to recover.

Notes

1. Ntozake Shange, "Unrecovered Losses / Black Theatre Traditions," *The Black Scholar* 10 (July-August 1979): 7-9.

2. Ntozake Shange, Interview, *In the Memory and Spirit of Frances, Zora, and Lorraine: Essays and Interviews on Black Women Writing,* ed. Juliette Bowles (Howard, Washington D.C.: Institute for the Arts and the Humanities, 1979) 24.

3. Shange, "Unrecovered Losses," 8.

4. Margaret Wilkerson, "Music as Metaphor: New Plays of Black Women" in *Making a Spectacle: Feminist Essays on Contemporary Women's Theatre,* ed. Lynda Hart (Ann Arbor: University of Michigan Press, 1989) 62.

5. Barbara Ann Teer, Interview, *Blacklines* 2 (Spring 1973): 25.

6. Elizabeth Brown-Guillory, *Their Place on the Stage: Black Women Playwrights in America* (New York: Greenwood Press, 1988) 41.

7. Sandra Richards, "Under the 'Trickster's' Sign: Towards a Reading of Ntozake Shange and Femi Osofisan" in *Critical Theory and Performance,* ed. Janelle Reinelt and Joseph Roach (Ann Arbor: University of Michigan Press, 1992) 68.

8. Shange, *Memory and Spirit,* 23.

9. Shange, "Unrecovered Losses," 8.

10. Shange, Preface, *for colored girls who have considered suicide / when the rainbow is enuf* (New York: Macmillan, 1975) xv-xvi.

11. Shange, "Unrecovered Losses," 8.

12. Ebonics is a combination of "ebony" and "phonics" or "Black Sounds." Popularized in the 1970s, Ebonics embraces the verbal, nonverbal, and gestural communicative patterns systematically employed by African-Americans.

13. Ntozake Shange, Foreword, *Three Pieces* (New York: St. Martin's Press, 1981) xii.

14. Sandra L. Richards, "Conflicting Impulses in the Plays of Ntozake Shange," *Black American Literature Forum* 17 (Summer 1983): 73.

15. Richards, "Conflicting Impulses," 76.

16. Wilkerson, 62.

17. Capitalization of titles and character names are consistent with those in Shange's published versions of her work.

18. Ortiz M. Walton, *Music: Black, White and Blue* (New York: William Morrow and Company, 1972) 31.

19. Layla is "attended" by six night-life companions (n.l.c.'s)—three women and three men—who represent her dream memories.

20. Shange, *Three Pieces,* xiv.

21. Ntozake Shange, *boogie woogie landscapes* (1979) in *Three Pieces* (New York: St. Martin's Press, 1981) 114. All subsequent references are to this edition.

22. Mary K. DeShazer, "Rejecting Necrophilia: Ntozake Shange and the Warrior Re-Visioned" in *Making a Spectacle: Feminist Essays on Contemporary Women's Theatre,* ed. Lynda Hart (Ann Arbor: University of Michigan Press, 1989) 87.

23. Richards, "Conflicting Impulses," 76.

24. Richards, "Conflicting Impulses," 76.

25. E. T. Kirby, "Indigenous African Theatre," *The Drama Review* 18 (December 1974): 24.

26. Jane Splawn, "Rites of Passage in the Writing of Ntozake Shange: The Poetry, Drama, and Novels" (Ph.D. diss., University of Wisconsin, 1988) 100.

Josephine Lee (review date December 1999)

SOURCE: Lee, Josephine. "Performance Review: *for colored girls who have considered suicide / when the rainbow is enuf.*" *Theatre Journal* 51, no. 4 (December 1999): 455-56.

[*In this review of the June 1999 Penumbra Theatre Company production of* for colored girls who have considered suicide / when the rainbow is enuf, *Lee offers a mixed assessment of the "multiracial" casting of the seven female characters, which included Asian Americans, African Americans, and one Latina actress.*]

By the time Ntozake Shange's Obie-winning *for colored girls who have considered suicide / when the rainbow is enuf* received national acclaim, in productions first at the Public Theater and then the Booth Theater on Broadway in 1976, its seven women characters were all played by African American actresses. But Shange described "the energy & part of the style that nurtured *for colored girls*" as inspired by, among other things, the multiracial feminist writing collectives in San Francisco during the early 1970s [Shange, *for colored girls* New York: Scribner, 1977), p. x]. Penumbra Theatre Company's production of *for colored girls* took these roots to heart, choosing three African Americans, two Asian Americans, and one Latina to sing different variations on "a black girl's song." By choosing a multiracial cast, director Kym Moore put a different spin on the terms of being "colored," opening up Shange's lyrical choreopoems to suggest their common terms of oppression, poverty, and racism, and showing that "bein' alive and bein' a woman and bein' colored is a metaphysical dilemma."

To its great credit, the production did not assign its parts indiscriminately; this perhaps might be better termed "color-sensitive" than "color-blind" casting. For the most part, the specific "color" of the actress merged with the characterization, adding complexity to a specific role rather than disguising the realities of race. African American actresses Aimee Bryant and Sharon Cage respectively performed rhapsodic reminiscences of sexual initiation on "graduation nite" in a New Jersey factory town and the story of a childhood adoration of Toussaint L'Overture. The poem **"somebody almost walked off wid alla my stuff,"** received a dynamic performance by Signe Harriday in the style of a black sermon. In one of the play's most interesting moments two Asian American actresses, Sun Mee Chomet and Jeany Park, enacted Shange's depiction of "the passion flower of southwest los angeles." Their casting transformed the story of a predatory woman who wears "orange butterflies & aqua sequins" to lure her male conquests into a more specific commentary on the exotic and sexualized stereotypes of the "Oriental" woman.

However, at times this choice of multiracial casting fell flat or became disorienting. Shange's choreopoem takes its force not only from the beauty of its poetry, music, and dance but also from its creation of an extraordinary sense of intimacy with its characters. This delicate familiarity rests in part on the assumption that only particular bodies are privy to certain experiences and can speak these lives truthfully. Occasionally, the production reminded us how difficult it is to translate specific and individual embodiments across the lines of racial and cultural difference: in moments, for instance, when an Asian American actress described her family as "just reglar niggahs with hints of spanish" or when actresses failed to render the rhythms of Shange's poetry without lapsing into patently artificial accents.

Other inconsistencies with the production were the fault of specific movement and design choices rather than casting. Sharon Cage's powerful rendition of "abortion cycle #1" was limited by trapping her in a large blue hemisphere (a multi-purpose receptacle also used in a number of other scenes), which reduced her body language to awkward and restricted pantomime. In the "latent rapists" sequence, the characters delivered their lines as if speaking at a tea party; again, an overly stylized effect ruined the power of Shange's disturbing poetry, rendering the confidential testimonial of "bein' betrayed by men who know us" too alienating. Movement and a use of crude gestural mimicry unfortunately became equally distracting in the "sechita" sequence. And the ending chorale's use of a circular translucent scrim that rose around the actresses became a gratuitous special effect.

At the same time, these momentary lapses did not interfere with a moving and honest set of performances, particularly in the second half. The best of these again reminded us of the play's roots in "an articulated female heritage & imperative" [Shange, xi]. Although the play does feature memorable diatribes against male abusers and oppressors, it idealizes women's relationships with other women in an equally compelling way. This note of colored feminist solidarity was sounded repeatedly through the production. Cast members murmured constant words of support for one another's stories. When the characters mourned "i usedta live in the world / then i moved to HARLEM," an image of "women hangin outta windows / like ol silk stockings" was accompanied by a smile rather than a pang of grief. And in the poem **"pyramid,"** which describes the desire felt by three friends for one faithless man, the poem concluded with the three women, played by Jeany Park,

Sharon Cage, and Julie Estrada, consoling one another. Momentarily, they froze in a tableaux with heads resting on one another's laps, a vision of "love like sisters."

Some of the production's most effective moments occurred towards the play's end. The ensemble's performance of "no more love poems" exemplified the force that Shange's melding of dance and poetry might have. By the time each member of the ensemble intoned that her love was too beautiful / sanctified / magic / Saturday nite / complicated / music "to have thrown back on my face," the entire theater beat to the rhythm of their words and feet. Likewise, the final harrowing solo, "a night with beau willie brown," received a heartbreakingly vivid performance by Sun Mee Chomet that left spectators in stunned silence. Chomet's vocal and physical expressiveness—demonstrating both great control and wild painful abandon—got to the heart of this story of brutal degradation and tragedy. This cathartic moment was followed by the final "laying on of hands," that ended the play on a more optimistic note of self-discovery: "i found god in myself / & i loved her / i loved her fiercely."

The Penumbra production gave a new face to Shange's first work for theatre, but preserved the vigor, intensity, and vitality that distinguished this groundbreaking piece. The enduring beauty and power of Shange's artistic imagination was not all we took away from this production of the play. The stories of hardship, emotion, endurance, and hunger for self revived by these seven colored women still very much speak to the unfortunate realities of today.

Carol Marsh-Lockett (essay date 1999)

SOURCE: Marsh-Lockett, Carol. "A Woman's Art; A Woman's Craft: The Self in Ntozake Shange's *Sassafras, Cypress, and Indigo.*" In *Arms Akimbo: Africana Women in Contemporary Literature,* edited by Janice Lee Liddell and Yakini Belinda Kemp, pp. 46-57. Gainesville: University Press of Florida, 1999.

[*In the essay below, Marsh-Lockett explores how Shange connected music, weaving, and dance with the exploration of African American female identity in the novel* Sassafras, Cypress, and Indigo.]

> *"If Black women don't say who they are, other people will and say it badly for them."*
>
> (Christian xii)

In the last lines of her choreopoem *for colored girls who have considered suicide / when the rainbow is enuf,* Ntozake Shange's characters declare the ultimate affirmation of their personhood: "i found god in myself / & i loved her / i loved her fiercely" (63). Such a potent utterance posits a viable solution to the problematic spiritual and psychological existence of African American women who have been forced to confront the vicissitudes of life in America and their particularly hostile implications for African American women from the seventeenth century to the present. Marginalized, therefore, by the triple hazard of gender, race, and class, the African American woman has continually been forced to define herself, to struggle against the stereotypes of mammy, matriarch, and jezebel to name herself and her place in society—indeed, the universe.

Ntozake Shange is one of several African American artists and intellectuals who have deconstructed the stereotypes. Confronting the inherent contradiction between the ideologies of womanhood and the devalued status of African American women, she has created works ultimately undergirded by a troubling and painful realization that in spite of the western patriarchal myth that women are supposed to be on a pedestal, African American women, left to the devices of larger society, are mistreated and assigned, as Zora Neale Hurston has written, the status of mules. She has, however, like the earliest of African American literary foremothers, continued in the tradition of countering the negative impact of life in America by developing or defining an African American female self—one that is not constricted by the influence and dictates of a white male power structure or its shadow, African American male prescriptions and assumptions. Thus, by defining and describing in her own terms an African American female experience and identity, Shange, who claimed her own power and personhood by renaming herself from Paulette Williams, suggests through her art that the African American woman derives her power through loving and claiming the divine in herself and expressing herself in her own terms. Shange's choice of the Zulu names— *Ntozake* ("she who comes with her own things") and *Shange* ("she who walks like a lion")—attests to her embracing and affirming her own power. More significantly, however, her name change and general aesthetic herald an evolution in the empowerment of African American women writers from the nineteenth century, when the polemic of the novel sought to appeal to the moral sense of white readers, to the current trend in the late twentieth century when African American women's novels address the African American community and a large African American female readership. For, like most contemporary African American female writers, Shange renders a distinct African American female self in all of its idealized and flawed dimensions.

Shange's **Sassafras, Cypress, and Indigo** is an example of an African American female text that identifies as its locus of power an African American sisterhood rather than white readers. Centered on a family of Charlestonian women, the novel is a verbal mosaic and a study in lyricism that celebrates womanhood, life, and art. As Barbara Christian observes, Shange "consciously uses a potpourri of forms primarily associated with women: recipes, potions, letters, as well as poetry and dance rhythms, to construct her novel" (185). In addition, she laces the novel with Afrocentric motifs and incorporates lush, powerful, and utilitarian vegetation imagery (sassafras, cypress, and indigo) in naming her major characters and in so doing shapes reader expectations of the strength, rootedness, and value of African American womanhood.

The novel has, moreover, a middle-class focus. The omniscient narrative voice is middle class and would seem to reflect cadences of Shange's own Paulette Williams background. Shange has, therefore, been able to easily portray the artistic and middle-class orientation of Hilda Effania and her three daughters as they discover themselves, define their womanhood, and work through the dynamics of the mother-daughter relationship. Further, the work is middle class in that it subordinates working class concerns to the artistic experience and at points in the text approaches but never embraces art for its own sake. But in so doing, the novel examines the quality of African American women's lives in the face of racism and sexism. For throughout the novel, despite their heightened spirituality and artistic sensibilities, the Effania women encounter instances of racism and sexism. Nevertheless, we can contrast the vivid portrayal of proletariat issues raised in much of African American literature, such as Richard Wright's *Native Son* or Ann Petry's *The Street*. A great achievement in the novel, then, is Shange's ultimate displacement of the European notion of art for art's sake with the traditional African perception of art's serving a functional and spiritual purpose in people's (here, Black women's) lives.

The artistic expression of the middle-class ethos comes through a triple plot structure in which there are three centrally linked stories, each exploring a sister's voyage into self-discovery through the medium of art. The three plots, in turn, are linked through the return structure of the mother-daughter relationship that is reminiscent of the pattern described by Myer Abrams in *Natural Supernaturalism*. This, according to Abrams, is a pattern that takes its philosophical origins from Hegel and Schelling, a structure that is aided in its support of the narrative by Shange's use of the arts, in this case, three—weaving, music, and dance. It is Shange's use of the arts metaphor in the exploration of African American female selfhood that I intend to examine in this essay.

In the novel, weaving occupies a central position, for it is the symbol of the mother-daughter relationship, and it maintains the unity of the novel. It also functions, as it has in much of Western literature, as a symbol of creation and life, of multiplicity and growth. We are reminded of the three fates: Atropos, who carried the shears and cut the thread of life; Clotho, who carried the spindle and spun the thread of life; and Lachesis, who carried the globe and scroll and determined the length of life. Weaving is a universal activity found also, for example, in African culture where, as opposed to European culture, it is not a gender-specific activity. However, in this instance, Shange transforms the motif and makes weaving a distinctly African American female activity and a means of exploring the essential self.

Early in the novel, weaving is a symbol of maturity or womanhood. It is, for example, an activity pursued by Hilda, Sassafras, and Cypress and does not include the prepubescent Indigo. We are told, "If the rhythm was interrupted, Sassafras would just stare at the loom. Cypress would look at her work and not know where to start or what gauge her stitches were. Mama would burn herself with some peculiarly tinted boiling water. Everybody would be mad and not working, so Indigo would be sent to talk to the dolls" (7). Weaving, here, becomes a nonverbal expression of sisterhood and a shared activity between women.

In the symbolism of weaving, we also find an exploration of Hilda Effania's consciousness and value system. For her, weaving is a source of joy and is the dominant motif of motherhood. Weaving features largely, for example, in the Christmas celebration in the Effania household. When the girls are home for Christmas, Hilda is weaving and enjoying the fullness of life. We are told that her most precious time "was spinning in the kitchen, while the girls did what they were going to do" (55). In this context, weaving is also associated with gift-giving and spiritual, psychic, and intellectual bonding between women. Her gifts to Sassafras and Cypress are handmade and consistent with each daughter's interest. To Sassafras she gives a woven blanket and eight skeins of "finest spun cotton dyed so many colors" (68), and to Cypress she gives a tutu. In turn, Sassafras's gift to Hilda is "a woven hanging called 'You Know Where We Came From Mama' & six amethysts with holes drilled thru for her mother's creative weaving" (70).

Juxtaposed to Sassafras's aesthetic preoccupation with weaving is Hilda's practical concern. Just as each daughter has artistic and spiritual dreams based on which she seeks to shape her being and her destiny, so we are told, "Hilda Effania had some dreams of her own. Not so much to change the world, but to change her daughters' lives. Make it so that they wouldn't have to do what she did. Listen to every syllable came out of

that white woman's mouth. It wasn't really distasteful to her. She liked her life. She liked making cloth: the touch, the rhythm of it, colors. What she wanted for her girls was more than that. She wanted happiness, however they could get it. Whatever it was. Whoever brought it" (57). In her pragmatism, Hilda, like many women in Western literature—Penelope and Anna come to mind—sees weaving as a means of constructing and maintaining a life-support system for the family and preserving the integrity of the kinship group. While she enjoys the craft, it is for her merely an occupation—a means of survival, and her desire for her daughters is a means of survival that would allow them their own direction and liberation from the dictates of the prevailing white power structure. This desire is especially clear in her reaction to Miz Fitzhugh's monetary gift to the girls. The annual gift comes with specific constraints, and we are mindful of Miz Fitzhugh's bigoted view of Hilda and her children and their "gall" as she sees it to seek existences as African American women outside of traditional "Negro" roles. Like the crafty Penelope, Hilda has a hidden set of motivations. While she preserves her positive relationship with Miz Fitzhugh, she also maintains her central position in her daughters' lives. That they have only one mother and that they will not be defined by white America is evident in Hilda's allowing the girls to spend the money exactly as they please.

Also significant to Hilda's identity as a mother is that, just as she literally weaves, she figuratively weaves a blanket of spiritual and emotional protection for her daughters. We are told, for example, of her concerns for Indigo, because the child even early in life pursues her own direction and defines for herself an identity and code of values out of deeply traditional southern folk beliefs and practices. The child, according to Hilda, "has too much of the South in her." We see this ever-spreading blanket of protection in her letters to the girls in which she expresses concern and passes judgment on their lifestyles, but pours out an incessant supply of loving support for them and their directions while expressing her desire that they acquire traditional American success in fine husbands and professions.

Weaving is also the axis of Sassafras's development as an African American woman. As a weaver, Sassafras comes into spiritual and emotional fruition through plying the craft she learned from Hilda. Ironically, Sassafras is the only one of Hilda's children whom Miz Fitzhugh attempts to appreciate. Out of this appreciation, she is motivated to finance Sassafras's prep school education. Her view of Sassafras and her weaving, however, is warped, since for Sassafras weaving is more than a mere honorable trade but is instead an affirmative merging of her artistic imagination and her womanhood. Miz Fitzhugh's presence, then, is significant to the dialogical relationship existing between the reader and the text, for she serves to remind the reader that for all their insulation, not even privileged African American women are immune to the intrusions of race and class; that only determination like Hilda's and firm self-definition like that of Sassafras can protect the African American woman from such intrusion.

Although Sassafras is eventually successful in her quest, her affirmation is not to be achieved without difficulties and frustrations as she finds herself thwarted and tested in the pursuit of her craft and in her attempt to reconcile her artistic and psychosexual beings. Sassafras endures these tests at the hands of her lover, Mitch, a musician who in his chauvinism seeks to undermine her talents and self-esteem and to denigrate her womanhood. Ignorant of the worth of her weaving, which she has to hide from him, he is by implication and deed insensitive to the full measure of her being. Weaving, then, is associated with Sassafras's assertion of selfhood as the activity becomes a retreat from the misogyny of Mitch and his two friends, Howard and Otis. Her weaving also allows her to absorb herself in the sanctity of her African American female heritage, which enables her to see herself in a positive light. We are told, "Sassafras had always been proud that her mother had a craft; that all the women in her family could make something besides a baby. . . . She had grown up in a room full of spinning wheels, table and floor looms, and her mother was always busy making cloth . . . but Sassafras had never wanted to weave, she just couldn't help. . . . It was as essential to her as dancing is to Carmen de Lavallade, or singing to Aretha Franklin. . . . Making cloth was the only tradition that Sassafras had inherited that gave her a sense of womanhood that was rich and sensuous, not tired and stingy" (91, 92). This insightful acknowledgment of her identity as a weaver is significant and necessary to her total well-being. It connects her to the larger tradition of womanhood. It ultimately creates for her a niche in the Black artists' and craftsmen's commune just outside New Orleans, and it allows her to merge spiritually with the Yoruba practices and value system of the commune. More important, it underlies her realization that she and Mitch can never reconcile their arts and spirits because they have divergent orientations and absolutely incongruous and disparate views of themselves and the world. Finally, in keeping with the association of weaving with reproduction, life, and growth, we find that this same realization, reinforced by the Afrocentric ethos of the commune and the growth Sassafras experiences there, gives her the strength she needs to shake the bonds of male dependency by ridding herself of Mitch, returning to Charleston to have a baby (the symbol of a new and healthy self), and, in Hilda's discourse, to "find the rest of [herself]" (220).

Like weaving, music in the novel is central to female development and identity. In the novel the music motif bears both positive and negative connotations as it assists in shaping the women's worldview and in defining for the reader and for the women themselves their place in the world.

First, music is the metaphor for Indigo's identity and her passage from childhood into African American womanhood. After her first menstrual period, Uncle John gives her a fiddle for which she demonstrates a natural love and talent. At the lower end of the socio-economic scale, Uncle John sees the fiddle as a means of connecting Indigo with her past and with the folk tradition. At this time, Uncle John becomes her mentor as he explains to her the link between music and the psychic survival of slaves:

> Them whites that owned slaves took everything was ourselves. . . . Just threw it on away. . . . Took them drums what they could . . . but they couldn't take our feet. Took them languages we speak. Took off wit our spirits & left us wit they Son. But the fiddle was the talkin one. The fiddle be callin' our gods what left us / be giving back some devilment & hope in our bodies worn down & lonely over these fields and kitchens. . . . What ya think music is, whatchu think the blues be, & them get happy church musics is about but talkin' wit the unreal what's mo' real than most folks ever gonna know.
>
> (27)

Here, Indigo learns that knowing the past is central to understanding the present, and music is integral to this lesson. Uncle John's influence remains dominant in Indigo's psyche as she continues to learn to play the fiddle with a view to retaining her link to the past and to the folk tradition. We also find that as she matures she remains steeped in the folk tradition and so defines her personhood.

Indigo's fiddle playing further facilitates her entree into local folk tradition when, as a result of her playing and the accompanying near mystical power, she acquires the friendship of Spats and Crunch, two Junior Geechee Captains, and is accepted and initiated as a Junior Geechee Captain herself. This evolving sense of folk identity also serves to shepherd Indigo out of childhood, as witnessed by her willingness to relinquish the childhood companionship of her dolls and pursue her music under the auspices of Sister Mary Louise, Uncle John, Spats and Crunch, and Pretty Man, the owner of a local tavern with a working-class clientele. It is this element of society that can relate to Indigo and her music. While they can perceive her genuine efforts to "play her own mind" and thus become increasingly steeped in the local folk tradition and her allegiance to the folk, Hilda, consistent with her middle-class dreams for her daughters, wants Indigo to have a conventional experience with music and encourages her to take traditional violin lessons. We note that at this stage of her development, Indigo's music lacks harmony; but as she becomes more personally integrated, her music becomes more melodious and less resembles the sounds of "banshees."

Music also becomes the metaphor for Indigo's maturation as she contemplates the meaning of womanhood. This is evident, for example, when Pretty Man's girlfriend, Mabel, fails to fully understand the implications of Indigo's experience with music and thus receives a beating from him. The reader is aware that Mabel and Indigo are motivated by two widely divergent sets of influences, Mabel by the profit motive and Indigo by the ancestral and folk spirits. Indigo, however, realizes only that she is responsible for Mabel's suffering. Through the medium of music she comes to understand the need for bonding between women, particularly African American women, because "the Colored had hurt enough already" (49). Later in the novel, music becomes the symbol of Indigo's full maturation and true identity as a midwife and folklorist on Difuskie Island, where she goes to live and study with her Aunt Haydee. There, Indigo studies and plays the violin and is able to contribute to and find her place among the folk. Music becomes the metaphor for Indigo's mode of expression and mystical powers—indeed, her psychic connection with her ancestral and folk past. Initially her fiddle playing serves to "soothe" the women in childbirth. Later, however, Indigo and her music become an institution as mothers and children seek spiritual refuge in her. Ultimately, Indigo and her music merge with the folk tradition on Difuskie Island. Through her powerful fiddle playing she is linked with the legend of the indomitable slave woman, Blue Sunday, who, as no one except Indigo had since done, moved the sea. Thus, armed with her talents and her spiritual and psychic connection with her folk past, Indigo assumes an easy and natural place among the folk and later inherits a position of responsibility when Aunt Haydee dies.

Shange also uses the music metaphor in her portrayal of African American male-female relationships. She demonstrates the developmental role of these relationships in the lives of African American women through the stark contrast between two significant relationships. On the one hand, there is the liaison between Sassafras and Mitch, in which music bears the Dionysian associations of destruction. In addition, just as in literature music has been associated with war, so the motif is used here to depict the battle between the sexes.

Mitch, a former juvenile delinquent, now a prison parolee, and worse yet, a junkie, is a musician. While he perceives himself to be an artist, music is, in his hands, a weapon and a means by which he can act out his brutally misogynistic tendencies. Part of this brutality is psychological, which we see in his efforts to negate Sassafras's creative impulses. He is, for example, intolerant of her weaving, for he does not fully understand its value as an art form. In addition, he does not allow her to display a sequin and feather hanging shaped like a vagina because, in his view, "it wasn't proper for a new African woman to make things of such a sexual nature" (78). He also tries to intimidate her into writing. The result is that she has to conceal her natural talents; but when, on one occasion, she does attempt to write and is meeting with success, he disrupts her first with sexual overtures and then by playing the Looney Tunes theme. He thus drives Sassafras into the kitchen to begin cooking. Perhaps, however, the most graphic example of the association between Mitch, misogyny, and music lies in the vivid scene in which Sassafras is subjected to Otis's poem "Ebony Cunt," which he reads, musically accompanied by Mitch and Howard. The poem celebrates African American men's sexual exploitation of African American women. When Sassafras voices her intolerance, she indicates in her rage the men's connection with African American women, and, consequently, embarrasses Mitch in front of his friends. His solution is violence. He beats her after the others leave and then plays the solo from Eric Dolphy's "Green Dolphin Street."

Because, as we can infer, Mitch is, for any number of reasons, detached from the feminine in himself; because he cannot see equality and harmony between the sexes; because, further, his consciousness is not Afrocentric, he lacks creativity. We note that the music he plays is not his own and that when he does offer love to Sassafras, it comes in the form of a "bewitched and tortuous mermaid song" (123). Music, then, becomes the metaphor for the cacophonous, nightmarish element of the male-female relationship that threatens the possibility of harmony and ultimately personhood.

In contrast, music celebrates the possibility of wholesomeness and fullness of life, the possibility of personhood, of light and hope, of union and harmony, as it shapes the context and structure of the relationship between Cypress and Leroy, which stands diametrically opposed to the lack of union between Sassafras and Mitch. Again, it is the music motif that establishes the dichotomy between Leroy and Mitch and their impact on the women's lives. Whereas Mitch has no worthwhile origins, no constructive present, and, hence, no potential for the future, Leroy is moral and disciplined, spiritually and emotionally integrated, and genuinely creative. He is well grounded in a past that has given him direction for a well-structured present and a productive and successful future. Moreover, throughout graduate school Leroy has endured the struggle to legitimize African American music and meets ultimately with success, as seen in the progress of his European tour. More important, as opposed to Mitch, Leroy is not misogynistic and sees in Cypress his chance for intimacy. He serves, then, as an enhancement to Cypress and an essential aid to her burgeoning selfhood.

Interconnected with the music motif is that of dance, which, like both weaving and music, bears an important association with female development and identity. Central to Cypress's existence, dance is the means by which she is able to assert her African American heritage, explore her womanhood, and eventually find her niche in the African American, albeit avant-garde middle class. Like Sassafras, however, Cypress finds that the pursuit of self-actualization is not an easy one. Initially, even Hilda is caustic about Cypress's heavy backside and suitability for ballet, but she eventually agrees to support Cypress's study of dance. In this context, dance features in the mother-daughter relationship and is the metaphor for psychic connection and shared values between Hilda and Cypress. It is significant that Hilda's initial views reflect the Euro-American view of the African American woman's body being unsuitable for the "high culture" of ballet. As Hilda grows in her relationship with Cypress, the reader would expect her to overcome the Euro-American view of the Black female body. On this point, however, the text remains silent. On the one hand, this silence underscores the generational distance between the two women, but on the other it reinforces the totality of Hilda's unconditional love and support for Cypress. Later, as Cypress begins to mature as a dancer, she benefits from the African influences brought to dance by Ariel Moroe and the Kushites Returned and the feminist interpretations brought by the lesbian troupe Azure Bosom. Both these troupes offer her options for self-definition. But her experiences with them leave her scarred, for she suffers as a result of Ariel's misogyny and Azure Bosom's emotional cannibalism.

Nevertheless, just as dance is associated with the pain necessary for Cypress's growth, so it is also the means by which she achieves affirmation. The reader is made aware of this affirmation through the combined motifs of music and dance, which are worked out through the perfect harmony she shares with Leroy. In this context music and dance converge into a cathartic, healing experience when, in a drunken, broken-hearted state after her lesbian affair with Idrina of Azure Bosom, Cypress finds herself in the Golden Onk. It is there that she enters a new realm and experiences a new universe where all is cosmic harmony. She hears Leroy's music and becomes "a dance of a new thing, her own spirit, loose, fecund, deep" (156).

In addition, the combined motifs of dance and music serve to dramatize the healing, restorative power of love as we follow the relationship of Cypress and Leroy and Cypress's increasing empowerment. Leroy inspires Cypress to dance, and she, in turn, learns through dance that she need not learn to read music—that she can "just climb into it" (196). As a result of Leroy's presence and influence, Cypress is able to expand her horizons through dance and resolve her questions about the ills of her past associations with Ariel and Idrina. Similarly, Cypress's presence and influence enable Leroy to face and dismiss the bitter memories of past racial injustices. In short, music and dance in the novel become symbols of the growth and emancipation of the human spirit. Such liberation can culminate only in joy and harmony, which in the novel is manifested in Leroy's proposal of marriage and Cypress's acceptance.

In what traditional American critical discourse might term this "highly experimental novel," each woman's voyage into self-discovery constitutes her story. Each woman's journey necessitates a return to the place which, for good or for ill, whether she will stay there or not, she must call home. Each returns to Charleston—Sassafras to give birth, the symbol of a new life, assisted in the act by her sisters; Indigo to carry out last rites for Aunt Haydee; and Cypress to begin a new life with Leroy. Facilitated by the arts motif, the return or circular plot structure is complete as each sister finds herself back in her Charleston origins, having explored her womanhood in distinctly African American terms through the medium of art.

In her construction of a narrative that outlines the development into womanhood of these three sisters, Shange has employed a dominant theme that surfaces in much of African American women's fiction: the quest theme that, according to Claudia Tate, is "a character's personal search for a meaningful identity and self-sustaining dignity in a world of growing isolation, meaninglessness, and moral decay" (xix). And in so doing, Shange, like many of her counterparts, has reconstructed the traditional Euro-American female bildungsroman, which typically depicts female growth *down* into womanhood and its life of privilege. Shange's novel gives us a new form that depicts one of several African American female patterns of growth into selfhood. These are, however, patterns that frequently challenge traditional American expectations. Their depiction involves the reader in a dialogical process with the reality external to the text that necessitates the reader's resistance of traditional Euro-American values, which have not only given rise to negative stereotypes of African American women but have also mandated an ideal African American female identity: a middle class, darker skinned, sometimes victimized, but otherwise identical version of a white woman. Shange's female characters, however, are far more than blackfaced white middle-class women, for they represent a distinct and affirming Afrocentric experience and value system that result from a successful fusion of African sensibilities and western culture.

Works Cited

Abrams, M. H. *Natural Supernaturalism: Tradition and Revolution in Romantic Literature.* New York: W. W. Norton, 1971.

Christian, Barbara. *Black Feminist Criticism: Perspectives on Black Women Writers.* New York: Pergamon Press, 1985.

Shange, Ntozake. *for colored girls who have considered suicide/ when the rainbow is enuf.* New York: Macmillan, 1975.

———. *Sassafras, Cypress, and Indigo.* New York: St. Martin's Press, 1982.

Tate, Claudia. *Black Women Writers at Work.* New York: Continuum, 1983.

FURTHER READING

Criticism

Kent, Assunta. "The Rich Multiplicity of *Betsey Brown.* *Journal of Dramatic Theory and Criticism* 7, no. 1 (fall 1992): 151-61.

Provides a detailed overview of the development of a script for the musical version of *Betsey Brown*; a summary of its story line; and a mixed review of the 1991 production of the play at the McCarter Theater.

Saldivar, José David. "The Real and the Marvelous in Charleston, South Carolina: Ntozake Shange's *Sassafrass, Cypress, and Indigo.* In *Genealogy and Literature,* edited by Lee Quinby, pp. 175-92. Minneapolis: University of Minnesota Press, 1995.

Studies Shange's use of Latin American and Afro-Caribbean magic realism in *Sassafrass, Cypress, and Indigo.*

Splawn, P. Jane. "'Change the Joke[r] and Slip the Yoke': Boal's 'Joker' System in Ntozake Shange's *for colored girls . . .* and *Spell #7.*" *Modern Drama* 41, no. 3 (fall 1998): 386-98.

Contends that in *for colored girls* and *Spell #7* "Shange change[d] the 'Joker' as manifested in the American minstrel tradition into a subversive 'in yr face' symbol of defiance—a contemporary version of Ellison's slipping of the yoke of oppression through the use of the mask."

Wole Soyinka
1934-

AP Images

(Full name Akinwande Oluwole Soyinka) Nigerian playwright, poet, novelist, essayist, memoirist, lecturer, librettist, biographer, and nonfiction and short story writer.

For additional information on Soyinka's career, see *Black Literature Criticism,* Ed. 1.

INTRODUCTION

Recipient of the 1986 Nobel Prize for Literature, Soyinka is regarded as one of Africa's finest contemporary writers. His plays, novels, and poetry blend elements of traditional Yoruban folk drama and European dramatic form to create both spectacle and penetrating satire. His narrative technique is based on the African cultural tradition, in which the artist functions as the recorder of the mores and experiences of his society. Soyinka's works reflect this philosophy, serving as a record of twentieth-century Africa's political turmoil and the continent's struggle to reconcile tradition with modernization. Through his nonfiction works and essay collections, Soyinka has established an international reputation as an unflinching commentator on political injustice and a sophisticated provocateur of social criticism.

BIOGRAPHICAL INFORMATION

Soyinka was born in 1934 in Ìsarà, Nigeria. As he grew older he became increasingly aware of the tension between African tradition and Western modernization, a theme that would appear in his later work. Aké, his village, was populated mainly by people from the Yoruba tribe and was presided over by the *ogboni,* or tribal elders. Soyinka's grandfather introduced him to the pantheon of Yoruba gods and other figures of tribal folklore. His parents, however, were representatives of colonial influence: his mother was a devout Christian convert, and his father was a headmaster at the village school established by the British. Soyinka published poems and short stories in *Black Orpheus,* a Nigerian literary magazine, before leaving Africa to attend the University of Leeds in England. He returned to Nigeria in 1960, shortly after the country's independence from colonial rule. In 1965 he was arrested by the Nigerian police, accused of using a gun to force a radio announcer to broadcast his satirical commentary on the fraudulent election. No evidence was ever produced, however, and the PEN writers' organization soon launched a protest campaign, headed by William Styron and Norman Mailer. Soyinka was eventually released after three months. He was arrested again two years later, during Nigeria's civil war, for his vocal opposition to the conflict. Soyinka was particularly angered by the Nigerian government's brutal policies toward the Ibo people, who were attempting to form their own country, Biafra. After he traveled to Biafra to establish a peace commission composed of leading intellectuals from both sides of the conflict, the Nigerian police accused Soyinka of helping the Biafrans to buy jet fighters. This time Soyinka was imprisoned for more than two years, although he was never formally charged with a crime. For the majority of his arrest, he was kept in solitary confinement. Denied reading and writing materials, Soyinka created his own ink and began to keep a prison diary, writing on toilet paper and cigarette packages.

This diary was published in 1972 as *The Man Died.* In the early 1990s, Soyinka opposed Nigerian General Ibrahim Babangida's refusal to allow a democratic government to take power. Babangida appointed General Sani Abacha as head of the Nigerian state and Soyinka, along with other pro-democracy activists, was charged with treason for his criticism of the military regime. Facing a death sentence, Soyinka left the country in 1994 to travel and lecture in Europe and the United States. Following the death of Abacha, who held control for five years, the new government, led by General Abdulsalem Abubakar, released numerous political prisoners and promised to hold civilian elections, prompting Soyinka to return to his homeland. He has held teaching positions at a number of prestigious universities, including the University of Ghana, Cornell University, and Yale University. He also served as the Goldwin Smith professor for African Studies and Theatre Arts at Cornell University from 1988 to 1991. Soyinka has received several awards for his work, including the Nobel Prize for Literature in 1986 and the Enrico Mattei Award for Humanities in 1986.

MAJOR WORKS

Soyinka's early plays focus on the dichotomies of good versus evil and progress versus tradition in African culture. For example, *The Swamp Dwellers* (1958) condemns African superstition by showing how religious leaders exploit the fears of their townspeople for personal gain. Commissioned as part of Nigeria's independence celebration in 1960, *A Dance of the Forests* (1960) warns the newly independent Nigerians that the end of colonial rule does not mean an end to their country's problems. The play features a bickering group of mortals who summon up the *egungun*—spirits of the dead, revered by the Yoruba people—for a festival. They have presumed the *egungun* to be noble and wise, but they discover that their ancestors are as petty and spiteful as anyone else. While Soyinka warned against sentimental yearning for Africa's past in *A Dance of the Forests,* he lampooned the indiscriminate embrace of Western modernization in *The Lion and the Jewel* (1959). The plot of this drama revolves around Sidi, the village beauty, and the rivalry between her two suitors. The story also follows Baroka, a village chief with many wives, and Lakunle, an enthusiastically Westernized schoolteacher who dreams of molding Sidi into a "civilized" woman. *The Trials of Brother Jero* (1960) was written in response to a request for a play that could be performed in a converted dining hall in Ibadan. Drawing on his observations of the separatist Christian churches of Nigeria, on Ijebu folk narratives, and on theatrical conventions used by dramatist Bertolt Brecht, Soyinka constructed a vigorous comedy around the character of a messianic beach prophet. Brother Jero—a trickster figure who sets up a shack on Bar Beach, Lagos, prophesying golden futures in return for

money—belongs to one of the revivalist Christian sects that existed at the time of Nigerian independence. In *Kongi's Harvest* (1965), the demented dictator of the state of Isma has imprisoned and dethroned its traditional chief, Oba Danlola. To legitimize his seizure of power, Kongi has laid claim to the Oba's spiritual authority through his consecration of the crops at the New Yam Festival.

Soyinka's later plays rely heavily on classical theatrical devices as a vehicle for the author's potent political and social satires. *The Bacchae of Euripides* (1973), an adaptation of the play by Euripides, reinvents the classic tale as a meditation on the nature of personal sacrifice within unjust societies. *Death and the King's Horseman* (1975) combines powerful dramatic verse and characterization with a structure that incorporates contrast and juxtaposition. The play is based on an actual 1945 incident of a colonial officer's intervention to prevent the royal horseman, the Elesin, from committing ritual suicide at his king's funeral, whereupon the Elesin's son would take his father's place in the rite. *A Play of Giants* (1984) is a surreal fantasy about international poetic justice in which an African dictator, on a visit to the United Nations in New York, takes a group of Russian and American delegates hostage. He threatens to release the Soviet-supplied rockets from his embassy arsenal unless an international force is sent to crush an uprising in his country. *The Beatification of Area Boy* (1995) centers around Sanda, a security guard at a Lagos shopping mall. Despite his position at the mall, the charming Sanda routinely organizes local scams and robberies. It is eventually revealed that Sanda is an ex-revolutionary who had sacrificed his higher education to organize political protests.

Soyinka's fiction expands on the themes expressed in his plays, constructing sweeping narratives of personal and political turmoil in Africa. His first novel, *The Interpreters* (1965), is essentially a plotless narrative loosely structured around the informal discussions between five young Nigerian intellectuals. Each has been educated in a foreign country and has returned on the eve of Nigerian independence, hoping to shape Nigeria's destiny. They are hampered by their own confused values, however, as well as by the corruption they encounter in their homeland. *Season of Anomy* (1973) takes the central concerns from *The Interpreters* and selects a new moment at which to consider the choices confronting those working for change. The plot follows a variety of characters including an artist named Ofeyi, a cold-blooded assassin named Isola Demakin, and a harmonious community called Aiyero in a narrative that is thematically linked to the myths of Orpheus and Euridice.

The prose in Soyinka's nonfiction works and essay collections is largely based on his own life and his personal political convictions. Besides *The Man Died,* he has also composed a series of memoirs—*Aké* (1981), *Ìsarà* (1989), *Ibadan* (1994), and *You Must Set forth at Dawn* (2006). While *Aké, Ibadan,* and *You Must Set Forth at Dawn* focus on Soyinka's personal life—*Aké* concerns his childhood, *Ibadan* recounts his teen years to his early twenties, and *You Must Set Forth at Dawn* chronicles his life as a public intellectual and his political struggles against the Nigerian government—*Ìsarà* is a biography of Soyinka's father. *Myth, Literature, and the African World* (1976), Soyinka's first essay collection, combines criticism of specific texts with discussions that reveal the scope of Soyinka's acquaintance with literary and theatrical traditions, as well as his search for a personal perspective. He further explored his interest in the role that politics and literature play in modern Africa in *Art, Dialogue, and Outrage* (1988). *The Open Sore of a Continent* (1996) reprints a series of vitriolic lectures in which Soyinka denounces the Nigerian government under the dictator Sani Abacha and laments the indifference of the West to the state of Nigerian politics. In *The Burden of Memory, the Muse of Forgiveness* (1999), Soyinka discussed the role of the South African Truth and Reconciliation Commission and questioned the nature of political truths. *Climate of Fear* (2005) is comprised of five lectures given by Soyinka at the Royal Institute of London in March 2004. In these works, Soyinka discusses the climate of fear that defines the political and social atmosphere of the early twenty-first century and the threat of terrorism on a worldwide scale.

Soyinka has also published several collections of poetry, including *Idanre and Other Poems* (1967), *Ogun Abibiman* (1976), and *Mandela's Earth and Other Poems* (1988). Composed over a period of twenty-four hours, *Idanre* collects a series of mythological poems that feature Yoruba terminology and display subtle manipulation of words, images, and idioms. Soyinka drew upon stories associated with the Yoruba mythological figures Ogun, Atunda, Sango, and Oya, and the Idanre Hills. In the twenty-two-page poem *Ogun Abibiman*, Soyinka combined a direct call for African states to take action against the apartheid movement in South Africa with a mythologized manifesto for the country's liberation. The treatise describes Ogun, Yoruba god of war, joining forces in a violent and mystical union with the legendary Zulu chieftain Shaka. In 2002 Soyinka published *Samarkand and Other Markets I Have Known,* a poetry collection that offers reflections on modern politics, his exile from Nigeria, and such writers as Josef Brodsky and Chinua Achebe.

CRITICAL RECEPTION

Soyinka's work has frequently been described as demanding but rewarding to read. Although his plays have been widely praised, they are seldom performed, especially outside of Africa. He has been acknowledged by many critics as Nigeria's finest contemporary dramatist and one of its most distinguished men of letters. While many critics have focused on Soyinka's strengths as a playwright, others have acknowledged his skill as a poet, novelist, and essayist as well. The most significant aspect of Soyinka's work, critics have noted, is in his approach to literature as a serious agent of social change and his commitment to promoting human rights in Nigeria and other nations. Commentators have maintained that the humor and compassion evident in his writings, as well as his chilling portrayals of the consequences of political greed and oppression, add a universal significance to his depictions of West African life. His incorporation of Yoruba mythology and ritual in his work has been a recurring topic of critical interest as well. His poetry, novels, and nonfiction works have attracted an international readership. Soyinka was the first African to win the Nobel Prize for Literature and he has been applauded by commentators for his versatility and the power of his works.

PRINCIPAL WORKS

The Invention (play) 1955
The Swamp Dwellers (play) 1958
The Lion and the Jewel (play) 1959
A Dance of the Forests (play) 1960
The Trials of Brother Jero (play) 1960
The Republican (play) 1963
The New Republican (play) 1964
Before the Blackout (play) 1965
The Interpreters (novel) 1965
Kongi's Harvest (play) 1965
The Road (play) 1965
The Strong Breed (play) 1966
Idanre and Other Poems (poetry) 1967
Poems from Prison (poetry) 1969; expanded edition published as *A Shuttle in the Crypt,* 1972
Madmen and Specialists (play) 1970
Plays from the Third World: An Anthology [editor] (plays) 1971
The Man Died: Prison Notes of Wole Soyinka (diary) 1972
The Bacchae of Euripides: A Communion Rite [adaptor, from the play by Euripides] (play) 1973
Collected Plays: Volume One (plays) 1973
Season of Anomy (novel) 1973
Death and the King's Horseman (play) 1975
Myth, Literature, and the African World (essays) 1976
Ogun Abibiman (poetry) 1976
Opera Wonyosi (libretto) 1977
Aké: The Years of Childhood (memoir) 1981
Priority Projects (play) 1982
Requiem for a Futurologist (play) 1983
A Play of Giants (play) 1984

Art, Dialogue, and Outrage: Essays on Literature and Culture (essays) 1988
Mandela's Earth and Other Poems (poetry) 1988
Ìsarà: A Voyage around Essay (biography) 1989
Before the Deluge (play) 1991
From Zia with Love (play) 1992
Ibadan: The Penkelemes Years: A Memoir, 1946-65 (memoir) 1994
The Beatification of Area Boy: A Lagosian Kaleido-scope (play) 1995
The Open Sore of a Continent: A Personal Narrative of the Nigerian Crisis (lectures) 1996
Early Poems (poetry) 1997
Arms and the Arts—A Continent's Unequal Dialogue (nonfiction) 1999
The Burden of Memory, the Muse of Forgiveness (non-fiction) 1999
King Baabu (play) 2001
Samarkand and Other Markets I Have Known (poetry) 2002
Climate of Fear: The Quest for Dignity in a Dehuman-ized World (lectures) 2005
You Must Set forth at Dawn (memoir) 2006

This volume includes The Swamp Dwellers, A Dance of the Forests, The Road, The Strong Breed, and The Bacchae of Euripides: A Communion Rite.

CRITICISM

Tejumola Olaniyan (essay date fall 2002)

SOURCE: Olaniyan, Tejumola. "Modernity and Its Mirages: Wole Soyinka and the African State." *Modern Drama* 45, no. 3 (fall 2002): 349-57.

[*In this essay, Olaniyan examines Soyinka's pragmatist critique of the African state, juxtaposing his* The Open Sore of a Continent *with Mahmood Mamdani's* Citizen and Subject: Contemporary Africa and the Legacy of Late Colonialism.]

We know that a broad and relentless interrogation of the African state constitutes the moral constant of Wole Soyinka's dramatic universe, whether he is employing the most arcane and ritualistic, or the most realistic and accessible, performance form. By the "African state" I mean both the established ruling institution and the existing social condition as a whole. This persistent critical interrogation has made Soyinka the foremost scourge of the seemingly perpetual state of anomie on the continent and those who manage and profit from it. Although this is less clearly articulated in the dramas than in Soyinka's other writings, I see the catalyst of the dramatist's huge exertions as one grand irony, a historical irony of epic proportion that serves as vast diorama: Af-

rica as living a modernity it practically financed with its blood and toil, its human and material resources, but whose direction it is powerless to chart and whose effect it is unable to control. If the acknowledged gains of that modernity in the West—stable, orderly government, accountability between the rulers and the ruled, entrenched striving for egalitarian relations, rationalized bureaucracy and economic system, optimum management of the population—continue to elude Africa, it is not because Africa is not part of that modernity but because it is part of it *unequally.*

What I want to do in these brief remarks is not, as my title might imply, to demonstrate how Soyinka's critique of the state in his works registers the illusions of modernity so far in Africa. As I have suggested above, such forceful registration is the constitutive fabric of Soyinka's exertions and, therefore, needs careful attention. Such an attention is indeed a substantial part of my larger project. Instead, what I want to do here is to raise a meta-query of Soyinka's critique of the African state. In other words, I am concerned here with frameworks of critique, with *modalities* rather than with mere examples.

There is a reason for my fixation with this kind of query. The African state as we have it today, we all know, is an outgrowth of the colonial state. It is a consequence of historical developments that actually circumscribed indigenous agency. Even now, forty years after independence, none of the institutions of the state—the party, the judiciary, the police, the bureaucracy, the language, and so on—has been decolonized enough to command the *affect* of the governed. This is the main source of the unending crisis of legitimacy facing the states. It has made them into perpetual states of "rule" with little hope of ever becoming states of "hegemony." Now, if this nutshell analytical history of the African state is accurate, then there are crucial implications for the kind of critique directed at it by would-be critics.

Two crystallized dominant paradigms are currently available for the critique of the African state: the *pragmatist* and the *foundationalist.* The pragmatist critique affirms the legality and authenticity of where the African state is here and now and insists that it could do much better by learning from its mistakes, as well as from successful examples worldwide, and by bringing uncorrupted reason and commitment to bear on the business of government. It foregrounds the necessity for managers of people and resources to be of unimpeachable character and avows that the soul of any institution is people of integrity. For the pragmatist, there is no human institution, no matter its wayward origins, that cannot be tamed under the proper direction. Behind this claim is a fierce belief in the endless capacity of individuals to make a difference in society; after all, the only dynamic factor in politics is the individual person. This mode of critique is dominant today among African writers and intellectuals, as well as among scholars of Africa. In addition to Soyinka, other leading writers whose works express the pragmatist view include Chinua Achebe, Nurrudin Farah, Peter Abraham, T. M. Aluko, and Athol Fugard, to cite only a few examples. This is also the reigning position in the social sciences, and has been so since the wave of independence in the 1960s.

The foundationalist critique, on the other hand, argues that the origin of the contemporary African state in the dictatorial colonial state compromises it so much that without a thoroughgoing decolonization of the instruments and procedures of rule, the African state cannot resolve its crisis of legitimacy. For the foundationalist, the problem is at the foundations; in other words, the problem is structural or systemic. While conscientious individuals are certainly needed to run institutions, the foundationalist holds that no amount of moral suasion can keep large numbers of people upright in circumstances that sneer at or even punish uprightness. Bad management of human and material resources, says the foundationalist, is not the root of the problem but merely a symptom. What can the best and most honest of men and women do, running a bureaucracy that speaks a language that 60 percent of the population they are governing cannot understand? Writers for whom only a fundamental critique of the state would suffice include Sembene Ousmane, Ngugi wa Thiong'O, and, in rare instances, Chinua Achebe (*Arrow of God* only) and Ayi Kwei Armah (*Two Thousand Seasons* only). In the last decade, a significant social science literature on the African crisis has begun to focus on foundations, after what seemed an exhaustion of its earlier fixation with lamenting the absence of "honest" and "good" leaders. Some of the scholars creating this literature are Basil Davidson, Crawford Young, Patrick Chabal, Claude Ake, Mahmood Mamdani, and Achille Mbembe.

The predominant mode of Soyinka's critique of the state, I suggest, is the pragmatist. In play after play, he is more interested in what is wrong now, and who is responsible, than in asking how things come to be what they are and what structured institutional and extra-institutional constraints and possibilities produce them. That is why his most favored generic mode in interrogating the state is satire. Satire, as we all know, derides and makes contemptible actions and behaviors that are aberrations or deviations from a desirable norm. But the emphasis is on the derision, not on investigating how an aberration came to be. What satire says is this: "Whatever the cause of your bad behavior, you would do well to change for the better." But satire does help the project of reform, even if it is uninterested in causes as such. And here is a defining ideological complexity at the heart of the genre. Satire aims to reform and thereby, according to the logic of reformation, make itself subsequently unnecessary; but precisely because its

province is more of manifestation than origins, its reappearance is virtually guaranteed.

But for my comparative critical assessment of both the pragmatist and foundationalist critiques of the African state here, I will be using, rather than any of Soyinka's classic dramatic satires, a non-fiction text in which he articulates the pragmatist view in elaborate detail. This is the important book *The Open Sore of a Continent: A Personal Narrative of the Nigerian Crisis,* published in 1996. For the sake of clarity, I will read this book alongside another significant book proposing a foundationalist critique, published in the same year by the notable political scientist Mahmood Mamdani: *Citizen and Subject: Contemporary Africa and the Legacy of Late Colonialism.*

There is a critical supplementary relationship between these two books. While Soyinka critically dissects a contemporary instance of the crisis of an African state, Mamdani's wide-ranging historicization shows how that crisis came about, how it could not have been otherwise. With perspicacious insight, Soyinka shows how the evil genie of tyranny, once set loose from its moorings, perpetuates itself and is perpetuated remorselessly even under different circumstances. Mamdani, on the other hand, gives us a persuasive account of the historical—specifically, colonial—origins of the evil specter: an account of "where the rain began to beat us," as Achebe would say (44). A similar supplementarity is evident in the respective styles of the two writers. Mamdani's is the clinical, sedate prose of the scholar-scientist; his sentences are rarely more than four lines long. On the other hand, what we get from the irrepressible wordsmith, Soyinka, is a near-average of seven lines per sentence, with not a few sentences running to twelve lines: a cascading, torrential prose of the embattled activist right in the thick of the struggle at the moment.

To say that a logic of supplementarity structures the two books is, also, of course, to say, clearly and simply, that they are different in stimulating ways.

Effectively, two of Soyinka's three chapters are devoted to meticulous interrogations of the nation-state form. Nigeria provides the specific point of departure, interspersed with theoretical reflections on general issues such as "nationhood" and "nationmaking," the nation and its boundaries, the nation and its constituent human groups, the nation and the state and their relations, national belonging and its modes, and the national will—the modes of its determination, and consequences of its conservation or subversion.

In all the observations and analyses, Soyinka is the clear-eyed pragmatist, keenly aware of the weak foundational structures of the nation called Nigeria—whether of awkward boundaries, the unseemly mixture of different ethnicities, or a score of other forms of colonial gerrymandering. At the same time, however, he is deeply affirmative that those are not, and ought not automatically to be, enough unmanageable reasons for the edifice to collapse. With true patriotism, the type that transparently promotes the mutual interests of all the constituent groups within the nation space, Soyinka suggests, it is actually possible to survive the affliction of rickety foundations.

The immediate backdrop of Soyinka's exertions is the structured inequality among the different ethnic groups in Nigeria regarding access to the common wealth, a structured inequality that has led to a civil war, judicial murders, and repeated crises of different varieties. Of the lessons of the late-1960s Biafran War for the present, Soyinka states that "every day still reminds us that the factors that led to Biafra neither were ephemeral nor can be held to be permanently exorcised. And instead of such evasive or pious devices, it would serve us better to think instead of what mutual interests need to be emphasized, promoted, and packaged with all the skill of first-class salesmen, in order to ground our nationalist sentiments in something more durable" (32). In other words, a nation is something not just more than but actually other than a geographical space, such that it is possible to have a geographical space called Nigeria that is really not a nation. But since nations are made and not divinely ordained, a geographical space can actually *be* a nation, *become* a nation—even one with strong foundations—through a thoroughgoing secular political act of articulating the "mutual interests" of the constituent groups. This, for Soyinka, is the "something more durable" that *makes* and *conserves* nations. This is the polemical pragmatism that subtends the title Soyinka gives to chapter one of his book: "A Flawed Origin—But No Worse Than Others," meaning that though the origin of the entity called Nigeria is defective, it is not thereby irredeemable.

Mahmood Mamdani would certainly agree with this assessment, though from an entirely different perspective. He is more interested in the contours of that form of rule specifically programmed to engender, among other things, endless ethnic competition and animosities, rather than in the specific manifestations of such ethnic rivalries within the nation space. This difference is significant. For Mamdani, the major legacy of colonial rule that has continued to impede democratic initiatives in Africa is the entrenchment of what he calls the "bifurcated state" (16-23), by which he means colonial rule through ethnically organized Native Authorities (NAs) enforcing "customary law," in the rural areas, and through a racially based supervisory central state in the urban centers. The NAs speak the language of custom as defined and enforced by the colonizers, while the central state speaks the language of civil society. Africans under the NAs were "subjects" under oppressive local "overseer" states, while their entrance into civil society where they could be "citizens" was jealously guarded by colonial racism.

At independence, the major reform carried out by the victorious nationalists was the Africanization or deracialization of the central state, while there was very little corresponding dismantling or "detribalization" of the NAs, much less the establishment of a non-coercive way of linking the rural and the urban. This, argues Mamdani, was ultimately the result, whether we are talking of "mainstream nationalists" (289-90) who came to power through multiparty elections or "radical nationalists" (290-91) who adopted the single party in order to detribalize the NAs. The result was "decentralized despotism" in one case (289) and "centralized despotism" in the other (291).

Within Mamdani's paradigm, the trajectory of Nigeria's decolonization is that of conservative, mainstream nationalism. The central state was deracialized and the civil society indigenized. But these democratic reforms were mainly urban-centered, as the rural power of the NAs was never detribalized. Electoral reform did not affect the appointment of the NAs and its chiefs (289). In such a context of bifurcation and decentralized despotism, electoral politics usually carries unduly high stakes, for victors will not only be the representatives of citizens in civil society but will also who have the right to rule over subjects through NAs, "for the winner would appoint chiefs, the Native Authority, everywhere. More than the rule of law, the issue in a civil society-centered contest comes to be who will be master of all tribes" (289). This is why, Mamdani says, "the ethnicity of the president is the surest clue to the ethnic tinge of the government of the day" (289).

In his book, Soyinka rails against what he calls the "spoils of office," which is transitory and position-based, and the "spoils of power," which is permanent and group- or ethnic-based (61-62). Mamdani's submission is that the entrenchment of these spoils could hardly have been otherwise, for two reasons: first, because "civil society politics where the rural is governed through customary authority is necessarily patrimonial: urban politicians harness rural constituencies through patron-client relations" (289); and, second, because the tribalized and undemocratized NAs, through the economy of patron-client relations, can only infect the deracialized civil society in the urban with its tribalism, which is why the nationalist deracialization of the central state on independence, in nearly all cases, wore an ethnic face.

One of Mamdani's great insights is the debunking of the opinion, commonly expressed in many circles, that decentralization equals democratization. The lesson of Nigeria is instructive indeed in its ironies. As part of the post-civil war strategies to decentralize government so that government, as the agent and bearer of "development" and "modernization," could reach the remote corners of the country, four large regions became twelve states. More than a decade later, twelve states became nineteen, ostensibly for the same noble goal of democratizing development. By this time, however, many discerning observers had begun to wonder if state creation was not just another ingenious white elephant to siphon the national wealth to line individual pockets, since the main attraction of state creation has turned out to be the endless lists of bureaucratic positions to fill and contracts to award. It matters little whether a state is economically viable or not, for, after all, the budget allocation comes from the almighty federal government, the central state. Today, the states are thirty-six, and more groups are still clamoring for states of their own.

But there is a further decentralization: each state is divided into "local government areas" or LGAs, each with its own local administration, which is entirely dependent on the state for sustenance, just in the same way in which that particular state depends on the federal government. In all this energetic decentralization, however, the model is that of the NA system set up by the colonizers, with its enforced tribalism and blighted notion of the customary. For not only are Nigerian states aggregations of supposedly related ethnic groups, but the LGA divisions further refine and tribalize, giving nearly every sub-ethnic group its own local government. The president, state governors, and chairs of LGAs are either appointed or elected, depending on whether the regime is military or elected. It is a testament to the enduring colonial legacy of the bifurcated state—or, in this Nigerian specificity, the triplicated state—that in spite of the extensive decentralization, the relationship of despotism along the chain of command remains firmly intact. States are merely autonomous, not independent of the federal government; and, in turn, the LGAs are autonomous but not independent of the state. Whether appointed or elected, the state governor depends on the goodwill of the president for prompt and adequate budgetary allocation, and many other things besides. In turn, the LGA chairs in the state must compete for the governor's favor by running their divisions in line with the governor's fancies. The old tyrannical relationship between the country and the city, the rural and the urban, that was established by the colonizers to serve the colonial dictatorship survives—even thrives,—under "democracy"!

Since what a military regime does is silence or at least depoliticize civil society, crises and violent disarticulations in the "triplicated state" occur mostly during electoral politics. Soyinka records for us in his book one especially unforgettable instance of the decentralized despotism at work. It happened in Ile-Ife, Oyo State, in 1982. Six members of a political party—the Unity Party of Nigeria (UPN)—were set on fire in a minivan as they drove to join a political rally. The perpetrators were thugs of a rival political party, the National Party of Nigeria (NPN), which is the party of the President but which lost Oyo State in the previous governorship elections and was determined to win at all

costs this time around. As this "daylight massacre" (67) went on, writes Soyinka, the police, "numbering over a hundred, sat on their hands in four open-sided vans, their rifles and teargas launchers between their legs" and simply watched "with emotions varying from impassivity to helpless horror" (66-67). The local police, it turned out, had advance orders from the federal government-controlled police national headquarters in Lagos to do nothing. The country's police everywhere in the nation had become an extension of the party in power at the centre, had become a tool for the entrenchment of the party of the incumbent president in every region of the country. The federal control of the police throughout the country was so total that even state governors, if they belonged to a different party from the President, had little control over the state branch of the police. Needless to say, the NPN did win the governorship elections in Oyo state, as had been predetermined and carefully executed!

The lesson of all this is, of course, that a system of electoral politics alone does not guarantee democracy. In fact, it had in many cases been what the late distinguished Nigerian political scientist Claude Ake called it: the "democratization of disempowerment." And specifically within the context of unreformed bifurcated or triplicated power structure, electoral politics can only produce inter-ethnic, inter-religious, and other kinds of factional struggles that provide the ideal thriving ground for the politics of clientelism. Soyinka's book is a passionate attack on the venal and ethnic character of this clientelism, while Mamdani's attention is on the embedded structures of the postcolonial state—and their historical origins—that cannot produce anything other than that clientelism. This returns us, then, to Soyinka's polemical title: "A Flawed Origin—But No Worse Than Others." Mamdani's foundationalist answer would be that a flawed origin cannot be so easily dismissed; that the implied meaning that Nigeria could do better, even with flawed origins, may be somewhat far-fetched; that other African countries that share similarly flawed origins are not necessarily doing better with democratic governance; that the question may be not so much being worse off than others as the historic challenge today of being better; and, finally, that there may be no real movement forward in democratization, no matter who wins elections, without our returning to revise that primal origin of colonially implanted impediments to democratization.

Soyinka, in exasperation at the inability of many committed people like him to turn the nation around, once described his generation as a *"wasted generation"* (emphasis added).[1] The hide of the rampaging elephant was just too tough for the available sharp knives. Soyinka's phrase gripped the Nigerian public imagination and was hotly debated in the papers. Critics borrowed the phrase to describe a new generation of much younger and obviously less patriotic Nigerian politicians and bureaucrats as the "*wasteful generation.*" By raising the sort of query I have raised in this [essay], and by seeming to lean more to the foundationalist than to the pragmatist view in thinking about the mirages of African modernity, I suppose I belong to a yet different and perhaps more dangerous generation: the pessimistic, skeptical, perhaps even a little bit cynical, generation. But I like to think that this is a pessimism of the intellect only, not of the will.

Note

1. "In a statement I made last year I referred to my generation as the wasted generation and I was thinking in terms of all fields, not just the literary: the technological talents that we have which are not being used; but I also had in mind our writers of course, the fact that a lot of our energy has really been devoted to coping with the oppressive political situation in which we find ourselves. A lot of our energies go into fighting unacceptable situations as they arise while at the same time trying to pursue a long-term approach to politics such as, for instance, joining progressive-looking political parties, but of course each step is always one step forwards and about ten backwards. I find the political situation very, very frustrating, personally frustrating. I mean, forget even the amount of let us say personal work one could have done, writing and so on, and just think in terms of the amount of time one could have spent on training, in theatre for instance, would-be actors, or devoting more time to would-be writers, many of whom are constantly inundating one with cries for help; the qualitatively different kind of creative community atmosphere, structures that one would really love to give more time to [. . .]. I know, very definitely, that I feel a great sense of deprivation in terms of what I could have contributed to the general productive atmosphere of the country in literary terms and I'm sure a lot of other writers feel the same. That is one of the penalties of the political situation we've been undergoing since independence and which has got *progressively* worse, progressively more lethal. The penalties for the wrong kind of political action in this situation have become far more depressing" (Wilkinson 92-93).

Works Cited

Achebe, Chinua. "The Novelist as Teacher." *Morning Yet on Creation Day: Essays.* London: Heinemann, 1965. 42-45.

Ake, Claude. *The Democratization of Disempowerment in Africa.* Lagos: Malthouse P, 1994.

Chabal, Patrick. *Power in Africa: An Essay in Political Interpretation.* New York: St. Martin's, 1992.

Davidson, Basil. *The Black Man's Burden: Africa and the Curse of the Nation State.* New York: Random, 1992.

Mamdani, Mahmood. *Citizen and Subject: Contemporary Africa and the Legacy of Late Colonialism.* Princeton, NJ: Princeton UP, 1996.

Mbembe, Achille. *On the Postcolony.* Berkeley: U of California P, 2001.

Soyinka, Wole. *The Open Sore of a Continent: A Personal Narrative of the Nigerian Crisis.* New York: Oxford UP, 1996.

Wilkinson, Jane, ed. *Talking with African Writers Interviews with African Poets, Playwrights and Novelists.* London: J. Currey, 1990.

Young, Crawford. *The African Colonial State in Comparative Perspective.* New Haven, CT: Yale UP, 1994.

Wale Oyedele (essay date 2004)

SOURCE: Oyedele, Wale. "*Season of Anomy—* Postmodernism and Development Discourse." *Neohelicon* 31, no. 2 (2004): 281-88.

[*In the essay that follows,* Oyedele discusses Season of Anomy *as a postmodernist text, focusing specifically on the narrative subtext, which emphasizes the themes of emancipation and progress.*]

I

Postmodernism and postcolonialism are relatively new concepts that have been put forth in the effort by different societies to come to terms with new realities. As theories and practice, they are about the present as they are about the past and its continuing effects. An important part of this effect is that contemporary life is lived as an intersection of diverse aspects that can no longer be taken for granted. The wider consequence is the rash of "posts" that characterizes contemporary discourse almost everywhere. "Post" has been prefixed to such diverse concepts as nation, Marxism, feminism, imperialism, ideology etc.

The dialogue of multiple heritage or multiculturalism that this has spun is extensive just as the scope of deployment of terminologies is quite vast. In literary expression, it is really interesting to find works done in Africa, other parts of the Third World and in the global West itself put under the postmodernist rubric. For instance, Chabal, in his discussion of the African crisis cites Rushdie's *Satanic Verses* and the works of Wole Soyinka and Ben Okri as postmodernist because they successfully combine the "art of the West and the inspiration from a non-Western culture." He draws attention to the wider import of this view when he says:

> regardless of the present condition of Africa, a genuinely creative African literature would be as resolutely postmodern as its Western counterpart. Or rather, that the two are no longer separate but part of one universal literary creation which can speak to us all.

(41)

We learn from Said in *Culture and Imperialism* that narratives ultimately claim social space for themselves and that right from its origins, the novel as a wholly Western cultural form has been imbricated with the space of imperialism (62; 70-71). In the counter-discursive tradition, African novels have operated largely in the same postcolonial space, with a more abiding interest in Africa's economic and cultural realities and social and ideological contradictions of contemporary postcolonial realities regardless of the rubric of categorization that critical reception ultimately invests such works with. Mutations of diverse configurations ultimately characterize contexts of interaction characterized by intersections. Gilbert and Tompkins have observed that in such developments, the centre/margin model canonized in postmodernism as a model for understanding imperialism can be problematic (256).

Chabal's opinion above leans heavily on the creative universe of literary expression. There is another universe, the universe of social action that is characterized by the social and cultural verities highlighted above. Both levels combine to give a picture of the marriage of the explicit with the implicit or the downright contemplative, all of which go to qualify the postmodern experience in postcolonial texts.

This arises largely because the Third World experience of multiculturalism is tied with a major quest for emancipation in which development and decolonization are important subtexts. This quest, and the insistent emphasis given to it, certainly modifies, if it does not even resist easy adoption into a single universal literary creation. We propose to examine Wole Soyinka's *Season of Anomy* as an example of this postmodernist thrust with a development subtext.

II

The disproportionate attention given to scatology and grotesquery, with additional force supplied by unindividuated characterization and naming are quite capable of taking the attention away from the rather subtle manner in which the emancipation discourse is conducted in *Season of Anomy*. Aiyero, in many senses a literary shorthand for Africa, can be put in the bracket of such communities as Ilmorog (*Petals of Blood*), Kameno and Makuyu ridges (*The River Between*), and Umuofia (*Things Fall Apart*) etc. The distinction of Aiyero lies in the fact that unlike these others whose participation in modern civilization is forced on them, Aiyero has so much of a leeway over its present and by its peculiar circumstances, can determine its future alliances and other directions. Seen this way, the sweeping orgy of killing and destruction that predominate show more clearly as a consequence of more overt actions which are themselves spin offs of other subtle but potentially irruptive choices in their epistemic ramifications. These irruptive choices border on the effort to make sense of the multiple heritage.

Wiredu's characterization of a communalist society appears to sit quite well with Aiyero's traditional state before its transformation:

> . . . one in which the individual is brought up to cultivate an ultimate sense of obligation and belonging to quite large groups of people . . . . This inculcation of an extensive sense of human bond provides a natural school for the enlargement of sympathies which stretches out beyond the limits of kinship to a wider community.
>
> (21)

The incidents and events in which we are permitted to see Aiyero in action are not many, but Pa Ahime comes across as its human embodiment, soul, and heartbeat. Aiyero offers a wholly homegrown model of politics, governance, economic and cultural structures and values. The common thread is collectivized relations. Property is jointly owned. Enterprise and the exercise of human talents are in the areas of fishing and farming. Boat building is the joint commercial venture and the income therefrom is complemented by the percentage sent home by Aiyero citizens that go to work in other places in the country.

The text's device for the summation of all that the community stands for is the scene of the burial of the commune's leader that goes by the interesting title of the Custodian of the Grain. The scene is remarkable not just for mass participation and involvement, it is vintage demonstration of the ascription, acceptance and performance of roles that have the appurtenances of choreography in socio-cultural terms. Guilds, groups, raconteurs, processions, rites, pungent smells and masks all fill the space. Man, nature and invisible forces form one cosmic bond. The objects of the elaborate sacrifice—bulls, blood, kolanut, oil, pigeons and others range beyond themselves and convey a mystical aura.

This is the state of affairs that Ofeyi, the sales promotion man describes with such expressions as "mould" and "stagnation" which appear to be implicated in the novel's more subtle resonances:

> . . . I don't know how to convey to you the smell of mould, stagnation which clings to places like this. It can prove paralyzing in a crisis and our generation appears to be born into one long crisis.
>
> (6)

The connection here established between mould, stagnation and paralysis is certainly interesting and such an observation must have been brought about in the first place because Aiyero has conducted its affairs in a manner that is largely oblivious of the developments taken for granted elsewhere in the 20th century of the novel's setting. But what is particularly striking is the conjunction of views between Ofeyi and the elders of the Aiyero commune which is unmistakable in the decision to offer Ofeyi the post of the Custodian of the Grain, the office of the commune's seniormost official:

Maybe the same thought has occurred to some among us. Have you thought of that? Why do you think the Founder began to think of a total stranger to succeed him as Custodian of the Grain? The meaning of the grain is not merely food but, germination . . .

(6)

The particulars of this conjunction of views relates to the identification of potential crisis with Aiyero's traditional state and an antithesis supplied to this by the ingestion or embrace of other realms and layers of experience. It should be noted here that there is an intention to come to terms with the multiple heritage of modern civilization or contemporary existence; an issue that is very much at the heart of the discourse of postmodernism.

The proposal for this ingestion and embrace comes in the form of making Aiyero a base for cocoa production which Ofeyi put to the elders. Indeed, Ofeyi's first contact with Aiyero is a result of a sales promotion campaign, his brief in the corporation where he works. Sales promotion is itself part of the complex process of an agricultural business which is intimately connected to influencing the behaviour of the end user or final consumer. Cash crop production is just one step. Other steps include processing by heavy equipment and machinery, packaging and distribution. Involved in this process is a whole order of personnel which performs diverse tasks. The name that the text calls this complex arrangement is the Cartel and its multi-regional and by extension multi-national dispersal is particularly emphasized in the novel's events.

This is a sharp departure from the collectivized near-agrarian farming to which Aiyero had been accustomed. But the people are ready for the necessary adjustments. The forest is cleared and the old founding ballads of Aiyero give way to a body of new work-songs which grows from the "grain of the vanguard idea" (20). Other expatriated Aiyero children are to shed the old tribal toga and embrace "new affinities, new working-class relationships" (170). At the maturation of the project, Aiyero is envisaged to be projected as a refreshing philosophy of new man, both in the material circumstances of the cocoa production and in the intangible but crucial proselytisation of this philosophy by Aiyero's expatriated children.

This then articulates an ancillary project that is grafted on the assumed economic success and consequent development that the cocoa project guarantees: Aiyero, the model of the new man and its expatriated children the hub of a model of liberation and development to be projected across the national commonwealth. According to the text:

> The goals were clear enough, the dream a new concept of labouring hands across artificial frontiers, the concrete affective presence of Aiyero throughout the land, undermining the Cartel's superstructure of robbery, indignities and murder, ending the new phase of slavery.
>
> (27)

Of course, it is good to bear in mind Hawthorn's observation on the limitless range of positive mischief that writers make out of free indirect discourse as above (79). But within the context of its deployment, it could only have been Ofeyi's thought.

III

We said earlier that novelistic space in *Season of Anomy* is shared between incidents and their agents according to the needs of the narrative. One immediate implication of this is that the postmodern discourse in the text is conducted at times in emblematic terms and at times explicitly especially if the substantial attention to the nature of evilry is seen as an effect.

Wider issues are woven into the text's conflicts at times by hints and allusions. Apart from its punitive intent, Ofeyi's forced leave is meant to tackle certain cognitive problems. We learn on page 21 that America, Japan and Germany are some of the countries that he will visit. Ofeyi's needs are articulated in terms of acquisition of more and presumably better professional know-how in the best places that they could be acquired. But in a genre that cuts its teeth in the postcolonial space, such choices even though it is in connection with advertising cannot but evoke the unequal relations brought in the wake of the mutation from global imperialism to global neo-imperialism.

Advertising itself has often thrived more in the competitive but often exploitative capitalist economic relations.

The relation between the Cartel, the Jeku Party, the Army, and the political leaders and the neo-imperial choices above can be seen in respect of their conscious and unconscious cooptation which they find convenient not least because it enables a reproduction of the neo-imperialist epistemology on a local scale. The internal forces coalesce around Zaki Amuri, around whom the others gravitate in a secondary interpellatory and cooptative process. It is in this sense that Aiyero reproduces a paradigm of cultural difference both within the nation and the wider world of the text.

Well, the motions are not just in one direction. For Ofeyi, Aiyero is an evident change of tack and strategy. He suddenly finds the practice of signifying through the copies and songs of his stage shows insufficient since as Lyne says in another context a ". . . carnival of signifying may point to the shortcomings of the status quo, but it does little to change them" (329). What results from all these however is the opposite: the deployment of an overkill of violence against Aiyero's men and others nationwide to serve the important notice that the critical and activist dispensation is not tolerated by the quad; the abduction of Iriyise, Ofeyi's lover and staff, which forces an abandonment of the project by Ofeyi as he searches for her for the rest of the novel; the retreat of Aiyero's men nationwide to scale down the loss etc.

The combination of the exercise of raw political power, and evilry may appear to confer invincibility on the quad and what it represents. This appears not too far fetched in Jones' conclusion on the Aiyero effort:

> it is difficult to imagine that the Cartel, having identified Aiyero as a source of dissidence, with its power still intact and its appetite for blood stimulated, would make this (i.e., Aiyero's decision to regroup and continue the fight) easy.

(210)

This is of course taking a view of the contest in near-exclusive military terms. But the action-reaction, wind-whirlwind dialectic offers us another view.

The violent backlash and clashes are just a more theatricalised effect of much deeper ideational clash and contradiction which perhaps becomes stark when placed in its discursive paradigm. The theoretical-conceptual paradigm has some unique features from which the action-reaction dialectic can be anticipated and is responsible for the especial tone, character and outcome of the contest. By extension, there is a sense in which Aiyero's moves and gestures can be anticipated and its containment similarly worked out. In short, the failure of the Aiyero project is the failure of a paradigm that cannot guarantee liberation and development by consequence.

Ofeyi's statement on page 27 quoted above offers us a view of the transformed Aiyero as having been tooled/retooled to be able to effect Ofeyi's envisaged emancipation. Before the transformation, Ofeyi perceives "mould" and "stagnation" as descriptive of Aiyero's traditional, isolated life. Stasis and regression are some of the connotations that these words evoke. It will not be far fetched to read linearity as lying behind this attitude to development for which Western industrialization provides an update or even growth and evolution. If "mould" escapes this charge because it is figural, "stagnation" hardly can. This embrace then signifies a combination of the poles but with a peculiar postcolonial inflection.

The situation becomes clearer when all this is considered in more practical terms. The substance of this envisaged change lies in the transposition of the cultural and ethical context that has embraced the economic and market relations of cocoa production. The ethical-political context represented by the quad appears to be the major source of grouse. In this transposition then, the whole gamut of the structured complex production process of cocoa industrialization with its further inner structure of unequal exchange relations, institutionalized racism, sexual bias and class divisions has been given a new ethical and cultural scaffold.

In his discussion of what he calls the postcolonial impasse in relation to emancipation discourse, Garuba, echoing George, identifies what he call the postcolonial condition:

> This condition is evidenced in the belief in the validity of traditional African culture with its customs, world view, and belief systems and a simultaneous acceptance of the idea of modernity as codified in the Enlightenment project with its emphasis on instrumental reason, science, progress and so on.

(9)

The Aiyero project as conceived by Ofeyi reproduces this in many respects. The Western arm of its embrace especially privileges instrumental reason, science and the linear conception of progress. When the brute force of this combination is left intact in this manner, its inherently monologic nature will only lead to closure by appropriating the other or at best, tolerate the other as opposite.

In its fully developed form, Garuba says further that this sort of contradiction leads to unimaginative mimicry on the one hand and uncreative violence on the other (5). It is most ironical to observe here the unconscious filiation of transformed Aiyero with Gborolu, the Cartle's cosmopolis of bipartite transformations in which both unimaginative mimicry and uncreative violence combine to manifest as social divisions. It is also instructive that the bulk of the text is taken up by ruminations on the mode of violence that will produce a more effective counter to the quad's mindless orgy of carnage and destruction.

For much of its verve, the Aiyero project only offers a more ethically upright version of the nationalist discourse. The evidence that this has always been contained lies in the fact that it cannot even influence or subvert the unfair exchange rate that has been the lot of most postcolonial societies playing on the global economic stage. They, like Aiyero, have always been on the fringe. Similarly, the activist programme is grounded before take off by these contradictions. If it becomes successful, then its end is already foregrounded in the beginning that is the Aiyero project, a rather ironical turn.

IV

One of the important effects in **Season of Anomy** is the relationship between cognition and development or rather, the repositioning of development as a cognitive matter. Given the nature of the public sphere, it is safe enough to say that our actions are implicated in concepts formulated consciously or unconsciously.

Emancipation and development will be possible by articulating what Garuba calls a "third text" which participates in but resists cooptation into either the binarism of postmodernism or postcolonialism. It entails embrace, disruption and critique at either ends. Part of the weaknesses of the Aiyero project is that the stability of economic and business relations is not disrupted and the whole development project cannot evolve its own logic of progression because of this. This simply leaves the initiative to the already powerful side that still recognizes itself in the famed transformation. This much can be felt in the statement by Batoki whom the text describes humorously as the "tunesmith of proverbs:" the child who swears his mother will not sleep, he must also pass a sleepless night" (86). The untamed power still looms large: "You can begin all over again . . . the idea is most valuable, but there are other lands beside Aiyero" (21). The biggest moral is that instrumental reason is most times amoral and will find cohabitation with such high egalitarianism difficult.

It does appear that for the postcolonial world that seeks genuine postmodernism, the development strategy will have to be articulated within two broad ideational paradigms that Baker has highlighted: on the one hand is the paradigm of *homo laborans* (man as labourer) which defines world trade, investment capitalism, market economy etc. On the other is the paradigm, *homo ludens* (man at play) which defines an aspect of modern experience that is not traditionally defined as essential to the processes of economic production and distribution (xi).

Such an approach is not readily embraced in contemporary times because the uni-polar construct has particularly strengthened American neo-imperialism which has been on the ascendant. This in turn receives additional impetus from the informal, interpellative powers of its cultural authority which is serviced by its control over information. There is equally enough informal political and economic compensation for the Ofeyi script in the politics of postcolonial societies to discourage such an ideological and altruistic intervention.

Let us say in summing up that postcolonial texts tell the story of postmodern possibilities for the black world implicitly through the creative universe of the texts. But in explicit thematisation, or even as an effect, what can be observed are the difficulties associated with accomplishing these possibilities and/or at times, the strategy that is required to bring this about. The narrative design of *Season of Anomy* seems to reproduce this disjoint in its own unique way. The incidents and events capture the frustrations of the postmodern discourse in the postcolonial world while the title of the sub-divisions—seminal, buds, tentacles, harvest and spores—signifying on the converse, appear to affirm the possibilities in figural, development terms.

Bibliography

Baker, H. A.: "Introduction" *Opening Up the Canon: Selected Papers from the English Institute, 1979.* Eds. Fiedler, A. and Baker, H. A. Baltimore and London: John Hopkins Press, 1981, x-xiii.

Chabal, P.: "The African Crisis: Context and Interpretation". *Postcolonial Identities in Africa.* London and New Jersey: Zed Books Limited, 1996, 29-54.

Garuba, H. "Negotiating the (Post) Colonial Impasse: Wole Soyinka's *The Lion and the Jewel* and Derek Walcott's *Ti-Jean and His Brothers*". Paper presented at the 1994/95 Department of English Staff Seminar Series, University of Ibadan.

Gilber, H. and Tompkins, J.: *Postcolonial Drama* London and New Jersey: Routledge, 1996.

Hawthorn, J.: *Studying the Novel: An Introduction.* London: Edward Arnold, 1992.

Jones, E. D.: *The Writing of Wole Soyinka* London: Heinemann, 1973.

Lyne, W.: "The Signifying Modernist and the Limits of Double Consciousness". *PMLA,* March, 1(7) (1992): 319-330.

Said, E. W.: *Culture and Imperialism.* New York: Vintage Books, 1992.

Soyinka, W.: *Season of Anomy.* London: Rex Collings, 1980.

Wiredu, K.: "Our Problem of Knowledge: Brief Reflection on Knowledge and Development in Africa". *Remaking Africa,* Ed. Oladipo, O. Ibadan: Hope Publications, 2002, 18-23.

Martin Banham (essay date 2005)

SOURCE: Banham, Martin. "Back to before: Soyinka's Stagecraft in *The Beatification of Area Boy & King Baabu.*" In *African Theatre: Blackout, Blowout & beyond: Wole Soyinka's Satirical Revue Sketches,* edited by Martin Banham, pp. 1-9. Trenton, N.J.: Africa World Press, 2005.

[*In the following excerpt, Banham contends that the subject matter and structure of* The Beatification of Area Boy *and* King Baabu *"indicate that Soyinka has returned enthusiastically and powerfully to the revue format that formed such a successful part of his early work."*]

Let's start with a song:

> The Russian astronauts flying in space
> Radioed a message to their Moscow base
> They said, we are flying over Nigeria
> And we see high mountains in built-up area
> Right in the middle of heavy traffic
> Is this space madness, tell us quick!
> The facts were fed to the Master Computer
> Which soon analysed the mystery factor.
> That ain't no mountain, the Computer said, snappish,
> It's just a load of their national rubbish.
>
> I love my country I no go lie
> Na inside am I go live and die
> I know my country, I no go lie
> Na im and me go yap till I die.

This is one of the verses of *Etike Revo Wetin?* from the revue *Unlimited Liability Company,* music and lyrics by Wole Soyinka, with Soyinka's great and long-time musical collaborator Tunji Oyelana. The revue was re-corded onto a long-playing record in 1983.[1] In 1995, in *The Beatification of Area Boy,* premiered in Leeds, a slightly altered version of the song emerges again—the Russian astronauts make their observation and 'the strange report was fed to computers / Which soon analysed the ponderous beauties / The computer re-plied, don't be snobbish / You know it's a load of their national rubbish.' The chorus, in line with the play's setting, substitutes Lagos for 'my country'.

> I love dis Lagos, I no go lie
> Na inside am I go live and die
> I know my city, I no go lie
> E fit in nation like coat and tie
> When Lagos belch, the nations swell
> When the nation shit, na Lagos dey smell.
> The river wey flow for Makurdi market
> You go find in deposit for Lagos bucket.[2]

The Beatification of Area Boy and Soyinka's most re-cent play *King Baabu,*[3] satirise respectively the Abacha regime in Nigeria and military tyrants generally. *King Baabu,* of course, takes its inspiration from Alfred Jarry's *Ubu Roi* and the form and stagecraft of both plays indicate that Soyinka has returned enthusiastically and powerfully to the revue format that formed such a successful part of his early work. This brief [essay] is entitled 'Back to Before' and you will recognise the 'Before' as being a reference to the various revues cre-ated by Soyinka and his colleagues in the late 1960s and early '70s, partially published in *Before the Black-out* in 1971.[4] Material from the Unife Theatre 'Guerilla Unit' 1978-9 under the general title of *Before the Blow-out* is also relevant here.[5] Those of us lucky (and old!) enough to have enjoyed *The Republican* and *New Re-publican* in 1964 and *Before the Blackout* in 1964 can share Soyinka's regret, voiced in the preface to the pub-lished review, that inevitably the mime sketches cannot be reproduced, but in fact they do resurface in—for in-stance—the postures of the Reformed Aweri Fraternity, the characters of the Right and Left Ears of State and in Kongi's assumption of 'unconscious' poses ('A Lead-er's Temptation', 'The Loneliness of the Pure', 'The Face of Benevolence') in *Kongi's Harvest* (1967) as well as in set pieces such as The Professor's praying duel with the Bishop in *The Road* (1965). Soyinka, in the same preface, argues for the effectiveness of the re-vue format as a counter to the amnesia created by 'the cosy, escapist air of formal theatres'.

Before the Blackout, the two available sketches from *Before the Blowout* and the recording of *Unlimited Li-ability Company* offer a range of examples of Soyinka's creative recycling of revue material into the two latest substantial plays. We have seen how a revue song re-emerges in *The Beatification of Area Boy. Before the Blackout* and *Before the Blowout* seem to me to con-tribute both characters and situations to *Beatification* and *King Baabu.* Both plays parade gross characters before us, in *Baabu*'s case a reincarnation of Jarry's

monstrous eponymous hero Ubu and his equally gro-tesque wife. But we have met them before. The two sketches from *Before the Blowout,* 'Home to Roost' and 'Big Game Safari' feature 'the famous Chief Theophilus Ajijebolorita Onikura and his wife Cecilia, known as "De Madame".' As they prepare for power they proclaim themselves 'The People's Couple'. In-flated only slightly they re-emerge in *King Baabu* as King Baabu the Bountiful, Baabu the Munificent, Fa-ther of the Nation, and his Queen consort Maariya. Their posturings on the balcony of the State House re-mind us of Kongi and mimed sketches from *Before the Blackout.* King Baabu's theatrical genesis can also, I suggest, be traced to Babuzu Lion Heart, 'the Papa Doc of the continent' in the *Before the Blackout* sketch 'Babuzu Lion Heart'. Soyinka describes him as 'a clear noon-day paranoid'. 'I am', he declaims to his sixteen year old 'popsy', 'Babuzu the Only, with a heart of a Lion. No, I *am* the Lion. Babuzu the Lion of Malladi. Grr-r-rrr!' *[He stops by a flowerpot, uproots the entire plant and squeezes it in his hand]* How I deal with plots against the state. Good! *[squeezes harder]* That juice is red, the blood of Babuzu's enemies. Gr-r-rr-! Animals!' The mixture of the absurd, the pathetic and the downright lethal embraces a wide bag of ty-rants. King Baabu himself eats his way through the wildlife of Africa and then, further to feast and satisfy himself, turns on his fellow men. Ubu has also been visited before by Soyinka. In another sketch from the same revue, 'Childe Internationale', 'Politician'—described as 'a "native-proper" self made business-man'—confronted by his 'been-to' wife, reminisces about a play he had been taken to see at the University and enjoyed. The only one, he observes, that he hadn't fallen asleep at. '. . . something like Yakubu . . . you know, the one I liked, where everybody was saying Shit.' The reference here to Ubu Roi's famous opening line—'Merde!'—confirms that Jarry's play was well es-tablished in Soyinka's creative consciousness long be-fore King Baabu emerged. (Astutely, James Gibbs iden-tifies another relative of Ubu in the 'malignant monster' Field Marshall Kamini, in *A Play of Giants,* who fa-mously tastes 'the elixir of power' when he seduces the wife of a man he is later to execute.[6] Incidentally, the University of Toronto also gets a mention in *Before the Blackout.* In the sketch 'Press Conference', The Min-ister deals with the Press confidently and without brook-ing interruption:

> Question: Now Sir, about the problems of this coalition Government. I wonder if . . .
>
> Answer: My friend, before you say anything else let me remind you that I am an M.A. Michigan. In fact, I got two B.A.s, you know: one at Toronto for Political Science and one for National Economics and Sociol-ogy, that was in Dublin . . . it was after that I went to Michigan to get my Masters . . . The B.A. Toronto was with honours you know. First class with honours. The B.A. Dublin had no honours but that was discrimi-nation. . . .

But to return to *Beatification* and *Baabu.* Both plays are broadly and vivaciously drawn pieces of popular theatre. *Beatification* has a range of scenes that could stand alone as revue sketches—the prisoners doing the 'army conga', the adoration of the bicycle, the military officer with his cry of 'DON'T TOUCH MY UNIFORM!!' plus strong musical elements. *Baabu* is constructed in a series of increasingly extravagant, fiercely satirical episodes tracking the career of Baabu from 'loyal' general to genocidal madman. *Beatification* is subtitled '*A Lagosian Kaleidoscope*'. In *King Baabu* the kaleidoscope tumbles ever more jagged and bloody images before us as this latter-day Ubu goes out of control and takes his country with him. The theatrical satire, playing to the eye as much as the ear, commences by entertaining the audience and culminates by confronting it. In the last moments of the play[7] (and here I'm quoting from the second draft of the manuscript) King Baabu, in a scene that may remind us of the despatch of another tyrant, is poisoned by a dose of doctored rhino powder—his preferred aphrodisiac. His Queen, Maariya looks on her collapsing world:

> And what are you all looking at? You think this is a freak show do you? It's not over. It's much too soon to crow. I know all your secrets and I won't go quietly. I know you're going to start lying to the people, lying, lying, lying, you fake redeemers. You want to settle accounts but your accounts are safely stashed away you know where. Now he's gone you'll all become butter-won't-melt-in-your-mouths latter-day saints. No, of course you never knew him, you never embraced him or sucked up to him, never used him when it suited you, you lying sycophants, you stinking collaborators, you slimy accomplices before, during and after the fact. Lying, lying . . . laundering your past so you can continue without shame in the public eye, shameless, shameless, shameless . . . of course now it was he who did it all, single-handed, no help from anyone, you never knew anything . . . oh yes you know how to renew yourselves so people begin to wonder if their memory has failed them, if you're not the same people who drove them into the wilderness, but oh yes you'll keep going and going and going on and on and on . . .
> *[As the lights dim slowly]*

It is, I believe, in the whole-hearted return to broad satirical theatre, growing from the fertile roots and means of the revue format, that Soyinka is seeking a new political engagement with contemporary audiences.

A song to finish with to remind us where Maariya's sentiments come from—another potential tyrant, petty-Ubu, lethal fool—again from *Before the Blackout*—'The Ogbugbu of Gbu'.[8]

> These trying times demand much care
> With crises, plots and tension
> From six hundred quid to a naira a year
> Is that a decent pension
>
> What matters if I sell my friends
> And lick some ass's arse-hole

> The new generation will make amends
> I'll stay on the government pay-roll.
>
> And this is the law I do maintain
> Till death, and so would you Sir
> That whatsoever Big Noise may reign
> I'll be the Ogbugbu of Gbu, sir.

The text of *Before the Blackout* that was published c. 1971 represented a range of materials first created for the revues of the 1960s—*The Republican, The (New) Republican* (1963) and *Before the Blackout* (1964). All were presented by companies Soyinka formed with colleagues, The 1960 Masks and the Orisun Players.

The programme of *The (New) Republican* . . . gives a taste of this early work and the performers who worked with Soyinka—many of them, including the musician Tunji Oyelana and the actor the late Wale Ogunyemi, becoming stalwarts of Soyinka's work thereafter. It describes the show as '1960 Masks in The (new) Republican and the Orisun Players'. Sketches were credited to Ralph Opara, Francesca Pereira, Yemi Lijadu, Olga Adeniyi-Jones and Wole Soyinka. The programme identifies writers through initials. Stage management was by Frank Aig-Imoukhuede and Kofi Pereira, and the production by Yemi Lijadu. The occasion was described as 'introducing the Orisun Players' and bore the following tongue-in-cheek disclaimer:

> The 1960 Masks solemnly declare that all the characters in this revue are wholly fictitious, and that any resemblances to man or woman, living or dead, are accidental and should be brought to their notice for further development.

In March/April 1964, six months after *The (New) Republican* was put on, Soyinka returned with *Before the Blackout,* presented in Lagos and Ibadan. The programme indicates the content, the running order and offers a few clues as to the targets of the sketches.

Of course the impact of the majority of these sketches in all the revues relied on their contemporary references and relevance, and a certain complicit familiarity with those lampooned on behalf of the audience generally (the Lagos and Ibadan middle class/university audience). The corruption and self-serving nature of politicians was a common topic. Some individuals are specifically targeted. For instance, in the 1971 text, as the note at the head of the sketch indicates, *Babuzu Lion Heart* was originally based on Kwame Nkrumah, but events between 1964 and the 1970s made it more pertinent to be updated to point to the Malawian 'President for Life' Dr Hastings Banda. *Vintage Scenes* is a grotesque comment on the cynical manipulation of the post-independence 1962 census in Nigeria, with voters being conjured back from the dead. *Childe Internationale* and, to a degree, *Death Before Discourtesy* made fun of the clash between generations and cultures in a rapidly changing world, again a theme well within the experience of the revues' audiences. . . .

Notes

1. Ewúro Productions EWP 001.
2. *The Beatification of Area Boy,* Methuen, London 1995, p. 17.
3. Performed 2001, published by Methuen 2002.
4. Orisun Acting Editions, Ibadan, 1971.
5. For information on *Before the Blowout* see Ahmed Yerimah, 'The Guerilla Theatre as a Tool for National Re-Awakening: A Study of the Soyinka Experiments', in Ebele Eko et al. (eds), *Literature and National Consciousness,* Heinemann, Ibadan, 1989 (I believe this article may have appeared originally in *Odu* 32, 1987).
6. James Gibbs, *Wole Soyinka,* Macmillan, London, 1986, p. 158.
7. Second draft of *King Baabu,* October 2000.
8. 'Ballad of Nigerian Philosophy', pp. 73-5.

FURTHER READING

Criticism

Adekoya, Olusegun. "A Picture of the Big Apple." *Research in African Literatures* 34, no. 2 (summer 2003): 183-91.

Discusses Soyinka's vision of New York City and his attitudes toward the United States through a reading of his poem "New York, U.S.A."

Ebewo, Patrick. *Barbs: A Study of Satire in the Plays of Wole Soyinka.* Kampala, Uganda: JANyeko Publishing Centre, 2002, 221 p.

Full-length examination of satire in Soyinka's plays, divided into sections including "The Socio-Political Scene: Comedy and Satire," "Religion and Superstition," "Tyrants and Military Dictators," and "Women and Sex."

Jeyifo, Biodun. *Wole Soyinka: Politics, Poetics, and Postcolonialism.* Cambridge: Cambridge University Press, 2004, 322 p.

Full-length study focusing on the relationship between Soyinka's body of work and his political and social views and activism.

McLuckie, Craig. "The Structural Coherence of Wole Soyinka's *Death and the King's Horseman.*" *College Literature* 31, no. 2 (spring 2004): 143-63.

Analyzes the function and significance of the peritexts—the title, subtitles, personal dedications, and author's note—in Soyinka's *Death and the King's Horseman.*

Additional coverage of Soyinka's life and career is contained in the following sources published by Gale: *African Writers*; *Black Literature Criticism,* Ed. 1:3; *Black Writers,* Eds. 2, 3; *Concise Dictionary of World Literary Biography,* Vol. 3; *Concise Major 21st-Century Writers,* Ed. 1; *Contemporary Authors,* Vol. 13-16R; *Contemporary Authors New Revision Series,* Vols. 27, 39, 82, 136; *Contemporary Dramatists,* Eds. 5, 6; *Contemporary Literary Criticism,* Vols. 3, 5, 14, 36, 44, 179; *Contemporary Novelists,* Eds. 6, 7; *Contemporary Poets,* Eds. 1, 2, 3, 4, 5, 6, 7; *Dictionary of Literary Biography,* Vols. 125, 332; *DISCovering Authors*; *DISCovering Authors 3.0*; *DISCovering Authors: British*; *DISCovering Authors: Canadian Edition*; *DISCovering Authors Modules: Dramatists, Most-Studied Writers, Multicultural Authors*; *Drama Criticism,* Vol. 2; *Drama for Students,* Vol. 10; *Encyclopedia of World Literature in the 20th Century,* Ed. 3; *Literature Resource Center*; *Major 20th-Century Writers,* Eds. 1, 2; *Major 21st-Century Writers* (eBook), 2005; *Reference Guide to English Literature,* Ed. 2; *Twayne's World Authors*; *World Literature and Its Times,* Ed. 2; *World Literature Criticism,* Vol. 5; and *World Writers in English,* Vol. 1.

Efua Sutherland
1924-1996

(Born Efua Theodora Morgue) Ghanian playwright and children's author.

INTRODUCTION

Sutherland was a pioneer of African theater, not only writing well-received plays but also founding the Ghana Experimental Theatre, which sought to expose both urban and rural Africans to drama. In her plays Sutherland foregrounds the role of women in modernizing Africa while they simultaneously nurture a sense of heritage.

BIOGRAPHICAL INFORMATION

Sutherland was born in 1924 in the Gold Coast region of western Africa—what is now the nation of Ghana—in 1924. She attended secondary school at St. Monica's College in Ashanti. Afterward she moved to England to attend Homerton College, Cambridge University, where she received a bachelor's degree in education before going to the University of London to study at the School of Oriental and African Studies. In 1951 she returned to Ghana and taught first at a secondary school in Takoradi, then at her alma mater, St. Monica's. She married William Sutherland, an African American, in 1954 and the two later founded a school in the Trans-Volta region in northern Ghana and established a theater for local productions in the central region. In 1958 Sutherland founded the Ghana Experimental Theatre in Accra. In 1960 Sutherland received funding from the U.S.-based Rockefeller Foundation and the Arts Council of Ghana to found the Ghana Drama Studio. The studio became part of the University of Ghana in 1963 and Sutherland was granted a long-term research position at the university's Institute of African Studies. At the Institute Sutherland founded the Ghana Society of Writers. Next she formed a community theater in Ekumfi-Atwian called Kodzidan and a traveling performance group called Kusum Agoromba. In 1962 Sutherland began working at the New School for Music and Drama, followed by positions with Ghana's National Commission on Children and the Du Bois Center for African Culture. Sutherland spent much of her career in theater traveling around Ghana with her performance groups. In the 1980s she served as an advisor to Ghana's President Jerry Rawlings. She died in 1996.

MAJOR WORKS

Having started out writing short stories, Sutherland turned to drama when she realized it would lend her works broader appeal in a country where so many citizens are illiterate. Sutherland's first major play, *Foriwa* (1962), originally appeared as a short story, entitled "New Life at Kyerefaso," in Langston Hughes's anthology *An African Treasury* in 1960. Based on a folktale, *Foriwa* is an allegory about a village called Kyerefaso, whose inhabitants refuse to accept changes to their way of life. It is not until the title character, who is the daughter of the town's "queen mother," marries a simple student named Labaran that the village is brought to enlightenment and a sense of its place in modernity. *Foriwa* is considered a metaphor for twentieth-century Ghana, with Sutherland advocating national unity regardless of gender, ethnic, or ideological differences. One of Sutherland's most acclaimed plays, *Edufa* (1962) is based on Greek dramatist Euripides's play *Alcestis*. When the play's title character—a vain, Western-educated, newly rich man—is told by an oracle that he will die unless he finds someone to take his place, he slyly convinces his wife to die for him. But while Euripides's version of the story was a "satyr play," or burlesque tragicomedy, Sutherland's is a tragedy, where trading in traditional values in favor of contemporary greed and narcissism brings about the downfall of Edufa and his culture. In *The Marriage of Anansewa* (1971), Sutherland used many techniques of traditional oral storytelling, including the involvement of the audience and a storyteller or narrator who serves as a mediator between actors and audience. For the story of her play, Sutherland returned to Ghanaian folklore, employing a trickster figure as the father of Anansewa, who is to be married. Seeking a high bride-price on his daughter, the father interrogates and manipulates her suitors mercilessly, unaware of the way he exploits his own daughter.

CRITICAL RECEPTION

Sutherland's major plays have been heralded for the innovation they demonstrate in adapting ancient sources and theatrical techniques to modern drama, as well as for their portrayal of women's roles in enacting social and political change in Africa. Sutherland is also admired for her commitment to take theater to people living in remote villages. Addressing Sutherland's legacy in the context of her interest in educating African children, the critic Gay Wilentz wrote: "Her performances and productions, her village education for children, and her plays themselves illustrate a playwright tied not only to the traditions and customs of the African continuum but secure in her place as an African woman passing on the values of her foremothers to the children."

PRINCIPAL WORKS

Odasani (drama) 1960

Playtime in Africa [photographs by Willis E. Bell] (children's verse) 1960

Edufa (drama) 1962

Foriwa (drama) 1962

Anansegoro: You Swore an Oath (drama) 1963

Tahinta (children's play) 1968

Vulture! Vulture! (children's play) 1968

The Original Bob: The Story of Bob Johnson, Ghana's Ace Comedian (biography) 1970

Ananse and the Dwarf Brigade (children's play) 1971

The Marriage of Anansewa: A Storytelling Drama (drama) 1971

The Voice in the Forest: A Tale from Ghana (fairy tales) 1983

CRITICISM

Lloyd W. Brown (essay date 1981)

SOURCE: Brown, Lloyd W. "Efua Sutherland." In *Women Writers in Black Africa*, pp. 61-83. Westport, Conn.: Greenwood Press, 1981.

[*In the following essay, Brown provides an overview of Sutherland's "idea of theatre," focusing on the role of women in her interpretation of the dramatic tradition in Ghana*]

In a discussion of the theater in Ghana, Efua Sutherland once declared that a truly vital theater should heed the example of oral literature by dealing directly with contemporary experience. Oral literature, she pointed out, "uses . . . experience artistically." By a similar token, a national theater should look at and utilize the repositories of a culture's experience, it should avoid the merely imitative art of "performing plays just because they exist in books already," and it therefore should depend on the willingness of the artist to create forms which can communicate both the contemporary experience and the historical process out of which it grew. In this sense, theater becomes a kind of immediate cultural exploration: "There are all sorts of exciting things to venture and I take a deep breath and venture forth, . . . I'm on a journey of discovery. I'm discovering my own

people." Sutherland's views and practice find a ready supporter in Ama Ata Aidoo: "What she conceives," Aidoo observes of Sutherland, "is that you take the narration—the traditional narration of a folktale. In the course of the narration, you get a whole lot of dramatic behaviour which one should use, in writing plays even in English. . . . I believe with her that in order for African drama to be valid, it has to derive lots of its impetus, its strength, from traditional African dramatic forms."[1]

The agreement between Sutherland and Aidoo on this point is appropriate. As dramatists they both represent an approach to theater that is based on a marked concern with the relationship between the arts of theater (writing, production and acting, for example) and the very idea of tradition in a culture. At their best, their works exemplify a highly effective combination of Western stage conventions and African (that is, Ghanaian) traditions of oral literature and ritual folk drama. They also envision theater of this kind as an ideal symbol, or microcosm, of Ghanaian culture as a whole, in so far as that culture exemplifies the interaction of Western and African values. Since the dramatist's dramatic forms are themselves the result of this historical interaction, the play does not simply describe cultural traditions as such; the play itself and the theatrical process as a whole are part of the cultural interaction that they describe. In this sense, it is useful to approach this kind of theater as an extension of its culture.

Neither Aidoo nor Sutherland is unique in this perception of African theater as living social experience. The works of Wole Soyinka and John Pepper Clark in Nigeria clearly reflect an interest in the relationship between theater as dramatic art and theater as an example of the kind of cultural synthesis that these dramatists perceive in their society. But on balance, both Sutherland and Aidoo occupy rather special places in West African theater. More than any other dramatists of comparable stature they have been involved in the kind of theater that, as social microcosm, is specifically concerned with the significance of sexual roles and relationships in their culture. Clark's *Song of a Goat* and Soyinka's *The Lion and the Jewel* are equally specific in this regard. The breakdown of the marriage in Clark's work disrupts the family structure, threatens the stability of the community, symbolizes crucial changes and fluctuations within the culture, and, by implication, represents a disturbing instability in the moral universe. In *The Lion and the Jewel,* Soyinka presents Baroka's sexual schemes against the background of a changing society. The chief relies on traditional ritual and on folk theater as symbols in weaving his schemes, and in the process the sexual role-playing that he exploits emerges as a dramatic art (in terms of the theater itself) and as extensions of social convention. But Aidoo and Sutherland return to this issue far more frequently and consistently than any other playwrights in Africa, emphasizing the integral relationship between the conventions of sexual role-playing and the conventions of dramatic role-playing on stage. In the process they develop their dramas as the means of questioning and analyzing the meaning of convention or social tradition. At the same time, they also stress that the woman's experience is the central, or at the very least, the major, subject of their dramatic analysis.

The prominence of the woman's role is clear enough in frankly domestic dramas like Sutherland's *Edufa* and *The Marriage of Anansewa.* Even in the relatively nondomestic context of her *Foriwa,* which is primarily a political play, there is a significant link between the woman's sense of her own identity and her awareness of changes taking place in her society.[2] In these plays the woman's awareness of self and social tradition is interwoven with the manner in which the dramatist presents her theater as an extension of the woman's culture as a whole. In this regard, we frequently find that Sutherland draws unmistakable parallels between the ingrained habits of sexual role-playing and the artistic conventions of the theater. In other words, sexual roles and dramatic roles are analogous to each other, because both have evolved within and have been shaped by specific historical conventions—sexual roles by social conventions and dramatic role-playing by the conventions of the theater.

The conventions of the theater are themselves treated as a symptom of the manner in which social conventions—in this case, Ghana's—have blended new and old values, non-African and African traditions. Consequently, the pointed analogies between the idea of sexual role-playing and the idea of theatrical role-playing, in dramatists like Sutherland and Aidoo, have a crucial implication. They suggest that the issues of sexual identity and role-playing have been radically affected by the same complex process of cultural conflict and cultural synthesis that the theater itself reflects.

All of this implies a certain interest in theater itself as a direct social experience. There is an implicit philosophical concept here that is comparable with Francis Fergusson's thesis when he expounds on what he describes as the "idea" of theater: "If Hamlet could ask the players to hold the mirror up to nature," he observes of Shakespeare's play, "it was because the Elizabethan theater was itself a mirror which had been formed at the center of the culture of its time, and at the center of the life and awareness of the community. We know now that such a mirror is rarely formed." In a different kind of society from Shakespeare's, the "very *idea* of a theater, as Hamlet assumed it, gets lost. . . . We do not have such a theater, nor do we see how to get it."[3]

Fergusson's "idea of a theater" is rooted in the notion that whenever the conventions of staging and play-acting reflect fundamental social and philosophical attitudes, then the theater itself—all the trappings of dra-

matic *representation*—is literally a microcosm of the universe as the dramatists and their society understand it. In the case of the Elizabethans, for example, the very location and structure of the stage itself reflected the Elizabethan assumptions about the ideal social order, about human life, and about the significance, as well as location, of heaven and hell. In the middle, the stage itself represented humanity; above the stage the typical Elizabethan superstructure could represent heaven, while the traditional trap-door in the stage floor opened down into Hell. In other words, the physical structure of the stage itself was an immediate projection of the Elizabethans' moral and physical concept of hell, humanity, and heaven. The same structure simultaneously reflected an accompanying social hierarchy: the superstructure could represent the court and the ruling nobility, the stage itself could be the landed and trading classes below, while the trap-door opened down to the cellar of the menial classes (*The Idea of a Theater,* p. 14).

One senses that in Sutherland and Aidoo there is such a shaping, controlling idea of theater. In their hands theater in contemporary Ghana emerges as the amalgamation of new and old forms that have been drawn from both Europe (ancient and modern) and Africa (traditional and "Westernized"). In turn, this fundamental perception of the nature of their theater is inextricable from their perception of modern Ghanaian society as a mosaic of new and old, alien and traditional—especially as this mosaic is exemplified by sexual identity and role-playing.

Of the two playwrights the older, Efua Sutherland, has been deeply involved with the mechanics of theater production for years. This involvement has had a clear impact on her interest, as dramatic writer, in the nature of dramatic conventions—and in European as well as African contributions to these conventions. Sutherland received her early education in Ghana before attending college in England. On returning home, she taught school in Ghana for some years and then launched the Ghana Society of Writers. In 1958 she established the Ghana Experimental Theatre, followed by the Ghana Drama Studio (for experimental productions). The Studio was subsequently incorporated into the University of Ghana's Institute of African Studies, and Sutherland herself has been a research fellow since then in the institute's School of Music, Dance, and Drama. In this capacity she has remained active in producing experimental plays and traditional theater, for adults as well as for children, promoting workshops that encourage writers and producers with interests in the relationship between traditional theater and contemporary Ghanaian life, and writing her own plays.

As writer, producer, and teacher, Sutherland has always been personally involved in the mechanics of theater, as well as the art of dramatic writing itself. Her career has enabled her to experiment with approaches to Ghanaian theater that explore the possible relevance of European models and the continuing vitality of indigenous folk drama and folktales. She has adapted Western drama (including her own adaptation of *Everyman*) to a Ghanaian context. At the same time, she has also been adapting Ghanaian tales to her contemporary theater. In fact, her career has been a "journey of discovery," to borrow her own words—a journey that has taken her from the adaptation of classical Greek drama (*Edufa*), to the distinctive milieu of rural life in modern Ghana (*Foriwa*), to the reliance on indigenous folk forms (*The Marriage of Anansewa*). These are not the only plays by Sutherland. Her other works have included *Odasani* (the *Everyman* production), *Nyamekye* (a production of dance, music and speech), and some children's plays (*The Pineapple Child, Ananse and the Dwarf Brigade,* and *Two Rhythm Plays*). But her three major, published plays exemplify at its best her continuing quest for certain dramatic forms—specifically, those forms which are analogous to the theme of sexual role-playing in the plays themselves.

In *Edufa* the classical Greek influence is represented by Euripides' *Alcestis*. As students of Greek drama are aware, Euripides' work is based on the legend of Admetus, king of Pherae, who has been doomed to death by Artemis for having offended the goddess. Admetus has been promised a reprieve if he can persuade someone to die on his behalf. After being rebuffed by other members of his family, including his parents, he accepts Alcestis' pledge to die in his stead. The grateful Admetus swears to remain a celibate after his wife's death. He promises her to give up his usual fondness for revelry—both vows being his assurance to Alcestis that he will mourn her for the rest of his own life.

Shortly after Alcestis dies Heracles, a friend of the family, pays a visit. Admetus is in a quandary at first. His responsibilities as a host do require him, as a matter of established custom, to entertain his guest, but this would mean breaking his solemn vows to his dead wife against revelry. He soon stifles his qualms and sets about entertaining Heracles. In return, Heracles undertakes to rescue Alcestis from death, and the play ends with her return as a silently mysterious figure who will only speak after a consecration period of three days. In Sutherland's play, death is not pronounced by an offended deity: Edufa simply learns that his death is imminent and that he can avert it by having someone die in his place. Edufa, a highly successful member of the nouveau riche, dupes his wife into taking his place by casually asking whether any member of his family loves him well enough to die for him. Ampoma says she does, thinking that she is responding to a purely hypothetical question, and in so doing dooms herself to death. Unlike Alcestis, her act of self-sacrifice is an unwitting one, but, like her Greek predecessor, Ampoma wrests the promise of life-

long celibacy from her husband. Unlike *Alcestis,* Sutherland's play ends on a note of tragic finality: there is no rescue from death here.

The thematic differences between *Alcestis* and *Edufa* shed significant light on some of the implications of Sutherland's play. Euripides invests his characters and their motives with a highly effective ambiguity. He underscores the complexity of the human personality, especially in the moment of that ultimate choice between life and death. Admetus' selfishness and his cowardice in the face of death are therefore counterbalanced by the equal selfishness of those who decline to die on his behalf. In turn, the self-serving narrowness on both sides is weighted against the understandable instinct for self-preservation. Admetus demonstrates his fickleness and insensitivity by the ease with which he breaks his vow to the dead Alcestis by ordering revels in honor of the visiting Heracles. But his hospitality is both a reflection of his genuine generosity and an observation of the strict laws of hospitality. As for Alcestis herself, the personality of the loving wife is matched by the inscrutable, even sinister, silence with which she returns from death; and the absolute selflessness which allows her to volunteer her own life for her husband's is equalled only by the ruthless single-mindedness with which she extracts from Admetus vows of life-long fidelity to her memory.

On the other hand, Sutherland's play prefers a less equivocal and more direct, satiric approach. Her Edufa is decidedly unambiguous, a grossly hypocritical man who is incapable even of the directness with which Euripides' Admetus requests his family to die for him. He represents a new breed that receives short shrift in the play, the new elite of educated and wealthy men who have adopted the worst features of Western culture (a cold-blooded materialism and a narrow individualism) and who demonstrate their "emancipation" by spurning African traditions of family, community, and religion, except in cases of emergency. Edufa symbolizes a debased and limiting notion of tradition: in his world the very idea of "tradition" has lost any connotation of the continuity of human values, and means simply the superficial forms that he has borrowed from the West and those few African conventions which he half-heartedly revives from time to time for his selfish needs.

Altogether, Edufa represents the moral anarchy that results from the rejection of a truly humane sense of society and its complex living traditions. It is significant, in this connection, that unlike Admetus, Edufa is offered an opportunity (by his father Kankam) to avert his wife's death by joining the entire family ("all of us whose souls are corporate in this household") in a collective beseeching of the gods (*Plays from Black Africa,* pp. 226-27). However, the selfish Edufa is too far removed from the traditionally communal values of family and religion, and he cannot respond to his father's appeal. Despite his shortcomings, Admetus has enough saving graces to merit his wife's reprieve from death, but when Edufa swears, in imitation of Euripides' Heracles, that he will force death to surrender up his wife, his futile threat is mere bombast: "I will bring Ampoma back. Forward, to the grave. . . . I will do it. I am conqueror. . . . Conqueror?" (*Plays from Black Africa,* p. 267).

Interestingly, Sutherland's work comes closest to the temper of her Greek predecessor's in the handling of Ampoma. Like Alcestis, Ampoma combines a capacity for loving self-sacrifice with a gentle but firm insistence on her own claims. She too exacts from her husband the promise that no other woman will share their children and their bed. As in *Alcestis,* the woman's frank self-interest implies a negative response to the husband's male selfishness. In this regard, Euripides' heroine is very skillful in the technique of using self-effacing devotion, not only as a genuine sentiment, but also as a firm, but covert, means of demanding her husband's respect.

This kind of claim is quite explicit in **Edufa,** especially when Ampoma reminds her husband that her impending death is really on his behalf, and that her love has been as self-destructive as it has been selfless. Her reminders to her husband and her claims on his fidelity seem to have a much more calculated effect than do Alcestis' demands on her husband in Euripides' play. This difference is largely due to the different circumstances under which the wives become sacrificial victims. In Alcestis' case it is a deliberate and informed act, taken with full knowledge of her husband's actual circumstances and the consequences for herself. In **Edufa,** however, the sincerity of Ampoma's offer to die on her husband's behalf does not really diminish the fact that she has really been duped into the role of sacrificial victim. In these circumstances, her reproofs to her husband imply a certain bitterness. In emphasizing the unselfish nature of her love, Ampoma is also subscribing to that strong sense of communal sharing which her husband has violated through his narrow selfishness and his greed. This is the same communality that her father-in-law invokes when he describes the family unit as a corporate body of souls.

Ampoma's invocation of the traditional ideals of a communal culture implies a certain sense of superiority to her destructively egocentric husband. In the process, she demonstrates that within this communal ideal sexual relationships enjoy a certain duality. They are a private, even intensely intimate, kind of personal sharing, but they are, simultaneously, a microcosm of that interdependence and sharing which is an intrinsical part of the communal tradition in society at large. It is therefore fitting that the chorus pays tribute, as it does, to these communal ideals when it comments on Ampoma's impending death:

Crying the death day of another
Is crying our own death day.
While we mourn for another,
We mourn for ourselves.
One's death is the death of all mankind.

(*Plays from Black Africa,* p. 234).

In Ampoma's personality this sense of tradition is a creative force rather than a merely narrow preoccupation with established forms. Her mind is flexible rather than static, growing to meet changes in her world. Consequently, she is committed to the ideal of sexual relationships as the outgrowth and reflection of communal ideas—and in this sense she reflects a strong sense of tradition. At the same time she is committed to a certain notion of female individualism: she does insist on the woman's need for a less restricted role in the society. She is therefore at pains to describe her public display of affection for her husband as a new female individualism. Women, she declares, spend most of their time concealing, and therefore restricting, their capacity for feeling—"preventing the heart from beating out its greatness." In fact "the things we would rather encourage lie choking among the weeds of our restrictions." There is not much time left for women to act, she adds chidingly, addressing the chorus of women, but instead of acting on the need for this kind of frank self-expression, women "sleep" half of the time (*Plays from Black Africa,* p. 261).

This kind of forthrightness against female restrictions is quite unmistakable, even in the work of a writer who does not think too highly of being regarded as a woman writer. Indeed, this forthrightness is even underscored by making Ampoma's sentiments representative rather than unusual, for the chorus of women agrees with Ampoma's argument. They clearly accept her analysis of women's roles in their society as the kind of truth that most women, including themselves, agree with without having the courage to voice on their own. Many women, they observe at the end of Ampoma's remark, would like to be able to say what Ampoma just said (p. 261). By extension, their agreement with Ampoma's crucial analysis suggests that they do regard her death as the symptom of a certain problem—that is, male selfishness—in the lives of women in their society, in much the same way that they have come to see her death as a communal and universal event ("One's death is the death of all mankind").

Ampoma's personality represents a complex awareness of certain traditions in her society. She is able to perceive sexual love in conjunction with those communal ideals that have persisted into the present and which she wishes to uphold. At the same time she is committed to traditions, not simply as set conventions for their own sake, but also as a growing and responsive set of values. She prizes privacy, as well as the communal implications of her sexual love. As a woman she insists upon a certain degree of independence, without espousing the kind of individualism that subverts a communal life style. This degree of individualism conforms with the degree of change she accepts as part of a continuing sense of tradition; for her individualism is clearly influenced by the West while remaining in close touch, as Edufa's does not, with their African culture. Finally, her sense of individualism remains sufficiently communal to ensure that she speaks on the subject as a representative voice—who is endorsed by the chorus of women—rather than as an eccentric outsider.

That choral endorsement is also significant in another, related sense. It exemplifies Sutherland's habit of integrating a theatrical convention (in this case the chorus) with social conventions that affect sexual relationships and identity. The convention of the chorus, borrowed from the classical Greek tradition, has been combined with the social milieu (a contemporary Ghanaian town) of Sutherland's play. As such, it appears as a group of women whose songs and chants stamp their classically derived role with a distinctively Ghanaian character. This kind of adaptation is not peculiar to Sutherland and other African dramatists, of course. But it is significant in Sutherland's work because it reflects her interest in the way in which current practices in the theater may symptomize, even reenact, cultural adaptations in the society. As a synthesis of themes and conventions from ancient Greece, old Africa, and modern Ghana, the play *Edufa* blends dramatic traditions. In turn, this blending reflects the cultural synthesis that is taking place in the changing society of which the theater is a part. In effect, the changes in Sutherland's own society have inspired her "journey of discovery" for new, expressive forms, just as much as they have sparked Ampoma's search for an expressive individualism that is compatible with established but constantly evolving customs.

While Ampoma's experience represents the search for humane social forms, her friend Senchi is the artist who is bent on a certain quest for moral order and for the appropriate means of expressing that moral vision. Her friendship with Senchi, wandering poet and singer, reinforces the impression that both personalities are brought together in the play to function as a composite character. Senchi feels uprooted and alienated, and, as such, he is an extreme form of the muted restiveness which Ampoma reveals in herself from time to time.

Senchi's role in *Edufa* is roughly analogous to Heracles' in Euripides' *Alcestis*. Senchi is a friend of both Ampoma and Edufa, just as Heracles is a friend of Admetus and Alcestis. Both Heracles and Senchi are travellers who just happen to visit their friends at a time of crisis. The similarity ends here. Senchi is a perpetual itinerant. Unlike the ebullient and gregarious Heracles, he is alienated and often cynical. His alienation as artist is more than the effect of his own critical and questioning intelligence. It is also the outcome of dislocating changes in his society, changes which have uprooted

the old African ways (respect for family, upholding of close-knit community ties, and so forth) in some quarters. Perpetual transient that he is, Senchi literally lives the experience of dislocation. Because he is repelled by the moral dislocations that he sees around him in the person of someone like Edufa, he is strongly committed to the idea of moral stability and to a social order that is stable while remaining flexible enough to accept orderly and humane change.

He shares this commitment with Ampoma. Therefore, her fate intensifies his barely concealed contempt for Edufa and for the new disruptiveness that is represented by Edufa's narrow selfishness and Western affectations. In Senchi's own words, both Edufa and himself make an odd pair, as friends, because Edufa's gross materialism is incompatible with Senchi's spiritual intensity as poet (*Plays from Black Africa,* pp. 246-47). Senchi's search for what he calls a kind and loving person (p. 238) is a quest for the kind of humaneness that could counteract Edufa's gross materialism. The circumstances of Ampoma's death represent another failure in that search. Her death means that he has ended up blank again (p. 268).

Senchi's role in the play also bears upon the relationship between artistic form and the social themes of the artist. In a personal sense, his itinerant habits and ill-fitting clothes are symbolic forms, reflecting the dislocation and disharmony which his satiric songs and stories describe. His language and the narrative style of his stories and social commentary are usually incomprehensible to everyone around him, but that very incomprehensibility underscores the sense of moral breakdown and emotional confusion he sees around him in Edufa's home and social class. Finally, the inability of others around him to understand much of what he says emphasizes his profound alienation from society in general.

Senchi's role and personality are as integral to the hybrid nature of Sutherland's theater as is his friend Ampoma. As we have already suggested, Ampoma's personality is an eclectic one, and it conforms with the hybrid nature of the play's forms, themes, and social environment. In Senchi's case, we have a rather ambiguous personality. He is repelled by Edufa's shallow imitation of Western individualism and materialism. At the same time, his own eccentricities as an alienated intellectual reflect his Westernization; for the spectacle of a poet who is deeply isolated from his own society is a familiar Western image rather than a traditional role for artists in the old Africa. He cherishes the communal humanism of old Africa, and this preference is clearly indicated by his scorn for Edufa's individualistic materialism. At the same time, his Western-style intellectuality and alienation, as poet, make it all but impossible for him to communicate his ideas to the women of the chorus, the very ones in the play whose lives are relatively close to that old communal lifestyle. In effect, he is a personal example of the ambiguities and patterns of conflict described by the play's themes, and symptomized by its form. To borrow Fergusson's idea of theater, Sutherland's sense of her social milieu, her characters and her dramatic form blends perfectly with a prevailing pattern of ambiguities and adaptations, inside and outside her theater.

There is a marked shift of emphasis in the next two major plays. Sutherland relies less heavily on adapting Western and Ghanaian forms into a hybrid pattern in *Foriwa* and *The Marriage of Anansewa*. In these two plays, there is a greater emphasis on reviving a sense of old African traditions, or celebrating the ones that have managed to survive into the modern world. There is a corresponding shift away from hybrid theatrical conventions towards the indigenous forms and conventions of the dramatist's own culture. In fact, the themes and the staging of a work like *Foriwa* do not simply describe the revitalization of indigenous forms and values. The play itself is a part of this process of revitalization, for its very existence reflects a vital and continuing interest, among the playwright and her audience, in the indigenous forms.

As theater, *Foriwa* incorporates the folk rituals of the community's traditional African culture and, in so doing, the play imbues these forms and rituals with a fresh, contemporary significance. This is comparable with the manner in which its themes call for a renewed commitment to the substance, rather than mere form, of indigenous conventions. At the same time, the play's themes emphasize only those aspects of Western culture that are compatible with Africa's sense of its own traditions and with its place in the modern world.

The play is based on the same materials Sutherland uses for her short story, **"New Life at Kyerefaso."**[4] After years of neglect and local apathy, the town of Kyerefaso is visited by Labaran, a young university graduate who is determined to prod the community away from its narrow conservatism and from its obsession with local forms and customs for their own sake. Their conservatism, and general indifference to improving their community in any progressive sense have led, over the years, to economic decline and the deterioration of the school system. Labaran's objectives are similar to those of the town's Queen Mother, for she has been trying unsuccessfully, for years, to lead her subjects out of their apathy. Her daughter Foriwa joins forces with the queen and with Labaran, and their crusade for change is climaxed by the town's annual festival in honor of the river Kyerefa. The Queen Mother successfully transforms the festival from the usual parade of meaningless rituals into a ceremony that actually inspires the community to rebuild itself in the spirit of its original founders.

This transformation of the festival from empty rhetoric into a vital force for change is fundamental to the play as a whole. The Queen Mother does not break with the villagers' traditions as such. Rather she insists that these traditions, particularly the annual ceremonies of birth and renewed life, become an actual experience in the life of the community itself. Thus, she mocks the traditional songs of praise to the ancestral founders of the town and to the river goddess, precisely because the present generation merely mouths the song while shunning the spirit of growth that it actually celebrates. The song has become a highly stylized and empty formality over the years, and the stilted style reflects the community's lack of spirit. The refrain promises that the singers will offer their "manliness to new life" in the river (p. 49), but Labaran, for one, is not convinced by the performance.

In his words, the river goddess should scream back a scathing response to the singers: "I am the lifestream of Kyerefaso. Your ancestors knew it when they chose to settle beside me. Are you going to do anything else besides dyeing my waters red from year to year with the blood of sheep?" (*Foriwa,* p. 35). When the Queen Mother repeats the traditional salute to the river-goddess, she transforms the language from a mechanical chant to a new and vibrant challenge: "Are your weapons from now on to be your minds' toil and your hands' toil?" she asks the men of Kyerefaso. "The men are tired of parading in the ashes of their grandfathers' glorious deeds. . . . They are tired of sitting like vultures upon the rubbish heap they have piled on the half-built walls of their grandfathers" (pp. 49-50).

In short, tradition ought not to be defined solely on the basis of a rigid loyalty to the achievements and symbols of the past. It should also incorporate a capacity for initiative and innovation, the kind of capacity that made the achievements of the past possible. The revitalized, direct language which the Queen Mother uses in her statement is part of a general revitalization (of forms, conventions, and language) which she perceives as integral to any living tradition. Since the prefestival ceremony at which she speaks and the rituals of the festival itself are forms of folk drama within the play as a whole, Sutherland has actually incorporated into her own theater the festival itself are forms of folk drama within the play as a whole, Sutherland has actually incorporated into her own theater the living, constantly renewed traditions of folk art. In effect, the structure and themes of the play exemplify the very principle that lies at the heart of the Queen Mother's argument. Traditional forms (folk art, in this case) are not simply antiquarian devices to be dusted off and used once a year; they should remain expressive and highly functional forms of communication.

The play's structure also depends on symbols and images that are integrated with the dominant theme of rebirth. These are drawn from the four-branched God-tree that dominates the town square and the setting of the play itself. The tree, near which Labaran has set up house, is actually described as a shrine. Its presence, throughout the play's action, is a highly visual example of what the Queen Mother and her allies are trying to achieve. It is old and a religious symbol and, on this basis, represents a very important link with the town's past. It is also alive and growing and, in this regard, it emphasizes the need to recognize traditions as living, growing conventions rather than static and antiquarian forms.

The tree's central location on stage, and its physical juxtaposition to the socially activist Labaran all have the effect of underscoring its significance as a symbol of social growth and change. At the same time, its religious significance reflects the degree to which social change should ideally be compatible with the deepest and most cherished of the community's religious and moral traditions. Finally, the "four-branched" design obviously emphasizes a sense of the universe (the four directions), indicating in the process that the tree's symbolism is both of local cultural significance and of universal implications. The kind of balance which Kyerefaso needs to strike between traditionalism and social growth is of immediate relevance to the community, to Africa as a whole, and to all cultures that hope to grow, and preserve their roots, in a changing world. By being located on stage the tree transforms the setting into a symbolic reflection of the community and the world view through which Sutherland presents the community. Given this centrality and dominance, the tree naturally makes its presence felt on the language of the play. Labaran describes himself and his mission as the scattering of seeds, in the manner of a forest tree (p. 34); and the Queen Mother herself exploits the tree image in defining custom as the "fruit" that the ancestors "picked from the living branches of life" (p. 25).

Significantly, this imaginative use of language and the capacity for growth which it represents, are also attributed to some of Kyerefaso's most apathetic residents, and in the process the dramatist hints at a dormant vitality, in the most unlikely society or individual, waiting to be released from static and unproductive notions of tradition. Thus, even the lazy draughts players who always ridicule Labaran's reformism are capable of a discriminating attitude towards expressive language, a sense of discrimination that bodes well for their ability to accept the challenges of expressive conventions in their community. The perpetual subject of Foriwa's beauty provides them with an opportunity to display the discriminating taste in language:

2ND DRAUGHTS PLAYER.

> She only needs to show her face in at the door, and like palm wine, the flies come swarming after it.

1ST DRAUGHTS PLAYER.

> How crude, Butterflies after a flower is much more like it.

(p. 16)

The new life at Kyerefaso flows not only from the revitalized conventions of tradition and language, but also from the personalities and symbolic roles of the main protagonists—Labaran, the Queen Mother, and Foriwa. Labaran is committed to the idea of reviving decaying communities, by way of new schools, new libraries, and agricultural reform, and he represents what a new generation of Ghanaians and their education should be. He combines a strong reverence for the community's past with a desire to see it benefit from the more useful and humane elements of Western culture. He embodies the dramatist's familiar ideal, a perception of tradition as continuing customs that are constantly renewed by being exposed to contemporary experience.

Labaran is the creative traditionalist, opposed both to the slavishly Western Scholar's Union and to those who are narrowly faithful to the externals of Ghana's communal institutions. Conversely his alliance with the old bookseller in pressing for a new library and a new school involves the ideal union of the old and the new in creative views of tradition. Labaran is a Hausa "from the north" who is initially suspected as an outsider, but his commitment to Kyerefaso, and his eventual acceptance by the town, suggest that the redefinition and revival of local traditions must take place as part of the forging of a new and broader, but ideally inclusive tradition—the tradition of contemporary Ghanaian nationhood as a whole. At this point Sutherland's dramatic art exemplifies not simply the idea of theater but the idea of national theater.

Labaran's most powerful ally is the Queen Mother herself. Her office links her securely with the past and its heritage, but her commitment to contemporary needs endows her with an evolutionary sense of tradition such as Labaran embodies. Throughout all of this, her identity as a woman is significant. Particularly on the basis of criticisms by older reactionaries like Sintim it is clear that the choice of a woman, and a literate one at that, has represented a radical departure from the customary method of choosing local rulers. Consequently, there is a significant link between the Queen Mother's views as ruler and the unusual fact that she is a woman who rules a reactionary community. She is not creative and progressive simply because she is a woman. However, as a ruler she offers a creative vision and a capacity for innovativeness that correspond with the kind of flexibility that made her accession to power possible in the first place. As a woman in the role of public leadership, the Queen Mother is one of the play's two examples of the manner in which Sutherland has linked the question of social customs with the issue of the woman's role. The restrictive sexual conventions which Sintim recalls with longing, are based on the narrow and static modes of tradition that are choking Kyerefaso, just as the Queen Mother's accession and rule exemplify a sociosexual liberality which is integral to the play's general emphasis on a progressive sense of tradition.

Foriwa is the second example of this sociosexual emphasis in the play. She is loyal to her mother's plans on behalf of Kyerefaso while demonstrating other levels of self-reliance and individualism. She is loudly determined to marry only someone of her own choosing, and, without being opposed to marriage as such, she remains detached from the mystique with which other women usually invest marriage. She has seen that for most of her married friends marriage has only been a dead-end which has dulled their eyes and slowed their "once lively" steps (pp. 6-8). Foriwa's active interest in marriage for herself (she is eventually betrothed to Labaran) and her capacity to criticize the stasis and narrowness that often afflict the tradition of marriage, all conform with that basic quality which she shares with Labaran and the Queen Mother, a deep respect for established conventions tempered by a critical awareness of the need to renew their meaning and form.

It is significant that Foriwa is assigned the leading role in the Queen Mother's formal challenge to the men of Kyerefaso that they give substance to their cherished customs. Foriwa is to dance with those men who are actually able to bring new life to the community. She declines to dance, on the ground that the men have not yet deserved the honor, but her refusal actually underlines the symbolism of the dance itself. It is a symbolic ritual, within the larger ritual of the festival and its preliminary ceremonies (such as the Queen Mother's challenge), and it represents the equal partnership of men and women in the (ideal) continuity of constantly renewed traditions.

The festival follows the confrontation between the Queen Mother and her foes. It is another symbolic ritual, for the eventual reconciliation between both sides is celebrated by the festival which represents the town's acceptance of her leadership and her challenge. They also accept Foriwa's role in all of this, for as a chastened Sintim remarks, Foriwa recalls the courage of those women who once made the ancestors men (p. 61). The symbolic celebrations of the festival are a prelude to yet another ritual, the impending marriage of Foriwa and Labaran. As a traditional ceremony, the marriage will confirm the continuity of established conventions. As the union of the two most innovative members of the community it celebrates the kind of progressiveness that must coexist with traditionalism.

On both counts, the impending marriage dramatizes the degree to which the new social experience envisioned by the play includes the ideal of sexual equality and independence for women as well as men. Finally, all of these conventions—the prefestival ceremony, the festival, and the impending marriage—are all forms of communal folk drama within the play. As a result, they allow Sutherland to integrate her vision of contemporary social changes with the continuity of folk art and folk traditions. Once again, her dramatic themes and conventions are a microcosm of the social order that she describes in her play.

The Marriage of Anansewa follows the direction of ***Foriwa***. In this later play there is a succession of social conventions presented as forms of folk drama, and these combine to make the play itself a social microcosm. These conventions fall into two categories. One set relates directly to the art of dramatic narrative itself (that is, the communal tradition of storytelling), and the other set centers upon marriage.

Sutherland's introduction to the published version of the play dwells at length on the oral traditions of Ashanti storytelling, especially in the case of Ananse stories. As performances, these stories are a species of folk drama, allowing for audience participation. The audience participates through the Mboguo, musical interludes in which the performers add to, or comment upon, the main tale itself. This kind of audience participation enhances the function of the story as a form of communal art. Even more explicitly than in ***Foriwa***, Sutherland is concerned with developing a kind of theater that is rooted in the established traditions of folk drama. The Anansegoro, as she describes this kind of theater, demands the ability of both dramatist and producer to invest the play with "some capacity for invoking this element of community participation" (p. vii).

The main plot of the play consists of the ingenious schemes through which Kweku Ananse secures money and other gifts from his daughter's suitors, encouraging each to send these gifts by leading him to believe that he is the favored suitor. Inevitably, the day arrives when all the suitors announce that they are on their way to meet Anansewa for a formal betrothal. Ananse averts disaster by announcing Anansewa's sudden death. All but one of the suitors send their regrets, in strict accordance with custom, but couched in terms which hint at difficulties that Anansewa might have encountered in their homes had the marriage actually taken place. The remaining suitor, Chief-Who-Is-Chief, goes beyond a literal adherence to the laws of custom. Since he has not been formally betrothed to Anansewa he is not obliged to assume responsibility for her "funeral," but he does precisely this, asserting the claims of husband on the sole basis of genuine feeling and loyalty. Overwhelmed by the Chief's generosity (not to mention his wealth), and released from his dilemma by the withdrawal of the other suitors, Ananse promptly announces the miraculous return of Anansewa from death, and the play ends with Anansewa's betrothal. Her marriage to the chief is in the immediate offing.

Within the structure of Sutherland's Anansegoro, the storyteller is both narrator and spectator, using the Mboguo to comment upon Ananse's schemes for the benefit of Sutherland's audience—while at the same time functioning as on-stage audience. This dual role underscores Sutherland's play-within-a-play structure.

In turn, this structure contributes to the kind of audience involvement that is demanded by the Anansegoro format, for the resulting impression of multiple action and multiple audience has the total effect of blurring the usual distinction between stage and audience, action and detached spectator. Ananse as schemer is really a perpetual actor whose schemes are witnessed, at first hand, by a selected audience—the storyteller himself. Then, in turn, the storyteller's relationship with Ananse's plots, as well as the plots themselves, comprise that overall dramatic plot—the "play"—that Sutherland's audience witnesses. Finally, this all has the effect of strongly implying that the theater as a whole, including the audience, is part of a larger theater—society—with its own patterns of social roles. Sutherland's idea of theater (as the extension or microcosm of social conventions and role-playing) has become clearly interchangeable with a certain idea of society (as a theater of traditionally defined roles).

Given this broadly representational nature of the play's action, it is appropriate that Sutherland conceives of Ananse himself as an "Everyman" (p. v). He is the consummate actor on this Ghanaian version of the world stage, spinning and acting out a succession of plots like the legendary Spider God after whom he is named and upon whom his character is based. He is the perennial trickster, well versed in the art of deception, and an expert without peer in the business of social intrigue and domestic plotting. His art of deception is therefore both an analogy and an integral part of theater itself, for dramatic art is really a convention of hoaxing an audience that is already predisposed to be deceived, and to be instructed in the truth by way of deception.

In the process, Ananse exemplifies the manner in which the theater is an extension or direct expression of the individual's personality and the individual's social experience. If his skills as a plotter and trickster reflect his personal greed and ambition, then the economic necessities that also contribute to this ambition reveal much about his immediate social conditions and the human condition in general—the condition of Everyman-Ananse. Therefore the song ("Oh Life Is a Struggle") which ushers him unto the stage also introduces the theme of adversity that justifies his schemes, at least in his own eyes. In his words, "While life is whipping you, rain also pours down to whip you some more. Whatever it was that man did wrong at the beginning of things must have been really awful for all of us to have to suffer so" (p. 1). Ananse's appeal to our sense of human history and to our awareness of traditional human suffering is important here. He is deliberately linking the moral justification of the trickster's role with the idea of tradition, claiming, in effect, that there is an intrinsic connection between his art as trickster and the history of human adversity.

His talents as actor are varied, ranging from an acutely discriminating use of language to his knowledge of established social conventions. The letters with which he flatters and cajoles money from the suitors are carefully composed in the long established, ego-massaging techniques of the praise-song. They are also shrewdly tailored to conform with the rules of courtship and marriage. His language is therefore generally encouraging, without offering the specific promise or undertaking that, according to the established custom, might commit Anansewa to any one of the suitors. The letter to the chief of Sapa is typical in this regard:

> Since forwardness has never been one of my faults, I will
> not even dare to drop a hint that the way is open for you now
> to begin oiling the wheels of custom. You who do not pay mere
> lip service to law and custom but really live by them, need no
> prompting from anyone.
>   Therefore I will only add that I'm very happy to be,
> Yours in the closest of links in the not too distant future.
>
> (p. 6)

As the storyteller remarks, it is clear that Ananse knows the customs very well (p. 16). Like the storyteller himself, Ananse judges others on the basis of their knowledge, and practice, of established customs. Thus, the final choice of a suitor for Anansewa is really made to depend on each suitor's attitude towards the appropriate customs of courtship, marriage and mourning. The ideal suitor is expected to know the customs, but he is also expected to use them in a flexible and humane way. Chief-Who-Is Chief is clearly the winner because he fits this ideal. He does not allow personal feelings of love and generosity to be thwarted by an overly literal attention to the conventions of courtship, betrothal, and mourning. On this basis, the chief represents the familiar Sutherland ideal of a flexible and creative traditionalism.

All of this brings us to the second group of conventions comprising the heart of the play—conventions that deal with marriage and other social institutions. Here Anansewa is a central character. Unlike her father and future husband, she is relatively inexperienced in the ways of the world and in the conventions through which one organizes, or copes with, those ways. An ingénue of sorts, she is really drafted by her father into his schemes before she is fully aware of his objectives. Her marriage is important in the play, not simply as an event towards which the plot is moving, but also as a process—or rather the culmination of a process. This is the process of education, her education. She has to be initiated into the ways of her world through a succession of conventions and rituals which represent certain experiences or values and which are to be climaxed by her impending marriage at the end of the play.

The first of these conventions is a formal education in certain Western skills that are necessary to modern society. Therefore, she is a trained secretary. Her secretarial role in her father's schemes (she types his letters to the suitors) initiates her into the formalities of traditional courtship—and in this regard she is yet another Sutherland character who combines the modern with the traditional. After her father announces her "miraculous" return from "death," she undergoes the "outdooring" ceremony. The ceremony is a necessary preliminary to her betrothal. It formally marks her growth into womanhood, establishing her as a debutante of sorts. It is part of a step-by-step education of a young woman in the traditions of her culture, including the tradition of marriage.

As a symbolic initiation into adulthood, that outdooring ceremony is also complemented by the ruse of her fake death. Followed as it is by the life-oriented ceremonies of "outdooring," betrothal, and marriage, her mock-death becomes, in retrospect, a ritualistic reminder that death itself, and the conventions that attend it (mourning, funeral, and the responsibilities of family and suitors) are intrinsic to life itself. In other words, Anansewa's growth as woman combines the customary patterns of initiation into adulthood with a growing awareness of harsh realities—like her father's poverty and death itself.

It is therefore appropriate that Ananse's schemes are interwoven with the conventions through which Anansewa is initiated into womanhood. She is thereby assured of an initiation or growth which is not simply based on a set of rituals observed for their own sake, but which imbue traditional patterns of womanhood (father's daughter growing into husband's wife) with an urgent awareness of life as a struggle. This process also endows her with a vital sense of her own personality and choices. Thus, she refuses to countenance her father's schemes if they were to bind her to a husband whom she would not choose.

Her education, like that of the audience itself, has proceeded through the hoaxes and disguises of Ananse's plots. In this respect, she is a highly personalized symbol of the way in which Sutherland's theater functions: she both reflects and experiences the social conventions of the audience's world. At this point Sutherland's social vision and her interest in the woman's role and identity have merged. They have become the central focus of her idea of theater.

Notes

1. *African Writers Talking: A Collection of Radio Interviews,* ed. Cosmo Pieterse and Dennis Duerden (New York: Africana Publishing Corporation, 1972), pp. 188-89, 22. Cited hereafter in the text as *African Writers Talking.*
2. References to Sutherland's plays are based on *Edufa* in *Plays from Black Africa,* ed. Frederic M. Litto, Mermaid Edition (New York: Hill & Wang, 1968), pp. 209-72; *Foriwa* (Accra: Ghana State Publishing Corporation, 1967) and *The Marriage of Anansewa,* African Creative Writing Series (London: Longman, 1975).
3. Francis Fergusson, *The Idea of a Theater.* Anchor Books Ed. (New York: Doubleday, 1953), pp. 14-15.
4. Efua Sutherland, "New Life at Kyerefaso," in *Modern African Prose,* ed. Richard Rive, African Writers Series (London: Heinemann, 1964), pp. 179-86.

Bibliography

Pieterse, Cosmo and Dennis Dverden, eds. *African Writers Talking: A Collection of Radio Interviews.* New York: Africana, 1972. Includes Interviews with Aidoo and Sutherland.

Sutherland, Efua. *Edufa.* In *Plays from Black Africa.* Ed. Frederic M. Litto. Mermaid Ed. New York: Hill & Wang, 1968, pp. 209-72.

———*Foriwa.* Accra, Ghana: State Publishing Corporation, 1967.

———"New Life at Kyerefaso." In *An African Treasury,* pp. 112-17.

———*The Marriage of Anansewa.* London: Longman, 1975.

Gay Wilentz (essay date summer 1988)

SOURCE: Wilentz, Gay. "Writing for the Children: Orature, Tradition, and Community in Efua Sutherland's *Foriwa.*" *Research in African Literatures* 19, no. 2 (summer 1988): 182-96.

[*In the following essay, Wilentz examines the ways in which Sutherland's play* Foriwa *seeks to reconcile Africa's traditional values with its emerging industrial modernity, with emphasis on the role of women in easing the cultural transition.*]

> I've heard a lot of people discussing at conferences the role of the [African] writer—all this rigmarole, well if there's any role, they should write for the children.
>
> —Efua Sutherland

Efua Sutherland, Ghanaian playwright, poet, and producer, is well known as one of Ghana's most active voices in utilizing traditional modes of theater to promote social change. Her goal has been to acknowledge traditional oral drama performed in villages, stimulate modern dramatic activities, and set up community theaters in rural areas. Moreover, she has been instrumental in fostering indigenous drama in both her theater groups and her plays.[1] Sutherland's plays have been integral to her concept of theater as a means of revitalizing rural life in African communities, and her impact has been felt through her plays for children as well as for adults.² Sutherland's best-known works, *Edufa* (1967), *Foriwa* (1967), and *The Marriage of Anansewa* (1975), are all directed toward reconciling the conflict of Western and African cultural values in modern-day African society; the latter two plays also satisfy her objective that written drama serve the community as the oral tradition has done.

This article focuses on Sutherland's play, *Foriwa,* in terms of its oral roots, the role of women in reviving the traditions, and Sutherland's use of two aspects of the oral tradition—the retelling of an African folktale and the presentation of a traditional ceremony—as a way to resolve cultural conflicts in modern African life. The play becomes an educational tool to unite traditional values and modern technology through the oral tradition and the collective process of the African community. Sutherland's desire to ensure that the traditions are passed on to the children, both rural and urban, and her vision of women as the moving force in revitalizing disintegrating rural communities illustrate how she has accepted and challenged the role designated to the African woman—to reflect and reform the orature of her foremothers. Sutherland has taken her drama back to the village communities from whence it came. Her open-air theaters for dramatic performances and storytelling reflect her commitment to educate future generations through the patterns and traditions of her ancestors.

Sutherland does not see dramatic works as taking the place of the oral tradition, but rather as part of the process in which the values and culture of her people and nation are to be transmitted to the children of the following generations. In an interview with Lee Nichols, Sutherland comments, "The traditional communities . . . have done a wonderful thing for the country: They have minded the culture. These are the people who ought to be thanked for what's been maintained of the culture" (107, 170). Her concern is for the children who will pass on both the traditional culture and the cultural conflicts of modern Africa; her fear has been that the clash of European and African cultures may break the continuum. Therefore, in her plays and productions, Sutherland has tried to capture the essence of traditional modes of oral performance, while promoting the storytelling that goes on at home. Her aim has been to expand on the tales told in village compounds and the stories told in village squares by bringing to her plays this "formidable frame of reference derived from [the people's] consciousness of that dramatic heritage" (Adedeji 76).³

Sutherland's play *Foriwa* is a later version of a short, allegorical tale called **"New Life in Kyerefaso"** (1960). Both pieces are based on the transformation of an African folktale used by mothers to warn their daughters away from unknown, handsome men. The folktale tells

of a beautiful and proud girl who refuses to marry any young man chosen by her family but decides instead to marry a handsome stranger. Whether the man turns into a python, a spirit, or a skull, the moral taught is that young women who disobey their families and do not listen to the wisdom of their elders will eventually meet disaster. This folktale has been reworked by numerous West African writers, yet Sutherland is unique in that the moral of the folktale in *Foriwa* is a positive one.⁴ The choice of a stranger brings "new life" to the town of Kyerefaso rather than devastation, altering the meaning of the old tale. In this way Sutherland expands the message of the folktale to illustrate a different dilemma: how to build a nation out of the different ethnic groups in Ghana.

In both the story and the play, Foriwa, a beautiful, articulate schoolteacher, has returned home to celebrate the "New Life" festival with her town and her mother, the Queen Mother of Kyerefaso. Like her mother, Foriwa is disappointed by the general apathy of the town. She tells her mother in despair, "Everyone is waiting for someone from somewhere to come and do this or that for Kyerefaso. Who, and from where?" (8). The people of Kyerefaso are not as interested in responding to Foriwa's questions as they are in whom she will marry. Everyone is happy about Foriwa's return but wonders when she will finally accept a suitor. Foriwa has many suitors, some very wealthy, yet—like the girl in the folktale—she is not interested in any of them. In the earlier short story, Foriwa's displeasure with her suitors is circulated around the town, and "that evening there was heard a new song in the village." The villagers use the well-known folktale to warn Foriwa of the possible repercussions of her proud behavior, and although the song does not refer specifically to Foriwa, everyone in the town knows who the "maid" is. I think it is worthwhile to quote this song in its entirety:

> There was a woman long ago
> Tell that maid, tell that maid,
> There was a woman long ago,
> She would not marry Kwesi
> She would not marry Kwaw
> She would not, would not, would not.
> One day she came home with hurrying feet,
> I've found the man, the man, the man,
> Tell that maid, tell that maid,
> Her man looked like a chief.
> Tell that maid, tell that maid,
> Her man looked like a chief,
> Most splendid to see,
> But he turned into a python,
> He turned into a python
> And swallowed her up.

(114)

The use of the oral tradition is apparent here in two ways. First, the community uses the folktale to try to "educate" Foriwa. Since her own mother and mother's family seem unable to control Foriwa, the community will take on that role to help her conform. Second, emphasizing their importance in eliciting proper behavior, songs are formulated quickly to pass judgment on a present situation.

Unlike the girl in the folktale, Foriwa has refused suitors not because of pride in her own beauty nor disrespect for her family but rather from a desire to work toward the improving of Kyerefaso and to find the man who will work with her. In Sutherland's reworking of an Ananse tale, *The Marriage of Anansewa,* the grandmother tells her granddaughter Anansewa that there are other important qualities a man should have besides wealth:

> My grandchild Anansewa, your old lady knows something about what is of real value in this world. You noticed that this outstretched hand of mine is empty, it contains nothing. And yet, this same empty hand will succeed in placing a gift into your brass bowl. What this hand is offering is this prayer of mine. May the man who comes to take you from our hands to his home be, above all things, a person with respect for the life of his fellow human beings.
>
> (41-42)

In *Foriwa,* as in *The Marriage of Anansewa,* what is of real value is not necessarily material. The grandmother gives Anansewa advice in the form of a riddle, an aspect of the oral tradition. Moreover, her values come from the traditional culture that has been distorted, in the present generation, by Western materialistic values, illustrated by the trickery of her son, Ananse. So when the Queen Mother asks Foriwa why she wants to refuse the present suitor, a man who "has salvaged his life from this decrepitude" by making a great success of his life materially, Foriwa answers that she will not join her life with a man who is interested merely in personal gain (6). She shudders at the kind of society he represents by ameliorating his own life at the expense of the community. She responds instead by approaching the subject of the town's deterioration and the Queen Mother's fights with the elders who care more for the words of the traditions than for what those words convey.

Foriwa is determined not to marry until she has helped rebuild the town and until both she and her mother agree on a man who has "respect for the life of his fellow human beings." Unlike the stranger in the folktale who is an evil, supernatural being, the stranger in this case is Labaran, an educated, socially active young man who is a Hausa from northern Ghana. Labaran, a university graduate, is dismayed by the life offered to him in the capital, and he wanders through the countryside hoping to find his place in society. He ends up in Kyerefaso and remains there to try to understand the changes in his country: "Anyone who thinks I have nothing to do deceives himself. Because he sees no office? This is my office, this street; the people who use it are my work and education" (2). Labaran is derisively called the "son of an unknown tribe" by Sintim, one of the elders (19), and both his education and his commitment are held suspect by the Akan people of Kyerefaso. When the postmaster, who is working with Labaran to start a bookstore and reopen the school, asks Sintim to request the land from the Queen Mother, Sintim flatly refuses to be an "emissary for an Itani" (a disparaging term for someone from Northern Ghana). The postmaster responds, "That's unfair. If this young man were a townsman, we could claim to be in possession of a man of real value" (18). The emphasis on what is of "real value" surfaces in all of Sutherland's writings. Finally, it is Foriwa who secures the land for the bookstore.

The friendship and ensuing love relationship between Labaran and Foriwa turn the folktale around, since their relationship does not presage disaster but rather the revitalization of the town of Kyerefaso. Moreover, the acceptance of Labaran by the Queen Mother and the town brings a new meaning to the tale; the stranger may not always be a villain, not when he is from your own country. The Queen Mother, who brings her community together, welcomes Labaran as her future son-in-law and son of the soil as she states: "They say that we see with our eyes. That is true. But we are not often able to say that we see with our hearts also. . . . I have come to thank you for having made your home on this foundation" (65). Rather than perceive Sutherland's reworking of the tale as a breakdown of the traditions, we can envision the moral of the tale as an even stronger reflection of the community's values and the community's health. The initial tale still represents the importance of the alliance of families in choosing a mate, but the tale is also broadened to express another alliance— that of all the people of Ghana.

Before exploring the roles of the women characters in the play itself, I would like to emphasize an aspect of Sutherland's drama that Lloyd Brown comments on in *Women Writers of Black Africa*—that the theater of *Foriwa* is an extension of the culture: "The play itself is a part of this process of revitalization, for its very existence reflects a vital and continuing interest, among the playwright and her audience, in the indigenous forms" (73). Therefore, we see Sutherland in the traditional role of the African woman, "minding the culture" as she calls it, making sure that what is meaningful in traditional life is maintained. In the process she moves beyond the mere recording of past traditions and helps to bring new life into the customs and rituals which have become as stale as the old men in the play. Sutherland alters traditions—instead of disrupting them—so as to communicate the cultural values of precolonial Africa with renewed meaning.

In an article exploring Sutherland's attempt to update traditional African modes of pedagogy for young children in a Ghanaian village, "The Atwia-Ekumfi

Kodzidan—An Experimental African Theatre," E. Ofori Okyea praises Sutherland for helping revitalize that village with her model theater and education project:

> The KODZIDAN in Atwia has had some effects on the life of the village generally. There is, for instance, a co-operative store started in the village as a result of the performances done in other villages and from filming fees. A new block of buildings is being added to the school to make it more presentable. Atwia has become the "eye" of villages around and *a few of the young men in Accra have returned to inject some new life into the village.*
>
> (83; emphasis added)[5]

Clearly, Atwia is the realized project that led Sutherland to rework her story, **"New Life in Kyerefaso,"** into the play, *Foriwa,* but the writer of the article seems to have missed an important aspect of the revitalization—the role of women. It is plausible to think that some of the young women from Accra have also joined hands to work in Atwia, but the writer has chosen, as usual, to mention only the young men. This misrepresentation of history (herstory) is typical of the neglect women as a group have suffered from historians, anthropologists, and politicians in terms of the role they have played in the past.[6] The point is pertinent here because it is precisely the young woman Foriwa, who, in the play, returns to Kyerefaso to "inject some new life in the village." Sutherland, in her choice of characters, emphasizes the role women have to play in the process of decolonization and the revitalization of communities through traditional customs and values. The function of the Queen Mother, the return of Foriwa, and the relationship between mother and daughter, exemplify Sutherland's intention to document women's unique contribution to the continuation of the traditional culture.

Although she is helped by her daughter Foriwa and the "stranger" Labaran, the Queen Mother is the moving force in the revitalization of the town of Kyerefaso. She brings her community together through a new interpretation of a traditional ritual. It is the Queen Mother's duty as "mother" to nurture her community and ensure that the values are maintained. In "Asante Queen Mothers in Government and Politics in the Nineteenth Century," Agnes Akosua Aidoo comments, "Like all Akan women, the Queen Mother derived her position from the matrilineal social organization. The Akan trace descent through the female line. The woman is the genetically significant link between successive generations" (65). The woman is also the valuational link between generations, so the role of Queen Mother is understood to include her ability to keep the culture's values alive. From precolonial times the Queen Mother has been the authority in the village in which she has resided, working with the elders of the village to govern the commu-

nity. As the "Ohemma" (the foremost authority on the genealogy of the royal matrilineage), the Queen Mother was considered "the custodian of the 'custom'" (Arhin 92-94). The authority of the Queen Mother—the most important female leader of the clan—was far greater in precolonial Africa, but she has remained an important figure in modern Ghana.[7]

In *Foriwa* the conflict between the Queen Mother and Sintim on her right as a woman to hold a position of authority does not, as some critics have suggested, arise from the unusual circumstances of having a woman in control; rather it stems from the colonial disruption of a traditional practice. When the Queen Mother attempts to revitalize the "path-clearing" ceremony, Sintim expresses his disgust at this woman acting as a leader:

> I am going to sprinkle ritual food all over Kyerefaso. I, Sintim. Son of the stalwart Odum tree. . . . I shall not stand by and see the town disgraced. How, when there are cocks here, should a hen be allowed to strut around in this manner, without getting her head pecked?
>
> (39)

Sintim represents the seemingly universal disdain for women that men have, but more important, he also reflects a colonialist view that women have no place in positions of authority.[8] The point is not that women were of equal status to men in precolonial Black Africa, but that their role in the political sphere was respected whether they governed over only the female population or the whole society. The determination displayed by women in responding to the conflicts in the play—the Queen Mother's opposition to the elders and the staleness of the traditions; Foriwa's desire to return home to help improve the community rather than to marry a rich man—does not necessarily arise from modern notions of feminism but stems from a traditional view of woman's place in society as wife, mother, and active member/leader of the community.

The Queen Mother, tired of the apathy of her town, decides to try to arouse the community by revitalizing an upcoming festival. Her aim is to demonstrate how far the society has strayed from the original spirit of the ceremony. The inability of the elders to adapt the values of the past to present experience disheartens her and makes her wonder why she does not go where she can breathe; "somewhere perhaps where, like a living tree, I can shed my wasted leaves to grow new ones, and flowers, and fruit." Yet when Foriwa asks her why she does not leave, she answers, "I'm rooted here. I agreed to be mounted like a gorgeous sacrifice to tradition" (8). Although the Queen Mother speaks negatively of being mounted like a sacrifice in her moment of distress, it is her appreciation of her roots that gives her the strength to reformulate the traditions of Kyerefaso. Sutherland utilizes the tree of life imagery (from the roots to the fruit on the branches) that adds to the perception of generational continuity in this play. The "four-branched

God-tree" across from the Queen's compound is one of the play's symbols of the dominant theme of rebirth: the God-tree is "alive and growing and, in this regard, it emphasizes the need to recognize traditions as living, growing conventions rather than static and antiquarian forms" (Brown 75). The Queen relates her own place in society to that of the shrine tree; she is rooted in her community, tied to the past, but also hopes to breathe life into the town so that it will bear fruit. Moreover, in her plan to revivify the festival, she describes this ritual as the fruit that has matured from the seeds of the ancients through the nurturing of each generation: "For a long time, I've been trying to find a way to make the people of Kyerefaso see; to see at least that for our ancestors, custom was the fruit they picked from the living branches of life" (25). The Queen's title as mother of the community and the references to the rebirth of the traditions in modern form illustrate how women utilize their role as mothers to include the nurturing of the land and the traditions of its people.

Filomina Steady, in *The Black Woman Cross-Culturally,* emphasizes that, for the black woman, being a childbearer is not necessarily a restrictive role but is one tied to land fertility and the oral tradition: "Women's role as child-bearers and food producers are often associated with fertility of the land, and this is implicit in much of the ritual. This life-giving quality endows women not only with much prestige but equates them with the life-giving force itself" (29-30). In the case of the Queen Mother, the role of the African woman is expanded to a nurturer of those she governs, and her responsibilities as the educator of her children extends to the entire community. It is the Queen Mother's function to bring her family (community) together to maintain the traditions for the generations to come.

Foriwa has many of the same characteristics as her mother, characteristics that enable her to accept the challenge of staying and helping rebuild the decaying town of Kyerefaso. Like her mother, she is independent and believes in her own opinions, but she also feels deeply for the community from whence she came and wants to be part of its rebirth. Her initial despair arises from the failure of the town to work out some compromise between the traditional values of the ancestors and the technological changes of modern Africa. It brings on a restlessness in her, but like the Atwia youths in Accra she hopes to "inject some new life" in her community:

> It's this place and you—pulling at my heart—making me restless. . . . When I come to the place where my mother is queen, I should proudly lift my head. I've listened to your misgivings about this town. All these years I've taken note of your futile arguments with the elders. You grieve when every meeting turns to litiga-

tion and obstruction. You fight, and that makes me proud of you, but you are alone, and you lose. Is this to be forever?

> (7-8)

It may appear on the surface that Foriwa disregards tradition by not marrying her rich suitor and by choosing to stay in Kyerefaso instead of making a better life for herself in Accra. However, one can argue that Foriwa is responding to the earlier traditions and values of her culture, values derived before Christian/Western doctrine categorized woman as "helpmate" rather than as a citizen in her own right. Maryse Condé comments, "African women stand at the very heart of the turmoil of the continent. Going back to colonialism, one is tempted to say that they were the principal victims of the encounter with the West. The missionaries did not understand the position they held in their families and societies" (133). Therefore, with a disruption of the culture as violent as that of colonialism, a strike against the atrophied traditions of a town might actually be closer at heart to the original cultural values than adherence to those distorted traditions. For this reason Foriwa rejects an easy solution for her individual life and remains at home as part of a communal effort to bring new life to Kyerefaso. Tired of being a "runaway daughter" (35), she chooses not to marry until she has fulfilled another commitment of the precolonial African woman, her responsibility to her community.

Foriwa's decision to remain in Kyerefaso is tied to her mother's reforming of the path-clearing festival. In terms of how mothers pass down cultural values to their daughters, the conflict between the Queen Mother's desire for what is best for her daughter and Foriwa's answer to her mother's call is an interesting example of how this play focuses on the reinterpretation of traditional culture. In spite of her mother's protests, Foriwa answers her mother's call (as Queen Mother) for *all* the children of Kyerefaso to return and help rebuild the town. During the ceremony Foriwa declares her intentions to the town: "When the Linguist tells this story, he shall also say, that I, your own daughter answered to your call" (53). And after the festival, she expresses her relief at finally making a commitment: "Mother, I have solved the conflict in myself. Your words down there today threw me up like a bird, and I have found my way home again." Her mother answers her with distress:

> I should have expected it. Oh, my child, why couldn't you have waited for some signs of promise in this place before you spoke. People don't change in a day, and our people may refuse to change. . . . I should praise you for it, *were I only Queen Mother, and not your mother also.*

> (55; emphasis added)

Foriwa does not accept her mother's advice to seek personal satisfaction, satisfying her individual desires. Instead, she listens to her mother in a much deeper way:

she listens to the words spoken by the mother of the community, the mother with wisdom handed down to her through the ancestors. As Foriwa's mother and as Queen Mother, she has passed on the values of her culture to her daughter so that Foriwa could not respond in any other way. Thus, the play portrays women as not only maintaining the customs but as actively altering and reforming these customs to make them applicable for modern Ghanaian life. Sutherland has documented women's important role in keeping the customs ripe and alive for the next generations to pick.

The climax of the play is the revitalization of an important traditional festival. The Queen Mother has chosen to revivify the annual "path-clearing" festival, a ceremony of new life. She decides to conduct a mock ceremony the evening before the festival to point out how far the town has strayed from its original meaning. The ritual glorifies the hard work that went into the founding of Kyerefaso and celebrates the beginning of the town. The mock festival is the turning point in the play because the community, and in a sense the audience, too, must choose whether to work for that new life or leave the ceremony as an empty ritual. This scene illustrates a dialectic between the action in the play and the aims of the playwright. Lloyd Brown refers to the simultaneous regeneration that the character Queen Mother and the playwright Sutherland create in the traditional culture: "Since the prefestival ceremony at which [the Queen Mother] speaks and the rituals of the festival are forms of folk drama within the play as a whole, Sutherland has actually incorporated into her own theatre living, constantly renewed traditions of folk art" (75).

The Queen Mother asks the people of the town to come as if to the festival. This causes much confusion in the town but the participants come. The Linguist, who is the oral historian of the town, explains, "We made her Queen because we love her; beyond the right of inheritance" (43). When everyone is assembled, the Queen Mother lets them go through the ceremony as they do each year, but she stops them in the middle of the ritual. She asks the community when will they live up to the words of the ceremony? She first addresses the male *asafo* dancers and then calls out to her daughter and the other women: "Where are you, women all. Come join the men in dance for they are offering themselves to new life" (49). Foriwa, who stands besides her mother, refuses to dance in the ceremony because she is unable to find anyone "with whom this new life shall be built." The Queen Mother, empowered by the truth of her daughter's statement, expresses her own feelings to the group:

> Sitting here, seeing Kyerefaso die, I am no longer able to bear the mockery of the fine, brave words of this ceremony of our festival. Our fathers earned the right

to utter them by their deeds. . . . But is this the way to praise them? Watching their walls crumbling around us. . . . Letting weeds choke the paths they made? Unwilling to open new paths ourselves, because it demands of us thought, and goodwill, and action? No, we have turned Kyerefaso into a death bed from which our young people run away to seek elsewhere, the promise of life we've failed to give them here.

(50-51)

The belief in the continuity of a culture from the ancestors to the descendants is a major aspect of African traditional society, and that belief is integrally related to the land. If the next generation leaves the land "to seek elsewhere the promise of a life," then the lineage will be broken and the fiber of the society destroyed. The Queen Mother realizes that the disintegration of her community is inevitable if the children leave and do not make a commitment to their culture. Through the shock of transforming the ritual, she attempts to incite the people of Kyerefaso to work toward creating a viable alternative to the city and its Western materialism.

Each of Sutherland's three plays deals with the conflict of Western and traditional values, specifically personal wealth in opposition to community responsibility. In *Edufa* the end result is tragic for the protagonists in that Edufa's wife Ampona dies as a result of his desire for material gain; the treatment of this theme is comic in *The Marriage of Anansewa,* although the message is the same. *Foriwa* takes a step beyond the critique and tries to create a performance atmosphere that reconciles these conflicting values in contemporary African life. In the play the educated individual is no more or less necessary to the revitalization of the town than the workers or dancers, and the Queen Mother's admonishment of the Scholars' Union for calling the *asafo* dancers illiterate clearly reflects this position (47).

The Queen Mother's reforming of the mock ceremony to awaken Kyerefaso to the real meaning of the festival reflects Sutherland's aim to arouse the audience so that they also will work to revitalize their own communities. The reconciliation of the Queen Mother and the elders, particularly the abrasive Sintim, her acceptance of Labaran into the community and her own home, and Foriwa's decision to remain in Kyerefaso all illustrate a positive step toward the revival of rural communities and the unity of all the people of Ghana. As I have mentioned earlier, the revitalization process of Kyerefaso is shared between the main protagonists—the Queen Mother, Foriwa, Labaran, and the postmaster; and it is their cooperation with the elders and the townsfolk that brings the town to life. Still, it is the Queen Mother, as nurturer of the town and the custodian of custom, who motivates the community through the transformation of the traditional festival. She tells her intention to the community through the Linguist: "Linguist, those are my thoughts. I knew no way of reaching my people better with such thoughts than to use this ceremony of our festival as my interpreter" (51). In this way the Queen Mother is passing on the customs of the ancestors to future generations not as archaic remnants of a time past but as part of a living tradition that keeps the culture itself alive. And her manner of renewing the rituals is in accordance with the way women have passed on the values of their cultures, by repetition and alteration, throughout generations. For, as feminist critic Jane Marcus states, it is the transformation, rather than the permanence of the creation, that is at the heart of most women's art.[9]

Although the Queen Mother's challenge to the community is the main motivating force in revitalizing Kyerefaso, Foriwa's participation—as daughter of the Queen Mother and daughter of the soil—is equally important because of her challenge to her own generation and her ability to take the leadership role from her mother. When Foriwa declines to dance in the mock ceremony because she does not find the young man with whom this new life could be built, she is actually taking up her mother's challenge and altering the ritual on her own. She tells the crowd, "He is not here, mother. I don't see him in these empty eyes. I see nothing alive here, mother, nothing alive" (50). Foriwa's declaration is important for two reasons: first, Foriwa emphasizes her mother's statement that until the community words "'I love my land' [cease] to be the empty croaking of a vulture on the rubbish heap," the festival and the traditions will mean nothing (50). Second, Foriwa ends up with Labaran, the stranger not included in the festival but instrumental in the revitalization process. Her comments foreshadow the time when all those who share the values of the society and want to work to improve it will be welcomed. Labaran, as one of the town's young men, must join the young women to build this new life, blending traditional values and modern experience. The acceptance of Labaran as Foriwa's husband-to-be presages the unity of Ghana's different ethnic groups, altering the folktale; yet, the original meaning of the tale also stands. Foriwa has chosen her own husband, but the marriage will be consecrated only with the Queen Mother's approval and by the traditions of her culture.

Foriwa's involvement in the process of revitalizing the town and Labaran's acknowledgment that their marriage will have to wait until their actions have proved true to the words spoken in the ceremony illustrate a renewed partnership in which the men and women of the community work together to improve their lives. Even Sintim, the antifeminist, responds to the power of both the Queen Mother and Foriwa; he comments that Foriwa has "the fire of those courageous women who made men of our ancestors" (61). Of course, he is only able to see women's strength in terms of what they do for men, but he plainly states that Foriwa's strength has been passed down to her through her foremothers.

One final comment on the play's use of modern technology to promote the oral tradition is in order here. After the challenge is taken up by the performers in the mock ceremony, the word is passed from compound to compound that the community will be prepared for both the festival the next day and the Queen's demand that they breathe new life into Kyerefaso. As the people disperse, the sound of the Queen's voice is heard once again from the foundation, challenging Kyerefaso to bring meaning and life to the words of the ceremony. But the Queen is not repeating herself; it is Labaran who has taped the Queen's voice with his "recording machine" (56). Again, in the final scene, Labaran plays the tape of Foriwa's speech as the others look on, recording this moment for posterity (64). The tape recorder documents the community's history in a more precise, though less creative, manner than the words of the orators, and it has a place in the society in terms of passing down the exact words of a speech or story. The recorder, as handled by Labaran, exemplifies a modern convenience utilized to enhance the oral traditions. In spite of its precision, neither the tape recorder nor the man who uses it can take the place of the oral tradition and the women who tell the tales to their children in every home, every compound. The art of the oral tradition depends upon the teller of the tale as well as the tale itself—whether it be a "master" teller or undocumented village women storytellers. Sutherland does not see literary drama taking the place of oral drama in the community, nor, one hopes, will the tape recorder replace the orature of the traditional culture.

In her three published plays for adults, Sutherland's aim has been to focus on the kind of values that are being passed on to the children: What will become of traditional culture, weakened by colonial domination, if the present generation does not continue their oral traditions and reform them to fit modern Ghanaian society? *Foriwa* works toward the resolution of these cultural conflicts by utilizing orature and literature as vehicles for the revitalization of rural communities. Sutherland's emphasis on women's role in "minding the culture" and bringing new life into old traditions, mirrors her own concern for and active participation in strengthening the bonds between the African past and future generations. Her performances and productions, her village education for children, and her plays themselves illustrate a playwright tied not only to the traditions and customs of the African continuum but secure in her place as an African woman passing on the values of her foremothers to the children.

Notes

1. Sutherland has been a motivating force in Ghanaian dramatic production. In 1958 she founded the Experimental Theatre Players, which became the

Ghana Drama Studio in 1960. She also organized the Kusum group which forms plays and improvisations in English and local languages.

2. Schmidt states that Sutherland has had a profound influence on children's literature through her children's plays and the theater group which she founded ("African Women Writers" 8).

3. Adedeji ("Theatre and Ideology") sees the role of modern African theater as fulfilling a cultural need on a national level that oral literature has done in local communities. For a more in-depth discussion on the dramatic heritage of both African orature and literature, see Awoonor's *The Breast of the Earth.*

4. Some of the writers who have utilized this folktale in their works are Ama Ata Aidoo, J. P. Clark, Flora Nwapa, and Amos Tutuola.

5. It is interesting to note that *kodzi* is one form of Akan folktale.

6. An excellent treatment of this topic is a paper by sociologist Mere, "The Unique Role of Women in Nation Building," which unfortunately is unpublished. See also "Women: The Neglected Human Resource for African Development."

7. In "The Black Woman in History," Clarke states that from the time of the traders, the colonialists "began a war on African customs, religion and cultures. In most cases, the first custom they attacked was the matriarchy" (17). See also Diop, *The Cultural Unity of Black Africa,* and Okonjo, "Sex Roles in Nigerian Politics."

8. For an unclouded treatment of the demise of the women's courts and women's political power under British occupation, see Leith-Ross's *African Women.*

9. I am liberally paraphrasing from Marcus's "Still Practice, A/Wrested Alphabet: Toward a Feminist Aesthetic."

Works Cited

Adedeji, Joel. "Theatre and Ideology in Africa." *Joliso* 2.1 (1974): 72-82.

Aidoo, Agnes Akosua. "Asante Queen Mothers in Government and Politics in the Nineteenth Century." *The Black Woman Cross-Culturally.* Ed. Filomina Steady. Cambridge, MA: Schenkman, 1981. 65-77.

Akyea, E. Ofori. "The Atwia-Ekumfi Kodzidan—An Experimental African Theatre." *Okyeame* 4.1 (1968): 82-84.

Arhin, Kwame. "The Political and Military Roles of Akan Women." *Female and Male in West Africa.* Ed. Christine Oppong. London: Allen and Unwin, 1983. 91-98.

Awoonor, Kofi. *The Breast of the Earth.* New York: Doubleday, 1975.

Brown, Lloyd. *Women Writers in Black Africa.* Westport, CT: Greenwood, 1981.

Clarke, John Henrik. "The Black Woman in History." *Black World* 24.4 (1975): 12-26.

Condé, Maryse. "Three Female Writers in Modern Africa." *Présence Africaine* 82 (1972): 132-43.

Diop, Cheikh Anta. *The Cultural Unity of Black Africa.* Chicago: Third World, 1959.

Leith-Ross, Sylvia. *African Women.* London: Routledge and Kegan Paul, 1939.

Marcus, Jane. "Still Practice, A/Wrested Alphabet: Toward a Feminine Aesthetic." *Tulsa Studies in Women's Literature* 3.1-2 (1984): 79-97.

Mere, Ada. "The Unique Role of Women in Nation Building." Unpublished paper, U of Nigeria, 1984.

Nichols, Lee. *African Writers at the Microphone.* Washington, DC: Three Continents, 1984.

Okonjo, Kamene. "Sex Roles in Nigerian Politics." *Female and Male in West Africa.* Ed. Christine Oppong. London: Allen and Unwin, 1983. 211-22.

Schmidt, Nancy. "African Women Writers of Literature for Children." *World Literature Written in English* 17.1 (1978): 7-21.

Steady, Filomina, ed. *The Black Woman Cross-Culturally.* Cambridge, MA: Schenkman, 1981.

Sutherland, Efua T. *Edufa. Plays from Black Africa.* Ed. Frederic M. Litto. New York: Hill and Wang, 1968. 209-72.

———. *Foriwa.* Accra: Ghana Publishing, 1967.

———. *The Marriage of Anansewa.* Washington, DC: Three Continents, 1975.

———. "New Life at Kyerefaso." *An African Treasury.* Ed. Langston Hughes. New York: Crown, 1960. 111-17.

"Women: The Neglected Human Resource for African Development." *Canadian Journal of African Studies* 6.2 (1972): 359-70.

FURTHER READING

Criticism

Ankumah, Adaku, T. "Efua Theodora Sutherland (1924-1996)." In *Postcolonial African Writers: A Bio-Bibliographical Critical Sourcebook,* edited by Pushpa Naidu Parekh and Siga Fatima Jagne, pp. 455-59. Westport, Conn.: Greenwood Press, 1998.

Critical and biographical overview.

July, Robert W. "The Independent African Theater." In *An African Voice: The Role of the Humanities in African Independence,* pp. 59-81. Durham, N.C.: Duke University Press, 1987.

> Includes Sutherland's works in a discussion of the history of African theater and the development of theater at Ibadan University in Nigeria.

Sutherland, Efua, and Maxine Lautré. "Efua Sutherland." In *African Writers Talking: A Collection of Inter-views,* edited by Dennis Duerden and Cosmo Pieterse, pp. 183-95. London: Heinemann, 1972.

> Interview from 1968 in which Sutherland discusses her experimental village theater and the state of African art in the late twentieth century.

Talbert, Linda Lee. "*Alcestis* and *Edufa*: The Transitional Individual." *World Literature Written in English* 22, no. 2 (autumn 1983): 183-90.

> Explores the common thematic concerns of Sutherland's *Edufa* and Euripides's *Alcestis.*

Véronique Tadjo
1955-

© Sophie Bassouls/Corbis

Côte d'Ivoirian novelist, poet, short story writer, prose writer, and author and illustrator of children's books.

INTRODUCTION

Considered radical and innovative, Tadjo is a Francophone African writer who has published in a variety of genres, including short stories, poetry, novels, and children's literature. A painter as well, Tadjo often illustrates her children's books and has exhibited her artwork in solo and group exhibitions. Among her writings that have been translated into English are the novel *A vol d'oiseau* (1986; *As the Crow Flies*) and *L'Ombre d'Imana* (2000; *The Shadow of Imana*), about the 1994 genocide in Rwanda. In 2005 Tadjo was awarded the prestigious Grand Prix Littéraire de l'Afrique Noire (The Grand Prize for African Literature) for *Reine Pokou* (2005; *Queen Pokou*), a novel about the legend of the mythical Queen Pokou and the establishment of the Baoulé kingdom, in present-day Côte d'Ivoire.

BIOGRAPHICAL INFORMATION

Born in Paris in 1955, Tadjo was raised in Abidjan, Côte d'Ivoire, by her father, a civil servant, and her mother, a sculptor and painter. She received her B.A. in English from the University of Abidjan, then entered the Sorbonne, earning a doctorate in African American literature and civilization. In 1983 she attended Howard University in Washington D.C. as a Fulbright scholar,

then later moved to the University of Abidjan, where she was a lecturer in the English department. In 1993 she became a full-time writer. She has traveled a great deal, including to Europe, the United States, Latin America, and West Africa, and has conducted workshops on such topics as literature for African youth and the illustrating of children's books. In 2000 and 2001 she served as a judge for the Caine Prize for African Writing. She resides in South Africa.

MAJOR WORKS

In the nonlinear and fragmented *As the Crow Flies,* the reader is encouraged to interact with the text from the perspective of a bird in flight, which swoops down sporadically into any number of tales, voices, moods, locations, and situations—including world disasters as well as everyday occurrences. Made up of several vignettes and told in a stream-of-consciousness style, the novel imitates the ancient art of storytelling and takes its inspiration from the African oral tradition, which utilizes an assortment of genres. Two main themes prevail throughout the novel: the value of love, and the importance of responding to social concerns, especially the needs of the poor. In one surreal vignette, a man and woman desperately in love conceive a son, whom they lovingly nurture and guide toward a social mission. Having been raised to have faith in himself, the son descends into despondency as he experiences the spiritual, physical, and intellectual desolation of society. While in this state he falls in love with an asexual woman, who has no use for passion and intimacy. Desperate to possess her, he drugs, then sexually assaults her. Her resulting pregnancy triggers an apocalypse in which people become stones, and the world is plunged into darkness. The tale contemplates how human virtue fails even when cultivated under the most ideal of circumstances, and reveals the central role of women in society, suggesting that to betray a woman is to invite destruction. Another vignette centers on the oppressive state of society, focusing on an actor, who represents the populace, and his relationship with the "enlightened" of society, who promote creativity and generosity, and with the repressive political leaders, who dismiss the arts and wield the powerful weapon of censorship. Other tales depict the poor, the "wretched of the earth"; the emotional and physical repercussions of abortion; a failed love affair between an African woman and a married man from America; a young girl who befriends a disabled boy, who then shuns her; the sexual violations of women; and the relationship between an elderly magician and a young woman who craves the gift of everlasting joy. In all, the text calls on individuals—especially women—to examine themselves in order to undergo a personal transformation and thus empower themselves to preserve and protect the moral order of society.

In 1989 Tadjo was invited by Tchadian writer Nocky Djedanoum to join a group of African writers who were to visit Rwanda in order to record their literary responses to the country's 1994 mass murders, in which the government advocated the extermination of almost one million Tutsis. Tadjo details her two trips to Rwanda in the nonfiction *The Shadow of Imana,* focusing on her encounters with orphans, despondent survivors, and sexual assault victims, and reflects on her witness of the brutalized and tortured remains of the victims. A sense of inquiry pervades the work, as the author contemplates such matters as the notion of man's inhumanity to man, the seemingly insurmountable task of forgiveness among Rwandans, and how to find the appropriate words to describe such atrocities.

CRITICAL RECEPTION

Having gained a reputation among French readers as an influential writer in the field of Francophone African literature, Tadjo has received a modest amount of critical attention among English-speaking scholars. Overall, she is recognized for her prose, which has been described as simple, poetic, and impressionistic. She is primarily lauded for the inventiveness of *As the Crow Flies,* which Irène Assiba D'Almeida called "one of the most original pieces of Francophone writing." Commenting favorably on such structural innovations as the blending together of several genres, the author's use of filmic techniques, and the novel's discontinuity and lack of a "typical" plot, some critics have focused on the sociopolitical criticism contained in the novel, pointing out that the narrator is a firm believer that social change must begin with the self-examination of the individual and that a return to traditional African beliefs and rituals can help cure society's ills. Others have lauded Tadjo's ability to achieve a sense of universality even while depicting individual characters and locations, and have singled out her emphasis on the importance of one's connection to his African culture and ancestry. The nonfiction work *The Shadow of Imana* has also generated critical discussion. Sonia Lee, for example, classified the book as "highly representative of the kind of Montaignean essay written by African women writers today," based in part on the fact that even though Tadjo visited Rwanda several years after the massacre, she considered herself connected with the tragedy because of the "collective memory" shared by all human beings. Claiming that Tadjo considered the act of writing *The Shadow of Imana* a political obligation, some

critics have contended that the author felt it her duty to write about and thereby preserve the events of the horrific past so as not only to give a voice to the past, but also to combat apathy, and to offer an attempt at comprehending how such inhumane violence could come to pass. Other commentators have assessed Tadjo's literary style in the work, finding it stark and somber, and have speculated that she utilized this spare style in order to deal with the atrocities and cope with her own raw emotional response.

PRINCIPAL WORKS

Latérite (poetry) 1984

A vol d'oiseau [*As the Crow Flies*] (novel) 1986

La Chanson de la vie et autres histoires [and illustrator; *The Song of Life and Other Stories*] (children's short stories) 1989

Le Seigneur de la danse [and illustrator; *Lord of the Dance: An African Retelling*] (for children) 1989

Le Royaume aveugle [*The Kingdom of the Blind*] (novel) 1990

Mamy Wata et le monstre [and illustrator; *Mamy Wata and the Monster*] (for children) 1993

Grand-mère Nanan [and illustrator] (for children) 1996

Champs de bataille et d'amour: Présence Africaine, Paris, and Les Nouvelles Editions Ivoiriennes [*Battlefields and Love*] (novel) 1999

A mi-chemin (poetry) 2000

L'Ombre d'Imana: voyages jusqu'au bout du Rwanda [*The Shadow of Imana: Travels in the Heart of Rwanda*] (prose) 2000

Talking Drums: A Selection of Poems from Africa South of the Sahara [editor and illustrator] (children's poetry) 2004

Reine Pokou: Concerto pour un sacrifice [*Queen Pokou*] (novel) 2005

Chasing the Sun: Stories from Africa [editor and illustrator] (short stories) 2008

CRITICISM

Irène Assiba D'Almeida (essay date 1994)

SOURCE: D'Almeida, Irène Assiba. "W/Riting Change: Women as Social Critics." In *Francophone African Women Writers: Destroying the Emptiness of Silence,* pp. 123-68. Gainesville: University Press of Florida, 1994.

[*In the excerpt that follows, D'Almeida offers a detailed reading of the structure, themes, and subject matter of* A vol d'oiseau, *commenting specifically on what the critic calls the novel's "femino-centric perspective" on social and political issues.*]

Véronique Tadjo, a poet and novelist from Côte d'Ivoire, entered the literary world with **Latérite,** a book that can be read either as a collection of poems or as a single long poem.[1] Her first novel, *A Vol d'oiseau* [*As the Crow Flies*], is one of the most original pieces of Francophone writing, and one that defies easy classification. It is surely a "text" in the primary meaning of the word, that is, "something woven." Tadjo's cloth is patterned from ninety-two independent yet related pieces, most accurately described as vignettes, that can stand on their own or be put together to form an immense appliqué representing an African social reality.[2] The vignettes are written mainly in prose, but Tadjo's language is never far from poetry, and here it exhibits her ability to use very simple words to create a superb poetic prose. The book comprises twenty-one chapters, each chapter containing a varied number of vignettes (one to eleven), ranging from one line to several pages in length, with each vignette assigned a roman numeral (I to XCII).

Like Werewere Liking, Véronique Tadjo often blurs the genres, and even within a genre she shows great originality in form and structure. In *A Vol d'oiseau,* there is no central figure, but a multiplicity of characters in different situations and belonging to different social classes. There is no single setting, but a variety of loci, no conventional plot, no real successiveness; only the main narrator serves as a unifying agent. This narrative technique, reminiscent of "stream of consciousness" and the *nouveau roman,* makes it possible for the writer to constantly shift directions, to move from one part of the world to another, to speak of the most diverse themes ranging from love and art to social and political issues. In addition, the vignette technique allows Tadjo to disregard the categories of time and space. She does not tell a story but a multitude of stories, some taken from personal life, news items, or reflections, some allegorical, constructed like a legend. Tadjo chooses to disregard chronology, which she views as artificial, distorted linearity and as a rearrangement of reality.[3] The reader is given a glimpse of her poetics when she says: "Bien sûr, j'aurais, moi aussi, aimé écrire une histoire sereine avec un début et une fin. Mais tu sais bien qu'il n'en est pas ainsi" [Of course, I too, would have liked to write a peaceful story with a beginning and an end. But you know that it does not work that way] (2). Even though literature is an imaginary construct, it has bearing on a tumultuous reality, and Tadjo uses it as an avenue for social criticism aiming at social change.

Two major themes of *A Vol d'oiseau* appear on the opening page, which functions as a kind of prologue. The first has to do with the importance and power of love, and the second with commitment to self and society. The prologue commences with a short poem, containing the title of the book, which reads like an epigraph: it urges that love be important enough to warrant total commitment, and that once set on its path, one must go the whole way, straight ahead, as the crow flies. Perhaps the metaphor can be extended to include not only love, but every human action:

> Si tu veux aimer
> Fais le
> Jusqu'au bout du monde
> Sans faire de détours
> A vol d'oiseau
>
> [If you want to love
> Do so
> To the end of the world
> With no false detours
> As the crow flies]

The beginning of the prologue is an invocation addressed to the reader in the second person *tu,* the informal, friendly form of "you." The usage of *tu*/you serves the phatic function of discourse by which the narrator maintains a constant contact with the reader, who is addressed directly and so drawn into the narrative.[4]

The second part of the prologue is written in prose rather than verse. It starts with the first person (*je*/I), then quickly moves to the second (*tu*/you), and back again to *je*/I. The recurrent use of the second person (*tu*/you) and its alternation with *je*/I complicates the relation between addresser and addressee. Indeed, according to various contexts, the *tu*/you refers to either the narrator/protagonist *or* the reader. The "I" is the producer of discourse, whereas the "you" is the receptor of the same discourse. Yet when the narrator says, "*Tu* dis en te regardant dans le miroir: '*Je* n'aime pas ce que *je* vois'" [In looking at the mirror *you* say, "*I* don't like what *I* see"] (2, emphasis added), there seems to be no difference between the "you" and the "I." Lafont and Gardès-Madray note: "Le passage dialectique du *je* au *tu* fait que *tu* est considéré . . . en *je* éventuel" [The dialectical passage from *I* to *you* results in *you* being considered . . . as a possible *I*] (93).[5] This technique of pronominal interpenetration indicates how there can be in Tadjo's text a double addressee; the addresser and the addressee of her own discourse. The narrator/protagonist is speaking to herself even while speaking to the reader.[6]

The second part of the prologue describes a character looking into a mirror, loathing a self-reflection marked by weaknesses and failures. Tadjo suggests that in order to overcome shortcomings one must be able to imagine one's own decomposition, or to face the idea of being cremated. The word *death* does not appear in the text, but it is generated connotatively with enough force to become the unspoken presence, the oppositional force against which the narrator sets herself. This resistance requires tremendous courage and strength, qualities necessary to survive in the world and to combat the forces that would thwart her life. And she goes on to prophesy: "Ta force surgira de tes faiblesses éparses et, de ton humanité commune, tu combattras les tares érigées en édifices royaux sur les dunes du silence" [Your strength will come from your scattered weaknesses and with your common humanity you will fight the corruption rising like a royal edifice on the dunes of silence] (2). The eye/I that is looking in the mirror does not settle on an uncritical acceptance of self, but aspires to and works for transcendence and seeks to develop a character strong enough to fight for voice and freedom. The phrase "the dunes of silence" suggests that when people are silenced for too long, that silence, which in principle is an abstraction, an absence, becomes concrete, a presence. It accumulates and solidifies like sand dunes on which the corrupt elements of society can erect their monuments of lies and abuse. Speaking up is a way to end this destructive masquerade and dislodge the abusers from their "royal" authority.[7]

The two major impulses of the novel announced in the prologue are woven throughout the text, variations on the two significant sentences, "L'histoire de la misère se raconte" [The story of poverty must be told] (22) and "L'amour est une histoire qu'on n'arrête pas de conter" [Love is a story that one never ceases to tell] (53), that summarize the themes. There exists, however, a third dimension, inseparably intermingled with love and social concerns. It is the pervasive inscription of women's experience that signals a female-authored text and a femino-centric perspective on social reality.

Vignette LXIII, which forms the whole of chapter sixteen, beautifully encapsulates *A Vol d'oiseau*'s tridimensional orientation. Drawing inspiration from the cultural reservoir of orature, Tadjo invents a tale of a man and a woman who love each other so deeply that they decide to have a child. No sooner have they made the decision than the woman becomes pregnant, giving birth to a son before the end of the day. In this legend, the importance of love and the positive impact it can have on individuals is exemplified by the degree of feeling shared by the young man's parents. Their commitment to each other does not undermine their commitment to society, manifested in the way they raise their son, patiently preparing him for a social mission: to travel and to teach. They tell him, "Reconstruis les cités détruites par la violence et l'oppression. Laisse pousser l'herbe folle et n'écrase pas les nuages. Parleleur de l'eau qui ne tarit pas. Plonge ta main dans la terre et respire son odeur et surtout, surtout, crois en toi-même" [Rebuild cities destroyed by violence. Let wild grass grow and do not crush the clouds. Tell them about the water that does not dry up. Dip your hand deep into the soil and inhale its fragrance. Above all, above all, believe in yourself] (69-70).

This is a message of justice, creativity, hope, and self-reliance, all positive values, but difficult to act on in a world whose social fabric has been badly damaged. The young man finds that the city he travels to is a locus of extreme contradictions. Bright lights inundate the rich

neighborhoods, and yet close by, there is nothing but mud and filth. People are dressed like royalty and parade their gold jewelry, but not far from them cripples in rags and abandoned children are a common sight. The teachings given by the young man's parents are difficult to pass on because skepticism and despair have settled in the city: "Le plus grave c'était que les habitants avaient perdu la foi. On parlait de liberté et de changement mais c'était des paroles inutiles. Personne n'y croyait" [What was most serious was that the people had lost faith. People talked of freedom and change but these were useless words. Nobody believed in them] (70). Indeed, the people have been deceived so many times with words emptied of meaning that they have lost all hope, becoming utterly apathetic. More devastating than physical destitution is the destitution of mind and spirit that becomes so contagious that the young man must fight to hold on to his own faith. Furthermore, he finds that the fulfillment of his mission is jeopardized by his own inability to establish contact with others, so that he soon feels estranged, suffering at the thought that he who was supposed to make a difference has become despondent like the rest.

He falls in love, but the relationship is very different from that of his parents because he and the woman he loves are very dissimilar people. The woman has a strong sense of who she is and of what she wants. She refuses to fit into accepted women's roles. Believing that what she can accomplish is limitless, she views love as secondary. She only agrees to a relationship with the young man to share a friendship: "Elle savait que ce qu'il disait faisait partie de la vie mais elle n'était pas prête. Il lui fallait encore du temps. Beaucoup de temps. Des années peut-être" [She knew that what he was saying was part of life, but she was not ready. She needed time. A lot of time. Years, perhaps] (71).

The young man does not have that patience. He is so taken by the woman, his desire so overwhelming, that one night he gives her a soporific drink, makes love to her, and conceives a child. The result of this betrayal is an extraordinary apocalypse: the world is plunged into profound darkness and silence, and people are turned into stone. The woman regaining consciousness immediately says: "Cet enfant n'est pas de moi. Il amènera le malheur" [This child is not mine. It will bring misfortune] (72). The young man, now panicked, places his hand on the woman's navel to see if the child is alive, but this touch unleashes a fury suggestive of nuclear disaster across the earth, laying waste the land and its people, as "un énorme nuage-champignon sculpta l'horizon incendié" [an enormous mushroom cloud was sculpted against the blazing horizon] (72).

This story is compelling in its force and effective brevity, and it illustrates some of the main ideological bearings of the novel. It is no accident that the young man was raised in the best possible conditions to fulfill his mission; similarly to Fall's Madiama, his failure indicates that the best conditions may not be sufficient to produce human virtue: something else is required. The young woman attempts to escape the stereotypical notion of womanhood, even disowning the child she is carrying because it was conceived against her will. Before that conception she had decreed that she had no gender, caring neither for skirts nor for breasts, significant symbols of rejection as they involve the semiotics of clothing and of gender difference. Most importantly, the story implies that to betray a woman, even in the name of love, is to risk total destruction, and Tadjo's surreal visions of the world's end emphasizes how the unhindered presence of women is vital to the survival of the cosmos itself. This deliberately grand vision of women's role and place in the world, though located at the phantasmagoric level of the tale, reflects the centrality given women in *A Vol d'oiseau.*

Tadjo's characters are generally nameless and often defined simply by their actions or function. The only exception to this is Akissi, and this is significant because Akissi is a woman, and she is going through an experience that affects women in the deepest way: an unwanted pregnancy and an illegal abortion.[8] Here, the use of a personal name specifies and makes intimate the vignette's action. In less than a page and with the economy of language characteristic of Tadjo's writing, the wide range of feelings agitating Akissi is evoked. Her unwillingness to accept this pregnancy is evident in her reaction to the transformations her body undergoes: "Jour après jour, elle sent ses seins gonfler. Son corps entier se transforme. Ele se voit devenir une autre. Elle ne comprend pas cette vie qui est entrée en elle et qui lui bouffe toutes ses forces. Elle n'est pas prête" [Day after day, she feels the swelling of her breasts. Her entire body is changing. She sees herself become another person. She does not understand the life that has slipped into her and is devouring all of her strength. She is not ready] (12).

In Akissi's case, pregnancy does not mean only a physical burden. It has serious psychological, emotional, and financial ramifications. The decision to terminate the pregnancy is in itself emotionally draining, all the more so because Akissi is forced into the back alleys filled with other women wanting to undergo the same operation. Like Ken Bugul in *The Abandoned Baobab,* Tadjo shows the common fate shared by all these women patiently waiting for their turn, alone (except for the man performing the abortion, men are conspicuously absent from the scene), turned into masks of stone, walled in by silence. And Tadjo makes this silence resound with unspeakable feelings generated by fear, by the anticipation of pain both physical and psychological, in an indifferent environment where no words are exchanged. Not the slightest sign of caring is shown here. On the contrary, it is a mere financial transaction, quick, cold, impersonal, made even more poignant as Akissi has to borrow the money for the operation. Tadjo does not speak directly for or against abortion. She simply presents a brief dramatization of a woman's experience that works very effectively to indict the laws of the land.

In other vignettes Tadjo describes more aggressively how the female body is constantly violated, even in public places. For the narrator, it happens in a movie theater where a fast and deft hand fondles her, painfully reminding her of a deeper wound—here again described with so few words as to heighten the drama: "Une main dans la pénombre d'un cinéma. Une main que je n'avais pas comprise. Une main qui prend la mienne. Brusquement, avec la musique du film, les paroles et le noir. Un pénis moite. Un homme qui se sauve. Une sensation irréparable" [A hand in the shadowy light of a theater. A hand that I did not understand. A hand taking mine. Suddenly with the music of the film, its words, the darkness. A wet penis. A man running away. An irreparable violation] (61).

The passage is spare but direct, disclosing clearly yet with calculated restraint how subject women are to casual molestation. The end of the vignette pinpoints the consequences of such acts for women: "an irreparable violation"; irreparable in the sense that it remains indelible. It can never be erased, only pushed into the recesses of memory, with the added agony that any similar occurrence may trigger the memory and make the woman live through the experience all over again, in pain and such rage that she is filled with the desire "de frapper, de casser un corps, d'anéantir une tête malade" [to hit, to smash a body, to destroy a sick mind] (61).

Worse still, the female body is violated irrespective of age or social competence. Even female children who are still too innocent to understand what is happening to them are the victims of such defilement, as Tadjo illustrates in the story of an older man and a girl still wearing a white and blue grade school uniform. Tadjo has the man entice the girl with candy, a double symbol of childhood and eroticism that he reinforces with sexual discourse: "Tiens, suce ce bonbon et ensuite embrasse moi" [Here, suck this candy and then kiss me] (32). His words and his actions leave no doubt that he is the seducer, yet in a cowardly reversal, while caressing her hair he compares her to Mamy Wata, the water goddess who in African mythology is the fatal seductress par excellence.[9] Identifying her in this way he shifts the responsibility for his actions onto the female child. In the end, however, after he asks her to take her clothes off and as she lies naked, he finds he cannot go through with the act. He redeems himself at least slightly by saying: "Je ne peux pas. Tu es encore trop jeune" [I can't, you are still too young] (32). The girl's innocence is again transparent in her reply: "Trop jeune, pour quoi faire? . . . Pour quoi faire?" [Too young to do what? To do what?] (32).

Tadjo is clear that women must assert themselves, taking more control over their destiny, instead of being "des femmes repliées sur elles-mêmes, léchant leurs plaies . . ." [women withdrawn into themselves, licking their wounds . . .] (54). They must put an end to any relationship that debases and devalues them and refuse to suffer any outrage on account of their gender. Such empowered women will no longer tolerate abuse, be it physical or verbal, and will refuse to understand "ces hommes qui veulent déchirer et qui donnent des coups de pieds dans le ventre des femmes avec des mots méchants, des mots qui blessent en plein coeur" [those men who want to tear and kick women's stomachs with harsh words, wounding words that hurt right into the center of the heart] (54). By using phrases such as "to tear" or "to kick," Tadjo suggests that verbal violence is no less damaging than physical violence. These observations don't mean that Tadjo rejects men entirely: her point finally is to say that love does not need to be hurtful, physically or otherwise.

Véronique Tadjo's treatment of female-male relationships here is closely akin to Werewere Liking's concept of the misovire, who, it must be remembered, is a woman unable to find an admirable man. This theoretical admirable man can only be born out of the transformation of the social self. Indeed, faced with women's formidable determination, men will have to change their behavior, discern the difference between loving and destroying, and realize that destruction is no proof of manhood. To make sure that this metamorphosis takes place, to help men as well as to protect themselves, Tadjo says women must also act: "Il faut leur dire d'arrêter. Les tenir à bout de bras et leur réapprendre l'alphabet" [We must tell them to stop. We must hold them at arm's length and teach them the alphabet all over again] (54). Reteaching the alphabet involves serious work on the part of both the teacher and the learner, but the work holds the promise of a new beginning, a new understanding, a new form of relationship between men and women. Women will not give up on the possibility of love. That is why Tadjo combines a resolute refusal to be abused in the name of love (or for any reason, for that matter) with an ardent desire for love, sensuality, and sexual fulfillment.

Writing has allowed women to speak the unspeakable, to utter words, ideas, concepts that are forbidden to them within the conventions laid out by patriarchal society. Sex, desire, passion, and love are topics that women are expected to pass over in silence. By transgressing these taboos through the medium of literature, writers such as Calixthe Beyala, Ken Bugul, Werewere Liking, and Véronique Tadjo break the unwritten conventions while still accepting, as positive value, the topology that regards women as emotionally sensitive; thus they reclaim the right to express their feelings. In *A Vol d'oiseau,* the protagonist admits to living through her skin. She does not hesitate to speak of the body as a seat of enjoyable sensations. She talks freely about everything from the tickle of water running on her skin in the shower to the intense pleasures of orgasm. The erotic sensuality of the following passage shows no recognition of the usual taboos that regulate the parameters of African women's discourse: "Je m'enveloppe de son odeur, mouille mon visage de sa sueur, touche sa peau, mords son épaule, avale son désir, ferme les yeux, tends mon corps, l'appelle et le rejette" [I wrap myself in his smell, wet my face with his sweat, touch his skin, bite his shoulder, swallow his desire, close my eyes, stretch my body, call and expel him] (80).

The quest for love is so central for Tadjo that she invents yet another story, which begins realistically and ends as a legend. The opening depicts a love between a sick woman and a man who shares her pain so deeply that "il aurait voulu hurler, transpercer les murs d'un son si puissant que la ville se serait tue et que le temps aurait reculé. Il aurait voulu vivre la même souffrance—dans sa chair, la douleur qui aujourd'hui remplaçait le plaisir" [he wished he could scream, pierce walls with a sound so powerful that the city would become silent and time would recede. He wished he could experience the same pain—in his flesh, experience the pain which today was replacing pleasure] (39). To save his beloved he attempts to pray, but finds he no longer knows how. He then makes the only choice he finds acceptable: "J'irai avec toi jusqu'à la mort . . . je veux t'aimer jusqu'au bout de ta souffrance" [I will travel with you until death comes. . . . I want to love you to the limits of your suffering] (40).

At this point the realistic setting is left behind and the story's action is transformed into myth. The lover takes the woman in his arms and crosses thousands of miles, finally arriving at the sea. She expresses the desire to die there and be buried by the waters, but he will not hear of it and resumes his journey, traveling until he reaches a white mountain. She expresses the desire to die there in a place peaceful, cold, and pure. Again he refuses, and resumes his journeying until he reaches a desert, where: "Ils surent . . . qu'ils avaient atteint le bout du monde et qu'il ne leur restait nulle part où aller" [They realized . . . that they had reached the end of the earth and there was no place else to go to] (41). The woman expresses her desire to die in the desert; having no choice, the man asks to make love to her for the last time, "et c'est là qu'entre ciel et terre ils s'aimèrent si fort que le soleil fit une éclipse et qu'un vent de fraîcheur balaya leurs corps" [and it is there, between sky and earth, that they loved each other so intensely that the sun was eclipsed and a cool breeze swept over their bodies] (41).[10]

This sad but beautiful story features a loving, compassionate companion, the very essence of the new man sought for by the misovire. So the greatest love story of the book is in the form of a mythological tale, the most compassionate man is a character in a tale, the woman who enjoys such compassion is on the verge of dying. Tadjo seems to suggest this conjunction of events might be possible only in an imaginary world; or she might mean that the power of imagination can be towering enough to accomplish the miracle of love. Yet love involves a wide array of relationships and the narrator extends it to her country as well as to individuals. She is connected to her country in an intimate manner, her feelings even strengthened by her exile in the "stone country"—an unnamed Western nation. In a three-line vignette (LV), she conveys this attachment with an exquisitely unexpected love metaphor: "Je songe à mon pays qui m'obsède chaque fois. Je le porte en moi, le jour. La nuit, il s'allonge à mes côtés et me fait l'amour" [I think of my country which, for me, has become a constant obsession. In the daytime I carry my country inside me. At night my country lies beside me and makes love to me] (64). It is easy to understand, then, the suffering she feels when confronting the ills of her society. Its problems are so glaringly present that they impose themselves on all the senses: "Faut-il être aveugle pour ne pas voir? / Sourd pour ne pas entendre? / Muet pour ne pas crier?" [Should one be blind not to see? / Deaf not to hear? / Dumb not to shout?] (66).

What the narrator sees is a society characterized by a profound sense of malaise, one she describes with phrases of disjunction: "la vie a dû rater une marche" [Life must have missed one step] (8); "on doit vivre un siècle crasseux" [we must be living in a filthy time] (21); "on doit vivre un monde sans queue ni tête" [we must be living in a senseless world] (29); "c'est vraiment un siècle qui baisse la tête" [it is really a century that walks with its head down] (29). This social malaise needs to be overcome, of course, because there is an enormous amount of work to be done, and her sense of urgency in this is moved by the seriousness of the problems to be dealt with: "Il n'y a pas de quoi avoir la tête en l'air. Il n'y a pas de quoi rire et se croiser les bras" [This is no time to be absentminded. This is no time to laugh and sit around idly] (65). Tadjo's narrator cannot afford to laugh in the face of the social injustice she describes with evocative force: "Je dis les inégalités qui croissent comme des margouillats sous les ruines des taudis" [I speak of the inequalities that grow like lizards under the ruins of slums] (65). Starting her sentence with the declarative "I speak," the narrator performs an act of language that, assuming the responsibility of enunciation, makes the statement stronger and the concern more acute. Describing inequalities as "lizards" emphasizes the proliferation of these inequalities, and the image of the "ruins of slums" conveys the sense of a double destruction.

Even within the fictional mode in which *A Vol d'oiseau* is cast, there is a dialectical motion between the purely "imaginary" tales, such as the one about the dying woman, and the putatively "real" *histoires vécues*—

stories lived, experienced by a character. Such an *histoire vécue* forms the background of chapter three, a long, first-person vignette. It tells the story of a young man who is at the same time the protagonist, focalizer, and narrator recounting his experiences as an actor. Within the story lies a depiction of the relationship that exists between intellectuals, politicians, and "ordinary" people. The young man is representative of the majority of the people as indicated by his modest background, his substandard living conditions, his speech patterns, his attitude toward education, and his aspirations. In fact, his representation of the people is doubled by the very role he acts within the play: "Je représente le peuple. Symboliquement. Je fais beaucoup de choses. Je cultive la terre. Je pêche. . . . Je danse. . . . Mes pas cadencés. Mon buste raidi. Mon cou cabré. Et puis 'Stop,' les bras en croix. Le héros se bat pour moi. Contre le monarque" [I represent the people. Symbolically. I do a lot of things. I till the land. I go fishing. . . . I dance. . . . In quick time. My chest stiffened. My neck taut. And then "Cut," arms in the form of the cross. The hero fights for me. Against the monarch] (15).

A variant of this speech is repeated at the end of the vignette: "Je représente le peuple. Symboliquement. J'ai les bras en croix. Le héros se bat pour moi. Contre le monarque" [I represent the people. Symbolically. My arms are in the form of the cross. The hero fights for me. Against the monarch] (20). Between this repeated quotation is Tadjo's generalized depiction of the state of African society. The young man simultaneously a representative of the people and representing them. Furthermore, his summary lines provide the reader with a vision of what life is like for the people he represents, an existence of hard labor that nonetheless finds some release in dance. Even that dance, though, is hampered by the strained positions of his body—positions symbolic of constraint and injustice. The phrase "my arms are in the form of a cross" suggests crucifixion, but the quotation goes on to describe a revolutionary mood personified by the "hero," who sides with the people, fighting with and for them against the monarch.

As there is a correlation between the "people" and the young man, a parallel can be drawn between the "hero" and the director of the theater company. The director represents an enlightened intellectual, one who turns ideas into action, and so commands the young man's admiration. He is intelligent, generous, and helpful in encouraging youngsters to use their creativity in acting. Creating a community of artists who can share all aspects of their lives, he develops a space where their talents can flourish. His home is opened to whoever needs a bed or food, and the visitor who happens to be there at lunch time is undoubtedly invited to share the meal.[11]

Not fully understanding the intricacies of the repressive system he is living in, the young man's innocent voice continuously makes remarks that are all the more powerful as they are understated. He laments the fact that arts are encouraged by neither politicians nor the public. At one performance there are only three rows of spectators, and, as participatory and encouraging as they are, the small audience points up the precariousness of artistic life in Africa. The young man observes: "Le théâtre, c'est pas un travail. Un jour on gagne, demain, on gagne rien. Ça me plaît, mais ce n'est vraiment pas un travail" [Acting is not a job. One day you earn some money, tomorrow, you earn nothing. I like acting, but really it is not a job] (18). In addition, theater is particularly censored because of its perceived potency. The director is constantly harassed by politicians, who see the plays as a threat, as again, the narrator ingenuously notes: "On dit qu'Il est un révolutionaire, que les pièces que nous on joue attaquent le gouvernement. Il y a toujours des problèmes" [They say He is a revolutionary, that the plays we perform are an attack against the government. We are always in trouble] (19).

One understands, then, why the people must have someone to fight for them, against the "monarch"—a living symbol of the oppressive political machinery.[12] It seems possible, however, that the people themselves will come to action because oppression cannot last for ever: "On en a tous marre de ce monarque qui s'assoit sur la tête de son peuple" [We are all fed up with this monarch who sits on his people's heads] (29). This image of sitting on someone's head, clearly an African idiom, takes on larger proportions because many African societies hold the belief that the head is the seat of life. Thus, to sit on people's heads is at worse to wish their death and at best to deprive them of all power. In search of inordinate power for himself, the monarch attempts to render his people powerless.

Powerlessness is also a characteristic of the poor, and poverty is personified by the mentally disturbed people who roam the streets, infested with lice, stinking so badly that their smell infests the whole city. The all-pervading stench shows that what happens to the "wretched of the earth" affects everybody. If those who exploit the people with detached indifference are blind to the crucial dimensions of human interdependency, violence will force them into such recognition. There will come a time when it will no longer be possible for them to count on their "lucky star." Their fat bank accounts and the endless privileges they enjoy will collapse with the rebellion of the down-trodden: "Vos jardins seront malmenés, vos autels sacrés assiégés et vos fétiches-idoles décapités. Vos demeures enfoncées. Vos livres jetés, vos maîtres à penser condamnés. Les traces de vos pas s'effaceront et sur une plage abandonnée, on transpercera vos poitrines de flèches empoisonnées" [Your gardens will be wrecked, your sacred shrines besieged and your fetish-idoles will be beheaded. Your homes smashed in. Your books thrown away, your intellectual guides condemned. The traces of

your steps will disappear and, on abandoned shores, your chests will be pierced with poisoned arrows] (66). If the exploiters retaliate, they will be unmasked by a mass media whose sophistication can now be used to the advantage of the voiceless majority: "Le monde entier verra les bouches tordues, le sang épaix et grotesque des corps aux derniers soubresauts" [The whole world will see the twisted mouths, and the thick, grotesque blood oozing out of bodies in their last convulsions] (66).

If her criticism of the sociopolitical structures and of the so-called leaders who maintain and enforce them is mordant, Tadjo still invites all individuals to work for a loftier ideal. That goal must be approached, not through complacency but through rigorous self-criticism: "Nous devons piétiner les mauvaises habitudes, déraciner les fausses théories et nous regarder face à face" [We must trample on bad habits, uproot false theories and look ourselves in the face] (65). All individuals have a responsibility both to themselves and to future generations, who eventually are going to ask: "Qu'avez-vous fait pour changer les choses?" [What have you done to change things?] (29). This is an interrogation that should spur the elders into reevaluating their acts, because "les actions que nous sculptons se cristallisent" [the actions that we take will crystalize] (65). And nothing would be more damaging than to crystallize the status quo for the younger generations.

Like Werewere Liking, Véronique Tadjo makes ancestral beliefs and rituals play an important role in the transformation of self and society. At the personal level, when the narrator cannot make sense of her love life, when the pain of separation is no longer bearable, she longs to go back to her ancestors' belief systems. She would like to call the Gods, say incantations, assemble healers, sorcerers, and spirits, and resort to magic to annihilate her memory. But she strives not for escape, but for empowerment and a new beginning.

At the social level, Tadjo emphasizes the necessity to revive cultural survival rites, and advocates ritual on a large scale, both in the city and in the country: "Il nous faut procéder aux rites de pureté. Faire les sacrifices nécessaires. Il faut replanter nos grands arbres arrachés, nos forêts sacrées décimées" [We must perform cleansing rites. We must make the necessary sacrifices. We must plant again our tall uprooted trees, our decimated sacred forests] (67). Tadjo puts ritual into a twofold play, making it perform its traditional function and serve as a cure for modern problems. The sacrifices refer to both ritual and the renunciation necessary to become agents of change. In the same way, the act of replanting trees constitutes at once a genealogical and ecological symbol, emphasizing a cultural continuum. On the other hand, it serves as a means to solve the urgent problem of deforestation facing the continent.

Also, because ritual valorizes speech and is articulated through speech, however esoteric, it will be possible to rediscover the significance of the word in "la parole complète. Celle qui est à la fois silence et verbe, action et inertie. Celle que seuls les grands initiés possèdent" [the completeness of the word that is both silence and speech, action and inertia. The word that only the great initiates possessed] (67). Thus, ritual can constitute the mediating process for a judicious balance between speech and action.

The novelists studied here [Werewere Liking, Aminata Sow Fall, and Véronique Tadjo] believe in a new sociopolitical order. Mostly, however, their fictions make it clear that *a new moral order* is desperately needed. Without it all other construction remains without foundation. The fictions also attest to the fact that this new moral order can only be turned into reality through individual commitment.

Notes

1. Tadjo's *Latérite* won the Agence de Coopération Culturelle et Technique prize in 1983. She wrote *Chanson de la vie* and *Lord of the Dance,* self-illustrated books of stories (some in prose, others in poetry) for children, inspired by African orature. Tadjo has also produced two novels: *A Vol d'oiseau* and *Le Royaume aveugle.*

2. My comparison of Tadjo's text as texture/textile is not meant to erase the writing subject in order to privilege the process of writing, as Nancy Miller's critique of Barthes's *Pleasure of the Text* suggests he does. (See "Arachnelogies: The Woman, the Text and the Critic," in Miller, *Poetics of Gender.*) My comparison is no doubt made in relation to etymology, but more so from a cultural standpoint that does not emphasize gender—the metaphor of weaving has been used by male and female writers alike. Charlotte H. Bruner entitles a book *Unwinding Threads,* an image borrowed from the Kabyle folk singers in the Algerian mountains who always begin their tales with the following formulaic phrase: "Que mon conte soit beau et se déroule comme un long fil . . ." [May my story be beautiful and unwind like a long thread . . .]. Also, in *Contes d'Amadou Koumba,* Diop describes himself as a weaver using threads to make a *pagne,* that is, a "cloth" or "wrapper" (12). Using the same metaphor, Dadié entitles his collection of folk stories *Le Pagne noir.*

3. For a discussion of chronology in fiction and as fiction, see Kermode's masterful analyses in *Sense of an Ending.*

4. The phatic function is also visible in the narrator's numerous interventions. For instance, after recounting the story of a woman who died in her bathroom because of poor construction caused by a dishonest architect, she says: "On m'a raconté cette histoire et c'est ainsi que je vous la livre" [I was told this story and I am passing it on to you

as it was told to me] (22). Further along, making a distinction between the leper who "licks the ground" and the fighter who, instead, has great pride, she tells the reader: "Ce n'est pas moi qui le dis. Je l'ai lu quelque part" [I am not the one who says so. I read that somewhere] (38). Also, speaking of the violence that men inflict on women she says: "Mais oublions tout cela et laissez-moi vous parler d'autre chose" [But let us forget all this and let me tell you about something else] (54).

5. Lafont and Gardès-Madray (*Introduction à l'analyse textuelle,* 93) analyze the dialectics of the *Je*/I and the *tu*/you in terms of temporality, which is not my purpose here. It is interesting, though, that they go on to say: "Il y a donc dans le mouvement par lequel *tu* devient *je* . . . un passage de l'éventualité à la réalité. Mais dans ce même mouvement, le *je* précédent devient un *tu.* Si l'on considère ce movement dans la fluence temporelle, on voit que *tu* est à la fois l'avenir et le passé du *je*" [Therefore, there exists in the motion through which *I* becomes *you* . . . a passage from a possibility to a reality. Yet, in the same motion, the preceding *I* becomes a *you.* If one considers the temporal flow in this motion, one sees that *you* is at once the future and the past of *I*].

6. The pronominal interpretation is further extended in the course of the narrative to include the third person, more often "she" than "he," and also a collective "we."

7. This is the only instance in which Tadjo uses the metaphor of silence for an act of "silencing." However, she often explores various aspects of silence, stressing the importance of silence and speech in human relationships. She muses over the potency of the word that, bringing to life that which is not, makes the difference between being and nothingness.

8. The name Akissi must have a special significance for Tadjo: Akissi is found in *Latérite* and also in *Le Royaume aveugle,* where she is King Ato V's rebellious daughter.

9. Mamy Wata, or Mami Wata, the water goddess or water spirit, is worshipped by many riverside communities in West Africa. She is said to attract men with her legendary beauty and bury them in the waters. She is mentioned in passing in Achebe's short story "Sacrificial Egg" and in Emecheta's *Joys of Motherhood.* Mamy Wata is central to Nwapa's *Efuru* and to Amadi's *Concubine.*

10. The end of this vignette is very reminiscent of one of the myths of creation among the Fon of Benin: "The Fon of Abomey. . . . speak of a supreme god (Mawu) and many other beings related to him. But Mawu is sometimes called male and some-

times female; Mawu has a partner called Lisa, and they may be spoken of as twins. One myth says that these twins were born from a primordial mother, Nana Buluku, who created the world and then retired. Mawu was the moon and female, controlling the night and dwelling in the west. Lisa was male, the sun, and lived in the east. They had no children when they first took up their stations, but eventually they came together in an eclipse. Whenever there is an eclipse of the sun or moon it is said that Mawu and Lisa are making love" (Parrinder, *African Mythology,* 23).

11. The description of this director is very reminiscent of Werewere Liking, who is also a theater director and has created a community of artists in her Villa Ki-yi in Abidjan. The artists also share everything and the villa is open to all. I had the good fortune of spending a day in the villa, where, in addition to interviewing Liking, I was invited to share a meal and see the rehearsal of *Singue Mura: Considérant que la femme,* a play that Liking was preparing for the Congrès de la Francophonie at Limoges, France. I also had the good fortune to see the play in its final form at Limoges in October 1990. It was a true spectacle, impressively presenting acting accompanied with song, dance, a display of living masks, and an epiphany of colorful and daring costume. The artistry of the cast was phenomenal.

12. Political oppression is for Tadjo a major preoccupation. She effectively denounces it in *Le Royaume aveugle* (meaning both "the kingdom of the blind" and "the blind kingdom"), an allegorical novel describing the iniquities of a totalitarian regime.

Bibliography

PRIMARY SOURCES

Beyala, Calixthe. *Tu t'appelleras Tanga* [Your name will be Tanga]. Paris: Stock, 1988.

Bugul, Ken. *The Abandoned Baobab: The Autobiography of a Senegalese Woman.* Translated by Marjoliyn de Jager. New York: Lawrence Hill Books, 1991. Originally published as *Le Baobab fou* (Dakar: NEA, 1983).

Liking, Werewere, and Manuna Ma-Njock. *"Orphée-Dafric" roman suivi de "Orphée d'Afrique."* Paris: L'Harmattan, 1981.

Tadjo, Véronique. *A Vol d'oiseau* [As the crow flies]. Paris: Editions Nathan, 1986.

SECONDARY SOURCES

Dadié, Bernard. *Le Pagne noir.* Paris: Présence Africaine, 1955.

Diop, Birago. *Tales of Amadou Koumba.* Translated by Dorothy S. Blair. London: Oxford University Press, 1966. Originally published as *Les Contes d'Amadou Koumba* (Paris: Présence Africaine, 1961).

Liking, Werewere, and Marie-José Hourantier. *A la rencontre de . . .* [Meeting with . . .]. Dakar: NEA, 1980.

———. *Contes d'initiation féminine du pays bassa* [Tales of female initiation among the Bassa people]. Paris: Editions St. Paul, 1981.

———. *Liboy li nkundung.* Conte initiatique [Initiation tale]. Paris: Editions St. Paul, 1980.

———. *Les Spectacles rituels* [Ritual theater]. Dakar: NEA, 1987.

Tadjo, Véronique. *La Chanson de la vie et autres histoires* [The song of life and other stories]. Paris: Hatier, Collection Monde Noir Jeunesse, 1989.

———. *Latérite.* Paris: Hatier, 1984.

———. *Lord of the Dance: An African Retelling.* New York: Lipp Jr. Books (Harper Collins Children's Books), 1989.

———. *Le Royaume aveugle* [The kingdom of the blind]. Paris: L'Harmattan, 1990.

CRITICAL SOURCES

Bruner, Charlotte H. *Unwinding Threads: Writing by Women In Africa.* London: Heinemann, 1983.

Kermode, Frank. *The Sense of an Ending: Studies in the Theory of Fiction.* London: Oxford University Press, 1966.

Lafont, Robert, and Françoise Gardès-Madray. *Introduction à l'analyse textuelle.* Paris: Larousse, 1976.

Miller, Nancy K., ed. *The Poetics of Gender.* New York: Columbia University Press, 1986.

Parrinder, Geoffrey. *African Mythology.* 1967. Reprint. New York: Peter Bedrick Books, 1987.

Véronique Tadjo with Stephen Gray (interview date 15 March 2002)

SOURCE: Tadjo, Véronique, and Stephen Gray. "Interview: Véronique Tadjo Speaks with Stephen Gray." *Research in African Literatures* 34, no. 3 (fall 2003): 142-47.

[In the following interview, conducted in Johannesburg, South Africa, on March 15, 2002, Tadjo reflects on such subjects as her relocation to South Africa, her work as a painter, her fondness for the short story genre, her thoughts on Western feminism and on censorship, and the genesis of her book The Shadow of Imana.*]*

In South Africa during the month of March writers are known to migrate to Durban for the annual "Time of the Writer" festival, where a meeting of anglophone and francophone African practitioners is generally an important theme. In 2002, as a spin-off event, the Alliance Française in Johannesburg organized a round-table discussion with several of the visitors from the French-speaking world, and included Véronique Tadjo, a previous guest at the Time of the Writer who recently became a resident of the city.

She was born in Paris in 1955, but she has lived most of her life and completed her studies in Côte d'Ivoire in West Africa, where she taught for some years in the National University in Abidjan. Further studies took her to the Sorbonne Paris IV and to Howard University in Washington, DC. Apart from the works for adults mentioned in the following interview, she has recently published an anthology of poems for children with her own illustrations, called *Talking Drums* (London: A. and C. Black, 2001), and her *Mamy Wata and the Monster* (in the original French version) has been listed as one of only four works for children chosen as among the best hundred African books of the twentieth century.

The following interchange took place at my home in Johannesburg on 15 March 2002, while preparations for the round-table were in progress.

[*Gray*]: *At the round-table session with francophone writers of Africa, held in Johannesburg's Alliance Française, the issue is to be problems of identity. Would you summarize what you wish to say on that score and about how your seven-month stay in South Africa has affected your sense of self so far?*

[Tadjo]: Well, I had always wanted to come to South Africa, and of course especially after those 1994 elections, because as you know we all celebrated—we celebrated something which was so amazing for all of us. So I will say I was happy when at last I was given the opportunity to come, because I must stress that I am absolutely sure that what I am getting here is transforming me and will transform me in many ways: in terms of ideas, debates, and so on, like that session itself at the Alliance Française. Because a lot of what is happening here in South Africa generally is very relevant to the rest of the continent. So I am here to look at how South Africans handle their big questions, try to find similarities with my particular country of Côte d'Ivoire, and try to understand where they're going and, if possible, how this may be applied to other places.

You're still staying "they" and "them," instead of "us."

Yes, but just because I'm so new here and it's only for the moment. I'm sure it will shortly shift to "we"! But also I don't want to presume and pretend I know so much, when in fact I have realized I know so little! There is the South Africa you dream of, when you're bored at home, seeing it through certain images . . . while there is quite another South Africa that you get to know when you live here. But I didn't come here directly, you follow?

Yes, a long wandering route.

And I'm very happy it went that way, because . . . well, let's not discuss now my life in the United States, in France, and then for some years in Britain; but within Africa first when I lived out of Côte d'Ivoire I moved to Nigeria, then to Kenya; especially the latter prepared me for South Africa. But I don't want to give the impression I have problems with Côte d'Ivoire as I don't, and I go back there regularly. If ever I think about my old age, well, I see myself probably settling down there finally, because there are a lot of things still to do there and to which I may contribute. Meanwhile I am happy to contribute wherever I find myself, but especially if it's Africa.

Do you find South Africans familiar with the kind of cultural background that you come from?

No, not at all. I'm just learning how big the continent is! With apartheid and having been cut off from the rest of the continent, in South Africa there is still a lot of ignorance and presumption and false ideas about, so it is quite interesting to try in a way to redress the balance a bit.

But during the bad years there were in fact very strong links between the apartheid system and your Côte d'Ivoire.

I know, and I'm not very proud of any of that. I think people at home knew about it somehow, but nobody ever talked about that. But once suddenly I jumped out and queried it—just in a conversational situation with some officials, during that length rule of President Houphouet-Boigny—and they were willing to discuss those links quite openly. But only if I brought it up; otherwise no, it was not an issue for everyone. As you surely know, political decisions have often been taken which do not coincide with what the people themselves would have wanted. But that is part of the dark side of our history, too; we have to understand all of that.

Currently you are engaged in a project to produce children's art at a studio complex called the Bag Factory in central Johannesburg. How do you with your strong French accent come across to them?

Well, I don't hide anything from them when I present my portfolio. For me, though, it has been like coming out a bit, reconciling two distinct aspects of my personality, because I appear before them both as a writer and as an artist. I am grateful for that experience because now I am made also to want to write about art. At the Bag Factory I was resident as a painter, which I have been since 1996, but I was made very welcome just for whatever I am. But it was a turning point for me in the sense that I saw I could work especially well here as a painter-illustrator, exactly because there are less language problems then. You see, I came to painting via illustrations, because I have always illustrated the children's books that I write, and I then needed to escape into bigger sizes. But it is not totally true that art appreciation is language-free, since you need to decipher a piece of art as well. But yes, art is an easier and more international language of its own, because people may just look at it for themselves. As you know, the writing life is quite a solitary one, so I do also enjoy a mode of expression that forces you to go out to people. I also think the writing and the painting are complementary; I may even be a better writer because I paint.

But your reputation does rest upon you as the writer and is well established in the francophone world. In English all we have is **As the Crow Flies,** *available to us in a complete translation only last year [in the Heinemann African Writers Series]; previously only two short excerpts from it were available in anthologies edited by Larson and by Vera.*

Yes, if we say Africa is divided mainly between French and English, without for the moment talking about the many other languages . . . let's say that there is a big problem between the two, as we are not communicating enough. And therefore, when we are faced with very similar problems, we are not talking about solutions together. With the francophone sphere and the anglophone sphere and rarely a bridge between the two, it is a big shame for the continent. We need to work at it much more.

But, being so bilingual, you are unusual among francophone writers, who are often completely lost here.

Well, speaking for myself, way back I did choose English as my scholarly profession, while keeping French as my creative profession. Everybody has their own reasons for making such choices, but in my case maybe it was that, coming from a mixed family—my mother was French, my father Ivoirien—I've always understood that I do not belong to just one place. And so I felt that English was going to help me understand the world outside the borders of the Ivory Coast, for example. My interest was at first in African American language and literature, and from that I realized I was extremely interested in African literature itself, giving me access to that which alongside French was written in English. So that route gave me a broader insight into what was happening to both sides of the language barrier. I stay in touch with the African American, though, because I see there is still a lot of relevance there for us in what is happening in their black community.

For the first two years of the Caine Prize, based in London, you served as a judge of the award for African writers. Has that proved sympathetic, as your note in front of their first anthology of winners called Tenderfoots *would indicate?*

Oh yes, because I could bring my side, that francophone world, to their attention. But what I especially like about the Caine Prize is the way it is targeted exclusively on

the short story. Short stories in Africa are—how can we say?—a very user-friendly genre, because at heart I am a type of short story writer myself. I like the fact that you can pick up a story, like it or leave it, and it doesn't present for the reader the kind of huge problems novels do. Being so condensed, it is quite amenable to Africans, almost an African type, just as we used to have from the oral tradition. When you're writing a short story you can even bring in poetry, for example, and so on, and I like its freedom. By contrast, the novel has become very hijacked, especially by the West, with the writer having to write only within certain confines. And I don't like the way they are telling you that, if you don't write a novel, you are not a serious writer. The novel has become a bit of a tyrannical genre.

Well, you have made your name with three novels, but we must also note that your debut was as a poet—with **Latérite** *of 1984.*

Some critics say that I just write poetic prose anyway, so in a sense it's all the same. But, much to my distress, I have crossed over from poetry into prose, because people have such a bad attitude towards poetry nowadays. Publishing poetry at all is a total, total nightmare, because it has wrongly come to be thought of as such an elitist genre. The educational system perhaps has traumatized people into reading poetry the wrong way and all that. So I turned to using poetry in a fresh way; I still function as a poet, yet within the prose medium, which is a bit more available to people.

That is why the first book which was called a novel, *A vol d'oiseau* of 1992, which you now have a decade later under the title *As the Crow Flies,* is a bit unconventional. It isn't an A to Z kind of narrative.

Since it is readily at hand to English speakers now, would you give some guidelines?

For a start the reader should use some imagination—to find the little threads that are running through the different stories within it. People say it is like the *nouveau roman,* very discontinuous, or consists of the prose-poems going back to Baudelaire and Max Jacob and all that sort of thing, but also it goes back to oral literature, which always used a melange of genres, freely switching from one mode to the other. That's how I view the work, as coming from that tradition rather than from any European one. I'm sorry, I have to resist the French tendency to claim everything that has been invented as their own. But, although I have read many French writers and so on, it is an African work. In reply to them I say I am heavily influenced by the African oral tradition, which has always been very innovative, always looking forward.

The work is extremely explicit on women's intimacies in Africa. How do you relate it to Western feminism?

Only with great, great caution, as I don't really buy into much of what is commonly thought of as orthodox feminism, the theory and the movement, outside Africa. But I think if you take the voices of women in Africa of the new generation, you'll see they express what African women are and like and want. I'm not trying to be provocative or anything, but it's just common sense: if you live in one particular environment, then your demands and needs are not the same as in another. You'll see that in *As the Crow Flies,* the translator was an African woman too—Wangui wa Goro from Kenya. That is not to say a translator always has to be of the same kind, but it does always have to be somebody with a certain inside knowledge.

Yes, but my question was: aren't you only too readily co-opted by feminists?

If they try to co-opt me I tell them—

What?

I tell them—hold it! I can't just take on all that Eurocentric terminology, no no. That doesn't mean I'm not going to read their material, think about it, etc., but I also have to think about how it's relevant to *our* situation, you see.

Because . . . look at *As the Crow Flies.* The essential thing is that I wanted to tell a story, but if you want to tell *one* story, you have to tell *many* stories. We women are not alone; we are made of many people. And you have to read *all* stories to get a better picture. It's like a puzzle with many pieces, but one where you have to work to put all the different pieces together.

Isn't one of the threads in the weave to do with censorship, as many of the vignettes concern characters confronting prohibitions?

Yes, and that is a general world problem, but also particularly acute in Africa. If you raise important questions, you can be censored and muzzled and all that. But often, as you know very well here in South Africa, you have to work within that context. But I meant especially when referring to censorship to show how a dream may be destroyed, and even how a dreamer who is driven to the wall may become an oppressor in turn. I have never experienced censorship myself directly, but I must say that with this particular novel, which was so obviously outspoken, I did experience the other danger—of being liked too much. They can also try to control you by bringing you in. Sometimes I think that that process can be worse, you know: so you always have to be alert. They gave me a small problem with *A vol d'oiseau* at the time, because of my not wanting to play their game. I didn't want them to make it a government thing in the end, whereby with speeches and the minister of this and that it could become something totally different. And then there was a big stink in the

press from the privileged elite who refused to see what needs to be seen. So I learnt my lesson. Although I was never physically threatened or anything like that, it was then that I thought maybe I should plan to take off, and look at a few things outside Côte d'Ivoire.

*Your most powerful recent work has been not about Côte d'Ivoire at all, but about Rwanda—with **L'ombre d'Imana,** published with Actes Sud in 2000.*

There I was a part of a project involving some dozen African writers, initiated by a Chadean friend, Nocky Djedanoum, at Lille's Fest'Africa festival in 1998, when we were to reside in Rwanda and respond to its recent genocide—because he thought not enough had been heard on that topic from Africa. It was something we thought could never happen on the continent and it had shaken us, deep down. We felt it was important to reflect on what had really happened. So we accepted to go there, with the only condition being that we should respond as writers—not like the many journalists or historians who dealt with the genocide, but in our capacity as pure writers. What I liked was that it was a big challenge and each one had an individual way of rendering what he or she saw. So that I think the project was successful for that reason. There wasn't one particular single thing to be said about what happened, but the project became hopeful in what each of us did: you'll find the different aspects which the journalists and historians did not cover, giving maybe a better understanding. . . . I also think all the writers involved have in one way or another been changed, in the sense in which they view their role as writers and their writing. It gave me a shot of maturity, that's for sure. It came at the right time for me as well, after I had written several books and, in terms of trying to understand life, that visit to Rwanda certainly has added a dark dimension, which was important for me to understand. It's a human problem; you have to prod and prod and prod at a thing like that. We knew of the Holocaust, thought it would never happen again—so it is important for a writer to continue to prod.

Your various publishers include those that specialize in African writers—in France they are L'Harmattan, Présence Africaine, and more. Are you going to go for more mainline publishers?

I'm quite content at the moment. I'll just have to play it as it comes. And I'm pleased to be in Heinemann, even if it's not mainline, because haven't we all read so many African writers thanks to the African Writers Series? But in Côte d'Ivoire I also have NEI—Nouvelles Editions Ivoiriennes—which gives me an African distribution too. I'm happy like that and I won't compromise in order to go for bigger publishers. That may be a bad career move. But my feeling is that, if you do what you want to do, after a while people will follow and find me.

You've said that in Côte d'Ivoire there is nowhere to hide, and there is still much to be done.

Yes, but that is must my personal statement. I do get very restless when I'm not there, even though I have to be in the West too and resource myself on a regular basis. But how can I leave it, since it is the main source of my writing, my painting, and—well, my creative being?

Sonia Lee (essay date 2005)

SOURCE: Lee, Sonia. "The Emergence of the Essayistic Voice in Francophone African Women Writers: Véronique Tadjo's *L'Ombre d'Imana*." In *The Modern Essay in French: Movement, Instability, Performance,* edited by Charles Forsdick and Andrew Stafford, pp. 77-86. Oxford: Peter Lang, 2005.

[*In this essay, Lee classifies Tadjo's* L'Ombre d'Imana *as a "Montaignean essay"—one influenced by Michel de Montaigne's* Essais—*in that it reflects Tadjo's subjective point of view and offers no solutions, but instead constantly questions the object of its inquiry.*]

What draws me to the essay resides in its paradoxical nature: it escapes any consensual structural definition, while sporting the greatest accountability for its content. Even if literary critics such as Adorno, Lukács, Genette, Barthes and others seem unable to agree on the components of the essay, they are of one mind as to the protean nature and fluidity of its form. It is safe to say that the only certainty of the genre is the undeniable paternity of Montaigne, whose *Essais* stand as the progenitor of this literary genre. In her excellent study, *The Essayistic Spirit,* Claire de Obaldia (1995, 40-41) points out that Montaigne's work remained unique and childless, but that it created a lawless genre, which marked French and world literature for ever 'whereas, England starting with Bacon started a tradition counting a long line of brilliant essayists' (Routh 1920, 33, quoted in Obaldia 37, n.1). Dudley Marchi (1994) in his analysis of *Montaigne Among the Moderns* differs on the matter of this childlessness as he demonstrates how the *Essais* have influenced many modern and postmodern writers. He states that:

> If the concepts on non-linearity, instability, and fluctuation, so diffuse today in literary but also scientific and social thinking, have any plausibility at all, then Chaillou, Sollers and others, with Montaigne as one of their guides, have certainly developed these qualities in key places in their work.

(309)

In step with Marchi, I, too, am about to differ on the matter of this childlessness: I feel that Montaigne's influence can be traced further in the work of many essays written by Francophone African women writers. It

may be true that in inventing a lawless genre Montaigne did not dictate a specific structure that would define it. But in describing the intent of his work, he gave us some clear indications as to what he meant to do, which are tantamount to a series of guidelines that may be applied to categorise as essays diverse contemporary texts not labelled as such by the literary establishment. In stating 'Je suis moi-même la matière de mon livre', Montaigne characterises his writing as self-referential and it is clear that the narrator's voice is that of the author expressing his subjective vision of reality and his readiness to be accountable for it. The narrator experiences an ever-changing world, through not only his intellect but also his emotions. As a result, the subject of his inquiry is never absolutely defined, there are no definite answers in Montaigne but a perpetual questioning which in turn pluralises the authorial voice. All this being said, it is precisely this Montaignean 'I', humanistic, subjective and accountable, that is emerging from several texts written by Francophone women writers, and, in the limited space allotted for this study, I propose to restrict my analysis to Véronique Tadjo's essay **L'Ombre d'Imana.**

Many prominent Francophone and Anglophone African male writers such as Chinua Achebe, Wole Soyinka, Mongo Beti, Léopold Senghor and Ngugi Wa Thiong'o have all written powerful essays about the many difficulties besieging their continent, and the ambiguous relationship that Africa entertains with the West. But to my knowledge, none of them is yet to write on the essay as a genre and how it can or should be Africanised. Therefore in my ongoing analysis of African women's essays I rely mostly on western methodology. Contrary to those in the West, most African writers started with fiction and produced great novels before engaging in the essay. In the Western literary tradition, it is commonly accepted that the essay preceded the novel and that in fact the novel exists 'latently in the essay'; Claire de Obaldia remarks (16) that the concept of the *Bildungsroman,* which explores the relationship between the self and the world in order to discover not only oneself but what one knows, recalling the Montaignean 'que sçay-je?', is in fact an essayistic form. It is interesting to note that many Francophone African writers (men and women) started their literary careers with what could be labelled a *Bildungsroman,* thus skipping a stage of Western literary evolution, a development which I think is directly linked to history. For contemporary African literature is a result of colonialism and its educational system, which in turn is a result of the rise of the bourgeois class and its literary embodiment, the novel. However, one can also argue that in Africa, the novel has borrowed from the folk tale, a prominent genre of oral literature, and thus infused this Western genre in its form and content with an indigenous literary praxis. But the Montaignean essay, whose basic tenet rests in the individual's gaze on the world and its relentless questioning, does not have its equivalent in the African oral tradition. What remains to be seen is how African writers, and in this case women writers, appropriate the genre to suit their needs.

In Africa, women's writing came on the wings of freedom. With the exception of South Africa and the Portuguese colonies, most African countries had liberated themselves from colonialism by the late 1950s or early 60s. A decade later, women writers had started to appear all over the continent, bringing for the first time to the public sphere the African woman's viewpoint, and thus breaking the ancestral custom that barred women from public speaking. Therefore, for African women, writing came as a double liberation, first from the oppression of colonialism, and secondly from the patriarchal imposition of silence. Like their male counterparts, they started mostly with the novelistic form and a few wrote autobiographies—*De Tilène au plateau* by Nafissatou Diallo (1975) and *Les Danseuses d'Impé-Eya* by Simone Kaya (1984). In 1979, the Senegalese Mariama Bâ published her watershed novel *Une si longue lettre* (1980), which represents a turning point in Francophone African literary history. The first person narrative through which a woman tells her personal drama in the form of a letter to a friend was seen as revolutionary because, contrary to the autobiographical 'I' that represents only the author's experience, the first-person narrative in this case expressed the anger and the sorrow of many African women and drew attention to the ills of Senegalese society from a woman's viewpoint. Bâ was the first writer to break the silence that tradition imposes on African women. Yet, in the novel the first person narrator is like a mask whose voice speaks from a fictional and unaccountable realm.

At the present time, many of the prominent women novelists have written interesting essays on a variety of subjects. To give a few examples, in Algeria several women, and among them the well-known Assia Djebar, have written courageous essays underlining the political reasons behind the blood bath which has been engulfing this society for the past decade. In Tunisia, Hélé Béji revisits the concept of culture in her post-colonial society. In Cameroon, Axelle Kabou accuses African societies of being mostly responsible for the economic and social chaos besieging their societies. But in Mali, Aminata Traoré, former minister of Culture, denounces the mystification of global economics and its negative effects on African development.

In the essay, the writer writes in her own voice, and therefore takes full responsibility for the opinions expressed, no longer hiding behind the mask of a fictional character. This accountability gives the writer's voice a tangible presence since it allows her to enter directly into the public forum to claim authority on social subjects, not only as a writer but also as a citizen, thus politicising the role of the woman artist. Therefore, the essayistic 'I' stands apart from the autobiographical first person narrator in that she does not contemplate only herself, although she does that as well, but more importantly she re-examines and re-negotiates her social position in a modern world that was not intended for her. The existential malaise of the African thrown into an alien world has been a recurrent theme of the African novel of the 1960s. Suffice it to quote Mongo Beti's famous novel *Mission terminée* (1957) where the young protagonist, after being educated in the French system, feels that the tragedy of his generation was like 'Celui d'un homme laissé à lui-même dans un monde qui ne lui appartient pas, un monde qu'il n'a pas fait, un monde où il ne comprend rien' (250-51). As a rule, African women do not resent the cultural interference of the Western school, but rather see education as the only way to free themselves from many of the burdens of tradition. However, they too are aware of having to decipher and appropriate for themselves a new world, 'a decolonized world' to quote Hélé Béji (1997), in which, as citizens of this decolonised global village, they must take their legitimate place.

Oral African literatures were the product of societies whose vision of the world corresponded with a way of life believed to be universally true. The moral order was respected and transmitted through the epic, through myths and folk tales. The intrusion of the Western world and its foreign brand of modernity transformed the ancient bard into a writer, as Roland Barthes suggested:

> Dès l'instant où l'écrivain a cessé d'être un témoin de l'universel pour devenir une conscience malheureuse (vers 1850), son premier geste a été de choisir l'engagement de sa forme, soit en assumant, soit en refusant l'écriture de son passé.

(1972, 8)

This tragic awareness, which characterises the modern writer, infuses most masculine African literature, which as a whole can be categorised as 'engagé' in the Sartrean sense. However, African women writers' social and political involvement seems closer to what Barthes called literature's *'engagement manqué'* (1964, 150). In effect, Barthes opposes to the Sartrean assertion the elusiveness of doubt and questioning which in itself is typical of Montaigne.

This political awareness and questioning of the world in which all women writers live results in what could be labelled a historical self-consciousness, in that the first person narrative is not only feminine but overtly African. Therefore, like their male counterparts, African women essayists are politically 'engagées' but their political intervention cannot be divorced from the form in which it is expressed. One cannot but be struck by the stylistic heterogeneity of African women essayists and their great preoccupation with language and writing as a means of action. In this regard they seem to partake of the notion espoused by many contemporary French thinkers, that a revolution can take place within language and consequently catalyze a rebirth of the human subject in its political existence, that significant ideological gestures can occur in discursive acts.

(Marchi 1994, 306)

Marchi remarks (1994, 306) that this is a notion that, according to Sollers, bears the influence of Montaigne.

In the light of the above, in the context of this collective study on the essay, I propose to analyze Véronique Tadjo's text *L'Ombre d'Imana: voyages jusqu'au bout du Rwanda,* which in my view is highly representative of the kind of Montaignean essay written by African women writers today. The publisher, as it is often the case for nonfiction texts, did not generically label Véronique Tadjo's work. So, to make my task easier, I will attempt to demonstrate that its proper classification should be that of an essay. Véronique Tadjo, who is from the Ivory Coast, wrote this piece in the context of a collective work on Rwanda called 'Rwanda: writing as a duty to memory', initiated by the Tchadian writer Nocky Djedanoum. Many writers from different African countries responded to the challenge and wrote their reactions to the genocide in a variety of forms such as essays, novels or poetry. Through the main title— *L'Ombre d'Imana*—Tadjo is alluding to the apparent unity between the Tutsis and the Hutus, since they share a common, unique God, Imana, as well as a common language, two powerful and rare assets for an African country. The text's sub-title *voyages jusqu'au bout du Rwanda,* which is a reference to Céline's novel *Voyage au bout de la nuit* (1934), negates the peaceful impression implied by the title to constitute a warning as to the subject of the book. Although her tone and intent differ from Céline's work, the two narratives share a horrific universe where humanity's inhumanity lies just beneath the surface, waiting to spring out at a moment's notice.

The book is dedicated to the memory of the dead 'but who remain forever in our hearts'. This is a way to involve the reader in a silent dialogue upon what happened in Rwanda:

> Je partais avec une hypothèse: ce qui s'était passé nous concernait tous. Ce n'était pas uniquement l'affaire d'un peuple perdu dans le cœur noir de l'Afrique. Oublier le Rwanda après le bruit et la fureur signifiait devenir borgne, aphone, handicappée.
>
> (13)

Tadjo's account of what happened is tightly organised as if to attempt to give order to the unimaginable. The text consists of six parts: the first and second voyages, both around forty pages in length, frame four short texts of about ten pages each. Furthermore, these six parts, which can be considered as chapters, are subdivided into shorter units each bearing a title announcing its particular subject. This systematic construct as to the

form contrasts with the fluidity of the content whose only organising thread is the author's ambulatory gaze as she visits the sites of the genocide.

As already mentioned, Véronique Tadjo's text is subtitled 'voyages' in the plural and it does describe two trips to Rwanda in the aftermath of the genocide. Yet, it can hardly be categorised as travel literature because the two voyages, which constitute the framework of the narrative, are in fact a long trip to hell written to exorcise horror and evil. How does one write that from April to July 1994 the government of Rwanda promoted genocide against a section of its own population, the Tutsis, which resulted in almost a million victims?

Similarly, it seems that the text distinguishes itself from what is usually referred to as 'testimonial literature' by the temporal and emotional distances that exist between the narrator and its subject. Tadjo did not witness the genocide first hand but only its aftermath. This distance makes possible the self-introspection and, paradoxically, the very Montaignean self-implication of the author into a tragedy that she views as an African and as a human being, as part of 'our collective memory'. Tadjo feels that 'Le silence est pire que tout. Détruire l'indifférence' (38). Because of this sense of accountability for what happened, Tadjo suggests that, above all, such crimes must be recorded by the written word in order to remain forever in the collective memory. Confronted with such deeds, the oral tradition will not do. 'L'oralité de l'Afrique est-elle un handicap pour la mémoire collective? Il faut écrire pour que l'information soit permanente' (38). To quote Roland Barthes once more 'l'écriture est un acte de solidarité historique' (1972, 14), in that it springs from a confrontation between the writer and her society, and for Tadjo this act must be written down, not simply to preserve the accuracy of the deeds—historians will do this—but in order to break the silence, to destroy indifference, to try to understand the emotions behind the massacre. Furthermore, to write, and in this instance to write about History, is to distance herself from the oral tradition and its communal mindset in order to exercise her freedom to think outside the group. Benoît Denis remarks that, in the essay:

> Ce qui littérarise ce type de textes, c'est l'importance qu'ils accordent à l'expérience sensible et à l'épaisseur affective du vécu. La subjectivité s'y donne comme fondatrice de la vision du monde proposée et l'énonciateur ne cesse de se mettre en jeu et en scène dans l'écriture.
>
> (2000, 90)

From the very beginning of the first 'voyage', the tone of the first person narrative oscillates between the personal and the interrogative mode without any incursion into indignation or moral judgment. The personal tone is Montaignean in its mundanity, in that Tadjo gives precise details of modern transportation with its escort of foreign airports, flight delays, lost luggage and the consideration that today's tourism can be a dangerous endeavour. Upon arriving in Kigali, the capital of Rwanda, the narrator is struck by the apparent tranquillity of the city, which goes on with the business of life as if nothing had happened. The physical scars of the city have disappeared, the traces of what took place in these now quiet streets are to be found only in the eyes of its inhabitants. The narrator feels that she is witnessing the realm of 'absolute evil,' an untranslatable world that she is paraphrasing for the reader because it must be told. She describes in a simple and sometimes poetic prose her tour of the strategic points of the genocide, which are now guarded by a caretaker who receives visitors and even tips. She cannot help wondering about this man's job; what must he be thinking of her who came from so far away to look at such horrors? She then puts into words the church of Ntarama where 5,000 people were massacred, the skulls and the bones of the victims, the traces of blood still visible on the walls, the tools of the crime, the tortured body of the young woman exposed for all to see, as an obscene reminder of human cruelty. What words should one use to tell such deeds? What is left of the dead is terrifying, but no more so than the testimony of those who survived, of those who managed to depart from the country, leaving loved ones to their death, of those who killed and are waiting to be judged and the knowledge that some of the killers are still at large. What is there to say of the children born of rape, born of hate, unloved and unwanted? The author asks the questions which are always posed after a genocide. How can this be? Who are these ordinary people who killed so willingly? Would I have been one of them? After all, it is ordinary people who commit genocides.

Thus ends the first of the three parts that constitute the first voyage. In the second part, Tadjo breaks with the testimonial mode and suspends the essayistic first person narrative to fantasise and imagine 'la colère des morts'. She invents a tale where the dead come back to haunt the living. They want to know why they were killed and why the living are unwilling or unable to answer their questions. In fact their anger stems from the apparent forgetfulness of the living. One particular man whose head had been cut off shows great frustration and refuses to leave. A wise man is called to appease the angry spirit. Through prayers, exhortations and sacrificial offerings he succeeds in defusing the desire for revenge of the dead: 'Nous supplions les morts de ne pas accroître la misère dans laquelle le pays se morfond, de ne pas venir tourmenter les vivants même s'ils ne méritent pas leur pardon' (59). Then, the sage addresses the living and warns them to rid themselves of the hate still present in their hearts, or else there will be no future for the country. The message of the tale is very clear and the question is: why did Tadjo decide to incorporate fiction into her essay? Before coming up with a possible hypothesis, I would like to point out that

Tadjo's fictional tale could be seen as an inter-textual reference to Sartre's *Les Mouches* and its political implication of the individual as independent thinker. This type of digression was much used by Montaigne whose *Essais* are full of quotations and references. The other possibility is an Africanisation of the essay through the use of the folktale to convey a message, a stylistic device much appreciated by an African public and used by other African women writers. It is also interesting to note that the tale is clearly didactic whereas the essayistic text is not. To complicate matters, Tadjo keeps the fictional mode for a while longer and the tale is followed by three short fictional narratives which personalise and attempt to understand some facets of the Rwandan drama, in particular the mindset of those who committed the atrocities. To try to enter into the human psyche, fiction is better equipped than rational and philosophical inquiry. The unthinkable can only be imagined. By fictionalising part of her essay, the author is simply enlarging her essayistic inquiry, thus modernising the genre but not betraying it.

Finally, the second voyage, which constitutes the final part of the text, goes back to the first-person narrative and the essayistic mode of commentary, statistical facts, philosophical digression and, in the case of this essay, individual testimony. Throughout the text and its generic lawlessness, Tadjo keeps weaving the same inquiring thread of trying to make sense of this senseless carnage. At the beginning of her essay, she poses the question: 'Si nous ne sommes absolument rien, pourquoi écrire?' (28), a question easily answered after reading, in the Human Rights Watch account of the genocide, that no witness was to survive the massacre, that no-one was to be left to testify. In this case, writing becomes an obligation, a political act: 'Oui, se souvenir. Témoigner. C'est ce qui nous reste pour combattre le passé et restaurer notre humanité' (97). Tadjo's hope that somehow to come to terms with such senseless cruelty is to write down the events as they were lived and recounted and without judgment. '"N'aie pas peur de savoir", dit une survivante' (117). Tadjo wrote this essay as a 'devoir de mémoire'; but through her travels around the country, her pertinent evaluation of the facts and the numerous encounters with both killers and victims, she concludes: 'Je ne suis pas guérie du Rwanda. On n'exorcise pas le Rwanda. Le danger est toujours là, tapi dans les mémoires, tapi dans la brousse, aux frontières du pays' (134). The author realises that Rwanda is part of her and part of us all as human beings, a discovery that Montaigne made four centuries ago: 'La nature a, je le crains, attaché elle-même à l'homme un instinct qui le porte à l'inhumanité' (1976, 119).

To conclude, one could argue that to realise the inhumanity of the human race is neither new nor original, and throughout the ages, countless writers have reflected upon it and wondered why. Tadjo brings no solution and no answer as to the reason for Rwanda's senseless massacre, but by refusing to forget, she keeps the question alive and her essay stands as one more warning that 'Notre humanité est en danger' (118). We can only hope that her voice will be heard.

Bibliography

Adorno, Theodor (1984 [1958]). 'L'essai comme forme'. In *Notes sur la littérature,* trans. Sibylle Muller. Paris: Flammarion, 5-29. 'The Essay as Form', trans. Bob Hullot-Kentor and Frederic Will. In *New German Critique,* 32 (Spring-Summer), 151-71.

Bâ, Mariama (1980). *Une si longue lettre.* Dakar: NEA.

Barthes, Roland (1964). *Essais critiques.* Paris: Seuil.

Barthes, Roland (1972 [1953]). *Le Degré zéro de l'écriture.* Paris: Seuil.

Barthes, Roland (1993-1995). *Oeuvres Complètes,* ed. Eric Marty, 3 vols. Paris: Seuil.

Béji, Hélé (1997). *L'Imposture culturelle.* Paris: Stock.

Beti, Mongo (1957). *Mission terminée.* Paris: Buchet; Chastel.

Céline, Louis-Ferdinand (1934). *Voyage au bout de la nuit.* Paris: Denoël et Steele.

Denis, Benoît (2000). *Littérature et engagement.* Paris: Seuil.

Diallo, Nafissatou (1975). *De Tilène au Plateau: une enfance dakaroise.* Dakar: NEA.

Genette, Gérard (1991). *Fiction et diction.* Paris: Seuil.

Kaya, Simone (1984). *Les Danseuses d'Impé-Ya, jeunes filles à Abidjan.* Abidjan: CEDA.

Lukács, Georg (1971/1974 [1911]). 'On the Nature and the Form of the Essay'. In *Soul and Form,* trans. Anna Bostock. Cambridge, MA: The MIT Press; London: Merlin Press; French trans. Guy Haarscher as *L'Ame et les formes,* Paris: Gallimard.

Marchi, Dudley (1994). *Montaigne Among the Moderns.* Oxford: Berghahn.

Montaigne, Michel de (1976). *Les Essais.* Paris: Hachette.

Obaldia, Claire de (1995). *The Essayistic Spirit: Literature, Modern Criticism, and the Essay.* Oxford: Clarendon Press.

Routh, H. V. (1920). 'The Origins of the Essay Compared in English and French Literature'. In *Modern Language Review,* 15, 23-40.

Sartre, Jean-Paul (1943). *Les Mouches.* Paris: Gallimard.

Tadjo, Véronique (2000). *L'Ombre d'Imana: voyages jusqu'au bout du Rwanda.* Arles: Actes Sud.

FURTHER READING

Criticism

Rice-Maximin, Micheline. "'Nouvelle écriture' from the Ivory Coast: A Reading of Véronique Tadjo's *A vol d'oiseau.*" In *Postcolonial Subjects: Francophone Women Writers,* edited by Mary Jean Green, Karen Gould, Micheline Rice-Maximin, Keith L. Walker, and Jack A. Yeager, pp. 157-72. Minneapolis: University of Minnesota Press, 1996.

> Focuses on the unconventional narrative structure of *A vol d'oiseau,* claiming that this fragmented text has revolutionized postcolonial African writing.

Additional coverage of Tadjo's life and career is contained in the following sources published by Gale: *Encyclopedia of World Literature in the 20th Century,* Ed. 3; and *Literature Resource Center.*

Quincy Troupe
1943-

(Full name Quincy Thomas Troupe, Jr.) American poet, biographer, editor, memoirist, and nonfiction and children's book author.

INTRODUCTION

Troupe is an acclaimed African American author whose jazz-inflected poems explore political and personal themes and celebrate the contribution of black artists, writers, musicians, and athletes. Many of his poems focus on racial themes, particularly the racial dynamic in contemporary America and the discrimination faced by marginalized people in society. His admiration for the jazz great Miles Davis has inspired several of Troupe's poems, led to his collaboration on Davis's autobiography, *Miles* (1989), and generated an account of that collaboration in *Miles and Me* (2000).

BIOGRAPHICAL INFORMATION

Troupe was born in 1943 in St. Louis, Missouri. His father was a catcher in the Negro baseball league, and the racial discrimination that limited his father's career and influenced his personal life became a key theme in Troupe's later work. Because of his father's career as an athlete, Troupe traveled to Cuba, Puerto Rico, and Venezuela as a young boy. His parents also introduced him to jazz and Latin music, and Troupe developed a lifelong passion for these styles. In high school he became acquainted with the music of Miles Davis, whose work would be a constant inspiration and influence on his work and life. After graduating from high school in 1959, he received an athletic scholarship to play baseball at Grambling College. He left college, however, and joined the army in 1961. A knee injury precipitated his release from military service and he began to write poetry. He moved to Los Angeles, and began teaching creative writing for the Watts Writers' Movement in 1966. He worked as an associate editor for *Shrewd* magazine and edited an anthology of poetry and essays, *Watts Poets* (1968). In 1972 his first collection of verse, *Embryo Poems, 1967-1971,* was published. Troupe received an International Institute of Education travel grant in 1972, which enabled him to go to the Ivory Coast, Nigeria, Senegal, Ghana, and Guinea. In 1975 he edited a collection of African, Caribbean, and Latin American writings, titled *Giant Talk.* Co-authored with David L. Wolper, *The Inside Story of TV's* Roots (1978)

chronicles the production of the renowned television miniseries about slavery in America, which was based on the book by Alex Haley. *The Inside Story* was a tremendous commercial success, selling more than one million copies. That same year Troupe was awarded the National Endowment of the Arts Award in poetry. His poetry collection *Snake-back Solos* (1978) received the American Book Award in 1980. After Troupe wrote a well-received article about the legendary musician Miles Davis in *Spin* magazine, Davis invited him to collaborate on his autobiography, *Miles,* which received an American Book Award in 1990. Troupe reflected on his experience working with Davis in *Miles and Me.* In 1991 he was appointed an instructor in creative writing and American, African American, and Caribbean literature at the University of California at San Diego. That same year he received the Peabody Award for coproducing and writing the radio show *The Miles Davis Radio Project.* He is also recognized as the two-time winner of the World Heavyweight Championship Poetry Bout in Taos, New Mexico. Troupe was named the first Poet Laureate of California in 2002, but was forced to resign the position when a background check revealed that the education credentials on his resume had been exaggerated. His 2002 collection of verse, *Transcircularities,* received the Binghamton University Milt Kessler Poetry Book Award in 2003; that same year he retired from teaching. In 2004 he was named editor of *Black Renaissance Noire.* He has taught creative writing and literature at several colleges and universities, including the University of California at Los Angeles, Ohio University, Columbia University, and the University of Ghana at Legon.

MAJOR WORKS

Troupe's verse is characterized by his use of jazz, bebop, blues, and rap music rhythms, and a variety of poetic forms, African and American myth, and black dialect. His first collection of poetry, *Embryo Poems, 1967-1971,* highlights the musical influences on his work, as several poems in the volume honor the African American creativity and spirituality that originated blues and jazz music. In addition, there are a number of dedicatory poems in the book that pay homage to influential figures in Troupe's life. Music is also a dominant theme in the poems of his next collection, *Snake-back Solos,* which contains poems praising the talent of St. Louis poet Eugene Redmond, writer Steve Cannon, Miles Davis, and Louis Armstrong. *Weather Reports* (1991) includes several poems from Troupe's first two collections as well as a few new poems. In *Avalanche* (1996), Troupe mixed poetic styles to explore the racial politics in America. The poems in *Choruses* (1999) touch on subjects such as religious cults, the basketball prowess of Michael Jordan, the greed of corporate America, and the masterful musical performances of Miles Davis. In this collection, Troupe utilized a variety of poetic forms—haiku, tanka, villanelle, sonnet, sestina, and free verse—and exhibited the influence of jazz rhythms on his verse. *Transcircularities,* a selection of Troupe's earlier poetry together with a few new verses, demonstrates his poetic development over the years and includes celebratory verses on such legendary musicians as John Coltrane, Duke Ellington, Bud Powell, and Miles Davis. Several political poems also appear in the volume. Troupe's 2006 collection *The Architecture of Language* celebrates the diverse linguistic influences that make up modern-day American language, touches on political and personal themes, and includes admiring poems on the golfer Tiger Woods and the late comedian Richard Pryor. *The Pursuit of Happyness* (2006) is the biography of once-homeless stockbroker Chris Gardner and was made into a motion picture that same year.

CRITICAL RECEPTION

Troupe is recognized as a talented and provocative poet, biographer, nonfiction writer, and editor. His poems are frequently anthologized, and his poetry and nonfiction work have received several awards, including two American Book Awards and a National Endowment of the Arts Award. Critics often praise him for providing a confrontational, unapologetic voice for marginalized peoples confronting a discriminatory society. In addition, scholars note his inclusion of contemporary issues and events in his poetry, finding his work a trenchant and relevant commentary on the state of politics, culture, and race relations in the United States. The influence of jazz, blues, bebop, and rap on Troupe's poetic style and subject matter is a recurring topic for critical discussion. Reviewers rarely fail to mention the musicality of his language, and many point out the variety of poetic styles he utilizes in his work. They praise his ability to infuse his poems with energy, vitality, and lyrical phrasing—remarking that many of the poems are intended for oral performance—and investigate the influence of art, music, literature, politics, and sports on his work. His verse is often compared to that of the great American poets Walt Whitman and Langston Hughes.

PRINCIPAL WORKS

Watts Poets: A Book of New Poetry and Essays [editor] (poetry and essays) 1968

Embryo Poems, 1967-1971 (poetry) 1972

Giant Talk: An Anthology of Third World Writings [editor with Rain Schulte] (poetry, short stories, folk tales, and excerpts from novels) 1975

The Inside Story of TV's Roots [with David L. Wolper] (nonfiction) 1978

Snake-Back Solos: Selected Poems, 1969-1977 (poetry) 1978

Skulls along the River (poetry) 1984

James Baldwin: The Legacy [editor] (essays and interview) 1989

Miles: The Autobiography [with Miles Davis] (autobiography) 1989

Weather Reports: New and Selected Poems (poetry) 1991

Avalanche: Poems (poetry) 1996

Choruses: Poems (poetry) 1999

Miles and Me (memoir) 2000

Take It to the Hoop, Magic Johnson [illustrated by Shane W. Evans] (juvenile poetry) 2000

Transcircularities: New and Selected Poems (poetry) 2002

Little Stevie Wonder [illustrated by Lisa Cohen] (juvenile poetry) 2005

The Architecture of Language: Poems (poetry) 2006

The Pursuit of Happyness [with Chris Gardner and Mim Eichler Rivas] (biography) 2006

CRITICISM

David Widgery (review date 5 January 1990)

SOURCE: Widgery, David. "Milestones in Music." *New Statesman & Society* 3, no. 82 (5 January 1990): 34-5.

[*In the following laudatory assessment of* Miles, *Widgery describes Troupe's collaboration with Miles Davis as a "wonderfully detailed, candid and informative" work.*]

The princely stare of the most influential jazz trumpeter in the latter half of the 20th century announces, from the cover of this enthralling autobiography, a seriously badassed mother-fucker. The baleful glare also reminds us of the uncompromising musical originality and political edge which have propelled Miles through four major phases of intense innovation now chronicled in this wonderfully detailed, candid and informative 400-page book.

Davis, son of a successful St Louis dentist, first came to light as the youngest member of the bebop revolutionaries who stormed the Winter Palace of Jazz between 1945-49. Officially studying at the Julliard School of Music, the 19-year-old tyro trumpeter not only succeeded in tracking down Charlie Parker but recording with him those haunting and expressive, if occasionally technically weak, solos on the Dial and Savoy albums of the late forties.

[In *Miles: The Autobiography,*] Davis's account of those dizzy years and the upsurge of post-war black self-confidence which they express is fresh, staccato and full of sharp judgments and warm affections. His portrait of Parker himself: on stage, in the studio, and gobbling chicken *à la pudenda* in the back of a taxi is simultaneously scabrous and deeply respectful. And he is both unsentimental and angry about the tragedies and desperation that dogged the beboppers: their financial exploitation, the lack of recognition by the white-dominated jazz establishment and the general horrors of marching through wintry Harlem slush to buy smack.

But it was after the first bebop wave had dissipated and his own five-year addiction to heroin had been conquered that Davis's brilliance as a composer and leader of improvising musicians became apparent with the series of quintets, most famously alongside John Coltrane, which between 1956 and 1960 produced classics like "Kinda Blue" and "Milestones".

Here too began his collaboration with that most delightful of men, Gil Evans, which was to produce "Sketches of Spain". The amount of musical intelligence packed into these recordings was immense and Miles recalls, for instance, that the drum voicings on the track "Saeta" derived not only from Arabic tonal scales of the black Moors but from the black bagpipers and drummers he had heard as a child at the Veiled Prophet Parades in St Louis. He clearly links the music of this period to the rise of the Civil Rights movement and documents the tremendous precision, not to say ruthlessness, with which he selected and instructed his musicians (the fraught relationship with Coltrane, who was still using heroin, is particularly interesting). As he says of the Sun Ra Orkestra tenor player John Gilmore, one of many Miles fired, "his sound wasn't what I heard for the band".

Before the sixties, therefore, the history of modern American music was being written by ex-Miles Davis sidemen. But this became even more marked in Miles's mid-sixties Third Period when he led the fusion bands (which effectively invented jazz-funk) with the infant protegé drummer Tony Williams, Herbie Hancock and Chick Corea, who Miles coaxed onto Fender Rhodes electric pianos, and Wayne Shorter.

By 1968 jazz was, in sales terms, largely eclipsed by rock music and, while scornful of the "hillbilly music" of the English rockers, Davis was alert to the changing audiences and appreciative of musicians like Hendrix and Sly Stone. He also had his own liking for black funk idioms: "Road house honky tonky funky thing that people used to dance to on Friday and Saturday nights." Here, to critical outrage, Miles's expressive lyricism

turned into something harsher and live-evil (as one of the fiercest albums of this period was palindromically entitled), the shards and angular rhythms of "Bitches Brew" and "On the Corner".

This epoch ended with Davis's infamous live non-appearances with plastic amplified trumpet and wah wah pedal barely discernible above electronic cacophones. The fusion period effectively ended in a mess of cocaine, sleepers, ill-health, car crashes and violence. Between 1975 and 1980 Davis didn't pick up a trumpet and seldom left the darkened rooms of his Manhattan town house where he orchestrated orgies beneath portraits of Bird, Trane and Max Roach and faux black marble.

But out of these ashes came, miraculously, a fourth renaissance in the eighties with superb albums like *We Want Miles* and *Tutu,* a new composing technique, a new career as a painter and, at last, a lifestyle compatible with his diabetes and sickle cell anaemia. And new collaborators like Marcus Miller and Palle Mikkelberg who composed the beautiful album *Aura,* recorded in 1985 but only recently released.

There are times in this journey from the world of Mintons and 52nd Street to that of Prince and the syndrum where Davis's account is coarse and inexpressive, and he is as weird as ever about women. But his tender account of Bud Powell in Paris and viciously funny transcription of his visit, in black leather pants, to a White House dinner in the Reagan era reveal his personal sensitivity and political sharpness. . . .

Gene Santoro (review date 29 January 1990)

SOURCE: Santoro, Gene. "The Serpent's Tooth." *Nation* 250, no. 4 (29 January 1990): 139-40.

[*In the following unfavorable appraisal of* Miles, *Santoro laments that the volume focuses more on Davis's personality and his private and business relationships and less on his significant contributions to the music industry.*]

Miles Davis is one of the only jazz musicians who could get away with putting just his first name and picture on the front of a book and still sell more than a few copies. After all, for the forty-plus years of his professional career Miles has been standing at or near the center of one musical earthquake after another.

If he came to New York on the pretext of studying at the Juilliard School of Music, he soon found his real mentors, Charlie Parker, Dizzy Gillespie and Thelonious Monk, and so from the age of 18 he worked with these bebop revolutionaries. By 1949 he'd decided to pursue a new musical direction with arranger Gil Evans and players like John Lewis and Gerry Mulligan; thus was born *Birth of the Cool* (Capitol). After kicking his drug habit in 1953 he gradually pulled together the landmark group that included John Coltrane, Cannonball Adderley and Bill Evans. This group worked modally, rather than simply cycling through chord changes as had been done since the beginning of jazz. A few years later his crackerjack outfit, with Wayne Shorter, Herbie Hancock, Ron Carter and Tony Williams, pushed that notion beyond its limits, and coincidentally launched what became known as fusion. In love with Jimi Hendrix's guitar and Sly and the Family Stone's straight-up funk, Miles went out *On the Corner,* which not only helped change the way jazz was recorded but earned the undying enmity of jazz critics, including Wynton Marsalis, who has loftily dismissed Miles's work after the 1950s, even though he obviously owes Miles an enormous musical debt. And so on.

Most jazz critics have been bad-mouthing Miles for decades, which is one of the major themes of his autobiography. If Miles is famous for anything outside his music, it's his continual putdown of the white-run jazz industry, from producers to critics, and his street-style mouth—and that language itself becomes another of the book's subjects.

Actually, *Miles: The Autobiography* reads as if Miles talked it into a tape machine, except for the set-piece opening chapter, a hackneyed prophetic epiphany involving a very young Miles and the blue flame of a gas jet. For the rest, Miles talks his way through his life, his music, his grudges, his fistfights, his persecutions, his addictions, his triumphs. That makes the book by turns fascinating and irritating, controversial and self-contradictory, lyrical and boring, pungent and self-aggrandizing—in other words, a lot like the man himself.

What most people want in star autobiographies are spicy revelations and settlement of old scores, and here Miles doesn't disappoint, even if some of the content does. Apparently, the hot-tempered Miles is as fast with his hands as he is with his mouth, and he doesn't seem to care which person or what gender he hits. Without trying to justify or excuse how disgustingly often he hits "upside the head" the women who pass through his life, I should point out that Miles—who has abused virtually every drug known—became a pimp during his period of heroin addiction in the early 1950s. A lot of his lingo and habits come from those dark days rather than from his relatively sunny, upper-middle-class upbringing in East St. Louis. Then too, he makes it plain how much he respected his father, who appears to have supported him emotionally and financially with virtually no strings attached, and how little he liked his mother, who fought with her husband continually and eventually divorced him. So there's plenty of fodder for would-be psychologists in Miles's antipathy toward women, the myriad casual affairs during his marriages, the recurrent brutality directed at wives and girlfriends (and for that matter

band members and friends) and his shrug-of-the-shoulders attitude about this subject.

Other musicians, even Miles's idols, also get brutalized, or are paid back for old grudges. For example, Charlie Parker, described as a brilliant musician and raconteur, is also depicted as a manipulative creep willing to shovel any mountain of shit, shortchange any friend or band mate, to feed his habits; the famously caustic Miles is remarkably unsentimental about either Bird's genius or his—and bebop's—excesses, musical or drug-related. Wynton Marsalis, too, gets some well-deserved lumps for his self-aggrandizing posturing.

Although the book definitely emphasizes personalities and events, the reader gets some sense of the dizzyingly varied musical styles Miles has pioneered or helped launch during his long career. That part of the trumpeter's life gets less attention than I'd expected, and it comes primarily in the form of anecdotal peeks behind the scenes—some fascinating, some rehashed from what look like other sources. And when strictly technical points are raised, they're often not properly explained.

But that's consistent with the way Miles's personality is presented here: cynical, largely unreflective, oddly vulnerable and shy, quick to anger and slow to forget. Away from the bandstand and recording studio, where he's plumbed the depths for sounds and ideas, he seems to keep himself deliberately visceral and shallow—as if too much reflection would dull his intuitive edge. That means, for instance, that his discussions of racism in the music business often become rhetorical or egocentric, rants rather than indictments. This is disappointing because Miles is one of the few jazzers who has had a large enough audience to make big bucks; his complaints of racist treatment could hardly be written off as economic sour grapes. Presented in a more informed and organized way, his attacks on racism in the music business and in society in general could have been deadly enough to extend the legacy of his father, a man active in African-American movements, and teach the rest of us a few things from the inside.

But that's like wishing Miles were Montaigne. For those who want more meat, there's always Jack Chambers's solid *Milestones*; for the rest, the music will have to continue to speak for itself, as it has done so eloquently for so long.

Susan Spilecki (review date fall 1998)

SOURCE: Spilecki, Susan. Review of *Avalanche,* by Quincy Troupe. *MELUS* 23, no. 3 (fall 1998): 216-18.

[*In the following favorable review of* Avalanche, *Spilecki praises Troupe's ability to combine personal observations with commentary on the politics of race, and for his awareness of those individuals who exist on the fringes of American society.*]

In his fifth book of poetry [*Avalanche*], Quincy Troupe stands before us as a versatile American poet, taking joy in the vast possibilities for motion in the avalanche of language and manipulating the violence of it to speak of life in America and in particular of racial politics. Troupe uses the three stages of an avalanche to "create new language / everywhere." In Section One, the poems mimic the "initial breaking away . . . in an awesome language of cacophony," their long lines injected with internal rhymes and convoluted jazz rhythms that drive the reader forward, as in **"The Sound, Breaking Away."**

> the assonance of sound breaking from ground
> breaking away from itself & found in the bounding
>   syllables of snow
> moving now beginning to roar above the cracking
> separation

But this is not simply language poetry. As one title states, Troupe spends his time "Slippin & Slidin' Over Syllables for Fun with some politics thrown in on the side." The separation of the avalanche is primarily a racial one. **"A Response to All You 'Angry White Males'"** is a carefully honed rant which asks who is to blame for the ills of the world, "who wins the title hands down for being the champion serial killer / on the planet, who lynched all those black & american indian people / just because they could, who's polluting, destroying the ecology of the planet." With controlled irony, the poem blasts the opponents of affirmative action, the proponents of proposition thirteen, and the "paper-pushing service empires / that put all you rust-belt blue-collar 'angry white male' workers / . . . out of work." Troupe is not afraid to confront readers politically, just as he is not afraid to create an angry tension through interminable sentences and increasing sarcasm:

> who took the whole nine yards & everything else
> that wasn't tied down, maybe it was some indian chief,
>   sioux perhaps . . .
> or a ching-chong-slick charlie-chan chinaman
> & his nefarious gang of thieves, maybe a mexican
>   "wetback" perhaps . . .
> who took away all your sweat, all your life savings,
>   but it wasn't buddy,
> no, it couldn't have been buddy, your next-door
>   neighbor,
> who looks just like you, & is you,
> could it

In this as in other poems, Troupe's taunting voice evokes from minority readers righteous indignation and from white readers, recognition and guilt.

Fusion, cross-fertilization and confluence are themes he returns to in order to break the tensions built by such poems. Yes, America is divided between conquerors and conquered, between races and religions, each with their own tongues. But, he reminds us at the beginning of **"Poem in Search of a Common Genetic,"** the addi-

tion of new accents changes a language, and the language changes the people who speak it, forcing them together in the act of communication.

It is not an easy change; it has all the force of a natural disaster. But Troupe presents his vision of it with a meditative, hopeful tone:

> . . . burning
> is where language springs from like lava erupting
> from a volcano, hot & luminous, powerful & new,
>   transforming
> as the crossfertilization of beliefs of priests & rabbis
>   & shaman
> holymen sitting across from preachers & medicine
>   men
> & imams & buddhists in america, the holy ghost
> crisscrossing tongues, this & that in a fusion of you &
>   me

> * * *

> the magic of singing in the flow of the mysterious ca-
>   dence
> inside the rowing consonance of the impudent river
> clean or dirty water washing smooth ripples across
>   our faces
> as we raise ourselves up clean inside our own
>   american voices
> holy throughout the sound of its utterance

The singing, the sharing of new language, sanctifies as it changes, bringing with it cleansing and hope.

The third section of the book mimics the third stage of the avalanche, after settling has occurred and the landscape appears new and clean. Troupe begins the section with half a dozen extremely short pieces focusing on people—including Tonya Harding and a homeless man—and places. The short lines and simple style bring readers up short after the lavishness of the previous two sections, but once Troupe has achieved this effect, he returns to his usual style.

There are weaknesses in the book of course, as in **"A Response to All You 'Angry White Males'"** when he suggests, "don't be so uptight, go out & get yourselves a good lay, grow up," thus objectifying women even as he fights against objectification on the basis of race and ethnicity. The same issue comes up in **"Male Springtime Ritual,"** where the speaker complains how hard it is on men in spring, with women "peeling off everything the hard winter forced them to put on / . . . eye-mean young men, too, fog up eyeglasses, contact lenses, shades—." But throughout the poem, the self-mocking tone with which he humorously accuses men of "eyeballing nipples" also absolves them of it: "it's all a part of the springtime ritual / & only the strongest eyeballs survive."

Throughout *Avalanche,* Troupe is consistently aware of his job as a poet fusing the personal and the political. He speaks not only for African Americans, although indeed he repeatedly draws on the imagery of jazz, voodoo, basketball and African myth. He also speaks for all of America's marginalized people, drawing them into the roar of the avalanche and theorizing new futures in the wake of his new "fissuring speech."

Quincy Troupe with Douglas Turner (interview date 25 October 2000)

SOURCE: Troupe, Quincy, and Douglas Turner. "Miles and Me: An Interview with Quincy Troupe." *African American Review* 36, no. 3 (fall 2002): 429-34.

[In the following interview, initially conducted during a Huntsville, Alabama, radio broadcast in October 2000, Troupe discusses his background, his perception of himself as an African American artist, and the central themes of Miles and Me.]

A Renaissance man for the twenty-first century, author and poet Quincy Troupe is Professor of Creative Writing and American and Caribbean Literature at the University of California, San Diego. A nationally recognized poet and biographer, he has authored twelve books and won two American Book Awards, in 1980 for **Snake-Back Solos,** a volume of poetry, and for **Miles: The Autobiography.** He wrote and co-produced **The Miles Davis Radio Project,** for which he received a Peabody Award; served as Editorial Director of *Code,* a national monthly magazine for men of color; and has edited **James Baldwin: The Legacy.** Troupe is also two-time Heavyweight Champion of Poetry, a title he won at the World Poetry Bout, a national competition that draws distinguished poets to Taos, New Mexico.

Troupe's latest work is **Miles and Me,** a candid account of his friendship with the enigmatic trumpeter. In it Troupe offers a glimpse into the inner sanctum of jazz's "Prince of Darkness." The book also shows the power of music—in particular, the music of Miles Davis—on Troupe's own development as an artist.

On October 25, 2000, Troupe appeared on *Return to the Source,* a jazz show I produce and host on WJAB 90.9FM in Huntsville, Alabama. What followed was a freewheeling, wide-ranging, engaging interview that covered **Miles and Me,** the impact of jazz and Miles's music on Troupe's own artistic development, the role of the African American artist, poetry, and Troupe's latest projects, including his first screenplay, for an upcoming movie on Miles Davis.

[*Turner*]: *Your new book is a much more personal account of your relationship with Miles, and in that sense it's as much about you as it is about Miles. We get a chance to see your background and your first exposure to jazz and Miles's music. What was your hometown, St. Louis, like when you were growing up?*

[Troupe]: When I grew up there it was segregated. I remember we didn't have a television, and going to listen to Joe Louis fight on the radio. When television came in, it was downtown at the department store, and the black people, including my dad and other black men, would take me down to the department store to watch Joe Louis on television. There would be a whole lot of black people, and white people too, on the sidewalk looking at Joe Louis knock somebody out. Other than that, we would sit around the radio and listen to those boxing matches and baseball games. The only thing we really had to do was to listen to the music, go to the movies, and play sports.

My father was a great baseball player, so I grew up between St. Louis, Mexico, Cuba, Puerto Rico, and Venezuela. He was the second greatest catcher of all-time in the old Negro Leagues. So in my house, we were listening to salsa and other Latin music. My mother liked Count Basie, Duke Ellington, Billy Eckstine, Charlie Parker. So I grew up around a lot of different stuff. The second man she married, after divorcing my father, was a blues musician. He played all the blues musicians—B. B. King, Muddy Waters, Bo Diddley.

Kids are always against what their parents like. I was listening to Johnny Ace and the Coasters . . . the Platters. I remember going into this fish joint one day in St. Louis. I was about 15 years old, and I saw these four black guys. I had transferred by that time to an all-white high school, and it was so square at that school. They were listening to Pat Boone covering black songs. I just wanted to be around something hip. These four black guys were sitting in a booth in the fish joint and they were really clean. They had on dark glasses, ascots. I had never seen a guy with an ascot, and a beret. They had their hats up on the three-pronged poles and they were smoking cigarettes, drinking soda, and eating fish sandwiches. I said, "Let me sit behind them and see if I can catch something." They were talking about "the homeboy across the river from East St. Louis" who was playing on the jukebox. It was Miles Davis. I had never heard of Miles Davis. And they talked about the guy on alto who "sounded like Charlie Parker, Bird," Jackie McLean. I didn't know who Bird was. They played the record two or three times. I thought they were pretty hip. Then they got up and left.

I remember going up to the jukebox and finding "Donna," because I remember them saying Miles Davis's "Donna." I put my nickel in and sat down and listened to it. It was great. I put another nickel in and listened to it again, and when I walked out of that fish joint, my life was kind of changed at that moment, hearing that music. From that point on, I was trying to learn everything I could about Miles Davis.

In the book you describe St. Louis and East St. Louis as great trumpet towns. Why?

Because we had these marching bands in St. Louis. We had all these German guys there who were teachers who were teaching the trumpet and the bugle. Out of that tradition came lead trumpet players like Clark Terry, Miles Davis, Shorty Baker, and a whole bunch of other guys; trumpet players are still coming out of St. Louis—Lester Bowie and Russell Gunn. A whole bunch of trumpet players have come out of St. Louis, and a lot of them were trained in those marching bands. The other thing was that East St. Louis stayed open all night long. People could go play in the bars on the weekends all night. You had this great musical milieu, and then you had the river where everybody was coming up in those riverboats and stopping in St. Louis. All those great bands, bringing Dizzy, Roy Eldridge, Louis Armstrong. They were all coming up from New Orleans. You also had people coming from Chicago and Kansas City. So at one time St. Louis was a hub where a lot of people were passing through from Oklahoma, from Kansas City, from the South, and from Chicago and New York. And St. Louis itself had great musicians like George Hudson, and my cousin Eddie Randall, who led the first band Miles played in. All this created a scene.

You describe the first time you heard Miles live and the incident in which Miles cracked the faces of a white couple who approached him in a way he felt was disrespectful. How much of Miles's surly nature was an attempt to live up to his reputation and how much was real?

Miles was a very complex person. He didn't like anybody, black or white, invading his space. He felt that if he wanted to talk to you he would talk to you. If he was having down time, relaxing at the bar, he didn't want people coming up to him. I remember people from St. Louis were just standing back observing him because we knew, but nobody told this white couple that Miles didn't want to meet them, so they got cursed out.

Miles did that when I met him. I saw him curse a big black guy out on the street who had come up to him to talk about a movie he was making. He wanted Miles to be in it. That's how he responded to stuff because he didn't know how to navigate that kind of stuff intellectually. The first thing that came into his mind, a lot of the time, that's what he said.

In the book you talk about Miles and Wynton Marsalis and their relationship, or lack of one. You mention Miles's observation that there was the potential for Wynton to become comfortable with where he was. What was their relationship like?

Wynton was influenced by Miles. When they first met, he was coming to Miles as a protégé in a sense, a young guy wanting to learn. And Miles was giving him as much as he wanted. I think the unfortunate thing that happened was that they were at the same record com-

pany, Columbia. Wynton was playing classical music, and then he was playing jazz, and he was starting to get this reputation. So I think he started to feel himself in competition with Miles, as they both played the same instrument. After a certain point, Wynton started to make these disparaging remarks about Miles. He started to say things in the press about the music Miles was playing after *Bitches Brew,* and certain kinds of music he didn't like. I've never really had a conversation with Wynton about that, but I thought it was kind of stupid for him to do that.

First it was a great relationship, and then it started to disintegrate. The low point came when Wynton and Miles were in Vancouver after Wynton had said this stupid stuff about Miles, and after he had come under the guidance of Stanley Crouch and Albert Murray. (Stanley hated Miles Davis because Miles had cursed him out when he approached Miles in the same way that the white couple had done earlier.) After saying these hateful things, Wynton came up to Miles in Vancouver in 1987 or '88 where Miles's group was playing, and he walked up on the stage like he was going to sit in without asking Miles if he could sit in. So when Miles saw him he went up to him—there are photographs of this encounter—and said something to him that no one could hear. I asked Miles what he said to him and Miles said he told Wynton, "If you play one note I'm hitting you upside the head with this trumpet. Get off my stage." After that, the whole relationship disintegrated.

How do you define yourself as an artist? Do you see yourself as an African American artist, and if you do, what does that mean?

I see myself as an artist and a poet. I'm basically influenced by and coming out of the African American, but American, tradition. I'm African American because I was born African American and proud of it. I don't run away from that. But as an artist, I see myself as a poet first, and then I see myself as a prose writer. I agree with Miles. He looked at himself as a musician and an artist. I don't hear white boys running around saying they're "white artists." I come out of St. Louis, the black culture there and the music there. I grew up in the church. I was a basketball player. I'm a poet. That's the way I approach myself.

Do you agree with Miles that "there is no honor in doing their . . ."

Miles was talking in terms of classical music. He was saying that he didn't see any honor in doing that and that we should be creating our own stuff. I feel that we should be creating our own stuff, too. But as a poet, I write in different ways. I can write a villanelle, a sestina, a haiku. I can write in those different forms. But I am about trying to raise up in the United States whatever cultural forms that we can raise up here. If I do work in another form, I'm about putting my own stamp on the form. For example, if I work in the French villanelle form, a nineteen-line poem where you pick two lines and repeat them four times throughout the poem, usually it's a kind of bland form, except for one by Dylan Thomas. I wrote a poem in my last book called **"Poem for Michael Jordan"** using that form. I think I've innovated it just by the sound.

In **Miles and Me** *you mention how you "came to know Miles as almost childlike, delicate, and much softer than [you] had ever imagined him being." Can you elaborate?*

Miles was a beautiful guy. When you got to know him, he was soft. Not "soft" soft. He was very sensitive. He was a very shy person. If he liked you a lot, he would do anything for you. He was generous. He would give you money. He was funny. He was a real guy, a human guy. He was always cracking on you, so you had to be ready. But I learned to crack back on him. He was childlike. He told me that great artists have to remain close to their childhood in order to let their imaginations flow, because as you grow older you become victim to all of these rules and regulations. But young children are not encumbered by all that, so their imaginations are free. They can create whatever they want to at that moment.

I agree with him. As an artist, if you can stay close to that sensibility without having all those rules and regulations, dos and don'ts, imprison you, then you're free to create a lot more. I think that's where he stayed in his imagination. That's why he was so fertile. That's why he was so protean.

I think it's hard for a lot of people to imagine Miles as being humorous. Most people could not see that in him.

Everybody that knows him knows that. I remember one time I got together with Santana and Miles's last drummer. We were sitting up there telling these Miles stories, and everybody was telling these funny stories and laughing. We laughed for about two hours. If he knew you, he was a funny guy. If he didn't, he had that mask up because he didn't want people to approach him.

I guess calling Miles "guarded" would be an understatement?

That's right. He definitely didn't want people invading his space. When I first met him, he reached out and grabbed my hair. I knocked his hand away. He was shocked. He looked at me so crazy and said, "What are you, crazy"? I said, "No. Just because I'm here to interview you doesn't mean that you can invade my space. That's your space over there, and this is my space. Miles's space. Quincy's space." His respect for me went up immediately as soon as I said that to him. And it stayed like that until he died.

I especially like the section of **Miles and Me** *called "Listening to Miles," your assessment of his music and how certain recordings were milestones in your development. What are some of your most memorable moments in terms of Miles's music?*

"Bag's Groove" blew me away. Then, when I first heard *Kind of Blue,* that blew me away. Two other memories. I had just started teaching at Ohio University when *Bitches Brew* came out. I remember going to the record store and I saw this album cover with this weird painting on the cover, and I said, "What is this?" I bought it and took it home. I didn't want to listen to it until I got my stuff together. So I got some food, some good wine, and I went in the front room. I put this record on, and it was so strange at first. It was kind of like an assault. I was stunned by it, but at the same time it was totally compelling. I listened to it from six or seven in the evening until after midnight. By the time I got up the next morning I was transformed. The same thing happened with *On the Corner.* A lot of my friends stopped listening to Miles after *Bitches Brew.* They said, "Man, that stuff's crazy." Then when *On the Corner* came out, the same thing happened. I was living in New York, and I put on *On the Corner* and had this amazing feeling about it. Miles was documenting the city and all those sounds and what those black people were doing up in Harlem.

It's interesting how music can impact a person's life. Most people think of music as background material, but music can have that kind of impact, can't it?

Yeah, I think that music has had a compelling influence on me. If I had not heard Miles's music in that fish joint, I don't think that I would be sitting here looking at this beautiful view I'm looking at now. Miles set me on a path that is remarkable in a lot of ways. He's the one that set me on the path to writing and using my imagination, and being creative. I just finished a screenplay based on **Miles and Me** that the people who produced *Hurricane* will produce. I would not have written that screenplay if I had not gone to that fish joint. That's what fate is. Because I heard that music, he propelled me into this thing that I do now. The end result, besides all the poetry I've written, is that now we're going to do this movie.

Who are they considering to play Miles?

There are a lot of names being thrown around. They've talked about Wesley Snipes, Samuel L. Jackson, Morgan Freeman. They talked about Danny Glover playing my character, and Forrest Whitaker.

Are you going to have any input into the final decision?

When they optioned it I asked to be one of the executive producers. But this is the way it is: Hollywood is run by who gets the money, and they make the final decisions. I'm not going to have a problem with that. First of all, I'm a novice when it comes to Hollywood. Plus, I trust the producer, Rudy Langlis, who was my editor at *The Village Voice* and *Spin*. He just did a movie about the Atlanta murders, and he's doing one on the Tulsa riots. He's a great editor and great person. I'm not going to tell him what to do, but I am going to put my two cents in.

In the book you describe Miles as an "unreconstructed" black man. What does that mean, and what does Miles mean to American culture? Will he ever be given the recognition he deserves?

By unreconstructed black guy, I meant that Miles was a black man who did not change for anybody. He was an African American man who came out of East St. Louis, and he wasn't going to kiss anybody's behind to get somewhere. He was going to be himself on all occasions. I think that in this country, because of the fact that we were slaves at one time, the dominant white culture feels that we have to become them. We have to talk in a certain way, dress in a certain way, talk calmly. We do that because we want to get ahead. I understand that. It's that middle-class thing. Miles was that unreconstructed black man who went on his own path.

I don't think people have to change. Picasso didn't change. The Kennedys don't change. Elvis Presley didn't change. Frank Sinatra didn't change. Why should Miles Davis or any African American guy have to change? We aren't running around murdering anybody. We aren't being like Jeffery Dahmer. African Americans are some of the most dedicated, loyal, patriotic people in the history of this country. Because of the fact that he didn't kowtow to a lot of white interests, a lot of people carry a grudge against Miles.

Miles Davis should have everything in this country. In the same way that France and Spain gave Picasso everything, Miles should have everything in this culture, because there's been no other person in this country that has changed the course of music six times. No one. And all the musicians respect him. He's absolutely an international icon. The cover of the January 2000 *GQ* issue in Japan read "Miles is God." We would never do that here.

Quincy Troupe with Jan Garden Castro (interview date March-April 2005)

SOURCE: Troupe, Quincy, and Jan Garden Castro. "Quincy Troupe: An Interview by Jan Garden Castro." *American Poetry Review* 34, no. 2 (March-April 2005): 49-57.

[*In the following interview, Troupe reflects on such topics as the lack of African American influence in the publishing industry; the personal, artistic, and geo-graphical inspirations for his work; the prevalent themes in his poetry; his approach to teaching poetry; and the controversy surrounding his being named poet laureate of California.*]

Quincy Troupe has been featured on two PBS television series on poetry. In 1991, he received the Peabody Award for co-producing and writing the radio show *The Miles Davis Radio Project.* Troupe is the author of fourteen books, including seven volumes of poetry: *Embryo, Snake-Back Solos* (winner of a 1980 American Book Award), *Skulls along the River, Choruses, Weather Reports, Avalanche,* and *Transcircularities,* which was selected by Publishers Weekly as one of the ten best books of poetry published in 2002 and which received the Binghamton University Milt Kessler Poetry Book Award in 2003. His nonfiction books include *Miles: The Autobiography* (winner of a 1990 American Book Award) and *Miles and Me.* He edited the 1975 anthology *Giant Talk* and *James Baldwin: The Legacy.* Troupe has taught at the University of California-San Diego (where he is Professor Emeritus), Ohio University, The College of Staten Island (CUNY) and Columbia University.

[*Castro*]: *Quincy, after James Baldwin died, you edited* **James Baldwin the Legacy,** *closing with his "Last interview" in 1987. Baldwin told you, ". . . I could see that there was something in Miles and me which was very much alike . . . something to do with extreme vulnerability . . . See, we evolve a kind of mask, a kind of persona . . . to protect us from all these people who were carnivorous and they think you're helpless. Miles does it one way, I do it another." I'd like to ask you the same question you asked Baldwin: "How do you do it?"*

[Troupe]: How do I mask?

Yes, How do you mask?

I think everyone that lives in the world wears a mask at some time or another in their lives. In the United States people wear masks because of various reasons. Sometimes they don't want to offend people they know; sometimes they don't want to offend certain religious or racial groups and they may temper what they say.

Sometimes artists wear masks when they're creating a persona. Some masks speak *for you.* Some artists wear a mask all the time and then sometimes take it *off.* And sometimes taking it off gets you into trouble. If I say something about white people, you know, or if I say something in New York about Jewish people, about what I don't like about Ariel Sharon, then it might get me in trouble, even if it's right, y'know what I mean, because some people might not want to hear it. If I say something about Jesse Jackson or Al Sharpton, black people might not want to hear it; you know, it gets you in trouble. Or if you say something about Bush today, some people will jump all over you. Religious fanatics jump all over if you say something unfavorable about religion.

In this neighborhood [Harlem]? In New York?

Anywhere, any where. You've got people of all political persuasions all over New York. You have this split culture now that's confused about many different things. People wear masks because of different reasons, sometimes artistic and sometimes political. If you say certain things, then you have vendettas coming at you: 'We won't publish his poems.' 'We won't publish his piece.' 'We won't invite him to do a reading here.' I think people wear masks because of those reasons . . . I wrote an editorial for *Black Renaissance Noire* [a journal at NYU; Q.T. is the new editor] talking about [sighs], basically, White Nationalism in this country. You don't see black people as talking heads on television; they have no pundits, perhaps a few.

What about Cornell West, Tavis Smiley . . .

They have a certain point of view. Tavis has his own show, basically a black talk show, mostly political, though he does have writers, poets and entertainers on. He's a great host and has a great, serious show, but it's viewed by most whites as a show for blacks. So we've gone back to . . . basically, a segregated situation. Not only in our schools, but in our political, social and cultural opinions, in our neighborhoods, and nobody thinks anything about it. I guess people just think it's normal.

You don't have people asking: Where are the serious African American movies? Why don't we have serious African American art shows? I mean, there are a lot of great African American, Caribbean and African scholars, thinkers, writers and poets. There are a plethora of fabulous, great black stories that great black actors can be in, great black painters and sculptors. But hardly anybody says anything about it, and if you do they think you're trying to make trouble. They think it's normal that the American Academy of Arts and Letters is mostly white people.

I thought you were a member of the Academy of American Poets. You're listed on their website.

I'm listed because of donations that I've given. I'm telling you, there are very few African Americans in the American Academy and Institute of Arts and Letters, very few. But nobody seems to mind; they think it's normal. I don't think it's normal. I think it's racist and creates a false image for the arts in the country. At this point in my life, I feel like I should say something. Whereas I used to wear a mask more, I'm taking the mask off, I'm taking the muzzle off now. If it offends people, then they should look at themselves and why it offends them. I mean, if something is wrong, we should be able to say so.

We should be able to say that for the most part the industry of poetry is racist. The industry of literature is racist. There are very few black editors, only a very few, who can green light a book—maybe one or two that I know of in the publishing industry. If you look at *Vanity Fair,* they have no black writers. If you look at all the major publications, they have few black writers, or editors, if any. You have very few blacks, Latinos, Native American Indians, or Asians in positions of authority. And people think that's normal. That's not normal when the country, in maybe twenty-five years, is going to be predominantly colored. We are going to be the majority in this country.

One other point about African American critics that John Wideman and I talked about—if you look at the *New York Times,* you have very few African American people critiquing books, even a black book. You know that they aren't going to let us criticize a white book. But they don't let us criticize African American books either. And then we have all of these white people, many of whom are newcomers who are being made into experts on African American music, books, art, dance and film. A lot of white music critics didn't like it that I wrote the Miles Davis book [***Miles: The Autobiography***]. And then I wrote ***Miles and Me.*** They just didn't like that I would become the expert . . . so they try to go around me all the time. They raid my book, you know, go through and take all the concepts out, without putting quotes around it, you know what I mean?

Plagiarize?

Yes, they're plagiarizing, they change a little bit, but no one says anything.

Part of it is our fault, too, because African Americans have to stop writing all their Ph.D. dissertations on Toni Morrison. I love Toni's writing, but you know, you have countless dissertations on Toni Morrison; why don't they write four on John Wideman, two on me, and three on Ishmael Reed? But everybody's writing dissertations on Toni Morrison or Maya Angelou. Come on, let's get serious. I think that we have a dearth of serious black critics. Why don't we have more African Americans writing about African American artists and sculptors? I used to tell my students, come on, let's get off the mark. Why don't you all write about all these other great writers, poets, artists and musicians? So black people bear part of the blame, but the establishment bears more.

You have touched on some aspects of many questions I want to ask. My next question revisits some of the landscapes you've opened up. Your poetry volumes each develop many extended metaphors, starting with the title poems: **Embryo, Snake Back Solos, Skulls along the River, Weather Reports, Avalanche,** *and* **Trans-**

circularities. *Could you talk about the holes in old people's eyes in "The Old People Speak of Death," ["turnstile holes the old folks ancestors left inside / their tunneling eyes for me to pass through" . . .] and the roles that eyes, the river, family, and memory play in your poems?*

That's a very good question, a poetic question. When I first wrote the part about the holes in old people's eyes, I was trying to talk about sorrow and loss, especially in black women's eyes—sorrow that these women, these people, these men did not have the opportunity to really exploit the full potential of their lives because they were African Americans living in this country. When I would look into my grandmother's eyes, and my uncles' eyes, and my dad's eyes, I would see these holes full of loss and sadness. My grandmother was a great woman, but she was a maid all her life. She worked for white people all her life, and she couldn't go to school and all of that, but she saved a lot of her money and bought houses in St. Louis and cared for my mother, my late Uncle Allen, and me and my younger brother, Timmy.

My father, on the other hand, was a great baseball player, probably the greatest athlete Missouri ever produced. He was the heavyweight national Golden Glove open division champion in boxing. He made all-state in football, basketball, and baseball. All three major sports. He was a dominant player, and a dominant boxer, and he spoke French and Spanish in addition to English. He could talk fluently about Latin, Cuban, Venezuelan, Puerto Rican, and Mexican culture. Yet he did not play in the major leagues, even though Roy Campanella, who is in the Major League Hall of Fame, was his substitute. My father, like Campanella, was a catcher.

My father, who was the second or third greatest catcher of all time in the old Negro Leagues, and probably the fourth, or fifth, or sixth greatest catcher of all time in the history of all of baseball, and also a great manager, could not exploit all the ability he had because of racism. Once a white man said to him, "Quincy, if you were a white man, you would be making a hundred thousand dollars a year now." Well, this only rubbed hot sauce or pepper into the open wound my father already carried. He didn't want to hear this. It was a cruel thing to say, because he couldn't be white. Ever. I wrote **"Poem for My Father"** [for Quincy T. Troupe, Sr., in *Transcircularities*] because he told me that story. I set the poem in the late forties. I realized the pain that he was going through—the fact that he could not play in the Major Leagues. And his team was regularly beating these great white teams, every time they would play. He was the catcher when Satchel Paige struck out nine, or six, or three white players in a row. He told the whole infield and outfield to sit down. It was just Satchel and my father. And he struck out the whole side. All-stars, white all-stars, and he struck them out.

What year was that?

It was in the early forties or late thirties. But I'm talking about the pain that my dad went through because of all of this. He had to play baseball the whole year round, you know, in the United States, Canada, Cuba, Puerto Rico, Venezuela, and Mexico. Here's a man who spoke three languages, knew all about Latin music, knew about Machito, could do all the dances, was brilliant mentally, a gentleman, and few whites took him seriously. When I looked into his eyes as he got older, I saw this sorrow there. And sometimes he would erupt into rage when you started talking about white players like Yogi Berra or Joe Garagiola. He was twenty times better than both of those guys, who are also from St. Louis. He didn't dislike them personally; he disliked what they exemplified. He was much better than them but couldn't play in the same league. He used to talk about this with me, almost on the verge of tears. So those poems are about sadness and unrealized potential.

You could multiply this by a lot of black people, such as Paul Robeson. This man was an absolute genius but couldn't get anything. It drove him into being what they call "an extreme left-leaning person" [laughs], a communist. Well, what do you expect when you graduate number one in your class at Rutgers, you graduate number one in your law school class, you're an All-American football player, you speak countless languages, and you're a black guy and you can't get the jobs that the people that graduated at the bottom of your class get, because they're white? How do you think he felt? I used to look into Robeson's eyes in his movies and in photos, and he had that same look that my Dad had.

Did you actually know Paul . . . ?

I didn't know him; I met his son. Paul (both of us are juniors, too) and I, we both had these famous dads, and we talked about the whole thing, at a party, about our dads. He said his dad used to be so angry about not only what they did to him, but what whites did to millions of black men and women. That poem for my father was trying to get to that deep image of rage and loss brought on by racism.

I have a St. Louis poetry question. Your poems cover the territory between life and death, from the smell of the St. Louis stockyards and the man swinging his hammer of death in "River Town Packin' House Blues" to the strong influence of sports, which we have talked about a little, and of St. Louis musicians, including Miles, John Hicks, and Lester Bowie. Could you talk about the disparate St. Louis influences on your poetics, starting with the poem "River Town Packin' House Blues" and its dedication to Sterling Brown?

I grew up on Delmar and Leonard, a few blocks from the packing houses on Vandeventer Avenue. Every time I left my house, I smelled this foul odor of burnt flesh in the air; I didn't know what it was at first. Then an old man told me, "Oh, that's the smell of them burning the flesh and skin of those cows and pigs that they kill over there on Vandeventer." And I said, "Ohh." And he said "That's the packing houses, the packing houses." And I said, "Ah, that's what that is."

I used to walk through the smell everyday. When I went to Carver Elementary School, I'd smell that smell, when I went to Vashon High School. Later, I got the chance to go into a packing house to see one of my friend's fathers, who was a packing house man. Before they developed these needles to kill them with, they used to hit the cows [sound of hands slapping] in the middle of the forehead with ball peen hammers. He'd hit them, BANG, as they passed by on both sides, and they'd fall down and someone else would cut their throats. And I saw this, all this blood, and the sound of the death cry and gurgle of the cow, pig, whatever, when they were dying. It was horrible. That's where that John Henry feeling in the poem came from.

You used the literary influence of the John Henry poem and your friend's father's example. Yet the poem ended up being about a murderous guy who wasn't necessarily your friend's father.

Oh it's the same guy! It's true, the guy was a killer, made that way by his experience working in the packing house everyday, killing all those cows and pigs. He lived down the street from me. His sons were friends of mine. One spring day, when I was young, I was running through their house—at this point, I lived at 3848 Ashland—and as I was running through their house . . . the next thing I knew I was flying into the wall. Their father hit me so hard I almost flew into the wall. When I jumped up, he looked at me and . . . I'll never forget those eyes when he looked at me and said, "Little Troupe, don't be running through my house like that. This ain't your house, so don't be running through my house like that." And I looked at him, and I saw this look in his eyes that was kinda like death. And I went, "Wow," inside my head. That was heavy!

How old were you?

I was thirteen, something like that. When I knew he was home, I never visited again until I was older, when I felt I could defend myself if he got upset. Over time I found out from his sons—this was before I wrote poetry—that he'd killed six men. He would go into taverns, have arguments and get into fights; he wouldn't start them, but he'd finish them. He worked every day, never missed work and was a great worker. At the bar, somebody might jump on him, and he'd just kill him—always with knives. You know, cut them to death or beat them to death with a bottle. And that's where that line came from about "Swingin his hammer named death." The whole idea was that there was too much

death to bring home to love. Because after you kill cows and pigs all day, you bring that brutality home with you. That's what I saw in him. Then I took a step back when I started writing poetry, because I remembered him. I went and visited with him again in the packing house and started looking at him closer. By this time he was getting older, but he was still the same guy, so I wrote this poem. I thought his image was a metaphor for black people in St. Louis—the way black people killed black people in St. Louis without any regard.

After I wrote the poem, I began to realize he was not just a metaphor for black people, but a metaphor for the way *all* people are in the United States, regardless of race. There is a metaphor of death hanging over the United States today. Many poets don't want to write about this: they'd rather write about something else that excludes politics. That's cool; I'm not against that. But the man in my **"River Town Packin' House Blues"** is both a murderer and a kind of anti-hero, because he went to work every day and didn't walk around picking on anyone. But he would put himself in these positions where violence occurred and he would kill anybody who messed with him at the drop of a hat. His employer supplied him with a lawyer because he came to work everyday, where he didn't cause any trouble. He'd always have a very good lawyer, who would help him beat the rap. After all he didn't *start* the fight. He would provoke somebody. He just didn't throw the first blow, but was just defending himself, like the United States says it is in Iraq: "We're just defending ourselves from terrorists." Even though they haven't found weapons of mass destruction, we were told Iraq was going to come over here and blow us all up, kill us on our own streets. What nonsense!

We've gotten off the beat of poetry . . .

I want to say why I dedicated the poem to Sterling Brown.

Good.

I dedicated the poem to Sterling because he really loved that poem, and because I learned so much about blues and folk poetry from him. He was a master poet and a master teacher. He taught Toni Morrison, Amiri Baraka, Ossie Davis, and Stokely Carmichal at Howard, along with many, many others. He was a great poet and a great man, in my opinion not mentioned enough as one of the true American master poets, just like Melvin Tolson isn't mentioned enough.

Good. Tell me how sports has influenced you.

I love most sports because it's pure expression. Nobody can take the fact that you're a great basketball player away from you. I played basketball and baseball in St.

Louis. I was a really good player, and it was a pure expression. The same thing is true in music although music can be a subjective thing, too.

In **Miles and Me,** *you compare Miles to Mozart and to Picasso and suggest that his style was criticized because he was black, saying, "He represented the best and worst of what we are, of our national character, whatever that is, just as Picasso and Mozart represented the best and worst of their national characters." That was pretty strong. I believe Miles invited you to write his autobiography because he admired the article you wrote about him for* Spin *magazine. And* **Miles The Autobiography** *reveals much more about Miles than most personalities would permit. Why did you decide not to censor Miles' voice and to reveal very intimate details? Did you, nevertheless, leave out some things that will be in your or Miles' archives?*

I will definitely have things in *The Accordion Years* that were left out of our book and *Miles and Me.* When Miles asked me to write his autobiography, I told him, "We have to tell the whole story, warts and all. We have to tell the story about your abuse of women. I disagree with the way you treated women personally. But it's your book; you can leave it out if you want. But I would suggest you take a hard look at yourself and tell the truth and it will make a greater book." And he agreed. That's another reason why I loved him so— because he was so truthful. Great literature comes from truth telling. Like Ted Joans once said, "All you have to fear from the poet is the truth."

The publisher also cut out some of his deep discussions of music. Critics criticized that. Well, it *was* there. I wanted to put an index and a discography in the hardback edition of the book. They wouldn't do it until the paperback came out.

Was race a factor in the editing?

I think so. The "bean counters" were trying to keep the hardback book under twenty five dollars. You see, they wanted his life in one volume. I thought it should have been two volumes. We're getting three volumes on Picasso. We have two volumes on W. E. B. DuBois by David Levering Lewis, and he's won two Pulitzer Prizes for his efforts. Miles Davis is extremely important to this culture, too, and our book should have been an in-depth look.

What's your role in the upcoming movie on Miles?

I was asked to write the screenplay by Rudy Langlais, who is a friend and the current producer. They are supposed to start filming at the end of 2004, or early 2005, but it's Hollywood and anything can happen.

Going back to poetry, your friend Eugene Redmond suggested I ask you to discuss the "notion of cross-fertilization of poetic forms, allied types of expressions and cultures" in your poems. How did you come up with—can I call this a juju mix?—early in your career? This has obviously inspired several generations of younger poets.

I was privileged to grow up in St. Louis, which is in its own space, culturally and geographically. It's in the middle of the country, and all kinds of things from the north, south, east and west pass through St. Louis. All kinds of music, all kinds of clothing styles and linguistic impulses pass through there. When I was young, my father played baseball in Mexico, Cuba, Puerto Rico, and Venezuela, and I was able to go with him to some of those places. So I didn't grow up in St. Louis exclusively, but was able to experience other cultures when I was little. I was able to listen to music from these places that my dad played around the house. So at a young age, without even knowing it, I was put on a path of appreciating different cultures. After a certain point, I hated the way St. Louis was set up. You know what I mean? Black and white. I always found it limiting to be in St. Louis.

I was always listening to music in my house—my mother playing Jackie Wilson, Duke Ellington, Count Basie, and Louis Armstrong; my father playing all those Latin musicians and Charlie Parker and others. I grew up to love Miles Davis and Chuck Berry, who lived down the street. All of this music, this mélange, influenced me greatly. Also, I grew up in the Baptist Church, and was a member of the choir, although I couldn't sing well. My first Choir director at First Baptist Church was Grace Bumbry [noted mezzo-soprano]. The second Choir Director was Olly Wilson [noted composer, now in California]. So we had this great Choir, these great singers, and the Church was always rocking. I grew up in the best of times. Later, I used to walk over to where Gaslight Square used to be; they had jazz clubs like . . .

The Dark Side?

Yeah, and that place where I saw Miles—Peacock Alley. I used to go across the river to see the great funk organist, Sam Lazar. And all those baseball players were coming to the house when my father was playing—Satchel Paige, Monte Irvin . . . I was meeting all those people when I was real little. And then after my mother divorced my father, she married a blues bass player named China Brown. And China Brown used to be in the house band at the Riviera, which was Jordan Chambers's club, who was St Louis's most powerful black politician. White powers conspired to tear down the Riviera because tearing it down ruined Jordan Chambers's political base. But they had the power to do it and so they did. In the meantime, all these musicians came through the house. I have been fortunate to have always lived in a very rich, cultural environment, which has, for me, over the years been very empowering.

How old were you when your parents divorced?

Maybe six or seven. When she married China Brown we were together until I graduated from high school. He used to work as a laundry man during the day and play blues on weekends. As I grew older, I always wanted to travel . . . and then I went to Paris in the army, and played basketball all over Europe.

Let's stop in Paris for a minute. You were playing basketball; how old were you?

I was in my early twenties. This was in the sixties, so I must have been around twenty-two. I was on the all-star basketball team. I was on a local army team in Metz, and then I was on a French team that played all over France, playing on Saturdays and Sundays. I learned about French food and French wine, being with these French people all the time. And then, traveling I got to see Sweden, Denmark, Germany, Greece, all these different places, at an early age. That's when I began to realize all whites were not bad. Growing up in the United States where they had lynchings, I felt most whites hated blacks. On top of that I went to Beaumont High School, which was an all white school.

So you had been in a mostly white high school?

I had gone to Vashon, which was an all black high school until I transferred to Beaumont High when I was thirteen or fourteen. It was not a good experience to go to Beaumont.

Switching from an all black school to a mostly white . . . ?

All white. There were seven black kids in my class. Seven black kids out of three thousand white kids. This was in the fifties—'56, '57, '58—the first years of integration and it was terrible. We used to fight all the time. I was the first black person on the basketball team at Beaumont.

France was the first place that accepted me as a black person. I had a French girlfriend named Carol. A French guy on the team with me came up and said, "You know, you'd make a good brother-in-law." I said, "What?" "You'd make a good brother-in-law," he said, "my sister adores you. Why don't you think about going out with her?" Now this is a white French guy telling me to go out with his sister. That was when I started really looking at France as being different in many ways from the United States. Now, France is racist, too, but I couldn't imagine this happening in the United States during this time. But it happened over there. I thought it was deep. So when I came back to the United States, I had a different view about whites, informed by my experience in France.

Talk about meeting Jean-Paul Sartre.

I met him through Carol. After I hurt my knee playing basketball, I started writing what I call an 'awesomely bad novel.' I don't know where it came from, but I always read books. I was one of the Book Worms [as a child] in St. Louis. My mother turned me on to books. In France I started writing this novel about this African American guy who makes sexual conquests all over Europe; I realized early on it was a silly novel. So I was telling Carol about it, and she says, "Oh, my family has a friend who is a writer: Jean-Paul Sartre." Well, I had no clue who Jean-Paul Sartre was. She says, "Maybe I can arrange a meeting with him and maybe he can help you." So she arranged a meeting with him. I think he wanted to meet me to talk about the race problem in the United States. Anyway, I meet this little guy with glasses: So I'm sitting there and he didn't want to read my novel after I told him I couldn't control the language. But he told me, "You ought to write poetry so you can get a grip on form and language. Distill your thoughts. Through poetry maybe you can get control of the language." The other thing he told me was to carry a notebook around with me all of the time, so I could write down whatever I saw or thought—and I still carry one. I saw him only a couple of times after that, and even though we talked I never knew him well. I was too young and silly!

*In your poetry, you've succeeded in addressing some issues of language as a deep metaphor for culture and other forms of communication. One of my favorite lines is from **Avalanche**, in the poem "& Syllables Grow Wings There." It says, in part, . . . "california earth-/ quakes trying to shake enjambed fault lines of minimalls / freeways & houses off their backs, rocks being pushed up there / by edges of colliding plates, rivers sliding down through yawning / cracks, pooling underneath speech, where worlds collide & sound cuts / deep fissures into language underneath the earth . . ." You are trying to communicate what is happening to the world today—the way that language is both uniting us and dividing us.*

In **"& Syllables Grow Wings"** I try to deal with the whole idea of language as it is impacted by geography and the physical space we live in and I try to use that as a mode of expression. To be able to explain a natural phenomenon, an earthquake, but at the same time try to use it emblematically to show the way language works in poetry. And also to explain how poetry works when caesuras, rhythm, and rupture are deployed in the language. I'm always trying to do that in my work now. I'm trying to get to another way of articulating and expressing myself and communicating the whole idea of where poetry and art come from. Art and poetry come from mysterious places inside the poet and artist, like earthquakes and tornadoes come from mysterious places in nature.

I'm trying to do it in a new poem I'm writing at the present time, one which I started in the late eighties but couldn't finish. It's titled **"The Architecture of Language,"** which I'm contemplating making the title of my next volume of poetry. I think it's going to be a long poem, perhaps twenty-five pages. At the present time I have about eight pages that I'm satisfied with: I have a habit of rewriting most poems twelve or fifteen times, which can be problematic. Anyway, in this poem I'm trying to bring all the "cross-fertilizing" aspects of language and forms together, as you brought up earlier in this interview, into something I hope will elevate the cross-cultural aspects of the American—not English—language. I believe in the poet being a neologist, which is one of the reasons I called my last book of poems *Transcircularities,* which you won't find in the dictionary because I made the word up. It's also one of the reasons I use "eye" instead of the first person pronoun "I" in my poems—but not in my prose writing. I use it also because of my embrace of the concept of the "third eye" in the center of the forehead that comes out of Egyptian philosophy and culture. Some people view the use of "eye" as pretentious, but its use allows me as a poet to get to a more spiritual dimension in the poem than using "I" would. But that's my personal choice and view. It's also philosophical. For the same reason, I try to infuse my poetry—and indeed, much of my writing—with elements of mystery, magic and so-called "duende," which is a concept I picked up from reading Garcia Lorca.

Where does your poetic language come from?

Poetic language comes from this mysterious place deep inside us, like earthquakes come from somewhere deep inside the earth, which is a body, some say a woman's body. Poetry also comes from a body of communal gestures and speech, fragments and words and sounds and rhythms, articulations and all of that. When we hear dogs barking, car horns honking, the sound of music, everything, even colors, that's all in the mix. For me it is miraculous that we can harness or attempt to harness the way that poetry and writing expresses itself—through people like James Joyce in *Ulysses,* Pablo Neruda, Lorca, Ezra Pound, T. S. Eliot and Aimé Cesaire, Derek Walcott and William Faulkner, Henry Dumas and Gabriel García Márquez—through a kind of natural, incredible use of language. Toni Morrison in *Jazz*—where she is trying to get to what jazz *is* through language. Allen Ginsberg in *Howl.*

We could talk about many poets of today who are trying to go beyond the whole idea that poetry is formalistic, like Jay Wright, Amiri Baraka, Wanda Coleman, Alice Fulton, Jayne Cortez, the early poetry of Jorie Graham, and others. These poets attempt to stretch the boundaries of language and marry it, perhaps attempt to create a new American improvisational form on the page and in the air. The sestina is a form. The villanelle a form, haikus and tankas are forms. Sonnets and odes are forms. As Octavio Paz writes in *The Bow and the*

Lyre, those are merely forms. What has to happen for form to come alive, to become poetry, is that the poet has to pour poetry into the form. It can't just be a line of iambic, or a nineteen-line villanelle. We are in a time of colliding cultures—computers, video games, television, music, assaults on our senses from everything imaginable—so how do you get all of that inside of a villanelle? How do you compose utterances that will fully express and communicate our visions inside fourteen or nineteen lines? That is a very difficult notion. And I'm speaking from the perspective of someone who has written forms and respects them. In the world we live in today, we need more symphonic ways of expressing ourselves in poetry, much in the way that Jimi Hendrix, John Coltrane, John Cage, or Miles Davis or somebody like that expressed themselves. I believe in this *and* that, rather than this *or* that. *And* being the operative word here. I believe people can write formal and also symphonic poems. Jazz suites. You can write symphonic, jazzy and at the same time switch, like I do sometimes, and write villanelles and sestinas. Listen, we are all schizophrenic.

I even ran a literary series in La Jolla called "Artists on the Cutting Edge: Cross Fertilizations." This series brought together poets, novelists, like Toni Morrison, John Ashbery, Derek Walcott, Sharon Olds, Victor Hernandez Cruz, Czeslaw Milosz, Gwendolyn Brooks, Galway Kinnell, Campbell McGrath, Denise Chavez, Yusef Komunyakaa, William Gass, W. S. Merwin, Kamau Braithwaite, Marilyn Chin, Jay Wright, Terry McMillan, Rita Dove and musicians Max Roach, George Lewis, Richard Muhal Abrams, Henry Threadgill, Wallace Roney, Sekou Sundiata, just to mention some. This series was wonderfully fulfilling because it served as a mirror that reflected a great cultural world. I loved mixing up everything because this is the way things truly are in the United States: mixed up. Plus the series always sold out.

That's quite a line-up; you should be planning programs for the Library of Congress. This makes me think of two different kinds of questions: first, what and how do you teach your students? And second, where does rap fit into this spectrum of sounds and language?

First, I teach my students . . . you know I retired from teaching, but I teach workshops from time to time. What I've always taught my students is to investigate their own possibilities. What is it that *they* hear? What do *they* think is important? As a person, as a poet who wants to write, what is important to *them*? And if *they* think it's important to write sestinas and villanelles, then that's what *they* ought to do. But I also tell them they ought to infuse that with as much energy, as much fun as they can. On the other hand, if you want to write both formalistically and the other way, then do that, too. If you don't want to write forms you don't have to. You can write whichever way you feel you can best express yourself. But in my beginning classes, the first thing they have to learn until they get to that point where I see they have it under control is blues, blues-sonnets, regular sonnets, villanelles, sestinas, haikus, tankas, and odes.

I believe poets should come to the table like musicians do. Most musicians know scales, know what they are doing technically [sings a scale]. Then if poets want to create and have an impact on the form, at least they know what it is. Don't talk about a subject if you don't know what it is. I tell young poets, first know what the subject is, know what the form is, what the history is, know the history of poetry, know who Pablo Neruda is, who Sylvia Plath is. You might not like him or her. You might not like Gwendolyn Brooks, but at least know who she is. I try to give my kids all of that information at the same time I'm trying to give the history of poetry and its forms.

In our second class together, they're going to learn more. When they get to the master level, I'll start to turn them loose [laughs], take my grip off them. Because by then I'll know they know a little about what poetry is, who Eliot, Pound, Tolson, Neruda, Gwendolyn Brooks, Sharon Olds, Lucille Clifton, Ginsberg, and Walcott are. But I don't let them fly until I know they know something about it all.

Going in the direction of rap . . .

Rap fits into my philosophy of this *and* that. What is rap? Rap is about rhythms, it's about syncopation and beats. It's also got a certain rhyme scheme, I call them modern day Popian couplets.

Whitman-esque.

Whitman-esque. If you listen to most rhymes of rappers they always remind me of the rhymes of Alexander Pope, the English poet. Rappers employ off-beat sprung rhymes and all that, but their base is still basically Popian couplets. I think rap with beats has a place in poetry. It has poetic properties. At the same time, the rhythms and beats are what's interesting to me, just like the rhythms and beats of Miles Davis. How do you scan a line or phrase of Miles Davis or Coltrane or Jimi Hendrix into a line of poetry? You do it by listening and mimicking the rhythms and beats. You can do the same thing with rap. You can mix it all up, iambic, hexameter, off-rhymes, scats, raps and syncopated accents; you can mix all that stuff up—which is very American.

When I was at Johns Hopkins studying 18th Century intellectual history, we had to read the complete works of the Marquis de Sade, a sadomasochist who wrote about infecting women's vaginas with gonorrhea and syphilis. This was justified at the highest intellectual levels as being a visceral expression which was new in the 18th Century. At the same time, it was obviously sexist and malevolent literature. What happens with rap? Is there the same problem that the message is not as good as the rhythm or the underbelly?

We used to have some very positive rap—Arrested Development and all those early, political groups. They just got swept aside by gangster rap and everybody—white kids mostly—wanting to hear that in the suburbs. The media especially likes to pigeonhole young and older African Americans. If they can pigeonhole a black rapper into a caricature or cartoon character calling women bitches and mother fuckers, posing with head rags, processed hair, baggy pants, goatees, humongous diamond necklaces and rings, horrific looking platinum teeth, they—the media—will, and will make them famous quicker than you can say "kill me." They will give them boatloads of money and media attention for being crass and stupid if you're black. That's the image they want out there. The message, especially the gangster rap thing, reinforces the idea that all black kids are beastly and heartless murderers in black communities. Some are, most aren't. I've never liked that message, but you have to understand it's just like rock and roll. Rock and roll's message for years was about teenage rebellion, about conquering women, and about hating grownups. It's like teenage rebellion. Rebellion has always been anti-parent, anti-social, for the most part, anti-control, and anti-establishment. That's what sells. Guns N' Roses, for example; the crazier they were, the more records they sold. Mick Jagger did all kinds of stuff. Madonna. So black rappers are just black young people doing the same thing so they can sell records.

Rapping fits into the mode of commercialization. You can buy into commercialism, buy four or five cars, diamonds, bracelets, even teeth. Rap beats are infectious, though; Max Roach says rap is the largest revolution in music since Be-bop. I believe that's true, because it has spread all over the world. It is the next step whether people like it or not. The beats are being overshadowed by silly, misogynistic, gangster, murderous, anti-social messages. The record producers don't want social protest or anybody conscious walking around. God forbid these kids start getting political and doing positive things for black communities, like some of them are as I speak, though not enough.

Your point about Arrested Development not making it and more violent groups making it is a really good one. How do you approach giving awards to deserving young writers?

I try to be as honest as I can. I was the Judge for the Cave Canem [Foundation Poetry] Award this year, and about fifty or sixty manuscripts came in without names. After looking through these, I narrowed it down to about twelve. I went through these real quick, because I've been an editor. Then I waited a day and read them again. I got down to six. There were three that stood out for me and one in particular . . . I gave that one a one and the others IAs. Then it was down to those three. It wasn't a choice about who was going to be first but who was going to be second and third. Then I picked second and third. I went back and looked at all of them again, and was comfortable. I sent in my choices, and everyone was happy with the choices, because these three poets had already been Cave Canem Fellows; they were up and coming poets that everybody loved. It turned out that the one who finished third had been a student of mine in Chicago. I try not to let my own stylistic preferences come into my decisions. Or race, or whether a poet writes politically or not. I pick the best person in the mix.

Were there any women in the mix?

Not in the top three.

The Cave Canem award was started by . . .

Cornelius Eady and Toi Derricotte. They built this organization. It's a big, wonderful organization.

*That's great . . . Two questions relating to literature. You were a pioneer in anthologizing black literature starting with **Giant Talk** in 1975. Are you satisfied with all of the black studies departments that have sprung up since then, including those at Harvard and Princeton? Is it good that we now have Chinese American, Latin, Latino, African American, Native American, and other sub-classifications of American literature?*

Giant Talk was an anthology of Third World writing, not just black. It was Latin Americans, Chinese, Indians, blacks, some people who would be thought of as white, Palestinians and Indians. I think "black studies" is an important, necessary component of higher education. I was a part of the Black Studies programs, having taught at UCLA, not so much in the Black Studies program but in the Upward Bound program, and then at Ohio University where I came and taught in the African American Studies department and was also Writer-in-Residence and taught English too. Anywhere I've taught I've always had a joint appointment, in English, Literature, African American studies and Creative Writing. I think that most white scholars who are European-based are not going to integrate most African Americans, or Native Americans, or Asians, or Latinos or anybody else into their normal pedagogy. Those programs are going to have to stand, because otherwise you wouldn't have black, white, Asian, Latino or Indian kids knowing anything other than white history.

I think the United States should be . . . again, this is where we get to what we call 'subjectivity posing as objectivity' in terms of evaluating literature or art. People come out and say that this is an objective choice and I like this person, this poet over that poet. Like Jasper Johns over Al Loving. It's not objective sometimes.

Certain people like certain writers and poets over other writers and poets because of taste and ethnicity. That's normal. I call it "ethnophobia," which is another of my neologisms. Most times their choices have something to do with their ethnicity, the way they've been brought up, whether they were brought up in Rochester or St. Louis. I like John Ashbery's poetry; he was brought up in Rochester, New York on a farm and went to Harvard. That informs the way he looks at culture. The way I look at culture and life is informed through the prism and fact that I was born and raised in St. Louis, Missouri and grew up there. Maybe Ashbery listens to Chopin, Beethoven, or Mozart, and maybe I listen to Chopin, Beethoven and Mozart, too, but I listen also to Youssou N' Dour, Jimi Hendrix, Miles, Coltrane, Howling Wolf, and Santana. You know what I mean? Does John listen to these musicians? Maybe. I don't know. But that's cool if he doesn't, but I know whatever either of us considers important *has* an important and profound impact on what we think and write. That's just the way it is.

This whole idea of objectivity informing the way we make critical choices in literature, in art and in culture is pervasive throughout our country. It's baloney; what's being passed off as objectivity is subjective. Why not say it out front? In terms of all these programs around the country, I think until white kids and kids of color can get to the point where we can move back and forth through all our cultures, and have all of this information right at our fingertips, which is going to be way off in the future, I would say that we have to keep these programs.

Would you like to talk about how Guadeloupe has influenced your work?

My poetry became very urban when I was living in Manhattan, which was a stretch of twenty years. Before New York I had lived in Paris, St. Louis, Los Angeles, other cities. I hadn't lived any place that was remotely suburban or country. So when I moved to La Jolla, California, from Manhattan I became aware, as I had not been when I first lived in California, in Los Angeles, of appreciating rural life. In La Jolla I became aware of the importance of nature, all kinds of natural life and the ocean. I started writing about that. I really enjoyed it . . . My work just flipped from being urban to being something else. I started writing long poems about nature and the ocean to the chagrin of some people who liked my writing before [laugh], who wanted to hear those urban, rhythmic poems, like the "Magic Johnson" poem and others. My new poems still had all this rhythmic stuff in them, but the imagery had changed; it wasn't about honking horns, city images and sounds, or people on the street. But when I retired from teaching at the University of California, San Diego in July of 2003, I decided I was not going to stay in California, but wanted to come back to New York.

So my wife and I moved back to New York, and decided to get a place in the West Indies, too. I wanted elasticity in my life, being able to be in New York City and someplace else remote. So my involvement in all of these sounds and looking at the world in a different way through the prism of vegetation, foliage, trees, and animals started in California.

When I started going down to Guadeloupe I realized that Derek Walcott had a step up on everybody because he grew up in St. Lucia, which is a gorgeous place. When I went to visit him a couple of times there, I remember looking at the trees and the leaves, saying, "Derek, it's incredible to live in a place with all this expansiveness and natural beauty." So we decided to live between New York and the Caribbean. In Guadeloupe I've been writing a lot, and my work has been totally influenced by this sensibility. It doesn't mean I'm not political, but my work has changed again, I think for the better. I've written about fifty poems. I love going there, to the beach in St. Anne. My wife Margaret and I have this little house in Montebello, and I write five feet from the outdoors. We open all the doors, and you can see hummingbirds, flowers, bananas and mango trees, frogs and lizards, everywhere! It's astonishing. And this is coming into my work in a real, positive way now. I like what I'm doing. When I introduced the Cave Canem poets, I had to read for twenty minutes, and I read these new poems. Yusef [Komunyakaa] came up to me and said, "Wow, those pieces were really different." Sharon Olds said the same thing. I love what I am doing now, in terms of the writing, what's happening with it.

I have to bring up something that clouded your distinguished career.

Go ahead.

You became the first official Poet Laureate of California, then were forced to resign after a background check revealed that you didn't have a college degree. The Chronicle of Higher Education *wrote an essay about this, and their printed opinions were largely that you were a successful professor and didn't need a degree, but the moral flag was raised. However, the moralists must realize that you never would have been hired without a degree. Did you feel set up when this all came down? Have you had further thoughts?*

First of all, I would have been hired without a degree, because Fanny Howe didn't have a degree, and she was teaching at the University of California, San Diego, along with other artists who didn't have one. We were all full Professors there because of our accomplishments. I don't feel bad about talking about it, because I felt liberated by saying, finally, that I didn't have a college degree. It has cleansed the rest of my life in many ways, and that's good for my mental health.

It happened when I was teaching at the College of Staten Island. Before that, I never had on my record that I had a college degree—didn't have it on my record when I was at UCLA, at USC, when I came to Ohio University, and when I came to the Richmond College, which then turned into the College of Staten Island. One day, this colleague—I refuse to use his name—came to me—he was familiar with my record—and said, "Quincy, all the things you've done, you would become a full professor if you were on the other track." I was on the lecturer's track. So I said, "What are you talking about?" and he says, "Well, you're on the lecturer's track, you should be over here on the track that leads to full professorship. Now you can't go any higher than being a lecturer." He said, "There would be a large difference in terms of pay for teaching the same classes." And I said, "Really?" I thought about that. So he said, "If I were you I would change that you don't have a degree, and put down that you have one."

So I did. I don't blame anybody for that. I did it knowing what I was doing. I regret what happened, but I don't regret it in the way a lot of people have discussed it, because of morality. I did become a full professor and when the students evaluated us, I was always in the top one percent of all professors on every campus where I taught. I didn't cheat any student out of anything. I was a great professor.

I was honored they selected me. Yet I didn't want to be Poet Laureate of California, because I didn't want to get involved in politics. Hugh Davies, who was the Director of the Contemporary Museum of San Diego, asked me to do it; I told him I didn't want to, but he kept asking me. Finally, I told him he could throw my name in the ring. Then one night, a guy called and said, "You are one of three finalists to be Poet Laureate of the State of California." I was stunned, I really was. The next thing I knew, I was *the* Poet Laureate of the State of California. I had to go through this background check by the Governor's office that took about two weeks. One Sunday I was in a New York restaurant having lunch with Walter Mosley, Clyde Taylor, Manthia Diawara, and my wife Margaret when the Governor's office called and said I was going to be named Poet Laureate that Monday.

I don't have the facts about what happened five months later. The attorney for the University of California, San Diego called me and asked, "Is it true you did not graduate from Grambling College?" And I said, "Yes." I never lied. I decided right then that I should resign. So I sat down and wrote a resignation letter that day—ten days before the news broke . . .

Then all of the stuff started. Some people came out and said I did the right thing: I faced the music. But some people of San Diego, which is a very conservative town, started attacking me left and right. Somebody said to me, "One thing you can say is that you were the first official Poet Laureate of the State of California. They can't take that away from you. It was a fair process, and they picked you because of what you had done, because of your achievements, not because of Grambling College. They picked you." And I said, "Yeah that's true."

The most horrible moment was when my mother started crying on the phone. My mother was eighty-five when that happened. Margaret [Quincy's wife] was crying, my son was crying because he was verbally accosted by a couple of young men at the college he was attending and almost got into a fight. For two months, it was terrible.

Through all of this, Margaret was great. One day she said to me, "You know, Quincy, in all the years I've known you, twenty-six years, except for Stanly Crouch, this is the only time you have gotten this kind of treatment in the press. You should be thankful." Which is true. And that kind of put it all into perspective.

That's how it happened. I was set to retire from the university in July 2003 until I was named Poet Laureate. After I resigned from the position, I went back to my original retirement date and moved back to New York City. In the end I thought it best to resign from both positions—the Poet Laureate-ship and the university—and to get on with my life. I haven't looked back because life goes on. But as I said earlier, it was an honor and privilege to be named the first official Poet Laureate of the state of California.

In the preface to **James Baldwin: The Legacy,** *you discuss Baldwin's genius: "The Baldwin sentence was muscular, compelling, collectable, musical, its own invention, but it was what he did that finally hypnotized us." How do you characterize literature written at the end of the 20th century and at the start of the 21st?*

I'll talk about the novelists I like and then talk about the poets. For me, García Márquez is the greatest writer living today. I just love García Márquez. I think John Wideman is an incredible prose stylist, as are Edward P. Jones and Ishmael Reed. Toni Morrison, at her best, can be a very compelling writer . . . I really liked *Texaco,* by Patrick Chamoiseau, the novels of Zakes Mda and one of my true heroes, Chinua Achebe, whom I just love, both as a writer and as a human being. As for poets, I think Derek Walcott is the greatest poet writing in the world today, bar none. He writes like a painter, which he is. Yusef Komunyakaa writes powerful poems, as do Sharon Olds, Alice Fulton, the early C. D. Wright and Jorie Graham, Thylias Moss, and Robert Pinsky. Recently, I was impressed by Rita Dove's poem "Hattie McDaniel Arrives at the Coconut Grove." There are many great writers today.

Let's talk about art in your spacious art-filled rooms. I love the piece behind you.

Yeah, that's the late Jacques Gabriel, a Haitian painter.

Your poetry is informed and inspired by many artists. Could you discuss some of these, including Oliver Jackson, José Bedia, and Romare Bearden and their impact on your voice and modes of expression?

The first painting that really impacted me was Picasso's *Guernica.* When I saw *Guernica* in New York that painting against war really made a big impact on me. When I came to New York, at first I really got influenced by people like Al Loving. I didn't know who Oliver Jackson was; I met Oliver when I was teaching at Ohio University. Then I discovered Romare Bearden and Jacob Lawrence. I always liked Raymond Saunders a lot, and Joe Overstreet, Ed Clark, and Al Loving. Margaret and I discovered José Bedia together in Miami. I started buying his work. He illustrated my book **Avalanche,** graced it with some of his drawings and paintings. There are so many artists . . . you just commented about the two pieces with the record with the hands on it—that's Mildred Howard. Mildred is a fabulous artist, like some of the Haitians—Jacques Gabriel, Edouard Duval-Carrié. Wilfredo Lam has had an impact on me. Hale Woodruff, the late Ethiopian Alexander Skunder Boghossian is one of my favorites. Sam Gilliam. These people have been big influences on my work. I also like people like Robert Rauschenberg, Jasper Johns, Vincent van Gogh, Elizabeth Murray, and Frank Stella. Melvin Edwards. Howardina Pindell, Frank Bowling. Charles Alston. There are so many painters and artists I love. All these people have influenced the way I think as an artist, the way I write poetry. Art has informed the visual and rhythmic aspects of my writing.

Frank Stella is another one who didn't have a college degree.

I know. College degrees work sometimes, and sometimes they aren't necessary. Having a college degree doesn't make you a great teacher. That's false, because it excludes a lot of great people, especially in the arts, and in other important areas, too, who would make great teachers. Would they have turned away Albert Einstein, Picasso, Miles Davis, John Coltrane, so many others? People should not be in the classroom just because they got a degree, but because they can teach and impart essential information.

Any closing thoughts? I haven't yet asked about your novel The Footmans, *which delves into St. Louis politics, including the dynasty of the Troupe family. How did you approach using your family history as fiction?*

The Footmans is the legacy of Charlie Footman. I've been writing it for a long time, because I just wanted to get it right. I never could find the form and structure that allowed the story to flow. Now I've found the structure and it's flowing and I'm going to finish it soon. I've got a grip on it now. One of the things that retiring from full-time teaching has done for me is that it has given me a lot of time, and that's what I needed to finish my novel. Time. I'm also writing what I call my auto-memoir, *The Accordion Years.* It's short of an autobiography, but longer than your traditional memoir. That's why I call it an auto-memoir. I'm writing about everything I think is important in my life. I feel if I can be as truthful as Miles Davis was in his autobiography, if I can tell the essential truths about my life in that way, then I will have a compelling book, because my life has been full of interesting stories.

Is The Footmans *scheduled for publication?*

No. First I'm going to turn in *The Accordion Years.* I'm going to hand in 250 pages to my agent this year and I'll probably turn in the whole book next year. Then I'll give them *The Footmans,* which I hope they will like. If they do then it will probably come out in three or four years. It's part of a strategy. I want the memoir to come out first and then the novel. I have a children's book called **Little Stevie Wonder** coming out from Houghton Mifflin in March. I'm turning in my book of essays and articles Coffee House is going to publish next year. It's called *Crossfertilizations*—pieces on music, culture, and politics. It's going to be about 300 pages, with the complete Miles Davis pieces, and all kinds of essays and articles about culture and politics. Then I'm going to publish an autobiography I'm co-writing with Chris Gardner, for Dawn Davis, the great editor over at Amistad/Harper Collins. This man rose from being a homeless African American to being a millionaire. He owns a company in Chicago.

How did you find him?

He found me! I turn down a lot of people. Chris has got a very rich book, funny, sad, with all kinds of compelling stuff. I like his story a lot, and he's willing to tell the truth.

I'm having fun now and like being editor (since January 2004) of *Black Renaissance Noire* at New York University's Africana Studies/Institute of African American Affairs. My first issue came out this August. The great lineup features new poetry by Derek Walcott, an interview with Aimé Cesaire at age 91, a poem by Kamau Braithwaite, part of Hugh Maskela's autobiography, fiction by Maryse Condé, an essay by Ishmael Reed on the treatment of black men by the media, and a piece by Robin Kelly on Cesaire, along with Eduoard Glissant. George Lewis does a piece on AACM in Chicago, and we have spreads on visual artists Al Loving and Anthony Barboza, who has a great cover photograph. The fabulous February 2005 issue includes Chinua Achebe, poetry by Yusef Komunyakaa, art by Jean Michel Basquiat, and the letters of Chester Himes and John A. Williams.

FURTHER READING

Criticism

Crouch, Stanley. "Play the Right Thing." *New Republic* 202, no. 7 (12 February 1990): 30-7.

> Detailed overview of *Miles* that includes a negative assessment of Troupe's use of vulgar language and, according to the critic, inconsistencies and inaccuracies.

Daniels, Douglas Henry. Review of *Miles and Me,* by Quincy Troupe. *African American Review* 35, no. 1 (spring 2001): 152-53.

> Generally positive evaluation of *Miles and Me* in which the critic delineates the predominant themes of the volume.

Review of *Little Stevie Wonder,* by Quincy Troupe. *Publishers Weekly* 252, no. 22 (30 May 2005): 60.

> Brief, favorable assessment that commends Troupe's "catchy" language, his clever blending of Wonder song titles into the biography's poetic text, and his inclusion of significant biographical details from Wonder's life.

Additional coverage of Troupe's life and career is contained in the following sources published by Gale: *Black Writers,* **Ed. 2;** *Contemporary Authors,* **Vols. 113, 124;** *Contemporary Authors New Revision Series,* **Vols. 43, 90, 126;** *Dictionary of Literary Biography,* **Vol. 41; and** *Literature Resource Center.*

Amos Tutuola
1920-1997

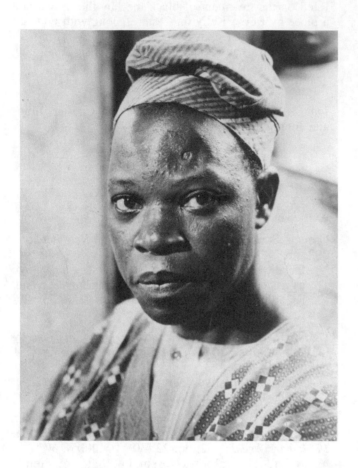

Harry Ransom Humanities Research Center, The Universtiy of Texas at Austin

Nigerian novelist, short story writer, and playwright.

For additional information on Tutuola's career, see *Black Literature Criticism*, Ed. 1.

INTRODUCTION

Generously praised by Western critics upon publication, Tutuola's novel *The Palm-Wine Drinkard and His Dead Palm-Wine Tapster in the Dead's Town* (1952) was derided among Nigerian scholars. Although it prominently features the folklore of Tutuola's homeland, some Nigerian critics despaired that Tutuola's nonstandard English, along with grammar and vocabulary derived from Tutuola's native language, Yoruba, reflected poorly on Nigerians and their literary potential. Tutuola's skillful

and innovative transformation of the themes and motifs of Yoruba oral narrative traditions became more widely appreciated among his own countrymen with the publication of his later works, although Tutuola's subsequent novels received less critical attention from Western critics than did *The Palm-Wine Drinkard*.

BIOGRAPHICAL INFORMATION

Tutuola was born in 1920 in Abeokuta, Nigeria, to a cocoa farmer, Charles Tutuola, and his wife, Esther. After attending missionary primary schools, Tutuola worked on his father's farm. He was trained as a coppersmith during the second World War and worked for the Royal Air Force from 1943 through 1945. Following the end of the war, Tutuola attempted unsuccessfully to establish his own blacksmith shop. In 1947 he married Alake Victoria. A year later, he secured a position as a messenger for the Labor Department in Lagos. Tutuola was inspired to write by his observation that local cultural traditions and stories were being forgotten. *The Palm-Wine Drinkard* was published in 1952 and immediately received favorable reviews. Tutuola continued write, attending evening classes and expanding the range of literature that he read. He also spent time traveling through Africa, Europe, and the United States. In 1979 he became a visiting research fellow at the University of Ile-Ife in Nigeria. By 1983, he was serving as an associate in the international writing program at the University of Iowa. Having published other novels and short stories, Tutuola returned to Nigeria and continued to write until his death in 1997.

MAJOR WORKS

Many of Tutuola's works share the common motif of the spiritual journey. During the journey, a typically weak character encounters dangers (often spirits from the underworld) and is transformed by the experience to lead a more meaningful life. *The Palm-Wine Drinkard*, Tutuola's best-known work, features such a journey and borrows subject matter and stylistic technique from Yoruba oral tradition. In the work, the Drinkard is driven on a quest to the land of the dead. Once tested, the changed man returns to his village, where he resolves a conflict between the Heavens and the Land. *Simbi and the Satyr of the Dark Jungle* (1956) is similar in format: the title character is a wealthy girl who decides that she must suffer and endure poverty. She is kidnapped and follows a fantastic path home through strange places such as "The Town of the Multi-Coloured People." The spiritual themes and allegorical nature of Tutuola's works have lead to their being described as mythologies or epics, rather than novels. *My Life in the Bush of Ghosts* (1954) similarly employs an episodic structure, with elements derived from Yoruba folklore, but rather than featuring a quest-driven character, this work involves a young protagonist who accidentally wanders into the realm known as the Bush of Ghosts following abuse and abandonment by his stepmothers. Once he has embarked on his journey through this realm, he experiences trials and transformations similar to those experienced by Tutuola's other protagonists. After twenty years, a goddess finally offers the boy the chance to return to an ordinary life with his mother and brother—an offer which the boy accepts.

CRITICAL RECEPTION

The techniques which Tutuola employs in *The Palm-Wine Drinkard* and his other works are praised for their ability to capture elements of oral tradition in written narrative. Tutuola repeats specific episodes for emphasis and embellishes well-known folktales with both personal interpretations and modern situations. Some works are concluded, in folklore tradition, with a moral or lesson, as in *My Life in the Bush of Ghosts*, in which Tutuola comments on the effects of hatred. Tutuola's unconventional usage of the English language—which includes unusual syntax, broken English, and idiosyncratic diction and grammar—is regarded by some scholars as integral to his oral style. Others have harshly criticized this approach as unpolished, claiming that it reflects negatively on West African culture. Still other critics have faulted Tutuola for the lack of development in his style over time and for his habitual reliance on episodic structure. Richard Bauerle favorably reviewed the collection of short stores that Tutuola published in 1990 (*The Village Witch Doctor and Other Stories*), observing that the stories, like Tutuola's earlier works, are based on traditional Yoruba folktales and feature themes of greed and betrayal. Describing the collection as "illuminating," the critic finds that Tutuola's style remains "fresh," even after so much time has passed since the appearance of his first novel. Other recent appraisals of Tutuola's work have gone back to *The Palm-Wine Drinkard* and offered reappraisals of this early and acclaimed novel. Steven M. Tobias has studied the book's anti-realism, finding that this style provides Tutuola with a unique tool for a subversive sociopolitical critique of colonialism. Examining Tutuola's unpublished plays, Chris Dunton has identified common themes in three of Tutuola's dramas. Dutton notes that Tutuola explored isolation, the problems associated with trust, and individual vulnerability, as he continually worked to improve his skills as a dramatist.

PRINCIPAL WORKS

The Palm-Wine Drinkard and His Dead Palm-Wine Tapster in the Dead's'Town (novel) 1952
My Life in the Bush of Ghosts (novel) 1954
Simbi and the Satyr of the Dark Jungle (novel) 1956
The Brave African Huntress (novel) 1958
The Palm-Wine Drinkard (drama) 1958
Feather Woman of the Jungle (novel) 1962
Ajaiyi and His Inherited Poverty (novel) 1967
The Witch-Herbalist of the Remote Town (novel) 1981
The Wild Hunter in the Bush of the Ghosts (short stories) 1982; revised edition, 1989
The Village Witch Doctor and Other Stories (short stories) 1990

CRITICISM

Richard Baurele (review date summer 1991)

SOURCE: Baurele, Richard. Review of *The Village Witch Doctor and Other Stories,* by Amos Tutuola. *World Literature Today* 65, no. 3 (summer 1991): 539.

[*In this review of Tutuola's* The Village Witch Doctor and Other Stories, *Baurele discusses the collection's basis in traditional Yoruba folktales and praises the work as "illuminating."*]

Amos Tutuola's new volume [***The Village Witch Doctor and Other Stories***] contributes eighteen more stories to his already large number, all based on traditional Yoruba folktales. His themes are much like those in his previous books: greed, thievery, betrayal, fraud, et cetera. However, the milieu is in some cases more modern. The major plot device is that of the trickster tricked. The title story is typical though more elaborate than most. The witch doctor keeps tricking his victim in different ways until finally the tables are turned. The characters in the tales include many familiar figures: the tortoise, the jungle drummer, the beetle lady, and people with regular Yoruba names.

Tutuola's manner of telling his stories is, as one would expect, closer to that of his later books than to that of his first and most famous work, ***The Palm-Wine Drinkard.*** There is more of the writer and less of the talker. Almost gone are such rich expressions as "He said whisperly" and "We took our fear back." Still, one occasionally encounters such fresh phrasing as "The priest lived lonely in the heart of the forest." It is gratifying to see Tutuola at age seventy still busy enriching African literature with his illuminating interpretations.

Steven M. Tobias (essay date summer 1999)

SOURCE: Tobias, Steven M. "Amos Tutuola and the Colonial Carnival." *Research in African Literatures* 30, no. 2 (summer 1999): 66-74.

[*In the essay that follows, Tobias contends that Tutuola's* The Palm-Wine Drinkard *is a subversive and complex analysis of Western colonialism, stressing that the anti-realism for which the work is often dismissed is an effective instrument for Tutuola's sociopolitical discourse.*]

> The truth is an offense but not a sin!
> Is he who laugh last, is he who win!
>
> —Bob Marley, "Jah Live" (1975)

From the time of its publication in 1952, the supernatural tale *The Palm-Wine Drinkard and His Dead Palm-Wine Tapster in the Dead's Town* by the Nigerian writer Amos Tutuola has generated an enormous amount of both critical confusion and controversy. Western critics initially reacted quite favorably towards the book and praised it for its rich, albeit "primitive," adherence to Yoruba oral, folk traditions. Perhaps its most well-known European proponent was the poet Dylan Thomas who described it in a review as a

> brief, thronged, grisly and bewitching story, or series of stories, written in young English by a West African, about the journey of an expert and devoted palm-wine drinkard through a nightmare of indescribable adventures.
>
> (qtd. in Lindfors 7)

Anthony West, a critic for *The New Yorker,* went so far as to say that in reading it, "[o]ne catches a glimpse of the very beginning of literature, that moment when writing at last seizes and pins down the myths and legends of an analphabetic culture" (222). Although most Western critics praised the book in a similar backhanded fashion for its freewheeling descriptions of exotic characters and situations, they ultimately found it lacking in "true" literary merit.

African reactions to the book were generally less favorable. Many educated Nigerians were highly incensed to discover that such a "primitive" book, written in broken English by a lowly messenger, was being lauded in European intellectual circles as the pinnacle of Nigerian culture. In particular, with Nigerian political independence nearly in sight in the early 1950s, Tutuola's world of bogey-men was one that most educated Nigerians would have liked to purge forever from global perceptions of their country (Lindfors 344). In addition, African critics were quick to point out that in many instances Tutuola outright botches his retelling of traditional folk tales or at best merely offers inferior English renditions of pre-existing Yoruba originals. All in all, the book proved something of a general embarrassment to the Nigerian intellectual establishment of 1952.[1]

In terms of its relationship to the discourse of Western colonialism, *The Palm-Wine Drinkard* is a far more complex and subversive book than it has generally been given credit for being. Admittedly, at first glance the story seems no more than a mythical romp by an unnamed, picaresque hero through a dream world in search of his dead palm-wine tapster. On this fairy tale quest, all normal laws of time, place, and nature are suspended. The hero changes his own physical form at will, moves effortlessly between the lands of the living and the dead, and encounters varied and wondrous creatures, many of whom he must fight and/or flee. What is to be made of this world and why would Tutuola choose it as his subject? More important, how could a such a fantastic story, one that would seem to have so little to say about the real world and its numerous problems, ever be called subversive?

It is important to pay close attention to the way in which Tutuola employs traditional folk tales in *The Palm-Wine Drinkard.* His retelling of these anecdotes has earned him the censure of African critics who argue that in many cases his stories deviate substantially from the Yoruba originals upon which they are based. However, Tutuola's retelling of these various stories may be regarded as instances of what Henry Louis Gates has dubbed "unmotivated signification" in his book *The Signifying Monkey* (xxvi). Gates suggests that in instances of "unmotivated signifyin(g)"—pastiche or noncritical parody—an established story or trope is not appropriated or echoed for the purpose of disparaging it. Rather, the intention behind this sort of signifyin(g) is to establish common cultural-narrative ground with a specific predicate work or literary tradition. Gates describes how this kind of signifyin(g) functions as

> a joyous proclamation of antecedent and descendant text. The most salient analogue for this unmotivated mode of revision in the broader black cultural tradition might be that between black jazz musicians who perform each other's standards . . . not to critique these but to engage in refiguration as an act of homage.
>
> (xxvii)

Historically, African oral tales have always been adapted and molded by their tellers so that they would have particular relevance to the specific social and moral climate in which they were told. Therefore Tutuola's modifications cannot be criticized legitimately for being either "untraditional" or "inaccurate." Admittedly, he alters traditional plots; however, he does this intentionally in order to speak more directly to the particularized concerns of the African setting in which he wrote. Despite the fact that most of the incidents of *The Palm-Wine Drinkard* appear to constitute little more than silly farce, many of them are in fact covert jibes at colonialism and the social conditions that it engendered. Through a sustained use of sublimation and metonymy, Tutuola creates an episodic allegory through which he can vent his personal frustrations with life under British domination.

For example, Tutuola did much of his writing while at his dull and bureaucratic British job and it can be argued that the episode of *The Pine-Wine Drinkard* in which his hero must turn himself into a canoe may be interpreted as an autobiographical confession of the real grief Tutuola felt at becoming a virtual object in service of an alien bureaucracy:

> I commanded one juju which was given me by a kind spirit who was a friend of mine and at once the juju changed me into a big canoe. Then my wife went inside the canoe with the paddle and paddling it, she used the canoe as a "ferry" to carry passengers across the river, the fare for adults was 3d (three pence) and half fare for children.
>
> (39)

Despite the great abilities and wondrous accomplishments of Tutuola's hero, in this incident he is reduced by an externally imposed economic system to struggling subhumanly—yet in a way that appears vaguely, almost cryptically bourgeois—for a modest sum of British money. Such a belittling and objectifying occupation is a severe drop in stature for Tutuola's hero: he has just a short time earlier not only done battle with powerful monsters but bravely conquered Death itself.[2]

The process in which Tutuola's hero and his wife are turned into various objects parallels the experience whereby colonized people lose their very sense of identity through the marginalization of their native languages and codes. Composing the canoe episode probably not only proved cathartic for Tutuola, but allowed him to examine and begin to redefine his own position in society during the transition to independence. This impulse to establish social positioning is a primary consideration of (post)colonial literature. According to theorists like D. E. S. Maxwell:

> A major feature of post-colonial literature is the concern with place and displacement. It is here that the special post-colonial crisis of identity comes into being; the concern with the development or recovery of an effective relationship between self and place.
>
> (qtd. in Ashcroft 9)

In a very real sense, the imposition of a foreign linguistic and cultural template onto his surroundings destabilizes the colonized or formerly colonized subject's context and, in so doing, renders his own identity uncertain.

Tutuola's true quest both for his hero's and his own identity, which he recaptures by taking charge of the alien environment established by colonial discourse, may help account for the fantastic and infinitely mutable landscape of *The Palm-Wine Drinkard.* In his book Tutuola struggles to mold and shape his hero's world into one that makes sense. Through the manipulation and reformulation of a foreign tongue Tutuola attempts to refamiliarize and reclaim the environment. This linguistic struggle is central for any colonized or formerly colonized culture whose language system has been supplanted by that of its colonizers. Typically, this process leads a colonized person to experience a sense of loss and alienation before he or she can develop an "appropriate" usage, or language system, with which to express the (post)colonial experience.

In developing such a usage, Tutuola invents and employs what can be described as an "interlanguage": a regionally specific version of English (Ashcroft 11). To Tutuola's initial Western readers and critics—such as Thomas and West—the author's English seemed incomplete, if not rather childish. And it is easy to come to this pate conclusion since Tutuola's book appears to be riddled with logical, grammatical, and syntactical errors as it seems to slip in and out of the author's textual grasp. For example, consider its opening paragraph:

> I was a palm-wine drinkard since I was a boy of ten years of age. I had no other work more than to drink palm-wine in my life. In those days we did not know other money, except for COWRIES, so that everything was very cheap, and my father was the richest man in our town.
>
> (7)

In answer to criticism that Tutuola's English is frequently "wrong," it can be countered that the writer's discourse constitutes a separate and genuine linguistic system (see Ashcroft 67). The development of such a system helps to displace standard English from its privileged place at a colonial or postcolonial country's cultural center. Tutuola's use and manipulation of both language and the fantastic play pivotal and complementary roles in his formulation of a discourse of resistance.

The critical writings of Mikhail Bakhtin help to explain the way that *The Palm-Wine Drinkard* most forcefully undermines and redefines the social context of its nascence: the colonially framed power structure of 1952 Nigeria. The struggle that exists between the two opposing forces—the colonizers and the colonized—of any colonial country is fundamentally dialogical. Quite obviously, the discourse and cultural codes of the colonizers occupy a place of privilege and control in a colonized country. There is very little that is secretive about colonial domination: the colonial machine is oiled by public, and quite frequently brutal, displays of power and discipline. Because the power structure of the colonial social order is, more or less, in plain sight—in contrast to the covert way in which power generally operates in the postcolonial world—Southern resistance can be directed at obvious targets.

Because it is such a jumbled and polysemous book, a central question begged by *The Palm-Wine Drinkard* is how to classify it. By no stretch of the imagination can *The Palm-Wine Drinkard* be considered a novel in the classical sense. As has already been noted, the book borrows heavily from traditional Yoruba orature. Antithetically, its plot's structural basis, that of an extended quest on which a hero must do battle with various allegorically conceived monsters, was probably derived from Western sources—possibly from Bunyan's *Pilgrim's Progress.* Conjecture that Tutuola was influenced by Bunyan is supported by his admission to having read the poet while a student at the British school where he was educated (Lindfors 336).

Pilgrim's Progress has seemingly influenced the organization as well as both the language and landscape of *The Palm-Wine Drinkard.* Note the epic, Bunyanesque quality of the following passage in which Tutuola's hero suffers in the African cousin of the Slough of Despond:

> As we had freed from the white creatures then we started our journey in that field. This field had no trees or palmtrees, only long wild grasses grew wild there, all resembled cornplants, the edges of its leaves were as sharp as razor blades and hairy. Then we traveled in that field till 5 o'clock [quitting time?] in the evening, after that, we began to look for a suitable place to sleep till morning.

(43)

This passage is a composite of influences, both Western and African, fantastic and starkly modern. Taken together, however, these diverse influences project an image of colonial oppression: they allegorically represent a hard day's labor in a Western-style plantation. In *The Palm-Wine Drinkard,* life becomes a mythic quest to flee toil amid foreign vegetation and to escape domination by "white monsters."

Tutuola's use of capitalized chapter headings such as "THE INVESTIGATOR'S WONDERFUL WORK IN THE SKULL'S FAMILY'S HOUSE," "OUR LIFE WITH THE FAITHFUL MOTHER IN THE WHITE TREE," and "TO SEE THE MOUNTAIN-CREATURES WAS NOT DANGEROUS BUT TO DANCE WITH THEM WAS THE MOST DANGEROUS" also hints at a Western influence. Tutuola probably derived this practice either from reading boy's adventure books or eighteenth-century novels, or quite possibly from reading English-style newspapers. The headings, as well as much of his phrasing throughout the book, without question possess both the appearance and tone of tabloid headlines.

Because *The Palm-Wine Drinkard* is infected with Yoruba as well as both British pop cultural and literary strains, it can be best conceived according to Bakhtin's idea of *heteroglossia.* It is truly a colonial romance in that it borrows both structurally and linguistically from the cultures of colonizer and colonized alike. In describing the ghost of his hero's child, Tutuola writes:

> When we reached there, she picked a stick and began to scratch the ashes with it, and there I saw that the

middle of the ashes rose up suddenly and at the same time there appeared a half-bodied baby, he was talking with a lower voice like a *telephone.*

(35; emphasis added)

Similarly, in describing a place outside a village the hostile inhabitants of which have captured his hero, Tutuola writes, "After that, they took us to a wide field which was in the full heat of the sun, there were no trees or shadows near there and it was cleared as a *football field*" (61).

Such hodge-podge cultural shifts are common throughout *The Palm-Wine Drinkard.* Frequently among ghosts, goblins, and enchanted villages, a seemingly out-of-place reference to a European object or concept such as a bomb, a razor blade, or soccer will appear. Tutuola's liberal cultural blending works hand-in-hand with his creation of a grotesquely "carnivalesque" atmosphere. The purpose of this is to subvert and undermine the privileged place that a foreign culture has come to occupy in his society. In *Rabelais and His World,* Bakhtin describes the way that invoking the carnivalesque challenges the dominant social-political paradigm, the *normal* way of living:

> As opposed to the official feast, one might say that the carnival celebrated temporary liberation from the prevailing truth and form of the established order; it marked the suspension of all hierarchical rank, privileges, norms, and prohibitions. Carnival was the true feast of time, the feast of becoming, change, and renewal. It was hostile to all that was immortalized and completed.

(10)

In *The Palm-Wine Drinkard* a monstrously distorted, nonsense view of the world becomes the norm. As a result, when an artifact of otherwise privileged English culture appears in the book, it in turn becomes something of an oddity. In this way Tutuola turns the colonial power structure on its ear in an attempt to reclaim the center for himself and his culture.

In *The Dialogical Imagination,* Bakhtin offers an explanation of the social function of parody, which hints at why Tutuola may have been attracted both to this genre and to discourse blending in general. Moreover, Bakhtin's theories may help account for the reason Tutuola chooses to adopt a comical anti-heroic character-narrator. Bakhtin suggests that in the parodic discourse of the public sphere, that of the street or marketplace, or in this particular case, quite possibly, the school yard or soccer field,

> the heteroglossia of the clown sounded forth, ridiculing all "languages" and dialects; there developed . . . street songs, folksayings, anecdotes, where there was no language-center at all, where there was to be found a lively play with the "languages" of poets, scholars, monks, knights and others, where all "languages" were masks and where no language could claim to be an authentic, incontestable face.

(273)

The establishment of such a climate and such a powerfully parodic language is central to Tutuola's anti-colonial project.

In its parodic rebellion, Tutuola's book has much in common with traditionally canonized novels such as *Gulliver's Travels, Moby-Dick,* and *Gargantua and Pantagruel.* Like its Western cousins, **The Palm-Wine Drinkard** was generated by a cultural context characterized by intense tension. Swift, Melville, and Rabelais all wrote in order to challenge and subvert the dominant morality, culture, and language of their respective eras, in the process trying to reinvent their societies' normative values. In attempting to critique and reform society, hyperbole, satire, and anti-logic often prove more forceful than direct assaults with realistic, customary literary weapons.

Perhaps the most striking and memorable of all the traditional folk tales recounted in **The Palm-Wine Drinkard** is that of the "beautiful complete gentleman." Variations of this story have appeared in at least seven different anthologies of Yoruba folk tales and it may be assumed that their word-of-mouth dissemination in Nigeria has been even more extensive (Lindfors 339). In this story a girl is enthralled by the physical beauty of a man she encounters in the marketplace. In framing this tale, Tutuola ironically confides in the reader:

> I could not blame the lady for following the Skull as a complete gentleman to his house at all. Because if I were a lady, no doubt I would follow him to wherever he would go, and still as I was a man I would jealous him more than that, because if this gentleman went to the battle field, surely, enemy would not kill him or capture him and if bombers saw him in a town which was to be bombed, they would not throw bombs on his presence, and if they did throw it, the bomb itself would not explode until this gentleman would leave that town, because of his beauty.
>
> (25)

Despite the man's apparent beauty, when the enamored woman follows him to his home she witnesses an amazing spectacle. Along the way, the man proceeds to remove various parts of his body—one by one—and return them to the people from whom he has rented them. Ultimately, the man is reduced to a terrifying, shrilly humming skull that takes the girl prisoner by tying a magical Cowrie to her neck. This enchanted bit of currency not only renders the girl unable to speak but emits an awful noise if she attempts to escape.

If Tutuola's version of this story is read allegorically, in a manner informed by the circumstances that surrounded it composition, then it can be interpreted as a warning about some of the dangers and temptations offered by colonial/transitional life in Nigeria. Through his retelling of this tale Tutuola suggests that although Western ideas and projects might at first seem tempting and attractive, these things ultimately prove little more than a deceptive facade. Once stripped away they reveal the true underlying structures of colonialism: death and enslavement. Through this tale Tutuola hints at the way in which colonial and, subsequently, postcolonial socio-economic systems serve to chain their African victims to money and other seemingly positive trappings while simultaneously trying to remove their ability to voice resistance.

Tutuola's story may be further elucidated by Bakhtin's discussion of the "Catchpole" incident from Rabelais's *Gargantua and Pantagruel.* In this episode a stand-in king rents his body to those who would pay to beat him. Bakhtin notes in *Rabelais and His World* that the theme of a ruler physically renting his body is particularly common in carnivalesque literature (197). Invariably, kings in such stories are unmasked and their true forms are revealed:

> In such a system the king is the clown. . . . The abuse and thrashing are equivalent to a change of costume, to a metamorphosis. Abuse reveals the other, true face of the abused, it tears off his disguise and mask. It is the king's uncrowning.
>
> (197)

The unmasking of the beautiful complete gentleman—his actual physical transformation to a diminished state—serves to undercut the dignity and control of this symbolic colonial ruler. Tutuola's story plays with this particular theme in order to subvert the colonial social hierarchy: the ruler is transformed into a fool and the palm-wine drinker escapes his clutches unscathed, ever the clever and victorious hero.

The effectiveness and legitimacy of employing the fantastic in culturally subversive art and literature has been attested to by various critics. Typically, they argue that

> [i]n cinematic as in novelistic discourse . . . realism operates as a form of fetishism, corresponding to the commodification of the novel and the film. That which seems most opposed to illusion or the fantastic—namely, mimetic representation—is from this perspective all the more illusory and powerful because it masks as truth its fetishized condition.
>
> (Brantlinger 168)

In other words, no matter how apparently damning an attack a realistic novel makes upon the society that has generated it, its very realism cannot help but partly reinforce dominant socio-political substructures. Realism does this by encouraging its readers to accept the conventional perspective it offers as the only appropriate way of decoding reality. In terms of Southern resistance literature, this interpretive habit could have negative repercussions. Primarily, it could encourage colonized and formerly colonized people to interpret their social milieu in terms of their colonizer's language/sign systems—the only *real* way of interpreting it. This practice could have the effect of reducing the likelihood that they will make a psychological break with their subservient role in the (post)colonial power structure.

Therefore, it may be argued that it is *The Palm-Wine Drinkard*'s monstrous anti-realism that makes it such a powerful vehicle for sociopolitical critique. The book's very absurdity is what frees it from the discursive and cultural center and challenges its readers to question the dominance of foreign paradigms. It is this quality that has made the book a classic of colonial literature despite initial criticism by both African and European reviewers. Unquestionably, the book is fantastical, but ultimately its carnivalesque qualities provide a useful and effective kind of "fantasy space" from which to critique the colonial world.

Notes

1. Chinua Achebe notes that not so long ago, many of his African students still showed displeasure that *The Palm-Wine Drinkard* was being given serious consideration as a work of literature. In his essay "Work and Play in Tutuola's *The Palm-Wine Drinkard*," Achebe recalls:

   > A young Nigerian woman doing a higher degree in American said to me when I taught there in the 1970s, 'I hear you teach Tutuola.' It was not a simple statement; her accent was heavy with accusation. We discussed the matter for a while and it became quite clear that she considered *The Palm-Wine Drinkard* to be childish and crude and certainly not the kind of thing a patriotic Nigerian should be exporting to America. Back in Nigeria a few years later I also noticed a certain condescension among my students towards the book and a clear indication that they did not consider it good enough to engage the serious attention of educated adults like themselves.

   (100)

2. I derived the original idea for the narrator-as-canoe segment of my essay from a series of lectures given by Patrick Scott at the University of South Carolina in the fall of 1993. I would like to thank Dr. Scott both for assisting me with this particular work and for helping to deepen my interest in and understanding of African literature in general.

Works Cited

Achebe, Chinua. "Work and Play in Tutuola's *The Palm-Wine Drinkard*." *Hopes and Impediments: Selected Essays*. New York: Doubleday, 1989. 100-12.

Ashcroft, Bill, Gareth Griffiths, and Helen Tiffin. *The Empire Writes Back*. New York: Routledge, 1989.

Bakhtin, Mikhail. "Discourse in the Novel." *The Dialogical Imagination: Four Essays*. 1975. Trans. Caryl Emerson and Michael Holquist. Austin: U of Texas P, 1981. 259-422.

———. *Rabelais and His World*. Trans. Helene Iswolsky. Cambridge: MIT P, 1968.

Brantlinger, Patrick. *Crusoe's Footprints*. New York: Routledge, Chapman and Hall, 1990.

Lindfors, Bernth. "Amos Tutuola." *Twentieth-Century Caribbean and Black African Writers*. Ed. Bernth Lindfors and Reinhard Sanders. Detroit: Gale Research, 1993. Vol. 125 of *Dictionary of Literary Biography*. 332-346. 148 vols. to date.

Gates, Henry Louis. *The Signifying Monkey*. New York: Oxford, 1988.

Tutuola, Amos. *The Palm-Wine Drinkard*. 1952. Westport: Greenwood, 1970.

West, Anthony. "Shadow and Substance." *The New Yorker* 5 Dec. 1953: 222-23.

Chris Dunton (essay date winter 2006)

SOURCE: Dunton, Chris. "Pupils, Witch Doctor, Vengeance: Amos Tutuola as Playwright." *Research in African Literatures* 37, no. 4 (winter 2006): 1-14.

[*In the following essay, Dunton relates the themes found in three of Tutuola's plays to similar thematic explorations in Tutuola's fiction and traces his attempts to improve his skill as a playwright.*]

1.

Between 1952 (*The Palm-Wine Drinkard*) and 1990 (*The Village Witch Doctor and Other Stories*), Amos Tutuola published eleven volumes of fiction and it is on this body of work that his reputation rests. Discussion of any involvement of Tutuola's in work for the stage, or of any aspiration he might have had to try his hand at dramatic literature, has focused largely on the dramatization of *The Palm-Wine Drinkard* staged by Kola Ogunmola in 1963. Yet Tutuola did complete at least three plays, all of which can be found in holograph and/or typescript form in the holdings of the Harry Ransom Humanities Research Center at the University of Texas at Austin. In this [essay] I analyze these three play texts and then focus on two questions, one of which has to do with Tutuola's working methods, the other with his thematic concerns. First, I suggest that throughout his working life Tutuola recycled material from one genre or subgenre to another to an even greater extent than has hitherto been acknowledged. Second, I highlight Tutuola's recurring preoccupation with the plight of individual characters who experience abandonment and marginalization. At this point, I broaden the scope of the discussion, to focus not only on the three plays but also on the novel *Ajaiyi and His Inherited Poverty*, to which all of the plays are closely related.[1]

That Tutuola should at some point have tried his hand at dramatic literature is, in one sense, not surprising, since he spent much of his working life in an environment in which the production of (broadcast) drama was part of the order of the day. From 1956 to 1976, Tutuola worked for the Nigerian Broadcasting Service (later, the Nigerian Broadcasting Corporation), where he was employed initially as Junior Stores Clerk and finally, after a series of promotions, as Senior Storekeeper. During the first year of this 20-year period he was at NBS Lagos, then in 1957 he transferred to Ibadan, which was to prove a major focal point for theater activity in South-West Nigeria during the 1960s and 70s. More or less from the outset of his time with the NBS/NBC Tutuola was working for an institution that concerned itself with radio drama: in 1959, for instance, the service pioneered *Save Journey,* a comedy series in Pidgin that became extremely popular (see Umokoro 124-25). Correspondence in the Tutuola collection of the Harry Ransom Center (HRC) traces Tutuola's advancement at the NBS/NBC, repeated suggestions that he be transferred back to Lagos (suggestions he resisted) and negotiations over his retirement (Folders 6.1-4; 7.4).[2] On the last issue, in an undated letter to Rosemary Goad, a board member at his British publishers, Faber and Faber, he writes: "This is to inform you that I have left the Nigerian Broadcasting Corporation voluntarily on health reason. But I simply mentioned 'health reason' just to say I was fed up to do government work" (Folder 7.4).

In an autobiographical note dated July 14, 1964, and held at the HRC, Tutuola states: "In 1957 I was transferred from Lagos to Ibadan in order to be in close with Prof. Collis of the University of Ibadan. In 1958, Prof. Collis who had interest in my books, taught me how to write The Palm Wine Drinkard in the form of a play" (Folder 10.5). This was not Tutuola's first contact with the University of Ibadan (then University College, Ibadan): correspondence from March 1953 shows that he arranged to meet there Geoffrey Parrinder of the Department of Religious Studies, who was advising Faber on plans to publish the novel *My Life in the Bush of Ghosts* (Folder 6.1). Further, Tutuola was clearly familiar with the possibility of disseminating his work other than through the print medium: from 1954 onwards several of his short stories were broadcast both by the BBC's West Africa Service and by the NBS/NBC (relevant correspondence is in Folder 6.1). Clearly, though, Tutuola's involvement in the stage adaptation of *The Palm-Wine Drinkard* was an important step in his career, although eventually, for him, not a fully satisfactory one. As documentation of the affair is quite extensive, but at points contradictory, with competing claims asserted for the authorship of the adaptation, the following is a summary account.

It appears that Tutuola first met Robert Collis, of the University College Hospital, Ibadan, in Lagos and that Collis suggested Tutuola come to Ibadan to work on a stage adaptation of his novel. The following year Collis introduced Tutuola to Geoffrey Axworthy, a highly in-

novative member of staff in the University College's School of Drama, responsible for such initiatives as the Theatre on Wheels project, and at that point Tutuola began work on his adaptation. Ajayi records that the task took around six months—considerably longer than Tutuola had originally estimated (Ajayi 80). When Tutuola did produce a script, it constituted what Axworthy refers to as "a libretto of Wagnerian proportions, raising technical problems far beyond the means of our university stage" (see Ogunmola ix; in my interpretation of Axworthy's account I am assuming that when commenting that in 1958 "Collis introduced me to Ogunmola, and it was agreed that the author should propose a sketch for a dramatization" (ix), the reference to "Ogunmola" should read "Tutuola"). Substantial editing work was carried out on the playscript, though to what extent Tutuola was involved in this—that is, to what extent Collis and/or Axworthy contributed—is not clear (in a letter of June 27, 1964, to Peter du Sautoy, then Vice Chairman of Faber and Faber, Tutuola claims that he wrote the original adaptation by himself and that "only my English was changed by the School"; see Folder 7.2). All of the major players in the story—Axworthy, Collis, Ogunmola, Tutuola—are now deceased. In his 1960 memoir of his time in Nigeria, Collis records his initial reading of *The Palm-Wine Drinkard* with great enthusiasm and how he arranged for a meeting with its author. After noting that "Amos Tutuola arrived on a bicycle from the Broadcasting Corporation where he holds the humble position of storekeeper" (Collis, *Doctor's* 81) he records his conversation with the author about the novel and his questioning Tutuola as to whether he himself had ever encountered spirits (82-3). There is, however, no reference to the stage adaptation. In a further volume published ten years later Collis does refer to the stage play, but only briefly, noting: "[W]hen I read [Tutuola's] 'Drinkard' I was completely enthralled. I got to know him and in the end I was responsible for getting the 'Drinkard' into dialogue so that it could be produced on the stage as something between a dramatic fantasia and an African ballet" (*Conflict* 16-17). Whatever the case—and what role, if any, was played in the preparation of the adaptation by Axworthy and/or Collis—although a workable script was arrived at, the project was shelved until 1962, when Kola Ogunmola was asked to work on the script; again, the extent to which Ogunmola departed from the text produced by Tutuola/Collis/ Axworthy seems not possible to determine, though in the letter to du Sautoy quoted above, Tutuola credits Ogunmola with doing no more than translating the play into Yoruba.[3]

When the Ogunmola Travelling Theatre revived their production of *The Palm-Wine Drinkard* for a gala performance at the Arts Theatre of the University of Ibadan (date uncertain), on the occasion of the installation of the University Chancellor, and in the presence of the Prime Minister, Sir Abubakar Tafawa Balewa, a lavish program brochure was produced. This includes an extended note by Wole Soyinka, hailing the production as a "bold experiment" and a successful one, "the fruition of a dangerous partnership in dramatic sensibilities," that is, between the academic institution (where Ogunmola had been resident dramatist) and a "people's theatre." While Soyinka's note praises Ogunmola and the play's director, Demas Nwoko, at length, no mention at all is made of Tutuola. Correspondence in the HRC shows that Tutuola came to feel that the (highly successful) adaptation had been hijacked by Ogunmola and that his own role—his ownership of the work—had been brushed aside. In the June 27, 1964, letter to du Sautoy, Tutuola complains that Axworthy and "his assistant," the theater activist Demas Nwoko, have failed to pay him royalties from performances of the *Drinkard* adaptation since its première a year before (he points out that the Ogunmola Theatre Party "has been acting this play in towns and villages since August 1963 both here in Nigeria and in Ghana" and that he has contacted a lawyer to make representation with them on his behalf; see Folder 7.2). Tutuola took the matter up again five years later when, in a memo dated 20th June 1969 (recipient unknown) he objected to plans to stage the play at the Algiers Festival of the Arts: "Mr Tutuola has declared that no permission has been sought for that purpose and anybody staging the play either in Nigeria or anywhere else without his permission as from now does so at his own risk" (Folder 6.2). Protracted and finally unsuccessful negotiations in the 1960s over the possibility of a film adaptation of the novel and the ugly imbroglio surrounding the intended staging of Bode Sowande's adaptation of *My Life in the Bush of Ghosts* in London at the Africa '95 Festival[4] cannot have enhanced Tutuola's optimism regarding the viability of his work on screen and stage. Nor had a response to Tutuola from Mary Treadgold, Talks Producer of the BBC African Service, dated May 15th 1959, been particularly encouraging (Tutuola's letter to Treadgold is not in the HRC holdings, but one can guess at its drift):

> I wish I could say, write us a play, but I can't. You see, we haven't enough really good African actors here to be able to produce such a play, as you would write. We couldn't use English actors for an African play, so I think that for the moment we shall have to stick to prose and poetry.

(Folder 6.1)

Yet there were more positive indicators. The HRC's Faber correspondence contains references to numerous stage adaptations of *The Palm-Wine Drinkard*—in, for example, Finland and Czechoslovakia—and in 1981 the South African writer John Matshikiza produced a dramatization of the short story "Ajantala, the Noxious Ghost" (Folders 7.3-6). In 1982, in correspondence with Anne Walmsley, there are references to discussions between Tutuola and Wole Soyinka on the possibility of a new stage adaptation of *Drinkard* (though Tutuola's letter of October 18th to Walmsley mentions this only as

a tentative possibility; see Folder 6.6). And despite the vicissitudes of Tutuola in his dealings with stage and film professionals and their agents, as the three playscripts in the HRC collection make clear, from 1959 to 1982, at least, he did attempt to write work for the stage.

2.

The earliest of the three plays under discussion is *The Pupils of the Eyes: A Yoruba Folk-Lore Written as a Short Play.* The HRC holds a holograph version of this play and also a typescript (Folders 3.6 and 2.7 respectively). Although the holograph is undated, the HRC correspondence contains a draft letter by Tutuola to the journal *Atlantic Monthly* offering for possible publication five short stories and the play (Folder 6.1); the letter is dated April 30th 1959, a date supported by the position of the holograph in the notebook in which it appears, sandwiched between texts dated 1959 and 1960 (the notebook is one of a series kept by Tutuola, some of them filled only over a period of years, as each new work was entered). Although it is also undated, from internal evidence (corrections and additions to the holograph) the typescript is later; it contains further corrections, written in by hand.[5]

A second play, *Ajaiyi and the Witch Doctor,* appears only in typescript form, dated 22/8/64; there are a few handwritten corrections, in Tutuola's hand (Folder 1.1). In the case of the third play, *The Sword of Vengeance,* the HRC holds the holograph and two typescripts, all of which are dated 16 /10 / 82 (Folders 3.7 and 3.8, respectively). I do not discuss here changes made to the text while Tutuola was in the process of writing the manuscript, changing his mind several times, for example, over the names given to characters. It is possible that the holograph does not represent Tutuola's first thoughts: the material on pages 2-5 is repeated, as if Tutuola were copying from an earlier draft and forgot that he had already covered this ground. *The Sword of Vengeance* is by some way the most substantial of the three plays, the typescripts of which number 18, 22, and 48 pages, respectively, and it is the only one of them, to my knowledge, to have been discussed in print hitherto. (In an interview with Molara Ogundipe-Leslie conducted by Alex Tetteh-Lartey for the BBC in 1983 it is referred to—by Tetteh-Lartey—as Tutuola's first dramatic work apart from the 1963 adaptation of *The Palm-Wine Drinkard.* Ogundipe-Leslie proceeds to give a synopsis of the dramatic action; Tetteh-Lartey 1-2). One of the typescripts bears numerous corrections in a hand other than Tutuola's; these emendations are incorporated in the other, "clean," typescript. In the context of the discussion that follows, Ogundipe-Leslie's record is significant:

> [T]he play is [. . .] not written in the usual format [. . .] for one thing [Tutuola] admits he doesn't know how to write a play. But he's just used his natural tal-

ent and all that. So it's like a combination of a novel and dialogue. So having finished the play he gave it to me. I looked at it and I thought it was very good and I handed it over to a playwright on the campus of the University of Ibadan who was very thrilled by it and who wants to produce it. So plans are on the ground to have it produced at Ibadan.

(Tetteh-Lartey 2)

After the passage of more than 20 years and with the understandable fading of memories, it has not yet been possible to establish the identity of the University of Ibadan dramatist to whom Ogundipe-Leslie passed on the typescript (pers. Comm.., Ogundipe-Leslie to CD, January 10th 2005; Dapo Adelugba to CD, January 22nd 2005). Further, whether that unnamed University of Ibadan playwright was responsible for the emendations on the earlier of the two typescripts I have not been able to determine.

3.

I wish now to give brief accounts of the three plays, focusing on their plots, their thematic preoccupations and on their approach to dramaturgy. The earliest of the three, *The Pupils of the Eyes,* is, by some way, the least assured. An incomplete handwritten note on the back of the cover page reads: "In the olden days there were no pupils in the eyes, but." The plot is thus identified as an etiological one (along the lines of "How the leopard got his spots"). Divided into nine short scenes the dramatic action corresponds to that of a central episode in Tutuola's 1967 novel *Ajaiyi and His Inherited Poverty* (see *Ajaiyi* 137-64: a discussion of Tutuola's recycling of materials is in the following section of this paper); the chief difference between play and novel is that in the earlier work the character Ajaiyi and his friends are absent—in other words, in the play the structure of (perilous) encounter and confrontation is less complex. The central character, Ishola, is instructed by his mother, Adeola, to take a dead rat to market to sell. There, three mysterious characters appear and bring the rat back to life, whereupon it runs away. When he returns home empty-handed, Adeola reveals to her son that she is a witch. The casual abruptness of this announcement is—presumably—unintentionally comic (devastating news is conveyed as if it were domestic trivia); a good example of Tutuola's strengthening of his materials as he recycled them can be seen through a comparison of this moment with its equivalent in the novel, where, given that Ajaiyi knows that Ishola's mother is a witch, while the boy remains ignorant of this, there is an element of dramatic irony. Subsequent scenes deal with Ishola's fear his mother plans to devour him—fears that are exacerbated by her dealings with other members of her coven—and with the revelation that the three strangers from the marketplace are powerful spirits. A drama of intrigue and counterintrigue ends with Ishola's escape from the forces of evil and with the mother seeking refuge in the eyes of the local

blacksmith (becoming—and here is the etiological "stinger"—the pupils in his eyes).

In terms of its dramaturgy, *Pupils* reveals a lack of awareness of the requirements of the dramatic text: that is, of those structural features and the conventions of stage directions that ensure the text provides materials and signals that might readily enable stage production. This is a problem that persists, to a greater or lesser extent, throughout Tutuola's career as an aspirant dramatist. Some scenes in *Pupils* are too brief to have any meaningful impact when staged: they constitute the bare bones of tale-telling (I am begging the question of how these scenes could be fleshed out—brought to life—by an innovative director). Similarly, much of the dialogue provides, in effect, a sketch for the more expansive and vital dialogue of the corresponding episodes in *Ajaiyi*: compare the exchange in which Adeola contrives to comfort her son (*Pupils* typescript 6-7; *Ajaiyi* 145-46)—237 words in the play text fleshed out to 322 words in the novel, the expansion allowing the dialogue to breathe and giving greater impact to characteristic verbal formulae. Yet a comparison of the holograph, the typescript, and revisions to the latter do show Tutuola grappling with the demands of effective dramaturgy. In the holograph version, for example, in scene 8 (when the spirits plot to kill Adeola) over the extent of a whole page Tutuola in effect abandons the format of the dramatic text and provides instead a narrative account of the incident. In the typescript this is corrected. Again, in the typescript the stage direction "Many people are going up and down in the market in buying articles" (*Pupils* typescript 11) appears canceled and replaced with the handwritten emendation "The noises of the people in the market are hearing loudly"—more manageable a direction for stage production. Likewise, with a handwritten addition to the end of scene 6 (typescript 12), which provides what would otherwise be absent, that is, continuity with the following scene.

As with *Pupils,* the dramatic action of the second of the three plays, *Ajaiyi and the Witch Doctor,* corresponds to one of the plot components of Tutuola's novel of 1967, although in this case the composition of the play text and that of the novel were closer chronologically: the typescript of the play is dated 1964 and a letter of Tutuola's to Bernth Lindfors dated 16th May 1968 confirms that the novel was written in 1965 (Folder 6.2). The dramatic action of the play relates to the framing action of the novel: that is, its first five scenes correspond to the opening action of the novel (*Ajaiyi* 11-40) and the closing two scenes to the novel's long-suspended denouement to that action (*Ajaiyi* 223-35). In this respect, a distinction can be drawn between the two plays *Ajaiyi* and *Pupils,* in that while the plot of the former corresponds to the base- or starter-material of *Ajaiyi*—the premise that generates the bulk of the action of the novel and its major thematic concerns (the struggle to achieve competence, to successfully confront evil and to escape from poverty)—in the case of **Pupils** the action corresponds to a single incident in the novel, one of that sequence of episodes that constitute the quest narrative, each of which episodes contributes to a broader understanding of Ajaiyi's protracted ordeal. If **Pupils** works at all it is at the level of marvel and wonder; thematically, it is relatively shallow.

Ajaiyi and the Witch Doctor opens, as does the novel, with Ajaiyi's parents discussing their poverty and its origin with the boy and his sister, Aina, and announcing that their own death is imminent. The dialogue here foregrounds more prominently than its equivalent in the novel the idea that the children are too immature to realize the full implications of their poverty: when they sing "How poor we are!" their naivety is marked through the direction that their voices should be "cheerful and melodious" (**Ajaiyi** typescript 1). The following four scenes correspond closely to the novel, dealing with the death of the parents, with Ajiyi's pawning of his labor, and with the kidnapping of the children, a misfortune that comes about as a result of their misunderstanding of their father's words and their consequent belief the kidnapper is their long-lost brother (a further pointer to their immaturity).[6] The moral object lesson here is to be careful to inquire into the true meaning of everything that is said, however clear its meaning may appear to be: a lesson that exemplifies one of Tutuola's main thematic preoccupations throughout his work, that even apparently secure circumstances may suddenly disintegrate, leaving an individual in extreme hardship or peril.

Ajaiyi and Aina are rescued from the kidnapper by a group of their home villagers (why these have come to the kidnapper's village is unexplained). In the novel the children effect their own rescue: the difference between the two texts here highlights the picaresque structure of the novel and its thematic concern with the testing of the individual, as Ajaiyi's escape initiates a period of wandering and perilous encounters culminating in his return to his village. In the play, with its much more restricted scope, Tutuola brings the children back to the village as quickly as possible, in order to re-engage with the problem of their negotiation of their poverty. This, as in the closing section of the novel, is effected through Ajaiyi's confrontation with the dishonest Witch Doctor whose trickery, it transpires, has been the cause of the family's poverty. As in the novel, this is the point at which Ajaiyi most definitively takes his fate into his own hands, the point at which he appears able to plan—to use deductive reasoning and decisive action—to resolve his crisis (another thematic feature characteristic of Tutuola's work, as I shall discuss below).[7]

As with the earlier play **Pupils,** the text of **Ajaiyi** shows Tutuola still not secure in his handling of conventions such as the viable stage direction. At several points what he offers is far more appropriate to narrative form. Thus: "The dead father is carried by the neighbours to the distance of half a mile" (**Ajaiyi** typescript 5); or the following passage of exegesis: "Ajaiyi does not know that it was not his father who had taken the first two rams but the Witch Doctor" (20). Elsewhere, an extended narrative passage indicates that a conversation is taking place without actually providing the dialogue ("After a few seconds [the father] tells [his children] to kneel down before him and then he is praying for them," 4). Nonetheless, Tutuola persisted in his efforts as a dramatist and in 1982 composed **The Sword of Vengeance,** the most assured of the three extant plays and, unlike its predecessors, a piece that merits stage production. As with the two earlier plays there is here a relationship with the **Ajaiyi** material (which by now had been published in novel form), although here only part of the dramatic action corresponds to this; other material in the play can either be viewed as a kind of excursus from the plot of **Ajaiyi** or does not correspond to this.

The play, which comprises 33 short scenes, begins with a party held by Owolabi and his friends, which is interrupted by the news that Owolabi's father has fainted. The emphasis here is very much on the irresponsibility of the group of young men:

> Gbotaye: (stops and shouts retighting the rope of his trousers as others were still running into the room) Ah! Yee! My trousers fall down from my buttock
>
> (**Sword** typescript 1)[8]

When the father dies, Owolabi, who is incapacitated by drink, drops his cup of wine on the old man's head. Each of the six friends takes his leave—with comic variants on the excuses they make—as soon as they realize the palm wine is finished.

Preparations for the burial are carried out—the wrapping of the body, performance of a funeral dirge, the placing of money in a plate: one of several set-pieces in the play that dramatize traditional observance. After the burial Owolabi rejoices in his inheritance, a sentiment echoed by his friends (as Owolabi is a rich man now, they realize "our palm wine will be increased by one hundred per cent," 4). The thematic motif of crass irresponsibility reaches its apex in the speech of the Cupbearer, who proclaims: "God has buttered my bread today! Look how the palm wine is full up on the floor. Now, I shall drink palm wine to excess today!" (7). Over the following scenes (nos. 3-8) Owolabi's wife gives birth to a son, Esan, and an unscrupulous witchdoctor, Osanyingbemi, contrives to steal Owolabi's inheritance (the emphasis here is on the hypocrisy of Osanyingbemi, who is "flattering Ifa continuously" (8) even as he steals, and on Owolabi's hedonism and lack of critical perception). Osanyingbemi reveals to

Owolabi that his dead father has stolen the money (10)—the first point at which the dramatic action corresponds to (an element in the climactic episode of) *Ajaiyi.* Owolabi swears on his "sword of vengeance" that either his son or his son's son will recover the money (10-11).

The action jumps forward several years, with Esan now a young man, asking his father for money to get married and with Owolabi's mournful response that their poverty is too great to allow for this ("that is the life of a man on earth. It is a pity, Esan, poverty has ruined us," 11). Esan—unlike his father, a model of responsibility—resolves to pawn his labor ("a poor person like me must work hard," 12). Though the pawnbroker is initially unwilling to take him on, he is vouchsafed for by Ajoke, who is now his fiancée ("though he is thin and weak on sight, he is able to work hard," 14). In this episode the emphasis on Esan's good faith, the motif of the helper (Ajoke) bolstering the courage and dedication of the hero, and the testing of the young man by the pawnbroker all correspond closely to the action of the third chapter of *Ajaiyi.* Following this, Tutuola departs from the novel, as the action develops with Esan and Ajoke's wedding (there is some telling parallelism here with the opening party scene of the play), the death of Owolabi, handing over to Esan his sword of vengeance, and—as his poverty worsens—the pawning by Esan of his labor to a second and then a third pawnbroker (again, the testing of his strength by these characters offers some dramatically effective parallelism, as the level of challenge increases).

In scene 19—the funeral of Owolabi—Osanyingbemi reappears, gloating in a melodramatic aside over Esan's ignorance of the whereabouts of his fortune (23). Dramatic irony is developed as Esan places his trust in Osanyingbemi ("as he was my father's close friend," 24). Esan continues to work for the pawnbrokers, leaving himself with insufficient time to work his own farm ("His inherited poverty began to grow from bad to worse"; 24). At this point the plot reverts to that of *Ajaiyi,* with Osanyingbemi convincing Esan to offer up rams placed in sacks on his father's grave, as propitiation required to insure the return of his fortune. The concluding scenes of the play are—assuming a fairly considerable degree of suspension of disbelief—dramatically effective, with a skillful concatenation of multiple pressures, as Esan is hounded by the pawnbrokers, whose demands he has not been able to fulfill, and as he continues to be manipulated by Osanyingbemi (once again, there is some effective dramatic irony here. At one point Osanyingbemi advises Esan "you can go back to your house now, because a young man like you must not keep too long in the dark!" 29). Eventually—though it has to be said, as much through luck as through judgment—Esan discovers how he has been tricked by

Osanyingbemi. Their eventual confrontation is, again, dramatically effective with the cut-and-thrust of variants of threat and attempted self-defense. With Esan's recovery of his fortune the play ends—parallelism, again—with a celebration, but one that is far more authentic than that which opened the play. As Esan forgives Osanyingbemi, as in the novel, the focus finally is on magnanimity and communal healing.

As regards the formatting of a dramatic text, Tutuola makes some advance here on his earlier efforts. While there are still occasional reversions to past tense narration, the holograph shows greater confidence in composing conventional stage directions.[9] In terms of the intrinsic interest of its materials, its skillful development of emblematic characterization (the irresponsible friend; the man of courage, good faith, and initiative; the loyal helper) and of dramatic intrigue and confrontation, *The Sword of Vengeance* is a substantially greater achievement than its predecessors.

4.

I wish finally to discuss those ways in which the three plays cast light on Tutuola's working methods, on his approach to form and on his thematic preoccupations. Bernth Lindfors has commented wittily on the relationship between the individual episodes that comprise Tutuola's works of extended fiction (in this case he is focusing specifically on *The Palm-Wine Drinkard*): "Like boxes of a freight train, they are independent units coupled with a minimum of apparatus and set in a seemingly random and interchangeable order" (*Folklore* 55). Or, putting it another way, the episodes constitute "a concatenation of discrete fictive units strung together on the lifeline of a fabulous hero in an almost random order" (Lindfors, *Early Nigerian* 31). Tutuola himself admitted as much: in a letter dated August 21st 1978 to Elena Borelli, an Italian student preparing a thesis on his work, he commented: "Everyone of my books comprises of many of Yoruba folk-tales which are extended. I cannot call my books Novels"; he goes on to add that the episodes in, for example, *The Palm-Wine Drinkard,* are "loosely strung together" (Folder 6.4).

The recognition that the extended fictional works comprise a sequence of, in Lindfors's words, "discrete fictive units" should caution against too confident an application to them of the term "novel" or, alternatively, too narrow a definition of what that term might cover. It also helps us to understand the ease with which Tutuola felt able to re-process his materials, as short story, extended fiction, play: he held, clearly, a very flexible idea as to the boundaries between genres.

Certainly the extent to which Tutuola recycled material is pretty remarkable. With a publication date of 1967 *Ajaiyi* draws on work written and/or published up to 13 years earlier. Its antecedents include the play *Ajaiyi and the Witch Doctor* and the published short story of the same title (1959: a highly condensed piece—just five pages—that covers what would eventually form two major episodes in the novel), as well as the play *The Pupils of the Eyes* and the story *Don't Pay Bad for Bad* (1960), an earlier version of which, *Dola with her Colanut Tree,* had been broadcast by the BBC's West Africa Service in 1954 (see Folder 6.1). Following the publication of the novel Tutuola drew on its materials for the play *The Sword of Vengeance* and for two pieces in his 1990 collection *The Village Witch Doctor and Other Stories,* namely, the title story and "Remember the Day After Tomorrow."[10] Given that this recycling was not unique to the *Ajaiyi* materials, Tutuola's desk seems to have functioned as a processing and reprocessing plant, with Tutuola first drawing on the Yoruba corpus as a primary source of material, and then reworking his own products as the opportunity arose.[11]

5.

Tutuola's imaginary is a world in which individual endeavor and, indeed, human existence itself are fragile in the extreme, a world in which supernatural forces and human frailty, and wickedness combine to threaten the individual and (in a work such as *Ajaiyi*) to render him or her in a state of constant anxiety. The commanding recognition for such an individual is, to quote one character in Tutuola's collection *Yoruba Folktales*: "'Ah, I am finished today!'" (Tutuola, *Yoruba* 38).

Tutuola was quick to acknowledge his recognition of the fragility of his own career. In a response to a question posed by the journalist Kristine McKenna (November 17th 1980) he refers to the death of his father—an event that brought Tutuola's education to an abrupt halt—as "the biggest and bitter obstacle which I have ever had in my life" (Folder 6.5). That this event was of cardinal—even paradigmatic—importance for him is suggested by the frequency with which the subject of poverty recurs in his work (poverty that can appear perpetual) and by his concern with the irresponsibility and / or powerlessness of parents and with the notion of the "lost" child.

In the novel *Ajaiyi* these concerns appear in a "darker proof" than in the rest of Tutuola's output.[12] This is not surprising, given that the novel was written during the Nigerian political crisis of 1965 (that is, at about the same time as Achebe's *A Man of the People*). As Nancy J. Schmidt observes: "the inclusion [in the novel's purgatory episode] of judges and politicians with liars and murderers is hardly surprising in terms of [the then] recent political events in Nigeria" (24). It is a novel in which the vulnerability of the individual is depicted relentlessly, as its dominant lexical cluster demonstrates: the words "poverty," "poor," "poorest" "poorness" appear no fewer than 169 times. There is an insistent, recurring emphasis on hunger and on hard work that

brings insufficient reward or none at all, so that the individual surrenders his autonomy to those more economically powerful ("we become the recluses of our creditors," *Ajaiyi* 88). Powerfully emphasized, too, right up until the novel's climactic episode, is a sense of confusion and of the sundering of the ability to read the world correctly: in, for example, the episode of the pupils of the eyes, in which three spirits kill their own mother (in a case of mistaken identity). The power of this episode lies not only in the unsettling nature of the explanation for the origin of the eyes' pupils (eyes that were clear before now have pupils that represent the sinister powers of a witch) but also in its narrative structure: as Ajaiyi and his companions seek refuge in a house that turns out to be that of a witch—fleeing from the frying-pan to the fire—as they then encounter threats even fiercer still, unfolding events are organized as a series of concentric circles, conveying a sense of deepening, helpless terror.

Tutuola's heroes find themselves alienated, cast adrift, with the rupture of relationships or of mechanisms of enablement through which a secure and fulfilling life might be sought. In Robert Plant Armstrong's words, the hero "endures by his own free will at least, even though in a world where freedom of will is abrogated, he submits to a moral order that is one of imposed and unpredictable outrage" (29). Remarkably, however—and this is at least as true of *Ajaiyi* as of Tutuola's other work—adversity is confronted and can be overcome. As B. M. Ibikotun has put it: "A reaching out to bring home what is lacking and good becomes imperative. Tutuola's heroes and heroines go out, come back and become forces to be reckoned with in their respective communities. They are never observers but participants and even makers" (30). If the two plays *The Pupils of the Eyes* and *Ajaiyi and the Witch Doctor* are decidedly minor works in Tutuola's output, in *The Sword of Vengeance* he depicts both extreme adversity and principled persistence in overcoming this, in a dramatic structure that is exciting and persuasive.

Notes

1. Research for this paper was supported by a Mellon Foundation scholarship and by a grant from the Research and Conferences Committee of the National University of Lesotho. My thanks are to these two bodies and to the Director of the Harry Ransom Center, Dr. Tom Staley, who with his administrators and library staff helped make my time there as Visiting Fellow so enjoyable. Thanks to Martin Banhma, who provided with a copy of the program brochure for the premiere production of the Ogunmola adaptation of *The Palm-Wine Drinkard*. Thanks also to Bernth Lindfors—that prime mover of so much work in African literary scholarship—who pointed me in the direction of this research.

2. All references to Folders are to the location of papers held in the Tutuola collection of the HRC.

3. Owomoyela (*Tutuola* 107) assertively contests Collins's assumptions about the extent of Tutuola's participation (in relation to that, variously, of Collis, Axworthy, and Ogunmola). For a further take on this controversy, see the comment made by Ulli Beier that "I still find it regrettable [. . .] that Ogunmola was not given a chance to create his own ply out of Tutuola's book, but that he was given someone else's dramatization that turned the realities of Tutuola's supernatural world into the feeble device of a dream" (Beier 114). See also Michael Etherton, who notes that "[The] prosaic attempt at providing some sort of naturalistic credibility reflects a deep-rooted misunderstanding of the bizarre but significant world of the original" (Etherton 49).

4. The Sowande play was withdrawn at the behest of Nigeria's then Minister for Information and Culture, Walter Ofonagoro, one of General Sani Abacha's most reviled henchmen. Ofonagoro's objections to *My Life* perpetuate familiar anxieties about the "primitivism" of Tutuola's work: "anything which promotes the largest African country should not be one that can ridicule it" (see Balogun). Femi Osofisan has commented eloquently on how Tutuola's "international success was [. . .] taken by the dominant Nigerian middle-class as a threat to their own social security" (Osofisan 27). Although both the Africa '95 Committee in London and the British Council supported the staging of *My Life,* after Ofonagoro's intervention it was replaced with Ola Rotimi's (in some respects) politically more acceptable *Ovonramwen Nogbaisi.*

5. Tutuola's handwriting is in a clear, easily readable, vertical cursive. There is a fair degree of variation in the formation of individual letters, depending on whether they are initial, medial, or final, and gradually developing changes in letter formation from the early 1950s to the late 1980s. Nonetheless, the basic features of Tutuola's handwriting remain distinctly recognizable. An important question in discussing Tutuola's development as a dramatist is the authorship of the handwritten emendations to the typescript of the latest of the three plays, "The Sword of Vengeance": though the hand here is not dissimilar to Tutuola's, there is sufficient, consistent variance to indicate it is not his.

6. Ajaiyi and Aina take their father's reference to "The Day after Tomorrow" to be the personal name of their absent elder brother, whereas it is intended to support a maxim along the lines "One will reap what one sows." The kidnapper taunts his victims by pointing out: "[I]t should have been better is you had asked for the meaning of it from your father before he died" ("Ajaiyi" typescript 10-11).

7. The play ends with an extravagant celebration, and with Ajaiyi and Aina singing "How rich we are!" (an inversion of the lament that opens the play: "How poor we are!"). The novel avoids this triumphant conclusion: here, the focus is on Ajaiyi's conscientiousness, on his repaying of debts, and on the consolidation of harmonious relationships in the village (*Ajaiyi* 233-35).

8. All quotations are from the "clean" typescript that incorporates emendations by someone other than Tutuola. Irrespective of the source of these changes, the typescript is approved by Tutuola, closing with his customary "The End / By Amos Tutuola / Copyright" and the date.

9. The anonymous changes made to the typescript are thoroughly professional, as in the opening general stage direction: "A bare stage is best suited for this drama so as to facilitate easy scene changes. [. . .] Noon. Owolabi and his six friends on chairs in the sitting room. [. . .]" (1).

10. The recycling of material did not always work to Tutuola's advantage. "The Village Witch Doctor" has few of the features that give, for example, "The Sword of Vengeance" its vitality, such as the inheritance of the sword, the role of the wife as helper, the use of parallelism to establish different levels of responsibility, and the use of dramatic irony.

11. This recognition is not original: see, for example, Owomoyela (*Tutuola* 128-30) on the relationship between *Ajaiyi* and the short stories. Consideration of the three play texts does, however, further highlight the case. For accounts of Tutuola's use of the Yoruba corpus, see, among others, Lindfors's "Debts" and Quayson. In an interview given in Palermo, Italy, in 1990, Tutuola lists fourteen categories of "materials which I use in my stories": thirteen of these refer to the Yoruba corpus (folktales, proverbs, riddles, legends, curses, and so on), while the remaining one refers to "My own imagination" (Di Maiao 40-50).

12. Very little critical attention has been paid to *Ajaiyi.* The first full-length study of Tutuola's work, by Harold R. Collins, gives only a brief summary account (ix-x—understandably, as the novel had appeared just as Collins was completing his study). Owomoyela pays the work some attention throughout his study *Amos Tutuola Revisited,* but no more than to any of the other novels; *The Palm-Wine Drinkard* is discussed in much greater detail here than are any of the works that followed. The volumes on Lindfors's *Black African Literature in*

English that cover the period 1936-1999 cite only one article devoted to *Ajaiyi* (that by Nancy J. Schmidt); of 49 articles listed that are devoted to specific works, 38 are on *Drinkard*). What critical attention has been paid to *Ajaiyi* is sharply divided as to its position within Tutuola's output. In a 1997 article, Owomoyela asserts that the novel "offers no appreciable departure form Tutuola's format or style" ("Tutuola" 873: a remark that recalls Lindfors's observation that "[Tutuola's] unkindest critics, denying he has written six novels [by 1973], insist that he has merely written one book six times," *Folklore* 61). By the time of his full-length study, published two years later, Owomoyela concedes that the extensive moralization in the novel marks "a spectacular exception" to the earlier work (*Tutuola* 79). Fred Akporobaro's assessment of the novel is similar to Owomoyela's: after noting that in Tutuola's work of the 1960s, "a new tone of strident satire and moralism has begun to emerge," he observes that "in spite of the new moralistic tone of *Ajaiyi* [. . .] the basic modes of hyperbolic and fantastic images, the technique of alogical predication, the exploitation of suspense and the embedding of situations and episodes remain still the characteristic features of his narrative art" (110-11). Perhaps the most perceptive commentary on the novel to date is that by Schmidt. While acknowledging continuities between *Ajaiyi* and the earlier work (in Tutuola's linguistic technique and in his use of fantastic elements, even if these are less extensively elaborated than previously), Schmidt notes the extent to which "Ajaiyi acts in terms of contemporary values" (22) and the unprecedented extent to which Tutuola in this novel "takes a definite stand in reference to some aspects of contemporary Nigerian life, namely, religion, kinship ties and politics" (24). Certainly Tutuola's publisher, Faber and Faber, seemed happy with *Ajaiyi*. Writing to the author on receiving the novel, Alan Pringle commented: "I think [*Ajaiyi*] is a splendid story, both exciting and moving, with so many variations of its theme—one of your best books and perhaps the best since *My Life in the Bush of Ghosts* and *The Palm-Wine Drinkard* (Folder 7.3). Schmidt's acknowledgment that Tutuola shows himself willing to pronounce on aspects of contemporary Nigerian life might appear surprising to those who have read only the earlier novels. In the later fiction that willingness is apparent and it shines through, too, in some of his correspondence. Witness a two-page typescript held in the HRC and headed "Below is my response to your letter of Dec. 30th 1986 (the identity of Tutuola's correspondent unknown) in which he comments on the need to resolve current crises in Africa (his examples show he is well informed)

and on the need to revive the Pan-Africanist project, and in which—at some length—he defends Soyinka, recently awarded the Nobel Prize, against the virulent critique made of his work by Chinweizu. In a fascinating comment on the alleged obscurity of Soyinka's language—fascinating because it reflects implicitly on charges leveled at Tutuola's own use of language—he states: "Though I strongly believe a writer is responsible to the public—(if you can define the Public)—that it should create for the public, the question of method (use of language inclusive) should strictly be left to him (the writer). For that makes the difference in writing" (Folder 6.7).

Works Cited

Ajayi, Jare. *Amos Tutuola: Factotum as a Pioneer.* Ibadan: Creative Books, 2003.

Akporobaro, Fred. "Narrative Form and Style in the Novels of Amos Tutuola." *Studies in the African Novel.* Ed. S. O. Asein and A. O. Ashaolu. Ibadan: Ibadan UP, 1986.

Armstrong, Robert Plant. "The Narrative and Intensive Continuity: *The Palm-Wine Drinkard.*" *Research in African Literatures* 1:1 (1970): 9-34.

Balogun, Sola. Report on Africa '95 Controversy. *Third Eye* (June 9, 1970).

Beier, Ulli. *The Hunter Thinks the Monkey is Not Wise.* Bayreuth: U of Bayreuth, 2001.

Collins, Harold R. *Amos Tutuola.* New York: Twayne, 1969.

Collis, Robert. *A Doctor's Nigeria.* London: Secker and Warburg, 1960.

———. *Nigeria in Conflict.* Lagos: John West Publications, 1970.

Di Maio, Alessandra. *Tutuola at the University.* Rome: Bulzoni, 2000.

Etherton, Michael. *The Development of African Drama.* London: Hutchinson, 1982.

Ibitokun, B. M. "Amos Tutuola." *Perspectives on Nigerian Literature: Volume Two.* Ed. Yemi Ogunbiyi. Lagos: Guardian Books, 1988: 28-30.

Lindfors, Bernth. *Folklore in Nigerian Literature.* New York: Africana Publishing, 1973.

———. "Amos Tutuola's Earliest Long Narrative." *Early Nigerian Literature.* New York: Africana Publishing, 1982.

———. "Amos Tutuola: Debts and Assets." *Critical Perspectives on Amos Tutuola.* Ed. Bernth Lindfors. London: Heinemann, 1980. 224-55.

Ogunmola, Kola. *The Palmwine Drinkard.* Ibadan: Institute of African Studies, U of Ibadan, 1972.

Osofisan, Femi. *The Nostalgic Drum: Essays on Literature, Drama and Culture.* Trenton and Asmara: Africa World P, 2001.

Owomoyela, Oyekan. "Amos Tutuola." *African Writers: Volume Two.* Ed. C. Brian Cox. New York: Scribner, 1997. 865-78.

———. *Amos Tutuola Revisited.* New York: Twayne, 1999.

Quayson, Ato. *Strategic Transformations in Nigerian Writing.* Bloomington: Indiana UP, 1997.

Schmidt, Nancy J. "Tutuola Joins the Mainstream of Nigerian Novelists." *Africa Today* 15 (1968): 22-24.

Tetteh-Lartey, Alex. Interview with Molara Ogundipe-Leslie. BBC *Arts and Africa* transcript 517G. 1983.

Tutuola, Amos. "Ajaiyi and the Witchdoctor" (short story). *Atlantic* 203 (1959): 78-80. Rpt. *Black Orpheus* 19 (1966): 10-14.

———. "Don't Pay Bad for Bad." *Présence Africaine* 30 (1960): 78-81. Rpt. *Reflections: Nigerian Prose and Verse.* Ed. Frances Ademola. Lagos: African Universities P, 1962. 33-6.

———. *Ajaiyi and His Inherited Poverty.* London: Faber and Faber, 1967.

———. *Yoruba Folktales.* Ibadan: Ibadan UP, 1986.

———. *The Village Witch Doctor and Other Stories.* London: Faber and Faber, 1990.

Umukoro, Matthew M. "Radio Drama in the Nigerian Theatrical Scene: Promise and Performance." *Theatre and Politics in Nigeria.* Ed. Jide Malomo and Saint Gbilekaa. Ibadan: Caltop, 1993. 123-37.

FURTHER READING

Asagba, O. A. "The Folktale Structure in Amos Tutuola's *The Palm-Wine Drinkard*." *Lore and Language,* 4, no. 1 (January 1985): 31-9.
> Identifies the folklore elements present in Tutuola's novel and defends Tutuola's work against accusations that the author plagiarized the work of D. O. Fagunwa, who, like Tutuola, drew from Yoruba folklore traditions in his writing.

Breitinger, Eckhard. "Images of Illness and Cultural Values in the Writings of Amos Tutuola." In *Health and Development in Africa: International, Interdisciplinary Symposium 2-4 June 1982, University of Bayreuth,* edited by Peter Oberender, Hans Jochen Diesfeld, and Wolfgang Gitter, pp. 64-72. Frankfurt: Verlag Peter Lang, 1983.
> Explores the ways in which African cultural ideas about illness are represented and reflected in Tutuola's writings.

Owomoyela, Oyekan. *Amos Tutuola Revisited.* New York: Twayne Publishers, 1999, 174 p.
> Study of Tutuola's writings, focusing on themes, inspiration, the author's exploration of and responses to colonialism, and the critical response to Tutuola's work.

Additional coverage of Tutuola's life and career is contained in the following sources published by Gale: *African Writers*; *Black Literature Criticism,* Ed. 1:3; *Black Writers,* Eds. 2, 3; *Concise Dictionary of World Literary Biography,* Vol. 3; *Contemporary Authors,* Vols. 9-12R; *Contemporary Authors—Obituary,* Vol. 159; *Contemporary Authors New Revision Series,* Vols. 27, 66; *Contemporary Literary Criticism,* Vols. 5, 14, 29; *Contemporary Novelists,* Eds. 1, 2, 3, 4, 5, 6; *Dictionary of Literary Biography,* Vol. 125; *DISCovering Authors 3.0*; *DISCovering Authors Modules,* Ed. MULT; *Encyclopedia of World Literature in the 20th Century,* Ed. 3; *Feminist Writers*; *Literature of Developing Nations for Students*; *Literature Resource Center*; *Major 20th-Century Writers,* Eds. 1, 2; *Major 21st-Century Writers* (eBook), Ed. 2005; *Reference Guide to Short Fiction,* Ed. 2; and *World Literature and Its Times,* Ed. 2.

Derek Walcott
1930-

AP Images

(Full name Derek Alton Walcott) St. Lucian poet, essayist, playwright, critic, and journalist.

For additional information on Walcott's career, see *Black Literature Criticism*, Ed. 1.

INTRODUCTION

A Nobel laureate and preeminent West Indian literary figure, Walcott is included among the leading contemporary English-language writers of poetry and drama. Born of mixed European and African heritage, Walcott uses literature to explore themes of ethnicity, cultural prejudice, and political inequality. Moreover, critics note that he examines these subjects in a manner that leads to psychological and moral insights pertinent not only to the clash between Western and Caribbean cul-

ture, but to the universal human condition. Having learned English as a second language, and acutely aware of its status as the language of colonial power, Walcott has assimilated the bulk of the Western literary canon—from Greek epics to modernism—skillfully employing its techniques and traditions in his works, while never losing sight of his Caribbean identity. Reviewers celebrate Walcott's poetry for its dazzling use of sophisticated poetic forms, heartfelt self-examination, and evocative descriptions of Caribbean life.

BIOGRAPHICAL INFORMATION

Walcott was born in 1930 in Castries, the capital city of the small Caribbean island of St. Lucia, a former British colony in the Lesser Antilles. Walcott and his twin brother, Roderick, were raised by their mother, Alix, a schoolteacher; their father, a civil servant and amateur artist and writer, died a year after their birth. Walcott's mother instilled a love of literature in her sons and encouraged their involvement in a local theater group. Walcott displayed an early talent for poetry and had work published by the time he was fourteen. Four years later, he self-published his first book, *25 Poems* (1948), and sold it on the streets of Castries. At the age of twenty, he wrote and staged *Henri Christophe* (1950), a play based on the life of the Haitian leader, and cofounded with his brother the Santa Lucia Arts Guild. The guild gave Walcott a means of producing and directing his own plays, such as *Robin and Andrea* (1950), *Three Assassins* (1951), and *The Price of Mercy* (1951). In 1953 he earned a bachelor's degree in English, French, and Latin at the University College of the West Indies in Mona, Jamaica, which he attended on a British government scholarship. In 1954 Walcott staged *The Sea at Dauphin,* one of his most acclaimed early works, and began teaching in West Indian schools. Over the next four years, he wrote several plays, including *The Charlatan* (1954), *The Wine of the Country* (1956), and *The Golden Lions* (1956). Walcott temporarily suspended his teaching career in 1958 when he accepted a Rockefeller fellowship to study drama in New York City. His next two plays, *Ti-Jean and His Brothers* (1957) and *Drums and Colours* (1958), focus on episodes from Caribbean myth and history.

In 1959 Walcott moved to Trinidad, where he started the Little Carib Theatre Workshop, which later became the Trinidad Theatre Workshop. For several years, he trained amateur actors and wrote poetry, as well as features and criticism for several Trinidadian newspapers. After writing and staging *Malcauchon* (1959), Walcott shifted his focus to poetry. He published four volumes of poems in 1962, including *In a Green Night,* which attracted overwhelmingly positive reviews throughout the English-speaking world. In 1967, a year after being named a fellow in the Royal Society of Literature, Walcott staged *Dream on Monkey Mountain* in the United States. The play won an Obie award in 1971 and became Walcott's first acknowledged masterpiece. After the success of *Another Life* in 1973, Walcott accepted a commission from the Royal Shakespeare Academy to rewrite the 1634 classic *El burlador de Sevilla,* by Spanish playwright Tirso de Molina, which resulted in the play *The Joker of Seville* (1974). In 1976 Walcott ended his tenure at the Trinidad Theatre Workshop, citing both professional and personal reasons. He received a Guggenheim fellowship in 1977, and in 1979 was named an honorary member of the American Academy of Arts and Letters. In the early 1980s, Walcott served as a visiting professor at several universities in the United States, including Columbia, Harvard, and Boston University, where he continued to teach through the 1990s. He began to divide his time between residences in the Caribbean and the United States, a practice that influenced his poetry collection *The Fortunate Traveller* (1981), which received the Heinemann Award from the Royal Society of Literature in 1983. In 1992 Walcott received the Nobel Prize for literature.

MAJOR WORKS

The central theme of Walcott's oeuvre is the dichotomy of the black and white races, the subject and ruler, and the Caribbean and the Western civilizations. His writing deals with the lasting scars—personal, cultural, and political—of British colonialism in his native land and the opposing African and European influences that characterize his West Indian heritage. Integrating the formal structure of English verse with the colorful dialect of St. Lucia, Walcott denounces colonial exploitation and suppression of Caribbean culture, while attempting to reconcile the disparate cultural legacies that inform his works and Caribbean history in general. Walcott's first major collection of poetry, *In a Green Night,* contains several early poems, such as "A City's Death by Fire" and "Epitaph for the Young," that reveal the considerable influence of Dylan Thomas and James Joyce, respectively. The volume also features Walcott's first mature poems, such as "Ruins of a Great House," in which he examined the decline of colonialism, and "A Far Cry from Africa," in which he explored his own mixed racial heritage. *The Gulf and Other Poems* (1969) is a stylistically diverse collection that is thematically unified by repeated examinations of separation and loss, featuring the autobiographical poem "Hic Jacet," in which Walcott contrasted his fascination with European poetry with his Caribbean roots. The book-length work

Another Life, (1973) is autobiographical. The poem's first three sections detail Walcott's youth, adolescence, and first love, while the last section portrays his painful effort to come to terms with not only his own past but the whole of Caribbean history.

The bulk of Walcott's poetic output is found in the five volumes he published between 1976 and 1987: *Sea Grapes* (1976), *The Star-Apple Kingdom* (1979), *The Fortunate Traveller, Midsummer* (1984), and *The Arkansas Testament* (1987). The first two collections contain lyrical poems largely centered on the Caribbean—particularly its history and culture—though *Sea Grapes* also includes several poems set in other locales. Walcott divided *The Fortunate Traveller* between poems inspired by his experiences in the United States and in the Caribbean. Though the dichotomy of settings is clear, the poems in both sections are an eclectic mix of barbed social criticism and personal confession. *Midsummer* is a lyrical and introspective collection; in many of the fifty-four poems, Walcott used his own life as a lens through which to view the intertwining of European and Caribbean cultures. *The Arkansas Testament* again emphasizes the theme of contrasting, yet related, cultures by organizing the poetry into two sections—"Here" and "Elsewhere." *Omeros* (1989), like *Another Life,* is a single book-length poem. In this work—whose title is the Greek word for "Homer"—Walcott paid homage to the ancient poet in an epic poem that substitutes the Antilles for the Homeric Cyclades. Two of the main characters, the West Indian fisherman Achille and Philoctete, set out on a journey to the land of their ancestors on the West African coast. The characters are concerned not with the events of the Trojan War, but rather with an array of civilizations, from African antiquity to frontier America and present-day Boston and London. *The Bounty* (1997) is a meditation on the passing of the author's mother. *Tiepolo's Hound* (2000) is another book-length poem, illustrated with the author's paintings, in which he examined the theme of exile while comparing his own life to that of Impressionist painter Camille Pissarro. In *The Prodigal* (2004), Walcott celebrated his return to St. Lucia after years of wandering. The book-length poem also reflects on the death of his twin brother, Roderick, in 2000.

Like his poetry, Walcott's plays are stylistically varied, but are united by themes of cross-cultural interaction. For instance, in *Dream on Monkey Mountain,* Walcott used highly stylized staging and characterization to evoke a dream world in which an escaped prisoner becomes the leader of an ill-fated religious movement. Many of Walcott's plays, often called folk-dramas, are firmly rooted in the common life and language of the West Indies and frequently incorporate Caribbean dialects and legends. They are also noteworthy for their advanced dramatic techniques, lyrical language, and the psychological depth of their characters. In *The Joker of Seville,* Walcott employed the refined wit and relaxed pacing of the seventeenth-century classic *El burlador de Sevilla* to examine the Dionysian aspects of social revolution. *O Babylon!* (1976) is primarily a musical—many of Walcott's plays include instrumental accompaniment—set in Jamaica in 1966, during the weeks surrounding Emperor Haile Selassie's visit to the island. In *Remembrance* (1977), Walcott focused on a single character, Albert Jordan, a teacher in colonial Trinidad, and used his story to examine the role of individual integrity and conviction in changing societies. In *Pantomime* (1978), which features only two actors, Walcott offered a revision of Daniel Defoe's *Robinson Crusoe,* presented through the eyes of a hotel manager and his assistant. *Beef, No Chicken* (1982) is a tragicomedy about a small town facing the encroachment of a six-lane highway. Walcott worked on a much broader canvas—both dramatically and thematically—in *A Branch of the Blue Nile* (1986). The play opens with a group of West Indian actors rehearsing a scene from William Shakespeare's *Antony and Cleopatra,* which Walcott used as a framework on which to hang several interior monologues concerning the relationship between life and fiction, religion, and a host of other topics. Walcott took on an even larger project in his next play, *The Odyssey* (1993), a stage version of the classic Greek epic poem. His production stays meticulously true to the original poem, but with small comic and socially relevant touches, such as Greek servants who speak in Caribbean dialect. Walcott has also collaborated with singer-songwriter Paul Simon to produce the unsuccessful Broadway musical *The Capeman* (1997). In addition to his poetry and plays, Walcott has also published a significant volume of essays with *What the Twilight Says* (1998). This collection brings together a number of Walcott's definitive statements on his aesthetic principles and historical perspective—which are found in his 1992 Nobel lecture, *Antilles* (1993)—as well as critical pieces on a variety of authors.

CRITICAL RECEPTION

Walcott has been widely praised as a virtuoso poet and a deeply committed postcolonial artist whose explorations of racial, cultural, and historical consciousness in the contemporary Caribbean are considered moving, erudite, and technically masterful. While Walcott's dramatic works have been highly regarded, his reputation rests more solidly on his poetry, which is generally considered to have reached a level of excellence that exceeds that of his plays. Among his volumes of poetry, *In a Green Night, Another Life,* and *Omeros* have been particularly acclaimed as his most important and successful works. However, Walcott's poetry and drama have not gone without marked criticism. One of the major complaints leveled against Walcott's poetry has been that his language is too refined. Critics have agreed that he is a highly accomplished wordsmith, but some feel that Walcott's wordplay can obscure his intended

meaning, making his verse appear to be a mere exercise in technique. Criticism of this type has appeared fairly consistently throughout Walcott's career. Similar claims of intellectual excess have been aimed at his plays. Criticism of his dramatic works has focused not only on his use of language, but also on his practice of weighing his plays down with expository passages. While this technique has allowed him to explore socially relevant topics, that comes at the expense of plot and character development, a number of reviewers have argued. Reviewers have also sometimes judged his plays as incoherent, tedious, and glib. Walcott has also garnered criticism for his tendency to use European forms to express Caribbean concerns; he is considered too Caribbean by some Eurocentric critics, and too European by some Afrocentric critics. Indeed, Walcott's deft use of complex rhyme and meter has been decried by some commentators as a coy affectation and by others as an act of "selling out." While this type of criticism has abated as Walcott's reputation has grown, his continued insistence on the interdependence of colonials and the colonized has remained a somewhat controversial position.

PRINCIPAL WORKS

25 Poems (poetry) 1948
Epitaph for the Young: XII Cantos (poetry) 1949
Cry for a Leader (play) 1950
Henri Christophe: A Chronicle in Seven Scenes (play) 1950
Robin and Andrea (play) 1950
Senza Alcum Sospetto [also produced as *Paolo and Francesca*] (radio play) 1950
Poems (poetry) 1951
The Price of Mercy (play) 1951
Three Assassins (play) 1951
Harry Dernier: A Play for Radio Production (radio play) 1952
The Charlatan (play) 1954
Crossroads (play) 1954
The Sea at Dauphin: A Play in One Act (play) 1954
The Golden Lions (play) 1956
The Wine of the Country (play) 1956
Ione: A Play with Music (play) 1957
Ti-Jean and His Brothers (play) 1957
Drums and Colours: An Epic Drama (play) 1958
Jourmard; or, A Comedy till the Last Minute (play) 1959
Malcauchon; or, The Six in the Rain (play) 1959
In a Green Night: Poems, 1948-1960 (poetry) 1962
Selected Poems (poetry) 1964
Batai (play) 1965
The Castaway and Other Poems (poetry) 1965
Dream on Monkey Mountain (play) 1967

Franklin: A Tale of the Islands (play) 1969

The Gulf and Other Poems (poetry) 1969

*Dream on Monkey Mountain and Other Plays (plays and essay) 1970

In a Fine Castle (play) 1970

Another Life (poetry) 1973

The Joker of Seville [with music by Galt MacDermot] (play) 1974

O Babylon! [with music by Galt MacDermot] (play) 1976

Sea Grapes (poetry) 1976

Selected Verse (poetry) 1976

Remembrance (play) 1977

Pantomime (play) 1978

Marie Laveau [with music by Galt MacDermot] (play) 1979

The Star-Apple Kingdom (poetry) 1979

The Fortunate Traveller (poetry) 1981

Beef, No Chicken (play) 1982

The Isle Is Full of Noises (play) 1982

The Caribbean Poetry of Derek Walcott and the Art of Romare Bearden (poetry) 1983

The Haitian Earth (play) 1984

Midsummer (poetry) 1984

A Branch of the Blue Nile (play) 1986

Collected Poems, 1948-1984 (poetry) 1986

†Three Plays (plays) 1986

The Arkansas Testament (poetry) 1987

Omeros (poetry) 1989

Steel [with music by Galt MacDermot] (play) 1991

Poems, 1965-1980 (poetry) 1992

‡Antilles: Fragments of Epic Memory: The Nobel Lecture (lecture) 1993

Derek Walcott: Selected Poems (poetry) 1993

§The Odyssey: A Stage Version (play) 1993

The Bounty (poetry) 1997

The Capeman: A Musical [with Paul Simon] (play) 1997

What the Twilight Says: Essays (essays) 1998

Tiepolo's Hound (poetry) 2000

‖The Haitian Trilogy (plays) 2001

Walker and Ghost Dance (plays) 2002

The Prodigal (poetry) 2004

Selected Poems (poetry) 2007

*Includes *Dream on Monkey Mountain, The Sea at Dauphin, Malcauchon, Ti-Jean and His Brothers,* and the essay "What the Twilight Says: An Overture."

†Includes *The Last Carnival; Beef, No Chicken;* and *A Branch of the Blue Nile.*

‡*Antilles* was originally delivered on December 7, 1992.

§This work is based on Homer's *The Odyssey.*

‖Includes *Henri Christophe, Drums and Colours,* and *The Haitian Earth.*

CRITICISM

Edward Baugh (essay date winter 2005)

SOURCE: Baugh, Edward. "Of Men and Heroes: Walcott and the Haitian Revolution." *Callaloo* 28, no. 1 (winter 2005): 45-54.

[*In the following essay, Baugh examines Walcott's dramatic portrayal of the Haitian revolution in three of his major plays:* Henri Christophe, Drums and Colours, *and* The Haitian Earth.]

The Haitian Revolution has exercised the Caribbean literary imagination to significant effect. It has spawned major works by some of the region's most distinguished writers. Outside of Haiti itself, there is the Cuban Alejo Carpentier's *El reino de este mundo* (1949), and, from the French Caribbean, two plays: Edouard Glissant's *Monsieur Toussaint* (1961) and Aimé Césaire's *La Tragédie du roi Christophe* (1970). Walcott has returned to the subject again and again, over a period of nearly forty years. His ***Henri Christophe: A Chronicle in Seven Scenes*** (1950), first produced in 1949, was his first substantial play. The Revolution provided one of the four major segments of his historical pageant ***Drums and Colours*** (1961), first produced in 1958. His major work on the Revolution, ***The Haitian Earth,*** was first produced in 1984. These works reward comparison, which, in a limited way, is the project of this paper. They constitute a fertile microcosm in which to explore Caribbean imagination, its continuities and variations. We must also put alongside these fictive works C. L. R. James's famous historical account, *Black Jacobins.* What is more, his little-known play of the same title was first produced even earlier, in 1936.

Walcott's ***The Haitian Trilogy*** conveniently collects all three of his dramatic engagements with the Revolution: ***Henri Christophe, Drums and Colours*** and ***The Haitian Earth.*** To compare his treatment of the Revolution in the three is to enhance understanding of his evolution as a dramatist, a Caribbean dramatist, both in content or world view and in style, as well as to enhance understanding of the hold of the Haitian Revolution on Caribbean imagination. The development reflects his foundational contribution to a Caribbean theater rooted in the experience of the common people, drawing on their arts of performance, including their language, and in the context of the colonial experience of the region. A central motive in this endeavor was to address the apparent or supposed absence or dearth of home-grown heroes.

In chapter 12 of ***Another Life,*** Walcott recalls how, still a teenager, he was fired by the dream and difficulty of making a new world of art in his island(s). It was to be an art made out of native materials, like the "plain wood" (*Collected Poems* 216) with which the carpenter, Dominic, worked, giving off "the smell of our own speech" (*Collected Poems* 217), and taking the Caribbean artist beyond a hankering after "the marble [of] Greece" (**"Ruins of a Great House," Collected Poems** 19) and all that it stood for, the hankering after "heroic palaces / netted in sea-green vines" (**"Royal Palms"** 16). The train of thought in chapter 12 of *Another Life* reaches a crucial point when the poet exclaims:

> Christ, to shake off the cerecloths,
> to stride from the magnetic sphere of legends.
> To change the marble sweat which pebbled
> the wave-blow of stone brows
> for the sweat-drop on the cedar plank,
> for a future without heroes,
> to make out of these foresters and fishermen
> heraldic men!

(*Collected Poems* 217)

The "gigantic myth" and "the stone brows" of Classical sculpture connote the heroics that attach to the "great tradition" of Classical art and literature.

It was in his plays that Walcott was most directly and definitively to take the "stride," a shaping movement in his effort to make a Caribbean drama. "To make of these foresters and fishermen / heraldic men," instead of "heroes," is "a succinct statement of what [Walcott] aimed to do in plays like *The Sea at Dauphin, Malcochon, Ti-Jean and His Brothers* and *Dream on Monkey Mountain*" (Baugh 43).[1] The stride may be traced in the movement from *Henri Christophe* and *Drums and Colours* to the four plays in *Dream on Monkey Mountain and Other Plays* (1970), as well as *The Haitian Earth,* even if the movement is not neatly chronological. Further, whatever meaning Walcott may be understanding from the term *heraldic man* will retain perhaps more than a trace of "hero." In other words, in resorting to the former term, Walcott retains some of the connotations of the latter, while eschewing others. Also, in *heraldic man* the word *man* in the sense of general, ordinary man, is no doubt almost as crucial as *heraldic,* as an aspect of the distinction between *heraldic man* and *hero.*

The passage quoted from *Another Life* is a rewrite of a passage from the unpublished manuscript of "Another Life," part prose, part verse, from which the published poem evolved. On October 17, 1965, Walcott wrote:

> The powerful truth is that no shadows haunt us now. We have moved away from the magnetic sphere of legends, giant stone statues and gesturing myths. We have a past without heroes. We can look back on servitude as natural and human without any desire for revenge.[2]

Whereas in chapter 12 of *Another Life* Walcott records how he had been haunted by the gigantic shadows of European art and literature, by 1965 he could say confidently that he had laid those ghosts. This does not mean that he had simply rejected them, but that he could now live easily with them, in a productive working relationship that might still involve a creative tension.

The quotation from the manuscript **"Another Life"** also helps to suggest how Walcott's desire to replace "heroes" with "heraldic men" connects with his quarrel with history. If heroes are towering men, larger than life, then the idea of history he counters is that of history as the deeds and impact of heroes. By contrast, heraldic men would be simple, ordinary persons ("foresters and fishermen"), close to the earth, the elements, who, by their experience and integrity, become icons representative of the generality, the common people, just as figures in heraldry, as on coats of arms, are symbolic, representative of a group, in some cases a nation. The heraldic figure calls attention not to itself but to what it stands for. As regards the genre of drama, the traditional hero connotes grandeur, size, expansiveness, grandiloquence, and in tragedy the will to power and the Aristotelian *hubris.*

Also pertinent here is Walcott's "confession" in his 1970 essay **"Meanings,"** an essay that explains his ambition as a West Indian dramatist as it had evolved up to *Dream on Monkey Mountain*:

> I am a kind of split writer. I have one tradition inside me going one way, and another tradition going another. The mimetic, the Narrative and dance element is strong on one side, and the literary, the classical tradition is strong on the other. In *Dream on Monkey Mountain* I tried to fuse them, but I am still after a kind of play that is essential and spare the same way woodcuts are clean, that dances are clean, and that Japanese cinema is so compressed that gesture does the same thing as speech.

(Hamner 48)

We may read in this statement rough equations between the heroic, the literary, the classical, and the grandiloquent on the one hand, and the heraldic, the indigenous, and the essential on the other. The dualism acknowledged in this passage is cognate with that between Walcott's yearning for a plain style in his poetry, and his instinct for metaphorical richness and elaboration. Whereas in this passage the expansive style is identified with the literary, and the spare style with gesture and physical presence, the polarities are also played out within the field of oral expression. Walcott's plays as a whole move between these two styles, or seek to make them work together. He never altogether eschews the literary and classical. One must also note that volubility and rhetoric as such are not alien to Caribbean oral tradition, where they have a different "color" from that which they have in the English literary and oratorical traditions, sometimes acting as parodic subversions of them.

Henri Christophe and *Drums and Colours* both invest (the latter in a pointedly qualified way) in the idea of the hero, the hero as great man. *Christophe* chronicles the Haitian Revolution from after the death of Toussaint L'Ouverture to the death of Christophe. The account centers on the two dominant men of that period: first on Dessalines, and then, after he has been assassinated at the behest of Christophe, on Christophe. As the title suggests, it is very much Christophe's play. The focus on the outstanding individual, the heroic hero, so to speak, is set in the epigraph to Part 1, a quotation from Shakespeare's *Hamlet* (act 3, scene 3):

> The cease of majesty
> Dies not alone but like a gulf doth draw
> What's near it with it; it is a massy wheel
> Fix'd on the summit of the highest mount,
> To whose huge spokes ten thousand lesser things
> Are mortis'd and adjoined, which, when it falls,
> Each small annexment, petty consequence,
> Attends the boist'rous ruin.

We are on familiar Aristotelian-Shakespearean ground, where the time-honored action is the ascendancy and fall of the great individual, the tragic hero, who towers above ordinary men, and whose fall, by reason of his greatness, brings the whole world crashing down with him.

The young Walcott, in his reaching after a theater that would speak to and for the West Indies, was excited to see in Christophe a Caribbean hero in the Classical-Elizabethan mould: "Full of precocious rage, I was drawn . . . to the Manichean conflicts of Haiti's history. The parallels were there in my own island, but not the heroes. . . ." (*Dream on* 11). He speaks of "their tragic bulk . . . massive as a citadel at twilight." "Their anguish was tragic . . . ;" "such heroes . . . had size, mania, the fire of great heretics" (*Dream on* 13). Nothing would have seemed amiss if Walcott had called this play a tragedy rather than a chronicle.

"Those first heroes of the Haitian Revolution," he writes, "to me, their tragedy lay in their blackness" (*Dream on* 12). He emphasizes that this is the central theme of *Henri Christophe,* and the play does advert to the race theme often enough, and it is imaged in the relationship between the black revolutionary leaders and the white Archbishop Brelle, who has a major part in the play. However, by and large, the race/color issue is treated as a given and invoked conveniently to explain motivation. It begins to take on a life of its own, a prickly vibrancy, only in the final confrontation between Brelle and Christophe.

The engine of the play's action is rather the sheer will to greatness of the "heroes," and, as a consequence, the passion of each, Dessalines and Christophe, to be absolute ruler, and the machinations they practice to attain their ends. Christophe boasts, "I am proud, I have worked and grown / This country to its stature. . . ." (*Trilogy* 91); "I shall build chateaux" (*Trilogy* 74); "I will be a king, a king flows in me" (*Trilogy* 68). We are told that Christophe is a more complex person than

Dessalines, that he has a conscience, and he professes, however fleetingly, a concern for the country. However, the energy of the portraiture is focused on, for example, his obsession with being made king, rather than president, and on his overweening desire to build monuments to his greatness, his Citadel and chateau. In this play, history is a mighty force, a great impersonal personality, a kind of metahero, with whom one can be on even terms if one is of like stature. For Christophe, history is his peer, his towering twin. His hubris is partly in his idea of his relationship to history: "I will make history, richer than all kings" (*Trilogy* 62); "It is I, who, history, gave them this vice to shout anarchy / Against the King" (*Trilogy* 101). The ambiguity afforded by the placing of the word *history* in this sentence underscores the nature of the presumed relationship. *History* may be read as either vocative (Christophe is addressing history) or in apposition to *I* (Christophe is history).

The fascination with heroes will also mean a fascination with the grand style, in language, verse form, and movement. As Walcott admitted, his "first poems and plays expressed [a] yearning to be adopted, as the bastard longs for his father's household. I saw myself legitimately prolonging the mighty line of Marlowe, of Milton. . . ." (*Dream on* 31). The appeal to Walcott of the heroes of the Haitian Revolution also lay in the fact that they afforded him a Caribbean story that would lend itself to the mighty line. The grand style of *Christophe* satisfies this project, but with a difference. Although it will recall the blank verse of Marlowe and Shakespeare and Milton, it is not blank verse, but free verse, with a recurring suggestion of iambic pentameter within a general dissolution of the iambic beat, and often a line that is longer than pentameter. The language, for all its grandeur, is appropriately modern, the heightening due partly to Walcott's characteristic metaphorical energy, which owes something to Shakespeare.

The play resonates with echoes of Shakespeare and Marlowe, whether in language or situation. For instance, Vastey's fatal and evil trapping of Brelle and infecting of Christophe's mind with the notion of Brelle's treachery through the business of the planted letters recalls Iago's manipulation of Othello and Desdemona. The speech in which Christophe expatiates on the lofty, wind-swept location of his Citadel (*Trilogy* 73) recalls the speech in *King Lear* in which Edgar evokes for the blind Gloucester the dangerously magnetic view from the cliff overlooking the beach. The Messenger's speech reporting the assassination of Dessalines is infused with the bloody excesses of Tamburlaine. Creole, a mild form, and in prose, is used only in the scene with the murderers in ambush preparing to kill Dessalines, and that is just as Shakespeare would have done, dialect prose for "low" characters. Again, the Africanness of Dessalines and Christophe, over and above the mere fact that they are blacks, is hardly considered, and that only ironically, when Christophe, dying, is attended by a witch doctor. Even so, Christophe has no faith in gods of any kind, whether Christ or Damballa, but he asks that the witch doctor "try again . . . / The old herbs, the antique magic . . ." (*Trilogy* 97).

Whereas *Christophe* begins with the news of Toussaint's death in exile, the Haitian segment of *Drums* ends with Dessalines and Christophe conspiring to betray Toussaint to Leclerc, the commander of the French forces. By shifting the focus from Dessalines and Christophe to Toussaint, Walcott goes beyond a youthful zest for the histrionic display of overweening egotistical ambition to consider a more complex, more humane, more reflective, and reasoning kind of leader. By using the Haitian Revolution as one of the four segments of his pageant-play, which was written and produced to mark the inauguration of the short-lived Federation of the West Indies, Walcott enhances the suggestion, incipient in *Christophe,* of the relevance of the Haitian experience to the idea and possibility of nationhood in the Caribbean.

Spanning the history of the West Indies since the arrival of Christopher Columbus, *Drums* was another ready-made vehicle to accommodate "heroes." It tells the story of "four heroes" (*Trilogy* 123): Columbus, Sir Walter Raleigh, Toussaint, and George William Gordon, each representing a different period in the history. The first two stand for imperialism and colonialism, the last two for resistance and revolt. But there is comparatively little heroics in *Drums.* For instance, in the Columbus segment, such heroics as emerge are no more than a nimbus of nostalgia exhaled by Columbus, now no longer "Admiral of ocean, and a tamer of tides" (*Trilogy* 145).

Although Toussaint is identified in the prologue as one of the play's four heroes, once again classical grand heroic is eschewed in what is shown. He is presented as a good man who had the courage to do what necessity and his conscience demanded, and who, in doing so, proved himself a great leader. His compassion and evenhandedness are made much of. We first see him overcome by dismay on discovering the body of Anton, mulatto son of Calixte-Breda, on whose estate he, Toussaint, had been a coachman-slave. Outstanding in warcraft, Toussaint is nonetheless the man of peace, concerned not with his own power, but with the well-being of the people after the revolution. Against Dessalines' vengeful bloodlust, he counsels: "Revenge is nothing. / Peace, the restoration of the burnt estates, the ultimate / Rebuilding of these towns war has destroyed, peace is harder" (*Trilogy* 241).

The first scene of the Haitian segment shows us the privileged whites, the slave-owning class. They behave in such a way as unwittingly to evoke our sympathy for the revolutionary cause of the blacks even before we meet them, by showing what they (the blacks) are up against. The issue of race and color thus becomes, more immediately than in *Christophe,* part of the dynamic of the action.

The setting is the mansion of Leclerc, the French General who has been sent by Napoleon to put down the rebellion. Present are Leclerc, General de Rouvray, whom he is replacing, Madame de Rouvray, Armand Calixte-Breda, the planter on whose estate Toussaint is slave and coachman, and Anton, Calixte-Breda's illegitimate son, whom he passes off as his nephew. Leclerc's wife, Pauline, Napoleon's sister, will join the group later. Liveried black slaves, voiceless and as if invisible, stand in the background and wait on the whites. The latter's casual dehumanizing of the blacks is nicely introduced. Calixte-Breda dismisses Anton's caution that he should "never underrate the authority of the people" with "Slaves are not people, they are intelligent animals" (218). Leclerc sneers amusedly at "Generals who were slaves. . . . / You know, Napoleon calls them 'gilded Africans'" (218); and Pauline intends to be witty and sophisticated when, having just been touring the slave compounds, she asks to be excused if she "reek[s] a little of the *parfum d'Afrique*" (221).

In this group, Anton, neither quite insider nor outsider, functions as a voice that can speak for the oppressed blacks. He has just returned from Paris, full of the spirit and ideals of the French Revolution. This idealism is in turn given a dimension of passionate, embattled personal interest, being an early manifestation of that mulatto angst which was to become a Walcott topos. When Anton tells Pauline that his mother was one of Calixte-Breda's house slaves, and that "He [Calixte-Breda] recognized her in darkness, in that republic / And that act in which complexions do not matter" (227), we hear the germ-sound of the idea that will develop, years later, into Shabine's brilliant formulation which begins, "I met History once, but he ain't recognise me. . . ." (*Collected Poems* 350). The recurrence of recognize deepens the resonance of the double meaning in each instance.

Anton functions as a link between the presentation of the whites and the presentation of the blacks, biologically (by virtue of his mixed blood) and in terms of plot, and metaphor. Empathizing with the slaves, he describes for Pauline the horrible acts of cruelty that are done to them in public spectacle. At the same time, foreshadowing Makak's bewitchment by the white moon-woman, he is smitten by Pauline, "White and lovely as the moon, and equally remote . . ." (229). Angry, bitter, confused, Anton exits, insisting on returning alone to the Calixte-Breda estate. The next, brief scene shows him walking through the cane fields, drunk. He is set upon by a group of rebellious slaves, and murdered for having the blood of his father in him.

The representation of the spirit of violent, bloody revolt in this scene is developed at the beginning of the next scene, with a ritualistic celebration of revolt, led by

Boukmann, who breaks the Christian cross as he invokes "serpent Damballa" (234) and exhorts his followers, "Kill everything white in Haiti today!" (235). Anticipation of Makak in his African dream scene! Boukmann and his followers then exit, leaving Anton's corpse. Toussaint, at this time still Calixte-Breda's coachman, enters and sees the corpse. He is overcome with anguish and the consciousness of his dilemma ("This poor boy hated nothing, nothing" [255]), but he also knows now that things have changed irrevocably and that his life must take on a new responsibility. Here, established in one quick stroke, is the dilemma of humanity that will distinguish Toussaint.

The next scene takes place some time later, when the revolutionary forces of Toussaint, Christophe and Dessalines are gaining ascendancy, with Toussaint *primus inter pares*. When the scene opens, Dessalines is looking down on Les Cayes, as that city is being sacked by Toussaint's troops. Dessalines gloats over the carnage, and at the fact that Toussaint has "scattered the forces of the mulatto Rigaud" (227). Christophe joins Dessalines, and later Toussaint. The very fact that we see them tired from battle, rain soaked and splattered with mud and gore, removes from them the ceremonial gloss they wore in *Christophe.* Although Christophe is not so elated as Dessalines by the bloodbath, and can say that "Revenge is tiring" (241), he is ready to begin plotting with Dessalines to betray Toussaint, whom Dessalines describes as "most power drunk" and having "monarchic aims" (240). This description fits Dessalines himself, and also Christophe, but does not accord with the Toussaint whom we hear in this scene—responsible and level headed, a man of action, but also a man of conscience and compassion.

The scene builds to a climax when soldiers bring before Toussaint his former master, Calixte-Breda, whom they have found "hiding in the ruins" (243). This confrontation opens up a volatile range of emotions, deep historical wounds, and prejudice. It is a confrontation that will recur and be artistically refashioned in subsequent Walcott works, notably *Pantomime.* Dessalines, impatient of the long, private audience that Toussaint is allowing to this enemy, seizes his pistol to shoot Calixte-Breda. Toussaint takes the pistol from him, as if to take responsibility for killing Calixte-Breda himself. But he cannot bring himself to do it. When, on his command, in which he takes no pleasure, a sergeant takes Calixte-Breda outside to shoot him, Toussaint is weeping. To Dessalines, this is only a sign of weakness, and encourages him to resume his effort to persuade Christophe that they should deliver Toussaint into the hands of Leclerc.

So the emphasis shifts from overweening personal ambition and boastful display of iron will. Toussaint's stature is measured by the width and depth of his humanity. In this regard, the fact of his weeping, his painful

understanding of the necessity demanded by "the times" (249), is to his credit. In *Ti-Jean and His Brothers* (written at much the same time as *Drums*), when, at the climax, Ti-Jean seems about to defeat the Devil, the latter pulls one of his devilish tricks and shows Ti-Jean a vision of his mother dying. Ti-Jean weakens, but the animals encourage him to stand firm, to sing in praise of life: "Sing, Ti-Jean, sing! / Show him you could win! / Show him what a man is!" (*Dream on* 162). Ti-Jean sings a song of thanksgiving to God, and as he sings he weeps. By his tears, as much as by his courage in adversity, he shows "what a man is." To the extent that he embodies the fullness and complexity of "what a man is," Toussaint proves himself a hero.

The de-emphasizing of heroics in *Drums* is enhanced by the Caribbean tone that Walcott gives to the play by framing it in a popular Caribbean performance mode. The prologue is given over to a Carnival band, led by Mano (a popular Trinidadian male nickname, but also a name suggesting "man," quintessential and unadorned man), and including Pompey, a calypsonian, who, by virtue of his name, is a kind of parody of the Classical heroic tradition. The band sets about to ambush, playfully, a road march coming down the street, and to change the theme of the march to "War and Rebellion" (119). The idea is of conscious role playing: the episodes from history, from the stories of heroes, are to be reenacted by the common people of the Carnival. The performance strategy implies the appropriation of the grand historical narrative by the grassroots tradition. The Carnival figures return at the end to bring the play to a close. Curiously though, they hardly engage in any direct winding up of the preceding action and, indeed, make hardly any reference to it. The Carnival group virtually takes over the play for the last two scenes and the epilogue. The play ends in a style quite different from that in which the four heroes were represented. Pompey is an anti-hero, but when he "dies," Mano's prayer over the body refers to him as "one significant fragment of this earth, no hero / But Pompey . . . Corporal Pompey, the hotheaded shoemaker. / But Pompey was as good as any hero that pass in history" (187).

The foregrounding of the common people is complete in *The Haitian Earth.* This play is Walcott's most comprehensive theatrical account of the Revolution, and the primary point of view is that of the people. The chronicle begins even earlier than it had begun in *Drums,* showing some of the events leading up to the Revolution. These include the torture and execution of Ogé and Chavannes, the mulattos who had dared to seek "rights for the mulattos" (309) from the French Assembly, and scenes showing the different local milieux out of which the three warrior-heroes of the Revolution—Dessalines, Christophe, and Toussaint—emerged, and the bursting of the seed of revolution in them. Anton's role changes somewhat in this account. He joins Rigaud's mulatto army to fight the blacks, thereby representing the fact that the blacks were up against the mulattos as well as the whites. Documentary material also becomes part of the action. Leclerc reads to the captured Toussaint a letter of instructions from Napoleon. Later, an aide reads to Napoleon a letter sent to him by the imprisoned Toussaint.

Various features of the composition of the play indicate a cinematic intention. The many brief scenes, some of which convey information by purely visual means, the quick cuts, time and space leaps, montage effects, stage directions that are really camera directions—these are all appropriate to a fluid representation of the varied, wide-ranging sweep of action. Space does not allow here for appreciation of how there is also a change in the style of the language to help convey the more stripped-down, earthy, unadorned quality of this play in comparison to *Drums* and even more so to *Christophe.* The point would be conveniently illustrated by comparing the two versions of the one scene from *Drums* that is repeated in *Earth,* the scene in which General Toussaint confronts his former owner, Calixte-Breda. We may also note in passing that the African factor in the blacks is more evident in *Earth* than it was in *Drums,* and that this is not unrelated to the relative prominence of the folk factor in *Earth,* as in the chorus of peasant women and the singing by which they express themselves.

The Haitian Earth is perhaps even less about the fortunes of the great men than it is about the common people, who do not appear as individual persons in the historical record. Pompey and Yette, fictional characters, are carried over (at least the names) from *Drums* and are now the true protagonists, perhaps even more so than Toussaint. Yette is now a mulatress of low social station, and Pompey a slave driver on the Calixte-Breda estate. The story of the vicissitudes of their romantic relationship, which represents the idea of harmony between blacks and mulattos, is interwoven with the chronicle of the historical figures, whose actions impact severely on the lives of the ordinary folk. The three "heroes" of the Revolution—Dessalines, Christophe, and Toussaint—still have their major roles, but they are now even more flesh and blood, more humanized than before, generally to their discredit in the case of Dessalines and Christophe, because what is represented, even more sharply than earlier, is their human weaknesses and maleficence, and to his credit in the case of Toussaint. The other two are granted their moments of grand self-assertion and heroism, as in Christophe's eloquent, lyrical recollection of Dessalines in battle at D'Ennery: "Across the ridges, the soldiers saw your body / Half-welded to its horse, like a black centaur" (423). But Walcott's presentation confirms the view that the first and greatest tragedy of the Revolution was the betrayal, banishment, and death of Toussaint, and his heroic stature is here configured in the extent to which he is a man with whom we can identify, and to which he meets his responsibilities as a man, especially those which require him to make hard, painful, even seemingly cruel decisions, in the interests of the discipline of his forces and the best interests, not of himself, but of Haiti.

The tragedy is not of the individual great man, but of Haiti itself, "the Haitian earth." Dessalines boasts, "I am the beginning, / And I am the end. Haiti is me" (426). The play persuades us of the common people's prior claim, whispered by Pompey to Yette in a moment when the future seems bleak: "But you and I, we is Haiti, Yette" (386). Christophe's final exit now is not that of the grand death speech, to a crescendo of drums, which concludes *Christophe,* but of his pathetic request to be helped into bed. In a final act of egotistic ill will, he had just ordered the execution of Yette, who had sought to place a curse on him for corrupting the Revolution. Right after Christophe's order, the play ends on a countervailing note, with Pompey, simple but strong, burying Yette's body and pronouncing his uplifting benediction on her.

Pompey's final entrance, carrying Yette's body, is to a single, stark drumbeat. The general paring down of things, of the reaching after heroics and grandiloquence, is reflected in the relatively down-to-earth style of the play. Against Christophe's dying boast to Pompey— "When men like you / Are tired, they will look up into the clouds / And see it [his Citadel], and take strength; the clouds themselves / Will have to look up to see it" (430)—Pompey replies:

> It had one talk then, I remember, under the old coachman [Toussaint], and that talk was not who was king but who would make each man a man, each man a king himself; but all that change. We see them turn and climb and burn and fall down like stars that tired, and cut my hand, my head, my tongue out if you want, Your Majesty, but my life is one long night. My country and your kingdom, Majesty. One long, long night. Is kings who do that.
>
> (431)

In that statement, which affirms Pompey's manhood, is the gravamen of the play and the culmination of the graph of its action. "My life is one long night"— Pompey speaks for Haiti. He articulates the bleak wisdom toward which Walcott's long artistic engagement with the Haitian Revolution has worked. This wisdom already existed in Vastey's epigrammatic reflection in *Christophe,* "We were a tragedy of success" (103), but now it is fully earned.

It is also a mark of Walcott's widened vision that *The Haitian Earth* ends holding up to our commendation, not a man, not Toussaint or Pompey, but a woman. The final speech is Pompey's tribute to Yette as he digs her grave: "You will be a country woman with a basket / Walking down a red road in the high mountains" (454). As Makak lives in the dream of his people, as Ti-Jean is the man in the moon. An icon. Heraldic woman.

Notes

1. This idea became a center-piece of Patrick Anthony's Ph.D. thesis "Symbol, Myth, and Ritual in Selected Plays of Derek Walcott."

2. The manuscript is housed in the West Indies Collection of the Library, University of the West Indies, Mona, Jamaica.

Works Cited

Anthony, Patrick. "Symbol, Myth, and Ritual in Selected Plays of Derek Walcott." Diss. University of the West Indies, St. Augustine, Trinidad and Tobago, 2000.

Baugh, Edward. *Derek Walcott: Memory as Vision: "Another Life."* London: Longman, 1978.

Carpentier, Alejo. *El reino de este mundo.* 1949.

Césaire, Aimé. *La Tragédie du roi Christophe.* 1970.

Glissant, Edouard. *Monsieur Toussaint.* 1961.

Hamner, Robert. Ed. *Critical Perspectives on Derek Walcott.* Boulder & London: Lynne Rienner, 1997.

James. C. L. R. *Black Jacobins.* 1938.

Shakespeare, William. *Hamlet.*

Walcott, Derek. "Another Life." *Collected Poems 1948-1984.* New York: Farrar, Straus & Giroux, 1986.

———. *Collected Poems 1948-1984.* New York: Farrar, Straus & Giroux, 1986.

———. *Dream on Monkey Mountain and Other Plays.* New York: Farrar, Straus & Giroux, 1970.

———. *Drums and Colours.* 1961.

———. *The Haitian Earth.*

———. *The Haitian Trilogy.* New York: Farrar, Straus & Giroux, 2002.

———. *Henri Christophe: A Chronicle in Seven Scenes.* 1950.

———. "The Royal Palms." *Negro Verse.* Ed. Anselm Hollo. London: Vista Books, 1964.

Fred D'Aguiar (essay date winter 2005)

SOURCE: D'Aguiar, Fred. "'In God We Troust': Derek Walcott and God." *Callaloo* 28, no. 1 (winter 2005): 216-23.

[*In the essay below, D'Aguiar investigates the role of religion in Walcott's verse.*]

"Do you believe in God?" I remember the interviewer in the company of another poet and me, asking Derek Walcott in the summer of 1986 at a BBC 2 Arena Caribbean Nights recording on the culture and arts of the Caribbean.[1] Derek Walcott paused for a moment and replied, "Only if God gets me another poem." Laughter erupted and with it a nod of recognition toward the contract with productivity every poet is sworn to at almost Mephistolian cost; laughter and a comic end to a serious subject. The idea of a poet selling a loved one for the price of a poem is not new. What is new or sounds like a new spin on an old thread is Derek Walcott's idea that the poem itself, namely poetics and poetry as a process, may contain God, indemnify spirituality, and enshrine faith in the middle of an absence of any obvious belief system, by investing in a formal procedure called the composed poem. If this is the case then the evidence should reside in the body of work. Nuggets of wisdom to do with a religious subject should be extractable from the work where the work functions as a surrogate cathedral for a missing conventional God worshipped in a conventional way.

As early as 1948 in **"A City's Death by Fire"** a poem preserved in his ***Collected Poems,*** Derek Walcott expresses a reverence for the trappings of the church that borders on religious conversion.

A City's Death by Fire

After that hot gospeller had leveled all but the
   churched sky,
I wrote the tale by tallow of a city's death by fire;
Under a candle's eye, that smoked in tears, I
Wanted to tell, in more than wax, of faiths that were
   snapped like wire.
All day I walked abroad among the rubbled tales,
Shocked at each wall that stood on the street like a
   liar;
Loud was the bird-rocked sky, and all the clouds were
   bales
Torn open by looting, and white, in spite of the fire.
By the smoking sea, where Christ walked, I asked,
   why
Should a man wax tears, when his wooden world fails?
In town, leaves were paper, but the hills were a flock
   of faiths;
To a boy who walked all day, each leaf was a green
   breath
Rebuilding a love I thought was dead as nails,
Blessing the death and the baptism by fire.

                    (***Collected Poems*** 6)

A religious vocabulary deployed at landscape, presented here as a cathedral, provides the poem's momentum. The poet ministers through song in a priestly way but without sermonizing. Philosophical enquiry works as gospel, rather than any declaration of faith or conventional belief. The presiding spirit is more Dylan Thomas than Christ. As a result, the benediction (a favorite word in the poet's lexicon) privileges art more than the life the art dramatizes God is present in what people do, in their patterns of behavior but God is absent in the behavior of the poet: there isn't a God as a given entity or assumed presence in the poet's procedure of writing the poem, although the language of God provides a vocabulary for the poet. This steers the reader toward the poetry as art and artifice, especially in the poem's metaphorical transformation of the ravaged city. The material reality of the city while reduced to ashes by the fire gives rise to the Phoenix of spiritual awakening. What the art achieves in the early poem is a sort of spiritual elation, and a peace in lieu of understanding but without the religious conversion of being saved, more like a drowning for the poet. The poem as a procedure carries with it a religiosity of a kind easily mistaken for faith in a conventional God. But it is more akin to the poet's identification with a literary tradition with Christianity as one of its cornerstones than any alignment with faith. A desecrated landscape becomes a shared terrain between this Christian frame and the formal devices of the poem engaged in a joint effort that utilizes the trappings of Christian iconography to shake off its influence. The poem's success is gauged by the tone of the address. A poem's tone is a property of the poet buried in the poet's architecture. Tone is tantamount to a point of view and an opinion held by the poet[2] and not necessary for the poem's success but which forms part of the poem's overall impact on the reader. Tone, as it stands in this early poem, expresses a need for a deeper meaning in existence beyond the physical and material facts of life. If progress could be measured in this lyric moment, outside of narrative time in its instantaneous marshalling of impulses, then it would move from a religious starting point and head toward the secular, not in a straight narrative line, but in its circuitous tonal progression (rather like this sentence!), its sense of shaking off religious influence for some quality to do with the formal rewards of the sonnet. The sonnet rebuilds the city destroyed by fire with a poetic structure that owes much of its form to an infusion of spiritual thought. Here Walcott functions as spiritual architect. His tone includes an expression of grief over the destruction of the city. The poem's double procedure is that it grieves for the perished city, while, simultaneously, it builds an alternate and imperishable edifice in the substitute form of a sonnet. This formal device shadows a religious experience and can easily be mistaken for one.

Both poem and religion promise knowledge beyond the known world. The religious promise is life after death. For the poem the buried meanings resonate far beyond the surface meanings of the words. Both arts (if I may so address religious belief) invest in a faith in the process: for religion it is worship, for poetry it is poetic practice. Doubt appears to govern both processes. A central tenet of religion—faith—circles the idea of doubt where doubt stars as the brink of faith before faith reasserts itself and casts off doubt. In the crucifixion, even if treated minimally as a parable, there is Christ in his supreme sacrifice on the cross wondering if God has forsaken him. In poetry doubt is necessary for poetic production. The poet doubts she or he is any good until the next poem and then doubts the worth of the thing and then writes another poem just to be sure, just because there is nothing else to be done and out of a compulsion for utterance and in service to the process

infected with doubt but resplendent in its routine of faithful repetition and life-affirming practice.

Landscape replaces the church and becomes for Derek Walcott a character, not a holy spirit, but flesh invested with spirituality, and that is how it earns his devotion. History relays story for the poet and as such history (with a degree of myth thrown into the mix) replaces the religious fable. Not a bad start for a young poet on an intuitive quest of understanding of his art and craft.

Derek Walcott's Methodist upbringing in St. Lucia placed him in a religious minority in a Catholic majority nation.[3] His Catholic schooling and veneration of his Irish Jesuit schoolmasters imbued him with an intuitive logic governed by religious praxis. But so did his use of English in a French Creole nation and his mixed-race background in a black majority country. Doubles typify his life and his search for a distance from each of them as he took what he could use from all of them. The experience made distancing into an art form for Derek Walcott at an early age. This formative experience planted a dichotomy in outlook that would constitute a challenge for the poet, namely, how to break out of a predictable binary dynamic way of thinking into more fruitful imaginative terrain.

In addition to his poetry Derek Walcott paints and tries to address painting as another expression of this spiritual quest. What seems to be behind both painting and poetry is a sensory frame at least as a starting off point, largely invested in narrative but not wholly so, which then spirals out into thoughts suggested by images and phrases as a method of moving from one line to another. This formal rigor resembles the trials of the Stations of the Cross, but only in its requirement of formalized difficulty as a necessary impediment before transcendence.

This formal rigor makes 1987 seem like a long way from 1948, but not really, if a reader subscribes to the notion of the poet as born not made ("born big so" as the Creole parlance would have it). Not just a struggle with craft but a struggle with place traps the poet in the poem, **"The Light of the World."** Strategically placed two thirds of the way into the "Here," first section of *The Arkansas Testament,* both a struggle with notions of craft and a wrestle with the idea of belonging to a place preoccupy the poet. The poem is a bus journey with the ordinary folk and the isolated poet ruminating on his place among them and what his art can offer them. Bob Marley, an artist like the poet, but one who has made it among the populous, frames the contemplative act by the poet. Marley is accepted among them, so why not the poet, the poem appears to ask the reader and the answer is an odd give and take of rejection and quiet acceptance, studied distance and guarded familiarity. The poet's desire for a woman provides an engine of sorts for the poet in his body. Art, in other words, if it is worth anything believes in the sensory as a gateway to the spiritual. In similar terms the woman the poet admires in the poem for her ordinary ripe flesh condition (as the ready-to-eat fruit analogy would have it) becomes transformed by that process of seeing, that particular metaphorical and transmogrifying lens, into a goddess. The poet sings her a hymn of his lust and in exchange her humble standing, plain but young, elevates to heraldic status. This transformative aspect of Derek Walcott's poetry with lust or desire as a springboard, Marley's "got to have kaya now" (an epigraph for the poem), serves as sex subordinated, desire deferred to the higher calling of poetry, and takes the poet into the realm of a process of thought and conjecture that easily trumps desire and grows to be an act of sublimated desire. The title of the poem[4] confers onto the people a humble gift—the transmutation of biography into art—that transforms their lives and opens a contemplative space that their busy routines appear not to make an allowance for. This twofold artistic benefit—a chronicling art and a transformative one—is bequeathed by the poet to the community that made him, or at least nurtured him, but one he is now distanced from to the point of silence and a near-voyeur's distance at that. It should be said that the poet is moved to tears by his yearning and his isolation, his love of the people and his loss of familial contact with them.

There is a cost to the poet for his artistic privilege and practice of artistic license. Life appears to be busily unfolding around him and he is seconded to it as a chronicler of events to do with it and as its philosopher. While he extracts pithy insights extrapolated from the situation of his body plunged into the environment, he remains mentally apart from it. The transport turns out to be wholly the poet's, his elevation of his surroundings from the quotidian to the heraldic plane. There is a concomitant teleportation of sorts involved whereby the ordinary and mundane give rise to the poetic and regal. That lust is transformed to desire and then metamorphosed once again into love results in a triple-layered unfolding of the poet's consciousness.

Another concern of the poem is framed by a woman vendor who wishes to board the bus and asks the driver in St. Lucian patois "*Pas quittez moi à terre.*" Walcott, in an almost DJ-inspired riff of verbal twists and turns by association of sound and meaning, runs with this for a few lines (in an artistic alignment of his prodigious gifts with Marley's):

> "which is, in her patios: "Don't leave me stranded,"
> which is, in her history and that of her people:
> "Don't leave me on earth," or, by a shift of stress:
> "Don't leave me the earth" [for an inheritance];
> "Pas quittez moi à terre, Heavenly transport,
> Don't leave me on earth, I've had enough of it."
> The bus filled in the dark with heavy shadows
> that would not be left on earth; no, that would be left

> on the earth, and would have to make out.
> Abandonment was something they had grown used
> to."

("Arkansas Testament," 49-50)

His lines hanker toward alexandrines but fall into a loose, because conversational, iambic hiatus typical of blank verse in general but idiosyncratic to Derek Walcott in particular in his mix of Standard English and French patwa[5] (with some English Creole) registers. That last line is at least double edged: a religious abandonment coupled to that of politics, nothing new about that twin configuration, but with a second betrayal on the part of the poet who is clearly concerned with the ways his calling as a poet leaves these people behind (those ordinary folk who are not passengers on his form of transport, so to speak) even as he seeks to sustain his vital creative links with them. Ironically, this is a success for the poet. He succeeds in devoting a poem about sex and desire to the ordinary subject, the common folk, who represent a yearning in him for acceptance among them. Their oblivious sense of getting on with life contrasts with his immobility in the face of overwhelming sensation. They occupy the poem just when the poem feels least in communion with them, as if to testify against his fears by invading his art. A potential religious frame is blown away for its profane alternative, not the Holy Spirit but common flesh takes care of this light, not the scripture of an all-powerful consciousness but the poetry generated by humble and vulnerable and culpable flesh and blood.

The senior Walcott resembles the young poetic novice and the middle-aged seer in terms of this toying with a Christian tradition in an effort to reach beyond it to poetry's secular, formal, and gravityless space. That space resides in the formal range of Derek Walcott's poems rather than as a statement of intent. God is not jettisoned so much as seen to have a built-in obsolescence as far as the craft of the art is concerned. At some point in the poem, once it progresses away from its originating impulses (say, in *Tiepolo's Hound,* which has many starts and stops into the Caribbean and Parisian life of Pissarro but then quickly settles into a contemplation about the rewards of artistic endeavor[6]). The delight resides in the local surprises to do with Derek Walcott's demonstration of a formal dexterity in and of itself rather than its being pressed into the service of any creed. He reconciles two art forms, painting and poetry. He examines his lifelong and double devotion as painter and poet to the two art forms as an artistic figure made in the Caribbean but mired in a Western Christian literary tradition by latching onto a precursor from the nineteenth century, the painter Pissarro.

The Bounty is not God but the manifestations of life on earth and the art of poetry, which seeks to articulate the character of that bounty, what Derek Walcott calls "the awe in the ordinary" (*The Bounty,* p.7 iii).[7] Derek Walcott as bounty hunter uses the bounty of his art and craft to understand nature's bounty. From one bounty, poetry, to another bounty, nature, Walcott devises the procedure that it takes a bounty to know a bounty. This declaration aligns him with the romantic tradition that saw reasons for religious belief in the obvious evidence of nature, or at least a redress between humanity's belief in its own superiority over nature and nature's self-evident magnificence.[8] But rather than the romance of Wordsworth to guide him, Walcott opts for a riskier spiritual precursor, in the person of John Clare. Mad John Clare throws into relief Walcott's own measured grief-ridden tones. Where Clare is mad, Walcott is sad. Walcott mourns his dead mother, "the rose of my life" (*The Bounty* 15), as though nature's reclamation of her body imbued all of nature with the love once associated with her body while she lived. But loss itself takes center stage rather than the character of his mother, which says more about the disparity between Clare and Walcott as Walcott positions himself in the poetic tradition than about a requiem for his mother; or put another way, both qualities, grief and loss, belong to the poem but in unequal measures that favor the mood of grief over the loss of the mother.

John Clare cuts a pitiful figure in the world of poetry not least because he died relatively young, incredibly poor, and in relative obscurity. The cost of a poetic consciousness out of sync with nature or driven mad by nature's bounty when it should have been in league with that largesse, qualifies Walcott's engagement with nature. Walcott's poetic consciousness is at least historical, whereas Clare's was most palpably not. Walcott understands Clare's sacrifice for the greater calling of art as too much of a cost to pay or cross to bear, and he qualifies his engagement as grief not rage, a mourning elegiac stance rather than any combative outlook. Nature is not out to defeat the poet, but must be a resource. Clare's recognition of a peace in death, after the fact of a life dedicated to poetry and the study of nature "the grass below—above the vaulted sky"[9] comes far too late for Walcott and it is swapped by Walcott for a communion between nature and the art of poetry. Whereas Clare went mad in his quest, Derek Walcott calls for repose in nature, a version, if ever there was one, of that line from Clare. But God is nowhere to be found, though, as in the earliest of Derek Walcott's poetry, the poetics is replete with the vocabulary of the church and therefore coterminous with a spiritual quest. Spirituality is supplied not by worship in a church but by poetic practice devoted to the study of nature. This places Walcott firmly in a romantic tradition with the obvious proviso of his historical consciousness as a necessary qualification of his engagement with Europe.

In God We Troust, the name and motto on the new boat or craft of Achille in *Omeros,* says much about the quality of this historical consciousness as it rubs up against notions of religious belief. The transfigured Greek hero in his commonplace Caribbean island backdrop is part of this elegy to the ordinary or the ordinary as imbued with the heroic. Myth is in cahoots with history—Greek myth meets an African and New World history. The misspelling, which Achille insists on keeping in obedience to his twin language loyalties (to French and English, patios and Creole), subverts the passive noun, trust, from the vessel in which the faithful place their faith to the much more troublesome verb equivalent and suggests a sort of quest or enquiry, or the continuous action of "throstle," and implies some as yet to be resolved relationship and search in the coalition between the divine spirit and human culpability. As Achille says to the priest who smiles at the name when he blesses the fishing boat, "Leave it! Is God's spelling and mine" (p 8).

The altered terms of engagement of high religion when embraced by the commoner equals the misspelling and required adjustment religion makes to survive as faith in a new setting. A similar adjustment is made to the spiritual quest retooled by the poetry kit: for God read poem.

I do not wish to argue that Derek Walcott is bigger than God but more to mean that poetry creates a secular space that replaces God. Poetry as a lifelong devotion takes the place of worship, and, at the expense of religion, poetry becomes the vessel for spiritual quest and fulfillment. More to the point, the formal devices of a poem carry with it inherent spiritual rewards, a deep confirmation of the sensuous life, and metaphorical contemplation as an end rather than a means. Reading Derek Walcott's lush rendition of this conjured spiritual space—its sheer metaphorical breadth and depth of tone—leaves me entirely convinced about the alternative religious truth in the claims made on his imagination by the Caribbean visual, or should that be victual. Probably both.

All this may be academic because the I-speaker in a Walcott poem may sound like the poet distributing the cornucopia of his tone when in fact the I-presence could easily be an assumed identity for the benefit of the poem's outcome and not the great man at all. Poets are commendably notorious for fronting their utterances, their poems as discourses, with a first-person speaker who has nothing to do with the actual lives of the poets and everything to do with the internal logic and dynamic of the independently spirited poem. I say this because *Omeros* is peppered with declarations of faith in God by the many dramatic players in the poem, from Philoctete, nursing his wise wound, to Helen in her haughty headdress, to the inebriated bit parts by the cast of outcast Europeans roasting in the Colonies as ex-pats. The tone of the I-speaker, cognizant as it is of the nuanced language of religion hankering after a hard-won spirituality in the middle of vapid materialism, borrows heavily on this religious diction and syntax, and conveys it into the libertarian territory of a veneration of nature. This borrowing from the church of God for the preferred altar of nature results in something lost in the translation. A reader may think Derek Walcott is mounting a sophisticated claim on nature as a part of the overall scheme of an inviolable church, all-encompassing even to the point of domesticating the poetic imagination.

Perhaps the safety valve against this sophist claim is the continuous energy of the bawdy calypsonian always rearing his head during the most pious of tones. Characters swear like troopers in *Omeros* and their bodies, their composed bodies, appear on the verge of spilling into pornographic revelation, stripping away decorum (helped by rum) for the common and sexually explicit, stripped down and bare, though not reduced body, invested in the sensuous. The senses, in at least one sense, do not take prisoners, appear classless and without gender bias, and in this sense alone stands for the libertarian ideal of a freed-up imagination, unmoored from the conventions of time and place through the very contraptions supplied by the poet's time and location. This contradiction of the senses as a gateway to some other place, using the constraints of time and place to gain ground beyond it, typifies the mission of writing invested in nature and the senses, but with a spiritual goal over and above the pleasures of the senses. And it is this creative impulse that takes Derek Walcott's poetry beyond the convention of God ("past faith" as he says in his most recent book-length poem, *The Prodigal*) and into the unusual sensuous realm of discovery, surprise and wonder.

Notes

1. During the break in a roundtable discussion with Derek Walcott, Linton Kwesi Johnson, and me, moderated by Darcus Howe.

2. The poet's limited understanding expressed in the poem's tone is delimited by the formal procedures of the poem (the poem's language, metrics, lines, imagery, stanzas, phrasing, voice, and so on).

3. See the early chapters in Bruce King's biography for more on Derek Walcott's childhood.

4. Find its religious basis in John 9:5, John 8:12, and John 12:46 among others.

5. There are more updated terms for this move away from the standard vernacular or received, official code of a language for its street or popular equivalent mixed as it is with West African grammar and diction and descended from the slaves as is the case for former British colonies in the Caribbean. Kamau Brathwaite in his monograph on the beginnings of Jamaica Creole Society introduced the idea of a "nation language" in an attempt to frame the majority use of this officially unwelcome mode of communication. In Trinidad and Guyana, for example, the contribution of South Asian languages to this English instigated by mid-nineteenth-century indentureship from India is another case in point (and subject for a different essay). Walcott's Nobel acceptance speech acknowledges this Indian influence on his imaginative. See too the enormous scholarship of the two editors of this Walcott Special, both of whom have made lasting contributions to these debates.

6. *Omeros* engages with myth even as the lives of its characters are circumscribed by religion. *Tiepolo's Hound* dispenses with this religious frame and opts for art instead.

7. The awesome list of nature aligns nature's behavior with poetic modes of enquiry; nature and poetry become synonymous. Walcott repeats the phrase with a slight variance "my awe of the ordinary" on page 8 of *Tiepolo's Hound* as emblematic of his epiphany and the premise for the book-length poem.

8. See Wordsworth's 'Lines: Composed a few miles above Tintern Abbey . . .' where he argues for nature as a force in the poet's life and a prime mover which shapes poetic thought—". . . sensations sweet, / Felt in the blood, and felt along the heart; / And passing even into my purer mind," (lines 27-9).

9. Clare (1793-1864), "The grass below—above the vaulted sky" (from his poem, "I Am")—a contemplative moment in poetry, if ever there was one, largely invested in stillness, it decrees a study of nature as the subject for the poet. The image also implies a posture of death in nature—the poet laid low but not yet buried.

Works Cited

Arena Caribbean Nights. BBC 2. Mod. Darcus Howe, prod. by Julien Henriques. June 1986.

Clare, John. (1793-1864). "I Am."

King, Bruce. *Derek Walcott: A Caribbean Life*. London: Oxford UP, 2000.

Walcott, Derek. *The Arkansas Testament*. London: Faber and Faber, 1998. American edition published in 1987 by Farrar, Straus & Giroux.

———. *The Bounty*. London: Faber and Faber, 1997. American edition published in 1997 by Farrar, Straus & Giroux.

———. *Collected Poems 1948-1984*. New York: Farrar, Straus, and Giroux, 1992.

———. *Omeros*. London: Faber and Faber, 1990. American edition published in 1990 by Farrar, Straus & Giroux.

———. *Tiepolo's Hound*. New York: Farrar, Straus & Giroux, 2000.

Wordsworth, William. (1770-1850). "Lines Composed a Few Miles above Tintern Abbey on Revisiting the Banks of the Wye During a Tour." July 13, 1798

Erik Martiny (essay date December 2006)

SOURCE: Martiny, Erik. "Multiplying Footprints: Alienation and Integration in Derek Walcott's Reworkings of the Robinson Crusoe Myth." *English Studies* 87, no. 6 (December 2006): 669-78.

[*In the essay that follows, Martiny traces the development of the Robinson Crusoe and Friday figures in Walcott's Crusoe trilogy—"The Castaway," "Crusoe's Island," and "Crusoe's Journal."*]

Unsurprisingly for a writer who is also a playwright, Derek Walcott's poetry is remarkably theatrical—the personae employed in his poems are so numerous and diverse that they form a complete cast of characters. I wish to examine the members of this populous troupe of speakers, in order to dwell on two recurrent personae: the avatars of Robinson Crusoe and his foil, Friday.

In fiction, Defoe's novel has spawned a multitude of imitations, creating the genre known as the Robinsonade. While eighteenth- and nineteenth-century versions tend to remain optimistic, twentieth-century revisions generally lay emphasis on the more sombre possibilities of the genre, its potential to explore the ravages of solitude or colonisation. Like most poets (*pace* the Francophone poet, St. John Perse), Walcott's poetic reworkings of the genre have echoed this trend. The purpose of the present essay is to examine Walcott's protean representation of Defoe's characters and to redress the fact that no full-length study has been carried out on the evolution of the Crusoe and Friday figures in his three-piece sequence. It has a corrective agenda also, in that it seeks to clear up some of the misunderstandings surrounding Walcott's rather elusive personae. I will show that these misconceptions stem in part from the gap separating Walcott's theoretical statements from his poetic practice.

As well as offering closer exegesis of Derek Walcott's Crusoe trilogy and reassessing **"The Castaway"** and **"Crusoe's Island"** as mid-life crisis lyrics, this study reads the Crusoe poems in the light of the Existentialist cultural landscape of the post-war period by relating Walcott to Samuel Beckett. I propose that one of the conflicts rehearsed in Walcott's Crusoe poems works through the debate between individualism and nationalism that set Beckett and the Celtic Revivalists at loggerheads. I read the Crusoe poems as a sequence which charts the development of Walcott's outlook from Beckettian alienation to a more communal integration. The poems' strong religious strain is also dwelt upon in order to show Walcott's theological oscillation between the poles of Existentialist atheism and paganised Christianity.

The term "postcolonial" has been the subject of some controversy in both academic and literary circles. J. M. Coetzee has condemned the catchall phrase for its im-plicitly "Western-centred" outlook.[1] While the term does reveal a European bias, I would argue that it is still an appellation of some critical viability and particularly appropriate where the Crusoe poems are concerned. Employed as a qualifier of varying intensity, postcolonialism is useful in defining a particular culture's "pre-occupations". If a nation's literature is dominated by reliance on such themes as history, marginality, hybridity, the reworking of the European canon and generally engaged in "writing back to the centre" through the colonial past, then it is still suffering from the imperial aftermath. According to this definition, it might be argued that Caribbean letters are, generally speaking, considerably more postcolonial than, for example, recent Irish literature, taken as a whole. In this sense, the fact that Coetzee's own novels are highly involved with the whole process of addressing the metropolitan (literary) centre (Coetzee's own novel, *Foe*, is itself a well-known reworking of *Robinson Crusoe*) frames them within the parameters of postcolonialism. A literature's "postcoloniality" is thus in direct proportion to the after-effects which the imperial disease has wreaked upon the national psyche. However, while I would argue that postcolonialism is currently still an appropriate term, it may not be a perennial one and should eventually fall into abeyance as a descriptive label for Caribbean literature. The enfranchised text will signal its Adamic liberation from colonial legacy and the term "postcolonial" will be used when periodising Antillean literary history.

Walcott's poetic is in fact a dialogic battleground for contending notions of identity. His personae never reveal Walcott's hard-and-fast positions. Rather, they embody respective donnings of a particular West Indian attitude: an exploration, rather than a ready-made expression of *esprit de corps*. Unlike Louise Bennett's Votin' Liz and her other female personae "of firm and militant convictions",[2] Walcott's personae are tentative dramatisations of potential areas of identity. It is therefore an error of interpretation to infer that the difference between the Negritudinist stance exuded in **"A Far Cry from Africa"** and Walcott's later condemnations of Africanism constitutes a contradiction.[3] Such a reading implies that poets operate in a temporal vacuum removed from change and that Walcott's statements are immutable utterances of adherence. It is important to note that even **"A Far Cry"** is set largely in the interrogative mode.

Despite Walcott's ultimate rejection of the African Aesthetic, much of his poetry also courts another historical idyll—the Cockaigne of the pre-colonial Carib, Friday before the arrival of Robinson Crusoe. Ultimately, however, these distinctions collapse when confronted by the more fundamental opposition between individualism and a sense of community. While the Crusoe-Friday poems deal with and do expurgate some of the more existentially disturbing aspects of the question, the conflict is never entirely resolved in Walcott's poetry. Shabine, the persona of **"The Schooner Flight",** can thus be read as an avatar of the castaway figure in Walcott's first collections. The male character of **"The Star-Apple Kingdom",** on the other hand, represents an attempt to become a unified nation-self. The psychic strain experienced by these personae is occasioned by an over-ambitious attempt to fill all communal deficiencies and, by the same token, cure all personal disorders, for this is their claim: "either I'm nobody, or I'm a nation" (346). Selfhood seems to be unattainable without a sense of nationhood. However, if identification with such a larger structure is self-aggrandising, it also involves the strain of a nation bearing down on the claims of the self. Spiritual nationalism entails both the glories of confraternity and the gargantuan sum of collective complexes. The greater one's sense of belonging, the more one is prone to assailments on the (national) ego. "Nobody" therefore characterises the under-identification of not knowing who one is through lack of nationality, while "nation" stresses the over-identification with nationhood that Beckett felt could not lead to adequate self-appraisal. The travel narrative of **"The Schooner Flight"** thus attempts to navigate between the twin poles of the almost autistic self-absorbtion the Castaway figure displays and the representative Author-of-the-nation that the Barbadian poet, Edward Kamau Brathwaite, exemplifies. These are the psychological stakes of **"The Castaway"**: the dichotomy between personal introspection and cultural extroversion.

Walcott's predicament can thus be formulated in the same terms as the clash between Samuel Beckett and the authors of the Celtic Revival in Ireland. Beckett's indictment of the Revivalist aesthetic centred on the premise that fusion with nationalist concerns prevented artists from apprehending their own individuated experiences. For Beckett, the glories of the Celtic Twilight were nothing more than an escape to a specious dignity. Perhaps the only major difference between Beckett and Walcott is that Beckett's starting and ending point is the given of individual estrangement whereas Walcott ceaselessly strives to depart from isolation. Characteristically, his is the half-way house between Beckett and the Celtic Revival.

Reiterating Yeats's well-known dictum according to which a man who is given a mask will talk the truth, Walcott has remarked that "one cannot avoid describing oneself in terms of masks".[4] While this theoretical absolute may be regarded as paradigmatic of his reliance on a theatrical mode of self-examination, it is by no means unproblematically so. The prototypal Robinson Crusoe-cum-Adam mask of the early poems sits somewhat uncomfortably on the young poet's face. If it at first appears to be grafted onto his features, it exfoliates upon examination and is eventually shed entirely. The mask therefore retains both the primary falseness one associates it with, as well as the apparently paradoxical necessity of revealing the self through emblematic disguise.

To trouble matters further, Walcott's programmatic reference to the persona in his critical essays does not always tally with the problematically composite "Adam/Crusoe" figure dramatised in the poems. This rift is one which critics have left largely unexamined. The Adamic vision Walcott yearns for in his theoretical works is fulfilled, if sporadically, only before and after this particular persona is invoked. As often, abstract edicts run at loggerheads with their praxis: Walcott's poetic practice strains to regain his limpid prescriptions. In his essay entitled **"What the Twilight Says",** he takes a nostalgic look at a youthful dream which led him to imagine a nation walking "like new Adams, in a nourishing ignorance which would name plants and people with a child's belief that the world is its own age".[5] Elsewhere, he describes the inherently Adamic nature of his juvenilia: "It was exhilarating to know that I was privileged to be the first one to put down the name of a certain town, or fisherman, or road."[6] The Crusoe poems themselves mark a strong qualification in this ideal. If Walcott's comments in the Hirsch interview do proceed to dichotomise Crusoe's condition in terms of fervent "creative possession" coupled to lonely despair,[7] the poems confront these dualities much more directly.

As the title of Walcott's 1965 collection suggests, his first Crusoe is a dispossessed castaway, cast out of the Eden of linguistic dominion. His disaffiliation has been effected by a deepening awareness of the disjunction between language, the socio-cultural reality it designates and its impotent desire to transmute the outside world through artistic production. This Sisyphus-like task is further troubled by the discomfiture of also having to borrow the oppressor's language. So much for Adamic naming. Instead of merely tasting the apple of experience, Walcott's Adam has, as it were, chewed off his own tongue. Much of Walcott's subsequent work may be seen as an attempt to breach the "gulf" (the title of his next collection) between the signifier and the signified.

The figure in **"The Castaway"** has little to define him. His linguistic depletion is such that he is even disinherited of his own name. This New World Adam cuts a poor figure as a broken old man marooned in the dustbin of his mind. Estranged from his own body and feelings, *ipso facto,* the speaker of this poem excludes the reader from emotive participation. Pathos, undermined by Beckettian bathos, remains the greatest absence of all in this poem. His is not a moving loneliness because the reader is debarred from anything other than intellectualised response. Self-pity is, if not ridiculed, then remorselessly suppressed. This stands in opposition to the Crusoe figure in Elizabeth Bishop's "Crusoe in England", who reflects that "'Pity should begin at home.' So the more / pity I felt, the more I felt at home" (121-2). Walcott's Castaway also stands as the antithesis of Defoe's proto-industrialist and Marx's vision of Crusoe as *homo economicus*. His affinities lie with his other contemporary incarnation as the idle animalistic islander in Coetzee's *Foe*: "pac[ing] about in his apeskin clothes, scanning the horizon for a sail" (18).[8]

This regression is accentuated by the distinctly faecal obsession evidenced in the poem. The Castaway is a West Indian Molloy speaking for the fundamental nature of the fundament: "Pleasures of an old man: / Morning: contemplative evacuation, considering / The dried leaf, nature's plan" (13-15). On the other side of the digestive tube, the food imagery suggests that his intake of nourishment is thwarted: "the morsel of a sail" (1-2) and "A net inches across nothing" (11) are his sole nutritional allowances.

In the poem, the defecatory act can be taken to represent a nihilistic view of artistic production ("contemplative evacuation", placed near "the dog's feces" (16) emphasises the link between thought and the excretory function). Nevertheless, while writerly endeavours seem doomed to faeces, there is an attempt, if not to transcend, then to revalue experience through the cyclical, alchemical processes whereby the "feces" are transmogrified to coral and rhymed with "genesis". The rhythm at this juncture becomes weightier as the tone heightens to biblical revelation: "In our own entrails, genesis" (19).

The poem might have ended at this point, but relentlessly pursues its course to reveal a full-length portrait of the estranged artist who is, in the double-edged words of the Irish writer Patrick Kavanagh's Alexander Selkirk figure, "king / Of banks and stones and every blooming thing".[9] If the first section of **"The Castaway"** stages the artist's inability to catch anything in his net "inches across nothing", or perceive meaning, the second part thickens his feeling of inadequacy. The artistic message he might have sent off lies, ineffectual, in a bottle "choked with sand" (29). The deromanticised, Beckettian natural world mocks his endeavours and provides no abiding solace: his rotting brain hatches nothing but a cacophony of insects. Similarly, the last line of the poem effects to sever the artist from his (writing) hand. One can almost picture a writing utensil instead of the nail in his Christ-like hand: "Clenched sea-wood nailed and white as a man's hand" (31).

It is therefore a moot point whether this last iconographic image is one of redemption or even renewal. The reader is witness to a disempowered, ship/shitwrecked Christ whose resurrection remains suspended in this passionless Passion. Suffering does not bear the comforting means of uplifting artistic insight: it is a

dead end in itself. The epiphanic genesis of the first section ends in the disappearance of hope. Clinched at this point, the poem appears to represent a bleak midlife crisis lyric (Walcott was also roughly the age of Christ crucified when he wrote it). This being said, the circumstances of its composition[10] do inform the view, expounded by Walcott, according to which complete annulment and depletion are sometimes necessary as creative rejuvenators. As he puts it, "If there was nothing, there was everything to be made".[11]

As one is about to conclude on the dubiousness of Adamic renewal, a single word in the last line qualifies the reader's previous perceptions (in a manner characteristic of the body of the Crusoe poems), and one is forced to reconsider the whole poem from the very specifically socio-cultural perspective of the Antillean world. The normative, Eurocentric universal implied in the use of "white as a man's hand" points to the racially exclusive quality of the statement. It is only at this point in the poem that it becomes clear that this crucified Crusoe is more than a general portrait of the artist as a future old man. Walcott's assertion that Crusoe is a specifically Caribbean writerly *doppelgänger* comes into focus. *Robinson Crusoe,* that central "colonial utopia", has, as Peter Hulme puts it, less to do with the historic world of the seventeenth-century Caribbean than with the "primary stuff of colonial ideology—the European hero's lonely first steps into the void of savagery".[12]

"Crusoe's Island", the second panel of the Crusoe triptych, refashions many of the same themes and motifs, marking a progression. The opening lines resurrect God after his annihilation in **"The Castaway"** only to announce His death some nineteen lines later. Nevertheless, Beckett's atheistic deicidal attitudes expressed in the Castaway's "Godlike, annihilating godhead" (23) give way in this poem to a kind of oscillatory agnosticism where artistic production depends on a sense of sacred communion but is ultimately denied such heightening by the absence of any divine prevention of human suffering. In the second part of the poem, we learn that the poet's compassion for others has gnawed away at his belief in God's solicitude. While the opening lines do image the Supreme Being steadfastly crafting his New World at the anvil, it is nonetheless a postlapsarian creation designed to exclude: "Hammers ocean to a blinding shield" (3). The image is later further qualified by the mention of "crippled Vulcan" (97), the artist's patron god, who was also excluded, cast over the side of Olympus for his ugliness, like Adam out of Eden.

Likewise, the "kiln" that Crusoe might have used to create his clay vessels is made (recurrently in the oeuvre) to connote Auschwitzian furnaces, in a characteristically anachronistic shock device. In Walcott's poetry, the apparently innocuous often assumes Plathian grimness. In this way, the poem seems to dramatise a contradictory wish to depose and reinstate God as the Prime Mover. Its confused theomachy is partially resolved through the *deus ex machina*-like bell that rings throughout the poem as a summons to communion. It resounds like John Donne's bell tolling and telling the poet-castaway that "no man is an island, entire of itself". It brings the poet to the realisation that despite his desire for the Transcendentalist self-reliance of the artist and his longing for a release from the stultifying tensions of domestic life, communion with the Other and with God lies at the heart of salvation. Walcott's Methodist upbringing, or one might say, more correctly, the longing for deist belief (to avoid the pitfalls of an over-insistent biographical reading as there is nothing "methodical" about the erratic religious impulses evidenced here) seems to reassert itself fitfully in the Crusoe sequence as it vies with paganism in an attempt to overthrow the atheistic nihilism of **"The Castaway"**. The original Crusoe's Puritan ethos is sapped from the outset of Walcott's trilateral sequence.

Like **"The Castaway"**, **"Crusoe's Island"** is clearly a mid-life crisis lyric which compounds existential *angst* with more theological doubt. The speaker of the second poem mentions his age twice: "Past thirty now" (20, "I stand at my life's noon" (91). The fact that these poems were written at the age at which Christ was crucified contributes to account for the references to crucifixion. Moreover, it might be pointed out that Walcott composed the Crusoe poems at the age at which not only Christ but also the poet's father, Warwick Walcott, died. It can be argued that these two deaths combine to generate much of the anguish evidenced in the sequence.

The final poem of the triptych, **"Crusoe's Journal"**, is tonally different to the first two poems of the sequence, displaying the poet's new-found ability to identify with his native Fridays through his use of the collective pronoun "we". This grammatical piece of wish-fulfilment seems to stem from a desire for a unitary national culture based ultimately not on racial or cultural homogeneity but on a sense of social cohesion. The poem's tone, diction and lineation all express a self-confident attitude to the role and place of Friday's nation. The regular, alternating length of the lines invites comparison to the beams of a staunch construction, especially in view of the irregular,[13] erratic morphology and rhythm of **"The Castaway"**'s lines, surrounded by the blank void of the aporias in between the spoliated stanzas. There has been some critical confusion concerning the speaker of this poem. Rita Dove, for instance, misreads the addresser as Crusoe.[14] Upon closer examination, it becomes clear that Crusoe has been debunked and is no longer the spokesman of the Caribbean Islands: his words have been appropriated by Walcott's spiritual ancestors, the Arawak Caribs. So, while the title and epigraph structurally provide an introduction to Crusoe's

private meditations, it is a group of Fridays who, as it were, snatch the microphone from his hands and seize on the means of production. Walcott's sequence thus stages a gradual distancing of the Crusoe figure in favour of the ever more powerful presence of Friday. If in **"The Castaway"**, Friday is little more than a footprint, "Friday's progeny", alluded to in **"Crusoe's Island"**, takes over the final part of the sequence. In theoretical terms, the hegemonic medium through which canonical conceptions of order, truth and reality are established is thus submitted to an aboriginal "abrogation" of "the categories of imperial culture [and] its assumption of the fixed meaning 'inscribed' in words".[15] Like the coloniser, the reader's expectations are thwarted into attention by this pronominal subversion of the "authorised" text. Adam Crusoe is now pictured as a merely fictional character in the natives' first recreational book: their "profane Genesis" (92). Walcott's dismantling of the colonial apparatus takes place most fully in this final part of the sequence in the speakers' counter-discursive utterances.

As the tourist-guide confidence of the opening lines suggest, these autochthones are not castaways; they reside on the *terra ferma* of home. Theirs is not the Castaway's rotting brain, but an "intellect [which] appraises / objects surely" (4-5). Walcott's vision and collective purpose are now clear as he launches into a swinging New Historicist indictment of Eurocentric religious, literary and racial hegemonic models. The guiding persona of the poem is a collective Friday writing back to the metropolitan centre and subverting its language through ironic punning and the use of modified repetition. He makes the colonial apparatus crawl with unmaking. The pun on "good Fridays" (21), for instance, raises Friday from apparent submission to deicidal poise, which reiterates the two other poems' references to Nietzsche-like deicide in another form: the anxiety-ridden loss of God in the first two poems is countered here by a gleeful subversion of Christianity. Similarly, the irony of anthropophagously eating Christ (in host form) contrives to foil the missionaries' attempts at evangelisation.[16] As in many contemporary renderings, Friday's ways confound his master's and ultimately prevail. Walcott himself has commented on this inversion: "People who come to the Caribbean from the cities and the continents go through a process of being recultured."[17] The subtle irony infused in an apparently innocuous line such as "we learn to shape from them [Crusoe's journals]" (56) is achieved through a previous echo of the deeply ironic "converted cannibals / we learn with him to eat the flesh of Christ" (24-5). Lack of attention to Walcott's sardonic strategies can lead to such reductive readings as Mervyn Morris's comment that "the persona identifies with Crusoe".[18] The potential irony inherent in "nothing was / the language of a race" has not been commented on. Of course, it is difficult to determine to what degree the collective Fridays' pronouncements are satirical denouncements of Defoe's hypotext, but their initially ironic debunking of Christianity should alert the reader to the possibility that anything they utter should be read with caution.

Ultimately, what makes the tone of this poem so confusing and difficult to apprehend is Walcott's own ambivalence to his material. His mixed feelings about *Robinson Crusoe* surface in Friday's approach to the coloniser's text. The journal novel is depicted as both destructive and creative. Its aesthetic value is extolled as being "odorous as raw wood to the adze" (9) and Walcott seems to envy Defoe's figurative minimalism, his novel's virtual eschewal of metaphor. Politically, however, the novel is presented as a legitimisation of European hegemony. In the final analysis therefore, I would argue that this poem has been partly misconstrued because Walcott's ambiguous hypertextual reworking of *Robinson Crusoe* is ultimately a satire laced with admiration for Defoe's innovatory masterpiece.

In the end, what makes this sequence so complex, and at times confusing, is its mixture of personal existential and aesthetic anxiety (at its height in, but never entirely defused by the opening poem) and a larger preoccupation with the dismantling of the colonial apparatus. The poems chart the search for the possible sources of this alienation in the fact of colonisation. The poet's sense of isolation in **"The Castaway"** is however only partially averted by his dive into the sea of history: individual loneliness is thus bartered for a warmer collective loneliness. The Beckettian sense of the artist's self-reliance as a guarantor of authenticity is finally worked through and relinquished in favour of a national cohesive definition of identity.

After these Crusoe and Friday-centred poems, Walcott largely forsakes the use of poetic masks in his next three collections, allowing only very thinly disguised autobiographical and biographical figures to people his poems. His cast of poetic personae resurfaces to receive its fullest development in **"The Star-Apple Kingdom"** and **"The Fortunate Traveller"**. In this dramatic heyday, spanning from 1979 to 1981, the avatars of Friday and Crusoe attempt to disencumber themselves from the trappings of a colonial legacy and struggle to merge into a single composite body.

Notes

1. Begam, 429.

2. Richards, 1207.

3. All line references are to be found in Derek Walcott, *Collected Poems 1948-1984,* London: Faber and Faber, 1992.

4. Walcott, "Walcott on Walcott," 82.

5. Walcott, "What the Twilight Says," 6.

6. Interview with Hirsch, 283.

7. Ibid., 292.

8. Most twentieth-century reworkings of the Robinson Crusoe theme have emphasised the physically degrading and morally disaffiliating aspects of the insular myth.

9. Muldoon, ed., 21. Robinson Crusoe is universally employed as a portrait-of-the-artist figure, and is of particular pertinence to West Indian artists since Defoe's desert isle has been situated on the Caribbean island of Tobago or its whereabouts.

10. "I stayed in a beachhouse by myself and I wrote them there. . . . The beaches around here are generally very empty—just you, the sea, and the vegetation around you, and you're very much by yourself" (Walcott, "The Art of Poetry XXXVII," 213).

11. Wyke, 66.

12. Hulme, 186.

13. Wayne Brown, 103, remarks that "a defining characteristic of *The Castaway* . . . is Walcott's struggle against his own predisposition towards the iambic pentameter, a struggle evident in the fact that many lines which were obviously composed as pentameters to begin with, are broken up or run on in the final version".

14. Dove, 70.

15. Ashcroft, 38.

16. In his history of colonial intervention in the West Indies, J. A. Froude, 115, relates the humorous anecdote according to which African slaves were willing to be baptised any number of times for a glass of brandy.

17. Walcott, "The Art of Poetry XXXVII," 214.

18. Morris, 149.

References

Ashcroft, Bill, Gareth Griffiths, and Helen Triffin, eds. *The Empire Writes Back.* London: Routledge, 1989.

Begam, Richard. "An Interview with J. M. Coetzee." *Contemporary Literature* 33, no. 3 (1992): 419-31.

Bishop, Elizabeth. *Complete Poems.* London: Chatto and Windus, 1983.

Brown, Lloyd W. *West Indian Poetry.* Berkeley: Twayne Publishers, 1978.

Coetzee, J. M. *Foe.* London: Everyman, 1994.

Defoe, Daniel. *Robinson Crusoe.* Rev. ed. London: Everyman, 1994.

Dove, Rita. "'Either I'm Nobody or I'm a Nation'. Review of *Collected Poems: 1948-1984.*" *Parnassus: Poetry in Review* 14, no. 1 (1987): 49-76.

Froude, J. A. *The English in the West Indies: The Bow of Ulysses.* London: Longmans, Green & Co., 1888.

Hulme, Peter. *Colonial Encounters: Europe and the Native Caribbean, 1492-1797.* London: Methuen, 1986.

Morris, Mervyn. "Derek Walcott." In *West Indian Literature,* edited by Bruce King. London: Macmillan, 1979.

Muldoon, Paul, ed. *The Faber Book of Contemporary Irish Poetry.* London: Faber and Faber, 1986.

Richards, David. "West Indian Literature." In *Encyclopedia of Literature and Criticism.* London: Routledge, 1991.

Walcott, Derek. Interview with Edward Hirsch. "The Art of Poetry XXXVII." *Paris Review* 101 (1986): 196-230.

———. *Collected Poems 1948-1984.* London: Faber and Faber, 1992.

———. "An Interview with Derek Walcott." *Contemporary Literature* 20 (1979): 279-92.

———. Interview with Dennis Scott. *Caribbean Quarterly* 14, nos. 1-2 (1968): 77-82.

———. "What the Twilight Says: An Overture." In *Dream on Monkey Mountain and Other Plays.* New York: Farrer, Strauss and Giroux, 1970.

Wyke, Clement H. "'Divided to the Vein': Patterns of Tormented Ambivalence in Walcott's *The Fortunate Traveller.*" *Ariel: A Review of International English Literature* 203 (1989): 55-71.

FURTHER READING

Criticism

Baer, William, ed. *Conversations with Derek Walcott.* Jackson: University Press of Mississippi, 1996, 211 p.

> Collects a number of interviews conducted by individuals including Dennis Scott, Carl Jacobs, Leif Sjöberg, Rebekah Presson, and David Montenegro.

Jay, Paul. "Fated to Unoriginality: The Politics of Mimicry in Derek Walcott's *Omeros.*" *Callaloo* 29, no. 2 (spring 2006): 545-59.

> Argues that Walcott designed *Omeros* specifically to address the array of critical debate about his work as a whole—especially disputes about his status within Caribbean literature.

MacDonald, Joyce Green. "Bodies, Race, and Performance in Derek Walcott's *A Branch of the Blue Nile.*" *Theatre Journal* 57, no. 2 (May 2005): 191-203.

> Contends that "in many ways *A Branch of the Blue Nile*—and the Shakespearean original behind it, *Antony and Cleopatra*—fulfills both Walcott's commitment to exposition and his acceptance of the Caribbean's status as a crucible of languages, races, and cultures, and his enduring belief that theatre can have the capacity to show a people to itself."

Additional coverage of Walcott's life and career is contained in the following sources published by Gale: *Black Literature Criticism,* Ed. 1:3; *Black Writers,* Ed. 2; *Concise Dictionary of World Literary Biography,* Vol. 3; *Concise Major 21st-Century Writers,* Ed. 1; *Contemporary Authors,* Vol. 89-92; *Contemporary Authors New Revision Series,* Vols. 26, 47, 75, 80, 130; *Contemporary British Dramatists; Contemporary Dramatists,* Eds. 5, 6; *Contemporary Literary Criticism,* Vols. 2, 4, 9, 14, 25, 42, 67, 76, 160; *Contemporary Poets,* Eds. 1, 2, 3, 4, 5, 6, 7; *Dictionary of Literary Biography,* Vols. 117, 332; *Dictionary of Literary Biography Yearbook,* 1981; *DISCovering Authors 3.0; DISCovering Authors: British; DISCovering Authors: Canadian Edition; DISCovering Authors Modules: Most-Studied Authors, Multicultural Writers, and Poets; Drama Criticism,* Vol. 7; *Encyclopedia of World Literature in the 20th Century,* Ed. 3; *Epics for Students,* Vol. 1; *Literary Movements for Students,* Vol. 2; *Literature of Developing Nations for Students,* Vol. 1; *Literature Resource Center; Major 20th-Century Writers,* Eds. 1, 2; *Major 21st-Century Writers* (eBook), 2005; *Poetry Criticism,* Vol. 46; *Poetry for Students,* Vol. 6; *Reference Guide to English Literature,* Ed. 2; *Twayne's World Authors;* and *World Writers in English,* Vol. 1.

Alice Walker
1944-

AP Images

(Full name Alice Malsenior Walker) American novelist, short story writer, essayist, poet, editor, and author of children's books.

For additional information on Walker's career, see *Black Literature Criticism,* Ed. 1.

INTRODUCTION

One of the most prolific black writers in America and among the most important contemporary American writers, Walker is the author of the Pulitzer Prize-winning novel *The Color Purple,* whose publication in 1982 made her an overnight literary celebrity. In novels, poetry, short stories, and essays, Walker writes about the black woman's struggle for spiritual wholeness and for sexual, political, and racial equality. Her work is an exploration of the individual identity of the black woman

and how embracing her identity and bonding with other women affects the health of her community at large. Walker describes this kinship among women as "womanism," as opposed to feminism, and sees herself as a "Womanist"—as someone who appreciates women's culture, emotions, and character. Critics have pointed out that her writings reflect not only this stance, but also, paradoxically, the universality of human experience. Though some critics have faulted Walker's fiction for its unflattering portraits of black men, most applaud her lyrical prose, her sensitive characterizations, and her gift for rendering beauty, grace, and dignity in ordinary people and places.

BIOGRAPHICAL INFORMATION

Walker was born in 1944 in Eatonton, Georgia, a rural southern town where her father was a sharecropper. When she was eight years old, she was accidentally shot in the eye by her brother, who was playing with a BB gun. Her parents, who could not afford a car, could not take her to a doctor for several days. By that time, her wound was so bad that she lost the use of her right eye. Permanently scarred, she spent most of her childhood withdrawn from others, writing poetry to ease her loneliness and becoming a meticulous observer of human relationships and interaction. The accident also had a lasting impact on her relationship with her father: his inability to obtain proper medical treatment for her colored her relationship with him, and they remained estranged for the rest of his life. In contrast, Walker has noted that she respected her mother's strength and perseverance in the face of poverty, recalling how hard her mother worked in her garden to create beauty in even the shabbiest of conditions. Despite her disadvantaged home life, Walker was an excellent student and in 1961 was awarded a scholarship to Spelman College in Atlanta, where she became involved in the civil rights movement and participated in sit-ins at local business establishments. In 1963 she transferred to Sarah Lawrence College in Bronxville, New York, where she began to work seriously on writing poetry, publishing her first collection, *Once* (1968), in reaction to a traumatic abortion. Walker shared the poems with one of her teachers, the poet Muriel Rukeyser, whose agent found a publisher for them. After earning her undergraduate degree in 1965, she moved to Mississippi to teach and continue her social activism, and she met and married Melvyn Leventhal, a Jewish civil rights lawyer. The two became the only legally married interracial couple living in Jackson, Mississippi. Since the couple's divorce in 1976, Walker has focused more on her writing and has taught at various colleges and universities. While working in Mississippi, she discovered the writings of Zora Neale Hurston, an author who would have a great influence on Walker's later work. Walker eventually edited a collection of Hurston's fiction called *I Love Myself When I'm Laughing . . . and Then again When I Am Looking Mean and Impressive* (1979). In addition to poetry, Walker has written short stories, essays, children's books, and several novels, most notably *The Color Purple,* which received both the Pulitzer Prize for fiction and the American Book Award, and was made into an award-winning film in 1985.

MAJOR WORKS

Walker's work consistently reflects her concern with racial, sexual, and political issues—particularly with the black woman's struggle for spiritual survival. Her writings are also infused with the idea of reformation, the sense of hope despite the brutal effects of sexism and racism suffered by her characters. Her first novel, *The Third Life of Grange Copeland* (1970), introduces many of her prevalent themes, particularly the domination of powerless women by equally powerless men. In the narrative, which spans the years between the Depression and the beginnings of the civil rights movement in the early 1960s, Walker chronicled three generations of a black sharecropping family and its patriarch, Grange Copeland, as they struggle with poverty and racism. Another theme in Walker's fiction is the way in which the black woman's attempt to be whole relates to the health of her community. The attempt at wholeness comes from remaining true to herself and fighting against the constraints of society, as in the stories from Walker's 1973 collection *In Love and Trouble.* In her 1973 poetry collection *Revolutionary Petunias and Other Poems,* Walker turned to the issues of civil and women's rights, maintaining a direct, personal voice in her focus on an individual's struggles on a daily basis to preserve dignity and liberty despite hardship and oppression. Her second novel, *Meridian* (1976), a tale of perseverance and personal sacrifice set during the 1960s, is generally regarded as one of the best novels about the civil rights movement. Considered autobiographical, *Meridian* explores conflicts between traditional African American values handed down through slavery and the revolutionary polemic espoused by the Black Power movement.

In her most highly acclaimed novel, *The Color Purple,* Walker used the form of letters in creating a black woman who is victimized physically and emotionally by her stepfather, who repeatedly rapes her and then takes her children away from her, and by her husband, an older widower who sees her more as a mule than as a wife. The letters are written to God and Celie's sister, Nettie, who escaped a similar life by becoming a missionary in Africa. Celie overcomes her oppression with

the intervention of an unlikely ally, her husband's mistress, Shug Avery. Walker's next novel, *The Temple of My Familiar* (1989) is an ambitious undertaking that records 500,000 years of human history. The novel's central character, Miss Lissie, is a goddess from primeval Africa who has been incarnated hundreds of times throughout history. She befriends Suwelo, a narcissistic university professor whose marriage is threatened by his need to dominate and sexually exploit his wife. Through a series of conversations with Miss Lissie and her friend Hal, Suwelo learns of Miss Lissie's innumerable lives and experiences—from the prehistoric world in which humans and animals lived in harmony under a matriarchal society to slavery in the United States—and regains his capacity to live, nurture, and respect himself and others. In her controversial fifth novel, *Possessing the Secret of Joy* (1992), Walker examined the practice of female genital mutilation in certain African, Asian, and Middle Eastern cultures. The novel focuses on Tashi, a woman who willingly requests the ritual, in part because she is unaware of what the ceremony involves. Since discussion of the ritual is taboo in her culture, Tashi is ignorant of the profound impact the procedure will have on her life. Walker's concerns about the international issue of female genital mutilation prompted her to further explore the subject, both on film and in the book *Warrior Marks* (1993). Written with film director Pratibha Parmar, *Warrior Marks* details how the two filmed a documentary on the ritual circumcision of African women. Walker published her sixth novel, *By the Light of My Father's Smile,* in 1998. Focusing on female sexuality and told in flashback, the novel centers on the Robinsons, a husband-and-wife team of anthropologists. Unable to secure funding for research in Mexico in the 1950s, the husband poses as a minister to study the Mundo, a mixed black and Indian tribe. When the couple's daughter becomes involved with a Mundo boy, the father reacts violently, a response that has repercussions throughout the novel. Walker experiments with points of view in the novel, even recounting the action through the eyes of the recently deceased patriarch of the Robinson clan.

Walker has continued to write in a variety of genres, from fiction to nonfiction and poetry. In 1997's *Anything We Love Can Be Saved,* she detailed her own political and social struggle, while in the short story collection *The Way Forward Is with a Broken Heart* (2000), she employed fiction to reflect on her own past, including her marriage, the birth of her daughter, and the creative life she built after her divorce. She returned to poetry with her 2003 collection *Absolute Trust in the Goodness of the Earth,* which was inspired by the terrorist attacks of September 11, 2001. Walker's seventh novel, *Now Is the Time to Open Your Heart,* (2004), recounts the tale of a successful African American novelist, Kate, and her search for new meaning as she approaches the age of sixty. In a long-time relationship with the artist Yolo, Kate decides to voyage down the

Colorado River and then down the Amazon, on trips of self-discovery. Yolo meanwhile goes on his own quest, to Hawaii, and to the woman he once loved.

CRITICAL RECEPTION

Walker earned high praise for *The Color Purple,* especially for her accurate rendering of black folk idioms and her characterization of Celie. Despite this almost unanimous praise for the novel, however, there are several widely debated aspects of Walker's writing as a whole. One such aspect is her portrayal of black male characters as archetypes of black men in modern society. Many reviewers condemn her portrayals of black men as overly negative, pointing to the vile characters in some of her work and to her own comments about black men as evidence of enmity on her part. Other critics assert that the author, in presenting flawed characters, reveals typical shortcomings in the hope that real people burdened with these flaws will recognize themselves in her stories and strive to change. Some reviewers also assert that Walker's work contains positive images of black men that are often ignored by critics. Beyond her portrayal of black men, some reviewers have found fault with Walker's characterization in general, opposing her tendency to refer to characters only with pronouns, thereby encouraging readers to consider the characters exemplary of anyone to whom that pronoun could apply. Finally, much of Walker's work is viewed as political in intent, at times to the detriment of its literary value. This negative assessment has been leveled in particular at *The Temple of My Familiar,* which has been described as a sociopolitical manifesto rather than a work of art. Considered a minor work at best, *The Temple of My Familiar* has also been criticized by commentators who took issue with Walker's speculative interpretation of the origins of patriarchal societies and found her discourses on racial and sexual relations pretentious and offensive. In contrast, reviewers praise works such as *In Love and Trouble* for balancing the art of storytelling with political concerns. Reviewers often laud Walker for her use of the oral storytelling tradition, finding her work most convincing when she employs anecdotal narrative. Critics have also given high praise to the nonfictional *Warrior Marks* for its exposure of the practice of female genital mutilation. In addition to the critical acclaim Walker has received as a major American novelist, she is also considered an accomplished poet. Though her poetry is occasionally described as overly strident and politicized, it has been praised for the intimate tone that often comes from her use of simple form and diction reminiscent of African American folk parables. Her poetry is admired, too, for its ability to tap into universal truths and emotions common to all people regardless of race or gender, and for its capacity to ennoble and dignify its subjects, who are typically regarded by society as insignificant and useless.

PRINCIPAL WORKS

Once: Poems (poetry) 1968

The Third Life of Grange Copeland (novel) 1970

Five Poems (poetry) 1972

In Love and Trouble: Stories of Black Women (short stories) 1973

Revolutionary Petunias and Other Poems (poetry) 1973

Langston Hughes: American Poet (children's biography) 1974; revised edition, 2002

Meridian (novel) 1976

Goodnight, Willie Lee, I'll See You in the Morning (poetry) 1979

I Love Myself When I'm Laughing . . . and Then again When I Am Looking Mean and Impressive: A Zora Neale Hurston Reader [editor] (fiction) 1979

You Can't Keep a Good Woman Down (short stories) 1981

The Color Purple (novel) 1982

In Search of Our Mothers' Gardens: Womanist Prose (essays) 1983

Horses Make a Landscape Look More Beautiful (poetry) 1984

Living by the Word: Selected Writings, 1973-1987 (essays) 1988

To Hell with Dying (children's fiction) 1988

The Temple of My Familiar (novel) 1989

Finding the Green Stone [with Catherine Deeter] (children's fiction) 1991

Her Blue Body Everything We Know: Earthling Poems, 1965-1990 (poetry) 1991

Possessing the Secret of Joy (novel) 1992

Warrior Marks: Female Genital Mutilation and the Sexual Blinding of Women [with Pratibha Parmar] (nonfiction) 1993

Alice Walker Banned (nonfiction) 1996

The Same River Twice: Honoring the Difficult; A Meditation on Life, Spirit, Art, and the Making of the Film The Color Purple, Ten Years Later (essays) 1996

Anything We Love Can Be Saved: A Writer's Activism (nonfiction) 1997

By the Light of My Father's Smile (novel) 1998

Dreads: Sacred Rites of the Natural Hair Revolution [with Francesco Mastalia and Alfonse Pagano] (nonfiction) 1999

The Way forward Is with a Broken Heart (short stories) 2000

Sent to Earth: A Message from the Grandmother Spirit: After the Attacks on the World Trade Center and the Pentagon (prose and poetry) 2001

Absolute Trust in the Goodness of the Earth: New Poems (poetry) 2003

A Poem Traveled down My Arm: Poems and Drawings (poetry) 2003

Now Is the Time to Open Your Heart (novel) 2004

We Are the Ones We Have Been Waiting for; Inner Light in a Time of Darkness: Meditations (essays) 2006

Why War Is Never a Good Idea (for children) 2007

CRITICISM

Ikenna Dieke (essay date 1999)

SOURCE: Dieke, Ikenna. "Alice Walker: Poesy and the Earthling Psyche." In *The Furious Flowering of African American Poetry,* edited by Joanne V. Gabbin, pp. 169-81. Charlottesville: University Press of Virginia, 1999.

[*In the essay that follows, Dieke considers Walker as an "earthling poet" based on her focus on everyday people and situations, her celebration of the relationship between humanity and the natural environment, and her attempts at self-analysis.*]

In what has now become one of the most significant books of essays in the rich repertoire of African American criticism, *In Search of Our Mothers' Gardens,* Alice Walker enunciates a preoccupation with the artistic imagination that might well be dubbed the earthling subjectivity. Reacting angrily to a reader's disparaging remark that "a farmer's daughter might not be the stuff of which poets are made,"[1] Walker insists that the raw material out of which the poet constructs the world of her art must necessarily originate from the common people for whom she clearly writes. "A shack with only a dozen or so books is an unlikely place to discover a young Keats. But it is narrow thinking, indeed, to believe that a Keats is the only kind of poet one would want to grow up to be. One wants to write poetry that is understood by one's people, not by the Queen of England."[2]

If we put aside the narrow context of this apparent though unintended slight against the English monarch, the expression "Queen of England" should be construed in a much wider sense, as an intentional trope by negation designed, first, to express the idea of art as the inspired response to the ordinary, the commonplace, the experiences of common people, and, second, to highlight the marked difference between this kind of art and that which has as its primary focus the high and mighty in society, the privileged elite. It is a distinction between high mimetic art and that of the low mimetic.[3] As Walker sees it, the enduring aspect of art is the artist's extraordinary capacity to hallow the commonplace, to imagine the limitless possibility of the extraordinary in the common run of affairs—in the words of Ralph Waldo Emerson, to see the miraculous in the ordinary everyday reality.[4] This sensibility is displayed at every level of her writing, but most energetically in her poetry. In fact, her poetry, from *Once* to *Revolutionary Petunias,* and from *Good Night, Willie Lee, I'll See You in the Morning* to *Horses Make a Landscape Look More Beautiful,* reads like one grand pastoral metaphor of the earthling consciousness, which attempts to redeem through the poetic medium a world thought to be of little worth. It is very much like dining with Keats

and being swept away by his doctrine of negative capability—"the abandoning of one's self to a selfless sympathy with common everyday things."[5]

Walker's poetry, therefore, like the verse of John Greenleaf Whittier, Thomas Gray, Robert Burns, Oliver Goldsmith, Henry David Thoreau, Walt Whitman, and William Wordsworth, does significantly share in many of the essential motifs of the earthling subjectivity, motifs neatly jelled and goulashed in the unique cadences of the familiar and the commonplace in the experiences of a woman of color in America and beyond. The essential characteristic elements of this earthling subjectivity are expressed through a preoccupation with certain themes and concerns.

First, the imagination that informs the earthling psyche is an imagination that originates from the artist-poet's concern with the affairs of common people. According to J. Bard McNulty, the earthling, or low mimetic, psyche is informed by a certain verisimilitude since the experiences it seeks to construct, or in some cases reconstruct, strike us as being true to life.[6] This quasi-populist realism intersects with feminism, or better yet "womanism," in that the focus of its subject now shifts from a concern with dominating powers and wills to an interest in, a sympathy with, the lowly and the commonalty, their hopes and aspirations, their secret dreams and disappointments, their sorrows and moments of incandescent joy, even personal triumphs. Appealing to the common run of people and things is for Walker a measure of power, both in a personal as well as in a political sense.

In **"Remember,"** the first poem in Walker's fourth poetry collection, *Horses Make a Landscape Look More Beautiful,* the poet assumes the persona of one who evokes and honors the memory of an unassuming, humble, almost self-effacing young girl "with dark skin / whose shoes are thin." With characteristic modesty, the girl declares: "I am the girl / with rotted teeth / I am the dark / rotten-toothed girl / with the wounded eye / and the melted ear." Her nobility and dignity come not from class or high birth but rather from her humanness; in other words, her capacity to respond to and satisfy human needs and desires. She is the one on whom we always call to hold our babies, to cook our meals, to sweep our yards, and to wash our clothes. But in spite of her meekness and lowly disposition, or perhaps because of them, she achieves, at least in the eyes of the poet, the highest honor and distinction as the repository of hope for humanity, hope for regenerative healing and wholeness.

In **"Ballad of the Brown Girl,"** the twenty-third poem in her first volume of poetry, *Once: Poems,* Walker writes about the tragic suicide of an ordinary girl of color. The reason for her suicide is that she lives in a society that does not tolerate interracial love relationships. The poet's sympathy is unquestionably with the girl. In fact, the last lines, a question, are meant to dramatize in bold relief the poet's anger and dismay, dismay at the fact that "here love fails to cross the racial barrier."

> "Question—
>
> did ever brown
> daughter to black
> father a white
> baby
>   take—?"

In the first movement/canto of **Revolutionary Petunias,** Walker's second poetry volume, the poems **"Burial"** and **"Women"** continue this sympathetic interest in the affairs of common people. In **"Burial,"** the occasion is a solemn one, the burial of the poet's father's grandmother, Sis Rachel Walker, alias "Oman." In a tone reminiscent of Thomas Gray's persona in "Elegy Written in a Country Church Yard," the speaker visits the gravesite of her departed immediate forebears and surveys the sense of neglect and desolation brought on by the passage of time. She grieves over the fact that she alone mourns amidst the crumbling tombstones that once "mark[ed] my family's graves." She is particularly distraught because what is supposed to be a final resting place of honor for the dead has now been turned into a place of near disuse and neglect. Where once stood the grieving mourners at the funeral ceremonies for her departed family members, the transhumant cattle now graze with ardent abandon in what has become a weft of weedy pasture. But the poet, despite all that, is still interested in renewing her contact with the dead, mindful of "the old, unalterable roots" that supply a large chunk of the emotional and social matrix that binds her to them.

In **"Women,"** the poet turns historicist and pays homage to a generation of black women, contemporaries of her mother, ordinary women with tireless industry who have achieved extraordinarily. Their raw physical strength, their fortitude and endurance expressed metaphorically as "Headragged Generals / Across mined / Fields / [and] Booby-trapped / Ditches," and their pioneering work in minority education, all are for the poet, decisive terms of personal endearment. The politics of ancestral memory and the passionate intensity of remembering these otherwise ordinary womenfolk are consistent with Walker's avowal to keep the tradition and memory of African American women alive and to let that be a constant source of inner strength and personal wholeness. In **In Search of Our Mothers' Gardens,** Walker writes: "There are countless vanished and forgotten women who are nonetheless eager to speak to her—from Frances Harper and Anne Spencer to Dorothy West—but she must work to find them, to free them from their neglect and the oppression of silence forced upon them because they were black and (also because) they were women.'"

In **"Did This Happen to Your Mother? Did Your Sister Throw up a Lot?,"** the first poem in Walker's third volume of poetry, **Good Night, Willie Lee, I'll See You in the Morning,** we have the simple tale of a colored woman forlorn of love. Deserted by a man she thought she loved, she swears that "I love a man who is not worth / my love," and that the same "love has made me sick." Love, that special sense of warm attachment and sympathetic tenderness has become instead one long, woebegone chapter of lies, deception, and cunning. As a result, she feels a gorgelike emptiness inside, an emptiness she compares to the massive depth of the Arizona Grand Canyon.

> My hand shakes before this killing.
> My stomach sits jumpy in my chest.
> My chest is the Grand Canyon
> sprawled empty
> over the world.

And yet her lovelornness is not hers alone. She shares the same fate with a host of other women, who at one point or another in their chequered lives have had to endure the unsettling disappointments and humiliations of faithless love.

Aside from depicting the ordinary scheme of everyday reality and the people that loom in it, another way in which Walker exemplifies her earthling subjectivity is through the hallowing of the place of nature in the lives of ordinary people. For Walker, the creative mind that perceives nature is an attingent traditional mind that hallows/celebrates the reciprocal dependence of internal and external natural processes. In other words, part of Walker's earthling subjectivity is focused on the sympathetic relationship between her creative intellect and the natural environment. In this relation, the natural environment is not perceived as Other, but instead as an essential part in the expression of one's individuality (in this case the individuality of the poet) as well as one's reciprocal relation to other people, that is, other members of one's community.

The one place where Alice Walker reflects this coordinate and organic perception of nature is in **"African Images, Glimpses from a Tiger's Back,"** one of the longest poems in **Once.** The poem begins:

> Beads around
> my neck
> Mt. Kenya away
> over pineappled hills
> Kikuyuland.

The proximity of Mt. Kenya and the pineappled hills to Kikuyu land is hardly fortuitous. It speaks to, as well as amplifies, the interfusion of nature in the lives of the people of Kenya. The poet is acutely aware of how closely human life here is integrated with physical nature. The pineappled hills, which appear as interlacing arches that weave the lives and destinies of the people, suggest that the people, autochthonous to the Kikuyu land, are farmers whose contact with the earth is fixed, almost like an ineluctable fate or inexorable necessity. The poet says:

> A book of poems
> Mt. Kenya's
> Bluish peaks
> "Wangari!"
> My new name.

She here suggests that from nature the woman artist draws everything, even herself. Consequently, the poetry that she composes is, like nature itself, ultimately concerned with the generative forces of being. For Walker this affinity between benign nature and artistic self situates and defines the matrix of her ecofeminist sensibility. We will return to this point a little later.

Meanwhile, the imposing majesty of Mt. Kenya, strewn across the elongated ridge of "pineappled hills," parallels the graceful charm, the virid brilliance of the "beads around my neck," offering the visiting poet to East Africa a conception of beauty as well as the language in which to express it. Besides, in an esemplastic imagination akin to Wordsworth's in "Tintern Abbey" and *The Prelude,* the conflation of "a book of poems" and the "bluish peaks" of Mt. Kenya suggests that nature is a creative force to which the human mind (but especially that of the earthling poet) is "exquisitely fitted."[8] It points up the manner in which nature goes about its kind of imaginative creation. According to McNulty, "The process is the 'express resemblance' of the process of imagination in the human mind."[9]

Furthermore, the act of taking on a new name suggests that nature provides the fundamental essence of the process of naming built into the consciousness of the indigenous people. The formal endowment of the praise/heroic epithet "Wangari" upon the visiting poet, apparently by the august assembly of the elders, and the cotangent and correlative processes of naming in the Kikuyu and Leopard clans underscore the unique ontological signification of nature in the thinking of traditional Africans, a thinking that Ernst Cassirer has described as "the myth-making consciousness."[10] This mythmaking consciousness further demonstrates how traditional peoples like the Kikuyus assign names that bear the tutelary influence of primogenitor/ancestor, and how the unique dimensions of clan psychology, which manifest in a variety of formal ritual inductions or initiation rites, all relate to the unique primitivization of nature.

The poet is so delighted, so enthralled by the majestic blossom, almost enchanting comeliness of the East African topography, the distant peaks and virid vistas spread before her very eyes, that she cannot help but catalogue its manifold beauty with a flurry of images. Walker's poetic intelligence is able to transform the grandeur of the manifold objects of sense into an expression of an indissoluble unity of universal poetic thought. This expression reminds us of Plato, for whom "the world of Nature . . . is the expression of an all-dissolving Unity of which the prevailing features are truth and beauty."[11]

With a technique akin to cinematography, the poet-visitor takes the reader on a guided panoramic tour of the East African landforms. First, the poet, from the relative security and comfort of her safari, peers at "a green copse" and "a shy gazelle" and an elephant bulldozing her way through the shifting rents of the morning mists. Next she looks out on "the clear Nile" inside of which "a fat crocodile / scratches his belly and yawns." Then the tropical evergreen woodland of the African rain forest comes clearly into view, lush with red orchids and the spinning cobra. From here, under the overarching blue sky, the poet sails gently on "a placid lake" in "a small boat," then through another "silent lake" along "bone strewn banks / Luminous / In the sun." Earlier the poet had stroked the water buffalo and the two ears of the mammoth hippopotamus with his hand, seen a leopard zap effortlessly through the branches of trees, a giraffe "munching his dinner," while off yonder on a high rise are Uganda mountains with their black soil and white snow, "and in the valley / Zebra."

There is hardly any doubt from the foregoing that our earthling poet on an exhilarating African safari reserves a deep appreciation and a respect for nature, its kaleidoscope of sights and sounds and colors, as well as the intense emotions they stir. The uniqueness of the verdant culture of an East African landscape is a source of incandescent joy for the poet. The safari itself amounts to a kind of initiatory rite. Besides, the topography, especially the verdure of the rain forest, reflects the culture of the indigenous people who occupy it and eke a livelihood out of it. All of that now unfolds before the traveling poet's eye in endless undulations of varying greens, all blending in a delightful, stark harmony of form and texture and color and atmosphere.

In **"Torture,"** the thirty-eighth poem in ***Horses Make a Landscape Look More Beautiful,*** nature takes on the function of the healer, the regenerative anodyne, serving to assuage the pain and trauma of life, to soothe, to calm and comfort in a moment of grief or seemingly irreparable loss.

> When they torture your mother
> plant a tree
> When they torture your father
> plant a tree
> When they torture your brother
> and your sister
> plant a tree
> When they assassinate
> your leaders
> and lovers
> plant a tree
> When they torture you

too bad
to talk
plant a tree.

The juxtaposition of dissimilar acts of torturing and soothing, of damage and reparation, in the process of self-renewal intensifies the healing and restorative power of nature. The poet ends her injunction with these words:

When they begin to torture
the trees
and cut down the forest
they have made
start another.

Here Walker's ecofeminist convictions ring loud and clear. The speaker is enjoining us to feel the life of the Other, the natural ambience. She is enjoining us to feel a compassion for nature of which the tree and the forest are but synecdoches. According to Judith Plant in *Healing the Wounds: The Promise of Ecofeminism,* "This compassion . . . is the essence of a new paradigm," of the moral necessity of grieving for the loss of our sisters and brothers who are the forests. "Our pain," continues Plant, "for the death of the forests is simply, and most fundamentally, compassion for the senseless destruction of life."[12]

The truth that the poet brings with her injunction is that we are part of this earth, and this fact must predispose us to see "how relations with each other are reflected in our relations with the natural world." Here Walker's message, like that of the ecofeminist spiritualists, becomes "a praxis of hope," the hope "that like the forests we destroy, or the rivers we tame, we are Nature."[13] In her prose work *Living by the Word,* Walker notes how, when she was residing in the northern hills of California, she had witnessed almost with helplessness the daily horror of the loggers' trucks (she calls them "hearses") as they felled the trees and carried, in her words, "the battered bodies of the old sisters and brothers." She also relates another incident at a national park during which she gazed at some gnarled, diseased old trees. "What the trees tell her," writes Winchell, "is that when it comes to human beings, trees do not discriminate; all people must share the guilt for the destruction being done to the planet and all its life forms." Again, Walker writes in *Living by the Word*: "Our thoughts must be on how to restore to the Earth its dignity as a living being; how to stop raping and plundering it as a matter of course. We must begin to develop the consciousness that everything has equal rights because existence itself is equal. In other words, we are all here: trees, people, snakes, alike."[14]

In fact, planting a tree, from the perspective of the poem **"Torture,"** has become for the speaker, in the words of Joanna Macy, "awakening to the ecological self," in which "conventional, customary notions of self and self-interest are being shed like an old skin or con-

fining shell."[15] And the person doing the planting itself has come into a new covenant that transcends separateness and fragmentation. By planting another tree or starting another forest, the planter is no longer just trying to secure it from mindless deforestation; rather, she herself has become a part of the forest protecting herself. She has become that part of nature recently emerged into human thinking.[16] The transition from the grisly scenarios of mindless sadists and assassins to the interdependent plane of regenerative nature is analogous to what Hazel Henderson has described as the shift in consciousness from "phenotype" to "genotype." Henderson writes: "We may be emerging from the 'age of the phenotype,' of separated ego awareness, which has now become amplified into untenable forms of dualism. . . . The emerging view is rebalancing toward concern for the genotype, protection of species and gene pools . . . and the new intergenerational risks being transferred to our progeny, about which economics says little."[17]

A third and final way in which Walker engages her earthling imagination is by a systematic attempt to understand her own personality, a kind of personalist idealism, beyond axiological or moral categories. She does that by asserting her own thoughts, feelings, perceptions, and valuations. The attempt also involves the unique interplay of character, ego, and circumstance vis-à-vis the workings of the artistic intelligence evincible within the processes of imaginative creation. In her essay, "The Black Woman Artist as Wayward," Barbara Christian suggests that what distinguishes Walker's poetry from her prose is that the former is a graph of Alice Walker's self. She writes: "In her poetry, Walker the wayward child challenges us to accept her as she is. Perhaps it is the stripping of bark from herself that enables us to feel that sound of the genuine in her scrutiny of easy positions advocated by progressive blacks and women."[18]

There are many poems in which Walker shows this interest in self and self-analysis. Six of them especially stand out as the most eloquent expression of the trinity of feeling, condition, and character of the poet's self. Each of them, by sheer eloquence of voice and candor, reveals an aspect of the poet's personality predominant at a given time and under certain definable conditions. That personality often is a unique mark of an individual who has grown, fashioned as it were by the processes of self-fertilization/self-pollination beyond easy categories of self-abasement or social adaption.

For Walker the graph of self that Christian speaks about is the ideology of the experience of the self as the essential arbiter of reality. That ideology celebrates autonomy as a fundamental individual right that must not be violated or vitiated by a sentimental or even the most pious appeal to collective experience. It is the ideology of self that Professor Mihaly Csikszentmihalyi has described as "'the autotelic self'—a self that has self-contained goals.''[19] It is a self that fiercely asserts and guards the validity and integrity of her own experience, a validity and integrity that requires no other validation, morally, socially, or culturally. The epitome of this self is revealed most trenchantly in Walker's **"On Stripping Bark from Myself,"** one of the most significant poems in *Good Night, Willie Lee, I'll See You in the Morning.*

The sheer audacity of voice with which this self announces her presence on this earth is unmistakable. The announcement, which sounds almost bellicose, comes down like a peel of thunder. It is as if out of the nebulous depths of social conformism and conditioned selves a new self emerges to claim her place in the world. The speaker says:

> I find my own
> small person
> a standing self
> against the world
> an equality of wills
> I finally understand.

But the audacity is somewhat weaned within the rhetoric of the underdog, which is intended not so much to elicit sympathy as it is to warn a world that is accustomed to taking advantage of small people that this time there is and must be a new deal. And the new deal, which in metaphorically coextensive terms subserves the agonistic mythos of David and Goliath, is a bold vision of the world as a level playing field where small people and big people, rich people and poor people, the advantaged and disadvantaged, live each in their own space as they see fit without any of them ever assuming for one moment that what is good and right for one is necessarily good and right for another. It is an intensely relativistic world in which one's responses need not be the responses of others dictated by society or political correctness, but instead responses shared with others dictated solely by the individual's defined needs and desires. In this regard, the self becomes the critical medium through which collective responses and sentiments are distilled or crystallized.

Thus, the self swears direly,

> No. I am finished with living
> for what my mother believes
> for what my brother and father defend
> for what my lover elevates
> for what my sister, blushing, denies or rushes
> to embrace.

Here she is warning that often what is passed off as the collective outlook of traditional phallocentric culture from which all reality must receive its legitimating authority is no longer tenable. Back in the days when women were "expected to keep silent about / their close escapes" and felt content living the lie that society's conditioning and customary sanctions had imposed on them, that silence might have appeared perfectly nor-mal. Back in the days when women could not see themselves outside of the assigned roles and normative constructs in society, and others could not see them independently of these roles and constructs, the kind of deviation and subversion of "the common will" contemplated by the Walker self here might have seemed too indefinable, even dangerous. Other poems in which Walker explores the assertive will of the self include, but are not limited to, **"So We've Come at Last to Freud"** and **"Mornings / of an Impossible Love"** (*Once*); **"Sunday School, Circa 1950," "Will," "Rage," "Beyond What,"** and **"Reassurance"** (*Revolutionary Petunias*); and **"On Stripping Bark from Myself"** and **"Early Losses: A Requiem"** (*Good Night, Willie Lee, I'll See You in the Morning*). In each of these poems, the capacity and freedom to launch a "ruthless" pursuit of one's inwardness is systematically vocalized. In other words, Walker's intent is to find her own personal turf, and ultimately, this turf is in accord with the thoughts of Hermann Hesse in *Demian*: "Each man had only one genuine vocation—to find the way to himself. He might end up as a poet or madman, as prophet or criminal—that was not his affair, ultimately it was of no concern. His task was to discover his own destiny—not an arbitrary one—and live it out wholly and resolutely within himself. Everything else was only a would-be existence, an attempt at evasion, a flight back to the ideas of the masses, conformity and fear of one's own inwardness."[20]

In closing, I want to return to the remark with which I began this essay, namely, Walker's angry response to the "white Northerner." It is not so much that John Keats was opposed to the earthling subjectivity. As a matter of fact, Keats, through his aesthetic doctrine of negative capability, not only preached about it but in fact practiced it in his poetry. It is not so much that Keats was white, and Alice Walker black. Instead it is that Walker was making a point about the immanent necessities of poetic thought: the contingent particularity of earthly experience that some people like the white northerner would rather ignore or relegate to the back yard. But Walker through her poetry reminds us of the ineluctability of poetic art as the immanent act of the mind and the relation of that mind to experience. What people mistakenly call transcendence with which they identify certain writings and writers is nothing but an epistemic category of a continuum involving a relationship with objects in the actual world and the transcendental universal forms or ideas of which they are embodiments.

Thus the earthling psyche can be appropriately defined as the act of the artistic mind that celebrates immanent reality, a consciousness of the pursuits and interests of earthly life, including the consciousness of essences captured in the objective, as well as those elements such as emotions, sentiments, thoughts, and sensations that constitute a person's unique individuality and identity. It embodies a somewhat primitivist theologic view of reality in which the earth itself is conceived as the primal source of numinous being. Its characteristic elements include, but are not limited to, a concern for the commonplace in the affairs of common people, an impassioned celebration of nature, an exploration of the self, and, sometimes, an engagement in a kind of mild, verbal satirical wit.[21]

Notes

1. Walker identifies this reader as "a white Northerner." As the daughter of indigent sharecropper parents from rural Eatonton, Georgia, Walker is naturally offended by the reader's reckless insensitivity and elitist pose. See Winchell, 15.

2. Walker, *In Search of Our Mothers' Gardens.*

3. For a note on the differences between the two, see McNulty, 104-5, 127. I would like to take the opportunity to acknowledge my indebtedness to McNulty's discussion of the low mimetic era in English and American literature. His discussion alone is the main inspiration for my theory of the earthling imagination.

4. Qtd. in McNulty, 114-15.

5. Ibid., 109.

6. Ibid., 108.

7. Walker, *In Search of Our Mothers' Gardens,* 36.

8. For a fuller discussion of the technique employed by low mimetic poets such as Wordsworth to explain the creative essence of nature, see McNulty, esp. 111-14, 118-25.

9. Ibid., 112.

10. Qtd. in Obiechina, 82.

11. Bryan, 2-3.

12. Plant, 1.

13. Griffin, 10.

14. Qtd. in Winchell, *Alice Walker,* 112.

15. Macy, 201.

16. Macy characterizes the understanding of the significance of this relationship as an "ecological sense of selfhood" (202). She also recalls, in particular, a walk through the jungle of eastern Australia: "One day, under the vine-strung jungle trees of eastern Australia, I was walking with my friend John Seed, director of the Rainforest Information Center. I asked him how he managed to overcome despair and sustain the struggle against the mammoth lumber interests. He said, 'I try to remember that it's not me, John Seed, trying to protect the rainforest. Rather I am part of the rainforest protecting myself. I am that part of the rainforest recently emerged into human thinking'" (202).

17. Qtd. in Macy, 210.

18. Christian, 53.

19. Csikszentmilhalyi, 207.

20. Qtd. in Miller, 112.

21. Some of the poems in which Walker displays her satirical wit include: "First They Said," "Listen," "We Alone," "Killers," "Songless," "A Few Sirens," "SM," "Attentiveness," and "The Diamonds on Liz's Bosom" (*Horses Make a Landscape Look More Beautiful*); "Sunday School, Circa 1950" (*Revolutionary Petunias*); "Janie Crawford" (*Good Night, Willie Lee, I'll See You in the Morning*); and "On Being Asked to Leave a Place of Honor for One of Comfort . . ." (*Once*).

Works Cited

Bloom, Harold, ed. *Alice Walker.* New York: Chelsea House, 1989.

Bryan, J. Ingram. *The Interpretation of Nature in English Poetry.* Tokyo: Folcroft, 1972.

Christian, Barbara. "The Black Woman Artist as Wayward." In Bloom, 39-58.

Csikszentmilhalyi, Mihaly. "The Autotelic Self." In *Reading Critically, Writing Well.* 3d ed. Ed. Rise B. Axelrod and Charles R. Cooper. New York: St. Martin's, 1993. 207-10.

Griffin, Susan. "Split Culture." In Plant, 7-17.

Macy, Joanna. "Awakening to the Ecological Self." In Plant, 201-11.

McNulty, J. Bard. *Modes of Literature.* Boston: Houghton, 1977.

Miller, James E. *Word, Self, Reality: The Rhetoric of Imagination.* New York: Dodd, 1974.

Obiechina, Emmanuel. *Culture, Tradition and Society in the West African Novel.* Cambridge: Cambridge University Press, 1975.

Plant, Judith, ed. *Healing the Wounds: The Promise of Ecofeminism.* Philadelphia: New Society, 1989.

Walker, Alice. *Good Night, Willie Lee, I'll See You in the Morning.* New York: Dial, 1979.

———. *Her Blue Body Everything We Know: Earthling Poems 1965-1990 Complete.* New York: Harcourt, 1983.

———. *In Search of Our Mothers' Gardens.* San Diego: Harcourt, 1983.

———. *Once: Poems.* New York: Harcourt, 1968.

———. *Revolutionary Petunias and Other Poems.* New York: Harcourt, 1973.

Winchell, Donna. *Alice Walker.* New York: Twayne, 1992.

Robyn R. Warhol (essay date May 2001)

SOURCE: Warhol, Robyn R. "How Narration Produces Gender: Femininity as Affect and Effect in Alice Walker's *The Color Purple.*" *Narrative* 9, no. 2 (May 2001): 182-87.

[*In this essay, Warhol examines the narrative strategies Walker employed in* The Color Purple *in order to emo-*

tionally move her readers, focusing in particular on the novelist's reliance on the first-person voice of the oppressed (Celie) and Walker's use of the epistolary form.]

Having a good cry is a feminine thing to do. In British and American mainstream culture of the nineteenth and twentieth centuries, weeping openly and emotionally—whether for grief, anger, frustration, sympathy, relief, joy, triumph, or gratitude—is an activity associated with girls and women, considered appropriate to their female frames and feminine feelings. Men cry, too, of course: if they are gay men, their tears are understood as part of the penchant they are supposed to share with feminine women for "making a spectacle" of their feelings;[1] if they are straight, they must be perceived as shedding "manly tears" or run the risk of compromising their masculinity. To have a *good* cry, though, is to indulge in one of the perquisites of this culture's version of femininity, whether the person doing the crying is male or female.

In this essay I will focus on the narrative strategies that produce the good cry in narrative fiction, using as my illustrative example Alice Walker's **The Color Purple** (1982), an unabashedly sentimental novel, notorious for making readers cry. For me and for many of my students and fellow readers over the past fifteen years, the last letter in Walker's epistolary novel functions to invoke a "good cry" that is identical to the impact of the classics of the feminine "good-cry" genre, from the climactic moments of Louisa May Alcott's *Little Women* and Harriet Beecher Stowe's *Uncle Tom's Cabin,* to the end of *It's a Wonderful Life.*[2] I will argue that the source of the novel's affective impact is not individual readers' personal (or somehow essentially "feminine") ability to identify with the characters but, rather, the novel's narrative technique, particularly the ways it uses focalization and address to underscore the novel's affirmation of what contemporary U.S. culture understands as feminine mythologies. My larger point is that readers' femininity does not preexist our repeated and habitual encounters with gendered cultural artifacts; rather, gender gets produced and reproduced through countless cultural patterns, including narrative strategies associated with texts that are marked within a given culture as "masculine" (such as adventure stories) or "feminine" (such as good-cry novels like **The Color Purple**). Narratology provides a useful vocabulary for describing the ways this works.

Sentimental narrative discourse requires a particular handling of "internal focalization," narratology's term for narrative discourse conveying the perceptions (vision, thoughts, feelings, etc.) not of the narrator but of a character, regardless of whether the discourse is in the narrator's or the character's voice. Scenes in sentimental novels tend to be focalized either through victims or triumphant figures who have formerly been represented as oppressed. This focalization invites the reader to participate emotionally from the subject-position of the oppressed, in the diegetic good times and the bad. Sentimental novels can use embedded first-person narratives to achieve this effect. More often, the "omniscient" (or in more properly narratological terms, "heterodiegetic") narrative focus simply shifts to the perspective of the sufferer, rendering the scene as he or she sees it. As Philip Fisher has pointed out, the focalization in sentimental narrative sometimes comes through sympathetic intermediary figures who are not, themselves, directly oppressed—such as Eva in *Uncle Tom*—but it is seldom if ever granted to those who oppress the protagonists in the fictional world. This careful limiting of the narrative point of view to those who suffer and triumph after tribulation can effect a powerful pull on the sensations of a susceptible, cooperative reader, regardless of the reader's historical orientation to the text (readers experiencing the novel twenty or a hundred years after its writing can have emotional reactions equal to those of the text's first readers).[3] In sentimental novels, moreover, the "good cry" is much more often evoked by scenes of triumph than by scenes of sadness.

Attention to the role narrative focalization plays in the affective dynamics of reading is important, as it presents a challenge to the idea that readers sympathize with suffering characters when they can "identify" with them. Michael Steig's remarkable reader-response study, *Stories of Reading* (1989), for example, attributes Steig's own crying over Charles Dickens's *Bleak House* to identification with the characters. Steig reports, "I still find my eyes filling with tears at the same old points. I have felt in the past that I must have some residue of sentimentality in my soul, and have been annoyed that Dickens manipulates me into that reaction, but that is probably unfair" (70). Steig finds the "coy" narrator, Esther Summerson, consistently irritating, "and yet at the same time I must be identifying with her strongly, on the evidence of the way my tears so easily flow" (70). Emphasizing the intrinsically personal psychology of such identification, Steig remarks, "To get at the reasons for this will require some digging into my past" (70). Of course, a model of identification like Steig's puts the crying reader in a position of enjoying pleasures that are both individualistic and masochistic. If we think about the feminine reader's tears as, in part, a consequence of the text's technical arrangement of perspective, rather than as a reflection of the reader's consciously or subconsciously feeling that the miserable or triumphant sufferer is "just like me," however, audiences' participation in sentimentalism becomes more positively performative, less revealing of some presumed hidden truth about the readers' "real feelings."

Epistolary fiction (the form of **The Color Purple**), with its shifts in narrative voice and in temporal perspective, brings the affective mechanics of focalization into especially vivid relief. As the letter-writer relates each segment of the story, she has access only to her own consciousness (like any conventionally realist first-person narrator, she cannot read other characters' minds, but can only report their actions and expressions, both verbal and physical). Her perspective is even more strictly limited, however, than that of the intradiegetic narrators of novels that are not epistolary, in that she only knows as much about the story as she *can* know at the time of composing the letter: she has not yet "lived" beyond the moment at which she is writing, and hence cannot foreshadow, in her narration, what is to happen after that moment.[4]

Since Samuel Richardson's *Pamela,* epistolary novelists have made the most of this technique's ability to build suspense and to heighten the affective impact of fictional narratives. Like Pamela, Celie does not know, in moments when she is writing in fear and anger, that her tribulations will end happily; unlike Jane Eyre, for example, she does not tell her story with the double consciousness (and the inevitably ironic distance between the "I" who speaks and the "I" who experiences) that comes from life-long retrospection.[5] Of course, epistolary narratives are usually written retrospectively, but the retrospection is in pieces, arranged serially as it were, rather than spanning the length of the diegetic time represented within the narrative. Hence, the telos in epistolary fiction is distinct from that of nonepistolary narrative, in that the epistolary narrator can reflect no sense of his or her final outcome in the narration, even if the author has used other means to establish foreshadows. The effect, for the willing or cooperative reader of the sentimental epistolary novel, is a heightened physical experience of reading that can be readily enlisted in the service of the good cry. The actual reader is "in the moment" with the epistolary narrator; the potential for detachment that is available to the authorial audience of retrospective or otherwise distanced narration is not available in epistolary form.

Critics commenting on **The Color Purple** take it for granted that this novel inspires readerly tears with moments of intensely rendered grief (as when the adolescent Celie mourns the two babies that were born to her and then brutally taken away; or when she is separated from Nettie, seemingly forever; or when she encounters the beautifully Amazonian Sophia, physically and emotionally diminished by her time in jail). But for me, the biggest cry comes at the novel's end, with a burst of joy peculiarly foregrounded by the focalizing effect of the epistolary form. The first fifty letters in the novel are addressed by Celie to "Dear God." Up to that point, the narrative form more closely resembles a diary than an epistolary fiction; the letters to God are a chronicle of Celie's isolation, inspired by her supposed-father's injunction against her reporting his repeated, incestuous rapes: "You better not never tell nobody but God" (11). At the novel's formal turning point, the diary form gets interrupted by eight of the letters Nettie has written to Celie from Africa, hidden until this point by Celie's abusive husband, Albert. Celie's rage against Albert and against that rapist who, she learns from Nettie's letters, was *not* in fact her own father, leads her to conclude

that God "must be [a]sleep" (163). At this point, with a third of the novel still to go, Celie changes her address from "Dear God" to "Dear Nettie," and though Nettie's subsequent letters are not answers to the letters Celie addresses to her, the remainder of the text takes the form of a correspondence (although it is undelivered and undeliverable) between the two sisters.

As commentators have observed, Nettie's letters serve the thematic purpose of broadening **The Color Purple**'s geographical and political horizons to include Africa and to connect that continent to Celie's little corner of the American South. The interpolation of Nettie's letters also serves a narrative function, though, as the letters provide Celie with an embodied narratee. Nettie's existence as narratee becomes the textual sign of Celie's relief from isolation, her coming into community as she comes out into her lesbian sexuality with Shug. When Celie grumbles to Shug about her religious disillusionment, Shug offers Celie an alternative view of God: "I believe God is everything, say Shug. Everything that is or ever was or ever will be. And when you can feel that, and be happy to feel that, you've found It. . . . She say, My first step from the old white man [image of God] was trees. Then air. Then birds. Then other people" (178).

As Celie renders it in a letter to Nettie, this scene's initial significance is in its romantic dimension, since it brings Celie closer to Shug. The Celie who relates this conversation cannot know how its vocabulary will return in the novel's last letter, or how the words' significance will shift, and so she cannot foreshadow its significance. The susceptible reader will be taken unawares, in the novel's final pages, by the scene's reprise.

Because the epistolary form focalizes the narrative through Celie's present state of feeling in each of her letters, the sudden happy ending does indeed carry heavy affective clout. But what makes me cry in Celie's last letter is not only—and, indeed, not primarily—the "happy-ending" events. I remain aware that these events, especially in combination, are so implausible as to be almost laughable. They include (1) the unexpected return of Nettie, who has been reunited in Africa with Celie's two lost children and has now brought them back, with their adoptive father (Nettie's own new husband) to live with Celie again; (2) the mother-and-child reunion that accompanies the sister's return; and (3) Celie's own new-found good fortune in having a place to welcome them to, having inherited the home her birth-father has left to her, thus solidifying the financial independence she has begun to establish with her pants-making business. No, it is not the situation itself that is the main source of the good cry for me. Instead, the main source is in the confluence of the narrative discourse with the novel's passionate endorsement of mythologies central to femininity (mythologies about sisters, mothers, children, and financial self-sufficiency, for instance), in the address of Celie's last letter. After having addressed fourteen consecutive letters to "Dear Nettie," Celie starts her last letter with a completely new beginning: "Dear God. Dear stars, dear trees, dear sky, dear peoples. Dear Everything. Dear God. Thank you for bringing my sister Nettie and our children home" (249). That passage gets me every time; for me, no other good-cry moment can surpass it. The way Celie's voice crosses the diegetic boundary, to include me in her address ("dear peoples. Dear Everything") and, in so doing, to assert my inclusion in Celie's newly minted concept of God; the way her address brings into being a moment of pure community embracing not just Nettie, as the previous letters had done, but all the characters and even me; the unmixed joy and triumph of the moment of ecstatic enunciation always make me cry. And that is why I'd call it a "feminine narrative," as it enforces and reinforces the physical experience of an emotion the culture marks as specifically feminine. The "femininity" of the text is not linked to the "femaleness" of the author or characters, nor to the sex of the presumed readers' bodies: it is a narrative effect.

To those who ask, "What's 'good' about 'the good cry'?" I respond (only somewhat self-consciously) that the ideals of sentimental culture—the affirmation of community, the persistence of hopefulness and of willingness, the belief that everyone matters, the sense that life has a purpose that can be traced to the links of affection between and among persons—are good ideals. Sentimentalism has a bad reputation, among general readers and critics alike; it is no coincidence that Steig, for one, reports resenting Dickens's "manipulation" of his tears. To be sure, sentimentalism is often exploited in order to promote agendas far less progressive than Walker's or even Dickens's. If manipulators of public sentiment unscrupulously deploy the narrative techniques of the sentimental tradition in the service of nationalism, capitalism, and commercialism, however, that does not drain the techniques themselves (or their potential affective impact upon actual audiences) of value. Becoming more conscious of how those techniques achieve their effects does not render readers immune to them, but it can offer us the opportunity to affirm "feelings" that constitute what is worth preserving from traditional feminine culture.

Notes

1. I am thinking of the links Joseph Litvak draws between spectacle, spectacular emotions, and homosexuality in *Caught in the Act*.

2. For an introduction to what I mean by the "goodcry genre," see my essay, "As You Stand, So You Feel and Are." That argument, and the general point I am making in the present essay, are elaborated in my book forthcoming from Ohio State University Press, *Having a Good Cry*.

3. See Sicherman for a rich account of Victorian-American feminine readers' reactions to reading sentimental fiction.

4. To be sure, the author of an epistolary narrative may foreshadow future diegetic events by including verbal details or patterns in the storyline that will recur, even though the narrator does not, at the moment of narration, realize that they will.

5. For more details on the retrospective impact of first-person narration, see my article entitled "Double Gender, Double Genre."

Works Cited

Fisher, Philip. *Hard Facts: Setting and Form in the American Novel.* New York: Oxford Univ. Press, 1987.

Litvak, Joseph. *Caught in the Act: Theatricality in the Nineteenth-Century English Novel.* Berkeley: Univ. of California Press, 1992.

Sicherman, Barbara. "Sense and Sensibility: A Case Study of Women's Reading in Late-Victorian America." In *Reading in America: Literature and Social History,* edited by Cathy N. Davidson, 201-25. Baltimore: Johns Hopkins Univ. Press, 1989.

Steig, Michael. *Stories of Reading: Subjectivity and Literary Understanding.* Baltimore: Johns Hopkins Univ. Press, 1989.

Walker, Alice. *The Color Purple.* New York: Harcourt Brace Jovanovich, 1982.

Warhol, Robyn R. "'As You Stand, So You Feel and Are': The Crying Body and the 19th-century Text." In *Tattoo, Torture, Mutilation, and Adornment: The De-Naturalization of the Body in Culture and Text,* edited by Fran Mascia-Lees and Patricia Sharpe, 100-25. Albany: State Univ. of New York Press, 1992.

———. "Double Gender, Double Genre in *Jane Eyre* and *Villette*." *Studies in English Literature* 36 (Fall 1996): 857-75.

———. *Having a Good Cry.* Columbus: Ohio State Univ. Press, forthcoming.

Pirjo Ahokas (essay date 2003)

SOURCE: Ahokas, Pirjo. "Hybridized Black Female Identity in Alice Walker's *Meridian*." In *America Today: Highways and Labyrinths,* edited by Gigliola Nocera, pp. 481-88. Siracusa, Italy: Grafia' Editrice, 2003.

[In the essay below, Ahokas contends that, "through a complex process of signification, Walker's novel [Meridian] not only suggests a more fluid, hybrid black identity but also charts a shift to the recognition of the heterogeneity of black identities."]

For many contemporary theoreticians, the border—present whenever two or more cultures edge each other (Anzaldúa ix)—has come to symbolize a promise or possibility of identity hybridization. As far as black cultural identity is concerned, this view questions the innocent notion of the essential black subject that characterized the identity construction and identity politics of black American cultural nationalism during the 1960s and early 1970s. It is true that the new essential black subject was a timely response to racism and marginalization (Hall 27, 28), and it managed to challenge the harmful, old stereotypes of black identity. Constructed exclusively around the dynamics of racial difference and put in the place of the so called "bad old essential white subject," it nevertheless suffered from many limitations as a strategy of black politics (Hall 28). Alice Walker's novel *Meridian* (1976) is regarded as one of the key novels about the Civil Rights movement and the new black militant front. I find the book very intriguing for the reason that, on the one hand, it is linked with black American nationalism, but, on the other hand, it also launches a powerful attack on the exclusionary discourses and practices within the movement during the most militant era of black politics.

In my paper, I will look at the different ways in which Walker's novel questions the narrow categories of identity which may seem necessary for political action, but which are based on far too restrictive and confining notions of identity. Challenging the fixed unitary subject proposed by black identity politics, Walker's book explores the differences within the group and individual identity. Moreover, crossing the rigidly constructed boundaries between "race," gender, ethnicity, and class, *Meridian* clearly alligns itself with the margin of hybridity that, according to Homi K. Bhabha, "resists the binary opposition of racial and cultural groups" (. . .) "as homogeneous polarized political consciousnesses" (Bhabha 207). Ultimately, through a complex process of signification, Walker's novel not only suggests a more fluid, hybrid black identity but also charts a shift to the recognition of the heterogeneity of black identities.

It is noteworthy that the novel's opening section takes place in the South in the mid-1970s when "militancy was no longer in the sidewalks" (Cooke 140), showing how, as a result of persistent racism, poor black people's lives have not changed much since the 1960s. The exaggerated opening scene in which the eponymous protagonist is introduced draws attention to its stage-like qualities, and it also seems to propose the idea of gender and ethnic performativity. Written in a very self-conscious mode, the novel's beginning foregrounds Meridian's—the black female protagonist's—lonely fight against the white townspeople's army tank. It also juxtaposes her with the grotesque, decaying body of a white woman that is publicly displayed by her husband for profit. Indeed, the notion of the performative aspects of gender and ethnicity is intensified when, a little later, the text goes as far as to make Meridian use the word "perform" about her own public appearances.

As Walker's novel progresses, it becomes quite clear that while the text raises critical questions about identity construction, it also suggests that by disrupting the performative aspects of identity construction, it becomes possible to destabilize fixed notions of identity to effect social change. Furthermore, the narrator's use of various black traditions also serves as an additional strategy of questioning the dominant discourse of black nationalism and its black subject.

Historically, black nationalism in America grew out of the American enslavement of Africans and, in its broadest sense, it presupposes the collective efforts of blacks to overcome their shared racial oppression. Opposed to the dominant white culture's reproduction of its hierarchical power, the black nationalists of the 1960s advocated a new, affirmative ideal of selfhood that, as they put it, could only be achieved through the repudiation of all aspects of American society that militated against a positive black self-image. Their emphasis on a "positive" black self, epitomized in the well-known politicized slogan "Black is beautiful," also tended to preclude those elements of the blacks' oppressive historical past in the United States that could not pass through the filter of black pride (Dubey 25-26). In addition to avoiding painful issues like slavery, black nationalist discourse tended to gender its racial subjects as masculine.

Some scholars have linked black women's marginalization in the black nationalist movement to these issues. During slavery black women were treated as breeders and slavery has also served as the source of the stereotype of the strong black matriarch (Dubey 19). New scholarship argues that these elements of the past could not be reconciled with the investment of black male nationalists in the powerful subject position of patriarchal masculinity (Dubey 18, 19). As far as the central issue of race was concerned, the same discourse conceived it in terms of simple, monolithic binary oppositions between white and black citizens and emphasized a mythical African origin common to all African-Americans.

The opening scene of Walker's novel bristles with multi-layered irony. In *Reconstructing Womanhood*, Hazel Carby argues that it is necessary to study ideologies of white Southern womanhood in order to be able to explain ideologies of black womanhood in the 19th century (20). It is evident from what follows in *Meridian* that the white mummy-woman's husband's definition of his ideal woman is in accordance to the 19th century cult of true womanhood. As a Southern prewar code of sexuality it glorified white women and excluded black slave women from the parameters of virtuous possibilities (Carby 27). When Walker contrasts Meridian's militant figure with the mummified corpse, she suggests "an alternative to the untenable roles of womanhood" (Nadel 159). By an ironic twist, however, the text shows that the postwar black community in the segregated south where Meridian grows up is committed to conventions of expected female behavior reminiscent of the white ideal. Within the old discourse of the cult of true womanhood, the prime objective of a woman was to be a mother, to manage a household, and to keep one's husband pleased (Carby 26). Imitating the white middle class, Meridian's black middle class surroundings stress the same self-sacrificial role expectations.

Even if Meridian manages to expose the double standard implicit in the dominant codes of femininity in her brief teen-marriage, depicted in the ironically named chapter "The Happy Mother," she is very successful in her repetition of the cultural conventions of what constitute good mothering. Compelled to approximate the ideal mother in spite of the fact that she harbors murderous and suicidal thoughts, "She was told by everyone that she was an exemplary young mother, so mature, so calm" (70). The text uses popular media to raise critical questions about the construction of female identity. While Meridian is not alone in looking for advice in fictional popular magazines," the way in which she reads their representations of women is far from confirming conventional expectations: "According to these magazines, Woman was a mindless body, a sex creature, something to hang false hair and nails on" (71).

The boundaries and borders of race and gender in the United States penetrate to the depths of Walker's female characters and even their bodies are inscribed with the prevailing ideological construction of femininity. In *Meridian,* the narrator calls attention to the fact that the fictional black women who accept white models from the fantasy world of movies wear them like masks: "their faces (old remembered faces now completely reconstructed by Max Factor and Maybelline) perfected masks through which the voice of some person formerly known came through" (109). Butler emphasizes the fact that gendering cannot be a willful appropriation and "it is certainly not a question of taking on a mask" (*Bodies* 7). Walker's narrator seems to be in tacit agreement by further extending the same critique to a willful attempt to appropriate white racial identity.

After the breakup of her marriage the protagonist studies at the aptly-named, all-female Saxon College, an elite institution for bright black girls where, ironically enough, "Most of the students—timid, imitative, bright enough but never daring, were being ushered nearer to Ladyhood every day" (39). In performative theory, identity construction is a temporal process in which gaps and fissures are opened up as the constitutive instabilities in the repetitive labor of a norm (Butler, *Bodies* 10). In *Meridian,* the possibility of destabilizing the dominant gender norms becomes evident when the protagonist sees a group of student activists—black and white, male and female—all dressed in workers' overalls with bibs, apparently performing gender differently from the absolute polarization of masculinity and femininity familiar to her from her immediate surroundings. The young civil rights workers' example makes the protagonist question the hierarchical division of gender and, inspired by her involvement in the movement, she subsequently wants to resist the prescribed feminine ideals.

In principle, the student movement of the 1960s was "group-centered" and egalitarian, and every activist who worked hard enough supposedly had some say in policy decisions (Giddings 300). Looking back, however, it is hardly surprising that the sexist treatment of female activists in *Meridian* had its counterpart in actual black militant organizations of which the most nationalistic are said to have been the most sexist (Giddings 316-317). As I have already mentioned, contemporary scholarship links the male activists' sexist attitudes to the construction of the revolutionary black subject. In Walker's novel, the tendency is traced even further back: Mr. Raymonds, a light-skinned, old fashioned "race man" and a radical nationalist of the 1920s, speaks about white violence against black women while, at the same time, he sexually harasses the young black protagonist.

The Black Aesthetic, developed by the Black Arts Movement of the 1960s, reflected black nationalist concerns. In *Meridian,* Truman Held, the ironically-named aspiring artist with whom Meridian falls in love, represents the advocates of a new revolutionary subjectivity. Sharing the gender assumptions of black nationalist discourse, he constructs black women as potential mothers and paints them "as magnificent giants, breeding forth the warriors of the universe" (168). The flip side of his idealizations is, of course, that in a direct reflection of black nationalist ideology, Truman wants to apply his womb-centered definition of black women to the protagonist whose black feminine identity is thereby constructed in explicit opposition to the revolutionary black subject (Dubey 20).

The body has not only been seen as a text of culture but also as a practical, direct locus of control (Bordo 13). One of the most remarkable features of Walker's novel are the depictions of Meridian's disintegrating body and the scenes in which she enters into paralyzed death-like coma. Madhu Dubey claims that, in Walker's book, "Meridian's skeletal frame is her most conspicious bodily mark of difference from (the) ideal black woman conceived as sheer bodily abundance" (Dubey 127). Meridian's fainting spells force a parallel between her and the mummy-woman, and it has also been argued that her catatonic trances mimic the white mummy-woman's paralysis (Dubey 127). Both Bhabha and Judith Butler have theorized the possibility of resisting the prevailing regimes of power, and each of them sees performative power as a discursive basis for opposition.

They emphasize the role of hyperbolic gestures of imitation and miming as a means of reversing discursive conventions (Bhabha 86; Butler, *Bodies* 232). In *Meridian,* the protagonist's hyperbolic "performance" of death-like inactivity effectively counters the dominant discourse of femininity as well as the Black Aesthetic conception of black feminine identity as an absence.

In sharp contrast to her former school friends' desire to possess white femininity, the protagonist begins to unsettle culturally specific gender expectations by wearing a railroad cap and dungarees as a signal of "her refusal of the conventional physical signs of femininity" (Dubey 127). Perhaps Meridian's choice of new clothes is more androgynous or even heterogeneous than masculine, but like cross dressing, her crossing of the border of gender "implicitly reveals the imitative structure of gender itself" and thereby suggests an openness to resignification and recontextualization (Butler 1990, 137, 138). Moreover, as a symbolic attempt to reconceptualize herself in terms of hybridity, Meridian's defiant gesture is also related to alternative role models offered by black history. These models point to the fact that race and gender are constituted through each other.

In the novel, a tree that grows on the college grounds is called the Sojourner. The name is an intertextual reference to Sojourner Truth, a former slave and one of the most famous female activists in black history. She not only questioned dominant gender assumptions, but her exposure of the concept "woman" as a construct has been summed up in the oft-quoted phrase "ar'n't I a woman." Harriet Tubman, a self-emancipated farm slave who dedicated her life to antislavery causes, is another historical figure explicitly connected with contemporary women's fight against racism: "black women are always imitating Harriet Tubman" (108). The fact that Tubman's narcoleptic seizures are echoed in Meridian's illness serves as a hint of their affinities for the reader. Like Sojourner Truth, Tubman is a very good vehicle for exploring the intersection of gender and race performativity: excluded from the 19th century white "cult of true womanhood" by race, she even executed an armed expedition against enemy forces.

According to Bhabha revision and reinscription belong to the process by which objectified others may be turned into subjects of their history and experience (191-192). Significantly enough, such a process is an integral part of *Meridian.* It is also worth bearing in mind that in Bhabha's theory the concept of the hybrid is linked to resistance. In the novel, Meridian criticizes Mr. Raymonds's talk about "The Race" as a monolithic entity, "as if it were a lump of homogenized matter that could be placed this way or that way, at will, to effect change" (111). Gradually, she also becomes aware of the dangers implicit in student activists' black nationalist construction of blackness as a unified essence.

While Meridian's understanding of her conventional mother increases when she relates Mrs. Hill's behavior to her enslaved maternal great-grandmother's and grandmother's fight for a better future, her father's Indian background gives her insight into the unfolding of complex relationships between different racialized identities. Even here Walker's narrator highlights the intersection of gender and race: the father figure's masculine identity is simultaneously positioned within African American history and Native American history that is symbolized by the ancient Indians' burial mound in the novel. Instead of excluding Meridian from his dual construction of ethnicity, the father tell her about the dispossession of the Indians and together they speak about Feather Mae, Meridian's paternal great-grandmother. Standing on the mound, Feather Mae is known to have experienced physical ecstasy in mystical trances through which she demonstrates, according to Rachel Stein, that her "spiritual legacy enabled the transformation of black women from sexually exploited objects into inspirited subjects" (97). It is important to notice that Meridian's trances also mimic Feather Mae's mystical experiences: she enters into a similar liminal state on the mound feeling that she is "a speck in the grand movement of time" (59). Looking for sites of resistance, hybridity theory has explored liminality and linked it with the transformational ability of cultural mixings and crossovers. Lacking fixity, Meridian's "rootedness" and committed positioning allow her to retain her respect for the justified interests of others.

The gender assumptions of black nationalist discourse also extended to white women, who were regarded as desirable sexual objects until 1967, when "Black Power called for Whites to be purged from the movement" (Giddings 303). Unlike Truman, Meridian manages to come to terms with her and his white, Jewish wife's shared past: "Look at it this way, black folks and Jews held out as long as they could" (181). Their reconciliation reveals that shared experiences of oppression can create bridges and serve as the basis for alliance.

The Black Aesthetic perceived artistic form as a transparent medium of ideological messages, whereas several critics have observed that because of its inventiveness, Walker's fragmentary novel that crosses genre boundaries seems to flaunt the structure of the text. Like the Black Aesthetic ideal, the form of Walker's novel can be discussed in relation to the construction of the black subject. The narrative self-reflexivity of *Meridian* helps to destabilize the categories of blackness and femininity, and this process is enhanced by the narrator's use of certain black oral, religious and musical traditions that were excluded from black nationalist discourse. Suffice it here to refer to the singing of Meridian's father that makes her connect the church music with the beliefs of American Indians, to Miss Winter's music classes where she teaches the blues, and to the

Baptist preacher who, among other things, asks "the young women to stop looking for husbands and try to get something more useful in their heads" (195).

In her study of black women novelists, Dubey argues that **Meridian** employs modes of psychological realism that are typical of the bildungsroman. She goes on to claim this reinstates the humanist model of the full integral self that she associates with the subject constructed by black nationalist discourse (156). According to Stuart Hall, the recognition of "blackness" as a construction portended the end of an innocent notion of the essential black subject (28). Walker's novel participates in this process by focusing on the negotiations at the borders of gender, race, and ethnicity. Samira Kawash links the insecurities of hybridity to the unknowable, the unforeseeable and the risky (217). In the end, the protagonist, who is recovering from her illness, leaves everything behind to become an engaged performer who sings from memory. Crucially, Walker's revision and hybridization of the traditional gender borders is not only limited to Meridian, but it also involves the self-centered black male protagonist indicating that he also has to change. Ultimately, Truman is left with the symbolic sleeping bag and the cap, both redolent of the possibility of an identity that may refuse to fit the traditional mold and suggestive of alternative hybrid sites of cultural negotiation.

Works Cited

Anzaldúa, Gloria. *Borderlands/Frontera: The New Mestiza.* San Francisco: Spinsters/Aunt Lute, 1987.

Bhabha, Homi K. *The Location of Culture.* London: Routledge, 1994.

Bordo, Susan R. "The Body and the Reproduction of Femininity: A Feminist Appropriation of Foucault." *Gender/ Body/Knowledge: Feminist Reconstructions of Being and Knowing.* Eds. Jaggar, Alison M. and Bordo, Susan R. New Brunswick: Rutgers University Press, 1989. 13-33.

Butler, Judith. *Bodies That Matter: On the Discursive Limits of "Sex."* New York: Routledge, 1993.

———. *Gender Trouble: Feminism and the Subversion of Identity.* New York: Routledge, 1990.

Carby, Hazel. *Reconstructing Womanhood: The Emergence of the Afro-American Woman Novelist.* New York: Oxford University Press, 1987.

Cooke, Michael. "Walker: The Centering Self." *Alice Walker: Critical Perspectives Past and Present.* Eds. Gates, Henry Louis Jr. and Appiah, K. A. New York: Amistad, 1993. 140-154.

Dubey, Madhu. *Black Women Novelists and the Nationalist Aesthetic.* Bloomington and Indianapolis: Indiana University Press, 1994.

Giddings, Paula. *When and Where I Enter: The Impact of Black Women on Race and Sex in America.* New York: Bantam Books, 1984.

Hall, Stuart, "New Ethnicities." *Black Film, British Cinema.* ICA Documents 7, 1988. 27-31.

Kawash, Samira. *Dislocating the Color Line: Identity, Hybridity, and Singularity in African-American Literature.* Stanford: Stanford University Press, 1997.

Nadel, Alan. "Reading the Body: Meridian and the Archeology of Self." *Alice Walker: Critical Perspectives.* Eds. Gates, Henry Louis Jr. and Appiah, K. A. New York: Amistad, 1993. 155-167.

Stein, Rachel. *Shifting the Ground: American Women Writers' Revisions of Nature, Gender, and Race.* Charlottesville: University Press of Virginia, 1997.

Walker, Alice. *Meridian.* New York: Washington Square Press/Pocket Books, 1977.

Ernece B. Kelly (essay date 2003)

SOURCE: Kelly, Ernece B. "Paths to Liberation in Alice Walker's *The Color Purple* (1982)." In *Women in Literature: Reading through the Lens of Gender,* edited by Jerilyn Fisher and Ellen S. Silber, pp. 75-8. Westport, Conn.: Greenwood Press, 2003.

[*In the following essay, Kelly details how Celie's capacity to express herself through letters, combined with her relationships with other women—who themselves are working toward liberation—helps her develop a sense of her own power.*]

Alice Walker's epistolary novel, **The Color Purple,** depicts African-American women in the early twentieth century striving to realize selfhood. Focusing on her protagonist's development, Walker shows Celie's progression from sexually abused child to less passive spouse to outspoken equal partner. Ultimately, Celie finds inner strength through the letters she writes, and through the influence and support of the women around her. Dramatizing the capacity for growth and redemption that comes from both self-expression and female bonding, Walker creates several characters who, in following their unique paths toward personal fulfillment, guide Celie to explore and honor her own.

After being raped and bearing her stepfather's two children, 14-year-old Celie fearfully heeds Alphonso's warning to "not never tell nobody but God" (1) and vents her troubles by writing letters addressed to an imagined white deity. For Celie, writing helps compensate for loss. At first, her letters to God ease her loneliness: when the cruel older man she is forced to marry, Mr.———, makes sexual advances toward Nettie, her sister, Nettie runs away. Before she and Nettie part company, Celie says to her, "'Write!'" Nettie responds: "Nothing but death can keep me from it" (19), foreshadowing the vital role that letters will play in these sisters' lives. Although she doesn't hear from Nettie for many years, Celie immediately takes pen to paper. Thus valuing her innermost thoughts, Celie eventually moves from being ashamed and silenced to living proud and in full possession of her voice.

As she records what she sees and knows, Celie also befriends Shug, Sofia, and Mary Agnes—each of whom insists on egalitarian love relationships. Fundamental to Celie's emergence is the self-assured Shug, an entertainer whose lifestyle contrasts vividly with Celie's. Shug urges Celie to "git man off [her] eyeball" (204), and so disrupts Celie's narrow world, consisting entirely of meeting her husband's excessive demands. Notwithstanding their differences, Shug sympathizes with Celie's abusive situation and her helplessness, insisting that Mr.———, known to Shug as Albert, treat Celie with respect, preparing Celie to assert her rights against his abuses.

Perhaps most importantly, Shug offers Celie emotional support and sincere declarations of love. Their physical intimacy seems natural, not controversial. Indeed, their caring sexual interactions, full of mutual admiration, enhance Celie's sense of self-worth, bolstering her resistance to Albert's domination. While Celie's distrust of men ("whenever there's a man, there's trouble" [212]), and Shug's bisexual orientation may be part of classroom discussion, students should observe that Walker eschews categories—thereby questioning social constructs such as heterosexuality, monogamy, and marriage—and instead delineates a relational universe in which the ability to give and experience love is more important to one's growth than *whom* one loves.

Most students become readily involved in debating Walker's depiction of Black men. Critics argue (for example, George Stade) whether Celie "redeems . . . men by releasing the woman already in them . . ." ultimately, depicting "the rejection of men and all their ways" (381-82). Certainly, as he sews in Celie's pants factory, Albert does sound and act sweet, utterly different from the brutal Mr.———. His son, Harpo, also softens; he has "learn something in life" (289), according to his no-nonsense, first wife Sofia. In the words of Trudier Harris, Walker has created "born again male feminists," redeemed by the novel's end (388). Sparking controversy, teachers may ask: Does Albert seem "feminized" or desexualized or genuinely "liberated" as he learns to sew, and for the first time becomes Celie's partner and friend?

Sofia, the first woman Celie meets who retaliates against anyone who tries to dominate her, responds to her own husband's ineffective attempts to rule by beating *him* up. While initially Harpo accepts the role reversal in their marriage, he eventually feels enfeebled by it, anxious about his manly image as he compares the indomitable Sofia to Celie, his father's obedient, and therefore enviable wife. Like Shug, Sofia rejects traditional female roles; with aplomb, she does the heavy domestic tasks—expertly repairing the roof and cutting wood.

Here, Walker makes an important point about a woman's abilities as equal to a man's, critiquing men's resistance to women's competence. Depicting tough-minded Sofia as perhaps the most courageous woman in the novel, Walker nonetheless has Sofia learn from Celie, using her friend's meekness as a model of how to behave in prison: "Every time they ast me to do something, Miss Celie, I act like I'm you. I jump up and do what they say" (93).

Mary Agnes—who becomes Harpo's wife when Sofia leaves him—finds her own voice when she intervenes to release Sofia from prison. Influenced by Mary Agnes' growth, Celie first sees her as "a nice girl, friendly and everything, but she like me. She do anything Harpo say" (83). Stronger than Celie, however, Mary Agnes fights for her man; symbolically, after acting on Sofia's behalf by satisfying her jailer's sexual demands, "Squeak" triumphantly discards her diminutive nickname. As Mary Agnes, she feels free to sing publicly with Shug. Letting loose her "funny" voice, she "come to life" (103). For both Mary Agnes and Celie, self-expression through the channel of musical or narrative voice augurs each woman's emancipation.

In the latter part of the novel, Walker uses Celie's sister's return from West Africa to advance Celie's liberation and Nettie's liberation as well. Shug's discovery of Nettie's unopened letters that Mr.———has vengefully stolen from the mailbox over many years, offers Celie an intimate audience to whom she can direct her correspondence. Writing to her sister, Celie begins to lay claim to her own authority: She no longer writes anonymously, as she did to God; now, Celie proudly signs her name.

Meanwhile, Nettie's letters allow her to gather and convey her understanding of cross-cultural gender parallels and differences that students are generally eager to discuss. During her years in West Africa, Nettie, on her own path to liberation, labors alongside the missionary couple Samuel and Corrine. In exchange, she requests—and receives—an education. In contrast, Olinka girls are denied education since "A girl is nothing to herself; only to her husband can she become something." Moreover, the Olinka maintain divisions between men's and women's work, and Nettie, who works hard and likes to learn, is considered a "drudge" (162). But from Nettie's viewpoint, the Olinka women are unhappy and "work like donkeys" (163). An Olinka man explains: "Our women are respected here. . . . There is always someone to look after the Olinka woman" (167).

Teachers may want to examine these paradoxes: In what ways can being well educated and "smart" sometimes create difficulties for girls and women in the supposedly progressive United States? What does it mean for a man to "look after" a woman in the Olinka culture and what does it mean in our culture? What are the costs of such protection? Interrogating Olinka and North American cultures by analyzing gender roles can help students of *The Color Purple* shape not only "womanist" (Walker's term, quoted in Abbandonato 297) but also multicultural, non-Western perspectives.

Works Cited

Abbandonato, Linda. "Rewriting the Heroine's Story in *The Color Purple.*" *Alice Walker: Critical Perspectives Past and Present.* Ed. Henry Louis Gates, Jr. and K. A. Appiah. New York: Amistad, 1993, 296-308.

Harris, Trudier. "*The Color Purple* as Fairy Tale." *Emerging Voices: A Cross-Cultural Reader.* Ed. Janet Madden-Simpson and Sara M. Blake. Fort Worth, TX: Holt, Rinehart and Winston, 1990, 386-88.

Stade, George. "Womanist Fiction and Male Characters." Madden-Simpson and Blake, 379-83.

Walker, Alice. *The Color Purple.* New York: Pocket Books, 1982.

FOR FURTHER READING

hooks, bell. "Writing the Subject: Reading *The Color Purple.*" *Reading Black, Reading Feminist.* Ed. Henry Louis Gates, Jr. New York: Meridian, 1990, 454-70.

FURTHER READING

Criticism

Heglar, Charles J. "Named and Namelessness: Alice Walker's Pattern of Surnames in *The Color Purple.*" *ANQ* 13, no. 1 (winter 2000): 38-41.

Finds that Walker's narrative strategy of either including or withholding the surnames of characters in *The Color Purple* relates to issues of male dominance and authority.

Newson-Horst, Adele S. Review of *The Way forward Is with a Broken Heart,* by Alice Walker. *World Literature Today* 75, no. 2 (spring 2001): 335-36.

Considers *The Way forward Is with a Broken Heart* as a revision of Zora Neale Hurston's *Dust Tracks on a Road,* and praises the characterizations in the former, judging them as essential to the collection's success.

Sol, Adam. "Questions of Mastery in Alice Walker's *The Temple of My Familiar.*" *Critique* 43, no. 4 (summer 2002): 393-404.

Argues that *The Temple of My Familiar* clearly is an attempt to redefine what a prodigious text is meant to do: how it is to confront history, to make a political stand, and to tell a story."

Winchell, Donna Haisty. "Beautiful, Whole, and Free: *You Can't Keep a Good Woman Down.*" In *Alice Walker,* pp. 72-84. New York: Twayne Publishers, 1992.

Identifies the search for self—for an identity defined by oneself, and not by others—as a main theme in the stories of *You Can't Keep a Good Woman Down.*

Additional coverage of Walker's life and career is contained in the following sources published by Gale: *African American Writers,* Eds. 1, 2; *American Writers Supplement,* Vol. 3; *Authors and Artists for Young Adults,* Vols. 3, 33; *Beacham's Encyclopedia of Popular Fiction: Biography & Resources,* Vol. 3; *Bestsellers,* Vol. 89:4; *Black Literature Criticism,* Ed. 1:3; *Black Writers,* Eds. 2, 3; *Concise Dictionary of American Literary Biography,* Vol. 1968-1988; *Concise Major 21st-Century Writers,* Ed. 1; *Contemporary Authors,* Vol. 37-40R; *Contemporary Authors New Revision Series,* Vols. 9, 27, 49, 66, 82, 131; *Contemporary Literary Criticism,* Vols. 5, 6, 9, 19, 27, 46, 58, 103, 167; *Contemporary Novelists,* Eds. 4, 5, 6, 7; *Contemporary Popular Writers; Contemporary Southern Writers; Dictionary of Literary Biography,* Vols. 6, 33, 143; *DISCovering Authors; DISCovering Authors 3.0; DISCovering Authors: British; DISCovering Authors: Canadian Edition; DISCovering Authors Modules,* Eds. MST, MULT, NOV, POET, POP; *Encyclopedia of World Literature in the 20th Century,* Ed. 3; *Exploring Novels; Exploring Short Stories; Feminism in Literature: A Gale Critical Companion,* Ed. 1:6; *Feminist Writers; Literature and Its Times,* Vol. 3; *Literature Resource Center; Major 20th-Century Writers,* Eds. 1, 2; *Major 21st-Century Writers* (eBook), Ed. 2005; *Modern American Literature,* Ed. 5; *Modern American Women Writers; Novels for Students,* Vol. 5; *Poetry Criticism,* Vol. 30; *Reference Guide to American Literature,* Ed. 4; *Reference Guide to Short Fiction,* Ed. 2; *Short Stories for Students,* Vols. 2, 11; *Short Story Criticism,* Vol. 5; *Something about the Author,* Vol. 31; *St. James Guide to Young Adult Writers; Twayne's United States Authors;* and *World Literature Criticism Supplement.*

Colson Whitehead
1969-

American novelist and nonfiction writer.

INTRODUCTION

Considered among America's most accomplished young authors, Whitehead is esteemed as a literary descendent of Ralph Ellison. While his work often defies genre categorization, it is characterized by a postmodern assessment of American tradition. His penetrating examinations of racial identity and modern culture, combined with the poetic sensibility of his prose, have placed Whitehead at the forefront of his generation of writers.

BIOGRAPHICAL INFORMATION

Whitehead was born in New York City in 1969. As a young boy, he decided that he wanted to be a writer after reading a Stephen King novel. He attended high school at the Trinity School in New York City and went on to attend Harvard University. After graduating from Harvard in 1991, he worked as a freelance writer and a television columnist for the *Village Voice*. His first novel, *The Intuitionist* (1999), was a Hemingway Foundation/PEN Award finalist. He received a Whiting Writers' Award in 2000, and earned an Anisfield-Wolf Book Award for his second novel, *John Henry Days* (2001). *John Henry Days* was also a finalist for the 2002 Pulitzer Prize for Fiction. That same year Whitehead was awarded a MacArthur Fellowship. Whitehead's work has appeared in such notable periodicals as *Granta,* the *New York Times Magazine, Harper's Magazine,* and the *New York Times*. He lives in Brooklyn.

MAJOR WORKS

Whitehead's writing is marked by a highly poetic prose style and a postmodern aesthetic. Frequently likened to works by Thomas Pynchon and Paul Auster, *The Intuitionist* is an allegory dealing with rival schools of elevator inspectors. The novel is set in a city that resembles modern New York but incorporates elements of nineteenth-century society. Modeled after the *noir* detective genre, *The Intuitionist* examines the insidious nature of institutionalized racism in a manner both realistic and fantastic. The epic scope and complex narrative structure of *John Henry Days* brings together a wide variety of fictional and historical figures, and re-volves around a festival honoring the legend of folk-hero John Henry. Shifting between disparate periods and locations, *John Henry Days* provides a satirical look at journalism and an examination of American history and popular culture. The nonfiction work *The Colossus of New York* (2003) consists of a series of impressionistic ruminations on the nature and character of New York City rendered in a manner reminiscent of prose poetry. Whitehead's third novel, *Apex Hides the Hurt* (2006), tells of a "nomenclature consultant" who is hired by the small community of Winthrop to help them decide whether they should revert to calling the town by its original name—chosen by its freed-slave founders—or adopt the name selected by a consumer-conscious software developer. The narrative relies upon humor and a peculiar premise to highlight concerns of racism and personal integrity in modern American society.

CRITICAL RECEPTION

Although Whitehead's first novel garnered widespread critical enthusiasm, his subsequent works have received mixed reactions. Scholars have hailed *The Intuitionist* as an off-beat, imaginative contribution to the tradition of African American literature, praising the novel for its rich insights into professionalism and physical disability. Despite a critical consensus that *John Henry Days* is an intelligent and ambitious work and despite favorable comparisons to Don DeLillo's *Underworld,* a number of reviewers have deemed Whitehead's second book convoluted and incoherent, censuring the author's extravagant prose. Some critics have derided *The Colossus of New York* for presenting an overly abstract, nearly unrecognizable version of New York City, though others have admired the book's descriptive passages. Still other reviewers have lauded the volume for providing a perspective on how the city has affected black culture and society. Extolled as a cutting social satire, *Apex Hides the Hurt* has nonetheless been faulted for its underdeveloped characters. Despite the mixed reviews of his literary oeuvre, commentators recognize Whitehead's ambition and talent and value his contribution to contemporary American literature.

PRINCIPAL WORKS

The Intuitionist (novel) 1999
John Henry Days: A Novel (novel) 2001

The Colossus of New York: A City in Thirteen Parts
  (nonfiction) 2003
Apex Hides the Hurt (novel) 2006

CRITICISM

Colson Whitehead with Suzan Sherman (interview date summer 2001)

SOURCE: Whitehead, Colson, and Suzan Sherman. "Colson Whitehead." *BOMB,* no. 76 (summer 2001): 74-80.

[*In the following interview, Whitehead discusses such topics as the central themes of his novels, his creative process, and his familial and educational background.*]

The Intuitionist, Colson Whitehead's acclaimed first novel, rests on a completely original premise—elevator inspectors split into two opposing camps. There are the Empiricists (the good-old-boy network of textbook followers) and the Intuitionists (who "intuit" elevator malfunctions, and are chided by the Empiricists as "voodoo men" and "witch doctors"). When a new elevator named for Fanny Briggs—a slave who taught herself to read—crashes, Intuitionist Lila Mae, the "first female colored elevator inspector," is scapegoated by the Empiricists for the free fall, and goes undercover to unravel what actually occurred. With consistently elegant prose Whitehead transforms the elevator into a multilayered metaphor for metropolis, religion, race and upward mobility. Painted in cool shades of gray, where urban grit, philosophy, and poetry quietly coexist, *The Intuitionist* is a stunning, mysterious world.

Whitehead continues to explore themes raised in *The Intuitionist* in his much anticipated new novel, *John Henry Days,* with the folk hero and former slave John Henry, who in the famous race of man versus machine, beats the steam drill and dies afterward. Henry converges with the present day at a John Henry festival, and with J., a black New York journalist who smugly covers the event. In this ambitious novel Whitehead presents a chorus of voices linked to John Henry, weaving the past and present together with confidence. Like the elevator in *The Intuitionist,* the John Henry myth is heightened to take on varied meanings and interpretations, as the recurring replacement of man with machine is explored. Whether it's the dishwasher, Victrola or the Internet, whether industrial or technological, whether John Henry or J., the question of "progress" and its startling affects on humanity is raised. Though *John Henry Days* is written in the third person, it contains the flavor of oral history, pointing to forgotten moments, gaps in American history, through Whitehead's extraordinary fiction.

[*Sherman*]: *There is a grandness, in both scale and subject matter, to* **John Henry Days.** *No stone is left unturned in tracing a huge chorus of characters who converge on the John Henry legacy. I am reminded of Robert-Altman's film* Short Cuts; *the splicing together of lives, a fantastically complex mosaic, though your characters cross centuries. I wonder how you began writing it; was it with the John Henry myth, or with J. the journalist, or was it more a conceptual idea?*

[Whitehead]: The book started off conceptually; I wasn't sure how to write about John Henry, though I knew I didn't want to do a historical novel. The early idea was very formal—five-page chapters dealing with different aspects: the history of the steam drill, the Altamont Speedway, and some modern trajectories such as the John Henry stamp ceremony. I plotted it out but it felt like I hadn't discovered anything new, it seemed too conceptual. I had the great myth of John Henry to jump off of, but no characters, no story. So the real-live historical event of the stamp ceremony became the backbone of the story, J. and his group of hack journalists erupted from there, solidifying the industrial age/ information age angle. I fleshed out the town and what would happen over the weekend of the stamp ceremony, and when I did, it became a pretty linear, contemporary story. By forcing these hacks to cover this relatively insignificant event, I found an entry. They were my modern equivalents of the railroad laborers, pick and shovel men of the information age. I wanted to break free of my previous novel, *The Intuitionist,* which is very hermetic; it takes place in one city and has a very small cast. In *John Henry Days* a lot of characters present themselves. As I started to think about the transmission of the John Henry myth and the theme of changing technology, I created characters who would provide footholds for discussing the oral ballad transmission, and then sheet music, the advent of vinyl, and then the late 20th century where we have all different technological formats for expression.

Initially, why didn't you want to write a historical novel?

It just didn't appeal to me. I wanted to do something where I could talk about modern pop culture. *The Intuitionist* had no pop culture references at all. From being a TV critic and a cultural critic, it felt like an obsession for me. With *John Henry* I got my history jones out by having chapters that take place in different time periods.

There is such loving reverence in **The Intuitionist** *for the elevator as a grand machine, and the swelling metropolis of skyscrapers it brings. Industry takes on a biological, almost human quality—"a tunnel like a throat," "a stone cocoon," "the skyline rows of broken teeth"—whereas in* **John Henry Days** *there is an overall disdain for the ever-advancing technology. From the steam drills to Web startups, it's like some sort of* *amorphous disease. In moving from* **The Intuitionist** *to writing* **John Henry Days,** *did you see a thread of continued interest in man's relationship to machine, but from an opposing perspective?*

I wasn't trying to make a counterpoint to *The Intuitionist.* I definitely have a fascination with machines, the sheer mechanism of the steam drill, the kind of obscure, random invention of the elevator. I like those weird, fun facts. It's only afterwards, now that the book is done and I've read it a couple times . . .

*A couple of times? (*laughter*)*

Well, yeah. You get a copy of the manuscript and then the galley, each a few months apart, so each reading is like a new experience. You start to love and hate different chapters, and you gain and lose favorite parts. In both cases there's an anxiety about progress and the advancement of machines. Everyone in *The Intuitionist* has all sorts of hopes and aspirations tied into the perfect elevator. In *John Henry Days* it's a lot more diffuse, where you have a songwriter threatened by the mechanization of sheet music, and a blues singer, who makes his living doing concert work, threatened by the advent of the Victrola. There's this anxiety and uneasiness, which I guess is a part of me since it's in both of my books. But technically and structurally I know exactly why those sections are there.

You mentioned there are parts of **John Henry Days** *that you love and parts that you hate. I'm wondering, what are they?*

Oh, it varies from week to week. Without getting specific, there are chapters that I can feel proud of because there's a new kind of sentence, it's like wow, that's a weird comma-clause-comma construction I haven't done before. Some chapters are just funny, light and lively, and it's a different kind of humor than the rest of the book and what I've done before. There's so many different voices in the book; the stream of consciousness voices were fun to do and worked well, but the following week I thought, nah, that's kind of mannered. Then next week I change my mind again and think it's great. So I still have a relationship with the book even though it's in the can.

A tremendous amount of research went into **John Henry Days.** *Historical references abound; from the steam drill to the Harlem Renaissance to the free Rolling Stones concert at Altamont. Was it a challenge to incorporate history into a fictional narrative without weighing it down; was it some sort of balancing act?*

It was definitely a balancing act. Since I didn't write it start-to-finish, I wrote different sections at different times, if I got bored I could take a break doing research for a month before writing another chapter. I'd get five stamp books out of the library and just have a stamp

week, or a Tin Pan Alley week. Even though I'm kind of a lazy person, I went down to the town of Talcott, West Virginia, where the actual John Henry Days festival takes place every year. I flew to Georgia and my friend picked me up and we drove around in his car for a day and a half. We got a small hotel room in Talcott and walked around, saw the Big Bend Tunnel named in the John Henry ballads. It wasn't something I normally do because I work out of my head. *The Intuitionist* is a book with a lot of small rooms, and *John Henry Days* is a lot bigger; I guess I had to break the mold.

John Henry Days *begins with people recounting their versions of who they think John Henry is. Each person has a different take on the man, in some cases their point of view is completely tied up with the color of their skin. By beginning the book in such a way, it clearly shows the subjective nature of history, the fluidity of truth, depending upon who tells the story. The idea of truth is also toyed with in* **The Intuitionist,** *when we learn that Fulton has been keeping the color of his skin a secret. Can you trace when your concern for that sort of truth emerged?*

I don't find history very reliable; there's a white history, and there's a black history. And I grew up at a time in college and right after college when there was this crazy deconstructionist sort of thing that nothing exists, everything is fluid, meaning in itself is fluid. It's hard to keep up with everyone's version of the truth; they cancel each other out.

In **John Henry Days** *slavery is referenced with a focus on emancipation; that's certainly not the whole truth of what happened in this country.*

The end of slavery is not a happy ending; it is not the complete triumph as it's presented in children's schoolbooks. In *The Intuitionist* I left a lot of things open, like the meaning of the perfect elevator. At different points in the book it means a literal transformation of the city, and then in other parts it's more of a personal transcendence. Then in *John Henry* there's the question of whether John Henry existed or not. In the book I talk about the two folklorists who went down to Talcott in the twenties; one guy came away talking to 40 people with the idea that he did exist, and two years later, another guy went down and talked to the same people and thought he didn't. The John Henry myth is so ambiguous. He challenges the mechanical steam drill that will replace him to a race; he drills faster and farther and wins, and then he dies from the exertion. So is that a triumph? Is it a defeat? Is it a triumph for the individual, a triumph for the machine, a necessary sacrifice that the community needs? I was trying to emphasize that kind of ambiguity.

Earlier, you said you consider yourself a lazy person. You don't seem that way at all, but of course I don't know what you do on a daily basis.

Yeah, you don't want to know. (*laughter*) I write very intensely for say, six months at a time. And then when I'm not writing, in between books, I take a lot of time off. I'm gestating, thinking about stuff. But I really do plumb the depths of complete slug labor, play a lot of computer solitaire and catch up on TV. The greatest compliment someone ever gave to me was, "You're the most productive lazy person I know."

In both books you delve into the self-consciousness of talking about color; not only in terms of white people, but black people as well. Here's quote: "The biracial who adopted a superficial militancy to overcompensate for light skin discussed the perfidy of ice people with gangster rapper ashamed of a placid upbringing in a middle-class suburb." Your books challenge white presumptions about blackness; I'm thinking about the marketing of your book in the predominantly white publishing industry. What have been your concerns in this regard?

It's being marketed as a literary novel, which is what it is, and what I want. Personally, I don't have any gripes the way things are going, though I definitely have gripes with the amount of black fiction being published. In my generation there's me, Paul Beatty, Danzy Senna and others, and we all do different things. And there are so few black editors around that certain voices aren't getting out there. Then on the other hand, I think there are five new black publishers opening up this year, putting out their particular flavors, so there are ways around the traditional outlets of the commercial publishers.

Were you working on **The Intuitionist** *when you were at the* Village Voice?

I had a TV column there, which gave me a lot of free time. At that point my living expenses were low and I had a really cheap-ass apartment, so I only had to work four days a month. I had time to do my fiction. I did the column for two years and then I ran out of things to say. I had become a hatchet man, criticizing shows that no one watched anyway; the unseen Fox "Married With Children" rip-off. So I quit that and started **The Intuitionist**. I was freelancing. I was definitely very broke, but I had a lot of time to work on the book.

What did you study at Harvard? Were you a philosophy major?

No, I was an English lit major. There weren't a lot of 20th-century fiction classes, just the classics. So I spent a lot of time going to the library to look up Ishmael Reed and Thomas Pynchon. Harvard has a really cool drama program with the American Repertory Theatre, so I took a lot of postmodern drama classes. I got this absurdist theater training, which, you know, comes out periodically in different things.

The postal workers.

Yeah, their humor, that Abbott and Costello back and forth.

Your writing makes achingly clear the complexities of black upward mobility. Lila Mae views the first elevator inspector as an Uncle Tom figure, while he feels she's made it because of him. In **John Henry Days,** *in the Harlem Renaissance scene, the mother is disgusted to discover her daughter's purchase of black folk music. Blackness is reinterpreted generationally; how heavy is this weight of reinterpretation when you yourself are writing about it?*

It's not so much a weight.

Is it a freedom then, to be writing it yourself?

Coming out of the post-Black Arts movement, and having blackness being reaffirmed in literature and drama, I think the young black writers of my generation have the freedom to do what we want. I can write a book that uses elevators to talk about race. Or I can talk about John Henry as a slave doing the only kind of work he can in 1873, and then talk about a privileged middle-class black man in 1996 who chooses his own numbing drudgery. I chose different moments in history to accentuate how issues of race and class have been dealt with; one example being the Strivers Row chapter in *John Henry,* where the bourgeois mom forbids any street Negroness in the house, to the point of erasing the black contribution to pop music.

There is no written account from that time of John Henry having beaten the steam drill—there is only oral history. For many reasons it's been imperative for blacks to assert what's been left out of history books. Were you thinking along those lines in terms of the Intuitionists, those who intuit what something is; they feel it, without relying on textbook facts?

Maybe, unconsciously.

Your narratives have a wonderful zigzagging quality. The plot moves in a progression, but it's not anything that's expected. There's a scene in **John Henry** *where a girl gets an internship at a newspaper, which she ends up resenting because all her friends go to Europe that summer. This girl does not show up again in the rest of the novel; I kept expecting her to reemerge. What was the decision in bringing her up and letting her go?*

In terms of the story itself, there are chapters that serve to further the story of what happened during the John Henry Days stamp festival weekend, and then there are chapters which serve to further the advancement of different notions of John Henry, what John Henry-ness is to different people.

And the notion of what journalism is becoming, its elitism.

Yeah, she's a part of the journalistic hackery world; the dilettante intern. She doesn't come back because I feel like she served her purpose. A lot of the characters show up and don't come back, or come back only in references, or come back as ghosts in other characters' stories.

You chose to center the book on a postage stamp festival honoring the John Henry stamp. Despite all the technological advances, there are still some things, like postage stamps, which are steeped in nostalgia. When you were writing were you thinking at all about this, as a contrast to the ever-advancing technology?

I think for me, the nostalgia comes out in different ways; the town of Talcott embraces the 120-year-old myth as a cause for celebration. The John Henry Days Festival actually exists.

Is that when you went down there?

No, I went down in the off-season. (*laughter*) I'm pretty sure the festival in my book is a lot bigger and definitely more lethal than theirs. In the face of rapid growth of these mono cities, these edge cities, where every town has a Gap, and we're all connected through the media. We're united in a mass-produced culture, and then there's this nostalgia for things we never had. You get that tension in Lucien, the PR guru who goes down to Talcott, he's not really sure what to make of all this authentic sentiment. He wants to embrace it, but can only think in a corrupt way. He doesn't know what to make of these strange feelings of community and loss. Because I grew up in Manhattan, I have a lot of weird notions about small town life. It was definitely fun for me to go to Talcott and try to create a few characters in opposition to the cynical, urban Lucien.

There's the husband and wife who run the motel that everyone stays in. Did these characters emerge as you were going along?

Yeah. I had a semi-outline. The more research I did, the more I wanted to expand on the myth. I put in Guy Johnson, the black folklorist who goes down there in the twenties, I put in Paul Robeson because he's such an incredible figure, and then I found out he was in a John Henry play on Broadway. I definitely had to reign myself in, because it just became a kitchen sink, anything that mentioned John Henry I wanted to put in. (*laughter*) The one thing I'm sorry I didn't put in was a Johnny Cash chapter, because he has this John Henry song which is pretty cool. He sang it one day on a variety show in the seventies and misidentified the town as Beckley, West Virginia. The residents of Talcott were very upset, and so he paid for the John Henry monument in Talcott. It would be incredibly cool to write about Johnny Cash, but it seemed like I had enough as it was.

Was it easier writing the second book with all the acclaim you received for **The Intuitionist,** *or did that make the writing, the living up to something, all the more difficult?*

I was lucky that I wrote half the book before *The Intuitionist* came out.

Lazy you!

Lazy me. (*laughter*) So what happened was I wrote half of **John Henry Days,** we moved back to New York, **The Intuitionist** came out, and I didn't actually work on the book for a year. I knew exactly what was going to happen in it, I had the voices down, though that wasn't what was weighing on my mind, anxiety-wise. **John Henry** is such a different book, stylistically and structurally, from **The Intuitionist,** I just hadn't done anything like it before; that was more my worry rather than can I live up to the good reviews of **The Intuitionist.**

In **John Henry Days** *you describe the writer Bob the newcomer, his debut, then Bob's return as, "the second novel, recapitulating some of the first's themes, somehow lacking—emboldened by success tries to tackle too much." Do you have different fears on the publication of your second book?*

I'm fearless. (*laughter*) I attracted a lot of mystery fans with **The Intuitionist,** because of its structure, so I'm not sure if they're going to be coming along for the ride this time. But I think it will attract different people for being a very different book.

Do you have an ideal audience?

I have a few friends who read all my stuff, works in progress. I think about what they might say, their predilections, but my ideal reader is me. (*laughter*) I guess the effort's wasted, since I'm actually writing it. But someone like me, or younger, who hasn't been exposed to crazy, more contemporary fiction, or who might want to start writing. For me, it's been important when I've encountered particular books in my life like *Invisible Man* at the age of 20, or *Gravity's Rainbow* as I started to write and to learn what I could and couldn't do.

Do you remember what you were told you couldn't do?

In sophomore English, reading Jane Austen all the time, you think that's what literature is. I don't worry about following some sort of Dickensian structure I learned in high school. The canon is not all that it's cracked up to be—there's a lot more out there.

Do you like Ben Katchor's cartoons?

Oh yeah, I've always felt a real affinity. His New York is the New York I love, the sort of fictional New York I never lived in; the buildings below 30th Street that I got from growing up with "The Twilight Zone," and the beleaguered guys in fedoras who are shoe salesmen and ventriloquists. All the weird, kind of Broadway, shticky 42nd Street, sad characters living in this sort of pug-nosed world. I'm not really sure why I latched onto that as an interesting place or landscape, but Ben Katchor really captures it.

I'm going to a lecture of his tomorrow night on museum cafeterias of the world. (laughter)

In **The Intuitionist** *Lila Mae is described as the first female colored elevator inspector. Do you see yourself as a "first" in some way?*

The first colored novelist to write about elevators.

Maybe on a more personal level?

Well, I think I'm trying to do what's not expected.

What do you think is expected?

When I started writing, the 20-something, angsty-struggle, first novel would come into the *Voice* all the time. It was the slacker moment. And that was what I didn't want to do; I wanted to make it new. It's the way my mind works; I can't write any other way. I don't worry about staking a claim for myself because what I end up writing is freaky in conception and readable in execution, at least I hope so.

Numerous male authors are accused of focusing predominantly on male characters and concerns in their books, but you've painted consistently strong, independent female characters. In an interview you gave for Salon *you mentioned that Lila Mae had initially been a man. Did you choose to make her a woman to further separate her from the good-old-boy world of the Empiricists?*

Once the character became female that came into play, but it was more just trying to not do what was comfortable. When I first finished the manuscript for *The Intuitionist* the main character was a wise-talking, young guy. And after reading a page of it, I was like, who cares? So I said, female character. Let's stretch it, not make it first person. Both those things, a third person book and a female character just seemed more interesting; it made the book more fun to do than something I already know. In the same way that *John Henry Days* started as gemlike essays on facets of John Henry. Once you think it up, why do something you already know you can do?

I imagine it would not be as fun for the reader either.

Yeah, that's more of a secondary concern. It's just less fun to write. If there's no challenge, there's no point in doing it.

Does being a writer make sense to you in relation to your familial history? Were you one of those people who planned on becoming a writer when they were six years old?

I was in the seventh or eighth grade. I thought it would be cool to write big geeky, slasher, horror, sci-fi movies: *Blade Runner, The Shining,* or be a comic book writer. I was living in a kind of fantasy world. My parents wanted me to do something more stable, lawyering or doctoring, but they got off my back when I started working for the *Voice*. As a kid in New York I always wanted to write for the *Voice*. Every week I went to the back pages to see which band was playing, and then went to Irving Plaza and the Ritz, and read the music reviews afterwards. I became a sort of *Voice* addict.

Intuitionism, the ability to feel without having to see is described by the Empiricists as "downright voodoo." I'm curious about your own religious upbringing.

Did we practice voodoo? I guess my mom went to church as a child, and started going again a few years ago. We were not a religious household when I was growing up. We were agnostics or atheists, I'm not sure which.

Skeptics.

We were a very skeptical household.

Why in **The Intuitionist** *did you choose to make the metropolis "the most famous city in the world," as opposed to simply Manhattan, and why not place it in a specific time? Did the choice of leaving it vague, sort of Kafkaesque, have to do with giving the story more reverberation in relationship to today?*

I wanted it to start as a parody of a detective story. I wanted this noirish city to work in, and then as different themes began to develop I started playing around with Lila Mae as a civil rights baby thrust into a completely male workplace. It became advantageous and fun to have a timeless locale where creatively I wasn't pinned down. Also the story is so fantastic, like a parallel world of New York that exists only on certain street corners at certain times of day. As the story became more allegorical, it seemed like the right choice.

Did it feel like a relief then, when **John Henry** *became incredibly specific?*

Oh, totally, yeah. There was one thing I couldn't figure out how to shoehorn in: Flight 800, the New York-to-Paris plane that went down in August of 1996. I thought it would be interesting to have one of the junketeers on that plane, since they're such doomed mercenaries. It fit in with the undercurrent of modern violence in *John Henry Days*. It was great to put real life names in the book instead; to be able to say he walked down Broadway as opposed to the great boulevard. And then being able to bring in Paul Robeson or the Eleanor Bumpers case or Altamont; real life scenes that glance off the themes in **John Henry.** It was totally fun, and liberating.

Here's a question about endings. **The Intuitionist** *concludes with Lila Mae sitting down to write her own words, and* **John Henry** *ends with J. almost certainly going off with the woman he's grown fond of—the "real story," as he calls it—as opposed to remaining on his sorry press junket. Do you consciously see your novels as ending on hopeful notes, and are you yourself hopeful in regard to the future?*

It's funny because in both books, different people interpret the endings in different ways. It seems that the more pessimistic you are, the more optimistic you find the endings of both books, and the more optimistic you are, the more pessimistic you find the endings.

Hmm. (laughter)

I thought of both J. and Lila Mae as writers; Lila Mae writing *The Last Elevator* and having a room of her own, being apart from the world in order to create, and J. having his existential dilemma about writing and if it's worthwhile. For me, personally, I summon those feelings for the books apart from their constructions. I find both endings to be both optimistic and open-ended, but then people read them and seem really upset.

What could possibly be upsetting about them?

Well, people say Lila Mae's all alone, everybody hates her, she has no friends, and she's stuck in this small room overlooking a factory and nobody understands what she's doing for many years—which is actually a writer's dilemma; you're writing something and it might get published, it might not, and if it does no one buys it and you struggle, and maybe one day someone will actually dig it. With **John Henry,** without trying to spell out the ending, it's a question of whether J. is fated in the same way John Henry is, to meet a certain course of action, or can J. escape the loop that seems to be his destiny? I got calls from some people who said, I finished the book and the ending is so sad. God, I'm so depressed. And other people said the complete opposite.

Do you like the variety of interpretation?

Yeah, I feel pretty hands-off once it's done.

But was that your intention?

Yeah, it was more intentional with **John Henry.** It's what I wanted.

In the face of all the acclaim you received with **The Intuitionist,** *and that you will certainly receive for* **John Henry Days,** *you have such a humbleness about you. How have you maintained this sense of yourself?*

Well, my attitude is that hopefully I'll be writing books for awhile, and they won't all be as well received as **The Intuitionist.** You have ups and downs. They'll all be received differently, I'll have different experiences writing them, and they'll serve different purposes for me creatively. I'm glad people can read them and have different responses.

Do you have another book in the works—being that you're so lazy?

I've started a book which you could say is about the Band-Aid industry. It's pretty fun, and I'll leave it at that.

Robert Butler (essay date September 2004)

SOURCE: Butler, Robert. "The Postmodern City in Colson Whitehead's *The Colossus of New York* and Jeffrey Renard Allen's *Rails under My Back.*" *CLA Journal* 48, no. 1 (September 2004): 71-87.

[*In the essay below, Butler contrasts the depictions of urban life and the social standing of city dwellers in* The Colossus of New York *and Jeffrey Renard Allen's* Rails under My Back, *while placing both works in the context of prominent African American urban narratives.*]

Twenty-eight years ago Blyden Jackson observed that "The Negro Novel is a city novel. It almost always has been" (80), and Amiri Baraka remarked a few years later that black literature has been "urban shaped" and has produced a "uniquely black urban consciousness" (148). Although many African American masterworks are clearly pastoral in outlook, such as Dunbar's *Lyrics from Lowly Life,* Washington's *Up from Slavery,* and Walker's *The Color Purple,* it remains generally true that African American fiction is largely urban and even anti-pastoral in nature, mainly because rural life has been so strongly linked in the black imagination with slavery and post-Civil War segregation and sharecropping. Wright's *Native Son,* Petry's *The Street,* Ellison's *Invisible Man,* Baldwin's *Go Tell It on the Mountain,* Naylor's *The Women of Brewster Place,* and Morrison's *Jazz,* to cite a few important texts, provide vivid examples of the strongly urban drive in African American literary tradition.

Colson Whitehead and Jeffrey Renard Allen, two black writers who have emerged in the past few years, have produced significant works which grow out of this rich tradition and have made important contributions to this tradition by providing fresh visions of the American city and how it impacts on black life. Whitehead's **The Colossus of New York** and Allen's *Rails under My Back* offer strikingly new interpretations of urban life and no doubt will exert a strong influence on subsequent African American writing. But what is the precise nature of the cities which these two writers present? How are their urban visions different from those contained in previous black masterworks? And what do their visions of city life reveal about black American life in the twenty-first century?

* * *

Unlike the cities in Wright's *Native Son,* Ellison's *Invisible Man,* Baldwin's *Go Tell It on the Mountain,* and Morrison's *Jazz,* which are clearly identifiable places that are easily visualized and located in a realistically presented time and culture, Whitehead's city is more of an indeterminate space than a fully reified place. As Kevin Larimer has observed, the city in *The Intuitionist* is "a non-specific setting—you don't know what year it is, where you are, or how long you've been there. With no cultural signifiers with which to identify, you accept the terms of its fictional world" (22).[1] In the same way, the city described in *The Colossus of New York* is more of a symbolic space than an actual place. A cauldron of perpetual change, it serves as a powerful reflection of the postmodern self, a provisional ego that is always in the process of ongoing and relentless transformation and always on the edge of extinction.

Indeed, nothing has any permanence or continuity in the city presented in *The Colossus of New York.* As Whitehead reveals in the opening paragraph, "You are a New Yorker the first time you say that used to be Munsey's or that used to be the Tic Tac Lounge" (3). The narrator describes his "home" in New York as a bewilderingly large number of apartments he once inhabited, each one signifying a temporary "identity" in a never-ending series of self-creations. Instead of providing its inhabitants with a stable place grounded in a shared history, common values, or genuine communal life, Colson's New York breaks down into the always shifting, subjective perceptions of the countless people who experience it:

> There are eight million naked cities in this naked city—they dispute and they disagree. The New York you live in is not my New York; how could it be? The place multiplies when you are not looking. We move over here, we move over there. Over a lifetime, that adds up to a lot of neighborhoods, the motley construction materials of your jerry-built metropolis.
>
> (6)

In such a wildly protean world, one can never define a single historical city which is an objectively real and stable place but can, instead, define only "his or her New York" (7), a "private New York" (4) that is a radically unstable process of change. Accordingly, the self which is generated in Colson's New York is always becoming, never settled into a stable condition of being. In this sense, his city bears close resemblance to the New York described in Jean-Paul Sartre's *Literary and*

Philosophical Essays, a "city in motion" (128) which is always changing, separating from the past and thus offering Americans the possibility of endless growth, ongoing self-invention. Unlike the "changeless cities" (118) of Europe, which are deeply rooted in place and tradition, American cities for Sartre were open spaces promising freedom but often delivering loneliness and alienation. In such a city, Sartre tells us, "you never lose your way, and you are always lost" (129).

Colson's "colossus," therefore, cannot be fictionally presented as a stable, solid setting which characterizes realistic novels such as Baldwin's *Go Tell It on the Mountain* or naturalistic fictions such as Petry's *The Street.* It is instead recreated surrealistically and impressionistically with images of endless motion. Most of the chapter titles are named after places of transit, for example, "The Port Authority," "Subway," "Broadway," "Brooklyn Bridge," "Times Square," and "JFK." The key actions present people in constant motion "runaways" (2) entering the city through the Port Authority Terminal, commuters using the subway to get to work and return home, a woman crossing the Brooklyn Bridge, and people exiting the city at JFK Airport. The chapter entitled "Rush Hour" best epitomizes Colson's protean city. Describing late afternoon "quitting time" when Manhattan's workers pack elevators and subways on their way "home" to a place which might offer some stability and connection with friends and loved ones, it envisions a world of "move, move, move" (151), where people get trampled and lost.

Indeed, the three inventions which make possible the modern skyscraper city, the elevator, the subway, and the commuter train, are seen as providing motion toward oblivion rather than movement toward a redemptive world of stable, fruitful relationships rooted in a coherent place. As people leave their highly pressured but meaningless jobs, they enter elevators which become striking symbols of their highly mobile but purposeless lives:

> People huddle into elevators and ride down to in-betweeness, into the space between work and home which is a kind of dreaming: it's where they go to make sense out of what just happened so they can go a little further.
>
> (113)

These are the kinds of elevators depicted so brilliantly in *The Intuitionist* which symbolize the modern world's promise of self-fulfillment by "elevation" into a world of existential freedom and individuality, but instead they deliver a terrifying postmodern "total free fall" (228) into self-destruction. The people huddled in the elevators depicted in *The Colossus of New York* want to move toward a place where they can "make sense of what has happened" to their restless and "elevated" lives but must settle instead for a liminal space that symbolizes their "in betweeness," nervous liminal existences characterized by pointless flux. Their desire for a stable "home" is always undercut and eventually destroyed by their aspiring to the American dream of endless mobility, always going "a little further" by moving perpetually to new jobs and more elegant apartments and houses.

Once off the elevators and making their way on streets filled with fast-moving crowds of people, "a grim procession of faces" (114), they enter subways which, like the elevators, are ingenious machines of constant motion which lead to no human destination. The subway is described as an "Abomination" of people who are packed together and bitterly competing for seats like pigeons squabbling over "stale crumbs" (119). Although one particular car is filled with people from the same office, they are essentially strangers who have nothing to say to each other, as each is locked in a private universe of economic competition and personal resentment. Emptying out into Grand Central Station and taking commuter trains to their widely spread-out suburban homes, they are "stupified" by the "spectacle and speed" (119) of their journey. They leave the train expecting solid family lives which will somehow redeem their empty work routines but find in the suburbs another purposeless existence on the margins of life:

> What waits for them across thresholds: marriages, mattresses, mortgages of all kinds . . . sleep the sleep of the successful because somehow you made it through the day without anyone finding out you are a complete fraud.
>
> (121)

Like the city which had earlier been compared to an elaborate theatrical spectacle, Colson's New Yorkers must live out fraudulent lives at work and in their homes because they are in both places expected to act out always changing roles while enunciating "lines" (120) which have no lasting meaning.

Colson's *The Colossus of New York,* like Phillip Roth's *The Human Stain* and Don DeLillo's *Colossus,* portrays the dark underside of the American myth of self-creation in the city. Colson's city, unlike the pragmatic city of Dreiser's *Sister Carrie* or the existential city of Ellison's *Invisible Man,* which envision the urban world as a protean setting inviting personal transformation, is, in fact, a firmly nihilistic world which promises the "elevation" of self but delivers instead self-annihilation. While Dreiser's Carrie becomes a more potent new person in Chicago and New York, and while Ellison's urban underground can become a womb offering new life, Colson's fast-moving metropolis is, paradoxically, an extremely fragile world in which human beings simply disappear.

Midway through *The Colossus of New York* the narrator imagines himself walking up Broadway and "disappearing with every step" (80) because he inhabits a world of narcissistic strangers who do not give a "damn" (80) about him. This feeling is particularly strong when he is "between corners" (80) and experiences the *anomie* of "in-betweeness" (113) which Colson's other New Yorkers feel when they ride elevators. Thus caught between two states of becoming but not anchored in any sense of stable being, Colson's narrator thinks, "This is Broadway after all and it will undo you bit by bit" (80). This fear of disappearance into an anonymous, always changing urban landscape runs throughout the entire book. At the beginning of the chapter on Coney Island, the narrator worries that "what people will find under their feet will not be pavement but something shiftier" (89) and that "everything disappears in the sand . . . the way people get lost in the streets" (90). In the cocktail party described in "Downtown," the two people nervously engaging in empty conversation remember that they were lured to New York from their "hometowns" by a "dream city" but could find "nothing solid beneath their feet" and "disappeared into the quicksand" (129) of a perpetually shifting urban world. Indeed, the entire book begins with "broken" (15) people leaving Port Authority Terminal, New York's "back entrance" (15), and disappearing into crowded streets. It concludes in precisely the same way with people leaving New York by one of its front entrances, JFK Airport, pursuing vaguely imagined destinations as the narrator intones, "Sometimes things disappear" (117).

Even the city itself is in danger of dissolving. A "make believe" (81) construction, which is constantly redefining itself as a work in progress, it is an unstable mixture of parts which can disintegrate. Apparently solid streets like Broadway have "fissures" (80) which Colson's New Yorkers worry will widen and bring about a general collapse. The Brooklyn Bridge "shakes in the wind" and the narrator reminds us that "[i]f it shakes it can fall" (104). Potholes and sewer lines, likewise, inspire anxieties that the city's "infrastructure is weak and aged and solid only in one place, under his feet" (84). Even New York's massive skyline is "fragile" and can "easily be destroyed" (92), a fear which Americans know all to well after the events of September 11, 2001.

* * *

The Colossus of New York, like *The Intuitionist,* is premised upon the belief that the postmodern American city is an infinitely complex technological system and, as such, is both extraordinarily powerful and perilously fragile. Contemplating the Ferris wheel at Coney Island, the narrator of *The Colossus of New York* muses that it is "a gear of the great engine of the metropolis" (94) and that such a "vertiginous city" (95) induces a "fearful sweat" (94) because it is the source of both wonder and terror as its riders move precariously "up and down" (95). Jeffrey Renard Allen's *Rails under My Back* is built upon a similar paradox which haunts modern and postmodern life since the Chicago it recreates is a city of wondrous power and terrifying fragility where its inhabitants are always in danger of "disappearing." Like Colson, Allen describes his city in terms of two central symbols, machines and "gravity," both of which are strongly deterministic forces which threaten to overwhelm his characters, making them literally and morally "disappear" into a postmodern environment characterized by social instability, random violence, and moral relativism.

At one point in *Rails under My Back* the narrator describes New York as "a great big machine" (359), and a character later describes it as "The city of trains" (410). A huge mechanical grid of high-rise buildings connected by subways and automobile-crammed highways, New York is a colossal mechanism which strips people of free will and eliminates them if they can not adjust to the city's highly restrictive routines. Allen's Chicago is also presented as an immense mechanical system which processes people, stripping them of their human qualities and then disposing of them. During the Great Migration large numbers of black people flooded into Chicago as they "followed the train" (271) from locations in the South, hoping to find an alternative to Southern racism and violence. But as Sheila McShane, the wife of one of the novel's central characters, eventually found out, the "rails" leading from Southern farms to Northern ghettos only gave them new forms of discrimination and injustice. Indeed, as she remembers her first ride to the North on a train also loaded with hogs destined for Chicago's slaughterhouses, she realizes that animals and people faced similar fates: "She remembers. Cows rode trains, passengers rode them here to the country's bumping, swinging heart . . . where they were slaughtered and butchered" (531). Many of the novel's black characters are indeed "slaughtered" and "butchered" by the lives they are forced to live in Allen's Chicago. The novel is densely populated by murdered and disfigured people. The aptly named "No Face" is missing an eye from a gang fight, and T Bone, a "crippled motherfucka" (22), operates an elaborate wheel chair after he has been paralyzed by the gun violence of gang warfare. Sam has had his legs literally sliced off by a train after he has fallen asleep on the tracks. The most hideous image of disfigurement appears at the end of the novel when at a funeral for a victim of gang violence the casket is opened to reveal that the corpse has been reduced to something resembling the by-products of a slaughterhouse, a "soup of ash, shit, and blood" (543).

Allen's Chicago is filled with machines which process and dehumanize its citizens. "Robotic surveillance cameras" (179) patrol its underground shopping mall and No Face is described as a similar kind of machine as his one functioning eye is described as a "surveillance camera" (181). Red Hook, the immense public housing project consisting of sixteen high-rise buildings which comprise a "massive grid" (377) trapping 9600 black families, is envisioned as a gigantic mechanical contraption, a huge "metal commode flooded with an invisible tide of heaving black brown and yellow flesh" (374). Although its broken elevators, inoperable stairwells, and impacted laundry chutes literally establish Red Hook as a dysfunctional mechanism, on a more important symbolic level, it is an intricate system which works all too well. A long train connects it with downtown Chicago, and the high-rises themselves are described as being built "rail upon rail" (374). And as Sheila McShan has earlier observed, "a train can't run a man but in one direction" (284). Just as Chicago's train system is a deterministic symbol placing Allen's characters on "rails" of environmental forces which control them, Red Hook and its sister project, Stonewall, is a massive machine dominating its inhabitants. Buried in an underground room at the center of Red Hook is a huge control center, "a maze of levers, buttons, gauges, meters, dials, switchboards, keyboards" (496). Red Hook, therefore, is described as an "inevitable" (495) universe, a series of deterministic forces which pull people into its orbit and reduces them to things.

Put another way, Chicago in general and Red Hook in particular symbolize what both Whitehead and Allen understand as "gravity," powerful forces which overwhelm people and strip them of human qualities. The first paragraph of *Rails under My Back* stresses that "nothing escapes the laws of gravity. We martyr to motion" (3), and throughout the novel a wide variety of characters are pulled down by inner compulsions and external forces which crush their most human impulses. Jesus Jones's bitterness toward his family compels him to kill his uncle and attempt to murder his father. After a dispute at his family's Christmas dinner, he disappears from their lives but then "orbite[s] back into their life like a red meteor" (353) when Freeze puts him on a "mission" (42) to kill his father. Indeed Freeze, himself frozen into the roles of Red Hook gang culture, eliminates all of Jesus's choices, making "all possible movements" gravitate toward "a single definitive act" (486). As he accepts the task given to him by Freeze, Jesus literally descends into the "spit mottled steps of the subway" and morally falls into the violent world controlled by this "Gravity" (48) of Red Hook culture. In a similar way, his father, John Jones, impulsively leaves his wife in Chicago and gravitates to New York, either to escape Freeze's murderous plan or to pursue a life free of family responsibilities and dwindling economic prospects. His brother Lucifer is quick to follow him, driven on by "the necessities of blood" (345).

At several points in the novel characters meditate on the force of gravity as it causes water to circle downward in various drains. When Lucifer returns home from New York and is completing his morning bath, he ponders the water as it "[loses] its battle against centripetal motion (force) and [circles] down the drain"

(341). Late in the novel when Birdleg is searching for a metaphor of ghetto life in order to warn the young Jesus and Hatch against succumbing to its pressures, he first of all illustrates his ideas with buzzards "flying in a circle," to suggest the predatory nature of street life, and then uses an even more revealing figure of speech: "Ain't you never looked in a sink and seen a drain? The water flying in circles?" (506). And Red Hook, Allen's ultimate symbol of the hell into which the black underclass falls, is seen as a gigantic "metal commode" which in a "toilet flush" (324) excretes "heaving black brown yellow flesh" (374). The horrific implication behind this pattern of drain metaphors is altogether clear— Allen's city, like Dante's circular Hell, is driven by a kind of relentless gravity which draws people into a downward spiral of deterministic behavior resulting in their elimination, figuratively "going down the drain" of ghetto life.

Rails under My Back, like Whitehead's **The Colossus of New York,** is filled with people who try to elevate themselves above their environment but who invariably fall victim to the worst forces in their surroundings and eventually disappear. Casy Love, the man with whom Lula Mae goes to Mexico, runs off and she never sees him again. R. L., who went West seeking a new life, is rarely heard from and is buried "somewhere in California on foreign soil" (452). Porsha falls in love with Deathrow, a resident of Red Hook, but he goes missing late in the novel due to mysterious circumstances and is not seen again. And John Jones, one of the novel's central characters, tells his wife he is leaving for a few days to attend an antiwar rally in Washington and to visit friends in New York, but he never returns and is not sighted in either city. His nephew Hatch regards his "disappearance" as a process which is both gradual and sudden, for John's entire life is a long process of depletion resulting in invisibility, "an oxidizing of a single cell, a single organ, a single limb, until—no more John" (352).

The Kafkaesque setting of the novel, like the city portrayed in **The Colossus of New York,** is an urban world where people disintegrate rather than grow, and disappear rather than develop continuous relationships which form the basis of meaningful social life and human identity. Two of Gracie's pregnancies produce stillborns, children who "disappeared" and "left no trace of their presence" (134). Porsha, who works as a "body model" whose face is deleted from the photographs for which she poses, fears that the biological force of aging, which she imagines as a kind of "gravity" (287), will eventually erode her beautiful body, thus reducing her to an insignificant cipher. Even after death, people in *Rails under My Back* simply vanish rather than become memorialized. A funeral home ironically named Sleepytime Incorporated often loses corpses in their immense warehouses and specializes in "mass incinerating" (228), strongly suggesting a version of the Holo-

caust. The recurrent disappearance of black people in a racist society regarding them as "invisible" is further underscored when Hatch remarks, "Nobody in our family had a gravestone" (227).

* * *

Whitehead and Allen, therefore, provide strikingly similar visions of the postmodern American city as centers of alienation and dehumanization. But a critically important difference between their urban visions is that Whitehead's city is an absolutely nihilistic world which defeats its people not only with various kinds of "gravity" but also their attempts to "elevate" themselves, both of which inevitably lead to "disappearance." But Allen's city offers a measured hope in urban sanctuaries which provide meaningful social experiences enabling his characters to salvage moral and spiritual meanings that allow them to construct human identities. While Whitehead's city condemns its inhabitants to a complete isolation which guarantees their destruction, Allen's city has significant pockets of social connectedness which empower people to resist the "gravity" that threatens to pull them down into circles of despair, leading to their disappearance.

This is true even in Red Hook, as Pool Webb's apartment provides a kind of "home" for him and his friends. Once he realizes that Hatch is related to John Jones, a fellow war veteran and a person with whom he has worked in developing a basketball program for the project's youth, he relaxes his gruff exterior and welcomes Hatch to "make yourself comfortable" (379) and talk. While most other locations in Red Hook are murderous places which threaten to "snuff" (380) people by throwing them off roofs or killing them in drive-by shootings, Pool's apartment is a place where Hatch and Pool can converse, share a meal, and help each other. The windows of his apartment look out to a stimulating vista offered by the lake, a sharp contrast to the dark, prison-like places which otherwise characterize Red Hook. And Pool's veranda has a full "garden" of "tomatoes, collard greens, and peppers" (379) which also serves as a dramatic contrast to the filth and sterility which afflict most of Red Hook.

A war veteran who was on the clean-up crew at Hiroshima and who in later years suffered a series of strokes, Pool does not succumb to the "gravity" of his old age and deteriorated social environment. Rather, he continues to struggle to maintain himself as a person and to help others. As the Superintendent of Red Hook, he operates a Community Center which tries to ameliorate the harsh lives of Red Hook's tenants. As his last name clearly suggests, he helps to create a "web" of positive social relationships which can catch a few people who are in danger of a "free fall" into oblivion.

The novel has several other important sanctuaries which also provide some relief from Allen's stark urban environment. The back yard of Nia's childhood home is a "private green haven" (293) where she and Porsha play, share, and become life-long friends. Her beauty shop, located in a very rough neighborhood filled with "beggars, bums, hoodlums" (295), is an oasis where people can relax, talk, and enjoy a physically beautiful environment. Her clients, who are treated like invisible people or inanimate objects in the outside world, get special attention in her shop, being treated individually by beauticians who operate in "the cool shade of a hidden grove" (297). The basketball courts at Red Hook and Stonewall also supply positive outlets for human energy in a world that has painfully few such outlets. At the beginning of the novel Jesus shows a humane side of himself as he plays a game of pick-up basketball at Red Hook. Moving like a "ballerina" (43), he literally resists gravity by spectacularly dunking a basketball and feeling connected to a team of friends. A flashback described toward the end of the novel depicts Jesus in a similarly humane way as he and Hatch are taught how to play basketball by Birdleg at a court in Stonewall. Here again, playing the game not only allows the boys to express themselves creatively but also to become part of a social unit, a team which they affectionately name the Stonewall Aces. As Birdleg instructs them in the game, he uses it as a metaphor of how to oppose the downward pull of their environment by using their "height" (500) and developing "wings" (499).

But by far the most substantial and significant sanctuary in the novel is the black church, an institution providing life-giving community, tradition, and spiritual growth. It empowers certain people to get off the "tracks" laid by others and achieve an important means of control over their lives. Gracie, whose external life has been dominated by her directionless husband and her volatile son, ultimately regards the Bible as a force which has "directed her life" (136) fruitfully. Religion tells her to "keep seeking, not only her own advantage, but that of the other person" (136). Lula Mae's church in West Memphis, Tennessee, performs a similar function, centering her life in stable values grounded in family and social activism. Towards the end of the novel, Porsha, who has despaired of locating Deathrow, after he has mysteriously vanished, attends the revival meeting in Reverend Rivers' church and is emotionally and spiritually lifted by the experience. Rivers' sermon envisions a fire and brimstone version of a postmodern Hell controlled by Satan's "engineering" (546). Cautioning his congregation to avoid "The quicksands and breakers of spiritual degradation" (548), he insists that "God is the only stability" (548) in a world where souls "dangle over the licking fires of hell" (548). Listening to this sermon, Porsha feels a "power" (549) rising within her, "radiating bright streams" (549) throughout her body. This elevating power arising from within, which is experienced by a congregation of people who share her values, offers some hope that she can resist the gravity of cultural forces which make her a faceless body model instead of a person capable of the "salvation" (548) preached by Rev. Rivers.

* * *

In post-9/11 America, Whitehead's and Allen's extraordinary visions of the postmodern city take on an especially compelling significance.[2] More than ever, we now realize how fragile are our apparently powerful cities and the culture which they so dramatically reflect. Colossal in design and intricate in the way they use a wide variety of interconnected technologies, American cities are vulnerable not only to spectacular terrorist attacks but also, as Whitehead and Allen stress, to failures brought out by systemic weaknesses deeply rooted in American history and culture. Whitehead's New York and Allen's Chicago are vulnerable monuments to American blindness, materialism, racism, and egoism. Housing projects like Red Hook are built with the hope that they will solve social problems, but they succeed only in making such problems worse by making people disappear into an urban design which renders them invisible. We have discovered that such a "city built into the sky" (372) is an extremely fragile construction and does not need a terrorist plot to destroy it since it can collapse from inherent weaknesses in its own design. Or to use the metaphor so brilliantly elaborated in *The Intuitionist* and strongly implied in *The Colossus of New York,* our very American impulse for "elevation" from the traditional values which put human limits on our desire for infinite personal development and economic growth may ultimately spell our doom as a nation, putting us in what Whitehead has so aptly termed a "total free fall" (228).

Notes

1. Walter Kirn's review of *The Intuitionist* makes a similar point, arguing that the novel's temporal setting is deliberately vague, being set in "either the near future or the distant past." Moreover, the Kafkaesque "unnamed Eastern city" in which the novel takes place is a "parallel universe" rather than an actual place. ("The Promise of Verticality," *Time* 153 [Jan. 25, 1999]: 78.) Phillip Lopate's review of *The Colossus of New York,* however, argues that the book's lack of "detailed, physical description" of actual places such as Broadway, Times Square, and Coney Island, is a serious artistic defect because it produces a confusing "hydra-headed subjectivity" ("New York State of Mind," *Nation* 227 [Dec. 1, 2003]: 34) rather than a vision of New York as an actual city. While this objection would make sense when applied to a "realistic" book about New York such as Alfred Kazin's *A Walker in the City,* it misses the point when applied to an impressionistic text like *Colossus,* which attempts to envision the postmodern city subjectively as a process which is experienced differently by different people.

2. Although the terrorist attacks of September 11, 2001, are not directly mentioned in *The Colossus of New York,* they loom large in the book's composition. Whitehead had done preliminary work on the book before September 11, taking extensive notes on his perceptions of New York, but his main focus as a writer consisted of working on a third novel. After observing and photographing the destruction of the World Trade Center from Fort Greene Park in Brooklyn, however, he put the novel aside and devoted himself to working full-time on *Colossus.* As Felicia Lee observes in her *New York Times* review of *Colossus,* the terrorist attack on New York compelled Whitehead "to tuck away the novel and delve into the essays about a city that suddenly felt more fragile, yet more solid." Realizing that New York, for all its impersonality and impermanence, was still the place he called "home," Whitehead pursued his book on New York with renewed energy and emotional commitment (E4).

Darryl Lorenzo Washington's review of *The Colossus of New York,* however, complains that the absence of any direct reference to the events of September 11 is a serious flaw in the book. He finds "such a significant omission" to be "confusing." Given Whitehead's postmodern outlook, such an omission makes sense. Envisioning a world of absence and disappearance, his decision to omit any direct reference to 9/11 is a clever literary strategy which dramatizes his vision of twenty-first century urban life.

Works Cited

Allen, Jeffrey Renard. *Rails under My Back.* New York: Harcourt, 2000.

Baraka, Amiri. "Black Literature and the Afro-American Nation: The Urban Voice," in *Urban Experience: Essays on the City and Literature.* New Brunswick: Rutgers UP, 1981.

Jackson, Blyden. *The Waiting Years: Essays on Negro Literature.* Baton Rouge: Louisiana State UP, 1976.

Kirn, Walter. "The Promise of Verticality." *Time* 153 (Jan. 25, 1999): 78.

Larimer, Kevin. "Industrial Strength of the Information Age: A Profile of Colson Whitehead." *Poets and Writers* July/August 2001: 21-25.

Lee, Felicia. "Singing the City Evanescent." *New York Times* 15 (Oct. 20, 2003): E1, E4.

Lopate, Phillip. "New York State of Mind." *Nation* 277 (Dec. 1, 2003): 31-35.

Sartre, Jean-Paul. *Literary and Philosophical Essays.* New York: Collier, 1962.

Wellington, Darryl Lorenzo. "New York Is the Only Thing on This Author's Mind." *The Crisis* 110 (Nov./Dec. 2003): 47.

Whitehead, Colson. *The Colossus of New York: A City in Thirteen Parts.* New York: Doubleday, 2003.

———. *The Intuitionist.* New York: Anchor, 1999.

Saundra Liggins (essay date summer 2006)

SOURCE: Liggins, Saundra. "The Urban Gothic Vision of Colson Whitehead's *The Intuitionist* (1999)." *African American Review* 40, no. 2 (summer 2006): 359-69.

[*In this essay, Liggins discusses* The Intuitionist *as a gothic novel, arguing that Whitehead chose the genre in order "to portray the alienation of the modern black American due to the progress in urban cities and to speculate on the future of U.S. race relations."*]

> But we do have in the Negro the embodiment of a past tragic enough to appease the spiritual hunger of even a James; and we have in the oppression of the Negro a shadow athwart our national life dense and heavy enough to satisfy even the gloomy broodings of a Hawthorne. And if Poe were alive, he would not have to invent horror; horror would invent him.
>
> —Richard Wright, *Native Son* xxxiv

By listing Henry James, Nathaniel Hawthorne, and Edgar Allan Poe as cultural references in his essay "How Bigger Was Born" Richard Wright does not merely address the similarities between the richness and depth of African American literature and the historical and cultural focus of these authors. As implicit in his use of the word "horror" to describe the racial history of the United States, Wright was also drawing an important connection between black America and the literary tradition known as the gothic. On its surface gothic literature seems an unlikely context in which to find a discussion of the African American experience. Originating as a formal literary tradition first in Europe with Horace Walpole's *The Castle of Otranto,* published in 1764, and consisting of such figures as castles and abbeys, tyrannical aristocrats, and damsels in distress, the genre's main purpose is to terrify, to reflect the threats and anxiety that individuals and societies often confront. With Charles Brockden Brown's *Wieland, or the Transformation* (1798), the American gothic literary tradition began, thus transplanting the genre onto US soil and transforming many of the earlier conventions. Rural towns and plantations replaced castles and abbeys, and landed gentry and slave owners stood in for European aristocracy. The gothic literature that would arise out of each of these contexts, even with their differences, took its inspiration from the social and political climates of the late eighteenth century.

Despite the temporal and contextual distance from its European and American gothic counterparts of the nineteenth and early twentieth centuries, contemporary African American literature resonates with many characteristics of the gothic aesthetic. The past still influences the present and future, and issues of identity still create conflicts within the individual. What contemporary African American gothic literature offers is a new set of questions: What does it mean to be a modern black American? Have class and gender differences replaced racial distinctions as the main threats to societal stability, for blacks and whites? How is future racial uplift to be achieved? In diverse ways, Wright and other novelists—Toni Morrison, Gloria Naylor, and Ralph Ellison, in particular—have widened the perception of the gothic genre.[1] Like these black authors before him, Colson Whitehead demonstrates a gothic sensibility in his 1999 novel *The Intuitionist*. Set against the unusual backdrop of an investigation into elevator operations, *The Intuitionist* is an allegorical tale of blacks' struggle for upward mobility. Whitehead uses an urban gothic landscape and traditional gothic conventions to portray the alienation of the modern black American due to the progress in urban cities and to speculate on the future of US race relations.

In *The Intuitionist* Lila Mae Watson is an elevator inspector who becomes embroiled in big-city politics when an elevator that she has passed free-falls, fortunately without any passenger injuries. Lila Mae's occupation as an elevator inspector, and her subsequent investigation into the accident, is a clever variance of the detective figure and the detective genre, seen throughout African American literature, but also closely tied to the gothic narrative.[2] As Lila Mae's inquiry deepens, she clashes with dangerous characters and learns of plans for a new elevator design called "the black box." These plans lie at the heart of a power struggle within the elevator industry, and underscore a much larger social battle. In this singular novel, Whitehead offers a tale that is part detective novel, part racial protest novel.[3]

For early American gothic writers the New World was a wild frontier. Novels such as Brockden Brown's *Edgar Huntly, or, Memoirs of a Sleepwalker* (1799), and James Fenimore Cooper's *The Last of the Mohicans* (1826) have depicted what Donald Ringe calls "the darker aspects of the American landscape—the terrible insecurity felt by the whites who find themselves alone in the threatening wilderness, the terror inspired in them by the hostile Indians" (109). Although rural environments have perhaps more often been the setting of American gothic literature, best exemplified in southern gothic novels by William Faulkner, Eudora Welty, and Flannery O'Connor, as urban cities developed, their concrete and steel terrains and turbulent social conditions provided a rich backdrop for the American gothic. Particularly during the 1930s and 1940s, the Los Angeles novel, represented by such texts as Nathanael West's *The Day of the Locust* and Raymond Chandler's *The Big Sleep,* and its cinematic counterpart, *film noir,* reflected an urban gothic sentiment. The US metropolis was brooding and pessimistic, rife with scandal, deception and treachery.

In keeping with this novelistic tradition, Whitehead displays his own vision of America's dismal landscape in *The Intuitionist.*

The northern city in particular has been the source of much inspiration in African American literature, codifying ideas of both hope and frustration. In the nineteenth century, slave narratives depicted the North as a refuge, a Heaven to which slaves escaped, if they could. In his 1845 narrative, Frederick Douglass describes his reaction to seeing New Bedford, Connecticut, for the first time: "From the wharves I strolled around and over the town, gazing with wonder and amazement. . . . Everything looked clean, new, and beautiful" (111). Into the twentieth century, the North was a land of disappointment and bitterness, as African Americans realized that the region was not completely free of racism or other forms of oppression. In his autobiographical *Black Boy* (1945), Wright describes his arrival in Chicago in 1927: "My first glimpse of the flat black stretches of Chicago depressed me and dismayed me, mocked all my fantasies. Chicago seemed an unreal city whose mythical houses were built of slabs of black coal wreathed in palls of gray smoke, houses whose foundations were sinking slowly into the dank prairie. . . . The din of the city entered my consciousness, entered to remain for years to come" (261). In *The Intuitionist,* Lila Mae's father, Marvin, likewise cautions his daughter about leaving their southern home for the North after she has been accepted into the Institute of Vertical Transport, a college for the study of elevators. "It's not so different up there, Lila Mae," he warns. "They have the same white people up there that they got down here. It might look different. It might feel different. But it's the same" (234). Despite this admonition, she sees the North as her opportunity to progress. She explains, "I moved up here because here is where the elevators are. The real elevators" (168).

The Intuitionist operates within two time periods. Its 1999 publication date, at the conclusion of arguably one of the most prosperous decades in American history, allows it to speak to the continuing alienation of the classes of people who were not the beneficiaries of social and economic gains. Whitehead portrays a northern city that was perhaps once a promising urban center but in the novel's present is a metropolis hit hard by economic downturns. Employment is scarce and influenced by racial and gender discrimination and the policies established at mid-century to counter this prejudice. Cronyism and patronage are rampant in business and politics. Minority groups and the poor struggle against social and economic repression that leaves them isolated and vulnerable to abuse. The contrast between economic prosperity and inner-city despair that the author depicts contributes to a gothic landscape infused with mystery, fear, and apprehension.

Without specifying the year in which this novel's story takes place, Whitehead uses subtle details of diction, automobile make, and dress styles, and so on, to depict a 1950's or 60's urban environment. In addition, the city setting is never named, although Whitehead coyly refers to it as "the most famous city in the world, with magnificent elevated trains, five daily newspapers, two baseball stadiums," and "the most famous street in the world" (12, 23, 163). The time of year, too, is ambiguous, the narrator revealing only that "everything in the garden is dying, that's what time of year it is" (58). One of the few references to the popular culture of the era comes from the appearance of a singing group called "Rick Raymond and the Moon-Rays," who performs "a song from a movie musical that was popular a few years back" at an elevator industry party (150). The history of the city and the larger surrounding area are referred to only by referring to "the infamous sale of the island" (47).

Whitehead delivers characters who are estranged from the majority of society. Reminiscent of Ellison's *Invisible Man*, another novel with (black) gothic overtones, the individuals who inhabit the fictional world of *The Intuitionist* only exist in surroundings that are hidden, underground, and peripheral. The hierarchy of the Department of Elevator Inspectors, for example, positions white employees above ground while black men are relegated to the motor pool in the "rank gloom of the garage" located at the bottom of the building: "This space in the garage is what the Department has allowed the colored men—it is underground, there are no windows permitting sky, and the sick light is all the more enervating for it—but the mechanics have done their best to make it their own" (18).

This description highlights the black American's relationship to the larger society. The dominant society is determined to keep African Americans, and perhaps all minorities—although no others are discussed in the text—at the bottom, in the dark, and out of sight. By making the most of their situation, "mak[ing] it their own," the black men take ownership of their work conditions, of their very existence, out of the hands of the white heads of the Department. They periodically revolt against their imposed subordination by defacing a poster depicting their boss, the chair of the Elevator Inspectors Guild. Whitehead writes:

> A close inspection of Chancre's campaign posters, which are taped to every other cement column despite regulations against campaign literature within a hundred yards of Headquarters, reveals myriad tiny insurrections, such as counterclockwise swirls in the middle of Chancre's pupils, an allusion to his famous nocturnal dipsomania. . . . Horns, boiling cysts, the occasional cussword inked in across Chancre's slat teeth—they add up after awhile. . . . No one notices them but they're there, near-invisible, and count for something.
>
> (18)

Whitehead presents a picture of subtle determination and resilience sustained by various characters throughout the text. This conflict between those who work underground in the garage and those who work in the building itself is symbolic of the larger struggle that gothic literature depicts. What Juliann Fleenor has written about the nightmare that the female gothic exhibits can equally be ascribed to Whitehead's presentation: the discord depicted in the literature is "created by the individual in conflict with the values of her society and her prescribed role" (10). The black workers at the Department of Elevator Inspectors are struggling within the confines of their position to find and reaffirm their voices and very identity.

Also linking *The Intuitionist* with the gothic tradition is the manner in which Whitehead molds the notion of evil into the shape of a modern patriarchy, producing a climate of terror and seclusion that devalues not only women but blacks as well. In becoming an elevator inspector—the first female and only the second black—Lila Mae has escaped the plight of those in the motor pool, only to face her own isolation. She experiences no camaraderie or even a professional rapport with her fellow inspectors. This separateness began even before Lila Mae joined the ranks of the elevator inspectors, however. As a student at the Institute for Vertical Transport, Lila Mae had to live in a converted janitor's closet above the gymnasium because there were no living quarters for "colored" students. She was a specter on campus, seen by other students and yet not acknowledged. Race relations at the school were characterized not only by whites' disregard for blacks, but by a blatant fear and hostility towards blacks. Using language that recalls the discourse of 19th-century slavery, the narrator tells us that "the admission of colored students to the Institute for Vertical Transport was staggered to prevent overlap and any possible fulminations or insurrections that might arise from that overlap" (44). Despite this staggered admission, the white faculty is unable to tell the black students apart, and they frequently call Lila Mae by the name of the previous black student, a male.

Lila Mae is able to use this invisibility to her advantage as she embarks on her own investigation into the crash of the elevator. At the Funicular Follies, the Department's annual banquet/variety show, she is mistaken for a maid and is therefore able to operate behind the scenes and witness the outlandish actions of her colleagues. Examining herself in the mirror after donning the maid's uniform that has been mistakenly thrust into her hands, and noting that she is not wearing shoes appropriate for such work, she shrugs off the contradiction, reminding herself that those in attendance "won't be looking at [my] shoes. They won't be looking at me at all." Throughout the night she repeats this observation, deciding not to put her hair back in a bun, more appropriate for her position as a waitress or maid, because "[t]hey do not see her." Even though these are the same men with whom she works side-by-side during the day, "[i]n here they do not see her. She is the colored help" (Whitehead 153).

Lila Mae's misidentification as a maid signifies what Hana Wirth-Nesher describes as "the paradox of the simultaneous visibility and invisibility of the black to the white in public space." In discussing the examination of double consciousness in Ellison's *Invisible Man,* Wirth-Nesher writes, "Although visible due to race, the black figure in the landscape is rendered invisible by being 'naturalized' into a familiar icon—the shoeshine boy, the 'Jolly Nigger,' or variations of Sambo" (96). Whitehead thus depicts the black female figure in white society rendered invisible and "naturalized" as a maid; thus, he illustrates the narrow-mindedness and racism within the Department and indeed within the larger US society.[4]

If race and gender erase Lila Mae, race distinguishes as hypervisible a blackface duo, "Mr. Gizzard and Hambone," actually two white elevator inspectors, who perform at the banquet. Their performance accentuates the dividing line between the predominantly white audience of elevator inspectors and the black waiters, waitresses, and busboys. The duo entertains the crowd in the traditional minstrel fashion: "The skinny man wears a white T-shirt and gray trousers. Clothespins hold his suspenders to his pants. The fat man wants to be a dandy, but his green and purple suit is too small for him, exposing his thick ankles and wrists. Their elbows row back and forth in unison and their feet skip 'cross the stage to the music. Their faces are smeared black with burnt cork, and white greasepaint circles their mouths in ridiculous lips" (154). To raucous applause, they perform a routine that includes dances and jokes, complete with requisite "Negro dialect" and pejorative stereotypes. One such joke: "Hambone, you ole niggah, where you git dat nice hat you got on yo head?" His partner answers, "I got it at dat new hat stoe on Elm Street." "Tell me, Hambone, did it cost much?" "I don know, Mr. Gizzard—de shopkeeper wasn't dar!" (154).

The response to this performance signals Whitehead's sense of the contrast between white and black. The world that Lila Mae and her fellow African Americans live in is one in which whites still accept such racial exhibitions as "Mr. Gizzard and Hambone" as accepted sources of entertainment, and as such, the white audience enthusiastically receives the minstrel performance. In appreciation, the elevator inspectors "[go] mad" and give the pair a standing ovation. In contrast, "the [. . .] colored workers do not speak on what they have just seen" (156). Lila Mae's reaction is similar to that of her fellow colored workers, reflecting their mutual disbelief, shame, and anger. Despite her seemingly outspoken personality and her more advanced position as an elevator inspector, she "does not mention it either, telling herself it is because she does not know the silent women she has been working with, whom she has not talked to all evening for her concentration on the Follies" (156). She rationalizes her silence, thinking to herself that her reticence "is because she is undercover and

speaking to them might trip her up, a dozen other reasons." Initially believing that "the other women are so beaten that they cannot speak of the incident," she finally realizes that "all of them, Lila Mae included, are silent for the same reason: because this is the world they have been born into, and there is no changing that" (157). Although she is verbally silent, like the men who work in the garage, Lila Mae also ultimately performs her own act of resistance. Before giving a new fork to one of the attendees of the dinner, she drags it through grease and the contents of the garbage can.

Included in the audience is Pompey, the city's first black elevator inspector, who "rub[s] laughter-tears from his eyes, [and] lean[s] against [another audience member] to steady himself" (157). Pompey's seemingly traitorous behavior, appearing to enjoy the blackface performance as much as his white co-workers, rather than being stunned into silence like the other African Americans, is understood when a clearer picture of Pompey develops. Called "little Pompey" (25) by the white inspectors, he has incurred the disdain of Lila Mae due to his "appalling obsequious nature, cultivated to exceptional degree" and a persistent rumor (or truth) that he, upon being invited to the office of the head of the inspectors, allowed himself to be kicked in the behind. "The next day," the story goes, "a small memo appeared on Pompey's desk informing him of his promotion to Inspector Second Grade."[5] Significantly, Pompey equally dislikes Lila Mae, declaring about the elevator accident and the impending investigation that threatens Lila Mae's career, "She's finally getting what's been coming to her for a long time" (26).

The smothered, growing conflict between Lila Mae and Pompey explodes when she visits his home to confront him regarding her suspicions that he is involved in inspecting the elevators of a mob-owned building and that he might have been responsible for sabotaging the elevator that she had inspected. She is surprised that he lives only two blocks from her, although his pleasant neighborhood is very different from her own desolate community; there are children playing in the street and people greet each other amiably. Unbeknownst to Lila Mae, Pompey has a wife and children, who are the motivation for his sycophantic actions. Confronting her accusations, he tells Lila Mae that he took the extra job because he needs the money to take his family out of the neighborhood that, while looking nice, is undergoing a change. "You see them kids play ball?" he asks Lila Mae. "Ten years from now half of them be in jail, or dead, and the other half working as slaves just to keep a roof over they heads. Ten years from now they won't even be kids playing ball on the street. Won't be safe enough even to do that" (194). He continues, defending his on-the-job demeanor, "how am I supposed to act, the way you carry yourself. Like you some queen. Your nose up in the air? I got two kids." And after Lila Mae criticizes Pompey for "shuffl[ing] for those white people like a slave," Pompey responds with his own critique. "What I done," he explains, "I done because I had no other choice. This is a white man's world. They make the rules. You come along, strutting like you own the place. Like they don't own you. But they do." He persists, frustrated by Lila Mae's unwillingness to appreciate his struggles with race and class as the first black inspector. "You had it easy, snot-nosed kid that you are," he states, "because of me. Because of what I did for you" (195).

This clash between Lila Mae and Pompey obviously echoes arguments between the early and later generations of African Americans who struggled for equal rights. Lila Mae feels embarrassed by Pompey's seemingly subservient behavior, behavior that she ultimately sees as part of very real sacrifices he has made. Pompey, on the other hand, is resentful of the ease with which Lila Mae has incorporated herself into the elevator industry, a progression perhaps made easier because she is female, and her appearance of having no regard for the path that was paved before her. Both characters are so concerned with their own agendas that neither of them can see their ultimate reliance on one another, or their place within a larger scheme set in motion by those looking for the missing elevator plans. As the novel draws to a close, one of the men who wants to find the plans to the black box tells Lila Mae how beneficial and utterly predictable it was for her to suspect Pompey, thereby steering her away from the real potential culprits. "Let one colored in and you're integrated," he says. "Let two in, you got a race war as they try to kiss up to whitey" (249).[6]

Whitehead offers no easy resolutions to this intergenerational conflict. Later in the novel, an unacknowledged, if one-sided, truce has been called. Lila Mae admits her misreading of Pompey, acknowledging that she was no better than her white co-workers. Whitehead describes the role that Pompey played in society:

> The Uncle Tom, the grinning nigger, the house nigger who is to blame for her debased place in this world. Pompey gave [whites] a blueprint for colored folk. How they acted. How they pleased white folks. How eager they would be for a piece of the dream that they would do anything for massa. She hated her place in the world, where she fell in the order of things, and blamed Pompey, her shucking shadow in the office. She could not see him any more than anyone else in the office saw him.
>
> (239)

Whitehead later adds that Lila Mae "hated something in herself and she took it out on Pompey" (240).

The divisiveness between Lila Mae and Pompey is a product of one of Whitehead's main tenets in *The Intuitionist,* what he calls "the lie of whiteness" (239). All of the characters, white and black, are afflicted by a blindness that prohibits them from realizing their position in society and from determining their own fate. All of them are searching for a means of escape, of rising above their present individual and social circumstances. The potential for this transformation might be found in the mysterious plans of the black box.

The very possibility of change informs Lila Mae's quest for the elusive black box. The search for the cause of the elevator's fall, and the resultant discovery of the plans for a potentially revolutionary elevator model—the black box—in the missing notebooks of a deceased inventor, could create a shift not only in the local politics of the city, but also in the city's and the nation's race relations. With this black box, Whitehead has created an ingenious metaphor for racial uplift. The investigation into the validity and location of the plans for the black box functions effectively as an exploration into the past, present, and future of racial progress, outlining the compromises, losses, and gains inherent in such an evolution.

Whitehead has created, then, an intricate postmodern tale, at the center of which is the symbol of the elevator. The structure of the elevator is an elaborate, mechanical, and philosophical fantasy, the design of which suggests the very opposite of the elevator's actual function. Of the form of the traditional elevator, the Arbo Smooth-Glide, Lila Mae notes: it was "equipped [. . .] with an oversized door to foster the illusion of space, to distract the passenger from what every passenger feels acutely about elevators. That they ride in a box on a rope in a pit. That they are in the void" (5). The elevator that Lila Mae describes is similar to the garage where the maintenance people work in the Department of Elevator Inspectors building: each is designed to give the appearance of openness—the elevator by its large doors, and the garage by its florescent lights—while masking the true intent and design of the space. On the one hand, the elevator is constructed to give the impression that it is not moving at all, all the while hurtling passengers through the heights and depths of a building. The Department's garage, on the other hand, while seemingly a blacks-only space where the workers experience freedom and autonomy, serves the white power structure as a perfect holding cell to the keep blacks in their place. Lila Mae and the other blacks in the city hope to find in the elusive black box an escape from the void of the garage.

The Arbo Smooth-Glide and the mechanics' garage further symbolize Whitehead's critique of late 20th-century US social and political programs that promise more than they actually deliver. The progress made by the 1960's civil rights movement and the subsequent passing of legislations beneficial to racial and ethnic minority groups was tempered by economic policies that kept any real progress to a minimum. Like dysfunctional social, political, and economic policies, the elevator and the garage offer the illusionary appeal of movement and progress, while simultaneously keeping things stagnant, or even moving them backwards.

Whitehead presents as an antidote to this conservative condition the mythological black box. To the novel's students of elevator science, the black box is more than another means of conveyance. It is "the perfect elevator," "one that will deliver [people] from the cities [they] suffer now, these stunted shacks" (61). The dueling national elevator companies, Arbo and American, are both in search of the plans for this project that holds such hope, not just for their respective companies and the industry as a whole, but for all people. Compared to the first elevator, invented by Elisha Otis in the early nineteenth century, which "delivered [people] from medieval five- and six-story constructions," this (post) modern invention, developed by James Fulton, "will grant [people] the sky, unreckoned towers: the second elevation. . . . [I]t's the future" (61). The second elevation represents unlimited potential and possibility for Lila Mae and the other residents of the city, if not the world. It suggests a lifting of the restrictions and constraints placed on black Americans in contemporary society.[7]

The inventor of the black box, James Fulton, was a black man who had passed for white, holding the position of outsider in the industry of elevator invention, as well as in the larger society. His is a dual presence throughout the novel, not only representing the evolution of the elevator industry, but also personifying the early days of race relations. When Lila Mae learns that Fulton was black, she perceives him as "a spy in white spaces, just like she is" (139).[8] Not only is Fulton a spy, but he also signifies the spectral presence so often present in the gothic. As such, throughout the text both he and his invention haunt the characters, especially Lila Mae. A unique bond develops between them, although they never meet in person. For several months, from the vantage point of her room at the Institute, Lila Mae would see a mysterious figure moving through the stacks of the library. On the last night that she was to see him, Fulton waved back to her, "communicat[ing] all he knew and what she already understood about the darkness" (46); the next day Fulton was found dead on the library floor. Fulton, in turn, had inquired about the girl he had seen through the window. When the Dean of the Institute identifies Lila Mae, Fulton senses an affinity as well, in part perhaps because of her race. He absentmindedly writes in the margin of his notebook, "*Lila Mae Watson is the one*" (253).

Fulton's imaginative theories on elevator construction and operation speak to the status of the black American in US society; they reflect the race's movement up—and down—the social order. In his seminal multivolume text, *Theoretical Elevators,* he writes that "*horizontal thinking in a vertical world is the race's curse,*"

thereby positing that what plagues the black race is a lack of upward vision, an inability to seek heights previously unreached (151). He further addresses this deficiency in Volume Two of his text: "*The race sleeps in this hectic and disordered century. Grim lids that will not open. Anxious retinas flit to and fro beneath them. They are stirred by dreaming. In this dream of uplift, they understand that they are dreaming the contract of the hallowed verticality, and hope to remember the terms on waking. The race never does, and that is our curse*" (186). With his innovative creation he proposes to lift this curse, thus realizing the dream of uplift, "the promise of verticality" (176). In truth, he writes of, in sociological, non-elevator, terms, racial uplift. One character says, in speaking of his search for the black box and its importance to the black community, "they always saying it's the future. It's the future of the cities. But it's our future, not theirs. It's ours. And we need to take it back. What he made, this elevator, colored people made that. It's ours. And I'm going to show that we ain't nothing. Show them . . . that we are alive" (140).

This second elevation, or black box, mirrors the gothic's function in philosophy in that it responds to traditional modes of thought. Just as the Fulton-designed elevator served as an improvement over the early Otis conception, so, too, did the gothic emerge in the eighteenth and nineteenth centuries as an improvement, or at least a change, over earlier philosophies. Gothic fiction, as J. Gerald Kennedy writes in his essay about Edgar Allan Poe, "enacts the radical uncertainty of an epoch of revolution in which nearly all forms of authority . . . came to be seen as constricting systems" (40). Fulton's design challenges not only the authority of the leaders of the elevator industry and their present theories of elevator inspection, but the dominance of traditional notions of race as well. Despite the vagueness of the novel's temporal setting, **The Intuitionist** clearly reflects a racial revolution. Like the gothic, the elevator responds to the fears of an industrial, urban, multiracial western society. Fulton has found a better way, and that way is the black box.

What makes Fulton's invention even more intriguing than its potential is that it is based on a joke, an attempt by Fulton to challenge traditional notions of elevator philosophy. Prior to Fulton's theories, elevator inspection was based on Empiricism, physical examinations of elevator machinery, its material components, to determine how the apparatus is working. As a means of revealing the deficiencies of this approach, Fulton writes a volume promoting an opposing ideology—one that he did not fully believe himself—based on sensing the elevator's movements and interior design. When investigating the elevator that eventually falls, Lila Mae "listens" and "concentrate[s] on the vibrations massaging her back." In her mind, the vibrations take the shape of an "aqua-blue cone," and she visualizes the upward movement of the elevator as "a red spike." Other shapes form as the elevator ascends. Lila Mae's intuition is innate and magical, for, the narrator tells us, "You don't pick the shapes and their behavior. Everyone has their own set of genies" (6). One critic would come to deem the practice "Intuitionist" and define it as "postrational, innate. Human" (238).

It is not accidental that the language that Whitehead uses to describe these differing philosophies evokes the dichotomy that exists between East and West, black and white. What Whitehead presents is not solely a potential technological shift, but ultimately an entire paradigm shift. Lila Mae's own description of the position of the early inspectors reveals the larger implications of the development of such a revolutionary approach as Intuitionism. "They looked at the skin of things," she says, further delineating the two methods not just along philosophical lines, but racial ones as well. "White people's reality is built on what things appear to be—that's the business of Empiricism" (239). The men at the Funicular Follies just "looked at the skin of things" when they failed to recognize Lila Mae in a maid's uniform, seeing her merely as a black servant, and not as their co-worker. Lila Mae shares their myopia when she initially suspects Pompey. The failure of Empiricism is that individuals don't see the subtle shadings, either of elevators or people. "Their sacred Empiricism has no meaning," Lila Mae concludes, "when they can't even see that this man [Fulton] is colored because he says he is not. Or doesn't even say it. They see his skin and see a white man."[9] Fulton's design suggests that Intuitionism, conversely, offers a new opportunity, a new *vision*, for both this city and for all of US society.

There are no clear conclusions at the end of Whitehead's novel. Lila Mae finds Fulton's notebooks that contain the plans for the black box, and she delivers them, incomplete, to both of the elevator companies. What is missing is the key that will break the code that Fulton used to design his elevator; only Lila Mae possesses the code. After she has completed Fulton's manuscripts, when she feels that the time is right, when society is ready to receive what the black box represents, Lila Mae will reveal the code to the rest of the world. It is then that Fulton's vision of the world will be transformed from a joke into a reality.

Notes

1. See *Native Son, Beloved* and *Song of Solomon, Mama Day* and *Linden Hills,* and *Invisible Man,* respectively.

2. For a discussion of the relationship between the detective and gothic novels, see, for example, Cawelti (27) and Day (*passim*).

3. Laura Miller cites Whitehead's influences as being Don DeLillo and "Ralph Ellison and Thomas Pynchon by way of Walter Mosley." Reviewer Shelley Ridenour sees traces of Ralph Ellison as well, but also includes George Orwell as an obvious inspiration. In an interview with Miller, Whitehead himself cites Stephen King, Ishmael Reed, and Jean Toomer as authors who have directly or indirectly inspired him.

4. As a courier, Lila Mae's father represents yet another familiar icon for whites. When he appears at an office building seeking a job interview for the position of elevator inspector, "[t]he secretary handed him a package when he walked in the door. He returned it to her thin white hands and informed her he was here for an interview. Wasn't a messenger boy" (161).

5. This scene replicates a scene in Wright's *Black Boy,* where Shortly lets a white man kick him in the behind for a quarter (227-29). Just as it is probably no coincidence that Wright's Shorty is also an elevator operator, Pompey is the name given, ironically or contemptuously, to an officious slave type in various antebellum slave narratives.

6. Racial politics had infused Lila Mae's career from the beginning. Lila Mae's assignment to the Fanny Briggs Memorial Building, named for a slave woman who had escaped to the North and taught herself how to read, was politically motivated. It was an election year, Lila Mae observes, and Chancre, the current Inspector Guild chair, "was so naked in his attempt to score points with the electorate," particularly the minority population, that he assigned her to that building (13).

7. So much is the elevator a symbol of (racial) progress, and therefore a threat to the white majority, that at the press conference following the accident, a reporter asks the city's mayor, "Do you think that a party or parties resistant to colored progress may be responsible?" (22)

8. When she discovers that Fulton was passing for white, she asks herself, perhaps reflecting upon her own experiences with her co-workers, "What did Fulton do when [other colored people] acted white? Talk about 'the colored problem' and how it is our duty to help the primitive race get in step with white civilization. Out of darkest Africa. Or did he remain silent, smile politely at their darkie jokes. Tell a few of his own" (139).

9. In discussing the potential impact of the discovery of Fulton's racial identity, one character remarks, "'I don't know if [the upper ranks of the Inspectors Guild] know he was colored, but if they do you know they ain't going to tell the truth. They would never admit that. . . . They'd die before they say that" (138).

Works Cited

Cawelti, John G. *Adventure, Mystery and Romance: Formula Stories as Art and Popular Culture.* Chicago: U of Chicago P, 1976.

Day, William Patrick. *In the Circles of Fear and Desire: A Study of Gothic Fantasy.* Chicago: U of Chicago P, 1985.

Douglass, Frederick. *Narrative of the Life of Frederick Douglass, An American Slave, Written by Himself.* 1845. Ed. David W. Blight. Boston: Bedford, 1993.

Fleenor, Juliann, ed. "The Female Gothic." *The Female Gothic.* Montreal: Eden P, 1983. 3-28.

Kennedy, J. Gerald. "Phantoms of Death in Poe's Fiction." *The Haunted Dusk: American Supernatural Fiction, 1820-1920.* Eds. Howard Kerr, John W. Crowley, and Charles L. Crow. Athens: U of Georgia P, 1983. 37-65.

Miller, Laura. "Colson Whitehead's Alternate New York." 12 Jan. 1999. *Salon.com.* 1 July 2006. <http://www.salon.com/books/feature/1999/01/cov_12featureb.html.

———. "The Salon Interview: Colson Whitehead." 12 Jan. 1999. *Salon.com.* 1 July 2006. <http://www.salon.com/books/int/1999/01/cov_si_12int.html.

Ridenour, Shelley. Rev. of *The Intuitionist,* by Colson Whitehead. 4 Oct. 1999. *Chicago Words Hub.* 1 July 2006. <http://newcitychicago.com/home/daily/book_reviews/intuitionist10499.html.

Ringe, Donald. *American Gothic: Imagination and Reason in Nineteenth Century Fiction.* Lexington: Kentucky UP, 1982.

Whitehead, Colson. *The Intuitionist.* New York: Anchor, 1999.

Wirth-Nesher, Hana. *City Codes: Reading the Modern Urban Novel.* Cambridge, MA: Cambridge UP, 1996.

Wright, Richard. *Black Boy.* 1945. New York: HarperCollins, 1991.

———. *Native Son.* 1940. New York: Harper & Row, 2001.

FURTHER READING

Criticism

Bérubé, Michael. "Race and Modernity in Colson Whitehead's *The Intuitionist.*" In *The Holodeck in the Garden: Science and Technology in Contemporary American Fiction,* edited by Peter Freese and Charles B. Harris, pp. 163-78. Normal, Ill.: Dalkey Archive Press, 2004.

Elucidates concepts of personal and professional identity, spatiotemporal setting, and physical disability in *The Intuitionist.*

Hill, Christopher Jack. "Literary Landscapes: Novels of Disparate Places, Themes and Souls." *Black Issues Book Review* 8, no. 3 (May-June 2006): 32.

Brief review that contends that Whitehead effectively satirizes corporate branding and society's penchant for empty and useless titles in *Apex Hides the Hurt.*

Whitehead, Colson, and Kevin Larimer. "Industrial Strength in the Information Age: A Profile of Colson Whitehead." *Poets & Writers Magazine* 29, no. 4 (July-August 2001): 20-6.

Provides a biographical sketch of Whitehead as well as an interview with the author.

Additional coverage of Whitehead's life and career is contained in the following sources published by Gale: *Contemporary Authors,* Vol. 202; *Contemporary Literary Criticism,* Vol. 232; and *Literature Resource Center.*

Zoë Wicomb
1948-

South African short story writer and novelist.

INTRODUCTION

Wicomb is an author and educator who is best known for the short story collection *You Can't Get Lost in Cape Town* (1987). Written during her self-imposed twenty-year exile from her native South Africa, the semi-autobiographical work is a collection of connected stories featuring mixed-race South Africans—called "coloured" by the apartheid government—and their lives and experiences somewhere between white and black society. Wicomb, who was herself labeled "coloured," writes out of her own experience as a black woman from South Africa, depicting her characters' search for identity amid the discrimination and the racial ambiguity they experience as members of the "coloured" community. Wicomb has also published two novels, *David's Story* (2001) and *Playing in the Light* (2006).

BIOGRAPHICAL INFORMATION

Wicomb was born in 1948 in rural Little Namaqualand, in a Griqua community in South Africa's Cape Province (now the Western Cape of South Africa). Her mother, Rachel Le Fleur, died when Wicomb was a young girl; she was subsequently raised by her father, Robert Wicomb, a schoolteacher who strongly encouraged his daughter to master the English language and assimilate into British society, believing these to be vital to her future success. At her father's urging, she attended an English secondary school in Cape Town, then the "coloured" University of the Western Cape (a school for mixed-race South Africans), where she received an undergraduate degree in English in 1968. In the early 1970s she left South Africa for England, where she completed a second B.A. at Reading University in 1973 and taught in Nottingham. Active in the anti-apartheid movement, she also embarked on a literary career, founding and editing the London-based *Southern African Review of Books* and writing her collection of short stories, *You Can't Get Lost in Cape Town*. After living in Glasgow for a time, earning a master's degree in 1989 from the University of Strathclyde, she returned to South Africa in the early 1990s, where she taught in the English department at the University of the Western Cape. She subsequently returned to Glasgow to lecture in English studies at the University of Strathclyde. She has also served as writer in residence at the universities of Strathclyde and Glasgow.

MAJOR WORKS

The semi-autobiographical *You Can't Get Lost in Cape Town* is narrated from the perspective of Frieda Shenton, a South African "coloured" woman who, throughout the course of the tales, grows from a young girl into an adult writer. Taking place between the 1950s and the 1980s, the ten stories are all set in either Cape Town or Namaqualand and revolve around how Frieda's identity is shaped by the race, class, and gender-based biases she faces, and how she attempts to bypass her classification as a lower-class, impure member of the "coloured" society in order to forge her own individuality. In the title story, Wicomb addresses relations between the races as the narrator tells of her abortion of the child she conceived with her white lover; "Home Sweet Home" recounts the alienation Frieda feels upon returning to her rural home after being educated in the city; "Ash on My Sleeve" tells of Frieda's visit to a friend who is content to live in a "coloured" section of Cape Town and participate in a cultural organization for blacks; and "A Trip to the Gifberge" turns on the themes of rediscovery, reconnection, and unification, as Frieda's mother imparts to her daughter her firm belief that colonialism has neither destroyed their connection to their homeland nor stripped them of their identity.

In 2002 Wicomb won the South African M-Net Literary Prize for her first novel, *David's Story*. Set in 1991, the novel opens as Nelson Mandela is being released from prison and the African National Congress has been legalized. The protagonist is David Dirkse, a "coloured" anti-apartheid activist married to fellow protester Sally. Leaving his wife and children for the town of Kokstad in order to research his roots, David takes a lover, Dulcie, who has suffered torture and rape. The history of Griqualand is revealed through David's discovery that he is descended from Andries Abraham Stockenstrom Le Fleur, who brought the Griqua tribe into the desert during the nineteenth century. Wicomb's second novel, *Playing in the Light*, is set in the post-apartheid Cape Town of the 1990s. Revolving around the search for identity and the metaphor of travel as a means to uncover the truth of one's roots and the reality of South Africa's past, the novel turns on the protagonist, Marion Campbell, owner of a travel agency, who eventually discovers that although she had thought of herself as white, she is in reality part "coloured."

CRITICAL RECEPTION

Overall, Wicomb's writings have received acclaim from critics. She has been called a talented storyteller whose prose is lyrical as well as tightly constructed, and has been regarded as part of a new trend in South African writing. According to critics, she opposes the impulse to view her fiction as autobiographical, and thwarts such attempts by using narrative strategies like the resurrection of characters—the mother in *You Can't Get Lost in Cape Town,* for instance, resurfaces in one of the last tales, after being thought dead in earlier stories. Focusing on the political nature of her writings, commentators have also assessed her work in relation to her perspective as a feminist writer from South Africa, with critical discussion revolving around her belief that the battle against the black patriarchy should coincide with the struggle against apartheid and other racial injustices. Her attitude toward her homeland has been analyzed as well; many commentators find that her writings evoke ambiguous feelings of both love and repulsion for the racially segregated country of her birth. Regarding *You Can't Get Lost in Cape Town* in particular, observers have commented favorably on her ability to mix personal stories with South African history and have noted that she uses everyday details in order to generate a new political consciousness among readers.

PRINCIPAL WORKS

You Can't Get Lost in Cape Town (short stories) 1987
David's Story (novel) 2001
Playing in the Light (novel) 2006

CRITICISM

Constance S. Richards (essay date 1995)

SOURCE: Richards, Constance S. "Transnational Feminist Reading; The Case of *Cape Town*." In *On the Winds and Waves of Imagination: Transnational Feminism and Literature*, pp. 73-102. New York: Garland Publishing, 2000.

[*In this essay, Richards discusses* You Can't Get Lost in Cape Town *in terms of South African postprotest literature, claiming that "politically committed writing such as Wicomb's in postcolonial South Africa acknowledges its dependence on protest literature, a counternarrative to colonialist representations which laid the groundwork for the institution of apartheid."*]

The act of reading is far from a passive process by which the reader absorbs the text like a sponge. Yet I can imagine a reading of texts that closely approximates such passivity, particularly when the world of the text is alien to the reader. But a passive reading like this, no matter how alien its subject matter, is not exempt from the de rigueur demand of a transnational feminist reading practice. In the postmodern epoch, postcolonial theorists of many disciplines make us aware that master narratives and nationalism fail to represent the nature of social and political movements. A reading practice that is not an aggressive pursuit of understanding multiple subjectivities will tend to rely on a myopic, ethnocentric narrative, and will fail to capture the nuances of experience that national allegory often masks. In the final analysis, there is no such thing as a passive reading. A reading that is not passionately engaged in "joining" with various subjectivities (particularly those hitherto obscured by canonical formations) can, at best, be described as passive. But such a reading of a text, however, may not be passive at all, but rather the conservative embrace of master narrative that works against postmodernist perspectives and interpretations of aesthetic expression.

The first time I read South African feminist and author Zoë Wicomb's *You Can't Get Lost in Cape Town* (1987), it became clear that the novel required of me, a white, U.S., academic, feminist reader, a politically engaged reading practice. Initially, my entry into the text seemed deceptively simple. I, too, grew up as a female in a patriarchal society; I could share the female narrator's resentment of her father's expectations and the contradictory desire to do well in school, to make him proud. I remember the dissatisfaction with my maturing female body and the adolescent approach-avoidance attitude toward "boys" which the young Frieda expresses. But details of the novel prevented my easy identification with the narrator. Something as simple as Frieda's anticipation of a new school year on the last day of her summer holiday left me feeling "othered." Frieda looks around at the heat-dried "succulents spent and shrivelled in autumn" (23), yet she also notes that, at eighty degrees, "it is unusually cool for January" (21). The disjuncture represented by autumn in a different hemisphere provides only one example of the way in which the setting of the novel disallows my passive reading and demands a more aggressive pursuit of the "joining." However, the master narrative models of my Western education, even the canonized feminist reworkings of them, do not seem to provide an adequate framework to facilitate this effort.

For example, we might read the novel using the Western model of bildungsroman (or more specifically, a *künstlerroman*): the narrator, Frieda, a writer, matures, leaves South Africa for England, and eventually returns home with the idea that South Africa may be where she belongs. The most common (white, Western) feminist approaches to subverting the bildungsroman, such as Virginia Woolf's *The Voyage Out* and Kate Chopin's *The Awakening,* create a female protagonist who seemingly comes to understand what patriarchy expects of a woman, and they refuse to continue the journey, "choosing" death instead. Frieda, however, matures and negotiates gender expectations, neither accepting nor rejecting a "proper" feminine role. To the end of the novel, she continues to actively negotiate what it means to be a woman, and as importantly, what it means to be a "Coloured" South African.

Even my reference to **You Can't Get Lost in Cape Town** as a "novel" reveals an imposed sense of cohesiveness. In his analysis of this text, André Viola refers to the structure as a "cycle of stories," characterized by discrete episodes which share a "unity of place and singleness of focus" (Viola 231). Viola's structuralist approach compares **Cape Town** to James Joyce's *A Portrait of the Artist as a Young Man,* identifying in the development of the artist (in Frieda's case, the writer) "five stages, each concluded by a highly deceptive climax" (234). However, Viola's insistence upon comparing the text to master narratives, underscored by the title of his essay, "Zoë Wicomb's **You Can't Get Lost in Cape Town**: A Portrait of the Artist as a Young Coloured Girl," fails to recognize that Wicomb complicates the bildungsroman with the possibility that her main character has invented an imaginary life and denies the disruptive potential of reimagining literary conventions. A reading of **Cape Town** that situates it in the field of South African literature might be more responsible. While literature in South Africa is certainly informed by Western tradition, colonial languages and education being deeply integrated throughout the empire, a reading that uses as its only measurement Western canonical texts automatically places **Cape Town** outside of its historical, political, and social context, and as in the case of some readings of Woolf's *Voyage,* reifies master narratives.

Contextualizing a contemporary South African novel in its national literary tradition poses some problems for a transnational feminist reading practice, however. One project of transnational feminism is to free feminisms from narrow forms of nationalist discourse. The critique of British colonialism that I read in Virginia Woolf's *The Voyage Out,* for example, emerges from my use of her feminist essays as a guide for interpreting the silence which she creates around the indigenous women of the novel. Woolf's claim that as a woman she has no country, as a woman her country is the world, is an attempt to distance herself from a long national history of imperialism and to imagine alliances on the basis of gender. Likewise, Alice Walker's essay "My Father's Country Is the Poor" will serve in chapter 4 [of *On the Winds and Waves of Imagination*] as a prime example of how she works against the narrow forms of black nationalism in the United States, itself a counterdiscourse,

constructed solely on the basis of racial identity. As we will see, even the Pan-Africanist stance in her later novels resists the tendency to ignore patriarchal oppression for the sake of African solidarity.

But in South Africa, the notion of nation is even more complicated. As in the United States, the black liberation struggle of South Africa is a counternarrative to the white power structure and at the same time a master narrative of racial solidarity. The black liberation movement in South Africa elides differences of gender, religion, ethnicity, and socioeconomic class, a tendency which feminists such as Wicomb resist. However, the concept of "race" has been complicated by the apartheid structure that separated (physically and socially) black South Africans from "Coloured" South Africans, affording a certain level of "privilege" to the latter, a standard divide-and-conquer technique. The politically progressive "Coloured" community has claimed black identity and committed to a unified struggle. But South Africa's recent transition to majority rule, ending the reign of apartheid, signals an opportunity to complicate the nationalist narrative with ethnic and religious difference, gender-related issues, and gay and lesbian identities.

A master narrative approach to the reading of South African texts in the epoch of a postapartheid South Africa fosters a dependency upon long-established assumptions about identity formation and location as determined by racial policies under apartheid, on the one hand, and resistance to such policies by the national liberation movement, on the other. The term "postmodern" shares a common space with "postcolonial," and the application of the two terms to Third World literatures signals the disintegration of the master narrative of nationalist discourses which fail, at the present time, to account for all the fragments that colonialism leaves behind. Zoë Wicomb cites such a moment of disintegrating identity in the South African theater in her unpublished essay **"Postcoloniality and Postmodernity: The Case of the Coloured in South Africa"**:[1]

> The resurgence of the term, Coloured, capitalised, without its prefix of *so-called* and without the disavowing scare-quotes earned during the period of revolutionary struggle when it was replaced by the word, black, has [much] in common with the condition of postmodernity: the successive adoption of names at various historical junctures; the failure of "coloured" to take on a fixed meaning; its shifting allegiances; and its typographic play of renaming whilst denying the act within an utterance that does not reveal capitalisation.

> (2)

Yet the strategic deployment of the term "Coloured" as a marker of postcolonial identity does not necessarily signal a politically progressive move. Wicomb's concern for the Cape coloureds of South Africa is, in part, motivated by their example as an instance of disintegrating identity vis-à-vis the "black" anti-apartheid movement and by their "shameful" support as a voting bloc supporting the Boer Party[2] platform during the first democratic elections on April 27, 1994:

> [T]he shame of [the vote] lies not only in what we have voted against—citizenship within a democratic constitution that ensures the protection of individual rights, the enshrinement of gay and lesbian rights, the abolition of censorship and blasphemy laws—but also in the amnesia with regard to the Nationalist Party's atrocities in maintaining Apartheid.
>
> (9)

The "we" in the above passage signifies Wicomb's membership in "Coloured" society, although this claiming is not her own but rather a category created by apartheid: Wicomb is a "Coloured" who identifies as black.[3] The example of Coloured identity and the disintegration of black nationalism which are Wicomb's concern also reveal the potential of postmodernity and postcoloniality to create new, reactionary forms of nationalism. As Wicomb puts it, "[W]ithin the new, exclusively coloured political organisations in the Cape, attempts at blurring differences of language, class and religion in the interest of an homogeneous ethnic group . . . defy the decentering thrust of postmodernism" (**"Postcoloniality and Postmodernity"** 2). Wicomb's valuing of the "decentering thrust of postmodernism" as a tactic of retaining the complexities of political and social identity in the postcolonial era provides a key to understanding identity construction in *Cape Town.* Even the structure of *Cape Town* demonstrates her postmodern tendency to destabilize the subject position. The text is a configuration of narrative fragments interrelated by a "Coloured" female narrator-protagonist, but otherwise disjunctured by the narrator-author's resistance to fixed locations. Such a text cannot be grasped by a passive or disinterested reading.

However, Wicomb's insistence that the conditions which gave rise to solidarity in black nationhood should not be forgotten must also shape a reading of her novel. Wicomb has been called a postprotest writer, "committed to democratic ideals but refusing a single ideological stance" (Sicherman 111). Politically committed writing such as Wicomb's in postcolonial South Africa acknowledges its dependence on protest literature, a counternarrative to colonialist representations which laid the groundwork for the institution of apartheid. The "protest" in "postprotest" is not a passive suffix paralyzed by an overdetermined prefix; nor is it a subordinate outdated appendage of South Africa's history. It acknowledges that the undoing of the symbolic features of apartheid South Africa has been no quick fix. The absence of de jure racial separation has not resolved the hegemony of white privilege, nor the uneven distribution of material wealth in postapartheid South Africa. Furthermore, a reading challenged by multiple subjectivities, and favoring fragmentation over unification, may be vulnerable to a kind of bourgeois academic and aesthetic opportunism suggesting that the celebration of difference is more important than the material well-being of the masses. A valuing of the postmodern, multivoicedness of postcoloniality should not be divorced from real conditions created by the white power structure. Hence, a reading of South African literature that aims to retain the social and political context of a text's creation would recognize that the protest model of South African literature is woven into postprotest writings such as Wicomb's *Cape Town.*

Further complicating the concept of a "new" South Africa is the idea that there is some moment of epiphany when "old" becomes "new." The first majority election in 1994 was certainly a milestone in an ongoing struggle. But the dividing line between apartheid and postapartheid is slippery. Prior to 1994, black South Africans saw a loosening of restrictions on cultural production, and some formerly white-only educational institutions were opened to controlled numbers of "nonwhite" students. The ideas that the new contains the old and that the transition from one to the other does not take place linearly but in fits and starts are demonstrated in the literature of this period of transition. For instance, Zoë Wicomb's *You Can't Get Lost in Cape Town,* published in 1987, seven years prior to this momentous election, brings the "new" to bear upon the "old." Wicomb sets her novel in a South Africa still functioning under the apartheid system as she moves our reading of South African literature beyond the single focus on racial oppression in the protest model but not beyond the politics of a "new" South Africa. Protest is a fundamental aspect of South Africa's present and future; it is always already present in her narrative.

The goal of a transnational feminist reading practice is to imagine, through the vehicle of literature, cross-cultural alliances among women. Such a desire demands that the reader examine his or her own political assumptions. My initial naive approach to Wicomb's *Cape Town* assumed that a desire to understand the concerns of a South African female writer and our shared claim to feminism were sufficient preparation for imagining coalition. After being brought up short by textual references which cast me as "other," I realized that I could not ethically read this novel outside of its historical particularity. Reading Woolf's *Voyage Out* as anticolonial requires contrasting it to the exoticizing tendencies of colonialist literature. Likewise, Wicomb's postmodern exploration of the female subject builds upon the postprotest counternarrative which attempts to reveal what protest literature strategically obscures in its binary vision of the oppressed resisting the oppressor. Hence, an ethically responsible construction of postprotest literature might begin by uncovering what it works against.

". . . LIKE LIVING ON SHIFTING SANDS"[4]:
PROTEST LITERATURE IN SOUTH AFRICA

A thorough examination of South African literature would recognize the colonialist writings that protest literature challenges. Titles of early English-language "ancestral novels" echo colonialist prejudices and concerns: *Makana: or, the Land of the Savages* (1832); *Jasper Lyle: A Tale of Kaffirland* (1852); *George Linten: or, the First Years of an English Colony* (1876); and *The Settler and the Savage* (1877). Sarah Christie, Geoffrey Hutchings, and Don Maclennan, coauthors of *Perspectives on South African Fiction,* suggest that early white South African writers who employed the novel form adopted English master narrative styles such as the pastoral, romance, and realism, and adapted them to the South African setting. Yet such classifications, which grow out of a literary tradition at the heart of the colonial project, do not sufficiently address the hegemonic place of race in South Africa.

What we now know as the state of South Africa began as a settler colony, established by the Dutch East India Company at the Cape in 1652 as a way station for eastbound traders. Dutch settlers displaced the indigenous Khoi,[5] then spread inland as "Trek-Boers," seeing themselves as early pioneers settling a savage land. As the Boer population increased, more and more farmland was required. Control of the Cape transferred from Dutch to British hands as a result of the Anglo-French wars of 1793-1815. Dutch descendants resisted British authority until they were granted "independence" from the British colonial administration in 1910. Caught in a litany of struggle between the two settler populations, the English and the Dutch, were numerous indigenous African cultural groups who suffered displacement and enslavement, and who sometimes fought back violently and were subsequently suppressed. Since the 1910 Act of Union until the granting of majority rule in 1994, the business of what to do with the African population was a major concern of the white power structure. All aspects of the lives of "nonwhite" inhabitants were subject to legislation: where they lived and worked, what they could and could not publish or say publicly, even what constituted immorality. The colonial settlers also legislated terms upon which the indigenous population surrendered to the white authorities the very land upon which they had lived for generations; white economic development took priority over African humanity. The structure of apartheid ("apartness") was built upon racial classifications which define Africans in negative terms. According to the Population Registration Act of 1950, "whites" are Afrikaans-speaking, English-speaking, or immigrants (usually identifying with English-speaking whites); "nonwhites" are comprised of "Coloureds," "Asiatics," and "Bantu." The Immorality Act (1949), pass laws, and land acts served to ensure separation of "whites" from "nonwhites" and to severely punish transgressors.

Given the implications of racial identity in such a setting, South African author and critic Lewis Nkosi comments in his critique of African literature, *Tasks and Masks* (1981), that

> with very few exceptions the literature of Southern Africa is wholly concerned with the theme of struggle and conflict—conflict between the white conquerors and the conquered blacks, between white masters and black servitors, between the village and the city. In particular, if South African literature seems unable to contemplate any kind of human action without first attempting to locate it within a precise social framework of racial conflict it is merely because very often colour differences provide the ultimate symbols which stand for those larger antagonisms which Southern African writers have always considered it their proper business to explain. . . . [W]hether written by white or by blacks the literature of Southern Africa is committed to the notion that certain 'tasks' are the legitimate function of socially responsible writers. Protest, commitment, explanation: Southern African readers and critics expect these qualities of their authors.

(76)

From its inception, the field of protest literature gives voice to a culture of resistance. The first black novel, *Mhudi* (1922), by Sol Plaatje, responds to the Land Act of 1913 which displaced the indigenous people from their farming and grazing lands and paved the way for the apartheid structure. Zoë Wicomb notes that Plaatje's literary prediction of the decimation wrought by this system and his appeal to black nationhood utilize the form of a traditional, orally transmitted folktale as an analogy ("Nation" 16). Later protest writers, however, "borrow their models from American literature, primarily that of black Americans" (Nkosi, *Tasks and Masks* 81). The appropriation of an African American literary model by South African authors confirms the hegemonic position of racial relations under apartheid, since it is race antagonism that has been the preoccupation of black American literature, and the African American protest model seems to be a pervasive and healthy response to racial oppression.

Nkosi's critical appraisal of South African writers such as Enver Carim, Nadine Gordimer, Alex La Guma, and Bessie Head favors "protest, commitment and explanation" as the appropriate focus of South African literature. Enver Carim's *A Dream Deferred* (1973), for example, provides for Nkosi "some grisly insights into the dialectical relationship between the conqueror and the conquered; and it is this relationship between the white rulers and their black subjects, the resultant corruption of one and the dehumanisation of the other, which absorbs and exhausts the energies of the South African writer" (*Tasks and Masks* 80).

Common themes echo through much of South Africa's protest literature. In his 1964 play *The Rhythm of Violence,* Nkosi utilizes the student protest movement as a vehicle for dramatizing organized militant resistance and exposing brutal repression on the part of the police. Two groups of characters enact the racial conflict. The play opens with a conversation between two machine gun-toting Boer policemen in the waiting room of Johannesburg city hall. Their presence is juxtaposed with an African freedom rally taking place outside. The physical location of the two groups immediately establishes the binary of race relations in the play. These two representatives of the white power structure are concerned with how best to contain the hated black freedom movement and still retain their own sense of "humanity." This internal discord, inherent in the psyche of the colonizer, serves as instance of diametrical conflict in protest literature. The author attempts to subvert the binary tendencies of the protest model by representing the student movement as a potential site of racial integration and political solidarity. One objective of protest literature is to overthrow the relations of antagonism that have made it necessary. With the introduction of white student activists, particularly the pivotal role played by the Afrikaner character Sarie, Nkosi weaves together the personal and political of apartheid South Africa using interracial relations as his vehicle. But his staging and the political affinity of the student activists retain an oppressor-oppressed duality.

In Nkosi's novel *Mating Birds* (1986), the suppression of student activism prefigures concern for what happens to the dispossessed black youth of South Africa. The narrator, Ndi, has been expelled from the University of Natal for protesting segregated classrooms and the kind of Afrikaner scholarship that teaches that "before the white man came there was no African history to speak of in this darkest of the Dark Continents. Whether we like it or not, African history commences with the arrival on African soil of the first white man" (104). Because Ndi lacks a student pass due to the expulsion, and is unable to obtain a work pass, he seeks out the safest place to spend his days, the "blacks only" side of the Durban beach which is "safe" because the presence of foreign tourists tends to curtail the public display of the brutal methods of the South African police.

In order to symbolize the "dehumanization" of the indigenous population resulting from the malevolent polices of the South African government, Nkosi uses interracial relations at their most intimate level in this novel. The first-person narrator is convicted of rape and sentenced to hang for breaching the Immorality Act, which forbids sexual contact between the races. The narrator's predicament resembles that of Bigger Thomas, who is also executed for his sexual transgressions, in the prototypical U.S. protest novel, *Native Son* (1940) by Richard Wright. The public beach in *Mating Birds* replicates the racial divide of South African society: the two main subjects face each other from opposite sides of the color line. Their publicly shared, yet separate, location becomes a place of sexual intrigue. In the private sphere, the bedroom of the white subject (Veronica),

mutual sexual desire is enacted. With the reimposition of the public, as their tryst is discovered by her Boer friends, sexual desire degenerates into racial betrayal through her accusation of rape. The public imposition of apartheid upon the private desires of the subjects exacts the betrayal of the black narrator by his white lover, and reflects the author's claim that the "relationship between the white rulers and their black subjects . . . [results in the] corruption of one and the dehumanisation of the other" (*Tasks and Masks* 80).

But while protest literature in Nkosi's hands eloquently demonstrates the insidious link that "apartness" constructs across racial classifications, it constructs race as the only basis for oppression in South Africa. A feminist reader might ask, "Where are the women in this version of protest?" In Nkosi's *Rhythm*, female student activists are a supporting cast, concerned with providing food and beer for the political meeting, and functioning as objects of sexual banter among the men. The only woman who is minimally developed is Sarie, and we are led to believe, at the conclusion of the play, that she will inadvertently betray the students. The female characters are not fully developed in Nkosi's novel *Mating Birds* either. In his reminiscences of her, the narrator's mother is constructed as a passive victim of the apartheid policies. Land "reform" acts have claimed ancestral land and have forced her to move into the city; pass laws restrict her residence to the townships and limit employment opportunities, forcing her into one of the more lucrative, though illegal, occupations available to African women, brewing and selling homemade beer. Likewise, Veronica appears only as the first-person narrator's story constructs her: an object of sexual desire. She never speaks except to betray him, and Nkosi offers little to suggest that the narrator's version of events is to be read as anything but the unequivocal truth.

Just as Lewis Nkosi's literary vision seems limited to a binary construction of race relations and fails to develop any gender concerns, Bessie Head, one of the few widely published female writers of color in South Africa, focuses on the effects of South African apartheid on the black man in her first novel, *When Rain Clouds Gather* (1969). *Rain Clouds* centers around a black South African, Makhaya, who has spent some time in jail and climbs a barbed wire fence to escape into Botswana. The rural village to which he flees seems to offer the "illusion of freedom" from the chaos of life as a black man in urban South Africa (7). The pastoral landscape and simple lifestyle provide a kind of peace for a community of exiles of various types, several from difficult personal situations in other parts of Botswana, one a refugee from an emotionless, middle-class English family. While Makhaya's escape testifies to the difficulty of life in South Africa, Head does not romanticize subsistence farming in rural Botswana. The protagonist's adjustment from urban to rural life and his alienation in exile are eased only somewhat by the communal interdependence that results from drought and the hard labor of cooperative agriculture.

The dearth of full-blown female characters in this early novel by Head and in the body of protest writing described thus far is attenuated somewhat by Miriam Tlali. Tlali's work can be called "protest" in terms of both content and style. Like Nkosi, she addresses the social and economic effects of a politics of racial domination. And unlike the approach of a postprotest writer like Zoë Wicomb, whose "novel" employs discursive strategies that suggest, insinuate, and open up spaces for negotiated readings, Tlali's approach is straightforward and explanatory. She constructs her first novel, *Muriel at Metropolitan,* completed in 1969 and banned until its publication in abbreviated and censored form in 1975, as highly autobiographical. Tlali presents the day-to-day life of Muriel, a black typist at Metropolitan Radio, a Johannesburg appliance store, and examines the intersecting sites of race and class oppression from the perspective of a female protagonist. *Muriel at Metropolitan* reveals the economic effects of apartheid by showing how the dubious system of "hire purchase" agreements further indebts and impoverishes the black population. The scenario Tlali creates would not be unfamiliar to the poor in any capitalist system, since the time-payment system is a pervasive practice serving to ensure economic dependence. Unlike Nkosi's approach of radical integrationism, Tlali's work seems concerned only with life within the black community. *Muriel at Metropolitan* echoes themes identifiable with the South African protest movement. Tlali's references to incarcerated leaders on Robben Island, the disintegration of the African family resulting from the policies of labor migration, loss of land and displacement of the black population due to land reform policies, and the call for collective action on the part of the black proletariat are signatures of the lived experience of a person of color in South Africa and define its protest literature.

A critique of apartheid is also articulated in protest literature written by white South Africans. Nadine Gordimer, for example, focuses on what seems appropriate: white complicity. Critic Robin Visel notes, "Gordimer's white South African women are in a sense outside the brutal pact between the male colonizer and the male colonized. But Gordimer refuses to let the white heroine off the hook as a fellow victim; she insists not on woman's passivity, but on her shared responsibility, her collusion in racism" (34). Like Lewis Nkosi's writing, a frequent concern throughout Gordimer's fiction is the taboo of black-white relations under apartheid. In her work, white South Africa is often associated with dryness, sterility, and death, while for her white heroines, "'blackness' is linked to sex, sensuality and imagination" (Visel 34); her tendency to sexualize black characters has been, at times, soundly criticized. From her early concern for the political re-

sponsibility of aesthetics in *The Late Bourgeois World* (1966), the ideological framework that Gordimer consistently brings to bear upon the South African situation is Marxism. In contrast to the above-mentioned examples of protest literature which utilize realist forms, Gordimer offers a more experimental style while still addressing themes of resistance.

Gordimer's style moves from modern Western literary forms like the bildungsroman in her earlier novels to a more postmodern narrative in her later work. Many critics identify *Burger's Daughter* (1979) as a point of stylistic transition with its "shift from the centrality of the subjective and individual to include South Africa in its various highly contested sets of relations, attitudes and voices" (King 6). For example, the novel includes actual police reports and "genuine black African student tracts, the mixing of the real with the imaginary" (King 6-7). But at its heart, *Burger's Daughter* is a bildungsroman concerned with Rosa Burger's struggle to find her own identity. Rosa has been raised in a socialist family and, upon the death of her parents, must work out her own place in the South African political landscape. Even the title "announces that at the novel's core there is a Freudian family saga" (King 7). Rosa's voluntary exile ends when she embraces the work of the ANC; *Burger's Daughter* imagines a place in South African protest for a white activist and so complements the protest literature written by South African writers of color.

But the project of constructing a literary history for Wicomb's 1987 novel defies this linear notion of literary development. South African protest literature does not transform into postprotest with any particular event in the struggle for independence. Lewis Nkosi's *Mating Birds* was published in 1989, for example, two years after Wicomb's *Cape Town,* yet his novel seems to be clearly consumed with the hegemony of racial oppression. Complicating the landscape of South African literary development are the flow of writers out of South Africa and the difficulties of publishing within the country under apartheid. Nkosi, Head, and Wicomb have written and published from locations of exile/expatriation. While Nkosi's play and novel do not address exile, Head's later novels and Wicomb's **Cape Town** bring this experience, as well as their "Coloured" identity, to bear to disrupt the protest form. For example, Miriam Tlali's 1989 collection *Soweto Stories* was written while she lived in South Africa, accounting perhaps for its stylistic similarity to the protest form—daily life in the townships, even in a changing South Africa, requires daily, direct resistance. Yet in this recent collection Tlali troubles the hegemony of race issues in protest literature with a critique of black patriarchy.

A reading practice concerned with contextualizing the work of a South African female writer of color must be cognizant that literary production in South Africa has been hampered by the effects of apartheid. Published works by South African women of color comprise a fairly small body of work. The daily lived experience of apartheid limits access to education and the material resources that facilitate the production of literature. Apartheid has brutally limited blacks' access to education, directly through withholding funding, and indirectly by making daily survival so difficult. Cultural banning, which restricted any work that was openly critical of the Boer government, has been particularly successful in discouraging the novel form. Many political writers living in South Africa have had to seek publishers outside of the country, often secretly, and poetry and short stories are easier to camouflage than book-length manuscripts. Because at present there are relatively few published black South African writers, I offer Miriam Tlali's *Soweto Stories* and Bessie Head's *Maru* (1972) and *A Question of Power* (1974) as available examples to which we might turn as a source of the issues raised in postprotest literature by South African female authors and which might inform a reading of ***You Can't Get Lost in Cape Town.*** Additionally, the postprotest visions of white South African authors whose creative production has not been limited in the same way as that of black South Africans may provide an interesting contrast.

Troubling Racial Hegemony: "Post"-Protest Literature

The short fiction collected in Miriam Tlali's *Soweto Stories* works against the "orthodox" anti-apartheid position which, while "celebrating the political activism of women, [claims] that the gender issue ought to be subsumed by the national liberation struggle" (Wicomb, **"To Hear"** 37). Tlali's short stories are peopled with female characters who resist apartheid as gendered beings. We see the migrant labor camps through the eyes of a wife who has had to leave her children and travel 150 miles from the "native reserve" to visit her husband to "'fetch' another child" (44). After her husband's arrest under the pass law, she is helped by strange women at the camp as she gives birth to a new child, far from her home and family support. In another story, a petit bourgeois man from Soweto is attacked and his car is stolen by *tsotsis*;[6] women flock out of the surrounding houses, blowing whistles and sending out the alarm; female community action proves the most effective way to deal with the errant youth.

In this collection, Tlali reveals the intersections of black patriarchy and racial oppression under apartheid. Displacement from ancestral lands leaves women caught in the conflict between rural and urban life, and traditional and modern culture. In several of her stories, overcrowding, housing restrictions, assignment to specified areas, alcoholism, and unemployment work against traditional support networks of extended family and male financial responsibility. For Paballo, the protagonist in "Mm'a-Lithoto," additional pregnancies are no longer a joy but a burden. The traditionally male-headed household means that it is her husband, Musi, who "owns" the home in the township; when his extended family are displaced from their farm, it is his responsibility to share his scant space. When her husband's expectations that she wait on his family, the crowded living conditions, and her advancing pregnancy become too much for Paballo, her only alternative is to take her child and leave. But her own extended family are also restricted to the townships; they have no room for her. Tlali's stories reveal that the support networks that were available to women within traditional, patriarchal rural life are rendered ineffective by city life; Paballo's male family members who would mediate such marital disputes, fining the husband in oxen for his failure to provide suitable housing for his wife, are powerless in the black urban township.

Tlali's women also suffer from modern sexism, intensified by the effects of apartheid. Sexual abuse on trains, extremely overcrowded by the politics of segregation, is so common that the women do not even need to name it to know they share the experience. Yet the white-only trains which run on parallel tracks are never full; everyone gets a seat. In "Devil at Dead End," negotiations required of a black female passenger to obtain a secondclass train ticket so that she will have a place to rest on her overnight journey, leave her vulnerable to the white ticket taker's sexual lust.

Both *Muriel at Metropolitan* and *Soweto Stories,* Tlali's earliest and latest published literature, respectively, share certain stylistic characteristics. Rather than the figurative language and literary tropes often identified with *l'art pour l'art,* we find unambiguous statements and calls to action. Both works frequently use the modifier "so-called" preceding terms like "coloured," "mine boys," "delivery-boys," and "boss-boy," throwing into question the legitimacy of the discourse of apartheid. Both works satisfy the "tasks," offered by Lewis Nkosi, of socially responsible literature: protest, commitment, and explanation. But Tlali's style has changed. *Soweto Stories* weaves together many and varied narrative voices, women of all ages and even men speak from its pages. This collection moves beyond the more straightforward autobiographical protest fiction of *Muriel at Metropolitan,* written twenty years before, by decentering the subject position, displacing it from an easy one-to-one correlation with the author. Furthermore, Tlali's use of footnotes and parenthetical explication in *Soweto Stories* might be read as a discursive strategy creating a more polemic feel and an appeal to a non-South African readership.[7] The meaning of characters' African names is translated; publication banning, border-crossing procedures, and university policies are explained. A consciously political reader might look to the context of the text's production to appreciate such authorial strategies. Between the time that Tlali wrote *Muriel at Metropolitan* and *Soweto Stories,* she had left southern Africa for the first time, visited the Iowa Writing Program in 1978, and become aware of a small but expanding international readership. Because the anti-apartheid movement has been, in part, carried out on a global stage, with local and international activists requesting economic sanctions against the nationalist government in support of majority rule in South Africa, the style of Tlali's later work might well be read as an appeal for transnational feminist protest.

Just as Miriam Tlali renders problematic the master narrative of South African protest literature on the basis of gender, her contemporary, Bessie Head, complicates the racial politics of this form. Born in Pietermaritzburg Mental Hospital in Natal, Head was the daughter of a white upper-class woman who was judged insane and committed to the mental hospital while pregnant. Her father was a black stable worker for her mother's family, and Head knew even less about him than she did about her mother, Bessie, after whom she was named. Sent immediately to a foster home, to English mission school at the age of thirteen, and then to train as a teacher, Head was a first-generation biracial child who grew up outside of the Cape Town "Coloured" community. She was one of the group of South African writers referred to as the *Drum* (magazine) school, and she lived in Cape Town's District Six for three and a half years while in her twenties. But the mere assignment of the classification "Coloured" did not buy her entry into the Afrikaans-speaking Cape "Coloured" community. "Coloured" identity in South Africa suggests images of the discursive stereotype of the tragic mulatto: a hybrid existing in the interstices of racial identity. To be "Coloured" is to be homeless (if you do not live in Cape Town), and for Bessie Head, homelessness was intensified by her exile in Botswana. Leaving marriage, family, and job, she left South Africa with her only son on a one-way, no-return exit visa and began a fifteen-year period of refugee status, until she was finally granted Botswana citizenship in 1979. It is the investigation of racial and geographic rootlessness in Head's novels which create gaps in what might seem like a seamless South African narrative of binary racial antagonism.

Head, like other *Drum* writers, was "educated, articulate, and well read" (MacKenzie xiv), but her regular contributions differed from theirs stylistically. Most *Drum* writers' work tended to be journalistic and overtly political; Head's more personal, often autobiographical style and avoidance of directly political topics foreshadowed the tone of her later novels. Like Head's earlier novel, *When Rain Clouds Gather, Maru* (1972) falls within the protest literature tradition but at the same time hints at the identity fragmentation which marks *A Question of Power* (1974) as a postprotest, postmodern novel.

Unlike *Rain Clouds* and *A Question of Power,* Head's second novel, *Maru,* does not have a South African pro-

tagonist, yet it takes up homelessness and the ambiguity of "Coloured" identity in the central character, Margaret Cadmore. Margaret was raised, as an "experiment," by an English missionary woman who took her as a newborn (her mother having died in childbirth), gave the child her own name, and raised her in the mission school. Young Margaret seemed to have "a big hole" in her identity because "she was never able to say: 'I am this or that. My parents are this or that'" (15). Yet race was imposed: "There was no one in later life who did not hesitate to tell her that she was a Bushman, mixed breed, half breed, low breed or bastard" (16-17). Margaret is a Masarwa, an ethnic group that functions as the servant class for the African people in the busy administrative village where Margaret is hired to teach. Her ethnic identity is obscured by her adopted English name, and upon arrival in the village, her appearance marks her as "Coloured" South African. With the abuse, discrimination, and alienation that Margaret suffers when she publicly claims her Masarwa identity, Head demonstrates a caste system which collapses rural/urban conflict, race/ethnicity, and socioeconomic class, a caste system that could equally well describe South Africa under apartheid.

While her first two novels complicate the racial politics of an anti-apartheid literary tradition, Head's third novel, *A Question of Power,* is the most highly autobiographical of her novels, yet it takes identity fragmentation to its limit. The novel centers around a "Coloured" protagonist, Elizabeth, who has "lived on the edge of South Africa's life" and leaves on a one-way visa to teach in rural Botswana (18). The bulk of the novel centers around Elizabeth's mental breakdown; she is caught in an internal struggle between two forces in male form who might be read as a Ghandi-like spiritualist (with a Medusa alter ego) and an African nationalist (and insatiable womanizer). The good versus evil allegory is racially marked by the white robes of the spiritualist and the very dark complexion of the nationalist. Through these two inner "demons," Elizabeth must sort out her feelings of not being a "proper African" as a mixed-race person with no clear sense of national identity. Elizabeth's location as a "Coloured" and her condition of exile offer us another vantage point from which to examine the effects of the experience of South African apartheid. But unlike protest writers whose focus continues to be determined by day-to-day struggle against apartheid, Head's *A Question of Power* suggests a more personal focus and potential resolution. The novel ends with Elizabeth's mental reintegration and her embrace of the communal farming project run by local women. The Cape gooseberry bush that they have transplanted to rural Botswana flourishes.

The discursive fracture of the hegemonic protest narrative by Head's insistence upon multiple subject positions and her correlation of mixed racial identity with the condition of exile will provide a literary context for reading the expatriation of Wicomb's "Coloured" protagonist. Likewise, the postprotest visions created by widely read authors Nadine Gordimer and J. M. Coetzee might provide insight into the postapartheid concerns of white writers, and a source of comparison for Wicomb's final vision in *Cape Town.*

In recent years, as it became apparent that majority rule in South Africa was inevitable, and particularly following the 1976 Soweto uprising, concern for what shape such a transition might take and what its effects might be on the minority population has been taken up in the fiction of Gordimer and other white South African writers. In his analysis of this literary trend, critic Bernth Lindfors refers to Gordimer's futuristic novel of South Africa, *July's People* (1981), and J. M. Coetzee's allegorical *Waiting for the Barbarians* (1980) as "apocalyptic." Gordimer's novel is set during an ongoing revolution; the Smales family have become dependent upon July, their former "houseboy," for survival. Gordimer focuses on the liberal white family's dilemma of being caught between different factions of the majority population struggling for control, yet her vision of post-"apocalypse" African life seems unsympathetic to black South Africans. Gordimer "concentrates mainly on the dirt, offering clinical descriptions of unhygienic conditions and unhealthy practices that make the Africans we see look obdurately backward. The coldness of Gordimer's view of Africa is disturbing . . . the future is memorable principally for its obsession with uncleanliness" (Lindfors 201-2). Lindfors moves from the futuristic *July's People* to the "apocalypse" of Coetzee's *Waiting for the Barbarians,* reading the last part of *Barbarians* as another kind of prediction for South Africa. The collapse of the frontier settlement finds the "human debris of empire [waiting] for the barbarians to arrive and obliterate their civilization" (203). While Lindfors notes that Coetzee's choice of allegory allows this ending to be read as the death throes of any "alien civilization" replaced through bloody revolution, he concludes by suggesting that, especially coming so quickly after Soweto, Coetzee may have written the novel "to remind his countrymen that someday soon the end will come, just as it has come to other peoples elsewhere in the world throughout recorded time" (203).

Although not necessarily chronological, my arrangement of South African writers suggests an increasingly fractured South African narrative—Nkosi by Tlali's feminism, Tlali and Nkosi by Head's racial ambiguity. Gordimer and Coetzee disrupt the realist narrative with their postmodern stylistics. Yet futuristic imaginings and apocalyptic allegories can aestheticize and universalize the literary political landscape to the point that the reader no longer knows who the enemy is. A transnational feminist reading practice demands that we resist a relativism that allows texts to be read as simply individual expression. Literature can provide one arena for doing the kind of comparative political work demanded of transnational feminism. The global oppression of women must be investigated as taking place in multiple sites which are both discrete and overlapping. A Western/First World reader who wants to imagine solidarity with South African women, utilizing a postmodern text such as *You Can't Get Lost in Cape Town,* would negotiate the conditions that give rise to difference at the same time as he or she desires the "joining."

A NOVEL FOR A NEW SOUTH AFRICA

Rather than uncritically embrace as integral to postcolonial literature postmodernism's tendency to break down subject-object and self-other binaries inherent in colonial representations and strategically adopted in nationalisms, a transnational feminist reader needs to look to a theory of subject construction that is not unitary or essentializing but is "heterogeneous as well as political, destroys binarism, and is inclusive. This subject provides a constant critique of nationalist and even insurgent agendas, of power relations that structure global economic flows, and will never be complete" (Grewal, "Autobiographic Subjects" 234). At the same time, transnational feminism wants to retain the conditions of that subject's emergence.

The South African master narrative of protest literature, with its binary construction of racial politics, has tended to obscure the multiple subject positions of South African women. But a postmodern aesthetic practice as an antidote should not erase the protest foundation from which postprotest literature springs. It was author James Baldwin who raised, in the arena of African American literature, the issue of aesthetic possibility in literature that is overtly political, a debate which is currently ongoing among South African writers and critics. According to Richard Barksdale and Keneth Kinnamon, Baldwin worried, "Does protest of any kind impair the artistic merit of a novel, a poem, or a short story?" Baldwin argued that "the best literature should deal with universals and rise above the mundane levels of social protest" (Barksdale and Kinnamon 656). Such questions suggest that protest literature, like other master narrative forms, tends to narrow the field of human experience and limit artistic possibilities. According to Baldwin: "The failure of the protest novel lies in its rejection of life, the human being, the denial of his beauty, dread, power, in its insistence that it is his [race] categorization alone which is real and which cannot be transcended" (Baldwin, *Notes* 17). Baldwin's openly gay identity often put him into conflict with the Civil Rights leadership of the 1950s (NAACP and SCLC) and the young militant leaders of the late 1960s black protest movement (Larry Neal, Eldridge Cleaver). Baldwin's "outsider" status as a homosexual was perhaps one of the motivations for his insistence on pushing the thematic limitations imposed by the protest novel form as defined by novels such as Richard Wright's *Native Son.* Despite his criticism of the protest novel form, however, Baldwin's novels and plays (like *Blues for Mister Charlie*) embrace and advance the struggle against race oppression in the United States. Baldwin simply expected more of literature than a binary, oppositional portrayal of human experience.

Like Baldwin, Zoë Wicomb is critical of the prescriptive form of protest literature which surfaces in the current debates among South African literary critics posed as "revolutionary vs. aesthetic or good vs. bad" (**"Agenda"** 15). And Wicomb is equally resistant to the suggestion that committed writing must be sacrificed to aesthetic development in a South Africa moving beyond apartheid. Her novel *You Can't Get Lost in Cape Town* acknowledges the "preoccupation with the liberation struggle" which has been the foundation of South African protest writing (**"Agenda"** 16). I return to Chela Sandoval's metaphor of the automobile's differential that allows the driver to disengage one gear and engage another. Such mobility recognizes tactical engagement of shifting arenas—now gender, now ethnicity, now class, now the politics of exile. This kind of strategic deployment of subjectivities is theorized in Zoë Wicomb's critical essays and given agency in the narrative of Frieda in *You Can't Get Lost in Cape Town*.

The form of Wicomb's novel resembles the fictionalized autobiography, a genre which is a part of South African protest/postprotest literature. Miriam Tlali's *Muriel at Metropolitan* and Bessie Head's *A Question of Power* utilize this form to tell highly personal stories about black life under apartheid and the alienation of exile. But Wicomb undercuts this resemblance with a series of strategies that challenge the reader's assumptions. Certainly there are compelling parallels between the narrator-writer, Frieda, and the author, Zoë Wicomb, as Carol Sicherman's essay "Zoë Wicomb's *You Can't Get Lost in Cape Town*: The Narrator's Identity" points out. Both narrator and author were born in rural Cape Province, to "Coloured," Afrikaans-speaking parents who valued the cultural capital of English and encouraged their daughter(s) to speak it. Both Frieda and Wicomb attended university in Cape Town and emigrated to England, where Frieda publishes some short stories in magazines, soon to be released "[a]s a book" (171). Similarly, Wicomb's collection of "stories" was published as a book while she was still living in England. Sicherman, however, turns to the differences in biographical facts between the author and narrator, responding to Wicomb's own stated preference for literature, that is, literature that offers its reader "the experience of discontinuity, ambiguity, violation of our expectations or irony" (**"Agenda"** 14). Sicherman goes on to suggest that *Cape Town* is not so much an autobiography as a broader "depiction of the formation of South African 'Colored' identity" (113).

Identity formation under an apartheid system built upon the white-nonwhite binary is certainly at the heart of this novel—Frieda and her college friend Moira are caught between "want[ing] to be white" in their teens and "want[ing] to be full-blooded Africans" as adults (*Cape Town* 156). But the development of a South African female *writer* of color is also crucial to *Cape Town*. Even in my initial reading of the text, it was the last chapter/story that prevented me from reading this collection as simply fictionalized autobiography.

The last chapter/story acts as a metanarrative on the process of writing autobiography. Ruptures in the plot do not allow the kind of historical linearity often expected of such first-person narratives. For example, the Mamma of Frieda's childhood seems to have died by chapter 3, where she is spoken of in the past tense. Yet the final chapter records Frieda's visit home following her father's death and her mother is still very much alive. This revelation then forces the reader to doubt the legitimacy of the earlier chapters as simply a writer's imagining of a young woman/writer's maturation. Frieda struggles to make her mother understand the nature of writing: "[T]hey're only stories. Made up. Everyone knows it's not real, not the truth" (172). "But you've used the real. If I can recognise places and people, so can others, and if you want to play around like that why don't you have the courage to tell the whole truth?" asks her mother. Her mother accuses Frieda of writing "from under [her] mother's skirts" (172). This discussion of the use of personal family history, by the "real" narrator in her made-up "stories," and the invention of her mother's death, "unnecessary" because she has killed her mother "over and over" with the publication of stories about such topics as abortion, insinuates into this fictional narrative the space to speculate on the narrator's identity as well as the boundaries between autobiography and fiction. Using this last chapter as a lens, subsequent readings reveal that Wicomb provides hints throughout that what we are reading are Frieda's "stories," not Frieda's or Wicomb's autobiography.

Early in the novel, Wicomb plants in the reader's mind a distrust of the reliability of writing. While at the university at Cape Town, Frieda struggles to write an essay on Thomas Hardy's *Tess of the D'Urbervilles* but is unable to express what she really feels. She imagines the confrontation with her Boer professor had she gone to his office asking for an extension; she studies the pen in her hand; she rereads her lecture notes: "The novel, he says, is about Fate. Alarmingly simple, but not quite how it strikes me, although I cannot offer an alternative. . . . Seduced, my notes say. Can you be seduced by someone you hate?" (41). Frieda longs to produce an essay that resists the professor's interpretation but opts instead for a "reworking of his notes" which will assure her a "mark qualifying for the examination" (55). Tess is "branded guilty and betrayed once more on this page," sacrificed to Frieda's pragmatic desire for academic success (56). Frieda's "betrayal" of Tess hinges on doing what is expedient rather than submitting a genuine expression of her opinion, warning the reader that we cannot always trust the written word or the professional expert.

Evidence that Frieda believes oral first-person narratives are also unreliable comes in a visit home prior to leaving for England; Frieda describes the way her family tell stories about themselves:

> They cut their stories from the gigantic watermelon that cannot be finished by the family in one sitting. They savour as if for the first time the pip-studded slices of the bright fruit and read the possibilities of konfyt in the tasteless flesh beneath the green. Their stories, whole as the watermelon that grows out of this arid earth, have come to replace the world.
>
>   (87)

She wants to expose the fallacy of wholeness shaped by these family stories:

> I would like to bring down my fist on that wholeness and watch the crack choose its wayward path across the melon, slowly exposing the icy pink of the slit. I would like to reveal myself now so that they will not await my return. But they will not like my stories, none of them.
>
>   (87-88)

The family stories deny aspects of Frieda's experience and her intent to leave South Africa and never return. Frieda's desire to smash this monochromatic representation of collective experience reveals a striving toward recognition of individual difference. But reading Frieda's desire for "truth" through the revelations in the final chapter of *Cape Town* reveals that Frieda's autobiography is as consciously constructed as is the family folklore: neither is to be trusted at face value.

Wicomb also blurs the boundaries of fiction and biography in the chapter/story titled **"A Fair Exchange."** This chapter begins like a fictional short story; through a male narrator's descriptions and through dialogue between characters, we read about rural life on the veld—his struggle to survive and the loss of his wife and children to another man. This tale of South African sheepherder Skitterboud seems to mark a jarring departure from the previous chapters which hitherto have shaped Frieda's autobiography. Near the end of the chapter, we discover that this is really one of Frieda's "stories," collected from Skitterboud on a trip home. The reader is warned that Skitterboud's first-person narrative is edited and revised in her reconstruction of it:

> Skitterboud's story is yellow with age. It curls without question at the edges. Many years have passed since the events settled into a picture which then was torn in sadness and rage so that now reassembled the cracks remain too clear. . . . A few fragments are irretrievably lost. Or are they? If I pressed even further . . . I am responsible for reassembling the bits released over the days that I sought him out.
>
>   (136)

Ownership of Skitterboud's story changes hands with the exchange of a pair of spectacles. Frieda is wearing at first them, but they also improve Skitterboud's vision when he tries them on. Frieda takes the spectacles back, insisting that he must have his own glasses/vision "specially prescribed" for him. But her lens(es) allows Skitterboud to "see" better and he insists that she leave the spectacles with him: "Who can know better than myself whether these glasses are good for me or not?" (139-40). The spectacles represent a narrative strategy that reconfigures Skitterboud's life. Frieda's narrative re-visioning of Skitterboud's story allows him to see the present better and to reconcile certain aspects of his past. The "whole truth" that Mamma wants Frieda to have the courage to tell consists in the negotiation between the subject and his biographer, the autobiographical writer and her reader.

Wicomb invokes distrust of discursive representation and provides a metanarrative discussion about writing in the final chapter of *You Can't Get Lost in Cape Town,* blurring the distinction between art and life: is this Frieda's story or is it her art (fiction)? The idea that the previous "chapters" can be read as Frieda's stories is not apparent until the final chapter, and this arrangement necessitates a second reading of the text. An actively engaged reading practice demands that, as readers, we allow ourselves to be drawn into the narrative and that we respond to the demands made on us by the text, that we be willing to negotiate with it. Wicomb's narrative arrangement in *Cape Town* is representative of the kind of postmodernist strategy developed by her South African literary constituency (Tlali, Head, Gordimer, Coetzee). But in the case of colonized artists, the tendency to push beyond established boundaries is also accompanied by the dialectics inherent in colonialism and the literature of protest which is its direct oppositional response.

Binary constructions limit our perceptions of the human experience in literature; an unsympathetic read of the binary relationships extant in postprotest literature of colonized people denies the context, the material context and objective reality, in which such literature is produced. Wicomb troubles the distinction between art and life, but a politically committed reader will not fail to situate her textual manipulations in the literary context against which such manipulations work. The intersecting sites of gender, race/ethnicity, and economic class provide Wicomb with a wedge with which to pry open the black versus white binary inherent in the discourses of the apartheid state and the anti-apartheid forces as portrayed in protest literature. Student protest in Lewis Nkosi's play *The Rhythm of Violence,* for instance, portrays activists of several racial groups, but the structure of its scenes suggests a typical two-sided struggle with a unified body of student anti-apartheid activists, on the one side, against the white administration, on the other. Similarly, in her chapter/story **"A**

Clearing in the Bush," Wicomb gives us an example of student protest at the "Coloured" university which her character Frieda attends. However, in order to show the ruptures within coalition politics, Wicomb's portrait moves beyond a depiction of a diverse but unified student body dedicated to a single cause.

In Wicomb's novel, the image of the student protest movement, as a kind of monolith, is challenged by gender politics. When the university is closed for a memorial service for the infamous and recently assassinated Prime Minister Verwoerd, the male students meet in the cafeteria to plan a boycott of the service and to determine the method by which all students should be notified of this political action. Frieda and her friend Moira observe the meeting and ask their friend James what it is about. Although James has been sent to enlist their support, he "nurse[s] the apple of knowledge in his lap," making the most of their anticipation, offering them "little lady-like bites," aware of "his power to withdraw it altogether" (53). The student action is planned and controlled by the men, and the cooperation of the women is assumed. James constructs the narrative; Frieda and Moira must be passive recipients. Such chasms between men and women are often concealed in the discursive representation of protest movements for the sake of unity. But Wicomb is clear that sexism need not be tolerated for the sake of black solidarity. In her contribution to a forum on feminism and writing in South Africa, sponsored by and published in *Current Writing: Text and Reception in Southern Africa* in 1990, Wicomb states: "I can think of no reason why black patriarchy should not be challenged alongside the fight against Apartheid" (**"To Hear"** 37). Wicomb's narrative portrayal of gender politics within the student protest movement reflects the disjunctures in hegemonic discourses, revealing one concern of postmodernity and post-coloniality in Third World texts and environments. Wicomb further complicates her portrait of the student body by challenging the assumed cohesion of colored identity and the anti-apartheid movement.

Despite the need for total support of the boycott in order to avoid reprisals for a few, some students attend the memorial. Several "Coloured" young men from the seminary, "future Dutch Reformed ministers," file in, dressed "in their Sunday suits. . . . They walk in silence, their chins lifted in a militaristic display of courage. . . . [T]hey . . . think their defiance heroic and stifle the unease by marching soldier-like to mourn the Prime Minister" (56). The action taken by the seminary students is a trope that seeks to provoke in the reader a distrust of nationalist propaganda that is always trying to cover up the cracks of dissension. Such disjunctures in postprotest narratives do not, however, diminish real oppositional relationships created by colonial and race oppression, but simply illuminate different subjectivities and the forces that determine them. In her essay **"Postcoloniality and Postmodernity,"** Wicomb dem-onstrates how ethnicity and linguistics determine shifting alliances across the spectrum of difference and disjuncture in the would-be unitary discourse of the anti-apartheid movement. The idea that the seminary students believe their action "heroic" indicates their co-optation by the very system that has allowed the white minority population to so successfully and brutally maintain control of the majority. Wicomb's essay points out that in the Cape, the "Coloured" population makes up a significant majority (52% compared with 25% African and 23% white). The Nationalist Party's about-face from a policy of racial separation to an appeal to this bloc of new voters on the basis of "shared culture centred in the Afrikaans language, the Dutch Reformed church and mutton bredie" and the majority Cape Coloured vote in favor of the Nationalist Party constitute, in Wicomb's words, a "postmodern effacement of history stretch[ing] back to the very practice of slavery" (9). Wicomb's discussion here calls attention to the way in which the pro-black and pro-English language position of the anti-apartheid movement, which is tantamount to a form of nationalism, erases and alienates some South Africans identified as "Coloured," particularly those whose mother tongue, Afrikaans, and whose religious customs originate in the Dutch Reformed Church.

While these seminary students represent a dissenting fracture within the student population, Wicomb also calls attention to the effacement of working-class "Coloured" from the student boycott. The narrative voice in this chapter switches back and forth between Frieda and an omniscient narrator who reveals the interior life of Tamieta, the lone female "Coloured" cook in the university's cafeteria. Her boss notifies her of the memorial ceremony, and Tamieta assumes that he means for her to attend the activity, only to discover that she is the only person there besides the Boers. She begins to fear that the memorial is for whites only, but she is somewhat comforted when the seminary students enter. When no other students arrive, Tamieta begins to understand that a boycott has been called. She thinks to herself, in a typical working-class female fashion: "If only there were other women working on the campus she would have known, someone would have told her" (60). Of course there are other women/people on campus, but they are the students who did not think to alert the cook whose labor sustains them daily. As the young "future Dutch Reformed ministers" call attention to the complexity of racial politics in South Africa, Tamieta reveals class as a blind spot in some versions of coalition. While Wicomb complicates Nkosi's version of the student struggle in South Africa with diverse subject positions, her inclusion of this movement in a chapter/story about Frieda's university experience signals its continuing import in South African fiction.

Likewise, the loss of South African land to Boer "land reform," with the resulting reservationlike townships and "native reserves," are insistent issues in protest and postprotest fiction alike. A reader who chooses active engagement as a reading practice might find Tlali's treatment of forced relocation and its effects on black South African women, for instance, a rich source for intertextual connections with Wicomb's *Cape Town.* Reading Wicomb's postprotest text against Tlali's depiction of black South African displacement raises questions about the intersections of economic class and racial classification under apartheid. Wicomb revisits the Group Areas Act in her portrait of the narrator's uncle, Jan Klinkies, who has lost his sanity and his wife along with his land. But Wicomb's narrator seems untroubled by her father's announcement that they must leave the veld for the village of Wesblok. The child's-eye view Frieda re-creates of her family's loss of ancestral home reveals the attenuating effect of middle-class status on personal suffering caused by displacement. Frieda's father is a rural schoolmaster who has a "nest egg" that will pay her tuition at the newly desegregated private school. Unlike Tlali's characters who live in labor camps and multifamily township houses, Frieda's father will buy a "little raw brick house [with] somewhere to tether a goat and keep a few chickens" (*Cape Town* 29). Young Frieda thinks that electric lights, indoor plumbing, and the proximity to friends provided by community housing might not be so bad. While many of Tlali's black female characters find limited options in urban life and must rely on the remnants of traditional support systems, Frieda leaves the village for university in Cape Town and then moves to England, where she becomes a writer. Class position, determined in part by apartheid's racial structure, allows Frieda opportunities to which Tlali's female characters do not have access. But at the same time, Wicomb's juxtaposition of Frieda with Tamieta, the cook at the university Frieda attends, disrupts the assumption that socioeconomic class marks the "Coloured" population of South Africa in any monolithic way.

Wicomb's novel also enacts the ethnic diversity obscured by apartheid's "Coloured" classification, the liberation movement's unifying embrace of "black," and the postapartheid adoption of "Coloured" by the reactionary forces at the Cape. Frieda grows up in a "Coloured" community, but ethnic bias marks this community. In *Cape Town,* it is Frieda's father who most often bears the burden of demonstrating it. When Frieda is a child, her father invokes ethnic difference in order to urge her to eat: "'Don't leave anything on your plate. You must grow up to be big and strong. . . . You don't want cheekbones that jut out like a Hottentot's. Fill them out until they're shiny and plump as pumpkins" (24). And when Frieda returns to South Africa after several years spent in England, he tells her that the formerly segregated doctor's office has changed: "[T]here's even a waiting room for us now with a nice clean water lavatory. Not that these Hotnos know how to use it" (105). The colonialist term for the indigenous South African population, "Hottentot," becomes an epithet of

ethnic prejudice. Most of Frieda's family are Namaqua, one of the subdivisions of the Khoi, the original Cape inhabitants, but her father values his "Scots blood" and his Shenton surname (29). When he first met Frieda's mother, she was disparaged by the Shentons as a "Griqua meid" (165), and she in turn uses the term "Griqua" to chastise a young Frieda who is misbehaving (9).

In addition to disrupting the homogeneity of "Coloured" identity with class and ethnicity, Wicomb's novel raises the issue of colonially imposed language. As a child, Frieda is forbidden to speak Afrikaans; both parents value English and model their pronunciation after an English mine owner who frequents the village. English language becomes cultural capital at Frieda's private high school and the university in Cape Town. I first read Wicomb's portrayal of the Shentons' veneration of English through what I knew at that time of the liberation movement's resistance, expressed during the 1976 Soweto uprising, to the imposition of Afrikaans language as the medium of instruction in South African schools. English language represented not only cultural capital but also an expression of solidarity with black resistance. But Wicomb's essay **"Postcoloniality and Postmodernity: The Case of the Coloured in South Africa"** complicates that assumption. Wicomb points out that Afrikaans was the first language of the "Cape coloureds," who originated as a product of sexual union between the Dutch settlers and indigenous inhabitants. Their response to the resistance movement's English language mandate was to embrace a nonstandard form of Afrikaans in a "flurry of coloured writing. . . . Renamed and revalorized as Kaaps, this local and racialised variety of Afrikaans as a literary language came to assert a discursive space for an oppositional colouredness that could be aligned to the black liberation struggle" (7). My assumption that textual cues signaled Wicomb's black solidarity obscured the complexity of the language issue among the "Coloured" community of South Africa. A reader who claims empathy with his or her reading subject, who is practicing a transnational feminist approach to reading, should be willing to engage in renegotiations with the text in light of such revelations.

The South African experience when organized as a narrative of protest "reflects a sort of weave of presence and absence," to borrow a phrase from Gayatri Spivak in her essay "The Problem of Cultural Self-Representation" (50). What is always present is the hegemonic binary of race, black versus white, or the binary of colonizer versus the colonized. But Wicomb's text restores many of the erasures imposed by colonial representations and strategically adopted by anticolonial resistance. With the anticipation of the demise of the apartheid structure, postprotest texts, like *You Can't Get Lost in Cape Town,* are opening up prescriptive forms of protest writing and binary representations.

While some writers such as Coetzee and Gordimer imagine apocalyptic endings to apartheid, Wicomb's postprotest text is set in a society still very much structured by it. Frieda has tried to escape to England, but Wicomb's text does not seem to support exile as a solution. Frieda's years in England constitute an erasure in the narrative. Frieda never writes any "stories" about it; her memories of life there conflate the uncomfortably cold winter and her sense of racial otherness. Like Bessie Head's Margaret (*Maru*) and Elizabeth (*A Question of Power*), whose ethnic difference isolates them from the larger communities in which they live, Frieda's period of expatriation is one of alienation. But unlike Head's texts, *Cape Town* leaves this period unexplored. Frieda returns to Cape Town and achieves a modified reconciliation with her mother, while insisting on her prerogative to write stories.

What Wicomb's postpartheid essays make clear is that, in her view, the end of apartheid has not yet been achieved. No revolution marks its passing. An essay in which Wicomb reflects about having been asked to judge an interracial literary competition expresses her concern for the brutal inequities which are the legacy of apartheid:

> In our situation, where apartheid conditions have militated against the linguistic development of black people, both in the imposition of European languages and the neglect of education, the function of the literary prize becomes obvious. Not only is it inappropriate or inadequate as a means of encouraging writing, but it actively perpetuates inequity by rewarding those who have been privileged.

("**Culture beyond Color?**" 28)

At the root of this issue is literacy. Wicomb calls for a "decent, compulsory, multilingual system of education for all" before any interracial construction of a new South Africa can be valid (32).

Wicomb suggests that instead of erasing a social history which reveals diversity and constructing nationalistic unities, South African "Coloured" identity could be staged as "multiple belongings" ("**Post-Coloniality**" 14). It is through Wicomb's representation of the tenuousness of "Coloured" identity that I have approached an analysis of her text. And it is this idea of "multiple belongings" that might serve as a metaphor for transnational feminist reading. An empathic desire to locate the fissures in hegemonic representations of "others" is one way to resist the generative power of colonial domination and capitalist exploitation. A reading practice that desires to find points of commonality across difference might want to examine, in the writing of South African female authors such as Wicomb, the discursive strategies which resist "hierarchising the evils of . . . society—racism, sexism, classism" and instead attend to the "ways in which the conflicting demands of representing these are textually articulated" ("**To Hear**" 42).

Notes

1. This essay was originally written as a conference paper and presented in abbreviated form as a plenary address at the African Language Association (ALA) conference in March 1995 (Columbus). Quotations here are from the original essay, kindly provided by the author.

2. Also known as the Nationalist Party of South Africa.

3. Wicomb lays claim to a black political identity in her essay "An Author's Agenda," published in 1990, prior to majority rule in South Africa; she reiterated this position at the 1995 ALA conference.

4. From Miriam Tlali, *Muriel at Metropolitan* (Essex: Longman, 1987) 169.

5. These indigenous people were referred to as "Hottentot," an infamous term in colonialist constructions of southern Africa.

6. These are urban street gangs of young people. The implication is that their intimidation tactics are not simply ignored by the justice system but that their guns and knives may be provided by corrupt police.

7. It is possible that the footnotes in particular are a result of choices on the part of the publisher rather than the author. The edition I am working from, *Soweto Stories,* was published by Pandora Press in London and perhaps targeted toward an international audience. This collection was also published in South Africa by David Phillip Publisher Ltd. under the title *Footprints in the Quag: Stories and Dialogues from Soweto.* Either way, the effect is the same. As a non-South African reader, I am left feeling that there is less investigation and negotiation required of me than when reading a postprotest/postmodernist work like Wicomb's *Cape Town.*

Bibliography

Tlali, Miriam. *Soweto Stories.* London: Pandora, 1989.

Wicomb, Zoë. "An Author's Agenda." *Critical Fictions.* Ed. Philomena Mariani. Seattle: Bay, 1991. 13-16.

———. "Culture Beyond Color? A South African Dilemma." *Transition* 60 (1993): 27-32.

———. "Postcoloniality and Postmodernity: The Case of the Coloured in South Africa." Unpublished essay, 1995.

———. "To Hear the Variety of Discourses." *Current Writing* 2 (1990): 35-44.

———. *You Can't Get Lost in Cape Town.* New York: Pantheon, 1987.

Constance S. Richards (essay date spring 2005)

SOURCE: Richards, Constance S. "Nationalism and the Development of Identity in Postcolonial Fiction: Zoë

Wicomb and Michelle Cliff." *Research in African Literatures* 36, no. 1 (spring 2005): 20-33.

[In the excerpt that follows, Richards uses the "phases in the process of cultural decolonization" that are spelled out in Frantz Fanon's The Wretched of the Earth *to examine how the development of a national consciousness affects the identity of the narrator-protagonist of* You Can't Get Lost in Cape Town.*]*

This essay will attempt to explain the role of nationalism as a site of awakening and identity formation in postcolonial literary texts. I have chosen to dislodge the "awakening" trope from a center of Western feminist literary studies, that is, from Kate Chopin's novella *The Awakening* (1899) and relocate it in other experiences of empire where awakenings also take place. This approach sees national consciousness as a transitional step, a site that provides a certain kind of awakening, and not as the end of a process. Nationalism, or national consciousness, in the Fanonian sense, is a phase leading to transnationalism. The movement from nationalism to internationalism, however, does not forsake the concern of local populations, but rather recognizes the systemic relationship of national causes to global capitalism.

This essay is particularly concerned with South African author Zoë Wicomb's *You Can't Get Lost in Cape Town* (1987) and West Indian writer Michelle Cliff's *No Telephone to Heaven* (1987). These texts represent, directly and indirectly, the role Black nationalism can play in the awakening phase of female literary characters in postcolonial texts by women writers. These works elucidate the fractured reality of national identity and women's struggle to negotiate the complexities of the postcolonial condition.[1]

In *Wretched of the Earth,* Frantz Fanon observes that the colonized indigenous writer/artist engages in certain phases in the process of cultural de-colonization, the first of these being a reification of European culture, the need to prove that she/he is capable of mastering these forms. Written literature is validated over oral; Western literary forms (the novel, for example) are preferred to indigenous orality; mastery of European language becomes a goal.

> Assimilation of the European culture is achieved, however, at the expense of the artist's connection to his/her own cultural history. The struggle between colonial and indigenous cultural identity moves the writer/artist to a romantic immersion into the precolonial stage of African identity, Fanon's second phase. Fanon suggests that the "native writer" turns to childhood memories—"old legends will be reinterpreted in the light of a borrowed estheticism and of a conception of the world which was discovered under other skies."
>
> (*Wretched* 222)

We see this focus in the work of some writers of African descent in the United States.[2] In *Praisesong for the Widow* (1983), for example, Caribbean American writer

Paule Marshall's protagonist Avey Johnson attempts to retrieve the past in order to make sense of her middle-class and middle-aged widowhood. Her interaction with Eebert Joseph and the Old People of Carriacou, who annually celebrate the remaining fragments of their African identity in the "nations dance," marks the beginning of Avey's immersion phase. Her awakening in Carriacou comes with the realization of a common history that connects what she sees on this island to her own family history. The root of her identity, compromised by her assimilation to middle-class America, she comes to understand, lies in the common struggle of Black people everywhere. With this knowledge she goes back to the cradle of her family history in the Black diaspora, to Tatem Island, the Sea Island land of her Aunt Cuney and her female ancestral community, where she must continue the struggle. A more localized model of the immersion phase can be seen in Janie Crawford's journey to the Black everglades community of Zora Neale Hurston's *Their Eyes Were Watching God* (1937). This journey marks Janie's rejection of the assimilationist preoccupation with northern urban capitalism, represented by the "male-centered, hierarchical values of [her] first two husbands, Logan Killicks and the 'citified' Joe Starks" (Rodgers 93). Janie's self-concept is predicated on membership in the community of rural Black folk whose culture, like that of the Carriacou people in Marshall's *Praisesong,* suggests a romanticized primordial African existence predating and existing outside of the internal colonization that has been the legacy of US slavery.

In terms of broad social formations, the Rastafanan movement in Jamaica utilized culture and history to affirm African identity and, in effect, revitalized the Ethopianism and Garveyism that were prominent among segments of the Black population in the late nineteenth and early twentieth centuries.[3] Culture flows between Jamaica and the US created a continuity that has, in part, shaped the imaginary of artists like Cliff and Marshall. The Black Arts Movement, the cultural arm of the Black struggle in the US in the 1960s and 70s, for example, often employed ancestral African as well as contemporary African-American images and expressions to instill racial pride and to legitimate African American cultural identity. Community-based art forms such as poetry readings and revolutionary "street" theater utilized African orality to heighten awareness of the concrete realities of the racialized system in the US.[4] The Black Consciousness movement in South Africa grew out of Black student resistance to apartheid and focused on a kind of psychological liberation, a rewriting of South African history from an African perspective, and a rethinking of what it meant to be Black that challenged extant racial categories.[5]

The third phase in Fanon's construction, the "fighting phase," moves the native intellectual from the celebration of indigenous culture to the development of a "revolutionary literature [. . .] a national literature" (*Wretched* 223). The development of a national consciousness and a national culture are seen by Fanon as inherent aspects of, and necessary steps toward, de-colonization. However, according to Fanon, "[i]t is around the peoples' struggles that African-Negro culture takes on substance, and not around songs, poems, or folklore. [. . .] Adherence to African-Negro culture and to the cultural unity of Africa is arrived at in the first place by upholding unconditionally the peoples' struggle for freedom" (*Wretched* 235). National culture and national consciousness in the Fanonian sense are not predicated on race or ethnicity but rather on the national interests and uplift of impoverished and oppressed populations in the cities and countryside across the whole continent of Africa. . . .

While Fanon constructs de-colonization as a series of developmental phases, we need to understand that this process is not teleological but dialectical and ongoing. Discourses of national liberation must be examined in terms of the environment in which and for which they are generated, the historical, political, social, and economic contexts that are often the product of antagonism and contestation in fragmented societies. At the same time, national consciousness must be able to move beyond the narrowly focused binary response that is the natural result of such antagonism. A progressive position on race, for example, does not guarantee any attention to the effect of other forms of human difference. My own feminist approach would lead me to critique Fanon's binary of colonizer-colonized (*Wretched of the Earth*) and his focus solely on cultural difference (*Black Skin, White Masks*) as ignoring the multiplicitous aspects of identity, in particular issues of gender. It has, indeed, been the tendency of some deconstructionists and postmodernists,[6] including some feminists and postcolonialists,[7] to dismiss discourses of national liberation on the grounds of their narrow preoccupation with binary relationships and perceived lack of tolerance for individual difference. The academic field of postcolonial studies is, to a great degree, born out of postmodernist theory and to some degree replicates this distrust of counterhegemonic master narratives of liberation such as Black nationalism and Marxism. My own approach to postcolonial studies, however, understands the field as offering a way to approach discourses of national liberation with a postmodern perspective that can engage with the various aspects of identity without denying the importance of specific experience.

Postcolonial novels, such as Zoë Wicomb's **You Can't Get Lost in Cape Town** and Michelle Cliff's *No Telephone to Heaven,* suggest the important role of Black liberation discourse in identity formation, while at the same time complicate the binary discourses of race (black/white) and colonialism (colonizer/colonized) with questions of gender, sexuality, and color privilege. In both novels, the protagonists represent racial ambiguity,

one a South African "coloured," Wicomb's Frida, and the other a Jamaican "mulatta," Cliff's Clare. This condition of being "not Black" and "not white," and what such liminality means in material terms in the respective sellings, provides the incentive to move the main characters through the phases that Fanon outlines. Black nationalism functions in *No Telephone* as a positive, though also problematic, answer to Clare Savage's childhood and adolescent sense of isolation. In **Cape Town,** however, protagonist Frida Shenton is left at an earlier stage of development.

Wicomb's novel is structured as a series of "story cycles" that share a setting, South Africa, a protagonist, Frida, and a focus, Frida's development as a young woman and a writer. Growing up in a South Africa still laboring under apartheid, Frida's racial identity is a matter of law; she is registered "Coloured," a category that privileges her above Black South Africans but subordinates her to whites. She is taught early on that mastery of English language and assimilation of British culture through education will be key to her success. The first chapter/story highlights around a family discussion about the correct pronunciation of an English word. Frida's parents are keen to impress upon her the importance of carefully imitating the "gentleman, a true Englishman" who owns the local gypsum mine but cannot speak a word of Afrikaans, necessitating the use of Mr. Shenton as an interpreter. Mastery of the colonial language represents cultural capital in the South Africa of Frida's childhood. The reader familiar with South African politics would also know that, as the student protest actions of the 1970s revealed, the embrace of English as a medium of instruction was a part of the Black liberation movement's program. Afrikaans was imposed upon the indigenous people and represented the brutal apartheid structure; as the language of instruction in the school system, it provided for an educated labor force whose opportunities for employment were limited to South Africa. The liberation movement understood that English, on the other hand, could open education and employment opportunities beyond those allotted by the Afrikaner regime. This politicization of English language, however, is not the Shenton's motivation; mastery of the King's English is the goal.

> It is not only in their embrace of English that Frida's parents represent the first of Fanon's phases. After their forced resettlement from the rural home of Frida's childhood, her father further facilitates her assimilation of British culture by sending her away to the newly integrated, formerly white, St. Mary's, even at great expense, as there is no high school available in the "Coloured" settlement He is heartily congratulated by his neighbors for "keep [ing] up with the Boers."
>
> (27)

By the time we see Frida as one of a small group of "Coloureds" at the University of Cape Town, a predominately white institution, she is beginning to question the hegemony of English culture and the white race. Her gender identity will not allow Frida to accept the interpretation of Thomas Hardy's *Tess of the D'Urbervilles* that her Boer professor imposes. "The novel, he says, is about Fate. [. . .] Seduced, my notes say [. . .]. Can you be seduced by someone you hate?" she wonders (41). At the university she also encounters firsthand the anti-apartheid struggle, though is not yet ready to identify with it. Student activists plan to boycott the mandatory memorial service which is to mark the assassination of Prime Minsiter Verwoerd (1966). While Frida and her friend Moira participate in the boycott, they are passive participants. The student group is led by men who assume without question the support of the two women in spreading the word about the boycott but not in the planning of the event, a critique Black feminists made of the US Black nationalist movement. Wicomb further complicates her portrait of Black nationalism by challenging the assumed unity of so-called "coloureds" with the anti-apartheid movement. Despite the need for total support of the boycott in order to avoid reprisals for a few, several "coloured" young men, "future Dutch Reformed ministers" attend the memorial ceremony (56). Wicomb refuses to romanticize the liberation struggle. Not only does she bring a feminist critique to bear on any notion of unquestioned solidarity among the anti-apartheid activists, she also makes clear the psychological effects an imposed racial hierarchy can have on some of those allowed a measure of racial privilege.

Further, Wicomb suggests that these student activists must examine their own class privilege. While the students have all been informed of the intention to boycott the service, no one has thought to tell Tamieta, the "coloured" canteen worker whose narrative voice frames this chapter. The students' academic matriculation marks their membership in petit bourgeois society. While they may recognize the plight of the Blacks in the townships and the workers in the gold and diamond mines, they fail to politically connect to the laborers who are closest to them and who facilitate their very presence in the university.

Frida's color privilege and class orientation preclude her from easy association with the increasingly insistent liberation struggle. On a trip home after living in England for an extended period, she encounters a childhood love, Henry Hendrikse, whom Frida's father had dismissed as "almost pure kaffir," not acceptable in the Shenton family where the memory of their British ancestor "must be kept sacred" (116). When the adult Frida meets Flenry, while waiting to be seen at a medical clinic, he is an activist in an unnamed underground liberation movement (the banned ANC or PAC perhaps?) and has been to Namibia for training, specifically to learn the languages of Black South Africa. Frida, distanced by British education and life in England, cannot distinguish between the Xhosa and Zulu

that is being spoken around them in the clinic. While Frida seems embarrassed by her discomfort among Black South Africans, she cannot see what Henry represents as a viable option. In her last interaction with Henry, he reminds her that in their youth, she publicly denied their friendship because of his color and the chapter ends with Frida's father repeating a rumor that Henry is a spy for the apartheid government. Although she has begun to feel alienated from any easy identification with England, Frida is not yet ready to relinquish the relative privilege that mixed race identity affords her in apartheid South Africa. Black nationalism, in this novel, is embodied in Henry who represents the progressive so-called "coloureds" who rejected this racial classification, embraced Black identity, and dedicated themselves to the liberation of all Black South Africans.

In terms of Fanons developmental phases, Frida cannot move directly from the reification of colonial culture, which is the stuff of her childhood, to the "fighting phase" that the adult Henry represents. Henry has immersed himself in the indigenous, precolonial culture and is now concerned with "us[ing] the past with the intention of opening up the future," to quote Fanon (232). When Frida becomes aware that his backpack contains both a map and a gun, she questions him about it. "In the bush," Henry reveals, "there's a war going on that you know nothing of, that no newspaper will tell you about" (*Capetown* 121). However, in *You Can't Get Lost in Cape Town*, we never see the protagonist awaken to the necessity of armed nationalist struggle in South Africa.

While Wicomb never moves her protagonist into direct participation in nationalism, she plants in her the seeds of distrust in the ideal of colonial culture and makes the discourse of liberation available to her. The novel closes with the suggestion, somewhat ironically from the mouth of Frida's mother, that an appreciation of indigenous culture is necessary. Frida's nascent nationalism leads her to be critical of her mother's desire for a "little white protea bush" for her garden, an indigenous plant and the official flower of the Afrikaner government (181). Her mother asserts that refusal to allow the colonial appropriation of indigenous culture is a form of resistance:

> You who're so clever ought to know thai proteas belong to the veld. Those who put their stamp on things may see in it their own histories and hopes. But a bush is a bush; it doesn't become what people think they inject into it. We know who lived in these mountains when the Europeans were still shivering in their own country. What they think of the veld and its flowers is of no interest to me.
>
> (181)

It is in the mother's words that we understand the single most important thing that all South Africans have in common. The land, and the political struggle over it, is the most basic unifying aspect of identity and, at the same time, remains the most contentious issue in South African politics today.

The 1994 national election, which brought into power a black majority government, signals the disintegration of a progressive political identity that had been based upon the rhetoric of black consciousness. While the discourses of postmodernism and postcolonialism emphasize this tendency of disintegration of national identity in postcolonial societies, they fail to account for the degree to which remnants of the colonial power structure remain, illuminating the continued relevance of some nationalist discourses, even in the present.

Zoë Wicomb cites an example of the perhaps premature embrace of postcolonial identity in the period immediately following independence in South Africa. She calls shameful the

> resurgence of the term Coloured, once more capitalized, without its old prefix of so-called and without the disavowing scare quotes earned during the period of revolutionary struggle when it was replaced by the work black, indicating both a rejection of apartheid nomenclature as well as inclusion in the national liberation movement.

("Shame and Identity" 93)

With the dismantling of the apartheid government, the formalized identity categories against which progressive mixed-race people stood in identifying themselves as Black, are gone. Yet, in postapartheid South Africa, the strategic deployment of the term Coloured as a marker of postcolonial identity did not necessarily signal a politically progressive move. Wicomb is also critical of some Cape Coloureds for their "shameful" support as a voting block supporting the Boer Party platform during the first democratic elections on April 27, 1994:

> [T]he shame of [the vote] lies not only in what we have voted against-citizenship within a democratic constitution that ensures the protection of individual rights, the enshrinement of gay and lesbian rights, the abolition of censorship and blasphemy laws—but in the amnesia with regard to the National Party's atrocities in maintaining apartheid.

("Shame and Identity" 99)

Postcolonial literatures can effectively use liminal categories like mixed-race identity to interrogate binary constructions in the society. In the case of Wicomb's South Africa, liminal racial categories not only serve as an instrument of discursive interrogation but also complicate social policy making and power sharing in the society . . . .

Although nationalism serves as a site of awakening, it does not rescue these characters from their liminal spaces; for Fanon, nationalism is itself liminal—a necessary phase. For Fanon, national consciousness is required for international consciousness: "Far from keeping aloof from other nations, therefore, it is national liberation which leads the nation to play on the stage of history. It is at the heart of national consciousness that international consciousness lives and grows" (*Wretched* 247-48). What Fanon is ultimately suggesting to us, if we consider the full development of his three phases, and what we can bring to our reading of postcolonial fiction, is that human struggle must move beyond local issues but not without first clearly identifying what those local issues are.

Notes

1. Referring to both novels as "postcolonial" requires some explanation of terminology. Wicomb's 1987 novel is not postindependence (1994 in South Africa) in the way Cliff's is. In her cogent discussion in "Notes on the 'Post-Colonial,'" Ella Shohal points out that critics often use the term "post" colonial to cover a variety of situations, sometimes masking distinctions between forms of colonialism (settler as opposed to internal) and suggesting the end of something. Yet the economic and social effects of colonialism often remain after independence. In their examination of the field of postcolonial literature, *The Empire Writes Back,* Ashcroft, Griffiths, and Tiffin suggest that "post" be taken to mean after the moment of colonization. This blurs the temporal distinction between the colonial and postindependence periods and at the same time acknowledges that anti-colonial resistance, the process of de-colonization, often begins long before independence is achieved. It is with this in mind that I use the term for Wicomb's novel.

2. Applying Fanon's phases of cultural decolonization to African American writers requires some attention again to definitions. Anne McClintock defines colonialism as "direct territorial appropriation of another geo-political entity, combined with forthright exploitation of its resources and labor, and systematic interference in the capacity of the appropriated culture to organize its dispensations of power" (88). Internal colonization, according to McClintock, "occurs where the dominant part of a country treats a group or region as it might a foreign colony" (88). As early as 1967, Stokely Carmichael (Kwame Touré) and Charles V. Hamilton articulated a theory of power relations in the US that clearly qualifies the history of people of African descent in the US as a colonial one. Even after the era of slavery, many African Americans lived in geographically segregated areas, economically and politically controlled from the outside. As yet, this population has neither emerged as an independent nation state nor become fully politically and economically integrated in the state which colonized it, either of which might qualify as "post independence." Hence the above definition of postcolonial

is also useful when applied to the African American literature cited here.

3. See Moses for a history of the nineteenth-century origins of what is often called "Afrocentrism."

4. See Neal for his discussion of the role of the artist in the transformation of society and a brief history of the US Black Arts Movement.

5. See Hirschmann for a tracking of the history of the Black Consciousness Movement and its impact on South African politics, in particular, the "Main Precepts" Hirschmann articulates from the 1969 founding of SASO (South African Students Organization).

6. Aijaz Ahmad, in his response to Fredric Jameson's "Third-World Literature in the Era of Multinational Capitalism," serves as a example. While praising Jameson's call for syllabus reform in academic literature departments to include "third world" literatures, Ahmad takes issue with Jameson's assertion that all "third world" literature is, by definition, national allegory, and that the "third world" is constituted solely by the "experience of colonialism and imperialism" (Jameson 67).

7. In the 1970s, a number of Black women, some of whom called themselves Black feminists, were critical of the focus and approach of US Black liberation movements such as the Black Panthers and Black nationalism. One of the best known is the manifesto compiled by the Combahee River Collective in 1977. Feminists and lesbians, the women of this collective had participated in these movements but were left frustrated by their inattention to the other sites of struggle they found important. Anthologies like Toni Cade's *The Black Woman* and Gloria Anzaldua and Cherrie Moraga's *This Bridge Called My Back: Writings by Radical Women of Color* also called attention to the need to attend to sexism, heterosexism, ablism, and classism within the struggle for Black liberation. More recently, transnational feminists call attention to the construct of the nation-state and the ways it may be outside of women's experience, even antithetical to the lives of women. For example, see essays by Mary Layoun, Lydia Liu, Nalini Natarajan, and Kamala Visweswaran in *Scattered Hegemonies: Postmodernity and Transnational Feminist Practices* (ed. Grewal and Kaplan).

Works Cited

Ahmad, Aijaz. "Jameson's Rhetoric of Otherness and the 'National Allegory.'" *Social Text* 17 (1987): 3-25.

Anzaldúa, Gloria, and Cherrie Moraga. *This Bridge Called My Back: Writings by Radical Women of Color* Watertown, MA: Persephone, 1981.

Ashcroft, Bill, Gareth Griffiths, and Helen Tiffin. *The Empire Writes Back: Theory and Practice in Post-Colonial Literatures.* London: Routledge, 1993.

Bilby, Kenneth, and Filomina Chioma Steady. "Black Women and Survival: A Maroon Case." *The Black Woman Cross-Culturally.* Ed. Filoma Chioma Steady. Rochester, VT: Schenkman, 1981. 451-67.

Cade, Toni. *The Black Woman.* New York: NAL, 1970.

Carmichael, Stokely, and Charles V. Hamilton. *Black Power: The Politics of Liberation in America.* New York: Random, 1967.

Cliff, Michelle. *Abeng.* 1984. New York: Penguin, 1995.

———. *No Telephone to Heaven.* 1987. New York: Vintage, 1989.

Combahee River Collective. "The Combahee River Collective Statement." *Capitalist Patriarchy and the Case for Socialist Feminism.* Ed. Zillah Eisenstein. New York: Monthly Review P, 1978. 362-72. Rpt. *Home Girls: A Black Feminist Anthology.* Ed. Barbara Smith. New York: Kitchen Table, Women of Color P, 1983. 272-82.

Fanon, Frantz. *Black Skin, White Masks.* 1952. Trans. Charles Lam Markmann. New York: Grove, 1967.

———. *The Wretched of the Earth.* 1963. Trans. Constance Farrington. New York: Grove, 1968.

Grewal, Inderpal, and Caren Kaplan, eds. *Scattered Hegemonies: Postmodernity and Transnational Feminist Practices.* Minneapolis: U of Minnesota P, 1994.

Hirschmann, David. "The Black Consciousness Movement in South Africa." *The Journal of Modern African Studies* 28.1 (1990): 1-22.

Hurston, Zora Neale. *Their Eyes Were Watching God.* 1937. Urbana: U of Illinois P, 1978.

Jameson, Fredric. "Third-World Literature in the Era of Multinational Capitalism." *Social Text* 15 (1986): 65-88.

Marshall, Paule. *Praisesong for the Widow.* New York: Penguin, 1983.

MacDonald-Smythe, Antonia. *Making Homes in the West/Indies: Constructions of Subjectivity in the Writings of Michelle Cliff and Jamaica Kincaid.* New York: Garland, 2001.

McClintock, Anne. "The Angel of Progress: Pitfalls of the Term 'Post-Colonialism.'" *Social Text* 31/32 (1992): 84-98.

Moses, Wilson Jeremiah. *Afrotopia: The Roots of African American Popular History.* Cambridge: Cambridge UP, 1998.

Neal, Larry. "The Black Arts Movement." *The Drama Review* 12.4 (1968). Rpt. In *The Norton Anthology of African American Literature.* Ed. Henry Louis Gates, Jr., and Nellie Y. McKey. New York: Norton, 1997. 1960-72.

Rodgers, Lawrence R. *Canaan Bound: The African-American Great Migration Novel.* Urbana: U of Illinois P, 1997.

Shoat, Ella. "Notes on the 'Post-Colonial.'" *Social Text* 31/32 (1992): 99-113.

Wicomb, Zoë. "Shame and Identity: The Case of the Coloured in South Africa." *Writing South Africa: Literature, Apartheid, and Democracy, 1970-1995.* Ed. Derek Attridge and Rosemary Jolly. Cambridge: Cambridge UP, 1998. 91-107.

———. *You Can't Get Lost in Cape Town.* 1987. New York: Feminist P, 2000.

FURTHER READING

Criticism

Sicherman, Carol. "Zoë Wicomb's *You Can't Get Lost in Cape Town*: The Narrator's Identity." In *Black/White Writing: Essays on South African Literature,* edited by Pauline Fletcher, pp. 111-22. Lewisburg, Penn.: Bucknell University Press, 1993.

Analyzes how Frieda Shenton's identity is shaped by her gender, race, ethnicity, and professional status as a writer.

Additional coverage of Wicomb's life and career is contained in the following sources published by Gale: *Contemporary Authors,* Vol. 127; *Contemporary Authors New Revision Series,* Vol. 106; *Dictionary of Literary Biography,* Vol. 22; and *Literature Resource Center.*

John Edgar Wideman
1941-

Ted Thai/Time and Life Pictures/Getty Images

American short story writer, novelist, essayist, and memoirist.

For additional information on Wideman's career, see *Black Literature Criticism*, Ed. 1.

INTRODUCTION

Wideman is best known for his short stories and novels that trace the lives of several generations of families in and around Homewood, a black ghetto district of Pittsburgh. In these fictional works, his dominant thematic concern involves the individual's quest for self-understanding amidst personal memories and African American experiences. Most critics assert that Wideman's blend of Western and African American literary traditions constitutes a distinctive voice in American literature.

BIOGRAPHICAL INFORMATION

Wideman was born in 1941 in Washington, D.C., and spent his early years in Homewood, a section of Pittsburgh, Pennsylvania. This area has been a recurring set-

ting for his later fiction. His family eventually moved to Shadyside, a more prosperous section of Pittsburgh, and he attended the integrated Peabody High School. After graduation, Wideman attended the University of Pennsylvania on a basketball scholarship, and received his B.A. in English in 1963. He was selected as the first black Rhodes scholar since Alain Locke in 1905. In England, Wideman studied eighteenth-century literature and the early development of the novel. He graduated from New College, Oxford University, in 1966, the same year he accepted a fellowship at the prestigious University of Iowa Writers' Workshop. In 1967, his first novel, *A Glance Away*, was published. During the late 1960s and early 1970s, Wideman was an assistant basketball coach, professor of English, and founder and director of the Afro-American studies program at the University of Pennsylvania; in fact, he became that university's first African American tenured professor. He has also served as a professor of English at the University of Wyoming and the University of Massachusetts. In addition to these duties, he has been a curriculum consultant to secondary schools nationwide since 1968. Wideman has received many awards for his work, including both the PEN/Faulkner Award and the American Book Award for his novel *Philadelphia Fire* (1990), and a MacArthur fellowship in 1993.

MAJOR WORKS

Wideman's first two novels, *A Glance Away* and *Hurry Home* (1970), center on protagonists who are haunted by their pasts and who engage in a search for self. Both novels emphasize the theme of isolation and the importance of friendship in achieving self-awareness. In *A Glance Away*, a rehabilitated drug addict returns to his home, where he renews family and social ties while trying to avoid re-addiction; in *Hurry Home*, a black law school graduate seeks cultural communion with white society by traveling to Europe, then reaffirms his black heritage in Africa. These characters find hope for the future only by confronting their personal and collective pasts. In *The Lynchers* (1973), a black activist group that plans to kill a white policeman in hopes of sparking widespread racial conflict is defeated by internal distrust and dissension. Wideman's *The Homewood Trilogy* (1985), which comprises the short story collection *Damballah* (1981) and the novels *Hiding Place* (1981) and *Sent for You Yesterday* (1983), utilizes deviating time frames, African American dialect, and rhythmic language to explore life in the Homewood area of Pittsburgh. The interrelated stories of *Damballah* feature several characters who reappear in the novels and relate tales of the descendants of Wideman's ancestor, Sybela Owens. *Hiding Place* concerns a boy's strong ties to his family and his involvement in a petty robbery that results in an accidental killing. In *Sent for You Yesterday,* Wideman put forth the argument that creativity and imagination are important means to transcend despair and strengthen the common bonds of race, culture, and class. The novel received the 1984 PEN/Faulkner Award for fiction. The eponymous narrator of Wideman's next novel, *Reuben* (1987), is an ambiguous and enigmatic figure who provides inexpensive legal aid to the residents of Homewood. These experiences provide insight into human relationships and the racial dynamic in twentieth-century America.

Race-related strife, violence, and identity are prominent themes in *Fever* (1989). In the collection's title story, Wideman juxtaposed present-day racism in Philadelphia, a city once offering freedom for slaves through the Underground Railroad, with a narrative set during the yellow fever epidemic of 1793. In the novel *Philadelphia Fire* (1990), Wideman combined fact and fiction to elaborate on an actual incident involving MOVE, a militant, heavily armed black commune that refused police orders to vacate a Philadelphia slum house in 1985. With the approval of W. Wilson Goode, the city's black mayor, police bombed the house from a helicopter, killing eleven commune members—including five children—and creating a fire that razed more than fifty houses. The book's narrator, Cudjoe, a writer and former Rhodes scholar living in self-imposed exile on a Greek island, returns to his native city upon hearing about the incident to search for a young boy who was seen fleeing the house following the bombing. This fictionalized narrative is juxtaposed with Wideman's address to his own son, who was sentenced to life in prison at eighteen years of age for killing another boy while on a camping trip. The tales in *All Stories Are True* (1992) are autobiographical in nature and concern such themes as storytelling, family history, and memory. In *Fatheralong* (1994), Wideman again juxtaposed his own personal life with universal concerns. In this volume, he examined his strained relationship with his father and his difficulties with his own son, then placed these interactions within the context of all father-son relationships and America's history of racism.

Wideman combined elements of history, religion, and race to form the story in his novel *The Cattle Killing* (1996); the narrator's memories of his childhood in Philadelphia are woven together with the plight of blacks in the city in the late eighteenth century and the story of the South African Xhosa tribe. His next novel, *Two Cities,* (1998), chronicles the story of Kassima, a widow still mourning the death of her two sons and husband on the streets of Pittsburgh. When she meets the mysterious Robert Jones, Kassima must confront her own pain and inability to open her heart again. Kassima's story is intertwined with that of her tenant's, Mr. Mallory, whose poignant photographs record the violence and despair that characterize black urban life in Philadelphia and Pittsburgh in the late twentieth century. *Hoop Roots* (2001) traces the development of basketball to a worldwide sports phenomenon and contains a meditation on the importance of basketball to the African American community. The stories of *God's Gym* (2005) provide an unadulterated and nuanced view of family, sexual, racial, and personal relationships. In his 2008 novel, *Fanon,* Wideman synthesized fiction, history, and memoir in a narrative revolving around the life of psychiatrist and revolutionary Frantz Fanon. The first section of the novel touches on aspects of Fanon's life story, including his experiences as an Algerian freedom fighter and his death in a Maryland hospital; in the second, Thomas, a novelist and screenwriter, struggles to write a screenplay based on Fanon's life; and in the final section, a character named John Edgar Wideman realizes his growing obsession with Fanon and reflects on events in his own life, such as the incarceration of his brother and his mother's declining health.

CRITICAL RECEPTION

Critics contend that Wideman's unique combination of fact, fiction, myth, and history has allied him with the modernist tradition and solidified his reputation as a leading American author. Many reviewers concur that his blending of European and black literary traditions constitutes a distinctive voice in American literature. Commentary on Wideman's strengths as a writer often focuses on the lyrical quality he manages to maintain in his prose even while he forges intricate layers of theme and plot and intermixes fact with fiction. This has led some critics to call his fiction complex and his technique experimental. Other scholars have praised his novels and short stories for the insight they provide not only into personal concerns but also into broad societal issues. In addition, his fiction has received acclaim for how it evidences his literary mastery over his material, with several critics remarking on how Wideman's highly literate style is in sharp contrast to his gritty subject matter. In assessing his short stories, numerous critics have compared Wideman to William Faulkner and have lauded the ways in which his novels and short fiction address both the role of the African American artist in society and the author's personal evolution as a writer and an individual.

PRINCIPAL WORKS

A Glance Away (novel) 1967
Hurry Home (novel) 1970
The Lynchers (novel) 1973

Damballah (short stories) 1981

Hiding Place (novel) 1981

Sent for You Yesterday (novel) 1983

Brothers and Keepers (memoir) 1984

*The Homewood Trilogy (novels and short fiction) 1985; also published as *The Homewood Books,* 1992

Reuben (novel) 1987

Fever: Twelve Stories (short stories) 1989

Philadelphia Fire (novel) 1990

The Stories of John Edgar Wideman (short stories) 1992; published as *All Stories Are True* 1993

Fatheralong: A Meditation on Fathers and Sons, Race and Society (nonfiction) 1994

The Cattle Killing (novel) 1996

Two Cities: A Love Story (novel) 1998

Hoop Roots: Basketball, Race, and Love (memoir) 2001

The Island: Martinique (travel memoir) 2003

God's Gym (short stories) 2005

Fanon: A Novel (novel) 2008

*Includes *Damballah, Hiding Place,* and *Sent for You Yesterday.*

CRITICISM

Jacqueline Berben-Masi (essay date summer 1999)

SOURCE: Berben-Masi, Jacqueline. "Prodigal and Prodigy: Fathers and Sons in Wideman's Work." *Callaloo* 22, no. 3 (summer 1999): 676-84.

[*In the essay below, Berben-Masi analyzes the function and significance of the father-prodigal son relationship in* Fatheralong.]

The current critical wave in France having recognized the autobiographical novel as its love child, I would like to extend the parameters to include a non-fictional work, albeit one whose material may well be transformed into fiction. My interest is the product of the writer's creative efforts in what is ostensibly an expository or a rhetorical domain. I want to study the figure of the author in the dialogue between himself and the reader, the roles the latter is implicitly expected to assume, and the outcome of this relationship in terms of a psychology of writing as well as an art. In adopting this approach, I closely follow François Dosse's study on Barthes, Lacan, and Foucault (11-43).

I set myself two tasks. The simpler is to identify the underlying structural patterns that give unity to the work as it echoes phenomena specific to the African-American experience. The more complex is to catch the author, or rather his persona, in the act of creating himself. Clues come from the primary experience he chooses to transcribe here, indicating selection and, at times, self-censure. In the role of chief enunciator of the text at the moment of its apprehension by the reader, the author persona operates within a traditional framework, one that lets me as reader anticipate implicit contracts. Following in the traces of Maurice Couturier, I take a fresh look at the implied author as a figure, a "fictional" construct insofar as he is the result of a filtering process, both conscious and unconscious (*La Figure de l'Auteur* 7-24, 59, 162, 167). How he manipulates the paradigms with which he has invested the genre, how he draws on different registers, crosses over categories, all to communicate his message, how he innovates his approach to direct interaction with the reader in a personalized essay form are all germane to my inquiry.

Perhaps as a result of rereading Mikhail Bakhtin, I found my two tasks overlapping. The deep pattern and the author-narrator persona influenced and enriched one another. Much like the earliest novels, *Fatheralong* accommodates many moods, modes, and styles. It combines sequences of provocation, self-searching, healing, and acceptance; it rallies support through the direct address to the reader who is apostrophized at every turn; it sounds a call to arms to unify the disparate readership into a militant corps; its modals of obligation repeatedly exhort us to face the challenge of eradicating race from the national consciousness, of establishing "terms of achievement not racially determined" (xxii). Added to this fiery sermon, there is an exemplum in confessional form: the genealogical search is a modest response to that challenge; the author-narrator urges others to tackle their own appointment with destiny, whether prosaic or epic, whether in the sense of what should or should not have happened. Like his own, their everyday life stories can "give race the lie." Race, which Wideman defines as "the doctrine of immutable difference and inferiority, the eternal strategic positioning of white over black" (xxii). He analyzes his advances and retreats, plumbs the *kairos,* those moments of axiological high tension that lead to an epiphany. He takes us to the crossroads where life and self meet in an encounter that alters the course of everything in its wake. Yet even minor events leave their permanent mark: each experience in life affects the makeup of the individual in the on-going rendezvous between self and life that German philosopher Gadamer termed *Erlebnis.* Or so literary convention would have it, from St. Augustin to the present day, as Georges Gusdorf shows us in *auto-bio-graphies* (447, 449).

Starting from one of Wideman's conventions, I would like to examine first how *Fatheralong* conforms to his now familiar tripartite structure, and then how the fable reinvests that structure. Theme, movement, and author persona depend upon a deeper triangle, presented from the unified perspective of the author persona, yes, but that of an author persona who shifts positions. Whereas in the novels *A Glance Away* and *Hiding Place,* three voices or character-focalizers develop parallel story lines which ultimately converge and inform one another, in the memoirs *Brothers and Keepers* and *Fatheralong* the writer necessarily abandons his internal focalization through several characters and limits his omniscience to his projected author figure, focalizing upon the others from without. While the words he reports as theirs are not purported to be fictional discourse, the parts that these individuals play in the general organization of the work conform to an archetypal pattern. I refer to the parable of the prodigal son, replete with its cloture of ultimate recovery. Three rhetorical styles—one polemic, one discursive, one lyrical—reflect different purposes, moods, and content. They also correspond to the author persona's relationship with the implied narratees, primary and secondary, and with the figures his persona takes, now as father, now as son, in a series of overlapping triangles.

It becomes difficult to deal continuously in terms of fathers and sons without paying service to the theological implications. Certainly, *Fatheralong* can be read as a redemption gospel. Appreciation of the father's position, understanding and reintegration ultimately become the task of John, a father himself with two sons, one a prodigal like John's brother Robby whom their father Edward cannot bring himself to visit in prison. As I read the text, the "lost" son's mortal fate is irrevocably determined, leading to Edward's despair. His refusal to visit Robby in prison is his only means to not ratify the judgment passed against his son by witnessing the latter's punishment and degradation. Brother (and father) John, in contrast, clings to hope for the moral destiny of all prisoners: those locked behind metal bars and also those imprisoned by social and psychological barriers erected by race, as defined above by Wideman.

Virtually, another world, another America than the one portrayed in official histories and popular culture alike, is mapped out here. Wideman's invoking this dark side of America invites a reconstruction of *Fatheralong* in the mode that Bill Marling adopts in his study of classic American detective fiction, *The American Roman Noir*. To be sure, I do not confuse *roman noir* with African-American literature. In contrast, there is common ground in the parallel universes and archetypal characters invested in both forms. In the works of Hammett, Cain, and Chandler, Marling finds that the plot reposes on an underlying triangle of father, elder son and younger son, each behaving in conformity with the roles established in Jesus' parable (x-xiii). Obviously, for sake of the comparisons that I draw, actual birth order is inconsequential. The genius of Marling's analysis is having shown the consistency with which these roles are played, each in accordance with the different axes subjected to his critical analysis. Consequently, the theme of the prodigal son embraces economic, religious, cultural, social, sexual and metaphoric aspects that collectively confirm its psychological valid-

ity and necessity to our Western notions of order. From an economic viewpoint, for example, the father offers his patrimony and self, the elder son as mirror image of the father works the land and increases the family wealth, and the younger son wastes the fruits of his father's industry and management. From the carnal perspective, the father is associated with the mother; together they form a stable nucleus. The elder brother marries and founds his own family, but the younger brother undermines and destabilizes the order by multiplying his conquests, thereby blurring the lineage, if not actually running with harlots. Morally, father and elder son have soul; they give and share themselves; they dedicate themselves to working and providing for others while the sibling gives in to self-gratification, to the temptation of egocentric activities which ultimately lead to his personal debacle.

The heart of the story, however, lies not here but in the conversion and redemption of the lost son who returns under his father's roof and authority. He who went astray can redeem himself by seeing the light, recognizing his error, taking his lesson to heart, and ultimately succeeding. His "return" restores the initial order or stability of the basic structure, perhaps setting the stage for a new cycle in which the younger son can become a patriarch in turn. For Marling, the return is interpreted as the success or failure of the prodigal in terms of the American Dream. For Wideman, the American Dream is problematic; what counts is the final assuagement of the father's loneliness and grief.

At this point, my reading of *Fatheralong* might seem contradicted by the facts of the Wideman saga. Given the incarceration of sons Robby and Jake, their appeals for freedom denied, their return to their fathers by their own power leads to an impasse. Circumventing this difficulty, Wideman ends the biblical father's patient wait by setting him out in active search. The real-life commitment to freeing those whom he sees as unjustly imprisoned is echoed in a journey. Thus Wideman *père et fils* symbolically don the mantle of the prodigal, and depart in the opposite direction to retrace John's grandfather's people, to find "the father's father," the illustrious ancestor who can confirm upon his descendants status, virtue, pride, and unity. And, yes, legitimacy as worthy heirs to the American Dream, but one that forsakes material gains for spiritual ones. Thus, by the grace of their fathers and their fathers before them, Robby and Jake can be reclaimed, their dignity restored, their "presence" renewed in the family consciousness, in the men's circle. Where seemingly it all began, since a well-defined paternal line leads back to Jordan Wideman as father of Tatum while the maternal line has paradoxically been lost (127).

Here is where I see a clear evolution between the two memoirs. In *Brothers and Keepers,* the mother assumes the traditional father's position: giving, loving, accepting, and supplying soul and stability. She occupies the position of the biblical patriarch in life and literature alike. Where is the father, we ask ourselves? Wideman has often alluded to a family rift; in *Fatheralong,* he tells us Littleman and all his father's relatives were somehow lacking in his mother's eyes. Again, as reader filling in the gaps in this tale, in the context of protest surrounding the book, I am tempted to see a more global cause than personal conflicts at work. A cause that embraces the full gamut of the rhetoric the writer engages in. My construction was inspired by reading the statistics and arguments that Jennifer Hochschild marshals in support of her theory that a chasm separates poor blacks from their middle-class or well-off brethren in their belief in the American Dream. I wonder if the irreconcilable differences that estrange the author's mother and father figures in *Fatheralong* might not be inscribed in this phenomenon. The parallel interpretations of the American Dream Hochschild outlines would partly elucidate John's father's leaving the family and fold to pursue his own fate alone. In *Fatheralong,* we learn why Edward, the real father, is circumvented; although unjudgmentally presented, he, too, is cast as a prodigal, destabilizing the family unit and confusing the lines of identity with a parallel family. Before the mother's reticence to deal with her husband, the elder son assumes the burden of reclaiming the lost father and restoring him to his natural position in the triangle. The task of "recovering" the prodigal father falls to the elder son, making him father to his father, so to speak, and displaces the dominant matriarchal focus which sociologists lament as the decline of the family unit. Reaffirmation of the patriarchal focus asserts the legitimacy of the father and upholds his right to enjoyment of the role history and biology have confirmed upon him. For this story is not just another tale of divorce, a broken home, and a child in trouble. Rather, it is an episode in the epic struggle between the sexes and the races in America: all black fathers are cut off from their offspring, "As long as injustice persists and with it the gross disparities between black communities and white communities on all the scales truly a measure of the right to life, the primal exchange, black father to son, son to father, will be obstructed, poisoned" (*F* 66).

Nothing short of heroic action is called for, but overtly transforming Edgar and John's trip to Greenwood into a heroic quest would run the risk of turning to parody. Granted, the pilgrimage to Promised Land does reenact the myth of the eternal return to the origins for the secret of the birth mystery, the identity of the father, ultimate reconciliation with him, and the granting of a boon. Nonetheless, the venture of discovery through male bonding constitutes a mere subplot, motivated by the prodigal son paradigm. Each must recover a lost ascendant and descendant. John soothes his feelings of guilt for former neglect and ingratitude for all Edgar has given him. Edgar rises in John's filial esteem and their difficulty in communicating subsides. Both their

internal journeys culminate in the recognition of alternative forms of success, proceeding from a core of great spiritual virtue, one that prepares the transcendental ascent into lyricism that concludes the book when John the father deals with the pain of losing his son Jake and applies the lesson learned "down home."

The quest as subplot to the return of the prodigal son reminds me of a Shakespearean device: the play-within-the play speaks an essential truth that the players themselves often fail to apprehend. For whose benefit—ourselves, Robby and Jake, the Wideman family, the author himself—does he relate the episode? Whereas Wideman's early fiction seemed to negate any hope for turning back once the connecting lines had been broken, here there seems to be a viable alternative, even if entirely in the mind. Especially if entirely in the mind, for Wideman sees the mind as the key:

> History is mind, is driven by mind in the same sense a flock of migratory birds, its configuration, destination, purpose, destiny are propelled, guided by the collective mind of members of the immediate flock and also the species, all kindred birds past and present inhabiting Great Time.
>
> (102)

We are dealing here with a story of a quest for the patrimony of "mind": family pride, identity, belonging, roots that paradoxically can only be reclaimed by physical displacement and male symbiosis. Like genetic traits such as body shape and size, common adversaries, albeit at different points in time, shared food, drink, talk, and time mingle the life-lines of fathers and sons, living and dead. The "return" to the origins in the South that grandfather Harry had begged the recalcitrant child John to make with him shifts gears from private time out for father and son to a drive to satisfy a mutual psychological need. The grandfather's wish at last granted becomes a consummate experience that perpetuates the family saga. Upon retrodding the ground of his father Harry's people, John's father Edgar plays Mentor and to the astonishment of his impatient son, makes meaning out of nonsense through persistence and by speaking in tongues of memory. The author paints an ironic self-portrait as an impatient man-child, tactfully trying to entice the father away from what the younger man perceives as foolishness, as squandering precious time. His realization that there is method to this madness enhances the older man's victory and stature. Edgar, as father, is in command, able once again to assume his role as provider. Together, they find "Littleman" whose circular South-North-South migration had once seemed tantamount to failure, but who now provides the key that unlocks the mystery John and Edgar need to unravel together. Together because their triangles overlap. Together because the success accrued here can remove the emotional blockages caused by physical prisons.

The symbiosis between author persona and father in *Fatheralong* reflects that between brothers in *Brothers and Keepers* with an important distinction. There, the link was more one of communicating vessels than Siamese twins: movements of improvement and failure constituted a double helix of ascent and descent; when one rose, the other fell. Author John needed to rehabilitate brother Robby in the eyes of a general reading public. Implicitly, he makes the analogy between his imprisoned brother and Malcolm X, whose discovery of religion and learning in prison ultimately freed him. Thus Robby's language evolves during the course of the book from street talk to standard American usage, demonstrating that he can, when he so chooses, operate like members of the mainstream. In addition, he has begun a technical course in preparation for a life outside confinement. Thus, he is ready for reinsertion. Not, however, without some "cost" to the author persona, for Robby's redemption sends John into a self-examination that instigates a private fall from grace. This downfall offsets his sibling's rise and recognizes the failed man's "success" which is prerequisite to his recovery by the family. Robby's bid for physical freedom having been refused, a suitable substitute must be found to conform to the parable. Idem for Jake in *Fatheralong.*

Earlier I spoke about what form this recovery had to take; now I would like to refine the notion of prodigality in the context of Wideman's book. It seems clear from his strong position on the catastrophe that race continues to wreak on the American society that the prodigal's self-exile need not be a sojourn in the moral or criminal underworld. Might it not be the African-American reinterpretation and adaptation of the American Dream to the structural differences in the socio-economic reality of the U.S. as theorized by Jennifer Hochschild? Does faithful son John, despite his vehement words of alienation, actually espouse a different value system that assimilates him to the white power structure? I hear his call to "transform ourselves, subdue our selfishness and shortsightedness, and thereby change the direction the country is going" (66) as addressed to all Americans, not just the black minority. Prodigal son Robby's exclusion depends on other factors than the inherent personality fault often attributed by American sociologists like Daniel Bell and Daniel Patrick Moynihan to those who transgress society's rules. In Wideman's words, "Difference becomes deviance becomes division becomes demonization. A campaign is mounted to deter, punish, exile, or eradicate the problem group" (67).

Robby and Jake do indeed belong to a problem group. Hochschild cites Pete Hamill's lament on the "Underclass . . . living in anarchic and murderous isolation . . . , [in a] ferocious subculture . . . [which is] the single most dangerous fact of ordinary life in the United States" (201). Moreover, she specifically refers to Robby Wideman. She in turn suggests that he is not an alien who rejects the tenets of the American Dream instructing our entire American society, that drug dealers and hustlers are also interested in achieving success, that equality of opportunity is there in the streets, and thus anyone might pursue it there, that wanting something badly enough leads one to the acts that ultimately deliver, that "virtue" is both tangible and intangible, that it can be seen by the outward signs of wealth as well as the "bad" reputation one can establish (200-13). Just as mainstream society concedes that success often means stepping over others, in the business of getting ahead in the world of hustlers and drug dealers, the ends also justify the means. Therefore, they do not preclude violence as a political weapon in this economic struggle. Robby had a legitimate, if self-aggrandized, vision of personal success which Hochschild quotes from *Brothers and Keepers*:

> I wanted to be a star. I wanted to make it big. My way. I wanted the glamour. I wanted to sit high up. . . . See, in my mind I was Superfly. I'd drive up slow to the curb. My hog be half a block long and these fine foxes in the back. Everybody looking when I ease out the door clean and mean. Got a check in my pocket to give to Mom. Buy her a new house with everything in it new. Pay her back for the hard times. I could see that happening as real as I can see your face right now. *Wasn't no way it wan't gon happen.* Rob was gon make it big.
>
> (191)

But then so perhaps was the prodigal son in the New Testament parable when he applied to his father for a premature share of the still-living father's assets. Gambling, frequenting other big spenders, create the illusion of having made it. Selling drugs and hustling are shortcuts. If hard work was primordial for new white immigrants to America in the 19th century to integrate the society, statistics on the high rates of violence and criminality among these groups reveal a similar perception of where to find the fast track to the relatively more easy life and work style that reigned among established Americans (225-49).

The Casuistic argument may run counter to the rule of law, but it does not contradict the drive for self-improvement that informs the national myth. *Fatheralong* is an impassioned plea for us all to reconsider our notion of the prodigal and to purge our society of the race issue that distorts our vision of certain Americans and short-circuits their access to the American Dream, leaving them no alternative but to evolve their own version thereof. And leaving us in a quandary as to our own reaction and response, active or passive, committed or detached. Not guilty, but responsible. We all face these choices.

In conclusion, what I had at first perceived to be an unresolved tension in *Fatheralong,* i.e., the adamant appeal, the imperious summons of the early sections of the book as opposed to the supplication for grace at its close, now appears to be the systolic and diastolic pressures that regulate the flow of the text. The change in diction as the author persona addresses himself to the faceless public multitude and then to the intimate private circle reveals an author persona engaged in paternal psychology, giving according to the needs of the receiver, and adopting a discourse proper to each. The public becomes like the stalwart, older son in the parable of whom the father expects nothing less than full compliance and support. In the intimacy of his direct, father-to-prodigal-son communication, however, poetry displaces the rhetoric of protest. Wideman has made his overture to universal suffering and can turn to fantasy, can refashion reality in a manner worthy of the pens of Borges and Rushdie. Moreover, I detect an intertextual allusion to the latter's *Haroun and the Sea of Stories* in Wideman's oft-repeated allegiance to the story as a prime necessity as well as a letter to his loved ones. Both come together in a theory that René Fuller maintained in an *Omnibus* article in the late 1970s: the story provides the smallest sense unit of communication; it is an engram, "a persistent protoplasmic alteration hypothesized to occur on stimulation of living neural tissue and to account for memory" (*American Heritage Dictionary* 434). In the ongoing Wideman saga and opus, I suggest that the story is the authorial presence, with its infinite potential to create anew, with its implied roles in relation to waiting audiences. Granting life by supplying the means to perpetuate the circle, giving life instead of imitating life. Is it coincidence that the story proper in **Fatheralong** ends in a marriage? As in Shakespearean comedy, the wedding that concludes the action can be read as a positive sign of stability for the reign. Despite having a video camera on hand to record the event, the storyteller is still indispensable to the event. Similarly, it is he who provides an "open cloture" to the work, he who composes an epilogue of lyrical flight that offers transcendence to a higher spiritual level where questions of race cannot camouflage virtue nor deny the right to succeed.

The *sotto voce* finale to **Fatheralong** lends an incantatory effect to the process we are witnessing. I hear the hymn that instructs the title. I feel the church-like atmosphere I felt at the end of **Hiding Place.** Wideman repeating a spiritual ritual. Can he conjure up the desired result? In my eyes he does. To compensate for the ephemeral nature of the epiphany, Wideman, like Joyce, resorts to recurrences of the event. In this manner, he sustains the father-son connection without betraying the militant posture of the opening. Indeed, this ambivalence between optimism and pessimism also makes the text advance. The word 'dread' punctuates the discourse, as the author persona shifts back and forth in his attitudes towards his own son-father relationship. Is the dread a threat lingering over our heads lest we drop the struggle, condemning the African-American experience to be forever one of exclusion, the minority man and woman denied participation in the myth, refused access to the normal order that rules the European-American universe? Or is it simply the inescapable necessity to begin afresh with each renewed contact, a Sisyphean task, but one that nonetheless confers meaning upon the lives of those who persevere?

Works Cited

The American Heritage Dictionary of the English Language. Boston: Houghton Mifflin, 1969, 1981. 434.

Couturier, Maurice. *La Figure de l'Auteur.* Paris: Seuil, collection Poétique, 1995, especially 7-24, 59, 162, 167.

Dosse, François. "Barthes, Lacan, Foucault: l'auteur, la structure." *De l'auteur à l'oeuvre.* Ed. Patrick Di Maschio. Paris: Ophrys, 1996.

Gusdorf, Georges. *Auto-bio-graphies.* Paris: Odile Jacob, 1991.

Hochschild, Jennifer. *Facing Up To the American Dream: Race, Class, and the Soul of the Nation.* Princeton: Princeton University Press, 1995.

Marling, William. *The American Roman Noir.* Athens and London: University of Georgia Press, 1995. x-xiii.

Wideman, John. *Brothers and Keepers.* London, Allison & Busby, 1985.

———. *Fatheralong.* New York and London: MacMillan, 1994.

Kimberly Ruffin (review date summer 2000)

SOURCE: Ruffin, Kimberly. Review of *Two Cities,* by John Edgar Wideman. *African American Review* 34, no. 2 (summer 2000): 368-69.

[*In the following favorable review, Ruffin highlights the significance of the Bible, the dictionary, and black English to* Two Cities.]

The Bible and the dictionary are not the typical cornerstones of love stories, but they rest at the foundation of John Edgar Wideman's **Two Cities** alongside the musicality of Black speech and the sounds of memory. This may be in part because Wideman explores, among other things, the kind of love James Baldwin called a "tough and universal sense of quest and daring and growth."

This Baldwin-esque notion of love foregrounds Wideman's most recent look at contemporary urban Pennsylvania via the two cities of Pittsburgh and Philadelphia. The three main characters in the novel, Kassima, Robert, and Mr. Mallory, deal simultaneously with repeated personal and community losses in addition to their longing not only for healing but also for the courage to love again. In weaving their stories together, Wideman expands our notion about what a love story may be as he advances the long history of African American orality and literacy with innovative stylistic choices.

Written texts such as the dictionary and the Bible are crucial to the narrative but play no more important role than Black vernacular speech, whether vocalized or only "uttered" in a character's memory. Wideman highlights the lyricism of Black speech in his text: His words seem well-suited to the page yet they resonate in the ear. The absence of quotation and question marks in *Two Cities* enhances the written word by forcing it to yield to the world of sound. A rhythmic labyrinthine effect results from Wideman's time-collapsed mixture of the narrator's voice, characters' voices, letters, seemingly unvocalized speech, and dialogue.

The struggles of enslaved Africans who used the Bible to obtain literacy echo in this novel. Kassima, following in her ancestors' footsteps, uses her literacy to re-claim this classic in Black letters. The younger member of a May-December romance, she must first wrestle the Bible from the "Bible crazy, church crazy" people who "hurt [her] bad as a child." Freed from their scriptural monopoly, she "finds her story" in the book of Lamentations. After Kassima uses a dictionary to complement her reading, she reflects on what she thought "Lamentations" meant, saying:

> Looking at the word, not having the slightest idea what it might mean, my guess was it might be something happy, a happy, dappy, fa-la-la ring to the word, something maybe to do with music, bells and tambourines and drums and long curvy goat-horns, you know, kind of stuff they play music with in the Bible days movies. Lester and the Lamentations, I thought that dumb thought too, thought the word sounded like Temptations or Sensations or Sweet Inspirations, the la-la-la names singing groups give themselves. Latin Lester and the Fabulous Lamentations. Little did I know, no clue what I was getting into when I started to read myself the book in the Bible with that name.

Although the actual biblical book "Lamentations" and Kassima's early associations share little similarity, they both return her to ritualistic places in human emotion: love and mourning. After her dictionary consultation and in-depth reading. Kassima rescues Lamentations from the all too righteous to address the mind-numbing grief following a ten-month span in which she loses her husband to AIDS, which he contracted in prison, and two sons, casualties of the inner-city plague of gang violence. Kassima soothes her wounds with the ancient sorrow songs "about people beat down so low they got to pray for a reason to pray."

Kassima's boarder and a veteran who never makes it back to his family after a traumatic tour of duty in World War II, Mr. Mallory is haunted by his war experiences and the bombing of the MOVE community. The remembered conversations between Mr. Mallory and John Africa, one of the victims of state-sanctioned violence, reads like a conversation between Lamentations' voice of mourning and a combination of Isaiah's prophetic alarm and Revelations' apocalyptic dirge.

Mr. Mallory, who travels around his community with a camera in a shopping bag, also writes to Italian artist Alberto Giocometti that his "work is taking pictures." In his letters (which result in a kind of one-sided conversation) to "Mr. G" he notes, "I'm not an artist but I'm learning from your art to use my camera in new ways. Difficult ways that will probably wear me out before they produce decent pictures. . . ." His passionate devotion to his art stems from his desire to create "one among countless ways of seeing, [a] density of appearances [his] goal" and an art that can speak "the language spoken by the people who taught [him] to feel, to live in a body." Mr. Mallory not only writes and paints but also fuses these two genres to reflect each other. His love for his art and attentiveness to mastery prompt his deathbed request that his unfinished project be burned, although Kassima's refusal to honor his request assists a community in crisis.

Robert reunites with Kassima when she requests his help after Mr. Mallory dies. He is elated that their breakup, prompted by Kassima's fears, has ended, and distantly sad about Mr. Mallory's demise, for he only knew him as an "old dude [with a] shopping bag" who was so common an appearance that he was "just part of the street."

Robert comforts Kassima as they take care of Mr. Mallory's arrangements, and he slips back into their relationship, which navigates the crossroad of his adult desire and his childhood memories. Just as quickly as Robert and Kassima's presumed one-night stand blossoms into a mature love between two people familiar with hurt, Robert surrenders to the remembrances that flood his childhood neighborhood of Cassina Way, the street on which Kassima lives. Understanding the power of this intersection of memory, love, desire, and awakening, Robert fortifies himself so that he can share his story without losing himself. He explains:

> Yes indeed, it was some night and quite a day too and everything that happened comes back when I let it come back but I'll only tell you bits and pieces. Turning it all loose would wear me out. couldn't stop it coming. Story catch me before I got to the end, swallow me in one bite.

The synchronicity of Wideman's multidirectional style and richly drawn characterizations make it worthwhile to read Robert's story, told in the "bits and pieces" he can offer. Because John Edgar Wideman finds a storytelling style that befits the characters' complexities, this "love story" has many textures. This love isn't satisfied with what's easy or necessarily comforting; it pushes those determined enough to keep it to strive for more.

Jacqueline Berben-Masi (essay date 2006)

SOURCE: Berben-Masi, Jacqueline. "Of Basketball and Beads: Following the Thread of One's Origins." In

Critical Essays on John Edgar Wideman, edited by Bonnie TuSmith and Keith E. Byerman, pp. 31-41. Knoxville: University of Tennessee Press, 2006.

[*In this essay, Berben-Masi asserts that* Hoop Roots *is not only about the evolution of basketball, but also centers on Wideman's connection to his African American heritage and community.*]

> The game a string of beads, bright and colorful. You dance them to catch the light, coil them, let them spill through your fingers, mound in your cupped hands. You play the beads, observe how each tiny sphere's a work of art in itself. Time's an invisible cord holding them together, what you can't touch, can't see, time connects glittering bead to bead, forms them into something tangible, a necklace, a gift.
>
> —John Wideman, *Hoop Roots*

Ostensibly about playground basketball and its evolution, John Edgar Wideman's nonfictional work ***Hoop Roots*** is a love song to an implied primary audience and a paean to an all-encompassing sport. We are dealing with a confessional exploration of the soul of the mature artist who is conscious of who he is—where he came from and how he got here—and desperate to keep in touch with his inner self. The author shares his universe directly with us, now as if they were his thoughts, now filtered through the device of a primary reader whom we must intuit. Textual clues indicate it is not the French journalist "Catherine" to whom the book is dedicated, but an African American lover lost, recovered, and volatile. The final chapter of the book becomes epistolary in a belated letter that hints that there was always another reader intended: namely, the deceased grandmother whose presence overshadows the work. Grandmother Freed adorns the book's dust-jacket photo where she stands with a child—the author's mother—in her arms. The latter, too, is meant to "receive" the tale. Hence, the "love song" is sung with a tripartite primary audience in mind.

That love is filial and romantic in turns. In keeping with this sense of an intimate communication, Wideman maintains a predominantly first- and second-person dialogue. This artistic choice accentuates the sensation of confidentiality and passion: we readers eavesdrop on a private conversation, perhaps put ourselves into the "you" or the "I" as we participate vicariously in the unfolding of the narrative. Experiential, composed of multiple segments, the book advances the basic themes set in the subtitle of the book—"basketball, race, and love"—plus one: the experience of writing. This is a highly self-conscious work wherein how the story gets told is as important as what it has to say. The various themes occur sequentially, but also simultaneously when they overlap in memory and time. Conversations minus the tags "he said, she said"—a trademark of Wideman's style—have the effect of speeding up the exchanges and making them seem less "contrived" or written. They in-

volve the reader by requiring a close following of the communication back and forth as each interlocutor "threads the pill," i.e., passes the ball back and forth to his or her teammate and adversary. A split-second's inattention and the identifying voice is a lost cause, like the pea in the shell game or the ace in the three-card shuffle that street hustlers ply. "Now you see me, now you don't" demands concentration beyond normal reader investment. Yet, read aloud, it makes for a more natural rendering of speech, and adds immediacy to the reader's participation in the event's unfolding.

The prefatory paragraph quoted above explicitly draws a parallel that is woven throughout the book and that we cannot avoid exploring ourselves. In short, basketball is as much a cultural ritual for the African American community as the intricate, patterned beadwork that retraces timeless symbols of the interpretation of life and the realms that constitute it among the Yoruba peoples of Africa.[1] Like beads, it has become part of Great Time: timeless, permanent, formative, defining. And like beads sewn into age-old designs of the cosmos that guide life in the here and now, the past, and the hereafter, Wideman implies that the movements on the basketball court, the apparel, the colors and textures, and the body language are all-determining for a lifetime in a black man's existence:

> If urban blight indeed a movable famine, playground ball the city's movable feast. Thesis and antithesis. Blight a sign of material decay; ball a sign of spiritual health rising from the rubble. One embodying apartheid, denial, and exclusion, the other in-your-face, finding, jacking what it needs to energize an independent space. The so-called mainstream stigmatizes the "ghetto" while it also celebrates and emulates hoop spawned in the "ghetto," discovering in playground basketball a fount of contemporary style and values. Feast and famine connected, disconnected, merging, conflicting in confounding ways, both equally, frustratingly expressive in their separate modes of the conundrum of "race."
>
> (50)

On the one hand, the basketball court is an escape valve from the ghetto conditions of life; on the other hand, it is a celebration of triumph in the creation of a counterculture adulated even by those who normally exclude the residents of the ghetto. There is a dimension that goes beyond mainstream's grasp of hoop: the basketball court is also the scene of an initiatory passage from adolescence to manhood, guided by the experts of the game. The initiates are both harassed and protected even as they are tested before being recognized and admitted to the fold. Wideman illustrates the process:

> My father . . . would have taken a prodigy like Ed Fleming under his wing, tested him, whipped on him unmercifully, protected him with hard stares if anybody got too close to actually damaging the precious talent, the fragile ego and vulnerable physique of a large, scrappy, tough kid just about but not quite ready to

handle the weight and anger of adult males who used the court to certify their deepest resources of skill, determination, heart, resources they could publicly exhibit and hone few other places in a Jim Crow society. . . . More abstractly applied, the lesson reminds you to take seriously your place in time, in tradition, within the community of players. Ed Fleming and the other vets teaching me to take my time, no matter the speed I'm traveling. Teaching me to be, not to underreach or overreach myself. Either way you cheated the game, cheated your name, the name in progress, the unfolding narrative, told and retold, backward, forward, sideways, inside out, of who you would turn out to be as you played.

(54-56)

On one level, battles are waged, and won or lost. The adversaries are racial and/or social discrimination: one must earn and establish a name, a reputation to be known by. The ultimate emergence and dominance of the jungle rules of playground ball in the professional domain bespeak the shift from one set of rules to another, from mainstream's monopoly over the game to begrudging acknowledgment of a different form, more improvisational, jazzlike, individualistic, calculated—and impulsive—rather than team coordinated. In parallel evolution with the author's own coming of age viewed at different periods of his life is the emergence of an alternative form of the game. The latter at last compensates for neglected homage to the long-overlooked role of the black minority in acculturating a homebred sport before its export around the world. That homage gets paid in a lyrical approximation of ghetto-speak—with rhymes, repetitions, and oppositions that suggest a musical theme, a backdrop against which to play the game, a fight song for the fans, a hymn to the heroes. On another, more personal level, this is the social finishing school whose unwritten rules convey the deeper sense of community values, of living together as a civilization. Basketball supplants the novels and films that teach the mainstream its mores and values, its "do's and don'ts," its rhythms of life, its manner of looking at itself in the mirror.

In brief, the basketball sequences are principally about the socialization of the author as youth: his ritualistic trials in the initiatory rite of becoming a black man in America, where the basketball court furnishes surrogate fathers and role models. In contrast, the episodes of the adolescent's patiently watching over his ailing grandmother define his relationship to the female element—running the gamut from male protector, respectful to the nth degree, to male predator of the desirable woman and her body. The two constitute a dual loss of innocence: learning the boundaries and limits, grasping when the latter can be bypassed to enable the necessary maturation of the author-subject. On another plane, the segments about the Aztec ruins at Chichén Itzá and the internal stories associated with this experience compose a single strand: it is the wooing of the ideal love and the struggle to hold on to her, as well as a dream of the

self that does not negate the effects of time's passage on the body and mind of the adult-implied author. The preoccupation with controlling all stories told opens onto the question of art itself:

> Art is someone speaking, making a case for survival. The art in our styles of playing hoop as eloquent as our styles of playing music. Art is what we experience, how we feel about being alive. Art's a medium for expressing what's crucial and worthy of being preserved, passed on. What works and doesn't. A culture's art shouts and whispers secrets the culture couldn't exist without, unveils its reasons for being.

(230)

In essence, basketball is art: it is a narrative of its own with a clear plot and development. Like jazz, it has its own rhythms and riffs. As a tradition, it preserves the culture. Ultimately, it provides the thread connecting the episodes of this book into a life, an autobiography based on relationships over time with family, game, and art. For basketball, over the centuries, over a lifetime, lets us step out of linear time and into Great Time. It inscribes itself into the cosmic sphere, where Wideman patiently tries to lead us. Basketball is a portal to another universe.

In a broad sense, **Hoop Roots** picks up where **Fatheralong** leaves off. The latter work portrays the author through the prism of his male genealogy: the missed occasions for cementing ties between father and son, the tantalizingly missing links and the attempts at compensating for what never happened but should have. **Brothers and Keepers** provides the first installment of John's autobiography based on the relationship between himself and his imprisoned younger brother Robby, but also between all black brothers and their prison guards, whether those brothers are incarcerated or simply visitors. Body language between the two camps communicates the patent demarcation between those in control and those who are controlled. There, too, basketball serves as a channel of understanding between the brothers, a glimmer of hope for change—leading the transgressor back to respect for the rules, back to a place on the team and in society. Wideman is rounding out his personal history not chronologically, nor methodically, but through exploring the formative and defining links most important to his adult life. Although the spotlight shines on another subject, the one we learn the most about in these three books is John Edgar Wideman. The practice is not unique—in *L'Afrique fantôme* (1934), *L'Age d'homme* (1939), and *La Règle du jeu* (1948-1976), Michel Leiris inscribed his autobiography thematically—but it is both unusual and effective as a form. By sharing his hobby horses, the author portrays himself riding them, allowing glimpses of the self that seem more natural, more candid, more complete than if he had written a classic, chronological history. As D. Bergez points out in an article on Leiris, the result of the displacement is a less narcissistic attitude of accommodation and a renewal of the genre as such.² It is my conviction that Wideman accomplishes the same in these nonfictional works, making a seamless piece of the three.

Like *Brothers and Keepers* and *Fatheralong,* part of *Hoop Roots* is written in Wideman's "other voice," what he sometimes refers to as his "other language." This is the blend of black English, street talk, scraps of black folklore, family tradition, skipped copulas, noun clauses rather than full sentences—or predicates without repeated subjects—punctuated with grunted expletives like "Uh huh!" or "Huh uh." There is an alternation between the scholarly and the colloquial, creating a linguistic blend that leaves the author's indelible mark on the work. At the same time, the coexistence of two voices allows both sides of the author's being to come to the fore and impress upon the reader a complicity that runs the gamut from the intensely personal to the strictly intellectual, from the women's domain to the men's. For Wideman's agenda restores the equilibrium to the purportedly matriarchal African American family unit by showing its protagonist participating in both domains, being deeply struck by the exquisite, life-catching moments that make up the daily routines of both sexes. Animus and anima are truly complementary, no matter what differences might pit seemingly opposing philosophies. *Hoop Roots* works in both directions: on the one hand, it delves into the roots of playground basketball; on the other, it clarifies basketball's role in helping a young man set down his own roots. It expands upon the book's introductory passage, underlining the need for separate interests to be shared at day's end by men and women (1). Between the lines, we intuit that this is a group history, one common to many African Americans. Indeed, setting down those roots is tantamount to claiming one's masculinity and black heritage with the encouragement of the women who surround and assist one. The women's role in John's upbringing (but also that of other young blacks in the ghetto) is germane to the love song the author sings in this book. His appreciation for the women's gifts, support, and understanding inform the intuited lover-reader, hence us as well, about the man courting her. It entices her into his world, implicates her in a social circle to which she is foreign and uninitiated—but not alien in the sense of a deliberate exclusion.

Highly diversified sequences are wound together, much like the grandmother's long braid of good hair. Arguably an African American obsession, that good hair intertwines the dark and the silver, all of it a shining mass offered to the lover like a string of multicolored beads, each hue rich in symbolic values such as virginity, fertility, and magic powers. In microcosm, the visit to Chichén Itzá with the mysterious re-found love repeats this pattern in the stories told by the lovers to mutually entertain and challenge one another, again much like the one-on-one of play-ground basketball. The true stories exchanged, like all nonfiction, involve the listener and invite contradiction. Between the lines the implied message reads as follows: You tell me a story that catches me by surprise; I one-up you by my own tale. If your story doesn't satisfy me, I recast it to correspond to my expectations and demands. Thus, one bare-bones account goes through four distinct versions or putative approximations of what really occurred. Here, the storytellers act as players in a simulated game of hoop: each tests the limits of the other's strategy, possessiveness, trust, and vision of life. They take on the accomplice-adversary and offer titillating episodes, but neither listener can resist intervening—challenging the teller's sincerity or objectivity. Both teller and listener reveal secrets that invite analysis and unveil deep feelings. Again, here is the indirect approach to the autobiography: we readers observe the subject interacting with others while reflecting upon his behavior and struggling to drop the mask even as he must retain a certain author persona—for the essence of truth cannot be unfiltered or unshaped, lest it lose its unity and impact.

Thus, as autobiographical treatise, *Hoop Roots* stretches the conventions of the genre: Wideman cannot resist revising the mythos of a fact to suit his own aesthetic needs, thereby fictionalizing the nonfictional and raising the text to the metafictional level. Dialogue between the teller and the listener heightens the antagonistic stance. As audience as well as artist in these sequences, Wideman can never drop his guard in the game because of his need to "score a point" on his partner. Why else invert the roles in her story about introducing a dog into an erotic scene—first assuming a macho subtext rather than a feminist reading, and then inserting a historically antiracist theme to subvert the entire anecdote? Her rejection of his interpretation signals the gulf in consciousness, each teller's take on life and time. While she can forget the past, he needs to insert all elements into an overall pattern of Great Time, because the "past is present," as Wideman reminds us time and again throughout his oeuvre. No incident is without universal significance. How a story is remembered and edited forges the links between yesterday and today and solders these links into a continuous chain. Again, as in *Brothers and Keepers,* the reader encounters a self-accusing narrator blaming his own spontaneous behavior for the consequences he has dreaded facing. Dread, guilt, and acceptance underpin the main themes in *Hoop Roots,* for love without betrayal of one kind or another requires a superhuman being. Such a creature's place is not in a realistic, nonfictional piece where the reader can challenge the text's authority, can exert his or her right to an opinion, and can exercise options as a caring agent with a stake in the tale.³ And Wideman is not indifferent to our having a stake in his tale, as the militant tone of the final pages makes clear. His autobiographical essays are a manifest polemic designed to draw the reader into either collaboration or confrontation.

Deliberately or not, the reader unwittingly dons the garments of "the other" and gradually slips into the "you" of the text. Like twin mirrors, each reflecting the perceived image of the other, we alternate in voyeuristic turns—just like the lovers spinning their tales: "Did I ask you to tell your stories so I could watch. Imagining myself a fly on the wall. Invisible, powerless, watching. Could I bear the sight of you in some white man's arms. A black man's" (124). The lover whose story unfolds is now the grandmother whose scrutinized body reveals her stories, now the younger woman lover. The "you" being spied upon through a crack in the door is also both women—one literally, the other figuratively. Moreover, we readers meld into that "you" in both directions. The author tests us, staring back at our "reflections" of the face he has chosen to uncover, at our reactions that he controls by his "now you see me, now you don't" style. In exchange, we train our vision on the man—relating experiences that are at times his own, at times fictionalized accounts that allow him to increase the distance between teller and tale, to change the vortex from centripetal to centrifugal, from inward to outward orientation. In these exchanges, the rule is the same as in basketball: "There are no shadows on the court. No place to hide. Everybody alone. Vertical" (108).[4] Before such exposure, we each contemplate the other, searching to recognize ourselves in the image. It is hardly coincidental that a mirror motif returns again and again throughout the text—the man trying to catch a glimpse of himself, turning the mirror to catch the other's, watching us watch him, perhaps judge his portrait. But also watching him watch us, gauge our reaction, anticipate our next move. The double mirror he invokes in **Brothers** allows constant surveillance. Meanwhile, he is both vulnerable and in control by choosing the information acquiesced: love and jealousy, sexual awareness and desire, racial identity and militancy—tricks and treats of reading African American culture in its multiple forms.

Admittedly, this book is a quest for self-knowledge in process, a confession that seeks first to bare, then to claim the self in the soul laid naked. So were **Brothers** and **Fatheralong.** As seen above, two voices relate the journey to the center of the man's private universe. I would now like to show how the two collaborate in a specific example. The colloquial style of the italicized first enunciation calls attention to itself and surprises the reader, heralding more intimate communication to come. It implies the reader is part of an inner circle. The more writerly style of the second passage, closer to Wideman's fictional voice, takes successive approximations of the truth to arrive at a precise rendering:

> One reason I'm telling all this old stuff, the hard stuff and silly kid stuff too, is because it ain't over yet.

(102; italics in text)

Have I harbored some deep, dark secret. Do I own a face I cannot bear to behold, a mask beneath the other masks that would turn a lover's heart to stone. Nothing so melodramatic, I hope. Rather a reckoning. A slow threshing. Grain by grain I must dig and sift, lift and comb. Not to censor or reveal things I've wished away. Not to confess or beg forgiveness. To see. To name. To enter the room, then begin to find my way safely out.

(103)

Note that there are inside voices and outside voices as well. In counterpoint to the adult voices tracing a pattern of proper conduct, which amounts to the internalization of other values, is the adolescent's discovery of an escape route that allows him to be simultaneously dutiful and prodigal. Creating a mental void, inner silence serves as a cosmic portal for safe entry into another dimension without abandoning his post at Grandmother Freeda's bedside. Just as the young author-would-be-ballplayer first watches and plays at a distance, wordlessly, he accompanies his grandmother for days on end in a state of suspended preoccupation:

> The quiet I carried with me from the room didn't fit in. I had to preserve a place within myself for silence, where I could steal away and be alone with it. Quiet a defense and refuge, a refusal to connect with everything it wasn't, couldn't be. . . . If I didn't let the quiet go, I could leave the house and not lose. And that was an immense relief, a freeing, even if maintaining inner silence exacted dues I've never, then or now, learned how to stop paying.

(98-99)

Quiet becomes a talisman for acceding to, then hanging on to, what counts most.[5] It is a means of reducing the distance between the I and the you as long as Wideman's lover persona takes precedence over the militant black rights activist. The latter stealthily emerges in the final chapters of the book: temporarily, the context shifts from the first- and second-person dialogue to a third-person narration resembling fiction. Under the title of "Who Invented the Jump Shot, A Fable," Wideman retraces a plausible, perhaps authentic, episode of the adventures of the early traveling Harlem Globetrotters basketball team. Their hectic, one-night stands in the heart of "cracker" America are juxtaposed with the static story of an archetypal ghetto figure, a slightly retarded black man who witnesses a racist pogrom and becomes the victim of a lynching.[6] His portrait is tenderly drawn; his ostracism from the white community painfully depicted. Once the atrocity of this innocent soul's being sacrificed to white racial prejudice has been touched upon, there is no avoiding a denunciation of the general appropriation of all things black by whites trying to make a buck, to rob the blacks, to exert and reassert their dominance. Here, too, is the author assuming his burden of social responsibility, championing lost causes like that of Mumia Abu-Jamal or of Robby Wideman. Instead of saying, "I am a militant!" he demonstrates his militancy directly. The autobiographical may seem to take a back seat to the oratorical, yet the confessional mode does not disappear. In this harangue, the author vents his outrage as if forgetting momentarily that he has another agenda to honor. Yet, he has revealed a great deal of himself even as he tries to recover from this lapse. A handy transition appears to end the digression as the author tosses in an admission: he is perhaps jealous of a ballplayer he and Catherine are watching. He is called back to the present moment and steps out of Great Time to reassume his role as wooer and "confessor," after having stepped up to challenge the evils of racism and the double standards imposed by the many upon the few. Somehow, though, his inner peace seems shattered. One wonders if the explosion is the price he refers to paying for his earlier silence. Or, is it more the turn he takes with the ball, scoring points as long as he can, having at last earned his chance by seizing the rebound from the shift to third-person voice in "Jumpshot"? There is an "in-your-face" quality to the opening and closing lines in that section, mocking scholarly attempts like the present essay to pin down the ephemeral so we can analyze, dissect, and discourse over it. The implication is that the truth lies in another dimension of reality. We university critics find ourselves under the microscope, find our pitiful efforts derided as we struggle with the pregnant silence a work like **Hoop Roots** leaves in our own minds. It seems insufficient to look at questions of voice, form, and style—of social, cultural, and racial grounding. Yet, it looks equally perilous to pursue further analysis and risk breaking a butterfly on the wheel. For such is the true nature of this text: real and imaginary, solid yet evanescent, permanent but temporal, strong and fragile. The book is a true reflection of the dust-jacket photo on its cover: deep emotions that emanate from the slightly faded images which, despite the uncompromising eye of the camera, maintain an aura of mystery.

Notes

1. See Drewal and Mason's *Beads, Body, and Soul.* Wideman prefaces his novel with a quote from this source and intersperses his text with brief excerpts. Read in conjunction with *Hoop Roots,* it becomes impossible not to see the deliberate thread spun between them.

2. On Leiris, see Bergez, 2024-25.

3. Here, we are following various theories on narrativity in nonfictional works, from Northrop Frye through James Phelan, David Lehman, and Eric Heyne. An interesting overview and criticism of the issue and the critics are to be found in a dialogue of three articles published by Heyne and Lehman.

4. "No place to hide" recalls the lyrics of a favorite hymn Wideman evokes in his 1981 novel, *Hiding Place.*

5. See "In Praise of Silence": "Silence times our habits of speech and non-speech, choreographs the intricate dance of oral tradition, marks who speaks first, last, how long and with what authority. Si-

lence indicates who is accorded respect, deference, modulates call-and-response, draws out the music in words and phrases. Silence a species of argument, logical and emotionally persuading, heightening what's at stake. Silence like Amen at the end of a prayer invokes the presence of invisible ancestors whose voices, though quiet now, permeate the stillness, quicken the ancient wisdom silence holds" (549).

6. Like the one encountered by Clement in *Hiding Place* or again in "Loon Man" in *All Stories Are True.* In a September/October 1984 National Public Radio interview, Wideman commented on the inescapable presence of such figures in every ghetto community.

Works Cited

Bergez, D. "Leiris Michel, 1901-1990." *Dictionnaire universel des littératures.* Paris: PUF, 1994.

Drewal, Henry John, and John Mason. *Beads, Body, and Soul: Art and Light in the Yoruba Universe.* Los Angeles: UCLA Fowler Museum, 1998.

Heyne, Eric. "Where Fiction Meets Nonfiction: Mapping a Rough Terrain." *Narrative* 9.3 (2001): 322-33.

———. "Mapping, Mining, Sorting." *Narrative* 9.3 (2001): 343-45.

Lehman, David. "Mining a Rough Terrain: Weighing the Implications of Nonfiction." *Narrative* 9.3 (2001): 334-42.

Wideman, John Edgar. *All Stories Are True.* New York: Pantheon, 1992.

———. *Brothers and Keepers.* New York: Holt, Rinehart and Winston, 1984.

———. *Fatheralong.* New York: Random, 1994.

———. *Hiding Place.* New York: Avon, 1981.

———. *Hoop Roots.* Boston, New York: Houghton, 2001.

———. "In Praise of Silence." *Callaloo* 22-3 (1999): 547-49.

FURTHER READING

Criticism

Dreiser, Petra. "Black, Not Blank: Photography's (Invisible) Archives in John Edgar Wideman's *Two Cities.*" *Mosaic* 37, no. 4 (December 2004): 185-201.
  Centers on the act of photographing in *Two Cities,* focusing specifically on how Mr. Mallory uses the camera "to create a counter-archive of lived black experience."

Grandjeat, Yves-Charles. "Brother Figures: The Rift and Riff in John E. Wideman's Fiction." *Callaloo* 22, no. 3 (summer 1999): 615-22.

Elucidates the function of the brother figure in Wideman's fiction.

TuSmith, Bonnie, ed. *Conversations with John Edgar Wideman.* Jackson: University Press of Mississippi, 1998, 224 p.

Collection of nineteen interviews with Wideman, conducted between 1963 and 1997.

Additional coverage of Wideman's life and career is contained in the following sources published by Gale: *African American Writers*, Eds. 1, 2; *American Writers Supplement*, Vol. 10; *Beacham's Encyclopedia of Popular Fiction: Biography & Resources*, Vol. 4; *Black Literature Criticism*, Ed. 1:3; *Black Writers*, Eds. 2, 3; *Concise Major 21st-Century Writers*, Ed. 1; *Contemporary Authors*, Vol. 85-88; *Contemporary Authors New Revision Series*, Vols. 14, 42, 67, 109, 140; *Contemporary Literary Criticism*, Vols. 5, 34, 36, 67, 122; *Contemporary Novelists*, Eds. 4, 5, 6, 7; *Dictionary of Literary Biography*, Vols. 33, 143; *DISCovering Authors Modules: Multicultural Writers*; *Literature Resource Center*; *Major 20th-Century Writers*, Ed. 2; *Major 21st-Century Writers*, (eBook) 2005; *Modern American Literature*, Ed. 5; *Reference Guide to American Literature*, Ed. 4; *Reference Guide to Short Fiction*, Ed. 2; *Short Stories for Students*, Vols. 6, 12, 24; *Short Story Criticism*, Vol. 62; and *Twayne Companion to Contemporary Literature in English*, Ed. 1:2.

August Wilson
1945-2005

AP Images

(Born Frederick August Kittel) American dramatist.

For additional information on Wilson's career, see *Black Literature Criticism*, Ed. 1.

INTRODUCTION

Widely regarded as one of the most notable African American playwrights of the twentieth century, Wilson is recognized for award-winning dramas that realistically portray the struggles of the black middle class in the United States. He reached a theatrical milestone in 2005 when he completed his ten-play cycle that depicts the history of the African American experience from the early 1900s to the late 1990s. Each play is set in a particular decade and the cycle includes two of his most acclaimed plays: *Fences* (1985), which won such coveted prizes as the Pulitzer Prize for drama, a Tony Award for best play, and the New York Drama Critics Circle Best Play Award; and *The Piano Lesson* (1987), which also garnered a Pulitzer Prize for drama as well as another New York Drama Critics Circle Best Play Award. His works, which are commended for their vivid characterizations and authentic-sounding dialogue, often center upon conflicts between blacks who embrace their African past and those who deny it. A talented storyteller, Wilson has been singled out for his efforts at preserving distinct elements of the African American oral tradition, and is much admired by a large segment of the theatrical community, which maintains that he

changed the landscape of American theater—thereby opening up new opportunities for other black playwrights. In the last ten years of his life he became known as a staunch defender of black theater and a strident opponent of the practice of colorblind casting. His racially and politically charged views prompted controversial debate in both the regional theater and theater-studies communities.

BIOGRAPHICAL INFORMATION

Wilson was born in 1945 in Philadelphia, Pennsylvania, to a white father, Frederick August, and a black mother, Daisy Wilson Kittel. Named for his father, who was largely absent during his childhood, Wilson took his mother's name when his parents divorced. He grew up in the impoverished Hill District in Pittsburgh, which he later used as the setting for many of his plays. He recalled encountering racism for the first time at the age of fourteen, when he entered Central Catholic High School, where for a time he was the only black student. Facing racial slurs and threats, he eventually transferred to a vocational school, then to the public high school, where, at the age of fifteen, he dropped out after a teacher falsely accused him of plagiarism. Thereafter he received his education from neighborhood experiences and at the local library. Excited at the prospect of choosing his own reading material, he discovered, in a collection marked "Negro," works of Harlem Renaissance and other African American writers. After reading pieces by Ralph Ellison, Langston Hughes, and Arna Bontemps, Wilson realized that blacks could be successful in artistic endeavors without compromising their traditions. In addition, he found inspiration in the work of poet Amiri Baraka, the Black Power Movement of the 1960s, and particularly in the work of collagist painter Romare Bearden. He subsequently pursued a literary career while working at menial jobs, successfully submitting poetry to small periodicals including *Connections* and *Black World*.

In 1968 he became active in the theater when he co-founded Black Horizons on the Hill, a theater company in Pittsburgh aimed at raising black consciousness in the area. Without any formal training, he began to direct plays and to occasionally act, using the theater as a forum for his early dramas. His first professional breakthrough occurred in 1978 when he was invited to write plays for a black theater founded by Claude Purdy, a former Pittsburgh director, in St. Paul, Minnesota. From there, Wilson moved to the Science Museum of Minnesota, where he was hired to write educational scripts for the internal theater group. He returned to drama in the late 1970s, writing *Jitney,* which was produced in Pittsburgh in 1982. In that same year his play *Ma Rainey's Black Bottom* (1984) was accepted at the Eugene O'Neill Theater Center for workshops and readings. While at the O'Neill Center, Wilson met Lloyd Richards, then dean of the Yale School of Drama and director of the original Broadway production of Lorraine Hansberry's *Raisin in the Sun.* The two became lifelong collaborators. Following the enormous success of *Ma Rainey's Black Bottom* after it opened on Broadway in 1984, Wilson was financially able to devote himself to writing full time. In the early 1990s he moved to Seattle, Washington. With the exception of *Jitney,* all of the plays in Wilson's cycle were ultimately produced on Broadway, including his last drama, *Radio Golf,* which he completed shortly before his death in 2005 and which premiered on Broadway two years later, in May 2007. Wilson died of liver cancer in 2005. In his honor, Broadway's Virginia Theater was renamed the August Wilson Theater, marking the first time in history that a theater was named for an African American.

MAJOR WORKS

While Wilson did not set out to create his plays in a series, it became clear to him over time that his plays in combination were creating a twentieth-century history of the black experience in America. *Jitney,* set in 1977, tells of a down-at-the-heels Pittsburgh gypsy cab company that is struggling for survival. Set in a Chicago recording studio in 1927, *Ma Rainey's Black Bottom* depicts the turbulent relationship between the legendary blues singer Gertrude "Ma" Rainey, her band, and exploitative white business managers and recording executives. One band member, the trumpeter Levee, desperately wants to succeed in the white-dominated world of commercial music, but his rage at the inherent injustice of a system controlled by whites leads to a shocking act of violence. Wilson next turned his attention to the 1950s as the setting for *Fences.* Earning Wilson his first Pulitzer Prize, *Fences* revolves around Troy Maxson, an outstanding high school athlete who was ignored by major league baseball because of his color. Struggling through middle age as a garbage collector, Troy experiences increasing bitterness, which results in clashes with family members, including his son, who also aspires to a career as an athlete.

A new play by Wilson, *Joe Turner's Come and Gone* (1986), debuted while *Fences* was still running on Broadway, an unprecedented accomplishment for a black playwright in the New York theatrical world. Regarded as more mystical than Wilson's other works, *Joe Turner's Come and Gone* is considered by many critics Wilson's finest work. Set in a Pittsburgh boardinghouse

in 1911, during the Great Migration of African Americans from the South, the play concerns the struggles of migrants in the post-Civil War North. Following seven years of illegal bondage, Herald Loomis, a black freedman, travels to Pennsylvania in search of his wife who fled north during his enslavement. The critical issue of white oppression is symbolized in Herald's haunted memories of Joe Turner, the infamous Southern bounty hunter who captured him. Herald's sojourn ends at the boardinghouse, whose black residents are also searching for wholeness in their lives. Wilson won his second Pulitzer Prize in 1990, for *The Piano Lesson.* Set during the Great Depression of the 1930s, the drama pits brother against sister in a dispute over the future of a treasured heirloom—a piano. Decades earlier, their grief-stricken grandfather, an enslaved carpenter, had etched African-style portraits of his wife and son into the piano's legs after the two were traded away in exchange for the instrument. In the play, the brother wants to sell the piano to buy land, while the sister adamantly insists on keeping it, revering the instrument as a means of preserving their family's history. Wilson's next play, *Two Trains Running* (1990) is set in a run-down diner on the verge of being sold. Reactions by the diner's regular patrons to the pending sale make up the body of the drama, which takes place on a single day in 1969. Set in the 1940s, *Seven Guitars* (1995) recounts the tragic story of blues guitarist Floyd Barton, whose funeral opens the play. Action then flashes back to recreate the events of Floyd's last week of life. In 2000, Wilson completed the eighth play in his cyclic history. *King Hedley II,* a dark retrospective, draws upon the life of the title character, an ex-convict attempting to rebuild his life in 1980s Pittsburgh. Hedley deals with his past while figuring out how to go "legit" in the midst of the brutality of a black ghetto. The play depicts the decline of the black family and the prevalence of violence and guns in contemporary inner-city neighborhoods.

In *Gem of the Ocean* (2003), set in Pittsburgh in 1904, audiences learn that spiritual healer Aunt Ester, a recurring matriarchal figure in Wilson's work, is over three hundred years old. Aunt Ester assists people who seek her guidance, allowing them to reconnect with the past, their history of slavery, and to draw strength from the experience. *Radio Golf,* set in 1997, is the last of the ten plays that constitute Wilson's cycle. In this work Wilson introduced Harmond Wilks, who, while on the threshold of success in the white-dominated world of business, struggles between the past that shaped him and the future that lures him. In 1996 Wilson laid out his views on race, theater funding, and multiculturalism in a keynote address to the Theatre Communications Group's annual conference. The speech, titled "The Ground on Which I Stand," was first published in *American Theatre* in 1996. Wilson's remarks created critical controversy and feud. A series of responses and counterattacks appeared in print both from Wilson and from *New Republic* critic Robert Brustein, culminating in a debate between the two on January 27, 1997, at the New York City Town Hall. Wilson's original speech appeared in book form in 2001.

CRITICAL RECEPTION

Wilson has achieved the stature of a preeminent dramatist in twentieth-century American theater. While his individual plays have garnered various critical responses, the scope of his ten-play historical cycle has received an overwhelmingly positive reception. Calling the sequence "epic," observers have remarked how, viewed together, the plays form a complete dramaturgical account of black American history. Overall, Wilson has been commended for his realistic depictions, multifaceted characters, and authentic and lively dialogue, which many critics note is a faithful rendering of black urban speech. He also has earned acclaim for his use of traditional African folklore, with scholars pointing out the "oral-history quality" of his dramatic works. His use of mystical and supernatural elements, especially in *Joe Turner's Come and Gone* and *The Piano Lesson,* has received a mixed response among critics, with some finding the elements "contrived" and superfluous, and others lauding the playwright's ability to dramatize the connection between twentieth-century African Americans and their enslaved ancestors. Another area of critical focus involves Wilson's presentation of the problematic dual nature of African Americans—the pressure to conform to white society while struggling to retain their African roots. Whether or not his works can be viewed as political has also inspired critical discussion. Some commentators have argued that even though on the surface Wilson's emphasis is on family and the details of everyday life, underneath, he presented the Western world as severe and unjust for blacks, who are displaced and separated from their African ancestry. They also note that Wilson suggested that by forging a renewed connection with their African culture and heritage, people of the African Diaspora can experience healing on an individual as well as on the communal level. Although the length of some of his plays and the frequency and duration of his characters' monologues have spurred some reviewers to call for a tightening of his works, critics are almost unanimous in lauding his dramatization of the twentieth-century experience of black Americans—a cycle Wilson was determined to finish even after he found out he had only a few more months to live. The ten plays serve "as regenerative models of healing," writes scholar Harry J. Elam, Jr., "integrat[ing] the political, the historical, and the spiritual in ways that push the realms of conventional realism and evoke a spirit that is both timeless and timely."

PRINCIPAL WORKS

Jitney (play) 1982

Ma Rainey's Black Bottom: A Play in Two Acts (play) 1984
Fences (play) 1985
Joe Turner's Come and Gone: A Play in Two Acts (play) 1986
The Piano Lesson (play) 1987
Two Trains Running (play) 1990
**August Wilson: Three Plays* [and author of preface] (plays) 1991
Seven Guitars (play) 1995
King Hedley II (play) 2000
†*The Ground on Which I Stand* (essay) 2001
Gem of the Ocean (play) 2003
Radio Golf (play) 2005

*This collection includes *Ma Rainey's Black Bottom, Fences,* and *Joe Turner's Come and Gone.*

†This is the text of Wilson's keyonote address at the Theatre Communications Group's annual conference in 1996. It was first published in *American Theatre* that same year.

CRITICISM

James R. Keller (essay date fall 2001)

SOURCE: Keller, James R. "The Shaman's Apprentice: Ecstasy and Economy in Wilson's *Joe Turner.*" *African American Review* 35, no. 3 (fall 2001): 471-79.

[*In this essay, Keller considers the role of the shaman in* Joe Turner's Come and Gone, *suggesting that Loomis's attainment of the vocation of shaman parallels the transformation experienced by African Americans after slavery, which the play suggests moves from restoration, to reunion, to religious and social emancipation.*]

In his book *August Wilson and the African American Odyssey,* Kim Pereira briefly engages the theories of the renowned anthropologist Mircea Eliade in order to understand the events and characters of Wilson's play ***Joe Turner's Come and Gone*** (82-83). Recognizing that the drama includes a search for self-actualization by a group of African Americans migrating north in the second decade of the twentieth century, Pereira asserts that it is only through the acceptance of their dual cultural heritage that the characters are able to recover from the degradations of their past and experience renewal (56). The allusion to shamanic rituals, for Pereira, signifies this cultural reconstitution. Loomis reconnects with his African self and thus "encapsulates the Black experience" (81). Pereira is certainly accurate in his recognition of the characters' quest for self-affirmation, as well as the importance of reconnecting with their non-Western cultural heritage, but he does not acknowledge the centrality of shamanism to the structure of the drama. The events of *Joe Turner* dramatize the election and education of a shaman, as the power to heal and to manipulate the spirit world is passed from one generation to the next.

The action of Wilson's play takes place in a Pittsburgh boarding house in 1911. The setting is appropriate to the subject matter since most of the characters are displaced people, whether uprooted by the desire to find economic opportunities in the industrial North or compelled to flee "the eyes of watchful tyranny" in the South. However, their search is not motivated entirely by practical considerations—sustenance and safety; they are also driven by the desire for spiritual renewal. The names of many of the characters reveal their longings for edification.

Bynum is a "conjure man" whose craft is devoted to the reunion of lost and separated persons whom he "binds" physically and spiritually. Having attained spiritual illumination, he is capable of facilitating the same in others. Yet the racial ideology of the play suggests that, in spite of his knowledge of the African folk and spiritual customs, he is nevertheless torn between two worlds. Bynum does not bind people exclusively; he also unifies cultures. His visionary sequence reveals the conjunction of African and Christian motifs (Pereira 71). His quest for the "shiny man" is the search for an individual whose own spiritual awakening exceeds his own, the uncompromising African Man.

This paradigm of cultural resurgence is, of course, Loomis, who recognizes Bynum's negotiation with the ideology that enthralls and exploits people of African descent and who lashes out at the conjure man's effort to bind him as he was bound to Joe Turner's chain gang for seven years: ". . . Harold Loomis ain't for no binding" (91). Loomis lost his religion when Turner captured him, depriving him of his family and his freedom. Loomis now recognizes the collusion between religion and the racist state and cannot bring himself to celebrate the white man's God, who has demanded such sacrifices from him. Thus he wanders, physically and spiritually, in search of his wife and his beginning. The "illumination" that is implicit in Loomis's name is not the divine madness of the Christian saints; it is derived from a more ancient source—the ecstasy of the shaman.

Loomis's refusal to remain in the company of his newly recovered wife, Martha Pentecost, reveals his aversion to Christianity and particularly to Western ecstatic traditions. The name *Pentecost,* of course, suggests the visitation of the Holy Ghost upon the disciples of Christ (Acts 2:1). Martha has maintained her faith in spite of the forced dissolution of her family. Loomis has sought her out only to deposit their child in her care and to make contact once again with the period of contentment and confidence that characterized their lives together. However, Loomis's journey into the past stretches beyond the gratifications of those happier times. He seeks

a spiritual healing that can only be achieved by an older ecstatic tradition. Martha recognizes that he is lost to Christianity and erroneously associates his new allegiances with evil: "You done gone over to the devil" (91).

Bynum and Loomis are foiled by those characters who have been more fully assimilated into white culture. The most stark contrast is with Seth, the boarding-house owner, who is determined to achieve material success and who has very little patience for those African Americans migrating north, looking for the same prosperity that Seth desires:

> These niggers coming up here with that old backward country style of living. It's hard enough now without all that ignorant kind of acting. Ever since slavery got over with there ain't been nothing but foolish-acting niggers.
>
> (6)

Seth is very demanding of his boarders, insisting on advanced payment in full, and is preoccupied with maintaining a respectable house. His callousness is antithetical to Bynum's selflessness. While Bynum counsels and guides Loomis through his visionary trance, demonstrating charity and grace, Seth is only concerned with ejecting Loomis from the premises for creating a disturbance. He haggles with all of the characters over their boarding fees and threatens to throw most of them out at one time or another.

The most revealing aspect of Seth's character is his scorn for Bynum's religious practices. The play opens with Seth's derisive account of Bynum's magical rituals, which he refers to as "all that old mumbo jumbo nonsense." The expression reveals Seth's refusal to acknowledge any affinity with his African past. He is a capitulationist who wants to blend into the white man's world. His ongoing negotiation with Rutherford Selig over the manufacture and sale of dustpans manifests his longing for the white man's success and for opportunities to exploit African Americans' labor potential. He fantasizes about hiring Jeremy to toil in his new dustpan business. However, he does not seem to realize the extent to which he is a victim of the white economy with which he longs to merge: The bank will not give him a loan to start a new business unless he offers his house as collateral, a request which within the context of the drama is unreasonable. The representation of white material success and independence that Seth longs to imitate is Rutherford Selig, the "people finder."

Selig, the only Caucasian character, possesses a name that, in German, means 'blessed' or 'ecstatic.' In combination with the verb *werden, selig* signifies the attainment of salvation—'to become saved.' It is something of a curiosity that the playwright would include the single white character in his visionary motif, particularly since Rutherford Selig is identified with those forces that have brought the African American characters to their current state of upheaval and degradation. Although Selig offers his services in the search for lost people, he is, by his own admission, associated with those who made it their business to separate Black families. Bertha remarks cynically that Selig "ain't never found nobody he ain't took away" (42). The association of his name with 'blessed' may suggest the opportunities that are inherent exclusively to whites in a racist culture. Selig obviates white cultural domination; his blessing is financial and entrepreneurial success, a condition that most of the characters wish to share, particularly Seth.

The play itself dramatizes the effort to introduce African Americans into the American industrial economy of the twentieth century, and Selig's role in the drama suggests that the most enduring link between the characters is the acquisition of material goods. The only Caucasian admits that his progenitors have always made their living pursuing African Americans: His great grandfather transported slaves from Africa; his father captured runaway slaves for their owners; and Selig himself locates displaced people for a fee. These practices reduce African Americans to commodities and are precursors to the assumption of Blacks into industry—the same process that characterizes the setting, both spatial and temporal, of the play. Selig's salvation is his own exclusion from racial oppression and his financial independence. Thus, his name is ironic. He attains his ecstasy through consumer capitalism, through the "selling" of material products. For him, African Americans are objects for exploitation and exchange in the new economy, as in the old. His efforts are thus another manifestation of Joe Turner's chain gang. He finds African Americans and binds them to the economic system, demanding payment for his services and products which, in turn, necessitates subsistence labor.

The mercantile obsessions of Seth and Selig, as well as the sensual preoccupations of Jeremy, Mattie, and Molly, are antithetical to the spiritual yearnings of the shamanic characters. Both Bynum and Loomis do no work within the play, and this refusal to labor is a truly revolutionary practice within a modern economy. While Bynum's motivations are not stated, Loomis specifically rejects the ideology that insists he labor on behalf of white men and their ideology:

> Great big old white man . . . your Mr. Jesus Christ. Standing there with a whip in one hand and tote board in another, and them niggers swimming in a sea of cotton.

> And he counting . . . what's the matter, you ain't picked but two hundred pounds of cotton today.

> (92)

Bynum's refusal to participate in the economy is a refusal to accept one of the most fundamental social structures of the modern state. His rejection of familial ties and obligations is yet another means of rejecting the same order. The obligation to the family necessitates labor in order to provide for the material needs of dependents. The shaman's path is solitary and anti-materialistic.

Eliade characterizes the shaman as a "specialist in the human soul" (8), the individual who is responsible for the spiritual and physical health of the tribe and who, in a visionary trance, journeys into spiritual realms to seek out and remove the sources of illness (5). Both Bynum and Loomis possess qualities associated with this shamanic legacy. However, Bynum's power is that of a fully realized medicine man, while Loomis is experiencing the agonizing transformations that will lead to his own shamanic vocation.

The initiation of a shaman can come about either through "hereditary transmission" or "spontaneous vocation" (Eliade 13). He does not choose his work, but is chosen by the spirits to pursue a life as a healer. The medicine men in *Joe Turner* seem to be the unwitting proselytes of the spirits. Bynum tells of his own election, which occurs on the road near Johnstown where he encounters a hungry man to whom he offers food and who, subsequently, promises to teach him the "meaning of life." The traveler rubs blood on Bynum's hands and encourages him to cleanse himself by smearing it on his face. Following this ritual, Bynum's companion begins to glow, and all of the objects in the vicinity grow to twice their normal size: "sparrows big as eagles!" Next Bynum encounters the distorted image of his dead father, who tells him that there are many "shiny men," and if Bynum ever sees another, his work will be complete; he can "die a happy man." Finally, the father urges Bynum to learn a curative song—the binding song (8-10).

The above narrative constitutes a clever mixture of pagan and Christian imagery. Bynum's shamanic powers are a negotiation between the religious heritage of Western culture and the practices of his African and Carribean ancestors. Bynum's experience is reminiscent of St. Paul's ecstasy on the road to Damascus, where he would encounter the crucified Christ and be converted to the new religion. The location itself near Johnstown may be a very subtle allusion to the *Revelation of St. John* (another scriptural ecstasy) as well as a reference to John the Baptist, who is cited specifically in the characterization of the "shiny man" as the "One Who Goes Before and Shows the Way" (10). The shiny man's blood that cleanses Bynum is, of course, an allusion to the redemptive qualities of Christ's blood, and the shiny man's glow may be an allusion to the transfiguration of Christ, still another ecstatic moment in the gospels.

However, the imagery of Bynum's ecstasy has a dual signification, one that yokes together historically antithetical religious traditions. Many of the same attributes associated with Christianity are decidedly shamanic.

The "shiny man" suggests the shamanic gods and spirits who are also associated with light. Fire is believed to be the easiest way to transform body into spirit (Townsend 440). Moreover, blood is integral to many ancient rituals, since it was believed to open the portal between worlds and nourish the spirits (Freidel, Schele, and Parker 201-02), and it is only after Bynum rubs himself in his companion's blood that his environment changes: His father's spirit appears; objects become larger than life; and his traveling companion begins to glow. The subsequent encounter with his father's spirit suggests the "hereditary transmission" of the shaman's vocation. Many shamanic (most notably Native American) ritual practices involve ancestor worship; the medicine man encountering the spirits of dead loved ones who inaugurate and direct his spiritual vocation (Schele and Freidel 202-03). It is his father's ghost who urges Bynum to find his song. Bynum reveals that his dead father was a "conjure man" whose song had the capacity to heal, a vocation consistent with the shaman's principal objective—to alleviate spiritual and physical suffering through interaction with the spiritual world (Eliade 28). In his effort to discover his own song, Bynum intentionally selects one that differs from his father's, but one that, nevertheless, possesses a philanthropic objective. He will bind those who have been separated, and he is likely to be very busy, since every character in the play is searching for a lost lover or family member.

In Bynum's ecstasy, the father reminds his son that if he (Bynum) ever sees another shiny man, he will know that his work has been successful. There is an element of finality to the father's promise, suggesting that Bynum's life and work will be finished (10). Thus the appearance of a "shiny man" at the conclusion of *Joe Turner* implies the consumation of Bynum's work and the passing on of his powers to the next generation, the obvious recipient being Loomis, who has been chosen to carry on the profession. Since shamanism is an oral tradition, it is necessary for the practitioner to initiate and train the next generation—those subsequent medicine men becoming the new repositories of the cultural wisdom (Ong 24). However, just as Bynum altered his father's craft, Loomis will also find a unique song, the "song of self-sufficiency . . . free from any encumbrances other than the workings of his own heart and the bonds of his flesh" (93-94). While Bynum's labors sought to reunite the fragmented and alienated African American population at both the individual and the cultural levels, Loomis's edification signifies the severing of the African from the American. His awakening is a refusal of the most basic tenets of the Western religious tradition. Unlike the other residents of the boarding house, Loomis no longer needs companionship to experience contentment, and he no longer needs the white man's religion to define his place within a culture. The binding of cultures that was a portion of Bynum's song is transcended by Loomis, who emerges as the new Af-

rican subject. His "shining" represents a new valuation—"a new money" (94). As indicated above, economics, the exchange of consumer goods and services for cash, is what unites all members of the modern state, but Loomis is a new currency, one that will not and cannot circulate within the white American economy. He is the resurrected African man, emerging from the degradation of abduction and bondage. Indeed, the unique goals of the play's three shamans signify the evolution of African Americans following emancipation: a movement from healing, to binding and reunion, and finally to cultural and spiritual self-sufficiency.

Loomis's edification as a shaman is a lengthy process, only the most crucial and auspicious moments of which are depicted in Wilson's play. The medicine man's craft frequently emerges from his efforts to heal his own suffering, and "the initiation of the candidate is equivalent to a cure." Indeed, his infirmity manifests his election (Eliade 27). Loomis is spiritually sick, wandering in search of his wife, who disappeared while he was in bondage to Joe Turner. He does not know how to renew his life in the wake of debilitating disillusionment and suffering, and his experiences with Bynum are pivotal. By reuniting Loomis's daughter Zonia with her mother, Bynum frees Loomis to pursue spiritual renewal: ". . . he is free to soar above the environs that weighed and pushed his spirit into terrifying contractions" (94). It is after this apotheosis that Loomis is finally able to say goodbye to his wife and to the memory of their lost happiness.

The playwright uses an image of flying to reveal Loomis's liberation from his mundane obligations. Loomis soars "above" his "environs." Soul flight is, of course, central to the shamanic experience. In the midst of his ecstasy, the holy man often possesses the spirit of a bird and describes his visionary flight above the earth (Harner 158).

> The Dyak shaman, who escorts the souls of the deceased to the other world, also takes the form of a bird. We have seen that the Vedic sacrificer, when he reaches the top of the ladder, spreads his arms as a bird does its wings and cries: "We have come to heaven". . . . The same rite is found in Melkula: at the culminating point of the sacrifice the sacrificer spreads his arms to imitate the falcon and sings a chant in honor of the stars.
>
> (Eliade 478)

The image of Loomis's soul flight is an unmistakable sign of his spiritual rejuvenation as well as his election to the shaman's vocation. Only now does he begin to shine. Eliade's association of the flight with sacrifice is also pivotal to understanding Loomis's apotheosis.

At the moment of his consecration, Loomis proclaims, "I'm standing! I'm standing! My legs stood up! I'm standing now!" (93). His elation over this simple task is the culmination of an image motif that began with Loomis's vision of the "bones people" at the end of Act

I. The vision of skeletal people drifting in ships, drowning in the ocean, and landing on the shore has proven a fruitful metaphor, signifying not only the slave trade and the displacement of African abductees to America, but also the disorientation experienced by the former slaves upon their emancipation and, by extension, the confusion and bewilderment experienced by Loomis following his release from seven years on a chain gang. However, Loomis's ecstasy is also related to the shaman's initiation. The dismemberment and evisceration of the neophyte body is a commonplace thematic in various accounts of the medicine man's genesis (Eliade 34). At his investiture, the novitiate describes being reduced to a skeleton by spirits who devour and then restore his flesh (Townsend 446). Among the Siberian Yakut shamans, the initiate dreams of being ripped apart by a giant "hook": "The bones are cleaned, the flesh scraped, the body fluids thrown away, and the eyes torn out of their sockets" (Eliade 36). In the genesis of the Tungus shaman, the novitiate is dismembered and consumed by spirits. Finally, they "throw his head into a cauldron where it is melted with certain metal pieces that will later form part of his ritual costume (43). The Malekula ritual is recounted in more detail:

> . . . the Bwili made himself a bamboo knife and[,] cutting off one of the young man's arms, placed it on two of the leaves. And he laughed at his nephew and the youth laughed back. Then he cut off the other arm and placed it on the leaves beside the first. And he came back and they both laughed again. Then he cut off his leg from the thigh and laid it alongside the arms. And he came and laughed and the youth laughed too. Then he cut off the other leg and laid it beside the first. . . .
>
> Lastly he cut off the head, held it out before him. And he laughed and the head laughed, too.
>
> Then he put the head back in its place and took the arms and legs that he had taken off and put them all back in their places.
>
> (Layard 65-66)

Loomis's vision of the "bones people" is instigated by the invocation to the Holy Ghost in the midst of the African Juba dance. Denouncing the characters' continued reverence for Christianity, Loomis "is thrown back and collapses, terror-stricken by his vision" (53). He sees himself reduced to bones and is particularly troubled by his inability to stand up and walk along the road. Thus the triumphant proclamation that he is standing at the conclusion of the drama suggests his restoration and his investiture as a shaman. He describes himself surrounded by "enemies picking" his "flesh." Yet despite his symbolic evisceration, Loomis is restored and is a "new" and better person. Asking incredulously if "blood make you clean," he slashes himself, rubs his blood on his face, and realizes that he is finally walking upright (93). Loomis's enlightenment involves a rejection of Christian salvation: He realizes that he can save himself, and this ability allows him to heal others as well.

Loomis's edification is managed and manipulated by Bynum, who questions the neophyte in the midst of his initial ecstasy and guides Loomis through a detailed account of the bones people. The play suggests that Bynum may have had a similar experience when he saw the shiny man:

> Then he carried me further into this big place until we come to this ocean. Then he showed me something I ain't got words to tell you. But if you stand to witness it, you done seen something there.
>
> (10)

The lack of details in Bynum's account leaves the interpretation of the passage open, but Bynum's prior knowledge of the content of Loomis's vision argues strongly that the events for which Bynum has no words include skeletons on the sea shore. Loomis recognizes Bynum as a kindred spirit: "You one of them bones people" (73). And just as his father introduced Bynum to the ocean of bodies, Bynum guides his own apprentice through this initiatory vision.

The conditions that instigate Loomis's ecstatic trance in the midst of the Juba dance are reminiscent of the shaman's possession that is an initial sign of election by the spirits. "Drumming, dancing, [and] chanting" are traditional means of invoking a mystical trance (Needham 505-14). When Loomis hears the Juba chanting, he dances, speaking in tongues. Just as the shamans of the Sudan become possessed by spirits, begin to tremble, and lapse into unconsciousness as a prelude to their visionary trance (Eliade 55), Loomis, at the conclusion of his dance, falls to the floor and begins to prophesy.

Bynum's preoccupation with helping others find their songs may also have its origin in the medicine man's ritual, where the song is frequently equivalent to the magic that the shaman practices (Eliade 98). One account of the role that song plays in the shamanic initiation is derived from the indigenous people of the Carribean: ". . . the first piai [shaman] was a man who, hearing a song rise from the stream, dived boldly in and did not come out again until he had memorized the song of the spirit women and received the implement of his profession from them" (qtd. in Eliade 97). "Each shaman," writes Eliade, "has his particular song that he intones to invoke spirits" (96).

It is not difficult to perceive the application of these ideas to Wilson's *Joe Turner.* Bynum's efforts to help the other boarders, particularly Loomis, find their songs is a definitively shamanic process. The conjure man has received his own song from the spirit of his father, a song that has a magical quality—the capacity to bind people together. His father's healing song was magical in a more traditional sense, and the song that Loomis learns at the conclusion of the play will teach others self-sufficiency. Bynum stipulates that he is not teaching new tunes, but helping others to rediscover the music that they have forgotten. In each case, he suggests that it is the domination of white European culture that has caused the African American characters to forget their songs. Thus the discovery of this music is a recovery of the past, the ante/anti-bondage consciousness. Loomis's reclamation and rehabilitation of his song is a call to evangelize once again, not advocating the Holy Spirit, but promoting self-sufficiency and a rediscovery of African cultural traditions. Loomis's current isolation was not always characteristic of him. He had once been a deacon in his church, and on the day he was captured by Joe Turner, he had stopped to preach to a group of men. Bynum tells Loomis that Joe Turner stole his song. Its recovery implies a renewal of his desire to guide and heal others.

A customary attribute of many shamanic rituals is the blood sacrifice of animals—pigs, goats, cows, etc. The blood served to nourish the gods or to transfer affliction and offense onto the sacrificial subject. Although the practice was uncommon, even human sacrifice might be conducted in a period of social crisis (Blacker 120-21). Initially, the blood imagery in Wilson's *Joe Turner* has a decidedly Christian quality. While both of the play's shamans experience a blood baptism as an introduction to their vocation, Bynum's clearly alludes to Christ's blood. The blood-covered hands of the "shiny man" suggest the stigmata, and he invites the neophyte to cleanse himself with that blood (9). The action results in an initiatory vision that launches his shamanic profession. In contrast, Loomis's blood ritual is a clear refusal of Christ as the sacrificial subject. While his wife prays for his soul, Loomis declaims against Christianity's false pledge to alleviate the suffering of African Americans. He identifies Christ as an instrument of domination, encouraging African Americans to abide their maltreatment patiently and offering little more than abstract promises of happiness after death. Dismissing the idea that Christ can atone for his sins, Loomis explains that he has done enough bleeding to warrant salvation on his own terms, and it is at this moment that the play declares Loomis's "self-sufficiency," his liberation from Western cultural and theological traditions. Loomis's transfiguration into the African medicine man is complete; he has gone beyond the negotiated shamanism of Bynum, who still allows Western culture to define his spirituality. Just as Bynum's "shiny man" "Goes Before and Shows the Way" (10), Bynum himself was merely a precursor to and facilitator of the newly enlightened African subject, and Loomis will light the way to the spiritual renewal of still others.

The passage of the shaman's vocation encompasses four generations in the play, revealing the means whereby African culture has been transmitted despite the cultural imperialism of white America. The embassy moves from Bynum's father, to Bynum, to Loomis, and, by implication, to the neighbor boy Reuben, who

also has a vision. He reveals his experience to Loomis's daughter Zonia. Reuben sees the spirit of Seth's dead mother near the pigeon coops; she is wearing a white dress and radiating light. She beats him with her cane and encourages him to release the caged birds. The spirit's visitation suggests spontaneous election: The beating implies the shaman's suffering and the pleasurable pain of the traditional ecstasy, and the charge that Reuben release the pigeons implies the liberation thematic that is closely related to the shamanic task within the drama. It looks forward to Loomis's liberation and subsequent flight following his final consecration.

The multiplying holy men within the text are set off in sharp contrast to the more mundane characters, who are preoccupied with material wealth, companionship, and sex. These individuals, who are more easily assimilated into white culture, are the very same subjects who must be enlightened and converted to an African consciousness by the play's wise men. Jay Plum describes the "black rite of passage" that is so common in African American literature:

> The initiand first rejects the socially fixed position of African Americans as a cultural "other" and withdraws from white society. He or she then moves through a timeless and statusless liminality in which he or she receives instruction, often in the form of ancestral wisdom. Finally, the initiand achieves a sense of self-sufficiency and is reincorporated into society.
>
> (564)

The neophyte recognizes that there is no place for him in white culture, so his reintroduction to society involves an embracing of his distinct differences as a man of African descent (565). It is easy to perceive the application of the above paradigm to the character Loomis in Wilson's play. However, the character's reawakening after his encounter with "cultural wisdom" is not the self-discovery of the average African American subject, but the creation of a new source of cultural wisdom, a new African holy man.

Wilson's play *Joe Turner* participates in the same process that it depicts. The audience experiences the transformation vicariously through the agonies and ecstasies of Harold Loomis. Wilson recognizes the antithetical influences that define African Americans—the impulse to assimilate into white culture and the impetus to extricate and maintain a distinct black culture. In his interview with Sandra Shannon, Wilson expresses his confidence in the viability of a distinctly African American spirituality and culture (546). In *Joe Turner,* even those characters most fully assimilated into white culture are familiar with and participate in the Juba dance and are sufficiently conversant with non-Western religious traditions to appreciate and fear Bynum's conjuring. However, the play stages an apotheosis which, by example, urges the audience to move toward an uncompromised African spirituality and consciousness. Thus the playwright himself becomes the shaman, manipulating the ghosts of our imaginations, healing the wounds created by four hundred years of racial oppression and cultural imperialism, and urging the audience to stand up and get back on the road.

Works Cited

Blacker, Carmen. *The Catalpa Bow: A Study of Shamanistic Practices in Japan*. London: George Allen and Urwin, 1975.

Eliade, Mircea. *Shamanism: Archaic Techniques of Ecstasy*. Trans. Willard R. Trask. Princeton: Princeton UP, 1972.

Freidel, David, Linda Schele, and Joy Parker. *Maya Cosmos: Three Thousand Years on the Shaman's Path*. New York: Morrow, 1993.

Harner, Micahel J. "Common Themes in South American Indian 'Yage' Experiences." *Hallucinogens and Shamanism*. Ed. Michael J. Harner. London: Oxford UP, 1973. 158-75.

Layard, John W. "Malekula: Flying Tricksters, Ghosts, Gods and Epileptics." *JRAI* [*Journal of the Royal Anthropological Institute of Great Britain and Ireland*] 60 (1930): 501-24.

Lewis, Joan. *Ecstatic Religion: An Anthropological Study of Spirit Possession and Shamanism*. Baltimore: Penguin, 1971.

Nadel, S. F. "A Study of Shamanism in the Nuba Mountains." *JRAI* 76 (1946): 25-37.

Needham, R. "Percussion and Transition." *Man* 2 (1967): 505-14.

Ong, Walter J. *Orality and Literacy: The Technologizing of the Word*. New York: Routledge, 1982.

Pereira, Kim. *August Wilson and the African American Odyssey*. Urbana: U of Illinois P, 1995.

Plum, Jay. "Blues, History, and the Dramaturgy of August Wilson." *African American Review* 27 (1993): 561-67.

Schele, Linda, and David Freidel. *A Forest of Kings: The Untold Story of the Ancient Maya*. New York: Morrow, 1990.

Shannon, Sandra G. "Blues, History, and the Dramaturgy: An Interview with August Wilson." *African American Review* 27 (1994): 593-59.

Townsend, Joan B. "Shamanism." *Anthropology of Religion: A Handbook*. Ed. Stephen D. Glazier. Westport: Greenwood P, 1997. 429-69.

Wilson, August. *Joe Turner's Come and Gone*. New York: Plume, 1988.

Harry J. Elam, Jr. (essay date 2004)

SOURCE: Elam, Harry J., Jr. "The Overture: 'To Disembark.'" In *The Past as Present in the Drama of August Wilson*, pp. ix-xix. Ann Arbor: University of Michigan Press, 2004.

[*In the essay below, Elam reflects on Wilson's historical cycle of plays within the larger framework of African American social, political, and cultural history.*]

> A series of wooden crates sits in the corner of a room. They emit barely audible sounds—Billie Holiday's "Strange Fruit" and "Travelling Light." A black man who bears a striking resemblance to Abraham Lincoln is shot by an assassin who shouts, "Thus, to Tyrants!"[1] A gay, black doctoral student and his 189-year-old grandfather travel back in time to slavery and the insurrection of Nat Turner; their vehicle is a bed that lands, *Wizard of Oz* style, on the evil "Massa Mo'tel," whose feet dangle from underneath it. Emerging from a watery grave, the ghost of a murdered baby haunts her mother's postemancipation home. Imagining himself the archangel Gabriel, a World War II veteran with a metal plate in his head performs a strange, possessed dance, and through it opens up the gates of Heaven for his deceased brother to enter.

These divergent images, produced in the 1980s and 1990s by African American artists, trouble the interconnections between the African American past and the present. The final reference comes from the Pulitzer Prize-winning play **Fences** by August Wilson, the author who is the focus of this study [*The Past as Present in the Drama of August Wilson*]. I set Wilson's work in relation to these other images in order to reinforce my contention that the creation of his twentieth-century cycle of plays does not happen in a vacuum, but within a confluence of artistic creation that includes visual, literary, and dramatic texts. The first representation cited is part of an installation included in conceptual artist Glen Ligon's exhibit at the Hirshhorn Museum in Washington, D.C., from November 1993 to February 1994 entitled "To Disembark." The crates, which vary slightly in size and design, approximate the proportions of the box in which the slave Henry "Box" Brown traveled from Richmond, Virginia, to freedom in Philadelphia in 1849. The title "To Disembark" connotes the transitional process of unloading at the end of the voyage, the impersonal disburdening of black Africans, like cargo from the hull of slave ships. In another section of the gallery hang lithographs that imitate nineteenth-century wanted posters for escaped slaves in which all the descriptions of the runaway slaves concern Ligon himself. Entitling this exhibition that visually foregrounds the impact of slavery on the contemporary African American subject "To Disembark," Ligon implies that African Americans are still in the process of disembarking, still discharging historic baggage, always and already on the physical and psychological journey toward liberated self-definition.

The texts from which the other images come also negotiate issues of disembarkation as they foreground the impact of the African American past on the present. Playwright Suzan-Lori Park's imaginative work, *The*

America Play (1990-93), which contemplates the profound effects that the myth and legacy of Lincoln's freeing the slaves continue to have on the African Americans, is the source of the second image. Irreverently questioning the lack of a gay presence in the history of slavery, Robert O'Hara's play *Insurrection: Holding History* (1999) is the source of the third. The fourth comes from Toni Morrison's now classic novel *Beloved* (1987). Set in the period of emancipation, Morrison's novel wakes the dead in order to provoke the processes of African American living. The last occurs during the climax of *Fences,* a play that explores and, with this final invocation of ritual, transcends the tensions of black family life in Pittsburgh, 1957.

I begin my examination of August Wilson's twentieth-century history cycle with this reference to *Fences* and to other African American works of the 1980s and 1990s in order to situate Wilson's historical cycle within a larger sociohistoric context. Throughout this volume [*The Past as Present in the Drama of August Wilson*], my allusions and references will not be limited to the African American dramatic canon but will draw from other genres of black cultural expression as well. Wilson's dramaturgy, like the cultural productions of all those mentioned above, depends on the circulation of images and conditions conducive to such historical explorations. In the 1980s and 1990s, as scholars and artists came increasingly to understand race as a social, political, and historical construction, they correspondingly came to consider how the political and cultural constructions of history helped to constitute the meanings of race.[2] And yet, concern for the politics of history and historiography is not particularly new within African American culture. The inability to suppress, control, manipulate, and right histories of race has repeatedly affected the social and cultural dynamics of African American life. W. E. B. Du Bois in his 1935 treatise *Black Reconstruction in America* took issue with the representation of race within American history at that time, arguing that "the story of Reconstruction from the point of view of the Negro is yet to be written. When it is written, one may read its tragedy and get its truth."[3] David Blight notes that the final chapter in Du Bois's work, "The Propaganda of History," served as "an indictment of American historiography and a probing statement of the meaning of race in American historical memory . . . the stakes in *Black Reconstruction* were the struggle over the nature of history itself."[4] Correspondingly, these artistic imaginings of history in the 1980s and 1990s, let me suggest, are part of a continuing battle over "the nature of history."

The emergence of this artistic return-to-the-past movement testifies to a present desire to reckon with unfinished business. Yet these artistic engagements do not simply offer a compensatory history for that which has been lost or omitted within the American historic lexicon. Rather, in keeping with the historical materialism expressed by Walter Benjamin in his "Theses on the Philosophy of History," they "brush history against the grain" not only to fill in gaps in historic knowledge but to expose history's relativism, as they explore how history means in the present.[5] In one of nine etchings with chin collé that mimic the frontispieces by white abolitionists of nineteenth-century slave narratives included in "To Disembark," Ligon writes, "The Narrative of the Life and Uncommon Sufferings of Glen Ligon, a colored man, who at a tender age discovered his affection for the bodies of other men, and has endured scorn and tribulations ever since."[6] The etching's style and words write Ligon's personal history into the slave past. Yet the etching also points to Ligon's own negotiations of identity in the present, how he is figured within a history, ghosted by the past. Critical to his and other interpretations of history, including that of Wilson, is an understanding that history is formulated in the now. According to James Baldwin, "If history were past, history wouldn't matter. History is the present. . . . You and I are history. We carry our history. We act our history."[7] With their fantastical, mystical, spiritual imaginings of the past, these artists see history not as static fact, but as malleable perceptions open to interpretation, as a place to envision the past as it ought to have been in order to understand the present and to achieve a future they desire.

Sparked in part by the sociopolitical circumstance of the times, this African American literary and theatrical archaeology in the 1980s and 1990s evidences an approach to the interaction between art, politics, and community more perhaps nuanced than that expressed in the Black Arts movement of the 1960s and 1970s. As Philip Bryan Harper notes, that movement "was characterized by a drive for nationalistic unity among people of African descent."[8] This mandate led in many cases to relational artistic practices that explicitly linked black advancement to the destruction of white hegemony, that sought to combat the "white thing," as Mike Sell calls it,[9] in terms of both form and content. The Black Arts orientation was decidedly presentist, critiquing Western aesthetics, challenging white privilege in order to effect immediate change. The movement preached a functional aesthetic that envisioned art as a powerful tool in the struggle for black liberation. Yet, writing in the early 1990s, after the black urgencies of the previous decades had largely dissipated, critics such as Harper and David Lionel Smith have pointed to the constraints that such an aesthetic imposed on black artists.[10] Rebelling against past, prescriptive paradigms that posited the fight against racism and white oppression at the center of all black artistic creation, playwright Suzan-Lori Parks writes:

> There are many ways of defining Blackness and there are many ways of presenting Blackness onstage. The Klan does not have to be outside the door for black people to have lives worthy of dramatic literature. . . . And what happens when we choose a concern other

than race to focus on? What kind of drama do we get? Let's do the math: BLACK PEOPLE + x = NEW DRAMATIC CONFLICT (NEW TERRITORY).[11]

The "new dramatic territory" that she imagines does not mean an art evacuated of social efficacy. Rather than an obliteration of the politics of race, Parks calls for a freedom to explore new visions of what constitutes black art and the liberty to discover how, within this art, the complex social dynamics and political impulses of black life find expression. Glen Ligon expresses a similar sentiment: "The work of artists of color is often reduced to being simply about race and nothing else as if our gender, sexual, class, and other identities didn't complicate any discussions of race as subject matter, or as if race was our natural subject matter."[12] Ligon speaks to the stereotypical expectations placed on black artists from external sources, while Parks discusses the agency of black artists themselves to create beyond the constraints of conventional racial politics. For both, as for Wilson, turning back toward history offers a place to construct "new dramatic territory," to disembark; to explore race and yet to operate seemingly removed from the immediacies of current racial contexts.

Significantly, the fire of the Black Arts movement of the 1960s—even as critics and artists assault its failures, its missed opportunities as well as applaud its successes—still haunts today's black artists. The movement calls out to Wilson and others to achieve its romanticized ideals of real social commitment, material social change, and a functional black unity. Its conjunction of arts and politics raises certain critical questions for artistic practice that challenge African American artists even now: How can we claim a racial unity, celebrate "black power," and cry out that "black is beautiful" without enforcing essentialism? How can we assert our collective blackness while allowing for intraracial differences? How can we marshal or recapture that sense of urgency that we found in black politics of the 1960s? Paradoxically, with such contemporary questions, historical analysis becomes increasingly important, and artists have turned to that past for answers. They seek to reevaluate that past in order to understand the present better. In such an effort, history serves not simply as the site of nostalgia and longing, nor only as progress or as rational, logical process. Rather, this return to the past in the present represents what Giorgio Agamben terms "a critical demolition of the ideas of process, development, and progress."[13] The result, then, is a new experience of history, a new contestatory and contingent engagement with the past that puts into question the historical categorization of race as it interrogates the meanings of blackness. For Parks, Ligon, O'Hara, Morrison, and Wilson, revisionist historicism has enabled complex renegotiations of blackness and new delineations of community.

Wilson's self-imposed project, to write a play for each decade of the twentieth century, both links him to and separates him from the other aforementioned history projects. With two Pulitzer Prizes, two Tony Awards and numerous other accolades, August Wilson stands out as one of the preeminent playwrights in contemporary American theater. He has changed the face of American theater, and his emergence has enabled other black writers to follow. As director Marion McClinton states, "A lot of black writers had doors opened to them basically because August Wilson knocked them out. . . . American theatre now looks toward African-Americans as viable members."[14] The viability of Africans in America, their place within the American dream, is central to Wilson's theatrical project. His singular commitment to exploring the experiences of African Americans over time has enabled him to delve into the particular, but also see the process of historic evolution. With this cycle he has shaped a history that is at once personal and collective, figurative and real. John Lahr writes that "his plays are not textbooks; they paint the big picture indirectly from the little incidents of life."[15] The plays explore African American history through Wilson's own memories, "his story." Ethics and aesthetics conjoin as the personal dynamics of his characters' lives have profound political consequences. He terms his project "a 400 year old autobiography, which is the black experience."[16] In this African American "autobiography," history both shackles his African American characters and empowers them. They must discover how both to embrace the past and to let it go. Because of Wilson's investment in "the souls of black folk" (as W. E. B. Du Bois would say), there is not simply a matter of unfinished business with the past but a hunger for redress and regeneration in the present. As regenerative models of healing, his cycle integrates the political, the historical, and the spiritual in ways that push the realms of conventional realism and evoke a spirit that is both timeless and timely.

Wilson's own movement in writing these plays in his cycle has been far from linear, moving back and forward through time and negotiating the past's impact on the present.[17] In fact, he did not originally set out to write a cycle, but in the process of writing discovered that this was exactly what he was doing.

> Somewhere along the way it dawned on me that I was writing one play for each decade. Once I became conscious of that, I realized I was trying to focus on what I felt were the important issues confronting Black Americans for that decade, so ultimately they could stand as a record of Black experience over the past hundred years presented in the form of dramatic literature.[18]

Although not written in chronological order, Wilson has to date completed plays on the 1900s, *Gem of the Ocean,* 1910s, *Joe Turner's Come and Gone* (1988), 1920s, *Ma Rainey's Black Bottom* (1984), 1930s, *The Piano Lesson* (1990), 1940s, *Seven Guitars* (1996), 1950s, *Fences* (1987), 1960s, *Two Trains Running* (1992), 1970s, *Jitney* (2000), and 1980s, *King Hedley II* (2001). His play of the century's first decade, *Gem of the Ocean,* premiered at the Goodman Theater in Chicago in April 2003 and moved from there to the Mark Taper Forum in Los Angeles in July 2003.

With each work, Wilson re-creates and reevaluates the choices that blacks have made in the past by refracting them through the lens of the present. In his most recent plays, he has decided not only to unearth the continuities and disjunctures of African American experience in time, but also to mine the relationship between his own texts. Wilson's *King Hedley II* explicitly revisits characters seen close to forty years earlier in *Seven Guitars.* In his final two plays of the cycle, *Gem of the Ocean* and a newer play to be set in 1999, Wilson intends to "build an umbrella under which the rest of the plays can sit. My relating the '00s to the '90s play should provide a bridge. The subject matter of these two plays is going to be very similar and connected thematically, meaning that the other eight will be part and parcel to these two. You should be able to see how they all fit inside these last two plays."[19] *Gem of the Ocean,* set in 1904, focuses on Aunt Ester, a character as old as the black presence in America, and the action that transpires when Citizen Barlow arrives at her house, seeking sanctuary from spiritual turmoil. While Wilson previously discusses Aunt Ester in *Two Trains Running* and *King Hedley II, Gem of the Ocean* marks the first appearance of this figure he now believes is "the most significant person of the cycle. The characters after all, are her children."[20] In this play that marks the ultimate inception and near culmination of the cycle, Wilson has worked his way around to staging Aunt Ester.

Because Wilson repeats and revises certain ideas, concepts, phrases, and ritualized actions within the plays—such as Aunt Ester—I have organized this book [*The Past as Present*] around key questions and critical thematic issues that evolve through his dramaturgy. Rather than constructing the chapters around individual plays, I examine Wilson's self-reflexive intertextuality. His plays purposefully speak to each other; they develop a common agenda. Therefore, examining them in consort and dialogue with each other is crucial. By considering the intersections and continuities across the cycle, I intend this analysis not only to provide insight into the individual plays but, more significantly, to explore how the cycle as whole makes meaning and to theorize how Wilson (w)rights history.

Invoking the concept of (w)righting, I consciously riff on the meanings of *writing, righting, right,* and *rites* to frame and analyze Wilson's processes of reckoning with the African American past. (W)righting underscores the etymology and the denotations of the word *playwright.* Just as a wheel*wright* makes wheels, a play*wright* functions not simply as *writer* but as a play *maker.* Playwriting is a selective and collective act of creation. "(W)righting history" implies that Wilson, through his three-dimensional constructions of the past, his meditations on black experiences in each decade of the twentieth century, is making history. Carefully situating each play at critical junctures in African American history, Wilson explores the pain and perseverance, the determination and dignity in these black lives. In the introduction that follows, "(W)righting History: A Meditation in Four Beats," I will further develop the concept of (w)righting, as I establish a theoretical overview around the concepts of history, memory, time, and ritual that will prove critical to this study and that are fundamental to an understanding of Wilson's dramaturgy.

Wilson's (w)righting history, his project of dramaturgically documenting the African American past, raises important questions of authenticity and essentialism in representation: How can one play capture, as Wilson proposes, "the most important issues confronting black Americans for that decade"?[21] Does Wilson's (w)righting therefore limit and essentialize blackness? Unlike Ligon's "To Disembark" or O'Hara's *Insurrection,* Wilson's African American history never refers to black homosexuality, nor does Wilson, like Lynn Nottage or Kathleen Collins, depict the historic images of the black bourgeoisie.[22] He intends to take up the subject of the black middle class in his final play of the cycle that he will set in 1999. Wilson has situated all his plays to date within very particular social, cultural, sexual, and even geographic spectrums. Can the Hill District of Pittsburgh serve as the symbolic home of all black America? Discussing his April 2001 production of Wilson's *Piano Lesson* for the San Jose Repertory Theatre, director Kenny Leon proclaimed, "It's like these characters represent all the African-Americans who have ever lived."[23] Certainly Leon is not alone in such contentions, as the very nature of Wilson's historical project lends itself to such generalizations. Given our current understanding of the diversity within African American life and of race and history as constructions, however, any criticism that takes Wilson's cycle simply as representative of all African Americans is problematic. Yet I would argue that the "limits" of Wilson representation do not need to be understood as essential, or romanticized as definitive portraits of authentic black experience. Rather, the critical task with Wilson's dramaturgy is that we recognize the utility of the representation without reading it as totalizing; that we note the possibility of responding to its symbolic meaning without corresponding absolutely to it or subordinating oneself to its authority. For theater and performance are always sites of surrogacy, where the figurative becomes charged increasingly with symbolic import and where collective recognition, empathy, and sentiment can be generated in the shared experience of spectatorship.[24]

One day as I was working on this Overture, my mother, whose social and educational background are very different from that of Wilson or his characters, remarked,

"August Wilson's theater makes me proud to be a black person." Not to be overly sentimental, I think her statement encapsulates complex relations of history, racial identity, and identification at play in Wilson's representation and reception. Wilson through his own style of realism, his three-dimensional portraits, his storytelling bravado, validates a history of black experience. Rather than locating blacks in positions of victimization, subordination, or objectification, Wilson places them as subjects of his drama. Given the history and politics of black representation in America, this is a significant move, as signaled by my mother's comment. She identifies with his creation. Even in her difference, it resonates. Wilson's imaginative, selective grounding of black America feels "real" and engenders racial pride. And yet my mother's remark, as well as Leon's, suggest the weight that Wilson bears in the public sphere. As the singular African American playwright, he must be responsible to all black people; he must uplift the race. Do we expect too much of him? Perhaps. Still, as evidenced by his interviews and speeches, Wilson takes on the mantle of social responsibility willingly. How Wilson, employing the vernacular, "keeps it real" historically, theatrically, and culturally is a question of critical import in this analysis of Wilson and his cycle.

Wilson writes that his "blood memory" is a guide for his creation.[25] Blood memory—the idea that there are some intrinsic experiences, some ontological knowledge that blacks remember just because they are black—also has the potential to seem essentialized. Suzan-Lori Parks, in her play *In the Blood* (2000), critiques the very notions of a fixed blackness. Her central character, Hester, is a black, homeless woman with a multicultural brood of children, each with a different father. Through her representation, Parks raises questions about what is in the blood and how blood is racialized. My sense is that Wilson's invocation of blood memory equally interrogates what is in the blood, functioning as a metaphor that is at once something and nothing. For memory is never a perfect mirror, and ideas of race are constantly in flux. Or as Ralph Ellison writes, "I said black is . . . an' black ain't."[26] Blood memory, in Wilson's theatrical construction, operates as a metaphor for his central idea of reimagining history and for appreciating how the African and African American past is implicated in the present. Wilson constructs blood memory on and through his dramas not as a biological essence but as a symbolic representation that dramaturgically blurs the lines between the figurative and the real.

Wilson's personal history, in fact, exemplifies the symbolic construction of blood memory operating in his cycle and testifies to the ways in which collective memory and race are the products of historical, cultural, and social construction. Wilson was born Frederick August Kittel on April 27, 1945. He was the fourth of six children. His father, Frederick Kittel, a white German

baker, hardly lived with the family. His mother, Daisy Wilson, worked as a cleaning woman and later married David Bedford, a black ex-convict and former high-school football star. As is signaled by his decision to change his surname from Kittel to his mother's name, August Wilson self-identifies as black, not as mixed. In his now famous speech to the Theatre Communications Group in January 1996 Wilson states,

> Growing up in my mother's house at 1727 Bedford Ave in Pittsburgh Pa., I learned the language, the eating habits, the religious beliefs, the notions of common sense, attitudes towards sex, concepts of beauty and justice, and the responses to pleasure and pain that my mother had learned from her mother, and which you could trace back to the first African who set foot on the continent. It is this culture that stands solidly on these shores today as a testament to the resiliency of the African-American spirit.[27]

Wilson notes that he constructs memory through the learned behaviors passed on in his mother's house. The meanings of the cultural traditions he describes in his mother's house, then, are produced in the present. How they come to signify on the past comes through current understandings of self, identity, and of subjectivity. "The resiliency of the African-American spirit" is a testimony to black endurance, adaptation, and the ability to evolve. Central to Wilson's dramaturgical project is the idea that one can move forward into the future only by first going back. Wilson's cycle suggests that African Americans need to confront more integrally the African dimension of their Du Boisian double consciousness, the penultimate principle of *both/and* in African American experience.[28] They must embrace the legacy of slavery, celebrate the African retentions that remain within African American cultural practices, and acknowledge the psychological scars that still endure.

Even as it starts with the 1900s and concludes with a play set in 1999, Wilson's history cycle reveals an African American continuum that is always in process, stretching back into Africa and reaching into the future. Within West African cultures, life is similarly imagined as a circular process that does not end but is linked in a continuum with the world of the ancestors as well as that of the unborn. Sandra Richards argues that for Wilson, the United States, like Africa, "is a site of cultural becomings . . . though the idea of democracy may be constant, its substantive meanings and referents are continually changing."[29] In the cross-cultural connections that Wilson develops, the notion of disembarking, of moving on toward liberated self-definition, is continuous. His cycle, then, does not constitute an end but a beginning. And so we disembark.

Notes

1. Suzan-Lori Parks, *The American Play,* in *The American Play and Other Works* (New York: Theatre Communications Group, 1995), 164, 171.

2. Certainly, this artistic attention to the political construction of history in this period correlates with the concurrent theoretical developments in poststructuralism and postmodernism from Roland Barthes to Jacques Derrida, from Hayden White to Frederic Jameson and others that interrogate history as discourse and question how history as narrative operates in relationship to the real. But rather than rehearse those arguments here, I want to turn to the particular interconnections of art, politics, and history in African American experience.

3. W. E. B. DuBois, quoted by David W. Blight, "W. E. B. DuBois and the Struggle for American Historical Memory," in *History and Memory in African-American Culture,* ed. Geneviève Fabre and Robert O'Meally (Oxford: Oxford University Press, 1994), 69.

4. Blight, "DuBois and the Struggle," 59.

5. Walter Benjamin, "These on the Philosophy of History," in *Illuminations,* ed. Hannah Arendt, trans. Harry Zohn, 1955 (New York: Schocken, 1978), 257.

6. Glen Ligon, "To Disembark," November 11, 1993-February 20, 1994, Hirshorn Museum, Washington, D.C.

7. James Baldwin and Margaret Meade, *A Rap on Race* (New York: Dell, 1971) quoted in Byron Kim, "An Interview with Glen Ligon," in *Glen Ligon Un/Becoming,* ed. Judith Tannenbaum (Philadelphia: Institute of Contemporary Art, University of Pennsylvania, 1998), 54.

8. Brian Philip Harper, "Nationalism and Social Division in Black Arts Poetry of the 1960s," in *African American Literary Theory: A Reader,* ed. Winston Napier (New York: NYU Press, 2000), 461.

9. See Mike Sell, "The Black Arts Movement: Performance, Neo-Orality, and the Destruction of the 'White Thing,'" in *African American Performance and Theater History: A Critical Reader,* ed. Harry J. Elam, Jr., and David Krasner (New York: Oxford University Press, 2001), 56-80.

10. See Harper, "Nationalism and Social Division," 460-74. See David Lionel Smith, "The Black Arts Movement and Its Critics," *American Literary History* 1 (spring 1991): 93-113.

11. Suzan-Lori Parks, "An Equation for Black People Onstage," in *The American Play and Other Works,* 20.

12. Byron Kim, "An Interview with Glen Ligon," in Tannenbaum, *Glen Ligon Un/Becoming,* 54.

13. Giorgio Agamben, "Project for a Review," in *Infancy and History: Essays on the Destruction of Experience,* trans. Liz Heron (London: Verso, 1993), 148.

14. Marion McClinton, quoted by John Lahr, "Been Here and Gone," *New Yorker,* April 16, 2001, 54.

15. Lahr, "Been Here and Gone," 54.

16. August Wilson, quoted by Sandra Shannon, "August Wilson's Autobiography," in *Memory and Cultural Politics,* ed. Amritjit Singh, Joseph T. Skerret, Jr., and Robert E. Hogan (Boston: Northeastern University Press, 1996), 179-180.

17. He wrote his play of the 1970s, *Jitney,* in 1979 and then revised it from 1996 to 2000; *Ma Rainey's Black Bottom,* set in 1927, was his first play to come to Broadway in 1984; *Fences,* which Wilson places in 1957, received the Pulitzer Prize in 1987; the action of *Joe Turner's Come and Gone,* occurs in 1911, but the play won the New York Drama Critics Circle Award for 1987-88; *Piano Lesson,* his play of the 1940s, won the Pulitzer Prize in 1990; while *Two Trains Running* is set in 1969, it premiered on Broadway in April 1992; *Seven Guitars* plays out in 1948 and won the New York Drama Critics Circle Award for 1996; *King Hedley II,* with its events transpiring during the decade of the 1980s, came to New York in April 2001; and *Gem of the Ocean,* set in 1904, premiered at the Goodman Theatre in Chicago in April 2003.

18. August Wilson, quoted by Kim Powers, "An Interview with August Wilson," *Theater* 16, no. 1 (1984): 52.

19. Chris Jones, "Homeward Bound: August Wilson," *American Theatre,* November 1999, 16.

20. August Wilson, "American Histories: Chasing Dreams and Nightmares; Sailing the Stream of Black Culture," *New York Times,* April 23, 2000, sec. 2.1.

21. August Wilson, quoted by John Lahr, "Been There and Gone," 54.

22. See Lynn Nottage, *Crumbs from the Table of Joy* (New York: Dramatist Play Service, 1998); Kathleen Collins, *The Brothers,* in *Nine Plays by Black Women,* ed. Margaret Wilkerson (New York: New American Library, 1986), 293-346.

23. Karen D'Souza, "Teaching the Fine Points of 'The Piano Lesson,'" *San Jose Mercury News,* March 25, 2001, sec. E.9.

24. My thanks to Ebony E. A. Coletu for her email conversation and her recommendations for this section.

25. See August Wilson, preface to *Three Plays by August Wilson* (Pittsburgh: University of Pittsburgh Press, 1991), xii.

26. Ralph Ellison, *The Invisible Man* (1947; rpt. New York: Vintage, 1995), 9.

27. August Wilson, "The Ground on Which I Stand," *American Theatre,* September 1996, 16.

28. Sandra Richards, "Yoruba Gods on the American Stage: August Wilson's *Joe Turner's Come and Gone,*" *Research in African Literatures* 30, no. 4 (1999): 100.

29. Richards, "Yoruba Gods," 101.

James Robert Saunders (essay date 2006)

SOURCE: Saunders, James Robert. "'I done seen a hundred niggers play baseball better than Jackie Robinson': Troy Maxson's Plea in August Wilson's *Fences*." In *Baseball/Literature/Culture: Essays, 2004-2005,* edited by Peter Carino, pp. 46-52. Jefferson, N.C.: McFarland and Company, 2006.

[*In the essay that follows, Saunders uses the character of Troy in* Fences *to comment on the opportunities available to blacks in the 1950s, comparing Troy with Josh Gibson, the real-life and exceptionally talented Negro League ballplayer who died at the age of thirty-five, never having been allowed to play in the major leagues.*]

It goes without saying that Jackie Robinson's entrance into Major League Baseball in 1947 was one of the most significant events in American cultural history. Prior to that time, blacks, even those who excelled mightily at the sport, were relegated to playing in a segregated baseball league without the fame or fortune that accrued to similarly gifted, and sometimes less gifted, white players of that era. But just as significant, as the event of Robinson breaking the color barrier, is the notion that he was not the best that the Negro leagues had to offer for what came to be known in some corners as baseball's "noble experiment."

Consider, for example, that on the same Kansas City Monarchs team where Dodgers general manager Branch Rickey found Robinson, there was also Satchel Paige, an incomparable pitcher so good, says historian Robert Peterson, that he pitched 100 no-hitters; so good that he would vow to strike out the opposing team's first six or nine men, and then promptly make good on that promise; so good that on occasion he would call in his entire outfield and then pitch without them, becoming in effect a one-man team daring the opposing batter to even be able to hit the ball past the infield, if he could hit the

ball at all (140-41). Such were the talents of Paige, a player whom Branch Rickey could not have helped being aware of, and yet he declined to make the pitcher an offer to join the Brooklyn Dodgers organization.

Among the numerous Negro League teams that Rickey could have chosen from were the Philadelphia Stars, the Newark Eagles, the Memphis Red Sox, the Cleveland Buckeyes, and the Birmingham Black Barons. Players he could have chosen ranged from Walter "Buck" Leonard, the black Lou Gehrig, to James "Cool Papa" Bell, who legend had it was so fast that he could click a light switch off and be in bed before it got dark. The list goes on in terms of other players who might have been chosen.

Many who played with Robinson in the Negro Leagues contend that he was not even close to being the best ballplayer among them. His Monarch teammate Othello Renfroe asserted, "We had a lot of ballplayers we thought were better ballplayers" (Heaphy 201). Buck Leonard declared, "We didn't think he was too good—at that time" (Heaphy 201). Rickey himself admitted that what he was looking for went beyond just the desire for a great ballplayer. He was in search of a person with the right disposition, someone who could withstand all the insults that the first black player in the majors was bound to face and turn the other cheek. Robinson's biographer Arnold Rampersad describes how, in interviewing the ballplayer, Rickey actually

> stripped off his coat and enacted out a variety of parts that portrayed examples of an offended Jim Crow. Now he was a white hotel clerk rudely refusing Jack accommodations; now a supercilious white waiter in a restaurant; now a brutish railroad conductor. He became a foul-mouthed opponent, Jack recalled, talking about "my race, my parents, in language that was almost unendurable." Now he was a vengeful base runner, vindictive spikes flashing in the sun, sliding into Jack's black flesh—"How do you like that, nigger boy?" At one point, he swung his pudgy fist at Jack's head. Above all, he insisted, Jack could not strike back. He could not explode in righteous indignation; only then would this experiment be likely to succeed.

[127]

In the interview, Robinson was able to convince Rickey that he was indeed the right choice. The interviewee was not only a ballplayer but also a graduate of UCLA and a retired Army officer. It is understandable how Rickey took everything into consideration and came to the conclusion that Robinson was the right man for the job in spite of not being the most gifted player that the Negro Leagues had to offer.

The irony of the situation was not lost on the playwright August Wilson, who grew up in Pittsburgh, and most certainly was familiar with the exploits of Josh

Gibson, the black Babe Ruth who, as Peterson reports, hit 89 home runs in a single season (158) and "hit the longest home run ever struck in Yankee Stadium" (160). And that's taking into consideration all the home runs that Ruth hit when he played for the Yankees. It is conceivable then that had he been able to play in the Major Leagues, Gibson might have proven to be even better than the Babe. Limited to playing in the Negro Leagues, though, Gibson was ultimately not allowed to fulfill his vast potential.

In the play *Fences,* Wilson has his main character, Troy Maxson, observe, "I saw Josh Gibson's daughter yesterday. She walking around with raggedy shoes on her feet" (9). The play is set in 1957, just ten years after Robinson broke the color line. Gibson had played out his years with the Negro League's Homestead Grays, Homestead being located just outside the Pittsburgh city limits. In spite of Robinson's great achievement in joining the majors, the tragedy that Wilson wants us to acknowledge is that so many other blacks, including Gibson, were denied that opportunity and the consequences go beyond just Gibson's generation but extend to at least one subsequent generation as symbolized by Troy's sighting of Gibson's daughter with her "raggedy shoes."

Troy's wife Rose tries to ease some of that sense of tragedy by pointing out, "They got a lot of colored baseball players now. Jackie Robinson was the first. Folks had to wait for Jackie Robinson" (9). Her fear, even as she reminds Troy of that positive development, is that her husband will soon drink himself to death, unable to bear the weight of the hand that fate has dealt him. In his prime, Troy batted .432 with 37 home runs in a single season, surely good enough to gain him a spot in the majors if he had only been a white man.

So when his wife, in an effort to ease her husband's torment, draws particular attention to the reality that *now* baseball's color line has been broken, her husband rails back at her with his own dose of reality that is just as crucial as the breaking of the color line was itself. To her assertion of what Robinson has done, Troy responds, "I done seen a hundred niggers play baseball better than Jackie Robinson. Hell, I know some teams Jackie Robinson couldn't even make!" (10). The statement that Troy makes is worthy of consideration. As I mentioned earlier, the great likelihood is that there were quite a few players in the Negro leagues who were better than Robinson. The question, however, concerns just how many were there? And were there actually teams in the Negro leagues that it would have been difficult for Robinson to make? These are questions that, however vital, will be extremely difficult to answer.

We will recall how Robinson's Kansas City teammate Buck Leonard did not think that he was all that good a player. But then in retrospect that teammate would admit, "Of course now we see what he really did. You know, you can be wrong about a ballplayer. You can look at him and don't think much of him, and then he turns out to be one of the best ballplayers of all time" (Heaphy 201). However, a retrospective of the sort that Leonard rendered was not so hard to do. In his first year with the Dodgers, Robinson batted .297, led the team both in stolen bases with 29, and in runs scored with 125. He also tied with teammate Pee Wee Reese for most home runs with 12. For those first-year feats, he was awarded Rookie of the Year. Before his career was over, he would win the Most Valuable Player award in 1949, play in six All-Star games and six World Series, and be elected into the Baseball Hall of Fame.

Still, the question remains as to how good he was compared to other Negro league players. When Troy says there were teams that Jackie Robinson could not have made, we suspect that this much is an exaggeration, more the grumblings of a person denied opportunity than an account of how things really were. Langston Hughes, in his poem "Harlem," warns of what might happen to a person whose dreams are left tragically unfulfilled. One possibility is that the dream dries up "like a raisin in the sun" (268). On the other hand, the unfulfilled dreamer might just explode, and this latter possibility is what Troy's life has in some sense become, a series of explosions evidenced, for example, by the manner that he responds to the mere mention of Robinson's name.

Jealousy is part of the reason that Troy is so angry. Who knows but that he might have been able to accomplish what Robinson achieved had he not, as Troy's friend Bono puts it, "come along too early" (9). One of Troy's difficulties is, just as the literary critic John Timpane describes, that he refuses to accept "that his own time has passed" (74). His baseball playing days are over, and he has been relegated to the sidelines for a front-seat view of changing times. Proud and joyous times, they may be for some; a terribly tragic trick is how Troy Maxson sees it.

It is interesting to note that Josh Gibson died in 1947, the same year that Robinson broke into the majors. That is quite a coincidence, and Robert Peterson informs us that "Gibson himself had had two tantalizing nibbles that suggested he might become the first to cross the line. In 1939, Wendell Smith of the *Pittsburgh Courier* reported that Bill Benswanger, president of the Pittsburgh Pirates, had promised a trial for Josh and Buck Leonard" (169). It is fascinating to contemplate the different course that baseball history would have taken had blacks broken the color barrier as early as 1939. It is equally fascinating to ponder what a difference it would have made in Gibson's own life if he had been the one chosen to do what Robinson would finally do eight years later.

Watching the actor James Earl Jones playing the part of Troy Maxson, as he did in the mid-1980s at the Yale Repertory Theatre and on Broadway, was like watching an aging Josh Gibson. At six-foot-one and well over 200 pounds, Gibson was a large man, especially for his times. Jones is similarly large and has added the weight that so often comes with the passing of the years. The spectacle of Jones, in his older years, standing on stage, wielding a baseball bat, that he purports to still be able to swing with some effectiveness, reminds us of the quintessential aging athlete lost in his own reveries of a time that has long since disappeared.

Like Troy Maxson, Gibson resorted to alcohol in an effort to alleviate the pain, the latter man ultimately dying as the result of what could be considered a stroke. Peterson is quick to add, however, that "there are those who believe his death was caused by his disappointment at being denied the opportunity to play in the big leagues" (168). In other words, having to watch Jackie Robinson get the once-in-a-lifetime chance to play in the major leagues, just at the time when he himself was playing out the last weeks of his own severely limited career, was more than he, even with his massive physical strength, could handle. Did he really die of a stroke at the age 35? Or did he die of a broken heart, more difficult to diagnose from a strictly medical standpoint, but just as deadly in the final analysis.

In Troy Maxson we are privy to a character of Gibson-like proportions, and through the playwright's art we are allowed to imagine how it might have been if Gibson, instead of dying at age 35, had lived to be age 53. When the play opens, it is the late 1950s, and Troy's son, Cory, is being recruited by a North Carolina college, to play football. In that situation, Troy's response to his son is: "I don't care where he coming from. The white man ain't gonna let you get nowhere with that football noway. You go on and get your book-learning so you can work yourself up in that A & P or learn how to fix cars or build houses or something, get you a trade. That way you have something can't nobody take away from you" (35).

Troy's experience with baseball has left him jaded, to say the least. And if the North Carolina institution is a white school, Troy is right to be very concerned. True, the *Brown v. Board of Education* decision had been rendered three years earlier. The Supreme Court had insisted that all public institutions be integrated. And now

this is Cory's chance. He is evidently a talented football player. But what will it be like when he arrives on that white college campus in the South in the late 1950s? Will he be allowed to perform up to his potential when the coaches will have so much pressure to play less talented white athletes? Will he and a handful of other black football players be the only blacks on campus? Will he even get his college degree? There are those who will argue that Troy is wrong to discourage his son from accepting the athletic scholarship. The father is jealous for having "come along too early" to have benefited from such an opportunity himself. It is as if he is being tormented by the Jackie Robinson phenomenon all over again.

But if one listens closely to Troy's demands on his son, one hears the intonations of Booker T. Washington who advocated industrial education as the necessary steppingstone for future black advancement. In his autobiography *Up From Slavery,* Washington defended his position, asserting

> one man may go into a community prepared to supply the people there with an analysis of Greek sentences. The community may not at that time be prepared for, or feel the need of, Greek analysis, but it may feel its need of bricks and houses and wagons. . . . Every student who came to Tuskegee, no matter what his financial ability might be, must learn some industry. . . . I lost no opportunity to go into as many parts of the state as I could, for the purpose of speaking to the parents, and showing them the value of industrial education. Besides, I talked to the students constantly on the subject. Notwithstanding the unpopularity of industrial work, the school continued to increase in numbers.

[109]

The Tuskegee principal was determined that his students be trained in fields that would make them useful once they graduated and had to fend for themselves out in society.

Similarly, Troy's main concern is with Cory's long-term survival. The father is trying to help his son avoid the pain of rejection that he himself experienced decades earlier. When Troy insists on auto mechanics or carpentry or grocery store employment as good options, he is urging his son to be safe, to build on a firmer foundation than what the dream of an athletic career generally allows. As a concerned father, he is an advocate for achieving some level of security as opposed to taking what he perceives as an unnecessary risk. And yet, just as was the case with Booker T. Washington, Troy can be viewed as significantly ambiguous. For example, at his public sanitation job, he is actually something of an activist, fighting to be a driver instead of a "lifter," fighting to dismantle a racist system where previously all the drivers had been white and all the lifters black. As jaded as he is, and perhaps much of that jadedness is a consequence of being a realist, he believes in the same cause for which Jackie Robinson stood—a society where equality of opportunity exists. The anguish comes, for Troy and others who are just like him, in waiting for that day to arrive.

Works Cited

Heaphy, Leslie. *The Negro Leagues, 1869-1960.* Jefferson, NC: McFarland, 2003.

Hughes, Langston. *Selected Poems of Langston Hughes.* 1959. New York: Alfred A. Knopf, 1988.

Peterson, Robert. *Only the Ball Was White.* New York: Oxford UP, 1992.

Rampersad, Arnold. *Jackie Robinson.* New York: Alfred A. Knopf, 1997.

Timpane, John, "Filling the Time: Reading History in the Drama of August Wilson." *May All Your Fences Have Gates: Essays on the Drama of August Wilson.* Ed. Alan Nadel. Iowa City: U of Iowa P, 1994. 67-85.

Washington, Booker T. *Up From Slavery.* 1901. New York: Bantam, 1970.

Wilson, August. *Fences.* New York: Plume, 1987.

FURTHER READING

Criticism

Jackson R. Bryer and Mary C. Hartig, eds. *Conversations with August Wilson.* Jackson: University Press of Mississippi, 2006, 260 p..
  Contains exchanges between Wilson and interviewers including Michael Feingold, Bill Moyers, Vera Sheppard, and Carol Rosen, conducted between 1984 and 2004.

Koprince, Susan. "Baseball as History and Myth in August Wilson's *Fences.*" *African American Review* 40, no. 2 (summer 2006): 349-58.
  Claims that in *Fences* Wilson used the metaphorical association between baseball and the notions of optimism and democratic freedom to subvert the idea of the American dream, which the play reveals as excluding African Americans.

Benjamin Zephaniah
1958-

Cambridge Jones/Getty Images Entertainment/Getty Images

(Full name Benjamin Obadiah Iqbal Zephaniah) English poet, playwright, children's book author, and writer of radio and television plays.

INTRODUCTION

Known as Britain's Rastafarian poet, Zephaniah writes political verse which advocates social justice and racial equality. He has made a name for himself with his high-energy and charismatic spoken-word and recorded performances, which have attracted popular and critical attention and are often broadcast on British television and radio. Zephaniah has also written several radio and television plays and children's books, and has recorded music.

BIOGRAPHICAL INFORMATION

Zephaniah was born in 1958 in Birmingham, England. He spent most of his youth in Jamaica, however, and was influenced by his mother's recitation of poetry and the tapes of Jamaican poets that were played in the household when he was a child. He began to perform in poetry competitions and became known for his ability to create poems that entertained audiences at churches, community centers, and on street corners. As a teen, he began to have discipline problems and left school at the age of fourteen. Around that time he was jailed for burglary. After being released, he decided to channel his energy into music and poetry. He worked as a reggae DJ in Handsworth, where he continued to develop his own poetic and performance style. In 1979 he moved to London and published his first poetry collection, *Pen Rhythm* (1980). Five years later, his first play, *Playing the Right Tune,* was staged in London. He was appointed writer-in-residence at the Africa Arts Collective in Liverpool in 1989 and has been a creative artist in residence at Cambridge University. A political activist, he became involved with the Rastafarian movement and adopted a vegan lifestyle, both of which profoundly affected his life and career. He also has worked as an actor on television shows and written several television and radio plays, one of which, *Listen to Your Parents* (2000), won the 2001 Race in the Media Radio Drama Award from the Commission for Racial Equality. In 1998 he became an advisor on the arts and music for the National Advisory Committee on Creative and Cultural Education. He has also made several well-received musical and spoken-word recordings. In 2003 he garnered much publicity for refusing to become an Officer of the Order of the British Empire (OBE), an award bestowed by the British government, explaining that the title reminded him of the brutality inflicted on his ancestors by imperialist powers. He has received several honorary doctorates, including from the University of North London and the University of Exeter.

MAJOR WORKS

Politics plays a central role in Zephaniah's work. As a prolific writer and well-known public figure, Zephaniah has written poetry, children's books, and plays that explore such topics as problems in Israel, the dangers of imperialism and capitalism, the evils of slavery, issues of national identity, and the need for social justice in contemporary society. Much of his work reflects his feelings about the racial discrimination encountered by minorities, especially by young black men in England. For example, in one of his young adult novels, *Refugee Boy* (2001), a young boy, Alem Kelo, is abandoned in London by his father, who hopes his son will escape the violence of the Ethiopian-Eritrean war. Placed with a kindly Irish foster family, Alem faces discrimination but perseveres despite legal troubles and the death of both of his parents. In one of Zephaniah's best-known poems, "Dis Policeman Keeps on Kicking Me to Death," he charged that black men are subject to police brutality; the issue is very personal for him, as his cousin, Michael Powell, was killed as a result of police brutality in Birmingham. Not only does Zephaniah denounce the racial discrimination black people experience in Britain, he also condemns the violence against women endemic in many cultures. His Rastafarian beliefs permeate his verse and many of his poems touch on animal rights, veganism, and the central role marijuana plays in the Rastafarian ideology. "Ganja Rock," for example, encourages believers to cultivate and smoke marijuana to attain mental emancipation and to fight for the legalization of the drug. Critics note that many of his poems are directly influenced by his involvement with music, particularly hip-hop and reggae, as well as the rhythms of his popular spoken-word poetry performances.

CRITICAL RECEPTION

Zephaniah has achieved prominence as a popular but controversial British poet and performer as well as a playwright, actor, and public figure. Reviewers have compared the explicit political content and highly charged anger in his verse to gangster rap, and praise his wit, intellectual rigor, and trenchant social and political commentary. Some recognize Zephaniah as a courageous and revolutionary voice for minorities experiencing racial, economic, and gender discrimination worldwide; others charge that his verse is shallow, childish doggerel that is cynically calculated to appeal to youthful sensibilities. These detractors unfavorably compare his verse and performances to Jamaican singer-songwriter Bob Marley and charge that, unlike Marley, Zephaniah is not fully committed to his revolutionary voice. Noting his association with the British literary establishment, they accuse Zephaniah of "selling out" to the very institution he criticizes. Despite the mixed critical reaction to his work, commentators agree that

Zephaniah is a charismatic poet and playwright who does not flinch from exploring controversial and sensitive issues.

PRINCIPAL WORKS

Pen Rhythm (poetry) 1980
The Dread Affair (poetry) 1985
Playing the Right Tune (play) 1985
Job Rocking (play) 1987
Hurricane Dub (radio play) 1988
Delirium (play) 1990
Our Teacher's Gone Crazy (television play) 1990
Streetwise (play) 1990
Dread Poets Society (television play) 1991
The Trial of Mickey Tekka (play) 1991
City Psalms (poetry) 1992
Out of the Night (poetry) 1994
Talking Turkeys (children's poetry) 1994
Funky Chickens (children's poetry) 1996
Propa Propaganda (poetry) 1996
School's Out (poetry) 1997
Face (young adult novel) 1999
Listen to Your Parents (radio play) 2000
The Little Book of Vegan Poems: Explicit Vegan Lyrics (poetry) 2000
Wicked World! (children's poetry) 2000
Refugee Boy (young adult novel) 2001
Too Black, Too Strong (poetry) 2001
We Are Britain! (poetry) 2002
Gangsta Rap (young adult novel) 2004
Prostate (play) 2006
J Is for Jamaica (juvenilia) 2007
Teacher's Dead (young adult novel) 2007

CRITICISM

Darren J. N. Middleton (essay date 1999)

SOURCE: Middleton, Darren J. N. "Chanting down Babylon: Three Rastafarian Dub Poets." In *'This Is How We Flow': Rhythm in Black Cultures,* edited by Angela M. S. Nelson, pp. 74-86. Columbia: University of South Carolina Press, 1999.

[*In the excerpt that follows, Middleton considers Zephaniah's Rastafarian beliefs through an examination of his religious verse.*]

Introduction

Fortified by a mighty arsenal of word and rhythm power, the Jamaican singer-songwriter Bob Marley used his Rastafarian religious beliefs in an often bitter and protracted campaign against Christian missionary propaganda and capitalist imperialism. That was in the sixties and seventies. Since then, however, Rastafarian reggae and "dub poetry" has catapulted to the status of popularist art form. Today, an ever-increasing plethora of Afro-Caribbean poets are mixing their own Molotov cocktails of trenchant social commentary with militant, black liberation theology. Armed with potent lyrical grenades, contemporary Rastafarian "dub poets" are now launching their own Marley-inspired musical call to resistance. In this essay, I briefly examine the religious poetry of three such Rastafarian dub poets: Mikey Smith, Mutabaruka, and Benjamin Zephaniah. Possessed with intense focus and singular purpose, their nontraditional verse and unique rhythmic expression seeks to raise the consciousness of the hearer in a manner not unlike the Hebrew prophets and psalmists of ages ago.

The Way of the Black Messiah: The Roots of Rastafari

At the height of his powers in the late twenties, Marcus Garvey urged the poor underclass of a tiny Caribbean isle fervently to look to their African homeland for the imminent crowning of a king. Like some latter-day John the Baptist, Garvey and his "prophecy" helped to lay the foundation for the man who was to come and save the African diaspora from physical and mental slavery. And so, when Ras Tafari, son of Ras Makonem of Harar, finally was crowned in Ethiopia in the early thirties, black nationalists and influential preachers in Jamaica found new meaning in timeworn biblical verses. Of particular importance is Psalm 68:31: "Princes shall soon come out of Egypt; Ethiopia shall stretch forth her hand unto God. Behold Philistine and Tyre with Ethiopia: my son was born there." This, along with a host of other biblical verses, served only to confirm that Ethiopia had a special relationship with God. Not everyone agreed with this hermeneutic, however, for it appeared severely to anger those Christian missionaries and white colonialists intent on believing in Africa as the primitive, dark continent.

At his coronation, Ras Tafari took a number of theological titles to go along with others of a more regal nature: King of Kings and Lord of Lords, Elect of God, the Conquering Lion of the Tribe of Judah, and Power of the Trinity: Haile Selassie I. Terms such as these recall famous verses from the Christian New Testament Book of Revelation and, in one way or another, they were used in preacherly discourse by Leonard Howell, Joseph Hibbert, and Archibald Dunkley to "verify" Haile Selassie's divine status. In time, of course, early

Rastafarian believers began to develop their credo to include the eschatological hope that Selassie I would help repatriate the black diaspora back to Ethiopia: the Black Man's Vine and Fig Tree.

Early Rastafarian preachment was enormously popular among the ghetto youth of Jamaica. A prototype of the liberation theology that is so vital in Latin America today, the Afrocentric thrust of Rastafarian beliefs initially provided much-needed hope and the possibility of improved life to a people long since marginalized and dispossessed by colonial rule. In the late thirties, then, Rastafarianism flourished throughout Jamaica with the force and veracity of a forest fire in summertime.

Since then, the mission field for Rastafarian preachers has extended beyond the boundaries of the crumbling and often violent projects of Western Kingston. Today, Rastafarianism is a worldwide phenomenon and is no longer confined to the lower socioeconomic classes.[1] In spite of this globalization, however, Rastafarian devotees continue to remember their humble roots. That is, contemporary Rastas continue to play an active part in Jamaican life by offering a social ministry for the poor. At the center of modern Rastafarianism, we could say, is an Africanized theology of hope for those caught up in a web of despondency: a Way of the Black Messiah. And nowhere is this ministerial vocation more dramatically worked out than in the lives of those Rastafarians dedicated to the use of language—revered today as a holy tool—to effect social and political *metanoia* in our time.

The Righteous Wail of the Soul: Origins of "Dub Poetry" in Jamaica

Jamaica's native tongue is a unique form of Creole patois. This is an elusive dialect of English that owes a great deal both to African tribal vernacular and to the colonial plantation owners of the eighteenth and nineteenth centuries. One person stands out, however, as the pioneer of poetry written in patois ("dub poetry"). She is Louise Coverley Bennett, a.k.a. "Miss Lou." Originally educated at London's Royal Academy of Dramatic Arts in the early decades of this century, Miss Lou is credited with introducing a language often considered by colonial educators as too "uncouth" for "genuine" creative writing. To this day, however, she defends her use of patois with the claim that it was the "ordinary" discourse of the influential oral storytellers of her youth. That is, it was the life's blood of a people run down by centuries of systemic oppression or, better put, the natural linguistic mode for men and women who knew the liberating power of parable and story in a time of harsh enslavement. Here is a brief quotation from her famous poem "Back to Africa":

> Back to Africa Miss Matty?
> Yuh no know wa yuh dah sey?
> Yuh haffe come from some weh fus,
> Before yuh go back deh?[2]

Of course, Miss Lou's preference for the "language of the people" has its parallels in non-Jamaican writing as well. Consider Nikos Kazantzakis, the Cretan novelist, and his controversial use of the "demotic" form of modern Greek in his epic tome *Odyssey: A Modern Sequel.* Kazantzakis delights in the use of words and phrases familiar to the peasants of Greece—the fisherman and the coppersmith—but which are disconcertingly unfamiliar to the intelligentsia.

A similar reverence for the oral tradition—with its own special lexicon, strange spelling, and unfamiliar idiom—continues to be the chosen form of Rastafarian poets today. As a corollary, Rastafarian poets hardly ever pay attention either to grammar or established laws of poetry. There are some, like the poet U-Roy, who possess a keen eye for "grammatical correctness," but for the most part it proves very difficult to find a Rastafarian poem that is written in traditional meter (in English, the ten-syllable unrhymed iambic line of five beats)! Why is this? There are at least two reasons. First, the "educated" concern for "correct" language use in creative writing is viewed as far too stylized, restrictive, and oppressively Western. By contrast, Jamaican dialect is seen as vibrant, alive, and unable to sustain an interest in so-called "grammatical exactness"; it is the dub poets who have always known how best to create strong messages out of patois' unique and powerful word stock. Second, Rastafarian dub poets consider social conscience to be a more pressing concern than any zeal for the "educated" observance of "acceptable" literary form; it is the dub poets who have always worked hard to keep the conflagration of social resistance and community rebellion burning. In short, Rastafarian dub poetry is not a refined, classically aesthetic product. It chiefly is an evolving and dynamic grasping and re-grasping of the theological significance of current events. Mikey Smith, the dub poet whose work I will examine, puts it this way:

> We haffi really look into the whole thing of the language thing, because sometime it is used in a negative sense as a hindrance to your progress, and people think seh, "Boy, why don't you communicate in Standard English?" Standard English is good to be communicated, but you must also communicate in what you also comfortable in. And what is widely being used by your own people from which you draw these source. So that's why me communicate da way deh. And if me can really spend some time fi try to learn the Englishman language and so, the Englishman can spend some time fi learn wha me seh too, you know.[3]

. . . . .

CAPITALISM IN A POETIC HEADLOCK: THE DUB POETRY OF BENJAMIN ZEPHANIAH

Although born in England, Benjamin Obadiah Iqbal Zephaniah spent the best part of his youth in Jamaica. His adolescent years, by all accounts, were traumatic and controversial. For example, he found himself taken out of his assigned comprehensive school at the tender age of twelve, largely because of discipline problems, and appeared then to have all the makings of an incorrigible ruffian. He arrived in London, however, at age twenty-two, and immediately set about writing verse for himself. Early books such as *Pen Rhythm* and *The Dread Affair* were received with critical acclaim, and this in spite of the fact that he sees his role chiefly as a "performance poet" rather than one who works with the page in mind.

Zephaniah has toured throughout the world, earning himself rave reviews for the dramatic manner in which he delivers his verse, and at one stage was shortlisted for two prestigious writing posts: Creative Artist in Residence at the University of Cambridge, and Regius Professor of Poetry at the University of Oxford. Sadly, he was forced to endure malicious treatment at the hands of the British tabloid media during the selection process for both positions. That is, the so-called "gutter-press" in the United Kingdom seized on Zephaniah's "approved school" background, seeking to create a climate of fear in the minds of the selection committee, yet the press omitted to mention that Zephaniah has spent many years visiting schools, youth clubs, and teacher-training centers in order to hold workshops in creative writing.

Like that of the other two poets in this survey, Benjamin Zephaniah's Rastafarian poetry fits hand in glove with his political interests. In Great Britain, for example, he has served as chairperson of a number of housing and workers cooperatives, women's refuge centers, and theater groups. Not surprisingly, in his poetry he refuses to shy away from a rigorous and forthright analysis of the current British cultural scene. In **"Dread John Counsel,"** he chronicles the slow, invidious decay of a political system that deprives black men and women of a genuine sense of identity and belonging:

> In this land my brothers and some sisters fight me down
> therefore in the dark place and the jailhouse I am found
> but I have a weapon that shall burn the enemy
> and it has a fallout that shall rule equality,
> the court is revolutionary the righteous ones shall stand
> and in the tabernacle there doth play a reggae band
> there is no House of Commons and everyone is high
> and this kingdom is governed by a upfull one called I,
> but I am here in exile so far away from home
> still in this sick captivity I will not use their comb.[4]

The comb reference requires some explanation. One of the most striking symbols of identity in the Rastafarian faith is the wearing of distinctive plaits or matted hair called dreadlocks. This brings to mind the Masai or Galla Warriors of Eastern Africa as well as the law in Leviticus 19:27. Rastafarians refuse to shave or cut their hair and, sometimes, will not use a comb either.

The net result is that to see a gathering of Rastas is like witnessing the mighty and gracious movement of a pride of lions—primary symbol of African strength. Here Zephaniah's reference to "their comb" is a symbol for his trenchant moral resistance—itself inspired by Leviticus 19:27—to Babylon, and its many instruments of oppression:

> we are not too fussy 'bout being British free
> the kingdom's international a kingdom we can see,
> they will never give us what we really earn
> come our liberation and see the table turn,
> still this is me in exile so far away from home
> still recruiting soldiers to break this modern Rome.[5]

One controversial aspect of Rastafarian belief is the frequent use of marijuana as a holy herb. It is often referred to as the "weed of wisdom." This is because of the legend that "ganja" purportedly was found on the grave of King Solomon, and because "sinsemillia" is thought to assist the believer in times of intense theological reflection, or "grounation" sessions. Rastas defend its use in three other ways.

First, the Bible appears to support the smoking of herb. Consider Genesis 1:29, "And God said, 'Behold, I have given you every herb bearing seed, which is upon the face of the earth, and every tree, in which is the fruit of a tree yielding seed; to you it shall be for meat.'" In addition, Revelation 22:2 speaks of "the leaves of the tree" that are for "the healing of the nations."

Second, this last verse underscores the general belief among Rastas that ganja has an enormous calming effect on the consumer, reducing psychological tension and helping the believer to acquire keenness of spiritual insight. The "healing of the nations" reference is often used by Rastas to refer to ganja's proven ability to assist in curing glaucoma and other illnesses.

Third, Rastas believe that ganja's functional purpose may be likened to the use of incense and/or bread and wine in the Christian church. That is, it is an aid to reflexive worship and sometimes takes on the quality of being a sacrament for the pious devotee. The believer is not obliged to use ganja if he or she does not wish to do so; rather, Rastas are encouraged to see its positive benefits and to decide for themselves.

Benjamin Zephaniah versifies this particular aspect of Rastafarian theology in his **"Ganja Rock."** That the holy herb inspires reflection ("third eyesight") is clear from the first stanza:

> Sip one time, sip two time
> 'til the mood is right,
> hold a cool meditation
> gain a third eyesight
> as from time begun show your love for the sun
> 'cause as you burn you learn,
> start from now for sure somehow
> everyone must get their turn.[6]

Not surprisingly, the public or private use of marijuana still is outlawed in most countries around the world. Against this practice, Zephaniah's **"Ganja Rock"** is an explicit preachment to cultivate, nurture, and smoke your own weed—all in the name of reverence for what nature supplies us with, and our own mental emancipation!

> lawmakers don't like ganja rock
> but if you look at the right clock
> I am sure you'll see it's ganja time,
> so liberate this ital weed
> it gives I headside vital feed
> and show them using herb is not no crime.[7]

As we have seen, the Christian New Testament Book of Revelation is often used by Rastafarians to "verify" many aspects of their theological beliefs. For instance, recall the connections between Haile Selassie's many regal titles and the apocalyptic figure of the Conquering Lion of the Tribe of Judah in Revelation 5:5, and the use of the "healing of the nations" reference in 22:2 to "support" the practice of smoking ganja in Rastafarian worship. In **"Dread Eyesight,"** Zephaniah crafts a poem based on the Final Judgment by transposing some of the familiar images from the Book of Revelation. The notorious "four horsemen of the apocalypse" are now the "four dreadlocks" who arrive at the End Times bearing a banner on which is written Selassie's name and many titles.[8] And it is the "elders" of the faithful Rastafarian community who herald the closing of history with life-giving words of inestimable salvational value:

> We are the children of slaves and the victims of oppression, so from the land in which we are removed to let us shout with a voice that vibrates with dread and say to them men of earth, it is JAH RASTAFARI who giveth wisdom and understanding, for the land of Ethiopia has lifted up her heart, and the power of the trinity has opened the gates of Zion for the spirits of children who lived earth lives of great tribulation to enter therein.[9]

To close this brief account of Zephaniah's Rastafarian poetry, it is fitting to highlight one of the more important parallels between Smith, Mutabaruka, and Zephaniah: the Rastafarian belief in the divinity of every man and woman. For the Rastafarian, the spirit of Ras Tafari applies to all creation—rainfall, sunshine, etc. Yet is most fully incarnate in righteous men and women who abandon all belief that "God" is some supernatural reality "beyond them" and instead grasp the presence of Ras Tafari in all living things. In **"Can't Keep a Good Dread Down,"** Zephaniah joins Smith and Mutabaruka in their theological immanentism:

> The Lion of Judah has prevailed
> the Seven Seals is I
> no living in the grave no more
> King Fari will not die,
> no brainwashed education

for wisdom must top rank
if you want riches
you must check Selassie I bank . . .
. . . Selassie I keeps on coming
can't keep a good dread down
those that stood start running
when JAH JAH comes to town,
greater love keeps coming
Alpha is here wid us,
so stop praying to polluted air
and give rasta your trust.[10]

These last two lines indicate Zephaniah's belief in the utter futility of praying to the Christian missionary God "up there," and is further proof of Rastafarianism's this-worldly nature. Finally, the line "King Fari will not die" must surely denote Zephaniah's outright rejection, as Western propaganda, of the reports of Haile Selassie's death in 1976. For Zephaniah, as for most Rastas, it is impossible for God, who holds the power of death in his hands, to suffer and die. And it is deeply incongruous for a holy man, a man who purportedly incarnated God Himself, to suffer the biblical "wages of sin." For Zephaniah as well as the other two poets in this brief study, Rastafari liveth!

CONCLUSION: DUB POETS AS CONTEMPORARY PSALMISTS

It is a well-known fact that the Rastafarian community does not possess anything like the Christian systematic theological tomes of either John Calvin, Friedrich Schleiermacher, or Karl Barth. They probably never will. In one sense, though, this need not prove to be a threat to the flourishing of their faith. On the contrary, the sure and inevitable decline of vibrant and dynamically evolving religious belief arguably occurs when believers busy themselves with the "central tenets" of their faith, and with the recording of these as numbered theses in weighty books! Against the propositionally oriented tradition of Christian theology, then, Rastafarianism has the distinct advantage of keeping what it believes "in solution" through the use of concrete images, metaphors, and parables. Like the psalmists of Hebrew antiquity, contemporary Rastafarians proffer spirited contextual wordscapes, imagistic litanies, and a sense of the holy eternally renewed in the common. Crying out against societal injustice and appealing for comprehensive urban renewal, the Rastafarian dub poets—especially the three I have examined in this essay—are modern, urban psalmists in a world seemingly unredeemed, paralyzed by hatred and violence. Michael Smith, Mutabaruka, and Benjamin Zephaniah—all three may be counted as Rastafarian liberation theologians on a spirit-driven, God-given mission to chant down Babylon!

Notes

1. In this essay, I wish not to enumerate Rastafarian belief by numbered theses. In one important sense, this would be antithetical to the very dynamism of Rastafarianism, which, despite the "-ism," is far from monolithic. Here I want to give a brief account of the early development of this rich and varied religion and then explore specific beliefs in the poetry of the three writers I touch upon. Readers interested in learning systematically, however, may consult two of my earlier articles: "Rastafarianism: A Ministry for Social Change?" *Modern Churchman* n.s. 31, no. 3 (1989): 45-48; and "Poetic Liberation: Rastafarianism, Poetry, and Social Change." *Modern Churchman* n.s. 34, no. 2 (1992): 16-21.

2. Louise Bennett, "Back to Africa," in *Black Youth, Rastafarianism, and the Identity Crisis in Britain,* ed. Len Garrison (London: ACER Project Publication, 1979), 8.

3. See Mervyn Morris, "Mikey Smith: Dub Poet," *Jamaican Journal* 18 (1985):42.

4. Benjamin Zephaniah, *The Dread Affair* (London: Arena Publications, 1985), 54.

5. Ibid., 55.

6. Ibid., 60.

7. Ibid., 61.

8. Ibid., 79.

9. Ibid., 81.

10. Ibid., 24, 25.

Kwame Dawes (review date spring 2002)

SOURCE: Dawes, Kwame. Review of *Too Black, Too Strong,* by Benjamin Zephaniah. *World Literature Today* 76, no. 2 (spring 2002): 159-60.

[*In the following mixed review of* Too Black, Too Strong, *Dawes unfavorably compares Zephaniah with Bob Marley and laments the fact that Zephaniah, in his official capacity with the British Council, does not "recognize that he may have actually been co-opted by the very system he denounces."*]

In his introduction to his newest collection of poetry, Benjamin Zephaniah, easily one of the most recognized of popular British poets, declares that he is not interested in winning awards and that he writes what he feels about being in a world in which a whole litany of abuses of humanity exist. He proposes that his poetry is not as important as many things in the world, but that he chooses to write because he cannot stay silent. The introduction does something else: it establishes clearly that Zephaniah understands himself to be thoroughly British—a man with no anxiety about declaring his Britishness and his willingness to own that identity.

Too Black, Too Strong is political. In a short note introducing the poem **"The Men from Jamaica Are Settling Down,"** Zephaniah lets us know that the piece was first commissioned by a BBC-linked film company which eventually turned down the piece because the last two stanzas were too political and too confrontational. The poet takes pride in declaring that he will not compromise on the struggle. And there is more: Zephaniah is daring in the collection in that he does take on, as he promises, some tough targets. His poem lampooning UB40, the popular British reggae group, pulls no punches: "You came, you saw, you copied, / And the record company loved you, / But you can't swing it / Like a buffalo soldier / Or a dreadlocks Rasta, / U.B. robbing we." But the dissing of UB40 is clearly too easily rendered, and one is not quite sure why he chooses to do that. The thing is that UB40, for all its limp cover songs, had a far from unrootsy beginning. And in a world in which the glorious power of reggae to touch all cultures is supposedly a good thing, their copying could be seen by some as flattery. Not Zephaniah.

Still, his targets are not all so easy. His poem **"Christmas Has Been Shot"** tackles the troubles in Israel, detailing the irony of the shutting down of Bethlehem for Christmas by the Israeli government. Zephaniah takes sides, and his reading of the politics of religion and race is complex in its daring even if his resolutions are not pat. But poetry cannot be pat. And the list of targets goes on. At times it is not clear where the revolution intends to go. Revolutionary poets are often faced with a troubling dilemma. What is the point of writing when fighting might be more useful? Christopher Okigbo decided to put away his pen and take up a rifle; he died fighting in Biafra after leaving us with a slim volume of tantalizingly brilliant poems. Bob Marley declared in his exile song, "Heathen," "He who fights and runs away / Lives to fight another day," but he had tasted bullets when he wrote that. Still, he declared the rationale for his art, his revolutionary art: "We free the people with music / With music, oh music, oh music" ("Trenchtown").

Marley saw it fit to make great art, art that was full of the genius of phrasing, of metaphor, of allusion and the grace of his honesty. His art sought to transform. But there is a rootedness to Marley's craft. It is grounded in a tradition of proverb-making, psalm-chanting, prophetic lamentation, folk interplay, blues resilience, griot storytelling and mythmaking that always grants his work the gravitas of age and wisdom: "Roots natty, roots / Dread bingy dread? I and I a de roots." It is not just the language; it is the relationship with history and tradition. In Marley it is rich. Zephaniah, on the other hand, seems to be attempting to make something out of nothing, or at best something shallow. He is not fully committed to a dialect voice, nor does he dialogue with voices that seem to share the tradition of revolutionary voice he espouses. If he borrows from a poetic tradition, it is in a thinly read British verse tradition that he never stretches or challenges. In a sense, Zephaniah

sees in himself an affinity to Marley; but where Marley's craft almost always seemed to triumph by offering a sophisticated vessel upon which his psalms were spoken, craft sometimes fails Zephaniah.

Of course, it is grossly unfair to compare Zephaniah with Marley—after all, must every playwright be compared with Shakespeare? Still, one wants to know what Zephaniah has done with his access to Marley's model, since he understands himself to be an inheritor of Marley's reggae esthetic. Sadly, the connections are superficial. This does not mean that Zephaniah does not produce some good poetry. He does sometimes, and only when neither wit nor intellectual rigor fires the poems does he fail; only when one senses the poet seeking for posturing rather than for deeply worked-through observation do we see these failings. Refreshingly, there are moments which suggest that when the elements are right and when Zephaniah has the capacity for irony (*not* antithetical to radical thought, as some like to argue), he can write strong poems, such as **"Going Cheap"** or **"Naked."**

One would assume, based on Zephaniah's notes and some of his complaints in the poems, that he is a poet struggling for attention and respect in England. Yet in the act of complaint, we realize that Zephaniah is a rather privileged poet in the UK: "On one hand I think it my duty to travel the world for the British Council and other organizations, speaking my mind as I go, ranting, praising, and criticizing everything that makes me who I am, but this is what Britain can do. It is probably one of the only places that can take an angry, illiterate, uneducated, exhustler, rebellious Rastafarian and give him the opportunity to represent the country." I know too many black British poets who would die for just one of the many British Council junkets that Zephaniah routinely gets. As a British representative he is a curiosity, a figure whose ranting against Britain allows Britain to declare its wonderful liberal sensibility. Where Linton Kwesi Johnson is sometimes vilified and feared for his hard-hitting reggae verse, Zephaniah is loved. Perhaps this may merely be a product of personality, but I suspect there is a great deal more going on there. One sometimes has the impression that Zephaniah is seen as harmless. Who knows if this is true? But what I miss in him is the irony to recognize that he may have actually been co-opted by the very system he denounces.

Zephaniah, though, remains mildly angry and deeply committed to speaking against the things that he sees as oppressive. And he has done quite well in the process. He has published two novels with the quite respectable Bloomsbury Press; five collections of poetry, four with Bloodaxe, one of the most important poetry presses in the UK; and three collections for children with Puffin/Penguin—all of this in the space of ten years. He continues to produce recordings of his work that are always quite popular. In this, he is assuring us that a legacy of work is bequeathed to his fellow Britishers and the world. The good news is that in every collection Zephaniah manages to spin out a few poems which have lasting genius and power. Of course, he lies about one thing: he is no "ex-hustler."

Christine Leahy (review date 29 September 2002)

SOURCE: Leahy, Christine. Review of *Refugee Boy,* by Benjamin Zephaniah. *New York Times Book Review* (29 September 2002): 27.

[*In the following brief review, Leahy describes the plot of* Refugee Boy.]

Alem Kelo's father is from Ethiopia and his mother is from Eritrea. It is the late 1990's, the two nations are at war, and the Kelos are persecuted in both places. Alem and his father travel to London for what is to be a brief holiday, but one morning the 14-year-old boy wakes up in their hotel room to find that he is alone, left with only a letter of explanation: "My dearest son: You have seen all the trouble that we have been going through back home. . . . Your mother and I think that it would be best if you stay in England. Here they have organizations that will help you, compassionate people who understand why people have to seek refuge from war."

Benjamin Zephaniah's chronicle of an East African in East London [*Refugee Boy*] sees Alem through relentless cycles of hardship and good fortune. Alem is taken into the care of the Refugee Council, which places him in a foster home and shepherds him through an application for political asylum. He faces culture shock, anxiety about his family and his application, neighborhood bullies and unpleasant cold weather. But there are also supportive new friends, piles of books to read and tasty English biscuits to eat.

Alem has an astonishing ability to cope, and a Dickensian heart of gold; he demonstrates exceptional thoughtfulness, good manners and determination, devot-

ing himself to schoolwork and to his kindly host family, who were themselves once refugees from Ireland. His foster parents, his schoolmates and his case workers at the Refugee Council all become so devoted to Alem that they are almost too nice to be believable. Alem feels "as if his life was a roller coaster." But "if good can come from bad," he vows, "I'll make it."

FURTHER READING

Criticism

Asoya, Sylvester. "A Writer's Rage." *Africa News Service* (25 February 2004): np.
Reviews the controversy surrounding Zephaniah's refusal to accept the OBE award, and offers a brief overview of the author's work with the British Council and his views on multiculturalism.

Carter, James. "An Introduction to . . . Benjamin Zephaniah." In *Talking Books: Children's Authors Talk about the Craft, Creativity, and Process of Writing,* pp. 19-39. New York: Routledge, 1999.
An account of Zephaniah's reflections on how he became a writer and performer, his creative process, and the importance of his children's poetry.

Harrison, Desireé. Review of *Gangsta Rap,* by Benjamin Zephaniah. *Black Issues Book Review* 6, no. 6 (November-December 2004): 75.
Brief favorable assessment of *Gangsta Rap.*

Zephaniah, Benjamin, Michael Rosen, and Lara Saguisag. "Performance, Politics, and Poetry for Children: Interviews with Michael Rosen and Benjamin Zephaniah." *Children's Literature Association Quarterly* 32, no. 1 (spring 2007): 3-31.
Zephaniah discusses such topics as his views on the United States and England, the political content of his verse, and his work as a performance poet.

Additional coverage of Zephaniah's life and career is contained in the following sources published by Gale: *Contemporary Authors,* Vol. 147; *Contemporary Authors New Revision Series,* Vols. 103, 156; *Contemporary Poets,* Eds. 5, 6, 7; *Literature Resource Center*; and *Something about the Author,* Vols. 86, 140.

Joseph Zobel
1915-2006

Martinican novelist and short story writer.

INTRODUCTION

Zobel is remembered for his 1950 novel *La Rue Cases-Nègres,* which was translated into English in 1980 as *Black Shack Alley.* Adapted into an award-winning film in 1983, *La Rue Cases-Nègres* is an autobiographically based novel about Zobel's impoverished childhood on a sugar-cane plantation and his eventual success as a writer. Often discussed as part of the Negritude tradition, *La Rue Cases-Nègres* won the 1950 Prix des Lecteurs.

BIOGRAPHICAL INFORMATION

Zobel was born in 1915 in Rivière-Salée, Martinique, an island in the French West Indies. Zobel's family, including his father, grandmother, and mother, were employed by the white Des Grottes family, owners of a sugar plantation. Since his mother worked as a wet nurse for the family, Zobel was cared for by his grandmother. An exceptional student, he excelled at the village school, earning entrance into the Lycée Schoelcher in the city of Fort-de-France. Obtaining his baccalauréat, he worked for a time for the local government before accepting a position in 1938 as a supervisor at the Lycée Schoelcher. During the repressive, pro-Vichy government of Martinique during World War II, Zobel began writing articles, short fiction, and autobiographical accounts of his youth. His first novel, *Diab'la* ("The Devil's Garden"), was rejected by censors, and only published in 1947 after the demise of the Vichy regime. By that time Zobel had entered the Sorbonne in order to study drama and ethnology, and had begun writing *La Rue Cases-Nègres.* At the prompting of the internationally known Negritude writer Léopold Sédar Senghor, whom Zobel met while in Paris, Zobel moved to Africa, teaching and working as an administrator at schools in Senegal. After Senegal won its independence in 1960, Zobel obtained a position with the state radio service, where he worked as a producer. Continuing to write, he completed two collections of short stories, *Et si la mer n'était pas bleue* and *Mas Badara,* which eventually were published in 1982 and 1983, respectively. In the mid-1970s he moved to a small village in southern France, writing poetry and opening a pottery shop with one of his sons. He achieved sudden celeb-

rity in 1983 with the release of the French film version of *La Rue Cases-Nègres,* which was awarded a Silver Lion from the Venice Film Festival, among numerous other awards. He continued writing poetry until his death in 2006 in Alès, France, at the age of ninety-one. A school in Rivière-Salée is named after him.

MAJOR WORKS

Zobel's first novel, *Diab'la,* treats the theme of colonial exploitation, detailing how a member of the proletariat escapes oppression by cultivating a garden. In Zobel's best-known work, *La Rue Cases-Nègres,* the author examined such motifs as race and class discrimination, the French colonial educational system, and cultural assimilation. Told from the perspective of José Hassam, the novel relates the extreme poverty of the narrator's childhood, when he was raised by his devoted and loving grandmother, M'man Tine, on a sugar-cane plantation. José has a strong support system in both M'man Tine and his own mother, Delia, both of whom sacrifice in order to give him the opportunity to escape the harsh and brutal realities of the plantation society through study at the lycée in Fort-de-France. By assimilating himself into the cultural system of the colonizer, José is able to break free from the confines of race and class discrimination and achieve the status of writer. A recurring motif in the novel is the contrast between orality and the written word: the literate (the white landowners) hold all the power, while the illiterate (the black peasantry) are subject to exploitation. Knowledge of the French language, therefore, is key to social and economic advancement. The novel also centers on liberation, as José refuses to remain trapped in a position of subjugation. In the sarcastic and critical *Fête à Paris* (1953), Zobel focused on race relations, colonialism, and French cultural values. Revolving around how a black colonial subject adjusts to city life, the novel has been linked to concepts of Negritude in its recognition of a purely African identity, its rejection of European values, and its condemnation of colonialism for both its financial exploitation and its efforts to erase black culture and identity.

CRITICAL RECEPTION

La Rue Cases-Nègres, which was banned in Martinique for two decades following its publication, surged in popularity in 1983, when fellow Martinican Euzhan

Palcy directed the film version of the novel. Released in the United States in 1984 under the title *Sugar Cane Alley,* the film has often been compared with the novel, with critics commenting specifically on how, in the thirty-three years between the release of the novel and the film, Caribbeans began to move away from an acceptance of cultural assimilation toward an opposition to it—an ideological shift that is reflected in the film. Scholars, including Ann Armstrong Scarboro, have considered Zobel a "modern-day maroon," linking the author with the West Indian folk hero of the runaway slave, who was revered for his bravery in surviving and resisting the brutality of slavery. Contemporary writers like Zobel, according to Scarboro, keep alive for Caribbeans the memories of the rebellions and revolts perpetrated by blacks, who actively challenged Western domination. In other critical discussions, commentators have debated whether or not the novel fits into the Negritude tradition, based on its depiction of a black hero who overcomes his destiny and on its expression of black pride. The contradictory forces under which Zobel wrote also have prompted discussion, with scholars recognizing the struggle French Caribbean writers faced in their attempts to reclaim their heritage while being forced to work within the confines of the Western literary community. Regarding the classification of the novel, critics are divided in their opinions: some call it a *bildungsroman,* since it traces the success of the protagonist despite the intrusion of the "Other," while others term it a psychological novel, based on its focus on the indoctrination of the colonial educational system, through which the narrator, in order to win his independence, must accept all things French.

PRINCIPAL WORKS

Diab'la (novel) 1947
La Rue Cases-Nègres [*Black Shack Alley*] (novel) 1950
Fête à Paris (novel) 1953
Soleil partagé (short stories) 1964
Laghia de la mort (short stories) 1978
Mains pleines d'oiseaux (novel) 1978
Et si la mer n'était pas bleue (short stories) 1982
Mas Badara (short stories) 1983

CRITICISM

Ann Armstrong Scarboro (essay date winter 1992)

SOURCE: Scarboro, Ann Armstrong. "A Shift toward the Inner Voice and *Créolité* in the French Caribbean Novel." *Callaloo* 15, no. 1 (winter 1992): 12-29.

[*In the essay below, Scarboro discusses three French Caribbean writers—Zobel, Simone Schwarz-Bart, and Daniel Maximin—as examples of "modern-day ma-*

roon[*s*]*," who "used their creative powers to claim authenticity and fashion pathways to freedom for the individual and the group."*]

> Ma bouche sera la bouche des malheurs qui n'ont point de bouche, ma voix, la liberté de celles qui s'affaissent au cachot du désespoir
>
> [My mouth will be the mouth of misfortunes that have no mouth, my voice, the freedom of those that sink in the prison of despair]
>
> —Aimé Césaire[1]

Privileging the writer as modern-day maroon and *porteparole* of the collectivity, I show in this article how Joseph Zobel, Simone Schwarz-Bart and Daniel Maximin have used their creative powers to claim authenticity and fashion pathways to freedom for the individual and the group, just as Aimé Césaire did in *Cahier d'un retour au pays natal.* I assert moreover that an evolution in form and content in the contemporary French Caribbean novel can be demonstrated by the juxtaposition of Zobel's **La Rue Cases-Nègres** (1950) with Schwarz-Bart's *Pluie et vent sur Télumée Miracle* (1972) and Maximin's *L'Isolé soleil* (1981).

"Le Grand Camouflage," Suzanne Césaire's essay in the last issue of *Tropiques* (1945), is a revolutionary document.[2] Sketching out the blueprint for a literature of liberation in a semi-cryptic fashion by incorporating descriptions of island beauty, Césaire proclaims a virtual manifesto of independence for the French Caribbean writer:

> Et maintenant lucidité totale. Mon regard par delà ces formes et ces couleurs parfaites, surprend, sur le très beau visage antillais, ses tourments intérieurs.
>
> Car la trame des désirs inassouvis a pris au piège les Antilles et l'Amérique. Depuis l'arrivée des conquistadors et l'essor de leurs techniques (à commencer par celle des armes à feu), les terres d'outre-Atlantique n'ont pas seulement changé de visage, mais de peur.
>
> (269)
>
> [And now complete lucidity. My gaze across these forms and perfect colors discovers her internal torments on the lovely West Indian face.
>
> For the web of unappeased desires has caught the West Indies and America in its trap. Since the arrival of the conquistadors and the proliferation of their techniques (firearms to begin with), the lands of the outer Atlantic have changed not only in appearance but in fear.]

Depicting the "tourments intérieurs" of her beloved Martinique, Césaire asserts the need to speak out, saying that writers must dare to depict discrimination in a way that allows the message of revolution to get through to those who are not free.

Césaire points out that French Caribbean writers have to play hide and seek so that the dominant Other does not silence the messenger with censure before s/he speaks. She also says that writers must encourage everyone to join the revolt. Uttering her own call to action to those who are afraid to speak/write, she reminds them of the power they used to possess. Her metaphor of strength, which recalls A. Césaire's poem, "Les pur sangs," is one to which all of us can respond:

> J'écoutais très attentivement, sans les entendre, vos voix perdues dans la symphonie carribbéene qui lançait les trombes à l'assaut des îles. Nous étions semblables à des purs-sangs, retenus, piaffant d'impatience, à la lisière de cette savane de sel.
>
> (270)

> [I listened very closely, without hearing them, to your voices lost in the Caribbean symphony that was hurling torrents to assault the islands. We were like thoroughbreds, restrained, pawing the ground with impatience, at the edge of this salt savannah.]

In writing her manifesto for a literature of liberation, Suzanne Césaire is like some of her ancestors—the maroons, runaway slaves who dared to proclaim their independence despite impossible circumstances and who used certain ploys of subterfuge to achieve their ends.

Edouard Glissant points out in *Le Discours antillais* that the group was deprived of a hero who could act as a catalyst for the collectivity when *marronnage* (cultural opposition) was treated as a deviation and punished. However, he also reminds us that the maroon is the only popular hero the French Caribbean people have ever had:

> Il n'en reste pas moins, nous ne le soulignerons jamais assez, que le Nègre marron est le seul vrai héros populaire des Antilles, dont les effroyables supplices qui marquaient sa capture donnent la mesure du courage et de la détermination. Il y a là un exemple incontestable d'opposition systématique, de refus total.
>
> (104)

> [It nevertheless remains true, we can never emphasize it enough, that the black maroon or runaway slave is the only real folk hero of the West Indies. The terrible tortures that marked his capture are a measure of his courage and determination. In his action we have an indisputable example of systematic opposition, of complete refusal.]

Today it is the writers who are the heroes and heroines as they thrust aside the domination of the Other and claim their territory anew. Maryse Condé affirms this notion that Caribbean writers must be modern-day maroons in *Le Roman antillais*:

> Le rôle de l'écrivain sera donc celui-là. Rappeler les révoltes, les soulèvements, les empoisonnements massifs des maîtres, en un mot la résistance et le marronage. . . . En fait, le marronage, c'est-à-dire le refus de la domination de l'Occident, symbolise une des constantes de l'attitude antillaise.
>
> (20)

> [The writer's role will thus be to remind us of the revolts, the uprisings, the massive poisonings of plantation owners, that is to remind us of resistance and rebellion. . . . In fact, *marronage,* i.e., the refusal of domination by the West, represents one of the constant aspects of the West Indian attitude.]

Glissant suggests that the contemporary artist is engaged in becoming the *porte-parole* of the collective consciousness of the people, recalling lived history and inspiring future action:

> La parole de l'artiste antillais ne provient donc pas de l'obsession de chanter son être intime; cet intime est inséparable du devenir de la communauté.
>
> Mais cela que l'artiste exprime, révèle et soutient, dans son oeuvre, les peuples n'ont pas cessé de la vivre dans le réel. Le problème est que cette vie collective a été contrainte dans la prise de conscience; l'artiste devient un réactiveur. C'est pourquoi il est à lui-même un ethnologue, un historien, un linguiste, un peintre des fresques, un architecte. L'art ne connaît pas ici la division des genres. Ce travail volontaire prépare aux floraisons communes. S'il est approximatif, il permet la réflexion critique; s'il réussit, il inspire.
>
> (439)

> [The language of the Caribbean artist does not originate in the obsession with celebrating his inner self; this inner self is inseparable from the future evolution of his community.
>
> But what the artist expresses, reveals, and argues in his work, the people have not ceased to live in reality. The problem is that this collective life has been constrained by the process of consciousness; the artist acquires a capacity to reactivate. That is why he is his own ethnologist, historian, linguist, painter of frescoes, architect. Art for us has no sense of the division of genres. This conscious research creates the possibility of a collective effervescence. If he more or less succeeds, he makes critical thought possible; if he succeeds completely, he can inspire.
>
> from *Caribbean Discourse,* trans. J. Michael Dash (1989), 236)]

The concept of the writer as modern-day maroon introduces the notion of becoming self-conscious, because the maroon had to assess his condition before he could run away. Jean Bernabé, Patrick Chamoiseau, and Raphaël Confiant suggest in *Eloge de la créolité* that contemporary writers have the opportunity and the obligation to reexamine their Caribbeanness, anchored in the richness of Creoleness:

> Ici, nous ne nous imaginons pas hors du monde, en banlieue de l'Univers. Notre ancrage dans cette terre n'est pas une plongée dans un fond sans pardon. Notre vision intérieure exercée, notre créolité mise comme centre de créativité, nous permet de réexaminer notre existence, d'y voir les mécanismes de l'aliénation, d'en percevoir surtout les beautés. L'écrivain est un renifleur d'existence. Plus que tout autre, il a pour vocation d'identifier ce qui, dans notre quotidien, détermine les

comportements et structure l'imaginaire. Voir notre existence c'est nous voir en situation dans notre histoire, dans notre quotidien, dans notre réel.

(39)

[Here we do not believe ourselves to be outside the world, in the suburbs of the Universe. Our anchoredness in this land is not a dive into the depths without forgiveness. Making use of our internal vision, putting our Creoleness at the center of our creativity, allows us to see the mechanisms of alienation, permits us to reexamine our existence, and especially permits us to perceive the beauty of that existence. The writer is one who breathes in existence and sniffs it. More than any other person, he has the task of identifying what it is in our daily lives that determines behavior and structures the imaginary. Seeing our existence means seeing ourselves in the context of our history, our daily life, our reality.]

In *La Rue Cases-Nègres* Zobel focuses on the external life of the collectivity rather than on his protagonists' inner lives, forcing his readers to see how racial and class prejudices dominate José's and M'man Tine's world. In *Pluie et vent sur Télumée Miracle*, Schwarz-Bart shows the development of an expanded self-awareness in both Reine Sans Nom and Télumée, and she portrays the group's life in detail. Rejuvenating the life of the collectivity through the exploration of its history, Maximin makes self-consciousness the primary focus in *L'Isolé soleil* because the protagonists' re-births structure the movement of the whole text.

As *romans d'initiation,* the three narratives teach lessons about how to live in a society where the presence of the Other, with its "mécanismes de l'aliénation" (*Eloge de la créolité* 39), has been a fundamental fact of daily life. Stressing the importance of the collectivity as a nourishing force for the individual, Zobel depicts young José's connection to M'man Tine and Medouze, Schwarz-Bart speaks of the invisible threads linking the village huts, and Maximin uses multiple excerpts from the works of previous generations of French Caribbean writers.

As *romans d'initiation* with an internal focus, *Pluie et vent sur Télumée Miracle* and *L'Isolé soleil* also teach the reader about the importance of the inner voice. Examining the relationship between the protagonist's internal, psychological growth and the world in which Télumée lives, *Pluie et vent sur Télumée Miracle* highlights the value of being true to oneself, staying in control of one's life, and keeping a secret part hidden, invulnerable to assault. As Maryse Condé put it in *La Parole des femmes,* Télumée "a su accepter la vie et par une secrète alchimie transfigurer les échecs, les angoisses et les souffrances" [knew how to accept life and by means of a secret alchemy transform its defeats, anguish and suffering] (36).

In *L'Isolé soleil,* Maximin tells us that the individual on his/her own path must look inside as deeply as possible to find his/her own voice if s/he wants real freedom:

"Brise ce premier miroir et écoute bien le silence de ton double devant ta main qui saigne et ton regard aveugle" [Break this first mirror and listen carefully to the silence of your double standing before your bleeding hand and blind gaze] (285). Valorizing the inner voice and creating the framework for journeys—journeys by both "le même" and "l'autre" [the one who is the same and the one who is similar]—are among Schwarz-Bart's and Maximin's most meaningful contributions.[3] The inner journey is essential to a literature of liberation, because only through such an exploration can the individual, and the collectivity, become free.

The novels also focus on how the individual can react against the Other. In *La Rue Cases-Nègres,* José appropriates the tool of the colonizer, the French language, using it to express his own value as a citizen and remaining in the white/black, master/slave world to make his statement. In *Pluie et vent sur Télumée Miracle,* Télumée learns to transcend suffering by creating her own space of spiritual peace, living apart from the world of the colonizer. In *L'Isolé soleil,* Marie-Gabriel recreates her roots by re-visioning her own history, freeing herself to journey forward in a world in which the Other can no longer hold all of the power.

José's journey of initiation moves outward toward the Other in confrontation, Télumée's moves inward toward her own center, and Marie-Gabriel's moves first inward and then outward, embracing the Other and celebrating communication. This evolution in movement reflects the change taking place in French Caribbean society today. In Zobel's era, the 1940s and 1950s, separation between classes and preferential treatment for the Other was the only way of life. Today, in Maximin's era of the 1980s and 1990s, the emphasis on multiplicity and diversity has created a climate where individual merit is appreciated with less regard to race and class, although economic and political independence have not yet been achieved.

When considered together as one unit, the novels portray an evolution in their relationship to cultural assimilation. Zobel's fictional world is based on assimilation—José works within the colonizer's system to proclaim his own identity by becoming a writer. Schwarz-Bart's characters reject cultural assimilation, but economic necessity forces them to labor for the Other whose presence continually limits their lives. Maximin's protagonists reject assimilation, creating their own psychological and economic independence. As the writers of *Eloge de la créolité* suggest, the new literature of liberation rejects assimilation, affirming instead Creoleness with its cultural difference and dynamic multiplicity:

Nous nous déclarons Créoles. Nous déclarons que la Créolité est le ciment de notre culture et qu'elle doit régir les fondations de notre antillanité. La Créolité est l'*agrégat interactionnel ou transactionnel,* des éléments culturels caraïbes, européens, africains, asiatiques, et levantins, que le joug de l'Histoire a réunis sur le même sol.

(26)

[We declare ourselves Creoles. We declare that Creoleness is the cement of our culture and that it should govern the foundations of our Caribbeanness. Creoleness is the *interactional or transactional substance* of cultural elements brought together on the same soil by the yoke of History, elements that are Caribbean, African, Asian and Levantine.]

The focus on social realism diminishes from ***La Rue Cases-Nègres*** to *L'Isolé soleil* as the emphasis on the inner journey and Creoleness expands. Not even addressing Creoleness, Zobel depicts the ravages created by the plantation society in extensive detail, and José's journey is primarily outward. While Schwarz-Bart's novel also portrays the poverty of rural society, her concentration is on Télumée's inner psychic journey. Maximin highlights the inner journey and Creoleness, privileging re-birth and bringing in international connections among black writers and musicians. His incorporation of history includes instances of social realism, but he concentrates on the collectivity and the individual's relationship to history rather than on the horrors of the past.

Taken as a unit, the three novels represent an evolution from a focus on confrontation to a focus on celebration of difference. This shift has been possible because writers like A. Césaire and Zobel set the stage for the newer generations by defining the reality that existed. Until that initial portrait had been made, no re-ordering of external reality could take place, because someone had to dare to be the first to proclaim the truth. Once the ravages of the plantation system had been depicted, authenticating the past experience of the collectivity, other writers could begin to focus on the individual as well as the group, describing the potential of the present-day situation.

Addressed to the writers' compatriots and to the literature's international audience, the call to action that characterizes the innovative force in French Caribbean literature springs from the protagonists' own private journeys. The texts of all three writers encourage the narratee to become a modern-day maroon him/herself, to take up the "conques de lambis" [conch shells] and signal revolt like Amboise and his fellow strikers in *Pluie et vent sur Télumée Miracle* (221). Although Zobel, Schwarz-Bart and Maximin use different narrative strategies, they all succeed in bringing about a new awareness for "le même," "l'autre" and perhaps even "l'Autre" [the one who is different].

Speaking through example, Zobel details the courage of M'man Tine's *prise de conscience* as she refuses to let her grandson work in the cane fields. José defines his own call to action: "C'est aux aveugles et à ceux qui se bouchent les oreilles qu'il me faudrait . . . crier cette histoire" [It is to those who are blind and those who block their ears that I must cry out this story] (311).

Schwarz-Bart embeds her challenge in Amboise's courage as head of the striking cane cutters and in Télumée's ability to persevere in the face of terrible losses:

> Mais pluies et vents ne sont rien si une première étoile se lève pour vous dans le ciel, et puis une seconde, une troisième, ainsi qu'il advint pour moi qui ai bien failli ravir tout le bonheur de la terre. Et même si les étoiles se couchent, elles ont brillé et leur lumière clignote, encore, là où elle est venue se déposer dans votre deuxième coeur.

(241)

> [But rains and winds are nothing. If first one star rises for you in the sky, then another, then another as happened to me, who very nearly carried off all the happiness in the world. And even if the stars set, they have shone, and their light still twinkles there where it has come to rest: in your second heart.

(from *Bridge of Beyond,* trans. Barbara Bray (1974), 167)]

Maximin's call to action is spoken by Marie-Gabriel:

> Accepte, accepte tout ce que tu peux de ton trésor. Ensuite, donne-le. Plus tu donnes, plus tu es. . . .
>
> Mais surtout ne donne jamais une miette de ce qu'en toi tu refuses ou n'acceptes pas encore. . . .
>
> Calcule tes forces et fais confiance à ta fragilité. Accepte la vie comme une vague. . . .
>
> Chaque vague touche au destin d'une autre.

(285-86)

> [Accept, accept all you can of your treasure. Then give it. The more you give, the more you are. . . .
>
> And especially don't ever give a crumb of something in yourself that you refuse or don't yet accept. . . .
>
> Calculate your strengths and trust your fragility.
>
> Accept life like a wave. . . .
>
> Each wave touches the destiny of another.

(from *Lone Sun,* ed. Clarisse Zimra (1989), 259-60)]

As with the focus on the inner voice, Maximin's call to action is stronger and more direct than are Zobel's and Schwarz-Bart's, because Maximin examines the inner voices of the individual and the history of the collectivity more deeply and then moves back out to the external world.

Embedded in Caribbeanness and Creoleness is the idea of an authentic, positive self-conscious expression of the collectivity and the individual. In *Eloge de la créolité* Bernabé, Chamoiseau and Confiant speak of a "regard libre":

Il émerge d'une projection de l'intime et traite chaque parcelle de notre réalité comme un événement dans la perspective d'en briser la vision traditionelle, en l'occurrence extérieure et soumise aux envoûtements de l'aliénation. . . . C'est en cela que la vision intérieure est révélatrice, donc révolutionnaire. Réapprendre à visualiser nos profondeurs. Réapprendre à regarder positivement ce qui palpite autour de nous. . . . C'est un bouleversement intérieur et sacré à la manière de Joyce. C'est dire: une liberté. Mais, tentant vainement de l'exercer, nous nous aperçûmes qu'il ne pouvait pas y avoir de vision intérieure sans une préalable acceptation de soi. On pourrait même dire que la vision intérieure en est la résultante.

(24)

[It emerges from a projection of the intimate and treats each fragment of our reality as an event from the perspective of breaking apart the established vision we have of that reality as external occurrence submissive to the bewitchment of alienation. . . . It is in this aspect that the internal vision is revealing, hence revolutionary. Relearning how to envision our own depths. Relearning to look positively at what palpates all around us. . . . It is an internal, sacred upheaval in the style of Joyce. That is to say: a freedom. And, trying in vain to use it, we perceived that there could be no internal vision without a prior acceptance of the self. One could even say that the internal vision is the direct result of this acceptance.]

This "acceptation de soi," which is precisely what Schwarz-Bart and Maximin's protagonists experience as the result of their inner journeys, is related to A. Césaire's positive vision of himself in *Cahier d'un retour au pays natal*:

Et nous sommes debout maintenant, mon pays et moi, les cheveux dans le vent, ma main petite maintenant dans son poing énorme et la force n'est pas en nous, mais au-dessus de nous, dans une voix qui vrille la nuit et l'audience comme la pénétrance d'une guêpe apocalyptique.

(57)

[And we are standing now, my country and I, hair in the wind, my hand puny in its enormous fist and now the strength is not in us but above us, in a voice that drills the night and the hearing like the penetrance of an apocalyptic wasp.

(from *Aimé Césaire, the Collected Poetry*, trans. Clayton Eshleman and Annette Smith (1983), 76-77)]

Coming to self-consciousness generates new freedom of action and creates new spaces for interaction. Télumée is free to use her healing arts to help her neighbors; Siméa, Marie-Gabriel's mother, can travel to Paris to help the Soledad brothers; Marie-Gabriel can write her novel. All of them are free to love and cherish other human beings and the land that surrounds them, carrying out the first steps of "le bouleversement intérieur" described by Bernabé, Chamoiseau and Confiant.

If Creoleness is to succeed, the "acceptation de soi" must characterize the group's attitude toward itself as well. *L'Isolé soleil* exemplifies this vision more fully than *La Rue Cases-Nègres* and *Pluie et vent sur Télumée Miracle,* because it affirms French Caribbean historical and literary figures, showing how extensive this heritage is. Maximin's second novel, *Soufrières,* affirms the group more completely, because it focuses on the group experience of enduring the eruption of Guadeloupe's volcano, La Soufrière.[4]

These three novels taken together also depict an evolution in the portrayal of female space, if we define that space in Hélène Cixous's terms as an aversion to fixed formulas, the celebration of openness and a renewed inner sensitivity.[5] Zobel tells M'man Tine's story as well as José's, but both are told by José's linear, factual voice in a setting where action takes precedence over feeling. Schwarz-Bart virtually omits male space, privileging female bonding, circular, mythical time and an emotional response to life. Maximin uses an androgynous combination, as he both affirms emotional sensitivity and invents his own version of Caribbean *écriture féminine* and as he uses action and linear thinking. Reflecting the hybrid, heteroglot reality of French Caribbean existence today, Maximin's androgynous fictional world exemplifies Caribbeanness and Creoleness.

A similar evolution from limitation to expansion appears in the way the three texts appropriate the world of nature and the world of the human body. All three novels use nature and the human body as "livres de lecture" [primers],[6] but Zobel's use of both is less frequent and less intense than are Schwarz-Bart's and Maximin's. Schwarz-Bart anchors her text in a specifically Caribbean space by using rivers, trees, flowers and natural phenomena as metaphoric representations of life patterns:

Toutes les rivières, même les plus éclatantes, celles qui prennent le soleil dans leur courant, toutes les rivières descendent dans la mer et se noient. Et la vie attend l'homme comme la mer attend la rivière. On peut prendre méandre sur méandre, tourner, contourner, s'insinuer dans la terre, vos méandres vous appartiennent mais la vie est là, patiente, sans commencement et sans fin, à vous attendre, pareille à l'océan.

(81)

[All rivers, even the most dazzling, those that catch the sun in their streams, go down to and are drowned in the sea. And life awaits man as the sea awaits the river. You can make meander after meander, twist, turn, seep into the earth—your meanders are your own affair. But life is there, patient, without beginning or end, waiting for you, like the ocean.

(from *Bridge of Beyond*, trans. Barbara Bray (1974), 52)]

Maximin's descriptions of trees, islands, cyclones and volcanic eruptions reflect the Caribbean landscape while they also mirror the condition of the Caribbean individual and the collectivity. Comparing her body to

Guadeloupe and the abortion forced upon her by her white lover (and her own mother) to a cyclone, Siméa shows us the power of the Other:

> Tout en déluge, en séisme et en raz-de-marée, le cyclone de 1928 vient de repasser onze ans après au pays de mon corps; la maison de mon ventre culbutée, son coeur éventré, mes rues encombrées de débris de toutes sortes, mes artères déracinées. Toute ma terre dévastée, vagin roussi. Ton cadavre arraché à mes décombres. Et maintenant, c'est l'isolement sans lumière, toutes les communications interrompues, la famine de toi parmi les fers tordus, les poutres rompues, mon visage renversé sur un sommier rouge de mes eaux et de ton sang mêlés.

> (123)

> [Deluge, quake, and tidal wave, the cyclone of 1928 has just hit again, eleven years later, passing right through my body: the house of my womb turned upside down, its heart gutted, my streets cluttered with every kind of debris, my arteries uprooted. My whole land devastated, my vagina pummeled. Your corpse ripped out of my ruins; and now, isolation and darkness; all communications disrupted; famine for you here among the twisted irons, broken beams, my head thrown back on a bedspring red with my waters mixed with your blood.

> (from *Lone Sun*, ed. Clarisse Zimra (1989), 111)]

The relationship of ***La Rue Cases-Nègres,*** *Pluie et vent sur Télumée Miracle* and *L'Isolé soleil* to history presents another shift in emphasis. José tells the story of his own life and his grandmother's *prise de conscience,* anchoring his text in realistic details. Schwarz-Bart depicts Télumée's quest for internal harmony, showing how she eventually exemplifies the wisdom of her community as she achieves individuation or self-understanding. Clearly, Zobel, Schwarz-Bart and Maximin all use real history to present the negative experience of colonial life. However, the third writer explores the resonance between the past and the present much more fully.

Maximin's protagonists journey to self-understanding and re-birth, but they engage as well in a quest to find the historical roots of the collectivity. The history of the collectivity is merged with Marie-Gabriel's personal story, because she re-creates herself in telling Siméa's story, and Siméa's story re-creates part of the collectivity's story. Making a double point about truth, Maximin shows that although a full-blown history written by Caribbean people cannot exist because those who would write it died long ago, the truth of the people's resistance to oppression can be affirmed by reading between the lines of colonial history books. This revisioning of French Caribbean history, which reflects the polyvalent dimension of contemporary life, fulfills the impetus of Caribbeanness and Creoleness, because it repairs gaping holes and redefines part of the fabric of Caribbean reality. Thomas Mpoyi-Buatu explains:

> Les Antilles constituent une société pluri-culturelle. Et l'émergence da sa spécificité culturelle a longtemps fait problème. En restituant les vertigineux méandres de l'émergence de l'identité antillaise, Maximin, à travers son roman, institue l'unique itinéraire que doit emprunter la mémoire critique.

> (31)

> [The West Indies constitute a pluricultural society. And the emergence of this society's cultural specificity has long been a problem. In restoring the dizzying meanders of the emergence of West Indian identity, Maximin, through his novel, institutes the unique itinerary that the critical memory should adopt.]

An evolution in form corresponds with the shifts in content I have just explored. With regard to physical structure, ***La Rue Cases-Nègres*** and *Pluie et vent sur Télumée Miracle* are divided into sections whose individual relationships to each other are logical and sequential. *L'Isolé soleil,* on the other hand, is composed of non-sequential fragments whose relationships seem to have little internal logic, but whose organization forces the reader to decipher what connections s/he can. This shift from easily accessible structure to labyrinthine form reflects the changes from external focus to internal focus, simplicity to complexity, and singularity to multiplicity that we have seen with regard to all elements of content—the inner journey, the call to action, the uses of social realism and writing, female space, the worlds of nature and the human body, and the portrayal of history.

A similar transformation appears when we compare other aspects of form—narrative voice, time and textual language. The traditional form of a first-person narrator and a linear time frame in ***La Rue Cases-Nègres*** and *Pluie et vent sur Télumée Miracle* is replaced in *L'Isolé soleil* with an innovative juxtaposition of multiple voices and a postmodern, zig-zagging, fragmented time frame. Moreover, the ramifications of Maximin's narrative strategy go far beyond the fact that it reflects the complicated, polymorphic nature of Creolized society today and marginalizes the reader.

Prohibiting easy entry into the text, Maximin's strategy limits his audience. In this cryptic design to confound readers and pay attention to multiple levels of meaning, Maximin is following the example set by A. Césaire in his poetry. Speaking of *Moi, laminaire . . . ,* the volume of poetry A. Césaire published in 1982, Jacques Rancourt asserts that the poet protects his writing from easy access by peeping toms:

> l'on dira que la communication n'est pas le principal de ce recueil.

> C'est vrai, mais c'est faux. Parlons plutôt d'une communication semée d'écueils. Propre à décourager quiconque aurait seulement envie d'aller fouiller dans l'intimité de Césaire. Et là, c'est l'intransigeance; les poèmes ne donnent pas prise à lecture voyeuse.

> (70)

> [One would say that communication is not the primary goal of this collection. This is true, but it is also false. Let us speak rather of a communication strewn with

reefs and stumbling blocks. Suitable for discouraging whoever desires only to go rummaging around in Césaire's intimacy. And therein lies the intransigence; the poems cannot be grasped by a voyeuristic reading.]

Rancourt's multivalent image of "une communication semée d'écueils" fits well with the works of both A. Césaire and Maximin, whose portrayals of island space are full of *reefs* and *stumbling blocks* that impede the reader from having a full understanding of the text on first encounter.

The variety of textual languages in these novels demonstrates a transition from classical French in **La Rue Cases-Nègres** to Creolized French in *Pluie et vent sur Télumée Miracle* to a combination of the two in *L'Isolé soleil*. Roger Toumson explains the history of the importance of language in the Caribbean setting:

> Dans l'espace énonciatif antillais, la parole est l'enjeu d'un conflit brutal entre deux histoires, deux cultures, deux pensées. Elle énonce une solution de continuité, une émergence.
>
> (131)

> [In the West Indian space of enunciation, the word is at stake in a brutal conflict between two histories, two cultures, two ways of thinking. It enunciates a solution of continuity, of emergence.]

Zobel uses a French language space to re-create himself as a separate, but still fundamentally Caribbean, individual, who dominates the language in order to celebrate his Caribbeanness and exhort others to action. The vocabulary he chooses, his sentence structure and his use of verbs illustrate his mastery of the language, while the details he depicts inscribe a Caribbean reality:

> Après tout, j'eus bientôt pour copain un chauffeur d'auto du quartier. Nous avions lié connaissance non pas dans le Petit-Fond, où il habitait pourtant, mais sur la route. . . .
>
> C'était chaque fois une bonne aubaine parce que, quatre fois par jour, je devais faire à pied, sous des averses pendant l'hivernage, et les soleils du Carême qui amollissaient le bitume, les deux kilomètres qui me séparaient de la ville.
>
> (255)

> [I soon had as a pal a car driver from the district. We had become acquainted not in Petit-Fond where he lived, however, but on the road. . . .
>
> On every occasion, it would be a godsend, because four times a day, either in the heavy rain during the rainy season or in the sun of the dry season that softened the asphalt, I would have to trudge on foot the two kilometers that separated me from the town.
>
> (from **Black Shack Alley,** trans. Keith Q. Warner (1980), 148)]

Schwarz-Bart incorporates mythical and philosophical language within the fabric of her Creolized and classical French, creating a multi-dimensional framework of

expression that invites the reader to explore hidden aspects of reality at the same time s/he is made aware of details of daily peasant life:

> Ainsi suis-je à mon rôle d'ancienne, faisant mon jardin, grillant mes cacahuètes, recevant les uns et les autres, debout sur mes deux jambes, toute garnie de jupons empesés pour leur masquer ma maigreur. Et puis le soir, tandis que le soleil décline, je réchauffe mon manger, j'arrache ici et là une mauvaise herbe, et je pense à la vie du nègre et à son mystère. Nous n'avons, pour nous aider, pas davantage de traces que l'oiseau dans l'air, le poisson dans l'eau, et au beau milieu de cette incertitude nous vivons, et certains rient et d'autres chantent.
>
> (243)

> [And so I have reached my role as an old woman, tending my garden, roasting my peanuts, receiving visitors standing up on my two legs, and decked in starched skirts so that they can't see how thin I am. And then in the evening as the sun goes down, I warm up my supper, I pull up a weed or two, and I think of the Negro's life and of its mystery. We have no more marks to guide us than the bird in the air or the fish in the water, and in the midst of this uncertainty we live, and some laugh and others sing.
>
> (from *Bridge of Beyond,* trans. Barbara Bray (1974), 168-69)]

The shift in language parallels the movement toward opacity noted by Toumson:

> L'évolution de la littérature antillaise, du mimétisme exotisant originel, tant décrié, à l'affirmation de leur originalité culturelle par les écrivains de la négritude et de l'après-négritude, marque un passage progressif d'une transparence maximale à une opacité maximale.
>
> (132)

> [The evolution of West Indian literature, from the early exotic mimicry that was disparaged to the affirmation of their cultural originality by the negritude and post-negritude writers, marks a progressive passage from maximum transparency to maximum opacity.]

Maximin's textual language functions to carry out his strategy of camouflage as well as to portray contemporary French Caribbean space. In the following conversation between Siméa and Louis Gabriel, Maximin criticizes André Breton, the first writer to bring A. Césaire's work to the attention of French readers,[7] he praises S. Césaire, he parodies exoticism, and he conveys a sense of place:

> —Vous connaissez Suzanne Césaire?
>
> —Non, je ne l'ai jamais vue. Je lui ai écrit une fois à propos de *Tropiques.* Vous connaissez cette revue qu'ils font à Fort-de-France?
>
> —Oui, moi aussi j'en possède des numéros, mais mon ami musicien dont je vous ai parlé tout à l'heure les connaît bien, puisqu'il vient lui-même du lycée de Fort-de-France où il était répétiteur. Il a même accompagné André Breton en excursion à la montagne Pelée! A

l'entendre, Breton s'émerveillait de tout comme un enfant: les colibris et les pommes-lianes, la statue bleue de Joséphine et les cheveux des écolières chabines, le *Cahier* de Césaire, les lucioles, les orchidées, le diamant vert au soleil couchant . . .

—Laissons Breton admirer et même recopier: les Antilles sont dix fois plus surréalistes que lui. . . . Pour en revenir à Suzanne, c'est le ton de ce qu'elle écrit que j'aime. Il est si rare qu'une femme épanouisse volontairement ses sentiments dans ses écrits.

(197-98)

["You know Suzanne Césaire?"

"No, I've never met her. I wrote to her once about *Tropiques*. You know, that magazine they're doing in Fort-de-France."

"Yes, I have a few issues, too. But the musician friend I told you about knows them well, he was a tutor at the lycée in Fort-de-France. He even accompanied André Breton on an excursion to Mount Pelée! The way he tells it, Breton was like a child, marveling at everything, the colibri and passionfruit, the blue statue of Josephine and the blond hair of chabine schoolchildren, Césaire's *Cahier*, lightning bugs, orchids, the last, emerald-green ray at sunset . . ."

"Let him admire. He can even copy. The Antilles are ten times more surrealistic than Breton. . . . To get back to Suzanne, what I like about her writing is the tone. It's so unusual to read a woman whose sentiments blossom in her writing."

(from *Lone Sun*, ed. Clarisse Zimra (1989), 177-78)]

Obscuring the criticism of Breton and the literature of exoticism, the flow of lighthearted conversation and colloquial language encourages the reader to focus on the relationship between the two speakers.

Just as the maroons of the French Caribbean had to hide in order to undermine the plantation system, these writers have to build opacity into their texts. Sometimes this is necessary for political reasons—the Vichy regime forbade the publication of Zobel's *Diab'là* in 1941, for instance, and the French climate during World War II was not friendly toward black writers who wanted to speak out. Jacqueline Leiner explains why this might be true:

Césaire, who has experienced unconditional European domination, obstinately seeks to recover the "West Indian self" smothered by colonization. He cannot view the latter as a valid matter of establishing contact between cultures; in fact "la colonisation ne réussit qu'à déciviliser le colonisateur" [colonialism succeeds only in uncivilizing the colonizer] as well as the colonized. The radicalism of Césaire and of the *Tropiques* contributors, which is characteristic of a number of West Indians, stands in stark opposition to the Senghorian compromise—which is not necessarily African.

(1145)

At other times, the camouflage hides part of the writer's meaning until the reader has been seduced by the narrative, as in the example quoted above from Maximin

about André Breton and the literature of exoticism. In this case, the delay in the reader's understanding of the full meaning magnifies the text's impact on the reader. Such is the situation in *Pluie et vent sur Télumée Miracle* where we do not realize at first that Schwarz-Bart is subverting the dominant orders of the male and the Other.

Secrecy can also function as a structural technique that reinforces the writer's meaning as in *L'Isolé soleil* where Maximin confuses the reader, forcing him/her to experience the difficulty of the protagonist's, and thus the collectivity's, search for his/her own roots. At other times, the opacity is used to reflect the reality that the French Caribbean individual's knowledge of history can never be fully known, as Glissant points out: "L'Histoire de la Martinique est une histoire perdue: oblitérée dans la conscience (la mémoire) collective par l'acte concerté du colonisateur" [The History of Martinique is a lost story: obliterated in the collective consciousness (memory) by the concerted act of the colonizer] (106).

Opacity in the text produces curious results. Writing in 1971, Jack Corzani described *La Rue Cases-Nègres* as a work that is "émouvante" [moving] but "souffre de son orientation populaire et paraît un peu prêcheur et larmoyant" [suffers from its popular orientation and seems a bit moralizing and maudlin] (194). Corzani's virtual dismissal of the text may well be related to Zobel's ability to use the tactics of the maroon—Zobel camouflages the narrative's intent so well, by a realistic depiction of Martinican life in the cane fields and Fort-de-France of the 1930s, that Corzani does not even perceive the novel for the document of liberation that it is, even though he has clearly studied it.

The circumstances of publishing this literature demonstrate the ambiguously dependent relationship between the French Caribbean and France. The firms of Éditions Caribéennes, Présence Africaine, l'Harmattan and Hâtier are bringing out the works of more and more writers today, but the large establishments like Seuil and Gallimard have greater power of dissemination. Although they do publish the novels of some of the new writers—Chamoiseau, Confiant and Maximin—they tend to focus on the well-established writers like Glissant and Condé, so that most new writers cannot reach the broadest audience.

The socio-political space from which French Caribbean writers speak today is evolving quickly. In 1979 Julie Lirus focused on assimilation in *Identité antillaise*:

Les questions que se posent les Antillais sur leur "être en situation" qu'on veuille l'entendre ou pas, prennent racines dans la société esclavagiste et coloniale. Elles se poursuivent de nos jours dans le cadre de la politique d'assimilation, qui tente de récupérer à son profit, c'est-à-dire au profit de la Métropole, toute action, organisation et idée pouvant aider au surgissement d'une identité antillaise nationale, envisageable malgré les différences dues à la spécificité de chaque île.

(11)

[The questions West Indians ask themselves about their "circumstances," whether one wants to acknowledge it or not, are rooted in colonial slave society. This continues today in the context of the politics of assimilation which tries to take over for the profit of the metropole every action, organization and idea that could lead to the sudden emergence of a national West Indian identity. Such an identity can be envisaged in spite of the differences emanating from the specificity of each island.]

In 1986, Micheline Rice-Maximin highlighted Caribbeanness in her study of Guadeloupean literature, "Koko sek toujou ni dlo":

Le désir d'assimilation a cédé le pas à l'Antillanité. C'est en cela que cette littérature fait preuve de plus d'autonomie, autre grand thème de la pensée guadeloupéenne. L'autonomie, qu'elle soit sociale ou politique est elle aussi reflétée dans le mouvement littéraire des dernières décennies où l'on voit les écrivains et les artistes prendre leur distance à l'égard de la métropole. Les liens et contacts intercaribéens par contre, se développement précisément grâce à cette distanciation.

(137-38)

[The desire for assimilation has given way to Caribbeanness. It is here that this literature demonstrates more autonomy, another important theme of Guadeloupean thought. Autonomy, whether it is social or political, is also reflected in the literary movement of recent decades where one sees writers and artists distancing themselves from the metropole. Inter-Caribbean links and contexts, on the other hand, are developing precisely because of this separation.]

Strongly implying that political and artistic independence are intimately intertwined for the Caribbean writer, Rice-Maximin presages what Bernabé, Chamoiseau and Confiant say in 1989 in *Eloge de la créolité*:

La Créolité dessine l'espoir d'un premier regroupement possible au sein de l'Archipel caribéen: celui des peuples créolophones d'Haïti, de Martinique, de Sainte-Lucie, de Dominique, de Guadeloupe et de Guyane, rapprochement qui n'est que le prélude à une union plus large avec nos voisins anglophones et hispanophones. C'est dire que pour nous, l'acquisition d'une éventuelle souveraineté monoinsulaire ne saurait être qu'une étape (que nous souhaiterions la plus brève possible) sur la route d'une fédération ou d'une confédération caraïbe, seul moyen de lutter efficacement contre les différents blocs à vocation hégémonique qui se partagent la planète. Dans cette perspective, nous affirmons notre opposition au processus actuel d'intégration sans consultation populaire des peuples desdits départements français d'Amérique au sein de la Communauté européenne. Notre première solidarité est d'abord avec nos frères des îles avoisinantes et dans un deuxième temps avec les nations d'Amérique du Sud.

(58)

[Creoleness sketches out the hope for a first possible regrouping at the center of the Caribbean archipelago, that of the Creole-speaking people of Haiti, Martinique,

St. Lucia, Dominica, Guadeloupe and Guyana, a drawing together which is only the prelude to a larger union with our English-speaking and Spanish-speaking neighbors. This is to say that for us, the acquisition of an eventual monoinsular sovereignty would only be one stage (which we hope would be as brief as possible) on the road toward a Caribbean federation or confederation. Such a union is the only means of fighting effectively against the different blocks of hegemonic calling that divide the planet among themselves. In this perspective we affirm our opposition to the present-day process of integration without popular consultation of the people who live in the French *départements* of America into the center of the European community. Our solidarity is first and foremost with our brothers of the neighboring islands and secondly with the countries of South America.]

The novels examined here differ in their relationships to the concepts of Negritude, Caribbeanness and Creoleness. Exemplifying the period in which it was engendered as well as the spirit of the particular writer, Zobel's novel belongs to Negritude, Schwarz-Bart's to Negritude and Caribbeanness and Maximin's to Negritude, Caribbeanness and Creoleness. Despite their differences, however, all three writers join in taking the kind of responsibility A. Césaire envisions in his interview with Daniel Maximin:

S'il y a, je crois, quelque chose qui s'impose, c'est de se convaincre encore une fois, chacun à notre niveau, chacun dans nos rôles respectifs, et cela dans tous les domaines, qu'il y a la nécessité de prendre conscience d'une *responsabilité*. Et une volonté non pas de détruire, c'est le plus facile, mais de construire précisément à partir de ce qui a été détruit par la violence de l'Histoire.

(17)

[If there is anything, I believe, that is important, it is to convince ourselves one more time, each at our own level, each in our respective roles and in all areas of endeavour, that there is a necessity to become conscious of a *responsibility*. And the desire not to destroy, that is the easiest, but to build precisely out of that which has been destroyed by the violence of History.]

In privileging the contemporary French Caribbean writer as modern-day maroon, I have emphasized the importance of the *prise de conscience,* the inner voice and a call to action. Each of the writers studied in this article participates in his/her own way in the development of a literature of liberation: Zobel's protagonist refuses condemnation to the cane fields, Schwarz-Bart's women triumph over crushing misfortunes, and Maximin's characters create renewal out of physical and historical losses.

Like their maroon ancestors, these writers respond to Suzanne Césaire's call to action, producing an "exemple incontestable d'opposition systématique, de refus total," [incontestable example of systematic opposition, of total refusal] (Glissant 104) and contribute to the "floraisons communes" [effervescence of the collective]

(Glissant 438) hoped for by Glissant when he wrote of the potential power of the Caribbean artist.[8] This literature, with its island shapes and forms, its dedication to breaking down barriers and its portrait of a multi-layered, multi-racial society, opens doors of discovery for everyone who reads it.

Notes

1. Aimé Césaire, *Cahier d'un retour au pays natal* (New York: Brentano, 1947; Paris: Présence Africaine, 1983), 22.

2. *Tropiques* is the magazine of Martinican culture which Aimé and Suzanne Césaire edited in Fortde-France with René Ménil from 1941 to 1945. In this journal, they and their closest collaborators "spelled out very clearly the ideological connections between the evolving Martinican version of negritude and the culture of European modernism" [A. James Arnold, *Negritude and Modernism: The Poetry and Poetics of Aimé Césaire* (Cambridge: Harvard UP, 1981), 13].

3. Daniel Maximin, personal interview, 19 April 1990. Maximin explains that he writes for several narratees, "le même," "l'autre" and "l'Autre." *My* interpretation of his comments is that "le même" is his Caribbean compatriot, "l'autre" is a person from another part of the world who has a sensitivity to the issues Maximin writes about, and "l'Autre" is the person who refuses to listen because s/he is not interested. Please note that the excerpts from this private interview convey certain of Daniel Maximin's ideas, but they are in unpolished form.

4. Daniel Maximin, *Soufrières* (Paris: Seuil, 1987). See, for example, his description of the residents fleeing the volcano's eruption which begins like this: "Seuls les yeux et les phares des voitures restent visibles. Noirs, Blancs, Indiens, Mulâtres, tous les visages sont de cendre. Les cris sont rares et les gestes sont glacés. L'heure est trop grave pour les terreurs paniques. . . . Comme tout peuple d'exilés, vous savez comment durer pour vaincre, fuir vers d'autres armes à forger dans le répit des frayeurs passagères, fissurer les héroïsmes pour la garde des enfants, aller vers la fin du monde toujours en avançant, plutôt déménager que couler le navire et capituler en pleine récolte. Les peuples trouvés ne savent pas se perdre" [Only the eyes and the lights of the cars remain visible. Blacks, whites, Indians, mulattoes, all the faces are made of ashes. Cries are rare and gestures are frozen. The moment is too serious for panic-stricken terror . . . as all exiled people, you know how to endure in order to conquer, to flee toward other weapons, to forge in the respite of temporary frights, to fissure heroisms in order to save children, to go toward the end of the world always moving forward, to move rather than to submerge the boat and to capitulate while in full harvest. People who have been found don't know how to lose themselves] (150).

5. See Hélène Cixous, "Castration or Decapitation?" *Signs* (Autumn 1981): 41-55.

6. Daniel Maximin, Personal interview, 19 April 1990. Maximin explained the genesis of the vital connection between Caribbean writers and the natural world: "Il y a un rapport élémentaire à la nature. L'air, l'eau, la terre, le feu, dans leur état pur, pas transformés ni ritualisés. . . . On retrouve des relais culturels pour exprimer les sentiments dans la littérature européenne. Ici on est nu. Le seul point de comparaison, c'est la nature. Le premier livre de lecture de l'écriture antillaise, c'est *la nature*. L'autre livre de lecture, c'est *le corps*" [There is an elementary relationship with nature. Air, water, earth, and fire, in their pure state, neither transformed nor ritualized. . . . You find cultural connections to express emotions in European literature. Here we are naked. The only point of comparison is nature. The first primer of Caribbean writing is nature. The other primer is the body].

7. See Arnold, 16-17. See also André Breton, "Un grand poète noir," preface, *Cahier d'un retour au pays natal* (1947; Paris: Présence Africaine, 1983), 77-87.

8. See Glissant's discussion of the artist's role in society, 438-39.

Works Cited

Arnold, A. James. *Modernism and Negritude: The Poetry and Poetics of Aimé Césaire*. Cambridge: Harvard UP, 1981.

Bernabé, Jean, Patrick Chamoiseau, and Raphaël Confiant. *Eloge de la Créolité*. Paris: Gallimard, 1989.

Breton, André. "Un grand poète noir." Preface. *Cahier d'un retour au pays natal*. 1947; Paris: Présence Africaine, 1983. 77-87.

Césaire, Aimé. *Cahier d'un retour au pays natal*. 1947; Paris: Présence Africaine, 1983.

Césaire, Suzanne. "Le Grand Camouflage." *Tropiques* 13-14 (1945): 267-73; Paris: Présence Africaine, 1978.

Cixous, Hélène. "Castration or Decapitation?" *Signs* (Autumn 1981): 41-55.

Condé, Maryse. *La Parole des femmes*. Paris: L'Harmattan, 1979.

———. *Le Roman antillais*. Paris: Fernand Nathan, 1977.

Corzani, Jack. *Prosateurs des Antilles et de la Guyane Françaises*. Fort-de France: Desormeaux, 1971.

Glissant, Edouard. *Le Discours antillais*. Paris: Seuil, 1981.

Leiner, Jacqueline. "Africa and the West Indies: Two Negritudes." *European Language Writing in Sub-Saharan Africa*. Ed. Albert S. Gerard. Budapest: Akadémiai Kiadó, 1986. 1135-53.

Lirus, Julie. *Identité antillaise*. Paris: Caribéennes, 1979.

Maximin, Daniel. "Aimé Césaire: La Poésie, parole essentielle." *Présence Africaine* 126 (1983): 7-23.

——. *L'Isolé soleil*. Paris: Seuil, 1981.

——. Personal interview. 19 April 1990.

——. *Soufrières*. Paris: Seuil, 1987.

Mpoyi-Buatu, Thomas. "Entretien avec Daniel Maximin." *Nouvelles du Sud* 3 (1986): 31-50.

Rancourt, Jacques. "*Moi, laminaire* . . . d'Aimé Césaire." *Notre Librairie* 104 (Jan.-Mar. 1991): 69-71.

Rice-Maximin, Micheline. "'Koko sek toujou ni dlo': Contribution à l'étude des caractères spécifiques de la littérature guadeloupéenne." Diss. U Texas at Austin, 1986.

Schwarz-Bart, Simone. *Pluie et vent sur Télumée Miracle*. Paris: Seuil, 1972.

Toumson, Roger. "La littérature antillaise d'expression française." *Présence Africaine* 121/122 (1982): 130-34.

Zobel, Joseph. *Diab'là*. Paris: Bellenand, 1946. Paris: Nouvelles Editions Latines, 1947.

——. *La Rue Cases-Nègres*. Paris: Froissart, 1950. Paris: Présence Africaine, 1974.

Haseenah Ebrahim (essay date 2002)

SOURCE: Ebrahim, Haseenah. "*Sugar Cane Alley*: Re-reading Race, Class and Identity in Zobel's *La Rue Cases Nègres*." *Literature/Film Quarterly* 30, no. 2 (2002): 146-53.

[*In the following essay, Ebrahim outlines the ideological changes director Euzhan Palcy incorporated into the 1983 film version of Zobel's* La Rue Cases Negres, *which the critic claims is told from a "pan-African feminist" viewpoint.*]

In this essay, I explore issues relating to race, gender, class and identity in the film adaptation of Joseph Zobel's novel, **La Rue Cases Negres** (translated, by Keith Warner, into English under the title **Black Shack Alley**). The film, *Rue Cases Negres* (released under the English title *Sugar Cane Alley*), was directed by Euzhan Palcy, a filmmaker who, like Zobel, was born and raised on the island of Martinique in the French West Indies. Zobel's novel was published in 1950, and banned on the island for 20 years after its publication. I argue that Palcy's film adaptation reflects ideological differences with the novel, differences that reveal a "pan-African feminist" perspective—albeit somewhat ambivalently at

times. Some of these ideological differences emerge from her identity as a woman with exposure to both Caribbean and other feminist/womanist discourses, and from having grown up in a post-departmentalization Martinique in which attitudes toward assimilation have become less optimistic.

Some characteristic features of a "pan-African feminist" critical praxis[1] include the recognition of the mutifaceted nature of black women's oppression, and consequently, the need to fight oppression on multiple fronts, involvement in the struggle for social transformation, the notion of "womanish" behavior (including the everyday defiances of oppression by ordinary black women), a form of feminism stressing male-female complementarity, and the totality of human experience (not just issues of gender). Other characteristics include values emphasizing survival, female autonomy and self-reliance, collectivity over individualism, recognition and respect for alternative systems of knowledge (such as the oral tradition), cultural expression as a major forum for political struggle for black women, and an emphasis on contextualization of cultural production, dissemination, and consumption.

The formulation of a pan-African feminist framework is intended to counter the tendency of mainstream Western feminists to dismiss work that does not privilege gender as the most worthy focus of analysis. For example, in one of the earliest film anthologies on women filmmakers to actually include women of color, Quart labels their work as "pre-feminist," remarking that for Third World women filmmakers, "often other social problems in these cultures seem more pressing" (241). Precisely. This accusation has been made against Palcy too; for example, Pallister criticizes Palcy for being insufficiently concerned with the alienation of black women. Such criticisms reflect a Western mainstream feminist perspective that is rooted in a dissatisfaction with those women directors who do not place gender issues at the center of their agendas. However, African/Diaspora feminisms attempt to integrate feminist activism with other struggles, and acknowledge the multiplicity of oppressions, and concerns, of black women.

In this essay, I will focus on questions of female autonomy and self-reliance, collectivity versus individualism, and recognition and respect for the oral tradition, as they relate to race, gender, class and issues of identity in the film, *Sugar Cane Alley,* and the novel on which it is based, **Black Shack Alley.**[2]

Palcy's first feature film, *Sugar Cane Alley,* is a story of colonial oppression in Martinique. It is based on Joseph Zobel's novel, **La Rue Cases Negres,** first published in 1950 and translated into English under the title, **Black Shack Alley.** Palcy's film adaptation, *Rue Cases Negres* (1983), was released in the United States under the catchier title, *Sugar Cane Alley* (1984), a title which, it may be argued, serves to "sweeten" (or, romanticize) the harsh material existence of black peasants in colonial Martinique.[3]

Sugar Cane Alley is set in the 1930s, and depicts a short period in the life of Jose Hassam, the grandson of a brusque but loving sugarcane worker on a Martinican plantation. The old lady, Ma Tine, is determined to give her grandson the formal education necessary to pull him out of the harsh world of material deprivation and physical labor that constitutes her own lot in life. As a result, she makes a number of sacrifices to ensure Jose is successful at school, including moving to the capital, Fort-de-France, a world of urban sophistication in which she herself is uncomfortable. Here, she has to take in washing to make enough money to supplement the meager scholarship Jose has received to attend the lycee, which would prepare him to either enter the civil service or further his education in France. Subplots include the story of a mulatto boy who is a classmate and friend of Jose's, and the deep bond between Jose and his spiritual father, the old man, Medouze.

In her analysis of three French Caribbean novels, Scarboro observes that in the novel, *Black Shack Alley* "Zobel's fictional world is based on assimilation, i.e., Josh works within the colonizer's system to proclaim his own identity by becoming a writer" (16). Palcy's version, however, minimizes this acceptance of cultural assimilation as the path to liberation from the canefields by enhancing the role of Medouze as the guardian of popular memory. Medouze's counternarratives of history draw on both his own experiences, and that of a popular collective memory, to challenge the emphasis on French history that the children of Martinique are inundated with at their local schools.

There are two, seemingly minor changes that Palcy makes to the role of Medouze. In the first, the novel has Medouze recounting to Jose tales told him by his own father. As a young man, Medouze's father had—together with all the other blacks—fled from the plantations upon hearing that slavery was over. However, they soon found themselves back in the position of having to work for the whites, for a pitiable wage, because the whites still owned the land (Zobel 32-33). In the film, however, Medouze's version of black Caribbean history gives agency to blacks themselves for their role in ending slavery through their rebellions, while also exposing the mechanisms by which the whites continue to wield power. During one of their regular conversations, the camera lingers on Jose's enraptured expression at the passion in old Medouze's voice as he explains (in the words of his father):

> I was a young boy like you, Medouze. All the blacks came down from the hills with sticks, machetes, guns, and torches. They invaded the town of St. Pierre. They burned all the homes. For the first time, blacks saw whites shake with fear, lock themselves in their mansions and die. That was how slavery ended [. . .].

> After slavery, the master had become the boss [. . .] Nothing has changed, son. The whites own all the land. The law forbids their beating us, but it doesn't force them to pay us a decent wage.

Both stories (i.e., as told in the novel and in the film) end by emphasizing how the basic economic relationship in which black labor produced profits for white owners remained the same after emancipation. The primary function of Medouze's storytelling in the film's version, however, is to develop a consciousness that challenges the immutability of official versions of history, versions that do not acknowledge the role of black resistance to slavery. Medouze's invocation of an antislavery rebellion attempts to develop a culture of questioning and of resistance. Palcy presents the act of storytelling, and this invocation of the antislavery rebellion of May 1848 (Herndon; Desalles), as an intervention in the colonial logic described by her countryman, Frantz Fanon, who noted that "colonialism is not simply content to impose its rule upon the present and the future. . . . By a kind of perverted logic, it turns to the past of the oppressed people, and distorts, disfigures, and destroys it" (210). Kubayanda notes that the history of slave rebellions and "marooning" or "marronage" has, in recent years, become an important paradigm in many Caribbean and Latin American nations in the effort to re-examine the history of Africans in the Americas. Palcy assigns this task to the village elder, Medouze.

Martinique had officially become an "overseas department" of France in 1946. The early years of departmentalization which occurred when the novel was written, brought with it a hope that assimilation into French society would bring escape from racial discrimination. The politics of this assimilationist approach, and resistances to it, would come later. Nevertheless, within the context of Martinique, Frenchness has always been considered a path to upward social mobility, with French schooling and fluency in—and use of—the French language being crucial to self-advancement (Burton). This, in fact, is the major theme of Zobel's *Black Shack Alley.*

Certainly, a celebration of the African-derived elements of black Martinican society is present in the novel. However, its value in the development of a unique Caribbean identity is strengthened by the changes made by Palcy. Medouze's stories provide the foundation for a strong sense of identity to counter the inroads made on the self-esteem of a young black child by the French educational system and by the Martinican social structure, both of which denigrate African heritage. Palcy's narrative strategy draws heavily on orality, storytelling and the elided historical consciousness, to reveal that Jose's identity—and Caribbean identity—requires negotiating a path between two cultures, an imperial one and an ancestral one. Cultural elements drawn from the African oral tradition, such as the laghia and the storytelling at wakes, compete with the elite's elevation of the French language, and of French customs and practices. Against French cultural imposition is juxtaposed the fabrication of charms, the singing of chants to ward off evil, work songs that ridicule "whitey," and the riddles and tales told by Medouze, all of which can be considered to constitute a discursive space representing what novelist Maryse Conde defines as "a pedagogy of survival in a hostile environment" (Shelton 718).

The second change Paley makes with regard to Medouze is that she retains his living influence on Jose for a more extended period. Indeed, the novel portrays Medouze in a similar manner to that in the film, but in the novel he dies before Jose even begins attending school. Palcy, however, presents Medouze as a countervailing force to that of the school and French colonial culture, so that Jose is able to move from one geographical/cultural space to the other with the fluidity of a hybridized identity. In doing so, Palcy engages in what Lionnet has referred to as "the deconstruction of hierarchies, not their reversal" (6). Thus, both Medouze—representing ancestral knowledge and memory—and Monsieur Stephen Roc—representing the world of colonial literacy and French culture—are presented as characters much admired by the young Jose.

Palcy's depiction of the continuing presence of the oral tradition in the New World echoes the childhood reminiscences of Kenyan writer, Ngugi wa Thiong'o:

> Our appreciation of the suggestive magical power of language was reinforced by the games we played with words through fiddles, proverbs, transposition of syllables. . . . So we learned the music of our language on top of the content . . . The home and the field were then our preprimary school but what is important . . . is that the language of our evening teach-ins, and the language of our immediate and wider community, and the language of our work in the fields were one.
>
> (10)

The novel, on the other hand, draws a clearer connection than does the film of the correlation between literacy and the ability to recognize one's oppression. In the novel, Jose's former schoolmate, Jojo, discovers that the manager's account books at the sugar factory have been doctored. He also understands that his ability to recognize the falsification of the records results from having retained some of his "learning" from his painful schooldays. Literacy and numeracy enable him to draw the workers' attention to their exploitation. As Kande notes, "orality in *Black Shack Alley,* imposed as a mode of exclusive knowledge by the peonage system, also perpetuates the segregation of bike landowners, who possess writing skills, and workers of African origin, who are illiterate and therefore subject to merciless pressures" (40). Ma Tine clearly recognizes the role of literacy in the social stratification of Martinican society, and in the mechanics of oppression, when she openly

proclaims her contempt for those blacks who condemn their children to a life of hardship in the canefields by pulling them out of school.

Menil observes that "one cannot help but be surprised by the fact that M'man Tine's discourse is received differently than in 1950. Emancipation through schooling was perhaps the only solution for the sons of slaves rejecting their disguised slave condition, but we also know the price that was paid, maybe the price of our country" (168-9). This difference in reception to the value placed on French schooling could be ascribed to the fact that the novel was written at a time when literacy could not be taken for granted by black Martinicans, whereas Palcy's generation does not have to question its right to an education. It is a generation which is, instead, highly conscious of the need to acknowledge the importance of orality in Martinican culture. Today, the hopes pinned on the French-imposed formal education as a means of empowerment may seem a little overoptimistic, even naive, with the hindsight that neo-colonialism has brought, but the significance of illiteracy as a tool in the maintenance of exploitation and oppression cannot be underestimated.

Noticeably more pronounced in the film, too, is the racialized nature of Martinican social stratification. Martinique's population has historically consisted of three principal strata: the white/bike upper class, the mulatto middle class and a predominantly black lower class. According to Burton "to be light-skinned still confers definite social and sexual advantages in Martinique (especially) and Guadeloupe, and, despite the rise of a substantial middle class since 1946, a high degree of correlation still obtains between class and colour" (11).

While racial and class issues are certainly addressed in the novel, the film chooses to confront the subject much more directly. Palcy creates a new character, Leopold, to illustrate the liminal political and social position occupied by the mulatto in Martinican society. Leopold, the child of a white Frenchman and his black mistress, is deeply hurt when he overhears his father, even as he lies on his deathbed, refusing to give his son his French family name, de Thorail. For the Frenchman, his name is too noble to be given to a mulatto, even if s/he is his own child.

Leopold's story combines—with some changes—what appears in the novel as scattered references to issues of racial and social stratification. By consolidating these elements into a coherent character and subplot, Palcy is able to develop a story which merely takes up a few paragraphs in the novel into an exploration of the contradictions of the mulatto experience, privileged in Martinican society as compared to blacks, but also—in the words of a worksong heard in the film—"whitey's nigger." The introduction of this subplot permits Palcy to portray the development of a color-based stratification through little vignettes in which both his black mother and his white father scold Leopold for playing with the black children. His parents' chastisements denigrate both blackness and the use of Creole, the language spoken by most blacks in 1930s Martinique. Menil notes that "Leopold challenges racial taboo, while Georges Roc [the character in the novel on whom Leopold is partially based] expresses only the rejection of social hierarchy" (170). Palcy also captures the complexity and irony of the position of Honorine, Leopold's mother, when she proudly puts on a new song by Josephine Baker, the black American singer who had achieved fame in Paris. As Pauly notes, "in two bars of a song, Palcy generates a multi-layered anti-colonial intertext with a legendary black female [also] caught between two worlds" (249).

Leopold exemplifies the hybrid but troubled nature of Caribbean identity. The film draws a direct connection between Leopold's coming to political consciousness and his white father's rejection. However, it is only after his father's betrayal that Leopold begins to identify with the oppressed segments of Martinican society, having up to this point steadfastly defended the reputation of whites against his little black friends' beliefs about their evil nature.

The character of Leopold—who is arrested after he attempts to steal the ledger at his father's sugar factory in order to expose the doctored books that deny the sugarcane workers their rightful pay—also departs from the archetypal mulatto-as-betrayer of blacks, as he himself becomes the one betrayed through the rejection of the white father he loves. While Zobel's novel was written at a time when Negritude was at its height in the black Francophone world, Palcy's film was made over 30 years later when cultural attitudes tended to emphasize Creolite as the synthesis of the various cultures that make up the Caribbean. While much of the celebratory discourse of Creolite tends to mask inequalities of power, it remains a concern of Palcy's. Although acknowledging the hybridity of Caribbean identity and culture, Paley is careful to expose the underlying biases against African cultural heritage concealed by the discourses of hybridity.

Cesar has noted that the representation of the social and racial environments in novel and film are further supported by the linguistic changes made by Paley. Shelton argues that the Caribbean has now entered an era that could be considered post-Negritude, one in which the Caribbean is increasingly being viewed as "neither a detached piece of Africa nor a remote province of France nor the backyard of the USA" (717). This view constitutes the foundation for the notion of antillanite, which reformulates historical agency in terms of metissage, one which emphasizes mixture and diversity, with its linguistic parallel in the concepts of creolite or oralite. While the language of the novel is French, with a few Creole expressions translated at the bottom of the pages, the film uses both French and Creole, acknowledging its prevalence among the non-elite of Martinique.

Paley expands Zobel's exploration of racial and class stratification in Martinican society to include gender. In the novel, Jose is the only child chosen to sit for the scholarship exam, but Paley includes the young girl, Tortilla, as one of two children invited by the teacher to do so. This allows Paley to address directly how Tortilla's experiences and opportunities differ from those afforded Jose. Gendered expectations with regard to education allow Tortilla to simply accept her father's decision not to let her continue with her education.

The depiction of women in *Sugar Cane Alley* generally reflects the pan-African feminist celebration of female autonomy and self-reliance through female networks, and collectivity over individualism. Generally, women play a prominent role in Jose's life—Madame Leonce, Mam'zelle Delice, Madame Fusil, etc., all take care of him from time to time. Except for Madame Leonce, the love of the women for Jose, as well as for each other, is reflected in the care that other women take of Ma Tine and of Jose when the former is ill. Paley has remarked that "women in Martinique are lovers, they are very kind, very lovely. But they are proud, very strong, very hard. They don't let you see their tenderness" (Linfield 44).

However, Paley's pan-African feminist sensibilities appear somewhat ambivalent at times. Perhaps the most interesting departure from the novel is one that is least explicable, except as a possible consequence of budgetary constraints. In the novel, two women, his mother (Delia) and grandmother (Ma Tine) feature prominently as pillars of strength and support in young Jose's life—the latter in the earlier years, and the former during the phase of city life. Both women are resolute in their determination to ensure social mobility for Jose through education. Ma Tine had ensured her daughter's life would not be as harsh as her own, by placing her to be trained in domestic duties in order to be employed in the homes of her employers instead of in their fields. But Paley combines their characters into one and focuses on the matriarchal figure of Ma Tine as the primary female source of the grit and determination crucial to Jose's success, thereby undermining—albeit to a limited extent—the pan-African feminist recognition of the importance of collective support. Nevertheless, the pan-African feminist notion of womanish defiance is unforgettably captured in Ma Tine's dismayed, but determined, retort upon hearing that the promised scholarship was only a fraction of the cost of Jose's schooling. "You will go to their school," she states, before embarking on a grueling life of washing and ironing in the city.

In addition, the novel describes the sexual harassment faced by Carmen, an older friend of Jose's. Carmen is forced to deal with the unwelcome sexual advances of the white mistress of the household in which he is employed. The film, however, depicts Carmen as a flighty young man who has no problem satisfying his white mistress's sexual needs—and who even revels in the affair—in a scene in which he displays great insensitivity to Jose's distress at being accused of cheating at school. The film's transformation of what is clearly a painful problem for Carmen in the novel ("It's bothering me a lot," Carmen says to Jose) into a frivolous interracial sexual dalliance, masks the racialized nature of sexual harassment, which makes both men and women its targets, in what is clearly a display of racial and class power. In the novel, Carmen reflects on the politeness that he must maintain in the face of his employer's sexual advances, politeness "due to a boss, politeness imposed by the whiteness of her skin" (Zobel 176). A pan-African feminist framework necessitates addressing the issues facing black men and women, not just women. Race and class privileges permit Carmen's mistress to circumvent the usual restraints imposed on white women by gender inequalities, in a clear illustration of both the potential, and historical reality, of the participation of white middle-and upper-class women in the oppression of blacks.

A pan-African feminist consciousness also shares with black men concerns regarding racial and other forms of oppression. Thus, when Tortilla's mother gives birth to a stillborn child, the event is met with the sentiment that another black child has been saved from the white man's canefields. However, Paley obviously shares with Zobel and her best known countryman, Frantz Fanon, a concern for the self-hatred or identity confusion of black Martinicans whose internalization of white racist ideologies leads them to aspire to marriage with whites and a desire to "lighten the race." The film reproduces a scene in the novel when Jose confronts a young woman employed at the local movie theater who declares that she may have a black skin, but that she is white inside—clearly an invocation of Fanon's analysis of questions of racial identity in *Black Skin, White Masks*.

Ultimately, Paley draws the protagonist in what one suspects is her own image rather than Zobel's. In the novel, Jose appears as a somewhat passive child, things happen to him. In Paley's portrayal, however, Jose is more than just a resilient child. He can be quite rebellious. Thus, an incident in the novel in which Jose flees in fear when a pitcher accidentally breaks in his hand at Madame Leonce's house is transformed into Jose's rebellion against his exploitation—he sneaks out of class to throw stones at her dishes drying out in the sun. In addition, Ma Tine chastises Jose for staring at her, arguing that children should not stare at adults—a reminder of bell hooks's idea of the "oppositional gaze" (116)— the looks of children at adults, and of slaves at slave owners—which hooks sees as constituting a form of resistance.

The changes Paley makes in the shift from novel to screen constitute a conscious—if not always cohesive or coherent—change in perspective, perhaps even inevitably so, considering that the feisty Paley is a product of a later generation than the novelist, of post-departmentalization Martinique, and of a generation of highly educated women who have been exposed to feminist and nationalist ideologies, as well as the paradigm of "marooning" in which the rebel figure becomes the icon of black Caribbean identity. Paley's pan-African feminist sensibilities once again motivate a re-reading of race and gender issues in her second feature film, *A Dry White Season,* an adaptation of the novel of the same name by the South African writer, Andre Brink.

Notes

1. I discuss the notion of a pan-African feminist critical praxis in much greater detail, and with greater contextualization, in my Ph.D. dissertation entitled *Re-Viewing the Tropical Paradise: Afro-Caribbean Women Filmmakers,* Northwestern University, 1998.

2. In this article, I use the English titles of both novel and film for consistency, and to avoid confusion.

3. I thank the anonymous reader who brought this to my attention.

Works Cited

Burac, Maurice. "The French Antilles and the Wider Caribbean." *French and West Indian: Martinique, Guadeloupe and French Guiana Today,* Ed. Richard D. E. Burton and Fred Reno. Charlottesville, VA: UP of Virginia, 1995.

Burton, Richard D. E. "The French West Indies d l'heure de l'Europe: An Overview." *French and West Indian: Martinique, Guadeloupe and French Guiana Today.* Ed. Richard D. E. Burton and Fred Reno. Charlottesville, VA: UP of Virginia, 1995.

Cesar, Sylvie. *"La Rue Cases-Negres": Du Roman au Film (bude Comparative).* Paris: Editions L'Harmattan, 1994.

Dessalles, Pierre. *Sugar and Slavery, Family and Race: The Letters and Diary of Pierre Dessalles, Planter in Martinique, 1808-1856.* Trans. Elborg Forster and Robert Forster. Baltimore: Johns Hopkins UP, 1996.

Fanon, Frantz. *The Wretched of the Earth.* New York: Grove Weidenfeld, 1963.

Glissant, Edouard. *Caribbean Discourse: Selected Essay.* Trans. J. Michael Dash. Charlottesville: UP of Virginia. [1981]

Herndon, Gerise. "Auto-Ethnographic Impulse in *Rue Cases-Negres.*" *Literature/Film Quarterly* 24.3 (1996): 261-266.

hooks, bell. *Black Looks: Race and Representation.* Boston: South End P, 1992.

Kubayanda, Joseph Bekunuru. "Minority Discourse and the African Collective: Some Examples from Latin American and Caribbean Literature." Ed. Abdul R. JanMohamed and David Lloyd. *The Nature and Context of Minority Discourse.* Oxford: Oxford UP, 1990.

Kande, Sylvie. "Renunication and Victory in *Black Shack Alley.*" *Research in African Literatures* 25.2 (1994): 33-50.

Linfield, Susan. "*Sugar Cane Alley:* An Interview with Euzhan Palcy." *Cineaste* 13.4 (1984): 43-44.

Lionnet, Franqoise. *Postcolonial Representations: Women, Literature, Identity.* Ithaca, NY: Cornell UP, 1995.

Menil, Alain. "*Rue Cases Negres,* or the Antilles from the Inside." Ed. Mbye B. Chan. *Ex-Iles: Essays on Caribbean Cinema.* Trenton, NJ: Africa World P, 1992.

Ngugi wa Thiong o. *Decolonizing the Mind: The Politics of Language in African Literature.* Naitobi: James Currey, 1986.

Ogunyemi. Chikweny Okonjo. "Womanism: The Dynamics of the Contemporary Black Female Novel in English." *Signs* 11.1 (1985): 63-80.

Pallister, Janis L. "From La Noire de . . . to Milk & Honey; Portraits of the Alienated African Women." Ed. Phanuel Akubueze Egejuru and Ketu H. Katrak. *Nwanyibu: Womanbeing and African Literature.* Trenton. NJ: Africa World P, 1997.

Pauly, Rebecca M. *The Transparent Illusion: Image and Ideology in French Text and Film.* New York: P. Lang, c 1993.

Quart, Barbara Koening. *Women Directors: The Emergence of a New Cinema.* New York: Praeger, 1988.

Searboro, Ann Armstrong. "A Shift Toward the Inner Voice and Creolite in the French Caribbean Novel." *Callaloo* 15.1 (1992): 12-29.

Shelton, Marie. "Conde': The Politics of Gender and Identity." *World Literature Today* 67.4 (1993): 717-722.

Walker, Alice. *In Search of Our Mothers' Gardens: Womanist Prose.* London: The Women's P, 1983.

Zobel. Joseph. *Black Shack Alley: La Rue Cases Negres.* Trans. Keith Q. Warner. Washington, DC: Three Continents P, 1980.

FURTHER READING

Criticism

Coulthard, G. R. "The West Indian Novel of Immigration." *Phylon Quarterly* 20, no. 1 (1959): 32-41.
> Assesses the manner in which Zobel treated themes of colonialism, race relations, and French culture in *Fête à Paris*.

Kande, Sylvie and Kwaku Gyasi. "Renunciation and Victory in *Black Shack Alley.*" *Research in African Literatures* 25, no. 2 (summer 1994): 33-52.
> Examining the novel as a communal autobiography, looks at orality and the written word within the context of societal oppression.

How to Use This Index

The main references

```
Calvino, Italo
    1923-1985 ....... CLC 5, 8, 11, 22, 33, 39,
                                    73; SSC 3, 48
```

list all author entries in the following Gale Literary Criticism series:

AAL = *Asian American Literature*
BG = *The Beat Generation: A Gale Critical Companion*
BLC = *Black Literature Criticism*
BLCS = *Black Literature Criticism Supplement*
CLC = *Contemporary Literary Criticism*
CLR = *Children's Literature Review*
CMLC = *Classical and Medieval Literature Criticism*
DC = *Drama Criticism*
FL = *Feminism in Literature: A Gale Critical Companion*
GL = *Gothic Literature: A Gale Critical Companion*
HLC = *Hispanic Literature Criticism*
HLCS = *Hispanic Literature Criticism Supplement*
HR = *Harlem Renaissance: A Gale Critical Companion*
LC = *Literature Criticism from 1400 to 1800*
NCLC = *Nineteenth-Century Literature Criticism*
NNAL = *Native North American Literature*
PC = *Poetry Criticism*
SSC = *Short Story Criticism*
TCLC = *Twentieth-Century Literary Criticism*
WLC = *World Literature Criticism, 1500 to the Present*
WLCS = *World Literature Criticism Supplement*

The cross-references

```
See also CA 85-88, 116; CANR 23, 61;
DAM NOV; DLB 196; EW 13; MTCW 1, 2;
RGSF 2; RGWL 2; SFW 4; SSFS 12
```

list all author entries in the following Gale biographical and literary sources:

AAYA = *Authors & Artists for Young Adults*
AFAW = *African American Writers*
AFW = *African Writers*
AITN = *Authors in the News*
AMW = *American Writers*
AMWR = *American Writers Retrospective Supplement*
AMWS = *American Writers Supplement*
ANW = *American Nature Writers*
AW = *Ancient Writers*
BEST = *Bestsellers*
BPFB = *Beacham's Encyclopedia of Popular Fiction: Biography and Resources*
BRW = *British Writers*
BRWS = *British Writers Supplement*
BW = *Black Writers*
BYA = *Beacham's Guide to Literature for Young Adults*
CA = *Contemporary Authors*
CAAS = *Contemporary Authors Autobiography Series*
CABS = *Contemporary Authors Bibliographical Series*
CAD = *Contemporary American Dramatists*
CANR = *Contemporary Authors New Revision Series*
CAP = *Contemporary Authors Permanent Series*
CBD = *Contemporary British Dramatists*
CCA = *Contemporary Canadian Authors*
CD = *Contemporary Dramatists*
CDALB = *Concise Dictionary of American Literary Biography*

CDALBS = *Concise Dictionary of American Literary Biography Supplement*

CDBLB = *Concise Dictionary of British Literary Biography*

CMW = *St. James Guide to Crime & Mystery Writers*

CN = *Contemporary Novelists*

CP = *Contemporary Poets*

CPW = *Contemporary Popular Writers*

CSW = *Contemporary Southern Writers*

CWD = *Contemporary Women Dramatists*

CWP = *Contemporary Women Poets*

CWRI = *St. James Guide to Children's Writers*

CWW = *Contemporary World Writers*

DA = *DISCovering Authors*

DA3 = *DISCovering Authors 3.0*

DAB = *DISCovering Authors: British Edition*

DAC = *DISCovering Authors: Canadian Edition*

DAM = *DISCovering Authors: Modules*

   DRAM: *Dramatists Module;* **MST:** *Most-studied Authors Module;*

   MULT: *Multicultural Authors Module;* **NOV:** *Novelists Module;*

   POET: *Poets Module;* **POP:** *Popular Fiction and Genre Authors Module*

DFS = *Drama for Students*

DLB = *Dictionary of Literary Biography*

DLBD = *Dictionary of Literary Biography Documentary Series*

DLBY = *Dictionary of Literary Biography Yearbook*

DNFS = *Literature of Developing Nations for Students*

EFS = *Epics for Students*

EXPN = *Exploring Novels*

EXPP = *Exploring Poetry*

EXPS = *Exploring Short Stories*

EW = *European Writers*

FANT = *St. James Guide to Fantasy Writers*

FW = *Feminist Writers*

GFL = *Guide to French Literature,* Beginnings to 1789, 1798 to the Present

GLL = *Gay and Lesbian Literature*

HGG = *St. James Guide to Horror, Ghost & Gothic Writers*

HW = *Hispanic Writers*

IDFW = *International Dictionary of Films and Filmmakers: Writers and Production Artists*

IDTP = *International Dictionary of Theatre: Playwrights*

LAIT = *Literature and Its Times*

LAW = *Latin American Writers*

JRDA = *Junior DISCovering Authors*

MAICYA = *Major Authors and Illustrators for Children and Young Adults*

MAICYAS = *Major Authors and Illustrators for Children and Young Adults Supplement*

MAWW = *Modern American Women Writers*

MJW = *Modern Japanese Writers*

MTCW = *Major 20th-Century Writers*

NCFS = *Nonfiction Classics for Students*

NFS = *Novels for Students*

PAB = *Poets: American and British*

PFS = *Poetry for Students*

RGAL = *Reference Guide to American Literature*

RGEL = *Reference Guide to English Literature*

RGSF = *Reference Guide to Short Fiction*

RGWL = *Reference Guide to World Literature*

RHW = *Twentieth-Century Romance and Historical Writers*

SAAS = *Something about the Author Autobiography Series*

SATA = *Something about the Author*

SFW = *St. James Guide to Science Fiction Writers*

SSFS = *Short Stories for Students*

TCWW = *Twentieth-Century Western Writers*

WLIT = *World Literature and Its Times*

WP = *World Poets*

YABC = *Yesterday's Authors of Books for Children*

YAW = *St. James Guide to Young Adult Writers*

Black Literature Criticism
Cumulative Author Index

Black Literature Criticism
Cumulative Nationality Index

Black Literature Criticism
Cumulative Title Index

Title Index

Narrative of the Life and Escape of William Wells Brown (Brown)
See *Narrative of William W. Brown, a Fugitive Slave, Written by Himself*
Narrative of the Life of Frederick Douglass, an American Slave, Written by Himself (Douglass) **1:1**:576–58, 581, 583–85, 588
Narrative of William W. Brown, a Fugitive Slave, Written by Himself (Brown) **1:1**:294–95, 297, 305
Natalie Mann (Toomer) **1:3**:1760
"Nation Time" (Baraka)
See "It's Nation Time"
"National Security" (Cortez) **2:1**:363
Native Labour in South Africa (Plaatje) **BLCS**:390
Native Life in South Africa (Plaatje) **BLCS**:390–91, 394–96, 401, 403–04
Native Son (Wright) **1:3**:1997, 1999, 2000–04, 2009–12, 2014–15, 2017–19
Natives of My Person (Lamming) **1:2**:1232–34, 1236–37; **2:2**:393, 400
"Nature for Nature's sake" (Mqhayi) **1:3**:1462
The Nature of Blood (Phillips) **BLCS**:382–85
The Nawal El Saadawi Reader (El Saadawi)
See *North/South: The Nawal El Saadawi Reader*
"Nayga Bikkle" (Goodison) **2:2**:95
Ne nous énervons pas (Himes) **1:2**:1010, 1016–17, 1019–20
"Near White" (Cullen) **1:1**:506
"Ned's Psalm of Life for the Negro" (Cotter) **1:1**:476
The Negro (Du Bois) **1:1**:606, 615
"The Negro Artist and the Racial Mountain" (Hughes) **1:2**:1059–60, 1064–65
"Negro bembón" (Guillén) **1:2**:916
"The Negro, Communism, Trade Unionism and His (?) Friend" (Garvey) **1:2**:874
"The Negro Hero" (Brooks) **1:1**:252
The Negro in Art (Locke) **BLCS**:277
The Negro in the American Rebellion: His Heroism and His Fidelity (Brown) **1:1**:294, 296–97
"The Negro in the Drawing Room" (Hughes) **1:2**:1047–48
The Negro in the Rebellion (Brown)
See *The Negro in the American Rebellion: His Heroism and His Fidelity*
"Negro Love Song" (Cotter) **1:1**:476
"A Negro Peddler's Song" (Johnson) **1:2**:1112
"A Negro Saw the Jewish Pageant, 'We Will Never Die'" (Dodson) **1:1**:572
"A Negro Speaks of Rivers" (Hughes) **1:2**:1056, 1063
Negro Tales (Cotter) **1:1**:479
"The Negro Woman" (Cotter) **1:1**:476
"The Negro Writer and His World" (Lamming) **1:2**:1235
"Negroes are anti-Semitic because they are anti-White" (Baldwin) **1:1**:96
"The Negro's Educational Creed" (Cotter) **1:1**:476
"The Negro's Ten Commandments" (Cotter) **1:1**:474
"Nelse Hatton's Revenge" (Dunbar) **1:1**:632, 636
"Nelse Hatton's Vengeance" (Dunbar)
See "Nelse Hatton's Revenge"
"Neo-HooDoo Manifesto" (Reed) **1:3**:1625
Neon Vernacular: New and Selected Poems (Komunyakaa) **BLCS**:218–219, 223, 225–227; **2:2**:365, 368, 372
Nervous Conditions (Dangarembga) **2:1**:412–20, 422
"Nestor's Bathtub" (Dove) **BLCS**:112
Never Again (Nwapa) **BLCS**:347–48
Never Die Alone (Goines) **1:2**:905
"Never Expect" (Goodison) **2:2**:91, 96
A New Battle in Woman's Cause (El Saadawi)
See *Ma'raka Jadîda fi Qadiyyat al-Mar'a*
"New Birth-Cords" (Anyidoho) **2:1**:89, 91

"A New Cologne" (Cortez) **2:1**:363
"The New Day" (Johnson) **1:2**:1112
"The New Farmer's Bank" (Osundare) **2:3**:183
"New Husband" (Adichie) **2:1**:29
"New Life at Kyerefaso" (Sutherland) **2:3**:279, 284, 286
"A New Man" (Jones) **2:2**:258–60
The New Nationalism (Baraka) **1:1**:146
The New Negro (Locke) **BLCS**:275, 280, 283, 291
"The New Negro in Literature, 1925-1955" (Brown) **1:1**:286
The New Republican (Soyinka) **2:3**:270–71
"The New Ships" (Brathwaite) **BLCS**:40
A New Song (Hughes) **1:2**:1050–51, 1062
"The New Woman" (Guillén)
See "Mujer nueva"
"The New Woman" (Randall) **1:3**:1606
"New World" (Madhubuti) **1:2**:1321
"New Year Letter" (Brathwaite) **BLCS**:38
"New York" (Senghor) **1:3**:1683
New York Head Shop and Museum (Lorde) **1:2**:1282
"Newcomer" (Okigbo) **1:3**:1526
"Newport Beach 1979" (Komunyakaa) **2:2**:367
"Newport Jazz Festival" (Jordan) **BLCS**:204
"News from Ethiopia and the Sudan" (Clark Bekederemo) **1:1**:428
"The News from Home" (Anyidoho) **2:1**:98
Next: New Poems (Clifton) **1:1**:467; **2:1**:315, 319
Ngaahika Ndeenda (Ngugi) **1:3**:1507
Niaye (Sembène) **1:3**:1533–34; **2:3**:237
A Nib in the Pond (Osundare) **2:3**:179–80, 188
The Nicholas Factor (Myers) **1:3**:1473, 1480
"Nigerian/American Relations" (Cortez) **2:1**:365, 388
"Nigerian Unity/or Little Niggers Killing Little Niggers" (Madhubuti) **1:2**:1315–16
"Nigger" (Sanchez) **1:3**:1661
"Nigger Lover" (McKay) **1:3**:1395
"Night of Sine" (Senghor)
See "Nuit de Sine"
Night of the Beast (Bullins) **1:1**:331–32, 334–35
"The Night Rhonda Ferguson Was Killed" (Jones) **2:2**:258
"Night Rain" (Clark Bekederemo) **1:1**:418, 422, 426–28
"Night Song" (Clark Bekederemo) **1:1**:421
The Night-Blooming Cereus (Hayden) **1:2**:988
Nightsong (Williams) **1:3**:1934, 1939, 1942–44
"Nightsong: City" (Brutus) **1:1**:311–13, 315, 317
"Nightsong: Country" (Brutus) **1:1**:310
"Nihilism in Black America" (West) **BLCS**:441
"Nikki-Rosa" (Giovanni) **1:2**:893
Nine Men Who Laughed (Clarke) **1:1**:443
"1955; or, You Can't Keep a Good Woman Down" (Walker)
See "Nineteen Fifty-Five"
"Nineteen Fifty-Five" (Walker) **1:3**:1817
19 Necromancers (Reed) **1:3**:1611
"1994" (Clifton) **2:1**:318
"1977: Poem for Mrs. Fannie Lou Hamer" (Jordan) **BLCS**:205
99 Years and a Dark Day (Andrews) **2:1**:41, 46
"Niobe in Distress for Her Children Slain by Apollo" (Wheatley) **1:3**:1894
Njamba Nene and the Flying Bus (Ngugi)
See *Njamba Nene na Mbaathi I Mathagu*
Njamba Nene na Mbaathi I Mathagu (Ngugi) **1:3**:1508; **2:3**:145
Nkrumah and the Ghana Revolution (James) **BLCS**:178
"No Assistance" (Shange) **1:3**:1694
"No Body No Place" (Baraka) **2:1**:177
"No Chocolates for Breakfast" (Jordan) **BLCS**:207–208
No Hidin Place (Brown) **1:1**:287
No Longer at Ease (Achebe) **1:1**:3, 5, 10–11; **2:1**:16–20

"No more love poems #1" (Shange) **1:3**:1694–95
"No More Marching" (Madhubuti) **1:2**:1313
No Place to Be Somebody (Gordone) **2:2**:102–4, 106, 109–14, 116–17
"No Simple Explanations (To the Memory of Larry Neal)" (Cortez) **2:1**:364–65
"No Sweetness Here" (Aidoo) **BLCS**:2
No Sweetness Here (Aidoo) **BLCS**:2, 6
No Telephone to Heaven (Cliff) **BLCS**:77, 79–87, 89–90
"Noah Built the Ark" (Johnson) **1:2**:1122, 1124
Nobody Knows My Name: More Notes of a Native Son (Baldwin) **1:1**:84–85, 93, 104
"Noche de negros junto a la catedral" (Guillén) **1:2**:920
"Nocturne" (La Guma) **BLCS**:246–47, 251
"Nocturne at Bethesda" (Bontemps) **1:1**:224
Nocturnes (Senghor) **1:3**:1675, 1677, 1683, 1686
"Noh Lickle Twang" (Bennett) **1:1**:185–86
La Noire de... (Sembène) **1:3**:1534
"Nokulunga's Wedding" (Mhlophe) **2:3**:67, 69
"North" (Walcott) **1:3**:1802
"North and South" (McKay) **1:3**:1380
"North and South" (Walcott) **1:3**:1798
North/South: The Nawal El Saadawi Reader (El Saadawi) **2:2**:29–30, 32–33
The Norton Anthology of African American Literature (Gates) **BLCS**:156–58, 161
"Nostalgia in Times Square" (Young) **1:3**:2044
"Not in My Season of Songs" (Osundare) **2:3**:188
"Not Sacco and Vanzetti" (Cullen) **1:1**:513
Not without Laughter (Hughes) **1:2**:1045–46, 1050, 1055, 1058
"Notebook of a Return to the Native Land" (Césaire)
See *Cahier d'un retour au pays natal*
"Notes d'un retour au pays natal" (Condé) **BLCS**:102
Notes of a Native Son (Baldwin) **1:1**:78, 85, 89, 93, 103
"Notes on a Native Son" (Cleaver) **1:1**:447
Notes on Dialectics: Hegel, Marx, Lenin (James) **BLCS**:192
"Notes on Speechlessness" (Cliff) **BLCS**:78
"Notes Towards Home" (Jordan) **BLCS**:205
"Nothing and Something" (Harper) **1:2**:977, 980
"Nothing Down" (Dove) **BLCS**:114, 125–126
Nothing Personal (Baldwin) **1:1**:93
"Nouveau sermon nègre" (Roumain) **1:3**:1631, 1635, 1645
Nova (Delany) **1:1**:530–31, 536–37
"November Cotton Flower" (Toomer) **1:3**:1759, 1763
"November 21, 1968" (Clifton) **2:1**:317
"Now" (Walker) **1:3**:1835
"now I love somebody more than" (Shange) **1:3**:1694
No. 1 with a Bullet (Elder) **1:1**:668
"Nude Interrogation" (Komunyakaa) **2:2**:371
"Nuit de Sine" (Senghor) **1:3**:1674
Les nuits de Strasbourg (Djebar) **2:1**:471–72, 474–76, 478
"Nullo" (Toomer) **1:3**:1763–64
Nyamekye (Sutherland) **2:3**:276
"Nympholepsy" (Braithwaite) **1:1**:243
"Ö" (Dove) **BLCS**:122–123, 126–127; **2:1**:494
O Babylon (Walcott) **1:3**:1801
"O Casa da Vara" (Machado de Assis) **1:2**:1294
"O espelho" (Machado de Assis) **1:2**:1299
O Pays, mon beau peuple! (Sembène) **1:3**:1532; **2:3**:228
"O, Roots!" (Soyinka) **1:3**:1719, 1721
Oak and Ivy (Dunbar) **1:1**:628, 630
"Obeah Win de War" (Bennett) **1:1**:185
"Obedience" (Dove) **2:1**:484
"Obituary for a Living Lady" (Brooks) **1:1**:261
Obra poética (Guillén) **1:2**:917
"Obsolete Geography" (Cliff) **BLCS**:78

Title Index

"To A Learned Lady" (Clark Bekederemo) **1:1**:424, 426

"To a Man" (Angelou) **1:1**:32–33

"To a Winter Squirrel" (Brooks) **1:1**:256

"To a Young Girl Leaving the Hill Country" (Bontemps) **1:1**:224

"To All Sisters" (Sanchez) **1:3**:1666

"To America" (Johnson) **1:2**:1135

"To an Old Man" (Randall) **1:3**:1606

"To an Unknown Poet" (Cullen) **1:1**:511

To Be a Slave (Lester) **2:2**:405, 409–12, 415, 417, 425

"To Be in Love" (Brooks) **1:1**:256–57

"To Be Quicker for Black Political Prisoners" (Madhubuti) **1:2**:1321

To Be Young, Gifted, and Black: A Portrait of Lorraine Hansberry in Her Own Words (Hansberry)
See *To Be Young, Gifted, and Black: The World of Lorraine Hansberry*

To Be Young, Gifted, and Black: Lorraine Hansberry in Her Own Words, An Informal Autobiography of Lorraine Hansberry (Hansberry)
See *To Be Young, Gifted, and Black: The World of Lorraine Hansberry*

To Be Young, Gifted, and Black: The World of Lorraine Hansberry (Hansberry) **1:2**:957; **2:2**:123–24

"To Blk/Record/Buyers" (Sanchez) **1:3**:1655

"To Certain Critics" (Cullen) **1:1**:504, 512

"To Chuck" (Sanchez) **1:3**:1662

"To Da-duh, In Memoriam" (Marshall) **1:3**:1371

"To Dante Gabriel Rossetti" (Braithwaite) **1:1**:244

To Disembark (Brooks) **1:1**:258

"To Don at Salaam" (Brooks) **1:1**:258

"To Endymion" (Cullen) **1:1**:509

"To France" (Cullen) **1:1**:511–12

"To Gurdjieff Dying" (Toomer) **1:3**:1766–67

"To Hear" (Wicomb) **2:3**:411, 416, 418

"To Hell with Dying" (Walker) **1:3**:1826

"To His Excellency General George Washington" (Wheatley) **1:3**:1883, 1889

"To John Keats, Poet: At Spring Time" (Cullen) **1:1**:493, 508

"To Kentucky" (Cotter) **1:1**:478

"To Keorapetse Kgositsile (Willie)" (Brooks) **1:1**:258

"To Lovers of Earth: Fair Warning" (Cullen) **1:1**:509

"To Mæcenas" (Wheatley)
See "Ode to Mæcenas"

"To Mr. William Wordsworth, Distributor of Stamps for Westmoreland" (Goodison) **2:2**:69

"To Ms. Ann" (Clifton) **1:1**:461

"To My Daughter the Junkie on a Train" (Lorde) **1:2**:1278

"To One Not There" (Cullen) **1:1**:512

"To One Who Said Me Nay" (Cullen) **1:1**:507

"To Plough" (Osundare) **2:3**:181

To Raise, Destroy and Create (Baraka) **1:1**:145

"To Ralph Crowder" (Anyidoho) **2:1**:98

"To S. M., A Young African Painter, on Seeing His Works" (Wheatley) **1:3**:1897

"To Sing a Song of Palestine" (Jordan) **BLCS**:205

To Smile in Autumn (Parks) **1:3**:1555–56

"To the Artist Who Just Happens to Be Black" (Cortez) **2:1**:379

"To the Dinosaur" (Osundare) **2:3**:180

"To the Diaspora" (Brooks) **1:1**:258

"To the Memory of Joseph S. Cotter Jr." (Cotter) **1:1**:477

"To the Mercy Killers" (Randall) **1:3**:1598, 1605

"To the New South" (Dunbar) **1:1**:639

"To the Rev. Mr. Pitkin on the Death of His Lady" (Wheatley) **1:3**:1884

"To the Right Honorable William, Earl of Dartmouth, His Majesty's Principal Secretary of State for North America" (Wheatley) **1:3**:1883, 1887, 1889, 1892, 1898

"To the Three for Whom the Book" (Cullen) **1:1**:510

"To the Union Savers of Cleveland" (Harper) **1:2**:980

"To the University of Cambridge, in New England" (Wheatley) **1:3**:1883, 1885, 1888, 1892, 1896, 1900

"To the White Fiends" (McKay) **1:3**:1385, 1389

"To Thelma Who Worried Because I Couldn't Cook" (Clifton) **2:1**:313–15

"To Those Who Sing America" (Davis) **1:1**:521

To Us, All Flowers Are Roses (Goodison) **2:2**:92–96

"To You" (Davis) **1:1**:524

"To You Who Read My Book" (Cullen) **1:1**:505, 508

"Today" (Walker) **1:3**:1842

"Today on This Day" (Cortez) **2:1**:362

"The Toilet" (Mhlophe) **2:3**:68

The Toilet: A Play in One Act (Baraka) **1:1**:126–27, 129, 139, 145–46; **2:1**:176

"Tom" (Brathwaite) **BLCS**:53

"Tommy" (Wideman) **1:3**:1923, 1926

"Tomorrow and the World" (Carter) **2:1**:278

"Tomorrow, Tomorrow" (Walcott) **1:3**:1804

"Tongue-Tied" (Cullen) **1:1**:511

"Tonton-Macoute" (Guillén) **1:2**:914

"The Torn Sky: Lesson #1" (Jordan) **BLCS**:205

"Tornado Blues" (Brown) **1:1**:290

Too Black, Too Strong (Zephaniah) **2:3**:462

"Torture" (Walker) **2:3**:371–72

"Tou Wan Speaks to Her Husband, Liu Sheng" (Dove) **BLCS**:112

"Touch-Up Man" (Komunyakaa) **2:2**:369

"Touris" (Bennett) **1:1**:182

"toussaint" (Shange) **1:3**:1694

Toussaint L'Ouverture (James) **BLCS**:193

"Towards a Personal Semantics" (Jordan) **BLCS**:201

Toys in a Field (Komunyakaa) **BLCS**:217; **2:2**:365

Trading Twelves: Selected Letters of Ralph Ellison and Albert Murray (Murray) **2:3**:96, 98

Tradition, the Writer, and Society (Harris) **2:2**:164, 168

La tragédie du Roi Christophe (Césaire) **1:1**:360–61, 364, 370–72

"The Tragedy at Three Corners" (Dunbar)
See "The Tragedy at Three Forks"

"The Tragedy at Three Forks" (Dunbar) **1:1**:628, 637, 639

The Tragedy of King Christophe (Césaire)
See *La tragédie du Roi Christophe*

"The Tragedy of Pete" (Cotter) **1:1**:477

Train Whistle Guitar (Murray) **2:3**:97

Transatlantic (Toomer) **1:3**:1758

Transbluesencey: The Selected Poems of Amiri Baraka/LeRoi Jones (Baraka) **2:1**:186–87

Transcircularities: New and Selected Poems (Troupe) **2:3**:318–20, 324

"Transition to Glory" (Adichie) **2:1**:29

"Translation from Chopin" (Randall) **1:3**:1606

"The Transmission" (Johnson) **2:2**:239–40

"The Transport of Slaves from Maryland to Mississippi" (Dove) **BLCS**:111, 121

"Travel from Home" (Bullins) **1:1**:336

The Traveller to the East (Mofolo)
See *Moeti oa bochabela*

Travelling Mercies (Goodison) **2:2**:62, 70, 72, 74, 76, 85, 91, 96–97

Traversée de la mangrove (Condé) **BLCS**:95, 97–101, 104, 106–107

The Treasure of Pleasant Valley (Yerby) **1:3**:2026

Tree of Life (Condé)
See *La vie scélérate*

The Trial of Dedan Kimathi (Ngugi) **1:3**:1507, 1509

"The Trial Sermon on Bull-Skin" (Dunbar) **1:1**:632, 636, 641

The Trials of Brother Jero (Soyinka) **1:3**:1710, 1712

Tribal Scars (Sembène)
See *Voltaïque*

"Trident" (Goodison) **2:2**:91

Trilogy (Walcott)
See *The Haitian Trilogy*

"Trilogy for Azania" (Busia) **2:1**:235

Triton (Delany) **1:1**:528, 537

"Triumph" (James) **BLCS**:187

The Triumph of Liberty (Bell)
See *A Poem Entitled "The Triumph of Liberty": Delivered April 7, 1870 at Detroit Opera House, on the Occasion of the Fifteenth Amendment to the Constitution of the United States*

"Triumphs of the Free" (Bell) **1:1**:177

"The Tropics in New York" (McKay) **1:3**:1396, 1398

"The Trouble about Sophiny" (Dunbar) **1:1**:637

Trouble in Mind (Childress) **1:1**:404, 406–07

"The Trouble with Intellectuals" (Randall) **1:3**:1597, 1605

"Trouble with the Angels" (Hughes) **1:2**:1048

"The Trousers" (Dunbar) **1:1**:637

"Truant" (McKay) **1:3**:1394–95

"The True Import of Present Dialogue, Black vs. Negro" (Giovanni) **1:2**:882, 885, 889, 893, 895–96

"The True Negro" (Cotter) **1:1**:476

"The Trustfulness of Polly" (Dunbar) **1:1**:630, 636

"Truth" (Harper) **1:2**:979

"Truth" (McKay) **1:3**:1388

The Truth About the West African Land Question (Casely-Hayford) **1:1**:346

"The Truth of Fiction" (Achebe) **1:1**:14

"Tu Do Street" (Komunyakaa) **BLCS**:217–218, 231, 233

Tu t'appelleras Tanga (Beyala) **2:1**:197–98, 202–4

Turn Thanks (Goodison) **2:2**:69–70, 72, 74–76, 92, 94, 97

"Turn Thanks to Grandmother Hannah" (Goodison) **2:2**:92

"The Turncoat" (Baraka) **1:1**:125

"turning" (Clifton) **1:1**:463

Turning the Wheel: Essays on Buddhism and Writing (Johnson) **2:2**:239, 248–54

"The Turtles" (Gaines) **1:2**:857

"Tuskegee" (Cotter) **1:1**:476

25 Poems (Walcott) **1:3**:1799

"Twilight Reverie" (Hughes) **1:2**:1052

Two Cities: A Love Story (Wideman) **2:3**:431–32

Two Love Stories (Lester) **2:2**:405

Two Rhythm Plays (Sutherland) **2:3**:276

"Two Seedings" (Clark Bekederemo) **1:1**:425

"Two Sisters" (Aidoo) **BLCS**:3

Two Songs: Song of Prisoner and Song of Malaya (p'Bitek) **1:3**:1562, 1567

"Two Thoughts on Death" (Cullen) **1:1**:504

Two Thousand Seasons (Armah) **2:1**:105, 108, 121

Two Trains Running (Wilson) **1:3**:1972–73; **2:3**:449

"Two Views of Marilyn Monroe" (Clark Bekederemo) **1:1**:426

"The Two Voices" (Forten) **1:2**:814, 817

"Two Who Crossed a Line (He Crosses)" (Cullen) **1:1**:508

Two Wings to Veil My Face (Forrest) **BLCS**:133, 138

Two Women in One (El Saadawi)
See *Emra'atan fi emra'ah*

"Two-an'-Six" (McKay) **1:3**:1382

Title Index

ISBN-13: 978-1-4144-3173-4
ISBN-10: 1-4144-3173-2

90000

9 781414 431734